THE DOCTRINE
OF THE
CHRISTIAN LIFE

A THEOLOGY OF LORDSHIP

A SERIES BY JOHN M. FRAME

The Doctrine of God

The Doctrine of the Christian Life

The Doctrine of the Knowledge of God

The Doctrine of the Word of God

THE DOCTRINE
OF THE
CHRISTIAN LIFE

JOHN M. FRAME

P&R
P U B L I S H I N G
P.O. BOX 817 • PHILLIPSBURG • NEW JERSEY 08865-0817

Library of Congress Cataloging-in-Publication Data

Frame, John M., 1939–
   The doctrine of the Christian life / John M. Frame.
      p. cm. — (A theology of lordship)
   Includes bibliographical references (p.   ) and indexes.
   ISBN 978-0-87552-796-3 (cloth)
1. Ethics in the Bible. 2. Christian ethics—Biblical teaching. 3. Christian ethics.
I. Title.
   BS680.E84F73 2008
   241—dc22
                                                    2008005337

To Johnny

And he said to him, "You shall love the Lord your God with all your heart and with all your soul and with all your mind. This is the great and first commandment. And a second is like it: You shall love your neighbor as yourself. On these two commandments depend all the Law and the Prophets." (Matt. 22:37–40)

Jesus said, "Truly, I say to you, there is no one who has left house or brothers or sisters or mother or father or children or lands, for my sake and for the gospel, who will not receive a hundredfold now in this time, houses and brothers and sisters and mothers and children and lands, with persecutions, and in the age to come eternal life. But many who are first will be last, and the last first." (Mark 10:29–31)

For by grace you have been saved through faith. And this is not your own doing; it is the gift of God, not a result of works, so that no one may boast. For we are his workmanship, created in Christ Jesus for good works, which God prepared beforehand, that we should walk in them. (Eph. 2:8–10)

So, whether you eat or drink, or whatever you do, do all to the glory of God. (1 Cor. 10:31)

Contents

SECTION THREE: THE EXISTENTIAL PERSPECTIVE

PART FOUR: THE TEN COMMANDMENTS

PART FIVE: CHRIST AND CULTURE

Analytical Outline

PART SIX: PERSONAL SPIRITUAL MATURITY

Preface

This volume will deal mostly with ethics, but also with a number of other subjects, grouped around the general title *The Doctrine of the Christian Life* (henceforth *DCL*). The ethics course I taught at Westminster Seminary had that title, but it was James Hurley, as I recall, who suggested to me that the Christian life was much more than ethics. The Christian life is not only a matter of following rules of morality, but a dynamic experience: living in the fallen world, in fellowship with the living God. So in this book I will discuss not only ethics (the normative perspective), but also the culture in which we live (the situational perspective) and the resources of redemption on which we draw daily (the existential perspective).[1]

I suppose, given my perspectival orientation, I could stretch the meaning of ethics to include the other two disciplines (and vice versa), but I should admit at the outset that this book does go beyond ethics as ethics is usually conceived.

Most of the book, however, will deal with ethics in the usual sense, for that is what I know most about. Yet I have always felt a certain uneasiness with the discipline.

I cringed a bit in 1968 when my senior colleague, Norman Shepherd, asked me to teach the course in ethics. But it was my first teaching job, at Westminster Seminary in Philadelphia, and I probably would not have refused any assignment. Shepherd evidently thought me qualified because ethics is partly a philosophical discipline, and I had studied philosophy at Princeton and Yale. Cornelius Van Til had, in past years, taught a philosophically oriented ethics course at Westminster, and I was much impressed

1. I shall discuss these "perspectives" in this volume, as I have in the other volumes of this series. The triperspectival scheme actually originated in my ethics teaching, and, in a way, ethics is its natural home. I have applied it to epistemology in *The Doctrine of the Knowledge of God*, because I believe that epistemology can be fruitfully analyzed as a subdivision of ethics. And many other applications of this approach have occurred to me, which I have presented in *The Doctrine of God* and intend to present in other books of this series. But readers who are not yet comfortable with this approach may find that the present volume presents it in areas where it is most clearly and obviously useful. And if you don't find it persuasive in this volume, you probably won't find it persuasive anywhere.

by his thinking.[2] I also believed that in ethics, as in all theological disciplines, biblical exegesis must have the final say. John Murray had taught an exegetically oriented ethics course at the seminary, and I greatly admired his writings in the field.[3] Even at that time, too, I was convinced that theology had to speak to the lives of people, not just to their intellectual conceptions. Shepherd knew these things about me, so he probably thought that I was suited to teach this kind of course.

As a matter of fact, however, I had always been rather uncomfortable in the field of ethics. As a philosophy major at Princeton, I had avoided every opportunity to take a course in ethics, even though I could have studied under Paul Ramsey, who had a huge reputation in the field. I likewise avoided ethics courses at Yale, though James Gustafson taught ethics during my years there. The only course in ethics I had ever taken was the two-credit-hour course I took at Westminster as part of the required curriculum. At that time, neither Van Til nor Murray was teaching the course, but rather Edwin H. Palmer. Palmer did what he could in the time he had available, but, though I loved him as a teacher and as a man, his course did not make much of an impression on me.

My aversion to ethics was mainly an aversion to the secular ethics literature, which, of course, even we nonsecularists are expected to read in preparing lectures and books. That literature seemed to me to be very confused indeed: overly dogmatic on some points (the pieties of liberalism) and relativistic on all others. I soon came to see this in the light of Van Til's insight that non-Christian thought is always both rationalistic and irrationalistic. But that insight left me with little motivation to study the literature on ethics, beyond the writings of Van Til, Murray, and others in the evangelical and Reformed theological traditions.

Over the years, however, I have gained a greater appreciation of the secular literature. Non-Christians often have a better grasp than Christians of the complications of ethical decision making. They may be ultimately confused, but at least they can help us define the options. And, given the multiplicity of options, this literature can help us to sympathize more with those who are wrestling with hard questions and can increase our humility as we come to admit our own uncertainty. Christianity, unlike any other ethical system, provides a solid basis for ethical decision making, but it does not make ethical decisions easy.

So here I am writing a book mostly on ethics, based on a love-hate relationship with the field that goes back forty-five years.

2. See his *Christian Theistic Ethics* ([Ripon, CA:] den Dulk Christian Foundation, 1971).
3. *Principles of Conduct* (Grand Rapids: Eerdmans, 1957); *Divorce* (Philadelphia: Presbyterian and Reformed, 1961).

In the Theology of Lordship series, I had intended this to be the fourth of four volumes (putting it off as long as possible). My original plan was to write *The Doctrine of the Word of God* (*DWG*) following *The Doctrine of God* (*DG*), which was published in 2002. But I decided to produce the present volume before *DWG*. I had already written much more material on ethics than on the Word of God. I had a 250-page lecture outline and maybe thirty supplementary papers that I had used in my classes. It seemed to me, therefore, that this book could be written much more quickly than *DWG*.

My original idea was to start the series with *DWG*, setting forth the basis for everything to come, followed by *The Doctrine of the Knowledge of God* (*DKG*), since our knowledge of God is based on his Word. Then would have come *DG*, giving the content of that knowledge, and finally the present volume, indicating the kind of life that is consistent with the knowledge of God.

More recently, however, I have been inclined toward a different order of topics:

1. *DG*, since God himself is the foundation of everything, including his Word
2. *DWG*, describing how he communicates with us
3. *DKG*, indicating how we gain knowledge from the Word
4. *DCL*, indicating the life that is warranted by this knowledge

But this order fails to indicate a major theme of this series, namely, that our knowledge of God is a subdivision of ethics (that is, thinking is part of life). That consideration would suggest a reversal of items 3 and 4 in the above list, putting *DKG* last. This is not to say that my other suggested orders are wrong. Rather, the point is that the four topics are interdependent, indeed "perspectival." If we put *DKG* last, for example, how can we account for the fact that the other three areas must be governed by a biblical epistemology?

I wish to express my thanks again to all who have encouraged and stimulated my thinking over the years, especially my students, who have been a captive audience for the testing of this material. I thank many for giving me criticism and other feedback on previous volumes in the series. Many offered kind words about *The Doctrine of God*, and I am especially thankful to the Evangelical Christian Booksellers Association for giving to that book their Gold Medallion award for 2003 in the area of theology and doctrine.

The only substantial negative criticism of *DG* among reviewers was that it made insufficient use of the historical tradition. That criticism leaves me a bit perplexed, because I cited a great many historical and contemporary sources in the volume. How much more of this should I have done in a volume that was already 888 pages long?

Is the point of that criticism that I did not include a thorough, systematic history of the doctrine of God? To that I answer simply that an author cannot do everything in one volume. *DG* was, of course, deeply influenced by many historical and contemporary currents of thought. But its purpose was to set forth biblical teaching, not to list all those currents. Surely it is not wrong for an author to write a book expounding biblical themes without also feeling it necessary to address historical themes and contemporary discussions in systematic detail.

My purpose in writing *DG* was not simply, or even primarily, to expound the doctrines, but mainly to establish their foundation, to persuade readers that they are true. *DG* is an argumentative book. Ultimately, for those who believe in *sola Scriptura*, the only way to establish the truth of doctrines is to appeal to Scripture. It might have been helpful for me to include more historical material to help people understand the doctrines better, to understand why they have been formulated as they have been. But I cannot think of a single instance where additional historical citations would have made my presentations of these doctrines more persuasive.

Given *sola Scriptura* (about which I will say more in chapter 11 of this book), even when a theologian does cite historical sources, including confessions, it is then necessary to go back to Scripture to establish the truth of what those sources say.[4] The main value of the confessions, then, is to mediate the biblical teaching. But is it too much to ask that in an 888-page book I might occasionally bypass the middle man?

Another question occurs: Is it possible that the desire of some for a more ecclesiastical and historical focus is related to the hyperhistorical trend in evangelical scholarship that I criticized in "*Sola Scriptura* in Theological Method"[5] and in "Traditionalism"?[6]

At any rate, readers and reviewers are advised that in this respect the present volume will be like *DG*. Although I shall include here many references to secular and Christian sources, historical and contemporary, my purpose, as in *DG*, is not to exposit the history of these doctrines, but to present and defend what I consider to be the biblical

---

4. A former colleague has described this procedure, not favorably, as "zero-based budgeting." If that is a fault, I plead guilty. Zero-based budgeting in theology is a good thing, a necessary consequence of *sola Scriptura*. I am thankful to Luther and Calvin that they did not merely assume the truth of their traditions, but brought them under the scrutiny of Scripture. They were zero-based budgeters with a vengeance.

5. Appendix 2 in Frame, *Contemporary Worship Music: A Biblical Defense* (Phillipsburg, NJ: P&R Publishing, 1997), 175–201.

6. Available at http://reformedperspectives.org and http://www.frame-poythress.org.

position. Everything else will serve that purpose, and thus the book will be inadequate for other purposes.

I should mention that the Bible quotations in this book come from the English Standard Version. This is a change from the previous books in the Lordship series.

I wish to thank Reformed Theological Seminary, which has provided the best possible working environment for me as a teacher and writer. I'm also grateful to Richard Pratt, Ra McLaughlin, and the staff of Third Millennium Ministries, for putting together a video series with me on the subject of ethics, helping me to rethink a number of formulations. I am also grateful to P&R Publishing, with whom I have had a great working relationship over the years, and especially to Jim Scott, who edited this book for them.

Abbreviations

I will refer to classical titles merely by title (or abbreviation). These can be found in a variety of editions. Other frequently cited titles are as follows:

AGG   John M. Frame, *Apologetics to the Glory of God* (Phillipsburg, NJ: P&R Publishing, 1994)

CVT   John M. Frame, *Cornelius Van Til: An Analysis of His Thought* (Phillipsburg, NJ: P&R Publishing, 1995)

DG   John M. Frame, *The Doctrine of God* (Phillipsburg, NJ: P&R Publishing, 2002)

DKG   John M. Frame, *The Doctrine of the Knowledge of God* (Phillipsburg, NJ: P&R Publishing, 1987)

WCF   Westminster Confession of Faith

WLC   Westminster Larger Catechism

WSC   Westminster Shorter Catechism

PART ONE

INTRODUCTORY CONSIDERATIONS

CHAPTER 1

Introduction

The Christian life is a rich journey, and it is not easy to describe. Without any pretense of comprehensiveness, I try to describe it in this volume as living under God's law, in God's world, in the presence of God himself. Those of you who have read other books of mine will recognize that triad as indicating what I call the normative, situational, and existential perspectives, respectively. Those of you who haven't read other books of mine can learn about that triad in the present volume.

We begin now with some introductory considerations. After defining terms and relating ethics to God's lordship, I shall discuss ethics itself from three perspectives: situational (the history of ethical thought), existential (a Christian ethical method), and normative (ethical principles, following the pattern of the Ten Commandments). But first we should address a couple of important introductory questions:

WHY STUDY ETHICS?

We should study ethics at least for the following reasons:

Servants of Jesus are people who have his commandments and keep them (John 14:21). Over and over again, Jesus tells us, "If you love me, you will keep my commandments" (John 14:15; cf. vv. 21, 23; 15:10; 1 John 2:3–5; 3:21–24; 5:3). Jesus' "new commandment" is "that you love one another:

3

just as I have loved you, you also are to love one another" (John 13:34). Love is to be the mark of the church, distinguishing it from the world: "By this all people will know that you are my disciples, if you have love for one another" (v. 35). This is not to say that we are saved by works, obedience, or keeping commandments. It is simply to say that if we want to be disciples of Jesus, we must be devoted to good works (Titus 3:8; cf. Matt. 5:16; Eph. 2:10; 1 Tim. 2:10; 5:10; 6:18; 2 Tim. 3:17; Titus 2:7, 14; 3:14; Heb. 10:24; 1 Peter 2:12). If we are to be devoted to good works, we must know what works are good and what ones are bad. So we need to study ethics.

One purpose of Scripture itself is to promote ethical behavior. The familiar passage 2 Timothy 3:16–17 reads, "All Scripture is breathed out by God and profitable for teaching, for reproof, for correction, and for training in righteousness, that the man of God may be competent, equipped for every good work." Note the ethical focus here. God breathed out the words of Scripture so that we may be trained in righteousness, so that we may be equipped for every good work. Of course, Scripture has other purposes as well. Many have emphasized that Scripture bears witness to Christ, and so it does (Luke 24:27; John 5:39). But Scripture presents Christ as one who equips us to be lights in the world (Matt. 5:14). Consequently, a great amount of Scripture is devoted to defining and motivating our good works.

In one sense, everything in the Bible is ethical. Even when Scripture expounds doctrinal propositions, it presents them as propositions that *ought* to be believed. That ought is an ethical ought. Indeed, all the content of Scripture ought to be believed and acted upon. The whole Bible is ethics. Of course, the Bible is not only ethics. It is also narrative, for to understand the history of redemption we must have recourse to everything in Scripture. So the whole Bible is narrative as well as ethics. Similarly, the whole Bible is doctrinal truth, wisdom, evangelism, apologetics, and so on.[1] But we have not understood the Bible until we have understood its ethic.

This is another way of saying, as I did in *The Doctrine of the Knowledge of God*, that theology is "the application of the Word of God by persons to all areas of life."[2] Any study or teaching of the Bible is an attempt to answer human questions, to meet human needs. Those questions or needs may be relatively theoretical (e.g., "What is the meaning of *ratzah* in the sixth

---

1. So I call all of these *perspectives* on the nature of Scripture. See *DKG*, 191–94. On apologetics as a perspective on the whole Bible, see Ezra Hyun Kim, "Biblical Preaching Is Apologia," a D.Min. project submitted to Westminster Theological Seminary in California, Spring, 2000.
2. *DKG*, 81.

commandment?") or relatively practical (e.g., "When should I remove life support from my dying father?"). But they are all practical in the sense that they deal with human questions and needs. In that sense, all theology is addressed to people to help them think and live to the glory of God.[3] So all theology involves ethics.

The study of ethics is enormously important for our witness to the world. We live in an age in which people are greatly concerned about ethics. Every day, the news media bring to mind issues of war and peace, the environment, the powers of government, abortion and euthanasia, genetic research, and so on. Many people seem very sure of the answers to these ethical questions. But when you probe deeply into their positions, you find that their conviction is often based on little more than partisan consensus or individual feeling. But the Bible does give us a basis for ethical judgments: the revelation of the living God. So discussions of ethical questions open a wide door for Christian witness.

People are far more open to discussing ethics than to discussing theistic proofs or even "transcendental arguments." Philosophy does not excite many people today, and many do not even want to hear personal testimony and the simple gospel. But they do care about right and wrong. Christians who can talk about ethics in a cogent way, therefore, have a great apologetic and evangelistic advantage.

It is true that many do not want to hear this witness today. They consider Christianity a "religious" position and therefore one that should not be discussed in the public square. But this view is utterly unreasonable, and that unreasonableness should be pressed. Why should religious positions be excluded from the debate, especially when secular positions have been unable to present a convincing basis for ethical judgments? As I shall indicate in this volume, the main currents of twentieth- and twenty-first-century thought have become bankrupt, confessedly unable to provide any basis for distinguishing right from wrong. I believe that many people today are hungering for answers and are willing to look even at religious positions to find them.

I shall argue as well that all ethics is religious, even when it tries hard to be secular. In the end, all ethics presupposes ultimate values. It requires allegiance to someone or something that demands devotion and governs all thinking. That kind of allegiance is indistinguishable from religious devotion, even if it doesn't involve liturgical practices. So the line between

---

3. Thinking is part of life, and so it too has an ethical dimension. It is subject to the authority of God's Word. Thus, epistemology can be understood as a subdivision of ethics. See *DKG*, 62–64.

religious and secular ethics is a fuzzy one, and it is arbitrary to use such a line to determine who is entitled to join a dialogue on ethics.

But more important than the ability to talk about ethics is the ability to live it. This is true of our witness to the world. People see how we live. Even Christians who are not articulate or eloquent can make, through their actions, a great impact on others. Jesus comments on the importance of our works to our witness: "Let your light shine before others, so that they may see your good works and give glory to your Father who is in heaven" (Matt. 5:16).

WHAT SHOULD BE OUR ETHICAL BIAS?

Before we begin our study, there is another question we need to ask. All of us are biased in favor of certain conclusions, even at the outset of our study. We cannot be neutral. But we ought to be self-conscious, even critical, of our biases.

There are those who enter the field of ethics with a goal of dispelling legalism. Perhaps they were raised in a church that imposed all sorts of rules on the kids and they didn't like it. So as ethicists they want to emphasize our freedom as individuals to make decisions for ourselves.

Others enter the field disgusted by the moral decline in our society. They may also be impressed by the rigorousness of Scripture and the high cost of discipleship. They are attracted to an ethic that does not compromise with worldliness, a radical ethic of discipline and self-control.

We tend to describe the first type of ethic as liberal, the second as conservative. Down through the years, ethicists have tended to divide into conservative and liberal parties. For example, in ancient Judaism there were the schools of Shammai (conservative) and Hillel (liberal). Catholicism has had Jesuits (liberal) and Jansenists (conservative). The liberal tendency to find loopholes in the moral law, to justify apparent sin, has given casuistry a bad name. The conservative tendency toward harshness and austerity has given moralism a bad name.

In this book, I urge readers not to side with either tendency. The point of Christian ethics is not to be as liberal as we can be, or as conservative. It is, rather, to be as biblical as we can be. So this book will seem to be more liberal than the majority on some issues (e.g., worship, cloning, just war, gambling, deceiving) and more conservative on others (e.g., the Sabbath, the roles of women, stem cell research). God's Word has a way of surprising us, of not fitting into our prearranged categories. Jesus rebuked both the conservative Pharisees and the liberal Sadducees; Paul rebuked both legalists and libertines. Understanding God's will rarely means falling into lockstep with some popular ideology. We need to think as part of a community, listening to our brothers and sisters, but we also need the courage to step aside from the crowd when God's Word directs us in that way.

So in this book I will be drawing some fine distinctions, as theologians are wont to do. I do this not to gain a reputation for subtlety and nuance, but simply to follow Scripture. My goal is to go as far as Scripture goes, and no farther, to follow its path without deviating to the left or the right. I trust God's Spirit to help us thread these needles, to help us find the biblical path, even when it is narrow and relatively untraveled. May he be with writer and reader as we seek to walk by the lamp of God's Word.

CHAPTER 2

An Ethical Glossary

Definitions are never a matter of life and death. Scripture gives us no directions for defining English words. So two people may use the same term with different meanings, without differing in their actual views. One theologian, for example, may define faith as intellectual assent, while insisting that trust always accompanies it. Another may define it as trust, while insisting that intellectual assent always accompanies it. The differences between these two theologians should not be considered significant at this particular point. We may define terms as we like, as long as our definitions don't confuse people or mislead them on substantive issues.[1]

In this chapter, I will define some important terms, indicating how I will use these terms in this particular book. These definitions are not necessarily best for all situations, even for all discussions of ethics.

ETHICS AND THEOLOGY

The first group of definitions will relate ethics to other theological disciplines. The earlier ones review discussions in *The Doctrine of the Knowledge of God*.

1. Compare the discussions in *DKG*, 76–77, 215–41.

8

KNOWLEDGE OF GOD

I use this phrase to mean a personal, covenantal relationship with God, involving awareness of his self-revelation, an obedient or disobedient response to that revelation, and the divine blessing or curse upon that response.[2]

This definition connects our knowledge of God to his lordship (see chapter 3) and to ethics, as I define it below.

DOCTRINE

Doctrine is the Word of God in use to create and deepen one's knowledge of God, and to encourage an obedient, rather than disobedient, response to his revelation. Or, more briefly, doctrine is the application of the Word of God to all areas of human life.

This definition is built upon the use of the Greek terms *didaskō*, *didachē*, and *didaskalia*, especially as Paul uses them in the Pastoral Epistles.[3] I prefer to define *doctrine*, therefore, not as theological propositions, but as an active process of teaching that leads to spiritual health: as Paul puts it, "sound (*hygiainousē*) doctrine" (1 Tim. 1:10; 2 Tim. 4:3; Titus 1:9; 2:1).

THEOLOGY

I define *theology* as a synonym of *doctrine*.[4]

So theology, too, is an active process of teaching, not first of all a collection of propositions. I am not opposed to theological propositions; there are quite a few of them in my books. But theological propositions are useful only in the context of teaching that leads to spiritual health.

In that sense, theology is a practical discipline, not merely a theoretical one.[5] I do not disparage theory; indeed, my own books are more theoretical than practical. But, in my definition, theory is not the only kind of theology there is, nor is it theology par excellence. Theology takes place, not only in technical books, but also in children's Sunday school classes, evangelistic meetings, preaching, and discipleship seminars. Theology is the application of the Word to all areas of life. Academic or theoretical

---

2. *DKG*, 11–49.
3. *DKG*, 81–85.
4. For the "traditional theological programs" of exegetical, biblical, systematic, and practical theology, see *DKG*, 206–14. For historical theology, see pp. 304–14. All of these are different ways of applying the whole Bible. They do not differ in subject matter, but in the questions we ask of Scripture in each program.
5. See *DKG*, 84–85, on the relationship between theory and practice.

theology is one kind of theology, not the only kind. And I shall argue later that theory is not more ultimate than practice, nor is it the basis of practice; rather, theory and practice are both applications of God's Word, and they enrich one another when they are biblical.

For that matter, the line between theory and practice is not sharp. Theory is one kind of practice, and *theoretical* and *practical* are relative terms that admit of degrees.

ETHICS

Ethics is theology, viewed as a means of determining which persons, acts, and attitudes receive God's blessing and which do not.

This formulation defines ethics as Christian ethics. Many will find this objectionable. Given this definition, for example, Aristotle's *Nicomachean Ethics* is not about ethics! Aristotle was not trying to determine what persons, acts, and attitudes are blessed by the God of the Bible. The same could be said of any non-Christian thinker.

It may seem absurd to define ethics in such a way as to exclude all non-Christian writers from the discipline. But, as I said earlier, I don't object to people using a different definition in a different context. If I were to discuss ethics with a disciple of Aristotle, for example, I would agree with him to define the topic as, say, the study of right and wrong.[6] But I mean my present book to be a distinctively Christian work, and I intend to show that non-Christian ethics is flawed, not only in its conclusions, but also in its initial understanding of its task. For that purpose, my theologically enhanced definition will be most serviceable.

Note also that on this definition ethics is not merely a branch of theology, but is in fact the whole of theology, viewed in a certain way. All theology answers ethical questions. Even the more theoretical kinds of theology, as we saw earlier, are explorations of what we *ought* to believe. That ought is an ethical ought. So, when we ask what we ought to believe about, say, the order of the divine decrees, we are asking an ethical question.[7]

All theology, then, has to do with ethics. It is also true that the subjects we usually treat in ethics, such as murder, stealing, and adultery, can be integrated with the rest of theology more thoroughly than in most theological systems. In a theological curriculum, it would be possible to deal with

---

6. Of course, at some point I would have to show the Aristotelian that his method of ethics is fundamentally flawed. But I would not insist on making that point at the beginning of a conversation.

7. Compare the argument in *DKG*, 62–64, 73–75, 108–9, 149–51, 247–48, that epistemology can be seen as a branch of ethics.

ethical issues (even those issues we normally think of as ethical) throughout, rather than postponing them to a special course. We could discuss the creation ordinances, the moral laws given to Adam and Eve before the fall, in the course of describing the original condition of the human race. Then we could teach the Decalogue in connection with the Mosaic covenant, ethical methodology in connection with theological prolegomena, and so on. But, in fact, theologians (including myself) have tended to avoid the more practical kinds of ethical questions in the main curriculum of systematic and biblical theology. So seminaries have come to offer courses in ethics as a separate discipline. In fact, however, ethics covers the whole range of human life and all the teaching of Scripture.

In this book, however, I will stick pretty much to the standard subject matter that theologians have called ethics, that is, the subject matter of the Ten Commandments, together with the presuppositions and applications of those commandments.

Finally, in this definition, take note of the triad of persons, acts, and attitudes.[8] These are the three subjects of ethical predication in the Bible. Only these can be ethically good, bad, right, or wrong. A rock can be good in a nonethical sense (e.g., good for use in construction). But a rock cannot make ethical choices; it cannot seek to bring itself, its actions, and its attitudes into conformity to God's will. So a rock is not a subject of ethical predication. Only rational creatures (God, angels, and human beings) are subjects of ethical predication, together with their actions and attitudes.[9]

METAETHICS

Metaethics is a second-order discipline, a theological reflection on the nature of ethics. Ethics is about good and bad, right and wrong, blessing and curse. Metaethics is about ethics. Metaethics discusses the nature of right and wrong, ethical methods, the presuppositions of ethics, and

8. I'm not sure whether this threefold distinction should be integrated with the other threefold distinctions of my Theology of Lordship books. And if it is to be so integrated, I'm not sure exactly how to do it. Both "persons" and "attitudes" are good candidates for the existential perspective. At the moment, I lean toward the following: person, normative; acts, situational; attitudes, existential. Of course, the beautiful thing about these triads is that they are perspectival, so that different arrangements are possible. For readers who are drawing a blank here, I will explain the perspectives in the following chapter.

9. Of course, we can make further distinctions within the categories of persons, actions, and attitudes. Actions, for example, can be divided into thoughts, words, and deeds, a distinction invoked, for example, in WLC, 149. These subdivisions are also subjects of ethical predication in Scripture.

so on. But, like Christian ethics, a Christian metaethic must be subject to Scripture and thus must be theological. In that way, metaethics is a part of theology, and therefore, according to my earlier definition, a part of ethics.

MORALITY

I will use the terms *morality* and *ethics* synonymously in this book, although they are often distinguished. Jochem Douma, for example, makes this distinction: "*Morality* consists of the entirety of traditional and dominant customs, while *ethics* is reflection upon those customs."[10] I think, however, that either term can refer (descriptively) to human customs[11] and (normatively) to the evaluation of those customs as right or wrong.

It is, of course, perfectly legitimate to reflect on the customs of human life, and I will be doing that in this book to some extent. But I believe that for Christians the work of ethics is essentially theological. Theology does, of course, reflect on human customs, as do many other disciplines. But theology reflects on those customs specifically for the sake of applying biblical standards to them. The same is true of ethics and morality in the normative sense, as I shall use the terms.

The two terms, also, can equally refer *de facto* to people's moral standards, or *de jure* to the standards they ought to have. Joe's ethics (*de facto*) are Joe's moral standards and/or the ways he applies those standards in his decisions. But from a normative standpoint (*de jure*), Joe's ethics may be wrong, unethical, or immoral.

VALUE TERMS

MORAL, ETHICAL

In light of the above discussion, I will treat the adjectives *moral* and *ethical*, like the corresponding nouns, synonymously. Both of the terms, however, can be used either descriptively or normatively. Descriptively, they mean "pertaining to the discipline of ethics," as in the sentence "This is an ethical, not an aesthetic, question." Normatively, they mean "conforming to ethical norms," as in the sentence "Senator Ridenhour is an ethical politician."

10. J. Douma, *Responsible Conduct* (Phillipsburg, NJ: P&R Publishing, 2003), 3.
11. As in the related terms *mores* and *ethos*.

IMMORAL, AMORAL, NONMORAL

The word *moral* can be negated in three different ways. *Immoral* is usually a normative term, used to criticize a person, act, or attitude as ethically bad or wrong. An *amoral* person is someone who is unable or unwilling to bring ethical considerations to bear on his decisions. *Nonmoral* is the opposite of the descriptive meaning of *moral* above, by which we distinguish ethical from nonethical topics of discussion. So the question of whether clam chowder should contain tomatoes is usually considered to be a nonmoral question, except occasionally by partisans on either side.

MORALISTIC

This term is vague, and I will not be using it much in this book. It can mean (a) trite or provincial in ethical attitude, (b) self-righteous, (c) putting too much emphasis on morality, (d) legalistic, putting works in the role that Scripture reserves for grace, or (e) (in preaching) failing to note or sufficiently emphasize the redemptive-historical purpose of a biblical text.[12] Usually the word is used as a term of reproach, but rarely with any precision or clarity. The word has bad connotations, and people seem to use it mainly for the sake of those connotations, to make an opponent look bad, rather than to bring clarity to a discussion. We should generally avoid using words in this way.

VALUE

A value is a quality of worth or merit. There are various kinds of value, including economic, aesthetic, medicinal, recreational, and ethical. So ethics may be regarded as a division of value theory. It is important to make distinctions between ethical values and other kinds of values. Writing a great symphony may be an act of great aesthetic value, but, depending on the composer's motive, it may be of no ethical value or even of negative ethical value.

FACT

Facts are states of affairs. Statements of fact (propositions) claim to assert what is the case. Philosophers commonly distinguish, sometimes very sharply, between facts and values, and those distinctions can be important

---

12. I have discussed redemptive history (that is, biblical theology) in *DKG*, 207–12, and I will try in chapter 16 in this book to show its role in ethics.

in ethical philosophy, as we shall see. However, it is also important to see the closeness of the relationship between fact and value. If a moral principle (e.g., "Stealing is wrong") is true, then it is a fact. Further, statements of fact presuppose moral values.[13] When someone says, "The book is on the table," he is implying that his hearers *ought* to believe that proposition. And that ought is an ethical ought.

NORM

A norm is a rule or standard that determines the ethical rightness or wrongness, the goodness or badness, of any person, action, or attitude. In biblical ethics, the ultimate norm is God's revelation.

VIRTUE

Virtues are grounds of praise for someone or something. There are non-moral virtues, such as efficiency, skill, and talent. Moral virtues, like love, kindness, fidelity, and integrity, are elements of a good moral character. Virtue ethics is a kind of ethics that focuses on these inward character traits. This type of ethics is often contrasted with command ethics (focusing on moral rules) and narrative ethics (focusing on a history or story that provides a context for ethical decision making). We shall see that as Christians we need not choose among these; Scripture provides us with divine commands, a narrative basis for moral choice, and a list of virtues, together with God's gracious means of conferring those virtues upon us.

GOOD

Good is the most general adjective of commendation. We use the term to ascribe any sort of value to anything: aesthetic, economic, etc., as well as ethical. So we should distinguish between moral goodness and nonmoral goodness. The most common form of nonmoral goodness may be described as teleological goodness. To be good in the teleological sense is simply to be useful—good for something, producing a desirable state of affairs. A good hammer is a tool that is useful for pounding nails into surfaces. Pounding nails is its purpose, its telos, its end. The hammer is not morally good, for moral goodness (in accord with our earlier definition of *ethics*) describes a person, action, or attitude that receives

---

13. See *DKG*, 140–41. See also pp. 71–73, on the relation of facts to interpretations. Note also the texts in *DKG* cited in footnote 7 to show that epistemology is part of ethics.

God's blessing. The hammer is not a person, so it does not receive God's blessing for the jobs it performs.

We do sometimes describe human beings as good in a teleological sense. A good plumber, for example, is someone who is skilled at fixing pipes. To say that Sid is a good plumber is not the same as saying that he is a good person. He may be skilled at fixing pipes, but otherwise a scoundrel. In such a case, we usually say he is a good plumber, but a bad person. To be sure, there is some overlap between the concepts. If Sid is skilled at fixing pipes, but he overcharges, steals objects from the kitchen, or makes an awful mess without cleaning it up, we probably would not call him a good plumber, for fear of being misunderstood. So there is a point where someone's ethics disqualifies him even from teleological commendations.

And in some cases moral turpitude compromises a person's skills. If skilled concert pianist Karl Konzertstück stays up partying all night and arrives at his recital with a hangover, with the result that he plays his music poorly, people will not recognize him that day as a good pianist. If such behavior becomes a habit, he may entirely lose his reputation, and his skills may also decline. So moral evil can imperil teleological goodness. Still, as a matter of definition, it is possible to speak of teleological goodness without reflecting on moral goodness.

Both teleological goodness and moral goodness are important to ethics. Morally good people seek in their actions to achieve goals that are teleologically good. For many philosophers, the highest goal (*summum bonum*) is happiness, either individual or corporate. Morally good acts, in their view, are acts that promote the happiness of oneself and others. So morally good actions are those that promote teleological goodness.

Scripture describes the highest good theologically: it is the glory of God (1 Cor. 10:31), the kingdom of God (Matt. 6:33). We shall see that these goals incorporate the happiness of people in various ways. But they are fundamentally theocentric, rather than anthropocentric. These provide the telos, the goal, of the believer's ethical actions: moral goodness seeks teleological goodness. For Christians, the teleological is theological, theistic, and theocentric.

Right

Right is generally synonymous with *moral goodness*: a good act is a right act. Its nuances, however, are somewhat different. *Right* belongs to the legal vocabulary. So when it describes moral goodness, it describes it as conformity to norms, laws, or standards. The corresponding biblical terms *tsaddiq* and *dikaios* have similar associations, and they can be translated "just" as well as "right."

In the triad mentioned earlier as the subjects of ethical predication, *good* applies equally to persons, acts, and attitudes, while *right* applies to actions and attitudes, but very rarely to persons. We often hear people described as "good guys," but not "right guys," though I often heard the latter phrase when I was growing up in the 1940s and 1950s. Scripture and theology, however, often refer to righteousness as a virtue, as conformity to God's standards.[14]

A common meaning of the noun *right* in ethics is "deserved privilege." We have a right when we have ethical and/or legal permission to do something or to possess something. In this sense, right is correlative with obligation. If Joey has a right to life, society has an obligation to protect his life. If Susanne has the right to an education, someone must provide her with that education. If Jerome has the right to free health care, then someone else has the obligation to provide him with it. Of course, it is possible to give up one's rights, as Paul does in 1 Corinthians 9:4–6, 12, 15. Rights in this sense are governed by moral and/or legal standards, and the emphasis on those standards is what connects this meaning of *right* with that of the previous paragraph.

OBLIGATION, DUTY, OUGHT

I shall use *obligation* and *duty* synonymously. These refer to actions we are required to do, commanded to do, by an ethical norm. *Ought* is a verbal form of *obligation*. What we *ought* to do is what the norm requires of us.

Some obligations are immediate, requiring us to carry them out right now, at the expense of anything else we may be doing or planning to do. For example, if we are in the midst of committing a sin, we are obligated to stop immediately. Other obligations are more general—things we must do at some time or within a certain time frame, but not necessarily right away. Later we shall discuss obligations that may legitimately be postponed in favor of other duties, such as the obligations to study the Scripture, to pray, to share the gospel with a neighbor, and so forth.

Some obligations are individual and some are corporate. For example, in Genesis 1:28, God tells the human race, represented by Adam, to replenish the earth and subdue it. This is not a command that Adam could have fulfilled by himself. He was to play a role, with others playing other roles, in the fulfillment of this command by the whole human race. Similarly, in the Great Commission in Matthew 28, Jesus commands the church, represented by the apostles, to make disciples of all the nations of the earth. Those eleven men, whether as individuals or as a group, could not carry out that

---

14. God is righteousness, not only in his character, his conformity to his own ethical standards, but also in his actions to redeem his people, his "righteous deeds." See *DG*, 451–58. Of course, those actions are righteous because they conform to his standards.

command by themselves. The command was given to the whole church, and each Christian is to fulfill a different role in the accomplishment of it.

Obligations include their applications. For example, if Sharon is obligated to go to a meeting on Wednesday, she is also obligated to find and utilize transportation that will get her to that meeting. So when God commands us to glorify him in all things (1 Cor. 10:31), everything we do ought to be an application of that command. Everything we do is either a fulfillment or a violation of that obligation. In that sense, all our actions are ethical. They are either good or bad, depending on whether they glorify God or not.

This is not to say that every choice is a choice between good and bad. We often make choices between two or more goods, as when choosing one cabbage or another at the grocery store.[15] But even the choice of a cabbage involves a choice to glorify God or not to; in that respect, it is an ethical choice. And of course in making that choice, as in making all choices, we have an obligation to choose the right rather than the wrong. In this situation, there are actually two choices being made at the same time: (1) the choice to glorify God, and (2) the choice of one good cabbage over another. The first is a choice between good and evil; the second is a choice between two goods.

Permission

Ethical norms regularly permit actions that they do not prohibit.[16] Permission, however, is not the same as commandment (1 Cor. 7:6). In my previous example, the ethical norm (God's word) does not command me to choose one cabbage over the other (assuming both are equal in all relevant respects). But since that norm does not forbid me, explicitly or implicitly, to buy that cabbage, it thereby permits that action. Permitted actions are good actions, and so we are inclined to say that some good actions are not obligatory. Obligated actions and permitted (but not obligated) actions form two separate classes of good actions.

In one sense, however, these classes of actions overlap. God does not command me to buy cabbage A rather than cabbage B. But he does command me to glorify him, and one way to apply that command is to supply nutritious food to my family. So my action is an application of a command, and, as we saw earlier, commands include their applications. In that sense, when I buy the cabbage I am carrying out a divine command. But making

---

15. I shall argue later that we are never called to choose between two or more wrongs, without the opportunity to choose a right alternative.

16. A prohibition is, of course, a negative command.

the purchase is not the only possible way to obey that command. I might equally well fulfill the command by buying a different cabbage, or by buying carrots or Brussels sprouts, or by buying nothing and getting food at another time.

GENERAL AND SPECIFIC OBLIGATIONS

We should distinguish between general and specific obligations. God's commands in Scripture are always to some extent general. For example, he says, "Honor your father and your mother" (Ex. 20:12). In that passage, he does not specify precisely how we are to honor them. Other divine commands supplement this general command by requiring more specific duties, such as providing for aged relatives (1 Tim. 5:3–8). But even those are not completely specific commands, for they must be applied to our own experience. For example, suppose that Jim must find a way to take care of his mother, who is blind and deaf. He could fulfill that obligation in several ways. Jim could take his mother into his own home. Or he could arrange for his sister to take their mother into her home, with Jim rendering financial assistance. Or he could arrange for some sort of institutional care. Any of these options, and others, might be a godly response to the situation.[17]

So there are different levels of generality and specificity in moral norms. As we apply the general norms, we usually find that there are a number of permissible ways to carry them out. But an obligation must be carried out in some way, not neglected altogether. So although any specific application may not be obligatory, we are still obligated to choose one or more of the permitted alternatives.

JUSTICE

The word *justice* brings us back to the legal vocabulary, which I mentioned in connection with the word *right*. In general, justice is that which is morally right. But the word tends to be used mostly in social contexts with the predominant meaning of "fairness" or "equity." More specifically, justice is the integrity of society's legal system. That includes especially the fairness of the courts, as they render verdicts and determine penalties.

People disagree, of course, on what constitutes justice or fairness. In today's political dialogue about economics, conservatives argue that justice is equality of opportunity, while liberals argue that justice is not achieved until there is also some level of equality of wealth.

17. I don't have the space here to argue my ethical evaluation of these alternatives.

CHAPTER 3

Ethics and Divine Lordship

I don't intend for this book to replace previous works on ethics written from a Reformed Christian viewpoint. John Murray's *Principles of Conduct*[1] and *Divorce*[2] still serve as benchmarks for exegetical depth in the field. John Jefferson Davis's *Evangelical Ethics*[3] continues to be an invaluable resource correlating biblical principles with historical and contemporary discussions of ethical problems. Readers will see that in this volume I have drawn freely from these books, as well as from Jochem Douma's *The Ten Commandments*[4] and *Responsible Conduct*.[5] Furthermore, my philosophical position is only an elaboration of Cornelius Van Til's *Christian Theistic Ethics*.[6]

The contribution I hope to make in this volume is to show the relationship of the Christian life, including ethics, to God's lordship. I have expounded the nature of lordship at length in *The Doctrine of God*, especially in chapters 1–7. In the present chapter, I will review that discussion and apply it to ethics in a general way, laying the foundation for what is to follow.

The name Lord (representing the Hebrew terms *yahweh* and *'adon* and the Greek *kyrios*) is found over seven thousand times in most English Bibles, usually referring to God or specifically to Jesus Christ. God's revelation of

---

1. Grand Rapids: Eerdmans, 1957.
2. Philadelphia: Presbyterian and Reformed, 1961.
3. Phillipsburg, NJ: P&R Publishing, 1985, 1993, 2004.
4. Phillipsburg, NJ: P&R Publishing, 1996.
5. Phillipsburg, NJ: P&R Publishing, 2003.
6. [Ripon, CA:] den Dulk Christian Foundation, 1971.

the name Yahweh to Moses in Exodus 3:14–15 is foundational to the biblical doctrine of God, for Yahweh is the name by which he wants especially to be remembered. The name Lord is found in the main confessions of faith of both testaments (see Deut. 6:4–5; Rom. 10:9; 1 Cor. 12:3; Phil. 2:11). God performs all his mighty works so that people will "know that I am the Lord" (Ex. 6:7; 7:5, 17; 8:22; 10:2; 14:4, and many other texts).

As Lord, God is, first of all, *personal, for Lord is a proper name.* Thus the Bible proclaims that the ultimate reality, the supreme being, is not an impersonal force like gravity or electromagnetism, or even a set of super-strings, but a person: one who thinks, speaks, feels, loves, and acts with purpose. As a person, he uses the impersonal realities of the universe for his own purposes and to his own glory. Modern secular thought is profoundly impersonalistic, holding that persons are ultimately reducible to things and forces, to matter, motion, time, and chance. Scripture denies this impersonalism, insisting that all reality, including all value, comes from a supreme personal being.

Second, the Lord is a supremely *holy* person. His personality shows his kinship with us, but his holiness shows his transcendence, his separation from us. God is above us, beyond us—not in the sense that he is far away, for he is intimately close; not in the sense that he is unknown or unknowable, for he clearly reveals himself to us; not in the sense that human language cannot describe him, for he describes himself to us in the human language of Scripture.[7] God is beyond us, rather, as the supreme person, the universal King, the Lord of all, before whom we cannot help but bow in awe and wonder. And, since our fall into sin, God is also separate from us, because ethical purity must be separate from ethical depravity (Isa. 6:5; Luke 5:8).

Third, God as Lord is head of a *covenant* relationship. In a covenant, God takes a people to be his, redeems them from death, demands certain behavior on their part, and declares his blessings and curses: blessings if they obey, but curses if they disobey. Parallels to this biblical concept of covenant can be found in ancient Near Eastern literature outside the Bible. A great king (the suzerain) would impose a treaty (or covenant) upon a lesser king (or vassal) and would author a document setting forth its terms. The document, typically, followed a standard literary form:

1. The name of the suzerain
2. Historical prologue: what the suzerain has done to benefit the vassal

7. This book, like all books in this series, assumes that Scripture is the Word of God and therefore infallible and inerrant in its original form. I plan to argue the point in *The Doctrine of the Word of God.*

3. Stipulations: commands specifying how the vassal king and his people must behave
   a. In general, the requirement of exclusive allegiance to the suzerain (sometimes called love)
   b. Specifically, laws indicating how the suzerain wants the vassal to behave
4. Sanctions
   a. Blessings: rewards for obeying the stipulations
   b. Curses: punishments for disobedience
5. Administration: dynastic succession, use of the treaty document, etc.

Except for section 5, this is the literary form of the Decalogue.[8] God comes to Israel and gives his name ("I am the LORD your God," Ex. 20:2a), identifying himself as the author of the covenant and of the covenant document. Then he tells Israel what he has done for them ("who brought you out of the land of Egypt, out of the house of slavery," v. 2b). Then come the commandments, with sanctions embedded in some of them (as in vv. 5–6, 7, 12). The first commandment demands exclusive covenant loyalty, and the others show what forms that loyalty is to take. As Lord, therefore, God is the suzerain, the head of the covenant relationship.

The heart of that relationship is: "I will be your God, and you shall be my people" (Jer. 7:23; cf. Ex. 6:7; Lev. 26:12; Rev. 21:3, and many other passages). It is amazing that the same Lord whose holiness separates us from him also reaches out to draw us into the circle of his holiness—indeed, to make us his holy people.

THE LORDSHIP ATTRIBUTES

My study of lordship indicates that the word *Lord* in Scripture has certain important connotations. That is, it is not only a name of God, but also a description. Among its connotations, three in particular stand out:

CONTROL

The Lord announces to Moses that he will deliver Israel from Egypt by a mighty hand and a strong arm. He shows his strength in the plagues and

8. For a more detailed discussion of this covenant structure and the literary form of the covenant document, see Meredith G. Kline, *The Structure of Biblical Authority* (Grand Rapids: Eerdmans, 1972). Kline maintains that, not only the Decalogue, but also the book of Deuteronomy, is in its literary form a covenant document.

in the deliverance of Israel through the sea on dry land, followed by the drowning of the Egyptian army. Thus God wins a decisive victory over Egypt, its ruler, and its gods (Ex. 12:12; 15:11; 18:11).

In his continuing relations with Israel, God regularly connects his lordship with his sovereign power, controlling all things. He is gracious to whom he will be gracious, and he shows mercy to whom he will show mercy (Ex. 33:19). What he intends to do, he accomplishes. Nothing is too hard for him (Jer. 32:17; Gen. 18:14). His word is never void of power (Isa. 55:11). His prophecies always come to pass. As I argue in *The Doctrine of God*, chapter 4, God controls the forces of nature, human history, and free human decisions (including sinful ones). It is he who gives faith to some and withholds it from others, so that he is completely sovereign over human salvation.[9] The following passages set forth the comprehensive reach of his sovereign power:

> Who has spoken and it came to pass,
>   unless the Lord has commanded it?
> Is it not from the mouth of the Most High
>   that good and bad come? (Lam. 3:37–38)

> And we know that for those who love God all things work together for good, for those who are called according to his purpose. (Rom. 8:28)

> In him we have obtained an inheritance, having been predestined according to the purpose of him who works all things according to the counsel of his will. (Eph. 1:11)

> Oh, the depth of the riches and wisdom and knowledge of God! How unsearchable are his judgments and how inscrutable his ways! "For who has known the mind of the Lord, or who has been his counselor?" "Or who has given a gift to him that he might be repaid?" For from him and through him and to him are all things. To him be glory forever. Amen. (Rom. 11:33–36)

Authority

God's authority is his right to tell his creatures what they must do. Control is about might; authority is about right. Control means that God makes

---

9. For discussions of how this divine control affects human freedom and moral responsibility, see *DG*, chapter 8. For a discussion of the problem of evil, see *DG*, chapter 9, and *AGG*, chapters 6 and 7.

everything happen; authority means that God has the right to be obeyed, and that therefore we have the obligation to obey him.

God's authority is part of his lordship. When God meets with Moses in Exodus 3, he gives him a message that has authority even over Pharaoh: Let my people go, that they may serve me. When God meets with Israel at Mt. Sinai, he identifies himself as Lord and then tells them to have no other gods before him. God's lordship means that we must obey his Ten Commandments and any other commandments he chooses to give to us. So Deuteronomy 6:4–6 confesses the lordship of God, and then goes on to tell us to obey all his commandments. Jesus, too, says over and over again, in various ways, "If you love me, keep my commandments" (John 14:15; cf. vv. 21, 23; 1 John 5:3). "Why do you call me 'Lord, Lord,'" he asks, "and not do what I tell you?" (Luke 6:46; cf. Matt. 7:21–22).

God's authority is absolute. That means, first, that we shouldn't doubt or question it. Paul says that Abraham did not waver in his belief in God's promise (Rom. 4:16–22). Abraham was certainly tempted to waver. God had promised him the land of Canaan, but he did not own one square inch of it. And God had promised him a son, who would in turn have more descendants than the sand of the sea. But Abraham's wife, Sarah, was beyond the age of childbearing, and Abraham was over one hundred years old before the promise was fulfilled. Nonetheless, Abraham clung to God's authoritative word; so should we.

Second, the absoluteness of God's authority means that his lordship transcends all our other loyalties. We are right to be loyal to our parents, our nation, our friends; but God calls us to love him with *all* our heart, that is, without any rival. Jesus told his disciples to honor their parents (Matt. 15:3–6), but he told them to honor him even more (Matt. 10:34–38).

Third, to say that God's authority is absolute means that it covers all areas of human life. Paul says, "Whether you eat or drink, or whatever you do, do all to the glory of God" (1 Cor. 10:31). Everything we do is either to God's glory or it is not. God has the right to order every aspect of human life.

COVENANT PRESENCE

So God's lordship means that he controls everything, and that he speaks with absolute authority. But there is also a third element to God's lordship, and in some ways this is the deepest and most precious. That element is his commitment to us, and therefore his presence with us.

The essence of the covenant, as we have seen, is God's promise, "I will be your God, and you shall be my people" (Jer. 7:23). God said that to

Abraham (Gen. 17:7), and he also said it to Israel under Moses (Ex. 6:7) and to the New Testament people of God (Rev. 21:3). He said this many times throughout Scripture. This means that the covenant Lord is one who takes people to be his.

When God takes us to be his people, he fights our battles, blesses us, loves us, and sometimes gives us special judgments because of our sins (as in Amos 3:2). But most importantly, he is *with* us. He places his name upon us (Num. 6:27), to brand us as his. Since we are his children, he dwells with us (Gen. 26:3, 24; 28:15; 31:3; Ex. 3:12; 4:12; Deut. 31:8, 23; Josh. 1:5; etc.), and we with him. In the Old Testament, God literally dwells with Israel, as he places his theophany in the tabernacle and the temple. In the New Testament, Jesus is "Immanuel," God with us (Matt. 1:23). He becomes flesh to dwell among us (John 1:14). And after his resurrection, he sends the Spirit to dwell in us, as in a temple.

Control, authority, presence. Those are the main biblical concepts that explain the meaning of God's lordship. We can see this triad in the literary form of the treaty document, mentioned a few pages ago. Recall that in the treaty the great king begins by giving his name (in the Decalogue, Lord). Then, in the historical prologue, he tells the vassal what he has done, how he has delivered them, emphasizing his might and power (control). Next he tells them how they should behave as a response to their deliverance (authority). Then he tells them the blessings for continued obedience and the curses for disobedience (covenant presence). God is not an absentee landlord. He will be present with Israel to bless, and, if necessary, to judge.

THE LORDSHIP ATTRIBUTES AND CHRISTIAN DECISION MAKING

The lordship attributes also help us to understand in more detail the structure of Christian ethics. In particular, they suggest a way for Christians to make ethical decisions.

HOW GOD GOVERNS OUR ETHICAL LIFE

First, by his *control*, God plans and rules nature and history, so that certain human acts are conducive to his glory and others are not.

Second, by his *authority*, he speaks to us clearly, telling us what norms govern our behavior.

Third, by his *covenant presence* he commits himself to be with us in our ethical walk, blessing our obedience and punishing our disobedience. But his presence also provides us with two important means of ethical guidance. First, because he is present with us, he is able to serve as a moral example: "You shall be holy, for I the LORD your God am holy" (Lev. 19:2; cf. Matt. 5:48). Second, he and he alone is able to provide sinners with the power to do good, to set us free from the power of sin (John 8:34–36).

THE DEMAND FOR APPROPRIATE RESPONSE

When we learn of God's *control*, we learn to trust in God's plan and his providence. God told Abraham that he would own the land of Canaan and have a huge number of descendants. But at the time he owned no land in Canaan, and his wife was far beyond the age of childbearing. Nevertheless, his overall attitude toward the promise was one of trust, or faith, as Paul says in Romans 4:20–21, "No distrust made him waver concerning the promise of God, but he grew strong in his faith as he gave glory to God, fully convinced that God was able to do what he had promised." Faith in Christ is faith in what he has done and what he has promised to do in the future. It is trust in God's sovereign care for us.

Next, when we learn of God's *authority*, we learn to obey him. Says God through Moses:

> Now this is the commandment, the statutes and the rules that the LORD your God commanded me to teach you, that you may do them in the land to which you are going over, to possess it, that you may fear the LORD your God, you and your son and your son's son, by keeping all his statutes and his commandments, which I command you, all the days of your life, and that your days may be long. Hear therefore, O Israel, and be careful to do them, that it may go well with you, and that you may multiply greatly, as the LORD, the God of your fathers, has promised you, in a land flowing with milk and honey. (Deut. 6:1–3; cf. vv. 6–9 and many similar verses in Deuteronomy)

The psalmist says:

> You have commanded your precepts
> 　to be kept diligently.
> Oh that my ways may be steadfast
> 　in keeping your statutes!
> Then I shall not be put to shame,
> 　having my eyes fixed on all your commandments. (Ps. 119:4–6)

God's control motivates us to trust; his authority motivates us to obey. "Trust and obey, for there's no other way to be happy in Jesus," as the hymn puts it.[10] David says, "Trust in the LORD, and do good; dwell in the land and befriend faithfulness" (Ps. 37:3).

Finally, when we become aware of God's *covenant presence,* we are moved to worship. Whenever God meets with human beings in Scripture, the situation immediately becomes one of worship: when the King enters, we bow down. Think of Moses at the burning bush (Ex. 3) or Isaiah meeting God in the temple:

> In the year that King Uzziah died I saw the Lord sitting upon a throne, high and lifted up; and the train of his robe filled the temple. Above him stood the seraphim. Each had six wings: with two he covered his face, and with two he covered his feet, and with two he flew. And one called to another and said:
>
> > "Holy, holy, holy is the LORD of hosts;
> > the whole earth is full of his glory!"
>
> And the foundations of the thresholds shook at the voice of him who called, and the house was filled with smoke. And I said: "Woe is me! For I am lost; for I am a man of unclean lips, and I dwell in the midst of a people of unclean lips; for my eyes have seen the King, the LORD of hosts!" (Isa. 6:1–5)

The apostle John tells that when the glorified Jesus appeared to him, "I fell at his feet as though dead" (Rev. 1:17).

Three lordship attributes, three mandatory responses: faith, obedience, worship. These responses are the foundation of our ethical life.[11]

THE THREE THEOLOGICAL VIRTUES

Faith, hope, and love are three virtues often brought together in the New Testament (1 Cor. 13:13; Gal. 5:5–6; Col. 1:4–5; 1 Thess. 1:3; 5:8; Heb. 6:9–11). Christian writers after the New Testament sometimes presented these "theological virtues" as supplements to the four "cardinal virtues" of Greek philosophy (prudence, justice, temperance, and courage). That gave them a total of seven, which, of course, is a desirable number.

10. Words by John H. Sammis, 1887.
11. Thanks to Mike Christ, who first suggested this triad to me. I've modified his formulation a bit, added exposition, and take full responsibility. Readers who are new to my triads will learn that they can be shuffled and rearranged without problem. Ultimately, as we shall see, each member of the triad includes the others. So different arrangements are possible and often edifying.

The idea that Christian morality is a supplement to pagan morality is an inadequate view, as I plan to argue in more detail at a later point. Scripture does affirm all seven of these virtues, but it gives some preeminence to faith, hope, and love. Love is the highest of these, according to 1 Corinthians 13:13, John 13:34–35, and other passages. Occasionally Paul speaks of faith and love, without referring to hope (Eph. 1:15; 3:17; 6:23; 1 Tim. 1:14; 6:11; 2 Tim. 1:13; Philem. 1:5). Faith includes hope, for hope is faith directed to God's promises for the future. And love, as the summation of Christian virtues, includes both faith and hope.

We can also look at this triad in terms of the lordship attributes. Faith trusts in God's revealed Word. Hope looks to God's controlling power, which will accomplish his purposes in the future, as in the past. And love treasures the presence of God in the intimate recesses of the heart and the new family into which God has adopted us.

NECESSARY AND SUFFICIENT CRITERIA OF GOOD WORKS

What is a good work? Reformed theologians have addressed this question in response to the problem of the so-called virtuous pagan. Reformed theology teaches that human beings are by nature totally depraved. This means, not that they are as bad as they could be, but that it is impossible for them to please God in any of their thoughts, words, or deeds (Rom. 8:8). Apart from grace, none of us can do anything good in the sight of God. Yet all around us we see non-Christians who seem to be doing good works: they love their families, work hard at their jobs, contribute to the needs of the poor, and show kindness to their neighbors. It seems that these people are virtuous apart from Christ.

Reformed theology, however, questions such virtue. It acknowledges that unbelievers often contribute to the betterment of society. These contributions are called civic righteousness. Their civic righteousness does not please God, however, because it is altogether devoid of three crucial characteristics:

> Works done by unregenerate men, although for the matter of them they may be things which God commands; and of good use both to themselves and others: yet, because they proceed not from an heart purified by faith; nor are done in a right manner, according to the Word; nor to a right end, the glory of God, they are therefore sinful, and cannot please God, or make a man meet to receive grace from God: and yet, their neglect of them is more sinful and displeasing unto God. (WCF, 16.7)

Note the three necessary ingredients: (1) a heart purified by faith, (2) obedience to God's Word, and (3) the right end, the glory of God.

The first is a plainly biblical emphasis. The Westminster Confession cites Hebrews 11:4 and some other texts. Romans 14:23 also comes to mind, which says, "For whatever does not proceed from faith is sin." In Jesus' arguments with the Pharisees, too, it is evident that our righteousness must not be merely external (see especially Matt. 23:25–26). In describing the necessity of an internal motive for good works, Scripture refers not only to faith, but especially to love, as in 1 Corinthians 13:1–3 and many other passages. We learn from these passages that love is not only necessary for good works, but also sufficient; that is, if our act is motivated by a true love of God and neighbor, we have fulfilled the law (Matt. 22:40; Rom. 13:8; Gal. 5:14).

The second element of good works, according to the Confession, is obedience to God's Word, to his law. Note the references in the previous section to the importance of obeying God's Word. Certainly obedience to God's Word is a necessary condition of good works, for disobedience to God's law is the very definition of sin (1 John 3:4). It is also a sufficient condition, for if we have obeyed God perfectly, we have done everything necessary to be good in his sight. Of course, among God's commands are his commands to love (see the above paragraph) and to seek his glory (see the next paragraph).

The third element is the right end, the glory of God. Ethical literature has often discussed the *summum bonum*, or highest good, for human beings. What is it that we are trying to achieve in our ethical actions? Many secular writers have said this goal is pleasure or human happiness. But Scripture says that in everything we do we should be seeking the glory of God (1 Cor. 10:31). Any act must glorify God if it is to be good, so seeking God's glory is a necessary condition of good works. And if an act does glorify God, then it is good; thus, glorifying God is a sufficient condition of good works.[12]

So there are three necessary and sufficient conditions of good works: right motive, right standard, and right goal.[13] Right motive corresponds to the lordship attribute of covenant presence, for it is God's Spirit dwelling in us who places faith and love in our hearts. Right standard corresponds

---

12. There is a sense, of course, in which even wicked acts bring glory to God, for God uses the wickedness of people to bring about his good purposes (Rom. 8:28). But the wicked person does not intend to glorify God by his actions. So 1 Corinthians 10:31 speaks of intent as well as action. Cf. Matt. 6:33.

13. Cornelius Van Til, in *Christian Theistic Ethics*, was the first to think through the significance of this confessional triad for ethical methodology. I gratefully acknowledge his influence upon my formulation here. In fact, Van Til's discussion was the seed thought for all my triadic thinking.

to God's lordship attribute of authority. And right goal corresponds to the lordship attribute of control, for it is God's creation and providence that determine what acts will and will not lead to God's glory. God determines the consequences of our actions, and he determines which actions lead to our *summum bonum*.

BIBLICAL REASONS TO DO GOOD WORKS

The history of redemption. There are basically three ways in which Scripture encourages believers to do good works. First, it appeals to the history of redemption. This is the chief motivation in the Decalogue itself: God has redeemed Israel from slavery in Egypt; therefore, his people should obey him.

In the New Testament, the writers often urge us to do good works because of what Christ did to redeem us. Jesus himself urges his disciples to "love one another: just as I have loved you, you also are to love one another" (John 13:34). Jesus' love, ultimately displayed on the cross, commands our response of love to one another. Another well-known appeal is found in Colossians 3:1–3: "If then you have been raised with Christ, seek the things that are above, where Christ is, seated at the right hand of God. Set your minds on things that are above, not on things that are on earth. For you have died, and your life is hidden with Christ in God."

When Christ died, we died to sin; when he rose, we rose to righteousness. We are one with Christ in his death and resurrection. So those historic facts have moral implications. We should live in accord with the new life, given to us by God's grace when we rose with Christ (see also Rom. 6:1–23; 13:11–12; 1 Cor. 6:20; 10:11; 15:58; Eph. 4:1–5, 25, 32; 5:25–33; Phil. 2:1–11; Heb. 12:1–28; 1 Peter 2:1–3; 4:1–6).

So the Heidelberg Catechism emphasizes that our good works come from gratitude. They are not attempts to gain God's favor, but rather are grateful responses to the favor he has already shown to us.[14]

But our focus on the history of redemption is not limited to the past. It is also an anticipation of what God will do for us in the future. God's promises of future blessing also motivate us to obey him. Jesus commands us, "Seek

---

14. This motivation is not what John Piper calls "the debtor's ethic," in which we do good works in a vain attempt to pay God back for our redemption. We can, of course, never do that, and we should not try to do it. See Piper, *The Purifying Power of Living by Faith in Future Grace* (Sisters, OR: Multnomah Books, 1995), 31–39, and the summary discussion in *Brothers, We Are Not Professionals* (Nashville: Broadman and Holman, 2002), 33–38. But gratefulness, nonetheless, is the only legitimate response to the grace God has given us in Christ.

first the kingdom of God and his righteousness, and all these things will be added to you" (Matt. 6:33).[15]

This motivation emphasizes God's control, for history is the sphere of God's control, the outworking of his eternal plan.

The authority of God's commands. Scripture also motivates our good works by calling attention to God's commands. Jesus said that he did not come to abrogate the law, but to fulfill it: "Therefore whoever relaxes one of the least of these commandments and teaches others to do the same will be called least in the kingdom of heaven, but whoever does them and teaches them will be called great in the kingdom of heaven" (Matt. 5:19). In their preaching, Jesus and the apostles often appeal to the commandments of the law and to their own commandments (see Matt. 7:12; 12:5; 19:18–19; 22:36–40; 23:23; Luke 10:26; John 8:17; 13:34–35; 14:15, 21; Rom. 8:4; 13:8–10; 1 Cor. 9:8–9; 14:34, 37; Gal. 4:21–22; Eph. 4:20–24; 6:1–3; 1 Thess. 4:1; 2 Tim. 3:16–17; Titus 2:1; James 1:22–25; 2:8–13; 1 Peter 1:16; 1 John 2:3–5; 3:24; 5:2).

God's commandment is sufficient to place an obligation upon us. We should need no other incentive. But God gives us other motivations as well, because we are fallen and because he loves us as his redeemed children.

This motivation reflects God's lordship attribute of authority. We should obey him, simply because he has the right to absolute obedience.

The presence of the Spirit. Scripture calls us to a godly life, based on the activity of the Spirit within us. This motivation is based on God's lordship attribute of presence. Paul says, "But I say, walk by the Spirit, and you will not gratify the desires of the flesh. For the desires of the flesh are against the Spirit, and the desires of the Spirit are against the flesh, for these are opposed to each other, to keep you from doing the things you want to do" (Gal. 5:16–17). God has placed his Spirit within us to give us new life and therefore new ethical inclinations. There is still conflict among our impulses, but we have the resources to follow the desires of the Spirit, rather than those of the flesh. So Paul appeals to the inner change that God has worked in us by regeneration and sanctification. In Ephesians 5:8–11, he puts it this way: "For at one time you were darkness, but now you are light in the Lord. Walk as children of light (for the fruit of light is found in all that is good and right and true), and try to discern what is pleasing to the Lord. Take no part in the unfruitful works of darkness, but instead expose them." In the verses that follow, Paul continues to

---

15. This is what Piper calls "future grace" in the works cited in the previous note.

expound on the ethical implications of this transformation (cf. Rom. 8:1–17; Gal. 5:22–26).

So Scripture motivates us to do good works by the history of redemption, the commandments of God, and the work of the Spirit within us, corresponding to God's lordship attributes of control, authority, and presence, respectively.

Types of Christian Ethics

These three motivations have led Christian thinkers to develop three main types of Christian ethics: command ethics, narrative ethics, and virtue ethics. Command ethics emphasizes the authority of God's moral law. Narrative ethics emphasizes the history of redemption. It teaches ethics by telling the story of salvation. Virtue ethics discusses the inner character of the regenerate person, focusing on virtues listed in passages like Romans 5:1–5, Galatians 5:22–23, and Colossians 3:12–17.

Sometimes a writer will pit these types of ethics against one another, designating one as superior to the others. I don't see any biblical justification for that kind of argument. As we saw, Scripture uses all of these methods to motivate righteous behavior. And it is hard to see how any of these could function without the others. It is God's commands that define the virtues and enable us to evaluate the behavior of characters in the narrative. It is the narrative that shows us how God saves us from sin and enables us to keep his law from the heart. And the virtues define what the redeemed person looks like when he obeys God from the heart.

What Really Matters

We can see the same triadic structure in the actual content of biblical ethics. I shall expound this structure at length later in the book. For now, let us note statements of the apostle Paul that intend to show the highest priorities of the Christian life. In these passages, he is opposing Judaizers, who think that one must be circumcised to enter the kingdom of God. He replies that neither circumcision nor uncircumcision is important, but rather something else:

> For neither circumcision counts for anything nor uncircumcision, but keeping the commandments of God. (1 Cor. 7:19)

> For in Christ Jesus neither circumcision nor uncircumcision counts for anything, but only faith working through love. (Gal. 5:6)

> For neither circumcision counts for anything, nor uncircumcision, but a new creation. (Gal. 6:15)

As mentioned earlier, there is a reference in 1 Corinthians 7:19 to keeping the commandments of God. It corresponds to God's lordship attribute of authority. "Faith working through love" in Galatians 5:6 is the work of the Spirit within us, and refers to God's covenant presence. "New creation" in Galatians 6:15 is the great redemptive-historical change brought about by Jesus' death and resurrection, the powerful work of God's sovereign control over history.[16]

FACTORS IN ETHICAL JUDGMENT

Imagine that you are a pastor or a counselor, and someone comes to your office with an ethical problem. Basically, there are three things that you will need to discuss: the situation, the Word of God, and the inquirer himself.

Normally, we ask first about the situation: "What's your problem? What brings you to see me?" This question is ultimately about God's lordship attribute of control, for God is the one who brings situations about.

Then we ask, "What does God's Word say about the problem?" This discussion invokes God's lordship attribute of authority.

Thirdly, we focus on the inquirer, asking how he or she needs to change in order to apply God's solution to the problem. At this point, we are thinking especially about God's presence within the individual. If the person is a non-Christian, then evidently he needs to be born again by God's Spirit before he can apply the Word of God to his life. If the person is a believer, he may need to grow in certain ways before he will be able to deal with the issue before him.

We note in such conversations that each of these subjects influences the other two. We may start with a presentation problem: "My wife is angry all the time." But as we move to a focus on God's Word, gaining a better understanding of Scripture, we may gain a better understanding of the problem as well. For example, Scripture tells us to remove the log from our own eye before trying to get the speck out of another's eye (Matt. 7:3). So the inquirer may come to see that his wife is angry because he has provoked her. So the problem now is not only in her, but in him as well. Reflection on God's Word has changed our understanding of the problem.

But this new understanding of the problem pushes us to look at more and different Scripture texts than we considered in the beginning. As we understand the problem better, we understand better how Scripture relates to it. Scripture and the situation illumine one another.

---

16. Thanks to my colleague, Prof. Reggie Kidd, for bringing these texts to my attention.

Then, when we move to the third question and ask the inquirer to look within, he may see even more things in himself that have provoked his wife's anger. So the problem, God's Word, and the inquirer have all illumined one another. You cannot understand your problem or yourself adequately until you have seen it through what Calvin calls "the spectacles of Scripture." And you can't understand the problem until you see yourself as a part of it.

And you can't understand God's Word rightly until you can use it, until you see how it applies to this situation and that. This is a more difficult point, but I think it is important. If someone says he understands "You shall not steal," but has no idea to what situations that commandment applies (such as embezzling, cheating on taxes, and shoplifting), then he hasn't really understood the biblical command. Understanding Scripture, understanding its meaning, involves *applying* it to situations. A person who understands the Bible is a person who is able to use it to answer his questions, to guide his life. As I argued in chapter 2, theology is application.

Perspectives on the Discipline of Ethics

In general, then, ethical judgment involves the application of a *norm* to a *situation* by a *person*. These three factors can also be seen as overall perspectives on the study of ethics:

The situational perspective. In this perspective, we examine situations, or problems. This study focuses on God's actions in creation and providence that have made the situations what they are, hence God's lordship attribute of control. The situational perspective asks, "What are the best means of accomplishing God's purposes?" That is, how can we take the present situation and change it so that more of God's purposes are achieved?

God's ultimate purpose is his own glory (1 Cor. 10:31). But God has more specific goals as well: the filling and subduing of the earth (Gen. 1:28), the evangelization and nurture of people of all nations (Matt. 28:19–20), and the success of his kingdom (Matt. 6:33).

The situational perspective explores the consequences of our actions. From this perspective, we ask, "If we do this, will it enhance the glory of God and his blessing on his people?" We seek the best means to achieve the ends that please God. We might describe ethics from this perspective as a Christian *teleological* or *consequential* ethic.

The normative perspective. From the normative perspective, we focus on Scripture more directly. Our purpose is to determine our duty, our ethical norm, our obligation. So we bring our problem to the Bible and ask, "What does Scripture say about this situation?" At this point, we invoke God's lordship attribute of authority. Since we are focusing on duties and obligations, we might call this perspective a Christian *deontological* ethic.

The existential perspective. The existential perspective focuses on the ethical agent, the person (or persons) who are trying to find out what to do. From this perspective, the ethical question becomes, "How must I change if I am to do God's will?" Here the focus is inward, examining our heart's relationship to God. It deals with our regeneration, our sanctification, our inner character. These are all the product of God's lordship attribute of presence within us.

INTERDEPENDENCE OF THE PERSPECTIVES

We have seen previously that knowledge of our situation, knowledge of our norm, and knowledge of our self are interdependent. You can't understand the situation fully until you know what Scripture says about it and until you understand your own role in the situation. You can't understand yourself fully, apart from Scripture or apart from the situation that is your environment. And you don't understand Scripture unless you can apply it to situations and to yourself.

So the situational perspective includes the other two. When we understand the situation rightly, we see that Scripture and the self are elements of that situation, facts to be taken account of. So we can't rightly assess the situation unless we assess the other two factors.

The same is true of the normative perspective. To understand Scripture is to understand its applications to the situation and the self.

Similarly with the existential perspective: as we ask questions about our inner life, we find that the situation and God's revelation are both elements of our personal experience, apart from which we cannot make sense of ourselves.

So each perspective necessitates consideration of the others. Each includes the others. Figure 1 pictures the content of ethics as a triangle. You can begin your study of ethics at any of the three corners. But as you advance through the triangle, you will eventually meet up with the other corners. For example, if you start to study the situation, you will eventually find yourself studying the norm and the ethical agent.

That's why I describe these approaches as "perspectives." I don't think of them as "parts" of ethics, as though you could divide the triangle into three distinct parts and then study each one separately. No, you can't really study the situation without the norm, and so on.

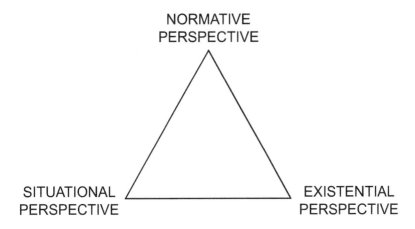

Fig. 1. The Triangle of Ethics

So the triangle represents the whole subject matter of ethics, and the corners represent different entrances to that subject matter, different emphases, different initial questions. But the goal is always to cover the whole triangle with regard to any ethical question.

In the end, then, the three perspectives coincide. A true understanding of the situation will not contradict a true understanding of the Word or the self. And a true understanding of each will include true understandings of the others.

But if the three are ultimately identical, why do we need three? Why not just one? The reason has to do with our finitude and sin. God knows all truth simultaneously, from every possible perspective. He knows what the whole universe looks like to the eye of the snail on my window ledge. But you and I are finite, not omniscient. We can only see a portion of reality at a time. That is to say, we can only see the world from one perspective at a time. For that reason, it is good for us to move from one perspective to another. Just as the blind man had to move from the elephant's leg to its trunk, to its torso, to its head, and finally to its tail in order to get an adequate picture of the elephant, so we need to move from one perspective to another in order to get a full understanding of God's world.

And we are sinners in Adam. According to Romans 1, that means that we have a tendency to suppress the truth, to exchange the truth for a lie, to try to push God out of our knowledge. Salvation turns us in a different direction, so that we are able to seek the truth. But the continued presence of sin in our minds and hearts means that we need to keep checking up on ourselves, and multiplying perspectives is one helpful way to do that.

In ethics, the three perspectives I have mentioned are especially helpful. The three perspectives serve as checks and balances on one another. The normative perspective can correct mistakes in my understanding of the situation. But the opposite is also true: my understanding of the norm can be improved when I better understand the situation to which the norm is to be applied. Likewise, *mutatis mutandis*, for the existential perspective.

Multiperspectivalism is not relativism. I am not saying that any viewpoint is a legitimate perspective. There is in ethics and in other disciplines an absolute right and wrong. The procedure I have outlined above is a means for us to discover that absolute right and wrong.

Scripture itself is absolutely right: inspired, infallible, inerrant. But we are fallible in our study of Scripture. To understand it rightly we need information outside the Bible, including knowledge of Hebrew and Greek grammar, knowledge of ancient history, and an understanding of those contemporary questions that people pose to Scripture.

TRIPERSPECTIVALISM AND THE REFORMED FAITH

In the next chapter, I shall apply this threefold scheme to debates between Christians and non-Christians on ethical matters. Here, briefly, I should like to speak about debates within the Christian fold.

I belong to the Reformed theological tradition, and I subscribe, with some exceptions, to the teachings of the Reformed confessions. Many of my readers (though I hope not all of them) come from that tradition as well. In this book, I shall often quote Reformed confessions, catechisms, and theologians. I don't think that the Reformed tradition has said the final word in theology, and there are some topics on which I disagree with many Reformed people. Some of those discussions will appear in this book. But in general I think that among all the traditions of Christian theology, the Reformed tradition is the closest to Scripture.

Some people in the Reformed tradition think that my triperspectival scheme is relativistic. I have responded to that criticism in the preceding section. Others think it is at best an innovation. I agree that the technical terms are new. But it seems to me that the basic ideas are an outworking of traditional Reformed theology.

The three categories first caught my interest when I read Cornelius Van Til's discussion of goal, motive, and standard.[17] As I mentioned earlier, Van Til derived that triad from the Westminster Confession of Faith. He

---

17. See the above discussion of the necessary and sufficient criteria of good works.

also spoke much about the interdependence of revelation from God, from nature, and from man: we get revelation from God about nature, revelation from nature about God, and so forth.[18]

More fundamentally, it is important to understand that Reformed theology has always strongly emphasized God's revelation in the creation and in human persons (God's image), as well as his revelation in Scripture.

Other branches of the church have often criticized Reformed ethics for being merely an ethics of law. Reformed theology has indeed had a more positive view of God's law than some other theological traditions, such as Lutheranism, dispensationalism, and charismatic theology. And occasionally Reformed writers have emphasized law in such a way as to detract from other aspects of biblical ethics. But in the debate between traditions it is important to make clear that the Reformed faith at its best has emphasized, not only law, but also a strong view of God's revelation in creation and in human beings. Calvin and the Reformed Confessions typically begin by invoking the teaching of Psalm 19 and Romans 1, the clarity of God's revelation throughout the universe. And Calvin, on the first page of his *Institutes*, notes that we cannot know God without knowing ourselves, or ourselves without knowing God.[19] And he disclaims knowledge of which comes first.

So in the theological debate, Reformed ethicists can rightly insist that their ethical tradition is not just an elaboration of God's law. God's law is our ultimate and sufficient ethical standard, but we must understand that standard by relating it to the divine revelation in the world and in ourselves. Reformed ethics can account for the nuances and subtleties of ethical decision making, without compromising the straightforward, simple unity of our obligation, namely, to obey God as he has revealed his will in Scripture.

18. Van Til, *An Introduction to Systematic Theology* (Nutley, NJ: Presbyterian and Reformed, 1974), 62–109.
19. 1.1.1.

PART TWO

NON-CHRISTIAN
ETHICS

CHAPTER 4

Lordship and Non-Christian Ethics

In chapter 3, I examined the general structure of a biblical ethic based on God's lordship, particularly his lordship attributes of control, authority, and presence. In this chapter, I will use that discussion to indicate the most important ways in which Christian ethics is different from non-Christian ethics.

In general, non-Christian ethics does not affirm the lordship of the God of the Bible.[1] I will seek to show here how a denial of divine lordship affects ethics. However, I will compare Christian and non-Christian thought in metaphysics and epistemology, before dealing specifically with ethics.

TRANSCENDENCE AND IMMANENCE[2]

The lordship attributes will help us to get a clear idea of the concepts of transcendence and immanence, which theologians often use to describe the biblical God. These are not biblical terms, but the Bible does speak of God being "on high" as well as "with us." He is both "up there" and "down here." He is exalted, and he is near. When Scripture speaks of God being up there, theologians call it transcendence. When Scripture speaks of God being down here with us, theologians speak of immanence.

1. I shall try to show that by specific examples in later chapters. I realize that the followers of such religions as Judaism and Islam would claim to worship the God of the Bible while denying the full supremacy of Christ. While opposing orthodox Christianity, they would claim to be serving the Lord. I will deal with that claim in chapter 5.
2. This section summarizes chapter 7 of DG.

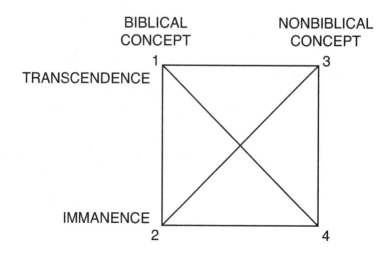

Fig. 2. The Square of Opposition: Transcendence and Immanence

There are dangers, however, in the concepts of transcendence and immanence. We can understand those dangers more clearly by looking at the
diagram in figure 2.[3]

Views 1 and 2, on the left side, represent a biblical understanding of
transcendence and immanence; views 3 and 4, on the right side, represent
common nonbiblical views.

In Scripture, God is transcendent (view 1) in that he is exalted as Lord,
as King. We should associate transcendence with the lordship attributes
of control and authority. He is immanent (view 2) in the sense that he is
covenantally present with us. So understood, there is no contradiction, not
even a tension, between divine transcendence and immanence.

Some, however, have misunderstood God's transcendence. They think
it means that God is so far away from us that we cannot really know him,
so far away that human language can't describe him accurately, so far away
that he's just a great heavenly blur, without any definite characteristics.
That view, that of nonbiblical transcendence, is view 3 on the diagram. If
God is transcendent in that way, how can he also be near to us? That kind
of transcendence is incompatible with biblical immanence (view 2). That
incompatibility is represented by a diagonal line between views 2 and 3.

Further, we *can* know definite things about God because they are revealed
to us in the Bible. Despite the limitations of human language, God is able
to use it to tell us clearly and accurately who he is and what he has done.

3. In the first printing of *DG*, p. 113, the diagram is misnumbered. It should be numbered as here. The diagram as presented on p. 14 of *DKG* is correct.

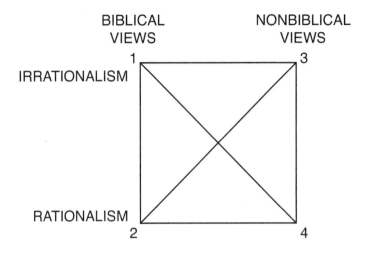

Fig. 3. The Square of Opposition: Irrationalism and Rationalism

These are aspects of God's immanence in the biblical sense (view 2), which are rejected by those who hold the nonbiblical concept of transcendence (view 3).

The term *immanence* is similarly misunderstood. Some theologians speak as though God's immanence immerses him in the world, hides him in the world, so that he can't be clearly distinguished from it (view 4). Some people even think that when you look deep down inside yourself, you discover that you are God and God is you. But that's not biblical. God is always distinct from the world, for he is the Creator and we are the creature. But God does come to be with us (the meaning of *Immanuel,* the name of Jesus in Matthew 1:23), and that's something wonderful and precious.

So the nonbiblical view of immanence (view 4) contradicts the biblical view of transcendence (view 1), confusing the Creator with the creature and giving God's sovereign control and authority to the world. The diagonal line between view 1 and view 4 indicates this contradiction.

IRRATIONALISM AND RATIONALISM

Let me now change the labels on the diagram, in order to present a similar argument about epistemology, or the theory of knowledge. In figure 3, I am replacing "transcendence" and "immanence" with "irrationalism" and "rationalism," respectively.[4]

4. For this discussion, compare *DKG,* 360–63, and *CVT,* 231–38.

Since Scripture teaches us that God is the ultimate controller and authority for human life, he is also the author of truth and the ultimate criterion of human knowledge. Therefore, our knowing is not ultimate, or, as Van Til liked to put it, autonomous. Human knowledge is "thinking God's thoughts after him," in submission to his revelation of the truth, recognizing his revelation as the supreme and final standard of truth and falsehood, right and wrong. Non-Christians (and Christians who compromise with secular ways of thinking) look at this principle as irrationalistic. They are appalled at the idea that we should renounce our intellectual autonomy and accept God's Word on his authority alone. To Christians, doing this is not irrationalistic at all; rather, it is the way God designed our minds to think. But it does involve confessing that human reason is limited, subordinate to God's perfect reason. So we can interpret view 1 of the rectangle as Christian "irrationalism" (note the quotation marks).

But we believe not only that human reason is limited, but also that under God our reason has great power. Since God has come into our world and has clearly revealed himself here, we are able to know many things with certainty. Non-Christians tend to see such claims of knowledge as rationalistic. How can anybody, they ask, be sure of anything in this confusing world? So I would label view 2 as Christian "rationalism." Again, note the quotation marks. Christians plead not guilty to the charge of rationalism, because they recognize that God's mind is far greater than ours, and therefore that the realm of mystery (view 1) is far greater than the realm of our knowledge. But they also recognize that through God's revelation they have access to real truth.

In the current debate between modernists and postmodernists, the modernists tend to accuse Christians of irrationalism—of believing biblical doctrines without sufficient reason. Postmodernists charge Christians with rationalism. They think Christians are arrogant to claim that they can know anything for sure.

But when we turn the tables, allowing ourselves as Christians to comment on non-Christian epistemology, we find ourselves saying about them what they say about us. That is, we say that they are irrationalistic and rationalistic. The nonbiblical view of transcendence holds that God either does not exist or is too far away from us to play a role in our reasoning. But if that is true, we have no access to an ultimate standard of truth. Such a view is skeptical or irrationalistic, as I would label view 3 on the diagram. The diagonal line between view 2 and view 3 shows the contradiction between them: the Christian says that God has come near us and has given us a clear revelation of truth; the non-Christian denies that and prefers skepticism.

But there is another side to non-Christian reasoning. For everyone who rejects divine authority must accept some other authority. Reasoning cannot be reasoning without some standard of truth and falsehood. The non-Christian either assumes the ultimate authority of his own reason (autonomy), or he accepts some authority other than that of the God of Scripture. In any case, he substitutes the authority of a creature for that of the Creator. He assumes that we have access apart from God to an authority that will allow our reasoning to be successful. That position (view 4) is rationalism, and it contradicts the limitations on reason asserted by view 1.

So Van Til argued that unregenerate human beings are rationalists and irrationalists at the same time. They claim that their own reason has ultimate authority (rationalism), but they acknowledge nothing that will connect human reason with objective truth (irrationalism).[5]

The rationalist-irrationalist dialectic of non-Christian thought bears on ethical reasoning, as well as on thinking about other matters. As we shall see, nonbiblical ethicists often oppose absolutes in general, but they forget their opposition to absolutes when they propose their own fundamental ethical principles, such as love or justice. One egregious example is provided by Joseph Fletcher. In his book *Situation Ethics*, he says that "for the situationist there are no rules—none at all," but in the same paragraph he proposes a "'general' proposition . . . namely, the commandment to love God through the neighbor." Is there a contradiction here between "no rules" and the rule of love? Fletcher replies enigmatically that the love commandment "is, be it noted, a normative ideal; it is *not* an operational directive."[6] Evidently he thinks that the love commandment is not a commandment, and therefore not a rule. But this distinction is quite implausible.

SPECIFICALLY ETHICAL INTERPRETATIONS OF THE RECTANGLE

I have used the rectangular diagram to illustrate the difference between those who accept the lordship of the biblical God and those who reject it, both in metaphysics (transcendence and immanence) and in epistemology (irrationalism and rationalism). I will refer to these metaphysical and epistemological interpretations in my critical evaluation of non-Christian

5. For more discussion of the rationalist-irrationalist dialectic in non-Christian thought, see my *CVT*, chapter 17, and *DKG*, 360–63.

6. Joseph F. Fletcher, *Situation Ethics: The New Morality* (Philadelphia: Westminster Press, 1966), 55.

ethical systems. There are, however, still other interpretations of the rectangle that are more specifically ethical in their meaning.

ABSOLUTENESS AND RELEVANCE OF THE MORAL LAW

Most writers on ethics would like to discover principles that are absolute (and so obligatory) and are also relevant (bearing on practical ethical decisions). In a biblical worldview, the law of God, our ethical standard, is absolute (view 1 on the diagram) because of God's absolute control and authority. Yet it is also relevant (view 2) because God reveals it to us in our experience through his covenant presence. He is with us in the ethical struggle. He knows the problems with which we must deal and has indeed designed the moral law with our situation fully in view.

But those who reject the biblical worldview find it difficult to achieve either absoluteness or relevance. The absoluteness of the moral law, for them, is the absoluteness of an opaque reality, which says nothing clearly (view 3). And relevance becomes the relevance of creatures talking to themselves (view 4). We shall see that among some non-Christian thinkers the authority of a moral principle is in proportion to its abstractness, that is, its irrelevance. The more specific and more relevant an ethical principle is, the less authority it has. For example, in Plato the highest ethical principle is abstract Goodness, which has no specific content at all. The same is true of Fletcher's view of love.

There is a religious reason for this antithesis between absoluteness and content. The non-Christian ethicist would like to believe, and would like others to believe, that he has moral standards and that it is possible to have moral standards without God. But he doesn't want to be bound by any rules. He wants to be autonomous. So he arrives at the paradoxical notion of absolutes without content: an appearance of moral principle, without any real moral principle at all. The alternative, of course, which has the same motive, is a moral content without authority. So in non-Christian ethics, there is an inverse relationship between the authority of a principle and its content, or relevance.

DIVINE SOVEREIGNTY AND HUMAN RESPONSIBILITY

In the Christian understanding, God's sovereignty is his lordship. So it entails his control and authority over all things (view 1 on the diagram).[7]

---

7. For a discussion of divine sovereignty and human freedom and responsibility, see *DG*, chapters 4, 8, and 9.

But his authority also entails human responsibility: what God says, we must do. And his authority is not a bare command, for he enters our history in Christ to live our lives and to redeem us. So our responsibility is not only a response to God's authority (view 1), but also to his covenant presence (view 2).

So human responsibility does not conflict with God's authority or presence. But what of his control? Does God's control of our actions compromise our responsibility? Those who reject this biblical world-view often argue that ethical responsibility presupposes total human autonomy to perform actions that are not caused by God, our environment, or even our own desires—actions that are totally uncaused. This view of freedom is sometimes called libertarianism. I have argued that libertarianism is incoherent and that it is not the ground of moral responsibility.[8] When a court examines whether Bill is responsible for committing murder, it cannot possibly use the libertarian criterion, for it would be impossible to prove that Bill's action is totally uncaused. Yet some such view is implicit in the idea that creatures are autonomous (view 4 on the diagram).

The only alternative, on a nonbiblical worldview, as I see it, is that our actions are controlled by some unknown reality (view 3 on the diagram). But a being of whom we are wholly ignorant cannot be the ground of our responsibility. Further, since we know nothing of such a force, we must regard it as impersonal. But an impersonal force cannot be the ground of ethical responsibility. We cannot incur ethical obligations to forces like gravity or electromagnetism. Ethical obligation is fundamentally personal, arising out of loyalty and love.[9]

So it is not the control of God over our actions that compromises our responsibility. Rather, it is worldviews that deny God's control and affirm libertarian freedom that destroy our responsibility. God's control supports our responsibility, by providing a personal context in which alone our choices can have meaning.

OBJECTIVITY AND INWARDNESS

The Bible teaches that the law of God is objective in the sense that its meaning does not depend on us. It comes from God's authoritative word (view 1). Yet God is not pleased with merely external obedience. He wants his word to be written on the human heart, where it motivates us from

---

8. *DG*, chapter 8.
9. Compare my "moral argument for the existence of God" in *AGG*, 93–102.

within. In the new covenant (Jer. 31:31–34), God writes his word, his moral law, on the hearts of his people. That is an aspect of his covenant presence (view 2). In the Christian worldview, moral standards are both objective and inward.

Those who deny that worldview must seek objectivity in an unknowable realm (view 3), where the moral standard cannot be known at all, let alone objectively. They seek inwardness by making each person his own moral standard (view 4). But that dispenses with all objectivity and leaves us with nothing to internalize.

HUMILITY AND HOPE

God's transcendence (view 1) shows us how small we are and promotes humility. But God has come into our history (view 2) to promise us, by grace, great blessings in Christ. We are indeed small, but we are God's people and therefore great. A non-Christian, however, is either driven to pride, because he is his own autonomous standard (view 4), or to despair, because he is lost in an unknown, uncaring universe (view 3).

FREEDOM AND AUTHORITY IN SOCIETY

We should also consider the implications of lordship in regard to social ethics. Most of those who write about the role of the state want to achieve a balance between law and order, on the one hand, and individual freedom, on the other. In Scripture, God gives control and authority to civil rulers in his name (Rom. 13:1–6), providing a basis for civil law and order. This view of civil authority can be placed in position 1 on our diagram. But the authority of the civil ruler is not absolute; it is limited by God's higher authority. Furthermore, God sets standards for civil rulers, as for all rulers. They are not to be tyrants, to "lord it over" people; rather, they are to serve those whom they rule, as Jesus himself came not to be served, but to serve (Matt. 20:25–28).[10] In this respect, they are to reflect God's own covenant presence, his covenant solidarity with his people. So they should seek what is best for their subjects. The ruler's power is also limited by the powers of other God-appointed authorities, as in the family and the church. So Scripture gives us a charter for limited government and personal liberty. We may place this teaching at point 2 of the diagram.

10. Jesus speaks here primarily of the apostles' role as leaders of the church. But since he compares their work to the work of Gentile civil authorities, he implicitly makes his own servanthood the model for Christian civil rulers as well. I shall consider the relation of church and state more fully under the fifth commandment.

Non-Christian social and political philosophy is also concerned about law and order, on the one hand, and personal liberty, on the other. But their arguments for law and order tend toward the extreme of totalitarianism (as in Plato, Hobbes, and Rousseau). They accept no revelation of God limiting the powers of government, and they have no other arguments sufficient to establish such limits. So government becomes an idol, a substitute for God himself. This teaching fits position 4 on our diagram.

But if the non-Christian thinker is more interested in personal liberty than in law and order, his argument for personal liberty leads naturally to anarchy. Again, non-Christian thought has no recourse to divine revelation that would affirm personal liberty while establishing a limit upon it. For the non-Christian defender of liberty, it must become an absolute, leaving government with no legitimate power at all. Thus, political chaos adds to the conceptual chaos implicit in position 3.

Of course, many non-Christian ethicists have sought a balance between law and liberty. John Locke is well known for his balanced approach in such matters. But although he was primarily a secular thinker, he may have been influenced by Christian writers, such as Samuel Rutherford, the author of *Lex, Rex*. Rutherford worked out a balance between the state and the people, mainly through biblical exegesis. Locke tried to accomplish the same balance through an empiricist epistemology. But David Hume later argued that one cannot derive moral obligations from empirical observation, an argument that made Locke's political philosophy far less plausible. I shall argue later in this book that no line can be drawn limiting the powers of government except by means of divine revelation. So the tension between irrationalism and rationalism in non-Christian thought can be seen also as a tension between anarchy and totalitarianism.

THREE ETHICAL PRINCIPLES

In this section, I will discuss another aspect of the ethical debate between Christians and non-Christians. This debate also concerns the lordship attributes.

Most people who think about ethics, Christian and non-Christian alike, are impressed by the teleological, deontological, and existential principles:

The teleological principle: A good act maximizes the happiness of living creatures. That is to say, a good act does good. Christians emphasize that a good act is one that is good for God, bringing him glory. But Scripture tells us that what brings glory to God also brings good to his people: "And the LORD commanded us to do all these statutes, to fear the LORD our God, for our good always, that he might preserve us alive, as we are this day" (Deut. 6:24; cf. 10:13). Non-Christian writers, like Aristotle, have also emphasized that doing good brings happiness, however that may be defined. The ethical life is the good life, the blessed life (Ps. 1; Matt. 5:1–11). And of course to live ethically is also to bring blessing to others.

In Christian ethics, this insight is based on God's lordship attribute of control. It is God who arranges nature and history so that good acts have beneficial consequences, to himself, to the ethical agent, and to other persons.

I call this the principle of *teleology*, for it declares that all our behavior should be goal oriented, that it should seek the glory of God and the happiness of people.

The deontological principle: A good act is a response to duty, even if it requires self-sacrifice. We admire people who follow their ethical principles, even at great cost. In the Bible, Abraham obeyed God's word, even though it meant leaving his home country and moving to a place where he was a complete stranger (Gen. 12:1), and even though it meant taking his son Isaac up to a mountain to be a human sacrifice (Gen. 22:1–19). To do his Father's will, the Lord Jesus gave his very life.

So God defines duties for us, absolute norms that take precedence over any other consideration. Our duties are what we must do, what we ought to do. They are necessary. And they are universal, for they apply to everyone. If it is wrong for me to steal, then it is wrong for you to steal in the same situation. Ethics is no respecter of persons.

This insight is based on God's lordship attribute of *authority*. The ultimate source of human duties is God's authoritative word. Some secular thinkers, such as Plato and Kant, have also acknowledged the importance of duty. But, as we shall see, they have had a difficult time determining where our duties are to be found and what our duties actually are.

I call this the principle of *deontology*, from the Greek verb translated "owe, ought, must." It states that ethics is a matter of duty, of obligation.

The existential principle: A good act comes from a good inner character. A good person is not a hypocrite. He does good works because he loves to do them, because his heart is good. Scripture emphasizes that the only righteousness that is worth anything is a righteousness of the heart. The Pharisees cleansed the outside of their cup, their outward acts, but not the inside, their heart-motives (Matt. 23:25). Non-Christian writers, such as Aristotle, have also frequently emphasized the importance of character, of virtue, of inner righteousness. But, as we shall see, they have not succeeded in showing what constitutes virtue or how such virtue may be attained.

This insight is based on God's lordship attribute of *presence*, "for it is God who works in you, both to will and to work for his good pleasure" (Phil. 2:13). Without inward regeneration and sanctification, our best works are hypocritical.

I call this the *existential* principle, for it says that morality is personal and inward, a matter of the heart.

ARE THE THREE PRINCIPLES CONSISTENT?

Christians can gladly accept all three of the principles listed above. The God of Scripture is the author of the situation, the Word, and the moral self, so that the three are fully consistent with one another. He ordains history, so that people will find their ultimate blessing in doing their duty. He has made us in his image, so that our greatest personal fulfillment occurs in seeking his glory in history, as his Word declares.

Many non-Christian writers appreciate the three principles, or at least one or two of them, even though they reject the God of the Bible. However, in the absence of the biblical God, these principles are in tension with one another.

The teleological principle says that ethical action leads to happiness. Yet the deontological principle says that in order to do our duty, we must sometimes sacrifice our happiness.

The teleological and deontological principles say that our ethical responsibility is objective, grounded outside ourselves. But the existential principle suggests that our goodness is inward and therefore subjective.

The deontological principle says that we are subject to a moral law that declares our duty, apart from our inclination or the consequences of our acts. But the teleological and existential principles measure our goodness by the consequences of our actions and our inner life, respectively.

The existential principle says that it is wrong to measure a person's goodness by anything external to him. But the teleological and deontological principles say that one may measure goodness by the consequences and norms of actions, respectively.

Non-Christian thinkers who appreciate the teleological principle tend to be empiricists in their epistemology (such as Jeremy Bentham and John Stuart Mill), basing human knowledge on sense perception.

But philosophers have generally recognized that sense perception does not reveal to us universal or necessary principles. It cannot reveal universal principles, because our senses cannot perceive the whole universe. And the world cannot reveal necessary principles to our senses, because necessity is not perceivable by the senses. At most, the senses tell us what happens, not what must happen, and certainly not what ought to happen. But the deontological principle says that ethics is based on principles that are universal, necessary, and obligatory.

So if one tries to hold these principles without God, they inevitably appear to be in tension with one another. With God, they cohere, for the same God who controls the consequences of our acts also declares our duties and also gives us a new inner life. But without God, it seems likely that in some situations one ethical principle will contradict another. We may, then, have to abandon our duty in order to maximize happiness or be as loving as possible (Joseph Fletcher) in a particular situation. Of course, we must then decide which principle will prevail. Non-Christian ethicists differ among themselves on this matter, forming three schools of thought.

THE THREE SCHOOLS OF NON-CHRISTIAN ETHICS

TELEOLOGICAL ETHICS

For some non-Christian ethicists, the teleological principle prevails. For them, what is important is the goal we are pursuing, usually defined as happiness or pleasure. That happiness can be individual (as in Epicurean hedonism) or both individual and corporate (as in Mill's utilitarianism). The ethical value of our actions is measured by the consequences of those actions—to what extent they maximize happiness and minimize unhappiness.

Teleological ethicists tend to be hostile to the idea that we are bound by absolute rules that take precedence over our happiness, as in deontological ethics. They also dislike the notion that ethics is subjective, as in existential ethics. Rather, they think it is something public—even subject to calculation. For they believe that we can determine what to do merely by calculating the consequences of our actions, the quantity and/or quality of pains and pleasures that our actions produce.

DEONTOLOGICAL ETHICS

For other non-Christian ethicists, the deontological principle prevails. For them, it is important above all to have access to authoritative norms that govern all human conduct. The teleological principle, that we should seek happiness, is insufficient, they say, even unethical. We admire, not those who seek their own happiness, but those who sacrifice that happiness for a higher principle. And to a deontologist, the existential idea that ethics is essentially subjective is destructive of ethics itself.

So the deontologist goes in search of absolute ethical principles. For him, a moral principle must be external to ourselves, universal, necessary, transcendent—indeed, godlike. Opponents of this approach believe that deontologists have failed to prove that such principles exist. But deontologists believe that without such principles there can be no ethics.

EXISTENTIAL ETHICS

I use the term *existential ethics* to refer to a broad movement, of which twentieth-century writers like Jean-Paul Sartre are only a part. Existential ethicists are those who are impressed most of all with the existential principle discussed in the last two sections. The most important thing about ethics, they say, is its inwardness. Goodness is of the heart, a matter of motive. A good act is an act that actualizes the true self (our essence, in Aristotle and idealism; our freedom, according to Sartre). If there are moral laws or principles, they must be affirmed from within. If we seek happiness, it is our own happiness, not a happiness defined by someone else. So it is wrong to judge anyone on the basis of external conduct alone.

In the chapters that follow, I will be discussing specific examples of these types of ethics, as well as some thinkers who attempt to combine them in various ways. Then I will discuss the general structure of Christian ethics as an ethic that recognizes all three principles as perspectives, an ethic in which the three principles are reconciled through divine lordship.

CHAPTER 5

Ethics and the World's Religions

In the first four chapters, I introduced the subject of ethics, relating it to the lordship of God. I suggested that we can fruitfully investigate ethics under three perspectives related to God's lordship attributes: the situational, the normative, and the existential. I also used the lordship attributes to distinguish in general between biblical and nonbiblical approaches to ethics.

OUTLINE OF THE TREATISE ON ETHICS

In the rest of my discussion of ethics, I will seek to do three things that roughly correlate with the triads previously expounded. First, I intend to show in more detail than was possible in chapters 3 and 4 why nonbiblical approaches to ethics are insufficient to guide our ethical decisions. In the remaining chapters of part 2, I will be discussing mainly non-Christian metaethical systems, rather than their specific ethical prescriptions, because that will enable me to focus more precisely on their presuppositions and methods.

Since most discussion of ethical issues today is based on these nonbiblical views, these chapters will indicate the context of current debate, the intellectual situation that Christian ethicists must address. So I associate the discussion of non-Christian ethics with the situational perspective.

Second, in part 3, I would like to set forth a biblical philosophy of ethics, a Christian metaethic, responding to the non-Christian metaethics discussed in part 2. We can think of this as a Christian method for making ethical decisions. That method is, of course, triperspectival. So in these chapters I will be looking in more detail at the three perspectives, trying to understand how each, with the others, helps us to analyze and resolve ethical issues. Since this method describes the actual subjective process by which we wrestle with ethical matters, I identify it with the existential perspective.[1]

Third, in part 4, I will try to formulate in general terms the actual content of a Christian ethic—the biblical norms that govern our lives. Here, following the traditions of many churches, I shall expound these norms under the headings of the Ten Commandments, relating them to ethical teachings throughout Scripture. In line with my general view of theology as application, this discussion will include, not only exegesis of the commandments in the usual sense, but also formulations of their applications to contemporary ethical issues. This discussion will represent the normative perspective on ethics.

The reader will note that the triperspectival system involves triads within triads within triads. This whole book is triperspectival. Part 3 provides the normative perspective to the whole book, but it is itself divided into perspectives, as are some of the subsections. This phenomenon reminds us that the perspectives are not sharply distinct from one another. Rather, each perspective includes the other two and therefore draws on the other two for its content and methodology. At times, it is difficult to say what topic should fall under which perspective. Indeed, most of the time it really doesn't matter, except for purposes of pedagogical organization. For example, you can think of a tree in the front yard as an element of your environment (situational), as a fact that demands your belief (normative), or as an element of your experience (existential). Each perspective brings out something important about the tree. None of them can adequately deal with the tree's reality without the help of the other two.

ETHICS AND RELIGION

First on our agenda is to discuss non-Christian approaches to ethics. Among the non-Christian approaches are some that are connected with

---

1. *DKG* was organized according to the objects of knowledge (situational), the justification of knowledge (normative), and the methods of knowledge (existential). So here again I identify methodology with the existential perspective. But in this case I use a different order of presentation: the existential second, and the normative third.

the great religions of the world, such as Hinduism, Buddhism, Islam, and Judaism. Others purport to be secular and nonreligious, such as the major schools of Western ethical philosophy: Aristotelianism, utilitarianism, deontologism, and so on.

Secular philosophies, of course, do not demand church attendance or participation in religious ceremonies. But in other respects they are religious. Roy Clouser, in his *The Myth of Religious Neutrality*,[2] discusses the difficulty of defining religion. What, he asks, do the great religions of the world have in common? That question is more difficult that it might seem, Clouser argues.[3] We might think that all religions include ethical codes, but Shinto does not. We might think that all religions acknowledge a personal supreme being, but Buddhism and Hinduism do not. Or we might propose that all religions demand worship, but Epicureanism and some forms of Buddhism and Hinduism do not. Clouser concludes, however, that it is possible to define religious belief, and he suggests the following:

A religious belief is any belief in something or other as divine.

"Divine" means having the status of not depending on anything else.[4]

Clouser's definition of *divine* is not sufficient for the biblical God, or, for that matter, the gods of other religions. But it does define an attribute of the biblical God, aseity,[5] which is also ascribed to the absolutes of other religious traditions. All systems of thought include belief in something that is self-sufficient, not dependent on anything else. In Christianity, the self-sufficient being is the biblical God. In Islam, it is Allah; in Hinduism, Brahma. Clouser points out that in Greek polytheism the gods are not divine according to his definition, because they depend on realities other than themselves. The flux from which all things come, called Chaos or Okeanos, is the true deity of the ancient Greek religion.[6] Even purportedly atheistic religions like Therevada Buddhism have deities in Clouser's sense. Therevada holds that the Void, the ultimate Nothingness, sometimes called Nirvana, is not dependent on anything else.[7]

But such a definition of religion makes it impossible for us to distinguish sharply between religion and philosophy, or indeed between religion and

2. Notre Dame, IN: University of Notre Dame Press, 1991.
3. See his discussion in ibid., 10–12.
4. Ibid., 21–22.
5. See *DG*, chapter 26.
6. Clouser, *Myth*, 25.
7. Ibid., 26–27.

any other area of human thought and life.[8] Philosophies also, however secular they may claim to be, always acknowledge something that is "not depending on anything else" and thus "divine" according to Clouser's definition. Examples would be Thales' water, Plato's Form of the Good, Aristotle's Prime Mover, Spinoza's "God or Nature," Kant's Noumenal, Hegel's Absolute, and the Mystical of Wittgenstein's *Tractatus*. In the epistemological sphere, also, philosophers typically acknowledge human reason as self-sufficient in the sense that it requires no justification from anything more ultimate than itself. When they appear to deny autonomous reason (as with the Sophists, Duns Scotus, Hume, existentialism, and postmodernism), they typically exalt autonomous will or feeling, as we shall see in the next chapters, which makes will or feeling divine.

The biblical point to be made here is that nobody is really an atheist, in the most serious sense of that term. When people turn away from worship of the true God, they don't reject absolutes in general. Rather, instead of the true God, they worship idols, as Paul teaches in Romans 1:18–32. The great division in mankind is not between those who worship a god and others who do not. Rather, it is between those who worship the true God and those who worship false gods, or idols. False worship may not involve rites or ceremonies, but it always involves the attribution of aseity to something.

In this chapter, I will discuss the ethics of what we usually call the world's religions, and then in the following chapters I will focus on what are usually called the traditions of secular ethics. As we've seen, there are no sharp distinctions between these. The systems discussed in this chapter might be called "more explicitly religious" and those in the next chapters "less explicitly religious," but the difference is in the trappings, not the essence. It is a difference of degree, not a radical difference. The more explicitly religious systems typically advocate worship, observe religious holidays, and promote prayer and ceremony. The less explicitly religious systems do not. But both of them base their thinking and living on something that is not dependent on anything else.

ETHICS BASED ON FATE

It should not surprise readers too much that I divide the ethical approaches of the world's religions into three types: ethics based on fate

---

8. The same result follows from some other recent attempts to define religion, such as Paul Tillich's definition of religion as "ultimate concern," and William Tremmel's "affirmation of unrestricted value." Clouser opposes these definitions in ibid., 12–16, but they also imply that all human thought is religious.

(situational), ethics as self-realization (existential), and ethics as law without the gospel (normative). These are perspectives, for each of the world's religions can be characterized in all three of these ways. But some religions emphasize one, some the other. The first type is impressed most by what we called in chapter 4 the teleological principle. The second type stresses the existential principle, and the third the normative principle. In this section, we will look at the first emphasis.

In polytheism, as Clouser points out, the gods themselves are not ultimate. They are not *a se*; that is, they do not exist independently. Nor do they serve as ultimate ethical authorities. Indeed, they are frequently guilty of ethical transgressions. They are jealous, angry, mischievous, rebellious, adulterous, and so on. What is actually divine in Clouser's sense is something impersonal. As we saw earlier, Clouser says that the self-existent being in Greek religion is that primal flux called Chaos or Okeanos. Greek literature also speaks of Fate (*moira, atē*) as the ultimate determiner of life and death.

Is Fate another name for Chaos, or is it something even more ultimate? It's hard to say. The literature speaks of Fate to indicate what directs nature and history, and of Chaos to indicate the unpredictable movement that is nature itself. But if there is no personal supreme being, what does it mean to say that Fate "directs" history? It seems that Fate is a name for "whatever happens," as in "Whatever will be, will be." And Chaos, or Chance, is another name for whatever happens. Fate is whatever happens, conceived as a rational process; Chance is whatever happens, conceived as an irrational process. Fate and Chance are the same, but they represent a rationalistic and an irrationalistic vocabulary, respectively.

Reference to impersonal fate as an ultimate can be found also in Egyptian (*maat*), Babylonian (*me*), and Confucian (*tien*, "heaven") texts. In Confucian (and some expressions of Greek) religion, fate is powerful in its own right, working vengeance against those who defy it. In Egypt, Babylon, and some other Greek sources, there is more of an emphasis on the enforcement of this impersonal law by gods and human rulers. That notion encourages hierarchicalism in society: In Egyptian religion, for example, Pharaoh is the link between heaven and earth, the absolute arbiter of right and wrong. Some Chinese texts regard the emperor similarly.

These systems tend to require an epistemology based in human authority. How do we know what is right and wrong? By the word of Pharaoh, the emperor, or perhaps the priests, scribes, or Confucian scholars. How do they know it? Either by revelation from a god or by their own observation of the processes of nature. If revelation comes from a god, it is based on the god's observations of these processes. For fate itself does not speak, since it is impersonal. It does not reveal anything. It just makes things happen—or is itself the sum total of what does happen.

So the epistemology of ethics in fatalistic systems is essentially empirical, based on experience of what happens in the world. When people do right, fate rewards them; when they do wrong, it punishes them. But then we must define right behavior as what gets rewarded by fate, and wrong behavior as what gets punished. This is how the teleological principle is taken by those who hold a fatalistic view of ethics. Right behavior brings happiness, and wrong behavior brings pain, because fate ensures it. Therefore, we should do right and avoid doing wrong. There are several serious problems with this view:

1. One problem with this epistemology is that fate, so far as anyone can observe it, is inconsistent. Sometimes people who seem to live moral lives are rewarded, but sometimes not. Sometimes the wicked are punished, but sometimes they are rewarded. These religions do sometimes posit afterlives in which such injustices are eliminated. But the afterlife is not an element of empirical knowledge for human beings. The gods, of course, may have some empirical knowledge of what happens to human beings in the afterlife. But until the gods themselves receive proper recompense for their own good and bad deeds, injustice continues. And as long as there is injustice, there is empirical uncertainty as to what fate decrees to be good and bad. So it is unclear how a god, or Pharaoh, or a priest, actually knows what fate has determined to be right or wrong.

2. But the problem is even worse than that. It is not only hard for people to learn right and wrong on this basis; it is impossible. As many have observed, ethical principles must be universal, necessary, and obligatory. A universal principle applies to everyone without respect of persons. If it is wrong for me to covet, it is also wrong for you (in the same situation) to covet. But empirical knowledge is never universal. Our experience is never omniscient; it never exhausts the universe.

A necessary principle must be obeyed. It is not optional. And it does not just happen to be mandatory. But empirical knowledge cannot discern necessity. As David Hume said, from sense experience you can discern that one billiard ball moves when another one hits it. But sense experience does not tell you that the second ball *had* to move.

If a principle is obligatory, those who violate it are ethically wrong and morally guilty. But this quality cannot be discerned through mere sense experience any more than the others.

3. But the problem is not just a weakness in our sense experience, as if our moral perception could be improved by better vision or hearing, or perhaps by the super vision and super hearing of a god. For the attempt

to derive moral principles from impersonal realities is also a violation of logic. Impersonalist views of ethics fall prey to what G. E. Moore called "the naturalistic fallacy."[9] Moore's discussion builds on an argument in David Hume's *Treatise of Human Nature*[10] to the effect that one cannot deduce *ought* from *is*. That is to say, from premises about what is, about factual observations, you cannot deduce conclusions about what you ought to do. For example, you cannot reason from "Ice cream tastes good" to "You ought to eat ice cream," or even from "Immunizations prevent disease" to "You ought to be immunized." According to Hume and Moore, facts of nature do not carry with them moral obligations.

Facts can be learned through observation and the scientific method. But moral obligations cannot be seen and heard. They cannot be observed. No scientific experiment can identify them. You can see a thief walk into a bank, put on a ski mask, take out his gun, demand money, put it in his bag, and walk out. When you see that, you say, "That was wrong." But you don't actually see the wrongness of it. You may believe strongly that what the thief did was wrong, but you cannot deduce the wrongness of his action from a description of what happened.

Some have directed this argument against Christian ethics. They have claimed that to reason from "God says stealing is wrong" to "Stealing is wrong" is an example of the naturalistic fallacy, since God's speaking is a fact, "Stealing is wrong" is a moral obligation, and we may never deduce obligations from mere facts.

That objection calls for more analysis. Why is the naturalistic fallacy a fallacy? Evidently, *is* does not imply *ought* because there is no *ought* in the premise, but there is one in the conclusion, as in:

Argument 1

> PREMISE: X is pleasurable.
> CONCLUSION: We ought to do x.

But consider the following argument, which is similar, though different:

Argument 2

> PREMISE: X is morally right.
> CONCLUSION: We ought to do x.

Argument 2 is not a fallacy because there are oughts in both the premise and the conclusion. That which is "morally right" is equivalent to what "we

9. Moore, *Principia Ethica* (Cambridge: Cambridge University Press, 1903).
10. 3.1.1.

ought to do." Argument 2, like argument 1, can be described as "deducing a value from a fact," but the factual premises of the two arguments are very different. In argument 2, the fact in the premise is, we might say, a moral fact. So we should formulate the naturalistic fallacy more precisely as follows: One may deduce moral conclusions from moral facts, but not from nonmoral facts.

Now consider this argument:

Argument 3

> PREMISE: God says stealing is wrong.
> CONCLUSION: Stealing is wrong.

The Christian claims that this argument does not commit the naturalistic fallacy, because the premise is a moral fact, not a nonmoral fact. There is an ought implicit in the premise. If God says something, it is never a mere fact; it is also a norm. God's word bears his lordship attributes of control, authority, and presence, and his authority makes whatever he says normative for us. So whatever he says, we are obligated to believe, and whatever he commands, we are obligated to do. Whatever God says, then, is normative. If he says something, there is an *ought* attached to it. Argument 3 does not commit the naturalistic fallacy, then, because it is an argument from moral fact to moral conclusion.

But what about religious fatalism, the type of ethical system we are discussing in this section? For a religious fatalist, we learn morality from this kind of argument:

Argument 4

> PREMISE: Fate rewards people who do *x*.
> CONCLUSION: People ought to do *x*.

Thus appears the teleological principle, as it fits into a fatalistic system. "A good act maximizes happiness" means that we determine the good by deciding what sorts of acts bring about a happy fate.

Does this argument commit the naturalistic fallacy, or does it reason from ought to ought? Well, there is no obvious ought in the premise. The fact that an impersonal process prospers people who behave in a certain way doesn't make that behavior obligatory or even right.

That is even true of personal processes of a similar kind. Think of persons who give rewards to people who serve them. Josef Stalin, for example, gave handsome rewards to many of those who murdered his enemies. Does that make their conduct morally right? Obviously not. Even less should we allow the apparent preferences of an impersonal fate (but how can an impersonal principle even have preferences?) to dictate our moral obligations.

Some writers, ancient and modern, have praised the courage of those who have defied what seemed to be their fate, however hopeless their defiance may have been. For these writers, it is opposition to fate, the struggle against it, that is morally praiseworthy. Prometheus became a hero by defying Zeus, and we admire Antigone for her hubris in opposing fate. So it seems to be at least an open question as to whether following fate, even if we could follow it, is a morally admirable course of action. But if fate, unlike the biblical God, is not fit to be a moral standard, then argument 4 commits the naturalistic fallacy.

The fundamental question is whether any impersonal principle provides a sufficient basis for morality. In my judgment, the answer is no. Even if the universe were governed by an impersonal principle, and even if it were possible for people to discern what kinds of behavior that principle rewarded or punished, it would remain an open question whether we ought to practice the rewarded behavior. And I cannot imagine any reason why we should feel morally bound by the dictates of any impersonal principle at all. Impersonal principles, like gravity, electromagnetism, and the like, have the power to push us around, but they don't have the power to tell us what we *ought* to do. To claim they do is to commit the naturalistic fallacy.

If morality cannot be based on anything impersonal, where can we find a basis for it? In the realm of the personal, of course. We learn our moral principles in a personal context: at mother's knee, in school, in church, in national celebrations. By their very nature, moral principles presuppose an interpersonal context. Virtues like loyalty, love, courage, and kindness presuppose a society. Typically, people come to believe in loyalty, for example, as a moral virtue, because they have grown up in a home in which parents were loyal to one another and to their children, and in which it therefore did not seem unreasonable for parents to expect the same from their children. The same is true of obedience and love. It should not be hard to understand how the modern breakdown of the family has led to uncertainty about obligations.

So children learn morality from their parents, not by appealing to some impersonal principle. But parents, of course, are morally fallible. So, as they mature, children often find themselves looking for a higher standard. If children learn morality from their parents, where did their parents learn it? How did our first parents learn it? And who makes the rules, ultimately, that govern all parents and all children? Evidently someone who is not fallible, for he or she must stand as the very criterion of right and wrong. But that criterion must be someone, not something, if it is to commend our ultimate loyalty, obedience, and love.[11]

The absolute moral standard must be an absolute person. And the only absolute person anybody knows about is the God of the Bible. The Bible is unique in teaching that the supreme moral authority is an absolute person. Other religions and philosophies proclaim absolutes, but those absolutes are not personal. Still other worldviews, like polytheism, teach the existence of supernatural persons, but these are not absolute. But if morality must be based on one who is both personal and absolute, then the God of the Bible is the only viable candidate.[12]

I conclude, then, that fatalist religions cannot supply an adequate basis for morality. It is not clear why anyone should think that the workings of fate are morally consistent, how one can know the dictates of fate, or, even if we could know those dictates, why they would have any moral authority at all.

To claim a knowledge of morality from observing fate is a rationalistic claim, for it exalts the powers of the human mind far beyond anything we can legitimately claim to know. It is also irrationalistic, because if the universe is ultimately impersonal (review chapter 3), then it is impossible to know anything about our moral responsibilities. So in this kind of ethic, we have a good illustration of Van Til's rationalist/irrationalist dialectic (review chapter 4).

ETHICS AS SELF-REALIZATION

Another type of more explicitly religious ethics can be found in the monist religions, such as Hinduism, Buddhism, and Taoism. Monism is the view that all things are ultimately one. In the West, ancient Gnosticism was essentially monistic, and that worldview is echoed in Neoplatonism and medieval mysticism. Peter R. Jones has also identified modern movements, known as "New Age" thinking in the 1980s and 1990s, which he now refers to as neo-paganism, as essentially monistic. Jones argues that these modern movements are virtually equivalent to Gnosticism.[13]

11. Note here an important triad indicating the nature of ethical obligation.

12. This paragraph summarizes the moral argument for the existence of God given in AGG, 89–118. Of course, in addition to Christianity, Islam and Judaism also worship gods that are absolute and, in some respects, personal. But that is because they are influenced by the Bible. In this respect, Islam and Judaism are "Christian heresies," like Sabellianism, Arianism, and the Jehovah's Witnesses. See the section "Ethics as Law Without Gospel," below.

13. See Peter Jones, *The Gnostic Empire Strikes Back* (Phillipsburg, NJ: P&R Publishing, 1992); idem, *Spirit Wars: Pagan Revival in Christian America* (Escondido, CA: Main Entry Editions, 1997); idem, *Capturing the Pagan Mind* (Escondido, CA: Main Entry Editions,

Since, on their view, everything is essentially one, monists believe that God, if he exists, is essentially one with the universe, not a being distinct from it. In Scripture, there is a sharp distinction between creator and creature. But monism denies that fundamental distinction. Indeed, for many monists, God is a name for our true inner self. When we gain a really deep insight into ourselves, we discover that we are God and he is us. This idea is what I described in chapter 4 as nonbiblical immanence (view 4 on the rectangular diagram). This view is generally called pantheism.

But monism also expresses itself in terms that suggest nonbiblical transcendence (view 3 on the rectangle), somewhat like the deism of the Enlightenment. For the Gnostics, the supreme being was so far from the world that he could not be named or known by human beings. He, or it,[14] is such a vast mystery that we can have nothing like a personal relationship with him. Indeed, he can have nothing at all to do with the material world, because any relationship with matter would compromise his perfect spirituality.

Clearly, such monism presents the sharpest possible contrast with biblical Christianity (see views 1 and 2 on the rectangle). Yet Elaine Pagels and others have tried to influence the church to accept ancient Gnostic texts as equal in authority to the canonical Scriptures.[15] The church should not accept such advice.

These twin emphases on transcendence and immanence formally contradict one another, and critics of Gnosticism from the church father Irenaeus to the present have pointed that out.[16] On the other hand, there is at another level a coherence between these two themes. For if God is

---

2003). Following the *Star Wars* theme, Jones originally considered calling the third book *The Return of the Rabbi*. He has also written various popular summaries of his thought, which are available at http://www.spirit-wars.com/index.html. I am greatly indebted to Jones for the ideas presented in this section, though I take full responsibility for their formulation.

14. Although monism sometimes describes its supreme being in personal terms, its basic view is that the supreme being is too transcendent for any human characterization to apply. That supreme being should not be considered either personal or impersonal. But since that supreme being is not clearly personal, monism involves the same difficulties that I ascribed to fatalism in the previous section. A basis for ethics must reside in a being who not only is personal, but who reveals himself as personal by, among other things, declaring to us his ethical standards. Or put it this way: like fatalism, monism basically tells us that the standard of ethics is "all of reality." But an examination of reality in general does not lead to conclusions about what we ought to do.

15. See Elaine Pagels, *The Gnostic Gospels* (New York: Vintage, 1989).

16. In *Against Heresies*, Irenaeus also criticized the Gnostic system in epistemological terms. If God is so mysterious that nobody can know him, then where do the Gnostics get their secret knowledge? And if the Gnostics are themselves divine, as we are all divine, then why do we need the knowledge that the Gnostics claim to provide? Thus he exposes the Gnostics as both rationalists and irrationalists at the same time. As we saw in chapter 4, rationalism and irrationalism emerge from unbiblical immanence and transcendence, respectively.

not distinct from the world (nonbiblical immanence), then of course we are unable to specify any distinctive characteristics that may belong to him (nonbiblical transcendence).

These forms of immanence and transcendence collaborate to destroy any biblical notion of ethical responsibility. If we are God (nonbiblical immanence), then we are responsible to nobody except ourselves. If we cannot know God (nonbiblical transcendence), then, again, we cannot be responsible to him. Thus, monistic systems erase all three perspectives of ethics. The normative perspective is lost because in monism there is no ultimate distinction between right and wrong. The situational perspective is lost because the world as we experience it is an illusion. So one seeks detachment from things, rather than a God-glorifying use of them. The existential perspective is lost because the self, and other selves, are also illusory. In this respect, too, monism emphasizes detachment rather than, as in Scripture, love. Thus, personal and social ethics become meaningless.

Nevertheless, Eastern religions and Western gnosticisms do emphasize ethics. As with religious fatalism, they teach many ethical precepts that are not too different from those in Scripture. We should not be embarrassed on this account, for Scripture itself tells us in Romans 1 and elsewhere that God has revealed the knowledge of his moral law to everyone in the world. Although people repress and disobey this law, they cannot escape it entirely.

But it is important for us to understand the role of ethics in monistic worldviews. Essentially, for these systems, ethics is a discipline by which we can escape from the illusion of plurality and can become conscious of our oneness with God and with the whole world. By means of ethical and other disciplines, we climb a ladder of knowledge to a realm above ethics. It is therefore a tool of self-realization, a means by which we can be aware of the real nature of the world.

Of the three principles we discussed in chapter 4, therefore, monists are most impressed with the existential principle, the principle that ethics is a matter of the inner life of the self, a means of self-enhancement.

The trouble is that these ethical disciplines, if successful, carry one to a realm in which ethical distinctions, like right and wrong, good and evil, have no meaning. If the world is one, then good and evil are one, and right and wrong are one. And without such contrasts, there is no such thing as good or evil, or right or wrong. On these views, ethics is part of our quest to transcend ethics.

Buddhism, for example, puts much emphasis on right living. But the goal of right living is to achieve Nirvana, a kind of nothingness, in which there is no more suffering. Nirvana takes away the curse of perpetual reincarnation, in which souls are born and reborn in different forms according to the *karma* gained from their good or bad deeds. We might be inclined to charge Buddhism with being egoistic in that it makes ethics a tool of personal salvation. We must remember, however, that the Mahayana tradition of Buddhism encourages altruism, saying that the Buddha, when he was about to enter Nirvana, turned around instead to offer assistance to others. Nevertheless, we should ask why the Buddha made that decision. If the whole point of ethics is to achieve Nirvana, why should any altruistic purpose deter one from that goal? We should commend the altruism of Mahayana. But Buddhism, in the final analysis, has no basis for altruism or any other moral principle.

As another example, consider the ancient Gnostics, who were divided into two ethical camps. Some were ascetic, denying to themselves pleasures and possessions, because they sought escape from the material world into the spiritual oneness of the supreme being. Others, however, were libertine, denying themselves no pleasures at all, because they believed that ultimately the material world was an illusion and unimportant. Doubtless some tried to find a happy medium between these extremes. But what principle could guide such a decision? Again, we see how monism makes it impossible to specify moral distinctions.

The root problem is that ethics, in monism, is subordinate to metaphysics and epistemology. For the monist, our problem is epistemological deception as to the metaphysical nature of the world and ourselves. The remedy is to overcome that deception and to recognize that we are essentially one with everything that is. For the Christian, the problem is very different: God made human beings different from himself, but reflecting his glory. But they disobeyed him, creating an enmity with God that must be relieved through sacrifice. In Christianity, there is a problem with an interpersonal relationship, a relationship between finite persons and the infinite person. It is about ethics: love, obedience, sin, redemption. In monism, the issue is fundamentally impersonal: dispelling illusions about metaphysical separations.

So, as with the religious fatalist, the monist has no personal basis for ethics. His sense of obligation must come from the impersonal nature of the universe itself. In the previous section of this chapter, however, we saw that an impersonal reality can provide no basis for ethical standards.

ETHICS AS LAW WITHOUT GOSPEL

My critique of fatalism and monism has centered on the impersonalism of those positions. A worldview in which the highest reality is impersonal is incapable of providing a basis for ethical decisions. But what of religions other than Christianity that do base their ethics on the revelation of a personal absolute? This would include traditional Judaism, Islam, and Christian heresies such as the Jehovah's Witnesses and theological liberalism.[17]

We should note that the reason why these religions affirm an absolute personal God is that they are influenced by the Bible. As I mentioned earlier, it is a remarkable fact that belief in a personal absolute is not found in any religion or philosophy except those influenced by the Bible. Traditional Judaism, of course, adheres to what Christians call the Old Testament. Christians and Jews disagree as to how that book should be interpreted, but they do share the belief that that book is the authoritative word of God.

From a Christian point of view, Judaism is a Christian heresy. Christian heretics (like Sabellians, Arians, Jehovah's Witnesses, and many in the tradition of theological liberalism) claim to believe the Bible, but they interpret it in ways that deny the essence of the gospel, or they pick and choose what to believe in Scripture, ending up with a deeply unbiblical theology. The dispute between Christians and Jews is in this respect the same.

Islam, too, may be understood as a Christian heresy. Its founder, Mohammed, initially respected the "peoples of the book," the Jews and Christians. He sought to promulgate the monotheism of Scripture among his own people. But eventually he produced another book, the Qur'an, which denied many fundamental teachings of Scripture, such as Jesus' deity and his atoning death. Even then, Muslims regarded Scripture as a divine revelation, but argued that it had been corrupted during the centuries of its transmission.[18] They respected Jesus as a prophet, believed in his virgin birth, his miracles, and his return at the final judgment.[19] Indeed, they turned to the Bible for their own apologetic purposes, arguing that Old Testament prophecies of the coming Messiah predicted the coming of Mohammed, not of Jesus.

But both Islam and Judaism do claim to base their ethics on the revelation of a personal absolute, indeed on the revelation of the God of

17. For an account of liberal Christianity as a heresy, indeed as a religion radically contrary to Christianity, see J. Gresham Machen, *Christianity and Liberalism* (New York: Macmillan, 1923). Although liberalism since Machen's time has taken on a more orthodox sound, it still falls prey to Machen's brilliant critique. I expect to develop an elaborate critique of theological liberalism in *The Doctrine of the Word of God* (forthcoming).

18. This claim, of course, is not easily defended. For example, it is extremely unlikely that *all* New Testament references to Jesus' atoning death are the result of textual corruption.

19. So it has been rightly said that Muslims believe more about Jesus than many liberal Protestants.

Scripture. So we cannot argue against Judaism and Islam in quite the same way that we argue against fatalism and monism. Theological liberals sometimes do and sometimes do not claim to believe in such a basis for ethics. When they do not, their positions amount to religious fatalism or monism. When they do, however, we must deal with them differently.

I say that we cannot argue against these positions in "quite" the same way that we argue against fatalism and monism. Nevertheless, there are significant parallels between fatalism and monism, on the one hand, and Judaism, Islam, and liberalism, on the other. The defections of these religions from Scripture affect their doctrine of God to some extent. Most obviously, these religions are Unitarian, not Trinitarian. They deny the full deity of Christ and therefore see God as a oneness without plurality.[20]

Without a doctrine of plurality in God, these religions have less ability to regard God as the ultimate ethical standard and exemplar. In discussing fatalism, I pointed out that virtues like loyalty, love, courage, and kindness require a society for their exhibition. They are interpersonal virtues, not merely personal ones. A Unitarian god cannot exemplify these until he creates finite persons to relate to. But when he does that, his virtues are relative to, and thus dependent upon, the creation. Thus, the Unitarian god is not the ultimate standard, and so is not even divine, in Clouser's sense.

Further, a Unitarian concept of God easily slips into an impersonal concept: (1) Theologies based on Judaism, Islam, and liberal Christianity commonly view God's transcendence in the nonbiblical way represented as position 3 in figure 2 of chapter 4. On this view, human concepts of God are, strictly speaking, impossible. We cannot regard God as personal or as impersonal. But we have seen that ethics requires a clearly personal concept of God.[21]

(2) In Islam, the biblical doctrine of predestination becomes a form of fatalism, in which free human choices have no ultimate effect on the course of events.[22] But such fatalism is mechanical, not personal.

---

20. In practice, of course, Unitarian religions almost always treat their god as impersonal. An unrevealed personal god is functionally equivalent to an unrevealed impersonal god. Unitarian religions veer toward impersonalism because to think of God as personal requires some detailed revelation expressing his attributes and actions. We cannot know that God is personal unless he speaks to us and shows us that he is personal. But Unitarianism's view of transcendence denies that such a revelation is possible.

21. According to Islam, we can know God's will, but cannot know God himself. But, as I have argued, the ethical authority of revelation is based on a personal relationship with its author. Islam does not offer such a personal relationship.

22. For my account of the relationship between divine foreordination and human freedom, see DG, chapters 4, 8, 9, and 16.

(3) In some Jewish and liberal theologies, the opposite problem occurs, in which God himself is so limited by human free will that he cannot know the future in an exhaustive way. In those theologies, God is not the sole origin of what occurs (contrary to Ephesians 1:11 and Romans 11:36). He is himself subject to the created world. Given such assumptions, it is gratuitous to posit God as the sole source of ethical standards.[23]

So Judaism, Islam, and the Christian heresies are not immune to the charge of impersonalism that I have brought against fatalism and monism. But even if we assume that these religions do believe (as they sometimes claim) in a personal God, there is yet more to be said.

These religions—indeed, all religions except biblical Christianity—are religions of works-righteousness. That is, they are religions whose members try to seek moral status by doing good works. This principle is directly opposed to the biblical gospel, which says that even our best works are insufficient to gain favor with God. Isaiah 64:6 reads, "We have all become like one who is unclean, and all our righteous deeds are like a polluted garment. We all fade like a leaf, and our iniquities, like the wind, take us away." In Romans 8:8, the apostle Paul says that those who are "in the flesh," that is, those who have not had their sins forgiven through the atonement of Christ, "cannot please God." Our only hope, therefore, is Christ. Paul says, "For all have sinned and fall short of the glory of God, and are justified by his grace as a gift, through the redemption that is in Christ Jesus, whom God put forward as a propitiation by his blood, to be received by faith" (Rom. 3:23–25).

So salvation is entirely by God's grace, his free gift, not by our works: "For by grace you have been saved through faith. And this is not your own doing; it is the gift of God, not a result of works, so that no one may boast. For we are his workmanship, created in Christ Jesus for good works, which God prepared beforehand, that we should walk in them" (Eph. 2:8–10).

In Judaism, Islam, and the Christian heresies (and also fatalism and monism), there is no doctrine of salvation by divine grace. Rather, people are expected to lead good lives, hoping that God will accept them. But this doctrine of works-righteousness leads to either pride or despair. It leads to pride on the part of those who think they can meet God's requirements on their own. This is, of course, a pride based on self-deception. People with this ambition are quite ignorant of God's standards, and they flatter themselves beyond measure to think they have measured up even to a minimal understanding of God's requirements. They have suppressed (Rom. 1:18)

---

23. I am here referring to the theological movement called open theism, which I have criticized extensively in *No Other God* (Phillipsburg, NJ: P&R Publishing, 2001).

their very knowledge of themselves, of the vast number of ways in which they have fallen short of God's perfection.

The doctrine of works-righteousness also leads to despair among those with better spiritual perception. They see the huge discrepancy between what God requires and what they have done, and they lose all hope of attaining fellowship with God.

It is only the cross of Christ that can put to rest that pride and despair. God's grace brings us fellowship with him that is not based on our works, so we may not boast (Eph. 2:9). And it brings us into deep fellowship with God as he sees us in his beloved Son, so we may not despair.

When Christians discuss ethics with Jews, Muslims, and liberals, as indeed with fatalists and monists, they should try hard to direct the conversation to the cross. For that is the most important issue, in the final analysis, and the most urgent for any inquirer. We should be willing to discuss metaphysics and epistemology as above, to question whether non-Christian religions have a basis for ethical claims. As Francis Schaeffer used to say, we should be ready to give honest answers to honest questions. But in the end the gospel is by far the most important thing.

All three types of non-Christian religions offer us, at most, law without gospel. Religions of the third type have a special focus on law, their application of the normative principle. As we shall see in later chapters, law and gospel are not separated in Scripture in the manner presented, for example, in Lutheran theology. In Scripture, the law is the law of the God who saves, the law of the kingdom of God. The gospel is the message that that kingdom is coming and that therefore God will save his people. But there is something of a law-gospel distinction between general and special revelation. Romans 1 teach us that God makes his moral standards, his law, known to all people through natural revelation. It does not teach that he also reveals therein the way of salvation. Rather, "faith comes from hearing, and hearing through the word of Christ" (Rom. 10:17). And of course our salvation comes, not through keeping the law, but by receiving the grace of Christ, known only through special revelation.[24]

Grace is only possible in a universe governed by an absolute person. Impersonal forces, like gravity and electromagnetism, treat everybody equally, according to the sheer force of whatever laws they obey. If you place your hand on a live wire, you will receive a shock, whether you are

---

24. I shall have more to say about the distinction between general and special revelation when we consider more fully the normative perspective of Christian ethics. Of course, special revelation presents the gospel, but it also presents law, integrated with gospel. We do not understand the full force and depth of the law except through the gospel, and we do not understand how good the good news is, apart from law.

righteous or wicked. The live wire does not make a loving decision to give some people a free gift of immunity to electrical shock. So impersonalist systems tend to be universalistic—to say that everyone will be saved in some way or other, or, as in secular impersonalisms, that we shall all be equally destroyed by natural forces. Christianity is not universalistic, for according to Scripture human beings are ultimately in the hands of a thoroughly personal God. He decides, for his own reasons and personal affections, who will be saved and who will be lost.[25]

So those apparently personalist religions that promulgate law without gospel have a view of ethics that is not much different from that of impersonalist religions. For all three forms of non-Christian religion, ethics is obedience to law without hope of forgiveness for sin. And in all three forms, even the law is questionable, because we cannot specify its content in an impersonalist universe.

---

25. I have addressed objections to predestination and reprobation in *DG*, chapters 9 and 16.

CHAPTER 6

The Existential Tradition

Having looked at three forms of more explicitly religious approaches to ethics, I now turn to less explicitly religious approaches, usually called secular ethics. I shall deal with these at somewhat greater length, since they dominate the ethical discussions of our own time.

PHILOSOPHY AND ETHICS[1]

Around 600 BC, an intellectual movement appeared in Miletus, in Asia Minor, that was eventually called philosophy. That movement spread widely throughout the Greek-speaking world and then to other nations. Philosophy means "love of wisdom," and in one sense it is the Greek heir to the genre of wisdom teaching that was common in the ancient Near East. The Bible contains wisdom literature, in the books of Job, Proverbs, the Song of Songs, and Ecclesiastes.

But there is a great difference between Greek philosophy and wisdom literature, particularly the wisdom literature of Scripture. The tradi-

1. In chapters 6–8, I draw on my essay "Greeks Bearing Gifts," in *Revolutions in Worldview: Understanding the Flow of Western Thought*, ed. W. Andrew Hoffecker (Phillipsburg, NJ: P&R Publishing, 2007), 1–36. That essay deals with the metaphysical and epistemological views of the Greek philosophers, as well as their ethical teaching, so readers may find it useful as a context for what I say here. I also recommend the other essays in this book, which deal in a similar way with other periods in the history of Western thought.

tional wisdom teachers sought to gather and catalogue the wise sayings of respected people. Biblical wisdom does this too, but emphasizes that there is an authority higher than any human teacher: "The fear of the LORD is the beginning of wisdom; all those who practice it have a good understanding. His praise endures forever!" (Ps. 111:10; cf. Prov. 1:7; 9:10; 15:33).

In contrast, the Greek philosophers sought to understand the world without reference to religion or tradition—and certainly without reference to the God of Scripture. Their chief authority was human reason, functioning independently of revelation and tradition. That view of reason I describe by the phrase *rational autonomy*. Although the Greek philosophers differed on a great many things, they all agreed on the principle of rational autonomy. For them, reason is the ultimate standard of all truth, and the good life is the rational life. Except during the medieval period, this principle of rational or intellectual autonomy has dominated the history of Western philosophy down to the present day.

Nevertheless, the Greeks also understood to some extent the limitations of human reason. They were concerned about the nature of error and deception. If human reason is the ultimate standard of truth, they asked, why isn't it omniscient? Why, indeed, is it so often mistaken? Their most common answer was that if reason itself is our ultimate guide, then its failures must be failures, not of reason itself, but of the universe. The problem is not in the knower, but in what he seeks to know; not in the subject, but in the object of knowledge.[2] We fall into error because the world in which we live is in some measure unknowable.

Here we see the rationalist and irrationalist motifs that we discussed in chapter 4, as they appear in Greek philosophy. Suppressing the revelation of God in the creation (Rom. 1), the Greeks give supreme authority to human reason. But when it fails, they attribute that failure to the nature of the world. But then the philosophical task proves impossibly difficult, for no rational account can be given of an irrational universe. Thus appears the rationalist-irrationalist dialectic.

The Greeks differed among themselves as to the balance between rationalism and irrationalism. Parmenides was a firm rationalist. He even denied the existence of anything that reason couldn't explain, such as, in his view, change. The Sophists, on the other hand, were irrationalists, holding that there is no objective truth at all, but only truth "for me" and "for you." But the Sophists nevertheless sought to live according to reason, at least

---

2. See the discussion of subject and object in *DKG*, 9–10, 69–71.

according to each person's individual reason. "Man is the measure of all things," said the Sophist Protagoras.

THE EXISTENTIAL FOCUS

In the next few chapters, I will focus on the views of ethics that have emerged in the history of philosophy. These chapters will discuss three traditions in philosophical ethics that correspond more or less to the three perspectives that we have been discussing. They also represent emphases on the existential, teleological, and deontological principles that I discussed in chapter 4.

This chapter discusses the existential tradition, which focuses on ethics as a phenomenon of the inner life. Of the three principles mentioned in chapter 4, the one valued the most by existential ethics is that a good act comes from a good inner character. This principle is biblical. We should affirm our ethical principles from within. Hypocritical obedience is not the obedience that God honors. He wants his word to be written on our heart. If it is written there, our behavior will be a kind of self-realization. Our behavior will display what we are, deep inside. As we saw in chapter 3, God motivates our behavior by encouraging us to become what we are: regenerate sons and daughters of God, dead to sin and alive in Christ. He wants our behavior to display what we are at the most fundamental level.

Secular forms of existential ethics honor these principles in some ways, but parody them in others. In secular forms of existential ethics, the existential principle tends to become an absolute, opposed to the teleological and deontological principles. Human subjectivity becomes the test of all moral truth, if such truth even exists.

No thinker is an absolutely pure example of any of these three tendencies. The reason is that ethics by its very nature requires all three perspectives. One can try to reject a perspective, but it always shows up somewhere. So, in secular existential ethics, our inner subjectivity is made to play all three roles: motive, goal, and standard. Existential ethicists make this move at the price of coherence, of course.

I shall discuss some secular thinkers like Aristotle, who actually try to provide a balance between the three perspectives. But without God, Aristotle fails to bring the perspectives into a coherent mutual relationship. And his example shows us why lesser thinkers have tried to eliminate one or two of the perspectives in favor of the third, even though in the end they have not been able to do so.

But for now we must look at the existential tradition, which focuses on the inner life and tends to see it as the whole of ethics.

THE SOPHISTS

The earliest Greek philosophers were not much interested in ethics, at least as far as we can tell from the texts available to us. They focused on metaphysics, and, especially with Parmenides, Heraclitus, and the atomists, on epistemology. But in the time of the Sophists, ethics became a subject of much interest.

The Sophists were educators in fifth- and fourth-century BC Greece who went from one city to another, teaching young men the skills needed for success in public life: rhetoric, grammar, history, science, art, and the virtues that lead to public admiration. These teachers had many clients, for the traditional aristocracy was losing ground to the mercantile class, creating opportunities for the upwardly mobile sons of wealthy families. Also, there was much political upheaval, raising philosophical questions about the ground and legitimacy of political rule.[3]

Thus, philosophy took a new turn. No longer were philosophers mainly concerned with the structure of the natural world. Now human nature and the problems of human society became prominent.

If one's main concern is to get along with various political factions, then relativism will have a strong appeal, as we know from contemporary politics. If there is no absolute or objective truth, no truth that everyone must acknowledge, then one's views are free to change with every wave of political opinion. So it is not surprising that the Sophists were relativists.

We learn about them mainly from the dialogues of Plato—an unsympathetic witness, to be sure, but most likely a fair one. According to Plato, for example, the Sophist Protagoras advocated acceptance of traditional ways of thinking, not because they were true, but because they are needed to gain power and acceptance. Gorgias denied the existence of objective truth and so wanted to substitute rhetoric for philosophy. Thrasymachus taught that "justice is the interest of the stronger," so that laws are (and should be) means by which the strong keep the masses subordinate. Callicles held, on the contrary, that laws are the means used by the masses to check the power of the strong. Critias, later described as the cruelest of the Thirty Tyrants of Athens, said that if a ruler wants

---

3. For more extensive discussion of the political and social background of Sophism, see Gordon H. Clark, *Thales to Dewey* (Boston: Houghton Mifflin, 1957), 46–48.

to control his subjects, he must encourage them to fear the gods, even though they are nonexistent.

Socrates, as Plato presents him in the same dialogues, replies that indifference or hostility to objective truth is unacceptable. For one thing, the Sophists themselves are making assertions of fact. If there is no objective truth, then the Sophists' positions are not objectively true, and there is no reason for anyone to listen to them. This argument has been a standard answer to relativism ever since, and we often hear it used today against postmodernism.

Further, Socrates argues, justice cannot merely be the interest of the stronger. For who stands to gain by something is not what makes it just, as opposed to unjust. There must be some quality in the thing itself that makes it just, that serves as a criterion to evaluate the conduct of rulers.

Thus Socrates refutes the irrationalism of the Sophists, or rather shows that such irrationalism is self-refuting. But the Sophists were also rationalists in the typical Greek way. Consider Protagoras's statement that "man is the measure of all things." This statement expresses the Sophists' irrationalism: reality is what any man thinks it is. But it is also rationalistic, for it makes human reason the ultimate criterion of truth and falsehood, of right and wrong. How could Protagoras know this, especially given his overall relativism? He asserts rational autonomy arbitrarily. That is, he asserts rationalism irrationalistically, as he asserts irrationalism rationalistically—by the measure of his own mind. No other course was open to the Sophists, for they were skeptical about the traditional gods and would not consider the God of biblical theism.

I describe the Sophists as representatives of the existential tradition of ethics. The existential principle links ethics with character and in general with human inwardness. But when non-Christian philosophers use this principle, they tend to absolutize human subjectivity and make it, not only essential to ethics, but the ultimate source of ethical norms. So the secular existential ethicist seeks to avoid any suggestion that ethical decisions must be based on an external, objective norm. The Sophists had no appreciation of the normative principle (that ethics seeks objective duties) or the situational principle (that ethics maximizes the happiness of human beings). As I argued in chapter 4, the three principles are in tension with one another, unless the biblical God holds them together. So non-Christian ethicists tend to deny one or two of these principles. The Sophists essentially denied all but the existential principle.

There is much that is attractive about the existential type of ethics. Indeed, if I weren't a Christian, I would probably be an existentialist, a kind of relativist or skeptic. In Dostoevsky's terms, if God doesn't exist, isn't everything permitted? Yet, because of Socrates' and Plato's arguments against it, the existential tradition has been the least popular among professional philosophers throughout the discipline's history, although in modern times it seems to have become a favorite of the man in the street. The more predominant schools of philosophical thought have taught that objective knowledge is indeed possible, though they have found it difficult to agree on how such knowledge is possible. But we shall look at those arguments in the next two chapters.

In the centuries following the Sophists, schools of skepticism emerged. Pyrrho (365–270 BC) argued for a kind of epistemological agnosticism, and the skeptics of the Academy (the school founded by Plato!) went even farther, arguing that truth could not be found. After that, skepticism virtually died out as an option for respectable philosophers.

HUME AND ROUSSEAU

But in the modern period, relativism and skepticism came again into their own. David Hume (1711–76), who was skeptical of many things, including the is-ought inference (see chapter 5), could find no basis for ethics except in "a moral sense" that generates feelings of approval and disapproval.[4] As with the Sophists, for Hume ethical standards are wholly inward, subjective rather than objective. Similarly, Jean-Jacques Rousseau (1712–78), the father of Romanticism, thought that everything good in the world is the outworking of good feelings.

KARL MARX

Karl Marx (1818–83) has perhaps had the greatest influence on politics and world history of any philosopher in the last two hundred years. Most people become Marxists, in my view, for ethical reasons. They find in Marx a thinker who cares about the poor and actually has a plan to do something for them.

But it is important to keep in mind that Marx is a thoroughgoing subjectivist. He thinks that ethical standards are relative to one's class. In his view, ethical systems are tools of political movements, aiming to promote the interest of one class against another. There is one ethic for

---

4. See Hume, *An Enquiry Concerning the Principles of Morals* (1751).

the bourgeois (the owners of the means of production) and another for the proletariat (the workers in the industrial plants). When the proletariat initiates revolution, whatever promotes that revolution is good and whatever hinders it is evil. And once the proletarian revolution is victorious, whatever promotes progress toward the classless society (the Marxist eschaton) is good, and whatever retards it is evil.

Specific ethical standards may change as the interests of one's class change. What is good today may be evil tomorrow. American Communists praised Hitler when he made a pact with Stalin. When Hitler broke that pact, everything he did was evil.

Which ethic is right? To Marx, there is no such thing as objective rightness in ethics, though he makes much of scientific objectivity in formulating his economic determinism. When idealistic young people are attracted to Marxism for ethical reasons, it is pastorally important to remind them that ethics is ultimately negotiable for a Marxist. Class interest is supreme, and ethics is a tool of class interest. When we look at Marxism from that perspective, it appears less than noble.

Nevertheless, Marx often speaks as though his ethical judgments were objective. For example, he famously condemns Christianity as "the opiate of the people." He regards it as an ideology concocted by the rich to keep the workers in their place, to make them satisfied with their presently wretched lot and heavenly reward, so that they do not resort to revolution. Christians may protest that the gospel has contributed much over the centuries to the welfare of the poor and of society in general. But Marx replies that even such "prophetic" Christianity should be opposed, for it does more harm than good. It kindles false hopes of reform, pacifies the masses, and therefore retards revolution, which is necessary for real change.

That sounds like an ethical critique of Christianity. Essentially he is saying that Christianity is the religious ethic that a particular class uses to oppress another class. But we must remember that Marx's alternative ethic is just an ethic of another particular class, designed, once that class comes to power, to oppress any rival class. Marx gives no reason except class allegiance to prefer his ethics to Christian ethics.

We can see in Marx the rationalist-irrationalist dialectic. Marx denies objective ethics (irrationalism), but he preaches a moralistic alternative, together with critiques of his opponents, with dogmatic assurance (rationalism).[5]

5. See Karl Marx and Friedrich Engels, *The Communist Manifesto* (1848); Marx, *Das Kapital* (1887).

FRIEDRICH NIETZSCHE

Nietzsche (1844–1900) has had a huge influence on twentieth-century thought, especially the postmodern movement. Like postmodernists, he was rather skeptical about the existence of ultimate truth (although he admitted the importance of the particular truths of ordinary life) and of the power of language to communicate it.[6] Like Marx, he believed that there is no disinterested search for truth. Intellectual inquiry is inevitably self-serving. We seek knowledge for its utility, but we cannot be sure even about the utility of knowledge. We must reconcile ourselves, therefore, to irresolvable disagreement.[7]

In the field of ethics, Nietzsche is well known for his view that traditional morality is not objectively true, but only a vehicle of the "will to power," by which some people oppress others. His position in this regard is identical to that of Marx, though Nietzsche does not share Marx's emphasis on class warfare. Nietzsche's own moral stance is, in his words, "beyond good and evil."[8] He urges a "transvaluation of all values." In his view, since God is "dead" as a factor in the lives of modern people, it is wrong for us to bind ourselves with moral traditions from the past. We should recognize that God is dead and be honest and joyful about the will to power.

It is interesting to compare Nietzsche with Marx on the subject of Christianity. Marx thought that Christianity was a religion of the rich, aiming to suppress the poor. Nietzsche, however, saw it as a "slave religion," arising from the self-interest of the weak and oppressed, expressing their secret hatred and envy of those more favored. Nietzsche's view is nearly the opposite of that of Marx, which suggests that the moral relativism of both men may be unsuited to making any cogent moral observations.

The difference between Marx and Nietzsche on Christianity is like the difference between the Sophists Thrasymachus and Callicles on the subject of justice and law. Thrasymachus taught that justice is the interest of the stronger, and Marx likewise taught that the strong classes of people use Christianity to keep workers in bondage. And as Callicles thought that laws are a device by which the masses could check the power of the

---

6. Friedrich Nietzsche, "On Truth and Lies in a Nonmoral Sense," in *Philosophy and Truth: Selections from Nietzsche's Notebooks of the Early 1870s*, trans. and ed. Daniel Breazeale (Atlantic Highlands, NJ: Humanities Press, 1990), 79–97.

7. Friedrich Nietzsche, *The Joyful Wisdom* (New York: Ungar, 1960).

8. Friedrich Nietzsche, *Beyond Good and Evil* (London: Allen and Unwin, 1967); idem, *On the Genealogy of Morals*, in *The Birth of Tragedy and the Genealogy of Morals* (New York: Anchor Books, 1990).

strong, so Nietzsche thought that Christianity was a slave religion, bent on frustrating the ambitions of superior people. Both wanted Christianity to be abolished. They wanted Christianity to be replaced by an ideology supporting class warfare (Marx) or the superman (Nietzsche).[9]

LUDWIG WITTGENSTEIN

Wittgenstein (1889–1951) was born in Austria, but taught at Cambridge in England. The only book he published during his lifetime was the *Tractatus Logico-Philosophicus*.[10] In that book, he argues that a language that is truly perfect, purified by the logical innovations of Bertrand Russell, could serve as a perfect picture of the world.

In the history of Western philosophy, the twentieth century was the century of language. In both Anglo-American and European philosophy (which were otherwise very different), language was the central item of discussion. The attention of philosophers shifted from the nature of the world as such to the language in which the world was discussed. They hoped that this shift of attention would enable them to make progress on issues where there had been a notable lack of progress since the time of the Greeks. Nietzsche had already made the study of language central to philosophy, and Wittgenstein pioneered this approach in the English-speaking world.

In Wittgenstein's approach, every sentence in a truly perfect language should refer to a fact in the universe, and he thought that we could identify facts only by sense experience. Our knowledge of facts, he thought, was built up, bit by bit, by simple ("atomic") sensations, leading to more and more complex ones. So in the perfect language, all complex sentences would be reducible to simple ones reporting simple facts, based on simple sensations.

This fundamentally empirical approach, of course, rendered ethics problematic (to say nothing of metaphysics and religion). For, as Hume and Moore had pointed out, the attempt to deduce ethical principles from empirical facts is a fallacy. So for Wittgenstein, ethical principles fell out-

9. The name of Kierkegaard also comes up in discussions of an existential approach to philosophy. Certainly Kierkegaard emphasized the importance of human subjectivity in the making of decisions. I am convinced, however, that Kierkegaard was first of all a Christian. It is difficult to relate the existential to the Christian elements of Kierkegaard's thought. So I reluctantly leave him out of this discussion, since my main purpose here is to mention thinkers who seem to be more or less pure examples of the existential tradition.

10. London: Routledge and Kegan Paul, 1921, 1963. Cf. his "Lecture on Ethics" (1929), available at http://www.kolumbus.fi/m.sipola/ethics.htm and other websites.

side the competence of the perfect language. And what cannot be said in the perfect language, Wittgenstein thought, cannot be said at all.

However, Wittgenstein was not willing to throw out ethics altogether. He was himself an ethically sensitive person. He described ethics (together with God, the self, and the world) as among those things that "can only be shown, not said." We feel, in other words, that ethical, religious, and metaphysical language is about something important, but we cannot really put that into words. These unsayable realities, for Wittgenstein, belong to the "mystical" realm.

Such is the place of ethics in the *Tractatus*. It is hard to imagine that from this system we could receive any assurance as to what is right or wrong. Essentially it is a form of what I have described as secular existential ethics, beset by the same problems as the ethics of the Sophists, Hume, Rousseau, Marx, and Nietzsche.

Wittgenstein himself saw the weaknesses in this approach. For technical reasons that I won't enter into here, Wittgenstein, even as he was writing his book, came to see that his own system was essentially contradictory. He had been trying to show the relationship between language and the world, but on the criteria he had developed for the perfect language, that relationship was one of those things that could not be spoken. It was unsayable, mystical. So Wittgenstein recognized that the whole *Tractatus* was basically an attempt to say something unsayable. Hence the famous closing lines:

> My propositions are elucidatory in this way: he who understands me finally recognizes them as senseless, when he has climbed out through them, on them, over them. (He must so to speak throw away the ladder, after he has climbed up on it.) He must surmount these propositions; then he sees the world rightly. Whereof one cannot speak, thereof must one be silent.[11]

Thus ethics, with metaphysics, religion, and the whole of philosophy, passes into silence.

The *Tractatus* is a remarkable example of how rationalism passes into irrationalism. Wittgenstein begins by trying to accommodate all reality into the form of a perfect language (rationalism), but he discovers that in this system nothing can be known or communicated (irrationalism).

But Wittgenstein eventually departed from this way of thinking and entered a new phase, sometimes called "the later Wittgenstein."[12] In his

---

11. *Tractatus*, 6.54; 7.0.

12. Many posthumously published texts of Wittgenstein reflect this later approach. The standard exposition is the *Philosophical Investigations* (New York: Macmillan, 1953, 1968), which Wittgenstein was actually preparing for publication at the time of his death. An easier

later thought, Wittgenstein abandoned the attempt to reduce all reality to the confines of a perfect language. Rather, he adopted a much more liberal view of language, noting that it has many functions, not only the function of stating facts. In most of the cases where we speak of "meaning," he says, we refer to the *use* of words in the activities of human life. So religion and ethics are no longer in the sphere of the unsayable. They can certainly be said. But Wittgenstein is rather dogmatic sometimes about the proper use of these words, insisting, for example, that religious language should never be used in critique of scientific language, or vice versa. His irrationalism continues in his new liberality, his rationalism in his often dogmatic insistence on propriety. In neither his earlier nor his later phases does Wittgenstein give us any help in determining standards of right and wrong. In the end, for him such standards are merely a component of our subjectivity.

EMOTIVISM

From about 1920 to 1950, the dominant philosophical movement in the English-speaking world was logical positivism. First formulated by a group of scientists and philosophers centered in Vienna ("the Vienna circle") and Berlin ("the Berlin circle"), it sought to limit knowledge to what could be learned through the scientific method. Many of these thinkers fled from the Nazis to the United States, including Rudolf Carnap, Herbert Feigl, Carl Hempel, and Moritz Schlick. The English philosopher A. J. Ayer popularized their work in his *Language, Truth, and Logic.*[13]

The logical positivists had read Wittgenstein's *Tractatus* with appreciation, but they were repelled by its mysticism and wanted instead to establish human knowledge on a scientific basis.

This group emphasized the "verification principle," namely, that a sentence has no "cognitive meaning" unless it can be verified by observations or the scientific method. Cognitive meaning is the ability of a sentence to state a fact, truly or falsely. So, the positivists reasoned, much language that we normally take to be factual, including the language of metaphysics, religion, and ethics, is cognitively meaningless. That is to say, such language is incapable of stating any fact, either truly or falsely. Wittgenstein's *Tractatus* had said that such language is mystical; the logical positivists thought that it was without cognitive meaning. In the end, the two positions were not far apart.

---

introduction is *The Blue and Brown Books* (Oxford: Blackwell, 1964), consisting of student transcripts of lectures that Wittgenstein dictated to his classes in the early 1930s.

13. New York: Oxford University Press, 1936.

Logical positivism appeared to be a radical challenge to Christian faith, and it instilled some fear in believers who were aware of the movement. The positivists were not just saying that Christianity was false. They were saying that it was neither true nor false, that it neither asserted nor denied any factual content.

What, then, happened to ethics in this philosophy? Like Wittgenstein, the logical positivists were not ready to dismiss ethics altogether, especially given the devastating evils of Nazism. But they could not admit that ethics was cognitively meaningful, that it was capable of stating facts. There could be no moral facts, because there was no observational or scientific way of verifying them. (Thus the logical positivists echoed the teaching of Hume and Moore that we cannot reason from "is" to "ought.")

Their approach was to reinterpret ethical language as something other than factual. Rudolf Carnap argued that ethical statements were disguised imperatives. Moritz Schlick said that ethical statements were rules for behavior, analogous to rules of procedure in science. But the most prevalent view in the movement came to be that of C. L. Stevenson's *Ethics and Language*.[14] Stevenson argued that ethical statements have two distinctive elements. First, they are expressions of emotion. When I say that stealing is wrong, for example, I am saying that I don't like stealing. Second, they recommend to others the feelings expressed. So "Stealing is wrong" means "I don't like stealing, and you shouldn't like it either." This view is not much different from Hume's attempt to base ethical judgments on "feelings of approbation."

So the predominant logical positivist view of ethics came to be called emotivism. But it never gained many followers, even in the philosophical community, for reasons such as these:

1. It became evident to most philosophers, secular as well as Christian, that the verification principle was deeply flawed. The positivists were not able to agree on a formulation of it. Some formulations seemed too narrow, for they ended up excluding some scientific language; other formulations seemed too broad, for they included some language of religion and metaphysics. Eventually it became obvious that the main goal of the positivists was not to understand how the term *meaning* is used in human life, but rather to come up with a "principle" that would glorify science and disparage metaphysics and religion. Philosophers came to see that the verification principle was an ideological tool, not an accurate reflection of what really constitutes meaning.

2. Further, like Wittgenstein's *Tractatus*, logical positivism fell into self-contradiction. The verification principle itself could not be verified by any

14. New Haven: Yale University Press, 1944.

kind of observation or scientific method. What observation or experiment could possibly verify the principle that cognitive meaning is limited to verifiable statements? The conclusion, then, is that the verification principle itself is cognitively meaningless—perhaps, like ethical language on this view, an expression of the positivists' emotions. As the *Tractatus* proved to be "unsayable," so logical positivism proved to be "emotive."

3. Emotivism itself, as a view of ethics, ran into many problems, chiefly that it abolished any kind of serious ethical discussion. In an ethical dispute one may, of course, on an emotivist view, debate the facts concerning which the feelings are expressed. And the disputants may draw one another's attention to features of those facts that might change attitudes. But in the end, once the facts are known and agreed to, if I like stealing and you don't, there is nothing more to be said. And why, on this view, should anybody ever agonize over a moral decision? If you know how you feel, but you are still uncertain of what is right, then you are simply confused. But this is a most implausible account of the moral life.

EXISTENTIALISM

During the twentieth century, language analysis was the dominant approach to philosophy in the English-speaking world. Wittgenstein and logical positivism were early examples. In the later part of the century, this emphasis continued, but with less extravagant claims. Anglo-American language analysts tend now to work in a more piecemeal way, trying to clarify this or that specific problem, without relying on big, global theories of the universe, of meaning, or of ethics.

Across the English Channel, a different type of philosophy emerged, called existentialism.[15] It is also concerned with language, but it has different emphases and preoccupations. With roots in the thought of Kierkegaard and Nietzsche, existentialism was developed by such thinkers as Martin Heidegger, Karl Jaspers, and Jean-Paul Sartre. There are significant differences between these thinkers, but I will confine myself to Sartre, who is by far the clearest writer of the group.[16]

15. Up to now, I have been using the term *existential* to designate a long tradition of philosophical ethics, a tradition in which "the existential principle" is valued over the normative and situational principles. Twentieth-century existentialism is a specific development in this tradition, but a development significant enough that I have given its name to the whole tradition of which it is a part.

16. See Sartre, *Being and Nothingness* (New York: Philosophical Library, 1956). A good introduction to the movement is Walter Kaufmann, ed., *Existentialism from Dostoyevsky to Sartre* (New York: New American Library, 1975).

Aristotle taught that when we make ethical choices, we seek to realize our essence. In his view, the essence of a human being is to be a rational animal. So in every decision and action (that is, in our "existence"), we should seek to express our rational nature. So in our ethical life we seek to realize our essence. Essence determines, or should determine, our existence. Thus, essence precedes existence.

I shall discuss Aristotle's view more thoroughly in chapter 7. I mention him here only by way of contrast with Sartre. Sartre defines existentialism as the view that, contrary to Aristotle, existence precedes essence. In his view, mankind has no essence, because there is no God. We have no defined purpose or nature. Therefore, we are thrown into existence without any manual to direct our lives. We simply act.

As the Greeks said to "count no man happy until he is dead," Sartre envisions that, after a person has lived his life, it will then be possible to describe him, indeed evaluate him. Only then can he be said to have an "essence" or "nature." We can speak similarly about the whole human race: only after the last human being has died, will it be possible (presumably, for another race) to describe the essence of humanity, what we really were.

According to Sartre, the notion that existence precedes essence results when we take atheism (Nietzsche's death of God) with proper seriousness. Sartre strives in his philosophy to develop a consistently atheistic view of things.

On this basis, he thinks, we are radically free. We are not determined by anything within us or outside of us. Nor are we subject to any authority outside of ourselves. Even if an angel tells us what to do, says Sartre, we must decide whether to obey or not, and we must decide how to interpret his words. So our thinking is autonomous, like the rational autonomy of the ancient Greeks.

Nevertheless, Sartre wants to make some general statements about how human beings are unique. What unique quality can we have, if we have no essence? Sartre answers that we are unique in that we incorporate nonbeing within ourselves—not being (that would be an essence), but nonbeing. We are unique in what we are not and in our relation to other things that are not.

The relationship between being and nonbeing has been a perplexing problem throughout the history of philosophy. Parmenides thought that the very idea of nonbeing was irrational: how can there *be* anything that *is not*? It seems that whenever you try to imagine or conceptualize nonbeing, you turn it into something, into being. The title of Sartre's main philosophical work, *Being and Nothingness*, indicates that he intends to deal with this problem in a fresh way.

For Sartre, nonbeing is a unique property of human beings. Among all beings, we alone are able to represent to ourselves things that "are not." We can conceive of the past, even the distant past, which of course no longer is. We can conceptualize and make plans for the future, which, as of now, is not.[17] We can also think about things that are possible, but which are not actual and may never be actual. Thus we employ our faculty of imagination creatively in art, science, and personal life. Through our interaction with nonbeing, we rise far above animals and plants in what we can accomplish.

Most significantly for Sartre's ethics, we are able to distinguish ourselves from what we are not, from our environment. The world exists *en soi*, "in itself." It is solid and definable. Rocks and trees can be defined and described. Of course, since God does not exist, they no more have predefined essences than human beings have. But they lack the human consciousness of nonbeing, so they play definable, predictable roles in the human universe. Only a human being exists *pour soi*, "for himself"—self-conscious and conscious of his uniqueness. So our relationship to nonbeing reinforces our lack of essence.

Thus, our decisions are radically free. We are never forced, by our essence or by our past, by our heredity, environment, or past experience, to choose in a certain way. At every moment, we freely choose to be what we are. There are limits, of course, but those limits themselves are chosen. If I choose to go to medical school and the admission requirements are too high, then I face a limit. But it is a limit only because it frustrates a desire that I have freely chosen. If I hadn't freely decided to seek medical training, my failure to be admitted would not be a limit to me.

Death is, of course, usually thought to be the ultimate limit. But, Sartre says, it is a limit only insofar as I freely choose to value life.

We usually think that an existential type of ethic will deny the notion of responsibility, since responsibility seems to presuppose an objective, external norm. Indeed, we wonder how there can be such a thing as responsibility with no God to be responsible to. But Sartre surprises us. Although he denies the objective norm, and although he denies God, he places a great emphasis on responsibility.

He says that since all our limits are freely chosen, we have no excuses for the things we do. We freely choose what we do—indeed, what we are. If someone grows up in a poor family and enters a life of crime, his poverty is

---

17. What, then, is the present? If we think of it as a knife-edge moment between past and present, then we cannot really think about it until it is past. That thought would suggest that past, present, and future are all nonbeing. We live in a universe of nonbeing, rather than being.

no excuse. He has freely chosen to violate the law. Although I disagree with his overall position, his discussion of responsibility is often illuminating.

We are not only responsible for our particular decisions and actions, but also responsible in a more general sense, according to Sartre. For in every choice we make, we choose a certain image of mankind. Our choices also affect the choices of other people, which can lead to serious consequences for the whole human race. Since the essence of mankind comes at the end of its history, rather than at the beginning, each of us contributes to that essence, in every choice we make. So we are responsible, not only for our own actions, but also for the ultimate value of mankind.

Yet few people recognize their vast responsibility or the extent of their freedom. Indeed, when we do glimpse our freedom, we sometimes recoil from it in fear. In some ways, we would rather be *en soi* than *pour soi*. We would rather be solid, definable, and predictable, than radically free. We like our excuses. We would prefer to think of ourselves as beings who are determined and defined by their past. That *en soi* character gives us status, a kind of dignity, a kind of power, and plenty of excuses. We would rather be beings than nonbeings.

It would be nice, of course, to be both *pour soi* and *en soi*, to have both pure being and pure nonbeing, both being and freedom, both essence and existence. But Sartre says this is impossible. In Christian theology, God has both essence and existence, and his essence is identical to his existence. But Sartre thinks that this concept of God is self-contradictory and therefore that this God cannot exist. No one can have both a perfectly defined nature (essence) and perfect freedom (existence).

But human beings try to be godlike, seeking essence along with their existence. In Sartre's view, this is *mauvaise foi* ("bad faith," sometimes translated "self-deception"). In bad faith, we deny our freedom. We pretend that we are mere objects, determined by our past or by our station in life.[18] We deceive ourselves into thinking that we are not responsible for our actions in Sartre's sense. To live like that is "inauthentic existence."

Sartre would have us live in an "authentic" way that expresses our freedom, our nonbeing.[19] In his novels, lead characters often act out of

18. According to the Idealist school of philosophy, which Sartre opposes, our ethical responsibilities can be deduced from our station in life. If you are a butler, you should behave as a butler; if a waiter, as a waiter, and so on.

19. Sartre again opposes Aristotle, but their principles are very similar. Aristotle calls on us to realize our essence. Sartre calls on us to realize our freedom. Sartre has, in effect, replaced Aristotle's "essence" with "freedom," namely, a lack of essence, a nonbeing. But is this freedom really something different from an essence? Has not Sartre made the old philosophical mistake of trying to define nonbeing (as freedom, in this case) and thus turning it into a kind of being?

character, violating the expectations of society. We need, he thinks, to overturn the conventions, to do things, occasionally at least, that the world will consider bizarre, even morally repugnant.

Some observations:

1. Sartre, no less than Gnosticism (see chapter 5), reduces ethics to metaphysics. For the Gnostics, our task is to rise to a higher level of being. For Sartre, it is to express our nonbeing. But both are impersonal characterizations of ethics. I have argued that ethics is essentially a matter of personal relationships: relationships between people and other people, and between people and God. Sartre's attempt to build a consistently atheistic ethic destroys any legitimate basis for ethical behavior. The notion that ethical behavior is acting out of character is ludicrous.

2. Contrary to Sartre's claim, his position is devastating to human responsibility. He is helpful in emphasizing the central role of free choice in our ethical decisions.[20] But why should we value one free choice above another? Contrary to Sartre, responsibility is necessarily answerability, which presupposes a personal relationship.

3. Sartre claims to set us free from all moral rules (irrationalism); yet, he stigmatizes a certain kind of behavior as inauthentic, thus claiming for himself the authority to legislate in the field of morals (rationalism).

POSTMODERNISM

The postmodern school (including such thinkers as Jean-Francois Lyotard, Jacques Derrida, Jacques Lacan, Roland Barthes, Michel Foucault, and Richard Rorty) has not focused much attention on ethics, but in the late twentieth century it became famous for its skepticism about "grand narratives" or worldview-based thinking. Certainly its influence on ethics, as on many other disciplines, is to commend what I have called the existential perspective, contrary to any notion of historical goals (the situational perspective) or transcendent norms (the normative perspective).

These thinkers come largely from backgrounds in linguistics, reacting against the structuralist linguistics of the 1960s and 1970s. In their view, there is no master structure common to human minds that generates all language. Nor does language refer to reality in any direct way. When we ask for the meaning of a word, we get, as a definition, other words. So words refer to other words, not to any objective reality.

---

20. However, his concept of libertarian freedom is unbiblical and incoherent. See *DG*, chapter 8.

So the task of the philosopher is "deconstruction": to break down the connections that people think they are making between language and reality. Indeed, nobody can serve as an authority as to the meaning of a piece of language. Even the author is incompetent to tell what his language means. For once he writes or speaks it, it enters into a community, and the meaning of his words is determined by the hearers. To people in that community, the text may convey much that is contrary to the author's intention, such as racial prejudice, gender oppression, and so forth. It may thus refute its own ostensible purpose, once deconstructed. Thus it is hopeless to try to find objective truth in language.

Like Nietzsche, postmodernist writers tend to see language as an expression of the will to power. Like Marx, they tend to read everything in the context of class warfare. Once deconstructed, language tends to be almost entirely about oppressors trying to dominate their victims and victims trying to fight back. So the discussion quickly turns to racism, feminism, speciesism, and so on.

These are, of course, ethical topics. But the views of postmodernists on these topics are rarely argued; they are merely presupposed. The postmodern conception of language rules out patient and careful argumentation about such topics, for every argument is a piece of language demanding deconstruction. Such arguments are dismissed as mere exercises of power.

The problem is not that postmodernists are skeptics in a general way. They oppose "grand narratives," but not "little narratives." They debunk large worldviews, but they claim to accept the simple facts of everyday experience. But ethics requires a worldview, a grand narrative. It is not just about the simple facts of everyday experience. Rather, as we have seen, it claims to deal with principles that are universal, necessary, and obligatory. If we reject worldview thinking, as postmodernism does, then we reject ethics in any meaningful sense of the word.

I do not deny that language expresses the will to power. Scripture often speaks of the power of God's word, not only its meaningful content (Isa. 55:11; Rom. 1:16). Human beings, created in God's image, use the power of their language both for good (Rom. 1:16) and for evil (Gen. 11:5–7), and they certainly have used it to oppress other people. It is also true that when people think they are simply stating facts objectively, they are often stating them in such a way as to increase their power over others.

But language is not only about power. It is also about meaning.[21] It not only makes things happen, but also communicates truth or falsehood from

---

21. In *Doctrine of the Word of God* I plan to explore the triad of power, meaning, and presence as it describes God's word and also as it describes human language generally. God's

one person to another.[22] The first does not in any way exclude the second. So we must not only observe what language does to people, as postmodernists do; we must also discuss in meaningful words what language *ought* to do.

Furthermore, postmodernism, like many other ideologies, tends to exempt itself from its own critique. If arguments against postmodernism must be deconstructed as attempts to gain power, why shouldn't arguments in favor of postmodernism be deconstructed in the same way? But if all such arguments are to be deconstructed, then truth about such issues (even the "little" ones, if postmodernists are willing to discuss them) will permanently elude us.

CONCLUSION

The existential tradition in secular ethics focuses on the inner life. That focus is legitimate in itself. Much of ethical importance takes place within us, in the heart, as Scripture says. But secular ethics misuses the existential perspective by absolutizing the authority of the human mind, will, and feelings. It affirms rational autonomy, and, when it sees the limitations of reason, it replaces or supplements it with autonomous human will or feeling. It is rationalistic when it claims authority for autonomous reason, but irrationalistic when it denies the knowability of the world and the accessibility of moral standards. Thus, this tradition is unable to provide any meaningful standards for ethics.

---

word is the power that creates and controls the world (Ps. 33:6), the communication of his truth (John 17:17), and the place of his dwelling with us (John 1:1–14).

22. To put it in technical philosophical terms, language is illocutionary as well as perlocutionary.

CHAPTER 7

The Teleological Tradition

The second major tradition in secular ethics is often called teleological. This term comes from the Greek word *telos*, which means "goal" or "purpose." This tradition understands ethics as a selection of goals and of means to reach those goals. In the secular version, the goal is usually human happiness or, more narrowly, pleasure.

Secular teleological ethics values what I called in chapter 4 the teleological principle: "A good act maximizes the happiness of living creatures." However, it is less impressed with the existential and deontological principles. Teleological thinkers are dissatisfied with the subjectivism of the existential approach. They are not content to rely on subjective feelings of approval and disapproval for ethical guidance; they seek something more objective, a basis for those feelings. But they are not impressed, either, by the abstruse reasonings or religious revelations that lead to the norms of deontological ethics, which we shall consider in the next chapter. Rather, they want a basis for ethics that is simple and practical, one that is easily explained and intuitively persuasive.

In their view, the goal of ethical decisions should be to achieve human happiness. An act is right if it maximizes happiness and minimizes suffering. So to determine what to do, we only need to anticipate the consequences of our proposed actions. Thus, teleological ethics is often called consequentialist. This seems to be a simple, practical, and persuasive method of evaluating decisions.

It is important here to review the distinction made in chapter 2 between moral and nonmoral senses of the word *good*. Only persons and their actions

91

and attitudes can be good in a moral sense. But happiness is a condition or state of affairs, so it can be considered good only in a nonmoral sense. In teleological ethics, the goal of happiness is called the *summum bonum*, or highest good.

In a teleological ethic, morally good decisions are means of achieving happiness. So moral goods are instruments to achieve nonmoral goods.

As we shall see, the Bible affirms the importance of considering the goals or purposes of our action. The highest goal, the *summum bonum*, is the glory of God (1 Cor. 10:31). Scripture also teaches us to consider the consequences of our choices (Luke 13:3, 5, for example). And it affirms the importance of maximizing the happiness of others (as in Luke 10:27). But unlike secular teleological ethics, Scripture also affirms the authority of God's moral norms and the importance of the character of the heart.

CYRENAICISM

Aristippus (b. 435 BC), founder of the Cyrenaic school, was one of the earliest teleological ethicists in ancient Greece. We don't know very much about his specific formulations, but the views developed in the Cyrenaic school represent a fairly crude teleological system, compared to the more nuanced approaches of Epicurus and Aristotle. The very simplicity of Cyrenaicism, however, makes it useful as an introduction to teleological ethics.

For the Cyrenaics, the highest good is the greatest amount of pleasure and the least amount of pain. This view is called hedonism, after the Greek word for pleasure. Now in teleological ethics, the most difficult question is how to evaluate different kinds of pleasure. How does one compare the pleasure of eating ice cream with the pleasure of listening to Beethoven or mastering golf?

The Cyrenaics faced this problem and answered it squarely: the best pleasures are the most intense. They saw pleasures as immediate sensations, as provided by food, sex, or drugs. Further, the Cyrenaics had no room for delayed gratification. According to them, short-term pleasures should not be sacrificed to the possibility of long-term pleasures. Naturally, rumors spread about immorality running rampant among the Cyrenaics.

EPICURUS

Epicurus (341–270 BC) presents a somewhat more sophisticated version of teleological ethics. Metaphysically, he was an atomist, following

Democritus (460–370 BC), who taught that reality is reducible to tiny bits of matter in motion. Democritus thought that atoms move in vertical tracks, parallel to one another. But if that is so, how do they ever collide to form objects? Epicurus answered that occasionally they "swerve" from the vertical. This swerving is unpredictable. In Epicurus's view, it explains not only the formation of objects, but also human free will.[1]

What place is there in such a materialistic system for ethics?[2] Essentially, Epicurus taught that we should avoid pain and seek pleasure (which he defined as the absence of pain). Unlike the Cyrenaics and some later Epicureans, Epicurus preferred long-term to short-term pleasures, mental to physical pleasures, and pleasures of rest to pleasures of movement. He especially valued *ataraxia*, calmness without disturbance from outside the self.

There are several problems with this view: (1) There are many things that human beings value more than pleasure. One example is sacrificing one's life to save the life of another. Epicurus gives us no good reason to pursue pleasure rather than some other value. (2) If we define *pleasure* so broadly as to include all other values, including self-sacrifice, then it loses its meaning. It doesn't distinguish pleasurable from nonpleasurable activities. (3) Even if it is true that people value pleasure in some sense above all else, it is a logical jump to say that we *ought* to value pleasure above all else.[3] But the ought is what ethics is all about. I doubt that anyone can derive an ethical ought from a materialistic philosophy. Matter in motion simply cannot tell us what we ought to do. It cannot motivate that loyalty, obedience, and love that are the ground of obligation.

Epicurus believed in the existence of the Olympian gods, but he held that they had achieved such bliss that they had no interest in getting involved in human history. So we need not fear them or expect any benefit from serving them.

1. This appears to be the origin of the concept of libertarian freedom, which I criticize extensively in *DG*, chapter 8. Many have argued that this kind of freedom is the ground of moral responsibility. But is that at all likely? Imagine that an atom swerved randomly somewhere in your head and made you steal $500. Would you feel guilty? More likely you would feel like the victim of a random event—like being struck by lightning. You didn't do anything to make the atom swerve. How can a human being be blamed for a mental accident? If libertarian freedom exists, it is not the ground of moral responsibility. Rather, it destroys responsibility.

2. You should not believe the rumors that the Greeks hated matter. Some of them did, among them the Platonists and Gnostics. But the Epicureans and Stoics were materialists.

3. Recall the discussion of the naturalistic fallacy in chapter 5.

ARISTOTLE

Aristotle (384–322 BC) is such a great thinker that he almost deserves a chapter to himself. It seems inappropriate to discuss him in a chapter along with Aristippus, Epicurus, and Mill, for his thought is far more sophisticated that theirs and much more influential. Aristotle's ethics is more than merely teleological, but it is essentially teleological. He makes the best case that can be made for a secular teleological ethic.

The greatest philosophers (among whom I would include Plato, Aristotle, Aquinas, and Kant, with honorable mention to Augustine and Hegel)[4] are thinkers who do not align themselves with one school of thought, but who creatively bring together ideas from many schools into impressive world-views. That was certainly true of both Aristotle and his teacher Plato.[5]

Aristotle accepts Plato's distinction between form and matter. Matter is the stuff of the world; form is what gives to that stuff its qualities: shape, color, truth, beauty, moral virtue, and especially purpose (telos). Plato separated form and matter into two worlds. Aristotle demythologizes Plato, teaching that form and matter are aspects of everything in this world, except for the Prime Mover, Aristotle's godlike first principle, which is pure form, without matter.

The forms in each thing define its essence, nature, and purpose. The nature of a human being is to be a "rational animal." Now the highest good (summum bonum) for any being is the realization or actualization of its particular nature. Aristotle, therefore, is a philosopher of self-realization, which we generally associate with the existential tradition. He is, as I said earlier, a complex thinker, rather than a follower of any single tradition. But I think that for him the teleological principle is more fundamental than the existential.

Since man's nature is to be a rational animal, Aristotle held the view (as did all Greek philosophers) that man's highest good is the life of reason. Complete, habitual exercise of our rational nature constitutes "happiness" (eudaimonia). Happiness is complete well-being.[6] Unlike the Cyrenaics and Epicureans, Aristotle says that happiness is not pleasure, though pleasure accompanies it as a secondary effect.

---

4. I am inclined to add Socrates to this list, but he wrote no books, and therefore his thoughts are difficult to disentangle from those of his student Plato, who is our main source of information about him.

5. Of Plato and Aristotle it has been said that no teacher ever had a greater student, and no student a greater teacher.

6. The Greek eudaimonia is perhaps more like our term "blessedness" than our "happiness." We usually think of happiness as an emotional state. But the Greeks took it more objectively: those benefits that entitle one to pleasant emotions.

Aristotle, like Plato, distinguishes three aspects of the soul, the vegeta-tive, the sensitive (perhaps roughly equivalent to Plato's "spirited"), and the rational. We share the first with plants, and the second with animals, but the third is unique to human beings. Moral virtues are qualities of the rational soul.

Aristotle distinguishes between moral and intellectual virtues. Moral vir-tues pertain to the will; intellectual virtues pertain to reason. We learn the moral virtues—courage, temperance, and justice—by imitating those who exemplify them. Such imitation leads us in time to form good habits, and those habits form a good character. The intellectual virtue is prudence,[7] and that comes from teaching. Aristotle distinguishes philosophical wis-dom (which is disinterested and contemplative) from practical wisdom (the ability to make decisions leading to happiness). One who has wisdom, Aristotle thinks, will seek moderation in all things.

So it is often possible to determine our specific duties by calculating the mean between two extremes. For example, a buffoon makes a joke out of everything; a boor takes everything too seriously. But wit is the "golden mean" between these extremes. Aristotle didn't offer any precise formula for defining the extremes or locating the mean. Doubtless he knew that with a bit of cleverness any act could be justified as being between two extremes (e.g., robbing one bank as the mean between robbing many and robbing none). And he did see that sometimes a right decision might be on one extreme, such as the very decision to do right rather than wrong. But he assumed that the wise man would be able to furnish a proper context for these judgments.

There is a question as to how we can begin to acquire moral virtues. Aristotle teaches that we need to have virtuous dispositions in order to perform virtuous acts, but we need to perform moral acts in order to form the habits that produce virtuous dispositions.[8] Aristotle is aware of this circularity and counsels readers to begin the process by doing things that "resemble" virtuous acts. But how one gets from resemblance to actuality is a mystery.

The Christian revelation has an answer: God's grace creates moral dis-positions in sinners and enables them to follow those dispositions. And it also answers another major problem in Aristotle's ethics. He assumes that we can learn our moral obligations simply by observing our own natures and what makes us happy. This is the root of the "natural law" tradition in

7. Prudence, courage, temperance, and justice are often called "the four cardinal vir-tues" of classical philosophy. Some Christians added to them faith, hope, and love, the "theological virtues," to make seven.

8. The emphasis on disposition is another existential element in Aristotle's thought.

ethics. But, as David Hume pointed out, one cannot derive moral obligations from natural facts. One cannot infer what we ought to do from what is the case. The fact that we are rational does not prove that we ought to live according to reason; the fact that we seek happiness does not imply that we ought to seek it. Scripture points to God's revelation as the source of our knowledge of ethical obligation. God is both fact and value. To know him is to know at the same time the ultimate source of reality and the ultimate source of ethical obligation.

Typical of the Greek philosophers, Aristotle thinks that human reason is sufficient to derive moral obligations from natural facts. That is the extent of his normative perspective. His emphasis on disposition and character is an element of existential ethics, within an overall teleological emphasis. For him, ethics is seeking happiness by rational cultivation of virtues. Aristotle has a better balance between the three perspectives than most secular thinkers. But the balance is precarious. He has no adequate way to derive moral principles (the normative perspective), so he has no sufficient justification for choosing happiness as a moral goal (the situational perspective) or for identifying the dispositions that the ethical agent should cultivate (the existential perspective).

UTILITARIANISM

The most influential modern version of teleological ethics is utilitarianism, the system developed by Jeremy Bentham (1748–1832)[9] and John Stuart Mill (1806–73).[10] Utilitarianism differs from Epicureanism chiefly in its view that the goal of ethics is not only the pleasure of the individual, but "the greatest pleasure for the greatest number." That is called "the principle of utility." For Bentham, this broader goal is a consequence of individual self-interest. For Mill, it is based on a social instinct common to mankind.

Bentham measures pleasures mainly in quantitative ways, as did the ancient Cyrenaics. Mill distinguishes qualities of pleasure, as did Epicurus.

In theory, utilitarianism is a simple, practical system. There is one principle, one goal to be sought, namely, the greatest pleasure for the greatest number. A good act furthers that principle; an evil act impedes it. A good act will maximize pleasure and minimize pain. An evil act will do the reverse.

9. Bentham's most accessible work is *An Introduction to the Principles of Morals and Legislation* (London: Athlone Press, 1970).

10. See especially his essay "Utilitarianism," published in many anthologies, such as Mill, *Utilitarianism and Other Essays* (London: Penguin Books, 1987).

It would seem, then, that we could simply "calculate" the goodness or badness of an act by calculating the pleasures and pains produced by it (especially now that we have computers). Indeed, Bentham spoke of a "hedonistic calculus." This emphasis is typically modern. It fits especially well into the political culture of democracy, in which the pleasures and pains of an electorate can be quantified by polls and votes.

Utilitarianism seems to be almost routinely assumed in contemporary discussion of ethical issues. And perhaps we should blame utilitarianism somewhat for the tendency of politicians to see their task to be that of providing more pleasures for particular groups in their constituency, such as the middle class, the poor, small businesses, women, minorities, and families.

One theoretical question discussed recently by utilitarians is whether the principle of utility should be applied to each of our individual actions or to the rules used to govern those actions. Does the principle ask us to judge what pains and pleasures each act brings about, or does it ask us merely to determine what general ethical rules will lead to the greatest predominance of pleasure over pain? Those who choose the first alternative are called act-utilitarians, and those who choose the second are called rule-utilitarians.[11]

Here are some evaluations of utilitarianism, which will overlap the comments made earlier about Epicurus:

1. Both Bentham and Mill assume that everyone by nature seeks pleasure and flees from pain. But is that true? People do sometimes sacrifice themselves for others, by an instinct that may be more fundamental than the desire to seek pleasure and avoid pain. According to Nietzsche, people really seek power more than they seek pleasure.

2. In the face of such objections, utilitarians are sometimes inclined to stretch the definition of pleasure to include such things as self-sacrifice and the exercise of power. But if that definition is stretched too far, everything we do becomes pleasure. And if everything is pleasure, then nothing is. And it becomes unclear just what we are trying to calculate when we seek to calculate pleasures.

3. Teleological ethics commits the naturalistic fallacy more obviously than other approaches. For even if it is obvious that human beings *do* seek pleasure in all their choices, it by no means follows that they *ought* to do so.

4. The move from an individualistic approach (Epicurus) to a corporate one (Bentham, Mill) requires justification. It certainly is not obvious, as Bentham thought, that maximization of everyone's pleasure is needed for

---

11. Richard B. Brandt introduced this distinction. See his *Ethical Theory* (Englewood Cliffs, NJ: Prentice Hall, 1959).

individual pleasure. Nor is it obvious, as Mill thought (reverting to the existential perspective), that we have a natural instinct to promote the collective pleasure of mankind. And even if we do seek the welfare of society, it is not thereby evident that we ought to do so.

5. Is it always right to maximize the happiness of a community? Most ethically reflective people would answer no, as in the situation where the majority group in a country takes great pleasure in murdering a minority group. But utilitarianism, taken consistently, would answer yes. For utilitarianism, in the final analysis, the end justifies the means. This is sometimes called the "swine trough" objection to utilitarianism, that it justifies behavior that any civilized person would deplore. The utilitarian Henry Sidgwick responded to this objection by adding to the principle of utility a principle of justice, or fairness.[12] This principle tells us to seek not only the maximum amount of pleasure, but also an equal distribution of it. However, this principle has no basis in the overall utilitarian scheme. It is a deontological principle, not a teleological one. Why should we seek fairness or equality? If not on a utilitarian basis, then on what basis? Furthermore, Sidgwick's principle of justice is not intuitively obvious. The argument between maximizing pleasures for the whole society and distributing them equally to all members of society continues today, notably in economic contexts: is it better to maximize opportunity or to insure equality of wealth? It is hard to see how this argument could ever be resolved apart from a religious revelation. Finally, Sidgwick does not provide an adequate method of resolving conflicts between his two principles—the conflicts that produced the very problem that the principle of justice was designed to resolve.

6. Utilitarians greatly underestimate the difficulty of calculating the pleasures and pains likely to result from an action. There are many kinds of pleasure and pain. Among pleasures, consider listening to Brahms, eating a cherry pie, running a marathon, falling in love, having your local baseball team win the World Series, and solving a philosophical problem. No method could quantify these pleasures so as to permit calculation. We can measure a feeling of cold or hot, by windchill calculations and such, but even that will vary from individual to individual. But how can we measure the pleasure of watching a sunset or looking at the Grand Canyon? Further, to measure the consequences of an action, we would have to trace its effects into the indefinite future and throughout the universe. One action, after all, can have enormous effects, years later and miles away. Imagine Columbus trying to calculate the effects of his decision to sail west.

12. See Sidgwick, *The Methods of Ethics* (New York: Macmillan, 1901).

It turns out, then, that utilitarianism, though advertised as a simple and practical method for evaluating courses of action, in fact requires divine omniscience. Only God can make the calculation required. Like the secular existential ethicist, the utilitarian ethicist must put himself in the place of God. We can now understand why many utilitarians retreat from act-utilitarianism to rule-utilitarianism: it seems so much easier to evaluate the consequences of rules than the consequences of individual acts. But unless the rules come from God, we have no reason to think that any rule will, throughout all history and throughout the entire universe, lead to more pleasure than pain.

JOHN DEWEY

John Dewey (1859–1952) is essentially a teleological ethicist, but he introduces much more flexibility into the traditional teleological concepts of means and ends.[13] In doing so, he reveals some of the complications that make hedonistic calculus impossible.

Dewey accepts the basic utilitarian model of ethics: choosing a goal and then the means to achieve it. But he rejects the idea that the goal must be pleasure or happiness. Dewey insists that pleasure is only one of many goals we seek, including health, wealth, power, learning, justice, entertainment, and friendship. Further, our goals change from time to time. And as our goals change, the means to achieve them also change.

Our ethical life is not, according to Dewey, a matter of choosing a goal and then enduring any means to achieve it. Some goals are highly desirable, but the means to achieve them are so difficult or unpleasant that we decide the goal is not worth the effort, and so we shift to another goal. Means and goals influence one another in a dialectical way. No goal is absolutely fixed.

So, in Dewey's view, ethics is not an orderly, simple process, such as that envisioned by Bentham and Mill. He sees goodness as the meaning experienced when a person wrestles with conflicting impulses, but somehow reaches a point of action.

I am tempted to describe Dewey's ethic as existential, because, as with Aristotle and Idealism, self-realization plays a major role. Self-realization describes the process of bringing together all the incompatible impulses into what he calls "an orderly release in action." But Dewey

---

13. See Dewey, *Ethics* (New York: Holt, 1932); see also his *Reconstruction in Philosophy* (New York: New American Library, 1950).

insists that even self-realization itself should not be considered a fixed goal, but only a criterion for evaluating other goals. Since he sees the decision-making process in terms of means and goals, I regard his ethics as primarily teleological.

But in a way his approach also serves as a refutation of teleological ethics, even a *reductio ad absurdum*. With ever-changing goals and ever-changing means leading to a flux of incompatible impulses that somehow leads to action (perhaps an axe murder), it is impossible to imagine what an ethical discussion could ever be about. Dewey is right to say that our goals change, and that with no revelation to guide us we cannot define happiness or pleasure as an absolute. But if he is right, his point serves as a deconstruction of teleological ethics and leaves little distance between teleological ethics and existential ethics. All of this leaves us hungry for an ethical norm. The philosophers to be considered in the next chapter earnestly try to supply one.

CHAPTER 8

The Deontological Tradition

In our survey of less explicitly religious non-Christian ethics, we now come to the last of the three major traditions. The word *deontological* comes from the Greek *deō*, translated "owe, ought, or must." So a deontological ethicist is concerned above all with the normative perspective of ethics, with ethics as obligation. He is impressed by what was called in chapter 4 "the deontological principle," namely, that a good act is a response to duty, even at the price of self-sacrifice. He is less impressed by the teleological and existential principles. Deontologists tend to be contemptuous of people who do good in order to gain pleasure or happiness (the teleological approach) or to express their inner inclinations (the existential approach). In the deontological view, seeking happiness is never morally virtuous; indeed, it detracts from the moral quality of any action. So when a writer despises pleasure and exalts principle or self-sacrifice, he is probably a deontologist.

Scripture also calls us to self-sacrifice (Matt. 16:24–26) and warns us against the deceits of pleasure (2 Tim. 3:4; Titus 3:3). But Scripture distinguishes between godly and ungodly pleasures. Godly pleasures are good, and they motivate us to pursue holiness. Often in the same passages where Scripture warns us against ungodly pleasures, it promises the rewards of the kingdom of God to those who obey (Matt. 6:28–33). So Scripture does not agree with secular deontologism. For Scripture, duty and happiness are not opposed, but in the long run reinforce one another.

101

Deontologists seek to find ethical norms that are universal, necessary, and obligatory. They usually accept the argument of Hume, Moore,[1] and others, that such norms cannot be found through sense experience (as in teleological ethics) or introspection (as in existential ethics). The problem set before the deontologist, therefore, is to find some other source of ethical knowledge. Christians have such a source in the revelation of God. But secular deontologists reject that possibility as well. As a result, they fail to find what they are seeking, and that failure is a main reason for the popularity of teleological and existential alternatives. Then the deontologist criticizes the other positions for their lack of any ethical norm at all, and the argument continues back and forth.

But there is more. Besides finding an absolute ethical standard, the deontologist must also show how that standard can be used to tell us in specific terms what is right and wrong. In other words, he must show how his standard contains ethical content. One major problem for the deontological movement is that once the philosopher identifies the source of ethical norms, that source turns out to be so abstract and vague that nothing specific can be derived from it. A norm that says nothing is, of course, no norm at all. But for deontologism, anything less than the ultimate source of norms lacks authority. So the more authority a norm has, the less content it has, and vice versa.

The problem is that when they deny the authority of God's revelation, secular deontologists cannot locate the ethical norm in a personal absolute. So they try in various ways to find impersonal sources of ethical authority. As I argued earlier and will continue to argue, that cannot be done. So the secular search for an absolute norm must inevitably fail. There will be either no norm at all (in existential ethics), or an inadequate one (in teleological ethics), or an authoritative norm with no content (in deontological ethics).

In the final analysis, this is a religious difficulty. Deontologists, like all those who lack the saving grace of God, do not really want to hear God's voice. With the pagans of Romans 1, they suppress divine revelation. You can suppress revelation by denying that there is an ultimate norm, by embracing an inadequate norm, or by embracing an "ultimate" norm that turns out to have no content. In each case, you are left alone to do what you want to do. Thus, deontological and teleological ethics revert to existential ethics. Rationalism reverts to irrationalism. Ethics reverts to human autonomy.

---

1. Moore's position will be discussed later in this chapter.

PLATO

In my view, the deontological tradition begins with Plato (427–347 BC), but, like his pupil Aristotle, he is much more than a member of a particular ethical tradition. Plato is one of the greatest thinkers in the history of philosophy, with interests in many questions of metaphysics, epistemology, and ethics. And he deals with many aspects of ethics other than the deontological. I will indicate teleological and existential themes in his ethical thought. (If the reader would like to begin with simpler versions of deontologism, I suggest that he move on to the next sections, on Cynicism and Stoicism, and come back to Plato later on.)

For all its complexity, Plato's thinking about ethics is essentially a deontological quest for an adequate ethical norm. Like his mentor, Socrates, he was stimulated to ethical reflection by the relativism of the Sophists, who were discussed in chapter 6. It cannot be true, he thought, that ethical virtue is whatever the individual wants it to be. But then what is it?

If we are to attain moral knowledge, we must be able, contrary to the Sophists, to attain knowledge. That knowledge must be objective, not relative to every knower.

Plato's epistemology begins with the observation that we can learn very little from our sense organs. So far, he agrees with the Sophists. Our eyes and ears easily deceive us. But the remarkable thing is that we have the rational ability to correct those deceptions and thus to find truth. It is by our reason also that we form concepts of things. We have never, for example, seen a perfect square. But somehow we know what a perfect square would be like, for we know the mathematical formula that generates one. Since we don't learn the concept of squareness by sense experience, we must learn it from reason. We similarly learn from reason the concepts of treeness, horseness, humanity, justice, virtue, goodness, etc. We don't see these, but somehow we know them.

These concepts Plato calls Forms or Ideas. Since we cannot find Forms on earth, he says, they must exist in another realm, a world of Forms, as opposed to the world of sense experience. But what are Forms, exactly? In reading Plato, we sometimes find ourselves thinking of the Form of treeness as a perfect, gigantic tree somewhere, which serves as a model for all trees on earth. But that can't be right. Given the many different kinds of trees, how could one tree serve as a perfect model for all of them? And even if there were a gigantic tree somewhere, how could there be a gigantic justice, or virtue, or goodness? Further, Plato says that the Forms are not objects of sensation (as a gigantic tree would be). Rather, they are known through intelligence alone, through reason. Perhaps Plato is following the

Pythagoreans here, conceiving the Forms as quasi-mathematical formulae, recipes that can be used to construct trees, horses, virtue, and justice, just as the Pythagorean theorem can be used to construct a triangle. I say "quasi" because Plato in the *Republic* said that "mathematicals are a class of entities *between* the sensibles and the Forms."[2] Nevertheless, he does believe that Forms are real things and are the models of which things on earth are copies.

The Forms, then, are perfect, immaterial, changeless, invisible, intangible objects. Although they are abstract, they are more real than the objects of our sense experience, for only a perfect triangle, for example, is a real triangle. And the Forms are also more knowable than things on earth. We may be uncertain as to whether a particular judge is just, but we cannot be uncertain as to the justice of the Form Justice. As such, the Forms serve as models, exemplars, and even criteria for earthly things. It is the Forms that enable us to know the earthly things that imitate them. We can know that someone is virtuous only by comparing him with the Form of Ideal Virtue.

The Forms exist in a hierarchy, the highest being the Form of the Good. For we learn what triangles, trees, human beings, and justice are when we learn what each is "good for," its purpose.[3] Everything is good for something, so everything that exists participates in the Form of the Good to some extent. The world of Forms, therefore, contains not only formulae for making objects, but also norms defining the purposes of objects. This is a teleological element in Plato's ethics, and it is not hard to see how it influenced his student Aristotle, whom we discussed in the previous chapter.

In *Euthyphro*, Socrates argues that piety cannot be defined as what the gods desire. For why should they desire it? They must desire it because it is good. So piety is a form of goodness, and goodness must exist independently of what gods or men may think or say about it. So it must be a Form. We should note, however, that if courage, virtue, goodness, etc., are abstract Forms, then they have no specific content. To know what is good, for Plato, is to know the Form of Goodness. But Goodness is what all individual examples of goodness have in common. How, then, does it help us to know specifically what is good and what is bad?

Whenever we try to define goodness in terms of specific qualities (justice, prudence, temperance, etc.), we have descended to something less than the Form of Goodness. The Form of Goodness serves as a norm for

---

2. Diogenes Allen, *Philosophy for Understanding Theology* (Atlanta: John Knox Press, 1985), 20. Allen's further comments on this issue are helpful.

3. As with Aristotle, Plato's Good is what I called in chapter 2 a nonmoral good. Yet, for Plato, moral goods like virtue are exemplifications of this nonmoral goodness.

human goodness, because it is utterly general and abstract. Any principle that is more specific is less normative, less authoritative. Such is the consequence of trying to understand goodness as an abstract Form, rather than, as in biblical theism, the will of a personal absolute.[4]

How do we know the Forms, located as we are in this defective, changing world? Here Plato reflects the subjectivism of the Sophists and Socrates: we look within. Here, Plato's ethic takes on an existential cast. We find within ourselves recollections of the Forms. That implies that at one time we must have had experience of the Forms. That could not have happened in this life, where our experiences are limited to imperfect and changing things. It must have happened in another life, before this one. So Plato embraces the Pythagorean-Orphic doctrine of reincarnation. We once lived in a world in which the Forms were directly accessible to us. Then we "fell" from that existence into the sense world, into bodies. Knowledge of the Forms remains in our memory, but sometimes it has to be coaxed out of us by Socratic questioning. One famous example is in Plato's *Meno*, where Socrates asks questions of an uneducated slave boy, leading him to display a knowledge of geometry nobody expected him to have.

But Plato's major interest, like that of Socrates, is to tell us how to live. His metaphysics and epistemology are all a prelude to his ethics and political theory. But it is in these areas that he is most disappointing. His Socrates discusses at length the nature of justice and courage, but comes to no firm conclusion. He does conclude that the definition of virtue is knowledge. One never does wrong, he determines, except out of ignorance. If one knows what is right, he will necessarily do it. But most of Plato's readers through the centuries (including his pupil Aristotle) have dismissed this statement as naïve, and Christians have found it superficial in comparison with the Bible's view of human depravity.

And if virtue is knowledge, what knowledge are we talking about? Knowledge of the Good? But the Good is more difficult to define than virtue is. Like all Forms, it is abstract. So how can it settle concrete ethical disputes, such as whether abortion is right or wrong? For Plato, to live right is to know the Good. But to say that is to leave all specific ethical questions unanswered.

Plato did come to some specific recommendations in the area of politics. But these recommendations have been almost universally rejected by

4. If anyone asks what the relationship of goodness to the God of the Bible is, the answer is that (1) goodness is not something above him, that he must submit to, (2) nor is it something below him, that he could alter at will, but (3) it is his own nature, his actions and attributes, given to human beings for imitation. "You therefore must be perfect, as your heavenly Father is perfect" (Matt. 5:48).

later thinkers. In the *Republic*, he divides the body politic into groups that correspond to the divisions of the soul. In his ideal state, the peasants are governed by the appetitive soul, the military by the spirited soul, and the rulers by the rational soul. So the rulers of the state must be philosophers, those who understand the Forms. Such a state will be totalitarian, claiming authority over all areas of life. The upper classes will share their women communally, and children will be raised by the rulers. Art will be severely restricted, because it is a kind of shadow of reality. It does not convey knowledge of the world, but only conjecture, the lowest form of opinion. Images detract from knowledge of Beauty (the Form), and they can incite to anarchy. Donald Palmer says that Plato's *Republic* "can be viewed as a plea that philosophy take over the role which art had hitherto played in Greek culture."[5]

Nearly all modern readers look at these ideas with distaste. Where did Plato get them? It would not be credible for him to claim that he got them by contemplating the Good. Rather, the whole business sounds like special pleading. Plato the philosopher thinks that philosophers should rule. He is rather like a Sophist here, claiming to be the expert in the means of governance. But he certainly has not shown that philosophers in general have any of the special qualities needed to govern. And the Sophists denied what Plato claims: access to absolute truth. We may applaud Plato's rejection of relativism. But his absolutism is what makes him a totalitarian. He thinks the philosophers have knowledge, so they must rule everything.

Plato engages in special pleading because he has no nonarbitrary way of determining what is right and wrong. But as we've seen, once one identifies Goodness as an abstract form, one cannot derive from it any specific content. So Plato's ideas about ethics and politics lack any firm basis or credibility.

The picture should be clear by now. Although Plato is more sophisticated than most secular thinkers, his position, like theirs, incorporates both rationalism and irrationalism. He is rationalistic about the Forms and irrationalistic about the sense world. For him, reason is totally competent to understand the Forms, but incompetent to make sense of the changing world of experience. Yet he tries to analyze the changing world by means of changeless Forms—an irrational world by a rationalistic principle. Eventually, in *Parmenides*, he admits that his fundamental questions remain unanswered.

With Plato, as with other philosophers we have considered, the tension between rationalism and irrationalism has a religious root. If Plato had

5. Palmer, *Looking at Philosophy* (Mountain View, CA: Mayfield Publishing Co., 1988), 73.

known the God of Scripture, he would have known in what fundamental ways our reason is competent, yet limited. And he would have understood that the world of change is knowable, but not exhaustively, because God made it that way. He would also have been able to consult God's revelation for ethical guidance, rather than teaching his students to rely on the abstract Form of the Good, which has nothing specific to say to them. The deficiencies of Plato's system reinforce my main thesis about ethics, that an adequate ethical norm can come only from an absolute person.

CYNICISM

In the last chapter, I described a rather crude version of teleological ethics, Cyrenaicism; here I will mention a rather crude version of deontological ethics, Cynicism. The relative simplicity of Cynicism may help to clarify the deontological approach.

Antisthenes (435–365 BC) is said to have founded this school of thought. The Cynics, like Plato, held that virtue is knowledge, and so they emphasized that it is worthwhile for its own sake, apart from any pleasure that may attend it. Doing good to achieve pleasure, they said, is morally worthless. So our task in life is to free ourselves from any desire for pleasure. The Cynics practiced self-discipline, renounced their possessions, and in some cases fled from civilization altogether, living out in the countryside. They seemed to insist on lives of nonconformity as a matter of principle.[6] Others charged that they were living like dogs. Thus they were called Cynics, from the Greek word meaning "dog."

I call this school deontological because it rejected pleasure (contrary to teleological ethics) and insisted on objective knowledge (contrary to existential ethics). But from the rather fragmentary accounts that we have of this movement, it is not clear where they sought to find the knowledge of virtue. Perhaps they attempted to derive their ethical norms from the negative proposition that pleasure is not a worthy goal of life.

Obviously, this is not a sufficient source of ethical norms, but in a way it provides a capsule view of the deontological movement. Lacking God's word, deontologists have sought ethical truth largely by negation. Plato sought it by negating the specificities of this changing world to posit an unchanging abstraction, the Form of Goodness. Kant, as we shall see, tried to derive moral norms from the very idea of universality, in contrast to nonuniversality.

6. Is this, after all, the "authentic existence" of Jean-Paul Sartre?

STOICISM

Stoicism was founded by Zeno of Cyprus (334–262 BC). Like the Epicureans, but unlike most other Greek philosophers, the Stoics were materialists, teaching that only physical objects were real. But they acknowledged many differences within the broad category of matter. The soul was made of very fine matter; rocks and dirt were made out of coarser matter. Even virtues are material, but they can exist in the same place as other matter, so virtues can be in the soul. Gordon Clark suggests that the Stoics' "matter" is more like a force field than a hard substance.[7] Or perhaps the Stoics meant that something is material if it really exists, if it has being. Perhaps for them (whether or not they were aware of it), the proposition "Reality is material" was tautological.

For the Stoics, knowledge begins with self-authenticating sensations. General skepticism about sense experience defeats itself, they thought, for it can be based only on the experiences it presumes to doubt. The combination of empirical epistemology and deontological ethics is unusual in the history of philosophy. But the Stoics also seek to do justice to the importance of reason. They teach that the mind must conceptualize its sense data, and, as it does, it reflects the rational order of the world itself (the *logos*).

The world is a single reality, governed by its own world-soul. This pantheistic God rules everything by natural law. As Plato's Republic is ruled by a philosopher-king, so the world of the Stoics is ruled by a divine philosopher-king.

Everything happens by law, so the Stoics took a fatalistic attitude toward life. Aristotle, like present-day open theists, had said that propositions about the future are neither true nor false, because the future is not an object of knowledge. The Stoics held, on the contrary, that if I say, "The sun will rise tomorrow," and it does, then that proposition was already true when I uttered it. Therefore, the sun had to rise. Furthermore, everything that has happened will happen again and again, ad infinitum, for, given infinite time, everything possible must take place, again and again. This is known as the eternal recurrence.

So the Stoics sought to act in accord with nature. That is, they resigned themselves to their fate. Their ethic was one of learning to want what one gets, rather than trying to get what one wants. As the Cynics had emphasized, pleasure, health, and life are good only insofar as they contribute to virtuous character. In themselves, they are worthless.

7. Clark, *Thales to Dewey* (Boston: Houghton Mifflin, 1957), 158–60.

Despite the fatalism of the Stoics, they did not advocate passivity. Contrary to Epicurus, they sought to be involved in public life. They taught, as did all Greek thinkers, that one should live according to reason, which is also according to nature and according to the universal structure of society. They considered human society to be a universal brotherhood, although we are told that the Stoic Roman emperor Marcus Aurelius did not treat his Christian subjects with much brotherly love.

Stoicism is one major source, after Aristotle, of ideas about natural law. But again, I ask David Hume's question: how does one reason from the facts of nature to conclusions about ethical obligation? The Stoics' lack of a truly theistic position made it impossible for them, as for Aristotle, to answer this question.

Some observations:

1. The Stoics, like all of the Greeks, urge us to live according to reason, but they don't show us why we *ought* to do so. If we are not to follow reason for pleasure's sake, why should we follow it?

2. What does reason actually tell us to do? I fear that Stoicism offers us an ethical norm (reason) with no specific content, just like Plato.

3. As a materialist, fatalistic system, Stoicism is not capable of finding an adequate moral norm. As I have been arguing, the ultimate moral norm must be personal.

IMMANUEL KANT

Kant (1724–1804)[8] is the most famous and influential modern advocate of deontology, just as Bentham and Mill are the most famous and influential modern advocates of teleology. Kant, however, is a great philosopher (like Plato and Aristotle) in a way that Bentham and Mill are not. Kant is important, not only for his ethical theory, but also for his metaphysics, his epistemology, and his theology.[9] It is not too much to say that Kant revolutionized all these disciplines, and that his work became the starting point of modern discussion of these subjects.

Kant might seem to be an unlikely deontologist. Deontologists tend to favor rationalism over irrationalism, as with Plato, Cynicism, and Stoicism. But Kant, at one level of his thought, is a skeptic. He holds that the world

---

8. Kant's ethical thought is found mainly in his *Foundations of the Metaphysics of Morals* and in his *Critique of Practical Reason*. These have appeared in many editions. For his metaphysical and epistemological thought, the standard works are his *Critique of Pure Reason* and the *Prolegomena to Any Future Metaphysic*.

9. His book *Religion Within the Limits of Reason Alone* is a landmark of liberal theology.

as it really is, apart from our experience, is unknowable. This real world he calls the "noumenal," or the "thing in itself" (*Ding an sich*).

Kant's early training in philosophy was in the circles of European rationalism, specifically under Christian Wolff, a disciple of Leibniz. The goal of the rationalistic tradition at the time was to reduce human knowledge to a deductive system following the model of mathematics. But Kant did something unusual for a continental European: he read the writings of a British philosopher, specifically David Hume.[10] Kant says that Hume roused him from his dogmatic slumbers. It seemed to Kant that Hume's skepticism threatened mathematics and science. From then on, his goal was to develop a philosophy that would rescue those disciplines.

He concedes to Hume that the world as such, the noumenal, cannot be known. But he insists that it is possible to know the world as it appears to us, the "phenomenal." As Plato divided the world into form and matter, Kant divided it into noumenal and phenomenal. Plato sought to do justice to both the rationalism and the irrationalism of his own time by distinguishing radically different realms, and so did Kant. Kant's distinction, however, is almost the opposite of Plato's. For Plato, the unknowable world is the world of our experience, but for Kant the world of experience is the knowable world. For Plato, the world beyond our experience is the world that is supremely knowable. For Kant, that world is not knowable at all.

How is it possible to know the world of our experience? Kant offers here a complicated discussion that would draw us far from ethics. Essentially, though, he argues that the basic structures of experience (essentially what Plato called the Forms) are the result of the human mind imposing its categories on the raw data of experience. Causality, identity, unity and plurality, and even space and time, are the work of the mind. The mind does not discover these in the real world; rather, it contributes them to its experience.[11]

In a sense, then, for Kant, the human mind replaces God as the creator of the world. Of course, the mind creates structure, not raw material; form, not matter. But nothing can be said about the raw material apart from its structure. Similarly, the Greeks found it difficult to distinguish between

10. Since the seventeenth century, the English Channel has proved to be a major dividing line between philosophical schools.

11. I forget where I heard or read this illustration, but it is a good one. A row of intelligent jelly jars are debating the philosophical question of why the jelly inside them always has a cylindrical shape. It seems that there are no physical or chemical properties in the jelly that necessitate that shape. But one jelly jar, more intelligent than the others, suggests that the jelly is cylindrical, not because of any property of the jelly, but because of the properties of the jars. Likewise, Immanuel Kant says that our experience is what it is, not because of something in it, but because of something in us.

matter and nothingness. So for Kant, the mind creates everything that can be spoken of. The rest is unknowable.[12]

Kant provides a clear example of the rationalist-irrationalist dialectic. He is rationalistic about the phenomena, but irrationalistic about the noumena. We know nothing about the real world, he says in effect, but we know perfectly the world of our experience, because we have created it. But if we have no knowledge of the noumena, how we can know what the phenomena "really" are? And does not Kant claim at least some knowledge of the noumenal world—namely, that it exists, that it serves as a limit to knowledge, and that it is that of which the phenomena are appearances? All the traditional arguments against skepticism can be brought against Kant's view of the noumena, and all the traditional arguments against rationalism can be brought against his view of the phenomena.

At any rate, we might expect from his epistemology and metaphysics that Kant would favor an extreme version of existential ethics, in which no knowledge is possible, but in which we may freely live according to our subjective preferences. And there is indeed an existential element in Kant's thought, as there was in Plato's. But Kant surprises us: the chief theme in his ethics is deontological.

For Kant, the important thing about ethics is duty. But how do we learn what our duties are, without a personal God to tell us?[13] The challenge for Kant is to find an impersonal source of ethical norms that contains specific content—what Plato's Form of the Good could not provide. And how can we find such a norm, given the rationalist-irrationalist thrust of Kant's epistemology?

Kant's argument is ingenious, if nothing else. He begins by asking an old philosophical question: is there anything that is good at all times, in all circumstances? The Greeks had noticed that boldness, for example, is sometimes good and sometimes bad. When it is good, we call it courage; when it is bad (as when a soldier decides to fight five hundred enemy soldiers single-handed), we call it foolishness. Pleasure, too, can be a good or bad thing, given the circumstances. But is there anything that is always good? Plato thought that the only reality in that category was the abstract Form of the Good. But we saw that this answer proved ethically unfruitful. Kant wants to do better.

Kant's answer is that the one thing that is always good is a good will. Nobody ever criticizes anybody for having a good will. The emphasis on

---

12. Kant's noumenal realm is much like Wittgenstein's "mystical" realm, which was discussed in chapter 6.

13. Kant explicitly rejects the idea of authoritative, divine revelation in *Religion Within the Limits of Reason Alone*. Indeed, that is the main point made in the book.

the good will is the existential element in Kant's ethics. Note that he seeks to improve on Plato by invoking a more personalistic concept. A good will must be the will of a person, not of an abstract reality.

But what is a good will? Kant says it is a will that does its duties; moreover, it does them for duty's sake. That is, a good will doesn't do its duty to gain pleasure or happiness (as in the teleological tradition), nor out of its own inclination (as in the existential tradition), but simply because it is its duty. Here Kant's deontology comes to the fore.

But then it becomes important to know what our duties are—again, without God to tell us. Kant, like the Greeks, thinks that we can find our duties by a rational process. For Kant, it goes like this. There are two kinds of imperatives, *hypothetical* and *categorical*. Hypothetical or conditional imperatives are "if . . . then" statements. For example, "If you want to paint the wall, you must put newspapers on the carpet." The imperative, "You must put newspapers on the carpet," is not for everyone, in all situations. Rather, it is only for people to whom the condition applies. If you don't want to paint the wall, you have no obligation to spread the newspapers.

In ethical discussion, we sometimes make use of hypothetical imperatives, such as, "If you want to prevent war, you should negotiate." Kant sees teleological ethics as relying on hypothetical imperatives, such as: "If you want happiness, you should avoid murder." But, in Kant's view, hypothetical imperatives are not fundamental to ethics. They are, if valid at all, applications of our basic duties, not the basic duties themselves.

The basic duties, the fundamental responsibilities from which all others are derived, are categorical, not hypothetical. That is, they are not based on any conditions or any particular life-situation. They are always binding, in every situation, under all conditions. That is to say, ethical principles must be universally and necessarily binding. If it is wrong to steal, then it is wrong for me, wrong for you, and wrong for every other rational agent anywhere in the universe.

But if ethical duties are unconditional and universally binding, then we cannot discover them through sense experience, which only discerns a small part of the universe and which cannot distinguish what is conditional from what is unconditional.

So how does Kant propose to discover categorical imperatives? He says that an ethical principle is categorical if someone can consistently will its universal application. As we saw above, Kant believes that ethical principles must be universally binding. Now we see that he wants to derive the content of those principles from the very idea of universality. Or, as your mother probably taught you, when you are considering a course of action, ask yourself, "What if everybody did it?"

Kant's clearest example concerns promises. Consider the principle that we may break promises whenever it is in our interest to do so. Can that principle be applied universally? Kant says no, because if everybody is free to break their promises, the very word *promise* would have no meaning. By definition, a promise is a pledge that we are obligated to keep. A pledge we are not obligated to keep is not a promise. If everybody thinks they can break their promises whenever they want, the concept of a promise becomes meaningless. So, Kant concludes, we may not break our promises when that is in our interest, and that implies the positive norm that we must keep our promises. That positive norm is a categorical imperative.

Another example concerns cruelty. Consider the principle that we may be cruel to others whenever we want. If that principle were universal, it would imply not only that I may be cruel to someone else when so inclined, but also that everyone else has the right to be cruel to me. That principle is intolerable; nobody desires to be treated cruelly, Kant argues. So the prohibition of cruelty is a categorical imperative.

These two examples are somewhat different. In the first, Kant's critique concerns the destruction of a concept, namely promise, rendering it meaningless. Someone might object that such a result is not a bad thing, that the idea of promises should indeed be banished from the world. A Nietzsche might chafe at the very idea that we should be expected to bind ourselves with words. We may disagree with Nietzsche, but such a view is not self-contradictory or meaningless in any obvious way, as Kant seems to think it is. Of course, it would be self-contradictory to bind oneself with a promise and then think oneself unbound by it. But it is not self-contradictory to oppose the very idea of promising, or to prefer to use the word *promise* in a weaker sense, for a relative commitment, not an absolute one.

The strength of Kant's argument, paradoxically, is really an appeal to inclination. Kant would evidently not like to live in a world without promises. I wouldn't either. But that inclination is emotional, not based on a logical argument.

The cruelty example is even more obviously an appeal to inclination. Of course I would not like to live in a world in which someone had the right to be cruel to me. Such a world would be unpleasant in the extreme. But I don't think it would be contradictory for someone else to prefer a world like that. Indeed, that seems to be precisely the sort of universe preferred by Mafia dons and drug lords: I have the right to torture and kill you, and if it turns out that you torture and kill me, well, that's just business. Also, sadomasochists would enjoy being in a world of cruelty.

Another problem is that Kant wants to avoid any appeal to the consequences of actions. But his arguments ask, "What would the world be like if this maxim were universalized?" To ask that is to ask about the consequences of universalizing the maxim in question.

Kant provides broader examples of categorical imperatives, which he considers summaries of all the others. They may be paraphrased as follows:

1. Act according to ethical principles that you can will to be universally followed.
2. Act according to principles that you could will to be universal laws of nature.
3. Act so as to treat human beings always as ends, never as mere means.

I will not try to explain the distinction between the first two. Essentially they indicate the principle described earlier, by which Kant tests ethical maxims. It is interesting, however, to see these principles laid out in this form. For it becomes clear that Kant is really asking us, in our moral judgments, to think like God. In traditional theology, it is God who wills principles to be universal, even to be laws of nature. In Kant's thought, man replaces God. We saw that earlier in his metaphysics, in which man's mind in effect creates the world. We see that here in his ethics as well.

The third principle shows that Kant would like to live in a world in which human beings are always treated as ends. But mobsters, to say nothing of Hitler, Stalin, Osama bin Laden, and Pol Pot, might prefer a different kind of world. Kant's argument, again, is more existential than deontological. It doesn't constitute a rigorous demonstration of any moral principle.

In the end, Kant's moral norm is as empty as Plato's Good. It cannot prove anything to be morally obligatory. Nor, argues Alasdair MacIntyre, is Kant's approach capable of establishing moral restrictions on anyone's conduct:

> In fact, . . . with sufficient ingenuity almost every precept can be consistently universalized. For all that I need to do is to characterize the proposed action in such a way that the maxim will permit me to do what I want while prohibiting others from doing what would nullify the maxim if universalized. Kant asks if I can consistently universalize the maxim that I may break my promises whenever it suits me. Suppose, however, he had inquired whether I can consistently universalize the maxim, "I may break my promises only when . . ." The gap is filled by a description devised so that it will apply to my present circumstances but to very few others, and to none such that if someone else obeyed the maxim, it would inconvenience me, let alone show the maxim incapable of

consistent universality. It follows that in practice the test of the categorical imperative imposes restrictions only on those insufficiently equipped with ingenuity. And this surely is scarcely what Kant intended.[14]

For example, let us test the maxim, "I may break my promises only when I promise my son Johnny to buy him a car for his birthday." Is that universally applicable? Sure. It's fine for absolutely anyone to break that particular promise to Johnny. Just kidding, son. But there is nothing logically contradictory in such a universalization.

Others have observed that Kant's method can be used to justify trivial duties. What about the maxim that everyone should wear red socks? There seems to be no contradiction in universalizing this principle. Does that mean that we have a duty to wear red socks? We could also argue similarly that we have a duty to wear blue socks. These principles together create a contradiction, but individually each one passes Kant's test.

So Kant's ingenious and strenuous effort to derive ethical norms from the principle of universality must be judged a failure. In the end, he gives us no more assurance of what is right or wrong than any other secular thinker. He tries to provide an absolute norm without God, which is to say, from impersonal principles. But once again impersonalism fails to provide universal, necessary, categorical imperatives.

There is a place for God in Kant's philosophy, but his God is not the source of moral norms. If God exists, for Kant, he exists in the noumenal realm, so nobody can know whether he exists or not. Nevertheless, Kant says, it is best for us to act *as if* God exists, for a number of reasons. One of these is that there is a connection between moral behavior and happiness. He rejects the notion that we should follow moral principles in order to achieve happiness. Rather, we should do our duty simply for duty's sake. But if we do our duty for duty's sake, then we deserve happiness. However, in this world, the righteous are often unhappy, while the wicked flourish. So Kant thinks we should assume the existence of an afterlife, in which a personal God rewards good and punishes evil. Again, he doesn't say that such a thing can be proved, but he recommends that we live as if it were true. Otherwise, he seems to think, morality itself is incoherent. This is sometimes called Kant's "moral argument for the existence of God." But, unlike the traditional theistic arguments, it does not purport to be a demonstration—only a piece of practical advice.

Here are some evaluative comments, by way of summary:

14. MacIntyre, *A Short History of Ethics* (New York: Macmillan, 1966), 197–98.

1. Kant pushes human autonomy to new heights, in effect identifying the mind of man with the mind of God—in his metaphysics, his epistemology, and his ethics.

2. The rationalism and irrationalism of Kant's distinction between the phenomenal and the noumenal affect his ethics. If we cannot know the real world, how can we be sure of what our duties are? If our experience is virtually created by the mind, how can ethical norms be anything more than the human mind proclaiming duties to itself?

3. Kant's principle that a good will does its duty for duty's sake, not for happiness or out of inclination, may sound pious, but it is not biblical. Scripture, as we saw in chapter 3 and earlier in this chapter, often motivates our ethical behavior by referring to its consequences (God's glory, human rewards and punishments) and by invoking the new inclinations given to us in regeneration.

4. Although Kant is right to say that moral principles must be universal, we have seen that we cannot discover those principles merely by testing each maxim for universal applicability.

5. The universality argument cannot justify any concrete moral norms. So Kant's deontology is as empty as that of the Greeks.

6. Kant claims to avoid any appeal to consequences (the teleological approach) or inclination (the existential approach). But he tests the universality of maxims precisely by showing the consequences of their universal affirmation. And in the end he judges these consequences according to his inclinations: his desire to live in a world in which promises exist, but cruelty does not, and everyone treats everyone else as an end.

IDEALISM

Idealism is the name usually given to the school of philosophy that followed Kant and had a large influence into the early twentieth century.[15] G. W. F. Hegel (1770–1831) is usually regarded as the leading figure in the movement, but Fichte and Schelling were also prominent names in Germany, as were T. H. Green, F. H. Bradley, and Bernard Bosanquet later in Britain.[16]

15. The influence extended to both sides of the English Channel! As I mentioned in an earlier note, it has been rare in the last few centuries for a philosophical movement to be prominent both on the Continent and in Britain.

16. It is interesting to note how many modern philosophical movements have three prominent members: Continental rationalists Descartes, Spinoza, Leibniz; British empiricists Locke, Berkeley, Hume; German idealists Fichte, Schelling, Hegel; British idealists Green, Bradley, Bosanquet; American idealists Royce, Bowman, Blanshard; pragmatists Peirce, James, Dewey; existentialists Heidegger, Jaspers, Sartre; process

As with Aristotle, Plato, and Kant, idealist philosophy is difficult to fit into any of our defined schools of ethics. It is an impressive blend of ideas, with affinities to many previous philosophical movements. For a secular system, it provides a remarkable balance among teleological, existential, and deontological themes. But I think the ethical appeal of idealism is its doctrine of the Absolute. This is an impersonal absolute, to be sure, but nevertheless a kind of absolute. And the idea of an absolute fits into deontological ethics far better than any other kind of ethics. Also, as we shall see, the notion of duty is important to idealist ethicists.

Idealism rejects the Kantian idea of the noumenal. Kant, as we saw, was inconsistent in his denial that we know the noumenal. But if the noumenal really is unknowable, then we cannot make any use of it in our philosophy. We cannot even affirm that it exists. So the idealists dropped that concept. But once you drop the noumenal, what is left? The phenomenal, of course. But then the phenomenal is no longer the appearance of the noumenal. Rather, it is reality. It is the "thing in itself." So the idealist rejects Kant's skepticism and adopts Hegel's affirmation of rationalism: the real is the rational, and the rational is the real.

Nevertheless, Hegel is chastened by Kant's critiques of reason. Reason discovers the truth, he tells us, not by simple observation (Hume) or by logical deduction of a mathematical-linear type (Leibniz), but by a method he calls dialectical. *Dialectic* is related to the concept of dialogue. Plato's dialogues seek to approach the truth by putting two or more viewpoints up against one another. As the deficiencies of each become evident, the truth begins to shine through. Similarly, Hegel's method seeks to find truth by self-criticism.

Here's how it works. You start with one idea, and then you begin to see defects in it, so that the opposite seems more adequate. But then you begin to see defects in the second idea as well, and more virtues in the first, and that meditation propels you to a third view that incorporates the truth of the first two ideas but also rises above them to show you more than you knew before.[17]

In other words, Hegel admits with Hume and Kant that our rational ideas have their inadequacies, that they are mixed with error. But he proposes that instead of falling into skepticism, we use these inadequacies to help

---

philosophers Alexander, Whitehead, Hartshorne; Boston personalists Bowne, Brightman, Bertocci. I haven't aligned these triads with my three perspectives, but I won't promise not to.

17. Hegel's disciples and interpreters labeled these three steps "thesis, antithesis, synthesis." Hegel himself used this language occasionally, but did not stress it.

us move on to greater levels of knowledge. Error, therefore, is a bad thing, but it also has its positive aspects.

Hegel develops a philosophy of vast complexity by using this method. He believes that he has discovered, not only a useful way to learn things, but the very mind of the universe itself. The dialectic is the road to absolute truth, so it reflects perfectly the movements of nature and history. Or, to put it better, the movements of nature and history reflect dialectical thought. (Historical events also proceed through conflict to resolution, making progress to higher and higher levels of civilization.) Indeed, the dialectic is the very mind of God, the mind of the Absolute. Hegel's Absolute is a pantheistic sort of deity, coming to self-consciousness through human thought. So the eventual outcome of the dialectic is that we will be identical with the divine mind.

One problem with this epistemology is that any idea we have today will be negated by another idea, so that today we do not have any ideas that we can call true. Hegel thought that the process of dialectical negation had ended in his philosophy, and that his philosophy would never be transcended by another. Similarly, he thought that the Prussian state had reached the pinnacle of historical development and would never be replaced by a superior order. But most readers have not accepted Hegel's claims in these regards. So we face the question, if nobody has reached the pinnacle, how do we know that our present ideas are anywhere near the truth? And how do we choose between one idea and another, if they are all (including idealism itself) subject to negation and synthesis? For idealism, there is a sense in which we will not have any truth until the end of the process (a kind of eschaton), when we achieve omniscience and our thought becomes fully identical to that of the Absolute. In other words, you can't know anything until you know everything. Thus, Hegel's rationalism devolves into irrationalism.

The specifically ethical teachings of idealism are presented more clearly among the British idealists than among the German ones. The following discussion is based on F. H. Bradley's *Ethical Studies*.[18] There is a large dose of existential ethics in Bradley, who emphasizes that morality is something irreducibly personal. Only persons have obligations; only persons can be obedient or disobedient to ethical norms. The reader will understand from earlier discussions that on this point I emphatically agree.

Bradley teaches that in ethics one is concerned primarily with developing inner character. How one changes the world or responds to moral principles is a secondary consideration. When I paint a fence, my ultimate

18. Oxford: Clarendon Press, 1927.

goal is not to have a painted fence, but rather to achieve inward satisfaction at completing my task. So, as Aristotle taught, ethical behavior is essentially self-realization. The point of ethics is not to change the world, but to change ourselves. As with Kant, the only unequivocal good is the good will. Ethical reflection and action can direct the will in a better direction.

But, unlike Kant, the idealists see the good will, not as a will that looks only to its duty in the abstract, but as one that also looks to its inclinations and environment. Self-realization involves all of these, which should not be set against one another, as in Kant. For example, should we not admire a person who enjoys doing right, who does it out of inclination, as much as, or more than, we admire someone who does his duty merely for duty's sake?

So for idealism, self-realization involves relating oneself to a context: to our own inclinations and happiness, to the needs of other people, to the physical environment (which can enable or prevent us from doing good), and ultimately to the whole universe. So, as in Hegel's metaphysics, in which you don't know one thing until you know how it is related to everything, so in ethics, you cannot attain your highest level of self-realization until you take into account your relation to the whole universe.

Bradley, however, narrows the context a bit in his chapter on "My Station and Its Duties." For him, the point of ethics is to find your station and to perform the duties associated with it. Your station may be your nationality, your occupation, your social class, or your place in a family or organization. Fathers have duties that are different from those of their children. The duties of kings are different from those of railroad engineers, and so on. In Bradley's view, you have some choice as to what station you occupy, but those choices are usually limited by birth, education, and economic status. But if you are a lieutenant in the navy, you must perform the duties prescribed for a lieutenant. If you are a butler, you must do the things butlers are supposed to do, and so on.

Since idealism, like Kant, focuses on duties, I call it deontological, even though idealists also speak positively about self-realization (the existential approach) and achieving happiness (the teleological approach). But it offers us no more reliable means of discovering our duties than did Kant. We may evaluate idealist ethics as a global epistemology (Hegel's dialectic) or as a view of individual vocation (Bradley). Hegel's dialectic seeks to bring about an identity between ourselves and the Absolute, but it devolves into rationalism and irrationalism. Hegel's Absolute is impersonal, so it is no better suited to be an ethical authority than is Plato's Good.

Bradley's theory of individual vocation appears to give us specific norms for conduct. But his view is obviously a reflection of his time. He wrote in England, at a time when social classes were rigidly defined and distinguished. Everyone knew how a king, or a prime minister, or a general, or a butler, or a street cleaner was supposed to behave. And if one stepped out of bounds, people shuddered over the impropriety. But in a time like ours, where people move rapidly upward and downward on the social scale, in a multiethnic and multicultural society, in an age where new vocations are being created every day, and where gender roles are disputed, it is not evident that the "duties" of particular "stations" have moral weight. Nor is it clear how Bradley's view helps us in trying to come to grips with the moral debates of our time—on abortion, preemptive war, women's rights, and so on. A follower of Bradley would probably take conservative positions on social issues generally. But if he wished to make a persuasive case, he would have to do more than just say that his position is dictated by his station in life. Conservative as its conclusions may be, that kind of argument is essentially relativistic, like Marx's view that morality is relative to one's social class.

MOORE AND PRICHARD

I have mentioned G. E. Moore (1873–1958) several times as the one who coined the term "naturalistic fallacy." Moore used the naturalistic fallacy argument mainly against utilitarianism. In its place, he adopted a kind of deontology known as intuitionism.

In *Principia Ethica*,[19] Moore wrestles with the definition of goodness.[20] We cannot define goodness as pleasure, as the utilitarians do, he says, because it always makes sense to ask if a particular pleasure is in fact good. He says the same thing about all other definitions that have been proposed. Again and again he reiterates that we cannot define goodness as x, because it is always an open question whether x is in fact good. This is Moore's famous "open question argument." So Moore concludes that goodness is indefinable.

I suspect that goodness is so difficult to define, not because it is indefinable, but because there are so many different sets of values in our society. If everyone agreed that goodness was pleasure, then it would not be an open question as to whether a pleasure was in fact good, though there would probably be open questions as to what was actually (or most) pleasurable. Similarly, if everybody agreed that goodness is what God approves, then it would not be an open question whether something approved by God was good.[21]

---

19. Cambridge: Cambridge University Press, 1903.
20. At this point, he is dealing with nonmoral goodness.
21. Some have suggested that if we define goodness as what God approves, then it is meaningless to say that what God approves is good. It would be as if I defined "world's great-

But let us follow Moore's argument further. Not only is goodness indefinable, he says, but it is impossible to derive goodness from any natural state of affairs. Any attempt to do so commits the naturalistic fallacy. Moore never quite defines what he means by "natural" in this context. Evidently, pleasure would be an example of such a natural state. But I have given reason to doubt whether a definition of goodness in terms of pleasure is necessarily wrong. In the end, Moore distinguishes between natural and nonnatural on the basis of intuition. But there are problems with his view of intuition, as we shall see below.

Still, as I've indicated often in the last few chapters, I do think that the naturalistic fallacy is a real problem in the secular ethical literature. Perhaps it could be better described more simply as a failure to justify the use of the word *ought*.

But Moore goes on: if goodness may not be derived from any natural state of affairs, what is it? He answers that it is a simple and unanalyzable (because indefinable) property of various states of affairs. And how do we discover goodness? Moore answers that we discover it by intuition.

However, Moore isn't very clear on how this is done. He speaks of holding something before the mind, contemplating it, and thereby identifying it as good or bad. The picture is somewhat analogous to sense experience. But of course Moore rejects the idea that goodness could be derived from sense experience. So his concept of intuition is mysterious.[22]

It is hard to imagine on this view how people could actually debate whether something is good. Once the parties "hold those facts before their minds," they can only report to one another what they intuit. Perhaps, as with emotivism, they can argue about the facts to which the intuitions are directed. But once everyone agrees about those facts, there can really be no argument about their goodness or badness, even though intuitions may disagree. Rather, each person can only appeal to his own intuition as a supreme authority.

---

est shortstop" as "RTS theologian," and then claimed to be the world's greatest shortstop. My statement would be true, given that definition, but it would also be silly and misleading. I think the problem is simply that in the shortstop/RTS case there is a blatant misuse of language. That is not evidently so in the first case. If we define goodness as what God approves, then of course all goodness, including God's own, will be judged according to his standards. I fail to see any problem in that. Someone might object that if God's acts are to be evaluated by his own standards, he could do something that to us would be monstrously wrong. However, Scripture tells us that God's goodness is similar to the goodness he requires of us, because we are made in his image. "You therefore must be perfect, as your heavenly Father is perfect" (Matt. 5:48).

22. I'm inclined to think that philosophers speak of intuition when they think they know something, but don't know how. Nevertheless, the concept of intuition is not entirely useless. See *DKG*, 345–46.

As did Bradley, intuitionism flourished in Britain at a time of strong moral consensus within the society. It was a post-Christian age, but an age in which traditional Christian morality ("borrowed capital," in Van Til's terms) continued to carry weight. So it is not surprising that when people discussed moral issues, holding the facts before their minds, their intuitions led to conclusions more or less in accord with the Bible. But when society became more pluralistic, leading to the extreme pluralism of today, that consensus broke down, and intuitionism became implausible.[23]

But the situation is even worse than that. Moore himself appeals to intuition mainly to establish the goal of behavior, that is, the good. He agrees with the utilitarians that ethics is a matter of choosing a goal and then the means to attain it, but he disagrees with them as to the manner of choosing the goal. Regarding the goal, Moore is deontological. But in choosing the means to achieve it, he follows the usual teleological-utilitarian pattern.

A student of Moore, H. A. Prichard,[24] argues that on this construction the end justifies the means. But (intuitively!) we know that cannot be right. A good end does not justify using wicked means to achieve it. So Prichard adopts a view even more consistently intuitionist: we need intuition, not only to evaluate the end, but also to evaluate the means. We need intuition all across the board, in any evaluation of any decision, action, or goal. This view implies, of course, that we must invoke intuition many times each day.

We should commend Moore and Prichard for understanding the importance of authoritative ethical norms. But their intuition is really an asylum of ignorance. In one sense, what they call intuition is really conscience, the faculty that God has given us for determining good and evil (see chapter 21). But conscience must be informed by God's revelation, lest it be ignorant, immature, or even "seared" (1 Tim. 4:2). In secular intuitionism, there is no objective source of ethical truth. Intuition becomes virtually a synonym for personal inclination, and this form of deontology becomes indistinguishable from existential ethics.

It is not surprising, then, that the philosophy of language analysis, of which Moore was a founder, led to Wittgenstein's mystical understanding of ethics and the positivists' emotivism, which we discussed in chapter 6.

---

23. I heard a story once, but have forgotten the source, about the chaos that ensued when D. H. Lawrence, an advocate of sexual liberation, visited a genteel ethical discussion group of Moore's time. Maybe the story is apocryphal, but imagining the clash of values helps us to see what the loss of consensus must have been like. After Lawrence and others like him, it was no longer possible to gain ethical assurance simply by holding a state of affairs before the mind.

24. See his *Moral Obligation* (London: Oxford, 1949).

Deontology continues to show up in ethical philosophy from time to time. For example, in *A Theory of Justice*, John Rawls (1921–2002) opposes utilitarianism and emphasizes the importance of "fairness."[25] Rawls argues that each person is entitled to the most extensive liberty compatible with the same liberty for others, and that inequalities are justified only to the extent that they are necessary to help the disadvantaged. Yet the foundation for these moral norms is unclear and unpersuasive. Deontology is right to say that we need to have moral norms beyond our individual subjectivity and the happiness of mankind. But it has no clear idea of how such knowledge can be gained.

CONCLUSIONS ON NON-CHRISTIAN ETHICAL PHILOSOPHY

We have investigated three types of non-Christian ethical philosophy, existential, teleological, and deontological. Permit me to summarize this material in the following comments:

1. We have seen that the better thinkers, like Plato, Aristotle, Kant, and Hegel, combine emphases from more than one of these perspectives. But even they tend to favor one and disparage the other two, and that tendency is even more pronounced among the lesser ethicists. This is understandable, because only God can guarantee the coherence of the three perspectives. The biblical God declares the moral law (the deontological perspective), and he creates human beings to find their happiness (the teleological perspective) in obeying that law. He also makes us so that at our best we will find God's law to be our chief delight (the existential perspective). So God made all three perspectives, and he made them to cohere. But if a thinker seeks to formulate ethics without God, he has no guarantee that the three perspectives will cohere. For all he knows, human happiness may require a life contrary to all moral rules. Or it may be that to keep the moral law, we must sacrifice all our happiness and inclination. So he must choose which perspective to follow in case of conflict, which will almost certainly take place. Thus, non-Christian thinkers tend to lose the unity and balance of the three perspectives.

2. Nevertheless, we have seen that each ethical thinker must deal with the three perspectives, even if he prefers one over the others. Kant, for example, seeks to avoid any teleological considerations. Yet to establish his categorical imperatives, he must consider the consequences of denying

25. Cambridge, MA: Harvard University Press, 1971.

them, and consequential reasoning is the essence of teleological ethics. Teleological thinkers, in turn, must give some consideration to moral norms, even though they tend to reduce these norms to happiness or pleasure, and even though they give no adequate account of why their norms are obligatory. Each ethicist must give some consideration to norms, goals, and feelings, whatever he may choose to emphasize. So there is a tension in each system between its focus on a particular perspective and its need to do justice to all of them.

3. No non-Christian ethicist does justice even to his own favorite perspective. Deontologists advocate an empty norm, one without definable content. That norm gives no clear guidance, and it prevents the lesser principles from giving us clear guidance, since they are relativized by the ultimate norm. Thus, there really is no norm at all, and we are no better off than we would be with a teleological or existential ethic.

Teleological ethics tries to be empirical, concrete, and practical. It wants to avoid any reference to mysterious, transcendent principles. But the basis for applying their principles, like the principle of utility, is ultimately mysterious. And the calculation involved in making ethical choices requires superhuman insight.

Existential ethics tries to do justice to the inner life, but it gives no guidance adequate for our self-realization.

4. All non-Christian systems involve rationalism and irrationalism: rationalism in the claim that the human mind can determine what to do without God's help, and irrationalism in claiming that ethics is ultimately based on unknowable chance or fate. Rationalism leads to dogmatic certainty about an absolute, but that absolute is empty and hence irrational. Irrationalism, however, is asserted by a would-be autonomous claim, and is therefore rationalistic. If irrationalism is true, then there is such a thing as truth, which means that irrationalism is false.

5. This epistemological confusion leads to a proliferation of different viewpoints as to the norms and goals of ethics. What is the goal of human life? Pleasure? Power? Self-realization? Contentment?

6. The non-Christian approach leads to the abandonment of ethics itself. The story of twentieth-century ethics is that philosophers have abandoned their traditional role (since Plato) of teaching us how to live. The main ethical thinkers of the twentieth century (with the exception of existentialism, which is inconsistent in this regard) don't try to tell us how to live; rather, they examine the language and reasoning of the discipline of ethics. In other words, they have given up ethics for metaethics. Their concern is not to defend ethical principles, but

rather to show us what an ethical principle is. Their message to us is, "If you happen to hold any ethical principles, here's what they are."

The reason for this development is not hard to see. If no norm or duty has been revealed to human beings by a personal God, then there is no way that any ethical philosopher, or anyone else, can tell us what to do.

7. Since non-Christian ethics is helpless to do justice to its own concerns, it is wholly unable to bring objections against Christianity. Traditionally, non-Christians have often objected to the morality of Scripture, even to God's actions (such as commanding Joshua to destroy the Canaanites). They have objected on ethical grounds to the imputation of Adam's sin, to election and reprobation, to the substitutionary atonement, and to hell. And they have vigorously argued "the problem of evil," insisting that a holy and all-powerful God would not have permitted evil in his universe.[26] But the non-Christian has no basis for raising these objections, since he cannot himself make a meaningful distinction between good and evil.

8. Yet there are elements in non-Christian ethical thought that can be useful for Christians. (a) Because of God's general revelation, the non-Christian has considerable knowledge of God's precepts (Rom. 1:32; 2:14–15) and sometimes sets forth that knowledge in spite of himself. (b) Non-Christian thought shows, as we have seen, the importance of doing justice to the three perspectives. (c) Non-Christian thought is often more sensitive than Christian thought to the complexities of the ethical life and of human decision making.

But, in the end, nobody has the right to argue an ethical principle unless he is willing to listen to the God of Scripture. Moral norms can come only from a personal absolute, and the Bible is the only written revelation that presents such a God to us. So we must now turn to Scripture to hear the word of the Lord.

---

26. For my response to the problem of evil, see *DG*, chapter 9.

PART THREE

CHRISTIAN ETHICAL METHODOLOGY

SECTION ONE

THE NORMATIVE PERSPECTIVE

CHAPTER 9

The Organism of Revelation

The main point of part 2 (chapters 4–8) is that non-Christian ethics is incapable of providing a basis for moral decision. Nevertheless, we live in a world dominated by non-Christian views of ethics. This world is our situation, our ethical environment. So I considered part 2 in terms of the situational perspective, though we also discussed other perspectives in that connection.

In this and the following chapters of part 3 of this treatise on ethics, I shall attempt to show how a Christian ethic provides the basis for ethical decisions that was lacking in non-Christian approaches.

Christian ethics, as I have indicated, is triperspectival. It seeks to honor all three perspectives—not just one or two, as is usually the case in non-Christian ethics. The three perspectives represent God's lordship. They are his lordship attributes—control, authority, and presence—manifest to us as his revelation. In part 3, I shall indicate how these perspectives function in our ethical decisions, particularly how they relate to one another in grounding these decisions. The subject of this discussion can be called methodology, or simply a Christian decision-making procedure. Since it describes a subjective process by which we make decisions, part 3 represents the existential perspective. But of course the decision-making procedure involves all three perspectives.

In general, a Christian ethical decision is the application of God's revelation (normative) to a problem (situational) by a person (existential). Recall the three factors in ethical judgment, discussed in chapter 3. There we considered as an example a counseling situation: the counselor must ask about the problem, about God's Word, and about the personal needs of the counselee. But we also saw there that the counselor cannot fully understand one of these factors without understanding the others. So each includes the other two. That is to say, they are perspectives.

In this chapter, I will begin with the normative perspective. From this perspective, the ethical question is, What does God's Word tell me to do? To answer that question, as we shall see, we will need to understand the situation about which the question is asked and the person who is asking it. But the focus will be on God's revelation, the source of the norms that will govern our decision.

This discussion could be called a Christian deontological ethic or command ethic. But unlike secular versions of deontology, our standard comes, not from an abstraction, an impersonal fate, or chance, but from the Word of the living God.

What is God's revelation? We evangelicals answer, almost involuntarily, Scripture. Certainly Scripture is God's word, his infallible and inerrant revelation.[1] And Scripture has a special place of prominence among other kinds of revelation, as we shall see. But Scripture is not all there is of revelation. There are words of God that are not in the Bible, such as (1) the words God speaks to all the forces of nature to direct their ways (Pss. 147:15–18; 148:7–8), (2) the living Word, Jesus, who is not contained within the Bible, though the Bible contains some of his words (John 1:1–14), (3) the words that Jesus spoke in the flesh that were not recorded in Scripture, and (4) the inspired words of prophets and apostles that were not recorded in Scripture.

I believe that the unique importance of Scripture can best be seen, not by denying the existence of other forms of revelation, but rather by showing the precise relationships between Scripture and those other forms. As we look at those other forms, we shall see that we cannot make adequate use of them apart from Scripture. So, by mentioning other forms, we do not detract from the uniqueness of Scripture; rather, we enhance it.

So God's revelation forms an organism, a unity of many self-manifestations, many norms. Ultimately, revelation includes everything, for all reality manifests God. So the normative perspective, like the other perspectives, is a perspective on everything. Yet we shall see

---

1. I cannot in this book discuss in detail the reasons for holding this fundamental article of faith. I hope to enter that discussion in *The Doctrine of the Word of God* (forthcoming). It should be evident, however, that if ethics is to be based on the will of a personal and absolute God, it must be possible for human beings to have access to his words. He must *speak* to us. And, as Cornelius Van Til pointed out, such a God can speak to us only with supreme authority.

that within that universal organism of revelation, Scripture plays a leading role. Let us now look at some aspects of that organism.

GOD HIMSELF AS ETHICAL NORM

In our discussion of the naturalistic fallacy in chapter 5 and later, I indicated that it is not a naturalistic fallacy to argue, "God commands *x*; therefore, we must do *x*." This argument might seem like a forbidden argument from what is to what ought to be, from fact to obligation. But that is not so, for God is not only a fact, but also a norm. That is so because anything God says is normative. His word is inherently authoritative, as well as powerful and present.

God's very nature is normative. That is to say, authority is an aspect of the lordship that defines him. This is evident from our previous discussions of the nature of lordship.

Scripture also teaches this fact by its identification of God as light: "This is the message we have heard from him and proclaim to you, that God is light, and in him is no darkness at all" (1 John 1:5). Note also the many applications to Jesus of the metaphor of light (Matt. 4:16; Luke 1:79; 2:32; John 1:4–9; 3:19–21; 8:12; 9:5; 12:46; 1 John 2:8; Rev. 21:23). When people see God, they see a great light, often described as his glory. That glory radiated from Jesus on the Mount of Transfiguration (Matt. 17:2). That physical light is associated with God's moral purity in 1 John 1:5.

But light does not refer only to God's moral excellence. It also refers to the communication of that excellence, the revelation of it, to human beings. The light of God's essence is a light that we are to walk in: "But if we walk in the light, as he is in the light, we have fellowship with one another, and the blood of Jesus his Son cleanses us from all sin" (1 John 1:7). The light is our ethical guide: "Your word is a lamp to my feet and a light to my path" (Ps. 119:105). The light reveals good and evil (John 3:19–21). So we should not walk in darkness (Matt. 6:22–23; John 8:12; 12:46; Rom. 13:12; 1 Cor. 4:5; 2 Cor. 6:14). To dwell in the light is to dwell with God; to dwell in darkness is to be apart from him. Indeed, we are to *be* the light (Matt. 5:14; Eph. 5:8).

By his very nature, God not only is ethically pure, but inevitably reveals his moral purity to human beings, calling them to live in accord with it. When sinners see a manifestation of deity, they are often filled with a sense of moral guilt (Isa. 6:5; Luke 5:8). God's very being is ethically normative.

In every form of revelation, God reveals himself. All revelation bears the lordship attribute of presence. So in every form of revelation, God reveals his ethically normative being. I have argued elsewhere that God's word is always one with God himself.[2] All revelations of God manifest his presence, as well as his authority and controlling power. The speech of God, his word, has divine attributes, attributes of righteousness (Ps. 119:7), faithfulness (v. 86), wonderfulness (v. 119), truth (v. 142; John 17:17), eternity (Ps. 119:89, 160), omnipotence (Gen. 18:14; Luke 1:37; Isa. 55:11), and perfection (Ps. 19:7–11). It is an object of worship (Pss. 56:4, 10; 119:120, 161–62; Isa. 66:5). And indeed, God's word is God (John 1:1).

So human ethical responsibility is essentially to imitate God. We are made in the image of God (Gen. 1:26–27). It is our nature, that which distinguishes us from all other creatures and gives us a special relationship to God. Rather than being "rational animals," as in Aristotle, our essence is to be like God. But just as God is both a fact and a norm, so our nature as his image is both a fact and a norm. Because God has dominion over all things, we are to have an analogous dominion, under him (Gen. 1:28). Even after the fall, we are to be holy as he is holy (Lev. 11:44; 1 Peter 1:15–16), perfect as he is perfect (Matt. 5:48). We are to work six days and rest the seventh, for that is what God did (Ex. 20:11). We are to reflect the light of God's moral purity (see above).

The imitation of Christ (*imitatio Christi*) is also a major theme in biblical ethics. We are to love one another, as Jesus first loved us (John 13:34–35; 1 John 4:9–11). We are to follow Jesus (Matt. 16:24; 19:21). We are to wash one another's feet, according to his example (John 13:14–15). We are to be sent into the world as he was sent (John 17:18; 20:21). We are to value one another above ourselves, as Jesus did (Phil. 2:5–11). Even Jesus' sufferings and death are exemplary (1 Peter 2:21; 1 John 3:16). So Paul speaks of himself as an imitator of Christ (1 Cor. 11:1).

We should carefully distinguish biblical imitation of God from coveting God's prerogatives. Recall that Satan tempted Eve by telling her, "You will be like God" (Gen. 3:5). In one sense, as we have seen above, being like God is the heart of godliness. But Satan was suggesting that Eve could be like God in another way, by rebelling against him and placing herself on the throne. There are some attributes and acts of God that we can never imitate. We are not omniscient or omnipotent; we cannot create a universe; we cannot redeem a race of sinners. None of us can ever be an ultimate ethical authority.[3]

At the most basic level, then, God himself is our source of ethical obligation. Our ultimate norm is personal, not impersonal. We have ethical

---

2. DG, 470–75. I will argue this in more detail in *The Doctrine of the Word of God*.

3. Cf. John Murray, *Principles of Conduct* (Grand Rapids: Eerdmans, 1957), 176–77.

duties, because God is intrinsically worthy of obedience and imitation, and because all creatures are inevitably confronted with the revelation of his standards.

THE WORD OF GOD AS NORM

How, then, does God reveal his ethical norms to us? God's revelation, his word, comes to us in a number of specific forms that we can summarize under three categories: the word that comes through nature and history, the word that comes through persons, and the word written—which correspond to the three perspectives: situational, existential, and normative, respectively.

The Word Through Nature and History

First, God's word is revealed through nature and history.[4] Scripture teaches that the heavens declare the glory of God (Ps. 19:1). Paul in Romans 1:18–21 says:

> For the wrath of God is revealed from heaven against all ungodliness and unrighteousness of men, who by their unrighteousness suppress the truth. For what can be known about God is plain to them, because God has shown it to them. For his invisible attributes, namely his eternal power and divine nature, have been clearly perceived, ever since the creation of the world, in the things that have been made. So they are without excuse. For although they knew God, they did not honor him as God.

So the creation clearly conveys some significant truths: God's existence, his nature, and his wrath against sin. Later Paul indicates that pagans know from God's revelation that those who do certain things are worthy of death (v. 32). So this revelation has ethical content.

Do people commit a naturalistic fallacy when they derive ethical content from the created world? No, because the ethical content is not derived from valueless facts, but from the authoritative revelation of God that comes to them through the creation. However, when non-Christians try to argue from the data of natural revelation to reach ethical conclusions, they typically omit any reference to God as the source of the data. And when the

---

4. The word "through" is important. We should not make the mistake of thinking that nature and history *are* the word of God. The word of God is God himself, not something in the creation. But the word makes itself known through creaturely means, including nature and history.

argument is presented simply as an argument from the facts and not from God, it is a naturalistic fallacy and should be dismissed on that account.

One thing is lacking in God's revelation through nature: it does not teach people the way of salvation. That knowledge comes from the gospel, and the gospel comes through preaching (Rom. 10:13–17). So we might say that nature teaches only law, not gospel.[5] Nevertheless, the gospel is revealed through history, specifically through redemptive history, those events by which God saves his people from sin. Those events form the content of gospel preaching. So history as a whole does convey the gospel. But only those in proximity to redemptive events can learn from them the way of salvation.[6]

Another limitation of natural revelation is that unregenerate people view it with hostility. They suppress the truth (Rom. 1:18) and exchange it for a lie (v. 25), and God gives them up to their depravity (vv. 24, 26, 28). So, without grace, general revelation does not help them. But natural revelation is sufficient to make them guilty, to take away all excuses (v. 20).

But for the believer, natural revelation is important also in other ways: (1) It gives us information that is useful in interpreting Scripture, such as information about ancient culture and languages. (2) It shows us the contemporary situation to which we must apply the Scriptures. (3) It gives us regular occasion to glorify God for his creation (Ps. 19) and providence (Pss. 104, 146, 147).

Note here the overlap between the normative and situational perspectives. When we ask where we go to find God's norms, one biblical answer is to go to the situation, namely, nature and history. As I said earlier, there is a sense in which everything is normative.

If the created world did not reveal God, Scripture itself would be useless. We cannot interpret Scripture unless we can understand the situations from which Scripture arose and the situations to which we seek to apply it. If the created world did not reveal God clearly, it would thereby cast doubt on the ethical con-

---

5. I shall discuss this topic at greater length in chapter 12.

6. On the whole, my category of "revelation given through nature and history" is identical to the traditional category of "general revelation." But there is a difference. Revelation given through nature and history, taken as a whole, includes both law and gospel, for the gospel is a segment of history, that segment we call redemptive history. But general revelation, understood in the traditional way, is that portion of God's revelation in nature and history that does not include the gospel. Redemptive history is hard to classify, either in the traditional scheme of general and special revelation, or in my scheme of general, special, and existential revelation. Since God's revelation in redemptive history is a revelation in event, rather than word, we are inclined to call it general. But since it has redemptive content, we are inclined to call it special. To some extent, these are artificial categories, and it doesn't matter much which we use to describe redemptive history. But we should be aware of the ambiguity of this category of revelation.

clusions we seek to derive from Scripture. So general revelation, like Scripture, is necessary, authoritative, clear, and sufficient for its own purposes.[7]

Revelation Through Persons

Since revelation is thoroughly personal, persons are fully appropriate media of God's revelation. As revelation through nature and history is sometimes called "general revelation,"[8] so I often describe revelation through persons as "existential revelation."

Some revelation comes to human beings through personal appearances of the divine persons of the Trinity. When God appears in visible form, that revelation is called theophany. When the Son of God took on flesh and dwelled among us (John 1:14), that revelation is called incarnation. When the Holy Spirit comes to reveal God in and to us, that revelation is called by various names, depending on its function: inspiration (2 Tim. 3:16), illumination (1 Cor. 2:9–12), demonstration (1 Thess. 1:5), revelation (Eph. 1:17).

Existential revelation, however, also includes revelation through human persons. Human beings are in God's image, so we *are* revelation. That image is not lost, but marred or defaced by the fall. But God's grace renews that image in the image of Christ. In this renewal, God writes his word on our heart (Jer. 31:33–34; cf. Deut. 6:6; Prov. 3:3). This means that there is a change in our most fundamental dispositions, so that our deepest desire is to serve God.

As the Spirit illumines the Scriptures and writes God's word on our heart, he truly reveals God to us. The term *reveal* in Scripture does sometimes refer, not to special revelation, nor to general revelation, but to the enlightenment of individuals, so that they actually come to know and appropriate God's truth (Matt. 11:25–27; Eph. 1:17).[9] This is an important form of existential revelation.

Because of redemption, human beings can serve as revelation in still another way: as examples for imitation. We saw earlier the importance of imitating God and Christ in our ethical lives. But one major means of growth for Christians is other Christians who serve as godly examples. Because he imitates Christ, Paul sets himself before us as someone we

---

7. An important article emphasizing this point is Cornelius Van Til, "Nature and Scripture," in *The Infallible Word*, ed. N. B. Stonehouse and Paul Woolley (Philadelphia: Presbyterian Guardian Publishing Corporation, 1946), 263–301.

8. But see note 6, above, explaining the difference between my concept of revelation through nature and history and the traditional concept of general revelation.

9. Evangelicals usually prefer the word *illumination* to the word *revelation* in describing this work of the Spirit. Thus they set themselves over against certain kinds of dialectic and charismatic theology. But the texts I have cited warrant the term *revelation* in this connection.

should imitate: "Be imitators of me, as I am of Christ" (1 Cor. 11:1; cf. 4:16; Phil. 3:17; 1 Thess. 1:6). He tells Timothy, in turn, to be an example for his congregation to follow (1 Tim. 4:12). The main requirements for elders and deacons in 1 Timothy 3:1–13 and Titus 1:5–9 are qualities of character, doubtless because these men are expected to serve as examples to the other members of the church. And Scripture mentions many Bible characters as positive or negative examples (1 Cor. 4:16; 10:1–12; Phil. 3:17; 1 Thess. 1:6; 2 Thess. 3:7–9; Heb. 6:11–12; 11:1–12:2; 13:7; James 5:17–18).

So imitation appears to be an important means of sanctification according to Scripture: imitating God, Jesus, Paul and other Bible characters, and one's own church officers. Of course, some discernment is needed. Human role models, even Bible characters apart from Christ, sometimes stray from God's path. Not everything they do is worth imitating. And some things they do are appropriate in their own situation, but should not be imitated in our own time, such as Joshua's ferocity in slaughtering Canaanites. But those facts do not discourage biblical writers from emphasizing the importance of imitation.

This is one reason why I dissent from the views of some who oppose exemplarism. They have argued that we should preach Scripture exclusively as a redemptive-historical narrative and never point to a Bible character as a moral example.[10] On the contrary, I think that biblical writers often present the characters in their narratives as positive or negative examples. Saul, for instance, is largely a negative example, and David is usually a positive one. God has given us these examples as an important means for our ethical and spiritual growth.

THE WORD AS SPOKEN AND WRITTEN LANGUAGE

God's word also comes to us as human words and sentences. This is sometimes called "special revelation."[11] This revelation includes, first, the divine voice, spoken directly to human beings, as to Adam and Eve, to patriarchs such as Noah and Abraham, to the people of Israel gathered around Mt. Sinai in Exodus 19–20, to Moses, to other prophets, and to the apostles.

10. See Sidney Greidanus, *Sola Scriptura: Problems and Principles in Preaching Historical Texts* (Toronto: Wedge Publishing Foundation, 1979). See also many articles and sermons in the publication *Kerux*.

11. Again, the triad I am using doesn't quite match the triad general/existential/special. Special revelation can refer to (1) any revelation in human words and sentences, or (2) revelation with redemptive content, whether in words or events. In the second sense, there was no special revelation before the fall; in the first sense, there was. In the second sense, the events of redemptive history (as distinguished from the written account of redemptive history) are part of special revelation; in the first sense, they are not. I hope to sort out these issues in *The Doctrine of the Word of God*. In this book, however, I will treat the two triads as roughly synonymous.

Clearly the revelation spoken directly from God's own mouth is of supreme authority. No one has a right to find fault with it. So it must be regarded as infallible and inerrant. Who would dare to stand before God at Mt. Sinai and criticize his words?

Second, verbal revelation includes the words that God speaks to us *through* the prophets and apostles. Theologians sometimes say that when God speaks through a human being, his words have less authority than when spoken directly. But according to Deuteronomy 18:18–19, God's word in the mouth of a prophet is truly God's word, with the full authority of God's word: "I will raise up for them a prophet like you [Moses] from among their brothers. And I will put my words in his mouth, and he shall speak to them all that I command him. And whoever will not listen to my words that he shall speak in my name, I myself will require it of him." According to Jeremiah 1:9–10, the word in the mouth of the prophet has authority even over "nations and kingdoms":

> Then the Lord put out his hand and touched my mouth. And the Lord said to me,
>
> > "Behold, I have put my words in your mouth.
> > See, I have set you this day over nations and over
> >   kingdoms,
> > to pluck up and to break down,
> > to destroy and to overthrow,
> > to build and to plant."

Third, verbal revelation includes the words that God speaks to us through the *written* words of prophets and apostles. Written revelation is part of the covenant that God made with Israel at Mt. Sinai in Exodus 19–20. In chapter 3, I mentioned the documents that had constitutional authority in ancient Near Eastern covenant arrangements. To violate the terms of the document was to violate the covenant. Similarly, the covenant between God and Israel under Moses included a document that served as Israel's fundamental law, namely, the Ten Commandments. When Moses returned from speaking with God, he brought with him two stone tablets containing those words. The Ten Commandments are, in literary form, an ancient Near Eastern suzerainty treaty.[12]

In this document, God speaks to Israel in the first person. He calls the document "the law and the commandment, which I have written for their instruction" (Ex. 24:12). Later we read, "And he [God] gave

12. For the elements of that literary form, see chapter 3.

to Moses, when he had finished speaking with him on Mount Sinai, the two tablets of the testimony, tablets of stone, written with the finger of God" (Ex. 31:18). Moses destroys the tablets to show God's anger over Israel's false worship in Exodus 32. But God replaces them, again emphasizing his authorship of them: "The LORD said to Moses, 'Cut for yourself two tablets of stone like the first, and I will write on the tablets the words that were on the first tablets, which you broke'" (Ex. 34:1; cf. Deut. 4:13). God ordered Moses to put this second edition of the Decalogue into the ark of the covenant (Ex. 25:16; 40:20), the holiest place in Israel. In the ancient Near East, covenant documents were traditionally placed in sanctuaries. So from the beginning, God's revelation was "holy" Scripture.

As theologians sometimes discount God's indirect revelation through prophets, they even more disparage written revelation, thinking that it has much less authority than the direct utterance of the divine voice or the oral voice of the prophet. But Scripture itself draws no distinction between the authority of oral and written revelation. The praises given to God's law, statutes, testimonies, words, and commandments in the Old Testament are directed to God's written word, the laws of Moses (Pss. 19:7; 119). Paul tells the Corinthians, "If anyone thinks that he is a prophet, or spiritual, he should acknowledge that the things I am writing to you are a command of the Lord" (1 Cor. 14:37), and so he places his written words on the highest level of authority. The famous New Testament passages on biblical authority only summarize this theme that goes back to Moses:

> All Scripture is breathed out by God and profitable for teaching, for reproof, for correction, and for training in righteousness, that the man of God may be competent, equipped for every good work. (2 Tim. 3:16–17)

> And we have something more sure, the prophetic word, to which you will do well to pay attention as to a lamp shining in a dark place, until the day dawns and the morning star rises in your hearts, knowing this first of all, that no prophecy of Scripture comes from someone's own interpretation. For no prophecy was ever produced by the will of man, but men spoke from God as they were carried along by the Holy Spirit. (2 Peter 1:19–21)

So Scripture, God's written word, is no less authoritative than the divine voice heard directly from God's lips. As such, it has a unique role in the organism of revelation. The point is not that the Bible is more authoritative than God's word in nature or through persons. Everything God says has the same authority, namely supreme authority. But the Bible has a unique role within the organism of revelation, in the following ways:

1. It is the document of the covenant and therefore the court of final appeal for God's people. Like the United States of America, and unlike the United Kingdom, the church has a written document as its fundamental law, its constitution.

2. Since Jesus ascended to heaven and the prophets and apostles have passed away, the Bible remains as our sole means of access to their words. We need their words to find eternal life (John 6:68) and to live lives useful to God (Matt. 7:24–27).

3. Without God's grace, we inevitably suppress and distort the truths of natural revelation (Rom. 1:18–32). We can interpret nature rightly, therefore, only when we hear and believe the message of the gospel. But that is available only in Scripture. So we need Scripture if we are rightly to interpret any other form of revelation. As Calvin says, we need Scripture as our "spectacles" to see the natural world correctly.[13]

THE UNITY OF THE WORD

The same God speaks in all forms of the word, and his message is consistent in all of them. In Psalm 19:1–11, we see the unity between natural revelation and the written word:

> The heavens declare the glory of God,
>   and the sky above proclaims his handiwork.
> Day to day pours out speech,
>   and night to night reveals knowledge.
> There is no speech, nor are there words,
>   whose voice is not heard.
> Their measuring line goes out through all the earth,
>   and their words to the end of the world.
> In them he has set a tent for the sun,
>   which comes out like a bridegroom leaving his chamber,
>   and, like a strong man, runs its course with joy.
> Its rising is from the end of the heavens,
>   and its circuit to the end of them,
>   and there is nothing hidden from its heat.

13. *Institutes*, 1.6.1.

> The law of the LORD is perfect,
>   reviving the soul;
> the testimony of the LORD is sure,
>   making wise the simple;
> the precepts of the LORD are right,
>   rejoicing the heart;
> the commandment of the LORD is pure,
>   enlightening the eyes;
> the fear of the LORD is clean,
>   enduring forever;
> the rules of the LORD are true,
>   and righteous altogether.
> More to be desired are they than gold,
>   even much fine gold;
> sweeter also than honey
>   and drippings of the honeycomb.
> Moreover, by them is your servant warned;
>   in keeping them there is great reward.

I think the point here is that Israel should keep the written law, because it is just as firmly established as God's revelation in the heavens and the earth. The two forms of revelation come from the same Creator, from the one who controls the whole world, from east to west. Note also Psalm 147:15–20:

> He sends out his command to the earth;
>   his word runs swiftly.
> He gives snow like wool;
>   he scatters hoarfrost like ashes.
> He hurls down his crystals of ice like crumbs;
>   who can stand before his cold?
> He sends out his word, and melts them;
>   he makes his wind blow and the waters flow.
> He declares his word to Jacob,
>   his statutes and rules to Israel.
> He has not dealt thus with any other nation;
>   they do not know his rules.
> Praise the LORD!

Again, God tells Israel that his word to Jacob has the same majesty and power as the workings of nature. Indeed, the written word, God's statutes and rules, are a great gift to Israel that God has not given to any other nation. All nations know of God's natural revelation, but only Israel has the privilege of knowing his written word.

Scripture also serves as the content of existential revelation. The "law" written on the heart is not something different from the law of Scripture. It is the content of Scripture itself, transferred to a new medium. So the example that godly people provide for us is the content of Scripture, translated into their decisions and actions, applied to their situations.

So the written word displays its prominence as the document of the covenant. But in other ways, the three forms of revelation are dependent on one another. Natural and personal revelation are dependent on Scripture, as explained above. But Scripture is also dependent on them in a way. We cannot understand Scripture without natural revelation, for to interpret the Bible we need to have a knowledge of ancient history, of language, and of the contemporary situations to which Scripture must be applied. And we cannot understand Scripture unless our minds and hearts are made ready for it, by natural ability and by the supernatural work of the Spirit.

CHAPTER 10

Attributes of Scripture

In chapter 9, I began to discuss the normative perspective of Christian ethics. I first discussed God himself as the fundamental norm. Then I discussed more specifically the word of God as norm and distinguished various forms of the word. We saw then that within the organism of revelation, a focal role is played by Scripture as the written constitution of God's covenant.

In this chapter, I will look at Scripture more specifically,[1] making ethical applications of its various attributes or qualities. In the Reformed tradition, writers have sometimes spoken of four of these attributes: necessity, authority, clarity,[2] and sufficiency.[3] Four is not a good number for me, since it is not evenly divisible by three. Of course, Scripture has a great many attributes, and if we need more, some are readily at hand. The point is to choose some that illumine important theological and ethical issues.

So I have settled on six—two triads[4]—adding power and comprehensiveness to the traditional list. The first triad consists of power, author-

---

1. Note the progression of discussion, from general to particular: God as norm, the word of God as norm, Scripture as norm, and (later) various parts and aspects of Scripture as norms.

2. Or, if you prefer a ten-dollar word, perspicuity.

3. See Cornelius Van Til, "Nature and Scripture," in *The Infallible Word*, ed. N. B. Stonehouse and Paul Woolley (Philadelphia: Presbyterian and Reformed, 1946), 263–301. Van Til also makes use of this foursome in *An Introduction to Systematic Theology* (Nutley, NJ: Presbyterian and Reformed, 1974), 133–36, and in *A Christian Theory of Knowledge* (Philadelphia: Presbyterian and Reformed, 1969), 41–71.

4. I should get some credit for resisting the temptation to make three triads.

ity, and clarity, three qualities of Scripture as God's speech. The second, showing the importance of Scripture to our decisions in life, consists of comprehensiveness, necessity, and sufficiency. In each triad, we may regard the first member as situational, the second as normative, and the third as existential, though I confess that the scheme gets stretched a bit in the second triad. In what follows, I shall discuss these qualities one by one, particularly as they bear on ethics.

POWER

God's word, according to Scripture, not only says things, but also does things. God's word brought the universe into being (Gen. 1; Ps. 33:6; John 1:3). It directs the course of nature (Pss. 147:15–18; 148:5–8; Heb. 1:3). No word of God will ever be void of power (Gen. 18:14; Luke 1:37).[5]

We see the power of the word also in the preaching of the prophets and apostles. Isaiah ascribes divine omnipotence to the word of prophecy (Isa. 55:11). Paul says that the word of the gospel is "the power of God for salvation to everyone who believes" (Rom. 1:16). Elsewhere, too, the New Testament speaks of the preached word as something living and growing (Acts 6:7; 12:24; 19:20; Heb. 4:12–13), accomplishing God's saving purpose (Acts 20:32; 1 Thess. 1:5; 2:13). The word also works powerfully at times to harden hearts (Isa. 6:9–13; Matt. 13:14–15; Acts 28:26–27).

Scripture is the place where we can find that preaching today. The word of God is no less powerful in written form than it was on the lips of the apostles. The message of Scripture still sanctifies, and sometimes it still hardens. The written word restores the soul and makes wise the simple (Ps. 19:7).

When we go to Scripture for ethical guidance, it is important for us to remember that it is not only a text, an object of academic study. As we saw in chapter 9, it is the presence of God among us and therefore a book that cannot be tamed. It will never leave us the same. If God's grace has gripped us, and we are ready to respond in faith and obedience, then God's Word will be powerful to sanctify our hearts. But if we come to Scripture with skepticism or indifference, or if we regard it as a mere object of academic inquiry, that experience will affect us for the worse.

So when we bring an ethical question to Scripture, we should not only exegete its passages carefully, but also be open to change. We should say to God in our hearts, "Speak, Lord, for your servant hears" (1 Sam.

---

5. This is the literal translation of these two texts.

3:9). We should go to Scripture for the power of the Word, not only for its instruction.

AUTHORITY

Since Scripture is God's word, it has supreme authority, for God cannot speak other than with supreme authority.

The story of redemptive history is the story of the authoritative word of God and man's response to it. In Genesis 1:28, Adam's first recorded experience is that of hearing the word of God define his nature and task. In Genesis 2:17, God's word utters the specific prohibition that will determine whether Adam and Eve are faithful children of God. They fall by their disobedient response to that word, and the rest of the biblical story shows how God deals with that fall.

All of God's redemptive promises and covenants come by word: to Adam, Noah, Abraham, Moses, David, the prophets, Jesus, and the apostles. When God delivers Israel from slavery in Egypt, he gives to them a written word, to be placed in the holiest part of the sanctuary. That written word stands as the ultimate standard of their covenant faithfulness. As we saw in chapter 9, it has no less authority than God's own voice, spoken directly from heaven.

But God's people sin again against God's law and reject his loving promises. So prophets bring more words of God to condemn their sin—and, amazingly, to reiterate the promises. In the death of Christ, God both judges sin and fulfills his promise. Jesus dies in the place of sinners and gains for them God's forgiveness and eternal life. The story of Jesus' redemption is the gospel, and that too is a word that comes with the supreme authority of God. Those who believe are saved; those who do not believe are condemned (John 3:18). Jesus' words are the words of eternal life (John 6:68).

Jesus' words are the supreme test of discipleship (John 12:47–48). If we love him, we will keep his commandments (John 14:15, 21, 23; 15:10; cf. 1 John 2:3; 5:3; 2 John 6).

Jesus wrote no books, but by sending the Holy Spirit he empowered his apostles to remember what he said (John 14:26), to learn all the truth, and to know what will happen in the future (John 16:13). The apostles proclaim the authoritative message of the gospel, demanding repentance and faith in God's name (Acts 2:38). The authority of their word is not limited to their oral preaching, but also attaches to their written words (1 Cor. 14:37; 2 Thess. 3:14).

The written word, therefore, is the word of God himself, breathed out of his mouth (2 Tim. 3:16). As such, it cannot be anything less than supremely authoritative. Such supreme authority certainly includes infallibility and inerrancy. It places upon us an ethical obligation to believe everything Scripture says and to obey everything Scripture commands.[6]

CLARITY

Since Scripture is God's word, it is his communication to us. In Scripture, God speaks, not primarily to himself or to the angels, or to the winds and waves, but to us human beings. God cannot fail to accomplish his purpose, so his communication cannot be anything less than successful. If words are unclear, they fail to communicate; they are not communication. So Scripture must be clear.

Scripture represents that clarity by describing how near God is to us in his Word. So the clarity of Scripture represents the existential perspective, the lordship attribute of divine presence. God says to Israel:

> For this commandment that I command you today is not too hard for you, neither is it far off. It is not in heaven, that you should say, "Who will ascend to heaven for us and bring it to us, that we may hear it and do it?" Neither is it beyond the sea, that you should say, "Who will go over the sea for us and bring it to us, that we may hear it and do it?" But the word is very near you. It is in your mouth and in your heart, so that you can do it. (Deut. 30:11–14)

Paul paraphrases this passage to speak of the presence of Christ in the gospel:

> But the righteousness based on faith says, "Do not say in your heart, 'Who will ascend into heaven?'" (that is, to bring Christ down) or "'Who will descend into the abyss?'" (that is, to bring Christ up from the dead). But what does it say? "The word is near you, in your mouth and in your heart" (that is, the word of faith that we proclaim). (Rom. 10:6–8)

In these passages, the clarity of God's word engages our responsibility. If we disobey or disbelieve, we cannot complain that God hasn't spoken clearly. Like God's word in nature (Rom. 1:20), the clarity of his word in the gospel implies that we are without excuse. So the clarity of God's word has an ethical thrust.

6. I shall, of course, have much more to say about the authority of Scripture in *The Doctrine of the Word of God* (forthcoming). So I have intentionally kept this section short, even though the matter is extremely important.

To speak this way, however, raises problems. For it seems that in some respects Scripture is unclear. Many people say that Scripture is too hard for them to understand, and that therefore it is unclear to them. And Scripture itself notes certain kinds of unclarity:

1. Scripture is unclear to the unregenerate. As I indicated earlier, the Word hardens them, until the Spirit changes their heart (Isa. 6:9–10; 28:9–13; 1 Cor. 2:6, 14–16; 14:21; 2 Cor. 3:14–16; 2 Peter 3:16).

2. Some doctrines of the faith are mysterious (Job 38–42; Rom. 11:33–36). Although we can speak of them, even regenerate people cannot understand them in depth. This is the limitation of our finitude.

3. All parts of Scripture are not equally clear. Peter says of Paul's letters, "There are some things in them that are hard to understand, which the ignorant and unstable twist to their own destruction, as they do the other Scriptures" (2 Peter 3:16). Of course, the ignorant and unstable are themselves responsible for twisting the teaching of Paul's letters. But Peter also says that the inherent difficulty of Paul's writing is a factor in the misunderstanding. So the WCF says, "All things in Scripture are not alike plain in themselves, nor alike clear unto all" (1.7).

How can we reconcile our confession of the clarity of Scripture with these senses in which Scripture is unclear? The Confession answers this way:

> All things in Scripture are not alike plain in themselves, nor alike clear unto all: yet those things which are necessary to be known, believed, and observed for salvation, are so clearly propounded, and opened in some place of Scripture or other, that not only the learned, but the unlearned, in a due use of the ordinary means, may attain unto a sufficient understanding of them. (1.7)

So the Confession makes a distinction between the things that are "necessary to be known, believed, and observed for salvation" and those that are not. The former must be clear; the latter may not be. And the Confession adds another limitation on the clarity of Scripture: many things in Scripture, even among those necessary for salvation, cannot be understood by everybody without help. Understanding in those cases comes through "a due use of the ordinary means." Those means presumably include the normal educational resources by which we learn to interpret language, and the special resources of the church, such as preaching, teaching, and prayer. So if you are a regenerate person, and there is something in Scripture you don't understand, that is either because (1) the matter is not necessary for salvation, or (2) you haven't made a due use of the ordinary means.

As to the first possible reason, I hesitate to try to distinguish in Scripture between what is necessary for salvation and what is not.[7] Certainly the atonement is necessary for salvation in a way that the number of David's troops is not. It seems that God could have redeemed us as easily if David had one hundred fewer troops, but he could not have redeemed us without the atonement. But there are certainly some gray areas here, such as the sacraments.

The second reason reflects the polemics of the Reformation period. The Roman Catholic Church withheld the Scriptures from the laity, thinking that the laity could not possibly understand them without the instruction of the church. The Confession does not deny the importance of teaching. It presupposes teaching in its reference to ordinary means. But it says that our need of teaching does not justify withholding the Scriptures from ordinary people. Any adult of normal intelligence can understand the basics of the atonement, for example, if he is willing to undergo some simple instruction.

But I would add a third reason why believers sometimes find Scripture to be unclear. That is that believers differ greatly from one another in their callings and responsibilities. When a child is four years old, there is not much of the Bible that he understands, even if he makes maximum use of the ordinary means of grace available to him. Even doctrines that are easily described as necessary for salvation, such as the doctrine of the atonement, may be obscure to our four-year-old believer.[8] How can it be that such a believer is baffled by the clear word of God? The answer should be obvious: a four-year-old child is not able to master the doctrine of the atonement, and he is not responsible to do that. He is not called to that kind of reflection. He is called to obey his parents, a biblical command that he can understand well enough, and with their guidance to grow in his knowledge of the Bible.

I noted earlier that the clarity of Scripture has an ethical application. It takes away excuses and establishes our responsibility to grasp what God's Word says. But a four-year-old child has much less responsibility of this sort, than, say, a twenty-year-old with normal mental gifts.

That reflection suggests a principle: the clarity of Scripture is relative to one's responsibilities. A fourteen-year-old has more responsibility than

7. Theologians have tried to make such distinctions also in regard to biblical inerrancy (teaching that the Bible is inerrant only in matters necessary to salvation) and, as we shall see, to biblical sufficiency. But since salvation in Scripture is a historical process, and most of the Bible narrates that history, it is very hard to draw lines in Scripture between what is necessary and not necessary for salvation.

8. He may well be able to sing, "Jesus loves me, he who died, heaven's gates to open wide." But the imputation of Christ's active righteousness, as distinguished from an infusion of righteousness, will probably escape his understanding.

he did ten years before. And he will find that Scripture is clear enough (with "a due use of the ordinary means") to advise him of those additional responsibilities. As he increases in age, he will increase in responsibility. And if he listens diligently to God's Word, he will find that Scripture becomes proportionately clearer to him.

Of course, responsibility changes, not only with age, but also with vocation. Ordinarily, a pastor is responsible to understand Scripture at a deeper level than the steelworker in his congregation. The pastor has been given greater opportunities to study Scripture, and to whom much is given, from him much is required (Luke 12:48). The steelworker is responsible to know Scripture well enough to carry out his responsibilities; the pastor must know more to carry out his responsibilities. Neither can claim as an excuse for dereliction that Scripture is unclear.

Scripture, then, is clear enough to make us responsible for carrying out our present duties to God. That principle seems to me to summarize what the Bible implies about its own clarity.

COMPREHENSIVENESS

Now let us move on to the second triad of attributes: comprehensiveness (situational), necessity (normative), and sufficiency (existential). As I indicated above, these express various kinds of importance that Scripture has for our lives, particularly for our ethical decisions. The first triad focuses more on the actual content of Scripture. The second triad shows how the first triad is important to us. In brief, then, the second triad asserts that the first triad is comprehensive, necessary, and sufficient. The power of the word is comprehensive, necessary, and sufficient; the same is true of the authority and clarity of the word.

The first attribute in the second triad is comprehensiveness, which I define as the relevance of all Scripture to all of life.[9] That is, God's truth is given to us in the whole Bible, not just parts of it, and that truth covers all of human life. Since the focus here is on the breadth of human life in all its contexts and environments, I link comprehensiveness with the situational perspective.

The first part of this definition is that *all* Scripture is our standard, not just part of it. So, when tempted by Satan, Jesus quotes Deuteronomy 8:3, "Man shall not live by bread alone, but by every word that comes from

9. Thanks to Noy Sparks, a student of mine, who suggested that I add comprehensiveness to necessity and sufficiency.

the mouth of God" (Matt. 4:4). And Paul says, "All Scripture is breathed out by God and profitable for teaching, for reproof, for correction, and for training in righteousness, that the man of God may be competent, equipped for every good work" (2 Tim. 3:16–17). This is true of "all" Scripture.

This concept is sometimes called *tota Scriptura*, "by all of Scripture," which correlates nicely with *sola Scriptura*, "by Scripture alone," which we will consider under sufficiency.

If Scripture were a merely human book, we could pick and choose what we find ethically useful. But since Scripture is the word of God, we may not do that. Rather, we must hunger for every word that comes from God's lips, as Peter said to Jesus: "Lord, to whom shall we go? You have the words of eternal life" (John 6:68). The word of the Lord should be our chief delight (Ps. 1:2), so that we hate to see any part of it fall to the ground.

Does this mean that we are to treasure the genealogies, the descriptions of rituals, and the mélanges of apocalyptic symbols? Yes. This does not mean that we need to pore over Leviticus, hunting for some kind of deep edification in each verse. Some texts do produce profound edification in a single verse, like John 3:16. Others edify chiefly by our consideration of the larger context. Leviticus 3:1–5 may not mean much to us today (though it meant a great deal to Aaron). But the Old Testament sacrificial system as a whole, of which Leviticus 3:1–5 is a part, is immensely important; it tells us what kind of death our Savior died.

So 2 Timothy 3:16–17 tells us that all Scripture is useful, and specifically that it is ethically useful. It is useful that we may be competent, equipped for every good work. We shall later discuss various parts and aspects of Scripture that have special importance for ethics: law, wisdom, and so on. But in that discussion we must be careful not to lose sight of the forest for the trees. Every particular statute or ethical maxim in Scripture must be related to the whole. For example, in Joshua 5:2, God calls Joshua to circumcise all the males in Israel. Does he call the church to do that today? No, because Paul says that neither circumcision nor uncircumcision matters now (1 Cor. 7:19; Gal. 5:6; 6:15). Evidently there has been a change in God's requirements. The question before us, then, in making our own decisions, is ultimately not what Joshua 5:2 says, but what the whole Bible says. All ethical questions, in the final analysis, are questions about what the whole Bible says to people about their situation.

The second aspect of the comprehensiveness of Scripture is that the Bible refers to all aspects of human life. In 1 Corinthians 10:31, Paul says, "So, whether you eat or drink, or whatever you do, do all to the glory of God." That "whatever" includes everything. Compare Romans 14:23, "*Whatever* does not proceed from faith is sin," and Colossians 3:17, "And *whatever* you do, in word or deed, do everything in the name of the Lord Jesus, giving thanks to God the Father through him." Another "whatever" occurs in Colossians 3:23.

This second aspect of comprehensiveness is related to the first. If only some passages or themes of Scripture were ethically useful, then Scripture would apply only to those parts of human life treated in those passages or themes. Conversely, if Scripture only addressed some aspects of human life, we would have to dismiss as irrelevant what it appears to say about other matters. But in Scripture's view of its own mission, the whole Word applies to the whole world.

God's lordship is comprehensive. He demands that every aspect of life be under his authority. Scripture also puts the same issue in terms of love: "You shall love the LORD your God with all your heart and with all your soul and with all your might" (Deut. 6:4–5; cf. Mark 12:30). God demands our complete allegiance, obedience, and passion. So everything we do should be done to his glory.

God's salvation is also comprehensive. "Therefore, if anyone is in Christ, he is a new creation. The old has passed away; behold, the new has come" (2 Cor. 5:17). Regeneration is radical, affecting our thinking, will, emotions, and actions. And redemption even stretches out to the cosmos:

> For I consider that the sufferings of this present time are not worth comparing with the glory that is to be revealed to us. For the creation waits with eager longing for the revealing of the sons of God. For the creation was subjected to futility, not willingly, but because of him who subjected it, in hope that the creation itself will be set free from its bondage to decay and obtain the freedom of the glory of the children of God. (Rom. 8:18–21)

> For in him [Christ] all the fullness of God was pleased to dwell, and through him to reconcile to himself all things, whether on earth or in heaven, making peace by the blood of his cross. (Col. 1:19–20)

Christians sometimes say that the Bible is silent on this or that matter: diet, exercise, tax increases, nuclear proliferation, auto repair, the need for stoplights, etc. But although there are many subjects that Scripture does not explicitly mention, it speaks of everything implicitly. It does that by providing principles for every ethical decision. Scripture doesn't mention abortion, for example, but it forbids murder and treats unborn children as human persons. So pro-life Christians rightly argue that the Bible prohibits abortion.

Often those principles are very general, of course. Scripture does not tell me, even implicitly, what brand of soap to buy. But it tells me that when I buy soap I should buy it to the glory of God. And by not prescribing a brand, it gives me the freedom to buy any of several brands. So even in this case, Scripture prescribes the difference between good and bad, defining the moral quality of my action.

Certainly the comprehensiveness of Scripture rules out attempts to limit the scope of biblical revelation. As I mentioned in the previous section, many theologians have tried to limit the content or authority of Scripture to narrowly religious matters (matters necessary for salvation). That would allow us to think autonomously in matters other than religion. So some have concluded that Scripture is not inerrant, clear, or sufficient, in matters other than salvation, narrowly conceived.

But Scripture will not be so confined. God is Lord over all, and salvation renews all areas of thought and life. So God's authority extends to anything he chooses to speak to us about. Scripture, as his word, also has comprehensive authority. If God wants to tell us in his Word some things about the history of Israel that contradict a scholarly consensus, he has the right to do so, and we should stand with him against the scholars. Changing our thinking about such matters may well be part of the comprehensive renewal that God brings to us in Christ. In any case, it is the word of our Lord, and he must be right, even if every man is wrong (Rom. 3:4). So if God wants to tell us in Scripture that evolution is false, we should stand with him and against the consensus of scientists.[10] If God wants to tell us that abortion is wrong, we should stand with him and not with contemporary opinion makers.

So to say that Scripture is comprehensive is to say that the whole Word applies to the whole world. We need to take a broad view of ethics, which encompasses the whole Bible and the whole creation.

NECESSITY

The second member of our second triad is the necessity of Scripture. The third will be the sufficiency of Scripture. Students of logic are familiar with the distinction between necessary and sufficient conditions. If A is a

---

10. This is not to say that Scripture is a "textbook of science." For the most part, Scripture does not focus on the usual subject matter of the sciences. And, as we shall see in the next chapter, we need both scriptural and extrascriptural data to do the work of science. But Scripture does say a number of things that are relevant to science, and what it says must be heeded.

necessary condition of B, then B can't exist without A. If A is a sufficient condition of B, then A can't exist without B. To say that Scripture is necessary for the Christian life is to say that we can't live without it. To say that Scripture is sufficient for the Christian life is to say that Scripture provides all the ultimate norms we need, so that if we don't have sufficient norms, it can only be because Scripture doesn't exist.

At this point, we shall look at the necessity of Scripture. The WCF presents the necessity of Scripture in the first section of its first chapter:

> Although the light of nature, and the works of creation and providence do so far manifest the goodness, wisdom, and power of God, as to leave men unexcusable; yet are they not sufficient to give that knowledge of God, and of his will, which is necessary unto salvation. Therefore it pleased the Lord, at sundry times, and in divers manners, to reveal himself, and to declare that his will unto his church; and afterwards, for the better preserving and propagating of the truth, and for the more sure establishment and comfort of the church against the corruption of the flesh, and the malice of Satan and of the world, to commit the same wholly unto writing: which maketh the Holy Scripture to be most necessary; those former ways of God's revealing his will unto his people being now ceased.

The Confession bases the necessity of Scripture on the inadequacies of natural revelation and the insecurities of other forms of verbal revelation. But I believe that the necessity of Scripture may also be derived from the very lordship of God in covenant with us.

The "necessity" of Scripture means simply that without Scripture we have nothing: no Lord or Savior; no faith, hope, or love. Remember that the Lord is an absolute, personal being, who makes a covenant with his people. That covenant takes the form of a written document. The Lord issues commands to other persons called servants. Immediately after the confession of God's lordship in Deuteronomy 6:4–5, God demands that the people of Israel study and obey his words (vv. 6–8):

> And these words that I command you today shall be on your heart. You shall teach them diligently to your children, and shall talk of them when you sit in your house, and when you walk by the way, and when you lie down, and when you rise. You shall bind them as a sign on your hand, and they shall be as frontlets between your eyes. You shall write them on the doorposts of your house and on your gates.

Similarly, Jesus asks in Luke 6:46, "Why do you call me 'Lord, Lord,' and not do what I tell you?"

Many would like to confess Jesus as Lord, without confessing the Bible as his word. But that is to empty the idea of lordship of meaning. Because the Lord is personal, he speaks to his creatures. Because he is supremely authoritative, he speaks to them with supreme authority. Because he is the covenant Lord, he speaks to us in a written document. Without that document, without Scripture, we cannot meaningfully say that God is our Lord.

As the Confession's statement indicates, God has also spoken directly to human beings, and he has spoken through the mouths of prophets and apostles. But written revelation has been, since the time of Moses, the primary means of covenant governance. And today we have access to God's direct speech and to his words spoken through the prophets only through Scripture. So without Scripture we have no Lord.

Similarly, without Scripture we have no salvation. For "salvation belongs to the LORD" (Jonah 2:9). Salvation in all its dimensions is the sovereign work of the Lord. We have access to it through the gospel, and the gospel is part of Scripture. Paul says, "So faith comes from hearing, and hearing through the word of Christ" (Rom. 10:17). Without that word, then, we are without hope. Consider again Peter's cry, "Lord, to whom shall we go? You have the words of eternal life" (John 6:68).

The Lord's promise of salvation to those who believe is a promise found in Scripture. If Scripture is not God's word, we have no reason to believe it, for a promise of salvation must necessarily come from God himself. If God doesn't warrant it, there is no reason to believe it. The promise is warranted only if it is a word from God. If the Bible is not the word of God, then there is no word of God, and there is no promise or gospel.

Since Scripture is necessary for the lordship relation itself (the covenant), and since it is necessary for salvation, it is necessary for the Christian life. In part 2, I argued that unless an absolute, personal God has spoken to us, there is no basis for ethics. The Bible is the only transcript of God's words, and hence it is the only source of absolute ethical norms.

As the Confession says, natural revelation is also a source of God's norms, of ethical content. But, as Paul says in Romans 1, apart from grace, sinners repress and distort that revelation, fleeing its implications. So we must heed Calvin, who said that we need the spectacles of Scripture to see natural revelation aright.

The remaining attribute of Scripture that I wish to discuss is its sufficiency. But I have so much to say on that subject that I will have to give sufficiency a chapter to itself.

CHAPTER 11

The Sufficiency of Scripture

The last of the six attributes of Scripture is sufficiency, sometimes called *sola Scriptura*, "by Scripture alone." The sufficiency of Scripture, particularly as applied to ethics, is a doctrine of immense importance and one that is frequently misunderstood. So I will discuss it at greater length than the other attributes. My basic definition: Scripture contains all the divine words needed for any aspect of human life.

CONFESSIONAL FORMULATION

The WCF formulates the doctrine thus:

> The whole counsel of God concerning all things necessary for his own glory, man's salvation, faith and life, is either expressly set down in Scripture, or by good and necessary consequence may be deduced from Scripture: unto which nothing at any time is to be added, whether by new revelations of the Spirit, or traditions of men. Nevertheless, we acknowledge the inward illumination of the Spirit of God to be necessary for the saving understanding of such things as are revealed in the Word: and that there are some circumstances concerning the worship of God, and government of the church, common to human actions and societies, which are to be ordered by the light of nature, and Christian prudence, according to the general rules of the Word, which are always to be observed. (1.6)

Below is a commentary on this statement, phrase by phrase:

"The whole counsel of God concerning all things necessary for his own glory, man's salvation, faith and life . . ." The sufficiency of Scripture is comprehensive, as explained in chapter 10. Everything we need to know for God's glory is in the Bible. The same is true for our own "salvation, faith and life." The Confession does not understand these terms in the narrow ways that I argued against in chapter 10. It sees salvation as comprehensive, as we can tell from the rest of the document. Similarly, "faith and life" is a comprehensive pair of concepts. WSC, 3, says, "The Scriptures principally teach what man is to believe concerning God, and what duty God requires of man." So it is reasonable to think that "faith and life" in WCF, 1.6, refers to everything we are to believe and do, the whole content of Scripture applied to the whole content of the Christian life.

Christians sometimes say that Scripture is sufficient for religion, or preaching, or theology, but not for auto repairs, plumbing, animal husbandry, dentistry, and so forth. And of course many argue that it is not sufficient for science, philosophy, or even ethics. That is to miss an important point. Certainly Scripture contains more specific information relevant to theology than to dentistry. But sufficiency in the present context is not sufficiency of specific information but sufficiency of divine words. Scripture contains divine words sufficient for all of life. It has all the divine words that the plumber needs, and all the divine words that the theologian needs. So it is just as sufficient for plumbing as it is for theology. And in that sense it is sufficient for science and ethics as well.

". . . is either expressly set down in Scripture, or by good and necessary consequence may be deduced from Scripture." The sufficient content of Scripture includes, not only its explicit teaching, but also what may be logically deduced from it. To be sure, logical deduction is a human activity, and it is fallible, as are all human activities. So when someone tries to deduce something from Scripture, he may err.[1] But the Westminster Confession speaks not of just any attempt to deduce conclusions from Scripture, but

---

1. This liability to error should caution us to be careful in the work of logical deduction. Certainly it must be done with hermeneutical wisdom. "All men have sinned (Rom. 3:23); Jesus is a man (1 Tim. 2:5); therefore, Jesus sinned" may seem like a valid syllogism, but of course it presupposes a defective Christology. (Thanks to Richard Pratt for this example.) So the right use of logic depends on many other kinds of skill and knowledge. On the other hand, the possibility of error should not lead us to abandon logical deduction. For error is not found only in logic, but also in every other activity by which we seek to understand Scripture: textual criticism, translation, interpretation, theology, preaching, and individual understanding. If our goal is to avoid making any error at all, we should not only avoid

of "good and necessary consequence." That phrase refers to logic done right, ideal logic. When deductive logic is done right, the conclusion of a syllogism does not add to its premises. It rather brings out content already there. In the classic syllogism, "All men are mortal; Socrates is a man; therefore, Socrates is mortal," the conclusion doesn't tell you anything that you couldn't find out from the premises themselves. What the syllogism does is to make the implicit content explicit. Logic is a hermeneutical tool,[2] a device for bringing out meaning that is already there in the text. So (1) the "content of Scripture" includes all the logical implications of Scripture, (2) the logical implications of Scripture have the same authority as Scripture, and (3) logical deductions from Scripture do not add anything to Scripture.

"... *unto which nothing at any time is to be added.*" Covenant documents in the ancient Near East often contained an inscriptional curse, a prohibition against adding to or subtracting from the document. Scripture, our covenant document, also contains such language (see Deut. 4:2; 12:32; Prov. 30:6; Rev. 22:18–19; cf. Josh. 1:7). These passages do not forbid seeking information outside of Scripture. Rather, they teach that we will never need any divine words in addition to God's written words, words that are available to us only in the Bible. That means as well that we should never place any human words on the same level of authority as those in Scripture. That would be, in effect, adding to God's words.

"... *whether by new revelations of the Spirit, or traditions of men.*" One can add to God's words either by claiming falsely to have new words from God, or by placing human tradition on the same level of authority as God's Word. The Confession ascribes these errors to its two main opponents, respectively: the enthusiasts and the Roman Catholics. The enthusiasts were largely Anabaptists, who held views similar to some modern charismatics. The Roman Catholics defended their tradition as a source of revelation equal to the Bible. Roman Catholic theology has since changed its formulations somewhat,[3] but it still regards tradition as highly as it regards Scripture. Since the writing of the Confession, it has become important also for Protestants to guard their respect for

---

logic, but we should avoid all these other activities as well. But that in itself would be an error of another kind.

2. See *DKG*, 242–301.

3. Roman Catholic theologians today tend to speak, not of "two sources" of revelation (Scripture and tradition), but of "one source," the stream of tradition of which Scripture is a part. Neither of these views, however, is compatible with the sufficiency of Scripture.

their own tradition, so that it doesn't compete with the unique respect due to Scripture.[4]

"Nevertheless, we acknowledge the inward illumination of the Spirit of God to be necessary for the saving understanding of such things as are revealed in the Word." To say that Scripture is sufficient is not to deny that other things may also be necessary. We should always remember that the sufficiency of Scripture is a sufficiency of divine words. It is a sufficient source of such words. But we need more than divine words if we are to be saved and to live holy lives. In particular, we need the Spirit to illumine the Word, if we are to understand it. So no one should object that the doctrine of the sufficiency of Scripture leaves no place for the Holy Spirit.

". . . and that there are some circumstances concerning the worship of God, and government of the church, common to human actions and societies, which are to be ordered by the light of nature, and Christian prudence, according to the general rules of the Word, which are always to be observed." I shall say more about these "circumstances" when I discuss the second commandment and the regulative principle of worship. For now, let us note that the sufficiency of Scripture does not rule out the use of natural revelation ("the light of nature") and human reasoning ("Christian prudence") in our decisions, even when those decisions concern the worship and government of the church.[5]

The reason for this, of course, is that Scripture doesn't speak specifically to every detail of human life, even of life in the church. We have seen that in one sense Scripture speaks of everything, for its principles are broad enough to cover all human actions. The principle of 1 Corinthians 10:31, that we should do all to the glory of God, speaks to every human activity and grades every human act as right or wrong.

But it is often difficult to determine in specific terms what actions will and will not bring glory to God. At that point, natural revelation and Christian prudence give us important guidance. For example, Scripture doesn't mention abortion. But natural revelation tells us that abortion is a procedure that takes innocent life. That shows us that the Bible's prohibition of murder is relevant to the matter of abortion.

Note that in this example, as the Confession says, there are "general rules of the Word" that are relevant to our decision. There are always general

4. See my articles, "*Sola Scriptura* in Theological Method," in my *Contemporary Worship Music* (Phillipsburg, NJ: P&R Publishing, 1997), and "Traditionalism," available at http://reformedperspectives.org, under "practical theology," and at www.frame-poythress.org.

5. Note the triad: Scripture, the light of nature, Christian prudence.

rules of the Word relevant to any human decision, as we have seen, such as the rule of 1 Corinthians 10:31. So to use the data of natural revelation in this way, though it is extrascriptural, is not to add to Scripture in the sense of Deuteronomy 4:2. To do this is not to add more divine words. It is, rather, a means of determining how the sufficient word of Scripture should be applied to a specific situation.

The fact that Scripture doesn't mention abortion, or nuclear war, or financial disclosure, or parking meters, therefore, does not mean that we may abandon Scripture in considering these issues. There is always a principle of Scripture that is relevant. The only question is: specifically, how does that principle apply? Recourse to natural revelation and human prudence can help to answer that question.

BIBLICAL BASIS

But is this confessional doctrine itself biblical? I believe it is. As we've seen, the covenant document contains an inscriptional curse, forbidding adding and subtracting. This is to say that God alone is to rule his people, and he will not share that rule with anyone else. If a human being presumes to add his own word to a book of divinely authoritative words, he thereby claims that his words have the authority of God himself. He claims in effect that he shares God's throne.

Nevertheless, during the history of Israel some did have the audacity to set their words alongside God's. False prophets claimed to speak in God's name, when God had not spoken to them (1 Kings 13:18; 22:5–12), a crime that deserved the death penalty (Deut. 18:20). And the people worshiped according to human commandments, rather than God's (Isa. 29:13–14):

> And the Lord said:
> "Because this people draw near with their mouth
>   and honor me with their lips,
>   while their hearts are far from me,
> and their fear of me is a commandment taught by men,
>   therefore, behold, I will again
>   do wonderful things with this people,
>   with wonder upon wonder;
> and the wisdom of their wise men shall perish,
>   and the discernment of their discerning men shall be hidden."

Jesus applied Isaiah's words to the Pharisees, adding, "You leave the commandment of God and hold to the tradition of men" (Mark 7:8). And it is likely that some people in Paul's time wrote letters forged in Paul's name, claiming his authority for their own ideas (2 Thess. 2:2).

God's own representatives, however, fearlessly set God's word against all merely human viewpoints. Think of Moses before Pharaoh, Elijah before Ahab, Isaiah before Ahaz, Jonah before Nineveh, and Paul before Agrippa, Felix, and Festus. Consider Jesus, who spoke with the same boldness before the Pharisees, the Sadducees, the scribes, Herod, and Pilate. Those who are armed with God's word, the sword of the Spirit, are free from the tyranny of human opinion!

Paul, in his famous statement about biblical inspiration, speaks of sufficiency as well: "All Scripture is breathed out by God and profitable for teaching, for reproof, for correction, and for training in righteousness, that the man of God may be competent, equipped for every good work" (2 Tim. 3:16–17). "Every" refers to sufficiency.

GENERAL AND PARTICULAR SUFFICIENCY

We should notice that 2 Timothy 3:16–17 ascribes sufficiency to the Old Testament. That is an interesting point, that the Old Testament is actually a sufficient moral guide for New Testament Christians. Why, then, does God give us the New Testament as well? That question leads to a distinction between general sufficiency and particular sufficiency:

GENERAL SUFFICIENCY

At any point in redemptive history, the revelation given at that time is sufficient. After Adam and Eve sinned, God revealed to them how they would be punished, and he also revealed to them the coming of a deliverer, the seed of the woman, who would crush the serpent's head (Gen. 3:15). This revelation, extensive as it is, is not nearly as extensive as the revelation available to us in the completed biblical canon. Was this revelation sufficient for them? Yes, it was. Had they failed to trust this revelation, they could not have used as an excuse the fact that it wasn't full enough. In this revelation, they had all the divine words they needed to have. So that revelation was sufficient.

Nevertheless, God added to that revelation, by speaking to Noah, Abraham, and others. Why did he add to a revelation that was already sufficient? Because Noah needed to know more than Adam did. The history of redemption is progressive. In Noah's time, God planned to judge the world by a flood, and Noah had to know that. The Adamic revelation was sufficient for Adam, but not for Noah.

Recall the principle I offered in chapter 10 regarding the clarity of Scripture: Scripture is clear enough to make us responsible for carrying out our present duties to God. Sufficiency should be understood in the same way. God's revelation to Adam was sufficient for him to carry out his duties, but Noah needed more, for he had additional duties. He needed more in order to do God's will in his time.

Similarly, the revelation of the Old Testament was sufficient for the first generation of Christians. But God graciously provided them with much more, including the letters of Paul. In God's judgment, these were necessary for the ongoing life of the young church, and when they were collected and distributed, believers recognized them as God's word. Once the New Testament began to function as God's word in the church, the Old Testament was no longer sufficient in itself, but it continued to function as part of the canon which was, as a whole, sufficient.

That consideration raises the question of whether God will add still more revelation to the canon. Sufficiency in itself, what I am calling "general sufficiency," does not preclude divine additions to Scripture, though it does preclude mere human additions.

PARTICULAR SUFFICIENCY

But there is an additional principle that should lead us not to expect any more divine words until the return of Christ. That principle is that Christ's redemption is final. When redemption is final, revelation is also final.

Hebrews 1:1–4 draws this parallel:

> Long ago, at many times and in many ways, God spoke to our fathers by the prophets, but in these last days he has spoken to us by his Son, whom he appointed the heir of all things, through whom also he created the world. He is the radiance of the glory of God and the exact imprint of his nature, and he upholds the universe by the word of his power. After making purification for sins, he sat down at the right hand of the Majesty on high, having become as much superior to angels as the name he has inherited is more excellent than theirs.

Verse 3 speaks of Jesus' purification for sins as final, for when finished, he sat down at God's right hand. Verse 2 speaks of God's speech through his Son as final, in comparison with the "many times" and "many ways" of the prophetic revelation. Note the past tense: "has spoken." The revelation of the Old Testament continued over many centuries; that of the Son came once for all. Nothing can be added to his redemptive work, and nothing can be added to the revelation of that redemptive work.

Hebrews 2:1–4 also contrasts the revelation of the old covenant with that of the new:

> Therefore we must pay much closer attention to what we have heard, lest we drift away from it. For since the message declared by angels proved to be reliable and every transgression or disobedience received a just retribution, how shall we escape if we neglect such a great salvation? It was declared at first by the Lord, and it was attested to us by those who heard, while God also bore witness by signs and wonders and various miracles and by gifts of the Holy Spirit distributed according to his will.

The "message declared by angels" is, of course, the Mosaic law. The "great salvation" in Christ is something far greater. The message of this salvation was declared first by Christ and then by the apostles ("those who heard"), with God himself bearing witness through signs and wonders. From the writer's standpoint, these declarations were all in the past. Even though part of that message (at least the letter to the Hebrews) was still being written, the bulk of it had already been completed.

Scripture is God's testimony to the redemption he has accomplished for us. Once that redemption is finished, and the apostolic testimony to it is finished, the Scriptures are complete, and we should expect no more additions to them. Scripture is the deposit of the apostolic testimony, its written record. It is the only form of that testimony passed on to us beyond the apostolic generation. Once that testimony is complete, Scripture, too, is complete.

The same conclusion follows from 2 Peter 1:3–11. There, Peter notes that Jesus' "divine power has granted to us all things that pertain to life and godliness, through the knowledge of him who called us to his own glory and excellence" (v. 3). All things that pertain to life and godliness, therefore, come from Jesus' redemption. After that redemption, evidently, there is nothing more that could contribute anything to our spiritual life and godliness. Peter then mentions various qualities that we receive through Jesus, concluding, "For in this way there will be richly provided for you an entrance into the eternal kingdom of our Lord and Savior Jesus Christ" (v. 11). This is the language of sufficiency. The virtues that come from redemption are sufficient for us to enter the final kingdom. Nothing more is needed.

So within the concept of sufficiency, I distinguish between general and particular sufficiency. As we saw earlier, the general sufficiency of Scripture excludes human additions, but is compatible with later additions by God himself. This is the sense in which the Old Testament is sufficient according to 2 Timothy 3:16–17. The particular sufficiency of Scripture is the sufficiency of the present canon to present Christ and all of his resources. God himself will not add to the work of Christ, and so we should not expect him to add to the message of Christ.

THE USE OF EXTRABIBLICAL DATA

If we remember that the sufficiency of Scripture is a sufficiency of divine words, that will help us to understand the role of extrabiblical data, both in ethics and in theology. People sometimes misunderstand the doctrine of sufficiency by thinking that it excludes the use of any extrabiblical information in reaching ethical conclusions. But if we exclude the use of extrabiblical information, then ethical reflection is next to impossible.

Scripture itself recognizes this point. As I said earlier, the inscriptional curses do not forbid seeking extrabiblical information. Rather, they forbid us to equate extrabiblical information with divine words. Scripture itself requires us to correlate what it says with general revelation. When God told Adam to abstain from the forbidden fruit, he assumed that Adam already had general knowledge, sufficient to apply that command to the trees that he could see and touch. God didn't need to tell Adam what a tree was, how to distinguish fruits from leaves, or what it meant to eat. These things were natural knowledge. So God expected Adam to correlate the specific divine prohibition concerning one tree to his natural knowledge of the trees in the garden. This is theology as application: applying God's word to our circumstances.

The same is true for all divine commands in Scripture. When God tells Israel to honor their fathers and mothers, he does not bother to define "father" and "mother" and to set forth an exhaustive list of things that may honor or dishonor them. Rather, God assumes that Israel has some general knowledge of family life, and he expects them to apply his command to that knowledge.

Jesus rebukes the Pharisees, not because they had no knowledge of the biblical text, but because they failed to apply that knowledge to the things that happened in their own experience. In Matthew 16:2–3, he says, "When it is evening, you say, 'It will be fair weather, for the sky is red.' And in the morning, 'It will be stormy today, for the sky is red and threatening.' You know how to interpret the appearance of the sky, but you cannot interpret the signs of the times." The chief deficiency in their application of Scripture was their failure to see Jesus as the promised Messiah, the central theme of the Hebrew Bible. In John 5:39–40, Jesus says, "You search the Scriptures because you think that in them you have eternal life; and it is they that bear witness about me, yet you refuse to come to me that you may have life."

Against the Sadducees, who deny the resurrection, Jesus quotes an Old Testament text that at first glance doesn't seem to speak to the point: "And as for the resurrection of the dead, have you not read what was said to you by God: 'I am the God of Abraham, and the God of Isaac, and the God of Jacob'? He is not God of the dead, but of the living" (Matt. 22:31–32).

That text (Ex. 3:6) was a famous one; every Jewish biblical scholar knew it well. The Sadducees' problem was not that they didn't know the text, but that they were unable or unwilling to apply it to the current discussion of resurrection. Jesus taught them that to the extent that one cannot apply Scripture, one is actually ignorant of Scripture. Knowing Scripture cannot be separated from knowing its applications.[6] But that is to say that one cannot know Scripture without understanding how it applies to extrabiblical data. Here, one cannot rightly understand the normative perspective without the situational perspective.

So Scripture itself says that Scripture has an ethical purpose. The right way to study Scripture is to apply it to the issues that face us in our own time. In Romans 15:4, Paul says, "For whatever was written in former days was written for our instruction, that through endurance and through the encouragement of the Scriptures we might have hope." Unlike any other ancient book, Scripture was written for the purpose of instructing those who would live many centuries in the future, to give them instruction, endurance, encouragement, and hope. Its own authors (divine and human) intended it to guide us in our ethical and spiritual struggles.

Similarly, the familiar passage in 2 Timothy 3:16–17, "All Scripture is breathed out by God and profitable for teaching, for reproof, for correction, and for training in righteousness, that the man of God may be competent, equipped for every good work," indicates not only that Scripture is God's word, but also that it has a practical and ethical purpose. Both this passage and the famous passage 2 Peter 1:19–21 were written by aged apostles, concerned about false teaching likely to enter the church after their deaths (2 Tim. 3:1–9; 2 Peter 2:1–22). Paul and Peter agree that Scripture contains the resources necessary to distinguish true from false teachers, both in their doctrine and in their character. (The ethics of the false teachers is a main emphasis of these contexts.) But to use Scripture that way is, of course, to apply it to the situations that the people encounter.

6. See *DKG*, 81–85, 95–98.

THE LOGIC OF APPLICATION

Ethical reasoning can often be expressed in the form of moral syllogisms. In a moral syllogism, the first premise states a principle, and the second states a fact to which the principle applies. Then the conclusion states the application. We might describe the first premise as normative, the second as situational, and the conclusion as existential, since it brings the principle to bear on our own ethical decision.[7] For example:

(1) Stealing is wrong (normative premise).
(2) Embezzling is stealing (situational premise).
Therefore, embezzling is wrong (existential conclusion).

In Christian ethics, the normative premise ultimately comes from God, for only he has the authority to define ethical norms for human beings. In principle, this premise may come from any kind of divine revelation. But we must remember the primacy of Scripture, which governs our understanding and interpretation of general and existential revelation. Our interpretations of general and existential revelation must be tested by Scripture. If someone claims that God wants me, say, to move to Paris, he needs to show me from Scripture that this is indeed God's will. But then the ultimate norm is Scripture, not general or existential revelation by itself.

We may state the sufficiency of Scripture for ethics as follows: Scripture is sufficient to provide all the ultimate norms, all the normative premises, that we need to make any ethical decision. It contains all the divine words we need to make our ethical decisions, and all ultimate ethical norms come from the mouth of God.

Then what use is general revelation? First of all, it is especially important in furnishing situational premises. Of course, the Bible also furnishes situational premises, as in:

(1) Adultery is wrong (Ex. 20:14).
(2) Lust is adultery (Matt. 5:27–28).
Therefore, lust is wrong.

But most of the time we need extrabiblical data to formulate the situation we are seeking to address, as in the following example:

(1) Stealing is wrong.

7. Within this general structure, subsidiary arguments are usually needed to establish the normative premise and the situational premise. So ethical arguments in practice have many premises and many twists and turns of logic. In the present discussion, I am presenting a general form that summarizes many arguments about ethics.

(2) Cheating on your income tax is stealing.

Therefore, cheating on your income tax is wrong.

The Bible, of course, does not mention the U.S. income tax, although it does mention taxes in general. What it says about taxes in general is relevant, of course. It is among the "general rules of the Word" mentioned in the Confession. But in order to evaluate the second premise, we need to know not only these biblical principles, but also some facts not mentioned in Scripture that tell us what the income tax is. Here is an even more obvious example:

(1) Sabbath breaking is wrong.

(2) Operating a tanning salon on Sunday is Sabbath breaking.

Therefore, operating a tanning salon on Sunday is wrong.

To establish the second premise, of course, we need to know some general principles of Scripture about the Sabbath. But Scripture doesn't mention tanning salons. So we need some specific information from outside the Bible to warrant the second premise.

Of course, to go "outside the Bible" is not to go outside of God's revelation. It is rather to move from the sphere of special revelation to the sphere of general revelation. So the whole syllogism utilizes general revelation, illumined and evaluated by special revelation.

Secondly, it should also be evident that even the normative premises of ethical syllogisms use extrabiblical data at some point. All our use of Scripture depends on our knowledge of extrabiblical data. Scripture contains no lessons in Hebrew or Greek grammar. To learn that, we must study extrabiblical information. Similarly, the other means that enable us to use Scripture, such as textual criticism, text editing, translation, publication, teaching, preaching, concordances, and commentaries, all depend on extrabiblical data. So in one sense even the first premises of moral syllogisms, the normative premises, depend on extrabiblical knowledge. Without extrabiblical premises, without general revelation, we cannot use Scripture at all. But Scripture is emphatically a book to be used.

None of these considerations detracts from the primacy of Scripture as we have described it. Once we have a settled conviction of what Scripture teaches, that conviction must prevail over all other sources of knowledge. Scripture must govern even the sciences that are used to analyze it: textual criticism, hermeneutics, and so forth. These sciences enable us to understand Scripture, but they must themselves be carried on in accord with Scripture. There is a hermeneutical circle here that cannot be avoided, and that circle shows how the normative and situational perspectives are interdependent. But in the hierarchy of norms, Scripture must remain primary.

ADIAPHORA

The Greek word *adiaphora* means literally "things indifferent," that is, things that make no difference. In theological ethics, people have sometimes used it to designate a class of actions that are neither right nor wrong, a third category of actions in addition to right ones and wrong ones. Some people have referred to eating meat and drinking wine (Rom. 14:21), for example, as adiaphora.

The question of adiaphora relates to the sufficiency of Scripture in this way: Scripture commands certain actions, and these are right. Scripture forbids certain actions, and these are wrong. But it seems as though there are many actions that Scripture neither commands nor forbids, such as eating meat and drinking wine. Scripture determines what is right and wrong, so when it is silent, neither category can apply. Thus, the argument goes, there must be a third category, the adiaphora.

Historically, this concept has been used most frequently in the area of worship. Luther applied the term to certain Roman Catholic forms of worship, which he thought were neither commanded nor forbidden by Scripture, and which the believer could therefore observe or not observe in good conscience. The Puritans and the Scottish Presbyterians, however, denied the existence of adiaphora in worship. For them, what God commands in worship is right; anything else is forbidden—there is no middle ground.[8]

I too reject the concept of adiaphora, not only in worship, but in ethics generally. My reasons, however, differ from those of the Puritans and the Scottish Presbyterians.

First, let us be clear that there are no *things* (i.e., material objects in the world) that are indifferent in any meaningful way, even though the literal meaning of the Greek term *adiaphora* is "things indifferent." People sometimes say, for example, that heroin is bad, peaches are good, but wine is indifferent. Remember, however, that such statements refer to nonmoral goodness, not moral goodness as I defined it in chapter 2. Also, Scripture tells us that in that nonmoral sense everything God created is good, not bad or indifferent (Gen. 1:31; 1 Tim. 4:4). I would judge from these passages that even heroin has a good use and is part of God's

---

8. I shall discuss this issue in more detail when we consider the second commandment.

good creation. In any case, these passages leave no room, in the world of material things, for adiaphora.

Those who have used the concept of adiaphora have generally applied it to human actions, rather than to material things. So applied, the concept deals with ethical goodness and badness. But are there any human actions that are ethically indifferent? When Paul says, "Whether you eat or drink, or whatever you do, do all to the glory of God" (1 Cor. 10:31), he implies that everything we do either brings glory to God or does not do so.[9] The "whatever" is universal. It includes our eating and drinking, sleeping, waking, bathing, working, marrying, entertaining ourselves—indeed, every human activity. When we glorify God, we are doing right, and when we do not glorify God, we are doing wrong. Here there is no room for a third category that we might call adiaphora. No human action is indifferent to God.

Why, then, has the concept of adiaphora become so popular in some circles? I think it has been confused with other concepts that are legitimate. These are:

1. Choices between two or more good things, rather than between good and evil. Certainly there are many choices of this kind in human life. But when we make a choice among equally good options, our choice is good, not indifferent.

2. Acts concerning which Scripture is silent. Now as we have seen, there are no human actions concerning which Scripture is absolutely silent. For 1 Corinthians 10:31 and similar passages cover everything. But there are human actions concerning which Scripture does not speak specifically. For example, Scripture doesn't specifically mention my use of a computer. It is addressed in 1 Corinthians 10:31 generally and implicitly, but not specifically. So we might be tempted to think that specific actions of this kind are adiaphora. However, my use of the computer is not ethically indifferent. It is either ethically good or ethically bad, for it is either to God's glory or not.

3. Acts neither commanded nor forbidden in Scripture. This is close to the previous category. But there are some acts that are mentioned in Scripture, and mentioned specifically, that are neither commanded nor forbidden. An example would be eating meat and drinking wine in Romans 14:21. We may be tempted to say that such actions are adiaphora. But we saw in chapter 2 that actions that are neither forbidden nor commanded are permitted (1 Cor. 7:6). What God permits us to do is good. So actions in this category are good, not bad or indifferent.

9. Earlier we cited other passages that also emphasize the universality of our responsibility to God: Rom. 14:23; Col. 3:17, 23.

4. Acts that are neither right nor wrong in themselves, but are right, or wrong in specific circumstances. Eating ice cream, for example, can be right in some circumstances, but wrong in others. Drinking a glass of wine may be a good thing to do in many circumstances, but not if one has already had ten glasses. Are such actions adiaphora? I would say not. Eating ice cream is not right or wrong "in itself," but no human action is ever performed in itself. It is always performed in one set of circumstances or another. Any specific act of eating ice cream will always be either right or wrong, never indifferent. That is true for any other act that is neither right nor wrong in itself.[10]

THE STRONG AND THE WEAK

Those defending the concept of adiaphora often mention Paul's discussions of the strong and the weak in Romans 14:1–15:13 and 1 Corinthians 8–10. The Roman and Corinthian churches were divided by controversies over vegetarianism (Rom. 14:2), the observing of special days (Rom. 14:5),[11] and the eating of food offered to idols (1 Cor. 8:1). The argument goes that these matters are adiaphora: it is a matter of indifference whether someone abstains from meat, or observes holidays, or eats food offered to idols.

In my view, it is misleading to describe these matters as adiaphora. The passages make clear that they are not matters of indifference. Rather, the choices that we make in these areas are either right or wrong. There is no middle ground.

The passages contrast two groups of Christians, whom Paul describes as "strong" and "weak." In 1 Corinthians, he describes the weak as those who lack knowledge (1 Cor. 8:1, 7, 10–11) and have a weak conscience (vv. 7, 9, 10–12). These groups were opponents, and on the specific issues of the controversy, Paul sides with the strong (Rom. 15:1), although he criticizes their behavior. Some readers are inclined to assume that God always favors those who have the most religious scruples. But in these passages, to the

10. If someone prefers to use the word "adiaphora" to refer to actions that are neither right nor wrong in themselves, I will not protest too much. Definitions are never a matter of life or death. Of course, in this case the term will refer only to general categories of these actions, not to specific examples of these categories. But I think that the use of this term always connotes the thought of moral neutrality, which is, in a Christian understanding, divine indifference. But God is never indifferent to what we do, as is plain from 1 Cor. 10:31 and similar texts. So I think even the most defensible uses of the term, such as this one, tend to mislead.

11. In my later discussion of the fourth commandment, I shall consider the implications of this passage for the keeping of the weekly Sabbath.

surprise of such readers, the strong are the ones without the scruples. The strong are the ones who eat meat, who think that observing special days is unnecessary, and who have no problem eating food offered to idols. The weak are the ones whose consciences are troubled by such practices.

Both groups are persuaded of the rightness of their positions. As Paul says, each carries out his practice "in honor of the Lord" (Rom. 14:6). And Paul honors the Christian professions of each. Although he disagrees with the weak, he describes them as brothers (v. 15) and as those "for whom Christ died" (v. 15; cf. 1 Cor. 8:11).

This division creates three problems in the churches, and it is important to keep these distinct in our minds:

1. The very fact that one group in the church is spiritually weak or lacks knowledge is a problem. People who are spiritually weak and ignorant need pastoral help to make them strong and knowledgeable. That help comes from the Lord, operating through the means of grace: the Word, the church, and prayer. Paul doesn't go into detail about what the strong should do to educate the weak, but he speaks elsewhere of teaching, nurturing, and restoring.

2. The two groups have bad attitudes toward each other. In this regard, both the strong and the weak are at fault. The strong "despise" the weak (Rom. 14:3, 10). The weak "pass judgment on" the strong (vv. 3–4, 10).[12] Passing judgment here probably means accusing of sin, perhaps even casting doubt on the other person's allegiance to Christ.

Paul's response to this problem is simply to forbid such attitudes: don't despise, don't judge. Both groups belong to Christ, and it is simply wrong for Christians to treat one another this way. Note that Paul never suggests in these passages that the strong should subject the weak to formal discipline, as he does with the incestuous man in 1 Corinthians 5. Rather, the two parties are to love one another as brothers within the church.[13] To say this is not to contradict the need for education and nurture, as noted above. Certainly the strong must seek to educate, nurture, and strengthen the weak. And, doubtless, the weak will continue for a time to seek to change the strong as well. But there are right and wrong ways to carry out this

12. First Cor. 8–10 doesn't include these specific expressions, but it is clear from 8:1–3 that Paul sees a lack of love in the whole controversy. In this passage, he mainly confronts those who have knowledge, the theologically stronger party. Although they have knowledge, they have not been using it in a loving way.

13. Evidently, then, not all differences within the church are subject to the formal procedures of church discipline. There are disagreements that may and ought to be tolerated. No church or denomination may demand complete agreement on all matters. For more discussion of this important subject, see my book *Evangelical Reunion* (Grand Rapids: Baker, 1991), now available at www.thirdmill.org and www.frame-poythress.org.

ministry to one another. Despising and passing judgment are not among them. The strong may not despise the weak, because the weak are fellow Christians. The weak may not judge the strong for the same reason—and, of course, because the strong are right.

3. But there is a third issue that Paul is mainly concerned with in these passages, and here the strong are at fault. The strong, by their behavior, are in danger of placing "a stumbling block or hindrance" (Rom. 14:13; cf. 1 Cor. 8:9) in the way of their weak brothers. This is a very serious matter. Paul describes the stumbling block as something that not only brings grief to the weak (Rom. 14:15), but defiles the weak conscience (1 Cor. 8:7), destroys the brother (Rom. 14:15; cf. 1 Cor. 8:11), even tends to "destroy the work of God" (Rom. 14:20),[14] and brings condemnation (v. 23). In placing a stumbling block before a weak brother, therefore, the strong brother himself sins against Christ (1 Cor. 8:12), even though, as we have seen, his convictions on these ethical issues are correct.

What kind of behavior by the strong could have such serious consequences? Evidently they were leading the weak into sin, for sin is the only thing with the spiritually destructive power that Paul describes. What kind of sin? The strong influenced the weak to sin against the dictates of his conscience (1 Cor. 8:7, 12). Conscience, as we shall see later, is our ability to tell right from wrong. People's consciences are not infallible. Sometimes a person's conscience tells him something is wrong when it is right, and vice versa. Consciences have to be taught and nurtured, by the means of grace, as we saw above.

Now a Christian's conscience tells him what is pleasing or displeasing to God. If that conscience is weak, it tells him that some actions displease God, when in fact they please God. If the weak Christian violates his conscience, then, he violates what he considers to be the dictates of God. To violate one's conscience, even when the conscience is wrong, is to rebel against God.[15]

The "stumbling block," then, is an inducement to sin against a weak conscience. Let's imagine that an elder of the church, a strong believer, invites a weak believer, a Christian who believes that God commands vegetarianism, to eat at his table. The strong believer serves meat, perhaps in

14. We should make allowance for hyperbole here. In the most important sense, the work of God cannot be overthrown. But the nature of sin, from Satan's first rebellion down to the present, is to destroy, particularly to destroy a person's spiritual life.

15. This is a sort of catch-22, to be sure. When one's conscience misleads, it may be wrong to follow it, for to follow it may lead to sin. But it may also be wrong to disobey conscience, for to disobey conscience is always to rebel against what one thinks is right. This dilemma shows the importance of educating the conscience according to God's Word.

part to pressure the weaker believer to become strong. The weak believer then is faced with the temptation to eat meat, which would violate his conscience. The temptation is all the greater because of his desire to please the elder and the general demands of hospitality. But if the weak believer eats the meat (without his conscience first being strengthened), he will be guilty of sin. Even though eating meat is not contrary to God's law, the weak believer is motivated by rebellion against God. He is placing the demands of hospitality, the demands of his host, over the demands of God, and therefore he sins. What is sinful is not the act itself, but the motive, the heart attitude.

At Corinth, the strong believers were actually going to feasts at idols' temples (1 Cor. 8:10). Paul's view is that the food itself is not a danger, even if it had at one point been offered to an idol (8:8; 10:25). But the religious context of a feast at an idol's temple could well be a danger to a weaker Christian. And if the weaker Christian hears that the food has been offered to an idol, and he sees the strong eating it (especially in the idol's temple), he may well be tempted to fall back into the actual worship of idols.

The strong, therefore, should avoid doing anything that might tempt the weak to sin against their conscience. The strong should certainly seek to educate the weak with the Word of God, to make them strong. But while the weak brother is weak, the strong should not tempt him to do things that violate his weak conscience or that might lead him back into an idolatrous religious system. The strong should teach, in other words, but should not exert pressure. We nurture the conscience, not by force or pressure, but by godly persuasion.

How do these passages apply to us today? People sometimes derive the lesson from these passages that a pastor should not drink alcoholic beverages in front of the teenagers in his church, for fear that he will encourage underage drinking. There is some wisdom in that advice, though it can be pressed too far. It might be better for the pastor to instruct the youth, so that they will not be tempted in that way. But that advice does not in any case arise from the passages we have discussed.

A better parallel involving the use of alcohol would be this: a pastor invites to his home for dinner a man who is conscientiously opposed to any use of alcoholic beverages. The pastor drinks wine himself and puts pressure on his guest to do the same. The example is a bit artificial. Most conscientious abstainers in our culture today are not likely to be influenced to violate their conscience by such an example. More likely, they will be inclined to "pass judgment on" the pastor in this case. That would be unfortunate, but that is not what Paul calls the "stumbling block." Nevertheless, that spiritual danger exists in some cases, and it is therefore wrong for the pastor to try to convert the abstainer to his position by using social pressure.

I hope it is evident now that the concept of adiaphora is inappropriate to describe the issues presented in these passages. It is true, of course, that eating meat, observing days, and eating idol food are not right or wrong in themselves, but become right and wrong in various circumstances. But, as I indicated earlier, all human acts take place in one set of circumstances or another. None occur simply in themselves. And in the circumstances described in these passages, the acts in view are right in some cases and wrong in others—never neutral. The strong are right to eat meat, for example, but they are wrong when they eat in such a way as to pressure the weak to violate their conscience. The weak are right to abstain, though not for the reasons they give. Both are wrong in their attitudes toward one another.

In these passages, it is plain that God's attitude toward these actions is not neutral at all. The passages have a pervasive emphasis on God's lordship, and it is because of God's lordship that Paul exhorts the people as he does. Note how many times the words *God* and *Lord* appear in these passages:

> Let not the one who eats despise the one who abstains, and let not the one who abstains pass judgment on the one who eats, for God has welcomed him. Who are you to pass judgment on the servant of another? It is before his own master that he stands or falls. And he will be upheld, for the Lord is able to make him stand. (Rom. 14:3–4)

> The one who observes the day, observes it in honor of the Lord. The one who eats, eats in honor of the Lord, since he gives thanks to God, while the one who abstains, abstains in honor of the Lord and gives thanks to God. For none of us lives to himself, and none of us dies to himself. If we live, we live to the Lord, and if we die, we die to the Lord. So then, whether we live or whether we die, we are the Lord's. For to this end Christ died and lived again, that he might be Lord both of the dead and of the living. Why do you pass judgment on your brother? Or you, why do you despise your brother? For we will all stand before the judgment seat of God; for it is written, "As I live, says the Lord, every knee shall bow to me, and every tongue shall confess to God." So then each of us will give an account of himself to God. (Rom. 14:6–12)

> Therefore, as to the eating of food offered to idols, we know that "an idol has no real existence," and that "there is no God but one." For although there may be so-called gods in heaven or on earth—as

indeed there are many "gods" and many "lords"—yet for us there is one God, the Father, from whom are all things and for whom we exist, and one Lord, Jesus Christ, through whom are all things and through whom we exist. (1 Cor. 8:4–6)

It is in the context of discussing these problems that Paul writes the verse that I have often been citing: "So, whether you eat or drink, or whatever you do, do all to the glory of God" (1 Cor. 10:31).

Paul commends mutual love in these situations because of the lordship of God. God is not neutral here. He cares what we do, and he cares about how we treat one another: not despising or judging, not setting a stumbling block in a brother's way. Partaking and abstaining are both good acts, when they are done in honor of the Lord. And they are good precisely because they honor God. There is no suggestion here of moral neutrality, nothing for which the term *adiaphora* might be appropriate.

But these passages are relevant to the sufficiency of Scripture, precisely because of the emphasis here on God's lordship. The prevailing issue here is God's honor, what pleases him. Human opinions must yield to God's words, which alone have ultimate authority. We find those words exclusively in Scripture.

CHAPTER 12

Law in Biblical Ethics

We have been studying the normative perspective on Christian ethics. In general, the normative perspective asks what God wants us to do. We saw that the ultimate norm is God himself. More specifically, we find his will for us in his word or revelation. We have looked at a number of forms that revelation takes, but we have focused on God's written word, the Scriptures, because of its primacy in the covenant that God made with us. In the previous two chapters, we discussed six attributes of Scripture that bear on ethics.

When we think of Scripture as an ethical norm, we are thinking about it as law. So it is important for us to give some attention to the concept of law in the Bible. From one perspective, law is a part of Scripture; from another perspective, it is the whole of Scripture.

In an obvious way, law is one part of Scripture that must be coordinated with other parts. The traditional Jewish divisions of the Hebrew Bible (the Christian Old Testament) were the Law, the Prophets, and the Writings. The Law, or Torah, consists of the first five books of Scripture, the Pentateuch. Christians have traditionally divided the Bible (both testaments) into law, history, poetry, prophecy, gospels, epistles, and apocalyptic. Like the Jews, Christians find law in the first five books.

Of course, the first five books contain not only law, but also other types of literature. Much of the Pentateuch is historical narrative, not divine commands. Many have translated *torah* as "instruction," rather than "law," and that seems appropriate, although the instruction in these books certainly includes a great deal of law in the literal sense. The centerpiece of the Pentateuch is the covenant that God made with Israel under Moses, which includes law as well as other elements, as we saw in chapter 3.

Divine commands are also found in many other parts of Scripture. Kings and Chronicles, for example, contain many divine commands for worship in the temple. The book of Proverbs contains advice from wise teachers that carries the force of divine commands. The prophets constantly command Israel to repent, at God's behest. Jesus shows the depth of the law in his teachings, such as the Sermon on the Mount (Matt. 5–7). The letters of the apostles contain much ethical instruction. In one sense, then, law is scattered throughout the Bible.

The element of law is important to Scripture, but Scripture contains many other elements as well. It contains imperatives, which we easily associate with law, but also indicatives, questions, promises, and exclamations.[1] It contains legal material, but also other genres, such as narrative, poetry, song, wisdom, parables, humor, and apocalyptic. We should note that all of these are God's authoritative word, and all of them are relevant to ethics, for according to 2 Timothy 3:16 *all* Scripture is breathed out by God and profitable for our instruction in righteousness, to equip us for good works.

It is interesting and important to consider how material in Scripture that is not legal in form can be relevant to ethics. Obviously, for instance, narrative is important because it tells the story of how God rescued us from sin and enabled us to do good works, and because it provides many examples of human behavior—some for our imitation, and some not. Poetry and song drive God's word (law and narrative) into our hearts, making it vivid, memorable, and motivating. Parables invite us to place ourselves in a provocative story that challenges our ethical complacency. Humor puts our pretensions into perspective. Apocalyptic stretches the imagination with symbolism about God's coming judgments and blessings.

As we see the variety of ways in which Scripture teaches ethics, we should be motivated to use similar variety in our own teaching. Ethical instruction is not just stating ethical norms. It is also singing, telling stories,[2] joking, exclaiming, and symbolizing.[3]

---

1. For another discussion of genres and speech acts, see *DKG*, 202–5.

2. Think, for example, of how Nathan confronted David using a parable to convict him of sin (2 Sam. 12:1–15). There will be more on this when we consider the existential perspective.

3. Obviously, I am not adept at these alternative ways of teaching ethics. But I would encourage others, with other gifts, to employ them for the edification of God's people. These are just as important as the writing of theology books.

So if we ask the normative question, "How does God want me to live?" we must look, not only at the specifically legal sections of Scripture, but through the whole Bible. This is only to say that the normative perspective is indeed a perspective, a perspective on the whole Bible.

In that sense, the whole Bible is law. For the whole Bible is God's authoritative word, given to us for our instruction in righteousness, to equip us for good works.[4] Everything in Scripture has the force of law. What it teaches, we are to believe; what it commands, we are to do.[5] We should take its wisdom to heart, imitate its heroes, stand in awe at its symbolism, laugh at its jokes, trust its promises, and sing its songs.

LAW AND GRACE

In what follows, I shall discuss relationships between the concept of law and other concepts in Scripture. First of all, it is important for us to understand the relationship between law and grace.

This relationship is, of course, an elementary aspect of the gospel. It is plain in Scripture that we cannot be saved from sin by obeying the law. Paul says:

> Now we know that whatever the law says it speaks to those who are under the law, so that every mouth may be stopped, and the whole world may be held accountable to God. For by works of the law no human being will be justified in his sight, since through the law comes knowledge of sin. But now the righteousness of God has been manifested apart from the law, although the Law and the Prophets bear witness to it—the righteousness of God through faith in Jesus Christ for all who believe. For there is no distinction: for all have sinned and fall short of the glory of God, and are justified by his grace as a gift, through the redemption that is in Christ Jesus, whom God put forward as a propitiation by his blood, to be received

---

4. The same thing can be said of narrative and the other forms of language as well. Some sections of Scripture are specifically narrative in form, but to know the whole narrative of the Bible you must consult the whole book. For that story includes the stories of God sending prophets, wisdom teachers, and so on. Similarly with other forms of speech and literature. See *DKG*, 202–5.

5. This is easier to understand if we recall a frequent theme of the Theology of Lordship series: epistemology is part of ethics. That is, there is an ethics of belief as well as an ethics of action. So even those parts of Scripture that seem to be given for our contemplation rather than our action are ethical: they tell us normatively what and how to contemplate.

by faith. (Rom. 3:19–25; cf. 4:1–8, 13–16; 11:6; Gal. 2:15–21; Eph. 2:8–10; Phil. 3:9; Titus 3:5)

Salvation, in other words, is not something we can earn by doing good works. It is, rather, God's free gift to us, given because of Christ's death for us. Our righteousness before God is the righteousness of Christ and him alone.

This has been the standard Protestant teaching since the Reformation, and it is enshrined in all the Protestant confessions. Recently, however, some have asked questions about Paul's teaching in this area. Some answers to those questions have been described as the New Perspective on Paul. That perspective is based on writings of Krister Stendahl, E. P. Sanders, James D. G. Dunn, N. T. Wright, and others. In that perspective, the problem with Judaism, according to Paul, was not works-righteousness, but its failure to accept God's new covenant in Christ, which embraced Gentiles as well as Jews. On this perspective, Paul's gospel is not an answer to the troubled conscience of someone (like Luther) who can't meet God's demands. Rather, it is the fulfillment of God's promise to Abraham to bless all nations. The "works of the law," against which Paul contends, are not man's attempts to satisfy God's moral law, but the distinctions between Jews and Gentiles, such as circumcision, food laws, and cleansings.

Discussions of the New Perspective are very complex, entering into details about the nature of Palestinian Judaism at the time of Paul, Paul's own history, and the exegesis of crucial texts. I cannot enter this controversy here. I do agree with those who believe that Sanders and others have been too selective in their references to Palestinian Judaism, and I believe that the New Perspective fails to deal adequately with a number of Pauline passages, such as Romans 4:4–5, Romans 11:6, Ephesians 2:8–10, and Philippians 3:9, which make plain that Paul rejects, not only legal barriers between Jew and Gentile, but also all attempts of people to save themselves by their works. Paul's argument in Romans 1–3, too, makes this clear: all people, Jew and Gentile alike, are guilty before God and cannot do anything to justify themselves. Their salvation comes only by God's grace, according to the passage in Romans 3 quoted above. So Luther's doctrines of *sola gratia* and *sola fide* are fully scriptural and fully Pauline.[6]

6. I recommend Kim Riddlebarger's essay, "Reformed Confessionalism and the 'New Perspective' on Paul," available at the website of the Alliance of Confessing Evangelicals, www.alliancenet.org, as an excellent introduction to this discussion. I fully endorse the conclusions of that article. I also commend a critical article, "N. T. Wright on Justification," by Charles E. Hill, available at http://www.thirdmill.org/files/english/html/nt/NT.h.Hill.Wright.html.

The New Perspective legitimately warns us against reducing Paul's gospel to soteric justification by faith. Paul's confrontation with the Jews was on several fronts. Nevertheless, it is important to insist that we are saved only by the grace of God in Christ, not by any works of our own.

In his chapter on "Law and Grace," John Murray summarizes well what law can and cannot do for us. Below are the main headings of his discussion:[7]

What Law Can Do

1. Law commands and demands; it propounds what the will of God is.

2. Law pronounces approval and blessing upon conformity to its demands (Rom. 7:10; Gal. 3:12).

3. Law pronounces the judgment of condemnation upon every infraction of its precept (Gal. 3:10).

4. Law exposes and convicts of sin (Rom. 7:7, 14; Heb. 4:12).

5. Law excites and incites sin to more virulent and violent transgression (Rom. 7:8, 9, 11, 13).

What Law Cannot Do

1. Law can do nothing to justify the person who in any particular has violated its sanctity and come under its curse.

2. It can do nothing to relieve the bondage of sin; it accentuates and confirms that bondage (Rom. 6:14).

GOD'S LAW AS THE CHRISTIAN'S NORM

But if law cannot justify us or relieve the bondage of sin, is it then obsolete to those who receive God's saving grace? Does the believer have nothing to do with law? Quite otherwise. Scripture is clear that the law has a positive role in the believer's life. The law is a gracious gift of God (Ps. 119:29). It is given for our good (Deut. 10:13). The psalmists express over and over again their delight in the law of the Lord (Pss. 1:2; 119:16, 24, 35, 47, 70, 77, 174). Jesus says:

Do not think that I have come to abolish the Law or the Proph-ets; I have not come to abolish them but to fulfill them. For truly, I say to you, until heaven and earth pass away, not an iota, not a dot, will pass from the Law until all is accomplished. Therefore whoever relaxes one of the least of these command-ments and teaches others to do the same will be called least in

7. John Murray, *Principles of Conduct* (Grand Rapids: Eerdmans, 1957), 184–85.

the kingdom of heaven, but whoever does them and teaches them will be called great in the kingdom of heaven. (Matt. 5:17–19)

And he adds to that law many of his own commandments, which he also expects us to keep: "If you love me, you will keep my commandments" (John 14:15; cf. vv. 21, 23; 15:10; 1 John 2:3; 5:3; 2 John 6).

Paul says that the law is "holy and righteous and good" (Rom. 7:12; cf. vv. 13–14, 16, 19, 21–22, 25), and he speaks of himself as "not being outside the law of God but under the law of Christ" (1 Cor. 9:21). He treats the basic principles of the Mosaic law as normative for Christians in passages like Romans 13:8–10, 1 Corinthians 7:19, and Galatians 5:13–14. And, like Jesus, he also sets forth ethical commands, as in Romans 12–16, Galatians 5:13–6:10, and Ephesians 4–6.

How is this positive emphasis on law compatible with grace? It is simply that those who are saved by God's grace will want to obey him. Obedience does not earn salvation for us; rather, it is the natural response of those who have become God's sons and daughters. As the Heidelberg Catechism puts it,

> Q. 86. *Since, then, we are redeemed from our misery by grace through Christ, without any merit of ours, why must we do good works?*
>
> A. Because Christ, having redeemed us by His blood, also renews us by His Holy Spirit after His own image, that with our whole life we show ourselves thankful to God for His blessing, and that He be glorified through us; then also, that we ourselves may be assured of our faith by the fruits thereof; and by our godly walk may win others also to Christ.

Now to obey someone, we must know what he wants of us. So to obey God, we must meditate on his law.

How, then, is this positive regard for the law compatible with Paul's statement in Romans 6:14, "For sin will have no dominion over you, since you are not under law but under grace"? In what sense are we "not under law"? Again, Murray's analysis is helpful. He argues that "under law" in the context of Paul's argument here refers to the bondage of sin:

> The person who is "under law", the person upon whom only law has been brought to bear, the person whose life has been determined exclusively by the resources and potencies of law, is the bondservant of sin. And the more intelligently and resolutely a person commits himself to law the more abandoned becomes his

slavery to sin. Hence deliverance from the bondage of sin must come from an entirely different source.[8]

That "entirely different source," of course, is God's grace. So Paul says, "You are not under law, but under grace." Grace, in Romans 6, particularly represents the fact that when Jesus died for our sins, we died to sin, and we were also raised with Christ to newness of life.

So, the expression "under law" has different meanings in Romans 6:14 and in 1 Corinthians 9:21. In Romans 6:14, Paul denies that believers are in bondage to sin, since they are not limited to what Murray calls "the resources and potencies of law." But in 1 Corinthians 9:21 Paul recognizes that the law continues to have authority over him, to show him how to obey the Lord who has saved him by grace.[9]

Paul also uses the phrase "under law" to refer to the distinctives of the Mosaic covenant, such as circumcision, temple sacrifices, the Aaronic priesthood, feast days, and so on—distinctives which the Judaizers were trying to impose upon Gentile Christians (Gal. 3:23). This is the theme that has become prominent in the writings of the New Perspective. The phrase in Galatians 3:23 has a meaning that is different from that of the phrase either in Romans 6:14 or in 1 Corinthians 9:21. In this sense, to be "under law" is to be under "the pedagogical nonage and tutelage of the Mosaic economy," in contrast to "the mature sonship and liberty enjoyed by the New Testament believer."[10] We should ascribe the same meaning to the "abolishing the law of commandments and ordinances" in Ephesians 2:15.

So Murray concludes that we are not under law in the sense of (1) being under the bondage of sin (Rom. 6:14) or (2) "being under the ritual law of the Mosaic economy" (Gal. 3:23). But we are under law in the sense of being obligated to obey our Lord (1 Cor. 9:21).[11]

LAW AND GOSPEL

I would now like to look at a distinction that is closely related to that between law and grace, but by no means identical to it. That is the distinction between law and gospel. As we have seen, we are saved by God's grace, not by our obedience to his law. So some have tried to draw a sharp distinction between two messages in Scripture. One message,

8. Ibid., 185–86.
9. See Murray's valuable discussion in ibid., 186–89.
10. Ibid., 188.
11. Ibid., 190.

"law," supposedly conveys law without grace, while the other, "gospel," conveys grace without law. In my judgment, it is not possible to make this distinction, even though Scripture does make a sharp distinction between works and grace.

It has become increasingly common in Reformed circles, as it has long been in Lutheran circles, to say that the distinction between law and gospel is the key to sound theology, even to say that to disagree with certain formulations of this distinction is to deny the gospel itself.

Sometimes this argument employs Scripture passages like Romans 3:21–31, emphasizing that we are saved by God's grace through faith alone, apart from the works of the law. In my judgment, however, none of the parties to the debate questions that justification is by grace alone, through faith alone. But it is one thing to distinguish between faith and works, a different thing to distinguish between law and gospel.

THE TRADITIONAL DISTINCTION

The distinction between law and gospel is not a distinction between a false way and a true way of salvation. Rather, it is a distinction between two messages, one that supposedly consists exclusively of commands, threats, and therefore terrors, and the other that consists exclusively of promises and comforts. Although we are saved entirely by God's grace and not by works, there are not two different messages of God in Scripture, one consisting exclusively of command ("law") and the other consisting exclusively of promise ("gospel"). In Scripture itself, commands and promises are typically found together. With God's promises come commands to repent of sin and believe the promise. The commands, typically, are not merely announcements of judgment, but God's gracious opportunities to repent of sin and believe in him. As the psalmist says, "Be gracious to me through your law" (Ps. 119:29 NIV).

The view that sharply separates the two messages comes mainly out of Lutheran theology, though similar statements can be found in Calvin and in other Reformed writers.[12] The Epitome of the Lutheran Formula of Concord, at 5.5, recognizes that *gospel* is used in different senses in Scripture,

---

12. Lutheran theologians frequently complain that Reformed theology "confuses" law and gospel, which, in the Lutheran view, is a grave error. The main difference is that in the Reformed view law is not merely an accuser, but also a message of divine comfort, a delight of the redeemed heart (Ps. 1:2). Also, the Reformed generally do not give the law/gospel distinction as much prominence within their systematic theological formulations. And, historically, they have been more open to the broader biblical language which the Lutheran Formula of Concord calls "correct" but not "proper" (see below).

and it cites Mark 1:15 and Acts 20:21 as passages in which gospel preaching "correctly" includes a command to repent of sin.[13]

But in section 6, it does something really strange. It says:

> But when the Law and the Gospel are compared together, as well as Moses himself, the teacher of the Law, and Christ the teacher of the Gospel, we believe, teach, and confess that the Gospel is not a preaching of repentance, convicting of sins, but that it is properly nothing else than a certain most joyful message and preaching full of consolation, not convicting or terrifying, inasmuch as it comforts the conscience against the terrors of the Law, and bids it look at the merit of Christ alone. . . .

I say this is strange, because the Formula gives no biblical support at all for this distinction,[14] and what it says here about the "gospel" flatly contradicts what it conceded earlier in section 5. What it describes as "correct" in section 5 contradicts what it calls "proper" in section 6. What section 6 does is to suggest that there is something "improper" about what it admits to be the biblical description of the content of the gospel in Mark 1:15 and Acts 14:15.[15] Mark 1:15 is "correct," but not "proper."

13. I am quoting the Epitome, a summary of the Formula, rather than the Solid Declaration, which deals with these matters at greater length. I think the argument of the Epitome is easier to follow, and I don't think the Solid Declaration adds anything important to the present discussion, though some Lutheran correspondents have told me otherwise.

14. The Solid Declaration (in section 6 of the chapter on "Law and Gospel") mentions Mark 1:15, in which "believing in the gospel" is distinguished from repenting. But especially in view of the use of "gospel" in verse 14, we may not take "gospel" in verse 15 to exclude any command. Indeed, "believe in the gospel" is itself a command. Section 26 of the Solid Declaration mentions also 2 Cor. 3:7–18 as a passage that "thoroughly and forcibly shows the distinction between the Law and the Gospel." That passage does not mention "law" or "gospel," but it does distinguish the Mosaic covenant as a "ministry of death" (v. 7) and a "ministry of condemnation" (v. 9) from the new covenant in Christ as a "ministry of righteousness" (v. 9). But the difference here is one of degree. Paul is comparing the relative glory of the two covenants. He is not teaching that the Mosaic covenant contains *only* condemnation. Indeed, not even Lutheran theologians believe that the gospel was absent from the Mosaic period or that it made its first appearance at the time of Christ. In all periods of redemptive history, God has renewed his promise of redemption.

15. The passage cited by the Formula, Acts 20:21, does not use the usual Greek verb for preaching the gospel (*euangelizō*), but the verb *diamartyromai*, "testify." But Acts 20:21 is nevertheless significant, since it gives a general description of what Paul declared in his preaching "both to Jews and to Greeks." That preaching was certainly gospel preaching. Paul resolved in his preaching to "know nothing among you except Jesus Christ and him crucified" (1 Cor. 2:2). Luke 24:47 is also significant, for it includes both repentance and forgiveness of sins as the content that Jesus gave to his disciples to preach (*kēryssō*) to all nations.

Law and Gospel in Scripture

I have been told that "proper" at this point in the Formula of Concord means, not "incorrect" or "wrong," but simply "more common or usual." However, I have looked through the uses of the *euangel-* terms in the New Testament, and I cannot find one instance in which the context *excludes* a demand for repentance (that is, a command of God, a law) as part of the content of the gospel. That is to say, I cannot find one instance of what the Formula calls the "proper" gospel, a message of pure comfort, without any suggestion of obligation. And there are important theological reasons why such a message cannot be found.

Essentially, the gospel in the New Testament is the good news that the kingdom of God has come in Jesus (Matt. 4:23; 9:35; Mark 1:14; Luke 4:43; Acts 20:24–25).[16] The kingdom is (1) God's sovereign power, (2) his sovereign authority, and (3) his coming into history to defeat Satan and bring about salvation with all its consequences.[17] God's kingdom power includes all his mighty acts in history, especially the resurrection of Christ.

God's kingdom authority is the reiteration of his commandments. When the kingdom appears in power, it is time for people to repent. They must obey (*hypakouō*) the gospel (2 Thess. 1:8; cf. *apeitheō* in 1 Peter 4:17). The gospel itself requires a certain kind of conduct (Acts 14:15; Gal. 2:14; Phil. 1:27; cf. Rom 2:16).

When God comes into history, he brings his power and authority to bear on his creatures. In kingdom power, he establishes peace. So New Testament writers frequently refer to "the gospel of peace" (Eph. 6:15; cf. Acts 10:36; Rom. 10:15), sometimes referring to the "mystery" of God bringing Gentiles and Jews together in one body (Rom. 16:25; Eph. 6:19).

The gospel is this whole complex: God's power to save, the reiteration of God's commands, and his coming into history to execute his plan. It is good news to know that God is bringing his good plans to fruition.

16. N. T. Wright believes that this use of *gospel* has a double root: "On the one hand, the gospel Paul preached was the fulfilment of the message of Isaiah 40 and 52, the message of comfort for Israel and of hope for the whole world, because YHWH, the god of Israel, was returning to Zion to judge and redeem. On the other hand, in the context into which Paul was speaking, 'gospel' would mean the celebration of the accession, or birth, of a king or emperor. Though no doubt petty kingdoms might use the word for themselves, in Paul's world the main 'gospel' was the news of, or the celebration of, Caesar." See "Paul's Gospel and Caesar's Empire," available at http://www.ctinquiry.org/publications/wright. htm. Of course, both of these uses focus on the rule of God as Lord, and both involve what is traditionally called law.

17. This is a triad of the sort discussed in this and other books in the Theology of Lordship series.

Consider Isaiah 52:7, one of the most important background passages for the New Testament concept of gospel: "How beautiful upon the mountains are the feet of him who brings good news, who publishes peace, who brings good news of happiness, who publishes salvation, who says to Zion, 'Your God reigns.'" It is the reign of God that is good news, news that ensures peace and salvation. Even the demand for repentance is good news, because in context it implies that God, though coming in power to claim his rights, is willing to forgive for Christ's sake. As God comes, he reigns, establishing his law throughout the earth.

In Isaiah 61:1–2, which Jesus quotes in his Capernaum sermon (Luke 4:18–19), Isaiah proclaims:

> The Spirit of the Lord GOD is upon me,
>   because the LORD has anointed me
> to bring good news to the poor;
>   he has sent me to bind up the brokenhearted,
> to proclaim liberty to the captives,
>   and the opening of the prison to those who are bound;
> to proclaim the year of the LORD's favor,
>   and the day of vengeance of our God;
> to comfort all who mourn.

This verse also provides important background to the New Testament use of *gospel*: note the "good news to the poor" in verse 1. This message too is the message of the coming of a king, a new administration of justice, even vengeance. This gospel, like that of Isaiah 52:7, is about the reestablishment of law.

So the gospel includes law in an important sense: God's kingdom authority, his demand to repent. And even on the view of those most committed to the law/gospel distinction, the gospel includes a command to believe. We tend to think of that command as being in a different class from the commands of the Decalogue. But that too is a command, after all. Generically it is law. And, like the Decalogue, that law can be terrifying to someone who wants to rely only on his own resources, rather than resting on the mercy of another. And the demand for faith includes other requirements: the conduct becoming the gospel that I mentioned earlier. Faith itself works through love (Gal. 5:6) and is dead without good works (James 2:17).

Having faith does not merit salvation for anyone, any more than any other human act merits salvation. Thus we speak of faith, not as the *ground* of salvation, but as the *instrument*.[18] Faith saves, not because it merits salva-

18. See, for example, WCF, 11.2.

tion, but because it reaches out to receive God's grace in Christ. Nevertheless, faith is an obligation, and in that respect the command to believe is
like other divine commands. So it is impossible to say that command, or
law, is excluded from the message of the gospel.

As gospel includes law, so does law include gospel. God gives his law as
part of a covenant, and that covenant is a gift of God's grace. The Decalogue begins, "I am the LORD your God, who brought you out of the land
of Egypt, out of the house of slavery" (Ex. 20:2). Only after proclaiming his
saving grace does God then issue his commands to Israel. So the Decalogue
as a whole has the function of offering Israel a new way of life, conferred by
grace (cf. Deut. 7:7–8; 9:4–6). Is the Decalogue "law" or "gospel"? Surely
it is both. Israel was terrified upon hearing it, to be sure (Ex. 20:18–21).
But in fact it offers blessing (note v. 6) and promise (v. 12). Moses and
the Prophets are sufficient to keep sinners from perishing in hell (Luke
16:30–31).

So the definitions that sharply separate law and gospel break down on
careful analysis. In both law and gospel, God proclaims his saving work
and demands that his people respond by obeying his commands. Law and
gospel differ in emphasis, but they overlap and intersect. They present the
whole Word of God from different perspectives. Indeed, we can say that
our Bible as a whole is both law (because as a whole it speaks with divine
authority and requires belief) and gospel (because as a whole it is good
news to fallen creatures). Each concept is meaningless apart from the other.
Each implies the other.

The law often brings terror, to be sure. Israel was frightened by God's
display of wrath against sin on Mt. Sinai (Ex. 20:18–21). But the law also
brings delight to the redeemed heart (Ps. 1:2; cf. 119:34–36, 47, 92, 93,
97, 130, 131; Rom. 7:22). Similarly, the gospel brings comfort and joy,
but (though less often noted in the theological literature) it also brings
condemnation. Paul says that his gospel preaching is, to those who perish,
"a fragrance from death to death" and, to those who believe, "a fragrance
from life to life" (2 Cor. 2:15–16; cf. 1 Cor. 1:18, 23, 27–29; 2 Cor. 4:3–4;
Rom. 9:32). The gospel is good news to those who believe. But to those
who are intent on saving themselves by their own righteousness, it is bad
news. It is God's condemnation of them, a rock of offense.

WHICH COMES FIRST?

In discussions of law and gospel, one commonly hears that it is important, not only to preach both law and gospel, but also to preach the law first
and the gospel second. We are told that people must be frightened by the

law before they can be driven to seek salvation in Christ. Certainly there is a great need to preach God's standards, man's disobedience, and God's wrath against sin, especially in an age such as ours, where people think that God will let them behave as they like. And very often people have been driven to their knees in repentance when the Spirit has convicted them of their transgressions of God's law.

But, as we have seen, it is really impossible truly to present law without gospel or gospel without law, though various relative emphases are possible. And among those relative emphases, the biblical pattern tends to put the gospel first. That is the pattern of the Decalogue, as we have seen: God proclaims that he has redeemed his people (gospel), and then tells them to behave as his covenant people (law). Since both gospel and law are aspects of all God's covenants, that pattern pervades Scripture.

Jesus reflects that pattern in his own evangelism. In John 4:1–42, he tells the Samaritan woman that he can give her living water that will take away all thirst. Only after offering that gift does he proclaim the law to her, exposing her adultery. Some have cited Luke 18:18–30 as an example of the contrary order: Jesus expounds the commandments and only afterward tells the rich ruler to follow him. But in this passage Jesus does not use the law alone to terrorize the man or to plunge him into despair. The man goes sadly away only after Jesus has called him to discipleship, which, though itself a command, is the gospel of this passage.

LEGITIMATE USE OF THE TRADITIONAL DISTINCTION

Now if people want to define *gospel* more narrowly for a specific theological purpose, I won't object too strongly. Scripture does not give us a glossary of English usage. A number of technical theological terms don't mean exactly what similar terms sometimes mean in the Bible. *Regeneration* and *election* are examples, as is *covenant*.[19] We can define our English terms pretty much as we like, as long as those definitions don't create confusion in our readers.

Over the years, we have come to think of *gospel* as correlative with *faith*, and *law* as correlative with *works*. In this usage, law is what condemns, and

19. The phrases "covenant of works" and "covenant of grace," found in WCF, 7.2–4, are not found anywhere in Scripture. *Covenant* in Scripture refers to particular historical relationships between God and his people, mediated by Noah, Abraham, Moses, David, and Jesus. "Covenant of grace" generalizes the common features of these historical covenants, seeing them as successive manifestations of God's redemptive lordship. "Covenant of works" finds in God's relation to our first parents features that are present in his later covenants (with significant differences, of course).

gospel is what saves. Although this distinction differs from the biblical uses of the terms, it does become useful in some contexts. For example, we all know a type of preaching that merely expounds moral obligations (as we usually think of them: don't kill, don't steal, etc.) and does not provide the knowledge of Christ that sinners need for salvation. That kind of preaching (especially when it is not balanced by other preaching emphases) we often describe as a preaching of *mere* law, legalism, or moralism. There is no good news in it. We are inclined to say that it is not preaching of the gospel. So, in this general way we come to distinguish the preaching of law from the preaching of gospel. That is, I think, the main concern of the Formula of Concord: to remind us that we need to preach both things.

We should be reminded, of course, that there is also an opposite extreme: preaching "gospel" in such a way as to suggest that Christ makes no demands on one's life. We call that "cheap grace" or "easy believism." We might also call it preaching "gospel without law." Taken to an extreme, it is antinomianism, the rejection of God's law. The traditional law/gospel distinction is not itself antinomian, but those who hold it tend to be more sensitive to the dangers of legalism than to the dangers of antinomianism.

Such considerations may lead us to distinguish in a rough-and-ready way between preaching law and preaching gospel. Of course, even in making that distinction, our intention ought to be to bring them together. None of these considerations requires us to posit a sharp distinction. And certainly, this rough-and-ready distinction should never be used to cast doubt on the integration of command and promise that pervades the Scriptures themselves.

It should be evident that "legalistic" preaching, as described above, is not true preaching of the law, any more than it is true preaching of the gospel. For as I indicated earlier, law itself in Scripture comes to us wrapped in grace.

Law/Gospel and the Christian Life

The Formula's distinction between law and gospel has unfortunate consequences for the Christian life. The document does warrant preaching of the law to the regenerate,[20] but only as threat and terror, to drive them to Christ

20. Theological literature speaks of three "uses of the law": (1) to restrain sin in society, (2) to terrorize people in order to drive them to Christ, and (3) to guide believers. In Lutheranism (not in Reformed circles), there has been controversy over the third use, though the Formula affirms it. But in Lutheranism it is often said that "the law always accuses." So the third use is essentially the second use directed at believers, driving us to Christ again and again and away from our residual unbelief. Reformed writers do not deny our continual

(Epitome, 6.4). There is nothing here about the law as the delight of the redeemed heart (Ps. 1:2; cf. 119:34–36, 47, 92, 93, 97, 130, 131; Rom. 7:22).

The Formula then goes on to say that believers do conform to the law under the influence of the Spirit, but it does so only as follows:

> Fruits of the Spirit, however, are the works which the Spirit of God who dwells in believers works through the regenerate, and which are done by believers so far as they are regenerate [spontaneously and freely], as though they knew of no command, threat, or reward; for in this manner the children of God live in the Law and walk according to the Law of God, which [mode of living] St. Paul in his epistles calls the Law of Christ and the Law of the mind, Rom. 7, 25; 8, 7; Rom. 8, 2; Gal. 6, 2. (Epitome, 6.5)

So the law may use threats to drive us to Christ. But truly good works are never motivated by any command, threat, or reward.[21]

In my view, this teaching is simply unbiblical. It suggests that when you do something in obedience to a divine command, threat, or promise of reward, it is to that extent tainted and unrighteous, something less than a truly good work. I agree that our best works are tainted by sin, but certainly not for this reason. When Scripture presents us with a command, obedience to that command is a righteous action. Indeed, our righteousness is measured by our obedience to God's commands. When God threatens punishment and we turn from wickedness to do what he commands, that is not a sin, but a righteous response. When God promises reward, it is a good thing for us to embrace that reward.[22]

The notion that we should conduct our lives completely apart from the admonitions of God's Word is a terrible notion. To ignore God's revelation of his righteousness is sinful. To read Scripture, but refuse to allow its commands to influence one's conduct, is the essence of sin.

---

need for Christ and the importance of hearing again and again that we are saved only by his grace. But in Reformed theology the law also plays a more direct role, giving us specific guidance in God's delightful paths.

21. We may question the consistency of this position. If the threats of the law drive someone to Christ, resulting in faith in Jesus, is that belief a good thing? One would be inclined to say yes, but it cannot be if actions motivated by threat are *ipso facto* sinful.

22. At this point, there is an odd convergence between traditional Lutheranism and secular deontology. Secular deontologists, like Kant, whom we considered in chapter 8, also reject ethical actions motivated by reward or punishment and say that one does good only by doing his duty "for duty's sake." As I indicated in my discussion of Kant, that position is unscriptural. Scripture often motivates our conduct by rewards and punishments, and it is not ethically right to shun these divine provisions. Kant also rejected ethical actions done in obedience to commands from someone outside the self, again violating Scripture, but strangely echoing the Formula of Concord.

And what, then, is supposed to motivate good works, if not the commands, threats, and promises of reward in Scripture? The Formula doesn't say. What it suggests is that the Spirit simply brings about obedience from within us. I believe the Spirit does exactly that. But the Formula seems to assume that the Spirit works that way without any decision on our part to act according to the commands of God. That I think is wrong. "Quietism" is the view that Christians should be entirely passive, waiting for the Spirit of God to act in them. This view of the Christian life is unbiblical. The Christian life is a battle, a race. It requires decision and effort. I am not saying that the Formula is quietist (Lutheranism rejected quietism after some controversy in its ranks), but as we read the position of the Formula, it does seem that quietism lies around the corner from it.

The Objective and the Subjective

Part of the motivation for this view of the Christian life, I believe, is the thought that one's life should be based on something objective, rather than on something subjective. On this view, our life is built on what Christ has done *for* us, objectively in history, not on anything arising from our own subjectivity or inwardness. On this view, the gospel is a recitation of what God has done for us, not a command to provoke our subjective response.

This understanding focuses on justification: God regards us as objectively righteous for Christ's sake, apart from anything in us. But it tends to neglect regeneration and sanctification: that God does work real subjective changes in the elect.

I have no quarrel with this understanding of justification. But in Scripture, though justification is based on the work of Christ external to us, it is embraced by faith, which is subjective. And faith, in turn, is the result of the Spirit's subjective work of regeneration (John 3:3).[23] So nobody is justified who has not been subjectively changed by God's grace.

Thus, the WCF, even in speaking of assurance of salvation, refers not only to the objective truth of God's promises, but also to "the inward evidence of those graces" and "the testimony of the Spirit of adoption" (18.2), which are in some measure subjective.

In fact, we cannot separate the objective from the subjective or, in the terminology of my earlier distinctions, the situational from the existential.

---

23. So, again, saving faith works through love (Gal. 5:6) and is dead without works (James 2:14–26).

Objective truths are subjectively apprehended. We cannot have objective knowledge, confidence, or assurance, unless we are subjectively enabled to perceive what God has objectively given us.

CONCLUDING OBSERVATION

Since the law/gospel distinction, as expressed in the Formula, is unscriptural, I do not commend it to Reformed believers. It is especially wrong to claim that this view is or should be a test of orthodoxy in Reformed churches.

LAW AND LOVE

Many discussions of ethics, especially by theologians, deal with the relationship between law and love. The question is important, because love is in some sense the central principle of Christian ethics. Some writers say that love somehow replaces law in the Christian life. But we should not accept that view without some reflection.

We saw in chapter 3 the centrality of the covenant relation in which God is lord and we are vassals, servants, sons, daughters, and bride. In the ancient Near East, *love* often refers to the allegiance of a vassal to his lord. Recall the elements of the suzerainty treaty that I listed in that chapter. In the treaty, the first stipulation, or law, is that of exclusive covenant allegiance, sometimes called love. In the Decalogue, that stipulation is the first commandment, "You shall have no other gods before me" (Ex. 20:3). Deuteronomy 6:4–5 expresses this stipulation with the term "love" in the Shema, the famous confession of the Jewish people: "Hear, O Israel: The LORD our God, the LORD is one. You shall love the LORD your God with all your heart and with all your soul and with all your might." Jesus calls this "the great commandment in the law" (Matt. 22:36), "the great and first commandment" (v. 38). In verse 39, he adds, "And a second is like it: You shall love your neighbor as yourself"—another commandment of love, this one from a more obscure Old Testament passage, Leviticus 19:18.

Jesus emphasizes the centrality of love in the believer's life. He stresses not only love of neighbors, but even love of enemies (Matt. 5:43–48), teaching that as God loves his enemies, we should also love ours. And love is his "new commandment": "A new commandment I give to you, that you love one another: just as I have loved you, you also are to love one another. By this all people will know that you are my disciples, if you have love for one another" (John 13:34–35; cf. 15:12, 17; 1 John 2:7–11; 3:11–24; 4:7–21). This commandment is "new" because it is based on the example of Jesus' own love for his people, a love, as the narrative later indicates, unto death. This love is to be the mark of the church, by which believers are to be distinguished from the world.[24]

Similarly, the apostles emphasize love in their ethical teaching (see Rom. 12:9–10; 15:30; 2 Cor. 8:7; Gal. 5:6, 22; Eph. 1:15; 3:17; 6:23; 1 Thess. 4:9; Heb. 13:1; 1 Peter 1:22). Love is the highest Christian virtue, according to 1 Corinthians 13 and 1 Peter 4:8. And as Jesus teaches (see Matt. 22:37–40; cf. also 7:12), so also does Paul teach that love fulfills the law (Rom. 13:8–10; Gal. 5:14; cf. 6:2).

What is love? I will discuss the nature of love more fully under the existential perspective. For the present, we may think of it triperspectivally: love is allegiance, action, and affection. As we have seen, within the covenant, love describes the exclusive allegiance of the vassal to the suzerain. Scripture also defines love by action, as by Jesus' atoning work in 1 John 4:10 and our actions toward others in Romans 13:10 and Ephesians 5:2. Biblical love is also affection, as indicated by references to romantic and sexual love (Gen. 29:20, 32; Prov. 5:19), the analogy therein to God's love (Hos. 3:1; 11:4; 14:4; Zeph. 3:17), close friendship (2 Sam. 1:26), and the believer's affection for God (Ps. 119:97) and for other believers (Rom. 12:10; 1 Peter 1:22; 1 John 3:17).

The following considerations are important in considering the relationship between love and law:

Love Is a Command, Part of the Law

Love is the great commandment, the greatest commandment, the highest virtue, the mark of the believer, the center of biblical ethics. But it is also, nevertheless, one command among others. Many thinkers, such as Friedrich

---

24. In the tradition of Reformed theology, the marks of the church are the preaching of the Word of God, the right administration of the sacraments, and church discipline. I believe it is biblical to speak of these as marks, but to do so requires a number of inferences. Scripture never directly refers to them as marks. But it does refer in that way to the love of Christ. It is unfortunate that this mark has been suppressed in favor of the others. And it is tragic that the world has often not been able to see this mark in us. Too often the church has not been a notable example of love, but has been more famous for its battles. See my paper, "Machen's Warrior Children," in *Alister E. McGrath and Evangelical Theology*, ed. Sung Wook Chung (Grand Rapids: Baker, 2003).

Schleiermacher,[25] Emil Brunner,[26] and Joseph Fletcher,[27] have tried to show that love is something other than a command. Fletcher says:

> Only one "general" proposition is prescribed, namely, the commandment to love God through the neighbor. . . . And this commandment is, be it noted, a normative ideal; it is *not* an operational directive. All else, all other generalities (e.g. "One should tell the truth" and "One should respect life") are at most only *maxims*, never rules. For the situationist there are no rules—none at all.[28]

Here Fletcher denies that love is a "rule." He admits that it is a general proposition, but he puts the word "general" in quotation marks. (And what is the difference between a rule and a proposition?) Then he says that love is a "normative ideal," not an "operational directive." If he has defined that distinction anywhere, I have not located the definition. Evidently he thinks that even love cannot direct us in all concrete ethical decisions, but serves only as an ideal.

Fletcher, of course, wants to deny that love is a rule or law, because he doesn't want us to be subject to rules at all, but he does want us to be subject to love, at least in an ideal way. But if "love only is always good,"[29] then it is hard to understand why it is not a law or a rule. So Fletcher denies the existence of rules and, like Plato, embraces, in effect, a rule that cannot be defined. The first is irrationalistic, in terms of our earlier analysis, and the second is rationalistic. But, as with Plato, since the rationalistic principle lacks content, it is essentially irrationalistic. And since Fletcher's denial of rules is a rational hypothesis,[30] his irrationalism is rationalistic.

In place of all this, Scripture clearly makes love a command of God. That fact immediately rules out any opposition or antithesis between love and commandments in general. Any arguments directed against the keeping of commandments in general carry equal weight against the keeping of the

25. Friedrich Schleiermacher, *The Christian Faith* (New York: Harper and Row, 1963). He thinks that love cannot be a law, since law is concerned only with outward acts. That may be true of human law, but it certainly is not true of the law of God.

26. Emil Brunner, *The Divine Imperative* (Philadelphia: Westminster Press, 1947). Brunner says that God's will for me, love, is absolutely concrete, while law deals only with general principles. But it certainly is not obvious that general principles can never dictate concrete decisions. Scripture itself assumes that God's commands do and ought to have this effect.

27. Joseph F. Fletcher, *Situation Ethics: The New Morality* (Philadelphia: Westminster Press, 1966).

28. Ibid., 55 (emphasis his).

29. Ibid., 57 (the title of chap. 3).

30. But how can one use reason to prove such a universal negative?

love commandment specifically. But in an ethic governed by Scripture, such arguments carry no weight at all.

THE LOVE COMMANDMENT REQUIRES OBEDIENCE TO THE WHOLE LAW OF GOD

In the suzerainty treaty structure of the covenant, the commandment to love the Lord (requiring exclusive covenant loyalty) precedes the detailed prescriptions of the law. We demonstrate our love by obeying the commandments. Such is the relationship in the Decalogue between the first commandment and the rest. Note also what follows the love commandment in Deuteronomy 6:4–9:

> Hear, O Israel: The LORD our God, the LORD is one. You shall love the LORD your God with all your heart and with all your soul and with all your might. And these words that I command you today shall be on your heart. You shall teach them diligently to your children, and shall talk of them when you sit in your house, and when you walk by the way, and when you lie down, and when you rise. You shall bind them as a sign on your hand, and they shall be as frontlets between your eyes. You shall write them on the doorposts of your house and on your gates.

To love God completely is to take heed to his words, to saturate one's mind and the minds of the others in one's family, with the commands of God. This is certainly at least part of what is meant by love fulfilling the law: love carries out the commandments of the Lord.

So Jesus says that those who love him will keep his commands. This is a major theme in the Johannine writings (John 14:15, 21, 23; 15:10; 1 John 2:3–5; 5:3; 2 John 5–6).[31] Unlike Fletcher, Scripture never suggests that one must disobey a divine command in order to fulfill the law of love.

LOVE IS A PROVOCATIVE CHARACTERIZATION OF THE LAW

We have seen that the law commands us to love, and that love commands us to keep God's commandments. Law requires love, and love requires law. But that relationship suggests synonymy: that law is love and love is law. Can that be right? And the question naturally arises: if love

---

31. Compare also the interplay between love and obedience in 1 John 3:19–24, where these are wrapped together in a uniquely Johannine way with the concepts of assurance, God's knowledge, answered prayer, believing in Christ, abiding in him, and the Spirit's witness.

and law impose on us the same obligations, how do they differ? Why do we need two categories, if each contains all the content of the other?

Readers of the Theology of Lordship series will not find it strange that I describe this relationship as perspectival. Love and law are the same content, considered from two different angles. But how do they differ as perspectives?

As perspectives, the difference between them is in focus or emphasis. Law focuses on the acts we are to perform, while love focuses on the heart-motives of these acts. Of course, godly heart-motives are themselves commanded by the law, and acts are part of the threefold definition of love that I presented earlier. But there is a difference of focus here.

To say that love is the central obligation of the Christian is to emphasize that slavish obedience (Kant's "duty for duty's sake") is not the goal of the law. Rather, that goal is to have a genuine passion for God and others that comes from the heart.[32] Biblical ethics is first of all personal, for God is the absolute person. It is behavior appropriate to a relationship with the one who created and redeemed us, our covenant Lord, a relationship that includes others made in his image.

But unlike Plato's Good, Kant's categorical imperative, and Fletcher's love, biblical love is not an abstract conceptual blank. It has definite content, and God specifies that content in his law. That is the principle we express best by describing our obligation from the perspective of law.

MORAL HEROISM

In this section, I will reflect further on the relationship between love and law, particularly in relation to the sufficiency of Scripture.

I have said that Scripture is sufficient for ethics in the sense that it includes all the divine words we will ever need to determine our obligations. And since God's word is the source of our obligations, we have none except those presented in the Word.

That might lead us to think that determining our obligation is fairly simple. If we are obligated to do something, there will be a biblical command to that effect. If there is no biblical command, there is no obligation. So it might seem possible to codify our obligations fairly concisely, just as the Jews found 613 commands in the Torah. Once we have obeyed all those specific commands, we might imagine, we will be right with God.

---

32. Recall our discussion in chapter 9 of God's word written on the heart.

But a number of incidents recorded in the Bible discourage such a project. For example, we read in 2 Samuel 23:13–17 that David longingly expressed a wish for some water from the well of Bethlehem, his hometown, then under the rule of the Philistines. In response, David's three mighty men

> broke through the camp of the Philistines and drew water out of the well of Bethlehem that was by the gate and carried and brought it to David. But he would not drink of it. He poured it out to the LORD and said, "Far be it from me, O LORD, that I should do this. Shall I drink the blood of the men who went at the risk of their lives?" Therefore he would not drink it.

Were these men ethically obligated to perform this action? One looks in vain for any text of the Torah or elsewhere in Scripture that commands such a thing. David did not command his men to do this, so they were not carrying out the will of a civil authority.

So it may seem that they were not obligated to do what they did. Nevertheless, the text agrees with David that what they did was something noble and wonderful. This was an action of surpassing valor. Scripture never suggests that they sinned by adding to the word of God. And it is hard for me to imagine that they would have done such a thing except out of great loyalty to their leader.

The same question can be asked about the story of the widow in Mark 12:44 who gave two small coins, all that she had, to the temple treasury. The law mandated only a tithe. Was she, then, performing a work of supererogation, doing more than the law requires, adding to God's word? Or was she doing something she was not actually obligated to do? And what about Barnabas, who sold his property and gave it to the church (Acts 4:37)? Peter told the liar Ananias that believers are not required to give their land to the church (Acts 5:4).

Some might be inclined to say that David's mighty men, the widow, and Barnabas were governed, not by obligation, but by some other motive. If they were not obligated to perform their works of heroism, they would not have sinned if they had chosen not to do those things.

But to say that these actions are not obligatory poses problems. Are these actions optional? Are they things that you can do or not do, at your own pleasure? Does such a category of actions really exist?

In 1 Corinthians 9, Paul describes all his exertions for the gospel, with all the "rights" he has relinquished so that the gospel might be made available without charge. If he had a right to be paid by the church, we are inclined to say, certainly he wasn't *obligated* to preach without pay. But there is a sense of obligation in the passage: "For if I preach the gospel, that gives me no ground for boasting. For necessity is laid upon me. Woe to me if I do not preach the gospel! For if I do this of my own will, I have a reward, but not of my own will, I am still entrusted with a stewardship" (vv. 16–17). Paul may have had a certain "right" not to preach without payment, but he had a definite *compulsion* to forego that payment. Further, his decision discharged a "stewardship entrusted" to him. What if he had refused to discharge that trust? Would he have sinned?

Before you answer, note that Paul says later, "I do it all for the sake of the gospel, that I may share with them in its blessings" (v. 23). Then he describes his compulsion as that of a runner with his eye on the victor's prize, concluding, "I discipline my body and keep it under control, lest after preaching to others I myself should be disqualified." In some sense, winning the prize depended on Paul's moral heroism.

This almost sounds like salvation by works. Of course, we know from other Scripture that it isn't that. What is it, then? Well, ultimately the prize is Jesus. It is his kingdom; it is the full blessing of knowing him. Compare what Paul says here with another passage reflecting his moral heroism, Philippians 3:7–11, 14:

> But whatever gain I had, I counted as loss for the sake of Christ. Indeed, I count everything as loss because of the surpassing worth of knowing Christ Jesus my Lord. For his sake I have suffered the loss of all things and count them as rubbish, in order that I may gain Christ and be found in him, not having a righteousness of my own that comes from the law, but that which comes through faith in Christ, the righteousness from God that depends on faith—that I may know him and the power of his resurrection, and may share his sufferings, becoming like him in his death, that by any means possible I may attain the resurrection from the dead. . . . I press on toward the goal for the prize of the upward call of God in Christ Jesus.

Paul is so passionate about Jesus that he wants to experience all the blessings that come to those who go all out for him. It's not that otherwise he will go to hell, or that there is some precise proportion between the merit of earthly works and heavenly reward. It is just that Paul wants to know Jesus as best he can. Compare 2 Corinthians 12, where Paul says that he endures his sufferings "for the sake of Christ" (v. 10), for in that weakness is his strength. Compare also 2 Corinthians 1:5–6, and the perplexing Colossians 1:24.

But aren't we *obligated*, in one sense, to know Jesus as best we can? Eternal life itself is knowing Jesus (John 17:3). God told Israel through Moses that they should come to know him (Deut. 7:9). He did his mighty deeds so that they "may know that I am the LORD" (Deut. 29:6). We are obligated not only to know him, but to *love* him, with all our heart, soul, strength, and mind (Matt. 22:37).

Paul's particular moral heroism is not obligatory for all of us. Preaching without charge was Paul's way of carrying out his passion for knowing and loving Jesus. Other apostles accepted payment for their ministry, as was their right. But they showed their passion for Christ in other ways. It is that passion that is obligatory, not a particular way of expressing it. It is the principle, not Paul's particular application of it, that is important.[33]

But God does expect some level of heroism from each of us. The great commandment, to love God with all we have, is an extreme demand. God may never call you to an act of military heroism like David's mighty men, or to give away all your belongings, like the poor widow, or to sell your property, like Barnabas. But he will ask you to make some kind of hard sacrifice, as he asked the rich young ruler to sell all his goods to feed the poor.

Moral heroism is an obligation, because our overall obligation is to be like Jesus: to love as he did (John 13:34–35; 1 John 4:9–12) in his most extreme sacrifice, and to serve others as he served us (Mark 10:45).

Moral heroism is another illustration of the fact, discussed in chapter 11, that the whole counsel of God for ethics includes, not only the explicit content of Scripture, but also what may be deduced or drawn from it by way of application. Moral heroism applies the law of love to situations in life that excite our admiration, even though the specific action may not be described explicitly in Scripture.

So moral heroism is part of our obligation. Of course, when we understand this obligation, we can see much more clearly why our good works can never measure up to God's standards. By comparison with the heroism of Christ, and even by comparison with some of his best followers, we fall far short. So we rely wholly on God's grace in Jesus for our salvation. But as we renounce our own righteousness for that of Christ (Philippians 3:9 again), we come to see Jesus' glory in comparison with our rubbish, and God plants in us that passion to run the race with Paul: to know the fullness of Christ's blessings and, above all, to know Christ himself.

33. Every commandment makes obligatory some specific applications. For example, Matt. 22:37 implies that we should not bow down to Baal or Zeus. But every commandment also allows a certain amount of leeway for individual application. For example, the fifth commandment requires Ruth Billingsley to honor her aging parents, Joe and Katherine Billingsley. But it doesn't specify precisely how she is to honor them with respect to financial support, living arrangements, personal visits, etc. We shall discuss this flexibility of application again in the next chapter, under "Priorities."

CHAPTER 13

Applying the Law

Under the normative perspective, we have considered the norms of Christian ethics from the most general to the most specific: God himself, his word, his written word, his law. As we saw in the previous chapter, law is both a part of Scripture and a way of looking at Scripture as a whole. Either way, God's law is normative for our lives. It tells us what to believe and what to do.

But we still need to get more specific. How shall we determine in specific terms what God's law has to say to us? In discussing moral heroism in the previous chapter, we saw that determining God's will is not a simple matter of looking things up in a list of commandments. God's commandments, particularly the law of love, are very broad. Their applications may take many forms that never appear on a list of commands—and indeed do not appear explicitly in any biblical text. As I indicated in chapter 11, most applications of Scripture require extrabiblical data, and they lead to conclusions that may not be stated explicitly in Scripture.

This situation is further complicated by the fact that Christians, rightly or wrongly, ignore many biblical laws. We don't offer animal sacrifices, but God commanded Israel to do that. The law of animal sacrifices is part of the law of God.

If we deny the necessity of animal sacrifices today, then we must distinguish between divine laws that are *currently* and *literally* normative, and others that are not. Everything in Scripture is normative in some way, because it comes from the mouth of God. Even those laws that we no longer observe literally, like those regulating animal sacrifices, have much to tell us about God's redemptive purpose, and what they teach us is divinely authoritative. But we believe that God no longer commands such sacrifices, and we believe that on the authority of the Word of God. So there is a difference in Scripture between what is generally normative and what is currently and literally normative.

How do we tell the difference? This is a hermeneutical question, a question of how we are to interpret the laws of the Bible. We may also describe it as a question of application: we are asking how the legal material in Scripture applies to us today.

When you think about it, it is fairly obvious that not every command in Scripture is normative for us today. As a rather absurd example, consider Jesus' command to his disciples in Luke 19:30, "Go into the village in front of you, where on entering you will find a colt tied, on which no one has ever yet sat. Untie it and bring it here." Jesus here instructs his disciples to bring him a colt on which to ride into Jerusalem on Palm Sunday. One can imagine a religious sect taking this verse as a literal demand on every Christian: every year, before Palm Sunday, every church member goes into town to fetch a colt for Jesus to ride.[1]

Such a practice is ludicrous, of course, because it is obvious from the context of Luke 19:30 that Jesus was not issuing this command as a perpetual ordinance for all time. Rather, this command was limited to a single instance, in a single, narrowly defined setting. How do we know that? Well, the passage doesn't say so explicitly. But to make the commandment broader than that defies good hermeneutics and even common sense.[2]

So it will not do for us to take every imperative in Scripture as a law to obey today. God has not given every biblical command to us so that we will carry it out immediately. Indeed, every command is directed to a particular situation that is both similar to, and different from, our situations today.[3] That fact introduces complications into the project of formulating an ethic based on biblical law.

When such complications appear in theology, it is often time to make distinctions. In this case, some distinctions within God's law will give us some guidance in determining what is currently normative. I shall

---

1. But we wonder, why only once a year? If Jesus commanded this act as a perpetual obligation, shouldn't we be doing it all the time—even at the cost of martyrdom (for some governments have been unkind to horse thieves)?

2. Common sense is not the chief rule of theology, but it is not to be routinely ignored.

3. Note again the overlap between the normative and situational perspectives. Without taking account of the situation in which the norm is given, we simply don't know what the norm is.

distinguish (1) between creation ordinances and later laws, (2) between the Decalogue and other legislation, (3) between the old and the new covenants, (4) between moral, civil, and ceremonial laws within the Old Testament, and (5) between certain kinds of priorities that exist in all biblical law. As in the previous chapters, we are moving from broad distinctions to more precise ones. Along the way, we shall look at the question of theonomy. And at the end we shall look at the concept of tragic moral choice, which claims that God's requirements for us are sometimes inconsistent.

CREATION ORDINANCES

Creation ordinances are laws that God gave to Adam and Eve before the fall. John Murray lists among them "the procreation of offspring, the replenishing of the earth, subduing of the same, dominion over the creatures, labour, the weekly Sabbath, and marriage."[4] These are taken from Genesis 1:28, 2:2–3,[5] 15, and 24. Of course, God also gave them the specific command not to eat of the tree of the knowledge of good and evil (Gen. 2:17), but that is not usually considered a creation ordinance, because God gave it only for one occasion, not as a perpetual ordinance for mankind.

I would add worship to this list. It is implicit in the Sabbath ordinance, but it is best to make it explicit. Although the term *worship* is not found in Genesis 1–3, it is inconceivable that Adam and Eve did not respond in worship to God's intimate and immediate presence in the garden. The garden is a sanctuary, a dwelling of God, and therefore holy ground. Like God's dwellings on Mt. Sinai and Mt. Zion, Eden is evidently a mountain dwelling of God.[6]

The teaching of Genesis 1:27–28, that man is the image of God, also has ethical implications, as in Genesis 9:6 and James 3:9. God's procedure in creating Adam (Gen. 1:26–28) and Eve (2:21–23) was different from the way he made other creatures. And to humans, but not to any other

---

4. John Murray, *Principles of Conduct* (Grand Rapids: Eerdmans, 1957), 27.

5. This treatment of the Sabbath ordinance is controversial. I shall argue its validity under the fourth commandment.

6. Gen. 2:10 describes a river originating in Eden and flowing downward, supplying current sufficient to carry four great rivers to the sea. This is parallel to "the river of the water of life, bright as crystal, flowing from the throne of God and of the lamb, through the middle of the street of the city" (Rev. 22:2). Eden's tree of life reappears in the holy city of Revelation, and the most prominent feature of the city is the presence of God himself, and the lamb.

creature, God assigned the godlike task and privilege of taking dominion over the whole earth (Gen. 1:26, 28). Given these honors, Adam surely knew that human life was something exceedingly precious to God, to be deeply respected. In Genesis 9:1–7, God renews the cultural mandate to Noah, with a reminder that man is made in God's image (v. 6). He thereby justifies the law against shedding man's blood. Certainly that law was known to Adam and Eve as well, heightening the tragedy of Cain's murder of Abel in Genesis 4.

So the creation ordinances, like other biblical laws, have a threefold, indeed a triperspectival, focus: on God (worship, Sabbath), on the natural world (replenishing, subduing, and dominating the earth), and on man himself (marriage, procreation, labor).

Creation ordinances are important, because they form the basic law of human existence. They do not presuppose any particular historical circumstances, as do, for example, the laws of Moses. Creation ordinances are given to man as man, presupposing only our creation in God's image and the earth as our created environment. So it is unlikely that God would abrogate or significantly modify any of these ordinances in the course of history.

After the consummation of history, of course, at least one of these ordinances will change. Jesus teaches that in the resurrection, human beings will neither marry nor give in marriage (Matt. 22:30). Evidently, then, procreation also ceases. Some have taught, too, that since Jesus has filled all things (Eph. 4:10) and has subdued all things to himself (Matt. 28:18), the cultural mandate is no longer in effect for New Testament believers. For the commandment is to fill and subdue the earth, and Jesus has already fulfilled both tasks. I disagree with this view, as I shall indicate under the situational perspective. But although the creation ordinances are, among biblical laws, the least problematic, there is room for discussion as to their present and future application.

THE DECALOGUE AND THE CASE LAWS

The Decalogue may be seen as a republication of the creation ordinances, applying them to Israel's life within the Mosaic covenant. The first four commandments deal with worship, including the Sabbath.[7]

7. In referring to the commandments in the Decalogue, I am using the numbering system common in Reformed (and most evangelical) circles, rather than the different systems used by Lutherans, Roman Catholics, and Jews. The first, then, is the prohibition of other gods, and the second is the prohibition of idol worship. The prohibition of coveting is all one commandment, the tenth.

If I am right to include worship as a creation ordinance, and Murray is right to include the Sabbath, then these four commandments are direct applications of these ordinances. The fifth and seventh commandments are based on the ordinances of marriage and family. The sixth and ninth commandments are based on the preciousness of human life in the image of God. The eighth and tenth commandments are based on God's command to labor, to subdue the earth, and to take dominion over it. God gives to us possessions, inheritances, and he calls us to increase these by the sweat of our brow, not by taking what belongs to others.

Certainly the commands of the Decalogue still bind believers under the new covenant, in general terms. Jesus' Sermon on the Mount contains extended exposition of some of the commands in the Decalogue. He condemns the oversimplifications and distortions of the scribes and Pharisees, but he affirms the commandments in their deepest significance. To the rich young man who asks Jesus what he must do to attain eternal life, Jesus presents commandments of the Decalogue (Matt. 19:16–19), before telling him to sell his goods and "follow me" (v. 21).[8] Paul cites commandments from the Decalogue when he seeks to show that love fulfills the law (Rom. 13:9–10). James also affirms commandments of the Decalogue as he demands that his readers fulfill the whole law, not just part of it (James 2:8–12).

So the whole church has recognized that the Decalogue remains normative for us, with the exception, according to some, of the fourth commandment. I shall address the controversy over the fourth commandment at a later point. But there are no changes in redemptive history sufficient to make adultery lawful or to render unnecessary the honoring of parents.

Nevertheless, there are some features in the Decalogue that refer specifically to Israel's situation as they wait in the wilderness to enter the Promised Land. In the Deuteronomic version of the fourth commandment, the people are told to keep the Sabbath because "you shall remember that you were a slave in the land of Egypt, and the LORD your God brought you out from there with a mighty hand and an outstretched arm" (Deut. 5:15). The fifth commandment promises to those who honor parents "that your days may be long in the land that the LORD your God is giving you" (Ex. 20:12). When we apply these commandments to our own situations, we need to

---

8. It may be significant that the commandments Jesus cites in verses 18–19 are from the "second table" of the law, dealing with our responsibilities to fellow human beings. The requirement to "follow me," then, in effect summarizes the first table, our responsibility toward God. So Jesus' use of the Decalogue may contain a startling testimony to his own deity. In any case, Jesus' directive to the rich man indicates the important role of moral heroism within the law.

apply these details in ways different from, though analogous to, Israel's situation. We keep the Sabbath, not because we were literally delivered from Egypt, but because Jesus delivered us from the greater bondage of which Egypt is a type: bondage to sin. And we honor parents, not literally to have long life in the land of Canaan, but to enjoy God's fullest blessings wherever we are "in the land," that is, "on the earth" (*epi tēs gēs*) (Eph. 6:3)[9]—and, beyond that, in the new heavens and new earth to come.

So it is not unthinkable that some elements of the Decalogue may change in their application, even though the basic obligations set forth bind all human beings until the last judgment.

Within the Pentateuch, it is also important for us to distinguish between fundamental law (creation ordinances, the Decalogue) and case law. Some scholars use the terms *apodictic* and *casuistic* to identify these two categories. Apodictic laws are, as Kant would say, categorical imperatives. They simply tell us what to do or not to do.

Casuistic laws are hypothetical imperatives. Typically, they begin with an "if," indicating the circumstances in which the law is applicable. For example, Exodus 22:1 reads, "If a man steals an ox or a sheep, and kills it or sells it, he shall repay five oxen for an ox, and four sheep for a sheep." The apodictic laws serve as the fundamental constitution of Israel. The case laws are judicial precedents, examples of how judges have applied the apodictic laws to various circumstances. God preserved them here to give to judges authoritative examples of how to apply the apodictic laws.

Of course, every situation is different. Exodus 21:33–34 says, "When a man opens a pit, or when a man digs a pit and does not cover it, and an ox or a donkey falls into it, the owner of the pit shall make restoration. He shall give money to its owner, and the dead beast shall be his." But what if the owner of the field has taken steps to cover his pit, but a storm weakens the cover? Then, presumably, the judge must assess (as judges must do today) how much of the responsibility belongs to the owner and how much he should pay, taking the circumstances into account. The case laws are not intended to refer specifically to every situation that may arise. Rather, they address representative situations, guiding judges in assessing responsibility.

9. This may be a bit of an exegetical stretch. Paul may simply be quoting the commandment, and *gē* may simply refer to the Promised Land, as the corresponding Hebrew term does in Ex. 20:12 and Deut. 5:16. But, as we shall see in the next section, the equivalent of the Promised Land in the new covenant is nothing less than the whole earth. By omitting "that the Lord your God is giving you" in his restatement of the commandment, Paul universalizes the place of blessing from "the land" of Israel under the old covenant to "the earth" in general under the new covenant.

The Decalogue leaves judges no discretion. They have no authority to make theft legal or to penalize people for worshiping the true God. But the case laws encourage judges to be flexible in considering how the principles of the Decalogue apply to each case. The judges may not contradict the case laws, any more than they may contradict the Decalogue. But since cases vary, God gives to judges discretion to relate the Decalogue to new cases in wise and creative ways. As in modern courts, the judges certainly had power to determine mitigating and aggravating circumstances, to assess motives, and to determine probabilities in the evidence.

The penalties attached to crimes in the case laws are also exemplary, not to be automatically applied. For example, it is evident that in many capital crimes there is provision to ransom the life of the criminal. Numbers 35:31 prohibits ransom for the life of a murderer. But that suggests that ransom was possible in other crimes for which the case laws specify the death penalty, even when the text does not specifically mention the possibility of ransom. Examples may be adultery, homosexuality, and blasphemy. Exodus 21:30 specifically mentions the possibility of ransom in an otherwise capital case. It may well be that judges in Israel had considerable liberty to determine penalties for crimes, following general principles of law found throughout the Pentateuch.

THE OLD AND NEW COVENANTS

When the New Testament refers to "the old covenant" (2 Cor. 3:14; cf. Heb. 8:13), it speaks of the covenant that God made with Israel, with Moses as mediator (Ex. 19–24). The "new covenant" is, in Hebrews 8 and 10, the covenant of which Jesus is the mediator, identified with the new covenant of Jeremiah 31:31–34.

God is the author of both covenants, and the covenant documents of each continue to be normative for God's people. Jesus proclaims the authority of the old covenant Scriptures in Matthew 5:17–20, as we've seen, and Paul says the same thing in 2 Timothy 3:16–17. The new covenant words of Jesus and the apostles come to us authoritatively through the New Testament Scriptures.

Both covenants continue the promise that God will bless all nations through Abraham's children (Gen. 12:3), a promise of God's grace. Both covenants also include divine commands. Murray argues that the demand for obedience and the promise of salvation by grace through faith are substantially the same in both covenants.[10] The demand for obedience in both covenants is not a demand that people earn their salvation through meritorious works (though the Jews sometimes misconstrued the Mosaic covenant as involving works-righteousness). Rather, it calls upon the believer to obey God (by God's grace) as the appropriate response to redemption. Murray quotes Geerhardus Vos in this connection:

> It is plain, then, that law-keeping did not figure at that juncture [the Mosaic covenant] as the meritorious ground of life-inheritance. The latter is based on grace alone, no less emphatically than Paul himself places salvation on that ground. But, while this is so, it might still be objected that law-observance, if not the ground for receiving, is yet made the ground for retention of the privileges inherited. Here it cannot, of course, be denied that a real connection exists. But the Judaizers went wrong in inferring that the connection must be *meritorious*, that, if Israel keeps the cherished gifts of Jehovah through obedience of His law, this must be so, because in strict justice they had earned them. The connection is of a totally different kind. It belongs not to the legal sphere of merit, but to the symbolico-typical sphere of *appropriateness of expression*.[11]

Nevertheless, Hebrews 7–10 does indicate substantial changes that come with the new covenant, changes so great that the author refers to the old covenant as "obsolete" (8:13). He adds, "And what is becoming obsolete and growing old is ready to vanish away." Those changes are:

A new priesthood (7:1–28). Jesus, the priest after the order of Melchizedek, replaces the Aaronic priesthood. This fact involves "a change in the law" (7:12), for the Mosaic law itself makes no provision for such a change. For this reason alone, many of the laws of the Pentateuch are no longer literally applicable: those that deal with the ordination of priests, their daily work of sacrifice, the cleansing rituals they must follow, their daily maintenance of the tabernacle and temple, and their yearly entrance into the holiest place.

A new sacrifice (8:1–10:18). By his sacrifice, Jesus deals with our sins "once for all" (9:26–28; 10:12–18). It was impossible for the blood of bulls and goats, under the old covenant, to take away sins (10:4), but

---

10. Murray, *Principles of Conduct*, 194–201. His whole discussion is valuable.

11. Geerhardus Vos, *Biblical Theology, Old and New Testaments* (Grand Rapids: Eerdmans, 1954), 143.

Jesus' sacrifice of himself dealt with the sins of his people completely and for all time, so that we need no additional sacrifice. So in the new covenant, sacrifices of animals, grain, oil, and wine play no further role. Laws requiring these are no longer literally normative, though we can learn much from them about the nature of Jesus' sacrifice.

Other passages in the New Testament mention three more changes that are also vitally important:

A new nation. The new covenant is not specifically between God and national Israel, as was the old. It is with a new family, a new nation, consisting of both Jews and Gentiles. Of course, even the old covenant was open to Gentiles who worshiped the God of Israel and accepted circumcision. And the new covenant is in a sense an extension of the old: the olive tree of Israel with some branches broken off and other (Gentile) branches grafted in (Rom. 11:17–24).

But the new covenant is nevertheless radically new. In the new covenant, "neither circumcision nor uncircumcision counts for anything, but only faith working through love" (Gal. 5:6; cf. 6:15; 1 Cor. 7:19). Because of this new family, the council of Jerusalem described in Acts 15 stated that Gentiles could be members of the church in good standing without being circumcised and without keeping all the laws of Moses. The council did ask that Gentiles abstain from "things polluted by idols, and from sexual immorality, and from what has been strangled, and from blood" (Acts 15:20, 29).[12] The reason given was not the intrinsic immorality of these actions, but because "from ancient generations Moses has had in every city those who proclaim him, for he is read every Sabbath in the synagogues" (v. 21). Of course, sexual immorality is to be avoided as something wrong in itself (as 1 Cor. 5:1–13). But the council was immediately concerned, evidently, not with morality as such, but with the offense that Gentile Christians might give to Jewish Christians.

So God has broken down "the dividing wall" (Eph. 2:14) between Jews and Gentiles, as Paul writes to Gentile Christians:

> Therefore remember that at one time you Gentiles in the flesh, called "the uncircumcision" by what is called the circumcision, which is made in the flesh by hands—remember that you were at that time separated from Christ, alienated from the common-

---

12. These are among the "Noachian commandments" recognized by Jewish tradition as pertaining to Gentiles as well as Jews. A good, brief introduction to this tradition can be found in J. Budziszewski, *Written on the Heart* (Downers Grove, IL: InterVarsity Press, 1997), 202–7.

wealth of Israel and strangers to the covenants of promise, having no hope and without God in the world. But now in Christ Jesus you who once were far off have been brought near by the blood of Christ. For he himself is our peace, who has made us both one and has broken down in his flesh the dividing wall of hostility by abolishing the law of commandments and ordinances, that he might create in himself one new man in place of the two, so making peace, and might reconcile us both to God in one body through the cross, thereby killing the hostility. And he came and preached peace to you who were far off and peace to those who were near. For through him we both have access in one Spirit to the Father. So then you are no longer strangers and aliens, but you are fellow citizens with the saints and members of the household of God, built on the foundation of the apostles and prophets, Christ Jesus himself being the cornerstone, in whom the whole structure, being joined together, grows into a holy temple in the Lord. In him you also are being built together into a dwelling place for God by the Spirit. (Eph. 2:11–22)

Note that breaking down the dividing wall leads to the abolition of commandments and ordinances (v. 15). Note also that there is a new temple (vv. 21–22).

In the new covenant, then, the temple in Jerusalem has lost its status as the unique dwelling place of God. Its veil was torn in two, from top to bottom, when Jesus was crucified (Mark 15:38). In AD 70, the building itself was destroyed, as Jesus had predicted (Matt. 24:1–2). God's dwelling is now in the heavenly tabernacle (Heb. 9:11), in Jesus (John 1:14), and in Jesus' people (1 Cor. 3:16).

And if God no longer dwells uniquely in the temple, the unique significance of the land of Palestine must change as well. The land was holy because the holy God dwelled in that land, with his holy people. But if there is a change in the holy people and the place of God's dwelling, then the land loses its special significance.

It is hard to say precisely what modifications these principles introduce into the law, but let me suggest the following:

1. Certainly this development does away with the requirement of circumcision, effectively replacing it with the new covenant sacrament of baptism. It vindicates the judgment of Acts 15.

2. I would assume that it also changes those provisions of the old covenant law that are primarily designed to defend the unique holiness of the temple, the land, and the nation of Israel. The new covenant church as

such possesses no land in Palestine. The annual feasts, which brought the Jews near to God's dwelling three times a year, are no longer appropriate to a truly international people of God. The laws such as the Jubilee that guarded the original divisions of the land of Palestine are not binding on Gentiles who never had such land rights.

3. Advocates of the New Perspective on Paul claim that certain laws had a particular importance in the conflict between Judaism and Hellenism, and therefore in the New Testament controversy over the "works of the law." Don Garlington describes the views of James D. G. Dunn: "Dunn does maintain that 'the works of the law' encompass the whole Torah, but within the period of the Second Temple certain aspects of the law became especially prominent as the boundary and identity markers of the Jewish people: prominently circumcision, food laws, purity laws, and sabbath."[13] It may well be that these are the laws that Paul especially considers to have been set aside by the work of Christ,[14] although, as Dunn implies, these are not the only laws, for Paul, that lack the power to save.

4. Vern S. Poythress argues that many other laws in the old covenant are, in part or in whole, means by which God guarded his unique relationship with the Jewish people in the holy land of Palestine. Israel, for example, was to purge the land of false religion. Deuteronomy 13:1–18 calls Israel to destroy unbelieving cities within the holy land as part of its holy war against the Canaanite tribes. But in the New Testament, God does not call the church to exterminate unbelievers for their unbelief, but rather to fight against the "ultimate opponents" of the Lord, Satan and his hosts (Eph. 6:12). And:

> Now during the New Testament era there is an advance. Holy war is waged through baptism and union with Christ. The flesh is crucified (Gal. 5:24). Human beings are not simply destroyed as were the Canaanites, but raised to life because of Christ's resurrection. This situation is the foundation for widespread evangelism.

13. Garlington, *Law and Gospel: The Contribution of the New Perspective on Paul* (forthcoming). The reference to sabbath will trouble some who follow the tradition of the Westminster standards. But of course that term is found in Col. 2:16, so there must be some sense in which the term *sabbath* can designate a law transcended by Christ. I shall discuss this issue under the fourth commandment.

14. In one sense, no law of God is ever set aside or abrogated (Matt. 5:17–20). But there are some laws that, because of events in redemptive history, we come to observe, in our new covenant age, in very different ways from what God asked of the old covenant Israelites. The commands to worship God by sacrifice, for example, continue to be normative, but we now worship by the sacrifice of Christ. Please insert this qualification whenever I use terms like *abrogated* or *set aside*. What I mean is that such laws are no longer to be *literally* obeyed. But I cannot state that qualification every time the issue comes up.

Now the whole inhabited earth has become the new land that is to be conquered in God's name (Matthew 28:18–20). We are to wage holy war. But the nature of that holy war is redefined because of Christ.[15]

So we should also take into account:

A new mission. As Poythress indicates, the new covenant requires a new conquest, not the military conquest of a piece of territory, but the conquest of the whole world through the preaching of the gospel. Like holy war in the Old Testament, this conquest brings God's judgment. But for those whom God has chosen, the judgment has fallen on Christ, and what remains is resurrection to new life. The Great Commission states the fundamental task of the church:

> And Jesus came and said to them, "All authority in heaven and on earth has been given to me. Go therefore and make disciples of all nations, baptizing them in the name of the Father and of the Son and of the Holy Spirit, teaching them to observe all that I have commanded you. And behold, I am with you always, to the end of the age." (Matt. 28:18–20)

As a result of this missionary conquest, God dwells in people all over the world, "from every nation, from all tribes and peoples and languages" (Rev. 7:9). In the Old Testament, there was also a concern for the nations of the world. God had promised Abraham that in him all the families of the earth would be blessed (Gen. 12:3). But in the Old Testament itself, the missionary direction was, as it has been called, predominantly "centripetal": the nations were to come to worship God in Jerusalem (as in Zech. 14:16–19). Isaiah anticipates a greater reality: altars to the Lord in foreign lands and equality among Egypt, Assyria, and Israel, as God's people (Isa. 19:23–25). But only in the New Testament, in Jesus' Great Commission of Matthew 28, does the movement of God become fully "centrifugal," moving outward to all the nations of the world.

This expansive mission reinforces the importance of the changes in law noted above. As the church moves to many nations, there is no place for laws mandating distinctive clothing or diet. Rather, Paul's rule is: "I have become all things to all people, that by all means I might save some" (1 Cor. 9:22). God no longer asks us to preserve the distinctiveness of our own national culture, but to sacrifice that distinctiveness to reach others

---

15. Vern S. Poythress, *The Shadow of Christ in the Law of Moses* (Brentwood, TN: Wolgemuth and Hyatt, 1991), 147–48.

for Christ. So the Lord admonishes Peter, when he resists reaching out to the Gentile Cornelius, that "what God has made clean, do not call common" (Acts 10:15). God drives home the point in a vision where he tells Peter to kill and eat all sorts of animals that the law describes as unclean.

So the cleansing laws and dietary laws no longer bind the Christian literally, though we may still learn much from them about God's desire for purity in his people:

> Therefore let no one pass judgment on you in questions of food and drink, or with regard to a festival or a new moon or a Sabbath. These are a shadow of the things to come, but the substance belongs to Christ. (Col. 2:16–17)[16]

> According to this arrangement [that of the Old Testament priesthood and temple], gifts and sacrifices are offered that cannot perfect the conscience of the worshiper, but deal only with food and drink and various washings, regulations for the body imposed until the time of reformation. (Heb. 9:9–10)

As for dietary laws, see Mark 7:14–23 (especially v. 19), Peter's vision in Acts 10:9–16 and 11:2–10, and the passages we considered earlier in Romans 14 and 1 Corinthians 8–10, which emphasize that "the kingdom of God is not a matter of eating and drinking but of righteousness and peace and joy in the Holy Spirit" (Rom. 14:17).

A new maturity. In Galatians 3:23–4:11, Paul compares our freedom from the law to the freedom of slaves liberated from their bondage. The law was "our guardian until Christ came" (3:24). The "guardian" (_paidagōgos_, translated "schoolmaster" in the KJV) was the servant who took the children to school, often giving them some harsh discipline along the way. But "now that faith has come, we are no longer under a guardian" (v. 25). This means that we are no longer slaves, but sons, crying "Abba! Father!" (4:6–7). This new relationship to God sets us free from "the weak and worthless elementary principles of the world" (4:9), such as the observance of "days and months and seasons and years" (v. 10).

It is difficult to determine precisely what laws Paul refers to here. I shall refer to this passage again under the fourth commandment. But here I want to observe that Paul regards the New Testament believer as more mature than believers under the old order. Children need constant restraint to keep them moving in the right direction. Adults, ideally at least, are expected

---

16. We shall discuss under the fourth commandment the specific teaching of this passage concerning Sabbath observance.

to discipline themselves from within. So it is right for them to have more freedom and responsibility. In the religious parallel, Christians are sons, rather than mere slaves. Our relation to God is more spontaneous.

This maturity comes from the work of Christ and the outpouring of the Spirit in a far greater fullness than was known under the old covenant. So, as we saw in chapter 3, the New Testament writers motivate us to good behavior, not only by citing the law, but by appealing to the work of Christ (Col. 3:1–3) and the presence of the Spirit (Gal. 5:16).

MORAL, CEREMONIAL, AND JUDICIAL LAW

WCF, 19.2–4, presents a distinction between various kinds of law:

> 2. This law, after [man's] fall, continued to be a perfect rule of righteousness; and, as such, was delivered by God upon Mount Sinai, in ten commandments, and written in two tables: the first four commandments containing our duty towards God; and the other six, our duty to man.
>
> 3. Beside this law, commonly called moral, God was pleased to give to the people of Israel, as a church under age, ceremonial laws, containing several typical ordinances, partly of worship, prefiguring Christ, his graces, actions, sufferings, and benefits; and partly, holding forth divers instructions of moral duties. All which ceremonial laws are now abrogated, under the new testament.
>
> 4. To them also, as a body politic, he gave sundry judicial laws, which expired together with the State of that people; not obliging any other now, further than the general equity thereof may require.

The moral law, then, is our fundamental responsibility toward God as set forth in the creation ordinances and, as we have seen, in the Decalogue. Ceremonial law has to do with the Aaronic priesthood, animal sacrifices, annual feasts, circumcision, the Day of Atonement, laws of uncleanness, and other matters. Judicial law (often called civil law) includes crimes punishable by the state and the penalties required for them.

The distinction is a good one, in a rough-and-ready way. As we have seen, there are such things as moral laws, that are based on our nature as creatures in the image of God, and are therefore literally normative for all history. It will never be right to steal or murder. It will always be right to worship the one true God exclusively and to honor one's parents. And, as we saw in the last section, there are many laws that should not be kept literally in the present period of redemptive history, and those are what the Confession calls ceremonial. Finally, there are laws given to guide the actions of civil magistrates in Israel, and those may be called civil.

But when we get into details, these designations are not as sharp or as helpful as we might like. For one thing, the laws of the Pentateuch are not clearly labeled as moral, civil, or ceremonial. In passages like Leviticus 19, laws that we group under different categories are mixed together. And the New Testament doesn't mention such distinctions either, typically referring simply to "the law." As we have seen, "the law" has various meanings in the New Testament, which must be determined by context. Our threefold distinction, though not found explicitly in Scripture, is a useful tool to analyze and classify the various laws in the Bible.

Further, there are problems with each of these designations:

The moral law. The creation ordinances and the Decalogue are surely the most obvious candidates for the status of "moral laws." But as we saw earlier, there are open questions as to their present applicability. Of course, if one believes, for example, that the cultural mandate is no longer normative, then he can relegate that commandment to the ceremonial category, rather than the moral category. But then, the distinction between "moral" and "ceremonial" is not as helpful as we might have thought. In these cases, we don't determine that a law is ceremonial and therefore not currently normative; rather, we follow the reverse procedure. Rather than determining that a law is abrogated because it is ceremonial, we determine that it is ceremonial because we believe it to be abrogated. So *moral* is just a label for those laws we believe to be currently normative, rather than a quality of the laws that leads us to that conclusion. The same is true for the label *ceremonial.* There is nothing particularly wrong with this procedure, as long as we understand what we are doing.

The ceremonial law. One might think that ceremonial laws are about ceremonies, particularly liturgies used in worship. Many of them are, including circumcision, the sacrifices, priestly ordination, priestly garments, feasts, perhaps cleansing laws, and so on. However, some laws about ceremonies are generally considered part of the moral law, rather than the ceremonial law. For example, the first four commandments of the Decalogue govern the worship of God's people. Also, some laws often called ceremonial have little to do with ceremonies, such as dietary laws, clothing laws (e.g., Num. 15:38), and laws concerning leprosy and other diseases. Again, it seems as though theologians call certain laws "ceremonial," not because they share a certain subject matter, but rather because they are judged not appropriate to the new covenant. The name *ceremonial*, therefore, is somewhat misleading. But I suppose we need some word to refer to laws that are not currently normative, and *ceremonial* is the word adopted by the Reformed tradition for that purpose.

The civil law. The civil laws are defined as the laws of the state of Israel as it existed in the Old Testament period. There are a number of problems, however, with this concept:

1. The laws of the Pentateuch rarely indicate precisely who is to enforce them. Some fall under the authority of judges (e.g., Ex. 21:22), while others are the province of the priests (e.g., Lev. 1–9). Sometimes the elders play a role (as in Deut. 19:12). But many others are not assigned to any government except that of God (as, we presume, Lev. 19:18), the self-government of individuals (e.g., the dietary laws), or the informal sanctions of the community.

2. In Reformed theology, as in the Westminster Confession, the distinction between civil law and moral law indicates that all the laws deemed civil are no longer normative. But that raises questions that deserve to be investigated. The Mosaic law contains the death penalty for the crime of murder, for example (Ex. 21:14; Deut. 19:11–13). But that law was not given merely to Israel. God gave it long before to Noah, and through him to the whole human race (Gen. 9:6). This law does not serve any purpose that is unique to the Israelite theocracy. Rather, it is an administration of simple justice. So among the civil laws are at least some that apply to nations other than Israel—that is, some that are not merely civil, but moral.

3. WCF, 19.4, quoted earlier, makes a significant exception to the "expiration" of the civil laws: "not obliging any other now [i.e., any state other than Old Testament Israel], further than the general equity thereof may require." What is this "general equity"? The precise meaning of this phrase has been the subject of considerable debate, but the basic idea is not difficult to ascertain.

God gives some laws to Israel that presuppose its unique status as God's chosen people. Among these are the laws concerning sacrifices, the tabernacle, and the priesthood. But he gives other laws that do not presuppose Israel's unique status, but which merely command basic justice. We saw this above with regard to the death penalty for murder. As another example, the basic penalty for theft is double restitution (Ex. 22:7). This penalty, again, is not based on Israel's unique status as God's holy people. Rather, it is a matter of simple justice: the thief must return what he stole, plus an equal amount, so that he loses what he hoped to gain. This law is normative, not only for Israel, but for any nation that seeks justice. That is to say, this particular civil law is a moral law.

All the laws that God gives to Israel are just, and in that sense they are a model for other nations. Moses says to Israel:

> See, I have taught you statutes and rules, as the LORD my God commanded me, that you should do them in the land that you are entering to take possession of it. Keep them and do them, for that will be your wisdom and your understanding in the sight of the peoples, who, when they hear all these statutes, will say, "Surely this great nation is a wise and understanding people." (Deut. 4:5–6)

That is to say, all the laws of God are perfectly just and right, given Israel's situation. Israel is God's holy people, and these laws are perfect laws for a holy people in the environment of the Promised Land. When Israel keeps these laws, the nations will see them as good and wise.

This does not mean that all the laws of Israel should have been copied verbatim into the law books of Egypt and Babylon. Egypt and Babylon were not holy peoples. Their culture and economies were different. But certainly some laws, like double restitution for theft, should have been adopted by those and other nations as well. Further, Leviticus 18:24–30, speaking of laws concerning sexual relations, indicates that nations other than Israel should have the same standards as Israel:

> Do not make yourselves unclean by any of these things, for by all these the nations I am driving out before you have become unclean, and the land became unclean, so that I punished its iniquity, and the land vomited out its inhabitants. But you shall keep my statutes and my rules and do none of these abominations, either the native or the stranger who sojourns among you (for the people of the land, who were before you, did all of these abominations, so that the land became unclean), lest the land vomit you out when you make it unclean, as it vomited out the nation that was before you. For everyone who does any of these abominations, the persons who do them shall be cut off from among their people. So keep my charge never to practice any of these abominable customs that were practiced before you, and never to make yourselves unclean by them: I am the LORD your God.[17]

17. For other evidence of the continuity between what God demands of Israel and what he demands of other nations, see Greg Bahnsen, *Theonomy in Christian Ethics* (Phillipsburg, NJ: Presbyterian and Reformed, 1977), 339–64.

So we should understand "general equity" to refer to the overlap between the civil law and the moral law. In the law of Israel, God enforces justice among his people. The law has other purposes as well, including ritual holiness, typology, and symbolism, that are not appropriate for other nations. But justice is appropriate for all nations, and the justice of the law of Moses is a model for justice in all nations.

The problem, then, in dealing with Israelite civil law, is to distinguish between the demands of justice as such and the special demands made of Israel as a holy people of God. The requirements for observing the Feast of Tabernacles are clearly for Israel alone, but the death penalty for murder is for all. But the two aren't always that easy to distinguish. What about the provision of cities of refuge for those accused of murder (Num. 35)? Is that a wise provision to protect the lives of those falsely accused, or is it a special provision for God's holy people (note that the slayer is released only at the death of the high priest, v. 28)? The student of the Mosaic law must think through each statute to determine what it means, asking why God gave that statute to Israel. Did God give it simply as justice? As a type of Christ? As a way to remind Israel of their special covenant? Or some combination of these? Students of the law must think through many possibilities.

THEONOMY

Theonomy, sometimes called Christian reconstruction, is a movement of Reformed thinkers dedicated to encourage observance of the Mosaic law by Christians. The patriarch of the movement was the late Rousas J. Rushdoony, who set forth his position in many writings, especially *The Institutes of Biblical Law*.[18] This position is also espoused in many writings by economic historian Gary North, Rushdoony's son-in-law. The most cogent exponent of theonomy was the late Greg L. Bahnsen, author of *Theonomy in Christian Ethics*.[19]

Bahnsen uses a phrase that expresses well the overall program of theonomy, as theonomists understand it: "the abiding validity of the law in exhaustive detail."[20] It appears to be a simple and radical proposal, telling us to hear God's law and do it, all of it. According to Bahnsen, this proposal is an implication of Matthew 5:17–20. So he and other

18. Nutley, NJ: Craig Press, 1973. See my review in appendix G to this volume.
19. Nutley, NJ: Craig Press, 1977.
20. Ibid., 39 (the title of chap. 2).

theonomists see their opponents as antinomian—as people who are not willing to obey God's commands.[21]

But, as we have seen, the question of obeying biblical laws is not simply whether we will obey them. It is also a question of how to interpret them and how to apply them. And theonomists are not oblivious to the hermeneutical questions. Indeed, they, like the majority of Christians, regard much of the law as no longer normative. When Bahnsen speaks of "the abiding validity of the law in exhaustive detail," he does not mean that we should follow the dietary laws or bring animal sacrifices to church with us. Rather, like most of us, he sees these laws as fulfilled in Christ, in such a way that they don't need to be kept literally today. The "abiding validity" of these laws means, rather, that we keep them by worshiping on the basis of Jesus' final sacrifice. When we bring the sacrifice of Christ before the Father, we are obeying the Old Testament command to bring sacrifices to God. So "the abiding validity of the law" is flexible enough to allow considerable change in the specific nature of our obligation. But understood in that flexible way, most orthodox Reformed thinkers would agree with the principle. Given that flexible understanding, the principle is not nearly as radical as it sounds.

So what is different about theonomy? I would say that theonomy is not absolutely different from other Reformed positions, but only relatively so. Theonomy is a school of thought within Reformed theology that prefers literal, specific, and detailed applications of Mosaic civil laws to modern civil government. The word "prefers" gives us some leeway. At points, the theonomists, like the rest of us, apply the law in general and nonliteral ways. But they tend more than the rest of us to prefer the specific and the literal.

In terms of our earlier discussion, theonomists tend to see a larger overlap between civil laws and moral laws than do other Reformed thinkers. Greg Bahnsen even rejects the distinction between civil law and moral law. For him, there is a major distinction in Scripture between moral laws and ceremonial laws (or "restorative laws," as he prefers to call them). And the civil laws, including the penalties for civil crimes, are not a third category. Rather, they are themselves either moral or ceremonial. In Bahnsen's view, they are largely moral.[22] In particular, Bahnsen and other theonomists insist that the penalties for civil crimes in the Pentateuch are normative for modern civil governments, including the death penalty for adultery, homosexuality, and blasphemy.

21. Bahnsen calls his opponents "latent antinomians" in ibid., 306–14.
22. Ibid., 207–16.

Theonomy appeals to many who are unhappy with the vagueness of much Christian ethics. Theonomy seems to promise them clear-cut answers to their ethical questions. But theonomists differ much among themselves as to how the civil laws are to be applied. In their movement, there is controversy, for example, over the status of dietary laws, the levirate, and long-term loans.

So the differences between theonomists and other Reformed thinkers are not sharp, but somewhat fuzzy. Theonomy, as defined above, is an emphasis, a tendency.

The opposite tendency is found in a number of other authors, notably Meredith G. Kline. Like Bahnsen, Kline makes a bold, programmatic statement, namely, "The Old Testament is not the canon of the Christian church."[23] By this statement, he does not intend to deny the authority of the Old Testament. Indeed, he recognizes the Old Testament to be God's word, inspired and infallible. But it is not *canon*, which means that it is "not a matter of faith-norms but of life-norms. More specifically, inasmuch as the nuclear function of each canonical Testament is to structure the polity of the covenant people, canonicity precisely and properly defined is a matter of *community* life-norms."[24] For Kline, the Old Testament is not part of the Christian canon, because it is the covenant document of the Mosaic covenant, not of the new covenant in Christ. The New Testament alone is the document of the new covenant. Although the Old Testament is normative for the faith of New Testament believers (i.e., for their "faith-norms"), it is not normative for its community life-norms (though presumably it is authoritative in some way for individual life-norms).

I find these distinctions unpersuasive. I grant that we should define the canon as those documents that God has given to govern the lives of the covenant people of God. But I don't see any biblical basis for the distinctions between life and faith, or individual and community, that Kline sets forth. Faith is part of life, and both individual and community life are under God's covenant.

But my main point is that Kline, like Bahnsen, is not as brash as his initial hypothesis might suggest. When Kline says that the Old Testament is not our canon, he does not mean what most of us think of when we hear the word *canon*. Rather, he has a technical concept of canon that doesn't exclude at all the authority of the Old Testament as the word of God. Further, Kline, like Bahnsen, is willing to apply Old Testament statutes

---

23. Meredith G. Kline, *The Structure of Biblical Authority* (Grand Rapids: Eerdmans, 1972), 99.

24. Ibid., 101–2.

to contemporary civil law, as in his discussion of Exodus 21:22–25.[25] In that article, he argues that the Israelite regard for the unborn rules out the practice of abortion. So Kline, like the theonomists, represents a tendency, not an extreme.

One gets the impression from reading Bahnsen and Kline that their principles are intended to determine our application of specific texts in the Mosaic law. Bahnsen's approach suggests that we should always, or most often, apply them literally; Kline's approach suggests the reverse. But since both principles have exceptions, we still need to give close attention to the application of each individual text. For example, as we examine the statute forbidding the eating of blood (Lev. 17:10–12), we must ask questions such as: What did this mean to its original audience? Why did God give them this rule? Does that reason make it appropriate to our situation, as it was in the situation in which it was written?

We must ask such questions of every statute, regardless of whether Bahnsen is right, or Kline, or some third alternative. That fact suggests to me that the exegesis of specific texts is more fundamental than the truth of any broad theological principle. That is, the exegesis determines the principle, rather than the other way around. That is always true in theology, and it is true in this case.

So whether the theonomist tendency, the Klinean tendency, or a more conventional Reformed approach is correct will depend not upon general theological principles, but on the exegesis of specific passages. If, on investigation, the best exegesis finds that most of the contested texts warrant highly specific, literal, and detailed applications, then we will have to say that the theonomists are most right. If exegesis more often points the other way, we will have to say that the theonomists are relatively wrong.[26]

I cannot exegete all the relevant passages here, but perhaps the following comments will be found helpful:

1. Historically, Reformed thought has shown elements of both relatively theonomic and relatively nontheonomic emphasis. I do not believe that either approach may claim unequivocally to be "the Reformed position." Of course, Reformed people are not antinomian. They believe that Christians are governed by God's law, and that includes the Old Testament. But Reformed exegetes, including Calvin, have varied greatly

25. Meredith G. Kline, "*Lex Talionis* and the Human Fetus," *Journal of the Evangelical Theological Society* 20 (1977): 193–201.

26. *The Shadow of Christ in the Law of Moses*, by Vern S. Poythress, is, in my judgment, the best attempt so far to analyze the meaning of the statutes of the law. After a comprehensive discussion of the laws themselves, Poythress presents, as an appendix, a critical analysis of theonomy.

as to how literally and specifically they apply the details of the Mosaic legislation to their own situations.

2. Kline's rejection of theonomy presupposes some ideas that are themselves controversial and in my opinion dubious: (a) the sharp distinction between "life-norms" and "faith-norms," (b) the derivation from the Noachic covenant of a religiously neutral state, and (c) his view of the New Testament as the sole canon of the Christian church. We should not, therefore, assume that Kline any more than theonomy represents the Reformed tradition unambiguously.

3. Other critics of theonomy tend to be vague in their arguments or even reveal a certain antipathy toward the Mosaic laws themselves (e.g., the horror displayed at the very idea of making homosexuality a capital crime).

4. Since both Bahnsen and Kline make broad, bold programmatic statements that they modify considerably in their detailed discussions, it seems to me that those bold statements do not really or fairly represent the views they are presenting. In actual fact, they are closer together than their rhetoric would suggest.[27]

5. In the application of Scripture, there is never unity without diversity, or diversity without unity. Every law of Scripture must be applied to situations. Since every situation is different, every application is somewhat different. On the other hand, since all Scripture is God's word, all applications are applications of the word of God, applications of a fundamental unity. Therefore, any rhetoric that denies unity or diversity is misleading. Contrary to theonomic rhetoric, there is always "change" from one application of a law to the next application of it. And contrary to antitheonomic rhetoric, all of God's Word must be brought to bear upon all of human life (Matt. 4:4).

6. "Change" in this discussion applies both to redemptive-historical change (e.g., old covenant to new covenant) and to cultural change (e.g., we no longer fence our roofs, as in Deuteronomy 22:8, because we no longer use the roof as space for living or entertaining guests). Assessing the relevance of all these forms of change is not always easy. Should believers wear tassels on their garments (Num. 15:38–39)? Is that ruled out by redemptive-historical change? Is it ruled out because the tassel has no symbolic value in the present-day world? How about head covering for women in worship (1 Cor. 11:2–16)? We should not assume that for each of these questions there is one obvious and easy answer, such that those who come to opposite conclusions from ours are fools or heretics. God has ordained, and therefore takes account of, our epistemological limitations.

27. See my "The One, the Many, and Theonomy," in *Theonomy: A Reformed Critique*, ed. William S. Barker and W. Robert Godfrey (Grand Rapids: Zondervan, 1990), 89–99.

7. Given the various changes from situation to situation in the application of the law, it is certainly not self-evident that God intended all of the civil laws given to Israel to bind all civil societies. If some of the statutes given to Israel are or are not also binding on other nations, that point must be demonstrated in piecemeal fashion, from one statute to the next.

8. Recall my earlier discussion of the relationship between the Decalogue and the case laws. Given the flexibility allowed to judges in Israel, it is not evident that the penalties of the case laws form a code to be mechanically imposed in each case. Every case is different. The penalties of the case laws are exemplary. And even if the case laws given to Israel are normative for modern civil governments, they do not present an exhaustive catalogue of penalties for every situation. There will always be a need for judicial flexibility. That flexibility will be all the more important in a modern society, in which judges must deal with many things unknown to ancient Israelites. What penalty should be given to Internet pornographers, for example? So even if the case laws are normative today, they would not preclude judicial flexibility; rather, they would necessitate it.

9. There is some confusion in theonomy between present and future application of the law. The rhetoric of theonomy is often calculated to arouse immediate action, and at least some of the appeal of the movement is that people see in it a practical political program for today's society. But others are horrified by the idea that theonomists, taking over government in these confused times, would immediately proceed to execute homosexuals, adulterers, and so on. Confronted with this objection, Bahnsen argues that the Mosaic laws should *not* be enforced today. They presuppose, he says, a people who understand and believe the law and who are committed to being God's people.[28]

But that changes theonomy from being a practical program for the present to being a future ideal. I suspect that few of us would disagree with theonomy, or would disagree as strongly, if it were simply presented as a future ideal. Sure, if the postmillennial hope is realized and the world is largely Christianized,[29] then most of us would find attractive the prospect of living under something like the Mosaic civil law.

---

28. Another theonomic reply has been that theonomists believe in limited government, so that a theonomic government would not have the power to conduct a reign of terror. That point is reassuring to some extent. But it is odd to hear that a theonomist government would deny to itself sufficient power to enforce what it considers to be biblical norms.

29. Most theonomists are postmillennialists. They believe that there may be a very long time before Jesus returns in glory. In that time, perhaps tens of thousands of years, it is not difficult for theonomists to envision the world becoming substantially Christian.

We can well agree that there are elements of the Mosaic law which would be enforceable and helpful in contemporary society, such as double restitution for theft without prison sentences. But the question of what is or is not to be implemented now is a difficult question, and it is made all the more difficult by Bahnsen's present/future distinction. We need not only determine how literally the law is to be applied in the ideal situation; we must also determine how it is to be applied in the nonideal situation of today.

To the extent that theonomy is a future ideal, rather than a present-day political program, it becomes less radical and more theoretical. To some readers, that makes theonomy more attractive; to others, less.

10. Much of the rhetoric of theonomy is based on the assumed need for certainty on specifics. I have often heard Bahnsen ask candidates for licensure or ordination in presbytery how they would argue against, say, bestiality, without referring to Old Testament case law. We need the case laws, his argument goes, because the other parts of Scripture are not sufficiently specific. Another example: theonomists typically deny the appeal to "natural light" (an appeal commonly made by Calvin and his successors) because the natural light is not sufficiently specific in its directives. The argument suggests that we need divine direction that is perfectly specific, that leaves no room for human reflection, lest we obey ourselves rather than God.

But in my view this is not the nature of Christian ethics. No command of Scripture is perfectly specific; all Scripture commands are general to some extent. Scripture does not tell me what key to press on my computer as I write this chapter. But it does tell me in general what I ought to say. Scripture does not anywhere specifically forbid abortion; we determine that abortion is wrong by applying the eighth commandment and the language of Scripture concerning the unborn. Scripture does not speak of nuclear war, of the use of artificial life support, and so on. So in Christian ethics there is always a situational perspective. To apply Scripture to specifics, we need to have knowledge of things outside the Bible.

Thus, we should not be frustrated that we do not have, say, a scripturally dictated maximum income tax rate. We will never escape the need to apply general principles to specific situations.

11. I have come to the conclusion that theonomy is a good case study of how theological ideas should *not* be introduced. The sharp polemics of the theonomic movement (and, to be sure, of its critics in return) have been, in my view, quite unnecessary and indeed counterproductive to its own purposes. People have a hard time seeing the important truths that theonomy communicates; it is hard to learn from someone who is always

accusing you of something. Reformed people have always had a high regard for God's law. They are not, on the whole, antinomians and should not be stigmatized as such. Theonomists should not attack them for "latent antinomianism," but rather should ask probing questions to gently guide them into more thoughtful and accurate applications of God's Word.

Am I condemning here the accusatory language used by the Reformers and indeed by Scripture itself? Doubtless there is a place for harsh language. Jesus was harsh with the Pharisees, but not with the woman of Samaria, although he certainly did convict her of sin. In general, I think the Reformers were justified in their polemics, but I have often wondered how much more persuasive they might have been if they had more regularly observed the adage that "you catch more flies with honey than with vinegar."

12. For all of this, I would say that theonomy has in many ways been a helpful movement. When I went to seminary, we had excellent courses in Old Testament history, poetry, and prophecy, but almost nothing on the law. My initial exposure to the details of the Mosaic law was through the theonomic literature. Further, the theonomists show how we can incorporate into Christian faith and life the *love* of God's law evident in Psalms 1, 19, 119, and elsewhere.

At the very least, the theonomic writings show us why the nations around Israel would marvel at the wisdom of the law (Deut. 4:6). Certainly, God gave these statutes for the good of his people (Deut. 10:13). Had Israel kept the law, she would have been far better off. And as we come better to appreciate the goodness of the law in its original context, we may come more to understand how it may be relevant to our own society, how it could be good for us as well.

PRIORITIES

We have been looking at various factors that determine whether particular biblical laws are currently normative. But even among laws that are normative at a particular time and place, there are priorities to be observed, and those priorities should also influence our decisions.

As we saw in chapter 9, our ultimate ethical authority is God himself. He is law in the highest sense. The law that he reveals to us is a system, a comprehensive way of life in which the supreme goal (*summum bonum*) is to bring glory to him (1 Cor. 10:31). Within that system, some elements are more important, more pressing, than others.

That is true in any system of law. In the United States, for example, there are many different kinds of law: the Constitution, federal statutes, orders from the executive branch, state constitutions and statutes, local laws, decisions of courts. Even the orders given by a policeman on his beat are law in a sense. But within this system, some kinds of law take precedence over others. When someone believes that a statute is unconstitutional, for example, he may appeal to the court system. The court's decision, for better or worse, takes precedence over the statute in question. When Paul, in Romans 13:1, tells us to be subject to "the governing authorities" (cf. 1 Peter 2:13), he means, therefore, to be subject to the entire system of law.

In American law, we may assume that there are contradictions within the system that have to be resolved by court appeals and such. We may not assume that in the case of God's law. Nevertheless, it too is a system, and there are parts of it that, at any given time, will take precedence over other parts. In what follows, I shall describe several kinds of priorities.

NORMATIVE PRIORITIES

There are some principles of God's law that Scripture explicitly states to be more important than others. In Matthew 23:23, Jesus says that justice, mercy, and faithfulness are "weightier matters of the law," compared with the Pharisees' concern with the tithing of mint, dill, and cumin. Significantly, Jesus affirms the tithing of herbs when he tells the Pharisees, "These you ought to have done, without neglecting the others" (v. 23). Both the more weighty and the less weighty matters are part of the law. But there is a difference between them.

Similar is God's statement in Hosea 6:6, "For I desire steadfast love and not sacrifice, the knowledge of God rather than burnt offerings" (cf. Mic. 6:6–8; Matt. 9:13; 12:7). In fact, God did desire burnt offerings, for he commanded them often in the Old Testament. The statement in Hosea is making a comparison, and it is to some extent hyperbolic. It means that God's desire for steadfast love is so much greater than his desire for sacrifice that in the context of such a comparison it seems that he does not desire sacrifice at all. Clearly these passages indicate not only normative principles, but normative emphases. The principles that God considers most weighty are the ones that should preoccupy us above all.

Similarly, WLC, 151–52, tells us that some sins are worse than others. That principle is implicit in the above references and in other passages (see Ezek. 8:6, 13, 15; Matt. 12:31–32; Luke 12:47–48; John 19:11; Heb. 10:29 [cf. 2:2–3]; 1 John 5:16). Any sin is sufficient to condemn us to hell. But even in hell there are degrees of punishment, as seems to be implicit in Luke 12:47–48.

These passages describe objective differences of importance among God's laws. The law itself declares these differences, and so I call them normative priorities.

SITUATIONAL PRIORITIES

In various situations in life, it becomes more important to follow one principle of the law than to follow another. Modern secular legal systems, for example, make special provision for emergencies. Normally, for example, we are expected to drive on the right side of the road and not to cross solid lines. But when Jim is driving and a sinkhole appears ahead, leaving him no room to drive on that side, it is legitimate for him to wait until a safe moment and then cross the solid line in order to drive around the sinkhole. The highest principle of the law is safety, and that takes precedence over the normal traffic rules. If Jim is arrested for breaking a traffic law, concern for safety can serve as a legal defense. In fact, in such a case, Jim has not violated the law. He has maintained its highest intention, which is to keep people safe.

Scripture also recognizes that emergencies can affect our relationship to God's law. Jesus notes how David and his men "entered the house of God, in the time of Abiathar the high priest, and ate the bread of the Presence, which it is not lawful for any but the priests to eat, and also gave it to those who were with him" (Mark 2:26). The reason, simply, was that they were hungry (v. 25). Jesus also defends his own disciples when they plucked grain to eat on the Sabbath: "The Sabbath was made for man, not man for the Sabbath. So the Son of Man is lord even of the Sabbath" (vv. 27–28). God did not make the Sabbath to starve human beings, says the lord of the Sabbath himself. If Sabbath restrictions prevent nourishment, they must yield. This is not Sabbath breaking, he says. It is, rather, a keeping of the Sabbath, as God intended it to be kept.

Similarly, the Bible's instruction to submit to human authorities (Rom. 13:1; 1 Peter 2:13; Heb. 13:17; cf. Ex. 20:12) is an important rule, but it is subordinate to our higher duty to obey God. So when the highest Jewish authority, the high priest, together with the Sanhedrin, ordered the apostles not to teach in the name of Jesus, they answered, "We must obey God rather than men" (Acts 5:29), and they violated the order "every day, in the temple and from house to house" (v. 42).

Philosophers have sometimes distinguished "prima facie duties" from "actual, present duties." Obedience to legitimate human authority is a prima facie duty in biblical ethics. We should practice such obedience except in the rare instance of an overriding consideration. One who argues that there is such an exception must bear the burden of proof. But there are indeed cases of such overriding considerations, where our actual, present duty is an exception to a prima facie duty.

To follow a legitimate exception, as the apostles did in Acts 5:29, is not to break the law of God. Taken as a whole system, the law requires that such exceptions be made.

We are on somewhat dangerous ground here. Ethicists are sometimes tempted to say, for example, that since love is the highest principle of Christian ethics, it warrants exceptions to laws of chastity. The argument is that one may have sexual relations outside marriage, as long as they are true expressions of love. Why should we accept Acts 5:29 as an exception to the general principle of Romans 13:1, and not accept loving fornication as an exception to, say, 1 Corinthians 6:18?

The answer is that the exception of Acts 5:29 comes from Scripture. It comes, not only from Acts 5:29 itself, but from the overall biblical teaching that God alone is the supreme authority. But Scripture never suggests that the law of love warrants fornication. To say that it does is to misunderstand biblical love. Love is first of all a love of God, a relationship of allegiance, action, and affection, as we saw in chapter 12. Those who love God will obey his standards for sexuality. Second, love is a relationship of allegiance, action, and affection between human beings, in which one seeks what is best for the other. Scripture teaches that fornication is never best for anybody.

So we should be able to see that "situational priorities" are never opportunities for us to deviate from Scripture. Rather, they inform us as to the complexity and depth of Scripture's own ethical standards. Indeed, as in other contexts, here the situational is the application of the normative, and therefore part of the normative. Normative and situational are never opposed; they always imply one another.

Existential Priorities

But there is yet a third kind of priority in our attempt to keep the law. That is the set of priorities related to our own callings.

Perhaps we can get at this issue by noticing that obeying God usually takes time and planning. We tend to think of obedience as an instant response to divine commands, as when Jesus called his disciples and they "immediately" followed him (Matt. 4:20, 22). And certainly, when God gives us a negative command, telling us to stop doing something, he gives us no opportunity to postpone our obedience.[30]

---

30. Someone once told me that a man in a church who had committed adultery claimed that he was "in the process of" repenting. I gathered that meant that he committed adultery less frequently than before. But repentance for a particular sin is not a process, but a decisive break.

Sermons sometimes suggest that to obey God means to drop everything we are doing and to do something else. If the sermon text calls for persistent prayer, we ought to stop everything else and pray. The preacher reminds us that Luther spent many hours in prayer, and we feel guilty that we have not done that.

But then the next sermon says the same thing about another duty, say, evangelizing your neighborhood. And then we are told to feed the poor, visit the sick, pursue social justice, study Scripture, parent our children, work on our marriage, attend worship services, and on and on. The guilt becomes greater than we can bear.

The fact is, however, that although all these are legitimate biblical duties, we cannot do them all at once. We are finite. Our schedules are limited. We must frequently stop obeying one command in order to carry out another. God understands our finitude. He does not assume that every command of his must be carried out immediately and continually. It is comforting and reassuring for us to realize that as well.

God also understands that Christians will vary from one another in the emphasis they place on each command. That emphasis will vary with gifts and calling. Those who are called to be full-time preachers will spend more time preaching than those who are called to be full-time homemakers. Even prayer varies among us. All of us are called to pray, but some of us, like the widows mentioned in 1 Timothy 5, may be called to continue "in supplications and prayers night and day" (v. 5).

So we are responsible to set priorities among divine commands. How arrogant that sounds! Who are we to determine how much time we are to spend carrying out each divine command? How can anyone presume to determine priorities among ultimates? But we must and we do.

We can understand this principle better when we see that many of God's commands are not given primarily to individuals, but to a corporate body—either to the human race as a whole or to the church as the body of Christ. For example, God gave the cultural mandate of Genesis 1:28 not to Adam and Eve as individuals, but to them as a corporate family, including their descendants. Adam could not have filled or subdued the earth as an individual. Only the human race as a whole could have any hope of carrying out that mandate. The same is true of the Great Commission (Matt. 28:18–20). Neither Peter nor Andrew could single-handedly make disciples of all nations. But the church, acting as a body under the impetus of God's Spirit, can and will.

So my individual responsibility is not to subdue the earth or to disciple all the nations. It is, rather, to find a specific role, for which God has gifted me, that will contribute something to those results. In my case, though some may disagree, God has called me to be a theologian. That calling requires me to study the Bible more than most, and to spend less time than others bringing the gospel door to door. It is that calling that determines, or should determine, my personal set of priorities. I must make a decision, but God offers his guidance for such decisions.

To speak of such a decision is merely to talk about applying God's Word to one's individual situation. We have seen over and over again that Scripture can do its work in our lives only as we apply it to our situations. Scripture itself requires it, and so existential prioritizing is a norm. Existential priorities, therefore, are not exceptions to divine norms, any more than situational priorities are. Indeed, at this point the existential and the normative coincide.

It is important that we recognize a legitimate diversity here within the body of Christ. The person who spends ten hours a week feeding the poor is not necessarily more faithful than the widow who spends those ten hours in prayer—or vice versa. We should be thankful to God for this diversity, for it is through this diversity of contributions that God accomplishes his great work.

People sometimes mistakenly think that if God has given a command, it must be given unlimited emphasis and time.[31] So, in some denominations, one commonly hears that since God requires sound doctrine, the church assemblies must give unlimited attention to doctrinal issues, even at the expense of missions, evangelism, and prayer. The problem is, of course, that God has also commanded missions, evangelism, and prayer. And if a denomination is to have a balanced view of things, it must at some point stop its doctrinal debates long enough to concentrate on other matters.

Imbalance sometimes occurs in the opposite direction, as well. Unfortunately, because of the denominational divisions of the church, people preoccupied with doctrinal matters tend to gravitate to certain denominations, and people preoccupied with practical ministry end up in others. It would be better to have people with both preoccupations in the same church.

But we should be clear that people preoccupied with doctrine are not necessarily more holy, more faithful, or more Reformed (!) than those who are preoccupied with missions. People with one group of priorities should

---

31. I belonged to a presbytery once that consumed enormous amounts of time on the reading and correcting of minutes, normally the first thing on the docket. When I asked why, I was told that God wants us to do all things decently and in order, and that entails a concern for accurate minutes. So God has ordained, the argument went, that the perfecting of minutes be given as much time as it takes—even if it squeezes out other matters, such as discussing church planting and evangelism. I didn't find the argument persuasive.

not criticize those who have a different emphasis. The difference is often a difference in divine calling.

The Orthodox Presbyterian Church is relatively preoccupied with issues of doctrinal purity, while the Presbyterian Church in America, holding to the same confessional standards, is relatively more preoccupied with church planting and missions. Some in each body are convinced that the other body is unfaithful to the Lord, because of its different emphasis. Attempts to merge the two denominations have not succeeded. In my judgment, part of the problem is that some in each group have confused their group's priorities with biblical principle.

A better way to look at it is this: the PCA is like a breadwinner, leaving the home each day to reach the world outside. The OPC is like a homemaker, keeping the house clean, determining who should be invited to dinner. Homemakers and breadwinners often get into arguments, but both are necessary to a good marriage. A church without breadwinners, or without homemakers, is a church that lacks some important gifts of God. So in my judgment the two denominations should not let the differences in their priorities interfere with their fellowship. They should rather be attracted to one another. Indeed, they should become one.[32]

TRAGIC MORAL CHOICE

We have been looking at various ways in which divine laws can lose their immediate, present normativity. But an important question remains, namely, whether two divine laws can ever make incompatible demands on us. This is the question of "conflict of duties," sometimes called "tragic moral choice." It is one of the most discussed questions in the ethical literature. You have probably thought about the famous illustration from World War II: You are hiding Jews in your basement. The Nazis come and ask you directly whether there are any Jews in your house. If you answer truly, you give innocent lives over to death. If you answer falsely, you tell a lie and violate God's standards of truthfulness. So in this case the sixth commandment, which prohibits murder, seems to impose on you a responsibility incompatible with the ninth commandment, which mandates telling the truth.

32. For more on the biblical mandate for church union, see my *Evangelical Reunion* (Grand Rapids: Baker, 1991), now available at www.thirdmill.org and at www.frame-poythress.org.

In this situation, it seems as though we must disobey one divine command in order to obey another, which is to say that at this point the demands of God's law are inconsistent. Or we can look at the problem from the situational perspective and say that in this situation there is no righteous alternative. In this situation, it is impossible not to sin.

Many ethicists assume that such conflicts exist. Liberal theologians have no problem affirming this, for they do not believe that the Bible teaches a consistent system of ethics. But even evangelicals sometimes affirm the existence of tragic moral choice. John Warwick Montgomery, who believes strongly in biblical inerrancy, writes:

> The Christian morality fully realizes the difficulty of moral decision, and frequently a Christian finds himself in a position where it is necessary to make a decision where moral principles must be violated in favor of other moral principles, but he never vindicates himself in this situation. He decides in terms of the lesser of evils or the greater of goods, and this drives him to the Cross to ask forgiveness for the human situation in which this kind of complication and ambiguity exists.[33]

Montgomery says here that sometimes we find ourselves in situations so difficult that we cannot avoid sinning. Doubtless he would say that this is one of the effects of the curse on the ground following Adam's sin. But though there is no righteous alternative available to us in such situations, we can nevertheless ask God's forgiveness through Christ.[34]

I must, however, take exception to this reasoning. I don't believe that the theory of tragic moral choice is compatible with Scripture, for the following reasons:

1. In Scripture, we have a moral duty to do what is right, and never to do what is wrong. But Montgomery seems to think that in situations of conflicting norms we have a moral duty to do something wrong, something for which we must afterward ask forgiveness. That notion is, in my judgment, morally confused.

2. In Scripture, ethical knowledge presupposes knowledge of what is right. God judges even pagans because they know what is right, but reject that knowledge (Rom. 1:18–23, 32). But on Montgomery's view, in certain situations there is no right alternative and therefore no possibility of knowing the right. By what standard, then, does God judge such conduct?

---

33. Montgomery, *The Suicide of Christian Theology* (Minneapolis: Bethany Fellowship, 1970), 69.

34. Montgomery is Lutheran, and we can hear in his words echoes of Luther's "sin boldly" and "*simul justus et peccator.*"

3. On this view, the law of God itself is contradictory, for it requires contradictory behavior.[35]

4. Indeed, on this view, Scripture counsels us to sin, contrary to Psalm 19:7–9, which says:

> The law of the LORD is perfect,
>   reviving the soul;
> the testimony of the LORD is sure,
>   making wise the simple;
> the precepts of the LORD are right,
>   rejoicing the heart;
> the commandment of the LORD is pure,
>   enlightening the eyes;
> the fear of the LORD is clean,
>   enduring forever;
> the rules of the LORD are true,
>   and righteous altogether.

5. And then, on this view, since Scripture is God's word, God himself counsels us to sin. That is a blasphemous supposition, rejected in the strongest terms by James 1:13–14.

6. It is also important to consider the Christological implications of this view. If Jesus faced conflicts of duties, then he was guilty of sin, for a conflict of duty is by definition one in which any choice is sinful. That conflicts with the biblical affirmation of Jesus' sinlessness (Heb. 4:15; 1 Peter 2:22; 1 John 3:5). On the other hand, if Jesus did not face tragic moral choices, and we do, then we cannot affirm that he "in every respect has been tempted as we are" (Heb. 4:15). If tragic moral choices exist, they are the toughest choices we have to make, the height of our moral and spiritual warfare. If Jesus did not have to make them, he did not endure our spiritual battle at its hardest point, and so the assurance of Hebrews 4:15 rings hollow. The only way to avoid this problem is to say that there are no tragic moral choices, that Jesus did not face them, and that neither do we.

7. God's Word gives us a specific promise concerning temptation in 1 Corinthians 10:13: "No temptation has overtaken you that is not common to man. God is faithful, and he will not let you be tempted beyond

---

35. Someone may want to argue that the law is consistent, but its applications are not. But I have argued that the applications of words are their very meanings (see *DKG*, 81–85, 93–98). And in this book I have argued in chapter 11 that the extrabiblical data by which we apply God's commands never subtract from the authority of those commands. Surely the consistency of Scripture is an empty concept if Scripture can command us to do contradictory things.

your ability, but with the temptation he will also provide the way of escape, that you may be able to endure it." This text says that no temptation is so great that the Christian cannot escape it. That is, even in the worst temptations, God gives us the resources to be faithful to him, to make right choices, to find ways of escaping from wickedness. Tragic moral choice, however, is a situation where by definition there is no way to escape. So this passage implies directly that there is no tragic moral choice.

This verse is, of course, a promise to Christian believers, not to others. But it would be odd to imagine a world in which every situation offers a right alternative to the Christian, but not to the non-Christian. It is true that non-Christians, lacking God's grace, commit sin in all they do. But that is not because there is no right alternative available for them. To the contrary, it is because they know what is right (Rom. 1) and refuse to do it.

So I must conclude that there are no tragic moral choices, no conflicts of duties. We should try to understand, however, why the theory of tragic moral choice is so plausible to many. The main reason, I think, is that many moral decisions are very difficult to make. Sometimes it is hard to find the way of escape, and people are tempted to think that such a way does not exist. Please don't think that in rejecting the theory of tragic moral choice I mean to imply that ethical decisions are easy to make. Rather, I encourage you to sympathize with those who wrestle with these issues, to pray for them, and to help them to find a godly solution.

Some alleged examples of tragic moral choice are really questions of priority within the divine law, such as we discussed earlier in the chapter. Others have to do with questions of interpretation. For example, as I shall argue later, I think a sound interpretation of the ninth commandment will allow us to withhold the truth from those who seek innocent life. So, rightly understood, the ninth commandment does not conflict with the sixth, and the example of the Nazis demanding information about Jews is not an example of tragic moral choice.

Another reason why people find this theory attractive is that they have found themselves in situations where they must choose "between two evils." As we recall, Montgomery used this as an example of tragic moral choice, but more analysis is needed. It is important to distinguish between "evils" and "wrongs." An evil is an event that brings suffering. A wrong is a moral evil, a sin against God, a violation of his law.

Now it is usually wrong to inflict evils on people, but not always. The punishment of criminals and just war bring suffering on those deemed to deserve it. But Scripture does not regard these as wrong. A surgeon may choose to inflict pain on a patient in order to heal him. The pain is an evil;

it exists only as part of the curse brought on the earth by sin. But it is not wrong for the surgeon to inflict pain for a good purpose. In doing this, he brings about evil, but he does not do wrong.

So it is sometimes necessary and right to choose the lesser of two or more evils. But it is never necessary or right to choose between two wrongs. The surgeon does no wrong when he inflicts evil on a patient for a good reason. Choosing between two evils, so understood, is not tragic moral choice. It may, indeed, be virtuous.

CASUISTRY

The application of Scripture to situations is sometimes called casuistry. Casuistry deals with cases, relating general ethical principles to the specifics of human life. Casuistry has gotten a bad name, because many have abused the process. For that reason, I prefer the term *application* to the term *casuistry*. But in fact we should recognize that, by whatever name, casuistry is unavoidable. Ethical norms, including those in Scripture, are always somewhat general. Scripture does not describe every situation in which we find ourselves each day, nor does it prescribe norms specifically for each of those situations. The work of applying its general norms to those specifics belongs to us, making use of both special and general revelation. And that work is called casuistry.

In casuistry, we see clearly the complexity of ethical decision making. The casuist must rightly interpret both the moral law and the situation to which the law will be applied. He must understand also people's motives (existential perspective), which can often affect or even determine the rightness or wrongness of their actions. He must understand mitigating circumstances and aggravating circumstances, which can also affect whether an action is right or wrong and the degree of rightness or wrongness.

The chief danger is that the casuist will replace or even contradict the moral law with his own (or a tradition of) interpretations. Jesus charged the Pharisees with breaking the commandment of God for the sake of their tradition (Matt. 15:3). Tradition is not in itself a bad thing. Used well, it makes the godly thinking of past generations useful to us today. But when used wrongly, it imposes barriers between the believer and God's Word.

This danger has taken two distinct forms in the history of ethics. Some casuists have been lax, using their interpretative powers to rationalize sin. Others have tried to be more rigorous, using casuistry to impose a burdensome yoke of regulations on God's people. So in ancient Judaism there was conflict between the lax school of Hillel and the rigorous school of Shammai. And in post-Reformation Roman Catholic circles there was debate between the lax Jesuits and the rigorous Jansenists.

The relatively lax parties have been famous for their justifications of apparently sinful conduct, such as (1) justifying a wrong action because it is more right than its opposite, (2) determining exceptions to general commands, (3) determining implicit qualifications for commands, and (4) excusing normally sinful actions if done from a good motive. These things are not always wrong. As we saw earlier, not every biblical command is to be fulfilled literally and immediately. There are exceptions and qualifications to some commands that Scripture presents implicitly or explicitly, as points 2 and 3 indicate. We shall see in our discussion of the existential perspective that motive does play a role in the moral quality of actions (cf. point 4). I have no sympathy for point 1, however, which either assumes tragic moral choice or assumes that in some other way a wrong action can be right. But even in areas 2–4, casuists of the lax sort have often gone too far, not observing the limits set by Scripture.

The rigorist schools of casuistry have added vast catalogues of moral restrictions to the relatively simple requirements of God's Word, leaving little freedom to the believer. Sometimes their motive in this has been to "fence" the law, adding extrabiblical restrictions to keep us from violating genuine biblical laws. Hence, to keep people from the possibility of boiling a young goat in its mother's milk (forbidden in Ex. 23:19), the Jews insisted that people not eat meat and dairy products at the same meal.

This encourages a nit-picking mentality, interest in minutiae, over against "the weightier matters of the law." There is nothing wrong with an interest in the minutiae of Scripture, unless, as with the Pharisees, that interest crowds out the things that are most important. Rigorism also obscures the clarity of Scripture, making it seem as though ethical questions can only be decided by experts.

To guard against the abuse of casuistry, we need to have (1) a firm, practical confidence in the Scriptures as the clear and sufficient word of God, (2) an awareness of what is more or less important within Scripture itself, and (3) a mature conscience, resisting rationalization and self-justification.

It is also important to know the limits of casuistry. Sometimes we dream of constructing a large book that would contain, not only all the ethical principles of the Bible (totaling 613, according to Jewish tradition), but also all the possible applications of those principles. But that dream is a delusion. The possible applications of the law of God can never be listed or written down. The number of them is far too large to be written in a book. With every breath we take, we are applying God's law. Every thought, word, and deed is done either to God's glory or to the glory of an idol (1 Cor. 10:31

again). And even if there were such a book, new situations would continue to arise. And then there would be questions about the application of that book itself—how it governs our conduct in those new situations.

Ethics books have their value, I hope, but that value is not to exhaustively describe our moral responsibilities. There will always be a need for individual application. Experts can help us in this task, but they cannot anticipate every fork in the road. God can, and his Spirit alone can equip us adequately for the moral journey.

THE SITUATIONAL PERSPECTIVE

CHAPTER 14

Situation and Norm

We will now begin to look at Christian ethical methodology from the situational perspective. Since it is a perspective, like the normative and existential perspectives, it covers the same subject matter as the other two, namely, the whole of ethics. Therefore, you can expect some overlap between the content of this section and that of the previous one. This section will not be a mere repetition, however, because it will look at the data from a different angle. Further, there are some subjects that I might have discussed under the normative or existential perspectives, but I have chosen to discuss them here instead, such as natural law and redemptive history.[1] The question of what one discusses under which perspective is largely pedagogical. Since the three perspectives cover the same ground, the question is not which choice is objectively true, but which choice is most helpful in presenting the material to people.[2] Theology is application!

Recall that, under the normative perspective, the ethical question can be formulated as "What does God tell us to do?" or "What is our duty?" Under the situational perspective, the question is "How can we change the world in order to bring glory to God?" As with the normative perspective,

---

1. Natural law could have been discussed under the normative perspective, because it deals with a means by which God reveals ethical truth. Or it could have been discussed under the existential perspective, since natural law theory places much weight on human nature and conscience.

2. In general, I don't take much interest in questions about which perspective is appropriate for a certain topic.

the situational perspective includes everything, but the focus is on the world, on the course of nature and history as the environment in which we make ethical decisions. It is focused less on the Bible than on extrabiblical data of importance to ethics. But it looks at those data in the light of the Bible. It is important to remember that the Bible (like everything else) is not only part of the normative perspective, but also an element of the other two perspectives. It is a norm of particular importance, but it is also an important fact of our situation (situational) and of our personal experience (existential).

As the normative perspective focuses on God's lordship attribute of authority, the situational perspective focuses on his lordship attribute of control. When we observe the course of nature and history, we are observing the outworking of God's eternal decree and his power to carry out that plan in creation and providence. It is God who has fashioned the world by his power, so that certain means lead to certain ends. This fact provides a basis for science in its examination of causes and effects. It also provides a basis for ethics as we attempt to accommodate means to ends.

As the normative perspective presents what may be called a Christian deontological ethic, so the situational perspective presents what may be called a Christian teleological ethic. In teleological ethics, one formulates goals for life and then determines means to reach those goals. Scripture also does this. As we shall see, it presents goals for human life and means of reaching them. And although Scripture is indispensable in revealing these goals to us, achieving them requires close attention to the situations in which we live. Those situations disclose to us many of the resources and opportunities we have for reaching godly goals.

Unlike secular forms of deontology and teleology, the normative and situational perspectives, when understood in a Christian way, are not inconsistent. A right understanding of God's norms and a right understanding of the situation in which we live are ultimately identical. Along the way, as the focus of our attention varies back and forth between the two perspectives, God's Word tells us much of what we need to know about the situation, and our observations of the situation tell us much about how we should be applying God's Word.

In chapter 11, I indicated that even though Scripture is sufficient to give us all the words of God that we need for any task, every moral decision requires a knowledge of extrabiblical data as well, so that the Word may be applied rightly to our circumstances. The situational perspective focuses on the use of that extrabiblical data, without forgetting that Scripture provides necessary directions for interpreting and using that data.

We can summarize the value of extrabiblical data in ethics in the following ways:

1. It provides many of the minor premises of moral syllogisms (chapter 11). Recall that the moral syllogism includes at least one normative premise, one situational premise, and a conclusion that is an applied norm. For example:

> (1) Lying is morally wrong (normative premise).
> (2) Bill's statement was a lie (situational premise).
> Therefore, Bill's statement was morally wrong (existential conclusion).

2. It poses moral questions. When God told Adam to fill and subdue the earth, that command gave moral significance to Adam's every experience. When Adam saw a snail crawling along the ground before the fall, his first concern would have been how to use this creature to subdue and fill the earth to God's glory. In that way, every fact of Adam's experience raised a moral issue, as it does for us as well.

3. It helps us to answer moral questions. Everything we learn about the facts helps us to answer the questions posed as in point 2 above. As Adam and other people studied snails, they would have discovered various nutritional uses of them, as well as the sheer aesthetic value of one of God's odder creations. This is simply to say that everything we experience in the world enables us in some way to apply God's norms to our lives.

In this chapter, we will consider the interface between the normative and situational perspectives. That is, we will consider further the ways in which the situation, particularly the data of our experience outside the Bible, helps us to learn God's norms for our lives.

In general, all the facts of our situation are normative. This is because God expects us to live lives in accord with reality, with the facts, with the world as he has made it. In Romans 1 and elsewhere, we learn that God reveals himself in the created world and therein communicates ethical content. This, as we saw in chapter 9, is natural or general revelation.

So the hierarchy of norms is also a hierarchy of facts. Under the normative perspective, in chapter 9, I discussed various kinds and levels of divine norms, ranging from God himself to persons and language. Our situation can also be described at various levels. As God is the supreme norm, so he is also our supreme situation, the supreme fact of our experience with which we must deal. More specifically, our situation is God's eternal plan, which directs the whole course of nature and history.[3] Still more specifically, our

---

3. For an account of God's eternal plan, or decrees, see *DG*, 313–39. If *DG* didn't exist, I would examine in the present volume the question of whether God's sovereign control of everything is compatible with human freedom and responsibility. That is an important

situation is nature itself, the general workings of the world perceived by our senses and reason and described by the physical sciences.

One subdivision of nature is what we call history, the events of human existence.[4] And one important subdivision of history is redemptive history, the story of creation, fall, and redemption.[5] Still more narrowly, we can focus on various phases of redemptive history. And one important part of that history is our own experience, what God is doing with us today. In our present experience, we deal with God, angels, other people (our social environment), and ourselves. Strange as it may seem, we ourselves are part of our environment, our situation, for in our decisions we must take into account our heredity, gifts, strengths, weaknesses, and so on. Here the situational and existential perspectives coincide.

NATURAL LAW

In the remainder of this chapter, I would like to examine a method of relating norms to situations that has enjoyed considerable prestige in the history of theological ethics. Traditional Roman Catholic theologians, together with many contemporary Protestant and Jewish thinkers, hold what they call a "natural law" theory of ethics. This idea can be traced from Aristotle and the Stoics to Aquinas, Hugo Grotius, and many modern thinkers, both religious and secular. Modern political conservatives, even some nonreligious ones, often appeal to natural law in their ethical judgments, because they believe

---

ethical question, because some have argued that our ethical responsibility depends on a certain kind of free will, a free will that is able to act apart from God's decree, a person's own character, even a person's own desires. That is the view called "libertarian free will." I believe that theory is wrong, unbiblical, incoherent, and actually destructive of moral responsibility. I have argued so at great length in *DG*, 119–59. The related question of how a good God could foreordain sin (given that libertarian freedom does not exist and therefore does not account for evil) is treated in *DG*, 160–82.

4. *History* refers either to the events themselves or to accounts of those events. In a broad sense, history includes everything that has ever happened to any human being. In a narrower sense, it includes only the most significant events: those most important to God's plan, the course of later events, and our present thoughts and feelings (note the triad). Naturally, historical literature deals with history in the narrower sense rather than the broad sense, because historians must deal with their finitude. But this fact opens areas of disagreement, for what is important to one historian may not be important to another. There are, therefore, differences of opinion, both about what history is and about what happened in history.

5. Some prefer a term like "covenant history" rather than "redemptive history," for the latter term literally embraces only events later than the fall. The former term would embrace creation and fall as well. But in common theological language, "redemptive history" covers the whole history narrated in Scripture, and I will maintain that common usage.

that such an appeal gives them an objective basis for moral judgments, contrary to the relativism of most contemporary thought.

One reason that religious conservatives often appeal to natural law is that it enables them to argue for their views without directly appealing to the Bible and church tradition. Secularists regularly attack Christians for "trying to impose religion on society." By appealing to natural law, rather than religion itself, the Christian can counter this criticism. For example, many Roman Catholics have argued that the case against abortion is not religious at all, but based only on scientific judgments about the nature of the unborn. So they oppose abortion by appealing to natural law.

Natural law is understood to be a moral order, found in nature and in man himself. It is accessible through reason and conscience. Knowledge of it does not require Scripture or God's saving grace. Following Aquinas, J. Budziszewski defines natural law as "moral principles that are both right for everybody and knowable to everybody by the ordinary exercise of human reason."[6]

Budziszewski says that reason comes to know natural law through God's general revelation.[7] He mentions five forms of general revelation: (1) creation's testimony to the existence of the true God, (2) "the fact that we are made in the image of God," (3) "the facts of our physical and emotional design," (4) "the law of conscience," (5) "the order of causality, which teaches us by linking every sin with consequences (Proverbs 1:31)."[8]

Several questions should occur to those who have accepted my own account of general revelation (chapter 9):

1. Scripture says that those who lack saving grace repress the truths of general revelation, exchanging them for a lie (Rom. 1:18, 25). Does that not make it impossible to base an ethic on general revelation alone? Budziszewski agrees that sinners hold down the truth, and that "persistence in such pretense darkens or perverts such natural knowledge as God has given us."[9] He says that "the human race has been in the condition psychologists call 'denial' ever since the Fall."[10] Nevertheless, Budziszewski

---

6. J. Budziszewski, *Written on the Heart: the Case for Natural Law* (Downers Grove, IL: InterVarsity Press, 1997), 109.

7. Recall my discussion of general revelation in chapter 9.

8. Budziszewski, *Written on the Heart*, 180–81. He says on 181: "The doctrine of natural law is grounded by the second, third, fourth and fifth of God's ways of general revelation." He does not explain his omission of the first form of general revelation. Elsewhere, as on p. 210, he argues that natural law loses its force if it is not seen as the law of a personal Creator, so the first form would seem to be as relevant as the others.

9. Ibid., 182.

10. Ibid., 183. See also his account of denial in *The Revenge of Conscience* (Dallas: Spence Publishing Co., 1999), 84–86.

notes that when the apostles in the New Testament confront Gentiles with the gospel, they appeal to the "testimony of creation."[11]

It is difficult to understand how best to coordinate depravity with common grace. But it is right to say that depravity is never so extreme that it entirely blots out God's law from the unbeliever's consciousness. Romans 1 teaches that the unbeliever knows it well enough that when he rebels against it, it leaves him without excuse (Rom. 1:20, 32). So I would say that the non-Christian both knows and suppresses the truth, and his knowledge of the truth may sometimes be conscious.[12] It is not wrong, therefore, to say that he is aware of God's moral standards through general revelation. Here I agree with Budziszewski.

But the rather precarious status of general revelation in the nonbeliever's consciousness calls in question the likelihood of that revelation producing a stable moral consensus in modern secular culture sufficient to govern nations.

2. What is the role of Scripture in natural law ethics? Obviously, for Aristotle, the Stoics, and other pagan predecessors of modern natural law theory, there is no role for Scripture at all. Aquinas, Grotius, and others, however, have had to deal with the relationship of natural law to Scripture. It has sometimes been tempting for natural law ethicists to leave Scripture out of the picture, regarding it as a theological, rather than an ethical, authority. But that won't do, if I have been right about the comprehensiveness of Scripture (see chapter 10).

Budziszewski, however, has a high view of biblical authority and often argues for the existence of natural law by appealing to Scripture. At one point, he relates natural law to Scripture as follows:

> There is a natural law, and it can be known and philosophically analyzed. But that which is beside the Scripture can be vindicated only with the help of Scripture; that which is revealed before the gospel can be secured against evasion only in the light of the gospel. The doctrine of natural law is best grounded not in the study of nature independent of God's Word but in the Word of God itself. I do not mean that natural law is the same as Divine law; I do mean that Scripture is our foremost authority about both.[13]

11. Budziszewski, *Written on the Heart*, 183.

12. The Pharisees who oppose Jesus in the Gospels would be an example of a conscious understanding of moral truth, accompanied by an unregenerate nature. For a fuller analysis of this question, see my *Cornelius Van Til* (Phillipsburg, NJ: P&R Publishing, 1995), 187–230.

13. Budziszewski, *Written on the Heart*, 183–84; cf. 186.

Budziszewski admits, however, that natural law theories often fail to be fully scriptural:

> Even among Christian philosophers the doctrine of natural law often fails to measure up. Either it focuses on matters peripheral to the text and the devices of our heart, or it wanders from its scriptural foundation. To one degree or another these have been flaws of almost all previous natural-law theorizing, including my own—and nearly all books about it, perhaps including the present one.[14]

This statement is a remarkable expression of candor. And I do appreciate Budziszewski's attempt to bring Scripture into his argument in a way that has not been common in the natural law tradition. But still more needs to be said.

If "that which is beside the Scripture can be vindicated only with the help of Scripture," then appeals to natural law depend on Scripture. If one presents a natural-law argument to someone who doesn't believe in natural law, who keeps challenging the authority on which the law is based, ultimately the argument must have recourse to Scripture. So natural-law arguments ultimately depend on arguments from Scripture. The argument is not merely "Play fair, because that is the natural law," or even "Play fair, because you cannot help believing in fair play," but "Play fair, because you cannot help believing in fair play, and we know that because the Bible says so."

Of course, to say that is to remove much of the appeal of the natural law tradition, which is the claim that we may argue objective principles of ethics without recourse to Scripture. If Budziszewski and I are right, there is no such thing as a natural-law argument apart from Scripture. Natural-law arguments are, in fact, natural-law arguments warranted by the Bible. That doesn't mean that every natural-law argument must be accompanied by Bible texts; rather, when an argument attempts to trace natural law back to its ultimate foundation, that foundation must be located in Scripture.

This is, in fact, what the Bible itself would lead us to expect. When God spoke with Adam in the garden, he presupposed that Adam had some natural knowledge of trees and animals and such. But he did not want Adam to interpret these objects autonomously, apart from God's own spoken word. Similarly, throughout the Bible, God expects human beings to interpret the world by his word, so that all human knowledge is a knowledge of world and word at the same time. This principle is especially important since the

14. Ibid., 186.

fall, though it would have been important even if Adam had not fallen. For since the fall, human beings do distort natural revelation (Rom. 1). That distortion can be removed only by saving grace, and saving grace comes through the gospel, the message of Scripture.

So, although nonbelievers have a certain knowledge of God apart from Scripture, which challenges them even though they repress it (as we saw above), that is not a desirable situation. It would be far better if they came to know God through the gospel and then learned to look at every fact in the world through the "spectacles" of Scripture.

3. But, given that Budziszewski recognizes a significant role for Scripture in warranting natural law, why do we need natural law at all? What use is natural law, when we have the Bible? Budziszewski answers, "The main use of general revelation, including the natural law, is apologetics: giving a reason for the hope that lies within us. I do not mean that in apologetics we always *refer* to the natural law but that we depend on its existence."[15] He mentions three forms of apologetics: evangelical, moral, and political. In evangelical apologetics, we seek to persuade people of the truth of the gospel. In moral apologetics, we "engage in ethical persuasion or counsel."[16] In political apologetics, we seek

> to leaven the civil law we share with our nonbelieving neighbors—for instance, when we seek agreement that life in the womb should not be destroyed, that sodomy should not be granted legal equivalence with marriage, or that sick people should be cared for and comforted instead of starved or pressured into suicide. In this area we can hardly get far by proclaiming to nonbelievers "The Bible says!" But we can get somewhere by proclaiming extrabiblical truths which we know, on biblical authority, that the nonbeliever really knows too.[17]

Budziszewski is himself a skillful and cogent apologist in moral and political matters. His *What We Can't Not Know*[18] is, on the whole, a brilliant defense of basic ethical norms. He is at his best with "the basics of right and wrong,"[19] such as "Play fair," "Don't murder," and "Take care of your family." Everyone, he says, acknowledges these standards. Even when people are unfair, they maintain that they are fair, rather than repudiate fairness. When they make excuses for their misdeeds, they appeal to these and other

---

15. Ibid, 184.
16. Ibid.
17. Ibid.
18. J. Budziszewski, *What We Can't Not Know* (Dallas: Spence Publishing Co., 2003). The dialogue on pp. 107–35 is an admirable example of that philosophical genre.
19. Budziszewski, *What We Can't Not Know*, 112.

basic ethical standards. In the few instances where they repudiate these ethical standards, they nevertheless use these standards to rebuke others.

In *The Revenge of Conscience*, Budziszewski takes another apologetic approach, showing how repressing the conscience leads to worse and worse moral conduct and to natural consequences, as when sexual immorality leads to sexually transmitted diseases.[20]

But when natural law thinkers get beyond these basics, I find them less persuasive. Roman Catholic writers often argue that since there is a natural connection between sexual relations and procreation, contraception is wrong. That argument seems to me to be a naturalistic fallacy (an argument from is to ought): sex leads to procreation, so sex *ought* to lead to procreation. Budziszewski defends natural law theory against the charge of naturalistic fallacy by saying,

> An "is" which merely "happens to be" has no moral significance because it is arbitrary; that's why it cannot imply an "ought." But an "is" which expresses the purposes of the Creator is fraught with an "ought" already. Such are the inbuilt features of our design, including the design of deep conscience.[21]

This argument is essentially the same as my own defense of Christian-theistic ethics against the charge of naturalistic fallacy (see chapter 5). And Budziszewski does show in various ways that natural law is a law of God, not merely a human conjecture about the natural purposes of things. But in the argument against contraception and in other arguments, it is difficult to show that the proposed restriction is in fact a law of God. I shall try to show under the seventh commandment that Scripture doesn't teach it. And in the absence of biblical support, I don't know how one could show that God forbids contraception. Opposition to contraception is not like opposition to murder, stealing, unfairness, or betraying friends. One can use means of birth control without evident inconsistency with universally acknowledged moral principles.[22]

The same is true in the argument over abortion. Later I shall try to present an argument against abortion from Scripture. But if we set Scripture aside, the natural-law argument runs like this:

(1) It is wrong to take the life of an innocent human person.
(2) Abortion takes the life of an innocent human person.
Therefore, abortion is wrong.

20. Budziszewski, *The Revenge of Conscience*, 20–38.
21. Budziszewski, *What We Can't Not Know*, 108.
22. I shall discuss this issue in more detail, including the possibility of a natural-law argument, under the seventh commandment.

But how do we establish from natural law alone the personhood of the unborn child, as presupposed in the second premise? Usually the argument is that the unborn child is genetically different from his parents and therefore not "a part of his mother's body." But there is a logical jump between genetic uniqueness and personhood. Genetic uniqueness is a physical property, but personhood is a moral one, implying moral rights. How can it be shown that genetic uniqueness conveys a right to life? I believe that Scripture teaches that the unborn child is a person, but it is by no means evident how that conclusion can be proved by natural law. So natural-law arguments often cry out for scriptural supplementation.

And if we can't argue an ethical point from Scripture, it would be best not to argue it at all. In chapter 11, on the sufficiency of Scripture, I tried to show that Scripture contains a complete transcript of God's will for ethics. So principles that cannot be established from Scripture cannot be established by natural-law arguments either. When people try to add to God's word by natural-law arguments, they violate the sufficiency of Scripture. This is not to say that it is wrong to use natural-law arguments. As Budziszewski shows, they can be very useful. But if I am right, these arguments have significant limitations.

I conclude, then, that natural law is an important apologetic tool, but it does not provide ethical norms in addition to those in Scripture. And those who use natural-law arguments need to beware of naturalistic fallacies.

4. A final question about natural law is whether it is adequate to govern civil society.

Aquinas distinguishes several kinds of law: (1) eternal law (God's own mind), (2) natural law ("the reflection of eternal law in the very structure of the created rational mind, directing us to our natural good"[23]), (3) divine law (Scripture), and (4) human law (laws of civil society). Aquinas says that human law should be derived from natural law, not divine law. Why? Budziszewski paraphrases Aquinas's answer: "Because government is charged with directing the community to its natural rather than its supernatural good, so God does not intend the enforcement of Divine law upon nonbelievers."[24] He adds, however, as Aquinas surely would, that "even if human law should not enforce Divine law, it should not *violate* it either—not any more than it may violate natural law."[25]

As an example, Budziszewski argues that the biblical principle, "I am prohibited from divorcing a faithful spouse," should not be imposed as law

---

23. Budziszewski, *Written on the Heart*, 61.
24. Ibid., 63.
25. Ibid.

on civil society without "a good deal of watering down."[26] The reason is that "before the coming of Christ not even believers were expected to understand the true nature of marriage" (cf. Matt. 19:8).[27]

I agree that we should exercise care when turning biblical principles into civil law. Not every command in Scripture is appropriate for civil law (for example, commands about the attitudes of our heart, as in Deut. 6:4–5). And not every command that is appropriate for civil law should be enacted in every nation, at least immediately. As I indicated in the discussion of theonomy, in chapter 13, some laws, like the death penalty for adultery, presuppose a national commitment to God's lordship and a population instructed in God's law.

But I cannot agree with Aquinas and Budziszewski that natural law alone, without the supplementation of Scripture, *should* determine the civil law. For one thing, I question Aquinas's distinction between natural and supernatural goods, and his limitation of the state's competence to the former, as I shall indicate in later discussions. And if that distinction cannot be maintained, then I see no reason to argue that Scripture should be excluded from influence on civil law.

This is not to say that I would necessarily quote Scripture texts in the context of political debate. As Budziszewski says, "In this area we can hardly get far by proclaiming to unbelievers 'The Bible says!' But we can get somewhere by proclaiming extrabiblical truths which we know, on biblical authority, that the nonbeliever really knows too."[28] But surely our goal is to get beyond these extrabiblical truths. As Budziszewski himself argued, natural laws are not fully warranted without an appeal to Scripture (as we saw above). And I have argued further that we should never investigate nature, except through the spectacles of Scripture.

The same conclusion follows from the very nature of politics, according to Scripture. The ultimate goal of political apologetics is nothing less than to present Christ as King of kings and Lord of lords. The political goal of biblical Christianity is a civil state that acknowledges him for who he is. Every institution of human culture, as well as every individual human being, is called to pay homage to King Jesus.[29] We may not reach that goal in the course of modern political debate, but that is where the debate should point, and we may well find occasion to tell nonbelievers, in all honesty, that this is the direction in which we would urge society to move.

26. Budziszewski, *The Revenge of Conscience*, 112.
27. Ibid.
28. Budziszewski, *Written on the Heart*, 184.
29. More will be said on this in our discussion of the fifth commandment.

And if the Lord tarries, it should not be unthinkable that one day our society could become predominantly Christian, so that the people will be, not only tolerant of biblical arguments, but eager to hear them. When and if that happens, we should certainly not refuse to bring the Bible into the public square.

Some readers, including some Christians, might disagree with this understanding of Jesus' lordship and its relevance to the state. But, at the very least, this is a view that many Christians have held. It would be wrong to limit political discourse so as to exclude such a view *a priori*. Secularists are eager to keep "religious" views out of the public square, an utterly undemocratic restriction. Christians should oppose all such limitations, even the exclusion of views they reject.

So although I would not insist on bringing up Bible passages in every political debate, I think we should not exclude them, either. Budziszewski says that "Scripture is our foremost authority about [natural law as well as divine law]."[30] There is no reason to deprive unbelieving society of this authoritative source, when they need it so badly, and when they need to know so much that natural law cannot supply.

In my judgment, the natural law tradition contains both bad and good. It is important for us to be discerning, here as always, to "take every thought captive to obey Christ" (2 Cor. 10:5).[31]

---

30. Budziszewski, *Written on the Heart*, 184.

31. For a more elaborate critique of natural law theory, as exemplified in writers such as John Courtney Murray, Jacques Maritain, and Ken Myers, see Peter J. Leithart, *Natural Law: A Reformed Critique* (Niceville, FL: Biblical Horizons, 1996). I think Leithart's treatment of human depravity needs more nuance, but he makes a powerful case for the use of Scripture in political discourse. At least some of the weaknesses that Leithart attributes to natural law thinkers have been overcome somewhat by Budziszewski, who has evidently been in correspondence with him (see Budziszewski, *The Revenge of Conscience*, xviii). That is why I have focused so closely on Budziszewski in this chapter. But Budziszewski has not come to see clearly the political claims of Christ in Scripture. For more on this subject, see my discussion of the fifth commandment.

CHAPTER 15

Our Ethical Situation

In this chapter, I will attempt to describe our ethical situation as Scripture presents it. That is, what are the chief facts that we must take into account when making ethical decisions? How does the Bible characterize our ethical environment?[1] As I indicated in the previous chapter, just as there are various levels within the normative perspective (God, revelation, verbal revelation, etc.), so there are various levels of facts that we deal with in the world. These include God, angels, human society, individual existence, and nature. Let us look at each one.

GOD

I have already said much about the role of God in our ethical decisions—both in this volume and, in effect, in *The Doctrine of God*—and I will say much more. So the present discussion will be much shorter than the subject warrants. But I will offer some summary thoughts.

Just as God himself is our chief norm, so also is he the chief fact of our experience, the chief person "with whom we have to do" (Heb. 4:13 KJV). He is our ultimate situation, for everything else in our environment,

---

1. Of course, it is also important to discuss the evidence of natural revelation about the facts that form our ethical environment. I shall try to do that a bit in my later chapters on Christ and culture. But natural revelation is so vast that it would be impossible to do justice to it in a single book.

including ourselves, comes from his eternal decree (Eph. 1:11), his creation (Neh. 9:6), and his providence (Acts 17:26; Heb. 1:3).

He is not just a fact among other facts. He is the all-conditioner,[2] the fact from which every other fact receives its existence and nature. So he is the fact that is revealed in every fact, the fact we encounter in every fact. As Calvin said, therefore, all that we do is *coram Deo*, "in the presence of God." Wherever we go, he is there (Ps. 139).

The biblical view of God is radically different from the views of God found in other religions, philosophies, and worldviews. That difference can be summarized under three headings:

The Creator. No other worldview presents us with a God who created all things out of nothing. Some worldviews are pantheistic, believing that the supreme being is the whole universe. Others offer no account of the origins of all things. For pantheistic and nonpantheistic alternatives to the biblical worldview, all reality is equal in dignity and authority. But in Scripture, there are two levels of reality, the divine and the nondivine, the Creator and the creatures. The Creator has ultimate power and authority; the creature does not. The ethical importance of this fact is staggering. In every ethical decision, the first consideration must be how that decision will affect our relation to God.

Absolute personality. It is also the case, as we saw in chapter 5, that only in Scripture is the supreme being an absolute person. There are personal gods in polytheistic religions, but they are not absolute. There are absolutes of a sort in worldviews like Hinduism and Hegelianism, but those absolutes are not personal. Only in biblical Christianity (and to some extent in religions influenced by the Bible) is there a being who is truly supreme, absolute, and personal. Our God is not only our Creator; he also knows, loves, feels, and speaks to his creatures. Life *coram Deo* is a fully personal relationship. So in our ethical decisions we are interested above all in what God thinks and how he feels about what we do.

Lordship. Again, I mention the importance of covenant lordship, the specific relationship that God has formed with his creatures. That relationship involves control, authority, and presence, and we have explored, in chapter 3 and elsewhere, the ethical implications of these lordship attributes.

2. Cornelius Van Til, *Why I Believe in God* (Philadelphia: Committee on Christian Education, Orthodox Presbyterian Church, n.d.). This pamphlet is available on various websites and in Greg Bahnsen, *Van Til's Apologetic* (Phillipsburg, NJ: P&R Publishing, 1998), 121–43.

1. God controls all there is, including our environment. Whether we find ourselves in happy or difficult situations, God has placed us there. So we should regard our situation, not as a predicament brought on us by impersonal fate, but as an opportunity and/or a challenge, brought to us by our covenant Lord.

2. God speaks to us with supreme authority. We have explored the implications of this fact under the normative perspective.

3. God is the ultimate presence, the one who is closest to us, the one with whom, of all persons, we have the most to do. He is not far away from us; indeed, he is always inescapable. We live *coram Deo*. So God sees all we do, and he evaluates all we do, in blessing and in judgment. Yet he not only evaluates our conduct, but also draws near to give grace, undeserved favor, beyond anything we can ask or think. He sent his Son to dwell among us (John 1:14) and to die the death we deserve. He sends his Spirit to comfort, sanctify, and lead us into all truth. Our ethical life is a deepening of that relationship, a walking together with God.

THE ANGELS

The Bible also presents angelic beings as beings "with whom we have to do," as one of the environments of the Christian life. It is hard for the modern Christian to know what to make of this. Believers in Bible times were deeply conscious of the presence of angels in their midst, as when Paul mentions that women should wear a head covering "because of the angels" (1 Cor. 11:10). Paul feels no need to explain this phrase. He assumes that the Corinthians will understand what he means. But I recall my revered professor of theology, John Murray, shaking his head sadly after reading this passage and confessing that he had no idea what it meant. Nor can I offer insight. Modern Christians, including myself, have lost the vivid consciousness of angelic beings that New Testament believers took for granted. Some popular writers and television shows have recently explored claims of angelic activity in our time, but these seem like cultural curiosities without much intellectual or spiritual weight.

Part of the problem is that modern people have lost touch with the supernatural and preternatural.[3] They have become skeptical of any world or any beings beyond those that are detectable by our senses. Christians believe in God, but they have absorbed enough of the antisupernaturalism

---

3. In traditional theology, God and his works are supernatural, "above nature"; angels and their works are preternatural, "beyond nature."

of modern culture that belief in angels seems foreign to them. It seems that belief in God is hard enough. Why add further difficulty by bringing angels into it? And if God is sovereign, what need do we have for preternatural beings? God is the one who judges and blesses us, sometimes in extraordinary ways. Why are angels important?

But Scripture itself mentions angels over three hundred times. This suggests that we need to take angels into account in our ethical decisions. Being a modern person myself, I don't pretend to have gotten very deeply into the doctrine of angels, but I would cautiously venture the following thoughts.

The doctrine of angels rebukes the smallness and impersonalism of our cosmology. Modern worldviews typically claim to have discovered a much larger universe than was known to the ancients and medievals. But they have a much smaller view of the universe of persons, having abandoned belief in God and in angels. According to Scripture, however, there are vast numbers of angels that inhabit the world. So we need to develop a larger perspective. In 2 Kings 6, Elisha's servant was terrified by the armies of Syria surrounding their city. Elisha comforted him with a vision of angels:

> He said, "Do not be afraid, for those who are with us are more than those who are with them." Then Elisha prayed and said, "O Lord, please open his eyes that he may see." So the Lord opened the eyes of the young man, and he saw, and behold, the mountain was full of horses and chariots of fire all around Elisha. (vv. 16–17)

Mysterious warriors—even mysterious horses!—were poised to bring victory to the prophet (in a most mysterious way, as the later verses indicate). Elisha's servant needed a larger cosmology, one allowing for more persons. He needed to understand, further, that the physical conflict is only part of a larger spiritual conflict, a larger warfare, as we will discuss further below.

So the doctrine of angels makes our worldview even more personalistic. It reminds us not only that God is a divine person, but that many of the means he uses to bring about events in the world are also personal, rather than impersonal. Scripture has little if anything to say about natural laws and forces, but much to say about God's personal agents, both angels and men. Typically, God does not press buttons; he sends messengers. This is important, because impersonalism always detracts from ethical responsibility.

The doctrine of angels shows us something of the dimensions of our ethical-spiritual warfare. We see this in at least three ways:

1. Angels participate in kingdom warfare. Above and around us are good and evil angels, engaged in spiritual warfare. Satan and his hosts engage human beings in the battle by tempting them to sin. The good angels, however, are "ministering spirits sent out to serve for the sake of those who are to inherit salvation" (Heb. 1:14). The two armies fight one another, as well as fighting against and for us (Dan. 10:13, 21; Jude 9; Rev. 12:7).

So Scripture urges us not to underestimate the difficulty of the struggle, as if we could succeed with human resources alone (Eph. 6:10–20). If we were fighting human beings, physical weapons would prevail, though even in human warfare God's will is decisive. But we are fighting beings who are far more intelligent, strong, and numerous than we are, and who, to us, are exceedingly mysterious.

On the other hand, we should not overestimate the difficulty, either, for there are angels fighting on our side (2 Kings 6:15–17) and the spiritual weapons of Ephesians 6 are sufficient.

It might seem uninteresting to conclude with the advice not to underestimate and not to overestimate the difficulty of the spiritual battle. But the main point here is that we should not base either our hopes or our fears on the empirical situation alone. News media and opinion makers in our culture seem to think that the most important issues are political, followed closely by entertainment. But Scripture says otherwise. The really decisive issues of human life are ethical and spiritual. And it is the religious and ethical equipment God gives us that will prevail over the hosts of evil.

2. Angels are witnesses to human salvation (Luke 12:8–9; 15:10; 1 Cor. 4:9; Eph. 3:10; 1 Tim. 3:16; 1 Peter 1:12; Rev. 4:6–8). Although angels participate in the redemptive drama, there is another sense in which they are spectators rather than participants. Redemption doesn't extend to them, for unfallen angels need no redemption, and fallen angels receive none (cf. Heb. 2:16). So, although the angels contend for God's redemptive purposes, they do not have the experience of being redeemed themselves. Scripture sometimes pictures them as standing in amazement, looking in from the outside, as it were. Remarkably, they even learn the wisdom of God from observing the church (Eph. 3:10). It is our privilege to teach the angels by our words and life!

3. The doctrine of angels is a measure of the greatness of our salvation in Christ, for salvation lifts us above the angels. According to Hebrews 2:9, Jesus was made, for a little while, lower than the angels for the suffering of death. But in his resurrection he is again exalted above them. The passage implies that Jesus' brothers, the church, share that exaltation with him, fulfilling man's dominion over the earth (Gen. 1:28; Ps. 8). Although we do not yet see everything subject to man, we see this dominion in Jesus (Heb. 2:8). So

the angels minister to us, not vice versa (Heb. 1:14). The world to come is not theirs, but ours (Heb. 2:5–8; cf. Paul's odd statement that we shall judge angels, 1 Cor. 6:3). It belongs to man, God's image, not the angels.

Scripture applies these facts by indicating that angel worship is not only a sin, but also a delusion, from which Christ has set us free (Col. 2:18–19; Rev. 19:10; 22:8–9). Further, because of redemption, the prince of the evil angels, Satan himself, is a defeated foe. We may resist him, and he will flee (1 Peter 5:8–9; James 4:7).

HUMAN SOCIETY

A much more visible dimension of our ethical environment is the social dimension. We live with other people. God expects us to take our fellow human beings into account when we make moral decisions. I shall say much more about social ethics in connection with the fifth through tenth commandments of the Decalogue. But here I wish to make some general observations.

THE CULTURAL MANDATE: A CORPORATE TASK

From the beginning of our existence, ethical life has presupposed a community. The first creation ordinance, the cultural mandate of Genesis 1:28, comes to Adam and Eve together ("And God blessed *them*. And God said to *them*"). Adam alone could not have filled and subdued the earth.[4] Since God made man male and female, and since reproduction is itself part of the cultural task, God evidently intended from the beginning that this work be carried out as a corporate task, a task for the whole human race. The individual is not responsible to fill and subdue the earth. His responsibility, rather, is to make the best contribution to this task that he can.

Thus, from the very beginning, God intended for us to make our individual decisions by taking other people into account, and specifically by seeking how we can best help our fellow human beings in their divinely ordained tasks.

THE FALL: A CORPORATE FAILURE

God made Eve to be a helper to Adam (Gen. 2:18) in every respect, and therefore also in the ethico-religious sphere. Both were to encourage one

4. Cf. the discussion in chapter 13, under "Existential Priorities."

another in keeping the commands of God. But in the fall, Eve took on the role of Satan, becoming a temptress rather than a helper to her husband. And Adam forsook his headship in the family, capitulating to the sinful request of his wife.

So the fall involved, not only individual sins on the part of Adam and Eve, but simultaneously a breakdown of their relationship with each other. God had intended human beings to have dominion over the animals, the man to have authority over his wife,[5] and all human beings to be subordinate to him. In the narrative of the fall, Satan inhabits an animal, who takes dominion of the woman, who usurps the authority of the man, who blames it all on God (Gen. 3:1). So Satan seeks an exact reversal of the authority structure.

We see the destruction of their relationship also in the sexual shame between the man and the woman (Gen. 3:7, 10–11, 21; cf. 2:25), in Adam's blaming of his wife for his sin (3:12), and in the further breakdown in family harmony implied in 3:16. By God's curse, both elements of the family task, childbearing and labor, are to be painful (3:16–19). So we see at the very beginning of the history of redemption that disobedience to God brought consequences upon corporate human society, as well as upon individuals.

FALLEN SOCIETY

People sometimes ask whether sin is a merely individual thing, or whether it has corporate dimensions. A related question is whether there are sinful structures in society. I believe that sin is basically individual, because it is personal. But sinful individuals contaminate the institutions they inhabit, and those institutions make the effects of sin even worse. When sinners gather together, they can accomplish more wickedness than they can individually.

In Genesis 4:17–24, the descendants of Cain develop the earliest forms of culture. These developments are not evil in themselves. But Moses chooses, as a paradigm of the moral quality of that culture, Lamech's song of vengeance (vv. 23–24).

It is hard to know what sin it was that so provoked the Lord in Genesis 6:1–7,[6] but evidently at that point human wickedness reached a zenith, so that "every intention of the thoughts of his heart was only evil continually"

5. I'll try to justify this nonfeminist reading at a later point. For now, consider 1 Cor. 11:3; Eph. 5:22–24; 1 Tim. 2:8–15.

6. Scholars have made various suggestions: (1) marriages between Sethites and Cainites, (2) sexual relationships between women and angelic beings, and (3) royal polygamy. I'm somewhat inclined toward the third suggestion.

(v. 5). God sent the great flood as a judgment. But the flood did not wash away sin. In Genesis 8:21, God in effect repeats the condemnation of 6:5: "The intention of man's heart is evil from his youth."

So in Genesis 11, there is another compounding of sin through corporate unity. People build a city and a tower "lest we be dispersed over the face of the whole earth" (v. 4), defying God, who had commanded the human race to be dispersed (1:28). In preparing his judgment, the Lord comments on the effect of this corporate enterprise on the moral character of the human race: "Behold, they are one people, and they have all one language, and this is only the beginning of what they will do. And nothing that they propose to do will now be impossible for them" (Gen. 11:6).

The compounding of evil through corporate units then becomes a common biblical theme. There are not only wicked people, but wicked cities: Sodom, Gomorrah, Tyre, Sidon, Chorazin, Bethsaida, Capernaum (Matt. 11:20–24). There are also wicked nations: the Canaanites, Moab, Edom, Ammon, Amalek, Assyria, Babylon, Egypt, etc. Here the sinful practices of individuals are reinforced by social agreements, covenants, and traditions. Sinful patterns of life become accepted by society, and therefore they are more easily accepted by individuals. So sinful individuals corrupt society and vice versa.

Biblical apocalyptic (Daniel; Matt. 24; Mark 13; Luke 21; Revelation) presents the ultimate spiritual battle as a battle between two kingdoms: the kingdom of God and the kingdom of human national-ecclesiastical units under the ultimate rule of Satan.

The Corporate Character of Redemption

But redemption, too, has a corporate dimension. As Satan works through institutions and groups, so does God. Even after the fall, the cultural mandate continues as our corporate task. Childbearing and labor bring toil and pain, but ultimately they succeed in keeping the human race alive until God sends the Redeemer.

And God redeems, not only individuals, but peoples. The book of Genesis describes the process of election,[7] in which God chooses one family and rejects another for his purposes of redemption. He chooses the family of Seth, rather than the family of Cain. He chooses Noah's family from all the others. He chooses the descendants of Shem over those of Ham and Japheth, Peleg over Joktan (Gen. 10:25?), Abraham over Nahor and

---

7. In terms of the distinction made in *DG*, chapter 16, I am speaking here primarily of historical election, not eternal election, though the former is an image of the latter.

Haran, Isaac over Ishmael, Jacob over Esau. In his covenant with Abraham, God ordains circumcision as a sign and seal of covenant membership, identifying the family of God and distinguishing them from all the other families of the world.

The equivalent to circumcision in the new covenant is baptism. Infant baptism is a controversial doctrine in the church today, but certainly the Jews of the first century who first heard the gospel would have assumed that their children were included in the new covenant, as in the Abrahamic covenant. That assumption would have been strengthened by Peter's statement that "the promise is for you and for your children" (Acts 2:39) and by the regular baptism of households (Acts 11:14; 16:15, 31–33; 1 Cor. 1:16). Nothing in the New Testament suggests a change from the Old Testament principle of family membership in the covenant. So we should recognize that in the New Testament too, God claims for himself, not only individuals, but also families.

After God claimed the family of Israel, it grew into a great nation. Additional institutions were needed to order different aspects of family life. So God gave to Israel prophetic, priestly, and kingly institutions. In the new covenant too there are apostles, prophets, pastor-teachers, elders, and deacons. As sinful institutions magnify the power of sin in the world, so godly institutions, working as God intends, magnify the influence of righteousness and grace.

In the consummation of history, there will be, not only a new heaven and a new earth, but also a city, the new Jerusalem. The goal of history is for God's righteousness to take institutional form, as well as to take root in the hearts of individuals.

Corporate Life and Moral Decisions (Summary)

God intends for us to help one another in our common task, not to try to do everything alone. He authorizes us to seek help and guidance from those equipped to give it. Because of sin, however, other people are not only helpers, but tempters as well. So there is a need for vigilance, testing, and proving, as well as for trust. The Russian proverb quoted often by President Reagan puts it well: "Trust, but verify." Temptation and sinful influence are compounded by the development of social institutions in unregenerate society.

But redemption builds a new society, in which we can again expect to work together with other people in a constructive way, carrying out God's commands. In that society, we can expect help, not only of a natural kind, but also help that comes from the gifts of the Holy Spirit. So we meet

Christ in our brothers and sisters. The highest gift is the highest task, to love one another.

The blessing of the Spirit is magnified in the development of godly institutions. Indeed, regenerate people cannot help but bring God's standards into their places of service: businesses, schools, the arts, technology, agriculture, labor, and even government (1 Cor. 10:31 again). Christians have an obligation to address all areas of human life, including all social institutions, with the commands of God. In some cases, as history has shown, this will lead to distinctively Christian institutions within the larger society. In other cases, it will bring about change in the secular institutions themselves.

LIVING WITH OURSELVES

But Christian ethics is individual as well as social. Even in deciding how to contribute to a corporate project, we must make individual decisions. And in doing so, each person should take account of his own strengths and weaknesses, opportunities and limitations.

In some ways, all human beings are alike, made in the image of God, under his lordship, responsible to him in every area of life, but fallen into sin. All Christians are also alike in that they are redeemed by Christ. They are new creatures in Christ, free from sin's dominion, filled with gifts of the Spirit. In all Christians, also, sin itself lingers until the consummation.

But in other respects, each of us differs from every other person, and every Christian differs from every other Christian. We have different personalities, different abilities and disabilities, different histories and experiences. In the body of Christ, each of us plays a unique role, with distinctive callings, gifts, and opportunities.

And each of us fights, in some ways, a unique spiritual battle. Generically, the temptations we face are "common to man" (1 Cor. 10:13). They can be summarized as temptations to violate any of the Ten Commandments. Hence, Hebrews 4:15 tells us that Jesus was tempted "in every respect . . . as we are." But these temptations take different forms in each person's life. All of us are tempted to steal, for example, but in different ways. Some are tempted to steal from individuals, others "only" from corporations or government, via such things as fraudulent use of warranties or tax evasion. Others of us are tempted mainly to steal honor that belongs to God.

All of us are tempted sexually. But some are tempted to homosexual sins, and others to heterosexual sins. All of us are tempted to dishonor our parents, but some are tempted to despise their counsel, while others are tempted to leave them without support in their old age.

Each of us has unique moral responsibilities, which are applications of our general moral responsibilities. Scripture teaches us to keep our contracts and work hard. For some, that will mean showing up regularly each day at a corporate office. For others, it will mean delivering a sermon each Sunday in a Presbyterian church. For others, it will mean doing the wash, cooking meals, and raising young children.

So moral decisions require us to take into account both the similarities and the differences between ourselves and others. That is to say that each of us must apply the Word of God to his own unique situation. Although we can and should seek help from others, no one else can do this for us.

Strange as it may sound, then, the self is a crucial element of its own environment. As we must learn to live with God, angels, and other people, so we must learn to live with ourselves. Here the situational and existential perspectives coincide.

I would now like to look more closely at two areas where living with ourselves is a crucial consideration.

LIVING WITH OUR GENES

One particular problem often discussed today in this area is the bearing of genetic inheritance upon moral responsibility. The rapid progress of genetic science has brought certain interesting facts to our attention. Some years ago, it was learned that an abnormally high proportion of boys with a double Y chromosome (XYY) engage in anti-social or criminal behavior. There was discussion of whether that discovery might help us in maintaining social stability. Should we abort children who have this genetic combination? Should we test children early for this condition and take special pains to steer XYY boys into constructive paths? Should we seek ways to change the genetic makeup of such children?

Later came the discovery that a certain gene is associated with a relatively high percentage of alcoholics. And then Simon LeVay, a gay activist and neuroscientist, published a paper in *Science* arguing that there are some minute but statistically significant differences between heterosexual and homosexual men in the size of the "INAH-3" region of the anterior hypothalamus, part of the brain.[8] Some have argued that this discovery tends to establish what gay activists have long been saying, namely, that

8. S. LeVay, "A Difference in Hypothalamic Structure Between Heterosexual and Homosexual Men," *Science* 253 (1991):1034–37.

homosexuality is an innate condition rather than a "choice," that it cannot be helped, and therefore that it should be accepted as normal.

I am not competent to evaluate LeVay's research. For a brief scientific critique by a Christian who appears at least to know what he's talking about, see P. D. Brown, "Science and Sodomy."[9] I do think that we are wise to suspend judgment until LeVay's work is corroborated by others who are more objective on the question. However, we should note, as others have, that there is an unanswered "chicken and egg" problem here: how do we know that this condition (or perhaps the larger unexplored physical basis for it) is the cause, and not the result, of homosexual thought and behavior?

And of course we must also remember that these discoveries were made through studies of the brains of people who were exclusively homosexual, compared with brains of people who were (I gather) exclusively heterosexual. But there is a wide spectrum between these two extremes. The exclusively homosexual population seems to be 1–3 percent of the population (the widely used Kinsey figure of 10 percent is now largely discredited). But many more people have bisexual inclinations, and still others are largely heterosexual, but willing to enter homosexual relationships under certain circumstances (experimentation, prison, etc.). Is there a genetic basis for these rather complicated patterns of behavior? Neither LeVay nor anyone else has offered data suggesting that.

But let's assume that there is an innate physical basis for homosexuality, and for alcoholism, and indeed for general criminality. As genetic science has developed over the years, there have been more and more correlations between genetics and behavior, and I expect that trend to continue. What ethical conclusions should we draw?

For one thing, we should not draw the conclusion that gay activists want to draw, namely, that any "innate" condition must therefore be accepted as natural, normal, and ethically right. As Charles Krauthammer points out, innateness has nothing to do with normality.[10] Many diseases, for example, are genetically determined. But we don't consider Tay-Sachs or sickle-cell anemia to be "normal" conditions, let alone to possess some ethical virtue. Nor do we consider alcoholism or XYY anti-social behavior to be normal

9. *Credenda Agenda* 5.3 (1993): 18. An unsigned article, "Is There a 'Gay Gene'?" in *Chalcedon Report*, issue no. 466 (September 2004), 14, says: "According to a March, 2004 report provided by the National Association of Research and Therapy of Homosexuality (NARTH): 'There is no evidence that shows that homosexuality is simply "genetic." . . . *And none of the research claims there is.* Only the press and certain researchers do, when speaking in sound bytes to the public.'"

10. Column in *Escondido Times-Advocate*, July 25, 1993.

and acceptable. Rather, we do all we can to fight them. Genetic discoveries, indeed, open up more possible weapons for this fight. Some have suggested, indeed, that the discovery of a "gay gene" would give us the opportunity, through abortion or genetic manipulation, to eliminate homosexuality (or at least one impulse toward it) from society altogether.[11]

And, of course, to say that innateness entails moral desirability is to commit a textbook example of the naturalistic fallacy.

Further, we must keep these discoveries in perspective. Not everyone who has the XYY genes becomes a criminal, and not everyone with a genetic risk factor for alcoholism actually becomes an alcoholic. Similarly, it is quite unlikely that a "gay gene," should it exist, would actually determine people to be homosexual. Although studies of twins do show a 20-percent correlation between genetics and homosexuality, that leaves a non-correlation of 80 percent. By far, most twin brothers of homosexuals are heterosexual. So the data suggest something less than genetic determinism. Indeed, they suggest that it is possible for someone to resist patterns of behavior to which he is genetically predisposed. Genes do determine eye color, sex, blood type, and so on, but patterns of behavior, although influenced by genetic makeup, do not seem to be controlled by it. The typical behavioral differences between males and females, for example, have a genetic basis, but (as feminists are quick to point out) that genetic basis does not determine how each person will behave in every situation. Some women behave in certain ways more typical of men, and vice versa. Astrologers like to say, "The stars impel, but they do not compel." The same thing (on a sounder scientific footing) would have to be said for the influence of genes on behavior.

Indeed, other sorts of influences are often more compelling than genetic inheritance. An unsigned editorial in *National Review* points out that "the effects of childhood brutalization can restrict one's freedom far more than does a physiological preference for sweets; and many purely biological impulses pale in strength before the smoker's need of a cigarette."[12] So if we excuse homosexuality on the basis of genetic predisposition, we should also excuse all acts resulting from environmental influence and from bad choices in the past. Clearly, however, we should deny the validity of any such excuses. We may not excuse otherwise wrong acts on the ground that they are influenced by "compulsions," hereditary or not.

Nor do we in other cases excuse acts committed on the basis of genetic predispositions. One who has a genetic propensity to alcoholism cannot

11. That is precisely what gay activists *don't* want to hear.
12. Aug. 9, 1993, 17.

excuse his alcoholism on that basis; nor can an XYY man excuse his criminality. These conditions do not force people to do anything contrary to their desires; thus, they do not compromise moral freedom.[13] They do create moral challenges, venues for moral temptation. But that, too, should be seen in perspective: all of us have moral "weak spots," areas where we are especially vulnerable to the devil's enticements. These areas of temptation have many sources, including heredity. Others would be environment, experiences, and our own past decisions. Thus, some have a particular problem with temptation to alcohol abuse; others, because of their early training, personal taste, or social attachments, are not often tempted to commit that particular sin. But they will certainly have other areas of temptation. This is true even for those who are most mature in the Christian faith: such maturity opens one to the temptation of spiritual pride. Thus, the person whose special moral challenges involve a genetic predisposition is not in a unique situation. We all face such challenges; they are never entirely under our control. For all of us, this world is a spiritually dangerous place. Truly, "your adversary the devil prowls around like a roaring lion, seeking someone to devour" (1 Peter 5:8). But thanks to God's grace, we may "resist him, firm in your faith, knowing that the same kinds of suffering are being experienced by your brotherhood throughout the world" (v. 9).

Would a genetic predisposition for homosexuality eliminate the element of choice? Certainly not. A person with a genetic propensity for alcoholism still makes a choice when he decides to take a drink, and then another, and then another. If there is a genetic propensity for homosexuality, then those with that makeup face greater temptation in this area than others. But those who succumb to the temptation do choose to yield to it, as do all of us when we succumb to our own besetting temptations. Homosexuals choose not to remain celibate, and they choose to have sexual relations. They are not forced to do this by their genes or by anything contrary to their own desires.

Is it possible for a homosexual to repent of his sin and, by God's grace, to become heterosexual? Christian ministries to homosexuals claim that this is possible and that it has happened, although they admit that this is a particularly difficult sin to deal with. Sexual orientation is something that goes very deeply into human personality, and we have an instinct to keep it relatively private. That instinct is a good one, but it does make counseling in this area especially difficult. Gay activists claim that transformation of sexual orientation is impossible, and they dispute alleged "ex-gay" testimonies. Indeed, some people who have professed deliverance

---

13. I am assuming here the view of free will developed in *DG*, 119–59.

from homosexuality have later returned to homosexual relationships. And many "ex-gays" have candidly admitted that they continue to experience homosexual attraction, which they now recognize as a moral and spiritual challenge. Pro-gay advocates argue that this lingering homosexual temptation proves that homosexuality is ineradicable.

I believe on faith that God can deliver homosexuals (1 Cor. 6:9–11), because Scripture teaches that his grace can deliver his people from all sin.[14] I haven't done firsthand research on the results of various ministries to homosexuals. It would certainly not surprise me to learn that many people who struggle by God's grace to overcome their homosexuality still experience homosexual temptations. People who have been addicted to alcohol often face continuing temptations in this area long after they have stopped drinking to excess. The same is true of those who have overcome the impulses of hot tempers, drugs, or heterosexual promiscuity. If that were true in regard to repentant homosexuals, it would not cast the slightest doubt on the power of God's grace to heal such people. Recurrent temptation is a problem for all of us, and will be until glory. One may not judge the fruits of Christian ministries on the assumption that deliverance from sin must remove all temptation toward that sin in this life.

The bottom line, however, is that the genetic element in sin does not excuse it. To see that, it is important to put the issue into an even wider perspective. Christianity forces us again and again to widen our viewpoint, for it forces us to see everything from the perspective of a transcendent God and from the standpoint of eternity. Such perspective helps us to see our trials as "slight" and "momentary" (2 Cor. 4:17) and our sins as greater than we normally admit. From a biblical perspective, the difficult fact is that in one sense all sin is inherited. From Adam come both our sin and our misery. We are guilty of Adam's transgression, and from him we ourselves inherit sinful natures. If a genetic predisposition excuses sodomy, then our inheritance from Adam excuses all sin! But that is clearly not the case.[15]

Is that fair? Well, here we resort to the usual defenses of the doctrine of original sin: Adam contained all the (genetic!) potentialities of all of us, and lived in a perfect environment, save one source of temptation. None of us could or would have done any better. And, American individualism to

---

14. John Jefferson Davis asks, "If Masters and Johnson can achieve a 66 percent success rate in dealing with homosexuals with purely secular techniques, can we doubt that with the power of God's Holy Spirit even more dramatic rates of transformation are possible?" *Evangelical Ethics* (Phillipsburg, NJ: P&R Publishing, 2004), 132.

15. Of course, Reformed theology construes our relationship to Adam as representative, rather than *merely* genetic, and that is important. But Adam represents all who are descended from him "by natural generation," so there is also an inevitable genetic element in human sin.

the contrary notwithstanding, the human race is one in important senses, and God is right to judge it as a single entity. In the final analysis, of course, we are his creations. He defines what is fair, and he has the right to do as he pleases with the work of his hands.

In this broad context, the argument that one sin should be declared normal on the basis of a genetic component appears entirely self-serving, and must be dismissed as invalid.

LIVING WITH OUR LIMITATIONS

Another area of current discussion that is related to living with ourselves is the question of accepting our limitations. The Bible teaches that we have two sources of weakness: finitude and sin. In the previous section, we explored one aspect of human sinfulness. In this one, we will explore a dimension of our finitude.

More and more, various groups within society are calling upon governments to remedy the disadvantages that they have relative to other groups. Thus there are today various "rights" movements, demanding remedies against real and alleged oppression based upon race, culture, sex, handicap, sexual orientation, and many other things, such as unusual height or weight. I shall deal with racism, sexism, and other such issues elsewhere. Homosexuality was discussed above and will be treated again in other connections.

For the present, let me use as an example the movement to accommodate persons with disabilities.[16] People with disabilities certainly have a special claim on Christian compassion. God tells Israel, "You shall not curse the deaf or put a stumbling block before the blind, but you shall fear your God: I am the LORD" (Lev. 19:14; cf. Deut. 27:18). Jesus showed his qualifications to be the Messiah by fulfilling Isaiah 35:4–6:

> Say to those who have an anxious heart, "Be strong; fear not! Behold, your God will come with vengeance, with the recompense of God. He will come and save you." Then the eyes of the blind shall be opened, and the ears of the deaf unstopped; then shall the lame man leap like a deer, and the tongue of the mute sing for joy. For waters break forth in the wilderness, and streams in the desert.

---

16. I know, certain people think you're supposed to say "challenges" or "different abilities," instead of "disabilities." I prefer the more honest and descriptive language, even if it is "politically incorrect." And I am quite ready to use it of my own present and future disabilities! Should I lose my sight, I would not want to be patronized by being called "perceptually challenged."

Jesus referred to this passage to show John the Baptist that he was indeed the one who was to come (Matt. 11:4–6). Jesus restored the disabled as a particularly vivid image of redemption from sin. For indeed in our moral and spiritual lives we are all disabled, and we need Jesus as our healer (Mark 2:17).[17]

The church has a major responsibility, therefore, to be a society that welcomes, values, and assists the disabled. Far too often, Christians have been unwilling to take the trouble to understand the needs of the disabled and then to treat them as valued and gifted members of Jesus' body.

Perhaps in part because of the church's failure, government has stepped in to remedy the needs of disabled people. The Americans with Disabilities Act of 1992 was a bold government plan to remove many types of impediments to the handicapped, mandating accommodations of various sorts to disabled employees, students, and customers. Since that time, most new buildings have become wheelchair accessible and many new employment opportunities have opened up.

Like most legislation, this has produced problems for some. Conservatives have objected to a number of provisions and judicial applications of the act. Llewellyn H. Rockwell argues that the act has had a crippling (!) effect on American business and, indeed, on the national economy. He lists a number of individual absurdities like wheelchairs at third base forced on the Little League, the use of Braille at automated drive-in (!) bank tellers, the forced rehiring of a blind fireman, accommodation for a man who failed his electrician certification test (because he was "no good at taking tests"), the forced rehiring of a postal worker fired for alcoholism.[18] But the broader picture is that "the number of complaints, however, will never measure the degree to which the act is radically changing American business. The threat of a complaint is as effective as the complaint itself. The hundreds of pages in the *Federal Register* spelling out what the ADA is supposed to mean don't come close to exhausting the possibilities."[19]

My own impression, more than a decade after the act, is that it has done much more good than harm. But we do need to look at this matter in broader perspective. We all have different levels of abilities in different areas of life, which means that each of us is relatively disabled in some way in comparison with others. Some kinds of disability are very visible. But less visible kinds of "disability" can be even more significant in

---

17. Thanks to my friend Michael S. Beates, who makes this point powerfully in his D.Min. dissertation project, "Wholeness from Brokenness: Disability as a Model of the Transforming Power of the Gospel" (Reformed Theological Seminary, Orlando, 2003).

18. "Wheelchairs at Third Base," *National Review*, July 7, 1993, 47–50.

19. Ibid., 50.

individual cases. Consider the boy who is poor at athletics and therefore finds it harder than most people to achieve his romantic and vocational goals. Consider the biologist whose Christian convictions keep him from achieving deserved prominence in his field. Consider the worker who loses his job because his employer must downsize in order to afford compliance with the ADA. Consider the people who are forced into poverty because of a recession prolonged by excessive government regulation of business. It would be utopian in the extreme to think that all of these complaints can be remedied by government edict.

Franklin Roosevelt was confined to a wheelchair by polio, long before anyone thought of the concept of "disability rights." There were many things he could not do that others could. Yet he was elected President of the United States for four terms, something that no one else has ever accomplished. People with disabilities also have abilities; indeed, their advocates keep reminding us of that, and rightfully so. A person with a visible handicap is not necessarily disabled in the more profound sense—that is, less able than others to achieve his goals. The Franklin Roosevelts of this world do not need government-mandated advantages in order to succeed. On the other hand, many of the "abled" find it hard to succeed without special help.

Therefore, laws like the ADA cannot succeed in creating ultimate equality. They give special help to many who don't need it and penalize people who, considered on an objective basis, do need help. This is, of course, the nature of government. It cannot make fine distinctions among individuals to determine who truly needs help and who doesn't. It can only mandate help to certain broad, visible groups. And when it does so, it inevitably creates injustice against those who are forced to sacrifice in order to help those whom the law defines as victims. And the more it tries to make finer and finer distinctions of this sort, the more injustice it brings about. The rationalist impulse, trying to produce perfect justice by fiat, almost necessarily increases injustice.

The church can do better, for the local church can look at each individual situation to see what a person's needs are and the resources he has for meeting those needs, and it can do this with the insight that the Word of God provides. Ultimately, however, only God can see the heart, and so only God can say definitively who is disabled and how badly, and who needs what.

As I shall indicate later, I do not oppose all government involvement in welfare. Governments are the ruling bodies of our extended family in Adam.[20] But I do believe that government should give families and churches the first opportunity to meet diaconal needs. And, when govern-

---

20. See my essay, "Toward a Theology of the State," *Westminster Theological Journal* 51 (1989): 199–226.

ment steps in, it should do so with a full understanding of its own limitations, particularly its inability to micromanage moral inequities. Government should enter the scene only when the families, churches, and other
private agencies have shown themselves clearly unwilling or incompetent
to do so. And in this enterprise, local government should have priority,
then regional/state, then federal; for the more local a government is, the
better position it is in to assess true need.

But the larger perspective is this: Scripture calls us to be content, not to
covet the advantages of others (see Ex. 20:17; Luke 3:14; Phil. 4:11; 1 Tim.
6:6–8; Heb. 13:5; 3 John 10). The early Christians, especially the apostles,
were the most disadvantaged of human beings, save Jesus. Yet, following
the path of the cross, they did not try to force others to "equalize" those
disadvantages. They accepted their disadvantages as part of their ethical
situation and sought to live in that situation so as to please Christ. New
Testament exhortations to citizens, slaves, wives, and children is entirely
contrary to the views of modern society (see Rom. 13; 1 Cor. 9; Eph.
5:22–6:9; Col. 3:18–4:1; 1 Peter 2:13–3:22). Of course, the Old Testament
prophets do teach us to fight against oppression. But our main weapon in
this battle is the Word of God. We are not to imagine that all problems
can be solved by an omniscient, all-benevolent state. Here the first commandment, as well as the tenth, becomes relevant.

OUR NATURAL ENVIRONMENT

The natural environment will claim our attention when we consider
the sixth commandment, but it is appropriate here to make some basic
observations.

Human beings are part of nature. Our very creatureliness is something we
have in common with nature, rather than with God. Further, God made
us from the dust of the ground (Gen. 2:7) and dependent on the ground
for our continued life (Gen. 1:29; 2:8–9, 15–17; 3:1–19). Therefore, there
are many obvious similarities and analogies between human and animal
life. And we must protect plant and animal life, and their habitats, if we
and our descendants are to survive.

Human beings are lords of nature. We are, nevertheless, radically different
from other forms of life in important ways. Our creation comes from a special
consultation of the divine council (Gen. 1:26). We are special creations, not
the products of evolution (Gen. 2:7, 21–23). We are the very image of God

(Gen. 1:26–28). Therefore, God has given us vassal lordship over the earth, to fill, subdue, and have dominion over it (Gen. 1:26–28; 2:19–20).

Our fall brought a curse on the natural world. In Genesis 3:17–19, God declares that the earth now will resist our attempts at dominion. Now the earth is a source of toil and weariness. God's declaration that all created things are good (Gen. 1:31) remains true even after the fall (1 Cor. 10:26; 1 Tim. 4:4). But human lust finds in things a source of temptation, as Eve found temptation in the forbidden fruit. And events in the natural world serve as means of divine judgment and chastening, as well as deliverance.

God uses nature in the history of redemption. God uses things in creation as signs of his redemptive activity, such as the rainbow (Gen. 9:13) and the star of Bethlehem (Matt. 2:2). Signs will also anticipate Jesus' return and the final judgment (Matt. 24:29–30). Although salvation itself is not a natural event, nature collaborates with God's redemptive purposes. Creation itself waits anxiously for the consummation (Rom. 8:19–23). So events in nature are not only occasions of temptation, but also of the believer's growth and victory. They work ultimately toward the accomplishment of God's purposes (Rom. 8:28). The consummation itself is, not only a new heavens, but a new earth, in which righteousness will dwell (2 Peter 3:13; Rev. 21:1).

God calls us to take nature into account when we make our moral decisions. From the beginning, God expected Adam to apply God's word to his natural environment. The cultural mandate challenged him to determine how every object could be used to subdue and fill the earth to God's glory. So did the commands to work and keep the garden (Gen. 2:15), to name the animals (2:19–20), and to abstain from the forbidden fruit (2:17). God still calls us to replenish and subdue the earth, and to deal with each part of creation in a way that honors him.

Such is the biblical mandate for ecological responsibility. God calls his people to have dominion over the earth, but that is not a license to exploit or destroy it. As God told Adam to "work" and "keep" the garden, so we are to work and keep the earth.[21] As God commanded Israel to give rest to the land (Lev. 25:4), so he calls us to maintain its vitality. And we are to be kind to animals as well (Deut. 5:14; 25:4).

---

21. "Work" and "keep" are used elsewhere for priestly functions. These priestly connotations are appropriate in Gen. 2:15, given that Eden is, as I said earlier, a sanctuary of God. "Keep" (*shamar*) can mean to guard the sanctuary against intruders. But, of course, given in the context of gardening (and the command about the fruit in vv. 16–17), these terms serve to make man's care of the earth part of his priestly responsibility to God.

CHAPTER 16

Redemptive History

The situational perspective deals with our ethical environment, which includes everything. By "everything," I mean God himself and the whole course of nature and history which he directs by his divine plan, his creation, and providence. In the previous chapter, I listed the elements of nature and history: God, the angels, human society, our individual makeup, and the natural world. That discussion was ontological in the sense that it focused on the *realities* (divine and human, persons and things) that participate in nature and history, rather than on the *events* of nature and history. But of course our ethical situation is constituted by events, not only by persons and things.

Events occur in the course of nature, which I defined in chapter 14 as "the general workings of the world perceived by our senses and reason and described by the physical sciences." A subdivision of nature is history, "the events of human existence." And an important subdivision of history is redemptive history, "the story of creation, fall, and redemption." In this book, I shall not try to describe the ethical significance of natural events in general. Although I will refer to natural history at appropriate times, the general subject exceeds my competence and the plan of this volume. But we must look carefully at human history as the Bible describes it. And according to Scripture the most important events of human history are those of redemptive history. When we make our ethical decisions, we must recognize that the world is created, fallen, and redeemed by Christ, and we must understand the ethical implications of those facts.

NARRATIVE

I have mentioned that the normative perspective presents us with a Christian "command ethic," that the situational perspective gives us a "narrative ethic," and that the existential perspective presents us with a "virtue ethic." Our concern now is narrative, the story of our life with God. The Bible contains many kinds of literature, as we have seen, but one of its most important genres is narrative. The biblical narrative tells us what God has done to secure the salvation of his fallen creatures. Centrally, that narrative presents Christ and tells us what he has done for us. It defines the content of faith and gives us assurance. It also defines our ethic, which is to respond appropriately to that story, to the One who has redeemed us.

The narrative genre has many advantages for preachers, teachers, and anyone else interested in communicating ethical content. People seem to enjoy listening to stories, rather than listening to commands or even descriptions of virtues. So we can understand why so much of the Bible is in narrative form. Jesus' own teaching is especially full of stories, many of them parables. We recall how God used Nathan's parable of the ewe lamb (2 Sam. 12:1–7) to convict David of sin. Narrative has a way of overtaking the listener by surprise, of involving him in the story.

Narrative is especially important in communicating gospel. Gospel is good news, and therefore it is a narrative of what God has done for us in Christ. In 1 Corinthians 15:1–11, Paul enumerated the elements of the gospel as a series of events, as a narrative. We might imagine, therefore, that narrative corresponds to gospel, and command to law. As I indicated in chapter 12, however, Scripture does not sharply distinguish between gospel and law. Law, among other things, tells us to believe in Jesus, and gospel narrates how the King came into the world to reimpose his law upon rebellious creatures.

In one sense, the narrative of creation, fall, and redemption includes the whole Bible. No part of Scripture is outside the story. The books of Psalms and Proverbs are not narrative in form, but they add to the narrative, telling us how God instructed his people Israel in piety and wisdom. To learn the whole story, we need the whole Bible. Without Psalms and Proverbs, we would not have the complete narrative. So the narrative is the whole Bible, and in that sense the whole Bible is narrative.

But it is also true to say that the whole Bible is divine command, for every passage is an authoritative word from God telling us what we must believe and/or do. So narrative and command (gospel and law, if you will) are complementary perspectives on the whole Bible. And the same may be said about the existential perspective, that the whole Bible is a description of virtue, showing us the virtues of God himself, Father, Son, and Spirit, and of those who belong to him by grace.

So narrative is important, but not all important. It is an important perspective on the whole Bible, but it is not the only perspective. The narrative is the whole Bible, and the whole Bible is narrative, but not to the exclusion of commands and virtues.

It is therefore important to note that although Psalms and Proverbs, for example, are aspects of narrative in a larger sense, they do not belong to the narrative genre. They have their own purposes, which are not merely to narrate events (although the poetry of the Psalms often does narrate redemptive history), but to inform the praises and the wisdom of God's people.

THE REDEMPTIVE STORY

The story of the Bible is the narrative of God coming to be with his people as their Lord, in his control, authority, and presence. After creation and fall, the story is about redemption, and thus about Jesus.[1]

Before the fall, Adam lived in God's garden-sanctuary, tending and guarding it as God's priest. God was Adam's friend, as well as his Lord. God spoke to Adam and Eve, defining their nature and task as human beings (Gen. 1:28) and granting them the blessings of the garden (1:29–31). He also gave to Adam the terms of a crucial test of covenant fellowship (2:15–17) and, through Eve's creation and the institution of marriage, constituted the human community (Gen. 2:18–25).

After the fall, God again came to be with Adam and Eve, this time in judgment, but also, surprisingly, with blessing. He cursed the serpent (Satan), Eve, and Adam, in the areas most appropriate to each. The serpent, who would exalt himself above God, will go on his belly and eat dust, awaiting his final destruction by the seed of the woman (Gen. 3:14–15). The woman will have pain in childbearing, and the rule of her husband will be frustrating to her (v. 16).[2] The man also will labor in pain, as the ground produces thorns and thistles. He will raise crops by the sweat of his face, looking toward his return to the ground from

1. I know of no better summary of the story than Edmund Clowney, *The Unfolding Mystery* (Colorado Springs: NavPress, 1988). Clowney's book shows, often in very striking ways, how Christ is the central subject of the Old Testament narrative.

2. I agree with Susan T. Foh that the "desire" Eve had for her husband was a desire to dominate him, a desire destined to be frustrated. See her *Women and the Word of God* (Phillipsburg, NJ: Presbyterian and Reformed, 1980).

which he came (vv. 17–19). Now human death enters the picture. But, we wonder, in terms of Genesis 2:17, why doesn't God execute the sentence of death immediately?

The postponement of death is God's redemptive grace. And there is yet more grace in the fall's aftermath. The curse on Satan is blessing to humanity: the promised seed will destroy him and will thus rid the world of evil. And the curse on the woman also hides a blessing. She is not to die immediately, but will continue to live and have children, one of whom will redeem the race. Similarly, the curse on the man's labor is also mixed with God's grace. His toil, though painful, will keep the human race alive until the coming of the deliverer.

Immediately, then, the narrative focuses on God's grace through the coming Messiah. Christ, even at the beginning, is the focus of the story. Human ethical life, then, is a response to God's grace that looks forward to final deliverance. Judgment occurs as well, in God's limitation of human life (Gen. 6:3), in the great flood (chaps. 6–9), and in the confusion of languages at Babel (11:1–9). These judgments indicate to believers that God will not be mocked, that his standards will prevail. Thus law and grace combine to guide the human race in the paths of God.

In the Abrahamic and Mosaic covenants, God comes to dwell with his chosen people (Gen. 26:3, 24; 28:15; 31:3; Ex. 3:12; 4:12; Deut. 31:8, 23; Josh. 1:5), anticipating the coming of Jesus, Immanuel (meaning "God with us," Isa. 7:14). In these covenants, the presence of the Lord governs all human life. God is the Holy One, who has called the family of Abraham, Isaac, and Jacob, from among all the nations of the earth, to be his holy people. They are to be holy, because he is holy (Ex. 19:6; Lev. 11:44–45; 19:2; 20:7, 26; 21:8; 1 Peter 1:16). So they are to live their lives as those who live on holy ground, who dwell in the closest proximity to God.

In one sense, to live in such fellowship with God is a wonderful thing. But that presence of God is also threatening. When God meets with Israel at Mt. Sinai, death awaits any human being or beast that touches the mountain (Ex. 19:12–13). When God comes to dwell in the holiest part of the tabernacle and temple, many barriers stand between the believer and that place. Death looms for those who violate the rules of approach.

But this fearsome God is also the Savior, the deliverer. Israel is to keep the law because of redemption, for the Decalogue begins, "I am the LORD your God, who brought you out of the land of Egypt, out of the house of slavery" (Ex. 20:2). And in the republication of the Decalogue in Deuteronomy 5, the Lord commands Israel to give rest to her households for the same reason: "You shall remember that you were a slave in the land of Egypt, and the LORD your God brought you out from there with a mighty hand and an outstretched arm. Therefore the LORD your God commanded you to keep the Sabbath day" (v. 15).

Throughout the Old Testament, God tells Israel to obey him, motivating them by his past deliverances and blessings. The prophecy of Isaiah begins with God lamenting that the children he has "reared and brought up" have rebelled against him (Isa. 1:2). He also mentions past judgments: because of Israel's sin, God has struck her down (v. 5), so she should know better than to defy the Lord. The judgments will cease if and when Israel repents (vv. 18–20), for God is ready to forgive those who are willing to obey him.

He also motivates their obedience by promises of future blessing (2:1–5) and judgment (2:12–22). He is the Lord of history, and he controls the fortunes of Israel. At the end, the Lord will be glorious, and his people will be holy (4:2–6). That movement of history is certain, and those who wish to share in that glory must return to God. So the situation, past, present, and future, motivates obedience.

Between the Old Testament and the final judgment, however, comes Jesus. The Old Testament foreshadows his work in the sacrificial system, in the lives of prophets, priests, and kings, and in specific prophecies of his coming. The Scriptures bear witness of him (John 5:39; cf. Luke 24:27, 44). Those who repent of sin and look to God in faith are at the same time looking forward to the Messiah. It is the prospect of his coming that encourages them to trust and obey the Lord, despite apparent defeats of his purposes.

When Jesus comes to accomplish our redemption from sin through his death and resurrection, these events give his people a fresh motivation for godly behavior (John 13:34; Rom. 6:1–23; 13:11–12; 1 Cor. 6:20; 10:11; 15:58; Eph. 4:1–5, 25, 32; 5:25–33; Phil. 2:1–11; Col. 3:1–3; Heb. 12:1–28; 1 Peter 2:1–3; 4:1–6; 1 John 3:16).[3] Jesus has loved us beyond measure by dying for our sins, and the only appropriate response is for us to love him and one another. Since he has died for our sins, and since we died with him to sin (Rom. 6), we should live as those who are alive to righteousness. Since we have been raised with him to newness of life, we should seek the things that are above (Col. 3:1–3).

So, as biblical theology emphasizes, imperatives in the New Testament flow from indicatives. Obligations follow from the narrative, from the story. This is not a naturalistic fallacy, because, as I said in chapters 5 and 9, everything that God is and does is ethically normative. And, of course, when a situation changes, appropriate behavior may change. On a warm

---

3. See the discussion in chapter 3 of the history of redemption as one of the Bible's "reasons to do good works."

day, it may be appropriate to wear short pants, but not when the temperature is ten below zero. When Jesus has died for our sins and has risen again, our only appropriate response is to love him. And if we love him, we will keep his commandments. Those who are convinced that Jesus has saved them will be powerfully moved to love and serve him. This fact underlies the structure of the Heidelberg Catechism, which moves from guilt to grace to gratitude. In the view of the Catechism, we keep the law out of gratitude, in response to grace.

To say this is not to contradict what I said earlier under the normative perspective. The simple fact that God commands me to do something is sufficient ground for me to do it. So far as sheer obligation is concerned, people should obey God whether they are redeemed or not. Even Satan and the fallen angels are under that obligation. Redemption adds a substantial motivation for obedience, but it does not create the obligation to obey. Further, even when we are serving Christ in response to his redemptive work, we need to know what he wants us to do. We continue to need the law to tell us what kind of behavior is appropriate for redeemed people. If we love him in response to his love, we will keep his commandments, but to do that we need to know what his commandments are.

THE TWO AGES

Biblical theology, which focuses on the history of redemption, has emphasized the "two-age" structure of the New Testament. In Matthew 12:32, Jesus speaks of a sin that will not be forgiven "either in this age or in the age to come." Paul also refers to these two ages in Ephesians 1:21. The first of the two ages is "this age" (*ho aiōn houtos*), the period of time in which we live, a period that is to end at the second coming of Christ and the final judgment (Matt. 13:39–40, 49; 24:3; 28:20). This is the age in which sin and the curse continue on the earth, before God's final victory. So Scripture describes this age in ethical terms as "the present evil age" (Gal. 1:4) from which Christ's redemption delivers us.

Nonbelievers are caught up in the affairs of this age, unwilling to be bothered by the demands and promises of God. Jesus speaks of "the sons of this age" (Luke 20:34). Paul refers to "the debater of this age" (1 Cor. 1:20), "the rulers of this age" (1 Cor. 2:8), and those who are "wise in this age" (1 Cor. 3:18).

Some Christians, to be sure, are numbered among "the rich in this present age" (1 Tim. 6:17); that is, they have acquired things that are valued by people in this age. That is not necessarily sinful, but Timothy must give them a special charge "not to be haughty, nor to set their hopes on the uncertainty of riches, but on God, who richly provides us with everything to enjoy." So all believers must take heed "to live self-controlled, upright, and godly lives in the present age" (Titus 2:12). The present age, even to believers, is a source of temptation.

The "age to come," however, is the age of fulfillment. Jesus contrasts "the sons of this age" (Luke 20:34) with "those who are considered worthy to attain to that age and to the resurrection from the dead" (v. 35). In the understanding of those Jews who believed in resurrection, "that age" follows our death and God's final judgment. In "the age to come," God's people have "eternal life" (Mark 10:30).

But the remarkable thing about New Testament teaching, in contrast with the Jewish conception, is that in one sense the "age to come" has already appeared in Christ. Believers in Christ are those "on whom the end of the ages has come" (1 Cor. 10:11). The closing of the holy places in the temple to worshipers is symbolic of the present age, so that when the veil is torn and we enter boldly into God's presence through Christ, another age has begun (Heb. 9:8–9). Christ "has appeared once for all at the end of the ages to put away sin by the sacrifice of himself" (Heb. 9:26). For believers, then, "the coming age" has begun in Christ. He has dealt with sin once for all.

The resurrection of Jesus is the crucial sign that "the last days" are here. The Pharisees associated the last days with the resurrection of the righteous and the wicked. So Jesus associates that time with resurrection in John 6:39–40, 44, 54. But when the grieving Martha says that her brother Lazarus "will rise again in the resurrection on the last day" (John 11:24), Jesus replies, "I am the resurrection and the life. Whoever believes in me, though he die, yet shall he live, and everyone who lives and believes in me shall never die" (vv. 25–26). Then he proceeds to raise Lazarus from the dead, indicating that the life-giving power of the age to come is present in himself. So in Luke 17:21 Jesus tells the Pharisees that the kingdom is already in their midst, certainly referring to himself. Wherever Jesus is, there is the age to come.[4]

After Jesus has risen, and signs of the Spirit's presence abound (sent from the throne of Christ), Peter proclaims that Joel's prophecy of "the last days" has been fulfilled (Acts 2:17). The writer to the Hebrews proclaims in the past tense that "in these last days [God] has spoken to us by his Son" (1:2).

---

4. The kingdom of God, mentioned often in the Gospels, is roughly synonymous with the "age to come," mentioned often in Paul and Hebrews. "Age to come" designates a time, and "kingdom of God" designates the new order of things to be established in that time.

The same conclusion follows from New Testament teaching on the kingdom of God. Geerhardus Vos defines the kingdom as follows: "To him [Jesus] the kingdom exists there, where not merely God is supreme, for that is true at all times and under all circumstances, but where God supernaturally carries through his supremacy against all opposing powers and brings man to the willing recognition of the same."[5] The kingdom of God, long awaited, has come in Christ (Matt. 3:2; 4:17; 12:28). The gospel is the gospel of the kingdom (Matt. 4:23; 9:35; 10:7). The Sermon on the Mount teaches the ethic of the kingdom (Matt. 5:3, 10, 19, 20; 6:33). The Lord's Prayer is the prayer of the kingdom (Matt. 6:10). The parables present the mysteries of the kingdom (Matt. 13:11). The church has the keys of the kingdom (Matt. 16:19; 18:18). The kingdom of God has come. Christ the king has been raised to God's right hand, where he has authority over all things (Matt. 28:18).

Yet there are also some biblical expectations for the last days and the kingdom that are still unfulfilled. The resurrection of the just and the unjust has not taken place. The return of Christ and the final judgment remain future. The saints pray, "Thy kingdom come" (Matt. 6:10), looking for the future manifestation of the kingdom. Sin and the curse continue on the earth. Indeed, these "last days" are "times of difficulty" (2 Tim. 3:1; cf. 2 Peter 3:3). It is a time in which false teaching abounds, in which unscrupulous people try to undermine the doctrine and holiness of God's people.

So the biblical data is somewhat paradoxical. On the one hand, the last days are here in Christ. On the other hand, much remains future. The age to come is present, yet the present age lingers. From Jesus' resurrection until his return, the two ages exist simultaneously. Our present existence is, as Vos puts it, "semieschatological."

Figure 4 shows Vos's diagram of the two ages.[6] "This age" runs from the fall of Adam to the return of Christ (the parousia). "The age to come" runs from the resurrection of Christ through all eternity. During the period between Christ's resurrection and the parousia, the two ages exist side-by-side.

It is important for us to understand the dynamic and the tension of the semieschatological age in which we live. Our salvation is complete in Christ, but sin will not be destroyed until his return. Or, as biblical theologians often put it, salvation is "already" here, but also "not yet" fully here. Christ has all authority, but Satan still has much power. We can draw

---

5. Vos, *The Teaching of Jesus Concerning the Kingdom of God and the Church* (Nutley, NJ: Presbyterian and Reformed, 1972), 50.

6. Vos, *The Pauline Eschatology* (Grand Rapids: Eerdmans, 1953; reprint, Phillipsburg, NJ: Presbyterian and Reformed, 1986), 38.

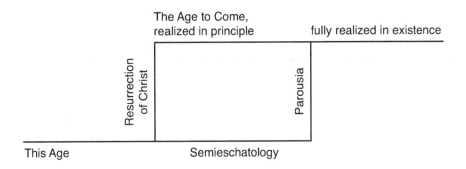

Fig. 4. Vos's Two-Age Diagram

confidently on the power and love of God, yet there are perils in the way. We have died to sin and have been raised to righteousness in Christ (Rom. 6), and yet we must "put to death . . . what is earthly in you" (Col. 3:5). The battle is won, but there is much mopping up to be done.[7]

This historical paradox is a current form of the larger paradox of the relation of divine sovereignty and human responsibility. God has saved us through Christ, by his own sovereign power. We must rely on him for all our provision. But this fact does not allow us to be passive. There is a battle to be fought (Eph. 6:10–20), a race to be run (1 Cor. 9:24–27). We are not to "let go and let God." Rather, as Paul says, "work out your own salvation with fear and trembling, for it is God who works in you, both to will and to work for his good pleasure" (Phil. 2:12–13). God's sovereign action does not discourage us; rather, it motivates us to fight the spiritual battle.

ETHICS AND THE MILLENNIUM

Having discussed the implications of semieschatology for the Christian life, let us now look at eschatology proper, that consummation of history that is still future, consisting of the return of Christ, the final judgment, and the eternal state.

I will not get into detailed discussions here about millennial positions and the order of events in the last days, but I will look briefly to see what ethical implications there may be to the three main millennial theories. Those theories are: premillennialism, the view that the return of Christ

---

7. I believe that it was Oscar Cullmann who referred to World War II to illustrate this paradox: Christ's atonement and resurrection are like D-day, while his return and the final judgment are like V-day. But of course the resurrection of Jesus guarantees its final outcome in a way that D-day could not.

precedes the thousand years of peace mentioned in Revelation 20; post-millennialism, the view that the return of Christ follows that period; and amillennialism, the view that this period is a symbol for the present age. In more recent discussion, postmillennialists (henceforth, "postmils," and similarly for the others) and amils have come to agree that the thousand years are a symbol of the present age. The two viewpoints differ, however, as to the degree to which Christianity becomes culturally and politically dominant during that period: postmils expect much cultural success, and amils expect little. Amils typically think that the gospel will be fruitful spiritually, but not culturally or politically.

The conventional wisdom is that premils and amils tend to be pessimistic about influencing society in biblical directions, while postmils tend to be optimistic. Of course, I have known some optimistic premils and amils, and some pessimistic postmils. Optimism and pessimism seem to me to have more to do with one's personality and spiritual maturity than with one's theology of the end times. And there are some types of postmillennialism that are actually conducive to pessimism. One postmillennialist thinks that Western civilization is doomed, at least in the near future; his optimism is for the long term only. But how long is that term?

The movement in the 1970s and 1980s toward greater Christian involvement in social issues was spearheaded, not by Reformed amils and postmils, but by Arminian premils like Jerry Falwell and Pat Robertson. This is an embarrassment for us Reformed people, who like to think that we have a corner on Christian political thought and action, and tend to look down our noses at "fundamentalists" for their lack of a "full-orbed Christian world-and-life view." Of course, fundamentalists like Falwell and Robertson may have been influenced, at third or fourth hand, by Reformed people like Rousas J. Rushdoony, Gary North, and Francis Schaeffer. But it was the evangelical premils who took the lead in the actual movements for social change, and we should give them credit. Here we see another reason why the church should reexamine its divisions. Full implementation of Christianity in our time requires the gifts given to people in all Christian traditions.[8]

Therefore, a premil commitment does not destroy all motivation for Christian social action, though perhaps one might still argue that from a strictly logical (as opposed to an emotional or empirical) standpoint postmillennialism *ought* to be a greater encouragement to such action. Thus would I resolve the argument between Gary North, who thinks one

---

8. See my *Evangelical Reunion* (Grand Rapids: Baker, 1991), available at www.thirdmill.org and www.frame-poythress.org.

must be postmillennial to be a theonomist, and Greg Bahnsen, who thinks postmillennialism is an advantage to a theonomist, but not a necessity.

Throughout my career, I have avoided the millennial question like the plague, thinking that Scripture does not clearly address it. Needless to say, I have never been asked to teach a course in eschatology. But let me try a perspectival approach, suggesting that all three views have some of the truth. I agree with the amils and premils that this age is an age of suffering and persecution for God's people (2 Tim. 3:12). I also agree with the postmils that in the long run this age can be seen as an age of Christian triumph, not only in narrowly "spiritual" matters, but in the church's social influence as well. That is in fact what we see in history: believers are always persecuted in some measure, but eventually Christianity triumphs and comes to profoundly influence the institutions of the societies it touches. And when Christianity declines, as in many parts of the world today, the institutions of those societies decline as well. To limit the church's triumph to a narrowly "spiritual" realm is, as postmils emphasize, Platonic rather than scriptural. When God saves a person, that person brings his regenerate values into every area of life (1 Cor. 10:31).[9]

Ethically, this approach saves us from premature triumphalism and from undue pessimism and frustration. Suffering comes first, then glory; but the blood of the martyrs is the seed of a great church. And as we look back over two thousand years of Christian history, it is wonderful to see how divine providence slowly but surely brings triumph out of dark circumstances. The church follows the path of the cross, and it shares in the glory of the cross. Here is another form of the paradox of the already and the not-yet.

The troubles of Christianity in our own time are not the worst troubles the church has experienced. The Roman persecutions, the barbarian invasions of Europe, the spiritual darkness preceding the Reformation, the religious wars following it, the secularist "Enlightenment" of the eighteenth century, and the totalitarian persecutions of Christians in the twentieth century were all more difficult challenges, in some respects, than we face today in modern Western civilization. But the church's persecutors are now obscured in historical dust, while the Christian church continues by God's grace as a powerful witness to Christ's lordship and salvation. The troubles we face today, including the attacks of militant Islam, will be similarly dispatched. In God we trust, and in him we are confident for the future. So I lean toward a short-term amillennialism and a long-term postmillennialism.

9. Recall our discussion of the comprehensiveness of Scripture in chapter 10.

Now, can I say anything in favor of premillennialism? Well, I believe that Jesus is coming visibly to earth to judge the living and the dead, and that that judgment just might take a thousand years![10] But I do not base that assertion on Revelation 20.

ETHICS AND ESCHATOLOGY IN SCRIPTURE

Scripture, as I pointed out, has little to say about the millennium and its supposed ethical implications. But it does say much about the ethical implications of the return of Christ and the final judgment. Indeed, Scripture's main use of these doctrines is ethical. It does not teach us about Jesus' return primarily to stimulate us to draw charts or to determine the precise order of events on the last day, but to show us how to live. It is remarkable that almost every text regarding the return of Jesus has an ethical thrust.[11]

These ethical applications are of several different kinds:

1. *Since this age is to end and the things of this world are to be dissolved, the Christian ought to have a set of priorities radically different from those who belong to "this age."* Peter says:

> But the day of the Lord will come like a thief, and then the heavens will pass away with a roar, and the heavenly bodies will be burned up and dissolved, and the earth and the works that are done on it will be exposed. Since all these things are thus to be dissolved, what sort of people ought you to be in lives of holiness and godliness, waiting for and hastening the coming of the day of God, because of which the heavens will be set on fire and dissolved, and the heavenly bodies will melt as they burn! But according to his promise we are waiting for new heavens and a new earth in which righteousness dwells. (2 Peter 3:10–13)

It is not appropriate to set our hearts on things that are doomed to be burnt up. Holiness and righteousness, however, last forever, and are therefore worth pursuing.

2. *As Christians, we eagerly await the return of Christ, praying, "Come, Lord Jesus!"* (Rev. 22:20). As we saw above, Peter calls us to "wait for"

---

10. S. Lewis Johnson, a premillennialist, taught, I'm told, that the millennium is essentially a thousand years of judgment.

11. I say "almost" here as a scholarly caution. I don't actually know of any exceptions. Of course, if *all* Scripture is given for ethical purposes (2 Tim. 3:16–17), then this narrower thesis follows as an implication.

and "hasten" the coming of Christ.[12] But so often we belie our eagerness by our preoccupation with this age. To authenticate our eagerness, we need to live "lives of holiness and godliness" (2 Peter 3:12). John tells us that when Jesus appears, "we will be like him, because we shall see him as he is" (1 John 3:2). The parousia will enable us much better to image the holiness of Jesus. If we are really eager to see Jesus, then, we should want to anticipate that new holiness as much as possible in this sinful age. So anyone with this hope "purifies himself as he is pure" (1 John 3:3).

3. *Since the resurrection of Christ has established the new age of the kingdom of God,*[13] *we are confident that our labors for Jesus will not be in vain, but will inevitably prevail.* Paul says, "Therefore, my beloved brothers, be steadfast, immovable, always abounding in the work of the Lord, knowing that in the Lord your labor is not in vain" (1 Cor. 15:58).

4. *We also look to the parousia as our deliverance from tribulation,* and therefore as a source of hope for Christians undergoing persecution (Luke 21:28).

5. *Since we know that Christ is coming, but we do not know the day or the hour, we must always be ready to meet him.* That means being up and about his business (Matt. 24:44–51; 1 Thess. 5:1–11; 1 Peter 1:7; 2 Peter 3:14).

6. *We also look forward to receiving our rewards on the last day.* God promises rewards to his people, and they receive those rewards when Jesus returns. That promise serves as an additional motivation (Ps. 19:11; Matt. 5:12, 46; 6:1–6; 10:41–42; Rom. 14:10; 1 Cor. 3:8–15; 9:17–25; 2 Cor. 5:10; Eph. 6:7–8; Col. 3:23–25; 2 Tim. 4:8; 1 Peter 5:4; James 1:12; 2 John 8; Rev. 11:18).

I confess that I was surprised by the number of times Scripture uses rewards to motivate obedience. Like many of us, I tend toward the Kantian notion that we should simply do our duty for duty's sake and never think about reward. But that notion is quite unbiblical. If God takes the trouble (this many times!) to urge our obedience by a promise of reward, we should embrace that promise with thanks, not despise it. That is, we should not only do good works, but we should do them for this reason.

This teaching, of course, is not salvation by works or merit. Although the word *reward* is used in these passages, there is no suggestion that we have

12. We "hasten" it, I presume, by praying for it and spreading the gospel, so that the full number of the elect are brought into the church. And, appropriate to the present discussion, evangelism is done by both word and deed.

13. Obviously, in this context, the "new age" refers to the biblical "age to come," discussed earlier, rather than to the occult new age of contemporary neopaganism. See Peter Jones, *Spirit Wars: Pagan Revival in Christian America* (Escondido, CA: Main Entry Editions, 1997).

earned the reward in the sense that we have paid God what the reward is worth. Jesus says that even when we have done everything commanded of us (and not one of us has done that), we have done no more than our duty (Luke 17:7–10). Indeed, in that case we are "unworthy" servants. Elsewhere, Scripture represents the reward as something out of all proportion to the service rendered (Matt. 19:29; 20:1–16; 24:45–47; 25:21–30; Luke 7:36–50; 12:37).

Nevertheless, there is some sort of gradation in the rewards given to individuals. Jesus says that the apostles will judge "the twelve tribes of Israel" (Matt. 19:28), suggesting that in the consummate kingdom there will be varying degrees of authority. But if the apostles have a special status, it is doubtful that they have it because they are more holy than all the saints in the succeeding centuries. Rather, they are the foundation on which the church is built (Eph. 2:20), and they continue in that role simply because Christ has called them to fill it. Some passages suggest degrees of blessing, as when Paul distinguishes those who build on the foundation of Christ with gold, silver, and precious stones from those who build with wood, hay, and stubble (1 Cor. 3:8–15), some of whom will be saved "only as through fire." But this passage deals with broad classes of Christians, not with some exact analysis of merits.

The parable of the talents (Matt. 25:14–30; cf. Luke 19:11–27) provides the best argument for proportionate rewards. One cannot argue, however, that the degree of investment success ascribed to the first two servants entitles them, as strict payment, to the master's rewards. Rather, the master acts generously, out of the goodness of his heart. This is to say that here, as with every transaction we have with God, we deal with him as a person, not with an impersonal principle of cause and effect.

Essentially, the reward is the kingdom itself (Matt. 5:3, 10; 25:34), which comes by electing grace (Matt. 25:34; Luke 12:31–32). Good works follow, rather than precede, this gift (Luke 12:33–48). To put it differently, the Lord himself is the inheritance of his people (Pss. 16:5; 73:24–26; Lam. 3:24). He is the inheritance of every believer. If there are differences of degree, they are differences of intimacy with the Lord himself. If some glorified saints lie closer than others to God's heart, no one else will be jealous or angry, for the eternal kingdom excludes such emotions. Rather, the lesser members of that kingdom will rejoice at the greater blessings given to others, and those who are greatest will serve the lesser—beginning with the Lord himself, as Jesus says in Luke 12:37, "Blessed are those servants whom the master finds awake when he comes. Truly, I say to you, he will dress himself for service and have them recline at table, and he will come and serve them."[14] Who would not want as much intimacy as possible with such a wonderful Lord? Here is a reward that profoundly motivates holiness of heart and life.

BETWEEN RESURRECTION AND PAROUSIA: THE BURDENS OF CHANGE AND KNOWLEDGE

As we have seen above, we live between the resurrection of Jesus and his return in glory. The apostles also lived in this period, toward its beginning. So our time is a continuation of theirs, and it is like the apostolic age in many ways: the already and the not-yet, the empowerment of the Spirit, the Great Commission mandate, looking forward to Jesus' return. It is also different in some ways: the charismatic gifts of prophecy and tongues (I believe) have ceased, being replaced in effect by the written canon of apostolic teaching. The apostles as leaders of the church have been replaced by elders and deacons, officers whose teaching does not have the foundational infallibility of the apostles, but which must be subject to that apostolic authority in the Word. There are also, of course, changes of culture and society, changes in science and technology, and so forth. Through all the changes, however, God is present with his people: in the Word, in the sacraments, in the body of believers, in the Spirit's inward witness.

Historical change is an important part of the ethical situation. As we apply the law of God, we must understand how it applies to each situation that comes before us. That work never ends. We may not assume that the Reformers or the Puritans, for example, finished the task, no matter how much we respect those great ministers of the Word. The Puritans did not have to evaluate nuclear warfare, genetic engineering, modern science, or neopaganism from Scripture, but we cannot avoid those tasks.

I must warn you against taking certain popular shortcuts. First of all, it is not scriptural to approach ethics with a mere traditionalism, a desire merely to emulate the Christianity of a past age. Whether or not we believe that past ages were "better" than this one, our mandate is not to repristinate or re-create a past situation; it is to apply the Scriptures to the situation of today. I fear that some Reformed churches seek to be mere museum pieces: historical artifacts where people can go to hear old-fashioned talk and experience older forms of church life—spiritual versions of Colonial Williamsburg. On the contrary, Christian worship is to be contemporary, in the sense of intelligible to people today (1 Cor. 14), and the church's

---

14. Thanks to Bill Crawford for bringing to my attention this amazing promise of our Lord.

preaching must adapt (insofar as Scripture permits) to the language and habits of the target population (1 Cor. 9).

The task of applying the Word of God to new situations is also avoided illegitimately by people who pit divine sovereignty against human responsibility and therefore refuse to make use of modern technology, science, medicine, communications, demographic studies, and so forth. All modern tools must be evaluated by the Scripture to determine which ones we should use and how we should use them. But the fact that God is sovereign in salvation does not invalidate human study, strategy, plans, techniques, and efforts. Otherwise there would be no point in seeking to communicate effectively at all; we could walk into a crowd, say any dumb thing we please, and wait for God to act. We all know that is not right. We all see the importance of studying the languages and culture of our target audiences, and in preaching classes those preparing for ministry learn to speak effectively. In doing so, we have no thought that such human preparation violates divine sovereignty. Why should we not extend this logic to demographic studies and modern techniques of communication?

If we avoid these shortcuts, we will have to face the fact that ethics in our time, as well as theology, to say nothing of church life and evangelistic strategy, should be different today, in important ways, from what it was in all past ages of church history, including the New Testament period. We face situations (both difficulties and opportunities) that were not faced by Machen, Kuyper, Hodge, Edwards, Owen, Calvin, Augustine, or Paul. The Word must be applied to those new situations. Of course, I grant that we are in the same warfare as the older saints, and that we must use the same spiritual weapons. But in its *specifics* that war is different now. Those who take the lazy way, the way of shortcuts, will be left behind. They may be instructive historical artifacts, but they will not be powerful instruments to bring people to Christ. God can, of course, use the feeblest instruments, but he typically honors the work of believers who count the costs and seize the opportunities.

Besides laziness, there is a certain selfishness about the shortcut mentality.[15] Shortcutters are those who feel comfortable with certain "tried and true" forms of life and witness—forms that God used in the past. Then they seek to produce a theological rationale for keeping those forms, even when times have changed. They talk as if they are fighting for biblical *principle*, but in fact they are merely arguing for a certain *application* of Scripture that was appropriate in a past situation.

15. Laziness is a form of selfishness, but the wider category also needs to be addressed in this context.

The debate is confused, of course, by labels like "conservative," which are applied both to defenders of scriptural principle and to those who merely defend past ways of doing things without scriptural justification. But defending authentic biblical principle is one thing; defending the continuance of outmoded applications is something very different. Both shortcutters and critics of shortcutters need to be more aware of this distinction.

What masquerades as a battle for biblical principle is often at bottom a mere rationalization of selfish impulses, a desire to stay comfortable, to avoid having to change familiar patterns. Often, however, Scripture itself is on the side of change! First Corinthians 9 is an important text in this respect. Paul was willing to be a Jew among the Jews and a Gentile among the Gentiles, so that some might be saved. He did not seek his own comfort, even his own rights. Indeed, he allowed his body to be buffeted, lest while preaching to others he himself should be a castaway. He tried "to please everyone in everything I do, not seeking my own advantage, but that of many, that they may be saved" (1 Cor. 10:33). And then he urges, "Be imitators of me, as I am of Christ" (11:1).

This means that in our evangelistic methodology, and indeed in our worship (for that also has an evangelistic element, 14:24–25), our goal must not be to please ourselves, but to bend and stretch, to accept discomfort and the trauma of change, in order to speak the Christian faith to the contemporary world.

There is another, rather different problem related to our distance from the New Testament. That problem is that our present historical situation is something of an epistemological burden. We are about 1,900 years removed from the completion of the New Testament canon. Now in some ways this is an advantage. We have had much more time to study Scripture than did the early church fathers like Clement and Justin Martyr. And in some ways, I think, contemporary orthodox Reformed theology has a far deeper and more precise understanding of the gospel than did the church fathers.[16] I say this contrary to those evangelicals who are joining Eastern Orthodox churches in order to return to the supposedly more profound teachings of the early church fathers. Although the Fathers did wonderful work in their day, standing heroically for the faith amid terrible oppressions, their writings were confused on many important points, such as the Trinity and justification by faith. And although it is valuable to read them today (often

16. One remarkable evidence of biblical inspiration is the incredible difference in spiritual understanding between the last books of the New Testament and the earliest writings of the postcanonical period. Clement, for example, is confused about all sorts of important things. Scripture, however, is so rich that it has taken 1,900 years for the church to learn many of its lessons.

they look at things from angles that are unusual today and edifying), we would be wise not to confuse their vagueness with profundity.

So in some ways our distance from the New Testament is an advantage. In other ways, however, it is a disadvantage. If I were a Christian church elder in, say, AD 62, and my church faced a controversy over, say, infant baptism, I could simply contact the nearest apostle (or his representative) and ask what the apostolic practice was. That would settle the question. In the early generations following the apostles, doubtless some reliable traditions dealing with matters not explicitly addressed in the New Testament were established. In my view, for instance, the early church did not need to have an explicit New Testament command to baptize infants. They just did it, for that was the apostolic practice, and the church had always done it that way.[17] But we do not have access today to the apostles, and we still have a lot of questions that we wish they were here to answer. In their absence, we must engage in a somewhat complicated process of theological reasoning. We would love to ask them about baptism, the nature of church government, the proper attitude toward war, the new covenant application of the Sabbath commandment, the style of worship, the grounds of divorce, the demands of Christ upon civil government, the proper criteria for determining physical death, and many other things. Some things mentioned in the New Testament, and evidently well understood by the original readers, are quite obscure to us, such as baptism for the dead (1 Cor. 15:29) and the covering of women "because of the angels" (1 Cor. 11:10).

Today, however, we are removed by many centuries from the time of the apostles. And controversy in the church, particularly during the time of the Reformation, has made it impossible to identify any single strain of church tradition as unambiguously apostolic. Thus, although we understand the central aspects of biblical teaching better than the church fathers did, there are other matters which we, perhaps, understand less well than they did.

It is also the case, as we mentioned before, that many issues of the modern day are not specifically discussed in Scripture. If we cannot contact the apostles to learn their view of baptism, much less can we determine directly what they would say about nuclear weaponry, the government's role in welfare, and the medical use of life-support equipment. Here too, there are biblical principles that apply, but the argument can be complicated. It is not as if the apostles were readily available for interviews, even on the issues of their day.

---

17. I am not, of course, advocating a Roman Catholic view of tradition. Scripture is the judge of all such traditions, and of course it is very difficult today to tell what traditions, if any, go back to apostolic times.

In facing our epistemological disadvantages, the first thing to be said is that God understands. He is the Lord of history. He has planned it and controls it providentially. It is no accident that we are in our present situation. That situation, uncomfortable as it may be at times, suits God's purposes perfectly, and we must be thankful for it. We should not murmur or complain, as did Israel in the wilderness. When someone calls and asks me a hard question, say, about whether they should remove life support systems from a dying relative, I usually begin by saying that these are, after all, hard questions, and that God understands how hard they are for us. We cannot contact the apostles, but he doesn't expect us to. He has left us with Scripture and the Spirit's illumination, and he has determined that that is enough. We may fumble around in searching for answers. We may make decisions that we regret later on, because we hadn't at first considered all the relevant principles and facts. But God understands.

In such situations, it is helpful to remember that we are justified by faith, not by works—nor, therefore, by ethical accuracy. That comfort does not, of course, excuse us from hard thinking. If God has justified us, we will want to please him, and we will make intellectual and other efforts to do what he wants. But the sincerity of such efforts is not measured by the perfection of the results. We may try very hard to apply biblical principles, and still come up with an answer that later proves inadequate. Yet God will honor our attempt. He knows the heart, and he takes into consideration the obstacles (including epistemological ones) that we must overcome.

Thus when, after prayerful, honest searching of Scripture you determine to let your mother die, and afterward wish that you had kept her alive longer on life support, do not be overcome with guilt. God still loves you, for Jesus' sake, more than you could ever love yourself.

Beyond that, I think that our "epistemological disadvantages" should give us more sympathy and forbearance for one another. If God still loves the believer who honestly makes a decision that proves wrong, we should also love and encourage that brother or sister. Sabbatarians and non-Sabbatarians, paedobaptists and believer's baptists, premillennialists and amillennialists, and pacifists and just war theorists should have greater love and understanding for each other. We should not pretend that everything is cut and dried, even though these issues may have been cut and dried in the New Testament period itself. We should agonize a bit with those who are wrestling with these issues. I am a paedobaptist, but what if I had been raised in a Baptist church? Would I have seen things the same way? Would the same arguments carry with me the weight they carry presently? I don't know. I believe I am right, and that Scripture teaches infant baptism. I will present that truth as God's truth. But I won't pretend that it is so plain that those on the other side must be either unintelligent or insincere.

God in his good providence has given us advantages and disadvantages, challenges and opportunities, which are not precisely the same as those of any past generation. He calls us to meet those challenges and seize the opportunities for Christ. The church of past ages can help us to avoid the mistakes of the past and to give us a platform on which to build the next story of God's temple. But we must not shirk our responsibility. We must be focused on the world of our own time and upon the Christ who is the same yesterday, today, and forever.

ETHICS, PREACHING, AND BIBLICAL THEOLOGY

At theological seminaries within the Reformed tradition, one of the most exciting discoveries that students make is the history of redemption. Biblical theology is the discipline that studies the Bible as a history of redemption. Many students become very excited about biblical theology. Many have done basic exegetical theology before coming to seminary, and many have experienced systematic theology in the form of confessions and catechisms. But biblical theology appears to them as something new.

The content of biblical theology is exciting to the believer. When we come to see Scripture as the history of redemption, we see far more clearly how all of Scripture bears witness to Christ. And biblical theology opens up to us a wonderful perspective on eschatology: that in Christ the last days are here, and that we are dwelling with him in the heavenly places. Redemption has been accomplished already, and its blessings are ours. There is, of course, a "not-yet" as well as an "already." The consummation has come, but it is still yet to come. We live as those who are sanctified, but not perfected.

As we have seen, the tension between the already and the not-yet is the setting of New Testament ethical reflection. God has justified us in Christ and has given us his Spirit, yet sin remains and will not be completely destroyed until the final day. Nevertheless, the "already," the definitive accomplishment of redemption in Christ, is our motivation for obedience. In our preaching and teaching, we should clearly set forth this framework as the context of ethical decision making.

I believe, however, that it is possible to go too far in our emphasis on the history of redemption. Some have claimed that the history of redemption is the primary context for theological reflection in Scripture, and that it must always be the primary subject matter of preaching. With this assertion

I must respectfully disagree. I have previously taken issue with these claims as applied to the concept and practice of theology and of preaching.[18] Here I will comment a bit on the implications of this view for ethics.

Although the two-age structure of Pauline ethics is important, it does not by any means exhaust the biblical teaching relevant to our ethical decisions. There are pages and pages of Scripture devoted to the details of God's law, to proverbs about the practical life of the believer, to the motivations of love and faith that should impel our passion for holiness.

Now some will point out that all these elements of biblical ethics are to be understood in the context of the two-age schema. That is true enough, but contextual arguments work both ways. If the law and the proverbs are to be understood in the context of the already and the not-yet, the opposite is also true: the semieschatological tension must be understood in terms of the law of God. It is the law that defines the sinfulness from which Christ redeemed us. And God saves us so that we may keep the law (Rom. 8:4). The law defines how we should express our gratitude for Jesus' redemption.

Preaching should certainly be redemptive-historical, but it should also expound God's laws and the new inner motivations to which we are called. In my terminology, redemptive history is the situational perspective, the situation in which we make ethical decisions. The law is the normative perspective, and the motive is the existential perspective. All three perspectives should be preached and taught, if Christians are to gain a balanced perspective on Christian ethics.

Should every sermon have redemptive history as its principal subject? I would say no. There is nothing in the Bible itself that requires us to restrict preaching in this way. It is common to develop a theology of preaching from the book of Acts, in which most of the preaching is evangelistic, given in marketplaces or synagogues. The preaching in Acts to Jews is quite overtly redemptive-historical, as the apostles and their colleagues (such as Stephen and Philip) present Christ as the fulfillment of Old Testament Scripture.

---

18. See *DKG*, 207–12. In footnotes there, I mention some of the authors who maintain the view I am contesting. Other sources would include Sidney Greidanus, *Sola Scriptura* (Toronto: Wedge Publishing Foundation, 1979); James T. Dennison, "What Is Biblical Theology?" in *Creator, Redeemer, Consummator*, ed. Howard Griffith and John Muether (Jackson, MS: Reformed Academic Press, 2000), 187–91; Richard B. Gaffin Jr., "Systematic Theology and Biblical Theology," in *The New Testament Student and Theology*, ed. John H. Skilton (Nutley, NJ: Presbyterian and Reformed, 1976), 32–50, and many articles at www.kerux.org and www.two-age.org. On the other side, I am pleased to see that Jay Adams has also registered protests against the extreme emphasis on biblical theology in some circles. See his "Reflections on Westminster Theology and Homiletics," in *The Pattern of Sound Doctrine*, ed. David VanDrunen (Phillipsburg, NJ: P&R Publishing, 2004), 261–68.

It is less so in the two instances where the apostles speak to crowds of unconverted Gentiles (Acts 14:8–18 and 17:16–34). In those passages, Paul bases his addresses on creation, on general revelation, to rebuke the idolatry of his audience. To be sure, there are allusions to Scripture, and in Acts 17:31 Paul does refer to Christ, without naming him. But neither of these addresses can be fairly described as redemptive-historical.

But in developing an understanding of preaching in Christian worship, we must go beyond the book of Acts. It is by no means clear that the preaching and teaching that went on in Christian worship services were significantly like the evangelistic preaching in Acts, either to Jews or to Gentiles. For one thing, references to teaching in such services are sparse in the New Testament. The only clear reference is 1 Corinthians 14:26, which refers to a "lesson" (*didachē*).[19] I am not inclined to draw a sharp distinction between preaching (*kerygma*) and teaching (*didachē*). Certainly, the two words can describe the same content. But I imagine that teaching in Christian worship was less evangelistic and more pedagogical in its main thrust, like the New Testament letters of the apostles, which were most likely read in worship (Col. 4:16; 1 Thess. 5:27). Although these letters take account of redemptive history, they also contain long sections of ethical exhortation, responses to specific questions, and so on.

There are some passages that are very confusing to modern congregations unless we say something about their redemptive-historical setting. God told Israel under Joshua to kill the Canaanites. Does he tell us to do the same? Certainly not, because the command presupposes a redemptive-historical setting very different from ours. The iniquity of the Canaanite was full; it was time for God's judgment against the Canaanite nations and the fulfillment of his promise to Abraham. Those conditions don't exist in our relationships with non-Christian neighbors. So every preacher must be aware of the redemptive-historical setting of his text. But that doesn't imply that the sermon must always be *about* that setting. There is no biblical rule that such settings are the only proper subject matter of sermons.

Indeed, there are many ethical passages in Scripture itself which do not explicitly focus on the redemptive-historical context. Proverbs, for example, says nothing about the semieschatological ethical tension, nor does the Mosaic law. We should not demand that a preacher emphasize something that is not emphasized in his text. If one argues that these texts must be seen in the light of the broader biblical principles of redemptive

---

19. Of course, there was also teaching in the worship services through tongues, interpretation of tongues, and prophecy (1 Cor. 14:26–33). I am assuming that these do not continue past the apostolic age. See Richard B. Gaffin Jr., *Perspectives on Pentecost* (Phillipsburg, NJ: Presbyterian and Reformed, 1979).

history, again I would reply that the reverse is also true. Surely we cannot maintain that *every* relevant theological context be brought into the exposition of every text.

I would also like to say a bit about the terms "moralist" and "exemplarist," used as deprecating terms for preachers and sermons deemed insufficiently redemptive-historical in focus. "Moralism" is, as I indicated in chapter 2, a very vague expression, mainly used as a term of abuse. It was used to describe the liberalism of Ritschl and his disciples. They had no gospel at all. To use the same term to describe principled evangelicals of our own time, I believe, is an injustice. *Moralism* also connotes legalism and salvation by works. I believe that if a preacher emphasizes grace in his overall ministry, including the proper relationship between grace and works, it is not wrong for him occasionally to preach on a proverb, a law, or a norm, without devoting his central attention to the structure of redemptive history or to the semieschatological ethical tension.

The use of the term "exemplarist" among advocates of redemptive history is, in my judgment, even more confused. It seems to mean that it is somehow wrong to refer to a Bible character as a moral example. On this view, preachers should refer to Bible characters only as plot devices, as means of advancing the narrative, not as positive or negative examples for our moral guidance.

It is true, of course, that Bible characters other than Jesus are sinful and therefore not always exemplary. It is also true to point out that when biblical characters are exemplary we must take into account their situation (i.e., their place in the history of redemption). The story of David and Goliath, for example, is not an exhortation to little boys to go out and kill bullies with slingshots, but it tells of David's courage in carrying out his responsibility as God's anointed, and thus points to Christ. But David's courage is exemplary nonetheless, and we may apply his example to our circumstances, making appropriate allowance for the difference between our calling and David's.

It is clearly wrong to say that there are in Scripture no moral examples.[20] We saw in chapter 9 that the imitation of God, of Christ, and of godly human beings is a major biblical mode of moral instruction.

Some redemptive-historical preachers seem to have an antipathy to the very idea of practical "application," preferring metaphors like "identification" and "participation." Here is an example:

20. One student actually told me that there are no moral examples in Heb. 11 for us to imitate. His argument was that in Heb. 12:2 we are told to look to Jesus, and, therefore, not to any of the saints mentioned in Heb. 11. In my judgment, commitment to an unbalanced kind of redemptive-historical emphasis had blinded that student to the obvious.

We are saying to the pew, "Come up to the heavenlies in Christ Jesus; come and find your life hidden with Christ in God in this text." Here is your life. We do not ask you to derive lessons from the life of Adam. We proclaim that your life is in Adam— miserable, sinful, rebellious, selfish, autonomous, hellish but we plead with men, women and children everywhere to find their life in that second Adam, to find themselves in Christ Jesus a new creation clothed upon with the righteousness of the Lamb of God, ushered into the paradise of God by the one who has tasted the flame and felt the edge of the sword of divine justice. We preach to you life in Christ Jesus—your life hidden with Christ in God—from first Adam to second Adam—from Adam protological to Adam eschatological—that is our method, that is our message.[21]

The rhetoric here is impressive. But what, concretely, is the difference between deriving "lessons" or "applications" from the life of Adam, and proclaiming "that your life is in Adam"? Most readers would think that our identification with Adam is one lesson we could derive from the story. Is the real point of this statement that this is the *only* application one can make? Should we never, for example, use the unfallen relationship of Adam and Eve as a model for Christian marriage?

I have heard some enthusiasts for redemptive-history complain that the term "application" has bad connotations, deriving from its use in theologies like Schleiermacher's and Bultmann's. But criticizing language on such grounds is an instance of the genetic fallacy. And the proposed alternatives, such as "participation" and "identification," have also been used in non-Christian philosophies, particularly those of Plato and the mystics. The alternative "living in the text" is really too vague to denote a preaching thrust that is purposeful and ethical.

If the argument about application were merely a terminological dispute, it would be of little importance. But I get the impression that some who stress redemptive history really want to avoid "practical" application. They want the whole sermon to focus on Christ, not on what works the believer should do. They want it to focus on gospel, not on law. They want the sermon to evoke praise of Christ, not to demand concrete change in people's behavior. In their mind, Christocentricity excludes any sustained focus on specific practical matters.

I agree that sermons should magnify Christ and evoke praise. But it is simply wrongheaded to deny the importance of concrete, practical, ethical

---

21. James T. Dennison, "Building the Biblical-Theological Sermon, Part One: Perspective," http://www.kerux.com/documents/KeruxV4N3A3.asp.

application. Such application is the purpose of Scripture itself, according to 2 Tim. 3:16–17. And since Scripture itself contains many practical exhortations, our preaching should include them too. To say that this emphasis detracts from Christocentricity is unscriptural.

Christ is central in Scripture as the Redeemer. But he is also the Word, Wisdom, the Lawgiver, the Lord of the covenant, the Lion of Judah, and the Shepherd who leads his people into the right paths. It is wrong to assume that an emphasis on Christ as Redeemer (redemptive history) excludes an emphasis on Christ as norm and motivator.

When a preacher avoids concrete ethical applications in his sermons, he is not preaching the whole counsel of God, and he is not adequately edifying his people. The best redemptive-historical preachers understand this. Some of the most powerful ethical preaching I have heard has come from Edmund Clowney and James Dennison. But in my judgment the concept of ethical preaching does not fit very well into their overall theory of preaching.

Let me also mention some dangers in the practice of preaching exclusively on redemptive-historical themes:

1. Much biblical truth can be left out or illegitimately deemphasized. The preacher may not feel free to dwell on the specifics, say, of Romans 12, if he feels that he must spend most of his time on the redemptive-historical setting of the passage (i.e., Romans 1–11).

2. Some redemptive-historical preachers develop a jargon-laden vocabulary. One recent seminary graduate preached a sermon in which he used the word *eschatological* about fifty times (at least it felt like that), besides a lot of other technical biblical-theological jargon. Maybe he thought that was all right, or even an advantage, with an audience of seminarians. My guess is that seminarians tend to tune out such discourses—they have heard all of that many times. But this language flowed so easily from this young preacher, that I feared he preached this way in his own congregation. If he did, anyone who visited the service would have been entirely bewildered.

In my view, it is best to avoid jargon in preaching. One can make the relevant points about redemptive history without all the technical terms. Most evangelical preachers emphasize (a) that God forgives all the sins of everyone who believes in Christ, (b) that we nevertheless need to continue fighting the spiritual warfare (in our hearts and our society) until the return of Jesus, and (c) that the redemptive work of Christ motivates us to pursue holiness. Those truths constitute the essence of the "already and not-yet," and this language communicates the truth far more effectively than does the jargon.

3. Excessive enthusiasm for redemptive history has sometimes produced division in churches and presbyteries. Some pastors not only preach redemptive history, but also condemn as "moralistic" anybody who fails to emphasize it as much as they do. So "redemptive history" becomes a party label, and factions battle over the concept. In my opinion, this partisanship is wrong.

Why is it, I wonder, that in our circles whenever anybody gets an interesting idea, it produces a party that makes it a test of orthodoxy, leading to another party that opposes it, and then to battles between these parties in the churches? Why can't those who think they have new insights quietly teach them to others while embracing them as brothers and sisters in Christ? If some don't "get it," why should that amount to heresy? Why not simply permit both views to be taught until the Spirit convinces God's people generally that one view is scriptural and the other is not?

In recent Reformed history, we have had these partisan battles over Van Til's apologetics (and now, different schools of Van Tillian apologetics), common grace, the incomprehensibility of God, supra- and infralapsarianism, theonomy, the relationship between grace and law in the covenants, Shepherd's view of justification, nouthetic counseling, exclusive psalmody, contemporary worship, means of church growth, and redemptive-historical preaching. None of these is resolved in our Reformed confessions, but partisans act as if they were. They think that their view alone is orthodox, and that their opponents are dangerous heretics. Can't we just lighten up a bit? Can we never admit our fallibility? Is there not a place, on some issues, for teachability, even tolerance? Can't we ever agree to disagree in peace and love, working together on those matters where we agree?[22]

4. For some reason, it seems to me that enthusiasts for redemptive history are often poor logicians. In some sermons, presbytery speeches, student papers, and even some published treatises, I have heard elaborate citations of Scripture, already and not-yets, messianic this and eschatological that, and then at the end some conclusion (a doctrinal, ethical, or procedural point) that doesn't have much to do with the redemptive-historical argumentation.

5. Young preachers who try to preach redemptive-historical sermons often spend so much time preparing the theology of their messages that they completely neglect rhetorical considerations—that is, communication. So their sermons come across as a lot of gobbledygook.

22. For more on this subject, see my article "Machen's Warrior Children," in *Alister E. McGrath and Evangelical Theology*, ed. Sung Wook Chung (Grand Rapids: Baker, 2003), 113–46.

The redemptive-historical method of preaching typically takes much more preparation time than others. And at its best it requires substantial intellectual and rhetorical gifts, which few seminarians and young pastors possess. When average preachers with busy schedules try to prepare redemptive-historical sermons, the result is often incomprehensible. Now, you can say what you like about the dangers of neglecting redemptive history, but a sermon that does not communicate with the people is not preaching at all.

So all I ask of a young preacher is that he preach clearly the gospel of grace, a proper relationship between grace and works, and no major errors stemming from redemptive-historical ignorance. These are simple goals, well within the abilities of seminary-trained young men whom God has called to the ministry. When a preacher accomplishes these goals, he may not fairly be accused of moralism. His preaching will be biblical and effective.

6. Young preachers often think that their sermons must not only be clear, but also profound and original. The redemptive-historical method often attracts them, because it encourages such creativity. The best of the redemptive-historical preachers, like Vos and Clowney, often lead the listener into unique biblical depth. But young preachers need to be more humble about what they can expect from their first sermons. It is better to realize one's own limitations and to seek what's most important: clear communication of the biblical gospel.

I will conclude by observing that I personally receive more benefit from redemptive-historically focused sermons than from any other kind. At best, redemptive-historical preaching exalts Christ and shows how all Scripture points to him. It also shows how Christ is relevant to all aspects of human life. So I hope that seminaries will continue to teach students how to preach on the history of redemption. What disturbs me is the recent movement to develop a redemptive-historical party in the Reformed churches, set over against other partisan groups, dividing the body of Christ.

CHAPTER 17

Our Chief End

In chapter 14, I indicated that the situational perspective is a sort of Christian teleological ethic. From the situational perspective, we ask how we should seek to change the world in order to bring glory to God. That question assumes that we are working toward a goal (the glory of God) and seeking means to reach it. Our situational ethics has a formal structure similar to secular teleological ethics, which seeks means to reach an end. In secular teleological systems, the end is usually human happiness or pleasure. Christian ethics does not ignore those goals, but makes them subordinate to the glory of God.

In this chapter, I will discuss several definitions of the goal of the Christian life, from the literature of Christian theology.

THE DOCTRINE OF THE TWOFOLD END

On the very first page of his *Summa theologica*, Thomas Aquinas presents his justification for a science of God (Scripture, theology) in addition to philosophy:

> It was necessary for man's salvation that there should be a knowledge revealed by God besides philosophical science built up by human reason. Firstly, indeed, because man is directed to God, as to an end that surpasses the grasp of his reason: "The eye hath not seen, O God, besides Thee, what things Thou hast prepared

for them that wait for Thee" (Is. 66:4). But the end must first be known by men who are to direct their thoughts and actions to the end. Hence it was necessary for the salvation of man that certain truths which exceed human reason should be made known to him by divine revelation.[1]

God has ordained that human beings, therefore, should pursue two ends, an earthly end and a heavenly one. Philosophy, without the aid of Scripture, enables us to understand our earthly end. Scripture and theology provide understanding of our heavenly end. Edmund Gardner finds the same duality in Dante's *De monarchia*:

> Man is ordained for two ends: blessedness of this life, which consists in the exercise of his natural powers and is figured in the terrestrial paradise; blessedness of life eternal, which consists in the fruition of the Divine aspect in the celestial paradise to which man's natural powers cannot ascend without the aid of the Divine light. To these two ends man must come by diverse means: "For to the first we attain by the teachings of philosophy, following them by acting in accordance with the moral and intellectual virtues. To the second by spiritual teachings, which transcend human reason, as we follow them by acting according to the theological virtues." But, although these ends and means are made plain to us by human reason and by revelation, men in their cupidity would reject them, were not they restrained by bit and rein. "Wherefore man had need of a twofold directive power according to his twofold end, to wit, the Supreme Pontiff, to lead the human race in accordance with things revealed, to eternal life; and the Emperor, to direct the human race to temporal felicity in accordance with the teachings of philosophy."[2]

This quotation adds to the first that (1) to each end correspond virtues: moral and intellectual virtues corresponding to our earthly end, and theological virtues (faith, hope, and love) to our spiritual end, and that (2) this duality implies a duality of institutions, the state to guide us to earthly happiness and the church to lead us to heaven.

These quotations represent the main thrust of Roman Catholic teaching concerning the ends or goals of human life. The view of Augustine and

---

1. Aquinas, *Summa theologica*, 1.1.1. English translation from the online version of the Christian Classics Ethereal Library, http://www.ccel.org/ccel/aquinas/summa. FP_Q1_A1.html.

2. Edmund G. Gardner, "Dante Alighieri," in *The Catholic Encyclopedia*, online edition, 2003, available at http://www.newadvent.org/cathen/04628a.htm.

other earlier church fathers was somewhat more otherworldly. Aquinas, under the influence of Aristotle, seeks balance between heavenly ends and earthly ones. Scripture also acknowledges the legitimacy of our earthly concerns. The things God created are good, even after the fall, according to Paul (1 Tim. 4:4). Jesus teaches that God is concerned to provide for all our physical needs (Matt. 6:33), but he places this teaching, as we shall see, in the context of a rather different view of the goal of human life.

For Aquinas, unaided human reason is sufficient to guide us toward earthly happiness, but not toward eternal life. We can see that this view of things fits in well with the traditional natural law approach to ethics, especially without the Budziszewski emendations. (Recall our discussion of this in chapter 14.) For Aquinas, natural reason (operating in accord with Aristotelian epistemology) is sufficient to direct the state, which in turn administers the affairs of earthly society. The church governs the spiritual sphere of life. Those who are most serious about seeking heaven take vows of poverty, chastity, and obedience and leave the sphere of earthly life for a "religious" vocation. These follow the *consilia evangelica*, the evangelical counsels.

We should also connect this view of things with our earlier discussion of the Lutheran law/gospel distinction (chapter 12). Although Lutherans and Roman Catholics have very different views of what constitutes the gospel, they share the notion that civil society should be governed apart from those teachings of Scripture that transcend natural revelation.

Aquinas's view should be understood as part of the larger distinction between nature and grace that underlies his thought. That distinction became the foundation of traditional Roman Catholic theology. Herman Dooyeweerd describes the "nature-grace motive" as follows:

> Within the natural sphere a relative autonomy was ascribed to human reason, which was supposed to be capable of discovering the natural truths by its own light. Within the supra-natural sphere of grace, on the contrary, human thought was considered to be dependent on the divine self-revelation. Philosophy was considered to belong to the natural sphere, dogmatical theology, on the other hand, to the supra-natural sphere. In consequence, there was no longer a question of Christian philosophy. Philosophical thought was, in fact, abandoned to the influence of the Greek and Humanist basic motives in their external accommodation to the doctrine of the Church. These motives were masked by the dogmatic acceptance of the autonomy of natural reason. . . . The Thomistic attempt at a synthesis of the opposite motives of nature

and grace, and the ascription of the primacy of the latter found a clear expression in the adage: *Gratia naturam non tollit, sed perfecit* (Grace does not cancel nature, but it perfects it).[3]

The nature-grace motive also appears in Roman Catholic anthropology, in which God supplements the natural gifts given to Adam at creation with a *donum superadditum*, a gift of divine grace, by which his senses are brought under the control of reason and thus Adam enters a deep fellowship with God. In the fall, Adam and Eve lose the superadded gifts, which must be restored through the operations of grace. Their natural gifts remain intact.

The picture is always one of supplementation. The fall has not radically disrupted the functions of nature. For the most part, those functions still operate pretty well. But human beings need something more, and grace provides what is lacking. Similarly, Aristotelian philosophy, to Aquinas, is sufficient for earthly happiness, though it must be supplemented by Scripture if we are to attain heaven. Occasionally, to be sure, Scripture must correct the conclusions of natural reason. Aristotle thought, for example, that the world was eternal. The Bible teaches otherwise. So Aquinas, who is first of all a Christian and only secondly an Aristotelian, gives Scripture veto power over philosophy. But Aquinas did not believe that philosophy, our study of the cosmos, had to be built upon Scripture from the outset. The foundations of philosophy, for Aquinas as for Aristotle, lie in would-be autonomous human reason.

But in Reformed thought there is a much deeper integration between nature and grace. As we saw in chapter 14, Calvin held that we cannot use natural revelation rightly, apart from the spectacles of Scripture. Scripture does not merely[4] supplement Aristotle and correct him here and there; rather, it challenges the non-Christian philosopher to place all of his thinking on a different basis, to bring every thought captive to Christ (2 Cor. 10:5).

In Reformed theology, there is no distinction in Adam's original constitution between natural and gracious gifts; rather, God constituted Adam as a good and righteous man. In the fall, Adam did not merely lose certain gifts;

---

3. Dooyeweerd, *In the Twilight of Western Thought* (Philadelphia: Presbyterian and Reformed, 1960), 44–45. Roman Catholic thinkers do in fact speak of "Christian philosophy" and of the thought of Aquinas as a notable example of it. They believe that Scripture and tradition actually encourage the kind of synthesis that Aquinas made between Christianity and Aristotle. Dooyeweerd denies that such a synthesis is legitimate.

4. Of course, this *merely* is important. Scripture does supplement the knowledge of God available in natural revelation. So to speak of supplementation is not necessarily wrong. But there is much more to be said. Talk of supplementation must be supplemented. See my *Cornelius Van Til* (Phillipsburg, NJ: P&R Publishing, 1995), 248–51, 260–61.

his whole life became corrupt. So saving grace does not merely add a supplement to fallen human life; rather, it restores it from the heart outward.

It should not surprise us that Reformed understandings of "man's chief end" tend to be unitary, rather than dualistic. Our goal is to glorify God in all of life. It is not that earthly happiness is unimportant. Our Father knows what we need to preserve and enjoy our earthly lives (Matt. 6:32–33). But our goal is not to attain these things, but rather to seek the kingdom of God (v. 33). The "religious" life is not a monastic existence, but human life as a whole, directed to God's glory.

TO GLORIFY GOD

The Shorter Catechism's answer to the question, "What is the chief end of man?" is, "Man's chief end is to glorify God, and to enjoy him forever."[5] This formula might seem to belie my last point, that Reformed concepts of the goal of ethics are unitary, rather than dualistic. The Catechism seems to call us to two things: glorifying God, and enjoying him forever. We shall see, however, that these two goals form a close unity. It should be immediately evident that they do not pertain to spiritual and earthly life, respectively, as on the Roman Catholic construction. Rather, both pertain to human life as a whole. There is no area of life where we are not called both to glorify God and to enjoy him forever.

Let us ask first what it means to glorify God.[6] The glory of God is literally the great light that shines forth when God makes his presence visible to human beings. As such, his glory is something physical, part of the creation. But glory is also a divine attribute, coordinate with greatness, power, majesty, and splendor in 1 Chronicles 29:11. As God, Jesus shares in the Father's glory (John 17:5). In Scripture, glory in this sense is more or less equivalent to the lordship attribute of divine presence. Wherever God is, even when he is invisible, there is glory. So the term can refer to God himself, his revelation of himself in the world, his reputation among human beings, or even the praise that human beings bring to him.[7]

His presence, in one sense, is throughout creation. So creation declares God's glory (Ps. 19:1). Human beings, his special image within creation, are also his special glory (Ps. 8:5; 1 Cor. 11:7). The image of God, as we saw in chapter 9, is both a fact and a norm. So is the glory in which God has made us. As God's image, we are made to reflect God's glory back to him. In one

---

5. WSC, 1.

6. This discussion summarizes, and occasionally quotes, a longer one in *DG*, 592–95.

7. *Doxa*, "glory," can also often be translated "praise."

sense, we do that by virtue of our creation. In another sense, to reflect that glory is a deliberate choice that we make or refuse to make.[8]

So Scripture calls us to glorify God in everything we do (1 Cor. 10:31). In one sense, we cannot increase God's glory. But when our lives image God, others see the presence of God in us. So we ourselves become part of that light from God that goes forth over the earth. When we speak truly of him and obey his Word, we enhance his reputation on the earth, his praise, so that we, like Jesus, become "the light of the world" (Matt. 5:14).

To glorify God is to recognize him as the chief fact of human life. He determines our purpose and governs our lives. The first four of the Ten Commandments focus on our duty toward him. Everything we do must take him into account, and whenever we properly take him into account, our actions are right (Rom. 14:23; Col. 3:17, 23).

TO ENJOY HIM FOREVER

But the Catechism adds a second phrase to its formulation of our chief end: "to enjoy him forever." At first it is difficult to see how these two phrases fit together. The first is theocentric, but the second appears to be anthropocentric. The first is distinctly biblical, but the second sounds rather like the goal of pleasure in secular teleological ethics.

It helps to notice, however, that even the second phrase is centered on God. We are not to enjoy ourselves, but to enjoy *him*. So the second phrase calls us to find our chief enjoyment in God, not in the world. To embrace the enjoyment of God as the goal of life is to sing with Asaph:

> Whom have I in heaven but you?
> And there is nothing on earth that I desire besides you.
> My flesh and my heart may fail,
> but God is the strength of my heart and my portion forever.
> For behold, those who are far from you shall perish;
> you put an end to everyone who is unfaithful to you.
> But for me it is good to be near God;
> I have made the Lord GOD my refuge,
> that I may tell of all your works. (Ps. 73:25–28)

8. These two senses correspond to the larger biblical distinction between God's decretive and preceptive wills (*DG*, 531–38). God has decreed that all creatures will glorify him, whether they are good or evil. But his precepts demand that creatures choose consciously to glorify him. Sometimes creatures obey those precepts, sometimes not. So in one sense everything glorifies God; in another sense, God receives glory only from what is holy and righteous.

Although Asaph uses forms of the first person pronoun ten times in this passage, and thirty-three times in the whole psalm, these verses are profoundly theocentric.[9] So when the Catechism moves from the first phrase to the second, it is not moving from God-centeredness to man-centeredness. Rather, it is looking at God-centeredness from two perspectives.

The second perspective is entirely scriptural. To redeemed human beings, glorifying God is a delight. In chapter 16, I showed how often Scripture mentions the rewards that God has promised to those who love him. Those rewards are delightful beyond our imagining, and they are a powerful motivation to obedience. In that chapter, I emphasized that the Christian ethic is far removed from Kantian deontology, in which we do our duty for duty's sake, with no thought of reward. Rather, in the Christian life, we seek to do God's will for God's rewards.

Even God's law, which we often regard as a stern taskmaster, is a delight to the redeemed heart (Pss. 1:2; 119:97; Rom. 7:22), a gift of God's grace (Ps. 119:29). It is our way of life, not in the sense that it brings us eternal life apart from grace, but in the sense that it brings fullness of blessing to those who are saved by grace, when they walk in God's ways (Lev. 18:5; Deut. 5:33; 8:3; 11:13–15; 28:1–4; 30:11–20). God has given the law for our good (Deut. 10:12–13; 4:40; 12:28).[10]

Scripture does condemn selfishness and preoccupation with our own comfort and pleasure (Matt. 6:24–34; 1 Cor. 6:13; Phil. 3:19; 1 Tim. 5:6; James 5:5). It demands self-sacrifice, even enduring hardship (Matt. 24:13; Mark 10:29–30; 2 Tim. 2:3; 4:5; Heb. 12:7; James 1:12; 1 Peter 2:19), and persecution (Matt. 5:10–12, 44; 10:23; 13:21; John 15:20; Rom. 8:35; 12:14; 1 Cor. 4:12; 2 Cor. 12:10; 2 Thess. 1:4; 2 Tim. 3:12). But some of the passages that describe most graphically the rigors and difficulties of the Christian life also emphasize its rewards. Matthew 5:10–12 reads:

> Blessed are those who are persecuted for righteousness' sake, for theirs is the kingdom of heaven. Blessed are you when others revile you and persecute you and utter all kinds of evil against you falsely on my account. Rejoice and be glad, for your reward is great in heaven, for so they persecuted the prophets who were before you.

9. It is still common for some to criticize contemporary worship songs for their overuse of first person pronouns. Critics often take this as a symptom of narcissism, evidence that these songs aim to glorify ourselves, rather than God. Let us be done with this kind of argument. The Psalms abound in first person references, but they are nonetheless profoundly God-centered. Compare my discussion of Ps. 18, in critique of Marva Dawn, in *Contemporary Worship Music* (Phillipsburg, NJ: P&R Publishing, 1997), 169–70.

10. This emphasis is, of course, contrary to the law/gospel view discussed in chapter 12, according to which the law includes no blessings and the gospel includes no obligations.

James 1:12 is a beatitude:

> Blessed is the man who remains steadfast under trial, for when he has stood the test he will receive the crown of life, which God has promised to those who love him.

Mark 10:29–30 promises blessings, not only in the next world, but in this one as well:

> Jesus said, "Truly, I say to you, there is no one who has left house or brothers or sisters or mother or father or children or lands, for my sake and for the gospel, who will not receive a hundredfold now in this time, houses and brothers and sisters and mothers and children and lands, with persecutions, and in the age to come eternal life.

And Paul, in 2 Corinthians 12:10, says:

> For the sake of Christ, then, I am content with weaknesses, insults, hardships, persecutions, and calamities. For when I am weak, then I am strong.

Evidently, then, the biblical principle is that the pleasures of serving God are not primarily short-term, but long-term, though of course God gives us many short-term blessings as well. Note the "little while" by which Peter describes the length of our hardship:

> Blessed be the God and Father of our Lord Jesus Christ! According to his great mercy, he has caused us to be born again to a living hope through the resurrection of Jesus Christ from the dead, to an inheritance that is imperishable, undefiled, and unfading, kept in heaven for you, who by God's power are being guarded through faith for a salvation ready to be revealed in the last time. In this you rejoice, though now for a little while, as was necessary, you have been grieved by various trials, so that the tested genuineness of your faith—more precious than gold that perishes though it is tested by fire—may be found to result in praise and glory and honor at the revelation of Jesus Christ. Though you have not seen him, you love him. Though you do not now see him, you believe in him and rejoice with joy that is inexpressible and filled with glory, obtaining the outcome of your faith, the salvation of your souls. (1 Peter 1:3–9)

Compare with this Paul's reference to his "slight momentary affliction" that is "preparing for us an eternal weight of glory beyond all comparison" (2 Cor. 4:17; cf. Rom. 8:18–25, 35–39). Although our suffering in the present may seem sometimes to outweigh the blessing of God, in eternity those troubles will seem tiny. And through God's Word we are able to view the present time in the light of eternity, recognizing the true proportions of things. In that light, those like Paul are able to say, even in the midst of terrible suffering, that it is light and momentary.[11]

In contrast, the pleasures of sin are fleeting (Heb. 11:25). Even pursuing the good things of God's creation is vain, outside the context of God's overall purpose for us (Eccl. 2:1–11; 12:13–14).

So our life with God is in the deepest sense an enjoyment of him. To say this may require us to look at life from perspectives that are different from our customary ones. But Scripture teaches us how to attain these perspectives, showing us how not to be anxious about anything, "but in everything by prayer and supplication with thanksgiving let your requests be made known to God. And the peace of God, which surpasses all understanding, will guard your hearts and your minds in Christ Jesus" (Phil. 4:6–7).[12]

In the end, one cannot glorify God without enjoying him. The goal expressed by WSC, 1, is, in the most profound sense, not twofold, but one. God desires to share his glory with his people, his image, his sons and daughters, his bride. He is not like Molech (Lev. 18:21), the false god who demanded human sacrifice. Rather, our God delights in the fulfillment of human potential.

Grudging obedience is not what he desires of us. It may be better than no obedience at all, but it is seriously defective. We should seek, not only to obey him, but also to delight in obedience. That delight comes from prayer and supplication with thanksgiving, through immersion in the words of Scripture and the hearts of the great saints of redemptive history, and through the fellowship of the church in Word and sacrament.

THE KINGDOM OF GOD

Another biblical formulation of the goal of human life is Matthew 6:33, "But seek first the kingdom of God and his righteousness, and all these things will be added to you." "These things" are the necessities of earthly life—food, drink, and clothing (v. 31). So in this text, as in the ones con-

---

11. Paul describes his "slight momentary affliction" in 2 Cor. 11:24–33. Most people would describe these sufferings as unbearable.

12. John Piper has rendered a valuable service to the church by his advocacy of "Christian hedonism." He shows powerfully and biblically that delight in God motivates the Christian life. See his *Desiring God* (Sisters, OR: Multnomah Publishers, 2003).

sidered above, God is concerned with human life and enjoyment. But here the Lord presents the goal from still another perspective.[13]

We discussed the kingdom of God in chapter 16. It is God's work in history by which he overcomes all his opponents and establishes his righteousness on the earth. We saw in chapter 12 that the gospel, the good news, is the declaration that God is bringing his kingdom to earth. In Matthew 6:33, we learn that the kingdom is what we should seek "first," that it should be the chief purpose governing our lives.

This goal shows further how our glorifying of God and our enjoying of him are related. For the kingdom is an institution that incorporates both God and his people. He is the king, and we are the subjects. In the kingdom, God and his people work together to bring transformation to people and to the world. Insofar as the kingdom prospers, God will be glorified and we will find our highest pleasure. We can think of glorifying God as normative, enjoying him as existential, and seeking his kingdom as historical and therefore situational.

So to speak of the kingdom as our ethical goal is to focus on the important factor of historical development. Our goal is not obedience in the abstract, but participation in a specific historical program. So everything we do should in some way contribute to the progress of that kingdom program. Not only should our own lives be righteous, but we should be seeking to establish God's righteousness on the earth.

THE CULTURAL MANDATE AND THE GREAT COMMISSION

The dynamism of the kingdom becomes even more evident when we consider two more specific forms of the biblical goal of human life. These are the cultural mandate of Genesis 1:28 and the Great Commission of Matthew 28:18–20. God gave the cultural mandate to Adam and Eve at their creation. He defined their task on earth as follows: "Be fruitful and multiply and fill the earth and subdue it and have dominion over the fish of the sea and over the birds of the heavens and over every living thing that moves on the earth."

Three things can be learned from this mandate. First, man's whole life is to be governed by God's commands. In this passage, God's word claims the right to govern the whole direction of human life. In terms of our three

13. Cornelius Van Til's favorite description of the goal of human life was "the kingdom of God as man's *summum bonum*." See *Christian Theistic Ethics* ([Ripon, CA]: den Dulk Christian Foundation, 1971), 44, cf. 41–151.

perspectives, this is the normative side of the mandate. Second, man is to subdue the earth and have dominion over all other creatures. Here, Adam and Eve are to image the power of God's lordship, taking control over the world to God's glory. This is the situational perspective of the mandate, showing how man is to use his power to bring his environment under his vassal lordship, ultimately to the glory of God.[14] Third, man is to be fruitful, multiply, and fill the earth with human beings, again imaging God, who fills the earth with his divine presence. This part of the mandate corresponds to the existential perspective.

Jesus gave the Great Commission to his disciples following his resurrection, preceding his ascension to God's right hand. This commission establishes the church as a missionary body:

> And Jesus came and said to them, "All authority in heaven and on earth has been given to me. Go therefore and make disciples of all nations, baptizing them in the name of the Father and of the Son and of the Holy Spirit, teaching them to observe all that I have commanded you. And behold, I am with you always, to the end of the age." (Matt. 28:18–20)

In the Old Testament too, God intended to bless all nations through his covenant with Abraham (Gen. 12:3). But the predominant imagery of that blessing (as in Isa. 2:1–4) was centripetal: the nations coming to Jerusalem to worship the Lord. The Great Commission begins a centrifugal movement: God's people going out from Jerusalem to Judea, Samaria, and "the end of the earth" (Acts 1:8), bringing the kingdom to all nations. The cultural mandate, as we have seen, is also centrifugal. So in the Great Commission Jesus renews God's original purpose to fill the earth with worshipers of the true God.

Of course, great events intervened between the cultural mandate and the Great Commission: the fall of man and the redemptive work of Christ. If the earth is to be filled with worshipers of the true God, they must first be saved from sin by the Word and Spirit of God. So, unlike the cultural mandate, the Great Commission is focused on the communication of the gospel, by which we are to make disciples, baptize them, and teach them a new way of living.

Otherwise, the two mandates cohere. The Great Commission, like the cultural mandate, can be described triperspectivally: it is based on

14. As I indicated in chapter 15, this does not mean that Adam should exploit the natural world. Of course, to exercise godly dominion, he must not only make use of the other creatures, but also preserve and nurture them, imaging the structure of God's own dominion.

Jesus' sovereign control of all things (the situational perspective).[15] It requires discipling, baptism, and teaching (the normative perspective). And it guarantees the presence of Jesus with his people for all time (the existential perspective).

We can also see a congruence between the two mandates in terms of another triad: seed, land, and divine promise. The divine promise is the norm that creates the obligation and insures the blessing (normative). Land is the territory that God has given for man to occupy (situational). Seed is the presence of man on the earth, analogous to God's presence in the creation (existential). The cultural mandate begins with God's word of blessing, which calls Adam and Eve to fill the earth with their seed and to take dominion over the land.

Scripture continues to stress this triad throughout redemptive history. In Genesis 3, God responds to the fall by giving promises encased in threats (see chapter 16), reiterating his normative will. Then he pronounces curses and blessings precisely in the areas of seed (childbearing) and land (man's toil). In these areas, man is to experience pain. But these are also to be God's means of preserving the human race until the child of the promise comes into the world.

All of the post-Adamic covenants are promises (normative) of land (situational) and seed (existential). God saves Noah by his word and renews the cultural mandate in Genesis 9:7. Abraham trusts in God's word to give him land (Canaan) and seed (descendants) through Isaac, as numerous as the sand and the stars (Gen. 22:17). In the Mosaic covenant, God renews the promise of land and chooses a people to fill that land. God promises David that a royal seed will always occupy the throne (2 Sam. 7:4–16), and that that seed will rule all the earth (Ps. 72).

The Great Commission carries this theme into the new covenant. Christ is himself the promised seed, the fulfillment of Genesis 3:15. He fills all things with his presence (Eph. 1:23; 4:10). And he takes title to all lands in God's creation (Matt. 28:18). It might seem, then, that there is nothing left for believers to do, since Jesus has fulfilled the terms of the cultural mandate. But we must not forget that we live in a semieschatological age, the age of the already and the not-yet. This is the age

---

15. Verse 18 uses the term "authority" (*exousia*), which I have usually associated with the normative perspective. In this context, however, I think that Jesus refers to his authority over all things to embolden his disciples, so that they will recognize that no disaster can prevent the success of their mission. That encouragement brings his control (situational) to the fore. But of course the situational and normative perspectives are inseparable. The situational is always normative in the sense that God's authority (normative) extends to all events of nature and history (situational).

in which Christ has fulfilled history, but in which nevertheless he calls his disciples to apply his finished work.

That call is the Great Commission. Believers are to fill the earth with worshipers of God and thus take dominion of all lands, using the resources that Christ gives them from heaven. Now the land is the whole earth, not just Palestine, and the seed consists of all those who have been begotten by God's Spirit. Thus will be fulfilled the prophecy of Isaiah that "the earth shall be full of the knowledge of the LORD as the waters cover the sea" (Isa. 11:9).

The Great Commission, therefore, can be understood as a republication of the cultural mandate for the semieschatological age. Unlike the original cultural mandate, it presupposes the existence of sin and the accomplishment of redemption. It recognizes that if the world is to be filled with worshipers of God, subduing the earth as his vassal kings, they must first be converted to Christ through the preaching of the gospel. But when the evangelization of the world is complete, the result will be that envisaged in the cultural mandate.

In Reformed circles, there have been different views concerning the relation of these two mandates. Some have thought that the cultural mandate is obsolete, because of the fall and redemption, and because Christ has already filled and subdued all things. On that view, Christians should be concerned only with the work of the gospel, not with bringing potentialities out of the earth for human dominion. Secular work is legitimate, on this view, but only as a means of supporting the work of the Great Commission.

Others believe that since the cultural mandate is the original mandate given to Adam, a creation ordinance (see chapter 13), it should be the main focus of human life. Some, indeed, on this view, are called to preach the gospel, but that is only one way of fulfilling the cultural mandate.

If, however, I am right about the conceptual congruence of these two mandates and the semieschatological nature of Christ's fulfillment of Genesis 1:28, then, first, the cultural mandate continues in force. It is right and good for us to explore and inhabit the earth and to use its resources for the glory of God and the betterment of human life. The works of science, art, technology, government, and so on are good, when done for God. These are good in themselves, not only as means to bring people to faith.

In the broadest sense, however, the cultural mandate cannot be fulfilled until the Great Commission is fulfilled. There cannot be a world full of worshipers of God until people repent of their sins and turn to Christ. So all of human life in this semieschatological age should have a redemptive focus. Everything we do should contribute in some way to the fulfillment of the Great Commission. The construction of an office building, for example, can be good in itself. But Christians involved in such a project should consider how that project can be used to turn hearts to Christ, as by contributing some profits to the work of the church.

So the goal of human life in this age always has a redemptive aspect. Scripture emphasizes this fact in a number of ways:

1. As we saw in chapter 16, the kingdom of God is not only the sovereign reign of God over creation, but specifically, as Vos said, "where God supernaturally carries through his supremacy against all opposing powers and brings man to the willing recognition of the same."[16] So the kingdom is redemptive in character, and that redemptive kingdom is the goal of human life in Matthew 6:33. Jesus there contrasts the kingdom with lesser priorities (which are nonetheless necessities!)—food, drink, and clothing. So it is the highest priority.

2. The love commandment in John 13:34–35 calls us to love as Christ loved us, and it says that this is the mark of those who are Jesus' disciples. But that love of Christ is distinctly redemptive.

3. In 1 Corinthians 9, Paul speaks of the goal of his life as saving human beings through the gospel (vv. 19–22, cf. 10:33), and indeed gaining his own share of the benefit of the gospel (vv. 23–27). We might think that these goals are unique to Paul's calling as an apostle. But in 9:24 and 10:31–11:1 he urges the Corinthians to have the same goals as he has. We saw earlier how 10:31 ("Do all to the glory of God") serves as a goal for all human life. Now we see the redemptive context of that goal.

4. In Philippians 3, Paul again sets forth the overall motivation of his life and ministry. He counts "everything" as loss for Christ (vv. 7–8), so everything in his life is now directed toward Christ. Pressing on toward "the prize of the upward call of God in Christ Jesus" (v. 14) is the "one thing" he does (v. 13), the "goal" he runs toward (v. 14). Again, Paul does not adopt this goal for himself alone, but he presents it as a model for us to imitate (vv. 15–17).

So everything we do should be done to advance, not only God's purposes in general, but specifically his program of redemption as presented in the Great Commission.

VOCATION

Thus far, I have discussed goals primarily of a corporate kind: goals for the human race as a whole and for the church as God's people. Glorifying

---

16. Vos, *The Teaching of Jesus Concerning the Kingdom of God and the Church* (Nutley, NJ: Presbyterian and Reformed, 1972), 50.

God, enjoying him, and seeking his kingdom are universal goals as well as individual goals. But the cultural mandate and the Great Commission are not really individual goals. As I indicated in chapter 15, neither of these presents a goal for each individual to attain. Adam could not have replenished and subdued the earth all by himself. This task presupposes a society in which each member plays a different role in achieving the result. The same is true of the Great Commission. No individual believer can "teach all nations," but the church as a body can do this with God's help. God has gifted individuals differently (Rom. 12:3–8; 1 Cor. 12:1–31; Eph. 4:1–16), so each believer must determine what specific role God has enabled him to play in the fulfillment of the Great Commission.

Specific roles entail specific goals. The teacher in the church must seek to achieve clarity and effectiveness in his teaching. Someone laboring in mercy ministry must seek the goal of meeting the needs of all whom God brings his way, expressing to them the love of Christ.

Protestantism has described these individual roles and goals as *vocations*, divine callings. In the medieval period, Christians applied the term to positions in the church: priests, monks, and nuns. The Reformation broadened the term to include all believers, so that even those doing secular work have divine callings.[17] Paul uses the term in this broad sense in 1 Corinthians 7:17.

Although the term *vocation* suggests a divine revelation to each individual of God's assignment to him, the Reformers did not consider vocation to be a special revelation. Special revelation is limited to Scripture. But God gives to each believer wisdom to discover how God has gifted him and how he can best use that gift in God's kingdom. That wisdom should of course be compared with the wisdom of other believers, who can help us to evaluate our gifts. It would not be wrong to describe this process as "existential revelation" (see chapter 9). In vocation, God enables us to apply the principles of Scripture to our own lives and to our circumstances. In this process, we come to see God's will for our lives[18] and to gain assurance that we are in the place where God wants us to be.

Vocation comes to us, then, by way of (1) God giving gifts to us, (2) the Spirit enabling us to discern those gifts through self-examination and

---

17. Calling in this sense differs from (1) "effectual calling," which is God's sovereign work of summoning elect people into union with Christ (as in Rom. 1:6–7), and from (2) the "gospel call" or "outward call," in which preachers of the gospel call their hearers to trust in Christ.

18. In *DG*, 539–42, I suggest that there is a third sense in which Scripture uses the phrase "will of God," alongside the decretive and preceptive senses. I think this is the case in Rom. 12:1–2, and similar expressions can be found in Eph. 5:8–10, Phil. 1:9–10, and Heb. 5:12–14. Vocation as discussed here is one kind of revelation of this will of God.

through the confirmation of others in the church, (3) God providing opportunities for us to develop and exercise those gifts, (4) God providing wisdom so that we can use those gifts in ways that glorify him, extend his kingdom, fulfill his mandates, and in the end enjoy him forever.

SHORT-RANGE GOALS

We continue to move from general to specific. As there are specific goals for each believer, so there are specific goals for each moment.

If Laura is asked to submit a report to her employer, she should do it "heartily, as for the Lord and not for men, knowing that from the Lord you will receive the inheritance as your reward. You are serving the Lord Christ" (Col. 3:23–24). Paul directs this admonition specifically to slaves. How much more does it apply to those who are voluntarily employed.

There is no Scripture passage that specifically requires her to submit that report, on time and in the form requested. But this is the application of many more general teachings of Scripture, such as those we have already considered. Glorifying God, enjoying him, seeking his kingdom, obeying his mandates—all of these things take place in thousands of individual decisions. The journey toward reaching the major goals of the Christian life requires many little steps.

Thus, for example, I have an obligation to teach a class in systematic theology in classroom 3 of Reformed Theological Seminary, Orlando, at 2 p.m. today, as I write. So far as I know, nobody else has that specific ethical obligation. But I have it, because of my individual calling and because of the specific tasks that that calling entails. And my goal is to cover certain subjects in that class in such a way as to help the students learn them. The big goals entail many little goals. We need to ask more often how our little tasks advance the big ones. And we need to consider whether the sublimity of the larger tasks gives shape to the details of our life, motivating us to seek God's glory again and again throughout the day.

THE EXISTENTIAL PERSPECTIVE

CHAPTER 18

Goodness and Being

We have seen that the normative perspective of Christian ethics asks, "What is my duty before God?" The situational perspective asks, "How should I change the world in order to achieve the goals that are pleasing to God?" Now we shall investigate the existential perspective, which asks, "How must I be changed, if I am to please God?" The question may also be asked from a corporate standpoint: "How must *we* be changed, if *we* are to please God?" The three questions are ultimately equivalent, but they present different perspectives on ethical choice, and each can sometimes help us to correct our misapprehensions of the others.

The normative perspective can be seen as a Christian deontological ethic, the situational perspective as a Christian teleological ethic, and the existential perspective as a Christian existential ethic. These reflect the emphases of their non-Christian counterparts (as we examined them in chapters 6–8), but they bring these emphases together into a more coherent and fruitful unity in the context of our covenant relationship to God.

I begin with some ontological observations, similar to those I made about the other two perspectives. Under the normative perspective (chapter 9), I showed how God's word is God himself, revealing himself through created media. Under the situational perspective (chapter 15), I indicated that our basic situation is God himself, together with all the persons and things he has made. Now again, under the existential perspective, we must consider the supremacy of God himself and his relationship to his creatures.

God is not only the chief norm and the chief fact, but also the chief person, the chief subjectivity. As such, he is not only our law and our situation, but also our example of holiness, righteousness, and love.[1] He is good, as only a person can be.[2] But to say that is not to say that he conforms to a standard of goodness imposed on him from above. Nor is it to say that he creates goodness as he creates the world, so that he could change it tomorrow. Goodness is neither above God nor below God. Rather, goodness is God. God is his own goodness. Goodness is God's eternal attribute. Without his goodness, he would not be God. So he will never be other than good. "God is light, and in him is no darkness at all" (1 John 1:5). And "anyone who does not love does not know God, because God is love" (1 John 4:8; cf. v. 16).[3]

This is to say that, like the highest being, the highest goodness is a person. He is not an impersonal, abstract form, like Plato's Good.[4] So our supreme standard of goodness, holiness, righteousness, and love is an absolute person. Since he is a person, he is not only a standard, but also an example to us of ethical perfection. He calls us to imitate what he is (Lev. 19:2) and what he does (Matt. 5:43–48; John 13:34–35).

God does not need anyone to tell him what to do. He does what is good because it is his character to do so. In the most important sense, he cannot do anything else. He does good because it is his deepest desire to do so. God's goodness and his being are one.

GOD'S IMAGE AND HUMAN GOODNESS

God has made human beings to be his image, and his intention is for his own union of goodness and being to be reflected in us. Of course, the image is never quite the same as the original reality. We know that human goodness is not inseparable from human nature, as God's goodness is from his, because we have indeed fallen from our original goodness. Neverthe-

---

1. I understand holiness, righteousness, and love as forms of divine goodness. See *DG*, 394–401.

2. This is true in both ethical and nonethical senses of goodness, but in this context I am thinking primarily of ethical goodness.

3. This is the doctrine of divine simplicity, that all of God's defining attributes are necessary to his being. For a general discussion of simplicity, see *DG*, 225–36 and passim through the chapters dealing with the divine attributes.

4. Cf. my discussion of Plato in chapter 8, especially on the dialogue *Euthyphro*. Also recall my discussion in chapter 3 of the importance of the fact that the Lord is a person, and the argument in chapter 4 and in *AGG*, 93–102, that the highest standard of ethics must be personal.

less, God made Adam to be a good person (Gen. 1:31); he gave him a good ethical character.[5] It is a great mystery how Adam, good as he was, came to sin against God.[6]

Besides being good, Adam was free and responsible before God.[7] Thus, Adam had to make his own decisions. He was responsible to obey God's norms, but to do that he had to adopt God's norms as his own. Adam had to decide whether he would make his decisions in accordance with God's standards.

A person can be obedient simply out of fear. But in our relationship to God, that is hardly the ideal. God wants us to obey him because we believe that his norms are *right*, that he is indeed the highest standard of goodness. One who obeys only out of fear might think that the one he obeys has false standards. But he obeys anyway, because he doesn't want to be hurt. But to obey God in the fullest sense is to confess that his standards are right and true. And to confess that is to adopt his standards as our own. And so a Christian who has faithfully internalized God's standards lives by standards that are both God's and his own. Such Christians do what they want to do, living by their own desires. That is the limited truth in the existential tradition of secular ethics (chapter 6).

Since there was no ethical tension within man, as originally created, Adam reflected God in the unity of his ethical commitment. He did not have to wrestle with tensions between will and intellect, between emotions and reason, or between heavenly ends and earthly ends. All of his being was an image of God's goodness.

Human beings reflect God's goodness in another way as well. As God's vassal kings, charged with exercising dominion over the earth (Gen. 1:28), we have the responsibility to apply God's norms to the rest of creation. Everything in creation is subject to us as we carry out our cultural task. So God intends us not only to be good in our inmost being, but also to be lawgivers to the rest of creation. As the image of God, we reflect God's ethical authority. As God is the ultimate lawgiver, so he has made us also

---

5. This is the common Reformed view, in contrast to the Roman Catholic position I discussed briefly in chapter 17. On the Roman view, Adam was created with an inner tension between his senses and reason, a tension that required a special gift of grace (*donum superadditum*) to relieve. Reformed theology does not recognize any such tension in Adam's original constitution. But the WCF does say that Adam was "yet under a possibility of transgressing" (4.2). It does not specify what it was in Adam that made sin to be possible.

6. John Murray calls this an "insoluble psychological and moral problem" in "The Fall of Man," in *Collected Writings of John Murray* (Edinburgh: Banner of Truth Trust, 1976–82), 2:75.

7. I discuss the nature of human freedom and responsibility in *DG*, 119–59.

to be lawgivers, as well as law keepers. As such, we are to fill the earth with the righteousness and love of God.

God created Adam to be something truly wonderful, a glorious image of God himself. Like God, though on a different level, Adam was worthy of respect and honor. The image of God is what makes human life exceedingly precious (Gen. 9:5–6; James 3:9).

GOD'S IMAGE AND THE FALL

There is controversy in the church as to whether in the fall the image of God was lost (as in Lutheran teaching) or merely defaced or marred (as in Reformed teaching). I hold to the latter view because of Bible references to the existence of the image in sinful people (Gen. 9:6; James 3:9). The continuance of the image implies that even after the fall, human beings are precious in God's sight and therefore ought to be precious in man's sight as well. Genesis 9:6 and James 3:9 invoke that preciousness as a principle that we are morally responsible to abide by. Clearly then, the fall takes nothing away from our moral responsibility, though it inhibits us from carrying out that responsibility.

So it remains true, even after the fall, that we are responsible to internalize the law of God, so that it becomes the law of our being as well. Our sinfulness will impede this process until we reach glory, but we should still seek that unity of goodness with all our being. As that unity increases, we will be more confident in deciding for ourselves what is right and wrong—that is, deciding according to our internalized divine standards.

We must never be satisfied with less than obedience to God from the heart. That is a large order, and it is a measure of our fallenness that we never do that perfectly in this life. Even when we conform outwardly to the law, we often note in ourselves some deficiency in inward motivation.

How does the fall affect the unity of human nature discussed earlier? As I said in the previous section, sin is not the result of inevitable conflict between various aspects of our being. Rather, it is the result of personal, willful choice, a choice of the whole person. It is true that following the fall, human beings often have to wrestle with ethical choices. A part of us wants to do right, another part to do wrong (Rom. 7). Sometimes we present this wrestling as a conflict between intellect and emotions, or between intellect and will. But, as we shall see later, this is not the best way to describe such moral instability. Intellect, emotions, and will, even assuming that they can be distinguished in the conventional way, are equally fallen, equally subject to regeneration.

So our struggle is not between our intellect and our emotions or our will, but between right and wrong.

All of our faculties and capacities are subject to temptation and therefore to inward ethical anxiety. We struggle between good and bad emotions, good and bad volitions, and good and bad thinking. These are different ways of saying that we struggle as whole persons between obedience and disobedience to our God. So, even as fallen creatures, there is a unity in human nature, though there is inward tension as well.

GOD'S IMAGE AND REDEMPTION

The atonement of Christ, applied to our hearts by the continuing work of the Spirit, renews us in the image of Christ (Eph. 4:24; Col. 3:10). This restores in principle the moral excellencies with which God originally created Adam. Sin does remain in the believer, not to be wholly eradicated until the return of Christ. But the *dominion* of sin is gone forever (Rom. 6:14).

The basis of Paul's confidence in Romans 6:14 is that when Jesus died, we died with him, and we were raised from the dead with him to newness of life (vv. 1–11). John Murray argues that the believer's "old man" (v. 6), the unregenerate self enslaved to sin, is dead once for all, never to be resuscitated. He is not "dead, but still alive," but simply dead.[8]

Our ethical struggle, then, is not a struggle to put to death our unregenerate self, but rather to grow as regenerate people. Murray says, "The definitive transformation, summed up in the putting off of the old man and the putting on of the new, does not remove the necessity or the fact of progressive renewal."[9] Referring to this progressive renewal, he cites Ephesians 4:23; Colossians. 3:10; 2 Corinthians 3:18; Romans 12:2. He continues:

> But this *progressive* renewal is not represented as the putting off of the old man and the putting on of the new, nor is it to be conceived of as the progressive crucifixion of the old man. It does mean the mortification of the deeds of the flesh and of all sin in heart and life. But it is the renewal of the "new man" unto the attainment of that glory for which he is destined, conformity to the image of God's Son.[10]

If, of course, the old man is simply dead, then it is something of a mystery as to why there is any sin in the new man—why anything remains to be

---

8. John Murray, *Principles of Conduct* (Grand Rapids: Eerdmans, 1957), 202–28.
9. Ibid., 218.
10. Ibid., 219.

mortified.[11] But this is the mystery of "the already and the not-yet," which we discussed in chapter 16. Our present concern, however, is to indicate the unity of goodness and being in the new man. Our union with Christ in his death and resurrection leads to a unity in our own being. The ethical struggle is anomalous. Our deepest desire as regenerate believers, and the Spirit's overall purpose for us, is to remove the remnants of sin from our hearts, so that our character is consistently righteous. The goal of God's dealing with us is that one day it will be impossible for anyone to conceive of us apart from our good character, that our goodness will become an essential and defining attribute of our being, as with God himself.

So Paul says that believers *are* light in the Lord (Eph. 5:8; cf. Matt. 5:14). As new covenant believers, the law is written on our hearts (Jer. 31:33; Heb. 8:10). We have God's word, not only as general and special revelation, but as existential revelation as well (see chapter 9): God's Word illumined by God's Spirit.

In the meantime, there is a battle to be fought. Scripture attributes sanctification to a work of God's grace that begins in our death and resurrection with Christ and continues as God constantly renews us in the image of Christ (Eph. 4:24; Col. 3:10), creating us as his workmanship for good works (Eph. 2:10; Titus 2:14). But this work of divine grace does not justify a passive attitude on our part. We are not to wait for the Holy Spirit to act in our lives. Rather, we are to take up arms against the forces of evil (Eph. 6:10–20) and to devote ourselves to good works (Titus 3:8). The Christian life is not a walk in the park. It is a war, a race (1 Cor. 9:24–27). We are not to "let go and let God," but rather to follow Paul's mandate: "Work out your own salvation with fear and trembling," not in spite of the fact, but because "it is God who works in you, both to will and to work for his good pleasure" (Phil. 2:12–13).

Sometimes the sovereignty of God excludes human responsibility. For example, because God alone is the Creator, we cannot create ourselves. Because God is absolutely sovereign in providing atonement, we cannot atone for ourselves. His sovereignty excludes any attempt on our part to claim

11. Strangely, Murray does not refer to the two passages in the New Testament that speak of mortification, Rom. 8:13 and Col. 3:5, although he does affirm the concept in the above quotes. But what is it that is mortified, if the old man is already dead? Perhaps we should recognize that although the teaching of Scripture is self-consistent, the metaphors in the Bible need not be perfectly consistent with each other. For example, Jesus is both "the foundation" of the church (1 Cor. 3:11) and "the cornerstone" (Eph. 2:20, where the apostles and prophets are "the foundation"). The point we should take from the mortification language of Scripture is that there is something in us that has irrevocably died with Christ, but there is also something in us that remains to be put to death. Mortification, like other aspects of the Christian life, is both already and not yet.

his distinctive prerogatives. But most often, God's sovereignty engages our responsibility, rather than detracting from it. So it is with sanctification.[12]

Cornelius Van Til, perhaps to the surprise of some of his readers, says that "the primary ethical duty for man is self-realization," for "when man becomes truly the king of the universe the kingdom of God is realized, and when the kingdom of God is realized, God is glorified."[13] Van Til expounds the concept of self-realization under three subheadings: (1) "Man's will needs to become increasingly *spontaneous* in its reactivity."[14] (2) "Man's will needs to become increasingly *fixed in its self-determination*."[15] (3) "Man's will must increase in *momentum*."[16] His illustration of momentum is a growing business: as the business increases, its managers need to increase in "alertness, stability, and comprehensiveness of decision."[17]

Here Van Til uses many bywords of the existential tradition. But he sees no tension between this language and his overall emphasis on the authority of God's law and the kingdom of God as man's *summum bonum*. For Van Til, as for Scripture, God's sovereign control and authority do not exclude, but encourage, a bracing sense of human responsibility and a deep reflection upon human ethical subjectivity. Note especially his emphasis on the freedom of the believer. Our trust in God does not extinguish our spontaneity, but rather fires it up. Our will is indeed God-determined, but also self-determined. And redemption creates within us a "momentum" toward godliness, a momentum that comes from within, as well as from without.

So we should not follow those who think that a proper emphasis on the objectivity of redemption excludes an emphasis on subjectivity. Divine grace, atonement, and justification are certainly objective—realities occurring outside ourselves, which we cannot change. But regeneration and sanctification are realities also. They too are objective works of God's grace, but they are also events that occur within us. And sanctification is a process for which we, together with God, must take responsibility. Christian ethics requires consideration of both the objective and the subjective, and of both divine sovereignty and human responsibility.

12. On the general relationship between divine sovereignty and human responsibility, see *DG*, 119–59. See also my comments on quietism in chapter 12 of the present volume. Quietism has appeared, not only in Lutheranism, but also in other Christian circles, such as the "victorious life" teaching of the Keswick Bible conferences. See B. B. Warfield, *Perfectionism* (Philadelphia: Presbyterian and Reformed, 1958).

13. Van Til, *Christian Theistic Ethics* ([Ripon, CA]: den Dulk Christian Foundation, 1971), 45.

14. Ibid.

15. Ibid.

16. Ibid., 46.

17. Ibid.

CHAPTER 19

Motives and Virtues

In chapter 3, I discussed the three necessary and sufficient conditions of good works that are mentioned in WCF, 16.7, namely, having the right standard, having the right goal, and having the right motive. Under the normative perspective (especially chapter 9), I discussed the standard, the word of God in its various forms. Under the situational perspective (especially chapter 17), I discussed the goal, the glory of God, which, like the word of God, can be particularized in various ways (as human enjoyment of God, the kingdom of God, the cultural mandate, and the Great Commission). In this chapter, as part of the existential perspective, I shall consider the motive of Christian ethics.

A motive is "an emotion, desire, physiological need, or similar impulse that acts as an incitement to action."[1] Some motives are desires to accomplish some specific result in the external world, as when a prosecutor says of a defendant, "His motive was revenge." In that context, *motive* becomes roughly synonymous with *goal.* We discussed goals under the situational perspective, but since the desire to achieve a goal is subjective, we might have carried on much of that discussion under the existential perspective. This is another example of how the three perspectives overlap.

But in the present discussion, I will focus on the inner, subjective dimensions of motive—those aspects of character, desire, and feeling that incite us to good or bad actions.

---

1. *The American Heritage College Dictionary*, 3d ed. (Boston: Houghton Mifflin Co., 2000), 890.

Scripture is clear in teaching that a right motive is necessary for a human action to be good. Both the Old Testament (Deut. 6:5–6) and the New Testament (Matt. 5:8, 28; 6:21; 12:34–35; 15:8, 18–19; 22:37; Rom. 6:17; 10:9–10) emphasize that true obedience to God is from the heart. As we have seen, God intends for his law to be written, not only on stone and paper, but also on the human heart (Jer. 31:33; Heb. 8:10). The heart is the center of human existence, the whole person as God sees him, the true self when all its masks are removed. So the heart is the motive of motives, the fundamental disposition of every person. The heart is the source of our most fundamental commitment, either to serve God or to serve an idol. It governs our actions (Matt. 15:19), words (Matt. 12:34), and thoughts (Matt. 9:4; 15:19).

Scripture strongly opposes hypocrisy (Isa. 29:13–14; Matt. 15:8–9). Jesus saw hypocrisy especially in the Pharisees, who did their good works to be seen by other people (Matt. 6:1–8; 23:5). External goodness is not enough, says Jesus. Not only the outside, but also the inside of the cup must be clean (Matt. 23:25–26).

The apostle Paul tells us that love is necessary for any work to be a truly good work (1 Cor. 13), and Hebrews 11:6 says that "without faith it is impossible to please [God]." WCF, 16.7, speaks of faith as that which purifies the heart, without mentioning any other motive for purity, evidently because faith is the sole instrument of justification. But Scripture, concerned not only with initial justification, but also with the continuing process of sanctification, mentions other motives as well, most notably love.

If love and faith are motives for good works, there is evidently a significant overlap between motives and virtues. That should not surprise us. Virtues, in Scripture, are the fruit of the Spirit (Gal. 5:22–23) applied to the heart (Eph. 6:6 and many other passages). For example, if the Spirit applies love to the heart of the believer, that believer becomes a loving person. He displays love in his behavior. Our behavior is always governed, motivated, by the character of our heart (Matt. 12:35). So the qualities of the regenerate character are motives, and our motives are virtues. This is to say that in a Christian view of things virtues never lie dormant. They are active and dynamic. They seek expression. They motivate. Motives are virtues, and virtues are motives.

A VIRTUE ETHIC THAT IS CHRISTIAN

The existential perspective on Christian ethics is not simply a Christian counterpart of secular existential ethics. It is also a virtue ethic that is

Christian. Recall the distinction between command ethics, narrative ethics, and virtue ethics, set forth in chapter 3. A complete Christian ethic contains all three of these, and each includes the others perspectivally. I have presented a command ethic under the normative perspective and a narrative ethic under the situational perspective. Now we should consider under the existential perspective what an ethic of virtue might mean in a covenantal Christian setting.

From what we have seen earlier, it is possible to teach ethics in several ways. In a command ethic, one sets forth the requirements of God's Word and seeks to apply those to all areas of human life. In a narrative ethic, we tell the story of God's people, from creation to the present day, as we anticipate the eschaton. There is no inconsistency between these two approaches, and they reinforce one another. The commands of God must be applied to the whole situation of mankind, which is described in the narrative. The narrative includes descriptions of events in which God gives commands to us, and it declares the resources that God has given to us by grace to keep those commands.[2]

A virtue ethic that is Christian will focus on a description of the regenerate heart. It will describe the biblical virtues and show how they motivate us to do good works. It will give examples of people who are loving, faithful, self-controlled, and so on. In doing so, of course, it will also expound God's commands, for the virtues are what God requires of us. And it will expound the Christian narrative, for that story tells us what God has done to plant such virtues in our hearts. Ultimately, then, a Christian virtue ethic will differ from the other two only in emphasis, in perspective. But that perspective is very important. It provides a window into the soul.

In this book, my main discussion of ethical issues will be an exposition of the Ten Commandments. There I will take a command approach. This is in line with the Reformed tradition, which typically expounds Christian ethics in terms of the law of God. But this is not the only biblical option. A command ethic operates in terms of the normative perspective, but it is also possible to teach ethics focusing on the situational (narrative ethics) and existential (virtue ethics) perspectives. I would hope that authors

---

2. "Narrative ethics" in recent theology sometimes means an ethic without commands, an ethic in which we tell the story only to encourage ethical action and to suggest ethical possibilities or "trajectories," but not to define our ethical responsibilities. But that is to eviscerate the narrative of Scripture. Scripture presents a narrative of God making demands on us, as well as making and fulfilling promises. To base ethics on a narrative devoid of revealed commands leaves us with no ethical standards except those derived from would-be autonomous human thought.

other than I will take up the challenge to write genuinely Reformed ethical treatises from situational and existential perspectives.

What follows will not be a complete virtue ethic or anything close to it. But it will attempt to list and describe some of the more important biblical virtues.

FAITH

WLC, 72, defines justifying (saving) faith as follows:

> Justifying faith is a saving grace, wrought in the heart of a sinner by the Spirit and word of God, whereby he, being convinced of his sin and misery, and of the disability in himself and all other creatures to recover him out of his lost condition, not only assenteth to the truth of the promise of the gospel, but receiveth and resteth upon Christ and his righteousness, therein held forth, for pardon of sin, and for the accepting and accounting of his person righteous in the sight of God for salvation.

Scripture emphasizes faith in two contexts: as the way in which we initially receive God's saving grace, and as a mentality that pervades the Christian life.[3] Initial saving faith is "the alone instrument of justification."[4] It is not the basis or ground of salvation; Christ's atonement is the only basis or ground of salvation. Nor is faith the efficient cause of salvation; that can only be the grace of God. Rather, we are justified by faith alone in an instrumental sense. Faith is the instrument, or means, by which we receive the grace of God in Christ.

There is nothing in our faith that deserves or merits salvation. We should not think that exercising faith is the one good work we can perform to earn God's favor. Nothing that we can do deserves his favor. Even our faith is weak and defiled, contaminated by sinful impulses. In that respect, faith is no different from any other work we perform. Why, then, are we saved by faith, rather than by love or by long-suffering? Because the nature of faith is to receive grace. What saves is not faith itself, but what faith receives.

---

3. Here I enumerate Scripture's most theologically significant uses of *faith* and the corresponding verb *believe*. But there are other uses of these terms that do not imply the salvation of the one who believes. For example, in John 8:31–59, Jesus addresses some Jews who are said to have "believed in him" (v. 31). The later conversation reveals, however, that they are in fact opposed to him. Here, belief or faith is a kind of initial and superficial commitment, not based on any inward change.

4. WCF, 11.2.

How does saving faith receive the grace of God? By believing God's promise.[5] *Believe* is the verb form of the noun *faith*. Paul says about Abraham, "No distrust made him waver concerning the promise of God, but he grew strong in his faith as he gave glory to God, fully convinced that God was able to do what he had promised" (Rom. 4:20–21). Paul adds, "That is why his faith was counted to him as righteousness" (v. 22), and he presents such faith as a model of saving faith in Christ (vv. 24–25).

The example of Abraham connects the two phases of faith that I mentioned in the first paragraph: initial saving faith and faith as a mentality that pervades the Christian life. Paul's concern in Romans 4 is the doctrine of justification by faith. But Abraham's faith did not occur only at the beginning of his relationship with God. It continued through his whole life. Romans 4 describes incidents that occurred long after he first responded to God's call in Genesis 12:1–4. So Hebrews 11 lists Abraham among the many Old Testament saints who lived by faith. Like them, he trusted God's promise, despite the fact that it went unfulfilled during his earthly life. He looked forward to "a better country, that is, a heavenly one" (Heb. 11:16).

So Paul contrasts living by faith with living by sight (2 Cor. 5:7; cf. Mark 10:52). Many of God's promises remain unfulfilled. We cannot verify them by our experience. But we look forward to their fulfillment because we trust God's word above all other sources of authority, even above our own eyes. So "faith is the assurance of things hoped for, the conviction of things not seen" (Heb. 11:1). We trust in God, who made the world from no visible source (v. 3). With Moses, we see "him who is invisible" (v. 27), so the visible challenges to our faith cannot prevail. The world says that seeing is believing. Jesus says, "Did I not tell you that if you believed you would see the glory of God?" (John 11:40).

So faith, in both its initial and its later expressions, is trusting God's promise above any other considerations.

That trust is shown through our works. To trust another person is not merely to commend his words, but to act on them. So James says, "But someone will say, 'You have faith and I have works.' Show me your faith apart from your works, and I will show you my faith by my works" (James 2:18). This is the

---

5. Following the main part of the Reformed tradition, I identify saving faith with trust, not merely with assent to propositions. See the relationship between them in the definition given earlier from the WLC. For the relationship between trust and assent to propositions, see *DKG*, 54–57. To summarize: it is not entirely wrong to identify faith with propositional assent, as long as that assent is strong enough to govern our behavior and attitudes. But it is far less confusing to say that faith is trust in Christ through his word. In our usual way of speaking, trust includes assent and more: covenant friendship, reliance, and a disposition to obey.

context of his later statement, "You see that a person is justified by works and not by faith alone" (v. 24). James is not contradicting Paul's statements that we are justified apart from works (e.g., Rom. 3:27; 4:2, 6; 9:11, 32; 11:6; Gal. 2:16; 3:5, 10). He is saying that saving faith is necessarily a living, working faith. Faith justifies, not because it brings about good works, but because it is the means of receiving God's grace. Yet it is not genuine unless it motivates good works. WCF, 11.2, tells us, "Faith, thus receiving and resting on Christ and his righteousness, is the alone instrument of justification: yet is it not alone in the person justified, but is ever accompanied with all other saving graces, and is no dead faith, but worketh by love."

That fact should not surprise us, and we should not regard it as some kind of theological puzzle. The grace that faith receives is a grace that leads to good works. Scripture emphasizes this:

> For by grace you have been saved through faith. And this is not your own doing; it is the gift of God, not a result of works, so that no one may boast. For we are his workmanship, created in Christ Jesus for good works, which God prepared beforehand, that we should walk in them. (Eph. 2:8–10)

> He saved us, not because of works done by us in righteousness, but according to his own mercy, by the washing of regeneration and renewal of the Holy Spirit, whom he poured out on us richly through Jesus Christ our Savior, so that being justified by his grace we might become heirs according to the hope of eternal life. The saying is trustworthy, and I want you to insist on these things, so that those who have believed in God may be careful to devote themselves to good works. These things are excellent and profitable for people. (Titus 3:5–8; cf. 2:14)

So in Galatians 5:6 Paul speaks of "faith working through love." God saves us by grace apart from works, but that grace produces works, for that is God's intent, his reason for saving us. Our faith receives this grace and through it we begin to do good works, as God has planned.

Evangelicals are sometimes inclined to think of faith as an event that takes place in the mind, perhaps the experience of saying inaudibly, "Yes, Lord, I believe." But when we say phrases like that in our heads, we may sometimes be deceiving ourselves. It is possible to say such phrases to ourselves as mere forms, without any intention of changing our behavior. In those cases, these words are not expressions of faith; much less can we identify them with faith. "Yes, Lord, I believe" may be an expression of true faith, or it may not be.

We should identify faith, not with that statement itself, but with the motive that underlies it, when it is uttered sincerely.[6] It is misleading, then, to say that faith is a "mental act,"[7] as much as it is misleading to call it a physical act (perhaps the act of coming forward in response to an altar call). It is rather a motivation underlying both mental and physical acts, when those are done to the glory of God. Faith can be seen equally, then, in faithful thoughts, words, or deeds. This analysis helps us to see more clearly both the distinction between faith and our other actions and the close relationship between them. They are not identical, for the motivation of an act is not identical to the act. But, as James teaches us, our only means of recognizing faith in ourselves and others is through good works. Or, as Jesus says of false teachers, "You will recognize them by their fruits" (Matt. 7:16).

Scripture tells us that faith is both necessary and sufficient for good works. It is necessary because "without faith it is impossible to please him, for whoever would draw near to God must believe that he exists and that he rewards those who seek him" (Heb. 11:6), and because "whatever does not proceed from faith is sin" (Rom. 14:23). It is sufficient because when we believe God, as did Abraham, God credits it to us for righteousness (Gen. 15:6). As Jesus said, "This is the work of God, that you believe in him whom he has sent" (John 6:29). When our works (thoughts, words, and deeds) are true expressions of faith, they cannot be anything other than good and right.

So, in a sense, it is true to say, "Believe God and do as you please." But, as we have seen, to believe God is always to believe his word, and that includes his law. So the existential perspective never permits us to transgress the normative.

But the existential perspective gives us an image of the Christian life that is different from the others. We are not only scribes, poring over God's statutes (normative), and pilgrims, walking toward a goal (situational), but also children, trusting their heavenly Father, knowing that he will prove true, though everyone else is a liar (Rom. 3:4). So Scripture regularly

6. Notice that I am not defining faith as a motive. My definition of faith is that of the WLC, cited earlier. I am only trying to indicate how faith is related to good works. Since saving faith receives and rests on Christ, it motivates us to live as Jesus does.

7. Here I take issue with the position of Gordon Clark, set forth in his *Religion, Reason, and Revelation* (Philadelphia: Presbyterian and Reformed, 1961), 94–100. If one wishes to divide the human being exhaustively into two parts, mental and physical, then faith, not being a physical action, would have to be in the mental category. But it is very different from those episodic experiences we usually call "mental acts"—experiences of visualizing things to ourselves, talking to ourselves, solving problems, etc. It rather seems that motivations, like faith, require another category in addition to the physical and the mental. But I am disinclined toward such categorizations in general (see *DKG*, 319–46, and the following chapter of this volume).

commends those who believe, who have faith, even amid temptations to disbelieve (Matt. 8:10; 9:2, 22; 17:20; 21:22; Rom. 4:20–21; Heb. 11). The Christian life is a wonderful adventure, as we live by God's promises, even when Satan tempts us to doubt and fear.

REPENTANCE

Repentance is not just believing that one is a sinner, or feeling sorry for one's sins, or even hating them.[8] It is the very act of turning away from them. To turn from sin is to turn to goodness. So there is a very close relationship between repentance and faith. "Repentance that leads to life" in Acts 11:18 is virtually a synonym of faith. And in WCF, 15.3, the relationship between repentance and pardon (part of justification) is the same as that between faith and justification: "Although repentance be not to be rested in, as any satisfaction for sin, or any cause of the pardon thereof, which is the act of God's free grace in Christ; yet it is of such necessity to all sinners, that none may expect pardon without it."

Repentance and faith are opposite sides of a coin. You can't have one without the other. Faith is turning to Christ, and repentance is turning away from sin. These two turnings are the same motion. You can't turn toward Christ without turning away from sin, and vice versa.

As faith is a motive for good works, so is repentance. When the Pharisees and Sadducees came for John's baptism, the Baptist exhorted them to "bear fruit in keeping with repentance" (Matt. 3:8). If repentance is true repentance, it issues in good deeds. Paul presented the same challenge to Gentile converts (Acts 26:20). See also 2 Timothy 2:25–26 and Revelation 2:5.

As the Christian life is a life of faith, so also is it a life of repentance. As we journey ahead by trusting in God's promises, so we look back from time to time, noting how we have offended God and others, and asking for forgiveness. All Christians confess in at least a theoretical way that repentance is important. We believe that all are sinners. Practically, however, we find it difficult to admit—whether to others, to ourselves, or to God—that we have personally done wrong and need to change. When someone criticizes our behavior, our first instinct is, too often, to defend ourselves. Although we confess in general terms that we have sinned, we don't want anyone to think that we have sinned in any specific way. That attitude is even more prominent among people in authority. For them, the

---

8. Nor is it the Roman Catholic concept of penance, which includes the idea that one may partially pay God back for transgressions by making sacrifices or engaging in various devotional exercises.

stakes are higher. For a prominent person, to admit to sin is to endanger the status that one may have carefully nurtured for a long time.

So when a Christian leader freely admits sin and asks for forgiveness, many of us find that strange. It is impressive, however, not only because of its rarity, but also because of its profoundly biblical character. It marks people who aim to lead as servants, rather than as masters (Matt. 20:25–28). It also enhances the leader's ability to deal with the sins of others, as Paul says in Galatians 6:1: "Brothers, if anyone is caught in any transgression, you who are spiritual should restore him in a spirit of gentleness. Keep watch on yourself, lest you too be tempted."[9]

HOPE

Having looked at faith, and repentance as an aspect of faith, we now look at the other two of the three "theological virtues" that I mentioned in chapter 3 and that occur together frequently in the New Testament. There I suggested that faith, hope, and love correspond to the three lordship attributes: faith focusing on the authority of God's Word, hope focusing on his control of the future, and love focusing on his intimate presence with us. Each of these involves the other two; neither can be practiced without the others.

Hope is faith directed toward the future aspect of salvation, the "not-yet." Like faith, it is firm and sure, not tentative and wishful, as our English usage often suggests. It is "a sure and steadfast anchor of the soul" (Heb. 6:19; cf. Rom. 5:5) based, like faith, on the revelation of God.

As such, hope, like faith, is a motive for good works. Our hope makes us bold (2 Cor. 3:12). The hope of salvation is the helmet that keeps us from the attacks of Satan (1 Thess. 5:8). In Colossians 1:4–5, hope motivates faith and love! These passages review for us the teaching we considered in chapter 16, that God's promises for the future motivate our behavior today. If we know that a wonderful reward awaits us, then we will let all our decisions be governed by that hope.

LOVE

In chapter 12, I mentioned that love is the center of biblical ethics. We saw there that the term *love* expresses the fundamental loyalty of the vassal

9. In this section, I have benefited greatly from the ministry of C. John Miller and his writings, particularly *Repentance and Twentieth-Century Man* (Fort Washington, PA: Christian Literature Crusade, 1980, 1998).

to the lord in a covenant. So love should be defined triperspectivally as allegiance (normative perspective), as well as action (situational perspective) and affection (existential perspective). In that chapter, my main concern was to show the relationship of love to law. My conclusion was that there is no conflict between them. The command of love requires obedience to God, though it also serves as a "provocative characterization" of the law. We also considered, under the heading of "moral heroism," the radicalism of love, that it goes beyond the surface meaning of the law to its depth, leading to extreme forms of obedience. The model is Christ's love, for he gave himself in death for his people, setting us a standard of love that is far beyond what we normally set for ourselves (John 13:34–35).

Here I will consider various characteristics of love as a motive for good works. Paul in 1 Corinthians 13:1–3 makes clear that no human work (including faith) can be good unless it is motivated by love:

> If I speak in the tongues of men and of angels, but have not love, I am a noisy gong or a clanging cymbal. And if I have prophetic powers, and understand all mysteries and all knowledge, and if I have all faith, so as to remove mountains, but have not love, I am nothing. If I give away all I have, and if I deliver up my body to be burned, but have not love, I gain nothing.

Without love, any attempt to do good will be a failure. Here are certain qualities of love that motivate good works:

COVENANT LOYALTY

As I indicated in chapter 12, the fundamental demand of a suzerainty treaty is love, in the sense of exclusive loyalty. The vassal is not to make treaties with any king other than his covenant lord. The same is true in the covenant between Yahweh and Israel. Notice how the term *love* is used in the great confession of the Mosaic covenant, the Shema: "Hear, O Israel: The LORD our God, the LORD is one. You shall love the LORD your God with all your heart and with all your soul and with all your might" (Deut. 6:4–5). Israel's love for Yahweh is one that allows no competition and tolerates no rivals. So in the covenant document called the Decalogue, the first commandment is "You shall have no other gods before me" (Ex. 20:3). This first commandment is, in effect, a law of love. In its exclusiveness, this love is closely parallel to marital love, so that in Scripture adultery and idolatry are symbols of one another.

In the New Testament as well, love is covenant loyalty to Christ as Lord. He has loved us in an exclusive way, by giving his life for his sheep (John

10:15). He gives that love to us (John 17:26), and we return that love to him and to one another as members of his body (1 John 4:19–21). Our love for Jesus and for one another distinguishes us from those who are outside the covenant (John 13:34–35).

Here we find prominently that element of love I earlier called "allegiance." God has chosen us, and we have chosen to be his servants, together with the body of his people. Love is being faithful to our covenant vows. Jochem Douma says, "We understand more clearly exactly what love toward God really is when we see *love is a choice*. Because only Yahweh is God, Israel and we must choose for Him. *To love means to stick with your choice*."[10] Douma also draws out well the parallel with marriage:

> When a marriage gets into trouble, the only path to resolution is the choice to love. The emotional element in that love may be wholly or partially absent, but faithfulness must come out. Concretely, then, love means that husband and wife form no relationships with third parties, but maintain the choice they made for each other with their wedding vows. The same is true with our relationship with the Lord.[11]

In both divine and human covenants, loyalty is not only a negative requirement, forbidding rival alliances, but also a positive virtue, motivating us to serve the one to whom we are committed. So allegiance leads to action. In the Decalogue, the first commandment motivates the remaining nine, and in the New Testament, Jesus tells his disciples that if they love him, they will keep his commandments (e.g., John 14:15).

GRATEFULNESS

In the suzerainty treaty structure of the covenant document (see chapter 3), the love command follows the historical prologue, which sets out the gracious deeds of the great king. So in the Decalogue, the first commandment, requiring exclusive love, follows the statement of Yahweh's deliverance: "I am the LORD your God, who brought you out of the land of Egypt, out of the house of slavery" (Ex. 20:2). Here love is Israel's grateful response to redemption.

Similarly, in the New Testament, we love because God first loved us in Christ (1 John 4:7–21), and we love *as* he loved us (John 13:34–35).

10. J. Douma, *The Ten Commandments* (Phillipsburg, NJ: P&R Publishing, 1996), 21.
11. Ibid.

So the Heidelberg Catechism treats the Decalogue under the category of "gratitude" in its general outline of guilt, grace, and gratitude:

> Q. 2. *How many things are necessary for you to know, that in this comfort you may live and die happily?*
> A. Three things: First, the greatness of my sin and misery. Second, how I am redeemed from all my sins and misery. Third, how I am to be thankful to God for such redemption.

It is not that we can pay God back for salvation, or even try to pay back a small portion. God's gift of salvation is too large for us even to begin to measure (Eph. 3:18–19). Nevertheless, the only appropriate attitude for those bought with so great a price is thankfulness (Luke 17:11–19). And thankfulness, like loyalty, is not only a feeling, but a disposition toward actions that express that thankfulness. Those who are thankful to God will not bow to idols, take his name in vain, violate his day, dishonor their parents, and so on.

Gratefulness and allegiance, therefore, are inseparable. But gratefulness adds to allegiance a further perspective on our love. Even on the human level, when someone gives us a large gift, we feel an obligation to please him. Ingratitude, though widely practiced, is universally despised. If our salvation is the greatest gift anyone has ever received, the greatest gift imaginable, then how can we do anything other than give ourselves wholeheartedly to our covenant Lord? How can we be other than deeply wounded at the very thought of betraying him?

COMPREHENSIVE REORIENTATION OF LIFE

The grateful allegiance we owe to God is comprehensive. That is, it reorients every aspect of life.[12] Earlier we saw in Deuteronomy 6:4–5 the command to love God with all of one's heart, soul, and might. Jesus replaces "might" with "mind" in Matthew 22:37, and he adds "mind" in Mark 12:30 and Luke 10:27. Certainly Jesus is not distorting the meaning of Deuteronomy 6:4–5. Love with the mind is implicit in that passage, the purpose of which is not to limit our love to certain specific human faculties, but to expand it to every area of life, centered in the heart. Similarly, we have seen the apostle Paul exhorting us, "Whether you eat or drink, or whatever you do, do all to the glory of God" (1 Cor. 10:31). Note also the comprehensiveness of love as a way of life in 1 Corinthians 13—its necessity for all other moral acts (vv. 1–3) and its connection with other

---

12. Recall the discussion of the comprehensiveness of Scripture in chapter 10.

moral virtues: "Love is patient and kind; love does not envy or boast; it is not arrogant or rude. It does not insist on its own way; it is not irritable or resentful; it does not rejoice at wrongdoing, but rejoices with the truth. Love bears all things, believes all things, hopes all things, endures all things" (1 Cor. 13:4–7).

So covenant love reorients everything we say, do, and feel. People have sometimes said that the love described in Deuteronomy is a kind of political allegiance, which does not gain any emotional content until later in Israel's history, as in Hosea's love for his unfaithful wife. Certainly covenant love is allegiance, and I don't object to the term *political*. But tension between the political and the emotional fails to account for the comprehensive language of Deuteronomy 6:4–5 and the nature of our "political" allegiance to Yahweh. The covenant is a political relationship, at least metaphorically, but a political relationship of a unique kind. If our exclusive love for the Lord permeates all of our existence from the heart, as in Deuteronomy 6, it certainly permeates all of life: our emotions, as our intellect and will. The heart governs all aspects of human life. And if God is the greatest allegiance of our heart, he is our greatest passion as well. Our greatest desire is to serve him. One cannot love another wholeheartedly while remaining emotionally cool toward him.

So it shouldn't surprise us when in Scripture God's love for us takes on a passionate character (Ezek. 16), with marital and even sexual imagery. Similarly, note fatherly and maternal figures of God's compassion in Psalm 103:13; Isaiah 49:15; 66:13; Hosea 11:3. Our allegiance to God should be equally passionate. A faithful heart creates faithful emotions. So, as I indicated earlier, biblical love is allegiance, action, and affection, existing together as a perspectival whole.

IMITATION OF GOD'S ATONING GRACE

We saw in chapter 9 that imitation of God is the fundamental principle of Christian ethics. We saw above how our love should image God's, in its depth, comprehensiveness, and passion.

In the history of redemption, God reveals himself particularly as the gracious God, the one who delivers those who have no claim on his mercy, even at the price of the death of his beloved Son. The love that Scripture commands is a love that images God's love, specifically his redemptive love. As he has given Israel rest in redeeming them from Egypt, so they should give rest to others (Deut. 5:14–15). As he has forgiven us, so we should forgive others (Matt. 6:12, 14–15; 18:21–35). And, more generally, as he has loved us, so we should love others (John 13:34–35; 1 John 4:7–21).

We might think that we can imitate Jesus in many ways, but not in his atoning love. After all, none of us can bring about the salvation of others by giving our lives. Remarkably, however, the atonement is the main point of comparison between Christ's love and the Christian's love. The love of God that we are to imitate is most fully displayed in the atonement, according to John 3:16; 15:13; Romans 5:8; 8:39 (in context); Ephesians 2:4–5; 2 Thessalonians 2:16; 1 John 3:16; 4:9–10; Revelation 1:5; cf. Mark 10:45; 1 Peter 2:18–25; Philippians 2:1–11.

God's love for us in the atonement is beyond measure (Eph. 3:18–19), in the depth of Jesus' suffering, including his estrangement from his Father, in the greatness of the blessing he bought for us, and also in our total lack of fitness for this blessing. As recipients of God's grace, we are supremely unattractive to him. We are the tax collectors and sinners (Matt. 9:9–13), "the poor and crippled and blind and lame" (Luke 14:21), those "still sinners" (Rom. 5:8) when Jesus came to die for us.

Truly, no sacrifice of ours can atone for the sins of someone else. But these passages make abundantly clear that our obligation is nothing less than to lay down our lives for one another, as Jesus did for us. Moral heroism, extreme self-sacrifice, as we discussed it in chapter 12, is the heart of the Christian's ethical obligation.

For examples, revisit the discussions in chapter 12 of the heroism of David's mighty men and of the poor widow who gave everything she had to the temple treasury. In general terms, to love in imitation of Christ is to put the interests of others ahead of our own: "Do nothing from rivalry or conceit, but in humility count others more significant than yourselves. Let each of you look not only to his own interests, but also to the interests of others" (Phil. 2:3–4). It is remarkable that he produces one of the richest Christological passages in Scripture in order to persuade people in the church to set aside their rivalries (perhaps especially Euodia and Syntyche, named specifically in 4:2).[13]

When we meditate on the cross, our rivalries with Christians of other traditions, denominations, and parties usually seem rather trivial. Jesus died for us; can we not just bend a little to accommodate a brother or sister? The demands of love upon us seem so little compared to what love demanded of him.

And when we consider how unattractive we were in God's eyes prior to the atonement, his love should move us especially to love the unlovely, especially those who don't seem to merit the compassion

---

13. This is another illustration of my general thesis (see chapter 16) that the redemptive-historical emphasis of Scripture is not opposed to ethical teaching, but is given for the purpose of ethical application, as is all Scripture (2 Tim. 3:16–17).

of the world: the poor, the weak, the disabled, hated minorities, and even the unborn.

IMITATION OF GOD'S COMMON GRACE: LOVING OUR ENEMIES

"Common grace," defined as God's kindness to the nonelect, is something of a misnomer, since the word *grace* in English translations of Scripture almost always has a redemptive meaning. Yet it is clear that God's love extends to the unregenerate and even to the nonelect.[14] In Matthew 5:43–48, Jesus says that God loves his enemies and gives them good gifts. God's enemies certainly include the unregenerate and the nonelect. And Jesus presents this expression of love as an example to us:

> You have heard that it was said, "You shall love your neighbor and hate your enemy." But I say to you, Love your enemies and pray for those who persecute you, so that you may be sons of your Father who is in heaven. For he makes his sun rise on the evil and on the good, and sends rain on the just and on the unjust. For if you love those who love you, what reward do you have? Do not even the tax collectors do the same? And if you greet only your brothers, what more are you doing than others? Do not even the Gentiles do the same? You therefore must be perfect, as your heavenly Father is perfect.

This teaching is not unique to the New Testament. In Exodus 23:4, God tells us to return our enemy's ox or donkey if we find it wandering away. Enmity toward someone else, for whatever cause, should not keep us from showing kindness to him.

The parable of the good Samaritan (Luke 10:29–37), following Jesus' affirmation of love as the heart of the law, shows that we are to offer help to people without putting them to a religious test. In Galatians 6:10, Paul says, "So then, as we have opportunity, let us do good to everyone, and especially to those who are of the household of faith." He says "especially," not "exclusively." The household of faith, the church as our extended family, has first claim on our resources. But our hearts should be generous enough to help those outside the fellowship as God gives us opportunity.

Jesus' teaching on the love of enemies faces a major problem: the imprecatory psalms and other imprecatory passages in Scripture. In imprecation, one calls down God's judgments on others. Some of these passages even

14. For a systematic discussion of the doctrine of common grace, see *DG*, 429–37.

commend hatred of the wicked (e.g., Pss. 119:113; 139:21–22). It would seem that such passages are incompatible with Jesus' teaching that we should love our enemies.

But imprecations are found in the New Testament, as well as in the Old—on the lips of Christ and the apostles, as well as on the lips of the psalmist (see Matt. 23:13–39; Gal. 1:8–9; Rev. 6:10; 18:20). On the other hand, as we have seen, the biblical ethic of love is also found in both testaments. Scripture always proscribes personal vengeance and calls us to love our enemies: Exodus 23:4–5; Leviticus 19:17–18; Psalm 7:4–5; Proverbs 20:22.[15] So the problem we have in reconciling these two biblical themes cannot be met by some view of dispensational change.

Jesus did refuse to exercise divine vengeance during his earthly life, because he came not to judge the world, but to save it. Thus, he rebuked his disciples who wanted to call down fire from heaven upon a city that rejected them (Luke 9:54–55), but he did promise judgment on unbelieving cities in the last day (Matt. 11:20–24). In these passages, we learn that Jesus' first advent was not to bring vengeance, but that ultimate vengeance is postponed until his return (2 Thess. 1:6–10). But these facts in themselves neither authorize nor forbid the use of imprecatory prayers today.

Nor is it a sufficient solution to say that the imprecatory psalms are prayers of Christ himself through his people.[16] While this is true in a sense, that merely raises the same question (the love/justice relationship) again with respect to Christ's own motives, and it renders problematic the use of such sentiments in free prayer.

Meredith G. Kline suggests that imprecatory psalms represent an "intrusion" of the end-time into the present.[17] In the final judgment, there will be no more common grace, but only eternal punishment for the wicked. In that day, we will not be called to love our enemies, for they will be manifested as God's eternal enemies, subject only to death. In imprecatory psalms, then, the speaker calls down God's final judgment upon his enemies.

Kline says that we may never call down God's wrath on people on our own initiative; the intrusion is exclusively God's prerogative. In the imprecatory psalms, God knows that David's enemies are eternally lost, so he inspires David to pronounce divine judgment upon them. But to make this view

---

15. Of course, the state is given the power to carry out divine vengeance in limited ways. See Rom. 13 and our later discussion of the fifth commandment.

16. As in James E. Adams, *War Psalms of the Prince of Peace* (Phillipsburg, NJ: P&R Publishing, 1991). There are, however, a number of useful observations in this book.

17. Kline, "The Intrusion and the Decalogue," *Westminster Theological Journal* 16 (1953–54): 1–22, reprinted in Kline, *The Structure of Biblical Authority* (Grand Rapids: Eerdmans, 1972), 154–71.

consistent, we should not apply the sentiments expressed in these psalms to anyone other than David's immediate enemies. And we should not compose other songs like them. Yet it seems obvious to most readers of Scripture that the book of Psalms is given for our present liturgical and devotional use, that they should be applied to analogous situations in our own experience, and that they serve as a model for our prayers and worship songs.

Imprecation does belong to the end-time, as an invocation of final judgment. Our own time is not that final time. But, as we saw in chapter 16, ours is a time in which the last days have begun. God's final dealing with mankind is, as of now, already as well as not-yet. Scripture sometimes seems to encourage, and sometimes to discourage, imprecation because of the tension between the fulfilled and the unfulfilled aspects of God's plan.[18] The problem is that, contrary to Kline, Scripture does not clearly tell us when to use imprecations and when not to. There is nothing in Scripture that says specifically that we may pray imprecatory prayers only when they are divinely inspired, and only when we are not applying them to anyone in our own time.

Helpful insight is provided by J. A. Motyer, who reminds us of the larger biblical pattern: "Vengeance is mine, says the Lord."[19] The imprecatory psalms, he points out, are prayers that call upon God to remedy those injustices that neither we as individuals, nor the state, are competent to remedy. They do not seek personal vengeance; rather, they leave vengeance to God, as God has demanded.

Imprecatory prayers, like all prayers, always carry the implicit qualification, "Thy will be done." When we ask for things, we should do so with the ultimate desire of glorifying God. If God will be glorified in giving us our request, then we thank him; if he is more glorified in denying our request, our prayer has not thereby become useless, for all prayer is a recommitment to God's purpose, his kingdom. The Lord's Prayer beautifully exemplifies this spirit.

Sometimes we are persuaded that someone is guilty of a great injustice that we are not able to deal with in our own strength. As in biblical imprecations, the believer is to share this concern with God. In doing so, he must share God's evaluation of injustice, that "because of these things the wrath

18. David's imprecations, of course, precede the resurrection of Christ, and so they cannot be analyzed in terms of two-age tension. In the Old Testament period, as Kline indicates, intrusion of the end-time was intermittent, occasional. But once the new age begins in Christ, the presence and absence of final judgment coexist in tension. One might even say that imprecation is therefore even more appropriate in the New Testament age, because there is a constant presence of the end-times.

19. Motyer, "Imprecatory Psalms," in *Evangelical Dictionary of Theology*, ed. Walter A. Elwell (Grand Rapids: Baker, 1984), 554.

of God comes upon the sons of disobedience" (Eph. 5:6). And so he calls for divine vengeance to be exercised—not by himself, but by God.

Can we *love* an enemy and still call for God's wrath against him? Is a desire for divine judgment consistent with a desire for our enemy's salvation? The psychology of it is difficult, to be sure. But consider this example: when Idi Amin went around in Uganda, killing Christians right and left, simply to satisfy his personal hatred, many Christians prayed that God would bring vengeance upon him. Such vengeance, of course, does not, either in the Psalms or in our example, necessarily entail ultimate damnation. The prayer is primarily for a *historical* judgment. Although historical judgment is not entirely divorced in the biblical mind from ultimate damnation, the two are not inseparably conjoined, either.

But what if God had converted Amin, instead of judging him? Would those Christians have been disappointed? Surely not; they would have glorified God for answering their prayer beyond their wildest expectations. Such a conversion would have brought vengeance against this man, a vengeance visited by God's grace upon Christ in his atoning sacrifice. Their prayer would also have been answered in that Amin the persecutor would have received the sharpest divine rebuke (cf. "Saul, why do you persecute me?") and a historical defeat for his murderous regime. Finally, their prayer would have been answered in that their deepest desire was the glory of God.

Should the Christians, then, have prayed for his salvation, rather than his judgment? No. Prayer is often somewhat immediate, and rightly so. Of course, Christians sometimes get into a mood where they start praying for all sorts of wild things: the conversion of people like Hitler, the conversion of all the members of the U.S. Congress, the coming of Christ this evening, and so on. I do not rebuke the naive, immature faith that motivates such prayers. God often gives special help to those who are children at heart. Indeed, there are even times when the prayer of mature believers properly anticipates the broad sweep of history: "Thy kingdom come, thy will be done, on earth as it is in heaven." But most often, prayer is based on our hopes for the near term. And biblical prayer follows this pattern; it is often realistically short-term in its expectations. We see a situation before us, and we make a tentative judgment, based on our understanding of God's usual workings (from Scripture and providence), as to what help we might reasonably expect. When Peter was in jail, the church prayed for his release, not for the conversion of everybody in the prison system.

When Amin was ravaging the church, the immediate need was for judgment. Although one with a childlike faith might have anticipated the possibility of Amin's conversion, to most Christians that was not a realistic expectation. Amin was a militant Muslim, a hater of all things Christian, and mentally irrational besides. Yes, God's grace has converted hopeless cases before, but this was not a time for considering extraordinary theological possibilities. It was time for an earnest cry for help, based on present realities in the light of Scripture. The best short-term possibility was judgment: the death of Amin or his expulsion from the country. So the prayer of these believers often did not explicitly include his conversion. But, as I said earlier, their prayer did not exclude that either. That possibility was always implicit in the nature of divine judgment (which provides for and offers atonement), in the nature of salvation (which is always a judgment upon sin), and in the qualification, "Thy will be done." I suspect that this is also the way the earliest believers prayed with regard to Saul the persecutor.

What about the "hatred" expressed in the imprecatory psalms (e.g., 139:21–22)? How is this compatible with Jesus's command to love, not hate, our enemies? Again, as we have distinguished between personal and divine vengeance, I think we must distinguish between two kinds of hatred. Love and hate in Scripture are patterns of behavior, as well as emotions.[20] To love is to seek another's benefit; to hate is to seek his destruction. When we pray for divine vengeance, granting all the above qualifications, we are seeking the destruction of an enemy of God. We are "hating" that person. But in our individual relationships with that person, in which vengeance is excluded, we are to love, to seek what is best for our enemy. So Scripture similarly distinguishes between good and bad anger: the quickly aroused, difficult to extinguish, murderous anger of personal vengeance (Matt. 5:22), and the slowly aroused, easily extinguished, righteous anger of God's servants defending his honor (Eph. 4:26)—like the anger of God himself. So hatred and love are not contrary to one another in every respect. It is possible to have a godly hatred and a godly love toward the same person, paradoxical as that seems.[21]

We today may be called to cry for divine justice: against abortionists and abortion advocates, against homosexual militants who try to destroy the church's freedom to proclaim God's Word, against the remaining anti-Christian dictators of the world, against those in bondage to false religions who think God has given them the right to kill innocent people. We crave great historical signs of God's displeasure with injustice. That desire is quite legitimate. But if God pleases instead to rebuke these movements by send-

20. In terms of our earlier analysis, love is action as well as affection, and hatred is action as well as revulsion.

21. For a more thorough analysis of the relationship between love and hatred, see the discussion of God's own love and hatred in DG, 460–63.

ing revival and converting the hearts of his enemies, our desire for divine judgment will be completely fulfilled. And in our cry for divine justice, the imprecatory psalms will rightly guide our prayers.

And, strange as it may sound, we do have a responsibility to cultivate the hatred of evil. In an age that takes the vilest behavior for granted, we are called to hate what God hates, as to love what God loves. Holy hatred and holy love are inseparable. If we love God, we will join him in his hatreds, both in our actions and in our feelings. So godly hatred, like godly love, is a virtue. And both serve as motives for Christian ethics.

SEEKING TO CARRY OUT OUR RESPONSIBILITY

In chapter 12, I emphasized that love is a disposition to keep all the commandments of God. If we love him, we should keep his commandments. So a characteristic of love is that it seeks to carry out our responsibility.

All the commandments of the Decalogue, except the fourth and fifth, are expressed in negative terms, and that is the predominant mode of legal instruction in Scripture. One might imagine, then, that Christian ethics is largely negative, that it is a matter of avoiding things. Now the negative focus of biblical law is not wrong. It provides a good warning that we live in a spiritually dangerous world, where temptation is rife. The Christian must learn to say no. However, the biblical ethic is very positive, and we learn that especially from the law of love. For love is, emphatically, not just a matter of avoiding this or that spiritual danger. Love seeks every possible way to serve God and one's neighbor. Love seeks, indeed, modes of moral heroism.

OTHER VIRTUES IN THE NEW TESTAMENT

The Scriptures refer to many other virtues as well. There are several long lists of them, and others are noted here and there. These lists are not intended to be exhaustive, nor is it possible to define each virtue in sharp distinction from all the rest. The virtues overlap considerably. Each one implies and presupposes many others, perhaps all the others, just as faith, hope, and love imply one another. So the virtues are more like multiple perspectives on the whole ethical life than like independent atomic constituents of ethical rectitude.

I have focused on the three "theological virtues"—faith, hope, and love. These include one another, as we've seen, and they include all the other biblical virtues as well. Someone with perfect love would also be perfectly joyful, peaceful, patient, kind, good, faithful, gentle, and self-controlled, to use the list of virtues in Galatians 5:22–23. Colossians 3:12–13 adds to this list compassion, humility, meekness, forbearance, and forgiveness, and then adds, "and above all these put on love, which binds everything together in perfect harmony" (v. 14). Compare 2 Peter 1:5–7: "For this very reason, make every effort to supplement your faith with virtue, and virtue with knowledge, and knowledge with self-control, and self-control with steadfastness, and steadfastness with godliness, and godliness with brotherly affection, and brotherly affection with love." Again, love is the conclusion and the summation. In each of these virtues, we see the workings of love, as in 1 Corinthians 13:4–7, which I quoted earlier in this chapter.

Any of these virtues would reward further study, study that could be supplemented by a survey of the various vices, with which Scripture contrasts the virtues (as in Rom. 1:29–31; Gal. 5:19–21; Eph. 5:3–5; Col. 3:5–10). I shall not go through these lists here. If I did, much of that discussion would overlap our later consideration of the Ten Commandments.

However, I should report some impressions that occurred to my hyper-triadic mind as I perused these virtues. I would suggest that there are three major emphases in these virtues that parallel the three perspectives based on the lordship attributes. Looking only at the lists of positive qualities, I am struck by the following themes:

Acceptance of God's promises (normative perspective). We saw earlier that faith is directed toward the promises of God and toward the fulfillment of those promises, as in Romans 4 and Hebrews 11. The godly person trusts God's word, even when it seems to conflict with other sorts of evidence, even the evidence of the senses. We see this theme also in the virtues of faithfulness, steadfastness, godliness (piety), patience, joy, and knowledge. We might call these the virtues of faith. Here the child of God continues steadfast in his trust, faithful to God's covenant, patient to the end. Having knowledge of God's revealed truth, he worships God in all of life (Rom. 12:1–2), recognizing God as Lord in everything.

Humility before other people (situational perspective). If God's promises govern our lives, they free us from making any attempts to create significance for ourselves. Such attempts are always at the expense of other people. With God as Lord, however, we need not fear man, and we need not define ourselves by dominating other people. Hence, in the list of biblical virtues we see a prominent emphasis on humility, under such names as meekness, forbearance, forgiveness, gentleness, and peace. In Jesus' teaching, accordingly, we return good for evil, turn the other cheek, and walk the second mile (Matt. 5:38–42; cf. Rom. 12:14–21).

Stretching our conceptual scheme a bit, these virtues might be called virtues of hope, which I connected earlier in this chapter with the situational perspective. The point is that God is in control of this world, and we are not. Therefore, we are free from the need to be in control of every situation and to dominate other people. We recognize ourselves as what we are, sinners saved by grace, and we honor one another, knowing that our own honor comes from God and not from any source in this world. We can be genuinely humble, knowing, as in the classic gag line, that we have a lot to be humble about. We can ignore offenses, be gentle in correcting others (considering our own proneness to temptation, Gal. 6:1–3), and seek peace with others, even when we are not entirely satisfied with the terms of peace.

Affection for others (existential perspective). As we trust in God and humble ourselves before him and other people, we find ourselves, not resenting others, but caring for them from the heart. So our list of virtues includes compassion, brotherly love, kindness, and goodness (benevolence). Although all the virtues display love in different ways, these affections seem to be most obviously virtues of love.

THE FEAR OF THE LORD

I have so far been restricting my consideration of biblical virtues mainly to the New Testament. Lists of virtues are rare or nonexistent in the Old. The Old Testament teaches godly living mainly through laws, applying them by narratives, psalmody, wisdom teaching, and the admonitions of the prophets. It does not focus much on virtues as subjective elements of godly character.

Yet there is one virtue that the Old Testament mentions very prominently, and which the New Testament also emphasizes: the fear of the Lord. In a profoundly enlightening discussion of the subject, John Murray says, "The fear of God is the soul of godliness. The emphasis of Scripture in both the Old Testament and the New requires no less significant a proposition."[22]

He mentions that in Scripture the fear of God is the beginning of knowledge (Prov. 1:7) and of wisdom (Ps. 111:10). Job's exemplary piety

22. John Murray, *Principles of Conduct* (Grand Rapids: Eerdmans, 1957), 229. Much of this section summarizes Murray's discussion.

is founded on the fear of God (Job 1:8). In Isaiah 11:2–3, the Messiah's unique endowment of the Spirit brings a delight in the fear of the Lord. The Preacher of Ecclesiastes, after describing alternative value systems, gives us his final word: "The end of the matter; all has been heard. Fear God and keep his commandments, for this is the whole duty of man" (12:13). In the New Testament as well, the fear of God sums up the godly life (Luke 1:50; Acts 9:31; 2 Cor. 7:1; Col. 3:22; 1 Peter 2:17). Murray observes:

> This emphasis which Scripture places upon the fear of God evinces the bond that exists between religion and ethics. The fear of God is essentially a religious concept; it refers to the conception we entertain of God and the attitude of heart and mind that is ours by reason of that conception. Since the biblical ethic is grounded in and is the fruit of the fear of the Lord, we are apprised again that ethics has its source in religion and as our religion is so will be our ethic. This is to say also that what or whom we worship determines our behavior.[23]

Murray then distinguishes between two senses of "the fear of God." The first is being afraid of God, which brings "terror and dread."[24] The second is "the fear of reverence" which "elicits confidence and love."[25] The first is appropriate when sinners stand in the presence of God, anticipating judgment. Murray says, "It is the essence of impiety not to be afraid of God when there is *reason* to be afraid."[26] He finds examples of this legitimate terror in Deuteronomy 17:13; 21:21; Psalm 119:120. This theme is not absent either from the New Testament (Matt. 10:28; Luke 12:4–5; Rom. 11:20–21; Heb. 4:1; 10:27, 31; Rev. 15:3–4). Considering how terrible the judgments of God are, it would be wrong for us not to dread them.

But this fear of judgment cannot of itself lead us to love God. It is not, Murray argues, the fear of God that is the soul of godliness. Rather, "the fear of God in which godliness consists is the fear which constrains adoration and love. It is the fear which consists in awe, reverence, honour, and worship, and all of these on the highest level of exercise."[27] Reverential fear of God is the sense of living in God's constant presence. In considering the life of Abraham, Murray argues that it was because Abraham feared

---

23. Ibid., 231. Note that Murray does not advocate an ethic of natural law, as that phrase is sometimes understood (see chapter 14).

24. Ibid., 232.

25. Ibid., 233.

26. Ibid.

27. Ibid., 236.

God that he obeyed God's commands, even the command to sacrifice his son Isaac (Gen. 22:11–12). He continues:

> The same relationship can be traced in the other virtues that adorned Abraham's character. Why could he have been so magnanimous to Lot? It was because he feared the Lord and trusted his promise and his providence. He had no need to be mean. He feared and trusted the Lord. Why could he have been magnanimous to the king of Sodom? It was because he feared the Lord, God Most High, possessor of heaven and earth, and might not allow the enrichment offered to prejudice the independence of his faith; he needed not to be graspingly acquisitive. . . . *That* is all-pervasive God-consciousness, and it is God-consciousness conditioned by covenant-consciousness. This is the fear of God, or its indispensable corollary.[28]

Murray concludes by presenting the fear of God as an antidote to the superficial Christianity of our time. The phrase "God-fearing" seems to have disappeared from the vocabulary of Christian virtues, reflecting a lack of understanding of God's majesty, glory, and holiness: "The fear of God in us is that frame of heart and mind which reflects our apprehension of who and what God is, and who and what God is will tolerate nothing less than totality commitment to him."[29]

I have expounded Murray at length, because I think he provides a necessary and neglected perspective on the Christian life. What he says here, of course, must be balanced by other emphases that we have already considered, the virtues of faith, hope, and love. Although there is no contradiction between fearing God and loving him, we often find it hard to achieve an emotional state that incorporates both and neglects neither. Another reason for the difficulty that Murray does not discuss is the problem of relating the fear of God to the New Testament concept of the friendship of God (John 15:13–15), based on the redemptive work of Christ. Because Jesus has torn the temple veil by his sacrifice of himself, believers have bold access into the holiest place, such as was not known in the Old Testament (Heb. 10:19). How is this new intimacy, conferred by grace, compatible with the fear of the Lord?

It erases the need for fear in the sense of terror and dread (1 John 4:18), but not the need for reverence as we stand in God's presence. At the present time, however, it is not always easy in our experience to separate the two

---

28. Ibid., 139–40. Murray follows this discussion with an interesting reflection on God as "the fear of Isaac" (Gen. 31:42, 53).

29. Ibid., 242.

kinds of fear. Until the consummation, I suspect, there will always be some element of terror in our reverence for God. Thus, there will always be some tension between the fear of the Lord and our experience of sonship.

But as for the relation between reverence and intimacy, we need to remind ourselves that our new friend Jesus, our heavenly Father, and the Spirit who dwells intimately within us are God indeed, the majestic, sovereign ruler of heaven and earth. The praise of God in the Psalms and in the book of Revelation expresses both intimacy and reverence. For many of us, there is tension here. But we do sometimes feel these two qualities fuse together in times of worship, sometimes in surprising ways. Christians are often overwhelmed with the consciousness that our Father God is the Holy One who works all things according to his eternal plan. May that unity of fear and love extend to all aspects of our lives.

CHAPTER 20

The New Life as a Source
of Ethical Knowledge

As I indicated in *The Doctrine of the Knowledge of God*, knowledge always involves a subject (the knower), an object (the known), and a norm (the standard or criterion). This triperspectival understanding of epistemology pertains to ethical knowledge, as well as to all other knowledge. In this book, from the normative perspective (chapters 9–13), I considered the criterion of ethical knowledge. From the situational perspective (chapters 14–17), I discussed the object of ethical knowledge, as well as such issues as general revelation, context, and goal.

Now, from the existential perspective, I shall talk about the subjective aspect of ethical knowledge. In this chapter, we shall see that the existential and normative perspectives overlap, for we shall see that the existential perspective is an indispensable means of coming to know ethical norms.

We cannot know anything without our minds, that is, without sense organs, reason, and other mental capacities. And we cannot know anything without these capacities functioning together in a subjective process by which we discover truth.

In one sense, these subjective capacities and processes are themselves revelational. In chapter 9, I argued that knowledge of God's revelation can be found through nature and history, through language, and through persons. Human beings are made in the image of God, and so they are themselves revelational. We find that revelation in everything human beings are and do, including their thought processes. So we need not fear that in investigating these thought processes we are abandoning revelation.

Further, as we have seen, Scripture teaches that God actually writes his words on our hearts—inwardly, subjectively. Without this divine act, we cannot understand, believe, or apply the revelation of Scripture itself. Traditionally, Reformed theology has described this divine work as illumination, but in chapter 9 I argued that it is equally biblical to call it "existential revelation," coordinated with "general revelation" and "special revelation" in a triperspectival set. So our own subjectivity is an important locus of divine revelation, and we examine that here from the existential perspective.

In all of this, we should not forget the primacy of Scripture, as I presented it when discussing the normative perspective. Although everything is revelational, including our own thought processes, Scripture plays a special role within the organism of revelation: (1) Scripture is the document of the covenant, the written constitution of the people of God. (2) It contains the gospel, which alone can enable us to see other forms of revelation rightly. (3) It alone is an infallible text, consisting of words and sentences authored by God himself. So, even though we come to know the content of Scripture through the processes of our own thinking, with the help of natural revelation (knowledge of languages, ancient culture, archaeology, etc.), the words of Scripture take precedence over any other source of knowledge. When, by responsible methods of exegesis, I come to believe that Scripture teaches a certain truth, I must believe it, even though other sources deny that truth.

So Scripture is our primary guide, even concerning the existential perspective, as it was concerning the situational and normative perspectives. But we have seen and shall see that Scripture gives great importance to the subjective side of knowledge.

ETHICAL KNOWLEDGE, A PRODUCT OF SANCTIFICATION

The Knowledge of God

In *The Doctrine of the Knowledge of God*, I argued that knowing God, in Scripture, is not merely learning additional facts or becoming familiar with an additional object. Rather, since God is a person, to know him is to enter into a personal relationship with him. His relationship to us is covenantal, for he is Lord. Therefore, to know him is to become his covenant servant.[1] Here the meaning of *know* is very close to "have as a friend," as in "I know Bill." In the covenant, we are God's people, and he is our God. He makes everything work for our good, and we seek to glorify him. Thus, obedience is a constituent aspect of this knowledge (see Jer. 22:16; Hos. 6:6).

As we grow in grace, we grow in the knowledge of God. We come to know God better as we become more obedient to him. Knowing God, therefore, is not merely an intellectual process, but an ethical one as well. And, as we shall see, the intellectual itself presupposes the ethical.

WISDOM

Wisdom is another virtue in Scripture that is both intellectual and ethical. Wisdom is a form of knowledge that penetrates to the deeper significance of things and therefore enables us to apply that knowledge to practical situations. Scripture often represents it as a skill, a knowing *how*, rather than knowing *that*. In Exodus 31:1–5, for example, Bezalel and Oholiab have wisdom (the ESV translates it "ability") from the Spirit of God to produce designs and crafts for the tabernacle. In James 3:13–17, wisdom is clearly ethical, the skill of godly living:

> Who is wise and understanding among you? By his good conduct let him show his works in the meekness of wisdom. But if you have bitter jealousy and selfish ambition in your hearts, do not boast and be false to the truth. This is not the wisdom that comes down from above, but is earthly, unspiritual, demonic. For where jealousy and selfish ambition exist, there will be disorder and every vile practice. But the wisdom from above is first pure, then peaceable, gentle, open to reason, full of mercy and good fruits, impartial and sincere.

Specifically, wisdom is the ability to do the right thing in difficult situations (Luke 21:14–15), especially to say the right thing (Acts 6:10; 1 Cor. 2:6 [cf. vv. 1, 4, 13]; 12:8; Col. 1:28; 2 Peter 3:15).

Wisdom, personified as the wisdom of God, serves as an ethical guide (Prov. 3:5–6, 21–26). Wisdom is God's own attribute, by which he made all things (Prov. 3:19; 8:22–31). He communicates it to us by his Word and Spirit (Deut. 34:9; Prov. 30:5; Jer. 8:8–9; Acts 6:3; 1 Cor. 2:6–16;

---

1. I am speaking here, of course, and throughout this chapter, of the believer's knowledge of God. Scripture teaches (Rom. 1:21) that unbelievers also "know God," but in a very different way: as an enemy, rather than as a friend. See *DKG*, 49–61.

Col. 3:16; 2 Tim. 3:16) on the basis of our union with Christ (1 Cor. 1:24, 30; Col. 2:3).

Like the knowledge of God, then, wisdom is ethical in character, and our progress in wisdom is parallel to our progress in sanctification.

TRUTH

Truth has several dimensions in Scripture. There is "metaphysical" truth, which John Murray defines as

> not so much the true in contrast with the false, or the real in contrast with the fictitious. It is the absolute as contrasted with the relative, the ultimate as contrasted with the derived, the eternal as contrasted with the temporal, the permanent as contrasted with the temporary, the complete in contrast with the partial, the substantial in contrast with the shadowy.[2]

Examples of this usage may be found in the Johannine literature, as in John 1:9, 17; 14:6; 17:3; 1 John 5:20, and in Hebrews 8:2.

The term *truth* is often used also in an epistemological sense, for statements that neither err nor deceive. This usage is far more common in our language. Note, for example, how the Johannine writings speak of an authentic witness as true, as in John 5:31–32; 8:13–14, 16–17; 10:41; 19:35; 21:34.

Then there is also an ethical meaning of truth. Truth is something we can walk in, according to 1 Kings 2:4; Psalm 86:11; 1 John 1:6–7; 3 John 3–4. To walk in the truth is to obey the commands of God. This language reflects the figure of the Word of God as a light on our path (Ps. 119:105). Because God's Word is true in the metaphysical and epistemological senses, it can keep us from stumbling in our ethical pilgrimage.

Here too, then, we can see an ethical dimension to an epistemological term. We do not respond adequately to the truth until we apply it to life, until that truth changes our lives.

DOCTRINE

The Greek terms based on *didaskō* typically refer in the Pastoral Epistles to a teaching of the word of God that leads to spiritual health. This is "sound" or "healthy" teaching (1 Tim. 1:10; 4:6; 6:3; 2 Tim. 1:13; 4:3; Titus 1:9). So doctrine, defined as this kind of teaching, also has an ethical goal. It is not given to us merely for intellectual contemplation.

2. John Murray, *Principles of Conduct* (Grand Rapids: Eerdmans, 1957), 123.

Doctrine, or theology in this sense, comes to us in all parts of Scripture, not only in formal propositions, but also in narratives, poetry, prophecy, letters, and apocalyptic. In Colossians 3:16, Paul says that we teach one another in song. What distinguishes doctrine, then, is not an academic style or an intellectually rigorous approach, though the academic approach should not be despised. What rather distinguishes theology is its ethical goal, to bring the biblical message to bear on people's lives. That indeed is the goal of Scripture itself (2 Tim. 3:16–17).

In this brief look at four terms that are important to theological epistemology, we have seen that knowledge has an ethical goal, and that therefore God's regenerating and sanctifying grace is active in the processes by which we gain and deepen such knowledge.

INTELLECTUAL KNOWLEDGE AND ETHICAL KNOWLEDGE

We have seen that the knowledge of God, together with wisdom, truth, and doctrine, is an ethical knowledge. But the same is true even of "intellectual" or propositional knowledge, such as the knowledge that there is a bookstore on the corner. There is, indeed, no propositional knowledge without ethical knowledge. Let us look at this matter from two perspectives.

THE ETHICAL PRESUPPOSES THE INTELLECTUAL

It is common to hear Christians of various traditions (especially the Reformed) say that life is built on doctrine.[3] This statement is based on passages like Hebrews 11:6 and 1 John 4:2–3. To live the Christian life, it is necessary (at least in the case of reasonably intelligent adults) to believe certain propositions: that God exists, that Jesus Christ has come in the flesh, that Jesus died for our sins, and that he has risen from the dead (1 Cor. 15:17–19).

The statement that life is built on doctrine misleads us, I think, by equating doctrine with a set of propositions. See the previous section

---

3. "Life is built on doctrine" was a slogan of J. Gresham Machen and his movement to restore biblical orthodoxy to American Presbyterianism. This needed to be said, over against the liberals of the day (taking their cue from Friedrich Schleiermacher), who maintained the opposite view. However, neither the liberals nor the Machenites, in my view, presented the full biblical picture, though the Machenites were, in their overall theology, far closer to the truth than the liberals. The present chapter is an attempt to restore balance.

for a broader understanding of doctrine. But the intent of this slogan is biblical. Even if we define doctrine in a more biblical way, it is true that propositional beliefs are part of doctrine, that God calls us to believe those propositions, and that belief in those propositions changes our lives.

If the intellect is the organ that evaluates, believes, and disbelieves propositions (and I shall question that definition also at a later point), then it follows that Christian ethics presupposes intellectual beliefs. Certainly, as we saw in chapter 16, Scripture regularly motivates us to obey God's word by a narrative, a set of historical facts. And we can receive that motivation only if we believe that the events of that narrative actually took place.

THE INTELLECTUAL PRESUPPOSES THE ETHICAL

But the opposite relationship also exists between obedience and propositional belief. It is also true that propositional belief, in the context of the Christian life, presupposes obedience. That is, it is not only true that life is built on doctrine, but also that doctrine is built on life.

Romans 1:18–32, 1 Corinthians 1:18–2:16, and other passages indicate that when people make an ethical decision to suppress the truth of God (Rom. 1:18), that leads them to believe lies (v. 25). So unbelief is defective, not only ethically, but intellectually as well. According to Romans 1:19–20, God makes himself clearly known through the creation. Those who refuse to acknowledge him are "without excuse" (v. 20). That response to revelation is stupid. Even Satan, who appears in Scripture to be intellectually superior to human beings, is a model of foolishness, when, knowing God's power, he seeks to supplant God's rule. Satan's disobedience infects his intellect and the intellects of all who follow him.

But if disobedience leads to stupidity, the opposite is also true: obedience leads to knowledge, to understanding. Jesus says, "If anyone's will is to do God's will, he will know whether the teaching is from God or whether I am speaking on my own authority" (John 7:17). Here Jesus teaches that an obedient disposition can lead to intellectual assurance. So begins a general theme of the Johannine writings, that to know God we must keep his commandments (1 John 2:3–6; 4:8; 5:2–3). Those who do not love their brothers are in darkness (1 John 2:9–11), a metaphor of both moral and intellectual privation. Knowledge is dependent on love, according to 1 Corinthians 8:1–4; 13:7, 11–13; 1 Timothy 1:5–11. Jesus makes knowledge of the glory of God to rest upon faith in John 11:40.

So the knowledge of God, even in its intellectual dimensions, requires the same work of the Spirit that brings ethical transformation (1 John 2:20–27; 4:2–3, 13–17; Eph. 1:17–18; 3:14–19).

In *The Doctrine of the Knowledge of God*, I discussed three passages that use the word *dokimazein*, meaning "to approve through testing": Romans 12:1–2, Ephesians 5:8–10, and Philippians 1:9–11.[4] In these passages, it is clear that we come to know the will of God, not only by reading the Bible or otherwise receiving propositional information, but through the process of ethical discipline: the sacrifice of our bodies (Rom. 12:1), nonconformity to the world, transformation by the renewal of our mind (Rom. 12:2), walking as children of light (Eph. 5:8), abounding in love (Phil. 1:9). In the Philippians passage, we learn again that love produces discernment.

Hebrews 5:11–14 makes a similar point, though it does not use the word *dokimazein*.[5] Deep doctrinal discussion (in context, the Melchizedekian priesthood of Jesus) can be appreciated only by those who are ethically and spiritually mature, "who have their powers of discernment trained by constant practice to distinguish good from evil." Theology is most helpful for people on the front lines of spiritual warfare, people who see in actual moral combat how important the doctrines are.

So sanctification presupposes knowing our duty; but the reverse is also the case.

The health of the intellect depends on the health of the whole person, both physically and ethically. As with all other human actions, intellectual actions are subject to the negative effects of sin and the positive effects of regeneration and sanctification. Thinking, like everything else we do, may be done in two ways: to the glory of God or to the glory of an idol. So thinking, like every other human act, is subject to God's norms, should seek the glory of God, and should be motivated by faith and love. The intellectual is ethical, and epistemology may be seen as a subdivision of ethics.[6]

We regularly use practical tests to determine if someone understands a concept. If someone has the right concept of a triangle, for example, we expect him to be able to draw one. Having a concept entails a disposition to action. This is especially true of religious knowledge. One does not fully understand who God is unless he regards God as the most important person in his life, unless he is prepared to sacrifice his own pleasures for the blessing of knowing God in Christ. Here concepts and passions are not easily separated. Life and doctrine are interdependent.

---

4. *DKG*, 154–55.
5. See discussion in *DKG*, 154–55.
6. Cf. *DKG*, 62–64.

MORAL DISCERNMENT

So we are prepared to look more closely at ethical epistemology, at the process by which we learn God's will for our actions. This is the process that we often refer to as ethical guidance.

We saw in chapters 9–13 the importance of Scripture as the law of God. I argued that we gain knowledge of God's will by applying that law to our own circumstances, circumstances that I focused on in chapters 14–17. Here I focus on the process of application, the subjective experience of applying God's Word to circumstances.

To apply the Word of God to circumstances requires a kind of moral vision. Such applications require the ability to *see the circumstances in the light of* biblical principles. In moral quandaries, we often ask questions such as "Is this act murder?" or "Is this act stealing?" For Christians, the challenge is to give biblical names to human actions. Sometimes it is obvious: taking money out of a friend's wallet without authorization is what the Bible calls stealing. Sometimes it is less obvious: is it murder to remove this terminal patient from life support?[7] Is it fornication for unmarried couples to engage in intimacies short of intercourse?

Although Scripture is sufficient as a source of God's words concerning our ethical life (chapter 11), it does not speak directly to every situation, especially to situations that are distinctive to modern life. It does not mention nuclear war, or Internet pornography, or even abortion. Hence, much of the work of application lies with us, led by the Spirit and by the general principles of Scripture. We also receive help from the church's traditional views, the preaching of the Word, parents, teachers, and friends. As we mature in the faith (Heb. 5:11–14, again), we are better able to make such judgments.

The process of learning how to apply the Word is somewhat mysterious, just as the workings of the Holy Spirit are always difficult to describe (John 3:8). But one crucial element is learning to see *analogies* between activities mentioned in Scripture and those of people today. Hijacking airplanes, for example, is different from stealing oxen, but the two activities are analogous. Similarly, we should ask how our dispositions compare with those

---

7. In chapter 11, I discussed moral syllogisms, in which the first premise is a moral principle, the second is a factual statement, and the conclusion is an application of the moral principle to the factual situation. For example: stealing is wrong; embezzling is stealing; therefore, embezzling is wrong. In the present context, I am referring to the same sort of application, but focusing on the formulation of the second premise. The question here, for example, is how we come to believe that embezzling is stealing, that abortion is murder, or that violating a speed limit is showing disrespect for our rulers?

of biblical characters who are positively or negatively exemplary: to what extent am I like Saul or David, or like Judas or Peter?

In the last paragraph, I mentioned "seeing" as the source of our knowledge of analogous moral patterns. But this seeing is not the same as physical sight. Rather, I am here using physical sight as a metaphor for the moral sensitivity described in Philippians 1:9 ("discernment") and Hebrews 5:11–14 ("powers of discernment").[8]

Even in nonmoral cases, there are forms of perception that transcend the powers of physical sight. In *The Doctrine of the Knowledge of God*, I referred to the "duck-rabbit," a drawing in which one can see a duck or a rabbit, depending on how one looks at it.[9] One can have 20/20 vision, seeing all the lines in the drawing, without being able to identify it as a picture of a duck, a rabbit, or both. Indeed, it is possible to look at the drawing without seeing it as a picture of anything.[10] So "seeing as" is different from seeing. One can look at the lines of a drawing without realizing how they together are analogous to a real animal.

The same is true in moral contexts. People with healthy sense organs may not be able to "see" moral patterns and analogies. Someone may be very much aware of something he has done, without being able to make the right moral evaluation of his act. For example, someone may assault another person, seriously injuring him, without understanding that what he did was wrong.

Even for believers, our inability to "see as" can lead to moral difficulty. Let's say that I have a feeling of rage. I know how I feel, and I know what actions that feeling has impelled me to do. But what is the moral evaluation of that feeling? That may not be obvious. In part, I resist any negative evaluation of my own actions because of my pride. But there is also ambiguity in the concept of rage itself. Scripture says that rage, or anger, comes in two forms. One is righteous indignation, such as Scripture attributes to God and to Jesus when he cleansed the temple (John 2:17). The other is an outworking of murderous hatred (Matt. 5:22). How should I evaluate my own rage? Is it righteous indignation or murderous hatred?

These questions cannot be answered by simple factual perceptions, in the usual sense. I may be aware of all the relevant passages of Scripture (such as the two mentioned above) without knowing how they apply in my case. Further, I may be aware of my own feelings and actions, and of

---

8. In Phil. 1:9, the Greek term is *aisthēsis*, from which we get English words like *aesthetic*. In Heb. 5:14, the word *aisthētērion* comes from the same root.

9. *DKG*, 157.

10. One can imagine such a response from members of a tribe that did not know about rabbits or ducks, or that did not use drawings to represent objects.

the circumstances of those actions, without being able to make the right moral judgments. These judgments, therefore, are not merely the result of sense perception or intellectual reasoning. One can know the facts of the situation, without seeing the relevant patterns and analogies.[11]

But it does often happen that moral discernment comes upon us, that we are compelled to note that something is good or bad, right or wrong. Sometimes that discernment coincides with the discovery of a Scripture text or a relevant fact, even though the discernment is not identical with such a discovery.

But sometimes moral discernment occurs in unexpected ways. In *The Doctrine of the Knowledge of God*,[12] I referred to David's adultery with Bathsheba, followed by his murder (in effect) of her husband Uriah (2 Sam. 11). After these events, David went through a period when he was complacent and unrepentant. We wonder how that can be. David, after all, was not ignorant of God's law (see Ps. 19:7–13, for example). And he certainly was not ignorant of what he had done with Bathsheba and Uriah. But somehow David did not make the connection between God's law and his own actions in a way that would impress upon him the wickedness of his actions and his obligation to repent.

What brought David to repentance was not the revelation of some fact about Scripture or the situation of which he was previously unaware, but an emotional shock. The prophet Nathan told him a story of a poor man who had one ewe lamb that he raised as a family pet. A rich man, who owned many sheep, stole the poor man's lamb and killed it to feed a guest. "Then David's anger was greatly kindled against the man, and he said to Nathan, 'As the LORD lives, the man who has done this deserves to die, and he shall restore the lamb fourfold, because he did this thing, and because he had no pity.' Nathan said to David, 'You are the man!'" (2 Sam. 12:5–7).

That story, with Nathan's application, drove David to repentance. Nathan presented no new facts, but he told a story that made evident to David the ethical pattern of his actions. David had behaved as the wicked rich man, as one who took what was not his and who had no pity. Now David could see. Now he was able to apply the principles of God's law to his own actions.

Ethical discourse, therefore, is never merely a matter of setting forth facts and Bible passages. It is also a matter of wise counseling, of dealing with the subjective issues that stand in the way of moral insight. Scrip-

---

11. This discussion is related to the naturalistic fallacy (see chapter 5). Moral values are mysterious in that they cannot be sensed, nor can they simply be deduced from factual premises. Attempts to derive them from nonmoral premises are fallacious.

12. *DKG*, 156–57.

ture, therefore, teaches ethics in many ways: through laws and through narrative, as we have seen, but also through proverbs, parables, songs, personal address (as in both the Prophets of the Old Testament and the letters of the New Testament), eschatological promises (see chapter 16), and apocalyptic vision.

We can also learn from such considerations that spiritual maturity plays a major role in ethical understanding. Two people may know the same Bible verses and the same facts, but they may disagree on the application of the former to the latter. That sort of disagreement may have many sources, but one may simply be that one person is more mature spiritually than the other. One, more than the other, may have his "powers of discernment trained by constant practice to distinguish good from evil" (Heb. 5:14). Such maturity comes through experience in fighting spiritual warfare, availing oneself of God's means of grace in the Word, the sacraments, worship, and fellowship.

Some ethical arguments can be resolved by Bible teaching, or by learning more about the circumstances involved. But others cannot be resolved until one or both parties develop more spiritual maturity. So perhaps the best way to deal with some ethical controversies is benign neglect: set them aside until one or both parties gain more spiritual maturity, that is, until God provides more resources for dealing with the problem.

It is wrong to suppose that we must get all the answers to ethical questions before we engage in spiritual warfare, as if the intellect were in every respect prior to life. Rather, there may well be some ethical questions (like the theological questions of Heb. 5:11–14) that we will not be able to answer (or even fully appreciate) until we have been in spiritual combat with the forces of darkness.

THE DOCTRINE OF GUIDANCE

In John 8:12, Jesus said, "I am the light of the world. Whoever follows me will not walk in darkness, but will have the light of life." Here and elsewhere, Scripture promises that God will guide his people. We have seen that Scripture is an important aspect of that guidance, as it is applied to natural revelation. If my previous discussion is correct, he also guides us subjectively, enabling us to apply Scripture to the circumstances of general revelation. This is part of the nature of "existential revelation" (see chapter 9).

This view of divine guidance contrasts with two others that are generally thought to be opposite to one another. One is an intellectualist view, that guidance is the process of studying the Scriptures. This view is often found, in practice if not in formulation, in Reformed circles. The other view is that God guides us by whispering in our ears, by giving us special revelation over and above the canon of Scripture. That view is often found among charismatics.

The interesting thing is that both of these views are intellectualist. Both agree that God guides mainly through revealing propositions and commands. On the first view, these are limited to those found in Scripture; on the second view, they are found outside of Scripture. Both views suppose that when we need guidance, what we need is more instruction.

But if I am right, then guidance also requires a subjective competence, the ability to recognize analogous patterns and to apply them to oneself. Scripture is a great help to us in this respect; after all, Nathan's parable is in the Bible. But the Spirit also operates on us from within, giving us new eyes and hearts, giving us spiritual perception.

So God's ethical guidance of his people does not add new sentences to the canon of Scripture. But neither is it necessarily an intellectual process. God deals with us personally, even inwardly. His operations within us are mysterious, not to be simply described or categorized. He can work through the subconscious, through dreams, through memory and intuition, as well as through what we usually call the intellect. Reformed theology has always acknowledged the necessity of the Spirit's illumination in enabling believers to understand the Word. But it is important that we see this illuminating work of God, not only enabling us to formulate doctrines, but also enabling us to apply Scripture to our circumstances, and to see our experiences and inner life in biblical terms.

CHAPTER 21

The Organs of Ethical Knowledge

When we think of ethics as a subjective process of decision making, we often consider various ethical "faculties," aspects of the mind that play important roles in ethical knowledge, decisions, actions, and character. In a Christian context, these capacities are ways in which God enables us to make the right choices. In chapter 20, we considered the process of gaining ethical knowledge in general terms. Here I shall become more specific and look at mental capacities that function in ethical thought and action.

It is sometimes thought that reason, emotion, conscience, imagination, will, and so forth, are more or less autonomous units, battling one another for supremacy in each human mind. But it is more scriptural to say that the whole person is the one who makes ethical decisions, and that the ethical faculties are ways of describing the person as he makes those decisions. In my view, reason, emotion, and so on are not conflicting voices within us, but rather are different ways of characterizing and describing the whole person. Reason is the whole person reasoning, emotion is the whole person feeling, and so forth. Further, each of these is dependent on the others. The best model, in my judgment, is perspectival. All these faculties are perspectives on one another and on the whole person.

I made the same argument in *The Doctrine of the Knowledge of God*, chapter 10, in regard to theology.[1] But on my definition (chapter 2), theology is ethics and ethics is theology. So what can be said about theological knowledge can also be said about ethical knowledge, with some difference of perspective.

---

1. *DKG*, 319–46.

THE HEART

In general, the heart is the "center" of man's being. It is what we are most fundamentally, as God sees us. It is what we are when all the masks are off. The heart is committed either to God (Deut. 6:4–5) or "hardened" and committed to an idol (Ex. 4:21; Deut. 15:7; 1 Sam. 6:6; 2 Chron. 36:13; Ps. 95:8; Mark 6:52; 8:17; Rom. 9:18; Heb. 3:8). That heart commitment governs the fundamental direction of human life. In Luke 6:45, Jesus teaches us, "The good person out of the good treasure of his heart produces good, and the evil person out of his evil treasure produces evil, for out of the abundance of the heart his mouth speaks."

The heart is the seat of honesty and goodness (Luke 8:15), as well as evil lusts (Matt. 5:28). When the heart is hardened, the result is not only wickedness, but also ignorance (Isa. 6:10; John 12:40). The hypocrite may profess allegiance to God, but his heart is far from him (Matt. 15:8). Yet God knows the heart and will judge it (Jer. 11:20; Rom. 2:5), disclosing its inmost secrets (1 Cor. 4:5).

As we have seen, God writes his word upon the hearts of the regenerate. This means not only that we know God's word, but also that our deepest inclination is to obey it.

So the heart is the chief organ of moral knowledge and of our moral will, our desire to obey. As we have seen throughout our discussion of the existential perspective, knowledge and obedience are inseparable. In the heart, God places knowledge and obedience, and they nourish one another.

To say that the heart discerns God's will is to say that the whole person discerns it. That being the case, we should not press too hard the various divisions of the human mind into faculties. Reason, will, and emotion are only aspects of the whole person as he thinks, decides, acts, and feels. Nevertheless, if the human person as a whole is the organ of ethical knowledge, then all aspects of that person are somehow involved in ethical knowledge. Thus, there is some value in making further distinctions to see in more detail how that knowledge arises and functions.

CONSCIENCE

Conscience is our God-given ability to discern good and evil.[2] Conscience convicts of sin (John 8:9 KJV) and commends us when we do right

---

2. Scholastic philosophy distinguished between *synderesis* (or *synteresis*), our natural tendency toward good, and *conscience* (sometimes called *syneidesis*), which applies that moral sense to practical actions. In terms of the moral syllogism, synderesis determines

(Rom. 2:15; 2 Cor. 1:12). A "good" or "clear" conscience is one that generally approves one's behavior and does so accurately (Acts 23:1; 24:16; 1 Tim. 1:5, 19; 3:9; 2 Tim. 1:3; Heb. 13:18; 1 Peter 3:16, 21); an "evil" conscience is one that condemns in some important way (Heb. 10:22).

So conscience is a source of ethical knowledge, of existential revelation. We may identify it with that moral sense that we discussed in chapter 20 in connection with Philippians 1:9 and Hebrews 5:14. It enables us to see the patterns and analogies we discussed in that chapter.

Nevertheless, conscience is not infallible. Paul speaks of some who have "weak" consciences (1 Cor. 8:7, 12). They have moral scruples (in this case, against the eating of food offered to idols) that are not based in God's Word. Compare also Paul's discussion in Romans 14. I discussed both of these passages in chapter 11.

Conscience can be even more deeply perverted. In 1 Timothy 4:2 (cf. Titus 1:15), Paul speaks of false teachers "whose consciences are seared." A seared conscience is nearly destroyed,[3] no longer a reliable moral guide. When people refuse again and again to follow God, and indulge in worse and worse sin, they may reach a point at which they have almost no consciousness of the difference between good and evil.

The perversion of the conscience leads to an ethical problem: should we always obey our conscience, or should we sometimes disobey it? We might say that if our conscience is weak or seared, we ought sometimes to disobey it. The problem, however, is that conscience defines for a person what is right. For a theist, conscience defines the will of God. So if we disobey our conscience, even when it misleads us, we see ourselves as doing what is wrong, even as violating the will of God. So if we violate a seared conscience, our action may be ethically right, but in our hearts, our intentions, we are choosing what is wrong. So the "strong" of Romans 14 must not induce the weak to act against their conscience, even though the consciences of the weak are misleading them. When you have a weak conscience, you can sin in one way by rejecting its dictates, and in another way by accepting them. I call this the paradox of ethical decision.

The only solution is a practical one: we need to train our consciences, so that they will rejoice in what is really good and condemn what is really evil,

---

the major premise, and conscience deduces the conclusion. (The minor premise comes from "an inferior sort of reason.") However, conscience certainly functions in other ways than in the production of syllogisms. In my vocabulary, and, I believe, that of Scripture, conscience includes synderesis and broadly indicates the source of all moral knowledge.

3. I don't believe that conscience can ever be totally destroyed. God always maintains his moral witness against sinners, as Rom. 1:18–32 indicates.

Translations of the Old Testament rarely use the term *conscience*. But in 2 Samuel 24:10, after David has sinfully conducted a census of the people, we read that his "heart struck him." Here, David's heart serves as what the New Testament calls conscience (cf. 1 Sam. 24:5; 1 Kings 9:4; 15:3, 14). So there is no metaphysical difference between the heart and the conscience. The two are perspectives on one another. The heart is the center of human personality. The conscience is the heart in its function as a moral guide. As we make moral decisions as whole persons, we gain moral knowledge as whole persons.

EXPERIENCE

In the history of philosophy, *experience* usually refers to knowledge gained from the senses. An *empiricist* (taken from a Latin word for "experience") believes that all human knowledge is based on sense experience.

English translations of Scripture rarely use the term *experience* or the various forms of *empirical*. But they do mention the sense organs of sight, hearing, smell, taste, and touch. Scripture sometimes speaks negatively of sensation, as when it contrasts faith with sight (see chapter 19). But for the most part, it regards the senses positively, even with regard to the knowledge of God. Hear the excitement of the aged apostle in 1 John 1:1–3, as he recalls the apostles' experience of Jesus:

> That which was from the beginning, which we have heard, which we have seen with our eyes, which we looked upon and have touched with our hands, concerning the word of life—the life was made manifest, and we have seen it, and testify to it and proclaim to you the eternal life, which was with the Father and was made manifest to us—that which we have seen and heard we proclaim also to you, so that you too may have fellowship with us; and indeed our fellowship is with the Father and with his Son Jesus Christ.

Of course, we do not have today that kind of sense experience of Jesus. But it is important to understand that our faith is based on eyewitness testimony. As Peter says, "We did not follow cleverly devised myths when we made known to you the power and coming of our Lord Jesus Christ, but we were eyewitnesses of his majesty" (2 Peter 1:16; cf. Luke 1:2; 1 Cor. 15:1–12). Although Jesus commends those who believe without seeing (John 20:29), he offers to Thomas the opportunity to believe through sight (v. 27). So, although we should not demand that God provide us with evidence of the senses, he has provided that to some people. And our faith rests upon the sense experience of those whom God has chosen to be eyewitnesses.

Although we today cannot be witnesses in the same sense, God nevertheless continues to use our senses to communicate his truth. We could not read the Bible, for example, without sense organs. And the sacraments are, as the Reformers called them, "visible words," revelation given by God to the eyes, and for us to touch, smell, and taste as well. The Lord's Supper fulfills in literal fashion the invitation of Psalm 34:8, "Oh, taste and see that the LORD is good! Blessed is the man who takes refuge in him!"

Further, it is through the senses that we encounter natural revelation and learn of the situations to which we must apply the Word of God. So the senses are not to be despised. God has given them to us as means of receiving his revelation, including moral revelation.

Of course, to deduce moral laws from sensations alone would be a naturalistic fallacy. But sensation is never alone. It is part of an epistemological complex. Critics of empiricism are right to say that we never learn anything from the senses by themselves. For one thing, there are such things as optical and aural illusions. To determine where the truth lies in the sensory world, we need minds, logical capacities, as well as sense organs. The senses provide data, but that data must be interpreted.

When I perceive a cow in the pasture, I do not only experience an image on the retina of my eye. I also relate that image to a package of mental concepts, one of which is "cow." "Cow," as an abstract universal concept, coming not from sense experience alone, but from a combination of sensation and other mental capacities. So perceiving a cow is an act of the whole mind, not only of the sense organs. Indeed, whenever we speak of "seeing" or "hearing" something, we are usually referring, not to the sheer physiological process of receiving sensory data, but to an interpretive action involving all the faculties of the mind.

We can understand further how experience has dimensions beyond the merely sensory. Seeing a cow in the field is an experience. But it is also an experience to observe one's own thinking processes, to sense God's presence in worship, to feel convicted of sin.

So experience provides an important perspective on ethical knowledge. Like conscience, experience is a concept that refers to the whole process of gaining ethical knowledge. As a perspective on this process, it focuses on one's introspective awareness of things that are happening within oneself and one's (particularly sensory) apprehension of one's environment. But that awareness in turn presupposes all other aspects of knowledge.

The obvious implication is that, as Hebrews 5:14 tells us, experience is important for ethical discernment. Believers learn to make the right decisions by wrestling with such decisions day by day. They learn to defeat Satan by engaging in spiritual warfare.

A respected teacher of mine once described a Sunday school program in which five-year-old children sang, "We are more than conquerors." My professor said that was cute, but somewhat laughable: they hadn't actually conquered anything. Well, I disagreed somewhat. As members of the body of Christ, these children had already conquered Satan, sin, and death, as surely as had the apostle Paul in Romans 8. Our conquest is not first an item of personal experience, but something accomplished by Christ and by ourselves in him. Still, my professor's point was not entirely wrong. "We are more than conquerors" (Rom. 8:37) means a lot more coming from Paul than coming from five-year-old kids. Paul actually experienced tribulation, distress, persecution, famine, nakedness, danger, and sword (v. 35). When a man goes through such experiences and emerges victorious in Christ, that is deeply edifying to other believers in a way that the testimony of inexperienced children can never be. Experience confers a degree of authority, to which Paul appeals often in his writings.

Experience, then, does not add to the canon of Scripture, but it does perform many positive functions in the Christian life. We can benefit greatly from the experiences of other believers and of ourselves.

So experience is another way to describe the process by which we learn to discern good and evil. As such, moral experience is virtually identical to conscience. And there is the same paradox with regard to experience that we saw with regard to conscience, the "paradox of ethical decision." We always ought to act according to our experience, just as we always ought to act according to conscience, because experience, like conscience, identifies what we regard as right or wrong. On the other hand, just as conscience can be defiled by sin, so our experience can be inadequate, misinterpreted, or misused. We sometimes make decisions, claiming that we have sufficient experience, when in fact we do not. Or we make decisions based on an inadequate portion of experience, as when we ignore our experience of God's word. Or we wrongly interpret and use our experience, because of our bent toward sin. Only God's grace can give us adequate experience to make right moral decisions. In this regard also, experience and conscience are the same.

REASON

Reason, or intellect, is the capacity to make logical inferences and to judge the logical consistency of ideas and behavior. We have seen that reason plays major roles in ethics: (1) formulating and evaluating moral syllogisms, (2) determining relations between means and ends, (3) exegeting and applying Scripture, (4) analyzing situations to which Scripture applies, and (5) understanding metaethics, the nature and methods of ethics.

Indeed, every aspect of ethical decision making uses reason in some way. We saw above that even perception is a rational process, not merely a sensory one. In perception, we connect our sense data with rational concepts from the mind. So perception is dependent on reason.

However, the reverse is also true. Reason cannot accomplish anything unless it has an object—something to reason about. For example, there can be no moral syllogisms without premises. And those premises require sensory knowledge; they cannot be derived from reason or logic alone. There can be no reasoning about means and ends without situations to analyze. There can be no reasoning about Scripture without Scripture.

So reason is dependent on the whole complex of factors within human knowledge. As sense experience depends on reason, the reverse is also true. True perception involves reason, and true reasoning involves perception. So reason and experience are in the fullest sense the same, and both are the same as conscience. These are three perspectives on our acts of ethical knowing. Reason may be described as the normative perspective, experience as the situational perspective, and conscience as the existential perspective.

Again, with reason as with the others, the paradox of ethical decision enters the discussion. In one sense, we should always follow our reason (as we follow our experience and our conscience), for reason identifies what we consider to be right. We have an ethical obligation, of course, not only to do what is right, but also to do *what we think* is right. But like conscience and experience, reason is not infallible. Sometimes it guides us wrongly. Sin infects our reasoning, as Paul teaches in Romans 1 and in 1 Corinthians 2:14. There is an antithesis between the wisdom of God and the wisdom of the world. So even though we are obligated to obey reason, we sometimes sin when we do so.

Like conscience and experience, reason requires God's grace to function rightly. God made our reason to function rightly only on the presupposition of the truth of his word. The authority of God's revelation is the highest of the laws of thought. By saving grace in Christ, God enables us to think according to that revelation.[4]

4. *DKG* argues this point at great length. That is the main theme of the book.

WILL

Will is our capacity for making decisions. So, by definition, the will is involved in all moral decisions and acts. Traditionally, will is contrasted with intellect (reason) and emotions. In some accounts, it almost seems as though will, intellect, and emotions are little beings up in our heads who vie for supremacy. Arguments have been made both about which of these three faculties is superior to the others and about which one *ought* to be superior. Philosophical movements have been identified by views on this alleged conflict: Aquinas has been called an intellectualist, Scotus a voluntarist, and Kierkegaard an emotionalist.[5]

My own view, however, is that we make decisions as whole persons, and that intellect, will, and emotions are perspectives on the whole persons, not subsistent entities. The intellect is the person's ability to think, the will is his capacity to decide, and the emotions are his capacity to feel. We are talking about three abilities that people have, not three independent entities within them. That I think is a more biblical perspective, for Scripture never distinguishes these three capacities or makes any general statements about the superiority of one or the other.

In my view, the three abilities are interdependent. You cannot make a decision (will) unless you judge (intellect) that it is the right thing to do. On the other hand, you cannot make the right judgment (intellect) unless you choose (will) to make it. The will is certainly involved in our intellectual judgments. As Paul teaches in Romans 1, certain people *choose* to disbelieve in God, despite the sufficiency of the evidence for his existence. Other people choose otherwise. In both cases, belief is a choice. The intellectual judgment is a decision of the will. That is one reason why I have emphasized that the intellectual realm has a moral dimension, that there is an ethics of knowledge.

So will and intellect are dependent on one another, and so are choice and reason. They are not independent entities, but perspectives on the mental acts of human beings. In everything we do, there is thought and choice. And we think about what to choose, and we choose what to think. And we choose what to think about what to choose. We accept reasons because we choose them, and we choose them because we find them reasonable.

We do sometimes think and do things without making conscious choices. In many cases, our choices are habitual, the product of choices made many years ago, which we follow today without reflection. In

---

5. Not to mention Hume, who taught that reason should be the slave of the passions.

other cases, our choices are virtually forced on us. We may not realize it, but most of us have made a choice to accept as real the world that our senses present to us. So even our most ordinary forms of knowledge are not independent of choice. That is even more obviously true with regard to ethical knowledge.

Our will, of course, must be purified by God's regenerating and sanctifying grace, just like our conscience, experience, and reason. God must teach us and enable us to choose good over evil, right over wrong. And as he does this, he also enables us to choose right reasons over wrong ones, good feelings over bad (see below), and good conscience over bad.[6] The paradox of ethical decision here is that we must follow our will (or can't help but follow it), but since our will has been corrupted by sin, we must seek God's grace to point our will in different directions.

IMAGINATION

Imagination has gained a bad reputation in some Christian circles, especially Reformed circles, because of a focus on negative uses of the term in Scripture. In the KJV, the word occurs in Jeremiah 3:17; 7:24; 9:14; 11:8, and elsewhere, to designate the origin of false worship. Significantly, modern translations avoid that translation. In Jeremiah 3:17, the KJV reads, "Neither shall they walk any more after the imagination of their evil heart." But the ESV says, "And they shall no more stubbornly follow their own evil heart." The term translated *imagination* in the KJV is regularly translated *stubbornness* in the ESV and the NIV. So these texts should not be taken, as they have in the past, as condemning imagination in some general way.

Nevertheless, Scripture does teach that idolatry is a product of the human mind or heart, and so it involves imagination even in our modern sense of the term. This connection with idolatry does indicate that there are dangers in the human imagination.

But these biblical references do not rule out positive uses of the imagination. I find it helpful to define imagination as our ability to think of things that are not. In a typical example, a sculptor conceptualizes a statue before he creates it. That conceptualizing is a work of imagination. The sculptor imagines something that is not, before he brings it into being. Similarly, imagination has many applications to the arts, science, and technology. As

---

6. It should be evident here that people (Arminians, hyper-Calvinists, and confused souls) who think that Calvinism denies the importance of human choice don't know what they're talking about. In Calvinism, all behavior is chosen and therefore responsible.

such, imagination is nearly the same thing as creativity, which is a reflection of God's own creative work and the working out of an imaginative plan.

But imagination has even broader functions. All of our thought and activity is a response to the past. But the past is no more. We remember it to some extent, but our overall conception of it is imaginative. Similarly, our thought and activity point toward the future, seeking to influence it. But the future, like the past, does not exist. Our knowledge of the future, such as it is, requires imagination. And what of the present? If the present is, as some have believed, a knife-edge between past and future, a moment to which we cannot meaningfully respond until it is past, then the present is nonbeing as well, to some extent a construction of the imagination. I don't mean to press this point as a philosophical position, but there is enough truth in it to warrant the conclusion that imagination functions in all knowledge, not just the arts, science, and technology. And it appears that we cannot know anything without it. As such, imagination is a further perspective on knowledge. It presupposes reason, experience, and conscience, and they presuppose it.[7]

As imagination fills in the temporal sequence, so it extends our spatial reach. Our knowledge of places far away is limited, but imagination takes the data we have and arranges it into a coherent mental picture of those locales.

In ethics, the imagination plays an important role in forming ethically significant patterns and analogies (see chapter 20). Further, imagination enables us to conceive of alternative courses of action as we ponder what to do in the future. And as we consider the validity of ethical principles, imagination helps us to form examples and counterexamples, case studies that may validate or invalidate the principles under consideration. Such illustrations are often useful in the teaching of ethics.

Scripture does not say in so many words that the imagination is fallen and must be redeemed. But clearly what we call imagination is an aspect of all ethical thinking and decision making. If the intellect and the will are fallen and in need of redemption, so is the imagination. The paradox of ethical decision is present here as well: we should follow our imaginations, but we must also correct our imaginations by God's Word, under the influence of his grace.

THE EMOTIONS

Scripture does not discuss the emotions as an independent item of concern, any more than it discusses the intellect or the will in such a way. Yet it says a great deal about particular emotions, such as grief, joy, anxiety, awe,

---

7. I consider imagination, like conscience, part of the existential perspective on knowledge.

terror, woe, and lust, and also about concepts that have a large emotional component, such as love, hate, and happiness.

Like the intellect and the will, the emotions are fallen and must be redeemed by God's grace. Unregenerate emotions are quite different from regenerate ones. Unregenerate people love wickedness and hate goodness. Through the Spirit, God gives us new dispositions, so that we feel very differently. We learn to love God and to hate evil, to rejoice in what is good, to be content in the face of difficulty, and so on.

Regeneration does not necessarily make us more or less emotional, any more than it makes us more or less intellectual or more or less decisive.[8] Like intelligence and decisiveness, emotion is a function of personality and gifts. The difference that regeneration really makes is that a believer's emotions (like his intellect and will) now belong to the Lord. Whether our emotions are strong or weak, and however they are distinctive in us, they are at his disposal, not our own.

When God gives us, upon regeneration, a new set of emotional dispositions, he commands us to develop them in the course of our sanctification. We need to grow spiritually in our emotional life, as in our intellectual life and volitional decisions, to conform more closely to the image of Christ. So in the realm of the emotions, as in others, there is both gift and task, both divine grace and human responsibility, both already and not yet. The Bible actually commands us to feel differently about things, as in Philippians 4:4, "Rejoice in the Lord always; again I will say, Rejoice," and in verse 6, "Do not be anxious about anything, but in everything by prayer and supplication with thanksgiving let your requests be made known to God." Hegel, in his *Early Theological Writings*,[9] said that Christianity was even more reprehensively authoritarian than Judaism, because, while Judaism commands actions, Christianity also commands feelings.[10] But of course even the Old Testament (and therefore Judaism) commands us to rejoice, to be calm in the face of difficulty, to fear and tremble (in some cases), to fear not (in other cases), and to love God with all our heart—which, as I have indicated, implies affection (chapters 12 and 19).

---

8. Charismatic Christians tend to think that regeneration makes a person more emotional, so that he is more inclined to yell, weep, and jump up and down. Reformed Christians, on the contrary, tend to think that regeneration makes one less emotional, so that one becomes calmer and makes one's decisions after careful thought. The Reformed like to sit still; the charismatics to dance around. These are, of course, traditional attitudes on both sides, not confessional positions, probably influenced by personality differences more than anything else. In my judgment, neither attitude is biblically warranted.

9. Chicago: University of Chicago Press, 1948.

10. I am using the words *emotions* and *feelings* interchangeably in this chapter.

But can we really control our emotions? Like beliefs, emotions often seem to come upon us unbidden. I cannot choose to hate my children, or to delight in the memory of Idi Amin. But Scripture assumes that in many cases, at least, we can play some role in changing our emotions. Like our intellect and our will, our emotions will not be perfectly pure until glory. But there are things we can do to better conform to God's standards in this area.

God's means of grace often have powerful effects on our emotions. When we read in Scripture of what God has done for us, we not only gain a better intellectual grasp of the events, but we come to feel as God feels about them. Scripture presents sin, not only as wrong, but also as something that is ugly. And it presents the new life as something beautiful. For example, when the angel tells the Virgin Mary that she is to bear God's child, and she replies, "Behold, I am the servant of the Lord; let it be to me according to your word" (Luke 1:38), the believing mind perceives her response as beautiful—however much some feminists may despise her submission.

Moses tells us that when Eve was tempted, her emotions led her into sin: "The woman saw that the tree was good for food, and that it was a delight to the eyes, and that the tree was to be desired to make one wise" (Gen. 3:6). Doubtless the fruit of the tree of the knowledge of good and evil was good, delightful, and desirable in these ways. But Eve imagined that the beauty of the tree would be hers if she took the fruit in disobedience. Scripture shows the ugliness of the results of that action.

The sacraments, worship, fellowship, and prayer also deeply affect our feelings. Even in secular society, people's emotions are deeply influenced by other people, by literature, institutions, arts, and media. Certainly the same thing happens as we fellowship in the body of Christ. In community, we develop affection for one another and loyalty to the Lord and his kingdom.

We usually cannot instantaneously change the way we feel, any more than we can immediately change our beliefs or our habits. But we can adopt general patterns of behavior that over time will lead to emotional change. And Scripture tells us what those general patterns of behavior are.

In this chapter, I am interested in how each of our faculties contributes to our ethical knowledge. Do the emotions make any contributions? I think so.

I realize that we often say to one another, "Don't follow your feelings." We often give such advice, especially to young people. But the intent of such advice is not to communicate a theory of human faculties, but rather to encourage reflection, especially on God's Word. What we mean to discourage is not reference to feelings in an abstract or general way, but making decisions on the basis of momentary feelings, rather than patiently waiting on God.

Certainly there are positive ways in which emotions can, do, and should influence our conduct. As I argued earlier that conscience, intellect, experience, and imagination are perspectives on the moral decisions of the whole person, so I will here argue the same for emotion.

Emotions, like conscience, reason, and experience, have a hermeneutical component. That is, they discover and express meaning in the situations of life. When I am angry, afraid, or delighted, I am responding to my situation and my understanding of it. But the emotion may hit me before I engage in any conscious interpretation or understanding.

It is possible to say in this case that the emotion is based on some subconscious form of reasoning. Certainly, emotions ought to be rational, as opposed to irrational. But it is hard in such cases to identify any rational process, conscious or otherwise, that precedes the emotion in time. Rather, the emotion itself often seems to be the first reaction (rational or otherwise) to the experience. Often the emotion is our initial interpretation of the facts, the beginning of rational evaluation, rather than an outcome of rational evaluation. When I am angry, I thereby interpret the situation, rightly or wrongly, to be deserving of anger. When I am sad, I thereby judge that the situation warrants sadness. If the emotion is rationally justified, it is part of the rational process leading to its own justification. If it is not rationally justified, then it involves a preliminary assessment that may be refuted by later reflection.[11]

So emotion includes implicit rational activity within it. But the reverse is also true. Reason presupposes emotions, because reasoning always involves evaluation. In reasoning, we try to evaluate ideas as true or false, adequate or inadequate for a task, profound or superficial, clear or unclear, interesting or dull, productive or inconsequential. Such judgments inevitably summarize, articulate, and defend feelings about those ideas. The process of reasoning is a dialogue between thoughts and emotions. Evaluation begins with feelings about a certain subject matter. Rational analysis may lead to more adequate emotions, and those more adequate emotions may lead to better analysis.[12]

11. When we speak of "rational" activity, sometimes we are referring to activity of the mind as such, that may or may not lead to knowledge. At other times, we are referring to mental activity that leads to knowledge. I am arguing that emotion always involves a rational element, at least in the first sense, and sometimes also in the second sense.

12. Note my illustration in *DKG*, 337, concerning the writing of book reviews. Although such writing is usually considered an intellectual task, emotions play a central role in the process. The reviewer usually begins by having certain feelings about the book, then refines those feelings by rational analysis, which refines the feelings, which refines the analysis, and so on. If the reviewer had no feelings about the book, there would be no review.

When do we know that we have completed our analytical task? When do we know that the job is done, that we have reached a conclusion, that we no longer need to research and analyze? The task is over when we have a sense of conviction within ourselves, and, at least in some cases, when we feel that we can defend the conclusion to others. But note the words "sense" and "feel" in the last sentence. That is the language of emotion. We know we have reached the conclusion of a rational inquiry when we *feel* satisfied. In *The Doctrine of the Knowledge of God*, I called this feeling "cognitive rest."[13]

So reasoning is an aspect of emotion, and emotion is an aspect of reasoning. This suggests that we should not draw a sharp line between the two, but should regard them as perspectives on one another—and on that larger complex, including conscience, experience, will, and imagination, centered in the heart. If we wish, we can see the emotions as the existential perspective of a triad including reason (normative perspective) and will (situational perspective).

It should not surprise us, therefore, that Scripture never says, as some Greek philosophers did, that reason should rule the emotions, or, as Hume did, that reason should be the slave of the passions. There is no hierarchical relation between the two. Both reason and emotions are equally aspects of the image of God in which we are created. Both are equally fallen; both are equally redeemed in Christ's people.

When we warn young people against fornication, we often tell them not to follow their feelings, for obvious reasons. But their problem is not just a problem of emotion. It is also a problem of reasoning. They are tempted to act according to unsanctified emotions, but also according to unsanctified reasoning. If they reasoned properly, they would put a higher priority on glorifying God and a lower priority on their present gratification. So they are wrong, not only in following their misguided emotions, but also in following their misguided reasoning. The remedy is not (as Plato thought) to bring emotions under the rule of reason, but to bring both emotions and reason under the rule of God's Word.

Sometimes, of course, it appears that rational processes can straighten out wayward emotions. A man who craves another drink may respond to rational arguments about the dangers of drinking and driving. But the opposite is also true. Sometimes we reject purportedly rational arguments because we *feel* that there is something wrong with them. When someone presents an elaborate, rational argument for bizarre conclusions, such as alien abductions, the nonoccurrence of the Holocaust, or Dwight Eisen-

---

13. *DKG*, 152–53. Note the context of this discussion to p. 162.

hower's membership in the Communist Party, we may not be able to refute all the evidence given, but we feel that something is amiss, and that feeling guides our rational process. That is a good thing.

Consider a believer, attending a worship service in a denomination other than his own, who is predisposed to criticize it. To his surprise, he finds himself feeling positive about the experience, delighting in the fellowship of the people and the presence of God. Perhaps his emotions have illegitimately suppressed his critical faculties, that he has wrongly "followed his feelings." It is also possible that the sanctification of his emotions has outpaced the sanctification of his intellect. He may have felt something that should lead to changes in his intellectual view of things. His emotions may be supplying him with new data that he needs to take into account.

To summarize, emotions are aspects of our God-given ethical sensitivity, our "powers of discernment" (Heb. 5:14). We dare not neglect them as we "try to discern what is pleasing to the Lord" (Eph. 5:10).

THE PATHOS GAME

In this section, I would like to follow up on the previous one with some homiletical observations, since I am concerned that evangelical theology, and especially Reformed theology, develop a more positive view of the emotions. Since this section makes some concrete applications, it will also serve as a transition to the next portion of the book, which focuses on the actual content of the Bible's teaching concerning ethics.

Is it wrong to hurt people's feelings? Most of our mothers told us so. But where does Scripture address this issue?[14]

I recently had an e-mail exchange with another teacher of theology, and I mentioned in a particular context the importance of being sensitive to the feelings of others. He replied to me that he didn't want to get into that. He said, "I am not equipped to play the pathos game."

This particular theologian is well known for his insistence that the gospel is objective, not subjective: that it is a message about what happens outside us, not what happens inside us. He criticizes the evangelical church for being focused on inwardness, on feelings. My own approach, in contrast to this, is that salvation (and therefore the gospel in the broadest sense) is both objective and subjective. It proclaims objectively that Christ has

---

14. I have given some thought to discussing this issue in connection with the Decalogue. But under which commandment would I place this topic? Probably the fifth or the sixth, which have to do with respecting and enhancing human life. But the connection between this topic and the preceding methodological discussion makes this the ideal location.

atoned for our sin, granting to us divine pardon, and it also proclaims that by trusting Christ we become new creatures. Christ grants to us what John Murray called a new "dispositional complex." We come to love righteousness and hate wickedness. We come to delight in God's law. We pant for God like thirsty deer for water. We gain new affections, new emotions. This is my "existential perspective."

NEGATIVE LESSONS FROM HISTORY

But this message has not always been accepted in Christian circles—hence my dialogue about "the pathos game." Christian theologians, following Plato and other Greek philosophers, have often seen emotions as something dangerous. Greek philosophy was hardly monolithic, and theologians have often exaggerated the agreement among Greek philosophers. But they did all agree that the good life is the life of reason. Reason should dominate human life, they thought, including the emotions. When the emotions rule, all goes askew. When reason rules the emotions (in some views, virtually extinguishing them), human life gets back on an even keel.

Music is particularly dangerous in this respect, since it rouses the emotions to such a degree. Plato warned us about it. Ulrich Zwingli, arguably the founder of the Reformed branch of Protestantism, eliminated music from worship, turning the weekly service into a teaching event. In this, it should be noted, he differed from Martin Luther, who said that music is the greatest thing next to theology.

We can be thankful that the other Reformed leaders, such as Bucer, Bullinger, and Calvin, did not follow Zwingli in this decision. But they were much more restrictive than Lutherans were about the type of music deemed appropriate for worship. Calvin had his congregations sing mostly (not exclusively) Psalm versions, and that became the rule in the Scottish churches (though not in the church of Cologne, for example).

The Reformation in general was a movement of scholars. Luther's view of justification began as a scholar's insight, a new understanding of righteousness in Romans 1:16–17. The event we celebrate as "Reformation Day" (October 31) was Luther's invitation to an academic disputation. This academic emphasis is one that Lutheran and especially Reformed theology continues to the present. Reformed worship continues to be centered on preaching, and often the preaching is of a rather academic sort. To supply congregations with pastors able to preach with such academic rigor, Reformed churches have emphasized the importance of a "learned ministry." Pastoral candidates must have college degrees and at least some postgraduate training, even though Scripture never hints at such educational requirements for pastors. They must know the original languages of Scripture and the fine distinctions of technical theology. The Reformed confessions are not basic summaries of faith like the Apostles' Creed and the Nicene Creed, but closely argued, miniature theological treatises, to which aspiring clergy are expected to subscribe in some detail, if not exhaustively.

The result is that Reformed churches have appealed mainly to people who have had some university or college training, and who therefore come from families economically able to provide such education. So Reformed church members tend to be educated and relatively wealthy.[15]

Among Reformed theologians, including J. Gresham Machen[16] and the authors of *Classical Apologetics*,[17] one often hears the view known as "the primacy of the intellect." What this seems to mean is that God's revelation addresses first of all the human intellect. The intellect, in turn, applies the truth to the will and to the emotions. At least this is what God, on this view, originally intended. One result of the fall, however, is that the hierarchy of intellect, will, and emotions was overturned, so that the intellect is now dominated by the will and the emotions. Salvation, then, returns human nature to its proper balance. The Christian life is, like the ideal life of the Greek philosophers, a life of reason, though of course it is a reason based on God's Word rather than on autonomous philosophy.

I disagree with Machen on this point, though I do sympathize with him. In the period following the Scopes trial, American evangelicalism went through a period of rather extreme anti-intellectualism. Many rejected scholarship in general, particularly science, as contrary to Scripture. Machen wanted to affirm that Christianity was rationally defensible, that it had nothing to fear from learned detractors. They were right to affirm the importance of the intellect, but not, in my judgment, at the expense of the will and the emotions.

I offer a similar evaluation of contemporary Reformed attempts to repress the passions. Feelings do play a positive role in the Christian life, as we have seen.

15. Arguably, it was because of this emphasis that the Reformed churches lost the American frontier. They were unable to supply enough pastors and were overtaken by Methodists and Baptists.

16. J. Gresham Machen, *What Is Faith?* (New York: Macmillan, 1925).

17. John Gerstner, Arthur Lindsley, and R. C. Sproul, *Classical Apologetics* (Grand Rapids: Zondervan, 1984). See my review of this book, published as appendixes to my *Apologetics to the Glory of God* (Phillipsburg, NJ: P&R Publishing, 1994) and *Cornelius Van Til* (Phillipsburg, NJ: P&R Publishing, 1995), and also my discussion of the primacy of reason in *DKG*, 331–32.

Other traditions have thought the Reformed emphasis to be one-sided. Anabaptists, Arminians, and charismatics of different stripes have held a more positive view of the emotions and a less positive view of academic attainment. This has given them a greater appeal to the poor, the uneducated, and the minorities of society.

SCRIPTURE ON THE EMOTIONS

Scripture does warn us against being driven back and forth by waves of emotion. Paul tells us to be anxious for nothing, and instead to pray (Phil. 4:6–7). Psalm 1 tells us to meditate on Scripture day and night, rather than being blown around like chaff.

But Scripture does not warrant any notion of "the primacy of the intellect." For one thing, Scripture does not even distinguish between intellect, will, and emotions, as distinct "faculties" of the mind. It talks about our thoughts, our decisions, and our feelings, but it never presents these as the products of three competing organs. Therefore, it never exhorts us to bring our decisions and feelings into conformity with our intellect.

For another thing, Scripture teaches that we are totally depraved, and that includes our intellectual, as well as our volitional and emotional aspects. Yes, our feelings sometimes lead us into sin, but the same is true of our intellect. If we seek to remedy our emotionalism by bringing our emotions into line with depraved intellectual concepts, there is no net gain.

Similarly, Scripture teaches that God's grace saves us as whole persons. Our thinking, acting, and feeling are all changed by regeneration. God's grace leads us to seek conformity with God's Word. The important thing is not to bring our emotions into line with our intellect, but to bring both our emotions and our intellect into line with God's Word.

I have set forth here and in *The Doctrine of the Knowledge of God* a perspectival model of intellect, emotions, and will: that these are three ways of speaking of the whole person thinking, acting, and feeling. I have argued that each of these "faculties" presupposes and influences the others, so that the three are not really separable. If it is important to bring our feelings into line with godly thinking, it is also important to bring our thinking into line with godly passions: our passion for God, his Word, and his righteousness.

Scripture also tells us that we should care about our own feelings and those of others. On the broadest level, Christian faith is a grand passion. If our faith embraces all of life ("whether you eat or drink, or whatever you do," 1 Cor. 10:31), then it embraces the emotions as well. If we are to love the Lord with all our heart, mind, soul, and strength, that covenant commitment will certainly be our greatest passion, as well as our most basic intellectual commitment and the dominant motivation for our will.

The Bible appeals to all these aspects of personality. It presents reasoned arguments to the mind, but it also exhorts the will, as in Ezekiel 33:11 NIV: "Turn! Turn from your evil ways! Why will you die, O house of Israel?" And it is full of godly passion. For example, hear this from Psalm 42:1–6:

> As a deer pants for flowing streams,
>   so pants my soul for you, O God.
> My soul thirsts for God,
>   for the living God.
> When shall I come and appear before God?
> My tears have been my food
>   day and night,
> while they say to me continually,
>   "Where is your God?"
> These things I remember,
>   as I pour out my soul:
> how I would go with the throng
>   and lead them in procession to the house of God
> with glad shouts and songs of praise,
>   a multitude keeping festival.
> Why are you cast down, O my soul,
>   and why are you in turmoil within me?
> Hope in God; for I shall again praise him,
>   my salvation and my God.
> My soul is cast down within me;
>   therefore I remember you
> from the land of Jordan and of Hermon,
>   from Mount Mizar.

The psalmist's grief at being away from the presence of God is an example to us. We too should pant, thirst, and cry for the presence of the living God. It is not enough to make intellectual theological observations about the different senses of his proximity and his absence. Nor is it enough to resolve to seek God's presence again. Rather, our emotions should desire God's nearness. If we don't desire him with such passion, there is something wrong.

The psalmist's anguish anticipates and reflects the agony of Jesus. As B. B. Warfield wrote in "The Emotional Life of Our Lord," Jesus was and is a man of passion.[18] He felt deeply about the Jews' desecration of his Father's house, about his rejection by Jerusalem, about the cup of suffering that the Father had set before him. And he felt compassion on the multitudes (Matt. 15:32; 20:34), reflecting God's own "tender mercy" (Luke 1:78). He says he has "earnestly desired" to eat the Passover with his disciples before his death (Luke 22:15). This language is highly emotional.

The apostle Paul speaks often of the "affection" he has for the churches. In Philippians 1:8, he says, "For God is my witness, how I yearn for you all with the affection of Christ Jesus." Like God himself, the apostle has compassion and affection for his brothers and sisters. He calls them to have the same compassion for one another (2:1–2; cf. Col. 3:12; Philem. 7, 12, 20).

Hear him again:

> For I wrote to you out of much affliction and anguish of heart and with many tears, not to cause you pain but to let you know the abundant love that I have for you. (2 Cor. 2:4)

> But we were gentle among you, like a nursing mother taking care of her own children. So, being affectionately desirous of you, we were ready to share with you not only the gospel of God but also our own selves, because you had become very dear to us. (1 Thess. 2:7–8)

> But since we were torn away from you, brothers, for a short time, in person not in heart, we endeavored the more eagerly and with great desire to see you face to face. (1 Thess. 2:17)

> Timothy has come to us from you, and has brought us the good news of your faith and love and reported that you always remember us kindly and long to see us, as we long to see you. . . . What thanksgiving can we return to God for you, for all the joy that we feel for your sake before our God . . . ? (1 Thess. 3:6–10)

> I am sending him [Onesimus] back to you, sending my very heart. I would have been glad to keep him with me, in order that he might serve me on your behalf during my imprisonment for the gospel, but I preferred to do nothing without your consent in order that your goodness might not be by compulsion but of your own free will. (Philem. 12–14)

18. In Benjamin Breckinridge Warfield, *The Person and Work of Christ* (Philadelphia: Presbyterian and Reformed, 1950), 98–145.

Again and again, Paul pours out his heart, expresses his own emotions, and expresses his deep care for the emotions of the people. Surely this is a model for us. Paul is playing the pathos game, if we may so trivialize what is happening here. He feels deeply for his people and wants them to feel deeply for one another.

Paul is grateful for those who "refreshed my spirit" (1 Cor. 16:18). He rejoices when a church longs to see him, as he longs to see them (2 Cor. 7:7, 11). He rebukes the Corinthians at another point for being "restricted in your own affections" (2 Cor. 6:12), and he counsels them to open their hearts wide (v. 13).

The apostle John also urges emotions of compassion: "But if anyone has the world's goods and sees his brother in need, yet closes his heart against him, how does God's love abide in him?" (1 John 3:17). He addresses the will: meet your brother's needs. But the lack of will is rooted in a lack of compassion, a lack of feeling.

Emotions also enter into the theology of the Bible in important ways. Consider Paul's hymn of praise to God's incomprehensibility:

> Oh, the depth of the riches and wisdom and knowledge of God! How unsearchable are his judgments and how inscrutable his ways!
>
> > "For who has known the mind of the Lord?
> >   or who has been his counselor?"
> > "Or who has given a gift to him
> >   that he might be repaid?"
>
> For from him and through him and to him are all things. To him be glory forever. Amen. (Rom. 11:33–36)

Can you feel the emotion pulsing through that passage? That passage is not meant only to inform you, but also to make you feel differently. The emotional content is part of the meaning of the text. If a preacher doesn't communicate that feeling, that emotion, he's depriving his congregation of an important element of the text. Imagine somebody reading this text in a monotone. That is a distortion of the text as much as a theological misinterpretation of it would be.

Again and again, Paul pours out his heart, expresses his emotions, and expresses his deep concern for the emotions of the people to whom he is writing.

The Reformed community needs to look at emotions much more positively, as the Bible does. We need to play the pathos game. There is no reason for us to disparage or try to dampen emotions in the Christian life, or even in worship. And if we don't have the resources in the Reformed tradition to express the profound emotions found in Scripture, then we should be humble enough to go beyond the Reformed tradition to find the resources we need.

We should counsel people not to act on momentary emotions. We should also counsel them not to act on every idea that pops into their heads, or on every desire or impulse. But ideas that are tempered and refined and prayed over to the point of cognitive rest (an emotion!) ought to be acted on. And emotions refined by thought, maturity, and good habits of decision making may well be reliable guides also.

HURTING PEOPLE'S FEELINGS

And it is wrong, as your mother said, to hurt people's feelings. That is true in many cases, at least. I grant that often it is impossible to avoid bringing grief to someone. People are often offended by the righteous actions of others. Not all emotions are regenerate. People are often too thin-skinned, too self-centered, to respond with proper emotions to the events of their lives.

Paul knew that he would have to cause some pain to some members of the Corinthian church (2 Cor. 2:1–5). In context, the "pain" is clearly emotional. But he is reluctant to cause such pain, and he speaks of his own pain in carrying out this duty. The duty was to discipline a member of the church. But in the passage, the offender has repented, and Paul calls the congregation to forgive—but not only to forgive, but also to "comfort him, or he may be overwhelmed by excessive sorrow" (v. 7). Paul wants the church to carry out its work so as to guard the feelings of one another.

The writer to the Hebrews urges his readers to obey their leaders, so that they can do their work "with joy and not with groaning, for that would be of no advantage to you" (Heb. 13:17–18). There are, of course, a variety of reasons why we should obey the leaders of the church. But the reason mentioned here is emotional. We obey our leaders for the sake of their emotional well-being, so they will be joyful. And, of course, their emotions are contagious. The writer implies that when they are unhappy, we will be unhappy too, and similarly when they are happy, we will be happy. A church with happy leaders is a happy church! To many, that sounds like a trivialization of the work of the church, but that is what the text says.

God wants us to care about how other people feel. He wants us to weep when others weep, and rejoice when they rejoice (Rom. 12:15). He sends us, as he sent Jesus, "to bind up the brokenhearted" (Isa. 61:1).

PART FOUR

THE TEN COMMANDMENTS

CHAPTER 22

Introduction to the Decalogue

In part 3 of this treatise on ethics, we discussed ethical methodology, the way Christians should make their ethical decisions. In part 4, we shall discuss the actual content of godly decisions, focusing on the Ten Commandments. Our progress has been from introduction (part 1) to non-Christian ethics (part 2) to Christian ethical methodology (part 3) and now to substantive ethical principles (part 4). Parts 2 and 3 deal mainly with metaethics (see chapter 2), and part 4 deals with ethics as such. So parts 2–4 represent the situational, existential, and normative perspectives, respectively, as I indicated in chapter 5.

Part 4 will present biblical ethics in the form of a command ethic (see chapter 3), rather than as a narrative ethic or a virtue ethic. I have decided on this approach partly because it is the dominant one in the Reformed tradition, to which I belong. The Reformed catechisms and many systematic theologies, including Calvin's *Institutes*, include exposi-tions of the Decalogue. I also think that it is easier (for writer and reader) to determine the applications of biblical commands than to work out the applications of the biblical narratives or to fully describe the biblical virtues. At least it is easier for me. But I reiterate that narrative ethics and virtue ethics are fully legitimate methods, and I hope that others will explore them, to supplement what follows in this book. Command ethics, however, is also legitimate. And, because it is a perspective, it is able in principle (whether or not I can bring it off) to cover all the ground that is covered by the other two approaches. Of course, to do that, it will be necessary for us to read the commandments in the light of the history of redemption (narrative) and of our subjectivity (virtues).

In this and the following chapters, we will be asking of Scripture the normative question: what does God want me to do? We will also be relating that question to situational and existential contexts. We will be discussing the Ten Commandments, explained and amplified by other parts of Scripture, and we will be applying them to questions of current interest.

THE DECALOGUE IN THE HISTORY OF REDEMPTION

We begin our consideration of the Decalogue by relating it to its situational context.

As I mentioned above, the Reformed tradition has regularly turned to the Decalogue to summarize the law of God, God's requirements for our lives. There are some limitations in all summaries. When we study the Decalogue, for example, we must consult the whole Bible to understand what murder and adultery are. The Old Testament itself supplements the Decalogue by the Book of the Covenant, the case laws of Exodus 21–24, and by many other statements of ethical principle. The New Testament provides necessary correlations between the law and the redemptive work of Christ.

The same is true of summaries, such as the law of love. Scripture teaches us the meaning of love, not only in summary verses, but in countless narratives, proverbs, poems, letters, etc., particularly the narrative of Jesus' death for us (John 13:34–35; 1 John 4:8–10). Summaries must always be supplemented, in the nature of the case.

Some might argue that even among summaries the Decalogue is not the best. It is not, of course, the only summary of the law in Scripture. Deuteronomy 6:5 and Leviticus 19:18 are the two great commandments of the law, according to Jesus (Matt. 22:37–40). Jesus says, "On these two commandments depend all the Law and the Prophets" (v. 40); so they serve to summarize all the commandments of the law. The two great commandments relate the law also to the virtue of love (see chapters 12 and 19), which is the center of biblical ethics, but not explicitly mentioned in the Decalogue.[1] Love fulfills the law, according to Romans 13:8–10, and it is Jesus' new commandment to his disciples (John 13:34–35). First Corinthians 13 makes love a necessary and sufficient condition of good works. So love is itself a summary of the law,

---

1. I shall argue, however, that the law of love is implicit in the first commandment.

sufficient to define good behavior. According to Colossians 3:14, love "binds everything together in perfect harmony."

Still other summaries of the law can be found in Ecclesiastes 12:13 ("the whole duty of man") and Micah 6:8 ("What does the LORD require of you?"). It is especially important to consider summaries of the law in the age of the new covenant, such as the references in the previous paragraph to the law of love. Matthew 5–7 presents Jesus' exposition of the law in its deepest meaning. And Matthew 7:12 presents a principle (the so-called golden rule) that "is the Law and the Prophets." Note also the list of the fruit of the Spirit in Galatians 5:22–23 and other lists of virtues that characterize the Christian life in general terms; we explored them briefly in chapter 19. We should ask, then, why we should use the Decalogue as a summary of the law, rather than another summary, especially one that is more recent in the history of redemption.

The Decalogue points beyond itself to wider contexts. It begins with the name of Yahweh and identifies him as the one who brought Israel out of slavery in Egypt (Ex. 20:1–2). So to rightly understand the Decalogue, it is important to understand the events that led to it and the covenant of which it is a part. And, as I discussed in chapter 19, it is important to understand that our place in the history of redemption is somewhat different than the place of Israel at the time God spoke these words. So some details of the Decalogue, at least, do not apply directly to us today. God did not lead us out of Egypt, as he did Israel (Ex. 20:2), and he does not promise us long lives in the land of Palestine for honoring our parents (Ex. 20:12).

Nevertheless, there are reasons in favor of using the Decalogue as our summary of God's law:

Its historical importance in the church. Both Roman Catholic and Protestant catechisms and theologies have traditionally dealt with ethics by expounding the Decalogue. So this method is a convenient way to reflect on what Christians of various persuasions have most wanted to say about ethics.

The uniqueness of the occasion on which it was promulgated. God commanded Pharaoh through Moses to release Israel, so that she might serve (worship) God (Ex. 4:22–23; 5:1–3). Pharaoh hardened his heart, but God set Israel free, and he led the nation to a place outside Egypt to worship him. So Israel's meeting with God at Mt. Sinai was a crucial aspect of her redemption.

Moses presents the setting dramatically: thunder and lightning (Ex. 19:16; 20:18), thick cloud and darkness (Ex. 19:16; 20:21; Deut. 4:11), a mysterious trumpet sound (Ex. 19:16; 20:18),[2] smoke and fire (Ex. 19:18) "to the heart of heaven" (Deut. 4:11),[3] and a quake (Ex. 19:18). Then came the most frightening thing of all, the voice of God himself (Ex. 19:9; Deut. 4:12, 33, 36; 5:22–26).

Like other miracles in Scripture, the Sinai phenomena did three things: they were exhibitions of divine power, they provided instruction, and they aroused fear.[4] As manifestations of divine power, the texts emphasize the sheer enormity of the phenomena (Ex. 19:18, 20; Deut. 4:11) and the uniqueness of this experience (Deut. 4:32–36). Thus, the events on the mountain revealed God's greatness and glory (Deut. 5:24).

As instruction, these phenomena reinforce God's words (Deut. 4:10, 36). They serve to confirm Moses as the mediator of God's covenant (Ex. 19:9; 20:18–19).[5] They also confirm the content of the law (Ex. 20:22–26; Deut. 4:10), the certainty of God's mercy and judgment (Deut. 4:24, 33 in context), and the identity of God himself (Deut. 4:35–36).

The phenomena also arouse fear, in the two senses that we considered in chapter 19: terror of judgment (Ex. 19:16; 20:18–19; Deut. 5:5, 25; Heb. 12:18–21) and sanctifying reverence (Ex. 20:20; Deut. 4:10; cf. v. 24).

So this particular occasion made a great impression on the Israelites. Deuteronomy reflects on this as the great "day of the assembly" (Deut. 9:10; 10:4; 18:16).

It is a great day also in the history of the New Testament church, for that event is also part of our own history. God has given to us the titles given to Israel in Exodus 19:6: see 1 Peter 2:9. We draw even closer to God in the new covenant, through Christ (Heb. 12:18–29), but this experience is parallel to that of Exodus 19. And Hebrews, like Exodus, reminds us that "our God is a consuming fire" (12:29).

The uniqueness of the relationship established by it. But the day of the assembly was important mainly because on it God established his covenant with the nation of Israel (Ex. 19:5–6). The frightening phenomena only reinforced the solemnity of this great event. God constituted them "a kingdom of priests and a holy nation" (v. 6). The people responded, "All that the LORD has spoken we will do" (v. 8). Then God established the

---

2. This was not the ram's horn (19:13), but another sound that grows louder as God draws near.

3. This is evidently something enormous and unearthly. Other passages emphasize the fire (Deut. 4:33, 36; 5:4–5), perhaps reminiscent of Ex. 3:2, or even Gen. 15:17. The fire in Gen. 15 pierces the "dreadful and great darkness" (v. 12).

4. See DG, 245–60, on miracles as "signs, wonders, and powers," reflecting God's lordship attributes of authority, presence, and control, respectively.

5. Compare the signs of the apostles given in the New Testament period (2 Cor. 12:12).

mountain as a holy place, a place of his presence. In Exodus 20, he speaks the law to his special covenant people.

We should not miss the important fact that this was the one occasion in redemptive history (since Genesis 3) in which all the people of God were gathered together in one place to hear the word of God directly from his lips.

The uniqueness of its publication. The Decalogue was written down by the very finger of God (Ex. 24:12; 31:18; 32:15–16; Deut. 5:22; 9:10) and put by the ark of the covenant, in the holiest place of the tabernacle (Ex. 40:20; Deut. 10:4–5; 31:26).[6] Other documents were added later (as Josh. 24:26), but the Decalogue was the seed of what became the biblical canon.

The uniqueness of its function in the covenant structure. The Decalogue is a covenant document, setting forth the terms of the covenant: the name of the Lord, the circumstances of the covenant, the laws Israel is to obey, and the blessings and curses that enforce those laws (see chapter 3). The Decalogue serves as the foundational document of the covenant between God and Israel under the mediatorship of Moses. It is Israel's written constitution, its highest law, the ultimate test of covenant faithfulness.

The uniqueness of its use in later Scripture. Although Scripture supplements the Decalogue, it nevertheless refers to it often as a foundational document of the people of God. As we have seen, Deuteronomy often refers to "the day of the assembly," and it refers specifically to the Ten Commandments (4:13; 10:1–5), even setting them forth a second time (5:1–27). Jesus' Sermon on the Mount expounds in depth the meaning of a number of the commandments (Matt. 5–7). When the rich young man asks Jesus what he must do to have eternal life, Jesus responds first by listing some of the commandments (Matt. 19:16–19). Paul lists several of them to show that they are fulfilled by love (Rom. 13:8–10). In James 2:8–13, the brother of Jesus cites Decalogue commandments to emphasize the unity of the law.

The uniqueness of its generality. As I indicated in chapter 13, the Decalogue represents an application of the creation ordinances to Israel's situation as God's covenant nation. As I mentioned earlier, there are a few details of the Decalogue that do not apply to us as new covenant Christians, but for the most part the Ten Commandments

---

6. The phrase "Book of the Law" in Deut. 31:26 suggests something more than just the Decalogue. But the Decalogue was certainly present, as the original document of the covenant between God and Israel under Moses.

express principles that will never change, that apply to all times and situations. The Decalogue presents these principles in general terms, thereby covering all of human life.

The uniqueness of its hermeneutical centrality. A general hermeneutical principle is that when we seek light on a biblical doctrine, we should first look at passages where that doctrine is most focally and clearly presented. So when we wish to study the doctrine of justification, we ought to focus on Romans and Galatians, though there is also relevant data elsewhere in Scripture. To understand Christology, we should focus on passages like John 1, Philippians 2, and Hebrews 1. For eschatology, Paul's epistles to the Thessalonians are a good place to begin. Then we can integrate other biblical data with the primary passages.

When we think about God's standards for ethics, therefore, we should look especially at parts of the Bible that are specifically and directly concerned with that. There is, of course, much teaching about ethics in the New Testament, but it tends to be unsystematic, and it is mainly concerned with the outworkings of salvation in Christ, rather than with defining right and wrong. Pursuing such definitions, the Old Testament often gives us more help. The Torah, of course, is the heart of the Old Testament law, and the Decalogue is the heart of the Torah. So it makes sense for those concerned with determining ethical standards to give special attention to the Decalogue.

So I will focus on the Decalogue, but I will also try to relate the commandments to many other parts of Scripture, in order to formulate the whole biblical teaching on these subjects. We should frankly acknowledge the limitations of any summary of the law. As we have seen, consideration of the Decalogue is not the only way to summarize biblical ethics, nor is it, in every respect, the best way. Yet it is one useful way, and, in some respects, it is uniquely useful.

DECALOGICAL HERMENEUTICS[7]

I intend in my discussion of the Decalogue to interact (sympathetically, for the most part) with Reformed catechetical formulations.[8] But to do that

---

7. I'm not sure that *decalogical* is an actual word, but part of the fun of being a theologian is being able to invent new words.

8. I am not a "strict" confessionalist. That is, I don't believe that either members or officers of the church should be required to endorse a confession in toto, especially confessions as elaborate and as old as those of the post-Reformation period. Such a requirement makes it impossible to reform the confessions according to the Word of God, and so it gives the confessions, in effect, authority equal to Scripture. Such a requirement violates *sola Scriptura*, and it seems to me absurd for anyone to think that 350-year-old confessions should continue

immediately leads to problems of a hermeneutical sort. The Larger Catechism proposes rules as follow for the interpretation of the Decalogue:

Q. 99. *What rules are to be observed for the right understanding of the ten commandments?*

A. For the right understanding of the ten commandments, these rules are to be observed:

1. That the law is perfect, and bindeth everyone to full conformity in the whole man unto the righteousness thereof, and unto entire obedience forever; so as to require the utmost perfection of every duty, and to forbid the least degree of every sin.

2. That it is spiritual, and so reacheth the understanding, will, affections, and all other powers of the soul; as well as words, works, and gestures.

3. That one and the same thing, in divers respects, is required or forbidden in several commandments.

4. That as, where a duty is commanded, the contrary sin is forbidden; and, where a sin is forbidden, the contrary duty is commanded: so, where a promise is annexed, the contrary threatening is included; and, where a threatening is annexed, the contrary promise is included.

5. That what God forbids, is at no time to be done; what he commands, is always our duty; and yet every particular duty is not to be done at all times.[9]

6. That under one sin or duty, all of the same kind are forbidden or commanded; together with all the causes, means, occasions, and appearances thereof, and provocations thereunto.

7. That what is forbidden or commanded to ourselves, we are bound, according to our places, to endeavor that it may be avoided or performed by others, according to the duty of their places.

8. That in what is commanded to others, we are bound, according to our places and callings, to be helpful to them; and to take heed of partaking with others in what is forbidden them.

---

to be regarded as inerrant statements of biblical doctrine. Nevertheless, I do subscribe to the Westminster standards, with a few exceptions that I deem minor. All this is to say that I do not feel bound by conscience or by ecclesiastical allegiance to defend the confessional documents at every point, and I will later be describing some of my exceptions. Nevertheless, in this section of the chapter, even though the Catechism's teaching seems quite vulnerable to modern criticism, I do think its teaching is biblical and should be defended.

9. I take this as confessional warrant for my comments about "priorities among ultimates" in chapter 13.

Seminarians who study biblical hermeneutics are likely to find these rules to be somewhat odd. The Catechism seems to be going far beyond the grammatical-historical meaning of the commandments. There is, for example, no statement in the Decalogue itself that it requires "the utmost perfection of every duty" and forbids "the least degree of every sin." Rather, it seems that the Decalogue deals with ten specific kinds of sin and obedience. By what logic does the Catechism generalize these commandments to cover the whole terrain of morality?

Rule 4 states, "Where a duty is commanded, the contrary sin is forbidden; and, where a sin is forbidden, the contrary duty is commanded: so, where a promise is annexed, the contrary threatening is included; and, where a threatening is annexed, the contrary promise is included." In some cases, this rule makes sense: for example, when Dad tells Johnny to mow the grass, the command implicitly forbids his failing to mow the grass. But it is sometimes difficult to reason in reverse fashion, to derive commands from prohibitions. When the teacher says "Don't write your name on the first line of the exam," what is the "contrary duty" that is commanded? Writing on the second line? Printing on the first line? Writing someone else's name on the first line? Writing somewhere else? However plausible the alternatives, none of them seems to be logically derived from the language of the prohibition. Another example: when a sign says "Keep off the grass," what "contrary duty" is commanded? Keeping on the sidewalk? One student of mine (now well known) suggested (rather in the spirit of the Catechism) that "Keep off the grass" requires us to give some positive encouragement to the growth of the grass. How? By applying fertilizer or water? These would be rather large orders for passersby and in any case not logically derivable from the language of the sign.

And then rule 6 says, "That under one sin or duty, all of the same kind are forbidden or commanded; together with all the causes, means, occasions, and appearances thereof, and provocations thereunto." Some might feel that to interpret the commands this way is going too far.

If I were writing a catechism for today, I would not write it in quite this way. But I do intend to defend the Catechism's procedure here. It reveals some important insights into the nature of biblical ethics. Note the following:

1. "Right understanding" in the answer should not be equated with the grammatical-historical method of exegesis typically taught in seminaries. To rightly understand the commandments of the Decalogue is to understand them in depth, to see how they apply to one's heart and life in all situations. At this point and others, the Catechism practices "theology as application" (chapter 2).

2. Whatever we may say about the Decalogue itself, rule 1 is certainly true of the law of God in general. It is "perfect, reviving the soul" (Ps. 19:7). In chapter 11, I argued that Scripture is sufficient as a moral guide. Since God's law in Scripture defines sin and righteousness, it therefore defines "the utmost perfection of every duty" and forbids "the least degree of every sin."

3. If the Decalogue is, as we have argued, a summary of the law of God, then it summarizes that sufficient standard. Compare the law of love, an even more concise summary of the law. If we truly love God and one another, we will certainly want to seek the utmost perfection of every duty and avoid the least degree of every sin. If we love God, we will keep his commandments (John 14:15 and elsewhere; see chapters 12 and 19). But the same is certainly true of the first commandment of the Ten. If we are to have no other gods before him (Ex. 20:3), then we should seek to do his will exclusively, both his positive commands and his negative prohibitions. The same is true with the other commandments of the Decalogue. Those who are in covenant with God should desire the utmost perfection of, say, Sabbath keeping and parental honor, and avoid the least degree of murder or adultery.[10]

4. So understood, the Ten Commandments (again, like the law of love) deal with the heart, with our basic dispositions to good and evil (see chapter 21). This is, of course, how Jesus himself expounded the Decalogue. For him, the sixth commandment forbids ungodly anger (Matt. 5:21–22), failure to seek reconciliation (vv. 23–26), and vengeance (vv. 38–42). The seventh forbids lust (vv. 27–30). If we want with all our hearts to obey the commandments, we will seek God's help, not only to avoid explicit, external sins, but also to avoid the attitudes of the heart that give rise to those sins. Thus, as the Catechism says, the Decalogue is a complete ethic, demanding purity of heart and all its external manifestations.

5. If we want to serve God, we will not only do what the commandments specifically say (determined by grammatical-historical exegesis), but will also seek, with God's help, the inner motives consistent with those commandments. We will also avoid acts of the "same kind" as those prohibited, not wanting to grieve our Lord (rule 6). It is not always easy to define what sins are of the "same kind," but Scripture usually gives us many examples. If I should honor parents (Ex. 20:12), I should also honor others God has put in authority (such as the emperor, mentioned in 1 Peter 2:17). Beyond the biblical examples, we should determine likenesses by "seeing as" (see chapter 20).

10. On how these can be matters of degree, see what follows.

6. If we love God, we should seek to avoid all "causes, means, occasions, and appearances" of sin, and "provocations thereto" (rule 6). Here the Catechism is on somewhat dangerous ground, though I am still inclined to defend it. The Pharisees sought to "fence the law" by adding all sorts of additional restrictions designed to keep people from any danger of sin—rules as to how far one may walk on the Sabbath, how heavy a load one may carry, and so forth.[11] The result was a loss of the sufficiency of Scripture. They erred in making these traditions equal in authority to God's Word. I do think that the Catechism, in its later application of the commandments, sometimes errs in the same way. For the most part, however, the Catechism fences the laws of the Decalogue by invoking other biblical laws.

But there are other problems here. Certainly if I know that doing A will cause me to commit B, a sin, I should avoid doing A. But it is rarely the case that one act directly causes another act. Anger does not cause murder in any obvious sense, for one can be angry with someone without murdering him. The same can be said about what the Catechism calls "provocations." Is anger an occasion of murder? *Occasion* can be a synonym of *cause*, but in the Catechism it most likely means "a favorable or appropriate time or juncture; an opportunity."[12] But *occasion* in this sense is difficult to assess ethically. If I carry a gun, I have the opportunity to murder many people. Does that make it wrong for me ever to carry a gun?

What Jesus is concerned about in Matthew 5, I think, are not causes, means, and occasions in general, but attitudes of the heart that lead to sins and are therefore sins themselves. Carrying a gun leads to murder only if the heart of the carrier is so disposed. But the connection of such dispositions with outward sin is not always easy to describe.[13] The language of cause, means, and occasion is somewhat inadequate. But attitudes are linked to actions, however difficult it may be to say how they are linked. A right attitude of the heart will lead us to form habits that make sin difficult and encourage righteousness.

Some actions are similarly linked to other actions. If Joe is beset by the sin of alcohol abuse, and if he regularly commits this sin when he enters a bar, he should prudently refrain from going into bars, though this might not be sinful for others. Entering the bar does not cause Joe to abuse alcohol, but it does present a source of temptation, given the dispositions of Joe's heart. So the Catechism would not be wrong to tell us that, for a time at

---

11. See my discussion of casuistry in chapter 13.

12. *The American Heritage College Dictionary*, 3d ed. (Boston: Houghton Mifflin, 2000), 943.

13. This is the famous mind-body problem: how does the mind influence the actions of the body?

least, someone might need to avoid situations in which he often commits sin, even though it is not unlawful for people in general to enter those situations. But that principle is not well described in the language of rule 6.

As for appearances, it is certainly biblical to seek, not only to be righteous in fact, but also to appear righteous to fellow believers and to the world (1 Tim. 3:7). Nevertheless, it is not always possible to avoid appearing evil to somebody. Jesus himself was called a glutton and a drunkard (Matt. 11:19). The Catechism writers probably had in mind 1 Thessalonians 5:22, which says in the KJV, "Abstain from all appearance of evil." But that is likely a mistranslation. The ESV reads, "Abstain from every form of evil."

THE UNITY OF THE LAW

I have offered a qualified defense of the Catechism's ethical hermeneutic. In short, the Catechism seeks to do what Jesus does in the Sermon on the Mount, linking each commandment with its heart-motive. The sixth commandment forbids murder, and also that anger which leads to murder.[14] But the only alternative to murderous anger is love. So to expound the sixth commandment fully, as Jesus did, it is important for us to relate it to the heart-motive, whether that motive is sinful anger or love.

But at the deepest level, there are only two heart-motives. Human beings either love God or they hate him. Those who love God also love their neighbors. Those who hate God hate their neighbors as well. When we trace out the inward "causes" of sinful and righteous acts, therefore, ultimately there are only two. One attitude (setting the mind on the things of the flesh, Rom. 8:5) leads invariably to sin: "Those who are in the flesh cannot please God" (Rom. 8:8). But setting the mind on the things of the Spirit (the "mind of Christ," 1 Cor. 2:16) leads to righteousness. Jesus reduces every sin to the mind of the flesh, and every righteous act to the mind of the Spirit.

So there is a unity to godly character and to the law that governs it. All righteous deeds arise from the same heart attitude, and all God's commands serve to commend that attitude. So love, the mind of the Spirit, inevitably fulfills the law (Rom. 8:10).

James says, "For whoever keeps the whole law but fails in one point has become accountable for all of it. For he who said, 'Do not commit adultery,' also said, 'Do not murder.' If you do not commit adultery but do murder, you have become a transgressor of the law" (James 2:10–11). This is a difficult passage, but I take it to mean that all obligations reduce to a single one.

---

14. There is also righteous anger, as we shall see.

Jesus describes that single obligation as the law of love. James describes it as "keeping the whole law." Love and obedience, as we have seen, imply one another. One who loves God will keep all his commandments, not just this one or that one. So disobeying even one violates our fundamental obligation. This is why the apparently minor issue of whether or not to eat the fruit of a tree destroyed the integrity of Adam's relationship to God. To disobey one command, even a minor one, was to become "a transgressor of the law," a violator of our fundamental moral obligation. The law is one. We may think that we are relatively obedient if we obey God 95 percent of the time. But the 5 percent convicts us as rebels, just as one adulterous liaison destroys the integrity of the marital relationship.

So the main issue before us is, not whether we will keep this law or that law, but whether we will be law keepers or lawbreakers. Decisions about individual laws, of course, though not the main issue, are nevertheless very important, since to break any one of them is to become a lawbreaker. And the issue of law keeping is identical with the issue of covenant loyalty (as we shall see in the discussion of the first commandment) and with the issue of love.

The practical import of this is that you cannot decide to work on one area of your ethical life (say, submission to authority) while ignoring the others. Since ethics is a matter of the heart, compromise in one area entails compromise in others. You won't be able to be fully subject to authority, in the biblical sense, unless you learn not to covet and not to lust. Positively, growth in holiness is holistic. It is a practice of the presence of God in all the situations of life, so that every decision becomes a godly response to his lordship.

TEN PERSPECTIVES ON ETHICAL LIFE

If the law is a unity, then in one sense each commandment requires of us the same thing. What each commandment requires is a loyalty toward God (i.e., a love for God) that issues in godly behavior. Of course, the commandments are not synonymous. Each one looks at the love of God from a different perspective. One focuses on one kind of behavior produced by love; another focuses on another kind of loving behavior. But we may expect that the content of each commandment considerably overlaps that of others. Keeping one commandment will lead us to keep others, and disobeying one will lead us to disobey others. For example, people who commit idolatry (disloyalty toward God), breaking the second commandment, are likely to commit adultery (disloyalty to their spouse), breaking the seventh commandment. Hence the Bible frequently uses adultery as an image of idolatry (e.g., Ezek. 16; Hos. 1–3).

Fig. 5. The Ten Commandments as Perspectives on the Whole Law*

Although this may be a bit of a stretch, it may be useful to see the Decalogue as containing ten perspectives on the ethical life. On this understanding, each commandment mandates the law of love (i.e., covenant loyalty) from a different perspective. So, as I illustrated the relationships of three perspectives by a triangular diagram in chapter 3, we might consider a decagon in the present instance (see fig. 5).

On this basis, each commandment requires complete righteousness (love) and forbids all sin, but each from its own particular angle. Each commandment describes from one perspective the nature of love and, at the same time, the nature of sin. In my expositions of the individual commandments, I shall show how this happens, but the following summaries may be useful at this point.

* Thanks to Linc Ashby for this artwork. I can draw triangles and rectangles with minor computer assistance, but I look in awe at people who can draw decagons.

1. In the first commandment, the "other gods" include mammon (money, Matt. 6:24) and anything else that competes with God for our ultimate loyalty. Since any sin is disloyalty to God, the violation of any commandment is also violation of the first. Thus, all sin violates the first commandment; or, to put it differently, the commandment forbids *all* sins.

2. In the second commandment, similarly, the sin of worshiping a graven image is the sin of worshiping anything (or worshiping *by means of* anything) of human devising. "Worship" can be a broad ethical concept in Scripture as well as a narrowly cultic one (cf. Rom. 12:1–2). Any sin involves following our own purposes, purposes of our own devising, instead of God's, and that is false worship.

3. In the third commandment, "the name of the Lord" can refer to God's entire self-revelation, and any disobedience of that revelation can be described as "vanity." Thus, all sin violates the third commandment.

4. The Sabbath commandment demands godly use of our entire calendar—six days to carry out our own work to God's glory, and the seventh to worship and rest. So the whole week is given to us to do God's will. Any disobedient or ungodly use of time, on the six days or the seventh, may be seen as transgression of the fourth commandment.

5. "Father and mother" in the fifth commandment can be read broadly to refer to all authority and even the authority of God himself (Mal. 1:6). Thus, all disobedience of God violates the fifth commandment.

6. Jesus interprets the sixth commandment to prohibit unrighteous anger (Matt. 5:22) because of its disrespect for life. Genesis 9:6 relates this principle to respect for man as God's image. Since all sin manifests such disrespect for life and for God's image, it violates the sixth commandment.

7. Adultery is frequently used in Scripture as a metaphor (indeed, more than a metaphor) for idolatry. Israel is pictured as the Lord's unfaithful wife. The marriage figure is a prominent biblical description of the covenant order. Breaking the covenant at any point is adultery.

8. Withholding tithes and offerings—God's due—is stealing (Mal. 3:8). Thus, to withhold any honor due to God falls under the same condemnation.

9. "Witnessing" in Scripture is something you *are*, more than something you do. It involves not only speech, but actions as well. It is comprehensive.

10. Coveting, like stealing, is involved in all sin. Sinful acts are the product of the selfish heart. This commandment speaks against the root of sin, and therefore against all sin.

So we have in the Decalogue ten perspectives on sin: as covenant disloyalty, as false worship, as misuse of God's revelation, as misuse of time, as disrespect for authority, and so on. And similarly, we have ten perspectives on love: covenant loyalty, true worship, and so on. To keep any one commandment, in its deepest meaning, is to keep all the others, and to love, as Scripture says, is to keep them all. This perspectival approach, then, helps us understand and appreciate the Catechism's view of the unity of God's law.

BROAD AND NARROW

So each commandment has a broad and a narrow meaning. The broad meanings are listed above under each commandment: the first commandment requires covenant loyalty to God, the fourth requires a godly use of time, the fifth requires respect for all authority, and so on. Each of these meanings covers all sins, all good acts, all moral decisions. Any decision I make can be described as respecting or violating covenant loyalty to God, as a godly or ungodly use of time, and so on.

But of course each commandment has a narrow meaning as well. These are the more obvious meanings. The fifth commandment tells us broadly to respect all authority, but narrowly it tells us to respect our fathers and mothers. The seventh commandment teaches us to be faithful to God in all we do, but it also tells us specifically not to have sexual relations with someone other than our spouse.

We should never pit the broad meanings against the narrow ones, or vice versa. People sometimes get the impression that since the seventh commandment has to do with covenant faithfulness, we should not invoke it for the mere purpose of evaluating sexual acts. Some writers seem to think that the broad meanings are glorious and deep, while the narrow ones are somehow trivial, or that to insist on the narrow meanings is somehow legalistic. On such a view, the narrow meanings are brushed aside by the broad meanings.

But that is to misunderstand both the broad and the narrow meanings of the commandments. To continue our discussion of the seventh commandment, covenant faithfulness is not a conceptual blank line, to be filled in as anybody likes. Covenant faithfulness, rather, governs specific sexual actions—excluding some, commending others. I argued in chapter 12 against Joseph Fletcher that love has specific content, for it is a disposition to keep God's commandments, specific as they are. What is true of the law of love is true of all the Ten Commandments. They all mandate love, and they also mandate the specific actions that are part of love. The eighth commandment, for example, forbids us to rob God of his honor, but it also forbids us to take donuts from the store without paying for them.

PREACHING CHRIST FROM THE DECALOGUE

If all Scripture testifies of Christ (Luke 24:27; John 5:39), then the law of God surely cannot be an exception. As we study the law, then, we should examine its witness to Christ. I assume that some readers of this book are preparing for Christian ministry. They especially need to know how to use the Decalogue in their preaching and teaching. But all of us need to learn how to see Christ in the law.

The law bears witness to Christ in a number of ways, some of which I shall discuss in the following points.

1. *The Decalogue presents the righteousness of Christ.* Jesus perfectly obeyed God's law. That is why he was the perfect lamb of God, why God imputes his active righteousness to us, and why he is the perfect example for the Christian life. He never put any god before his Father. He never worshiped idols or took God's name in vain. Despite what the Pharisees said, he never violated the Sabbath command. So the Decalogue tells us what Jesus was like. It shows us his perfect character.

2. *The Decalogue shows our need of Christ.* God's law convicts us of sin and drives us to Jesus. It shows us who we are, apart from Christ. We are idolaters, blasphemers, Sabbath breakers, and so on.

3. *The Decalogue shows the righteousness of Christ imputed to us.* In him we are holy. God sees us in Christ, as law keepers.

4. *The Decalogue shows us how God wants us to give thanks for Christ.* In the Decalogue, as we shall see below, obedience follows redemption. God tells his people that he has brought them out of Egypt. The law is not something they must keep to merit redemption. God *has* redeemed them. Keeping the law is the way they thank God for salvation freely given. So the Heidelberg Confession expounds the law under the category of gratefulness.

5. *Christ is the substance of the law.* This point is related to the first, but it is not quite the same. Here I wish to say that Jesus is not only a perfect law keeper, according to his humanity, but also the one we honor and worship, according to his deity, when we keep the law.

(a) The first commandment teaches us to worship Jesus as the one and only Lord, Savior, and mediator (Acts 4:12; 1 Tim. 2:5).

(b) In the second commandment, Jesus is the one perfect image of God (Col. 1:15; Heb. 1:3). Our devotion to him precludes worship of any other image.

(c) In the third commandment, Jesus is the name of God, that name to which every knee shall bow (Phil. 2:10–11; cf. Isa. 45:23).

(d) In the fourth commandment, Jesus is our Sabbath rest. In his presence, we cease our daily duties and hear his voice (Luke 10:38–42). He is

Lord of the Sabbath as well (Matt. 12:8), who makes the Sabbath his own Lord's Day (Rev. 1:10).

(e) In the fifth commandment, we honor Jesus, who restores us to the divine family as he submits himself entirely to the will of the Father (John 5:19–24).

(f) In the sixth commandment, we honor him as our life (John 10:10; 14:6; Gal. 2:20; Col. 3:4), the Lord of life (Acts 3:15), the one who gave his life that we might live (Mark 10:45).

(g) In the seventh commandment, we honor him as our bridegroom, who gave himself to cleanse us, to make us his pure, spotless bride (Eph. 5:22–33). We love him as no other.

(h) In the eighth commandment, we honor Jesus as the source of our inheritance (Eph. 1:11), as the one who provides everything that his people need in this world and beyond.

(i) In the ninth commandment, we honor him as God's truth (John 1:17; 14:6), in whom all the promises of God are Yes and Amen (2 Cor. 1:20).

(j) In the tenth commandment, we honor him as our complete sufficiency (2 Cor. 3:5; 12:9) to meet both our external needs and the renewed desires of our hearts. In him we can be content with what we have, thankful for his present and future gifts.

THE PREFACES TO THE COMMANDMENTS

As I indicated in chapter 3, the Decalogue is in its literary form a suzerainty treaty or covenant document. To review its structure:

1. Name of the great king (Ex. 20:2a)
2. Historical prologue (v. 2b)
3. Stipulations (vv. 3–17)
    a. General stipulation: exclusive covenant loyalty (love) (v. 3)
    b. Specific stipulations: the specific content of love (vv. 4–17)
4. Sanctions
    a. Blessings for obedience (vv. 6, 12)
    b. Curses for disobedience (vv. 5b, 7)

The fifth main section, called "administration" or "covenant continuity" is not present in the Decalogue, but it is a part of Deuteronomy, which Kline also identifies as a suzerainty treaty.

The bulk of our discussion in the remainder of this book will deal with the stipulations and sanctions, the commandments themselves, seeking to determine how these apply to our lives today. But we should not neglect sections 1 and 2, for they place sections 3 and 4 in a proper context. We have looked at the overall context of Israel's meeting with God, "the day of the assembly." Now we should look at the context of the commandments in the Decalogue itself.

God's Name

The document begins with God's name: Yahweh, the Lord. As God so identified himself to Moses in Exodus 3:14–15, so he now identifies himself in the direct hearing of all his people. This identification ensures, first, that the covenant is a *personal* relationship.[15] Ultimately, we are to obey the law, not just because its principles are true, but because of the one who commanded them. I have argued that the personality of God is indispensable to ethics. Worldviews that reduce the personal to the impersonal (as we saw in chapters 3–8, especially 5) lose any basis for ethics. Ethics is based on a family relationship. In this world, we learn ethical standards in the family, in a context of love and loyalty.[16] Similarly at the ultimate level, we learn right and wrong from a heavenly Father, an absolute personality. Only such a personal relationship can communicate principles that are absolutely authoritative.

Notice also that Yahweh here is "the LORD thy God" (v. 2).[17] First of all, this expression in effect makes Israel part of God's own name. Yahweh is "Yahweh thy God," Yahweh the God of Israel. How remarkable it is that the Lord of glory so profoundly identifies himself with his sinful people!

Second, this expression is the first of many uses of the second person singular pronoun throughout the document. God gives his commands, therefore, in an "I-thou" relationship. This language emphasizes both the unity of the people (as if they were one person) and the intimacy of their relationship to God.

So although the Decalogue is a legal and even political document, it is also a loving self-communication between the Lord and the people he has chosen to be his.

15. In chapter 3, I indicated that the Lord is a person, and also that he is supremely holy. Earlier in this chapter, we explored the holiness of the Lord by looking at the terrifying phenomena that kept Israel away from the mountain. So Ex. 19–20 is quite parallel to Ex. 3 in presenting God as holy, as personal, and as the head of the covenant.

16. This is, of course, a statement of an ideal, given the many disruptions of the family structure in our fallen world. But this is what God designed as a means of ethical instruction, and many of us have experienced it in some measure. If one has not experienced such bonds of loyalty and love in a home, perhaps one has experienced them in school, church, a sports team, or other group.

17. I use the KJV here, which, unlike modern translations, is able to render the difference between second person singular and plural.

Third, "Lord" calls to mind again the lordship attributes of control, authority, and presence. The treaty form can be analyzed in this way: the historical prologue emphasizes the Lord's control over history; the stipulations emphasize his authority; the sanctions emphasize his presence in blessing and judgment. The Lord, then, presents himself to Israel as one who is sovereign over all things in heaven and on earth, whose word must be obeyed without objection, and who will be with his people to fulfill his promises and threats.

THE HISTORICAL PROLOGUE

In the historical prologue, God reminds Israel that he brought them "out of the land of Egypt, out of the house of slavery" (v. 2). This statement makes the important point that God's gracious deliverance *precedes* the demands of the law, and it forms the basis for Israel's obedience. Grace precedes and motivates works. This relationship between grace and works is substantially the same as that in the new covenant.

Scripture emphasizes (similarly to the parallel secular treaties) that the making of the covenant *follows* the divine victory (Deut. 1:1–5; 4:44–49; 29:1–3). God's grace is the cause of that victory (Deut. 4:20; 6:10–12; 7:6–8; 8:17; 9:1–6). He has sovereignly elected Israel, not because of her merits, but in spite of her stubbornness and disobedience (Deut. 7:6–8; 9:4–7; 10:14–17). Israel should obey because she is God's elect (Deut. 27:9–10), and because God has delivered and blessed her (Lev. 19:36–37; 20:8; 22:31–33; Deut. 6:20–25; 8:1–6, 11–18; 10:21–11:7; 29:2–9).

This does not mean that these laws bind Israel only, and not other nations. As I argued in chapter 13, the laws of the Decalogue are, for the most part, identical to the creation ordinances that bind all mankind. The mere fact that God commands something is sufficient reason to obey.[18] But the fact that God has delivered Israel gives them an additional reason to obey, the motive of gratitude. That God has given us an even greater deliverance in Christ should motivate our obedience all the more.

So God's gracious blessing precedes Israel's obedience. Nevertheless, there is also a sense in which blessing *follows* obedience. In Exodus 19:5–6, we read, "Now therefore, if you will indeed obey my voice and keep my covenant, you shall be my treasured possession among all peoples, for all the earth is mine; and you shall be to me a kingdom of priests and a holy nation." Here Israel's special relationship to God is conditional upon her obedience. Israel will not be God's treasured possession if she does not keep

---

18. See chapter 3, under "Biblical Reasons to Do Good Works."

the covenant. Even here, the covenant is in place before God even gives this admonition. Israel is to keep a covenant that already exists. But Israel's continuation in this favored position depends on her faithfulness.

And the blessings of the covenant, the favorable sanctions, also depend on Israel's obedience (Ex. 20:6, 12; 23:22–33; Deut. 5:32–33; 6:1–3, 17–19; 8:7–10; 11:10–12; 13:18; cf. Ps. 1). This is true also of the new covenant in Christ (Matt. 6:33; Mark 10:29; Eph. 6:1–3; 1 Tim. 4:8). As we saw in chapter 16, there are rewards for Christian believers, contingent upon their obedience.

So God's blessing appears twice in the treaty structure: the historical prologue (section 2) describes a blessing that precedes the covenant making itself, God's grace apart from works. But the sanctions (section 4) describe further blessings that are contingent upon obedience, with curses for disobedience. Ideally, grace leads to human good works, which bring further blessing (Eph. 2:8–10). But in fact, those who are initially chosen sometimes disobey and are subject to final rejection.[19]

19. When I speak here of a divine choice that can be rescinded, I am talking, of course, not about election as God's eternal plan for the salvation of individuals ("eternal election"), but about God's election of people in history to serve his purposes, which I call "historical election" in *DG*, 317–25. Those whom God elects for salvation in Christ before the foundation of the world (Eph. 1:4), the "eternally elect," cannot lose their salvation. Their salvation is contingent only on God's unchanging purpose.

CHAPTER 23

The First Commandment: No Other Gods

We come now to our exposition of the Ten Commandments.[1] Following the Westminster Larger Catechism, we can divide them into one group of four, pertaining to "our duty to God," and a group of six, describing "our duty to man."[2] So the structure of the Decalogue parallels Jesus' "two great

---

1. Scripture refers to "the Ten Commandments" (see Ex. 34:28; Deut. 4:13; 10:4), but never numbers the individual commandments. There are several different numbering systems. Roman Catholics and Lutherans combine the commandment to have no other gods with the commandment forbidding graven images into one commandment, calling that the first, and then split the prohibition of coveting into two: the ninth being about coveting your neighbor's house, and the tenth being about coveting his wife, servants, or animals. I will be using the form of numbering common in the Reformed tradition, which sees the prohibition of other gods as the first, the exclusion of idols as the second, and the prohibition of all coveting as the tenth. Choice of a numbering system is not of much theological importance. The Roman-Lutheran system does give less prominence than the Reformed to the command concerning the worship of idols, reflecting a difference in theological emphasis that I will discuss under the second commandment. Nevertheless, their numbering system may be correct. The blessing and curse in Ex. 20:5b–6 appropriately attach to all of verses 3–5a, not just to verses 4–5a. On the other hand, the Roman-Lutheran division of the prohibition of coveting into two commandments is quite implausible. Another possibility is that the references in Ex. 34:28 and elsewhere include the preface of 20:2 as the first. That verse is not, of course, a command-ment, but the Hebrew term translated "commandment" in Ex. 34:28 is *dabar*, "word." In the traditional Jewish numbering, verse 2 is combined with verse 3 to constitute the first word, and the other commands are numbered as in the Reformed view. But if verse 2 is taken to be the first word, then verses 3–6 could be taken together as the second, and from then on the numbering would work as in the Reformed tradition. That seems to me to be the most likely alternative, but I will follow the standard Reformed numbering.
2. WLC, 98.

commandments," to love God and to love one's neighbor (Matt. 22:36–40). This is something of a rough-and-ready distinction, however, since the last six commandments certainly describe duties to God as well as to man, and since the first four have implications for our conduct toward other people as well as toward God.[3] As I indicated in chapter 22, the law is a unity.

My discussions of the commandments will move, as a rule, from theological background to specific applications, from narrow meanings to broad meanings (see chapter 22), from positive to negative.

The first commandment reads simply, "You shall have no other gods before me." Confessional expositions have been as concise as that of Luther's Small Catechism: "We must fear, love, and trust God more than anything else."[4] And they have been as elaborate as this from the WLC:

> Q. 104. *What are the duties required in the first commandment?*
> A. The duties required in the first commandment are, the knowing and acknowledging of God to be the only true God, and our God; and to worship and glorify him accordingly, by thinking, meditating, remembering, highly esteeming, honoring, adoring, choosing, loving, desiring, fearing of him; believing him; trusting, hoping, delighting, rejoicing in him; being zealous for him; calling upon him, giving all praise and thanks, and yielding all obedience and submission to him with the whole man; being careful in all things to please him, and sorrowful when in anything he is offended; and walking humbly with him.

> Q. 105. *What are the sins forbidden in the first commandment?*
> A. The sins forbidden in the first commandment are, atheism, in denying or not having a God; idolatry, in having or worshiping more gods than one, or any with or instead of the true God; the not having and avouching him for God, and our God; the omission or neglect of anything due to him, required in this commandment; ignorance, forgetfulness, misapprehensions, false opinions, unworthy and wicked thoughts of him; bold and curious searching into his secrets; all profaneness, hatred of God; self-love, self-seeking,

---

3. Traditionally, it has been held that the two groups of four and six commandments are the "two tablets" of the original edition (Ex. 31:18; 32:15; 34:1, 4, 29; Deut. 4:13; 5:22; etc.). But I agree with Meredith G. Kline's argument that the two tablets each included all ten. In the Near Eastern treaties, two copies were made, one for the sanctuary of the great king and one for the sanctuary of the vassal king. In Israel, however, there was only one sanctuary, and both copies were placed there. See Kline, *The Structure of Biblical Authority* (Grand Rapids: Eerdmans, 1972), 113–30.

4. Luther's Small Catechism, I, A.

and all other inordinate and immoderate setting of our mind, will, or affections upon other things, and taking them off from him in whole or in part; vain credulity, unbelief, heresy, misbelief, distrust, despair, incorrigibleness, and insensibleness under judgments, hardness of heart, pride, presumption, carnal security, tempting of God; using unlawful means, and trusting in lawful means; carnal delights and joys; corrupt, blind, and indiscreet zeal; lukewarmness, and deadness in the things of God; estranging ourselves, and apostatizing from God; praying, or giving any religious worship, to saints, angels, or any other creatures; all compacts and consulting with the devil, and hearkening to his suggestions; making men the lords of our faith and conscience; slighting and despising God and his commands; resisting and grieving of his Spirit, discontent and impatience at his dispensations, charging him foolishly for the evils he inflicts on us; and ascribing the praise of any good we either are, have, or can do, to fortune, idols, ourselves, or any other creature.[5]

Both Luther and the Larger Catechism find in the first commandment an issue of the heart. For both, the commandment does not tell us only to avoid worshiping other gods, like Baal, Moloch, Chemosh, Astarte, Zeus, Hera, Apollo, and so on. It also teaches us to avoid placing anything other than the true God ahead of him in our thoughts, actions, and affections. The forbidding of literal polytheism is the "narrow" meaning of this command (chapter 22). The forbidding of any competition at all with the true God for our allegiance, obedience, and affection is the broader meaning. As with all biblical ethics, the first commandment is a matter of lordship. We are to recognize from the heart that God is Lord of all things and that therefore he will tolerate no rivals.

The difference between Luther's exposition and that of the Larger Catechism is that the latter tries to enumerate, as exhaustively as possible, the attitudes of heart and the physical actions that are appropriate to this command and the would-be rivals of God that tempt us to violate it. I find the long lists of virtues and sins in the Larger Catechism amusing at times. I can almost picture a committee sitting around a table, with various people putting up their hands to inject this or that item ("Oh, we must not forget 'highly esteeming'!"), leading to a list of gargantuan proportions and literary disaster. The Heidelberg Catechism, as usual, is far more graceful:

5. Luther's Large Catechism is even more elaborate, but its answers, here and elsewhere, are sermonic essays on the text. The Larger Catechism, on the other hand, is a list of mandatory applications, without sermonic discussion. It is more like a legal document.

Q. 94. *What does God require in the first Commandment?*

A. That, on peril of my soul's salvation, I avoid and flee all idolatry, sorcery, enchantments, invocation of saints or of other creatures; and that I rightly acknowledge the only true God, trust in Him alone, with all humility and patience expect all good from Him only, and love, fear and honor Him with my whole heart; so as rather to renounce all creatures than to do the least thing against His will.

In this catechism, there is also a list, but it makes no attempt to be exhaustive, and the first person language (echoing the second person, singular language of the Decalogue itself), along with the rhetorically powerful final clause, engages the heart as well as the mind. The Larger Catechism also tries to engage the heart, but it always seems to have in mind the model of a legal document, multiplying citations as if to close every loophole. The Larger Catechism wants to ensure that "having another god before me" will be *illegal* in the church, and that nobody will have any excuse.

Nevertheless, I actually find the Larger Catechism more edifying than the Heidelberg Catechism, because of its breadth and depth. Whatever we may think of the long lists, the items are almost always biblical (I have chosen not to list the proof texts), and they enable us to dig deeply into the nature of our exclusive allegiance to the Lord. Did it occur to you that "lukewarmness" was a violation of the first commandment?[6] It didn't occur to me, either, before reading it here. But when you think about it, that correlation is a profound insight. To the extent that we are lukewarm in our attitude toward God, we are putting other things ahead of him. Like other Bible passages (see chapter 21), the first commandment makes demands upon our emotional life. So for those who have the patience to actually meditate on the lists of the Larger Catechism and compare each item with Scripture, there is great spiritual profit here.

Note also little touches like the opening of Answer 104, where we are urged to recognize God as "the only true God, *and our God*" (emphasis added). That picks up the language of Exodus 20:2, where God identifies himself as "the LORD your God." This language excludes any merely theoretical acknowledgment of God's existence. This confession, as much as that of the Heidelberg, is a personal confession, one of covenant allegiance. The Larger Catechism repeats that point in Answer 105, where atheism is either denying (the existence of) God or "not having a God." So an atheist may be someone who believes that God exists, but who refuses to be his covenant servant.

6. Or "bold and curious searching into his secrets"? Or "vain credulity"? Or "charging him foolishly for the evils he inflicts on us"?

The lists show us, in practice, what it means to interpret the Decalogue according to the principles of WLC, 99, which I discussed in chapter 22. In the lists, the Larger Catechism considers how each commandment "requires the utmost perfection of every duty" and "forbids the least degree of every sin" (rule 1). The lists also show the "spirituality of the law," how it extends to "understanding, will, and affections," and also to "words, works, and gestures" (rule 2). And they show how each prohibition also forbids all "causes, means, occasions, and appearances thereof, and provocations thereunto" (rule 6). In the end, they show that each commandment commands all righteousness and forbids all sin. If you or I can measure up to the standards of WLC, 104 and 105 (and of course we will not measure up, short of glory), then we will be completely sinless. For one who is not disloyal to God in any way, in any degree, will surely not do anything contrary to his will. All sin is disloyalty to God. All sin is putting something else before him. So the first commandment defines all sin and all righteousness, from its particular perspective of covenant loyalty.

LOVE

The Larger Catechism makes a huge number of connections between the first commandment and various virtues and sins. In what follows, I will focus on some of the more obvious virtues implied by the first commandment, perhaps adding some structure and organization to the lists in the Catechism. I shall thereby try to show that the Catechism's perspective is warranted by Scripture itself, for it summarizes the ways in which Scripture applies this commandment to our ethical life.

In chapters 3 and 22, I described the suzerainty treaty as an ancient Near Eastern literary form, of which the Decalogue and the book of Deuteronomy are examples. In the secular treaties, following the name of the great king and the historical prologue, came the stipulations. The first stipulation, typically, was the requirement of exclusive loyalty. The vassal is not to make similar treaties with any other king. In Exodus 20:3, the first commandment makes that same requirement of Israel. Israel is not to give its ultimate loyalty to any other god.

In the secular treaties, such exclusive covenant loyalty was sometimes called love. Deuteronomy 6:4–5 also expresses covenant loyalty in the language of love: "Hear, O Israel: The LORD our God, the LORD is one. You shall love the LORD your God with all your heart and with all your soul and with all your might." This is, of course, Jesus' first great commandment (Matt. 22:36–38). This loyalty-love is the center of the believer's relationship with God.

I discussed the nature of love in chapters 12 and 19, so I won't say much more at this point, except to reiterate that in the Decalogue, as well as in the rest of the Bible, love is central to the lives of God's people. It summarizes our entire obligation.

In the context of the Decalogue, this law of love follows the historical prologue ("who brought you out of the land of Egypt, out of the house of slavery"), so we see that grace precedes obedience, and that love is the first response of a person whom God has redeemed. And the command to love God precedes the other commandments, indicating that love is the motivation for keeping the rest of the law.

The New Testament realization of this commandment is that Jesus demands the same exclusive covenant loyalty that the Lord demands in the Decalogue. Jesus says that loyalty to him is a higher obligation than loyalty to our parents (Matt. 10:34–37). He did defend the fifth commandment as well, charging that the scribes and Pharisees did not honor their parents (Mark 7:9–13), but he nevertheless placed himself ahead of parents in our hierarchy of ethical obligations. But who deserves a loyalty higher than our parents except the Lord himself?

Jesus should be more important to us than our own lives (Matt. 16:24–27). Indeed, Paul says, "But whatever gain I had, I counted as loss for the sake of Christ. Indeed, I count everything as loss because of the surpassing worth of knowing Christ Jesus my Lord. For his sake I have suffered the loss of all things and count them as rubbish, in order that I may gain Christ" (Phil. 3:7–8). None of this makes any sense unless Jesus is indeed God. As God demanded exclusive covenant loyalty of Israel under Moses, so Jesus demands no less from us in the new covenant.

When the rich young ruler asked Jesus what he should do to attain eternal life, Jesus mentioned several commandments of the Decalogue. He mentioned only commandments from "the second table," the commandments emphasizing our responsibility to our fellow man. When the ruler asked, "What do I still lack?" the reader might expect that Jesus would cite the first table, our responsibility to God. Instead, Jesus said, "If you would be perfect, go, sell what you possess and give to the poor, and you will have treasure in heaven; and come, follow me" (Matt. 19:21). Jesus here demanded a radical renunciation of the ruler's besetting sin, coveting wealth. And, in effect, he replaced the first table of the law with the commandment to follow him. To be perfect, we must be exclusively loyal, not only to God, but specifically to Jesus. Exclusive loyalty to Jesus does not detract from exclusive loyalty to God, only because Jesus is God.

So the first commandment of the Decalogue is first of all a demand for exclusive loyalty to God—Father, Son, and Holy Spirit—which is another way of stating the law of love.

WORSHIP

Another way to look at the first commandment is to say that it is about worship. The first four commandments deal especially with our relationship to God. But in all our relationships to God, we stand as worshipers. When people meet God in the Bible, they bow down; they are moved to worship. So the first four commandments serve as rules for worship. The first commandment deals with the object of worship, the second with the manner of worship, the third with the language of worship, and the fourth with the time of worship.

People who take courses on ethics usually don't expect to have to study worship as well. Students usually like to focus on second-table issues like abortion, war, and divorce. But in a Christian ethic, we must focus also on our duty to God. Indeed, that must be our primary focus. And the term *worship* is shorthand for "our duty to God."

In Scripture, worship is both a broad concept and a narrow concept. Narrowly, worship is what we do on certain occasions. In the Old Testament, it includes the offering of sacrifices of animals, flour, oil, and wine. In both testaments, it includes meetings for prayer, praise, the reading and teaching of Scripture, and observing sacraments. The people of God carry out similar activities in families and privately. The word *cultic* is sometimes used to describe such activities.[7] The first commandment requires, of course, that such worship be given only to the one true God.[8]

Remarkably, however, Jesus also accepts worship from human beings (Matt. 28:9, 17; John 9:35–38), and he demands that we honor him as we honor the Father (John 5:23). Even the angels worship him (Heb. 1:6). One day all will bow before the name of Jesus (Phil. 2:10). The hymns of Revelation are directed to him (Rev. 5:11–12; 7:10).[9] So first-commandment language applies to the worship of Jesus: his is the only name on which we should call for salvation (John 14:6; Acts 4:12). As the Lord is our exclusive object of worship, so is Jesus, rendering an identity

---

7. Do not confuse this use of the term *cultic* with its use to designate heretical and non-Christian sects.

8. For a more elaborate account of worship in Scripture, see my *Worship in Spirit and Truth* (Phillipsburg, NJ: P&R Publishing, 1996).

9. For additional references, see *DG*, 679–80.

between the two inevitable. As we are to love Jesus above all others, so we are to worship him as we worship God.

Worship in Scripture also has a broader meaning, as indicated in Romans 12:1–2:

> I appeal to you therefore, brothers, by the mercies of God, to present your bodies as a living sacrifice, holy and acceptable to God, which is your spiritual worship. Do not be conformed to this world, but be transformed by the renewal of your mind, that by testing you may discern what is the will of God, what is good and acceptable and perfect.

Here the "living sacrifice," the "spiritual worship," is to live lives in the world that are transformed by God's Spirit. Here, worship is ethics. In the Old Testament, too, there was a close relationship between worship and purity of life. One could approach God only with "clean hands and a pure heart" (Ps. 24:4; cf. Luke 1:74; Acts 24:16; 2 Tim. 1:3). When we come before God, he must deal with our sins. Hence, Old Testament worship emphasizes sacrifice, and New Testament worship celebrates the finished sacrifice of Christ.

The biblical vocabulary of worship (as *'abad, latreuein, douleuein, leitourgein*) uses terminology that can refer either to secular or to religious service. And cultic language often applies to ethical purity in general (Matt. 6:24; James 1:27; Heb. 12:28). Paul uses such language also in connection with his mission to the Gentiles. "For God is my witness," he says, "whom I serve (*latreuein*) with my spirit in the gospel of his Son" (Rom. 1:9). In Philippians 2:17, he says, "Even if I am to be poured out as a drink offering upon the sacrificial offering of your faith, I am glad and rejoice with you all."

I shall therefore distinguish between worship in the broad sense and worship in the narrow sense. In the broad sense, worship is a perspective on all of biblical ethics. To worship is to obey God, and vice versa. All of life is worship, an offering to him, the living sacrifice of our body. Thinking of our lives in that way is a motivation to godly behavior. And this image shows us again how all sin violates the First Commandment, and how all righteous actions fulfill it.

CONSECRATION

Consecration is an aspect of worship—setting ourselves and all our possessions apart for God's use. In a sense, all worship is consecration and vice versa, so consecration is another perspective on the first commandment and on the Christian life as a whole.

Note the many laws in the Pentateuch requiring the sanctification of individuals and things: the firstborn child (Ex. 13), the ransom of individuals for the census (Ex. 30:11–17), the consecration of the Nazirite (Num. 6:1–21), the consecration of firstfruits (Deut. 26:1–19). In circumcision (Gen. 17:9–14; Lev. 12:3) and the Passover (Ex. 12; Num. 9; Deut. 16), God's people recognize that he has set them apart (consecrated them) from other nations and made them his "holy" people (Lev. 20:26; Deut. 7:6; 14:2, 21; etc.). Similarly, when a person is baptized, he takes upon himself the name of the Father, the Son, and the Holy Spirit (Matt. 28:19): he becomes God's person, distinguished from all the other families of the earth. And the Lord's Supper signs and seals the new covenant in Jesus' blood, by which we are separated from the world (Matt. 26:28; 1 Cor. 11:25).

So God separates his people from the world to be distinctly his. In covenant, he is our God and we are his people. We have seen in previous sections of this chapter that the first commandment is grounded in who God is, as the Creator, in contrast to us, as creatures. By the fact of our creation, we are bound to love, serve, and worship God above all others. But our obligation is also grounded in what God has done in history, namely, his redemption (Ex. 20:2) and his choice of us as his people, taking us from all the other nations to be holy in him. He is our Lord by creation and redemption.

SEPARATION

In discussing love, worship, and consecration, I have linked the first commandment to three positive biblical concepts.[10] But the language of the commandment itself, like most of the commands of the Decalogue, is negative: "You shall have *no* other gods before me." So we should look also at the negative thrust of the commandment.

Why is the Decalogue so largely negative? All of the commandments except the fourth and fifth are stated as prohibitions, and the fourth contains much negative language. It is, of course, a matter of emphasis. As we have seen (and as the Catechism emphasizes), negative formulations do not rule out positive paraphrases and applications. Positive and negative are matters more of phrasing than of meaning. But why all the negative phrasing?

The very notion of exclusive covenant loyalty requires us to refuse rival loyalties. And there are rivals, others who tempt us to abandon our

---

10. Recall my argument in chapter 19 that love gives a positive thrust to biblical ethics, even though Scripture often states its commands negatively.

covenant with God.[11] God has made covenant with us in a fallen world. So the negative focus reflects the reality of sin and temptation. Obedience to God in a fallen world always involves saying no—to Satan, the world, and our own lusts (1 John 2:15–16). And it requires us to take up arms against wickedness (Eph. 6:10–20). So the ethical life is a conflict, a battle. Scripture calls us to repentance (turning away from a sinful course), self-denial (taking up our cross to follow Christ), and separation (breaking away from associations that compromise our loyalty to God). The New Testament in this regard is no less negative than the Old Testament, the Sermon on the Mount being a case in point. And even love, that most positive of virtues, is described negatively in 1 Corinthians 13.

There is a strong tendency in modern evangelicalism to stick to the positive and avoid the negative. We can argue about the rhetorical issues, but we should be reminded that Scripture, God's own communication to us, often stresses the negative. Sometimes we need rebuke; we need to be told no. Sometimes we need to reject false doctrine because it is false. Sometimes we must present God's standards in contrast to the standards of the world, if they are even to be understood.

So the first commandment implies a doctrine of separation, of exclusion, of denial. It tells us to say no. From what are we called to separate? Here, as in all matters, Scripture is our sufficient guide. The concept of separation has been prominent in evangelical writings about the Christian life. Such writings have described "the separated life" as one without alcohol, tobacco, dancing, card playing, and so forth. I shall say more about these issues, but for now we should note that such things are not the focus of biblical separation. Scripture itself focuses, rather, on separation from the following:

FALSE GODS

The narrow teaching of the commandment is that we should not worship beings other than Yahweh (cf. Deut. 6:13–15; 12:29–32). Scripture mentions many such beings that demand and receive worship from humans: Baal, Astarte, Moloch, Chemosh, Dagon, Rimmon, etc. These gods may be fictions, or they may be supernatural beings (demons, 1 Cor. 10:20) who wrongly claim the prerogatives of Yahweh. When tempting Jesus, Satan himself demands worship, and Jesus rebukes him by quoting Deuteronomy 6:13, which reflects the first commandment (Matt. 4:9–10).[12]

---

11. Hence there is the frequent biblical parallel between our covenant with God and the marriage covenant. See chapter 19 and our later discussion of the seventh commandment.

12. The Syrian general Naaman, healed of leprosy by Yahweh, determined from that time forward to worship only the God of Israel. But he told the prophet Elisha that he would still be

God tells Israel to be literally iconoclastic, to break down the pillars and altars of false gods, to destroy every vestige of Canaanite religion (Ex. 23:24; 34:13; Deut. 12:2–3). Israel's separation from false worship is to be drastic, radical, and complete.

If exclusive covenant loyalty-love is the root of all righteousness, then to give that love to someone else is the root of all sin. The true God is a jealous God, as the second commandment tells us, and he will not give his glory to someone else (Isa. 42:8; 48:11). As the unfaithfulness of adultery betrays a marriage, so false worship violates the covenant at its heart. Thus, Scripture often draws parallels between adultery and idolatry (Lev. 20:5; Jer. 3:9; Ezek. 16; Hos. 1–4) and between faithfulness in marriage and faithfulness to the Lord (Eph. 5:22–33).

God-Substitutes

Worship of Baal and Astarte violates the narrow meaning of the first commandment. But the command also has a broader meaning. It is wrong also to worship our own power (Hab. 1:11), money (Job 31:24; Matt. 6:24), possessions (Luke 12:16–21; Col. 3:5), politics (Dan. 2:21), pleasure and entertainment (2 Tim. 3:4), food (Phil. 3:19), or self (Deut. 8:17; Dan. 4:30). Surely, if it is wrong to worship Baal, it is also wrong to worship something that is even less than Baal pretends to be. And yet that is what we often do. People who would never dream of bowing down in an idol's temple put other things ahead of God in their lives. Here the temptation is more subtle, and the rationalizations are more readily at hand. Often we just slip into these patterns, rather than making a conscious decision. So the Bible warns us, using language inspired by the first commandment.[13]

Practices of False Religions

God's people must abstain from divination, sorcery, necromancy, human sacrifice, and superstitions (Lev. 18:21–30; 19:26, 31; 20:6, 27; Deut. 16:21; 18:9–14). Only the true God knows the future, and he is the only one to whom the believer should turn for supernatural help.

---

required to escort the king of Syria into the temple of Rimmon for worship. The king would lean on his arm, forcing him into a bowing position! He asked pardon in advance for this, and Elisha appears to have granted it (2 Kings 5:1–19). In these bows, Naaman would not actually be worshiping Rimmon, for worship is a matter of the heart. But the physical act of bowing is something that both Naaman and Elisha took seriously: it requires a pardon, divine forgiveness.

13. "Mammon," in Matt. 6:24 and Luke 16:9–13 in some translations, simply means "wealth" or "money." But Jesus personifies it, as if it were the name of a god, enhancing the allusion to the first commandment.

FALSE PROPHETS AND RELIGIOUS FIGURES

The Old Testament provides the death penalty for sorcerers (Ex. 22:18), those who tempt Israelites to worship other gods (Deut. 13), and false prophets (Deut. 18). If a city in Israel becomes a center for false worship, other Israelites must make war against that city and destroy it completely (Deut. 13:12–18). False prophets include both those who speak in the name of other gods and those who falsely claim to speak the words of the true God (Deut. 18:20). God's people are not to give heed to such (Deut. 18:14), but only to the word of God (Deut. 18:18–19).

The death penalties here must be understood in the context of Israel's unique status as God's covenant people, in his holy land, with his holy presence dwelling among them. Vern Poythress argues that the destruction of an idolatrous city in Deuteronomy 13:12–18 is in effect part of the holy war of Israel against the Canaanite cities in the time of Joshua.[14] When Israelites behave like Canaanites, they must be treated like Canaanites. But Deuteronomy 20 distinguishes between Israel's wars against cities within the Promised Land and its wars with cities outside. So the issue in these passages is not idolatry per se, but idolatry within the precincts of God's holy presence. We should not assume, therefore, that the death penalty should be applied to all idolaters everywhere or in our modern nations. Nor is the radical iconoclasm that God demanded of Israel normative for new covenant believers.

Nevertheless, the death penalties indicate even to us today that idolatry is serious business, and that we should be concerned not only with false religion, but also with people who practice it, lest they influence us to be unfaithful to the Lord (Ex. 23:31–33; Deut. 13:6–8; Josh. 23:7–8; Ezra 4:1–3). That God's people should shun false prophecy and false teaching is also a New Testament principle. Jesus tells us to beware of false prophets (Matt. 7:15; cf. 24:11, 24), and the apostles oppose them (Acts 13:6–12; 2 Cor. 11:13; 2 Tim. 3:1–9; 2 Peter 2:1–22; 1 John 4:1; Rev. 16:13).

UNHOLINESS AND UNCLEANNESS

The objects of Israel's world were divided into three categories: holy, clean, and unclean. The tabernacle, the temple, and the furniture of these buildings are holy. Cattle are clean animals, suitable for food, but pigs are unclean. God intended his people to give special reverence to holy things and to avoid unclean things.

14. Vern S. Poythress, *The Shadow of Christ in the Law of Moses* (Phillipsburg, NJ: P&R Publishing, 1995), 141–42.

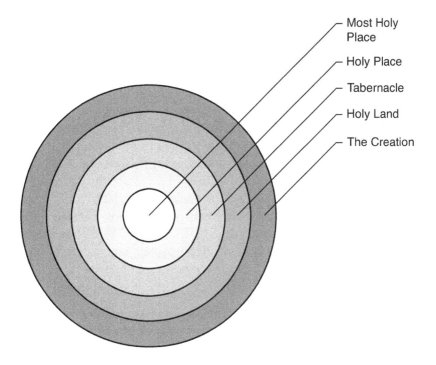

Most Holy
Place

Holy Place

Tabernacle

Holy Land

The Creation

Fig. 6. Degrees of Holiness

God himself is supremely holy,[15] and holy things are things that have
a special relationship to God. The tabernacle, God's house, is holy, but
its holiness admits of degrees. The innermost room is the Most Holy
Place, entered through another room called merely the Holy Place (Ex.
26:33–34). Compared to the Most Holy Place, the Holy Place is common
(the usual opposite of holy). Compared to the Holy Place, the rest of the
tabernacle is common. But compared to the area outside, the whole tabernacle is holy. There is even a sense in which the whole Promised Land
is holy (Zech. 2:12), the place that God has chosen for his name to dwell
in. And in a still broader sense, the whole creation is holy (see fig. 6). The
Lord says, "Heaven is my throne, and the earth is my footstool" (Isa. 66:1),
relativizing the value of any temple that men might build for him.

The priests are holy people, with holy garments (Ex. 29:29). But, in a
broader sense, the whole nation of Israel is holy. God's own people, separated from all the other nations, are to be "a kingdom of priests and a holy

15. For the meaning of holiness, see *DG*, 27–29. On p. 28, I define it as "God's capacity
and right to arouse our reverent awe and wonder."

nation" (Ex. 19:6). They perform holy actions, primarily the sacrificial offerings given to the Lord.

Certain times are holy: the Sabbath and the feasts of the Lord. So, as Tremper Longman points out, God gives to Israel holy places, holy times, holy people, and holy events.[16] The opposite of *holy* is *profane* or *common,* and these terms also admit of degrees. Compared to the Most Holy Place, the Holy Place is common; compared to the Holy Place, the rest of the tabernacle is common, and so forth. God does not tell Israel to avoid the profane or common. Such a prohibition would take Israel out of the world entirely. But he does urge Israel to distinguish between the holy and the common, as between the clean and the unclean (Lev. 10:10).

God revealed to Israel distinctions between clean and unclean things, animals, and people (e.g., Num. 19; Deut. 23:1–14). Poythress believes that cleanness has to do with God's righteousness and orderliness, and with his desire to illustrate to Israel the importance of separation from sin and death:

> Dead bodies are unclean both because of the immediate connection with death and because they degrade the order of living things back to the relative disorder of the nonliving earth. Birds that feed on carrion (dead bodies) are unclean. Things that are somehow defective or deviate from a paradigmatic order are also unclean. Fish with scales are the paradigmatic form of water creature; hence, all water creatures without scales or fins are deviant and unclean.[17]

He subsequently discusses other instances of holiness, cleanness, and uncleanness. These laws do seem to have some connection with hygiene. Many of them mandate practices that modern medical science recognizes as conducive to good health. This may be one means by which God fulfilled his promise to deliver Israel from "the evil diseases of Egypt" (Deut. 7:15; cf. 28:60–61). It shouldn't surprise us that obeying God tends toward life, rather than toward death. But, Poythress adds, the context of the laws themselves

> says nothing about hygiene but stresses the need of Israel to "be holy, because I, the LORD your God, am holy" (Lev. 19:2). The entire system is a pervasive expression of the orderliness and separation required of a people who have fellowship with God the Holy

---

16. Tremper Longman III, *Immanuel in Our Place: Seeing Christ in Israel's Worship* (Phillipsburg, NJ: P&R Publishing, 2001).

17. Poythress, *The Shadow of Christ in the Law of Moses*, 81–82.

One, the Creator of all order. As Gordon Wenham says, "Theology, not hygiene, is the reason for this provision."[18]

The language of clean and unclean can also take on a broadly ethical meaning. Psalm 24:3–4 reads, "Who shall ascend the hill of the LORD? And who shall stand in his holy place? He who has clean hands and a pure heart, who does not lift up his soul to what is false and does not swear deceitfully." Here it is difficult to tell where the ceremonial ends and the ethical begins, but both are certainly present.

The broadly ethical meaning is prominent in the New Testament. God has cleansed the Gentile nations by the grace of Christ, so that they may enter the covenant people on the same terms as the Jews (Acts 10:15; 11:9). In teaching this lesson to Peter, God tells him in a dream to kill and eat unclean animals. In the Old Testament, the pagan nations were the paradigm of uncleanness. God wanted Israel to be separate from them. But in the New Testament, the grace of God abounds to send Christians out to the nations, taking the gospel to them (Matt. 28:19–20). Association with pagans is now mandatory, not discouraged.

In the Old Testament, the assumption was that association with pagans would lead Israel into sin (see Ex. 23:33). Indeed, God instructed Israel to annihilate the Canaanite tribes within the Holy Land (Deut. 7:1–4, 16–26). In the New Testament, however, the assumption is that the power of the gospel will lead pagans into the worship of the true God and Jesus his Son. Even in a marriage between a believer and an unbeliever, God encourages us to hope that the believer's faith will prevail (1 Cor. 7:12–16; 1 Peter 3:1–6). This doesn't always happen, but God often works this way, and we are encouraged to pray for this result. As I mentioned earlier, Christians are to shun false teachers, as in the Old Testament. But the fullness of grace in the new covenant gives us freedom from fear and anxiety about the power of Satan.

So, in one sense, God through Christ has cleansed the nations: not that every pagan will be saved, but that the power of Satan to deceive the nations has been so weakened (Rev. 20:3) that paganism is no match for the power of the gospel, and Christians should seek to become fully involved in the lives of pagans, without participating in their sin. And if the nations themselves are now clean, then there is no need to continue the system of clean and unclean objects. So Jesus teaches his disciples that food cannot defile them, and Mark adds, "Thus he declared all foods clean" (Mark 7:19; cf. v. 15; Acts 10:15; Rom. 14:14, 20).

---

18. Ibid., 83. Poythress cites Gordon J. Wenham, *The Book of Leviticus* (Grand Rapids: Eerdmans, 1979), 21.

So, in the New Testament, cleanliness (or purity) is ethical, as in 2 Corinthians 7:1, "Since we have these promises, beloved, let us cleanse ourselves from every defilement of body and spirit, bringing holiness to completion in the fear of God" (cf. Eph. 5:5; Col. 3:5).

Holiness and cleanness, then, follow the larger pattern in the biblical applications of the first commandment. Narrowly, they describe the ceremonial requirements for living in the place of God's special presence. Broadly, they describe our overall ethical relationship to God. The former symbolize the latter, and they also apply the latter to Israel's unique role in the history of redemption. When the new covenant sets aside that unique role, fulfilling and setting aside the Holy Land, the temple, and the Aaronic priesthood, the ceremonial requirements change. But in the broader sense, we are still in the presence of God, wherever we are in the world, for heaven is his throne and earth is his footstool. And, in his broader presence, it is still important that we have clean hands and a pure heart, that we be separate from the defilements of sin, and that we be holy, as he is holy.

CHAPTER 24

The First Commandment: Contemporary Issues

We are living in a time when the worship of false gods abounds. Although Baal, Astarte, Moloch, Chemosh, and Rimmon have disappeared, we still have Allah, Brahma, and various tribal deities with us. We should remind ourselves also of the discussion in chapter 5, that impersonal philosophical or religious principles are also in effect objects of worship.[1] And of course the modern world has developed many God-substitutes that tempt people to forsake their Creator.

In chapter 23, I discussed how the Bible itself applies the teaching of the first commandment. Here I shall make some applications to contemporary issues.

THEOLOGICAL CONTROVERSIES

It may well be asked, If we cannot stand for the true God in theological discussions, where can we stand for him? But false concepts of God

---

1. On Roy Clouser's definition, as we saw, religion is belief in something as divine, that is, something "not dependent on anything else." So even in atheistic forms of Buddhism, there is a God-substitute, namely Nirvana, which does not depend on anything outside itself. And the impersonal absolutes of professedly secular philosophy, such as Plato's Good, Aristotle's Prime Mover, Spinoza's *Deus sive Natura*, and Hegel's Absolute must also be considered false gods.

abound, even in Christian circles, and even among theologians, who certainly should know better. These certainly include the views of God in process theology and open theism[2] and the views of extreme feminists who want to describe God exclusively as a feminine figure.[3] Also included are the traditional and more recent forms of monism, in which God and the world are equated, as well as the views that make God so transcendent that even the language of the Bible cannot truly describe him.[4]

The question does arise, however, as to the difference between believing in a false god and having an erroneous view of the true God. Does every error concerning God constitute worship of a false god? Do Arminians and Calvinists, for example, worship different gods? Normally we would say that Arminians and Calvinists worship the same God, though they disagree as to some of his decisions and actions. On a Calvinist view, God foreordains everything that comes to pass. On an Arminian view, God does not foreordain human free decisions, though he knows in advance what they will be.[5] But what about Christianity and Islam? Both religions claim to worship the God of Abraham, but Muslims reject the Trinity and espouse a fatalistic view of God's sovereignty.

The line between worshiping a false god and having false beliefs about the true God is not sharp. In the end, whether or not we worship the true God is a matter of the heart, which only God himself can read infallibly. Scripture certainly presents to us many examples of simple believers, such as the Samaritan woman of John 4, the blind man of John 9, and the Roman centurion in Matthew 8:5–13, who doubtless had some false concepts of God, but were accepted by God's grace. The Pharisees, on the other hand, apparently held orthodox theological views of God, but violated his word in so many other ways that Jesus regularly presents them as reprobate and, specifically, as false worshipers (Matt. 15:7–9).

The first commandment, as I have noted, speaks of the *object* of worship, while the second commandment speaks of the *way* of worship. The second, as we shall see, urges us to worship only according to God's revelation of himself. But the object and the way can never be entirely separated. If we worship God without taking any heed to God's revelation of himself, we are certainly worshiping a product of our own minds, not the true God at all. So it is important that we worship according to

---

2. See my book, *No Other God* (Phillipsburg, NJ: P&R Publishing, 2001), a critique of open theism.

3. See my critique of these views in *DG*, 378–86.

4. For these false views of transcendence and immanence, see chapter 4. See also Peter Jones's critique of neopagan monism in chapter 5.

5. In *DG*, chapter 8, I defend the Calvinistic position.

truth, even though the theological errors of those who trust Christ as their Savior and Lord can be forgiven.

At the extremes, these distinctions are not difficult to make. I would not hesitate to say that Christians and Hindus worship different gods. I also believe that the Muslims' Allah, though he shares some historical continuity with Yahweh, is a different god. The only true God is the God and Father of our Lord Jesus Christ (1 Cor. 8:6). In second-commandment terms, that means that we must worship God only in the name of Jesus Christ (Matt. 28:19–20; John 3:36; 5:23–24; 14:6; Acts 4:12). In first-commandment terms, this means that to worship a non-Trinitarian God is not to worship the true God. Contemporary Judaism, therefore, also worships a god other than the God of Scripture, though Jews living before Jesus' resurrection worshiped according to a true knowledge of God's revelation (John 4:22).

But there are issues of less consequence than that of the Trinity, such as the differences between Arminians and Calvinists, or supralapsarians and infralapsarians. In these cases, I think we should give one another the benefit of the doubt, recognizing our own theological fallibility. In between the less and the more serious differences are the differences between orthodox theology and such views as open theism and mother-goddess feminism. Here too I tend toward judgments of charity, while condemning these errors in strong terms.

It is not always easy to say, based only on a person's theology, whether he worships the true God or some other god. But the first commandment is relevant to our theological reflection in other ways as well. It is remarkable that theological errors, including errors about God's being and actions, are often reflexes of movements in the secular culture. For example, the concept of libertarian free will has dominated philosophy (both process and analytic schools of thought) in the late twentieth century. Process theology and open theism followed in the wake of that movement. Secular feminism made great gains in the general culture in the 1960s and 1970s. Following that, theologians tried to show that they could be feminists too. Today there is a trend in theology to say that the Scripture blesses homosexual relationships, following the secular movement toward homosexual rights. To a distressing extent, new theological movements follow fashionable secular trends. When a position becomes popular in secular politics and culture, it seems quite certain that some theologians will discover that position in the Bible and church tradition.

At this point, the first commandment becomes especially relevant. One must ask, Who or what are we worshiping: the God of Scripture or the fashionable trends of secular culture? In my judgment, for example, the Bible clearly declares homosexual activity to be sinful.[6] Others have argued differently, and I try to take those arguments seriously. But I cannot help but feel that some are resolving these issues, not on the basis of honest exegesis, but rather because a pro-homosexual position is required in some circles for academic, political, and cultural respectability. It seems almost too coincidental that theologians began to question the traditional exegesis of these passages in the wake of the secular gay rights movement. I do agree that secular ideas may legitimately move Christians to reconsider their exegetical findings. But in my judgment the pro-homosexual exegesis of these passages is so unpersuasive that it is hard to take as anything other than a cultural reflex.

In many ways, Christians have an easy time in the modern West. For the most part, we aren't asked to die or to suffer physically for our faith. But God does call us, on occasion, to hold unpopular beliefs. Can we not do even this much for Jesus? And if not, can we really claim to love God with all our heart? At this point, our theology becomes a first commandment issue.[7] It is a question of whether we value cultural trends more highly than God.

The spirit of the time challenges our first-commandment observance in other theological areas as well. Jochem Douma brings up the issue of our submission to God in suffering.[8] Much popular theology, aided and abetted by process theology and open theism, says that God is not the cause of suffering.[9] But Scripture teaches otherwise (see Deut. 8:5; the book of Job; Heb. 12:6; James 1:2–4; Rev. 3:19).[10] It is difficult to reconcile God's sovereignty over suffering with his holiness and hatred of evil. But here, as in other areas, we must confess the truth, even when it is unpopular and difficult to defend. And so our patience in suffering becomes a first-commandment issue.

Even more obviously contrary to the first commandment is religious pluralism, the view that all the world's religions (and nonreligions!) are pathways to the true God. On this view, Brahma and Allah are among the "many names" of the true God.[11] But the first commandment requires exclusive allegiance and love. The only true God, as we have seen, is the Father of our Lord Jesus Christ. The only way to the Father is through him (John 1:18; 14:6; Acts 4:12).

---

6. See the discussion below under the seventh commandment.

7. This is another application of the central principle of DKG, that the epistemological is ethical.

8. J. Douma, The Ten Commandments (Phillipsburg, NJ: P&R Publishing, 1996), 27–29. He cites Answer 94 of the Heidelberg Catechism's exposition of the first commandment.

9. E.g., Harold S. Kushner, When Bad Things Happen to Good People (New York: Schocken Books, 1981).

10. See DG, chapter 9.

11. John Hick, God Has Many Names (Philadelphia: Westminster Press, 1982).

So the Christian faith is of necessity evangelistic. The Bible defines evangelism (broadly—including nurture) as the fundamental task of the church (Matt. 28:18–20). Evangelism is not an expression of hatred to non-Christians, as many have charged. It expresses the love of Christ, warning people of danger and offering them liberation from sin.

Related to the error of pluralism is the error of supposing that God will never judge or condemn any of his creatures. But such a sentimentalist concept of God, though popular today, is not true to Scripture. Again, the first commandment calls Christians to stand against such distortions and for the one true God alone.

THE OCCULT

Earlier, I cited Deuteronomy 18:9–14, which reads:

> When you come into the land that the LORD your God is giving you, you shall not learn to follow the abominable practices of those nations. There shall not be found among you anyone who burns his son or his daughter as an offering, anyone who practices divination or tells fortunes or interprets omens, or a sorcerer or a charmer or a medium or a wizard or a necromancer, for whoever does these things is an abomination to the LORD. And because of these abominations the LORD your God is driving them out before you. You shall be blameless before the LORD your God, for these nations, which you are about to dispossess, listen to fortune-tellers and to diviners. But as for you, the LORD your God has not allowed you to do this.

It is not easy to determine the precise meanings of the Hebrew words here translated "sorcerer," "charmer," "wizard," and so on. Nevertheless, the basic meaning is clear: believers are not to seek supernatural help from anybody but the one true God. Specifically, they are not to seek from wizards and fortune-tellers information about the future.

Although the Canaanite religions are no longer with us, diviners abound in every city today. People seek guidance from astrologers, fortune-tellers, psychic mediums, Ouija boards, those who claim to contact the dead, and so on. Even professing Christians sometimes dabble in such superstitions, as a kind of supplement to an inadequate relationship with God or out of dissatisfaction with the simplicity of the gospel.

The above passage from Deuteronomy, along with others, connects these occult practices with false worship, thus condemning them under the first commandment. The list begins with human sacrifice, an abomination under the law of God (Lev. 18:21; 20:2–5), but a common way of appeasing false deities in the ancient world. But many of the practices later in this list focus on something less obviously cultic: wrong attempts to gain knowledge, especially knowledge of the future. God not only forbids us to worship false gods, but also forbids us to "listen" to their prophets (cf. Lev. 19:31; 20:6, 27).

So the passage in Deuteronomy goes on to speak of how God will raise up true prophets for the people of Israel: "The LORD your God will raise up for you a prophet like me from among you, from your brothers—it is to him you shall listen" (18:15). The word translated "listen" in this context does not mean merely to hear what someone has to say. Like the older English term "hearken," it connotes hearing with a disposition to believe or obey. Compare "Hear, O Israel" in Deuteronomy 6:4.

So Deuteronomy 18:9–22 contrasts two alleged sources of supernatural knowledge: one false, one true. It tells us today that we must seek divinely authoritative guidance from Scripture alone (compare the discussion of the sufficiency of Scripture in chapter 11).

The passage does not justify a kind of reverse superstition, in which Christians avoid any contact with the occult or with practitioners of it. Believers are sometimes afraid even to look at horoscopes, for example, for fear that they will somehow be contaminated. But Deuteronomy 18 itself assumes some knowledge of the occult, at least on Moses' part. Paul tells us, moreover, that he and the other apostles are "not ignorant of [Satan's] designs" (2 Cor. 2:11). One must know something about the claims of the wicked, even in order to reject those claims and to expose them to the Christian public for what they are. Of course, young and immature Christians should not immerse themselves in occult literature and movements. But some spiritually mature people in the church should be aware of what the occultists are saying and doing, so that they can give biblical guidance to fellow believers.

Similarly, I do not think we should, as a general rule, forbid believers to watch films or read novels about ghosts, wizards, and the like, even when those media treat the occult favorably. To view such a film, for example, is not necessarily to "hearken" to a false revelation. Again, for immature Christians, there is some danger of being sucked into a false worldview from overexposure or uncritical exposure to such media. But those with a good grounding in the Word of God should not be fearful. In chapter 23, I argued that the main rule for New Testament Christians is not physical separation from evil, but conquest of it.

People often ask whether Christians should celebrate Halloween. I myself prefer to celebrate Reformation Day at that time of year. But the word *Halloween* is a form of "All Hallows Eve," the evening that precedes All Saints Day in the church calendar. In its missionary labors in Europe, the church substituted its own holiday for some pagan observances. In the modern West, Halloween is essentially a mockery of ancient paganism. It is not paganism, but a celebration of the gospel's victory over paganism. I see no spiritual danger in observing that celebration, as long as we, and our children, understand the difference between mocking paganism and endorsing it.[12]

Christians should understand that false gods and demons have no power over the Christian. We may resist even Satan and he will flee (James 4:7; cf. 1 Cor. 8:4).

Scripture does not claim that false religions contain no truth at all. Practitioners of false religions and the occult know God in the same paradoxical way that all unbelievers do (Rom. 1:18–32), and they gain from God's general revelation much knowledge of the created world. So non-Christian religions do contain some ethical maxims that are true (chapter 5). And occasionally some useful knowledge can be found even in the context of false worship: an herb used in witch medicine, for example, may prove effective in treating illness. Yoga, removed from its religious context, may contain useful techniques for relaxation. Acupuncture and martial arts are often beneficial, though their origin is deeply religious and pagan.

What we must deny is that false religions are a source of supernatural guidance, particularly knowledge of the future. In chapter 11, I indicated that the sufficiency of Scripture does not mean that Scripture contains all the truth that we need for human life, but only that it contains all the divine words that we need. That is, Scripture is our only supernatural source of knowledge. Knowledge of other sorts is also necessary to us, and it is available through general revelation and existential revelation—through the world, our senses, our reason, and the help of other people. We should test such subordinate sources of knowledge by the Bible, but we should not reject them in general. The knowledge of non-Christians from common grace is one such subordinate source. We should not "hearken" to it, as an authoritative supernatural message, but we should use it for what it is worth.

Notice here the principle I mentioned in chapter 1: our goal in ethics is not to be as liberal as possible (i.e., to accept false religions as alternative sources of divine truth), or as conservative as possible (i.e., to avoid all contact with anything linked to false worship), but to be as

---

12. I agree with James B. Jordan, "Concerning Halloween," *Open Book*, no. 28 (August 1996), available at http://www.biblicalhorizons.com/ob/ob028.htm.

biblical as possible (i.e., not to worship false gods or to accept anything but Scripture as supernatural revelation).

SECRET SOCIETIES

Christians have long discussed secret societies, such as the Freemasons, the Odd Fellows, and the Rosicrucians, in connection with the first commandment. Many have argued that these associations are religious in character and that their religion is non-Christian. Yet many people have been members both of churches and of secret societies.

A number of churches and denominations have made official statements to the effect that Masonic Lodge membership is incompatible with the Christian faith.[13] After a thorough study of the literature of Freemasonry, Steven Tsoukalas concludes,

> Freemasonry is much more than a fraternal order. It is a religion—one that is diametrically opposed to Christianity. Several reasons have been offered here to demonstrate that Freemasonry is a religion. First, it possesses a dogma concerning God. The Masonic God, T.G.A.O.T.U.,[14] subsumes the various deities of its initiates. He is addressed, prayed to, and relied upon. Second, the Lodge possesses a dogma about the immortality of the soul and life after death. It defines the soul, and it promises in its burial and memorial services that the soul of a departed brother is in the presence of God, regardless of whether he believed in Buddha, Krishna, Jesus, Brahman, Allah, or Confucius. Third, its symbolism of the Apron [and other symbols] has theological—specifically salvific—overtones. Though a Mason is free to believe in Jesus Christ as the foundation of this symbolic teaching, Christ is viewed as only one of many saviors or exemplars of the principle of good that initiates may choose. Fourth, the Scottish Rite homogenizes Christianity, Islam, Qabbalah, Hinduism, Zoroastrianism, and other religions into a religious ritualistic system that "gleans the truths" from all

13. See, e.g., the written statements of the Orthodox Presbyterian Church (*Christ or the Lodge*, available at http://opc.org/GA/masonry.html), and the Presbyterian Church in America ("The Report of the Ad Interim Committee to Study Freemasonry," report to the 15th General Assembly [1987], available at http://www.pcanet.org/history/pca/2-300.pdf). The Roman Catholic Church, the Lutheran Church—Missouri Synod, the Christian Reformed Church, and the Reformed Presbyterian Church of North America have also stated that Freemasonry is incompatible with Christianity.

14. I.e., the great architect of the universe.

of these traditions, thereby restoring the "great primitive religion" originally given to all humanity. For these reasons and others, Freemasonry must be considered a religion. For these reasons also, I cannot see how a man can be a Christian and an *informed* Mason at the same time.[15]

Tsoukalas and others mention other criticisms of Freemasonry: (1) Initiation requires an oath to keep the secrets of the Lodge. But "the Christian, bound as he is to maintain justice and equity before God and man to the best of his powers, has no right to pledge himself in advance to keep secret something the bearing of which on questions of justice and morals he cannot know."[16] Further, some of these secrets bear upon the salvation of human beings. In such areas, secrecy is inappropriate; everybody should know the way of salvation. (2) The way of salvation in Masonry is essentially works-righteousness. (3) Masonic rituals use Scripture with a distorted meaning. In Psalm 118:22, for example, "The stone that the builders rejected" represents the Lodge, not Christ, in Masonic theology.

I must agree with these arguments and conclude that Lodge membership is contrary to the first commandment. The same must be said of any other society that requires adherence to a religion other than the exclusive worship of the Lord.

Christians who belong to such organizations sometimes defend them by observing that they carry on philanthropic activities and that they discourage certain types of sin among their members. But the same can be said of Islam or Buddhism or any number of other false religions. Non-Christian religions, like non-Christian individuals, are able by God's common grace to perform acts of civic righteousness, acts that benefit society.[17] But they do not please God, nor should they be supported by God's people.

FALSE RELIGION IN THE CHURCH[18]

Scripture teaches, and history confirms, that even in the church there can be false religion. We recall that God's Old Testament people fell into

---

15. Steven Tsoukalas, *Masonic Rites and Wrongs* (Phillipsburg, NJ: P&R Publishing, 1997), 225.

16. "Christ or the Lodge."

17. Cf. the section on "Necessary and Sufficient Criteria of Good Works" in chapter 3.

18. Much of this section paraphrases and condenses material from my book *Evangelical Reunion: Denominations and the Body of Christ* (Grand Rapids: Baker, 1991), now available at www.thirdmill.org.

the worship of false gods, violating their covenant with the Lord. But the same unfaithfulness has been present in the New Testament church. Peter says, "But false prophets also arose among the people, just as there will be false teachers among you, who will secretly bring in destructive heresies, even denying the Master who bought them, bringing upon themselves swift destruction" (2 Peter 2:1).

Peter continues through the chapter with a devastating exposé of these teachers, describing their theology, especially their morals, and the divine judgment awaiting them. Jesus similarly attacked the scribes and Pharisees (Matt. 23 and elsewhere), and Paul speaks of immoral church leaders who are "lovers of pleasure rather than lovers of God, having the appearance of godliness, but denying its power" (2 Tim. 3:4–5).[19] He adds, "Avoid such people" (v. 5; cf. Phil. 3:17–19; 2 Thess. 2:3–12; 1 Tim. 4:1–5). In Galatians 1, Paul says that Judaizing teachers are leading Christians away from the authentic gospel of Christ. Against them he pronounces an anathema: "But even if we or an angel from heaven should preach to you a gospel contrary to the one we preached to you, let him be accursed. As we have said before, so now I say again: If anyone is preaching to you a gospel contrary to the one you received, let him be accursed" (Gal. 1:8–9). The heresies mentioned in such passages are not minor errors, but false teachings that contradict the gospel itself. They amount to another religion and so violate the first commandment.

In our own time, we are familiar with unbelief in the church. J. Gresham Machen's masterful Christianity and Liberalism demonstrates that liberal or modernist theology is not Christianity at all, but a different religion, another gospel.[20] Carefully, Machen discusses liberal views of doctrine, God, man, the Bible, Christ, salvation, and the church, and finds that at each of those points there is, not only a discrepancy, but an antithesis between liberalism and authentic biblical teaching. But even in Machen's time, liberalism had come to dominate major denominations, including their colleges, seminaries, mission agencies, and publication boards. Since Machen's time, liberalism has changed its terminology, but not its substance. Van Til's The New Modernism[21] and Christianity and Barthianism[22] make a similar case against neoorthodoxy.

19. It is important to notice here, because the apostles make so much of it, the correlation between heresy and immorality. The kind of false teaching condemned here is not minor theological mistakes made by otherwise godly people. Rather, it is rejection of the biblical faith, leading to an obvious reversion to unregenerate habits. It would be even more in accord with the apostles' emphasis to put it this way: the false theology of these teachers is an aspect of their ungodly life. Again, we see how our use of the intellect is part of our ethical life.

20. New York: Macmillan, 1923.

21. Philadelphia: Presbyterian and Reformed, 1946.

22. Philadelphia: Presbyterian and Reformed, 1962.

What should we do about this serious matter? Machen, in 1936, left the Presbyterian Church, USA. The denomination suspended him from the ministry for refusing to resign from a mission board that was independent of the denominational board. Machen saw this as a triumph of unbelief in the denomination. He, and others who left with him, started a new denomination, the Presbyterian Church of America, later renamed the Orthodox Presbyterian Church. Other denominations have been formed for similar reasons.

Remarkably, Scripture itself never says that believers should leave a church organization and form a new one because of false teaching. Israel in the Old Testament was often guilty of idolatry. Revivals of true worship occurred from time to time, but the nation, including the religious establishment, relapsed. After the exile, the scribes and Pharisees represented movements toward religious purity, but Jesus said they "shut the kingdom of heaven in people's faces" (Matt. 23:13) and made each proselyte "twice as much a child of hell as yourselves" (v. 15). They were "full of hypocrisy and lawlessness" (v. 28). Jesus says that God will judge these religious leaders (vv. 32–36), a threat fulfilled in the destruction of the temple in AD 70.

But nowhere in the Old Testament, nor in Jesus' teaching, does God command believers to abandon Israel and to form a new nation, church, or denomination. God himself brings a separation between the followers of Christ and Judaism when the synagogues expel Christians from their fellowship, and when the temple is destroyed. But there is no exhortation in the New Testament for Jewish Christians voluntarily to leave the synagogues. Rather, it is assumed that believers, like the apostles, will bear witness within the synagogues to God's grace in Christ, as long as they are able to do so. This was the practice of the apostle Paul, who preached the gospel in the synagogues wherever he traveled.

As we have seen, there is doctrinal and practical corruption in the New Testament church as well. But again, the apostles do not call on believers to leave their churches and form new ones because of corruption. Rather, the churches themselves are to take action against it (as in 1 Cor. 5). Even the church at Laodicea, which Jesus threatens to spit out of his mouth (Rev. 3:16), is still a church (v. 14), and Jesus does not counsel true believers to leave it. Rather, he tells the whole church to repent.

The apostolic church of the New Testament is not a voluntary association. Every believer is joined to it in the body of Christ. That church is both organism and organization: it is a body, held together by the Spirit, and it is an organization, ruled by apostles, prophets, elders, and deacons. Where disputes exist, there is an orderly pattern for resolving them (Matt. 18:15–20), including provision for excommunication (v. 17; 1 Cor. 5) in extreme cases. Rightly appointed leaders are to be obeyed (Heb. 13:17). In the first century, nobody had the right to leave the apostolic church and start a new denomination.

But schisms did later take place. Churches separate from the original church organization were founded by the heretic Marcion in the second century and by the more orthodox figures Novatian (third century) and Donatus (fourth century), who thought the existing church was guilty of intolerable compromise. The Egyptian and Syrian churches broke fellowship with the rest of the church in the wake of the Council of Chalcedon (451), and the Eastern and Western churches separated in 1054. The excommunication of Martin Luther in 1521 began a proliferation of divisions: Protestant from Catholic, Protestant from Protestant, sectarian from sectarian, churches of one nation from those of another, leading to the thousands of denominations existing today. Some of the Reformers, such as Bucer, Melancthon, Oecolampadius, and Calvin, sought unity among the Reformation churches, but without success. Afterward, it became commonplace for churches to divide over doctrinal and practical issues. And it was assumed that churches of different ethnic background would remain distinct, even when they agreed on matters of doctrine and practice. In the United States, some Reformed denominations are of Dutch background, others of Scottish, and it is inconceivable to many that these churches could ever be united.

In my view, the breakdown of the one, true church of the apostolic period into a plethora of denominations today has been a great tragedy. The vast number of denominations testifies to the vast extent of sin in the church. For when people leave one denomination to start another, sin is always involved, either in those who leave or in those who force them to leave, or (more likely) on both sides.

No denomination is a church in the New Testament sense. In the New Testament, the word *church* refers to the universal body of believers (as in Matt. 16:18), to citywide organizations of churches (such as the churches at Philippi, Rome, Jerusalem, Antioch, and Corinth), and to house churches (Rom. 16:5; 1 Cor. 16:19; Col. 4:15). The term never refers to anything like a denomination, that is, to a group of churches separate from others in government, doctrine, practice, and/or ethnicity.

The one, true church still exists, nevertheless. There is still one head of the universal church, Jesus Christ, and the apostles still rule the church through their inspired writings. Local congregations that are subject to Christ and the apostles may legitimately continue to claim the title of *church*. So the true church continues to function biblically at the universal level and the local level. But the middle levels have been disrupted by the sin of schism.

Christians have tried to replace these middle-level structures with denominations. Denominations are not the church, but they try to function as churches as much as possible. Denominations are a poor substitute for the middle-level structures of the New Testament church, but for the present they are the only structures we have. So we should thank God for these weak instruments and try to make the best of them.[23]

But this creates problems, for example, in church discipline. The church at Antioch in the New Testament period could deal with sin and controversy by bringing the leaders of all the local churches together.[24] But in modern cities, one cannot gather together representatives of all the Christian churches for official business. If there is a problem in an Episcopal church, only Episcopalians will be called to deal with it. If an offender appeals a verdict against him in a Presbyterian church, he can file his appeal only with Presbyterians—indeed, only with Presbyterians of a single denomination. He cannot appeal to the wisdom of Presbyterians outside his denomination, let alone to that of Baptists, Independents, Methodists, and others. Thus, a portion of the church tries to do the work of the whole church, contrary to New Testament ecclesiology. And when a denomination does discipline an offender, it is usually fairly easy for him to leave that denomination and join another.

Denominationalism, therefore, cripples the church in its battle with false religion in its midst. The church cannot speak with one voice against error, as it could in the first century. What, then, should we do, when false religion overtakes the life of a church or denomination?

First, we should continue to follow the directions of Matthew 18:15–20, 1 Corinthians 5, and other passages dealing with church discipline. The offenders should be challenged to repent and, in extreme cases, they need to be excommunicated.[25]

But what if such efforts fail, and a false religion like liberalism becomes dominant in a denomination or church? In the one, true church of the first century, it would have been a sin for believers to leave the church because they judged it to be theologically or morally corrupt. Their only choice, I believe, was to stay indefinitely, praying and working for reformation.

---

23. I am speaking here as a Presbyterian. In other traditions, there are "independent" or "nondenominational" churches. Those churches are, in effect, denominations unto themselves. They should seek connections with other Christian bodies, but, failing that, should try as best they can to replicate in themselves what I have called the middle-level structures of the body of Christ.

24. In my tradition, such gatherings are known as presbyteries.

25. Not every difference of opinion in the church, of course, is a cause for formal discipline. Paul does not recommend discipline for the minority parties discussed in Rom. 14 and 1 Cor. 8–10.

Difficult as this course of action may have been, they could count on Jesus' promise that the church would stand on the rock of the confessing apostle, and "the gates of hell shall not prevail against it" (Matt. 16:18).

But no denomination, in my judgment has the right to claim that promise. Jesus does not promise that the gates of hell will never prevail against the Presbyterian Church in America, or the Baptist General Conference, or the Church of God in Prophecy. Denominations come and go. Denominations that for a time are useful instruments of the kingdom of God do succumb to sin and error. When that happens, we may speak of an "apostate" denomination.[26]

Individual congregations, too, sometimes lose their grip on the gospel, so that they can no longer be considered churches in the New Testament sense. We have seen that the New Testament regards as true churches even bodies with severe problems, such as the church in Laodicea. But Jesus does threaten to spit this congregation out of his mouth if they do not repent (Rev. 3:16), just as he threatens to remove the lampstand of the church of Ephesus (Rev. 2:5).

An apostate church or denomination is an organization currently based on a false religion, though its heritage is Christian. If believers should not be members of religious secret societies, even more should they avoid membership in an apostate body that calls itself a church. Positively, believers should be members of bodies that honor Christ and his Word, so that they can serve God as he intends, and so they can have all the blessings of the means of God's grace. So there are times at which believers are obligated to leave one religious organization and join another.

But how do we determine when a professing church body has become apostate? The Reformers developed three "marks of the true church," namely, the true preaching of the Word, the right administration of the sacraments, and church discipline. These are not explicitly listed anywhere in Scripture as marks of the church, and one may argue that the most fundamental biblical mark, love (John 13:34–35), should be on this list. But certainly, to be called a church, a body must proclaim the gospel truly, observe the sacraments instituted by Christ, and have a system of discipline that is effective enough to guard the preaching and sacraments. Discipline is important so that true preaching and true observing of the sacraments take place regularly and reliably. Whenever any of those marks is lacking, the body is apostate; it should no longer be considered a church.

---

26. I don't speak of an apostate denomination as an "apostate church." Denominations are not churches.

But it is not always easy to apply these marks. The WCF recognizes that purity in these matters is a matter of degree (25.4). With regard to preaching: what errors are serious enough to warrant the conclusion that the church's preaching is not sound? If Pastor Smith is amillennial and I am postmillennial, should I regard his preaching as unsound and his church as apostate? I should think not. What makes preaching apostate, surely, are errors that pertain to the essential nature of the church's proclamation, the gospel of Christ. The "destructive heresies" mentioned in 2 Peter 2:1 include "denying the Master who bought them." Must a Calvinist, then, regard Arminian preaching as apostate because it calls people to accept Christ by their libertarian free will?

So far as I know, nobody has ever made a serious theological study of the level of error that renders a church apostate or, to put it differently, the kinds of theological differences that are tolerable or intolerable within a church body. I commend that study to theologians younger and more astute than I. I see this as a daunting task. Perhaps it is not possible to determine such levels objectively.

Alternatively, we may need to resolve such questions by "seeing as" (chapter 20): if Pastor Jones preaches what I think is an error, I need to ask God to show me whether this error is a "destructive heresy" (2 Peter 2:1), a "quarrel over opinions" (Rom. 14:1), a "vain discussion" (1 Tim. 1:6), or, perhaps, not an error at all. And of course I need to correct my own perceptions by the perceptions of others in the body and, if necessary, by corporate church discipline. In any case, it is not always easy to make decisions concerning the soundness of preaching and teaching, the first mark of the church.

The same is true of the second mark. Should Presbyterians and Baptists regard each other as apostate because they disagree about baptizing infants? Should the differences between Reformed and Lutherans about the Lord's Supper necessitate a breaking of fellowship? Generally, Reformed churches have been willing to recognize Bible-believing Baptist and Lutheran churches as true churches, although they have not been willing to form unions with such churches.[27] Reformed churches have not always recognized the Roman Catholic Church as a true church, but they have generally accepted Roman Catholic baptism as valid.[28] Here, as with

27. In my judgment, this is not a coherent position. All true churches ought to be one. Bodies that recognize one another as true churches should seek to restore the oneness of the New Testament church. I grant, of course, that such a process of reunion may take much time and discussion.

28. Respected Princeton theologian Charles Hodge rejected the rebaptism of Roman Catholics in the section on "Romish Baptism" (pp. 444–71) in "The General

the first mark, we have not reached a consensus. There is no theological treatment of these matters generally recognized as cogent.

The third mark, church discipline, can be judged by its ability to maintain the first two. But then the ambiguities of the first two marks attach to the third as well. An additional ambiguity is this: Let's say that a local church maintains well the three marks of the church, but it belongs to an apostate denomination. May a Christian belong to that congregation? One could argue that sound discipline at the local level could at some later time be aborted at the denominational level, so as to invalidate the discipline of the local church which is otherwise sound.

In my view, the local church has erred by continuing to belong to such a denomination. And if its discipline is interlocked with that of the denomination, that is a potential problem for its own discipline. But unless that potential problem has become actual, I would not regard the error of its denominational membership as one that renders the local church itself apostate. I believe a Christian could be a member of that local church, while urging it toward a more consistently biblical denominational alignment.

SECULARISM

Secularism, with its variant, secular humanism, is today the most powerful rival of the Christian religion. It holds that there is no God and that human beings live best when they do not call on supernatural help. It claims, therefore, to be nonreligious. However, secularism is a religion, according to Clouser's definition (see chapter 5), for it believes in something "not dependent on anything else," namely, the natural world itself, together with human thought or conscience. And certainly, if belief in God is a religious position, then denial of God is as well. Both views require faith, and both choose to reason according to the presuppositions of that faith. Agnosticism is not a coherent compromise. Agnostics choose to live, and therefore to think, as unbelievers, though in some cases they allow that the existence of God is possible.

Assembly," *Biblical Repertory and Princeton Review* 17 (1845): 428–71, available as "Do Roman Catholic Clergy Count as Ministers of the Gospel?" at http://www.hornes.org/theologia/content/charles_hodge/do_rc_clergy_count_as_gospel_ministers.htm. Hodge answered affirmatively the question, "Is the Church of Rome a Part of the Visible Church?" in *Biblical Repertory and Princeton Review* 18 (April 1846): 320–44, available at http://www.hornes.org/theologia/content/charles_hodge/is_the_church_of_rome_a_part_of_the_visible_church.htm.

So agnosticism is a form of atheism, and atheists and agnostics may both be considered secularists.[29]

But although secularism is a religion, secularists typically present themselves as nonreligious. On their view, the secularist makes his decisions by reason alone, while religious persons make theirs by faith, or by faith-informed reason. Therefore, they would say, religious views are not relevant to rational discussions, especially in science, ethics, or politics. This secular point of view has come to dominate the thinking of the opinion-forming institutions in the West, particularly major universities, the mass media, and many areas of government, especially bureaucracies and the courts. To them, religious views do not deserve a respectful hearing. Secularists have gained the power to forbid religious expression in public schools and other government contexts.[30] They have demanded the right not to be offended by public expressions of views that challenge secularism.

The privileged position of secularism is a manifest injustice. In a free society, all points of view should contend in the marketplace of ideas. That some ideas come out of a theistic worldview should not be a disadvantage, unless there are cogent reasons for thinking that theism is absurd. But there are no such reasons, and indeed it is secularism that faces insuperable objections. As I argued in chapters 4–8, ethics is meaningless apart from the presupposition of an absolute, personal God. And, as I argued in *The Doctrine of the Knowledge of God* and *Apologetics to the Glory of God*, knowledge is impossible apart from ethics. The most that secularism can justly demand is a place at the table to argue its case. It has no standing to deny such a place to Christian theism. It is ridiculous to claim, for example, that the denial of intelligent design in biology is scientific, while the affirmation of it is not scientific.

In any case, secularism has come to dominate many aspects of Western society, and that dominance provides the greatest challenge to Christians who seek to live by the first commandment. These challenges occur in

---

29. I summarize here a point from AGG, 92–93, 204–6.

30. Their pretext in the United States has been the separation of church and state. But the U.S. Constitution does not prohibit religious expression in government. It requires only, in the First Amendment, that Congress shall not create a national established church. When the Constitution was passed, there were established churches in various colonies. They did not want their established churches threatened by a national established church. The consensus was that state-level establishments could continue, but that there should be no nationally established church. So the First Amendment was not intended to prohibit even government-established churches at the state level, let alone the expression of religious views in government contexts, such as displays of the Ten Commandments in courts. Court decisions in recent decades have, to be sure, taken a much more radical view, but we should pray that the courts will return to the original intent of the Constitution.

many areas. In business, for example, an employee can sometimes lose his job for trying to maintain Christian standards, such as by telling the truth to customers. In that case, he must decide what he values most, his job or the Lord God.

In some countries, Christians have had a problem of conscience in joining secular labor unions. Such unions have sometimes demanded of workers an affirmation of the Marxist ideology of class warfare. So in the Netherlands and Canada, believers have formed Christian labor unions.

I also have difficulties with the practice of Christian theological seminaries (including my own) seeking accreditation from secular agencies. How can a secular organization be qualified to judge the competence of a school for Christian ministry? In my judgment, the only organization qualified to judge the performance of a seminary is the church. It is, I think, legitimate for seminaries to seek outside help to warrant their financial accountability,[31] and secular affirmations of the academic qualifications of professors is a valuable thing.[32] But I bristle at the huge efforts required of a seminary to gain secular approval, and the changes that seminaries sometimes make in their programs to get that approval. Seeking such accreditation is not sinful in itself, but it certainly poses challenges to schools that seek to keep the first commandment.

In my opinion, the biggest challenge to modern Christians, in the area of the first commandment, is that of secular schools, to which I will devote the rest of this chapter. This discussion will serve as a case study, from which I shall draw principles that may apply to other areas in which the Christian must deal with secular institutions.

Scripture makes it clear that education, like every other area of human life, must be done to the glory of God (1 Cor. 10:31) and in the name of Christ (Col. 3:17). Therefore, it must be done in accordance with the Word of God, the Scriptures (2 Tim. 3:16–17). Scripture not only is a standard for education, but pervades the content of a godly education. Deuteronomy 6:6–9 reads:

> These words that I command you today shall be on your heart. You shall teach them diligently to your children, and shall talk of them when you sit in your house, and when you walk by the way, and when you lie down, and when you rise. You shall bind them as a sign on your hand, and they shall be as frontlets between your eyes. You shall write them on the doorposts of your house and on your gates.

31. There are, however, nonsecular agencies that provide such help.
32. In most cases, no more warrant is required than a degree from an accredited institution.

"God-centered" is really too weak a term to describe this kind of education. "God-saturated" is more like it. Children are to grow up in an environment where they cannot avoid the Word of God; it is always there, searching them, admonishing them, instructing them in the truth.

It follows that everything the child learns about the world should be related to God's Word. And, in a way, Scripture speaks about *everything*. It doesn't give us detailed instruction about plumbing, or British history, or auto repair, but it does teach us how to relate all these things to God, how to study them, and how to implement our studies in practical life, so that God is pleased. We cannot, for example, study history while ignoring divine providence, let alone (as in many secular curricula) ignoring the substantial role of religion in forming the culture and politics of nations. We cannot teach science without emphasizing that this world is created and directed by God. It is God's providence that makes the world an orderly place that we can understand and dominate (Gen. 1:28–30). So, historically, Christian theism has given great encouragement to the development of science, and children need to be taught about that.[33] We cannot teach modern music and film without teaching children how to evaluate them from God's perspective.

God has placed children in important relationships within the family, the church, and the state. God intends for adults to take responsibility for the education of their children. Here, obviously, the family plays the crucial role. Note that the passage in Deuteronomy above tells us to "teach them diligently to *your children*," an expression which gives special responsibility to parents. In the book of Proverbs, also, instruction in God's wisdom comes from parents: "Hear, my son, your father's instruction, and forsake not your mother's teaching" (Prov. 1:8; cf. 2:1; 3:1; 4:1; 5:1; 6:1; 7:1; 19:27; 23:19, 22, 26–28).

It would certainly be wrong, however, to think that Scripture *restricts* education to the family. I know of no Scripture text or principle that forbids parents to delegate some of the education of their children to others. Certainly in Bible times apprenticeship was common, and God's Word says nothing against it. And obviously it is not wrong for parents to ask their children to read books written by others, allowing the author of the book to assist them in their work of education. Nor is it wrong for parents to send their children to piano teachers or carpenters for tutoring in specialized areas—of course, under proper parental supervision. The passage in

33. See, e.g., R. Hooykaas, *Religion and the Rise of Modern Science* (Grand Rapids: Eerdmans, 1972).

Deuteronomy is not interested in the fine points of how the education is carried out. It certainly cannot be pressed to imply that every bit of teaching must be done by the parent. It simply places the overall responsibility for education upon the parent.

In the discussion of schools, it is important to consider the distinct roles of family, church, and state in the education of children. First, the state. Does it have any business in the education of children? To answer this question, we must ask what the state is in scriptural terms. In my analysis (and I realize this is controversial), Scripture does not describe the divine appointment of the state as an institution separate from the family and the church.[34] Rather, the state emerges naturally from the family when the family becomes too large to be governed patriarchally.

So the state is family government, the government of extended families. On a broader level, the states of the world represent the government of the family of the human race, the family of Adam. The church, too, is an extended family. It is the community formed by the redeemed family of God; it is our family in Jesus. The old family, the family of Adam, fell into sin, so God established on earth a new family in his Son. Jesus died on the cross for his "brothers" (Heb. 2:11–12), the "children" of God (vv. 13–14). So we become brothers and sisters of one another through Christ. Paradoxically, Christians are members of both families.

Now there is no question but that the church has an important role in the education of our children. The church has a teaching and discipling ministry (Matt. 28:19; Acts 5:42; 1 Cor. 12:28–29; 14:19; Eph. 4:11; Col. 1:28; 3:16; 1 Tim. 4:11; 6:2; 2 Tim. 2:2; Titus 2:3–4; Heb. 5:12; James 3:1) and that is certainly not restricted to the teaching of adults. God charges the church to teach the Scriptures to everyone. Some portions of Scripture are addressed specifically to children (as Eph. 6:1–3), and all of it is relevant to them. The church should support the parents (and vice versa) in teaching the Word of God to children, as their age and level of understanding permits. Church and family should not compete with one another, but should work together. That is implicit in the context of Deuteronomy 6:6–9, for that passage is part of the covenant between God and the whole nation of Israel. The whole nation, as the people of God, was to maintain this commitment to teach the children whom God had given them. The commandment is given to families, but the whole nation has an interest in bringing this about.

---

34. For a more detailed discussion, see my article, "Toward a Theology of the State," *Westminster Theological Journal* 51 (1989): 199–226. I shall summarize this article later in this volume under the fifth commandment.

Does the state have any role in education? As we have seen, family and state are not radically separate in Scripture. If the state is an extended family, then it does have an interest in the education of children. At least, the state should carry out its duties in a way that helps, rather than hinders, the people in carrying out their divine obligations. And certainly the state has educational functions, in the training of soldiers, in the preparation of people for governmental functions, in teaching people their civic responsibilities.

However, Christians should be very critical of the role of the state in educating children. Although nothing in Scripture prohibits a role for the state in the teaching of children, there are, nevertheless, obvious disadvantages in the concept of a state school:

1. The state, as state, is not particularly competent to educate children. The work of the state, in Scripture and in contemporary society, is focused on the maintenance of law and order. Government bears the sword against wrongdoers and against aggression from outside the nation (Rom. 13:1–7). Government is in the business of using force to make people do what is right. But although corporal punishment may sometimes be necessary in education, the primary tool of education is not compulsion, but instruction. There is no reason, therefore, to assume that government schools will be competent, or more competent than private schools or home schools. As a matter of fact, most observers think that some public schools are excellent, but that others are abysmal.

2. The state governs the family of Adam, which has fallen into sin. Although there have been godly rulers in history, they have been the exception rather than the rule, and even the godliest rulers have usually been surrounded by other officials who have not shared their love of God. So the state has typically, from Bible times to the present, reinforced the worst trends in society, which is another reason to question its role in the education of children.

3. In the United States and many other countries, the state is prohibited from encouraging any religion. Arguably this was not the original intent of those who wrote the U.S. Constitution, but the "wall of separation" between the state and religion has been the consistent view of the courts in recent times. We should, I believe, seek to change this by legal means. But, humanly speaking, we are not likely to succeed in the near future. Therefore, no state school can legally provide the kind of education described in Deuteronomy 6:6–9.

4. Indeed, state schools regularly *oppose* the Christian view of the world and human life. For it is impossible to be neutral between Christ and

unbelief (Matt. 6:24; 12:30). As the state schools try to exclude "religious" views, they end up by default teaching secular humanism. Secular humanism is itself a religion in the sense that it demands total allegiance and presents a distinct set of standards for all of human life, but standards contrary to Scripture. It teaches that the human mind is the ultimate standard of truth and right. At the same time, it teaches (inconsistently) that there are no ultimate standards. So secular humanism is both irrationalist and rationalist, relativistic and tyrannical. There are no absolute truths, but secular humanism is the absolute truth.

5. The irrationalist side of secular humanism is detrimental to education as such. If there is no absolute truth, then why should students even bother with learning? If there are no absolute standards of right and wrong, how can the schools establish codes of behavior and tests of academic performance? Confusion about the goals of education is obvious in the various kinds of "new new math," "social promotion," and in general the substitution of self-esteem for academic standards.

6. The rationalist side of secular humanism is no better. The state schools frequently teach positions that are contrary to God's Word on many particular matters. They regularly teach that naturalistic evolution is a fact, that biblical sexual standards are outmoded, that Christianity has played a negligible role in world history, that all cultures are equally good, that people are naturally good, that socialism is the best form of government, that abortion is a woman's right, and that "safe sex" is the best way to prevent unwanted pregnancies and sexually transmitted diseases. In short, state schools teach that one may ignore God in every area of life without consequences. And the recent tendency is for school advocates of "political correctness" to stifle any dissent against radical feminism and egalitarianism. The result is the substitution of brainwashing for education.

7. In schools, peer relationships are often as important as the content of the curriculum. Therefore, it is important that teachers exercise godly discipline over their students and seek to train them in godly character. State schools are unable to do this, because of their commitment to secular humanism. Therefore, Christian students attending state schools are often exposed to the worst values and behavior among their peers. And typically they face temptations to explore drugs, illicit sex, gang violence, and so forth. Further, secular humanism encourages the autonomy of children from the authority of parents and teachers. Children typically adopt the values of their peers, rather than those of their teachers (let alone parents).

8. State school teachers and administrators often see it as their mission to rescue students from the antiquated views of their parents and

churches. Typically they resent attempts by parents to influence their teaching. Indeed, for example, by providing condoms and abortions without notifying parents, they place themselves above the parents and even drive wedges between parents and children.

9. Since state schools are usually run by people who have no sympathy for Christians or for others who dissent from the secular humanist consensus, they seek in various ways to oppose and even intimidate Christian and home schools, and to encourage Christians to enter the state school system, so that the children of Christians can to some extent be brought under the influence of the state system. Once Christian families are committed to the state system, the system seeks to increase its influence on them.

These arguments are pretty formidable, and every Christian should take them seriously before deciding to send children to state schools. Nevertheless, I think these arguments are not strong enough to prevent us from ever making use of state educational facilities. I will make that case below.

A Christian education should prepare children to live in the unbelieving world, not only in the Christian subculture. Jesus told his disciples to "go therefore and make disciples of all nations" (Matt. 28:19). The Old Testament also had a missionary aspect, since God intended to bless all nations through Abraham's seed. But, for the most part in the Old Testament (Jonah's mission being one exception), the emphasis was on Israel remaining separate from foreign nations, which would defile them and lead them astray to worship other gods. Not until Jesus sent the Holy Spirit with power did the worldwide missionary movement begin in earnest. In Acts 2, the Spirit came on the church, and three thousand speakers of many languages became believers (Acts 2:41). After that, the apostles preached the gospel to Gentiles as well as Jews (Acts 10–11).

So, in the New Testament, the rule is not to isolate oneself from the world, though we must continue to beware of the temptations that the world sets before us. Jesus intends us to remain "in" the world, but not to be "of" the world (John 17:11, 15–16). Satan is a defeated enemy; we may resist him, and he will flee from us (James 4:7). The gates of hell cannot defeat the church (Matt. 16:18).

Children, of course, need to be isolated in the early years of their lives. They are not mature enough then to march by themselves into battle against the hosts of Satan, to withstand all the evils of our time. But the home and the church should be preparing them for this very battle.

If they are to fight strongly against wickedness, they must have some knowledge of the world. Paul was not ignorant of Satan's devices (2 Cor. 2:11); we should not allow our children to be ignorant of them either.

Further, as they grow older, they need to enter into relationships with non-Christians in which they can learn to stand for the truth and to lead others to Christ. Once they leave home, they will be exposed to non-Christian peers and culture on a regular basis. They should be prepared for that gradually, when they have access to parental supervision. We do not want Satan's devices to catch them by surprise.

There is room for debate, of course, as to how early, how quickly, and by what means we should expose our children to the world. Some things are obvious. Five-year-olds should not be exposed to a steady stream of pagan rock music, R-rated films, and sociopathic companions. On the other hand, however, a Christian college graduate ought to be able to attend a secular university graduate program without undergoing spiritual upheaval. Between those obvious points, many others are debatable. Children, after all, are very different from one another, and Christian children mature spiritually at different rates. I have known some who have gone to public high schools and given powerful witness of Christ to their classmates, without compromising either their beliefs or their standards of behavior. Others have suffered spiritual shipwreck in such contexts. Parents need to make wise judgments regarding their own children.

My point, however, is that we should not only seek to shelter children from evil influences, but should also give them opportunities to test themselves in the world. And it is much better that they undergo these tests when they still have parents nearby to counsel them, than if they wait and face the tests alone.

This argument suggests that for some families, it might be a good idea to give their children a limited exposure to the teaching and culture of state schools. Many homeschoolers, for example, send their children to take classes at local community colleges when they reach high school years or beyond. But community colleges are state schools, with all the problems of state schools mentioned above. Yet the parents believe that when their children reach the college level, they are mature enough to handle the spiritual problems of a secular college, especially when they can live at home, under continued parental supervision.

Usually Christian homeschoolers don't criticize one another for taking the community college option, but they tend to become very critical of fellow Christians who send their children to public schools for elementary and high school. Granted, that is more dangerous. It is right for us to ask one another hard questions about such decisions. But we should be slow to judge. Parents ordinarily know better than outsiders what their children are able to do, or what resources are available to a child to repel the attacks of Satan.

I have noted that a state school can never provide the type of education described in Deuteronomy 6:6–9, and that is a crucial point. Nevertheless, I believe that some exposure to the state system may be a legitimate *part* of a Deuteronomy 6 education. For an education saturated with God's Word must provide laboratory experiences in which the child is trained to *apply* the principles of Scripture to the world in which he lives. If the child cannot *apply* the Word, he does not really understand it. He must learn how to identify sin and righteousness, truth and falsity, testing everything by the Scriptures, like the noble people of Berea (Acts 17:11). To do that, he must gradually be exposed to the world and its thinking—both through books and through practical experiences.

If the reader has been persuaded by my argument so far, he should be interested to know that there are ways in which parents can expose their children *gradually* to the state school system, without allowing that system to dominate their children's education. That is, there are ways in which parents can give their children a taste of the public schools without giving the children up to the state. And when parents use the public schools in these ways, they gain some educational and financial benefits.

There are, for example, public school programs intended to help students with special needs. There are also independent study programs administered by public school districts, through which children can be homeschooled, with some level of participation in the school system. And there are also charter schools, some of which are founded and administered by Christians. A Christian-friendly charter school may not legally teach Christian values in an explicit way, but it can avoid the methods of secularist indoctrination common to other state schools, and it can provide students with Christian role models.

All of these options have disadvantages as means of Christian education. But they have advantages as well.

SOME OBJECTIONS AND REPLIES

I have argued that in some cases public schools may be helpful to parents who are seeking to educate their children according to God's Word. Some, however, have taken the position that Christian parents should *never* make use of public school programs of any sort. Their arguments are expressed in italics below, and my replies follow:

God does not permit the state to be involved in education. By using public schools, Christian parents support the state in its disobedience. As I said above,

I know of no way to show from Scripture that God absolutely forbids state-sponsored education. There are many problems with state education, especially in our present situation, which I have noted above. But I think that they are not sufficient to warrant an absolute prohibition of Christian involvement in the public schools. There are best-case scenarios, such as charter schools organized largely by Christian parents, which support the rights of parents to give Christian education to their children. Such charter schools avoid most (but not all) of the problems of the public schools. I have yet to see a cogent argument that absolutely forbids parents from taking part in such endeavors.

But let's assume that God does forbid the state to be involved in any kind of education. Does that imply that Christians should make no use of public schools? Perhaps an illustration may help: A thief takes all my money, and then offers me five dollars for bus fare home. Should I refuse to take it?

It can just as easily be argued that the state should not be involved in the retirement savings of its citizens. Does this imply that I should refuse my Social Security checks when they come? Certainly not. They are mine. One may argue that the state stole the money from me in the first place, but when the state offers to return some, I am certainly not obligated to turn it down. To accept the money is not to acknowledge the state's right to have taken it in the first place. It is not to be complicit in the sin of the state.

In the church at Corinth, some were evidently arguing that Christians should not buy food in the marketplace, since some of it may have been dedicated to idols. Paul responds that they should abandon that scruple. Offering the food to idols is a sin, but Christians don't become sinful by buying and eating the food (1 Cor. 8–10).

Similarly, if the state has sinned in establishing the public school system, Christians do not sin by making use of its benefits, any more than they sin by using state highways, accepting Social Security checks, or even paying taxes (which Jesus commands, Matt. 22:21).

There may sometimes be sins connected with our participation in the state. Parents who give to the state schools free rein over their children, without making any attempt to counteract the secularism of the public schools, in my opinion are guilty of serious sin. But the sin in that case is not the sin of using public school facilities. It is the sin of failing to take parental responsibility. Using state facilities, in and of itself, is not sinful.

To send a child to public school is to place him under the authority of the godless state. To do so is idolatry. I have heard this kind of language often from earnest opponents of state-sponsored education, but I confess I do not understand it. After all, we and our children are already under the authority of the state, whether we like it or not. The state already imposes restrictions upon us, some unjust, which we may seek to change by legal means, but may not disobey. I fail to see how placing a child in a public school (especially a Christian-friendly charter school, such as I have described above) changes that situation for the worse.

Certainly children who attend any school face a new set of rules and restrictions that they have to follow. But in many situations (especially in Christian-friendly charter schools), those restrictions are bound to be largely helpful, to both the parents and the child.

When we send children to public school, it gives the state a "foot in the door" to gain more and more power over us. I have heard that public school boards sometimes make use of their independent study programs to get information on families and other homeschoolers, so as to bring unjust legal actions against them. But of course, anything we do can be investigated by an authority that is willing to bend the laws governing privacy and religious freedom.

Is there a danger to homeschoolers receiving assistance from public schools that someone will take legal action against them for including religious elements in their teaching? In my view, that would be contrary to the First Amendment. If it happens, one can simply drop out of such a program, or fight it in the courts.

But participation in state schools is unwise for Christians. It aids and abets a movement toward greater state power, and hence toward a greater domination of unbelief in our society. I respect this argument, but we must understand the true force of it. It is a strategic argument, recommending a particular tactic in the cultural warfare of our time. The argument is that we can do more good for society in general if we simply boycott the public schools than if we make use of them. That may be true, but in this instance I am not convinced.

Christians are often asked to boycott things in order to send a message to organizations and to society in general. Some years ago, the Southern Baptist Convention and other Christian organizations promoted a boycott of entertainment produced by the Disney Corporation. Certainly this recommendation does not have the status of a biblical command. If it did, we would have to boycott any corporation that contributed in any way to immorality in society. On that basis, we would have to boycott nearly every business, withdrawing almost entirely from the world of commerce.

Scripture never takes that approach. The pagan food vendors at Corinth doubtless used their profits in all sorts of idolatrous and immoral ways.

Certainly they promoted a kind of worship (often immoral) that did great harm to society. But Paul does not tell Christians to boycott them. On the contrary, they are to "eat whatever is sold in the meat market without raising any question on the ground of conscience" (1 Cor. 10:25).

Nevertheless, if great numbers of Christians were to boycott Disney, the boycott would "send a message" that could do some good. The proposal deserves serious consideration, but it is not the word of God. So boycott proposals are strategic suggestions, not biblical norms. Perhaps a Christian boycott of the entire public school system would send a useful message. But such a boycott is not likely to take place. And the first responsibility of Christians is to their own children, not someone's broad strategy for social improvement. Christian parents should consider such boycott proposals seriously, but they are not obligated by God to participate in them, and it may be to their children's advantage if they do not participate in them.

The use of secular textbooks and teaching that is not explicitly Christian is a violation of Deuteronomy 6:6–9. To say this is to say that Christian children should never be exposed firsthand to the ideas of the unbelieving world. I do not believe that such a conclusion can be reached from Deuteronomy 6. As I have said, one does not properly understand God's Word until he can apply it to the affairs of life. If a student knows nothing of unbelieving thought, he cannot use the Word as the sword of the Spirit, and he has not had a truly Christian education. If he has not had a firsthand exposure to unbelieving ideas, he has not gained an adequate exposure to the power of those ideas. He will then not be ready to deal with these ideas when he leaves the home.

Certainly an exclusive and pervasive use of non-Christian texts and teaching would be wrong. But we are speaking here about a controlled, gradual exposure of children to the broader educational culture (unbelieving, to be sure), by means of intensive parental teaching and some exposure to the secular educational world. It seems to me that such an arrangement, carefully planned and carried out, is very much in accord with Deuteronomy 6:6–9.

CONCLUSION

Planning our children's education includes many difficult decisions. Those who oppose any involvement in secular schools have impressive arguments, because they put the most important consideration first: that education must be based on God's Word. Certainly these people have, for the most part, the best interests of children at heart. The most important part of education is that our children be taught to think and live according to God's Word.

I do believe, however, that parents committed to this goal may, in some cases, make good use of public schools. In these cases, I believe that the use of these will contribute to, not detract from, the goal of a God-saturated Christian education.

But surely every Christian parent should consider seriously the alternatives of homeschooling and private Christian schooling. These forms of schooling are the best equipped to help parents reach biblical goals, though they may often need supplementation. Secularism is a great danger, and every Christian parent must consider it seriously in deciding how to prepare children to live in the world, but not be part of it.

CHAPTER 25

The Second Commandment: Prohibited Images

The second commandment is one of the longer ones.[1] It is interesting that the commandments expressed at greatest length in Scripture (the second and fourth) are the ones whose meaning is most debated in the church today. Here is the statement of the commandment in Exodus 20:4–6:

> You shall not make for yourself a carved image, or any likeness of anything that is in heaven above, or that is in the earth beneath, or that is in the water under the earth. You shall not bow down to them or serve them, for I the LORD your God am a jealous God, visiting the iniquity of the fathers on the children to the third and the fourth generation of those who hate me, but showing steadfast love to thousands of those who love me and keep my commandments.

Here is the exposition of the commandment in the WLC:

> Q. 108. *What are the duties required in the second commandment?*
> A. The duties required in the second commandment are, the receiving, observing, and keeping pure and entire, all such religious worship and ordinances as God hath instituted in his word;

---

1. I think it likely that the curse of verses 5 and 6 is intended to apply to the first commandment as well as the second. (Note that God's jealousy applies to the content of the first commandment in Ex. 34:14 and Deut. 6:13–15.) But even without that addition, the second commandment is one of the longer ones of the Decalogue.

particularly prayer and thanksgiving in the name of Christ; the reading, preaching, and hearing of the word; the administration and receiving of the sacraments; church government and discipline; the ministry and maintenance thereof; religious fasting; swearing by the name of God, and vowing unto him: as also the disapproving, detesting, opposing all false worship; and, according to each one's place and calling, removing it, and all monuments of idolatry.

Q. 109. *What are the sins forbidden in the second commandment?*
A. The sins forbidden in the second commandment are, all devising, counseling, commanding, using, and anywise approving, any religious worship not instituted by God himself; tolerating a false religion; the making any representation of God, of all or of any of the three persons, either inwardly in our mind, or outwardly in any kind of image or likeness of any creature whatsoever; all worshiping of it, or God in it or by it; the making of any representation of feigned deities, and all worship of them, or service belonging to them; all superstitious devices, corrupting the worship of God, adding to it, or taking from it, whether invented and taken up of ourselves, or received by tradition from others, though under the title of antiquity, custom, devotion, good intent, or any other pretense whatsoever; simony; sacrilege; all neglect, contempt, hindering, and opposing the worship and ordinances which God hath appointed.[2]

As with the first commandment, we see here an elaborate list of applications, one that provokes self-examination. The applications cover a broad territory, including actions that we do not usually associate closely with the second commandment. Do we often think of receiving the sacraments, for example, as an application of the second commandment? Or how is religious fasting related to the prohibition of using carved images in worship? I shall explore these and other questions in the following discussion.

ARE IMAGES ALWAYS BAD?

A literal reading of verse 4 in typical English translations suggests that the commandment forbids the making of any image at all, of anything. On

2. In the following discussion, I will take issue with some of the points in WLC, 109. As I have mentioned before, although I subscribe to the Catechism, I do not thereby endorse every word of it. I have communicated my disclaimers to my presbytery, and they have expressed no objection to me teaching my view. They and I believe that these differences do not affect my affirmation of the system of doctrine taught in the Westminster standards.

that understanding, the commandment forbids all representative art, as is the view of Islam. But that interpretation is most unlikely. Nothing else in the Bible suggests that making images is always wrong. Indeed, God himself requires the making of images in the very context of worship. In Exodus 25:18–20, God commands Moses to make "two cherubim of gold" to put at the two ends of the mercy seat, in the holiest part of the tabernacle. Cherubim are also supposed to decorate the curtains of the tabernacle (36:8). The lampstand in the Holy Place is to have six branches (like a tree), and the cups are to be "like almond blossoms" (25:33–34). The hem of the priest's garments contains images of bells and pomegranates (28:33–34). Solomon's temple was even more embellished, with cedar "carved in the form of gourds and open flowers" (1 Kings 6:18). The temple also included images of cherubim in the inner sanctuary (1 Kings 6:23–28), and "around all the walls of the house [Solomon] carved engraved figures of cherubim and palm trees and open flowers, in the inner and outer rooms" (v. 29; cf. vv. 32, 35). The palm trees and cherubim recur in Ezekiel's vision of a future temple (Ezek. 41:17–20), and God tells Ezekiel that the cherubim each have two faces, one of a man and another of a lion.

These images recall the garden of Eden: its beautiful growing things and the cherubim that barred man's return after the fall (Gen. 3:24). So the tabernacle and the temple serve as images of the garden. Indeed, we are told in Hebrews 8:5 that the whole tabernacle is also an image of heaven, the antitype of Eden. It is an image, a likeness, of the heavenly tabernacle. It is for this reason that Moses was to make everything precisely according to the pattern that God gave him on the mountain (Ex. 25:40; Heb. 8:5).

When Israel complained about the food that God provided for them in the wilderness, God sent "fiery serpents" among them, so that many died (Num. 21:6). When the people repented, God commanded through Moses: "Make a fiery serpent and set it on a pole, and everyone who is bitten, when he sees it, shall live" (v. 8). Here again, God commands the making of an image, and he even calls the people to look to that image for healing. In John 3:14–15, the serpent becomes a symbol of Jesus, lifted up to die, "that whoever believes in him may have eternal life."

It is inconceivable that God would command the making of images on these occasions, if making images were intrinsically sinful.

Someone might argue that images are legitimate only when God directly commands them to be made. But there is no reason to suppose that God directly commanded the images of a calf's head and lions on Solomon's throne (1 Kings 10:19–20), and Scripture does not suggest that there was anything wrong with those images. More to the point is that the actual language of the second commandment makes no such qualification, and there is no suggestion elsewhere in Scripture that art in general requires a direct divine warrant.

Others have suggested that though it is not wrong to make images, it is wrong to allow them to be displayed in a place of worship. But that view is refuted by the many texts listed above, in which God requires the making of images precisely for Israel's place of worship, even the most holy place of God's presence. And the second commandment itself does not contain any reference to location, nor do other texts that reflect the teaching of that commandment.

What Exodus 20:4–5 teaches, rather, is that we should not make images *for the purpose of* bowing down to them and serving them. That is plain from the use of the word *pesel* (translated "carved image") in verse 4. A *pesel* in Scripture is never simply a piece of artwork. It is always an image used for idolatrous purposes. Further, the connection between verses 4 and 5 shows implicitly that what God forbids is not art in itself, or even art located in a place of worship, but art made as an object of worship. Although this relationship between the two verses is not explicit, it is grammatically possible and necessary in this context. Hebrew does not always state explicitly the relationship between one clause and the next, so we must determine that connection by the context (and, of course, by the overall context of Scripture).

The implicit relationship between making images and worshiping them becomes explicit in Leviticus 26:1, "You shall not make idols for yourselves or erect an image or pillar, and you shall not set up a figured stone in your land to bow down to it, for I am the LORD your God." Here again, what God forbids is not the making of any image for any purpose, but rather the making of an idol (*elil*), an object to be worshiped. Leviticus 26:1 also mentions images (*pesel*, see above) and "figured stones" (*matstsebah*). The word *matstsebah* can be used in a good sense, as in Genesis 28:18, when Jacob set up a stone as a "pillar" to memorialize his meeting with God at Bethel. But Leviticus 26:1 only mentions the wrongful use. So, Leviticus, more explicitly than Exodus 20:4–5, relates the prohibition of images to their use as objects of worship.

This understanding correlates with biblical descriptions of idols as "gods of silver" and "gods of gold" (Ex. 20:23), "gods of cast metal" (34:17; Lev. 19:4). These expressions refer not to images as such, but to images used as objects of worship.

In 2 Kings 18:4, we learn that King Hezekiah destroyed the bronze serpent that Moses had made, because the people had begun to make offerings to it. Again, the pattern is that an image is legitimate as a mere representation, or even, in this case, as a means of divine healing. But worshiping the bronze serpent was sinful, and to prevent that worship, the object itself had to be destroyed. It is the *misuse* of an image that God condemns, not its existence or presence.

This is the sin condemned over and over in Scripture: making idols as objects of false worship. This is the narrow meaning of the second commandment.

OBJECTS OF WORSHIP

In the above discussion, I say that the second commandment forbids the use of images as "objects of worship." That phrase needs some more explanation.

In paganism, the relationship between the image and the god is more than merely pictorial, or even representative. Something of the sanctity of the god attaches to the image itself. The connection between the image and the god can be so close that the worshiper regards the material object as itself divine in some way. This concept is implicit in Exodus 20:23, Exodus 34:17 (mentioned above), and also in Isaiah 44:12–20, where God ridicules the man who uses half his wood to build a fire and the other half to make an idol to worship. Absurd as it is, the pagan calls out to his wood to deliver him.

In other kinds of paganism, the relation between image and god may be more subtle. The image may be thought of as a sacramental conduit of divine influence, or as a representation of the divine, in which case the image deserves reverence because of what it represents.

When I say, then, that the second commandment forbids the use of images as "objects of worship," I mean to include all these forms of paganism. Any view that justifies bowing down to an image is wrong, and bowing to an image, whatever the rationale, is also wrong.

IMAGES OF THE TRUE GOD

Discussion of this commandment in the church has often focused on the question of whether we may represent the true God by an image. Initially, we may be disconcerted by the fact that the commandment says nothing specific about images of God. It mentions only images of things in the creation—in heaven, in the earth, or in the sea.

But of course the whole point, as I've indicated above, is that in idolatry images of earthly things are used to represent the supernatural, so that the images themselves become objects of worship. So idolatry involves both the image itself and what the image is thought to represent. In idolatry, the image of something earthly represents a god.

So the commandment forbids the worship of images representing any god whatever, whether false or true. Indeed, later biblical allusions to the second commandment often focus on attempts to worship the true God by means of images. Exodus 32 is perhaps the paradigm of idolatry practiced by the people of God. Moses has been delayed in returning from the presence of God, and the people ask his brother Aaron, the high priest, to "make us gods who shall go before us" (v. 1). With gold donated by the people, he makes a golden calf and says, "These are your gods, O Israel, who brought you up out of the land of Egypt!" (v. 4). Then he builds an altar before it and proclaims, "Tomorrow shall be a feast to the Lord [Yahweh]" (v. 5). The grammar has some odd features here. There is one calf, but a plural pronoun refers to it in verse 4 (recalling the "gods" of v. 1). So there seem to be polytheistic aspects of the people's false worship. On the other hand, Aaron ascribes to the "gods" the act of bringing the people out of Egypt (v. 4), quoting the preface of the Decalogue itself. Further, Aaron declares a feast of Yahweh. So amid some polytheistic confusion, it seems evident that Aaron and the people consider the golden calf to be an image of Yahweh (perhaps in company with some other beings).[3]

The same thing is evidently the case in 1 Kings 12:25–33, which the biblical writer certainly considers parallel to Exodus 32. God made Jeroboam king over ten northern tribes of Israel, leaving Solomon's son Rehoboam to be king over two southern tribes. To prevent the northern tribes from worshiping in the temple of Jerusalem (ruled by Rehoboam), Jeroboam erected new places of worship in Bethel and Dan, where he placed "calves of gold." Of these, he said, echoing Aaron's words in Exodus 32, "Behold your gods, O Israel, who brought you up out of the land of Egypt" (v. 28). The narrator comments, "Then this thing became a sin" (v. 30). Again, amid polytheistic language (now there are two calves as well as the plural reference to the divine deliverer), Jeroboam wants to connect his new religion with Yahweh, the God who led Israel out of Egypt.

So in the two paradigm cases of Exodus 32 and 1 Kings 12:25–33, Israel sinned, not only by worshiping images, but specifically by worshiping the

---

3. There are plural aspects to Yahweh as he is presented in the Old Testament that anticipate the doctrine of the Trinity: see *DG*, 631–37. So the confusion between singular and plural references here is not without some rationale. Yahweh is not a bare oneness, like the Islamic Allah, but a God who is multipersonal and therefore complex. In addition, he often appears in a "glory-cloud" (Kline), surrounded by angelic beings. Still the Old Testament, like the New, is clear in teaching that there is only one God (Deut. 6:4).

true God by means of images.[4] The worship of false gods by images is, of course, already condemned by the first commandment. So the second commandment has a special interest in removing idolatry from the worship of Yahweh.

Idolatry has two senses: (1) worshiping a false god, and (2) worshiping any god by means of an idol. The first commandment deals primarily with the first form of idolatry, while the second commandment deals with the second form of it. But of course the two are intimately connected. To worship a false god (first commandment) is to direct our worship to something creaturely, namely an idol (second commandment). And to worship an idol (second commandment) is to rob God of worship that he alone deserves (first commandment). So the two commandments imply one another and serve as two perspectives on our worship. In that way, the second commandment, like the first, covers all aspects of human life. That is the broad meaning of the second commandment.

GROUNDS FOR THE COMMANDMENT

Why is it that God disapproves of the worship of images, or even the worship of himself by means of an image? There are at least four reasons that have been put forward:

GOD'S REDEMPTIVE-HISTORICAL INVISIBILITY

People have often cited God's invisibility as a ground for the prohibition of idolatry, the idea being that an invisible God should not be worshiped under a visible form. On this view, the visible image inevitably distorts the nature of the invisible God, and therefore cannot represent him truly.

Scripture itself, however, does not endorse this argument. It is true that God is invisible (Rom. 1:20; Col. 1:15; 1 Tim. 1:17; Heb. 11:27) and that no one has ever seen him (John 1:18; 5:37; 6:46; 1 John 4:12, 20). However, God often reveals himself in Scripture by visible means, namely, theophany and incarnation. Jacob saw God "face to face" (Gen. 32:30; cf. 16:13; Ex. 24:10; Num. 12:8; Judg. 13:22). The New Testament, further, uses strongly visual language to indicate God's revelation of himself in

---

4. For another case of the use of idols among ostensible Yahweh worshipers (also connected with the tribe and city of Dan), see Judg. 17–18. Cf. also the narrative in Gen. 31 about Rachel's theft of "household gods" (vv. 19, 32, 34–35) from Laban. But by Gen. 35:1–4, Jacob calls his household to "put away the foreign gods that are among you," and he buries their idols under a tree.

Christ (John 14:9; 1 John 1:1–3). Other passages emphasize the visibility of Christ in his transfiguration and resurrection (Acts 1:3; 1 Cor. 15:3–8; 2 Peter 1:16–18).[5]

Man himself is God's image (Gen. 1:26–27), and Christ is the image of God par excellence (2 Cor. 4:4; Col. 1:15; Heb. 1:3). So it is simply wrong to claim that God cannot be imaged. It does seem counterintuitive to say that an invisible being can be imaged by visible things. But to see how this is possible, consider Psalm 94:9: "He who planted the ear, does he not hear? He who formed the eye, does he not see?" The functions of our ears and eyes image the powers of God, who hears and sees without ears and eyes. So God's invisibility does not entail that there are no images of him, or that every image of him is misleading.

So the divine attribute of invisibility as such is not relevant to the second commandment. What is relevant is that God determined to hide himself at a particular point in Israel's history. Deuteronomy 4:15–19 reads:

> Therefore watch yourselves very carefully. Since you saw no form on the day that the LORD spoke to you at Horeb out of the midst of the fire, beware lest you act corruptly by making a carved image for yourselves, in the form of any figure, the likeness of male or female, the likeness of any animal that is on the earth, the likeness of any winged bird that flies in the air, the likeness of anything that creeps on the ground, the likeness of any fish that is in the water under the earth. And beware lest you raise your eyes to heaven, and when you see the sun and the moon and the stars, all the host of heaven, you be drawn away and bow down to them and serve them, things that the LORD your God has allotted to all the peoples under the whole heaven.

Israel is not to worship images because God chose, on the day of the assembly recorded in Exodus 19–20, to reveal himself invisibly, by word rather than by visible form: "Then the LORD spoke to you out of the midst of the fire. You heard the sound of words, but saw no form; there was only a voice" (Deut. 4:12). The word translated "form" here and in verse 15 is *temunah*. The point is not that God has no *temunah*, or that God's *temunah* can never be seen. In fact, Moses saw God's *temunah* (Num. 12:8), and David anticipates one day awakening to behold God's "likeness" (*temunah*) (Ps. 17:15). God might also have shown his *temunah* to Israel on the day of the assembly, but he chose not to.

---

5. In this paragraph, I summarize *DG*, 587–89. The entire section there on God's invisibility is relevant to the present discussion.

So God's formlessness, as a ground of the second commandment, is not metaphysical, but redemptive-historical. God revealed himself formlessly to Israel at the inauguration of the Mosaic covenant, and so he forbade them to use any material or visible thing as an object of worship. He could have made a material thing that so perfectly represented him that it deserved worship. Indeed, that is what he did in the incarnation of Christ. But he chose not to provide such an object for Israel's worship during the Old Testament period.

The new covenant is different in this respect. Under the new covenant, God does reveal himself in a material and visible form. Recall John 14:9, where Jesus says, "Whoever has seen me has seen the Father." And 1 John 1:1–3:

> That which was from the beginning, which we have heard, which we have seen with our eyes, which we looked upon and have touched with our hands, concerning the word of life—the life was made manifest, and we have seen it, and testify to it and proclaim to you the eternal life, which was with the Father and was made manifest to us—that which we have seen and heard we proclaim also to you, so that you too may have fellowship with us; and indeed our fellowship is with the Father and with his Son Jesus Christ.

Note how the apostle rejoices in the visibility of the revelation of the Word of life. In this passage, there are many references to the senses: hearing, seeing, touching. To John, the concrete visibility of new covenant revelation is important in itself, and also as polemic against the Docetists who deny that "Jesus Christ has come in the flesh" (1 John 4:2).

The visibility of God's form is, in Scripture, an eschatological concept. When Jesus returns, "every eye will see him" (Rev. 1:7). He shall return visibly, as he ascended to heaven (Acts 1:11). In glory, the pure in heart "shall see God" (Matt. 5:8). Paul says, "For now we see in a mirror dimly, but then face to face" (1 Cor. 13:12). The writer to the Hebrews says that we need "the holiness without which no one will see the Lord" (12:14). John promises, "When he appears we will be like him, because we shall see him as he is" (1 John 3:2). David expects to see God's *temunah* at his final awakening (Ps. 17:15). A few, like Moses, have had the privilege of seeing God's *temunah* while on earth. That is an anticipation of the end.

Jesus' incarnate glory is the beginning of the end, the beginning of the new heavens and the new earth. But the time between his ascension and his return is "semieschatological."[6] During this period, Scripture presents

---

6. See chapter 16.

the invisibility of God in paradoxical terms:[7] "We look not to the things that are seen but to the things that are unseen" (2 Cor. 4:18), "seeing him who is invisible" (Heb. 11:27). There is a kind of seeing, even though we walk by faith and not by sight (Rom. 8:24; 2 Cor. 5:7; Heb. 11:1, 13). Even though we do not now see Jesus, others have, and so, in a sense, we see him too (Heb. 2:9).

Is it, then, proper to use images in new covenant worship? In the most obvious sense, no. The New Testament also opposes idolatry strongly and often (Acts 15:20, 29; 17:16–31; Rom. 2:22; 1 Cor. 5:10–11; 6:9; 10:7, 14; 12:2; 2 Cor. 6:16; Gal. 5:20; 1 Thess. 1:9; 1 Peter 4:3; 1 John 5:21; Rev. 9:20; 21:8; 22:15). But we are to worship God's image par excellence, the Lord Jesus Christ. Should we worship pictures of Jesus? No. Scripture never suggests such a thing, and we are bound to biblical norms. Jesus himself is the image we worship, not some picture of him.

We cannot, like the apostles, see Jesus with our eyes today. We see him through his Word and sacrament. In this respect, our worship is much like that of the old covenant. But our worship now recalls a time when God was visible on earth in the person of Jesus, and it draws us to heaven, in which Christ, still visible, sits at the right hand of God. The New Testament presents vividly the story of Jesus—teaching, working miracles, hungering, thirsting, praying, resisting temptation, loving us beyond measure in his death and resurrection, and ascending bodily to the heavenly glory. The text does not just give us propositional information, but through its language it creates images in our minds—images that draw us to the visible Jesus as the object of our worship. We are not to worship those images—even the images of our minds. But we are to worship the one whose images they are.

So I must respectfully take issue with Larger Catechism 109, when it proscribes "the making any representation of God, of all or of any of the three persons, either inwardly in our mind, or outwardly in any kind of image or likeness of any creature whatsoever." The Catechism here forbids making images, even of Jesus, even in the mind. For one thing, as I have indicated, the second commandment does not forbid *making* images, even representations of God. It only forbids making them for the purpose of bowing to them in worship. In the second place, the Scripture certainly intends to provide for its readers mental pictures of Jesus. It is, for most of us, psychologically impossible to read the New Testament (or even portions of the Old Testament like Psalm 22 or Isaiah 53) without

---

7. Knowing that some Reformed people like to pounce on any use of the word *paradox*, let me say that in my usage (here and elsewhere in my writings) it does not imply logical contradiction.

forming such pictures. To forbid mental pictures of Jesus, while allowing mental pictures of other things in the gospel narrative, promotes Docetism, a view in which the Son of God did not really take on flesh. But our faith is to be focused on the real Jesus, whom, though unseen, we love: "Though you have not seen him, you love him. Though you do not now see him, you believe in him and rejoice with joy that is inexpressible and filled with glory, obtaining the outcome of your faith, the salvation of your souls" (1 Peter 1:8–9).

GOD AS THE LIVING GOD

A second biblical ground for this commandment is that idols, as objects of worship, are impersonal. As I indicated in chapter 3, a fundamental distinctive of biblical teaching is that the supreme being is personal, not impersonal. Scripture emphasizes that the true God is "the living God" (Deut. 5:26; Josh. 3:10; 1 Sam. 17:26, 36; 2 Kings 19:4, 16; Pss. 42:2; 84:2; Jer. 10:10; etc.). But all religions and philosophies operating without biblical influence teach that reality is fundamentally impersonal.

Correspondingly, a common biblical critique of idols is that they cannot see, hear, eat, smell, or speak. They are "mute" (1 Cor. 12:2—"dumb" in the KJV). (See also Deut. 4:28; Pss. 115:5–8; 135:15–18; Isa. 40–48, esp. 46:7; Jer. 10:5; Hab. 2:18–19.) They are made of impersonal stuff: gold, silver, wood, stone (Ex. 20:23; Deut. 4:28; 28:36, 64; 29:17; Isa. 40:18–20[8]). Those who make them or worship them become like them (Pss. 115:8; 135:18). People become like the gods they worship, and idol worship depersonalizes.

So idols are lies, not because God is invisible or cannot be pictured, but because idols fail to picture what is most important about him—his personality, his ability to see, hear, speak, and interact with his creatures. Without personality, God cannot judge—good news for unbelieving hedonists, but bad news for the universe. And without personality, God cannot love—bad news for everybody.

RESPECT FOR GOD'S TRUE IMAGE

This may be a bit of a stretch, but it seems to me that the triad of heaven, earth, and sea in the second commandment suggests another ground. This

---

8. Don't miss the exquisite satire here. The craftsman has to be very careful in his choice of wood. You don't want your god to rot. Recall again the absurdity of Isa. 44:12–20, in which the carpenter warms himself with one piece of wood and worships the other piece.

triad is a common biblical way of describing the whole creation, hearkening back to Genesis 1:26. The point, therefore, is that worship should be given to the Creator, rather than to anything he has created (cf. the description of idolatry in Rom. 1:25).

But in Genesis 1, where is "the image of God"? Of course, that image is man himself (Gen. 1:26–27). This fact suggests that the commandment intends, not only to guard the dignity of God, but also the dignity of God's true image, mankind. For man to bow down to an idol is not only to worship something less than God, but also to worship something less than himself. It is an affront to God's dignity and also an affront to man's.

In the texts cited in the previous subsection, idols are weaker than man. The carpenter who makes the idol then bows down to his own handiwork (Isa. 44:12–20). To say that idols cannot see, hear, smell, or speak is to distance them, not only from God, but also from man. So those who make idols destroy themselves, becoming like them (Pss. 115:8; 135:18).

Only Jesus Christ fulfills the criteria of an image of God to whom man should bow down. He is personality in its fullness: seeing, hearing, smelling, speaking, judging, loving. He is our Creator, not a mere creature. Worship of him brings salvation, not destruction. Those who bow down to him become like him—in abundant life, rather than death, and in the fulfillment of personality, rather than its destruction.

God's Covenant Jealousy

The ground that is most prominent in the language of the commandment itself is: "For I the LORD your God am a jealous God, visiting the iniquity of the fathers on the children to the third and the fourth generation of those who hate me, but showing steadfast love to thousands of those who love me and keep my commandments" (Ex. 20:5–6). As I suggested earlier, these covenant sanctions may belong to the first two commandments together and in effect to all the commandments. But it is significant that this section follows specifically the prohibition of worship by idols. When discussing the first commandment (chapter 23), I mentioned the biblical parallel between idolatry and adultery. I shall return to that theme under the seventh commandment. For both marriage and our relation to God are covenantal and require exclusive loyalty. When we are disloyal, jealousy rightly ensues.

In the covenant, God's name is Jealous (Ex. 34:14). Worship of idols, like illicit sexual intercourse, is perhaps the most concrete, blatant form of covenant disloyalty. So: "Take care, lest you forget the covenant of the LORD your God, which he made with you, and make a carved image, the form of anything that the LORD your God has forbidden you. For the LORD your God is a consuming fire, a jealous God" (Deut. 4:23–24).[9] Second Kings 21:7–8 also describes idolatry as a flagrant violation of the covenant, and Ezekiel 8:3 refers to an "image of jealousy, which provokes to jealousy."[10]

In the second commandment, God's jealousy leads to judgment: "For I the LORD your God am a jealous God, visiting the iniquity of the fathers on the children to the third and the fourth generation of those who hate me" (v. 5). Violation of the covenant law leads to curse.

It might seem as though God here threatens to punish children for the sins of their fathers, contrary to Ezekiel 18, in which God promises not to do this. According to Ezekiel 18:14–18, a son whose father is unfaithful to God may turn from his father's ways, turn to the Lord, and be saved. Repentance and life are possible, even for a son who comes from an ungodly family.

What Exodus 20:5 teaches is not that children are punished for the sins of their parents, but that idolatrous parents create an atmosphere in their families that encourages their children, even later generations, also to be idolatrous. The "third and fourth generation" are also generations "of them that hate me." They hate God as much as the first generation did, and they die for their own sin, as Ezekiel 18:20 teaches.[11] Part of the punishment of the parents is that they live to see the awful consequences of their sin in their children and grandchildren.[12]

The latter often suffer the consequences of their parents' sins. And as God brings a punishment upon the parents, the children suffer as well. But this punishment does not necessarily involve damnation. Such children can still repent and be saved. Ezekiel 18 has to do with life and death punishment: salvation, damnation. Exodus 20 includes that for the damned, but involves only temporal visitation for the elect children of lost parents.

There is nothing deterministic about this process. What God says through Ezekiel (18:14–18) is that if a child turns away from the sinful behavior of his father, he will live and not die. Scripture often speaks of

9. Similarly, God's jealousy forbids Israel from making covenants with the pagan inhabitants of the Promised Land (Ex. 34:14).

10. On jealousy as an attribute of God, see *DG*, 458–59.

11. In Scripture, nobody ever dies for the sins of someone else, with two exceptions: (1) We are all directly guilty of the sin of Adam (Rom. 5:12–21). (2) Jesus died for our sins (1 Cor. 15:3). In these two cases, God judges people by their union with a federal head. But these two cases are unique. The general rule is that of Ezek. 18:20: everyone dies for his own sin. Even in the two "exceptions," the principle is the same, for, by God's imputation, Adam's sin is our sin, and our sin becomes the sin of Jesus (2 Cor. 5:21).

12. Thanks to Bruce Waltke, who makes this point in his *Biblical Theology* (forthcoming).

a remnant that shall escape God's judgment. The converts at Pentecost heeded the apostolic injunction to "save yourselves from this crooked generation" (Acts 2:40). Repentance is always possible, by God's grace.

But the terrible reality is that often the iniquity of the fathers begins a process by which the wrath of God is stored up, to be released perhaps generations later in terrible fury (Lev. 26:39; 2 Kings 17:7–23; Isa. 65:7; Jer. 16:11–13; Dan. 9:16; Amos 7:17; Matt. 23:32–33; Rom. 1:24–32).

On the other hand, God promises to show "steadfast love to thousands of those who love me and keep my commandments" (Ex. 20:6). The "thousands," most likely, are thousands of generations, as in Deuteronomy 7:9. "Generations" is found in Deuteronomy 7:9, though not in Exodus 20:6, but the two verses are otherwise parallel, describing the nature of God's blessing sanction within the covenant.

On this understanding, God's mercy is broader than his wrath: thousands of generations, rather than a mere three or four. Since "there is no one who does not sin" (2 Chron. 6:36), this blessing speaks of God's grace. Again, however, there is nothing deterministic here. A father who, by grace, is faithful to the Lord, creates an atmosphere in his family that leads his children and grandchildren to be faithful. But faithful men sometimes have ungodly sons (Ezek. 18:5–13), and they will die in their sin. This does not invalidate the promise of God's favor to "thousands of generations," for his intent throughout history is to bring to himself a vast number of people from every nation to enjoy his favor. In his covenants, he gives grace that draws people to himself. Although some apostatize, God will fully accomplish his loving purpose:

> After this I looked, and behold, a great multitude that no one could number, from every nation, from all tribes and peoples and languages, standing before the throne and before the Lamb, clothed in white robes, with palm branches in their hands, and crying out with a loud voice, "Salvation belongs to our God who sits on the throne, and to the Lamb!" (Rev. 7:9–10; cf. 19:6)

This blessing comes through Jesus, who served his Father exclusively and faithfully. He refused to commit idolatry, even to gain all the blessings of this world (Matt. 4:8–10). He won, for thousands of generations of his children, the eternal blessings of God.

CHAPTER 26

The Second Commandment: Regulating Worship

In chapter 25, I discussed the basic exegesis of the second commandment. In that commandment, God forbids the making of images for the purpose of worshiping them. That is the narrow meaning of the commandment. But, as we saw from WLC, 108 and 109, the Reformed tradition has made broader applications. In the view of the Westminster divines, the commandment applies not only to the worship of images as such, but also to other issues concerning the regulation of worship. In their view, even churches that forbid the worship of images can violate the commandment in various ways.

We should take this argument seriously. In chapter 22, I defended the Larger Catechism's method of drawing broad principles from the specifics of the Decalogue. The commandments have both narrow and broad meanings, so we should assume that this one does too. Having looked at the narrow meaning in chapter 25, I shall investigate possible broader meanings here.

THE REGULATIVE PRINCIPLE

The Reformed tradition has derived, from the second commandment and related texts, a distinctive view of how God regulates his worship. That view has been called "the regulative principle." In brief, that principle is that worship is by divine warrant, command, prescription. In worship, that is to say, we should do only what God requires us to do, and we learn his requirements only from Scripture. This principle begins WLC, 109, which I cited in the previous chapter: "The sins forbidden in the second commandment are, all devising, counseling, commanding, using, and anywise approving, any religious worship not instituted by God himself." Note also the following statement from WCF, 21.1:

> But the acceptable way of worshiping the true God is instituted by himself, and so limited by his own revealed will, that he may not be worshiped according to the imaginations and devices of men, or the suggestions of Satan, under any visible representation, or any other way not prescribed in the Holy Scripture.

In these quotations, note the operative words "instituted" and "prescribed." In Reformed churches, worship is a command performance. The popular summary is that whatever is not commanded is forbidden.

Reformed writers often compare this regulative principle with the view of Lutherans and Anglicans, that whatever is not forbidden is permitted.[1] That presents a nice theoretical contrast between two views. It is, however, a bit unfair to Lutherans and Anglicans. This way of putting it suggests that for them anything goes in worship, as long as Scripture does not forbid it. One can imagine worship services featuring three-legged races, lectures on mathematics, readings from Jane Austen, rock concerts, and ballroom dancing, all justified because Scripture doesn't forbid them. But of course that is not the way Lutherans and Anglicans think about worship or practice it. Indeed, they are, compared to other Protestants, exceptionally principled, highly resistant to activities in worship considered inappropriate, irreverent, or undignified. Most everything in Lutheran and Anglican worship, even things that Presbyterians most object to, such as vestments, processionals, and incense, arise from some theological reflection, including a biblical rationale. So Lutherans and Anglicans too, in the final analysis, want worship that is justified by Scripture, and they reject activities that in their judgment do not conform to biblical norms. They do not typically affirm that elements of worship must be prescribed by Scripture, but, as we shall see, the Reformed tradition also qualifies the notion of prescription by its views of circumstances and expressions. So

---

1. One could say that Roman Catholics also hold this view, but I prefer to leave them out of the present discussion. The reason is that they hold a view of tradition different from Protestants, leading to a denial of the Protestant doctrine of *sola Scriptura*. To show how that view complicates their approach to the regulation of worship would take us too far afield. I have defended *sola Scriptura* in chapter 11 of this book.

the Lutherans and Anglicans apply Scripture to worship differently than Presbyterians do, but this may be a hermeneutical/exegetical issue, more than one of fundamental principle.

So we need to continue our exposition of the Reformed position, attending to qualifications of the prescription formula. Note the following from WCF, 1.6:

> The whole counsel of God concerning all things necessary for his own glory, man's salvation, faith and life, is either expressly set down in Scripture, or by good and necessary consequence may be deduced from Scripture: unto which nothing at any time is to be added, whether by new revelations of the Spirit, or traditions of men. Nevertheless, we acknowledge the inward illumination of the Spirit of God to be necessary for the saving understanding of such things as are revealed in the Word: and that there are some circumstances concerning the worship of God, and government of the church, common to human actions and societies, which are to be ordered by the light of nature, and Christian prudence, according to the general rules of the Word, which are always to be observed.

This passage begins by stating the sufficiency of Scripture, or *sola Scriptura*. But, as we saw in chapter 11, it qualifies that doctrine by saying that besides Scripture we need (1) the inward illumination of the Spirit of God and (2) understanding of "circumstances." These circumstances are aspects of worship and church government, "common to human actions and societies," that cannot be settled either by explicit or implicit biblical teaching. Rather, they are to be ordered by general revelation ("the light of nature"), Christian wisdom ("prudence"), and the general rules of Scripture.[2]

A traditional example of a circumstance in the area of worship is the time at which worship takes place. God in Scripture prescribes public worship, but he does not tell us the time of day at which it must occur. Still, if we are to worship at all, we must do so at a particular time. So in order to do something prescribed in Scripture, we must do something not prescribed in Scripture, namely, make a decision on the time at which we will worship. The Confession explains this apparent deviation from the regulative principle as a "circumstance" of worship. In making this decision, we employ our own human wisdom ("prudence"). But even in making this human judgment, we are not autonomous. We must give attention to the light of

---

2. These three factors form a triad: the general rules of Scripture are normative, general revelation is situational, and wisdom is existential.

nature and the general rules of the Word. For example, it would ordinarily be wrong for a church to schedule its Sunday morning worship service at 4 a.m. That violates the sleep patterns of most people (the light of nature), and it violates the law of love (the general rules of the Word).

Other obvious examples of circumstances would be the place of worship, the number of songs, the language of communication, the times at which the people sit, stand, or kneel, and the use of seats or pews. These are the sorts of issues that arise, not only for church worship, but for any kind of public meeting. The Rotary Club and the Oviedo City Council also have to decide on the times of meetings, the place of meeting, and so forth. So the Confession describes circumstances as "common to human actions and societies."

Thus we get the distinction between "elements" and "circumstances" that is common in Reformed discussions of worship. Elements are those aspects of worship that Scripture commands. Circumstances are those things we must do in order to perform the elements. The Westminster Confession does not itself use the term "elements," but it does speak of "parts of the ordinary religious worship of God," among which it includes prayer, preaching, singing of psalms, administration of the sacraments, religious oaths, vows, solemn fastings, and thanksgivings on special occasions (21.5).

The Westminster divines also believed that the regulative principle as formulated above is distinctive to matters of faith or worship. Note the following: "God alone is Lord of the conscience, and hath left it free from the doctrines and commandments of men, which are, in anything, contrary to his Word; or beside it, if matters of faith, or worship" (WCF, 20.2). Here they distinguish between two different regulative principles: one for human life in general, and a different one for faith and worship. In human life in general, we are free from any doctrine or commandment of men that is contrary to God's Word. But in matters of faith and worship, we have a greater liberty, a freedom from any human commandment in addition to God's Word. So for the Westminster Confession, the principle of *sola Scriptura* applies to faith and worship in a stronger sense than to other areas of life.[3]

EVALUATING THE REGULATIVE PRINCIPLE

The regulative principle is biblical in its insistence that worship is by divine warrant. The purpose of worship, of course, is to acknowledge the

---

3. I gather that "faith" here refers to theological doctrine. I will be focusing more directly on worship in this discussion, since that is the narrow concern of the second commandment.

greatness of God, to honor him for who he is and for what he has done. We want first of all to please God. There are in worship also benefits for the worshipers, which Paul sums up in 1 Corinthians 14:26 as "building up." But those benefits come when people are gathered together to glorify God. "Building up," or edification, is building up in the Word, in the grace of Christ, and in the Christian virtues.

How do we determine what glorifies God in worship? No doubt we can obtain some knowledge of this from natural revelation, for Paul teaches that on the basis of natural revelation human beings should have engaged in true worship: their idolatry is culpable (Rom. 1:21–23). But Paul also shows us clearly how sinners suppress that revelation apart from God's saving grace and the knowledge of him given in the gospel that we have in Scripture. So it is evident that Scripture must be our guide, in worship as in all of life. Scripture is the only revelation of God given in words and sentences. It is there that God tells us how he would like to be worshiped, and in Scripture he corrects our faulty understanding of natural revelation.

I might try to discover what would please God in worship by sitting in my easy chair and imagining what would please me if I were God. But such a method would leave me with no assurance that I am worshiping rightly. It is, indeed, important to be assured in this respect. Contrary to our usual modern way of thinking, God is not always pleased when people decide to worship him. God takes false worship very seriously. In Genesis 4:5, we learn that "for Cain and his offering [God] had no regard." In Leviticus 10:1–2, we read, "Now Nadab and Abihu, the sons of Aaron, each took his censer and put fire in it and laid incense on it and offered unauthorized fire before the LORD, which he had not commanded them.[4] And fire came out from before the LORD and consumed them, and they died before the LORD." Note also the following passages in which people suffer severe penalties for defective worship: 1 Samuel 13:8–14; 2 Samuel 6:6–7; 1 Kings 12:32–33; 15:30; 2 Chronicles 26:16–23; 28:3; Jeremiah 7:31; 1 Corinthians 11:29–30. So it is literally a life-and-death matter to worship God according to his command. For us today, that means deriving our worship from the Bible.

I have based my defense of the regulative principle on fairly general considerations: the nature of worship as homage to God, the nature of revelation, the sufficiency of Scripture. Other defenses of the regulative principle, in my judgment, are less successful:

The Westminster divines derived the regulative principle from the second commandment, believing that the prohibition of idolatry was based

---

4. The NIV translates "contrary to his command." The ESV is more literal. The NIV (evidently assuming a connection with Ex. 30) brings out the fact that these priests were not simply adding to God's word, but contradicting it.

on a broader principle: that worship should not be based on human imagination. Certainly, idolatry does elevate human craftsmanship, speculation, imagination, and creativity above God's word. The Confession itself recognizes, however, that there is a place for human wisdom to function in worship, under the category of circumstances. And those who seek to employ the Confession's regulative principle find that they must use their human wisdom in other ways as well, as we shall see below.

The second commandment does indeed forbid worship based on human reason alone. Thus, it is relevant to the regulative principle. Indeed, what it says pertains not only to worship in the narrow sense, but to all of human life, worship in the broad sense (chapter 23). It is a foundation for *sola Scriptura*, the sufficiency of Scripture, as the principle of all human decisions.

But the second commandment does not distinguish between elements and circumstances, nor does it distinguish right from wrong uses of reason in worship. Insofar as the regulative principle depends on such distinctions, it must rely on portions of Scripture other than the second commandment.

Reformed theologians have also tried to derive the regulative principle from the list of passages I mentioned above, beginning with Genesis 4:5 and Leviticus 10:1–2. But I doubt that can be done. To derive the regulative principle from these passages, one must show that God judges worshipers, not only for violating his commands, but for adding to them, that is, for doing things in worship that God has not commanded. But in the list of passages I have cited, the issue is disobedience to revealed commands, not merely doing things that God has not commanded. In Genesis 4:5, for example, God disapproves of Cain's offering, but nothing is said relevant to the regulative principle. We cannot tell from the passage whether Cain's sin was adding to God's commands (which would violate the regulative principle) or simply violating them (which would be sinful whether or not the regulative principle is true).

Leviticus 10:1–2 seems more relevant to the regulative principle, because Nadab and Abihu offered "unauthorized" incense. This may seem to mean that God judged them for doing something he had not commanded, rather than violating a command he had given. On that reading, they sinned by violating the regulative principle: doing something in worship that God has not commanded. But more likely, Nadab and Abihu violated the Exodus 30:9 prohibition of "unauthorized incense." In Exodus 30:22–38, God gives the recipe for a unique kind of incense to be used only for holy purposes. Evidently, the sons of Aaron used some other kind of incense. So they sinned, not by adding to the command of God, but by violating his command. The regulative principle, as defined above, is not the issue.

In 1 Samuel 13:13, Samuel clearly says that Saul's sin was a violation of God's command: "You have not kept the command of the LORD your God, with which he commanded you." The same is true of the other passages in my list. In these, God condemns people, not for doing things he hasn't commanded, but for violating commands he has given.

The most likely exception is Jeremiah 7:31, "And they have built the high places of Topheth, which is in the Valley of the Son of Hinnom, to burn their sons and their daughters in the fire, which I did not command, nor did it come into my mind."[5] Here God states explicitly that the people's sin is something he did not command. But of course "which I did not command, nor did it come into my mind" is an understatement. He hadn't commanded human sacrifice, or even thought about commanding it, because of the enormity of his revulsion against the practice. He had, in fact, explicitly forbidden it, as in Deuteronomy 18:10. In Jeremiah 7:31, the sin of the people was not to add a element of worship that God had never spoken of before, but rather to violate requirements that God had given very clearly and emphatically.

So these passages do not prove the regulative principle specifically. They do not prove that whatever is not prescribed is forbidden. They do show that God takes violations of his rules for worship very seriously.

I do believe, however, that the regulative principle is solidly grounded in the more general considerations noted earlier. Whatever we do in worship must have biblical warrant.

PROBLEMS IN APPLYING THE REGULATIVE PRINCIPLE

Although the regulative principle is biblical, applications of it to specific matters are sometimes difficult. Consider the following questions:

How do we determine the elements of worship? Some formulations of the regulative principle (outside the confessions) demand that elements of worship be based on "express commands" or explicit biblical warrants. But even the most conservative Reformed churches include elements of worship that are not directly commanded in Scripture. There is no explicit command, for example, to have a benediction in a worship service, or even a baptism. Baptisms in the New Testament are performed outdoors or in homes. There is no command to perform them in weekly worship services.

---

5. Open theists take this passage as an expression of divine ignorance. That is what it says, if we take it literally.

So most Reformed treatments of the regulative principle list more than one source for biblical warrants: (1) explicit commands, (2) approved examples (as the hymns and lessons in 1 Corinthians 14:26), and (3) theological inferences (e.g., from the nature of baptism as a sacrament, it is evidently appropriate for worship).[6] To allow the second and third categories is to remove some of the simplicity from the principle, and it does create room for controversy. To allow them is to give considerable scope for human reflection, even in determining "elements"—a disturbing result, since many revere the regulative principle precisely because it minimizes (or even eliminates) such reflection. But it is not clear how the regulative principle can function without this kind of reflection.

Examples in the second category are certainly the equivalent of divine commands. If the Corinthians included lessons and hymns in their worship, and Paul approves of what they are doing, then he must have recognized that God approved of the practice. As for the third category, recall that WCF, 1.6, does say that the whole counsel of God is found not only in the explicit, but also in the implicit, teaching of Scripture ("good and necessary consequence").[7] Certainly if God commands A, and A implies B, then God also commands B.

But then it is wrong to defend the regulative principle as a means of eliminating human reflection from worship. Human reflection plays a vital role in all worship, whether or not that worship affirms the regulative principle.

Do we need a third category of worship actions? The categories of elements and circumstances, as defined earlier, do not exhaust what we do in worship. For example, prayer is an element of worship. But the specific words used in prayers are not commanded in Scripture, either by explicit commands, approved examples, or theological inference. Scripture includes general principles of prayer and many sample prayers that must govern our own prayer life, but it does not prescribe the words to be prayed in a given worship service.

Are these specific words circumstances then? Not according to the Confession, which defines circumstances as matters that are "common to human actions and societies" (1.6). Circumstances are matters that the church shares in common with all other organizations, sacred and secular. But the specific words of prayers are not shared in this way. Prayer is not common to human actions and societies.

---

6. For a defense of this wider understanding by a conservative writer, see Michael Bushell, *The Songs of Zion* (Pittsburgh, PA: Crown and Covenant Publications, 1980), 21–25.

7. For a defense of this principle, see *DKG*, 251–54.

So some Reformed writers have added to elements and circumstances a third category, sometimes called "expressions" or "forms." Michael Bushell, who holds a traditional view of the regulative principle, expands the category of circumstances to include these, but that creates a problem for him. He then must distinguish between circumstances that have "spiritual meaning" or "sacred significance," such as the words of prayers, and those that don't, such as the time and place of worship.[8] But on his view, anything with "sacred meaning" or "spiritual significance" is an element. So Bushell's proposal leads to an overlap between elements and circumstances. The specific words of prayers, in Bushell's view, are both circumstances and elements.

As a result, Bushell has in effect repudiated the most basic assertion of the regulative principle, namely, that elements of worship must be prescribed by Scripture. If the specific words of prayers are elements, and they are not prescribed by Scripture, then there are some elements of worship to which the regulative principle does not apply.

In my view, the problem lies in Bushell's identification of elements with "spiritual significance," which I will discuss under the next question. In the meantime, I prefer to describe the specific words of prayers, etc., as expressions or forms, rather than circumstances or elements.

Can we distinguish sharply between spiritual and nonspiritual significance?
As we saw with Bushell, some have tried to define elements of worship by identifying them with matters of "sacred" or "spiritual" significance. Is that a helpful criterion?

In the Old Testament, as we saw in chapter 23, there are various degrees of sacredness or holiness, from the most holy place of the temple to the holiness of the whole people of God in the whole Land of Promise, to the whole earth as God's footstool. Priests are holy compared with other Israelites, but every Israelite is holy compared to Edomites and Egyptians. So holiness is not a sharp line that can be drawn through the whole creation.

In one sense, everything we do has spiritual significance: "Whether you eat or drink, or whatever you do, do all to the glory of God" (1 Cor. 10:31; cf. Rom. 14:23; 2 Cor. 10:5; Col. 3:17). As I indicated in chapter 23, there is a sense in Scripture in which everything is worship—worship in the broad sense, as in Romans 12:1. So Abraham Kuyper taught that "life is religion."

Of course, there is also worship in the narrow sense, which is what we are presently concerned with. Scripture does tell us in general terms what

8. Bushell, *The Songs of Zion*, 30. On p. 28, he uses "forms" as a synonym for "elements," which indicates some diversity in the tradition in the use of these terms.

belongs in worship in that narrow sense, such as prayer, teaching, and sacraments. But it does not base this teaching on any general category of holiness or spirituality. We should not define *element* by the concept of holiness, because in Scripture many activities that are holy in some sense (worship in the broad sense) are not components of worship in the narrow sense.

It is tempting for us to regard circumstances of worship as somehow "secular," common rather than holy, irrelevant to matters of the spirit. But take the question of the time of worship as an example. As I mentioned earlier, if the leaders of a church schedule a worship service at an inappropriate time, say 4:00 a.m., this decision may greatly affect the quality of worship. The human spirit in Scripture is not something totally disconnected from the body. Think also of the effect on worship of the type of seating, the length of the meeting, the clothing people wear, and the language in which the sermon is preached. So even those aspects of worship that are "common to human actions and societies" can make a spiritual difference.

So although the distinction between holy and common is important in Scripture, I do not think it is helpful in distinguishing between elements, forms, and circumstances of worship. This does not mean that we can do anything in worship services that we can do in other contexts (three-legged races, etc.). Scripture gives us clear direction as to what sorts of activities are appropriate to worship services. My point here is that its direction is not based on the holy/common distinction, and that that distinction, therefore, is not a good way to define the regulative principle.

Are there two regulative principles? As I mentioned earlier, WCF, 20.2, teaches that God regulates "faith and worship" more strictly than he governs the rest of life. The elements of faith and worship must be prescribed in Scripture, though the elements of other areas of human life need not be. This section of the Confession seems to say that in matters of faith and worship (in the narrow sense), whatever is not prescribed is forbidden, but that in other areas of life (i.e., worship in the broad sense), whatever is not forbidden is permitted.

It is certainly true that worship in the narrow sense is of special concern to God.[9] We have seen a long list of passages, beginning with Genesis 4:5 and Leviticus 10:1–2, that describe God's severity with those who worship him wrongly. But this is not to say that the area of worship is subject to a regulative principle different from that governing other areas of life. It is

9. Again, I focus on worship, rather than on "faith" (here, doctrinal orthodoxy), because that is the focus of the second commandment. But the same principles, in general, apply to faith.

only to say that God has a special concern with violations of his regulations for worship in the narrow sense.

Consider the regulative principle in the form "Whatever is not prescribed is forbidden." Does this principle apply only to worship in the narrow sense, or also in the broad sense, to all of human life? Given that all of life *is* worship in a sense, it would be odd if the two kinds of worship were governed differently.

As a matter of fact, God governs the two realms in the same way. In ordinary life, everything we do is subject to divine commands. God's commands are broad, as we have seen; they stretch out across the whole range of human decisions. So 1 Corinthians 10:31, for example, "Whether you eat or drink, or whatever you do, do all to the glory of God," covers absolutely everything we do. In every decision we make, we either obey that command or violate it. Every good thing we do is, in effect, commanded by 1 Corinthians 10:31. Anything we do that is not commanded by 1 Corinthians 10:31 is forbidden.[10]

The case can be made similarly for other universal commands in the Bible, such as Romans 14:23, 2 Corinthians 10:5, Colossians 3:17, and, as we have seen, the first commandment. Anything we do that is not prescribed by these and other passages is forbidden. The regulative principle of worship, therefore, bears on all of life, not only on worship in the narrow sense.

This result is to be expected from our previous discussion of the sufficiency of Scripture (in chapter 11). The Confession itself recognizes that the sufficiency of Scripture bears on all of life.[11] But the regulative principle is simply the application of the sufficiency of Scripture to worship. So if we are to recognize the universality of *sola Scriptura* as taught in the Confession, we should reject the distinction between two regulative principles taught in WCF, 20.2.

Someone may object that there are many specific things we do in ordinary life that God has not commanded: getting up in the morning, brushing our teeth, having breakfast, unlocking the front door, etc. But we have seen that in worship services as well we rightly do things that Scripture does not specifically command. Hence we have the categories of circumstances, expressions, and forms. So the two realms are in fact parallel. In both spheres, God tells us in general what he wants us to do. We try to decide, through sanctified wisdom, how to carry out those

---

10. Cf. my critique of the concept of adiaphora in chapter 11. Everything we do makes a difference to God. Nothing is morally neutral.

11. According to WCF, 1.6, Scripture is sufficient for "all things necessary for [God's] own glory, man's salvation, faith and life."

commands. In both spheres, there are divine commands and human applications, elements and nonelements, if you will.

What is the authority of human officers, in the church and other institutions? The Westminster divines, in their formulation of the regulative principle, were very much concerned about "liberty of conscience" (WCF, 20.2). They objected to the imposition of worship forms in the Church of England that violated their conscience. So the regulative principle is, in part, an attempt to define what officers (primarily in church and state) may and may not do to govern human life. Through it, the divines meant to subject officers to the higher authority of God's Word. So the regulative principle says in effect that officers of the church may require church members to follow God's commandments in Scripture for worship ("elements"), and they may require worshipers to follow these commandments in various ways ("forms," "circumstances") that agree with the general rules of the Word, even if they are not commanded there. But they may not command practices contrary to Scripture, nor may they require the addition of elements not commanded in Scripture.

Officers of the state may also require their citizens to obey them in matters Scripture assigns to the state.[12] This is parallel to the "elements" we have discussed under worship. These officers may also require citizens to carry out these civic duties in various ways not prescribed by Scripture, but compatible with its general rules. This is parallel to the "forms" and "circumstances" of worship. But these officers may not command anything on divine (or other ultimate) authority that is not found in Scripture.

In this way too, then, it becomes evident that the regulative principle is the same for all spheres of human life, and for worship both in the broad sense and in the narrow sense.

How specific are God's commands for worship? Arguments over the regulative principle, especially in the Puritan and Scottish Reformed traditions, are not so much about whether Scripture is sufficient for worship (in the narrow sense), but *how* it is sufficient. I am suggesting that Scripture is sufficient for worship in the same way it is sufficient for everything else. That is, God gives general principles, and we seek to apply these principles. But this view is unsatisfying to those who treasure the more traditional formulations of the principle. For it seems to them that if God only gives general principles, that leaves too much room for human thought, reflection, and imagination.

---

12. WCF, 23.1–4. Cf. my discussion of family, church, and state in chapter 32.

But we have seen that human thought is inescapable in worship, just as everywhere else. We need human thought to read the Bible, and we need it to engage in the exegetical and logical processes that will identify for us the elements of worship. We need human reflection, further, to determine how to carry out the circumstances of worship within the general boundaries of Scripture.

But the tradition has attempted to minimize human input, by declaring that God's commands for worship are not only general, but also specific, in the following ways:

1. Some have claimed that each element of worship requires a specific biblical rationale. For example, John Murray, convinced that song is an element of worship, says this with regard to the question of whether we should sing only the Psalms in worship:

> In dealing with this question, it should be appreciated that the singing of God's praise is a distinct act of worship. It is to be distinguished, for example, from the reading of Scripture and from the offering of prayer to God. It is, of course, true that songs of praise often include what is of the nature of prayer to God, as it is also true that in the offering of prayer to God there is much that is of the nature of praise and thanksgiving. But it is not proper to appeal to the divine authorization or warrant we possess as to the content of prayer in order to determine the question as to the content of song. Prayer is one element of worship, singing is another.

He then gives examples "of the necessity and importance of guarding the distinctiveness of each of the several parts of worship and of determining from the Scripture what its prescriptions are respecting each element."[13] In other words, on Murray's view, it is wrong to argue that since many hymns are prayers, their content should be determined by the Bible's teaching about prayer.[14] Rather, since song is an "element" distinct from prayer, it requires an independent scriptural warrant specifying its distinct content.

13. John Murray, "Song in Public Worship," in *Worship in the Presence of God*, ed. Frank J. Smith and David C. Lachman (Greenville, SC: Greenville Presbyterian Theological Seminary Press, 1992), 179–80. This article is reprinted from "Minority Report of the Committee on Song in the Public Worship of God," *Minutes of the Fourteenth General Assembly of the Orthodox Presbyterian Church* (1947), 58–66, available at www.opc.org/GA/song.html#Minority.

14. This position is taken in the committee's majority report (see Smith and Lachman, *Worship in the Presence of God*, 375–92), "Report of the Committee on Song in the Public Worship of God," *Minutes of the Thirteen General Assembly of the Orthodox Presbyterian Church* (1946), 101–7, and *Minutes of the Fourteenth General Assembly of the Orthodox Presbyterian Church* (1947), 58–66. This report is available at www.opc.org/GA/song.html.

I would question whether song is indeed an element in Murray's sense. It seems more biblical to me to regard song as a circumstance—that is, as a way of praying, a way of teaching, and so on. Further, the argument that each element of worship requires a biblical rationale independent of the others seems to me to lack biblical support or even confessional support.

I believe that there is considerable overlap among the elements of worship. Song is a form of teaching, prayer, and praise. Teaching should also be a form of praise, as we teach one another in God's very presence. Praise should be a form of teaching, for it should edify the congregation as to God's worthiness for praise. Indeed, the whole service is prayer, because it is presented in God's presence. And the whole service is teaching, for every element of worship serves to edify the people. The notion that worship can be neatly broken up into independent units is based more on philosophical atomism than on Scripture.

We should allow Scripture itself to tell us how the elements of worship are related, rather than assume an atomistic structure. Hymns that are also prayers should be governed both by God's rules for hymns and by his rules for prayer.

2. A more plausible hypothesis is that God's commandments for worship must be specific to each redemptive era. For example, God's commandments to bring animal sacrifices to the temple do not apply specifically to the New Testament age. Therefore, on this view, we cannot justify a practice in New Testament worship unless God specifically commands it for New Testament worship. On this view, for example, choirs are excluded, for God commanded them for Old Testament temple worship, not specifically for New Testament worship.

Certainly it is true that God's commandments for worship vary from age to age. God abrogates older practices (such as animal sacrifices) and replaces them with newer ones (such as the Lord's Supper). But Scripture does not suggest that these changes have a general rationale such as the previous paragraph describes. In Scripture, the abrogation of animal sacrifices under the new covenant is not based on the mere absence of a specific divine command. Rather, it is based on the finality of the sacrifice of the Son of God. Scripture never says that worship under each new covenant requires a completely new set of divine commands.

Significantly, there are no recorded divine commands specifically listing the elements of synagogue worship. God evidently approved that worship, as it was Jesus' custom to attend it (Luke 4:16). Worship in the synagogue was evidently based on general principles, not specific ones. It is obvious throughout Scripture that God wants people to gather in his name, to read his Word, and to pray. Those who formed synagogues worshiped according to those general principles, not according to some revelation specific to the synagogue.

The same has been true in all covenantal eras with regard to private and family worship. For such worship, God has never given a specific list of elements. Rather, individuals and families worship according to general principles, assuming that in all ages God desires our prayer, praise, and reading of his Word.

New Testament corporate worship, unlike synagogue, private, and family worship, is governed by some principles and ordinances specific to the era of the new covenant. Baptism and the Lord's Supper, together with the overall pattern of celebrating the resurrection of Jesus, are examples. And, as we have seen, the New Testament does abrogate some previous practices. But there is no suggestion in the New Testament that the fulfillment of redemption in Christ abrogates all previous practices that are not specifically reauthorized for the new covenant.[15]

Some Reformed people have argued, for example, that the new covenant excludes the use of orchestras and choirs because these were aspects of temple worship, and that form of worship is completely abrogated. But Scripture never says that temple worship is completely abrogated. Christ's sacrifice makes an end to animal sacrifices, but not to everything that went on in the temple. Temple worship contained not only animal sacrifices, but also prayer (as Acts 3:1), teaching (Acts 5:25), and praise. There is no biblical reason to suppose that these elements (along with choirs and orchestras) require specific renewals for the new covenant age.

3. Another way of making God's prescriptions for worship overly specific is to demand specific biblical warrant even for the means of carrying out the elements of worship. Bushell, for example, demands, not only a specific biblical rationale for the use of songs in worship,[16] but also specific biblical instruction telling us which songs are to be used. One is inclined to say that at least the choice of songs is circumstantial, rather than elemental. Nobody says that the specific words of prayers or the specific words of sermons require specific biblical commands. But in the case of songs, Bushell says that a specific biblical command is required, because "the specific content of worship-song is determinable from Scripture, while the specific content of preaching is not."[17] That is to say, if Scripture commanded us to use certain prayers, sermons, or songs in worship, we could not then use any others. But

---

15. The notion that all previous practices are implicitly abrogated unless renewed is more like dispensationalist exegesis than the exegesis typical of covenant theology.

16. He believes that songs are an "element" of worship, a view that I questioned earlier.

17. Bushell, The Songs of Zion, 32.

in fact, Bushell thinks, Scripture does not command us to use specific prayers or sermons, but does for songs.

Now, I don't think Scripture commands us what to sing in specific terms.[18] But at the moment I want to respond to Bushell's more general principle. Let's consider a parallel example. In Colossians 4:16–17, Paul authorizes the public reading of his letter, both in the church at Colossae and in other churches, and also the public reading of "the letter from Laodicea."[19] He similarly instructed that 1 Thessalonians be read publicly (see 1 Thess. 5:27). So we may say that there are biblical commands to read three of Paul's letters in church (I presume, in the worship meeting). But what about Romans or 1 Corinthians? On Bushell's principle, the specific commandments of Colossians 4:16–17 and 1 Thessalonians 5:27 imply that we are forbidden to read any other Pauline letters in church. Since there are biblical commands to read three of Paul's letters, we are forbidden to read any others. To read others would be a violation of the regulative principle, an addition to God's Word.

But that is absurd, and I think we should simply reject the principle that generates such an absurdity. Scripture gives us the general principle that we should read Scripture in worship, and applications of that principle in Colossians 4 and 1 Thessalonians 5. There is no reason to think that Scripture implicitly or explicitly forbids additional applications. Similarly, even if Scripture specifically authorized, say, the Psalms as worship songs, that would not forbid us to sing other worship songs that meet biblical criteria.

This is the general pattern of biblical ethics. For example, the eighth commandment says, "You shall not steal" (Ex. 20:15). Scripture gives us this general principle. It also gives us some specific applications: Do not steal an ox or a sheep (Ex. 22:1). But the applications of this command are not at all limited to the specific examples found in Scripture. The commandment forbids us to steal anything—including Samoan currency, automobiles, race horses, and candy bars—whether or not Scripture mentions those applications specifically.

So I reject all three attempts to require certain levels of specificity for divine commands under the regulative principle. God is free to regulate worship, as the rest of life, as generally or as specifically as he chooses. Our responsibility is to accept his prescriptions as they are, not to demand something he has not chosen to give. The regulative principle

18. Scripture does command us to sing "psalms," but I take that term to be a general reference to worship songs, rather than a specific reference to the biblical book of Psalms. See my *Worship in Spirit and Truth* (Phillipsburg, NJ: P&R Publishing, 1996), 123–27.

19. This may be a lost Pauline letter or another canonical letter, possibly Ephesians, that circulated through several churches.

itself demands that we recognize God's freedom in revelation. When God reveals his will at a general level, we should try to implement the specifics by our sanctified human wisdom. When he reveals his will more specifically, we should be grateful for that additional guidance. But we should not try to dictate to God how generally or how specifically he may speak to us.

Some may think that without specific divine commands, worship has no meaningful limits. Similarly, some theonomists (see chapter 13) have argued that unless God dictates to us specific civil penalties for every infraction of his law, then his law is useless. But that argument is inadequate, both for theonomy and for the regulative principle. There are some areas of life that are governed specifically by God's Word, but others that are not. God has chosen to rule his world, and his worship, in that way. And in making that choice, he rules us very well indeed.

So the regulative principle for worship is no different from the regulative principle for the rest of life. In both cases, God gives us his sufficient will in the Bible, and we apply Scripture to our specific situations by the general principles of his Word and the inward work of the Spirit.

Does the regulative principle require traditionalist worship? Both defenders and critics of the regulative principle have sometimes said that observing the principle will lead to a worship that is traditionalist, even archaic. That is not the case. In fact, the regulative principle is primarily a means of criticizing tradition. This is true in the Bible passages that warrant the principle. Recall, for example, Jesus' attack on the Pharisaic traditions (Matt. 15:1–9), using Isaiah 29:13. Through Isaiah, God charged Israel with worshiping according to the commandments of men—using the regulative principle against them. The Reformers also used the regulative principle to counter the traditionalism of the Roman church. In our own time as well, we should use the regulative principle as needed to counter the dead weight of tradition. Tradition can be a good thing, but not when it denies us the freedom to worship according to Scripture.

Worship according to Scripture is always contemporary in one sense. First Corinthians 14, the only extended passage in the New Testament dealing with Christian worship after the resurrection of Jesus, has as its main theme the importance of intelligibility in worship. Paul urges the church not to allow in worship services the use of uninterpreted tongues, for those cannot be understood by people and are therefore not edifying. All worship should be edifying (1 Cor. 14:26). The Reformers applied this principle by worshiping in common languages rather than Latin. For us, this principle certainly excludes worship that is primarily archaic.[20] And, in my judgment, it also warrants contemporary music, when it is appropriate to the purposes of worship.[21]

So the regulative principle guards, not only the authority of God and the sufficiency of his Word, but the freedom of the Christian as well. It is always true that the authority of God frees us from the tyranny of human beings. It is "the perfect law, the law of liberty" (James 1:25; cf. 2:12). The regulative principle is another example of how God's Word sets us free.[22]

CONCLUSIONS ON THE REGULATIVE PRINCIPLE

Although I have affirmed what I take to be the main thrust of the regulative principle, I have objected to some of the elaborations of it found in the Reformed tradition, including a few in the confessions themselves. To summarize: in worship, as in all of life, we live by God's commands. His commands cover everything we do, so that whatever he does not command is prohibited. The proper applications of these commands, however, require human thought, consideration of the broader principles of Scripture, and the work of the Holy Spirit in our hearts.[23]

IMAGES IN WORSHIP

I have discussed elsewhere a number of applications of the regulative principle to specific areas of worship, dealing with controversies over exclusive psalmody, the legitimacy of musical instruments, choirs and soloists, lifting hands, clapping, drama and dance, observance of Christmas and Easter, etc.[24] I would like to consider here another controversy that relates

20. Note the word "primarily." A little archaism isn't bad, if it's explained sufficiently and used to connect modern worshipers with the saints of old.

21. See my *Contemporary Worship Music: A Biblical Defense* (Phillipsburg, NJ: P&R Publishing, 1997).

22. Some of the arguments in this discussion are taken from my unpublished essay, "A Fresh Look at the Regulative Principle," which goes into more depth at some points and responds to objections by T. David Gordon. For still more discussion, see my book *Worship in Spirit and Truth.*

23. After all is said and done, I think the term *applications* is better than the more traditional terms *circumstances, expressions,* and *forms.* The traditional terms, as we've seen, lead to unnecessary complications. The term *application* shows that decisions about worship should be made the same way as decisions in other areas of life. I have discussed the methodology of application in the earlier chapters of this book.

24. *Worship in Spirit and Truth,* esp. chapters 6, 8, and 11.

more closely to the specific concerns of the second commandment. That issue concerns the uses of images in worship. Should we allow pictures in a place of worship? If so, of what kind?

I argued in chapter 25 that the second commandment does not forbid the making of images or the presence of images in places of worship. Indeed, the Lord himself commanded the use of images in the tabernacle and the temple. The commandment excludes only the worshiping of images and the making of images for the purpose of worshiping them.

Clearly, God did not intend for the images of cherubim, trees, and flowers in the tabernacle and the temple to be objects of worship. What, then, was their purpose? Evidently these were symbols intended to teach Israel, to remind them of the Lord's dealing with them. Teaching is a major aspect of worship under the new covenant as well, as we have seen in 1 Corinthians 14.

There have been discussions in the church as to whether it is legitimate under the new covenant to use images in places of worship for the purpose of teaching. The iconoclastic controversy, largely in the Eastern Church, was resolved in 787 by the Second Council of Nicaea, sometimes called the Seventh Ecumenical Council. The council determined that the presence of images in places of worship was legitimate and beneficial, as long as the images were not worshiped. Those favoring the use of images claimed that they were a valuable teaching tool. We recall that literacy and the distribution of literature in those days was nowhere near as extensive as today. So it is understandable that many felt the need for a visual type of teaching, in addition to oral instruction.

This view has prevailed in the Eastern Orthodox and Roman Catholic communions, but some Protestants have questioned it. Martin Luther opposed the violent iconoclasm of Karlstadt and others, and he approved, with many cautions, the pedagogical use of images: "If the worship of images be avoided, we may use them as we do the words of Scripture, which bring things before the mind and cause us to remember them."[25] Reformed confessions, however, explicitly reject the pedagogical use of images. The Heidelberg Catechism is the most forthright:

> Q. 98. *But may not pictures be tolerated in churches as books for the people?*
>
> A. No, for we should not be wiser than God, who will not have His people taught by dumb idols, but by the lively preaching of His Word.[26]

25. Cited by Charles Hodge, *Systematic Theology* (reprint, Grand Rapids: Eerdmans, n.d.), 3:303–4, adding two other citations from Luther to the same effect.
26. Cf. the Second Helvetic Confession, 4.

I know of no Bible passage, however, that restricts teaching in the church to oral and written communication. People sometimes appeal to 1 Corinthians 1:21, which the KJV translates, "It pleased God by the foolishness of preaching to save them that believe." But this passage is better rendered in the ESV, "It pleased God through the folly of what we preach to save those who believe." God's powerful "foolishness" in this verse is not the oral medium, but the content proclaimed through that medium, the gospel itself. The issue confronting the unbelieving world is not the medium of preaching, as opposed to images, drama, a written text, or something else. It is rather a specific message, communicated by means of Paul's preaching, but which can also be communicated in a variety of other media.

Under the old covenant, God did in fact choose to instruct his people by means of images as well as words. I know of nothing in the new covenant that would make this impossible.[27] There is, of course, no specific command of God to use images as teaching aids in new covenant worship. But, as I indicated in the previous section, the biblical regulative principle does not require us to have specific commands for worship pertaining to each covenant. Rather, there are general principles that pertain equally to all covenants, and it seems to me that the pedagogical use of images is one of them.

When images are put in a place of worship, there is sometimes the danger that people will worship them. That was especially true in the Reformation period, when converts from Roman Catholicism to Protestantism had been accustomed to paying homage to pictures and statues. In a situation where people are coming into the church from a background of idolatry, there is much wisdom in eliminating images from the worship area. But this is a decision based on wisdom, not a divine mandate binding in all situations. Charles Hodge says, "No one who has ever seen any of the masterpieces of Christian art, whether of the pencil or of the chisel, and felt how hard it is to resist the impulse to 'bow down to them and serve them,' can doubt the wisdom of their exclusion from places of public worship."[28] That may be true, though I include myself among those who have never felt this impulse. But even Hodge presents this exclusion as an exercise of wisdom, rather than a universal divine mandate.

27. The notion that worship without images is somehow simpler, purer, or more spiritual has appeared in theological literature. But I know of no biblical basis for this assertion. Even under the new covenant, God provides the visual imagery of the sacraments. Prejudices against the material and visual have more in common with Gnosticism than with anything in Scripture.

28. Hodge, *Systematic Theology*, 3:304–5.

I think that in most Protestant churches in the modern West, there is little danger of pictures becoming temptations to idolatry. I am even more certain that this danger does not exist with regard to symbols: crosses, doves, the Christian fish, decorated banners, and so on. Certainly we cannot fault God for minimizing this danger in his directions for decorating the tabernacle and the temple, even though Israel lived in the midst of idolatrous nations. The presumption, therefore, should be in favor of the use of such symbolism for teaching.

We have learned much in our time about how people have different learning styles. Some people are more oriented to listening and reading, others to visual images, others to activities. I know of no biblical reason to confine the teaching of the Word of God to the verbal medium, depriving worshipers whose learning styles are more visual.

IMAGES OF JESUS

Even granting the legitimacy of having some images in the church, many have balked at having images of Jesus. Jesus is God incarnate, so an image of Jesus is an image of God himself. As we have seen, the Larger Catechism forbids "the making any representation of God, of all or of any of the three persons" (WLC, 109). That certainly includes Jesus, the second person of the Trinity.

But again I must differ with the Catechism. As we saw in chapter 25, the second commandment does not forbid the making of images, even of God. It forbids making images for the purpose of worshiping them. Below I will reply to some arguments against the pedagogical use of pictures of Jesus.

Since Jesus is God, and God cannot be pictured, Jesus cannot be pictured either. In this argument, I reject the premise that God cannot be pictured. Although God is immaterial and invisible, he has many images. Each human being images him, and Jesus is God's image par excellence, "the image of the invisible God" (Col. 1:15; cf. Heb. 1:3). Jesus images God, not only in his powers and character, but also in his physical being. He said to Philip, "Whoever has seen me has seen the Father" (John 14:9).[29]

So there is no reason to assume that Jesus cannot be pictured. The apostles recalled the ministry of the incarnate Christ as a lavish visual feast

29. Review also the discussion of God's redemptive-historical invisibility in chapter 25. God sometimes chooses to use a *temunah*, a visible form, to reveal himself. The prohibition of images in Deut. 4 is not because God has no *temunah*, but because he chose not to reveal his *temunah* to Israel on the day of the assembly.

(1 John 1:1–3). They saw him, they looked on him, he was made manifest to them. The visual nature of the incarnation was something precious to them. And when Docetists denied that Jesus came in the flesh, John identified that view as a terrible heresy (1 John 4:2–3; 2 John 7). If cameras had been available in that day, one could have taken a photograph of Jesus. If the Shroud of Turin should ever prove authentic, it would bear a true likeness of our Lord.

Since we don't know what Jesus looked like, any image of him is necessarily a lie. In fact, we do know some things about Jesus' appearance. He was male, in his early thirties during his ministry, and Semitic. He sometimes wore a robe. We don't know further details (though, again, if the Shroud of Turin proves to be authentic, it could reveal much more information).[30]

But of course no image, not even a photograph, reveals everything about a person. Formal portraits reveal only the front, not the back, and of course no internal organs. To say that a picture is a lie because it excludes some detail is unfair. People usually understand the amount of detail that an artist claims for his image, and they don't hold him accountable for anything more than that. A cartoon caricature of a political leader may look different from the politician himself, but people who understand the conventions governing cartoons will recognize the image as capturing truth. Nobody ever suggests that good caricaturists tell lies because their pictures differ markedly from their subjects.

Sometimes the relationship between an image and its subject is almost purely conventional. Cornelius Van Til represented God by a circle, placed above a smaller circle representing creation. The circle does not look like God, or even like a theophany. But people are usually willing to accept the conventions warranting this sort of diagram, and nobody ever calls it a lie.

So it is possible to make a genuine picture of Jesus, even if the image turns out not to look very much like Jesus. What use is this? It reminds us that Jesus was a real, visible person, come in the flesh.

Some Sunday school materials, seeking to respect the Larger Catechism, have included pictures of Bible characters and places, but not of Jesus. This practice gives the student the impression that Jesus during his earthly ministry was an invisible presence. But that encourages Docetism, the heresy the apostle John warned us against in the texts cited earlier. Docetism says that Jesus did not really come in the flesh. That is a very serious error, not one that we should encourage in our children. Rather, we should include

---

30. People have sometimes taken Isa. 53:2–3 as a physical description of Jesus. I think it is that, but it presents mainly the physical effects of his suffering, rather than his appearance apart from that.

pictures of Jesus in our teaching materials, so as to give our students some sense of the profound visibility of God's coming into our midst.

Images of Jesus circumscribe his divine nature or separate it from his human nature. The iconoclasts of the Eastern Church argued that an image of Jesus attempts to picture either his divine nature or his human nature. If it pictures his divine nature, they argued, then it tries to make that nature finite, circumscribing it by the artistic medium. But if it pictures his human nature alone, then it makes a separation between the two natures, the heresy ascribed to Nestorius and condemned by the Council of Chalcedon in 451.

The answer to this dilemma, I think, is that a picture of Jesus is a picture neither of his divine nature nor of his human nature, but of his person. The Council of Chalcedon declared that Jesus had two natures in one person. A nature cannot be the subject of a photograph. Natures are abstract properties. When people looked at Jesus on earth, what they saw was his person, a man with two natures, a man who was also God. And certainly they did see him, which is to say that there were images of Jesus upon their retinas and in their minds. That fact in itself shows that images of Jesus were possible (indeed inevitable) and legitimate.

If his divine nature was circumscribed in some way,[31] it was circumscribed by his incarnate flesh, not by any artist. Someone taking a picture of Jesus with a camera would have simply recorded the result of that circumscription, the divine-human person Jesus, on film. The question of how the divine nature could be limited by flesh is a mystery of the faith, but it remains equally mysterious whether or not there are pictures of Jesus.[32]

So I know of no reason to forbid pictures of Jesus. Of course, we should be cautious in the use of such pictures, just as with the other kinds of pictures discussed in the previous section. People who are inclined to worship images may be especially inclined to worship pictures of Jesus. But in many situations today (such as the average children's Sunday school in present-day America) that danger is minimal or nonexistent. And there are positive reasons to use pictures of Jesus in the church's pedagogy.

---

31. I put the matter hypothetically, because I hesitate to say that the divine nature was "circumscribed" by the incarnation. Indeed, I'm not sure what "circumscribed" would mean in this connection. Jesus' body was finite, but as God he continued to rule throughout the universe. But perhaps "circumscribed" can be taken as follows: Jesus' body was a special location of deity, like the holiest part of the temple. That use of the term is acceptable.

32. For a fuller discussion of these issues, grounded exegetically and historically, see Jeffrey J. Meyers, *"Vere Homo*: The Case *for* Pictures of the Lord Jesus Christ" (Niceville, FL: Biblical Horizons, 1993), available at http://www.hornes.org/theologia/content/jeffrey_meyers/vere_homo_the_case_for_pictures_of_jesus.htm.

CHAPTER 27

The Third Commandment:
Reverence for God's Name

The third commandment reads, "You shall not take the name of the LORD your God in vain, for the LORD will not hold him guiltless who takes his name in vain" (Ex. 20:7). The name Yahweh, the name of our covenant Lord, is holy, and our use of that name should reflect his holiness. We should not utter his name without expressing in some measure the reverence and awe that are due to him, for that would be to speak in a way that denies his nature.

The use of God's name, therefore, constitutes worship, either broad or narrow, true or false. When we use God's name, we must remember that we stand in his holy presence, and his presence always creates a situation of worship, of reverence and awe. So the third commandment continues the emphasis on worship that we have seen especially in the first four commandments. The first commandment deals with the object of worship (situational perspective), the second with the regulation of worship (normative perspective), and the third with the attitude toward worship (existential perspective).

As with the other commandments, the fundamental idea of the third commandment has many implications. Note the applications made in WLC, 112–13:

Q. 112. *What is required in the third commandment?*

A. The third commandment requires, that the name of God, his titles, attributes, ordinances, the word, sacraments, prayer, oaths, vows, lots, his works, and whatsoever else there is whereby he makes himself known, be holily and reverently used in thought, meditation, word, and writing; by an holy profession, and answerable conversation, to the glory of God, and the good of ourselves, and others.

Q. 113. *What are the sins forbidden in the third commandment?*

A. The sins forbidden in the third commandment are, the not using of God's name as is required; and the abuse of it in an ignorant, vain, irreverent, profane, superstitious, or wicked mentioning, or otherwise using his titles, attributes, ordinances, or works, by blasphemy, perjury; all sinful cursing, oaths, vows, and lots; violating of our oaths and vows, if lawful; and fulfilling them, if of things unlawful; murmuring and quarreling at, curious prying into, and misapplying of God's decrees and providences; misinterpreting, misapplying, or any way perverting the word, or any part of it, to profane jests, curious or unprofitable questions, vain janglings,[1] or the maintaining of false doctrines; abusing it, the creatures, or anything contained under the name of God, to charms, or sinful lusts and practices; the maligning, scorning, reviling, or any wise opposing of God's truth, grace, and ways; making profession of religion in hypocrisy, or for sinister ends; being ashamed of it, or a shame to it, by unconformable, unwise, unfruitful, and offensive walking, or backsliding from it.

The Westminster divines believed that the third commandment, like the other commandments, presents a broad perspective on the Christian life that in effect defines all virtues and all sins. And, of course, it also focuses on a number of specific sins. So the commandment has a broad meaning and a narrow meaning.

THE NAME OF THE LORD

I shall try to define the breadth and narrowness of the commandment first by looking at the significant terms in the text: "the name of the Lord," "take," "in vain," and the concluding curse sanction.

---

1. In case any readers are not convicted of the sin of vain jangling, the phrase is from the KJV translation of 1 Tim. 1:6. The Greek term is also translated "vain discussion" (ESV) and "meaningless talk" (NIV).

First, let us consider the name of the Lord.[2] Naming in Scripture accomplishes three purposes: exercising sovereignty (control), giving revelation (authority), and locating (presence).

NAMING IS EXERCISING SOVEREIGNTY (CONTROL)

First, naming is an exercise of sovereign control. The one who gives a name to someone else has some measure of control over the one who receives it. The parent names the child, the conqueror names the conquered city, and the Lord names his people. Yahweh names himself, for there is no one higher than him. This fact indicates his aseity, his self-sufficiency, his control over all things pertaining to himself.

It has been thought that to know someone's name is to have some power over that person. In paganism, this belief underlies the use of names in curses to bring injury. As with all pagan beliefs, this one is parasitic on the truth. Knowing someone's name does give us an advantage in our dealings with him. Even today, we exchange names with strangers by a somewhat formal style of introduction, understanding that the exchange of names initiates a relationship that can bring benefits or burdens.

Remarkably, in Scripture, God does share his name with his people. This fact underscores the fundamentally personal character of our relationship with the Supreme Being (chapter 3).[3] In revealing his name, he does not relinquish any of his own power or control. But knowing his name enables his people to call upon him (Ps. 20:1; Prov. 18:10), thus availing themselves of his power. As Jacob discovered through his wrestling with God at Peniel, this is much like having power over God (Gen. 32:22–32, esp. v. 29). According to Hosea 12:4, Jacob was, at Peniel, both a victor and a petitioner at the same time: "He strove with the angel and prevailed; he wept and sought his favor."[4]

---

2. For more discussion of God's name and names, see *DG*, 343–61.

3. Ben Kim, a former student, pointed out to me that in Confucian societies one may not call a superior by his name, only by a title. In the West, that principle exists in military discipline ("Yes, Sir!") and in other areas such as the use of "Majesty" and "Highness" in royal etiquette. Fathers and mothers, also, for good reasons, discourage their children from addressing them by name. These facts underscore the greatness of the privilege we have of addressing God by his personal name Yahweh (Lord) and by the name Jesus. Certainly, Judaism lost something important when it came to regard *Yahweh* as too holy to be pronounced. I will say much in this chapter on the importance of reverence for the divine name. Reverence stresses the transcendence of God. We should not forget, however, that the very fact that God has given us his name is a remarkable expression of his immanence, his covenant friendship with us.

4. The "angel" is God himself, as we see in Gen. 32:28–30.

God also places his name upon his people (Num. 6:27; Deut. 28:10; 2 Chron. 7:14; Dan. 9:18–19; Rev. 13:6), identifying his future with theirs. As long as they bear his name rightly, not in vain, he will protect them by his power.

Naming Is Characterizing (Authority)

Names in Scripture both denote and describe; that is, they have both denotation and connotation. To name somebody is to say something about him. A father would express in the child's name his hopes for the child, some circumstances of the child's birth, or his feelings about the event. *Abraham* is a proper noun, designating a particular human being, and it also describes him as "father of a multitude." *Yahweh*, as we have seen, is also a proper name, designating the one true God.[5] But it also describes God as the ultimate Lord, focusing on his attributes of control, authority, and presence. God names himself, and in doing so he presents to us an authoritative declaration of who he is and what he does.

In that way, his names are revelational. *Yahweh* connotes God's lordship attributes, *Elohim* his creative power, *El Shaddai* his might, *El Elyon* his transcendence, *Yahweh Sabaoth*, his lordship over the armies of heaven.

So we sometimes use the term *name* broadly to mean "reputation," as when we speak of "Peter's good name." First Kings 4:31 says that Solomon's name (translated "fame" in the ESV) "was in all the surrounding nations." Proverbs 22:1 says, "A good name is to be chosen rather than great riches, and favor is better than silver or gold." It is in this sense that Psalm 8:1 says, "O LORD, our Lord, how majestic is your name in all the earth!" God has revealed his greatness in the heavens, in the earth, and in man, his image; so his fame, his reputation, is great.

Naming Is Locating (Presence)

A name also serves to mark a person. It furnishes a way of locating a person in a crowd. We can find him by calling his name, because it distinguishes him from other people. Where the name is, he is.

Our names become closely identified with us. When someone forgets your name, or laughs at it, or mispronounces it, you feel slighted. This is even more obviously the case in the broader use of *name* to mean

---

5. Of the various names of God, only *Yahweh* refers exclusively to the true God. *Elohim*, for example, can refer both to the true God and to false gods. So *Yahweh* is the proper name of God in a unique sense. Other names can become exclusive by compounding, as *Elohim Yisrael*, God of Israel (Ex. 5:1).

"reputation." To injure Tom's good name is to injure him. To revere his name is to revere him.

God is also identified with his name. To praise his name is to praise him; to despise his name is to despise him. Glory is due his name (Pss. 29:2; 66:2; 96:8). We are saved for "his name's sake" (Ps. 106:8; cf. 1 Sam. 12:22; Pss. 23:3; 25:11; 79:9), because, as we saw above, we bear his name. We give thanks to his name (Ps. 140:13) and trust his holy name (Ps. 33:21). God redeems his people for the sake of his own reputation, his glory, his name.

Indeed, God's name has divine attributes. It is glorious and awesome (Deut. 28:58), majestic (Ps. 8:1, 9), and holy (Lev. 20:3; Pss. 33:21; 99:3; etc.). So, like the word of God, God's name is God himself.[6] This helps us to understand why the names of God should always be used in a reverent way. For when we deal with God's name or names, we are dealing with God himself.

I have been correlating God's name with his lordship attributes of control, authority, and presence. We should now be able to show how the name of God is both narrow and broad. Moving from narrow to broad, God's name is (1) the proper name Yahweh, (2) other names like Elohim, El Shaddai, and El Elyon, (3) his whole revelation of himself and the human reception of that revelation (i.e., his reputation), and (4) Yahweh himself.

BEARERS OF GOD'S NAME

Obviously there is a sense in which Yahweh uniquely bears his own name. He alone is Yahweh. But, remarkably, as we have seen, he appoints others to share his name in certain ways. His name dwells in the tabernacle and in the temple (Deut. 12:11; Ezra 6:12; cf. Ezek. 43:7). It is located in the special angel who led Israel to the Promised Land (Ex. 23:20–21), who is certainly the same angel elsewhere identified with Yahweh himself (Gen. 32:22–32; Hos. 12:3–4). As we have mentioned, God also places his name on his people, whom he identifies with his dwelling in Revelation 13:6. And his name is located, par excellence, in Jesus Christ, the only name given by which we must be saved (Acts 4:12), to which every knee shall bow (Phil. 2:9–11). So the third commandment is fulfilled in Jesus. We have seen that he is our exclusive object of worship (first commandment) and the true image of God (second commandment). Now

6. Cf. the discussion in chapter 9 that God himself is our revealed standard for ethics, and *DG*, 470–75, which argues that God's word is identical with God himself. I plan to develop that point in greater depth in *The Doctrine of the Word of God* (forthcoming).

we see that he is the name of God par excellence. To despise the name of God is to despise Jesus, and vice versa.

God's name is also in the gospel of Christ, according to Acts 9:15. For there the Lord says that Paul will carry his name "before the Gentiles and kings and the children of Israel." God's plan is for Gentiles, as well as Jews, to bear his name, as they come to bear the name of Jesus.

And there is a sense in which the whole creation bears the name of God. As we saw in chapter 23, the heaven and the earth are God's throne and footstool (Isa. 66:1; Acts 7:49) and therefore his temple. In Matthew 23:16–22, there is an interesting variation on this theme. There, Jesus accuses the scribes and Pharisees of trying to find loopholes to mitigate the force of their oaths:

> Woe to you, blind guides, who say, "If anyone swears by the temple, it is nothing, but if anyone swears by the gold of the temple, he is bound by his oath." You blind fools! For which is greater, the gold or the temple that has made the gold sacred? And you say, "If anyone swears by the altar, it is nothing, but if anyone swears by the gift that is on the altar, he is bound by his oath." You blind men! For which is greater, the gift or the altar that makes the gift sacred? So whoever swears by the altar swears by it and by everything on it. And whoever swears by the temple swears by it and by him who dwells in it. And whoever swears by heaven swears by the throne of God and by him who sits upon it.

Jesus had addressed the same issue earlier, in Matthew 5:33–37:

> Again you have heard that it was said to those of old, "You shall not swear falsely, but shall perform to the Lord what you have sworn." But I say to you, Do not take an oath at all, either by heaven, for it is the throne of God, or by the earth, for it is his footstool, or by Jerusalem, for it is the city of the great King. And do not take an oath by your head, for you cannot make one hair white or black. Let what you say be simply "Yes" or "No"; anything more than this comes from evil.

I shall discuss later whether the latter passage forbids all oaths. For the moment, let us consider the issue common to these two texts. The Jews hesitated to use the name of God in their oaths, fearing his wrath if they failed to do what they had sworn. So they used other names, hoping that the consequences of failure would not be as bad. But Jesus says that when we swear by anything at all—by the gold in the temple, the temple itself, the altar, the gift on the altar, or by heaven, by earth, by Jerusalem, or even by our own head—we are in effect swearing by God. The holiness of the temple, for example, depends on God. When we swear by the temple, we call on God to continue maintaining its holiness, so as to bring curses on the one who swears falsely by it. But the same is true of our own heads. If we swear by our own head (e.g., "May my hair turn white if I don't perform my oath"), we are swearing by God, for only God can determine our hair color. Only he, therefore, can administer the oath sanction.

I conclude that because God has created all things and remains sovereign over them, to swear by anything is to swear by him. That is to say that in one sense the whole creation bears his name. The whole creation is under his control, it authoritatively reveals his nature, and God is present throughout it.

To bear God's name is to be a location of his presence. There are different ways in which God can be present, and therefore different ways of bearing his name: (1) In the broadest sense, God's presence is everywhere. (2) God locates himself in special places, where his presence is felt intensely, as in his theophanies and in the tabernacle and the temple. (3) God's name dwells in himself, one God, with all his Trinitarian distinctions; therefore, in the divine angel of the Lord, the Holy Spirit, and Jesus Christ. (4) God's name dwells in his covenant people, his church. These different types of name-bearing correspond to the senses of holiness that I distinguished in figure 6 of chapter 23.

So both the nature of God's name and the range of its bearers show us that the commandment is both narrow and broad. It is sinful to use divine names such as Yahweh irreverently, and it is also wrong to misuse anything in the whole creation. All sin, therefore, can be seen as a violation of the third commandment.

"TAKING" THE NAME

The same conclusion follows from the verb of the main clause. We usually think of the commandment as a commandment about language, about what we may say and how we should say it. Certainly that is an important part of our obligation, since God's "name," literally and narrowly understood, is a piece of language. But the verb here is not *amar* or *davar*, one of the common Hebrew words translated "speak." Rather, it is *nasa'*, a term usually translated "lift up, bear, carry."

So the commandment is not only about speaking God's name, but, more broadly, bearing it. What does it mean to bear God's name? I indicated earlier that God places his name upon his people (as in Num. 6:27). So we

belong to him. Our identity is to be the people of God. We take that identity with us wherever we go. Whenever we violate his covenant, we bring
dishonor on the name of God that we bear. We injure God's reputation, his
good name. So, again, any sin is a violation of the third commandment.

It is interesting to note a parallel between the third commandment and
Psalm 24:3–4:

> Who shall ascend the hill of the LORD?
>   And who shall stand in his holy place?
> He who has clean hands and a pure heart,
>   who does not lift up his soul to what is false
>   and does not swear deceitfully.

One of the moral qualifications for standing in God's presence is not to
"lift up" one's soul to what is false. "Lift up" here is *nasa'*, as in the third
commandment, and "what is false" is *shav'*, translated "in vain" in the third
commandment. The psalm likely alludes to the commandment. Interestingly, however, in the psalm "his soul" replaces "the name of the LORD your
God." Here in the context of temple worship, to lift one's soul to vanity
is the equivalent of lifting God's name to vanity, indicating a close connection between the soul and the name of God. God is so identified with
believers that to defile our own lives ("soul") is to defile his name. So again
we see that the commandment governs all of life.

VANITY

The term *shav'*, translated "in vain," has several meanings in the Old
Testament. It can mean "empty, trivial, meaningless," as in Job 7:3.[7] It often
refers to unsuccessful action (Job 15:31; 35:13; Pss. 60:11; 89:47; Jer. 2:30;
4:30; 6:29; 46:11; etc.). It refers generally to human wickedness in Job 11:11
and 31:5, and specifically to lies in Deuteronomy 5:20 (the Deuteronomic
version of the ninth commandment),[8] Psalm 12:2, and Job 31:5.

Sometimes it is not clear which of these meanings best fits the context, as in Psalms 26:4 and 41:6, since meaninglessness and falsehood are
closely related in Scripture.[9] In Psalm 24:4, which I mentioned above as
an allusion to the third commandment, lifting up one's soul to vanity is

---

7. *Hevel*, a different term, is found in the famous texts in Ecclesiastes (1:2, 14; 2:1,
etc.), which proclaim that all is vanity.

8. The Exodus version, 20:16, uses a different Hebrew term, *sheqer*.

9. In some ways, of course, false statements are meaningful, as most philosophers would
assert. But false statements fail to connect with reality. They fail to guide us in the right

parallel to swearing deceitfully. Leviticus 19:12 indicates that swearing falsely by God's name profanes that name. A chief example of both falsehood and meaninglessness is idolatry, which is called *shav'* in Psalm 31:6 and Jeremiah 18:15.

Meaninglessness is a form of falsehood, for the name of God is itself rich in meaning. When we trivialize that name, we attempt to dilute that meaning and therefore falsify or distort it. And falsehood is certainly one form of vanity, a use of the divine name that reduces its significance and power. So meaninglessness and falsehood include one another as misuses of God's name.

If the central idea here is falsehood, then the commandment envisages a legal context in which someone swears to tell the truth using God's name. In that situation, the commandment enjoins true witness. Other applications would be built on that foundation. But it seems to me that on this understanding the ninth commandment, which more clearly focuses on the legal process, becomes superfluous. For that reason, and on account of the broader use of *shav'* in Scripture, I prefer to read the commandment as a prohibition of "vain" or "empty" use of the divine name. Certainly that includes lying oaths, but the initial focus of the commandment is broader.

THE SANCTION

"For the LORD will not hold him guiltless . . ." The commandment adds here a sanction, as does the second commandment, but a much shorter one, without a blessing.

Blasphemy, the violation of the third commandment, is considered a particularly serious crime in Scripture. It is a capital crime, for "sojourners" as well as the people of Israel (Lev. 24:15–16). Scripture describes this evil also as reviling God's name (Ps. 74:10, 18), despising his name (Isa. 52:5–6), and cursing his name (Rev. 16:9; cf. vv. 11, 21).

The Jewish charge against Jesus, which led to his crucifixion, was a charge of blasphemy, because he made himself out to be God (Matt. 26:65).[10] The worst sin that Jesus himself refers to is "blasphemy against

---

direction. So in false statements the overall purpose of language fails. Perhaps that is the insight that lies behind the biblical treatment of these concepts.

10. Note that in the words of Jesus in verse 64, which the high priest considered blasphemous, there is no use of the divine name as such. The priest thought that Jesus had blasphemed, not because he literally misused the divine name, but because he

the Holy Spirit." That sin "will not be forgiven, either in this age or in the age to come" (Matt. 12:32). Douma explains:

> This particular form of blasphemy must be understood, in our judgment, as *willfully* misunderstanding and branding as *devilish* what in fact comes from the Holy Spirit. With your own eyes you see the work of the Holy Spirit, so clear that you cannot miss it—but then you proceed to ascribe the work of the Holy Spirit to the Devil! God does forgive sins—even sins committed against the Son of man will be forgiven—but *this* is going too far.[11]

Douma connects this passage with Hebrews 10:26–31. In general, Scripture teaches that by grace we can repent of even the worst sins and expect God's forgiveness. David committed adultery and murder; Paul before his conversion was an accessory to the murder of Stephen (Acts 22:20). But Scripture indicates that some sorts of sins mark a point beyond which repentance is impossible (Matt. 12:22–32; Mark 3:22–30; Heb. 6:4–10; 10:26–31). That is to say, some sins mark a level of disobedience at which God will not bring the grace of repentance and forgiveness. Looking at it from a human perspective, we could say that people who commit such sins are so hardened to God that they will never want to repent and so will never be forgiven. Therefore, if anyone is truly sorry for a sin and willing to repent before God and ask forgiveness, that is a sure sign that he has not committed blasphemy against the Holy Spirit.

THE NAME OF GOD IN WORSHIP

As we come to more specific applications, let us remember that this commandment, like the first, second, and fourth, focuses on worship. We have seen that our use of God's name is always in God's presence. And when God is present, we bow down, we engage in worship. Hence, we should always use God's name in reverence, the attitude of worship. To use God's name is always an act of worship, whether in a church service or outside.

Let us look first at the use of God's name in a context of worship. In worship, there are three prominent uses of his name: in oaths, confessions, and blessing. Oaths are an element of religious worship, according to WCF,

---

equated himself, a mere man, with God. So the concept of blasphemy extends beyond language to ideas and beliefs.

11. J. Douma, *The Ten Commandments* (Phillipsburg, NJ: P&R Publishing, 1996), 80 (emphasis his).

22.1.[12] Confessions have a place in worship, particularly as the congregation recites historic creeds. And blessing commonly occurs at the end of a service, in the benediction.[13] But, as we shall see, there are also appropriate roles for oaths, confessions, and blessings outside of formal worship, in other spheres of life. That is to say, these uses of the divine name occur in worship in the broad sense as well as in the narrow sense.[14] These three uses of God's name correspond roughly to the church's kingly, prophetic, and priestly ministries, respectively, and therefore to the situational, normative, and existential perspectives.

OATHS AND VOWS

In an oath, we call God to witness concerning the truth of a statement ("assertory") or a promise ("promissory"). A vow is a kind of promissory oath, promising to God that we will do something. It is possible to be under oath, in effect, without uttering the name of God,[15] though in general oaths involve such utterances. In an adjuration, for example, we are placed under oath by another party, usually someone in authority (Josh. 7:19; Matt. 26:63–64). There are also many cases in Scripture of a solemn attestation without specific use of the divine name, as when Joseph tells his brothers, "By this you shall be tested: by the life of Pharaoh, you shall not go from this place unless your youngest brother comes here" (Gen. 42:15; cf. 31:53; Deut. 27:11–26; Josh. 24:19–22; 1 Sam. 1:26). Jesus often underscores his teaching by the expression "truly, I say to you" (e.g., Matt. 5:18, 26; 6:2). The gospel of John typically represents Jesus uttering "truly" twice (e.g., 1:51; 3:3, 5).

Calling God to witness is asking him to use his power against us if we lie. So I connect oaths with God's lordship attribute of control and with the situational perspective. Hebrews 6:16 emphasizes that in oaths "people swear by something greater than themselves," something powerful enough to administer a sanction such as the third commandment contains. So the third commandment has a Godward reference. It is concerned especially with the honor of God. But there is also a manward reference: oaths help

12. In worship, oaths are present, e.g., in membership vows, the ordination of officers, and marriage vows.

13. Many churches also employ an "apostolic greeting" at the beginning of the service, such as "Grace to you and peace from God our Father and the Lord Jesus Christ" (Rom. 1:7). This too is a benediction, a blessing.

14. Recall the distinction between worship in the broad sense and worship in the narrow sense, from chapter 23.

15. In this regard, compare our earlier discussion of Matt. 23:16–22.

to maintain stability in a fallen world. Under certain circumstances, a person's word was to be accepted without corroboration on the basis of an oath (Ex. 22:10–11). So the oath has always been a vital aspect of civil law. When the oath is despised, the result is government corruption, civil injustice, and cultural chaos.

In modern Western society, people often take oaths and vows without seriousness, as the divorce rate attests. Some years ago, when the union of American air traffic controllers violated their oath not to strike, the news media saw the oath breaking as no great matter. When President Reagan fired all the controllers who had violated their oaths, the media almost universally condemned his action. Many worried that air disasters would ensue, or that air traffic would come to a standstill. That did not happen. Reagan's action provided a valuable countercultural impetus, though present-day cultural respect for oaths does not seem to have grown much since then. But legal penalties for lying under oath still remain, so that oaths are still taken seriously in formal legal processes.

In the Bible, the oath is serious business indeed. Scripture often commands us to take oaths and vows in the name of God (e.g., Ex. 22:10–11; Pss. 22:25; 50:14; 61:8; 65:1). Taking oaths in God's name, not in the name of another god, is a mark of allegiance to him (Deut. 6:13; 10:20; Isa. 19:18; 65:16; Jer. 12:16). The covenant itself is a relationship of oath-bound commitment, on God's part (Gen. 26:3; Deut. 7:8; 29:12, 14; Heb. 6:17) and on the part of the vassal (Ex. 24:3; Deut. 27–28). In the Psalms texts cited here, the taking and paying of vows is a synecdoche for the worship of God as a whole.

Many oaths and vows appear in the narrative of Scripture. God himself takes oaths in many places (Gen. 22:16 [cf. Heb. 6:13–17]; 26:3; Pss. 89:3, 49; 110:4; 132:11; Jer. 11:5; Ezek. 33:11; Luke 1:73). Jesus accepted the adjuration of the high priest in Matthew 26:63–64. He had been silent up to this point in his trial, but in response to the adjuration he spoke plainly of his divine power as Son of Man. An angel takes an oath in Revelation 10:5–6. Paul often appeals to God as witness to his teaching (Rom. 1:9; 9:1–2; 2 Cor. 1:23; 11:31; Gal. 1:20; Phil. 1:8; 1 Thess. 2:5, 10), and he places others under oath (1 Thess. 5:27). Other biblical characters take oaths (Gen. 14:22–23; 21:23–24), and the writer to the Hebrews tells us, without any criticism, that this is a common practice among people (Heb. 6:16).

Scripture often refers to oaths as legitimate, useful, and important. They are central to our covenant relationship with God and important to maintaining godly relationships with other people. A problem arises, therefore, when Jesus appears to prohibit oaths altogether:

> Again you have heard that it was said to those of old, "You shall not swear falsely, but shall perform to the Lord what you have sworn." But I say to you, Do not take an oath at all, either by heaven, for it is the throne of God, or by the earth, for it is his footstool, or by Jerusalem, for it is the city of the great King. And do not take an oath by your head, for you cannot make one hair white or black. Let what you say be simply "Yes" or "No"; anything more than this comes from evil. (Matt. 5:33–37; cf. James 5:12)

In view of what we have seen above, it would be very strange if Jesus intended to forbid oaths as such. Nowhere else in Scripture is there any hint of rebuke to anyone for the mere act of taking an oath (though of course there are examples of false and unwise oaths). The fact that oath-bound commitment is essential to our relationship with God is an especially telling datum. The fact that God himself swears is also important—more important than it might appear on the surface. It might be argued that God's right to swear does not imply *our* right to swear. On the other hand, in the context of Scripture, it is clear that God has far less reason to swear than we do. As the ultimate standard of truth, his yes is necessarily always yes and his no is always no. If he, who is perfectly trustworthy and even self-attesting, sometimes confirms his word with an oath, surely there are times when we ought to do the same.

To interpret Matthew 5:33–37 properly, we must remember that the Sermon on the Mount is not only an exposition of the law of God, but also a critique of Jewish distortions of it. Jesus here is not talking about all oaths, but oaths taken "by heaven," "by earth," "by Jerusalem," etc. Such oaths were often taken to escape the solemn responsibility that went with an oath in the name of Yahweh. As I mentioned earlier, Jesus teaches here (and in Matt. 23:16–22) that to swear by anything in creation is to swear by God, for God's name dwells in all creation. It is to those who misuse oaths in this way that Jesus says, "Do not take an oath at all" (5:34). But he does not intend to restrict the use of oaths by people who are aware of the solemnity and omnipresence of God's holy name. James 5:12 likely summarizes this teaching for people who are already aware of the context.[16]

So Matthew 5:33–37, Matthew 23:16–22, and James 5:12 do not forbid all use of oaths. Rather, they remind us of the seriousness of oaths, that God's involvement is inescapable, and that there are divine sanctions for failing to keep our commitments.

---

16. Rabbinic literature also teaches, "Let your yes be yes and your no, no," to discourage people from making frivolous or unnecessary oaths, without casting any aspersions on serious, solemn oaths.

The larger biblical teaching calls believers to form communities in which oaths will not be necessary, or, to put it differently, in which we will be constantly under oath. As we have seen, adjurations and informal oaths like "truly, truly" do obligate, as do "by Jerusalem" and "by my head." And a simple yes or no also obligates us before God.

In the new heavens and new earth, oaths will be unnecessary. So I suspect that in the present time it pleases God when we speak the truth to one another without oaths, except in cases where trust has broken down. In the family of God, it is best that oaths be rare. When we take them, we should speak with full awareness of the solemnity of God's name.

OATHS AND SIN

Oaths can be occasions of sin in several ways:

OATHS WITH WRONG CONTENT (NORMATIVE)

There are some oaths we should not take. These include, obviously, oaths taken to false gods (Ex. 23:13; cf. Deut. 6:13; 10:20; etc.). Oaths of allegiance to false religious organizations (including secret societies: see chapter 24) violate the third commandment as well as the first. Oaths can also go wrong when we pledge something unlawful. In Matthew 14:1–12, Herod takes an oath to give to the daughter of Herodias anything she wants, and she asks for the head of John the Baptist on a platter. (For other examples, see 1 Sam. 14:24–30 and Acts 23:12).

In general, we should never take an oath that obliges us to commit sin. The Larger Catechism takes this principle a step further and says that we should not even keep an existing oath if it is "of things unlawful" (WCL, 113). 1 Samuel 25 supports this principle. In verses 21–22, David takes an oath to kill every male in Nabal's household for his insulting breach of hospitality. Nabal's wife Abigail intercedes, and David reverses course:

> And David said to Abigail, "Blessed be the LORD, the God of Israel, who sent you this day to meet me! Blessed be your discretion, and blessed be you, who have kept me this day from bloodguilt and from avenging myself with my own hand! For as surely as the LORD the God of Israel lives, who has restrained me from hurting you, unless you had hurried and come to meet me, truly by morning there had not been left to Nabal so much as one male. (vv. 32–34)

Here, David does not keep his original oath. He recognizes that if he had kept it, it would have been contrary to God's will. The narrative certainly implies that this reversal was a good thing, that David's oath should not have been kept. The principle certainly makes sense, even apart from this proof text. To commit an atrocity is wrong, even if one has taken an oath to commit it. Further, one can imagine situations in which carrying out one oath might be contrary to another oath, which would require the breaking of one of them. In the above example, we saw that David's oath to destroy Nabal's family was contrary to his covenant oath to serve the Lord.

Another example can be found in 1 Samuel 14:24–46, where Saul takes an oath and curses anyone who eats food until he is avenged on his enemies. His son Jonathan, not knowing of the oath, eats some honey. Saul is about to kill Jonathan, but the people intercede on his behalf, ransoming his life (v. 45). The mechanics and theology of the ransom are not clear. What is clear is that Saul did not literally carry out his foolish vow, and that was a good thing.

In this connection, I should also make some reference to the vow of Jephthah in Judges 11:29–40. In this passage, Jephthah prepares to fight the Ammonites. "And Jephthah made a vow to the LORD and said, "If you will give the Ammonites into my hand, then whatever comes out from the doors of my house to meet me when I return in peace from the Ammonites shall be the LORD's, and I will offer it up for a burnt offering" (vv. 30–31). When he arrives home, his daughter comes out "to meet him with tambourines and with dances" (v. 34). Jephthah mourns, "Alas, my daughter! You have brought me very low, and you have become the cause of great trouble to me. For I have opened my mouth to the LORD, and I cannot take back my vow" (v. 35). With Jephthah's permission, his daughter spends two months in the hills with her companions weeping "for her virginity" (v. 38). Jephthah then keeps his vow (v. 39).

The implication seems to be that Jephthah sacrificed his daughter as a burnt offering. If that is what he did, he was certainly guilty of sin. God had strongly condemned human sacrifice (Lev. 18:21; Deut. 18:10), so Jephthah was certainly free to violate his vow when he saw that it would require him to sin; indeed, he was obligated to violate it. The fact that he preferred to keep the vow rather than to save his daughter would underscore one major theme of the book of Judges: the low spiritual state of the people when they lived without a king (Judg. 17:6; 21:25).

Others have taken the view that Jephthah did not kill his daughter in this way, but dedicated her to serve God in the sanctuary in perpetual virginity.[17] In favor of this view is the fact that *'olah*, translated "burnt offering" in verse 31, does not literally refer to burning. It comes from the verb *'alah*, "to go up," and evidently refers to the ascending of the smoke of the offering. Ascension offerings, as we may call them,[18] emphasize the total consecration of the offerer to God. To symbolize total consecration, the ascension offering of an animal must be thoroughly burnt, except for the skin (Lev. 1; 7:8). Might it be possible also to bring a human being to God as an *'olah*?[19] If so, he or she could not be burned, because of the strong divine prohibition of human sacrifice. The offering would have to consist of some other form of total consecration. Since the daughter wept for her virginity (vv. 37–38), some have thought that her father consigned her to a celibate life of sanctuary service. In this case, Jephthah's vow was not necessarily wrong, though it may have required a greater sacrifice than he intended to make, and it was not wrong for him to carry it out.

OATHS NOT KEPT (SITUATIONAL)

Scripture makes clear that our oaths should be true and our vows must be kept (Lev. 19:12; Num. 30:1–2; Deut. 23:21–23; Mark 14:71; Acts 5:4), even when made to our enemies (Josh. 9:1–27; 2 Sam. 21:1–14). We should keep our oaths, even when it hurts us to do so (Ps. 15:4). There are two biblical qualifications to this requirement. One is that we should not keep an oath when it requires us to sin (see discussion above). The other is that under some conditions an oath can be voided by a higher authority. Numbers 30:3–16 says that a woman's vow can be voided by her father (if she is young and living in his house) or by her husband. Perhaps the principle of this passage would also apply to young boys living at home, or to people in other authority relationships. Thus Scripture strengthens relationships of authority. Without this provision, those under authority could evade any responsibility simply by taking a vow conflicting with that responsibility.

17. See C. F. Keil and F. Delitzsch, *Commentary on the Old Testament* (reprint, Grand Rapids: Eerdmans, 1949), on Judg. 11:34–40. See also a thorough argument by James B. Jordan in *Judges: God's War Against Humanism* (Tyler, TX: Geneva Ministries, 1985), and his "Jephthah's Daughter," *Biblical Horizons* no. 86 (June 1996), available at http://www.biblicalhorizons.com/bh/bh086.htm.

18. As Jordan indicates, "ascension offering" is probably a better title for the offering than "burnt offering." The names of other offerings (sin, trespass, guilt, fellowship) refer to their function, not the means of their consumption. So the *'olah* should be translated "ascension offering" or perhaps "consecration offering."

19. When Paul asks his readers to give their bodies as "a living sacrifice" in Rom. 12:1, he seems to have the ascension offering in mind.

Oaths Arising from Wrong Attitudes (Existential)

We have seen in examples above that oaths and vows sometimes arise out of rashness. People swear carelessly without considering the likely effects of their oaths (e.g., as in Lev. 5:4). Isaiah 48:1 speaks also of presumptuous swearing. The people of Israel swore by God's name, assuming their right to invoke him by name, though in fact they were obstinate (v. 4) and idolatrous (v. 5).

We also considered earlier the attempts of some Jews to mitigate the force of oaths by substituting other names for the name of God. The purpose of their heart was not to keep their oaths, but to do whatever they wished. As with all the commandments, keeping or violating them begins in the heart.

CONFESSION

I mentioned that there are three principal uses of the name of God in worship: in oaths, confessions, and blessings. We now consider the second of these. In confession, we acknowledge that God has placed his covenant name upon us, making it our own. We identify ourselves as God's covenant servants. We confess, therefore, before three audiences: to God, as we accept the terms of his covenant; to ourselves, as we willingly accept our new identity as God's people; and to the world, as we proclaim where we stand in the spiritual warfare and invite others to stand with us.

It is important, not only to trust in Christ, but also to confess him before men. Jesus said, "So everyone who acknowledges me before men, I also will acknowledge before my Father who is in heaven, but whoever denies me before men, I also will deny before my Father who is in heaven" (Matt. 10:32–33). Here, a good confession is a condition of salvation. Everyone saved by the grace of God will confess Jesus publicly and will not deny him.[20] Paul makes the same point in Romans 10:9–10: "If you confess with your mouth that Jesus is Lord and believe in your heart that God raised him from the dead, you will be saved. For with the heart one believes and is justified, and with the mouth one confesses and is saved."

So Christianity is a public faith. As the Great Commission implies, it is to be carried out in workplaces and marketplaces as well as in churches and homes. God gives us his name to be proclaimed, not to be hidden as a private treasure. The Christian should always be prepared to speak about

20. Jesus of course is speaking of adults with normal capacities. The same condition certainly does not apply, for example, to babies dying in infancy.

Christ and on his behalf, whenever an unbeliever asks him to give a reason for his faith (1 Peter 3:15). Certainly, some are more gifted at this than others. But anyone can say, with the blind man of John 9:25, "Though I was blind, now I see."

However, this does not mean that the believer should be talking about God all the time, in all situations. Jesus tells us not to cast our pearls before swine (Matt. 7:6). There are times to be silent. Although Jesus made "the good confession" (1 Tim. 6:13), he was silent in some situations (Matt. 26:63; 27:14). Silence is appropriate when to speak would be counterproductive to our witness, especially when it is likely to lead only to ridicule or blasphemy.

Today, we often use the term *confession* to refer to written doctrinal statements that have authority in the church. One of the purposes of such confessions is to give a witness to the world of our Christian faith, and historically they have been useful for this purpose.[21] Scripture itself contains a number of summaries of the gospel that we would today describe as confessions, as in 1 Corinthians 15:1–11 and Philippians 2:6–11. But in Scripture itself the term *confession* does not refer to such summaries, or to any particular written document. Confession is a confession of God himself, and, in the New Testament, specifically of Jesus Christ as Lord. Written confessions are a means to the end of confessing Christ.

Scripture specifies a number of sins that violate our confessional obligation. Contrary to confessing Christ is concealing our allegiance (John 12:42) or even denying him, as did Peter (Matt. 26:69–75). More broadly, it is wrong to behave in such a way as to injure the reputation of our Lord, to profane his name (2 Sam. 12:14; Ezek. 36:20–32).

BLESSING

Given to God by man, blessing is equivalent to praise. So "bless the Lord" in Psalm 103:1 is translated "praise the Lord" in the NIV. When one human being blesses another, he calls on God to give redemptive benefits. So a blessing is a prayer. But the most prominent blessings in Scripture, the Aaronic benediction of Numbers 6:23–27 and the apostolic benediction of 2 Corinthians 13:14, are more than that.[22] In Numbers 6:27, God says that the benediction is an occasion for the priest to place God's name upon the people. Second Corinthians 13:14, similarly, blesses

---

21. Other purposes for confessions are the instruction of believers and the maintenance of doctrinal discipline within the church.

22. *Benediction* and *blessing* are equivalent terms.

the church in the threefold name of the triune God. So the name of God is a prominent aspect of blessing. In the deepest sense, blessing identifies people with God's name, as his covenant people, with the right to inherit all the promises of the covenant. It is this richer concept of blessing that underlies the custom in churches today for the pastor to pronounce a benediction at the end of a service.

But, in a more general way, Scripture calls on believers to bless all people, even those who persecute them (Rom. 12:14; cf. 1 Cor. 4:12; 1 Peter 3:9). To bless in this sense, of course, is not to place upon all people the name of God, with all the benefits of salvation. But we should desire that salvation for everybody. We should pray for "all people" (1 Tim. 2:1). Obviously, these prayers cannot always be specific! But we should genuinely desire God's blessing upon all, for God has charged us with bringing Christ to people of all nations, kingdoms, and languages.[23]

The opposite of blessing is cursing (Rom. 12:14; James 3:10). Scripture rebukes those who love to curse (Ps. 109:17–19), and who, more generally, revile other people. This sin is especially wicked when directed against the helpless, such as the poor (Prov. 17:5) and the deaf (Lev. 19:14).

In Matthew 5:21–22, Jesus condemns the use of language to bring curses on others:

> You have heard that it was said to those of old, "You shall not murder; and whoever murders will be liable to judgment." But I say to you that everyone who is angry with his brother will be liable to judgment; whoever insults his brother will be liable to the council; and whoever says, "You fool!" will be liable to the hell of fire.

We should not take this passage as a general condemnation of all strong language in our interpersonal life. The prophets and apostles frequently use strong language against their hearers (as in Gal. 1:8). Remarkably, Jesus himself, having condemned some for calling other people fools (*mōros*) in the passage cited above, uses the same term against the scribes and Pharisees (Matt. 23:17–19). The point is that condemnatory language, no less than murder, is not ethically neutral. Rather, both are matters for divine judgment (i.e., they make us liable to judgment). In some cases, that judgment may be favorable to us, though Jesus implies that in many other cases the judgment will be negative.

Evidently, just as there is a righteous and an unrighteous anger (see our discussion of the sixth commandment), so there is a righteous and an

---

23. For more on the obligation of universal love, and the question of the imprecatory psalms, see chapter 19.

unrighteous use of strong, denunciatory language. The question is always a question of heart attitude: are we venting our own (murderous) anger (Matt. 5:21), or are we being zealous for the honor of God?

HUMOR IN RELIGION

Having considered the main biblical themes related to the third commandment, I would like to apply these teachings to several issues of modern life. First, let us consider humor, especially as it is sometimes used in religious contexts.

Our exposition of the third commandment indicates that God's name is something sacred. There is a solemnity about it, something that ought to generate reverence and awe. Many have thought that such reverence and awe is incompatible with humor, and that therefore anytime we speak the divine name, or even speak more broadly of biblical teaching, we should be deadly serious.

To be consistent, people holding this view would have to condemn humor altogether, for, as we have seen, all creation bears God's name. To laugh at anything is, in a way, to laugh at God, for everything is God's creation.

But Scripture itself contains humor. God laughs at the wicked in Psalm 2:4, and he declares the wisdom of the world to be foolishness in 1 Corinthians 1:20, something worthy of derision. Proverbs too identifies wickedness with foolishness. And although it condemns inappropriate jokes in 10:23, it contains some comical images, such as the sluggard who "buries his hand in the dish and will not even bring it back to his mouth" (19:24; cf. 26:15), or the wealth of the rich that "sprouts wings, flying like an eagle toward heaven" (23:5), or the quarrelsome woman who is "a continual dripping on a rainy day "(27:15). The recurring theme that "whoever digs a pit will fall into it, and a stone will come back on him who starts it rolling" (26:27; cf. 28:10; Pss. 7:15; 9:15; 57:6; Eccl. 10:8) can hardly be read today without evoking Road Runner cartoons.

Sin in Scripture is tragic, but it is also comic. The seriousness of it should not detract from our ability to laugh at it. This laughter is edifying. It shows us how pitiful are man's efforts to oppose almighty God. That Satan himself should imagine that he can overturn God's throne is the height of absurdity. That mere human beings join his rebellion is even more ridiculous. The point of comedy is often disproportion, and if we don't see the disproportion here enough to laugh at it, we have not quite caught the point. And the disproportion between the Creator and his creatures can lead to a holy laughter, in which reverence and amusement coincide.

Scripture contains other jokes as well. That God chose a donkey to speak to Balaam (Num. 22:22–41) probably struck the ancient Hebrews as funny, just as it strikes us. Jesus' own humor includes the camel trying to go through the eye of the needle (Matt. 19:24), the Pharisees who strain at gnats and swallow camels (Matt. 23:24).[24] We don't laugh at these passages, I suppose, because the jokes are so old. But they are funny, when you think about them afresh. Again, Scripture emphasizes disproportion, as it seeks to teach us to view the world in the right perspective.

I am often amused by Acts 12:12–17, in which the church is praying earnestly for Peter's release from prison. God answers their prayers miraculously, and Peter goes to the prayer meeting. Rhoda, the servant girl, hears him knocking, but does not open the door. Rather, she reports to the prayer meeting that Peter is there. Rather than letting him in, they get into an argument about whether he could really be there, while he keeps knocking. That is all too typical of theological and ecclesiastical assemblies! Eventually he comes in and tells what God has done. So God gently mocks his people, who cannot believe that he would actually answer their prayers.

Scripture speaks well of a cheerful, merry, or glad heart (Prov. 15:13; 2 Cor. 9:7). That should not surprise us. Laughter is close to cheer, and cheer is close to joy. Christianity is about serious matters, but it does not make us glum.

So it does not seem wrong to me to include humor in theology, preaching, counseling, and general speech about the things of God. That does not seem to me to compromise God's holiness. Rather, done in the right way, it increases our appreciation for God's greatness, by showing the disproportion between the Creator and the creation. Of course, humor that demeans God or his image in man is wrong. But good humor is a wonderful remedy to human pride and despair.

PROFANITY

In our society, words like *God*, *Christ*, and *Jesus* often appear as exclamations, to express surprise or anger. The very solemnity of these terms underlies this usage: people want to use strong expressions in these situations, and the divine names are the strongest expressions they can find. If these expressions represented cries for divine help in a difficult situation, there could be no objection to them. But many people use these terms,

---

24. For other examples of Jesus' jokes, see D. Elton Trueblood, *The Humor of Christ* (New York: Harper, 1964).

aware of their sacredness, without any godly intent. Rather, their purpose is to express their resentment against a situation, against other people, and ultimately against God himself.

These uses of the terms border on oaths. The speaker may wish to bring down the wrath of God on someone who has offended him. Or he may resent some situation that no human being has brought about, so that in effect he is cursing God when he uses God's name.

But in some social usage, the solemnity of the divine names is largely forgotten. In much profanity, the divine name could be exchanged for "shucks" or "fiddlesticks" with less force, but not much change of meaning. We might be inclined to think that such nearly unintentional profanity is less serious than a false oath. But we should lament the history that has brought cultures to evacuate the very meaning of the divine name. Surely that is an example of the "vanity," the "meaninglessness," that the third commandment condemns.

What of such terms as *gosh, golly*, and *gee?* Historically and etymologically, these are substitutes for the divine names, invoked to avoid the possible devastating results of taking God's name in vain. As we have seen, however, Jesus' teaching is that substituting some other expression for the divine name in no way lessens the seriousness of an oath.

Still, in many subcultures, the connection between these and the divine name is not recognized, and the meaning of terms, after all, is determined by use, not etymology. It could be argued that in some cultures these terms are not divine names at all, or even conscious substitutes for the divine names. Nor do such uses constitute oaths in any meaningful sense. They are nothing but exclamations.

The application of the third commandment is certainly less clear in these cases. I used these words while growing up in an evangelical church; all my teachers and pastors used them too. However, we avoided profane uses of the literal divine names like the plague. The whole point was to avoid using the actual divine names in vain. Were we guilty, then, of "substituting" something else for the divine name in order to escape God's judgment? Well, that's hard to say. Of course, the etymology is irrelevant. If *golly* and *gee* function as substitutes for the divine name, then *shucks* and *fiddlesticks* can as well. We have seen that all creation bears God's name. "By the temple" and "by my head" are not etymologically related to God's names, but the Jews of Matthew 23 used these terms as substitutes nonetheless. Should we then exclude all language that might function as a strong exclamation? But there is a place for exclamation in language, as we find in Scripture itself.

I cannot charge someone with sin for using these terms as we did years ago, given the nature of our subculture. But there are other subcultures in which these terms are understood differently. When I left my boyhood church and joined the Orthodox Presbyterian Church, I discovered a very different subculture, a subculture in which the etymologies of *gosh*, etc., were taken very seriously. In that subculture, the meanings of these terms were different. And, wishing to maintain fellowship with these brothers and sisters, I soon eliminated these terms from my vocabulary. In matters of language and vocabulary, we should certainly be as Jews among the Jews and as Gentiles among the Gentiles (1 Cor. 9).

BATHROOM AND SEXUAL SLANG

Bathroom and sexual slang, especially as put-downs, are also third commandment issues. These terms are not etymologically related to the divine names, but, like *golly* and *gee*, they are commonly used as expletives in general culture.

One cannot make an absolute prohibition of such language, for Scripture doesn't prohibit it. Indeed, one finds it in Scripture. In Philippians 3:8, Paul considers his works-righteousness to be *skubala*, "dung." As for sexual slang as reproach, consider Galatians, where the enemies of Paul are *tous ek peritomēs* (2:12), "the circumcision guys." Paul expresses the angry wish that they would "go the whole way and emasculate themselves!" (Gal. 5:12 NIV). In Philippians 3:2, he calls them "dogs" and *katatomē*, a play on *peritomē* that might be rendered in English as "deconcision." Perhaps that term, like the language in Galatians 5:12, suggested castration to Paul.

Yet we must be aware that such instances are rare in Scripture. They occur in cases where extreme judgment must be expressed and where there is justified anger. And they always make a godly point. Further, Paul's sexual references are relevant to the precise subject he is dealing with, namely, circumcision.

In these ways, of course, scriptural language is worlds apart from the street language of today, perhaps from the street language of its own time as well. We all know people who cannot utter a sentence without including a sexual or bathroom reproach, and this kind of talk has been immortalized in the current genre of ghetto movies.

The problem with that is not the utterance of a word that should be taboo. As we've seen, there are situations where such language is appropriate. But this language today is vastly overused, and in terribly inappropriate ways. The problem with excrement language in our society is that it describes human beings, God's image, as one of the ugliest, most unpleasant substances imaginable, proverbially the lowest level of being. And the problem with sexual slang is that it shows contempt, not only for people, but for the precious heart of marital love (see later discussion of the seventh commandment).

This is not the language of love, joy, peace, patience, kindness, goodness, faithfulness, gentleness, and self-control (Gal. 5:22). There is no thankfulness here. This is the coarse language condemned in Ephesians 5:4.

This language proliferates, to be sure, in subcultures mired in poverty and the legacy of oppression. Still, even granting the grimness of the conditions in which many of these people live, and granting our responsibility to help in some way, we cannot condone the hatred that often festers in their hearts. The "poor" in Scripture are righteous, though oppressed. Their remedy is not to hate, but to cry out to the Lord. And he delivers them. Their language is not profane, although it is frequently imprecatory!

Between the extreme of the street language and the extreme of a total abstinence from such expressions, there are lines that are hard to draw.

As in all questions of linguistic usage, much depends on one's upbringing and the perceptions of one's culture and subculture. What is seen as coarse in one society will be routinely accepted in another; what is seen in one society as a Christian "given" will be seen in another society as self-righteous. There is a place for flexibility and sensitivity, as we seek to contextualize the gospel in all cultures and subcultures. Perhaps the absolute principle is this: The Christian should always be, and be perceived as, one who, while not self-righteous and legalistic, nevertheless avoids contemptuous or irreverent attitudes and the language by which his culture or subculture expresses those attitudes.

LANGUAGE IN LITERATURE AND DRAMA

I once received a letter from a student who had written a play to be performed at his Christian college. He had included profanity in the dialogue. The college administration refused to let the play be performed, on the ground of Ephesians 4:29, "Let no corrupting talk come out of your mouths, but only such as is good for building up, as fits the occasion, that it may give grace to those who hear." The question is whether it is ever legitimate for a Christian actor to utter blasphemies or profanity, e.g., while impersonating a character, or for a Christian writer to put such language in the mouth of a character.

Clearly it would be wrong for an actor to do something on stage that is wrong in itself, such as to perform a sex act. Even if the act is with his spouse, the stage is an inappropriate place for it; see my later discussion of the seventh commandment. But speaking unedifying or blasphemous words is, I think, in a different category. What is wrong is not the vocables themselves, but using them to express our own thoughts and feelings. A particular expression, say *blig*, might be blasphemous in one language, profane in another, genteel in a third. And even in cultures where *blig* is profane or blasphemous, it is possible to utter the word (as when compiling a dictionary) without committing profanity or blasphemy.

Ephesians 4:29 clearly does not mean to forbid the mere physical act of uttering an unedifying expression. Scripture itself records (and when we read Scripture, we read) the unedifying and even blasphemous words of God's enemies. Consider also Lamech's song of defiance (Gen. 4:23–24) and the fool's saying "There is no God" (Ps. 14:1). Paul in 1 Corinthians 12:3 quotes a blasphemy: "Jesus is accursed!" and Matthew 12:24 quotes the words "It is only by Beelzebul, the prince of demons, that this man casts out demons," words which Jesus in verses 31–32 describes as the unforgivable blasphemy against the Holy Spirit.

Of course, Scripture records these words for our edification: unedifying words in an edifying context. The question, then, becomes: does a literary or dramatic blasphemy serve an edifying purpose in its larger context? It does, I think, when (as in Scripture) it aims to portray wickedness as wickedness, that is, when its portrayal is, on Christian criteria, true. The challenge to the Christian artist is to present sin in its true colors—as something ugly, destructive, and, in a certain way, ridiculous (Ps. 2:4; 1 Cor. 1:20).

Now when an actor, in a performance, gives a speech containing offensive language, he is not necessarily expressing his own thoughts or emotions, but those of the character he plays. To put this matter into perspective, consider that Jesus himself took foolish, sinful words on his own lips. In Luke 12:19, Jesus quotes the words of the rich fool, rebuked by God in verse 20. In effect, Jesus is an actor here, playing a role. The rich fool sins in uttering these words, but Jesus does not. For Jesus is not defying God, as the fool does; he is rather portraying the fool, for our benefit. Other biblical writers do the same, in the passages listed above and elsewhere.

Sometimes, to be sure, actors are urged to feel the very emotions they portray. Certain kinds of "method" acting—where an actor motivates himself to portray, e.g., hate by generating feelings of hate within himself—are problematic. Christians should not seek to generate within themselves ungodly emotions. Yet I suspect that morality and dramatic effectiveness are not necessarily opposed to one another. A good artist must maintain both empathy with, and distance from, his subject, as did Jesus when he loved and suffered for sinners, without losing his own identity as the sinless, divine Savior. A "method" which insists on identification without distance cannot express redemptive involvement.

But it is not wrong in itself to speak unedifying words in the course of portraying another person. To do that is not to perform sinful speech-acts, but to ascribe those speech-acts to someone else.

On this criterion, one could argue that there ought to be more blasphemy and vulgarity in Christian drama than there usually is. These sins utterly pervade our society today, and any truthful portrayal of that society ought to be consistent with that pervasiveness. We should also note, however, that Scripture rarely quotes words of defiance to God, and when it does, it rarely quotes vain use of the literal divine name. ("Jesus is accursed!" in 1 Cor. 12:3 is the only instance I can think of.) Scripture presents fallen society as it is, therefore at its worst. But it does this without wallowing in filth. Christian drama should have a similar reticence. It is possible to describe evil accurately without wallowing in it. It is even possible to suggest pervasive linguistic sin without giving extensive examples of it, as David does in Psalm 12:

> Save, O LORD, for the godly one is gone;
>   for the faithful have vanished from among the children of man.
> Everyone utters lies to his neighbor;
>   with flattering lips and a double heart they speak.
> May the LORD cut off all flattering lips,
>   the tongue that makes great boasts,
> those who say, "With our tongue we will prevail,
>   our lips are with us; who is master over us?"
> "Because the poor are plundered, because the needy groan,
>   I will now arise," says the LORD;
>   "I will place him in the safety for which he longs."
> The words of the LORD are pure words,
>   like silver refined in a furnace on the ground,
>   purified seven times.
> You, O LORD, will keep them;
>   you will guard us from this generation forever.
> On every side the wicked prowl,
>   as vileness is exalted among the children of man.

This is a picture of a godless society that uses the great gift of language to rebel against the Lord.[25] The solution, now as then, is the words of the Lord, pure words, purified seven times.

---

25. Such rebellion was present at the Tower of Babel (Gen. 11:1–9, esp. v. 7).

CHAPTER 28

The Fourth Commandment:
Views of Sabbath Keeping

The fourth commandment, like the second, is one of the longer commandments and also one of the most controversial as to its application.

The versions of this commandment in Exodus and Deuteronomy differ more significantly than do the versions of the other commandments. So I will include both passages here:

> Remember the Sabbath day, to keep it holy. Six days you shall labor, and do all your work, but the seventh day is a Sabbath to the LORD your God. On it you shall not do any work, you, or your son, or your daughter, your male servant, or your female servant, or your livestock, or the sojourner who is within your gates. For in six days the LORD made heaven and earth, the sea, and all that is in them, and rested the seventh day. Therefore the LORD blessed the Sabbath day and made it holy. (Ex. 20:8–11)

> Observe the Sabbath day, to keep it holy, as the LORD your God commanded you. Six days you shall labor and do all your work, but the seventh day is a Sabbath to the LORD your God. On it you shall not do any work, you or your son or your daughter or your male servant or your female servant, or your ox or your donkey or any of your livestock, or the sojourner who is within your gates, that your male servant and your female servant may rest as well as you. You shall remember that you were a slave in the land of

Egypt, and the LORD your God brought you out from there with a mighty hand and an outstretched arm. Therefore the LORD your God commanded you to keep the Sabbath day. (Deut. 5:12–15)

The chief difference is that the second formulation replaces the reference to God's creation rest with a reference to God's deliverance of Israel from Egypt. So in Exodus, the chief reason for keeping the Sabbath is imitation of God's creative work and rest. In Deuteronomy, it is celebration of God's giving Israel rest from the bondage of Egypt. The motive of Sabbath keeping in the Exodus passage is creation; in Deuteronomy, redemption.

However, we should not think that Deuteronomy revokes the earlier creation motive. The Decalogue as recorded in Exodus is Israel's holy covenant document, written by the finger of God. Its content cannot be revoked, at least within that covenant structure.[1] The Deuteronomic formulation affirms the earlier Exodus language by the phrase "as the LORD your God commanded you." Furthermore, in Scripture, creation and redemption are not antagonistic. Redemption is the work of the Creator. Creation and redemption do not generate two different ethics, but rather the same one. Imaging the Creator (chapter 9) involves imitating his work of redemption (chapter 16), loving others as he has loved us (John 13:34–35). Also, the Exodus Decalogue, as we have noted, begins with the preface, "I am the LORD your God, who brought you out of the land of Egypt, out of the house of slavery." So in Exodus, redemption is a motive for keeping all the commandments, including the fourth. Thus, the two formulations of the fourth commandment are complementary.

VIEWS OF THE SABBATH

Of all the Ten Commandments, the fourth is the most visibly rejected in modern society. Although many people still have a day off on Sunday, relatively few attend church. Rather, Sunday has become the chief day of the week for shopping and professional sports. Or Sunday can be just another day on the job. For many, Sunday has become no different from any other day.

Among evangelical Christians, the situation is not much different, though of course many more of these attend church. Most evangelicals

---

1. I shall give reasons later for believing that the Sabbath commandment is not merely a part of the Mosaic covenant, but that it is a creation ordinance. But even if it is only an ordinance of the Mosaic covenant, it has such a status that it cannot be repealed by a later Mosaic ordinance.

feel no obligation to cease working in order to devote a whole day to God. By way of justification, they say that the fourth commandment is "Old Testament, not New Testament"—an argument rarely given to justify violations of the other nine, and, in any case, as we shall see, biblically inaccurate. The prevalence of dispensational theology has contributed to this kind of thinking and practice.

In the Reformed community, one would expect a greater respect for the fourth commandment, because of the distinctly positive attitude toward the law in Reformed theology (chapters 12, 13). Indeed, there are in the Reformed community proportionately more serious Sabbath keepers than in other Christian traditions, and there are affirmations of Sabbath keeping in the Reformed confessions. But the Reformed community too is divided on this issue, not only in practice, but also in theology. And the theological difference goes back to the time of Calvin.

Reformed theologians have taught at least six views of Sabbath observance. In describing them, I shall begin with the least restrictive and move toward the most restrictive, or, as we tend to put it, from "least Sabbatarian" to "most Sabbatarian."

From Sabbath to Lord's Day

One of the most impressive recent scholarly treatments of the Sabbath doctrine is *From Sabbath to Lord's Day*, a collaborative effort by a number of evangelical writers of generally Reformed persuasion.[2] In the introduction, the editor, D. A. Carson, summarizes the book's distinctive position:

> First, we are not persuaded that the New Testament unambiguously develops a "transfer theology," according to which the Sabbath moves from the seventh day to the first day of the week. We are not persuaded that Sabbath keeping is presented in the Old Testament as the norm from the time of creation onward. Nor are we persuaded that the New Testament develops patterns of continuity and discontinuity on the basis of moral/civil/ceremonial distinctions. . . . We think . . . that although Sunday worship arose in New Testament times, it was not perceived as a Christian Sabbath.[3]

Carson and the other writers of this volume deny that the Sabbath is a creation ordinance as I defined it in chapter 13. Nor are they willing to distinguish, as the Reformed tradition has done since Calvin, between aspects of

2. Carson, D. A., ed., *From Sabbath to Lord's Day* (Grand Rapids: Zondervan, 1982).
3. Ibid., 16.

the Sabbath commandment that are ceremonial and others that are moral.[4] Essentially, for them, no part of the fourth commandment is "moral" in the sense of binding the consciences of believers through all eras of history.

Positively, they do hold to a New Testament origin for Sunday worship, and they identify the first day of the week with "the Lord's day" of Revelation 1:10. But Andrew Lincoln argues:

> The Lord's Day need not be understood in terms of a sacred day. . . . The day can be said to be the Lord's because it is the appropriate day for worshiping Him, and this is significantly different from the view that sees the day, by analogy with the Jewish Sabbath, as a full twenty-four hour period belonging to the Lord in a distinct way from that in which all the Christian's time belongs to the Lord. . . . To claim that specifically Sunday is the appropriate day for a gathering of the Christian community for worship is not to imply that somehow in itself that day is holy.[5]

John Calvin

It might surprise some readers to note that John Calvin's view is one of the least restrictive of the six. He requires somewhat more of new covenant believers than does the Carson volume, but he agrees with Carson more than he disagrees. His understanding of the fourth commandment follows:

> First, under the repose of the seventh day the heavenly Lawgiver meant to represent to the people of Israel spiritual rest, in which believers ought to lay aside their own works to allow God to work in them. Secondly, he meant that there was to be a stated day for them to assemble to hear the law and perform the rites, or at least to devote it particularly to meditation upon his works, and thus through this remembrance to be trained in piety. Thirdly, he resolved to give a day of rest to servants and those who are under the authority of others, in order that they should have some respite from toil.[6]

The first of these three purposes (the chief in Calvin's view) regards the Sabbath as a type of redemption, under the figure of rest. As a farmer rests

---

4. Chapter 13 also discusses this distinction.

5. A. T. Lincoln, "From Sabbath to Lord's Day: A Biblical and Theological Perspective," in *From Sabbath to Lord's Day*, ed. Carson, 389–90.

6. John Calvin, *Institutes of the Christian Religion*, ed. John T. McNeill, trans. Ford Lewis Battles (Philadelphia: Westminster Press, 1960), 2.8.28.

from toil, so in dealing with sin God calls us to turn from our works to his grace: salvation is by rest, not work. God required the Jews to rest one day in seven in order to anticipate that rest. But we now have that rest in Christ. We have put away our evil works and now rest in the salvation of Christ. Since we have the reality, we no longer need to carry on this symbolic observance. So this aspect of the Sabbath is a ceremonial provision not literally applicable in the new covenant.[7] This aspect of the Sabbath is a shadow that passes away in Christ. In this connection, Calvin cites Colossians 2:17 and asks, "Who but madmen cannot see what observance the apostle means?"[8]

Nevertheless, the second and third purposes of the fourth commandment continue to bind us, in a somewhat more literal way. In the new covenant, as in the old, we need to have stated times for worship, and we should give rest to our servants. Even in these cases, however, Calvin is flexible. In his view, God does not require that new covenant worship be held on a particular day of the week, or even weekly interval; nor is there a particular day of the week on which we must give rest to workers. Calvin wishes that Christians would worship every day, but he recognizes that is unlikely to be widely accepted. So he commends the practical wisdom of weekly worship as a church ordinance, and he appreciates the value of first-day worship as a memorial of the resurrection of Christ. But he insists that the weekly interval is only a practical measure.[9] It is not sacramental; it does not represent a spiritual mystery. To regard it that way is superstition, as in Romans 14:5.

But even though weekly worship is a church requirement, not a divine requirement, Calvin urges us to take it seriously. Bauckham says that for Calvin,

> Unlike the Jew on the Mosaic Sabbath, the Christian is required to rest only in order to be free to worship. But Calvin sometimes interprets this requirement with surprising strictness. Both daily work and recreation should be suspended for the whole duration of

---

7. Unlike the authors of *From Sabbath to Lord's Day*, Calvin does distinguish between moral and ceremonial laws and puts considerable emphasis on this distinction. For a discussion of this issue, see chapter 13 of this book. He also states, contrary to them, in his commentary on Gen. 2:3, that the Sabbath (the moral aspect of it, anyway) is a creation ordinance, though he does not, in my view, do justice to the implications of this fact. (See Richard B. Gaffin Jr., *Calvin and the Sabbath* [Fearn, Ross-shire: Christian Focus, 1998]). For these reasons, I list Calvin as "more Sabbatarian" than the authors of the Carson book.

8. *Institutes*, 2.8.33.

9. At this point, Lincoln's article in the Carson volume, cited above, is actually somewhat more Sabbatarian than Calvin, since Lincoln sees the first day as uniquely appropriate to Christian worship, though not a holy day.

the day in order that the whole day should be devoted to corporate and private worship and religious instruction.[10]

Bauckham here paraphrases material from Calvin's *Sermons on Deuteronomy*, which Bauckham describes as "Calvin at his most Sabbatarian"[11]— material that influenced Puritan writers in a more Sabbatarian direction. But, I reiterate, for Calvin, these arrangements for the day are not divine requirements in themselves, but appropriate accommodations to activities sanctioned by the church. The particular day is not the point, for the church, within its rights, could summon us to worship on some other day, or at some other interval.

The Heidelberg Catechism reflects Calvin's view of the Sabbath:

> Q. 103. *What does God require in the fourth Commandment?*
> A. In the first place, God wills that the ministry of the Gospel and schools be maintained, and that I, especially on the day of rest, diligently attend church to learn the Word of God, to use the holy sacraments, to call publicly upon the Lord, and to give Christian alms. In the second place, that all the days of my life I rest from my evil works, allow the Lord to work in me by His Spirit, and thus begin in this life the everlasting sabbath.

Like Calvin, the Catechism focuses on the Sabbath as a symbol of redemption. We keep the fourth commandment by resting from sinful works and receiving the grace of God's Spirit. Calvin's second priority is the Catechism's first: God mandates public worship and instruction. But, like Calvin, it does not say that this worship must take place every seventh day or that believers are under a divine obligation to cease all daily work and recreation in order to participate in the work of the church.

The Decrees of Dort

The Synod of Dort (1618–19) adopted a somewhat more Sabbatarian position in response to issues raised among the Dutch churches. The main purpose of the Synod was to deal with Arminian doctrine, the subject of their famous Canons. But they also made pronouncements on some other matters, known as the "Post-Acta." Their statements on the Sabbath follow:

10. R. J. Bauckham, "Sabbath and Sunday in the Protestant Tradition," in *From Sabbath to Lord's Day*, ed. Carson, 317.
11. Ibid., 336, n. 29. The *Institutes*, he says, represent Calvin at his "least Sabbatarian."

I. There is both a ceremonial and a moral element in the fourth commandment of the divine law.

II. The ceremonial [element] is the rest of the seventh day after creation, and the strict observance of the same day was especially enjoined upon the Jewish people.

III. The moral [element] is that a certain and definite day be set aside for worship, and for the purpose that as much rest as is necessary for worship and for pious reflection upon it [be provided].

IV. The Jewish Sabbath having been abolished, Christians must solemnly keep Sunday holy.

V. This day has always been observed from the time of the apostles in the ancient Catholic Church.

VI. This day must be so set aside for worship that on it people may rest from all ordinary labors (excluding those which love and present necessity demand) together with all such recreations that hinder worship.

These statements reflect Calvin's view that the prohibition of Sabbath labor in the Old Testament is a ceremonial aspect of the law that is abolished in the new covenant.[12] With Calvin, they also say that the commandment requires the setting of a day for worship, and they approve Sunday for that purpose. What Calvin probably would not have said, however, is that Christians must "solemnly keep Sunday holy." To Calvin, I suspect, that language would have sounded "superstitious."

As Calvin granted that we should arrange the other activities of the day to facilitate worship, so Dort emphasized rest from ordinary labors for the purpose of worship. But the language of article VI is more like Calvin's *Sermons on Deuteronomy* than like the *Institutes*, and its classifications (worship, rest, works of necessity, works of love, recreations) anticipate the language of the Westminster standards.

The doctrine of Calvin, the Heidelberg Catechism, and the Synod of Dort is sometimes described as "the Continental view" of the Sabbath. Its most striking feature is the new covenant abolition of the weekly Sabbath, and of the Old Testament prohibition of work every seventh day. Although Reformed theology is generally positive toward biblical law, especially the Decalogue, the continental branch of the Reformed tradition relegates the chief requirements of the fourth commandment to ceremonial status.

12. Or is it only the strict observance of the *seventh* day that is abolished as ceremonial, opening the way for a first-day Sabbath (as in the Westminster standards) that should be observed as strictly as the Mosaic Sabbath? The articles are not clear at this point.

Nevertheless, as we move historically from Calvin to Dort, this tradition tends to bring in through the back door what it has expelled through the front. As a practical necessity, Calvin himself recognizes that we need to cease work in order to prepare for and attend worship. Dort goes further, recognizing this cessation as a solemn responsibility to keep a "holy" day, bringing the church far closer to the literal meaning of the fourth commandment. This movement is understandable: if we have a holy obligation to worship God, then we have an equally holy obligation to eliminate anything in our lives that conflicts with this worship. But then how does this holy obligation differ from that which God imposed on the Jews? Calvin would argue that at least the actual day is now optional. But Dort does not seem to recognize the church's freedom to choose the day. Andrew Lincoln, in the Carson volume, thinks that Sunday is the most appropriate time to worship, but not a holy day. Dort, however, says that it is holy.

The Westminster standards develop a clearer view of these matters, as we shall see, whether or not we find their position persuasive. But I have observed that, as a rule, members of Reformed churches of Continental background, who subscribe to the Heidelberg Catechism and the Decrees of Dort, tend to be more Sabbatarian in practice than members of Presbyterian churches who subscribe to the Westminster standards, even though the latter documents are themselves far more restrictive. In this case, the teaching of confessions does not seem to be the main determining factor in the behavior of church members.

KLINE'S LATER VIEW

References to Meredith G. Kline's writings are a frequent feature of the Theology of Lordship series. I regard him as the most impressive biblical theologian of my lifetime, and his teaching and writing have greatly influenced my own thinking. His work is orthodox, yet often original, and it always provides us with rich analysis of Scripture. I do not, however, follow him uncritically, as will be evident.

His view of the Sabbath has changed somewhat over the years, enough that I will distinguish his "early" from his "later" view. The early view, which he taught during my student years, will be discussed in the next subsection. Here I shall mention his later and, I believe, final position. I invert these positions chronologically to satisfy my general plan: this view is "less Sabbatarian" than the next, but "more Sabbatarian" than the Continental positions.

Kline moves toward a stronger Sabbatarianism in that he sees an essential continuity between the Sabbath given to Adam in Genesis 2:3, the

Sabbath of the Decalogue, and the New Testament Lord's Day. He also sees major discontinuities among these. But he believes that these are all Sabbaths, and that they have essentially the same meaning: they celebrate God as the Consummator of his creative work. God not only begins, but also sovereignly completes, his work.

Celebration of a completed divine work is called "rest." As an eternal, omnipotent being, God does not need to rest in a literal sense. But he does finish tasks, and the completion of his major tasks is important to him, a matter for celebration. At creation, God looked at all he had done, called it good (Gen. 1:31), and then rested (2:3). At the completion of redemption, there will be a final Sabbath rest for the people of God (Heb. 4:9), the consummation of the heavenly kingdom, anticipated by Israel's conquest of the Promised Land (Deut. 3:20; 12:9; 1 Kings 8:56). So, "observation of the Sabbath by man is thus a confession that Yahweh is his Lord and the Lord of all lords."[13]

The major discontinuities in Sabbath administration, for Kline, arise from a distinction that is very important to his theology, that between the holy and the common. After the fall, Kline says, God instituted an order of common grace that mitigates the effects of the curse on the earth, but does not bring salvation. This includes the general culture, shared by believer and nonbeliever alike, particularly the institution of the state. He says:

> This sphere is common not only in the sense that its benefits are shared by the generality of mankind, the just and unjust alike, but in the sense that it is nonsacred. Particular emphasis needs to be given to the fact that the political, institutional aspect of common grace culture is not holy, but profane.
>
> Significantly, when the Lord republished the cultural ordinances within the historical framework of his common grace for the generality of fallen mankind, he did not attach his Sabbath promise to this common grace order. The ordinance of the Sabbath was not reissued in the revelation of the common grace order either in Genesis 3:16–19 or in the covenantal promulgation of it in Genesis 9. The withholding of the Sabbath sign from common grace culture is a clear indication of the secular, nonholy character of that culture.[14]

The Sabbath ordinance is renewed, however, in the Decalogue. The reason, on Kline's view, is that the Mosaic theocracy is very different from the

---

13. Meredith G. Kline, *Kingdom Prologue* (privately published, 1991), 25–26. My exposition of Kline so far summarizes pp. 21–26 of this book.

14. Ibid., 96.

common grace order that existed from Adam to Moses. In the theocracy, all is holy, not common. So the Israelite's daily work, as well as his worship, has a Sabbatarian structure and the promise of Sabbath rest. It is for this reason, Kline thinks, that God tells Israel, not only to worship God every seventh day, but also to cease work on that day. Both cult and culture, both worship and work, are oriented toward consummation fulfillment.

Kline believes, however, that in the new covenant there is no more theocracy. Although God remains sovereign, he no longer attaches himself to a single nation, covenanted to them, dwelling with them in a temple, rendering their entire culture holy. Rather, in the new covenant, culture reverts to the common grace status it had from Adam to Moses, and in the nations outside Israel. It is no longer holy, but common.[15] God gives no covenant promise to the common culture today. Therefore, the Sabbath must take a different form. New covenant worship continues to be under God's covenant promise and follows a Sabbatarian pattern, based on the weekly Lord's Day. But cultural labor, even of the believer, is part of the common grace order and therefore is not bound to a Sabbatarian pattern.

The practical conclusion is that under the new covenant we keep the Sabbath by worshiping God weekly, but we have no obligation to cease from the work or recreation of the six days, except, presumably, to facilitate worship.

Of the views we have considered so far, Kline's is the first to be overtly "Sabbatarian."[16] He holds that the Lord's Day is not only a holy day (as in the Post-Acta of Dort), but a Sabbath. He believes that it is a Sabbath because of the continuity of its meaning with the other Sabbaths of Scripture, from Genesis 2:3 forward.[17]

Nevertheless, he also agrees with the first three views, and against the last two, that the new covenant believer is under no obligation to rest on the Sabbath from his weekday labors. His argument for this proposition, however, is very different from those who hold the first three views. According to them, we need not stop our daily work, because the Lord's Day is not a Sabbath at all. For Kline, it is a Sabbath, but our daily work now has a different character from its character under the Mosaic theocracy.

15. Culture becomes holy again in the new heavens and the new earth, the consummation of redemption.

16. Nevertheless, as we shall see, his view is far from that of the Westminster standards. The many ostensibly strict confessionalists who subscribe to Kline's view should be more troubled by that fact than they are.

17. Kline believes with Calvin that the Sabbath is not only a Mosaic ordinance, but also a creation ordinance. But he develops this point in much more depth than does Calvin.

The chief point in Kline's argument is that we need not cease work on the Sabbath day, because work is common, not holy.

Although Kline and his disciples are almost alone in making this argument, his distinction has affinities with others I have discussed in this book: (1) the distinction between law and gospel in the Formula of Concord (chapter 12), (2) the distinction between natural law and Scripture as bases for ethics (chapter 14), (3) the Roman Catholic distinction between nature and grace and the corresponding doctrine of the twofold end (chapter 17), and (4) the distinction between religious and nonreligious activities in connection with the regulative principle (chapter 26). These discussions will continue when I consider the fifth commandment (with respect to the relation of church and state, chapter 32), and when I consider the relation of Christ and culture (appendix E).[18] I have consistently rejected this series of twofold distinctions, and for similar reasons I find Kline's distinction unconvincing, as I will indicate.

KLINE'S EARLIER VIEW

Kline's later view is almost the opposite of the one he taught in his class lectures in the early 1960s, when I was his student. Later he held that we are to worship on the Sabbath, but have no obligation to rest. Earlier he argued that our primary responsibility is to rest on the Sabbath, and that worship is a subordinate aspect of Sabbath activity. I found Kline's earlier view persuasive during my student years, and unlike Kline I continue to defend it today, with some qualifications.

In his earlier years, he questioned the position agreed to by the first three views we have considered, namely, that God designed the Sabbath mainly for worship, not for rest.[19] In the first four views, Sabbath (or Sunday) rest is primarily a means of preparing for worship.[20] But in Scripture itself, rest is a far more prominent element of Sabbath celebration. One may even say that the essence of Sabbath (from *shabbat*, "to cease, desist, rest") is rest. Genesis 2:3 describes God's rest. It does not mention worship, of course, since God is not a worshiper, but the supreme object of worship. The fourth

18. Kline's distinction is most amenable to the Lutheran "two kingdoms" view of Christ and culture.

19. Kline's later view also makes rest an important feature of the Sabbath doctrine, but as with the first three views, it is for him mainly a type of redemptive consummation. He also recognizes the requirement of literal rest within a theocratic order. But in our present, nontheocratic situation, we are required to worship on the Sabbath, not literally to rest.

20. In Kline's later view, since new covenant believers are not called literally to rest on the Sabbath, whatever rest we enjoy is by way of preparing for and facilitating worship, as on the first three views.

commandment tells Israel to cease work, without mentioning worship explicitly (though to keep a day "holy" is certainly an act of worship). God typically judges Sabbath breakers (as in Num. 15:32–36), not for failing to worship on the Sabbath, but for doing inappropriate work. Similarly, Jesus' argument with the Pharisees was not over Sabbath worship, but over Sabbath work (as in Matt. 12:1–8).

So the early Kline finds the essence of the Sabbath in rest, rather than in worship. Of course, when we rest from our weekly labors in honor of God, it is an especially appropriate time for worship, and Kline is well aware of the biblical emphasis on Sabbath worship that I shall later describe. But he is unpersuaded of the Westminster standards' view that the day is to be spent entirely in public and private worship, together with deeds of necessity and mercy. Plain physical rest, like a long nap (what the Westminster divines may well have considered "idleness": see WLC, 119), is also appropriate, as is noncommercial recreation,[21] such as taking walks, swimming, biking, or neighborhood games (contrary to the prohibition of "recreations" in WCL, 119).[22]

I have observed that when candidates for ministry in the Presbyterian Church in America are asked to state their exceptions to the Westminster standards, the most common exception by far is to the prohibition of recreation on the Sabbath in WCF, 21.8, and WLC, 119. In fact, it has seemed of late that nearly every candidate has taken such an exception. So this view appears to be gaining strength in confessional Presbyterianism, almost to the extent that the Westminster standards' prohibition of recreation has become a dead letter.

THE WESTMINSTER STANDARDS

Finally we come to the most Sabbatarian of the six views we have considered. I shall quote the relevant texts here:

> 7. As it is the law of nature, that, in general, a due proportion of time be set apart for the worship of God; so, in his Word, by a positive, moral, and perpetual commandment binding all men in all ages, he hath particularly appointed one day in seven, for a Sabbath, to be kept holy unto him: which, from the beginning of the world to the resurrection of Christ, was the last day of the week,

---

21. Commercial recreation (professional sports, entertainment, etc.) is in a different category, for it requires someone to perform their weekly occupations on the Sabbath day.

22. Even in his earlier teaching, Kline was not a strict subscriptionist to the Westminster standards.

and, from the resurrection of Christ, was changed into the first day of the week, which, in Scripture, is called the Lord's day, and is to be continued to the end of the world, as the Christian Sabbath.

8. This Sabbath is then kept holy unto the Lord, when men, after a due preparing of their hearts, and ordering of their common affairs beforehand, do not only observe an holy rest, all the day, from their own works, words, and thoughts about their worldly employments and recreations, but also are taken up, the whole time, in the public and private exercises of his worship, and in the duties of necessity and mercy. (WCF, 21.7–8)

Q. 116. *What is required in the fourth commandment?*

A. The fourth commandment requires of all men the sanctifying or keeping holy to God such set times as he hath appointed in his word, expressly one whole day in seven; which was the seventh from the beginning of the world to the resurrection of Christ, and the first day of the week ever since, and so to continue to the end of the world; which is the Christian sabbath, and in the New Testament called the Lord's day.

Q. 117. *How is the sabbath or the Lord's day to be sanctified?*

A. The sabbath or Lord's day is to be sanctified by an holy resting all the day, not only from such works as are at all times sinful, but even from such worldly employments and recreations as are on other days lawful; and making it our delight to spend the whole time (except so much of it as is to be taken up in works of necessity and mercy) in the public and private exercises of God's worship: and, to that end, we are to prepare our hearts, and with such foresight, diligence, and moderation, to dispose and seasonably dispatch our worldly business, that we may be the more free and fit for the duties of that day.

Q. 118. *Why is the charge of keeping the sabbath more specially directed to governors of families, and other superiors?*

A. The charge of keeping the sabbath is more specially directed to governors of families, and other superiors, because they are bound not only to keep it themselves, but to see that it be observed by all those that are under their charge; and because they are prone ofttimes to hinder them by employments of their own.

Q. 119. *What are the sins forbidden in the fourth commandment?*

A. The sins forbidden in the fourth commandment are, all omissions of the duties required, all careless, negligent, and unprofitable performing of them, and being weary of them; all profaning the day by idleness, and doing that which is in itself sinful; and by all needless works, words, and thoughts, about our worldly employments and recreations.

Q. 120. *What are the reasons annexed to the fourth commandment, the more to enforce it?*

A. The reasons annexed to the fourth commandment, the more to enforce it, are taken from the equity of it, God allowing us six days of seven for our own affairs, and reserving but one for himself, in these words, Six days shalt thou labor, and do all thy work: from God's challenging a special propriety in that day, The seventh day is the sabbath of the Lord thy God: from the example of God, who in six days made heaven and earth, the sea, and all that in them is, and rested the seventh day: and from that blessing which God put upon that day, not only in sanctifying it to be a day for his service, but in ordaining it to be a means of blessing to us in our sanctifying it; Wherefore the Lord blessed the sabbath day, and hallowed it.

Q. 121. *Why is the word Remember set in the beginning of the fourth commandment?*

A. The word Remember is set in the beginning of the fourth commandment, partly, because of the great benefit of remembering it, we being thereby helped in our preparation to keep it, and, in keeping it, better to keep all the rest of the commandments, and to continue a thankful remembrance of the two great benefits of creation and redemption, which contain a short abridgment of religion; and partly, because we are very ready to forget it, for that there is less light of nature for it, and yet it restraineth our natural liberty in things at other times lawful; that it cometh but once in seven days, and many worldly businesses come between, and too often take off our minds from thinking of it, either to prepare for it, or to sanctify it; and that Satan with his instruments much labor to blot out the glory, and even the memory of it, to bring in all irreligion and impiety. (WLC, 116–121)

According to these documents, God gave the Sabbath at creation, and it continues through the Old and New Testament periods to the consummation, with only one change: the change from the seventh day of the week to the first day. The New Testament Lord's Day is not only a holy day, as in the Post-Acta of Dort, but "the Christian sabbath" (WLC, 116).

The Sabbath command is "a positive, moral, and perpetual commandment binding all men in all ages" (WCF, 21.7). The Sabbath day is a holy day, to be observed by people of all nations and religions.

On the Sabbath day, human beings are to rest from "their own works, words, and thoughts about their worldly employments and recreations" (WCF 21.8). As in the case of the prohibition of images in the second commandment, the Westminster divines are concerned not only with actions, but also with thoughts. Again, they focus on attitudes of the heart that can lead to sin.[23]

Positively, on the Westminster view, the "whole time" of the Sabbath is to be taken up "in the public and private exercises of his worship, and in the duties of necessity and mercy" (WCF, 21.8). As with the first three views we have considered, worship is the main point of the Sabbath ordinance (note how WCF, 21.7, begins). We rest, basically, in order to have time to worship. There is nothing in these documents suggesting that rest has any theological significance apart from the pragmatics of worship. There is here no consideration of rest as a symbol or type, either of redemption from sin (Calvin, Heidelberg Catechism) or more generally as celebration of a completed divine work (as in Kline's views, both earlier and later). But, as a practical matter, the Westminster standards require strict resting on the Sabbath from the work of the six days.

---

23. WLC, 119, qualifies the prohibition of "thoughts about their worldly employments and recreations" by inserting "needless." Evidently the writers of the Catechism recognized the psychological impossibility of following literally the requirement of WCF, 21.8.

CHAPTER 29

The Fourth Commandment: Theology of the Sabbath

In this chapter, I will evaluate the six views of the Sabbath described in chapter 28 by looking more carefully at the biblical teaching on the subject. My own position is more like the fifth view, the early Kline view, than like any of the others,[1] although I will be adding some idiosyncratic thoughts from time to time.

THE SABBATH AND CREATION

We shall look first at the Sabbath in the biblical creation narrative. That narrative refers to the Sabbath as follows: "And on the seventh day God finished his work that he had done, and he rested on the seventh day from all his work that he had done. So God blessed the seventh day and made it holy, because on it God rested from all his work that he had done in creation" (Gen. 2:2–3). Relating this passage to the six earlier days of

---

1. I should warn the reader, as I did in the discussion of the second commandment (chapters 25–26), that I am here taking some exceptions to the teaching of the Westminster standards, to which I have subscribed as a teaching elder of my denomination and a professor at Reformed Theological Seminary. Neither of these bodies requires "strict" subscription, both are aware of my exceptions, and neither has raised any objection to my teaching in these areas.

creation, Kline finds here consummation, enthronement, and consecration.[2] He says regarding consummation:

> First and most obvious, the Sabbath marks the completion of God's work of creation. As a celebration of the finishing of the world-temple, the Sabbath proclaims the name of the Creator to be Consummator. To be the builder who arrives at the seventh day of completion, to be the Sabbath attaining Creator, is to bear the name "the Last" along with the name "the First."[3]

God's lordship enables him to complete what he starts. He can, of course, bring about the fulfillment of his purposes in an instant. But he has chosen to deal with his creatures in a temporal, historical process, in which his purposes take time to be accomplished. That is true throughout redemptive history and is true today. So there is an already (what God has accomplished in the past) and a not-yet (what remains to be fulfilled) (see chapter 16). But because of who God is, the ultimate fulfillment is not in doubt. God's sabbath rest in Genesis 2:2 points forward to the certain completion of all of God's works. The Sabbath introduces eschatology into Scripture for the first time.

The second principle that Kline finds in this passage is divine enthronement: "God created the heaven and the earth to be his cosmic palace and accordingly his resting is an occupying of his palace, a royal session. The dawning of the Sabbath witnesses a new enthronement of Elohim."[4] God has been king from the beginning of the narrative, displayed in his sovereign power to bring the earth out of nothing, and specifically in the presence of the Spirit in Genesis 1:2, which Kline identifies as God's glory-throne. But God's mighty acts bring him new honors, and Genesis 2:2–3 shows him inhabiting a new temple and throne, the earth itself.

God has always been Lord (i.e., King), but each mighty act he performs creates new territories, new dominions, over which to exercise his lordship. The Sabbath, then, celebrates God's lordship, in its essence, but also in its continued historical expansions. So the fourth commandment in Deuteronomy 5, as we have seen, adds a second motivation to that of the Exodus version: keep the Sabbath because God redeemed you from Egypt.

---

2. Kline is not known as a triperspectivalist, but I think it would not be wrong to see these categories in our customary triadic pattern. Enthronement is normative, consummation is situational (having to do with the flow of events), and consecration is existential, for it "expresses man's commitment to the service of his Lord." Meredith G. Kline, *Kingdom Prologue* (privately printed, 1991), 26.

3. Ibid., 22.

4. Ibid., 22–23.

Redemption from Egypt marks a further expansion of God's lordship: a victory over his enemies, and his taking a people for himself. The covenant with Israel declares him to be Lord, not only of all creation, but specifically over this people he has chosen to be his. So the Sabbath celebrates both God's lordship over creation (Gen. 2:2; Ex. 20:11) and his specific lordship over Israel, his redeemed people (Deut. 5:15).[5]

Similarly, Jesus, who is Lord even before he is born (Luke 1:43), becomes Lord again by virtue of his atoning death and victorious resurrection (Acts 2:36; Rom. 1:4). As the Lord's Day in the New Testament celebrates Jesus' resurrection, the new creation, it also celebrates an advance in his historical lordship: ultimate victory over Satan, sin, and death. As such, there is a deep analogy between the meaning of the Sabbath in Genesis 2:2 and that of the Lord's Day in the New Testament.

Third, Kline relates the Sabbath to consecration. As he understands Genesis 1, God on the first three days creates realms, and on the next three creates the rulers of these realms. But then "we observe the glory of all the creature-kingdoms of all six days being carried along as a tributary offering within the gates of the Sabbath day to be laid at the feet of the Creator-King, now beheld in the brilliance of his epiphany as Sabbath Lord."[6]

Consecration here means, then, that all creation recognizes, affirms, and honors God's lordship and behaves accordingly. What does this consecration mean for human beings? Adam and Eve are present at the beginning of the Sabbath, having been made on the sixth day. Kline says, "All the creation of the six days is consecrated to man as the one set over all the works of God's hand, as the hierarchical structure of Genesis 1 shows, but man himself in turn is consecrated to the One who set all things under his feet."

So man is part of the holy celebration of God's lordship. He is one of those creatures consecrated to God on the seventh day, and, as God's vassal king, the rest of creation is consecrated to him. He acknowledges God's lordship, and he gratefully accepts God's gift of vassal kingship, taking on himself the responsibility to carry out the cultural mandate of Genesis 1:28 (see chapters 13, 17).

It should not surprise us, then, that when God gives the Sabbath to Israel he makes it a "sign" of the covenant between him and them:

> And the LORD said to Moses, "You are to speak to the people of Israel and say, 'Above all you shall keep my Sabbaths, for this is a sign between me and you throughout your generations, that you

5. Note the parallels between creation and redemption in Isa. 43:1, 7, 15; 2 Cor. 5:17; Gal. 6:15; Eph. 2:10; 4:24. Redemption is like creating anew. See DG, 295–98.
6. Kline, *Kingdom Prologue*, 25.

may know that I, the LORD, sanctify you. . . . It is a sign forever between me and the people of Israel that in six days the LORD made heaven and earth, and on the seventh day he rested and was refreshed.'" (Ex. 31:12–13, 17)

Here the Sabbath is a covenant sign which serves to consecrate the people of Israel to the service of their Lord.

Now we should consider a major point of contention among the six views of the Sabbath: does Genesis 2:2–3 obligate Adam and Eve to keep the Sabbath weekly, to imitate God's own cycle of work and rest? *From Sabbath to Lord's Day* argues in the negative. An initial look at the Genesis text might seem to support that view, for the passage speaks of God's rest, not about any analogous rest for man. It may seem that man's role here is to celebrate God's work, not his own—to acknowledge God's rest, not to rest himself.

But I believe that implicitly the text does require human Sabbath observance, for the reasons stated below. I shall move from the least to the most persuasive, but the earlier reasons provide a foundation for the others.

1. As God's image, man has a fundamental ethical responsibility to imitate God, as we saw in chapter 9. This does not necessarily mean that we must imitate everything God does. God does many things that we cannot do, and he has many prerogatives that we don't have. Sometimes the difference between Creator and creature makes imitation impossible—or even forbids imitation, as when Scripture tells us to leave vengeance to God alone. Sometimes redemptive-historical development makes it wrong for us to imitate what God did in a time that was different from our own. For example, God destroyed the firstborn of Egypt in Exodus, but it would be wrong for us to do any such thing today. But in the absence of such considerations, our bias should be in favor of imitation, not against it. In Genesis 2:2–3, there does not seem to be any metaphysical, ethical, or historical reason why we should not imitate God's cycle of work and rest. That is not, I think, a watertight argument for a Sabbath obligation in this passage. But it does warrant a more favorable attitude toward other arguments than some interpreters and theologians have shown.

2. Although the Sabbath here is God's rest, not man's, it is hard to understand why God would have structured his work in a six-plus-one pattern if not as a model for creatures. The day of rest by itself can be understood (as I indicated above) as a celebration of God's completed work, pure and simple. But, given that God does not actually grow weary so as to need literal rest, the celebratory rest might have as easily occurred after three days, or after two, or even after one. That is to say, God's celebratory rest

does not in itself presuppose any particular numerical scheme. So why the six days? It seems obvious to me that God intended the six-plus-one pattern for man's edification and imitation.[7]

3. We should remember that Moses is the primary author of Genesis[8] and that he wrote it for the Israelites who came out of Egypt by God's mighty hand, who became God's special people through the covenant of Exodus 19–24. Part of that covenant is the fourth commandment. Surely a Jewish reader of Genesis during the wilderness period would see Genesis 2:2–3 as the beginning of Sabbath observance, the background of the fourth commandment. The six-plus-one pattern, the cycle of work and rest, and the holiness of the seventh day all parallel the language of the fourth commandment. The Jewish reader would see that, as in the fourth commandment, God in Genesis 2 institutes a day of rest, which he blesses and makes holy.

4. But the clinching argument is the language of the fourth commandment itself. There the Lord says that Israel should keep the Sabbath *because* of the event of Genesis 2:2–3: "For in six days the LORD made heaven and earth, the sea, and all that is in them, and rested the seventh day. Therefore the LORD blessed the Sabbath day and made it holy" (Ex. 20:11).

It is important to ask, What Sabbath does Exodus 20:11 refer to? Does "Sabbath" here refer to God's rest after creating the world or to man's own Sabbath rest? It must refer to both. The first sentence of Exodus 20:11 refers to God's own rest, but "Sabbath" in the second sentence must refer to the "Sabbath" of verse 8, the weekly Sabbath that God requires of Israel. Exodus 20:11 sees an identity between these. It teaches that when God took his own rest from his creative labors and rested on the seventh day, which he hallowed and blessed, he also hallowed and blessed a human Sabbath, a Sabbath for man (Mark 2:27). In other words, when God blessed his own Sabbath rest in Genesis 2:3, he blessed it as a model for human imitation. So Israel is to keep the

---

7. I will not here enter into the question of whether the six days should be taken literally, as long ages, or as a literary framework. I don't think that question is relevant here. Even if the six days are a literary framework, God clearly intended to create the world in a way that was amenable to such a framework and to inspire Moses to present it that way. So the question still arises as to why God used that framework rather than some other one. For an inadequate discussion of the length of the days, see *DG*, 302–6.

8. I cannot argue this point here, but it is assumed by most evangelicals. The many parallels between the events of Genesis and those of Exodus verify Mosaic authorship of both books. In Genesis, Moses chooses and describes events that resonate with the experiences of the wilderness generation, such as God's dividing the waters in creation (Gen. 1:7; Ex. 14:21) and bringing plagues upon Egypt (Gen. 12:17; Ex. 7–12).

Sabbath, because in Genesis 2:2–3 God hallowed and blessed man's Sabbath as well as his own.

In my judgment, this argument establishes that the Sabbath is a creation ordinance (cf. chapter 13). It is one of those institutions like marriage, labor, and the cultural mandate given to Adam and Eve before the fall and therefore to all mankind. Although it is not unthinkable that God might change a creation ordinance at some time in history, such changes are very unlikely. For creation ordinances are given to man as man (Mark 2:27, again). They are not given merely as symbols of redemption, and therefore they are not "ceremonial." Rather, they express the basic relationship between Creator and creature.

Of course, as we have seen, the Sabbath in Genesis 2 does have an eschatological meaning. It looks forward to the conclusion of God's purposes. It may look forward to a future rest for man as well. So even before the fall, the Sabbath symbolized the reward that would have awaited Adam and Eve had they not sinned.[9] Certainly in the postfall period it symbolizes the completion of God's redemptive purposes. But what it symbolizes as a redemptive ordinance does not come to pass until the final judgment. So there is little likelihood that Sabbath observance will ever be abrogated between creation and consummation. Indeed, on this understanding it is likely that Sabbath observance will still be a norm for human beings even in the eternal state following the last judgment, for it is given to man as man. In that eternal state, it will celebrate continuing works of God and provide a weekly opportunity for man to consecrate to God the fruit of his labors.[10]

---

9. Richard B. Gaffin comments: "Given both the typology inherent in the original creation and the eschatological reference of the Sabbath, the following picture of the prefall Sabbath emerges. Genesis 2:2–3, together with their commentary in the fourth commandment, show that the weekly Sabbath given to Adam served a function in the creaturely realm similar to the seventh day of the creation week for the Creator. As God rested from his completed work of creation, so man would enter into his rest after completing his God-given tasks as vicegerent over the creation (cf. Heb. 4:10). This analogy between Creator and image-bearing creature involves an important difference. The creating work of God had been completed and his rest begun (cf. Heb. 4:3b–4). The task entrusted to Adam/man had yet to be performed; his rest was still future (cf. Heb. 4:9)." *Calvin and the Sabbath* (Fearn, Ross-shire: Christian Focus, 1998), 154.

10. I grant that the continuance of creation ordinances after the final judgment is a bit speculative. Certainly marriage does not continue then (Matt. 22:30). And certainly, when we reach our heavenly rest, the symbolic-typical functions of the Sabbath will cease. But there seems to be no reason why the Sabbath should not continue. Most likely there will still be work for human beings to do, in finite (though glorified) bodies that continue to need rest. And I see no reason why worship in the new heavens and the new earth should not have a weekly rhythm as it does today. The Sabbath in the eternal state would also be a reminder that God's work and man's have a structure and meaning, whereby everything that happens is periodically consecrated to God's glory.

The chief biblical argument for Sabbath observance today is that it is a creation ordinance given to man as man, and therefore appropriate for every age. The Sabbath takes on various additional meanings throughout history as it celebrates God's continuing series of mighty works, especially mighty works of redemption. But the obligation to celebrate God's works and anticipate further ones is integral to the very distinction between Creator and creature. Exodus 20:11 says that our very nature as images of God is *sufficient* reason to observe the Sabbath, whatever additional reasons may arise in redemptive history.

So the meaning of the Sabbath is not primarily or exclusively redemptive, as Calvin and some of his followers have thought.[11] And the completion of redemption in Christ does not bring an end to Sabbath observance, as in the first three views I discussed in chapter 28.

THE SABBATH AND COMMON GRACE

As I mentioned in the last chapter, Meredith G. Kline finds in Genesis 3:14–9:17 the establishment of a "sphere" or "order" of common grace, which he describes as follows:

> This sphere is common not only in the sense that its benefits are shared by the generality of mankind, the just and unjust alike, but in the sense that it is nonsacred. Particular emphasis needs to be given to the fact that the political, institutional aspect of common grace culture is not holy, but profane.[12]

He notes that in establishing this order of common grace in Genesis 3:16–19 and 9:1–17, God reiterates some creation ordinances: labor, childbearing, and the cultural mandate. But he does not reinstitute the Sabbath. Kline comments:

> The withholding of the Sabbath sign from common grace culture is a clear indication of the secular, nonholy character of that culture. For to put the stamp of the Sabbath on a cultural program is to set it apart as holy to God, as a bearer of the divine name and of the promise of being crowned with consummation glory. Accordingly, in the postlapsarian context the Scriptures relate the Sabbath sign of sanctification and consummation to the redemptive

---

11. Gaffin's analysis is helpful. He concludes, "A basic error is Calvin's failure to reckon adequately with the Sabbath institution as a creation ordinance" (*Calvin and the Sabbath*, 146).

12. Kline, *Kingdom Prologue*, 96.

program exclusively. The only culture on which the sabbatical sign is explicitly impressed is the theocratic kingdom-culture of Israel under the old covenant.[13]

The command to rest weekly from one's daily work, in Kline's view, is only valid in contexts where such work is holy. Work was holy, he thinks, in Eden before the fall and in the Israelite theocracy, and it will be holy again in the new heavens and new earth. It was not holy in the common grace order that prevailed before the Mosaic covenant, that continued after that covenant among the nations outside Israel, and that prevails in all nations in the period between Jesus' ascension and his coming again. This is what I earlier called Kline's later view of the Sabbath, the fourth view we considered in chapter 28. He concludes that in the present time we have no obligation to cease work on the Sabbath, but only to worship (a holy activity) on that day.

I agree with Kline that God gave common grace to people after the fall. He provided benefits to his enemies, even to those whom he would never save from sin. However, I do not see biblical evidence of an "order" or "sphere" of common grace. Now if a "common grace sphere" is merely a time or place where God is acting in common grace, then that sphere covers all times and places from fall to consummation. Even in theocratic Israel, God gave blessings of common grace to the wicked as well as the blessings of special, saving grace to the elect. But Kline's reference to the "political, institutional aspect of common grace culture" seems to suggest that he is thinking primarily of government, together with other "cultural programs," when he speaks of the common grace sphere.

So his argument is that after the fall God established nonholy governments and cultural programs in the world. But how are they nonholy, as opposed to those of the Israelite theocracy, which he believes to be holy? A holy government, in his view, is "a bearer of the divine name and of the promise of being crowned with consummation glory."

We can understand what it means for an individual to be holy in this sense. Scripture also describes as "holy" the good angels, the tabernacle, the temple, priests, offerings, Israel itself, the Promised Land, Sabbaths and feasts, the church, Jesus, and God himself. But I don't think Scripture ever describes a government or a cultural program, in itself, in Israel or outside Israel, as either holy or nonholy. King David, of course, was anointed by the Lord; King Nebuchadnezzar was not. Anointing might suggest a holy status. But Elijah anointed Hazael to be king of Syria (1 Kings 19:15), and God refers to Cyrus, king of Persia, as "my anointed" (Isa. 45:1), so if anointing

---

13. Ibid.

suggests holiness, that holiness existed outside the Israelite theocracy. Note also Paul's reference in Romans 13:4 to the civil magistrate as a "servant" (*diakonos*, sometimes translated "minister") of God, "instituted" (v. 1) and "appointed" (v. 2) by God. In Paul's time, these magistrates were mostly Roman pagans.

Certainly nothing in Genesis 4–9 suggests that God made any distinction between holy and nonholy governments and cultural movements, though he certainly made distinctions between righteous and wicked ones. As I shall indicate in my discussion of the fifth commandment, I don't even see in this passage the establishment of the state as an institution, let alone a distinctively nonholy institution. These chapters do not mention any institutions beyond the family. God gives to Cain protection from his relatives in 4:14–15. He gives to Noah's family the power to shed the blood of those who shed the blood of others (9:6).

As for "cultural programs," it is not entirely clear what the difference is between one that is holy and one that is righteous, but not holy. Clearly, for Kline, a holy program is not merely a program that conforms to God's standards, but one that somehow has the promise of consummation glory. Does that mean that God will give it a special covenant blessing—that it will continue past the final judgment? Where would we even turn in Scripture for answers to such questions?

Is a holy program a means of salvation from sin (Kline's "promise of being crowned with consummation glory")? It is true that Adam does not earn his salvation by his toil in the fields (Gen. 3:17–19), but in this respect his labor is no different from that of workers who lived in the Israelite theocracy. So on this definition Adam's labor and that of the Israelite are equally nonholy.

Is a holy program a kind of labor that is consecrated to God? Farmers and herdsmen in Israel were expected to bring their firstfruits to God, but so were Cain and Abel (Gen. 4:3–4) and others living before the theocracy (as Abram in Gen. 14:19–20). God asks us today, as well, to perform our cultural labors to God's glory (1 Cor. 10:31).

So Kline's contrast between holy and nonholy governments and cultural programs does not exist in Genesis 3:16–9:17 (or, I suspect, anywhere else in Scripture). Certainly in these chapters God never founds an institution or cultural program and declares that it is, and should be, nonholy. God establishes culture before the fall, in Genesis 1:28. In 3:16–9:17, he expects people to carry out these duties in faithfulness to him. That's all there is to it.

Now it is a fair question, and germane, to ask why God does not reiterate the Sabbath command in the Noachic covenant of Genesis 9. The flood is like a de-creation and re-creation.[14] So, as after the original creation, God gives the cultural mandate to the new creation after the flood. He tells Noah and his family, as he told Adam and Eve, to "be fruitful and multiply" (vv. 1, 7) and to take dominion of other life (vv. 2–6). Why, then, does he not renew the Sabbath commandment as well?

It is also the case that God gave to Noah's family a wonderful deliverance, comparable in scope to his deliverance of Israel from Egypt. But after Israel's deliverance from Egypt, God reiterated the Sabbath command, and he presented that deliverance as an additional motivation for them to keep the Sabbath (Deut. 5:15). So why does he not do the same after the deliverance of Noah and his family from the great flood? Some answers to these questions follow:

1. Although there is an analogy between creation and the flood, there are also differences. For one thing, God does not rest after the flood, as he did after creation. So there is no new occasion for a Sabbath blessing on the order of that in Genesis 2:2–3.

2. As we have seen, God does not explicitly command Adam and Eve to keep the Sabbath in Genesis 2:2–3, though a Sabbath obligation is implicit. So, in literary terms, there is no Sabbath commandment in Genesis 2 that could be echoed in Genesis 9.

3. The redemption of Genesis 6–9 differs from that of Israel's exodus in that the latter singles out Israel from all the nations as God's holy people. God reiterates the Sabbath as a seal of their distinctiveness (Ex. 31:12–17). But the covenant of Genesis 8:20–9:17 is with the entire human race (and with all flesh, besides). Noah's family is not a special, holy people. So there is no need in the Noachic covenant for the Sabbath to take on the role of a special covenant seal.

4. Genesis 9 deals with the immediate situation of Noah and his family. Upon leaving the ark, they may well have wondered what they were to do next. Was the earth still a fit place for human habitation? Had God given them power to subdue the whole earth, or had he only provided them a small sanctuary? Had he, perhaps, restricted their territory because their numbers were small or because human beings had shown themselves to be incapable of subduing the earth to the glory of God (Gen. 8:21)? The Noachic covenant clarifies that, despite their small numbers and their sinful bent, God still wanted them to exercise dominion over the whole earth. There is, however, no special question about Sabbath observance that arises at this time. Noah and his family doubtless kept the Sabbath aboard the ark, and they did not need to be reminded of it.

14. See *DG*, 278–82.

Certainly there is no suggestion here that the Sabbath command is omitted because Noah's culture is a "common grace order." Genesis 8–9 does say much about common grace: the promise of regular seasons (8:22) and the promise that God will never again destroy all flesh by a flood (9:11–17). But there is here no reference to a common grace *sphere* as opposed to a holy sphere, to a common grace culture or government, as opposed to a holy culture or government. To say that the lack of a Sabbath command proves the existence of such an order is at best an argument from silence and at worst speculation.

5. Kline wants to say that the Sabbath commandment, as a creation ordinance, always governs worship, since worship is always a holy enterprise, as opposed to culture and government. Yet we should note that in Genesis 3:14–9:17 God does not republish the Sabbath ordinance either for culture or for worship. If the absence of a Sabbath ordinance for culture means that culture should not follow a sabbatical pattern, then the consequences are the same for worship. But neither Kline nor any other Sabbatarian would admit that. This is just another way of saying that these chapters do not make the kind of distinction that Kline tries to find in them.

So I believe that the Sabbath ordinance of Genesis 2:2–3 was in force from Adam to Moses and then was renewed in the Decalogue. I cannot establish the extent to which people actually observed the Sabbath during this period. There are no clear references to Sabbath observance until Exodus 16, four chapters before the Decalogue, where God tells Israel to gather a double portion of manna on the sixth day and the following day to observe "a day of solemn rest, a holy Sabbath to the Lord" (v. 23). Clearly, Exodus 16:23 assumes that Israel knew what a Sabbath was, however much they were able or unable to celebrate it during their slavery in Egypt. In any case, whether people during this period actually observed the Sabbath or not, they were under obligation to do so.[15] John Murray comments,

> The silence of Genesis subsequent to Genesis 2:2, 3 proves nothing as to the desuetude of the institution during patriarchal times, nor does it prove ignorance of the ordinance on the part of the patriarchs. But even if we suppose that the remembrance of this institution did pass away and that the patriarchs did not observe the weekly Sabbath, it is no more difficult to explain this lapse from the creation ordinance than it is to explain the lapse from

15. Here are other examples of this principle: (1) Most likely, Israel never kept the Jubilee after God commanded them to keep it. But that fact did not erase their obligation (Lev. 25:9–10). (2) Israel failed to allow the land to lie fallow every seventh (sabbatical!) year, as God commanded them. This is one reason why God sent them into exile (2 Chron. 36:21).

the principle of monogamy so clearly implied in Genesis 2:24. It is precarious to base too much on silence. But even if the silence indicates declension, ignorance, and non-observance, this does not remove the creation ordinance nor does it disestablish its binding obligation.[16]

So I do not agree with Meredith Kline's view that the prohibition of Sabbath labor pertains only to "holy" work. I cannot find any justification for this claim, implicit or explicit, in the text of Scripture.

Some have used Kline's distinction between holy and common spheres as an argument to support some of the twofold distinctions that I have rejected earlier in this book: law/gospel, natural law/Scripture, nature/grace, religious/nonreligious, and so on. I hope my discussion of Kline has further weakened the argument for these positions. Kline does reply to criticisms from the Kuyperian-Dooyeweerdian tradition that rejects these twofold distinctions:

> Characteristically, members of that [Dooyeweerdian] school have been critical of schematizations that distinguish between the city of man and the city of God. In particular they would frown on the suggestion that the city of man is common, in the sense of nonholy. They believe they can detect a scholastic nature-grace dualism lurking in any such approach. But to dismiss every two-cities scheme on the grounds of such a suspicion is too hasty and undiscriminating. . . . The Scriptures compel us to distinguish between the kingdom of God as realm and reign and to recognize that though everything is embraced under the reign of God, not everything can be identified as part of the kingdom of God viewed as a holy realm.[17]

I agree entirely that a comprehensive view of God's sovereignty does not exclude distinctions within creation. And there are distinctions between holy and nonholy (as with the priests and the temple) that have a legitimate biblical basis.[18] But Kline and others must bear the burden of proof if they wish to extend the holy/common distinction to spheres of culture

---

16. John Murray, *Principles of Conduct* (Grand Rapids: Eerdmans, 1957), 34–35.

17. Kline, *Kingdom Prologue*, 105. In my judgment, there is a biblical distinction (and antithesis) between the city of God and the city of Satan, but not between the city of God and "the city of man."

18. I am inclined, however, to see the holy/common distinction as a difference in degree. See chapter 23, especially the diagram in the discussion of unholiness and uncleanness. The distinction between righteousness and wickedness, however, is absolute, exclusive, and antithetical.

and government. Because of the argumentation above, I do not believe that Kline has satisfied that burden.

Having dealt with Genesis 2:2–3 and Genesis 3:16–9:17, I believe that I have refuted the main arguments for the first four views discussed in chapter 28. That leaves the final two views as serious contenders.

THE SABBATH AND REDEMPTION

The biblical reasons for keeping the Sabbath are (1) creation and (2) redemption. As we have seen, God calls us to keep the Sabbath in imitation of his creative work and as a memorial of his redemptive deliverance. Exodus 20 emphasizes the first, but does not neglect the second, for our observance of the whole Decalogue is based on the fact that "I am the LORD your God, who brought you out of the land of Egypt, out of the house of slavery" (v. 2). Deuteronomy 5:15 underscores that ground: "You shall remember that you were a slave in the land of Egypt, and the LORD your God brought you out from there with a mighty hand and an outstretched arm. Therefore the LORD your God commanded you to keep the Sabbath day." We shall see that the Lord's Day in the New Testament is also a response to redemption, in this case a celebration of the resurrection of Jesus.

The eschatology that the Sabbath brings even into the prefall world (see above) extends to the consummation of redemption. We shall see this in Hebrews 3–4, in which "Sabbath rest" is a name for the final reward of the believing Christian.

As we shall see, the meaning of this redemptive rest is not specifically the forgiveness of sins, but it is the rest from toil brought about by God's curse on the ground. (God doesn't tell us to sin for six days and to find forgiveness on the seventh, but to work six days and rest on the seventh.) As such, the Sabbath well defines, not specifically the work of Jesus' atonement, but the final state of the church. This fact suggests that the Sabbath will not be abrogated with the completion of Jesus' atonement, but will continue to symbolize and anticipate our heavenly rest until the last day. There is nothing in the relation of the Sabbath to redemption that suggests that the Sabbath will ever be abrogated.

WORK AND REST

The main differences between views five and six have to do with the relation of worship to rest on the Sabbath and the nature of the Sabbath rest. The Westminster standards (view six), following Calvin and others in the Reformed tradition (though differing with them in important ways), see worship as the primary activity of the Sabbath. For them, to rest is mainly to set aside other responsibilities in order to have time for worship. The early Kline view (view five) sees rest as the fundamental meaning of the Sabbath. The day of rest, on this view, does facilitate worship, but rest is the Sabbath's essence.

I believe that the early Kline was right on this score. Scripture always defines the Sabbath as a day of rest, rather than a day of worship. God's Sabbath in Genesis 2:2–3 is a time of rest from his labors. The fourth commandment calls on Israel to work for six days and rest for one.[19] When Scripture mentions specific violations of the Sabbath, they are in the category of illegitimate work, not failure to engage in Sabbath worship (Ex. 31:13–17; 34:21; 35:3; Num. 15:32–36; Neh. 13:15–18; Jer. 17:21–22; Amos 8:4–6). Jesus' confrontations with the Pharisees on the Sabbath concerned work rather than worship, as in Matthew 12:1–14.

The Sabbath rest is physical, not merely a ceasing of one activity in order to perform another, as some Reformed writers have represented it. Scripture often condemns burdensome activity on the Sabbath, even when there is no question of people missing worship activities (Neh. 13:15–18; Jer. 17:21–22). The Sabbath is a day on which to be "refreshed" (Ex. 23:12; 31:17), a "delight" (Isa. 58:13). I therefore believe it is legitimate to spend part of the Sabbath day in sheer physical rest. A nap on that day should not be disparaged as idleness, as might be supposed from the language of WLC, 119.[20]

The "work" from which we should rest on the Sabbath is particularly our daily labors, from which we earn our living. Exodus 34:21 mentions plowing and harvesting. Nehemiah 13:15–18 condemns the treading of winepresses and the transportation of goods for sale (cf. 10:31). Amos 8:4–6 also implies that buying and selling are inappropriate on the Sabbath,

---

19. Bible students are sometimes surprised to learn that the fourth commandment requires them to work for six days! There is a work ethic in the fourth commandment that appears also, implicitly, in the eighth, ninth, and tenth commandments. Rest is the central meaning of the commandment, but rest has no meaning if it is not a rest from work.

20. If readers will excuse a personal note, I feel, as I grow older, a need for a special rest period weekly. I don't seem to need naps on most days, but my body tends to wilt on Sunday afternoon. I suspect that God has made the human body to operate on a weekly calendar. It shouldn't be surprising that obeying God's laws is physically beneficial as well as morally right, since God is the author of the human body as well as the moral order. As I observed earlier, the Sabbath is made for man as man. As a general rule, obeying God's law has good consequences; it brings blessing, rather than curse (Deut. 10:13; cf. chapters 14–17 of this volume). The good life and the obedient life are, in the long run, identical.

though the main burden of this passage is different. But Jeremiah 17:22 forbids the carrying of heavy burdens "out of your houses" on the Sabbath, suggesting that such hard work is inappropriate even when it does not have a commercial purpose.

The case of the man gathering sticks in Numbers 15:32–36 has occasioned much discussion:

> While the people of Israel were in the wilderness, they found a man gathering sticks on the Sabbath day. And those who found him gathering sticks brought him to Moses and Aaron and to all the congregation. They put him in custody, because it had not been made clear what should be done to him. And the LORD said to Moses, "The man shall be put to death; all the congregation shall stone him with stones outside the camp." And all the congregation brought him outside the camp and stoned him to death with stones, as the LORD commanded Moses.

Exodus 35:3 forbids kindling fires in homes on the Sabbath day, so it is natural to assume that the man in Numbers 15 was preparing to violate that provision. Exodus 35:2 does specify the death penalty for people who work on the Sabbath.[21] But if it were that simple, it is hard to understand why Moses didn't carry out the penalty immediately, rather than waiting for further revelation. Many commentators think that what Exodus 35:3 forbids is not the burning of wood on the Sabbath, but "kindling" a fire in the sense of starting one from scratch. One could add wood to a fire that had been started earlier, to keep warm, but one could not start up a new fire. Perhaps revelation was needed to determine the motive of the stick gatherer, that he gathered the sticks to kindle a new fire, or even to sell them, or for other business purposes. Divine revelation may also have been necessary to determine whether the suspect had merely made a mistake, or whether he was defying God. The immediately preceding context, verses 22–31, distinguishes unintentional sins (a "mistake," v. 26) from sins done "with a high hand" (v. 30) and specifies that one who commits the latter be "cut off from among his people." (This expression may refer either to death or to exile.) God may have revealed to Moses that the stick gatherer had sinned with a high hand.[22]

21. For a general discussion of death penalties in the law, see chapter 13.

22. James B. Jordan, in *Sabbath Keeping and the Death Penalty* (privately printed), available at http://www.biblicalhorizons.com/catalogue.htm, takes a very different approach. In his view, the stick gatherer of Num. 15 committed the crime of despising God's sanctuary: "It seems that there was no death penalty for ordinary work done on the sabbath, but only for certain liturgical crimes connected with causing one's own fire to blaze up at the time

The net result of this teaching is that work forbidden on the Sabbath includes (1) daily business, whether agricultural or commercial, and (2) hard labor at home, such as lifting heavy loads or starting a new fire. We may presume, too, that God frowns on labor that limits attendance at worship, or activities that encourage or require others to break the Sabbath. All of these prohibitions, however, are to be modified by the biblical teachings about deeds of necessity and mercy, which we shall take up shortly.

Rest is fundamental also to the theological symbolism of the Sabbath. In Genesis 2:2–3, as we saw, it represents a completion and celebration of man's cultural labors (and of course a successful completion of the probation of Genesis 2:17). In Psalm 95:7–11, rest represents the Promised Land, the fulfillment of God's promise to Abraham, which Israel in the wilderness forfeited by its covenant disobedience. But the psalm also widens the scope of the promised rest. Even as the Israelites dwell in the land, another rest awaits them. So the psalmist urges the people not again to forfeit the rest that God has promised. Hebrews 3:1–4:10 explains that this rest is the final eschatological promise, the promise of the new heaven and new earth. The writer urges the Hebrew Christians, as in Psalm 95:7–11, not to forfeit this rest by going back to Judaism. The Sabbath rest awaits the people of God.

The theme of redemption as rest is especially appropriate since the fall brought about a curse on the earth and made man's labor a hard task (Gen. 3:17–19). Even before the fall, Adam would have known the difference between work and rest, for he would have observed that distinction in keeping the Sabbath. But after the fall, work became painful and toilsome, and rest became a partial relief from the curse. In Deuteronomy 5:15, the Sabbath command recalls the rigors of slavery in Egypt, from which God gave rest to his people. So Ecclesiastes 2:9–11 speaks of man's toil as "vanity," and Psalm 90 expresses similar weariness of the world. The wicked, indeed, have no genuine peace or rest (Isa. 48:22; 57:21), but God gives rest to his people as a redemptive blessing (Ps. 127:2). Jesus promises rest to those who come to him (Matt. 11:28) (rest by taking on a yoke!), and God gives rest from their labors to the glorified saints (Rev. 14:13).

In all of this, the biblical emphasis is not on rest as a symbol of grace (with work as a symbol of sin), as Calvin and others supposed. The rest is not a rest from sin as such, but a rest from the toil that sin has brought upon our working life. God's rest temporarily lifts the curse from our labors—and

---

God's hearthfire was to be magnified." On this view, as on the more traditional views, Moses needed to seek God's revelation to determine the motive of the stick gatherer. Gathering sticks on the Sabbath is not a capital crime in itself, but it is a capital crime if done for certain purposes.

eventually permanently. It is a redemptive symbol, but not a symbol of grace as opposed to works. Rather, it symbolizes our final reward as a rest from our labors.

It is important that we understand that, as an aspect of the theology of the Sabbath. The Sabbath command is not that we sin for six days and receive grace on the seventh. Rather, it is that we toil for six days and rest from that toil on the seventh. If the Sabbath symbolized primarily a rest from sin, then it would be plausible to construct an argument like Calvin's to the effect that the Sabbath is now abrogated, since what it symbolized has now come to pass in reality. But since the Sabbath rather symbolizes rest from toil and curse, there is no reason to expect its abrogation until the curse is removed from the earth.[23]

RECREATION

One question often discussed today among Sabbatarian Christians is whether recreation is appropriate on the Sabbath. That is, is recreation an aspect of Sabbath rest or a form of work appropriate only on the other six days? The Larger Catechism favors the latter view, forbidding "all needless works, words, and thoughts, about our worldly employments and recreations" (WLC, 119).[24]

But we have seen that the prohibitions of Scripture are directed to work, not recreation as such. Some have thought that Isaiah 58:13–14 includes a prohibition of recreation:

> If you turn back your foot from the Sabbath,
>   from doing your pleasure on my holy day,
> and call the Sabbath a delight
>   and the holy day of the LORD honorable;
> if you honor it, not going your own ways,
>   or seeking your own pleasure, or talking idly;
> then you shall take delight in the LORD,
>   and I will make you ride on the heights of the earth;
> I will feed you with the heritage of Jacob your father,
>   for the mouth of the LORD has spoken.

23. The Sabbath may not be abrogated even then; recall my earlier argument that the Sabbath may well extend into the eternal state. For it had meaning even before God placed a curse on the ground.

24. The Catechism does distinguish between "employments" and "recreations." But it evidently assumes that "your work" in Ex. 20:8 includes recreation. That inclusion is not intuitively obvious.

Note that the word "pleasure" occurs twice in verse 13. If we equate "pleasure" with "recreation," the passage would seem to exclude recreation. But that is not what the passage means. "Pleasure" here comes from the Hebrew *hefets*, which often refers simply to the will of a human being or God (as in Isa. 44:28; 46:10; 48:14; 53:10). The contrast in Isaiah 58:13–14 is not between doing pleasant things and unpleasant things, but between doing our will and God's. Indeed, the passage itself emphasizes that the Sabbath is to be a pleasant experience, a "delight." If recreation is pleasant, enjoyable activity, as opposed to toil, then the Sabbath itself is by nature recreational (cf. the references to being "refreshed" in Ex. 23:12 and 31:17). Recreation, then, is a form of rest.

Now that does not settle the issue of what kinds of activities are permitted on the Sabbath. Isaiah 58:13–14 distinguishes only between God's will (i.e., his pleasure) and our own desires that conflict with his. It does not tell us in detail what God's will is for our Sabbath activities. There is in Isaiah 58:1–12 at least the suggestion that some Sabbath activities are especially pleasing to God. These are the works of mercy for the poor and needy, which I shall discuss later. Verse 3 uses the phrase "your own pleasure," the same language as in verse 13, to refer to oppression of the poor. Clearly that is the burden of Isaiah 58: to condemn those who oppress the poor and even have the audacity to do that on God's own day. Rather, God's Sabbath is a time to show mercy.

But there is no reason to think that God through Isaiah is telling the people to forsake Sabbath recreation. To determine what God specifically forbids and permits, we must go to other passages, as we did in the previous section. But as we have seen, the focus of these other passages is to forbid work: daily business and heavy lifting. These passages do not forbid pleasurable activities as a distinct category. So we may conclude that Scripture permits Sabbath recreation, since there is no reason to think that recreation is a form of work appropriate only to the other six days. This is a negative argument.

But does Scripture merely permit recreation on the Sabbath, or is there some positive value to Sabbath recreation in keeping with the nature of the day? I have been greatly helped to see its positive value by Charles L. Jacob's article, "Eat the Fat, Drink the Sweet, and Be Merry."[25] The title is based on Nehemiah 8:9–10, where the Levites are teaching the law to Israel, newly regathered from exile. It is a "holy" day (v. 9), like a Sabbath. There is a solemnity about it, as God convicts the people of sin. But the

---

25. Jacob's article can be read at http://reformedperspectives.org/newfiles/cha_jaboc/TH.Jacob.Sabbath.html.

Levites urge the people to make a feast of it, to enjoy good food and drink and not to mourn. Jacob points out how often God's holy days are feasts, times of recreation, as well as times of learning and worship. The Sabbath, we have seen, celebrates God as Creator, Redeemer, and Consummator of history. Jacob shows that whenever God's people celebrate these great events, they *play*. Compare the dancing accompanying the bringing of the ark to Jerusalem (2 Sam. 6:12–23), the emphasis in the Psalms on rejoicing before God, the singing and dancing following the deliverance from Egypt (Ex. 15), the rejoicing in the New Testament over sinners being found (Luke 15), and Jesus' partying in the gospels. The eschatological passages of Scripture are full of feasting and song. How can the Sabbath, which celebrates creation, redemption, and consummation, be any different?

So it is important to keep in mind that by its very nature the Sabbath is a feast, not a fast. It is a time of abundance, not deprivation. It should be a delight, a time of play and joy. There is of course a difference between feasting before the Lord and mere secular entertainment. Since the Sabbath is a holy day unto the Lord (note: a day, not just an hour or two), Sabbath recreation should be focused on him. But there is also a circle around the focus. When people dance before the Lord, they do it in honor of him. But this doesn't mean that every foot movement carries religious symbolism. The dance is simply the outworking of a joyful disposition—a playful, happy response to God's goodness.[26] That circle naturally extends to congregational meals (like the New Testament agape), games for children and adults, times to swim and hike, laughing and sharing.

On Independence Day, many Americans really do celebrate the founding of the United States. In doing so, they enjoy barbecues together, watch fireworks, play ball games, go to the beach, and salute the flag as it passes. Celebration of the nation's founding is the focus; other activities revolve around that focal point. The Sabbath, I think, is much like that, though with a more intense focus on its object. God is the focus, but there is enjoyment also in the dancing, feasting, and making merry, in the circle around the focal point. And in that enjoyment, we anticipate the prosperity promised in God's covenant, the delights awaiting us in the new heavens and the new earth.

This doesn't mean that all forms of recreation are appropriate for the Sabbath day. Some kinds of recreation require other people to carry on

---

26. In *Contemporary Worship Music* (Phillipsburg, NJ: P&R Publishing, 1997), 59–61, I argue that there is a great difference between worship and musical entertainment, in regard to both goal and means. Nevertheless, there is some overlap in the values of these two spheres. Both worship and entertainment require clear communication, good preparation, skillful musicians, emotional impact, memorability, and positive social interaction.

their daily labors, such as commercial sports and entertainments. To attend these, we must engage in buying and selling, which God forbade to Israel on the Sabbath.

Some forms of recreation promote values opposed to God's Word, such as certain kinds of music recordings and videos. If we listen to such things, we should be self-conscious in our Christian values, seeking to undermine unbelief and to rescue those caught up in it, while thanking God for his common grace to unbelieving entertainers. This counsel is valid for every day of the week, of course, not just the Sabbath. But we may well choose to limit our exposure to worldly entertainment on the Sabbath more than during the rest of the week, to maintain the distinctive character of the day.

For the rest, one would be hard-pressed to come up with a list of Sabbath recreations that are always or never appropriate. Much of our ethical thinking in this area should be about goals and motives (the situational and existential perspectives). Dance on the Sabbath can be appropriate, but it is possible for people to idolize the dance, as an escape from God rather than a tribute to him. The same is true for athletics, meals, naps, and so on.

We should plan the Sabbath day as a total experience for ourselves and our families, including worship, recreation, and deeds of necessity and mercy (see below). There ought to be a balance in these activities that enables us to say at the end that we have been with God in a special way—that we have worshiped him, enjoyed his creation, and loved the people he has made in his image. This total experience may well be different from week to week, from family to family, from church to church, from culture to culture.

WORKS OF NECESSITY

The Westminster standards, as I have noted, see the Sabbath primarily as a time of public and private worship, but they do acknowledge some exceptions: works of necessity and mercy. I shall consider here the former category.

An example of a work of necessity is given in Matthew 12:1, where Jesus' disciples, on a Sabbath, pick heads of grain to eat. Now there is much more to be said about this passage, which we will discuss later, but for now we should note what is most obvious: that nothing in Scripture forbids eating on the Sabbath or preparing food to eat.[27] As I indicated earlier, the

27. Luke 6:1 tells us that the disciples rubbed the grain in their hands to separate out the kernels.

Sabbath is not a fast. It is made for man, not man for the Sabbath (Mark 2:27). Like the rest of the law, God intends it to enrich human life, not to destroy it. The Pharisees, evidently, following various traditions, associated the disciples' actions with harvesting, a form of work. But Jesus, as always, takes his cue from Scripture, rather than from tradition.

Other examples of works of necessity include the priests making arrangements for worship (Matt. 12:5–6). It was generally understood also that warfare could take place on the Sabbath. In Joshua 6:12–20, Israel blew trumpets for seven days as they surrounded Jericho. In 2 Kings 11 and 2 Chronicles 22:10–23:15 we read of the plot of Jehoiada against the wicked queen Athaliah to install the rightful king Joash, which took place on a Sabbath.[28]

Another biblical example of a work of necessity is the rescue of a person or animal (Luke 14:5). This may be considered a work of mercy, but, viewed as the preservation of life, it is also a work of necessity.

The mention of an animal leads us to consider a more general observation: that farming and herding, even though they are businesses, require some attention on the Sabbath day. Animals must be milked and fed each day. Now God might have taught Israel that agriculture was an ungodly way of life, since it requires some Sabbath labor. But he did not, in effect warranting certain kinds of minimal maintenance, even of one's business, on the Sabbath.

One can easily understand that matters of life and death must be dealt with on the Sabbath day. (Hence physicians and nurses, police and fire-fighters, must work on the Sabbath.) But works of necessity are not limited to such life-and-death situations. Most people would survive if they went without food one day a week. But the Sabbath does not require that. People could survive without agricultural businesses—by retreating to a hunter-gatherer lifestyle. But God does not require that of us. Works of necessity are not just works that are necessary to keep us alive. They are works that keep human life on an even keel.

Gary North, oddly a theonomist but not a Sabbatarian, published an article called "The Economics of Sabbath Keeping,"[29] in which he argues that keeping the Sabbath is incompatible with the structure of modern civilization. Many modern industries cannot be shut down for one day a week. Steel mills, for example, take several days to be shut down and started up. So, North argues, on a strictly Sabbatarian basis the steel business must

28. The extracanonical book 1 Maccabees (2:41) speaks of the defense of a people being legitimate on the Sabbath, expressing the usual Jewish understanding.

29. Appendix 4 to Rousas J. Rushdoony, *The Institutes of Biblical Law* (Nutley, NJ: Craig Press, 1973), 824–36.

be abandoned as ungodly. And if Sabbatarians were consistent in their position, North argues, they would shut down the electricity and heat to their homes on the Sabbath day, for delivery of that electricity and heat requires people to work in factories. If we use electricity and heat, we are in effect paying someone to gather sticks on the Sabbath, for which the man in Numbers 15:32–36 was executed.[30]

Brian Schwertley, a conservative Sabbatarian, argues to the contrary that maintenance of steel mills and electric plants should be considered works of necessity.[31] Because of "the huge increases of population since ancient times, and the massive population centers that have arisen with industrialization," he says, the human race now requires centralized forms of energy distribution. "The medical and environmental benefits alone render a central, dependable, clean source of energy a necessity."[32]

I agree. But Schwertley still seems to have in mind the idea that works of necessity are strictly to preserve the lives of people. For North, evidently, a work of necessity is necessary to preserve individual lives; on this basis, the use of electricity is not a work of necessity. For Schwertley, it is necessary from a more corporate standpoint, to preserve lives generally in society. I doubt, however, that raising cattle in the Old Testament period was absolutely necessary to preserve life, individually or corporately. Nor is the steel industry today strictly necessary for human survival. My view is that the necessity here is not a necessity for human survival, but a necessity for maintaining the general *quality* of human life as it exists in our time and culture.

So, just as in biblical times it was not wrong to milk one's cows on the Sabbath, it is not wrong on that day to maintain the furnaces in a steel mill.

Nor, I think, is it always wrong to go to a restaurant to eat on the Sabbath. We must eat, and we must prepare the food we eat. We can either do that ourselves or pay someone to do that for us; so far as the theology of the Sabbath is concerned, it doesn't matter. Of course, when we buy restaurant meals we are paying people to do work by which they make their living. I would be pleased if fewer restaurants were open on Sunday, but some should be open, since food is as much of a necessity as medical care. For my own family, I prefer that restaurant meals on the Sabbath be rare, for I prefer

30. Perhaps from the same reasoning, newspapers reported that Sen. Joseph Lieberman, an orthodox Jew, turns out all electric lights in his home on the Jewish Sabbath. But, regarding Numbers 15, review my discussion earlier in this chapter.

31. Schwertley, "The Sabbath and Modern Industrial Civilization," *The Counsel of Chalcedon* 23.5–6 (October–November, 2001): 36–40. Available at http://www.reformedonline.com/view/reformedonline/sabbathciv.htm. I often disagree with Schwertley, but this article is a good one.

32. Ibid., 38.

to discourage the massive Sunday commercialism of our time. But I don't believe that it is a sin to eat out, as part of the Sabbath feast.

Is it ever legitimate for a Christian Sabbatarian to take a job that requires Sunday work? As we have seen, a number of businesses carry on activities that are unquestionably appropriate for the Sabbath: police and fire departments, physicians, nurses, and other medical personnel. And we have also seen that other sorts of businesses have legitimate needs for Sunday workers: steel mills, farms, and so forth. But what of other kinds of employment? The general rule, certainly, is that that is forbidden by the fourth commandment. But what if a Christian can find no way of supporting himself and his family, other than by taking on Sunday work that is not a work of necessity in the ways that police and farm work are necessary?

I would say that supporting one's family is also a work of necessity. One should certainly not decide hastily to take such a job, and if one has such a job he should seek to find other employment as soon as possible. But the Sabbath is made for man, not man for the Sabbath (Mark 2:27). As we have seen, eating is a work of necessity, and if Sunday work is necessary to provide food, that is a necessity as well.

I suspect that during Israel's Egyptian bondage they did not keep the Sabbath. Their overseers, doubtless, were not Sabbath observers, and the picture we receive from the early chapters of Exodus is that Egyptian masters worked Israelite slaves to the bone. They had no choice. Perhaps they could have opted to die rather than to break the Sabbath, but Scripture never presents that as a desirable option. Again, the Sabbath is made for man, not man for the Sabbath. So Deuteronomy 5:15 motivates Israel to keep the Sabbath by remembering their time as slaves. God delivered them from that, and he expects Israelite masters to deliver their servants from toil on that day.

A Christian who can support his family in no other way than by Sabbath work is in bondage, in a way. He should seek to be free (1 Cor. 7:21), but while in bondage he should serve his master faithfully.

WORKS OF MERCY

In addition to works of necessity, the Westminster standards identify works of mercy as an exception to the Sabbath rest. The Larger Catechism speaks of "our delight to spend the whole time (except so much of it as is to be taken up in works of necessity and mercy) in the public and private exercises of God's worship" (WLC, 117). On this view, God permits works of mercy in addition to worship, but the former are less in keeping with the fundamental meaning of the day.

I agree that works of mercy are appropriate on the Sabbath day, but I do not regard these as exceptions to the biblical meaning of the Sabbath. Rather, deeds of mercy are central to that meaning. We can see that easily if we recognize that the fourth commandment tells us, not only to rest ourselves, but to *give* rest to others: "you, or your son, or your daughter, your male servant, or your female servant, or your livestock, or the sojourner who is within your gates" (Ex. 20:10; cf. 23:12). Deuteronomy 5:14 gives particular emphasis to this point: "that your male servant and your female servant may rest as well as you." Then verse 15 adds, "You shall remember that you were a slave in the land of Egypt, and the LORD your God brought you out from there with a mighty hand and an outstretched arm. Therefore the LORD your God commanded you to keep the Sabbath day." The connection is that since God delivered Israel from the toil of slavery, they should also relieve the toil of others. So by its very nature, the Sabbath is a time for giving mercy.

Mercy is also prominent in the system of sabbatical years. In the seventh year, Israel is to give rest to the land (Ex. 23:10–11), allowing it to lie fallow. This provision shows mercy, in a way, to the land, but it also gives consideration to the poor and to the animals: "that the poor of your people may eat; and what they leave the beasts of the field may eat" (v. 11; cf. Lev. 25:1–7). Also, during the sabbatical year, Israelites were to "release" debts owed to them (Deut. 15:1–11). The seventh year also provided release for Hebrew slaves (Ex. 21:1–6; Deut. 15:12–18; cf. Jer. 34:8–22).[33] And in the Jubilee year, following seven sevens of years, property was to revert to the families that owned it originally (Lev. 25:8–17).

So the Pharisees should not have been surprised that Jesus made the Sabbath a day of healing (Matt. 12:9–13; Mark 3:1–5; Luke 6:6–10; John 5:1–17; 9:13–16). These were not emergency healings; they could have waited another day, with no tragic consequences. (And John 11 shows that even when Jesus did wait, and apparent tragedy resulted, he was able to put it right.) So Jesus evidently made a definite decision to heal on the Sabbath, regarding it as a particularly appropriate time for such healings. He asks his opponents, "Is it lawful on the Sabbath to do good or to do harm, to save life or to kill?" (Mark 3:3). Clearly, it is his view that it is lawful to "do good." In this context, "good" does not mean "morally right," but rather "benevolent." The Pharisees had put

---

33. It is not clear whether this seventh year is the same seventh year on which the land was to rest, or whether it represents the seventh year from the beginning of the slave's service. In either case, the figure seven represents liberation.

so much emphasis on physical rest that they had missed this weightier matter of the law.

So it is not accidental that the great plea for justice and mercy for the oppressed in Isaiah 58:1–12 immediately precedes the plea for Sabbath observance in verses 13–14. The Sabbath is a time "to loose the bonds of wickedness, to undo the straps of the yoke, to let the oppressed go free, and to break every yoke . . . to share your bread with the hungry and bring the homeless poor into your house; when you see the naked, to cover him, and not to hide yourself from your own flesh" (vv. 6–7).[34]

The Sabbath is fundamentally a day of rest, but it is a communal rest, a shared rest. It is a rest that we give to one another, in imitation of the Lord who gave rest to us in Jesus, and in anticipation of the consummation of that rest. So it is a day of mercy. We may show mercy on any day of the week, but we should make special efforts on the Sabbath to extend God's love to all who are in need.

WORSHIP

I have differed with the Reformed tradition by saying that the fundamental meaning of the Sabbath is rest, rather than worship. Nevertheless, the Sabbath is a day of rest on which worship is profoundly appropriate. Note the following considerations.

1. In the fourth commandment, God tells Israel to "remember" the Sabbath day, to keep it "holy." Remembering here is not merely recollecting, but active memorializing. Compare the references to "keeping" the Sabbath in Exodus 31:14, 16; Leviticus 19:3; Isaiah 56:4. To remember or keep the Sabbath as a holy day is an act of worship.

2. As a holy day, the Sabbath has a special relation to God. Again and again, Scripture says that the Sabbath day is God's in a special sense: it is "a Sabbath to the LORD your God" (Ex. 20:10; cf. Isa. 58:13). The six days are our days; the Sabbath is God's. So we can understand how momentous was Jesus' claim that "the Son of Man is lord of the Sabbath" (Matt. 12:8). Since the Sabbath belongs to God alone, this saying can be nothing less than a claim to deity. But the point I wish to make here is that to consecrate a day to God alone is to worship.

---

34. The text in Isaiah speaks in verse 6 (as in vv. 3–5) of fast days, rather than the Sabbath, which, as I indicated earlier, is a feast rather than a fast. But in this context, God's will for the fast days and for the Sabbath day (v. 13) is identical. So I do not hesitate to apply verses 6–7 to the Sabbath, as well as to fast days.

3. So, as the temple was God's dwelling in space, we might say, the Sabbath is God's dwelling in time.[35] It is a day on which God is specially present to his people. But when God is present, when we meet with God, our stance must be that of worshipers.

4. Richard Gaffin argues from Psalm 95 and Hebrews 3–4 that there is an identity between the rest of God at creation and the future rest that believers enjoy as their final inheritance:

> The rest of God, the consummation of redemption mentioned in Ps. 95:11, of which the eventual possession of Canaan was only a shadow or type, and which the new covenant people of God are presently striving to enter—this rest is none other than the rest of God at creation. Eschatological redemption-rest is not merely an analogue of God's creation-rest; the latter is not simply the model for the former. Rather, the writer knows of only one rest, "my rest," entered by God at creation and by believers at consummation.[36]

The Sabbath day anticipates that rest, the consummation of redemption. To celebrate the consummation of redemption in advance is an act of worship.

5. But our Sabbath is not only a celebration in advance of the consummation. It is a foretaste of it. We noted earlier that Exodus 20:11 identifies Israel's Sabbath with God's creation rest. When God blessed the latter, he blessed the former as well. Indeed, the verse does not distinguish between the two. It suggests that the two are inseparable. To observe the Sabbath is to share for a day in God's creation rest. So to observe the Sabbath is to enjoy in advance the blessings of eternity in the presence of God. In this respect, the Sabbath is like the Holy Spirit, a "guarantee" of our final inheritance (2 Cor. 1:22; 5:5; Eph. 1:14). It is like the Lord's Supper, which is a foretaste of the messianic banquet (Rev. 19:9) in the last day.[37] To enjoy such a foretaste is to worship.

6. In Matthew 12:3–5, Jesus compares his disciples eating grain on the Sabbath to David's men eating the holy bread of the Presence in 1 Samuel

35. Note parallels between the Sabbath and the sanctuary in Lev. 19:30 and 26:2, and also the proximity between legislation on the sanctification of the Sabbath (Ex. 31:12–17) and legislation pertaining to the tabernacle and the priesthood (25:1–31:11).

36. Richard B. Gaffin Jr., "A Sabbath Rest Still Awaits the People of God," in *Pressing Toward the Mark*, ed. Charles G. Dennison and Richard C. Gamble (Philadelphia: Committee for the Historian of the Orthodox Presbyterian Church, 1986), 39.

37. The Sabbath, like the sacraments, is also a "sign" of the relationship between God and his people (Ex. 31:13). I do not, however, agree with those who would like to make the Sabbath a third sacrament, alongside baptism and the Lord's Supper. Gaffin's arguments in *Calvin and the Sabbath*, 161–63, are decisive in my view.

21:1–6. Now Jesus did not need to defend his disciples in this way. It would have been simpler for him to say merely that the law did not forbid the preparation and eating of food on the Sabbath. But here, as elsewhere, Jesus "overanswers" in a way that draws attention to himself as the son of David: as the high priest had the right to give David's men permission to take the holy bread, so Jesus has the right to give his disciples permission to take grain from the fields. Then he compares his behavior with the holy labors of priests and says, "Something greater than the temple is here" (v. 6). So Jesus teaches that Sabbath conduct, for himself and believers, is holy. Even our eating and drinking, at his behest, is holy. To observe the Sabbath through holy behavior is to worship.

7. So the Sabbath naturally becomes a day of worship as well as a day of rest. On the Sabbath is "a holy convocation" (Lev. 23:3; cf. Ezek. 46:3). The synagogue meets on the Sabbath, a pattern of worship that Jesus endorsed by his attendance and participation (Luke 4:15–16). Psalm 92 is called "a Song for the Sabbath." Sabbath offerings were brought to God (Num. 28:9–10; Neh. 10:32–33; Ezek. 45:17).

8. And, as we shall see in the next chapter, the Lord's Day (Rev. 1:10), the first day of the week, becomes the Christian day of worship following the resurrection of Jesus. If the Lord's Day is a Sabbath, as I believe it is, that also marks an occasion of Sabbath worship.

So our Sabbath rest is a rest in the presence of God. He has been resting from his creative work, and for one day a week we join him, looking forward to the fullness of that rest on the last day. To rest in God's holy presence is to worship. During that rest, it is appropriate that we also meet for worship in the narrower sense, for times of praise, prayer, teaching, sacrament, and fellowship.

SUMMARY

The Sabbath is a celebration of God's lordship: both of his lordship attributes (control, authority, presence) and of his lordly deeds (creation, redemption, consummation). On the Sabbath, we celebrate God's lordship by meeting with him (worship) and by imitating him. We imitate his control by imaging his cycle of work and rest (Ex. 20:9–10). We imitate his authority by affirming his covenant sign (Ex. 31:13, 17) and by declaring his revelation in preaching, teaching, and sacrament. We imitate his gracious presence through works of mercy.

CHAPTER 30

The Fourth Commandment:
The Sabbath in the New Covenant

In the previous chapter, we explored the general meaning of the Sabbath as Scripture presents it. We looked at this largely in Old Testament terms, not considering the role of the Sabbath in the new covenant. I did argue, however, that there is nothing about the Old Testament Sabbath that anticipates future abrogation. As a celebration of God's lordship in creation, we can expect the Sabbath to continue as a marker of the Creator-creature relation. As a rest from the toil brought about by God's curse on the ground, we can expect the Sabbath to continue at least until the consummation of redemption.

We saw that the Sabbath in Scripture is not a rest from our own attempts to earn salvation by our works, but a respite from the toil brought on by God's curse upon the ground. If it symbolized the abandonment of works as a means of salvation, then we might imagine that the Sabbath would be abrogated when salvation by grace is finally accomplished. But that reason for abrogation is not valid.

So our discussion so far suggests that the Sabbath will continue into the time of the new covenant. In the previous chapter, I also gave reasons for thinking that the basic character of Sabbath observance will not change until the last day. In this regard, I argued against Meredith Kline's contention that weekly cessation of work is appropriate only in certain redemptive-historical settings.

But in this chapter we must look more specifically at the new covenant in Christ, asking what role the Sabbath plays in it, focusing more sharply on New Testament teaching.

THE TEACHING OF JESUS

In chapter 29, I considered Matthew 12:1–14 as an example of Jesus' controversy with the Pharisees over Sabbath observance. We saw then that, on Jesus' view, (1) eating and preparing food on the Sabbath are works of necessity, (2) Jesus governs the Sabbath as the chief priest, one greater than the temple (v. 6), and as the lord of the Sabbath (v. 7), and (3) healing, a work of mercy, is especially appropriate on the Sabbath day (vv. 9–14).

We should note also the parallel passage in Mark 2:23–28, which adds another note to the discussion. Note verses 27–28: "And he said to them, 'The Sabbath was made for man, not man for the Sabbath. So the Son of Man is lord even of the Sabbath.'" Here, as in Matthew 12, Jesus grounds the Sabbath ordinance in the needs of man as man, not in anything distinctive to the Mosaic economy. "Man" in verse 27 is *anthropos*, generic man, man as created by God. This term and the verb "was made" (from *ginomai*) take us back to creation, when God originated the Sabbath. So Jesus in this verse finds the origin of the Sabbath in creation, rather than in God's covenant with Israel. This saying, then, validates our emphasis on the Sabbath as a creation ordinance.

This understanding fits Jesus' overall argument in the passage, that God did not intend the Sabbath to make us hungry. Eating, including the preparation of food, is a proper Sabbath activity. God's concern for human health and strength even takes precedence over the holiness of the tabernacle's bread of the Presence (vv. 25–26).[1] The Sabbath, indeed, is "made for" man: it is God's blessing on us. Our bodies need rest, just as we need food, and the Sabbath provides it.[2]

When the wicked use the Sabbath as a means of oppressing people, God sends a champion to defend the weak. Jesus is the "Son of Man," one who is himself man and who has a special sympathy for human need (Heb. 2:10–18; 4:15). But as Son of Man he also represents human beings before God and rules over all aspects of human life.[3] So the Son of Man is "lord even of the Sabbath" (Mark 2:28). I noted earlier the momentousness of

1. Recall the discussion of priorities in chapter 13.
2. Recall footnote 20 in chapter 29 in which I emphasized that God's law not only honors himself, but also suits the needs of human beings, including the needs of the body.
3. For a discussion of the title Son of Man, see *DG*, 672–73.

this claim. The Sabbath is the Sabbath of "the LORD your God," not the Sabbath of any mere created being. Jesus' claim to this particular lordship is a striking claim to deity. But the humanity of Jesus assures us that God will administer the Sabbath with an understanding of our needs and weaknesses. The Sabbath is mercy, not oppression.

So in this passage Jesus underscores the foundation of the Sabbath in creation and the importance of the Sabbath to man as God's creation. So works of necessity and mercy are appropriate.

Similarly, in John 5:1–17, Jesus heals on the Sabbath a man who has been an invalid for thirty-eight years. The Jews object both to the healing itself and to the fact that Jesus told the man to carry his bed.[4] In this case, Jesus appeals, not specifically to his office as Son of Man or as High Priest, but simply to his identity with God: "My Father is working until now, and I am working" (v. 17). As with Mark 2:28, this is a claim to deity. Jesus claims the right to do whatever his father does (cf. vv. 19–24). The Jews understand, and they seek to kill him for making himself equal with God (v. 18). Jesus here appeals only to his own divine status, not, as in Mark 2:27, to the nature of the Sabbath as a gift to man as man. Jesus here invokes a rationale for his Sabbath activity that no other human being could invoke.[5] None of us can say with Jesus that he has a right to do on the Sabbath anything that God does. But we do have the right and the obligation to do on the Sabbath what Jesus did as man, insofar as we are able. And here again Jesus' example of showing mercy is a model for us.

We also read that Jesus attended Sabbath worship in the synagogues (Mark 1:21; 6:2; Luke 13:10). This was his "custom" (Luke 4:16). There is no record of Jesus ever violating any biblical ordinance concerning the Sabbath, though he had no respect for the traditions of the Pharisees.

So there is no suggestion here or anywhere in the gospels that Jesus intended to abrogate the Sabbath in the new covenant. This is an argument from silence, of course. But during his earthly ministry Jesus often indicated the changes that would come after his resurrection, how believers would serve him in that new era. He taught, for example, that in that day

---

4. As we have seen, the Sabbath ordinance does forbid heavy lifting, but "heavy" is a relative term. In any case, it boggles the mind that the Jews were more preoccupied with the weight of the bed than with the mercy of God in healing this sick man. Surely, to say the least, their priorities were badly distorted (see chapter 13).

5. I mentioned in chapter 29 that in Matt. 12 Jesus "overanswers" the Pharisees' question. I think that is true here in John 5:17 as well. It would have been sufficient for Jesus to say that healing is appropriate on the Sabbath, or, as in Matt. 12, that basic human need transcends the demand for Sabbath rest (even if the Pharisees had rightly construed that rest). Here, anticipating the great Christological discourse in verses 19–47, he gives an answer that tells us more about his own nature and authority than about the Sabbath as such.

worship would not be centered in Jerusalem (John 4:21–24). He declared that the Old Testament dietary laws would no longer be binding (Mark 7:19). He predicted the destruction of the temple (Matt. 24:1–2). He established sacraments for the postresurrection church (Matt. 26:26–28; 28:19). He defined the authority of the apostles (Matt. 16:13–19; 18:18–20). He presented the worldwide task of the church (Matt. 28:18–20). Given the many times he clashed with the Pharisees over the Sabbath, he certainly had many opportunities to declare a coming end of Sabbath observance, if indeed he intended that. So it is significant that he did not make such a declaration. Rather, he affirmed the Sabbath as a blessing to man, a time of resting, worshiping, eating, drinking, and healing.

Jesus did not say specifically that the Sabbath would continue. But by his words and deeds he suggested that it would, and he never suggested the contrary. As in the case of infant baptism, Reformed theology assumes continuity between the covenants, except where Scripture clearly indicates discontinuity. So the overall pattern of Jesus' life and words should lead us to expect that the Sabbath will continue in the new covenant, under Jesus' lordship as Son of Man (Mark 2:28) and as God in the flesh (John 5:17).

HEBREWS 3:7–4:13

Beyond the teaching of Jesus, there is little explicit reflection in the New Testament on the Sabbath. Hebrews 3–4, however, is significant for our understanding of how New Testament Christians should understand the Sabbath in relation to Christ.

The purpose of the letter is to discourage Hebrew Christians from returning to Judaism. So the first two chapters emphasize that Christ is far greater than the angels who delivered the Mosaic law. Hebrews 3:1–6 adds that Jesus is also greater than Moses, who by God's power led Israel from Egypt nearly to the Promised Land. Moses died without seeing that land, as did a whole generation of Israelites, because they did not trust God's provision or believe his promises. They had tested God, even though God had done miracles for forty years in their midst (3:8–9, quoting Ps. 95:8–10). So God swore against that generation, "They shall not enter my rest" (Heb. 3:10, quoting Ps. 95:11). The psalmist, writing long after the wilderness years, admonishes Israelites of his own time, "Today, if you hear his voice, do not harden your hearts as in the rebellion" (Heb. 3:15, quoting Ps. 95:7–8). So, even after Israel had entered the Promised Land, a further rest awaited them. (Joshua's conquests had not given them the fullness of God's rest [Heb. 4:8].) If they hardened their hearts, as did the wilderness generation, they would not enter that second rest.

Now the writer to the Hebrews sees a parallel with the Jewish Christians of his audience. Like the Israelites of Moses' time, and the time of the anonymous psalmist, Christians have a rest to look forward to, and they are in danger of losing that rest by hardening their hearts (4:1–3). In 4:3–4, a new note enters: this rest is nothing other than God's own rest, the rest of Genesis 2:2, which God entered following the creation. "For we who have believed enter that rest, as he has said, 'As I swore in my wrath, "They shall not enter my rest,"' although his works were finished from the foundation of the world. For he has somewhere spoken of the seventh day in this way: 'And God rested on the seventh day from all his works.'"

God began his rest after creation. He invited Adam to join him. But because of the fall and the delay of redemption, man has not yet entered that rest. So for Israel in the wilderness, Israel at the time of Psalm 95, and New Testament Christians, our final Sabbath rest is still future. God still exhorts his people to enter that rest, which is a sharing of his own creation rest. "Today" (Ps. 95:7) is when we should "strive to enter that rest" (Heb. 4:11).

So "there remains a Sabbath rest for the people of God" (4:9). "Sabbath rest" here is *sabbatismos*, which can be translated "Sabbath keeping," but here the term evidently refers to the future rest, of which Canaan is a type, the final reward of the believer. This final reward is to join God in the rest he entered into at creation.

This passage does not, therefore, tell believers explicitly to keep the weekly Sabbath in the new covenant age. The *sabbatismos* is future, not weekly. But that future rest is called *sabbatismos*, and the writer identifies it with God's creation rest, which we have seen to be the basis of Sabbath keeping in the fourth commandment. So we should see the future *sabbatismos* as the fulfillment of the weekly Sabbath. It is what the weekly Sabbath anticipates, the ultimate blessing of which the weekly Sabbath is a foretaste.

The *sabbatismos*, therefore, is not completed by Jesus' first coming, his atonement and resurrection. It is, rather, a future blessing, something we have yet to experience. If it were perhaps a symbol of the forgiveness of our sins in Christ, then it would be plausible to say that what the Sabbath symbolizes is already here, and therefore that no more symbol is necessary. If the symbolism of the Sabbath were exhausted in the past and present reality of redemption, then one could argue that it is no longer necessary to keep the weekly Sabbath.[6] But if what the Sabbath symbolizes is still future, then weekly Sabbath observance performs a vital function: it is a reminder of and participation in that final reality. Hebrews 4 tells us that what the Sabbath symbolizes and anticipates is still future.[7] Thus, it establishes the continuing appropriateness of weekly Sabbath keeping.

Certainly nothing in these chapters suggests that the Sabbath is abrogated in the new covenant. That is an argument from silence, but, like my earlier argument from silence, it is significant. One major theme of Hebrews is that the new covenant is different from and better than the old. Christ is better than the angels, Moses, or Aaron. The sacrifice of Christ brings an end to the sacrifices of bulls and goats (10:4). So great is this disparity that the former covenant is "becoming obsolete and growing old." It is "ready to vanish away" (8:13). So Hebrews is preoccupied with *discontinuities* between the old and new orders. If the Sabbath were abrogated during the new covenant period, it would be very strange that Hebrews takes no notice of it and indeed presents an argument congenial to the continuation of Sabbath observance.[8]

THE LORD'S DAY

As in Old Testament times, so in New Testament times believers observed a special day each week. John refers to it in Revelation 1:10: "I was in the Spirit on the Lord's day." Christian writers following the time of the apostles tell us that the Lord's Day is the first day of the week, our Sunday, in which believers gathered to celebrate the resurrection of

6. Even this argument would not be ultimately persuasive. For the ground for keeping the Sabbath is not found exclusively in redemption. As I indicated in chapter 29, we keep the Sabbath to join God in his celebration of creation (Ex. 20:11; Gen. 2:2–3).

7. This coheres with my former point that the Sabbath symbolizes, not forgiveness of sins as such, but the release from toil that comes from redemption. The release from toil is still future.

8. In this section, I am much indebted to Richard B. Gaffin Jr., "A Sabbath Rest Still Awaits the People of God," in *Pressing Toward the Mark*, ed. Charles G. Dennison and Richard C. Gamble (Philadelphia: Committee for the Historian of the Orthodox Presbyterian Church, 1986), 33–51. In this article, Gaffin counters the position of A. T. Lincoln in "Sabbath, Rest, and Eschatology in the New Testament." The latter article is part of the book I mentioned in chapter 28 as representing the most anti-Sabbatarian of the six views discussed: D. A. Carson, ed., *From Sabbath to Lord's Day* (Grand Rapids: Zondervan, 1982), 197–220. See also Lincoln's "From Sabbath to Lord's Day: A Biblical and Theological Perspective," in the same volume, pp. 343–412. Heb. 3–4 is prominent in Lincoln's argument, hence in Gaffin's. Lincoln argues that the "rest" in view is not entirely future, but that it is present now in the believer's experience.

Jesus.[9] These first-day meetings began with the resurrection appearances themselves (Matt. 28:1–10; Luke 24:13–49; John 20:1, 19, 26). These were, of course, times of worship, as is always the case when believers meet with the Lord.

On the day of Pentecost, the disciples gathered to await the promise of the Spirit (Acts 2:1). This was also most likely on the first day of the week. The wave and meal offerings for the Pentecost feast were made "on the day after the Sabbath" (Lev. 23:11, 16). Acts 20:7 indicates an occasion when the Christians at Troas gathered to break bread "on the first day of the week." The apostles stayed seven days at Troas (v. 6). It is natural to assume that with this schedule they were able to attend two weekly meetings of the church. The first day is also mentioned in 1 Corinthians 16:1–2: "Now concerning the collection for the saints: as I directed the churches of Galatia, so you also are to do. On the first day of every week, each of you is to put something aside and store it up, as he may prosper, so that there will be no collecting when I come." Evidently, people in the churches of Galatia and Corinth were to bring their contributions to the meeting on the first day of the week. These biblical data are somewhat sketchy, to be sure, but there is no reason to doubt the church fathers' account that the first day of the week, the Lord's Day, was the regular time of Christian worship.

These references to the Lord's Day have raised three major questions in the discussion about the Sabbath: (1) Is the Lord's Day a Sabbath? (2) If so, on what authority is the Sabbath changed from the seventh day to the first day? (3) Given that the change of day is legitimate, what is the meaning of the change?

Is the Lord's Day a Sabbath?

Andrew Lincoln, whose articles in *From Sabbath to Lord's Day* I have cited earlier, grants that the Lord's Day is the first day of the week, the Christian day of worship, the celebration of Jesus' resurrection.[10] He denies, however, that the New Testament regards the Lord's Day as a Sabbath. He finds no evidence that the New Testament regards this day as a day of rest or as a successor to the Jewish observance. He says,

> The day can be said to be the Lord's because it is the appropriate
> day for worshiping Him, and this is significantly different from the

9. *Didache*, 14:1; Ignatius, *To the Magnesians*, 9:1. For other references, see G. W. H. Lampe, *A Patristic Greek Lexicon* (Oxford: Clarendon Press, 1961), under *kyriakos*.

10. Lincoln, "From Sabbath to Lord's Day," 383–86. He cites a number of patristic writers in addition to those I have mentioned above.

view that sees the day, by analogy with the Jewish Sabbath, as a full twenty-four hour period belonging to the Lord in a distinct way from that in which all the Christian's time belongs to the Lord.[11]

On the other hand, there is the evidence from the term *Lord's Day* itself. It translates *kyriakē hēmera* in Revelation 1:10, indicating a day that has a special relationship to the Lord. The only similar construction in the New Testament is *kyriakon deipnon* (1 Cor. 11:20), translated "Lord's Supper." The supper is, of course, different from all other meals, a meal that belongs to the Lord in a unique way. So I believe that *kyriakē* implies more than that this day "is the appropriate day for worshiping Him."

This is evident, not only from the parallel to the Lord's Supper, but also from the many Old Testament passages that speak of the Sabbath as specifically the Lord's day. It is "a Sabbath to the LORD your God" (Ex. 20:10). God says it is "my holy day" (Isa. 58:13), as opposed to man's; it is "the holy day of the LORD" (same verse). It is hard for me to imagine that people in the first century with a background in Judaism would not see the parallel between the Lord's day in Old Testament and the New Testament's Lord's Day. As the supper is a meal that belongs uniquely to the Lord, so the Lord's Day is a day that belongs uniquely to the Lord.

Consider also that the Lord's Day is, after all, a day, not merely a shorter period. Jesus' meetings with disciples on the day of his resurrection occurred both at dawn (Matt. 28:1–10) and in the evening (Luke 24:29). The church's meetings on the first day occurred in the morning, as the church fathers indicate, but also in the evening, as in Acts 20:7. So the Lord's Day involved activities that, like the Sabbath, must have required the setting aside of other responsibilities.

Further, if my earlier argument is right that the Sabbath is a creation ordinance and, with the other nine commandments of the Decalogue, a moral law, and if I am right to say that there is no reason why the Sabbath should be abolished under the new covenant, then there must be a place for the Sabbath in the new covenant. Either the Jewish seventh-day Sabbath continues into the new covenant (as is the view of Seventh-day Adventists and others) or (what seems to be the only other alternative) the Sabbath continues in the form of the Lord's Day. I shall defend the latter position in the next section.

Still, there are formidable problems in the claim that the Lord's Day is a Sabbath. For one thing, three Pauline passages speak against the observance of days; I shall discuss them later. For another, it is clear that the early Christians did not immediately recognize the Lord's Day as a day of

---

11. Ibid., 389.

rest. The early Jewish Christians observed the Sabbath on the seventh day and then joined in distinctively Christian worship on the first. Lincoln summarizes the historical evidence: "The majority of Jewish Christians in Palestine and many in the diaspora may well have kept the Sabbath and also met with their fellow believers in Christ for worship at some time on the following day."[12]

The seventh day was the day of rest and of the synagogue service. The first day was the celebration of Jesus' resurrection. But there was, of course, a contradiction in this dual practice. Lord's Day worship was the true worship, the worship of God's own Son. How could that day of worship be separated from the day of rest? We saw earlier that the two should coincide, for it is by enjoying God's rest in his presence that we bow down before him.

Paul and other believers hoped initially that the Jews as a body could be won to Christ. Had that taken place, all Jews would have worshiped Jesus on the first day. But, in God's providence, the mass conversion did not take place. Like Jesus, Paul attended the synagogue services and presented the gospel there (e.g., Acts 13:14–15; 14:1; 17:1, 10). But the number of Jewish converts was a disappointment, which brought much agony to Paul (Rom. 9:1–3). The hostile response of the Jews led him to take the gospel to Gentiles (Acts 13:42–48; 18:6; 28:28). So the churches outside Israel became increasingly Gentile churches, churches made up of people who had not historically kept the Jewish Sabbath. Further, Jewish Christians were either expelled from the synagogues or left voluntarily. So Christianity became less a sect of Judaism, more a faith independent of Judaism. The Lord's Day became, increasingly, the main time of worship for believers, and observance among them of the seventh-day Sabbath declined. But how could this practice be reconciled with the fourth commandment?

For some centuries, it was not. In the time of the apostles, the church lived with the ambiguity; many Christians recognized the seventh day as the Sabbath and the first day as the Lord's Day. It may be that Romans 14:5, Galatians 4:9–10, and Colossians 2:16–17 refer to a controversy between Jewish and Gentile Christians over the observance of the seventh-day Sabbath.[13] If this is the case, we should read Paul as saying that the seventh-day Sabbath is no longer required. The Lord's Day is its replacement, in effect, though Paul does not mention that in these contexts. But it is hard to tell what thought processes on either side lie behind these three passages. More will be said on this in a later section of this chapter.

---

12. Ibid., 384.
13. There are other ways, however, of dealing with these passages, which we shall explore later.

After the apostolic age, when the enmity between Christianity and Judaism became more pointed, Christians regarded the seventh-day Sabbath as something "Jewish," which Christians should eschew, while embracing the Lord's Day. Ignatius's letter to the Magnesians says that Christians "no longer observe the Sabbath, but direct their lives to the Lord's Day, on which our life is refreshed by him and his death." The writings of the church fathers are interestingly parallel to the developments we noted (in chapter 28) from Calvin to Dort. They gradually begin to treat the Lord's Day as a Sabbath. Dionysius of Corinth (170), like the Synod of Dort, speaks of the Lord's Day as holy.[14] Tertullian (160–225) describes Sunday observance as "a distinguishing mark of Christians," and he is the first known Christian writer to speak about "laying aside daily business on Sunday."[15] The Council of Laodicea (360), like the Westminster standards, formalizes the Sabbatarian character of the Lord's Day: "Christians must not live according to Jewish patterns, and therefore they perform work on Saturday; but they must respect Sunday and as Christians they should quit their work, if possible."[16]

Does this history show that Christians generally violated the fourth commandment during the first four centuries? In observing this development, it is important to keep in mind that in the early centuries of the church, Christian believers, like the Israelites in Egypt (see my argument in chapter 29), were rarely *able* to set aside Sunday work altogether. Christians had to support themselves and their families, what I have identified as a work of necessity. Being largely poor and often persecuted, they could not simply take off a day of their choosing for worship and rest. Jewish Christians, at least, had support from the Jewish community and tradition to rest on the seventh day. But no one had such support for a first-day Sabbatarian observance. So Paul did not make an issue of this in the first century, though he may have defended Christians against those who would require them to rest on the seventh day.

It was not until later, when Christianity had grown more influential in society (and especially after Constantine became the first Christian emperor), that theologians and church leaders began to treat the Lord's Day fully as a Sabbath and demand cessation of work on that day. This development, I think, largely accounts for the relative silence in the early centuries on the Sabbatarian character of the Lord's Day. And, in my judgment, there is nothing in that development that undermines the fun-

14. Cited in J. Douma, *The Ten Commandments* (Phillipsburg, NJ: P&R Publishing, 1996), 139.
15. Ibid. Quotations are of Douma's paraphrases.
16. Ibid.

damental obligation of the fourth commandment, or the view that the Lord's Day is in fact the Christian Sabbath. Theologically, the case for a first-day Sabbath is strong. The historical facts can be understood in a way that does not contradict that theological understanding.

THE CHANGE OF DAY

But who authorized the change from the seventh day to the first? Jesus did, by rising from the dead on the first day and meeting his disciples on this and subsequent first days. And the apostles did also, by adopting Lord's Day worship and by failing to impose a seventh-day rest upon Gentile Christians.

This change of day does not represent a violation of the fourth commandment or an abrogation of its terms. The fourth commandment speaks of the Sabbath as "the seventh day," but Hebrew uses ordinal numbers (first, second, etc.) both as names for the days (like our Sunday, Monday, etc.) and also as numbers designating a sequence. Context determines which of these meanings is right. If someone is told on Wednesday to work six days and rest on "the seventh," the word "seventh" does not mean Saturday. Rather, in this context, it refers to Tuesday, the seventh day in the sequence beginning on Wednesday.

In Exodus 20:9–10, "seventh" is ambiguous; it could have either of these two meanings. It is natural to assume that the starting point is the first day of the week (Sunday), which would make the seventh day Saturday. But in fact the fourth commandment does not specify any starting point. It refers only to sequence: work six days and rest on the seventh.[17]

Is there reason to think that the sequence always began on Sunday, so as to end on Saturday? I think not. Consider the following points:

1. The commandment does not say specifically on what day of the week the sequence was to begin.

2. It is difficult for us today to know, given all the changes in the calendar over thousands of years, precisely what day of our modern week was the Jewish Sabbath in the time of Moses.

3. The sequence of Sabbaths may have begun on a different day each year. Curtis and Charles Ewing, for example, argue that the first day of Passover each year, the fifteenth day of Abib, is a Sabbath (Lev. 23:6–7).[18] The

---

17. Ra McLaughlin's response to the question "Is the Sabbath Saturday or Sunday?" is very helpful here. See http://reformedanswers.org/answer.asp/file/99959.qna/category/th/page/questions.

18. Curtis Clair Ewing and Charles Wesley Ewing, *Israel's Calendar and the True Sabbath* (Velma, OK: National Message Ministry, 1958). Rousas J. Rushdoony accepts the Ewings' account in *The Institutes of Biblical Law* (Nutley, NJ: Craig Press, 1973), 134–36.

seventh day after that is another Sabbath (v. 8), and the weekly Sabbaths for the rest of the year are counted from that (vv. 15–16). Now the fifteenth day of Abib occurs, of course, on the same day of the month each year, but on a different day of the week—like your birthday. So, on the Ewing hypothesis, the Sabbath occurs on a different day of the week each year. This view is somewhat speculative. It is not plain on the face of Leviticus 23.[19] But Scripture doesn't rule it out either. So we cannot say dogmatically that the Sabbath always fell on the seventh day of the week during the Old Testament period, though it did always mark the end of a seven-day sequence.[20] Of course, at a later time, at least during the time of Jesus' earthly ministry, it did fall regularly on the seventh day of the week.

4. The Ewings thought that God had at least required the Jews to begin the sequence of Sabbaths on a certain day of a month. But it may be that the calendar is a human decision, not given by divine revelation. Indeed it is impossible to exclude a human element in the determination of the calendar. For one thing, God has not revealed to us where to put the International Date Line. Human beings made that decision. But a day that is Sabbath on one side of the line will not be Sabbath on the other side.[21] So, at this point, human beings decide what day is to be the Sabbath. The same happens whenever the calendar is changed.

Imagine people lost on a desert island, who have forgotten what day of the week it is. Surely it would not be wrong for them to choose a day, any day, and make that the Sabbath for that community, even if that day turned out to be Thursday elsewhere in the world, or even if that day happened to be the third day in the calendar used by Moses. But that kind of choice has been made whenever people have adopted a new calendar.

My conclusion is that human beings choose the days of the week, month, and year on which the Sabbath is to fall. This choice is not made by divine revelation. Divine revelation tells us only to observe the Sabbath as the seventh day after six days of work.

So Jesus and the apostles, by changing the day from seventh to first, were not contradicting the terms of the fourth commandment, which tells us

19. My own view, which is the common one, is that the Passover and Pentecost Sabbaths in Lev. 23 are first-day Sabbaths, in addition to the weekly Sabbaths, not replacements for the weekly Sabbath, nor points of beginning for the sequence of Sabbaths.

20. Several special ceremonial Sabbaths in Leviticus are clearly identified by day of the month, not day of the week: (1) the Sabbath connected with the Feast of Trumpets (Lev. 23:24–25), and (2) that connected with the Day of Atonement, which is nine days later (Lev. 23:26–32).

21. Some Westminster Seminary students once put out a joke seminary catalogue, describing one course as "Problems of Sabbath Observance When Crossing the International Date Line."

only to work for six days and to rest for one. God still calls us to keep that commandment literally in the new covenant.

THE MEANING OF THE CHANGE

But why the first day? Did Jesus choose it arbitrarily to be the resurrection day and the postresurrection Sabbath day? I think not. The Old Testament already contains much symbolism concerning the first day, which the New Testament fulfills. Note the following:

1. Adam's first full day of life occurred on God's seventh day, God's Sabbath (Gen. 2:2–3). So God's seventh-day Sabbath (which he shared with Adam, as we have seen) coincided with Adam's first day. The completion of God's creative work was the beginning for Adam, the foundation of man's earthly life, just as the resurrection of Jesus is the foundation of our new lives in him, the new creation (cf. 2 Cor. 5:17). In both cases, the Sabbath is associated with the first day.

2. The Pentecost wave and meal offerings occur on days "after the Sabbath" (Lev. 23:11, 16), that is, on first days of the week. The day of the meal offering is itself a Sabbath, though it is not called that. Israel is to hold a holy convocation on that day and is not to do "any ordinary work" (v. 21). So on this feast of the firstfruits, we are reminded of Jesus, the firstfruits of the dead (1 Cor. 15:20, 23). Like the Lord's Day, Pentecost celebrates resurrection.

3. In the Feast of Tabernacles as well, there are first- and eighth-day Sabbaths (Lev. 23:35, 39).

4. Now, since Pentecost and Tabernacles each includes two first-day Sabbaths, it is likely that the two Sabbaths in the Passover feast are also on the first day (vv. 6–8). So all three of the annual feasts which look forward to the redemption of Christ feature first-day Sabbaths.

5. The Jubilee is most likely a year following a Sabbath year, culminating the system of years with a first-year symbol: a Sabbath after a Sabbath.

The Old Testament symbolism, therefore, tells us that when God fulfills his redemptive purpose, the first day will have some special significance. It will mark a new beginning, a new creation, new life from the dead. When redemption is accomplished, there will be an emphasis on looking back, not only on looking forward.

Even as symbolism, the difference is a matter of degree. In the Old Testament, there was a looking back (to creation and deliverance from Egypt) as well as a looking forward (to Christ). And in looking forward, the Israelites anticipated something new taking place, to which they would afterward look back. So there were both seventh-day and first-day Sabbaths. In the

New Testament, there is only a first-day Sabbath, indicating the overwhelming significance of the finished work of Christ. But there is still the pattern of six days of work and one day of rest. It is still literally true, as the fourth commandment says, that we work for six days and look forward to the Sabbath as a rest from that toil. There is still a looking forward as well as a looking back: a looking back to the resurrection and a looking forward to Jesus' return and the consummation of all things. But the symbolism in the Old Testament is weighted somewhat toward looking ahead, and in the New Testament toward looking back. The change between seventh-day and first-day Sabbaths is essentially *a change in symbolic weight*.

THE KEEPING OF DAYS IN THE NEW COVENANT

I have postponed as long as possible a discussion of three Pauline passages that have played a major role in the discussion of the Sabbath in the New Testament. But now we must look at them. They are:

> One person esteems one day as better than another, while another esteems all days alike. Each one should be fully convinced in his own mind. (Rom. 14:5)

> But now that you have come to know God, or rather to be known by God, how can you turn back again to the weak and worthless elementary principles of the world, whose slaves you want to be once more? You observe days and months and seasons and years! I am afraid I may have labored over you in vain. (Gal. 4:9–11)

> Therefore let no one pass judgment on you in questions of food and drink, or with regard to a festival or a new moon or a Sabbath. These are a shadow of the things to come, but the substance belongs to Christ. (Col. 2:16–17)

These texts represent the most persuasive rebuttal to the Sabbatarian position. To many, it is obvious that these texts are incompatible with Sabbath keeping. We recall Calvin's statement, "Who but madmen cannot see what observance the apostle means?"[22]

But to others Paul's meaning here is not so obvious. Certainly, if the reader agrees with the argument so far—(1) that the Sabbath is a creation

---

22. John Calvin, *Institutes of the Christian Religion*, ed. John T. McNeill, trans. Ford Lewis Battles (Philadelphia: Westminster Press, 1960), 2.8.33. I confess I often enjoy Calvin's invective when it is directed against views other than my own. When he attacks my own positions, however, I consider him immoderate.

ordinance, (2) that it is affirmed by Jesus, (3) that the Lord's Day is a Sabbath, and (4) that there are no other suggestions in Scripture that Sabbath observance is to be abolished in the new covenant—then these statements of Paul are somewhat perplexing. Even on the anti-Sabbatarian position of Andrew Lincoln, the Lord's Day is the "appropriate" day of worship, as opposed to other days. But that is itself a kind of day keeping. To recognize the Lord's Day as uniquely appropriate for worship could well be construed as "esteeming one day better than another" (as Rom. 14:5) or "observing days" (Gal. 4:10). But Lincoln insists that his view of the Lord's Day does not contradict the strictures of the three passages. For him, these passages do not ban every kind of day keeping, only the keeping of a day as holy, or as a Sabbath. But the passages themselves make no such distinction. Lincoln, like Sabbatarian interpreters, is forced to assume that Paul's original readers would have understood his words in a more precise sense than is obvious on the surface.

One of the frequent problems we have in interpreting Paul is that we hear only one side of the conversation. We often wish that we had not only Paul's letters to the churches, but also their letters to him, so that we could better understand what questions he is responding to, what controversies he is seeking to resolve. God in his good providence has chosen not to give us that information, so we often have to try to extrapolate from what Paul says the likely motivations of his remarks. The difficulty of that task should be taken more seriously than it often has been among interpreters of the three passages before us.

As I mentioned briefly at an earlier point, I think the best suggestion is that Paul is here addressing a controversy over the Jewish seventh-day Sabbath. The Jewish Christians generally observed the seventh-day Sabbath and then worshiped Jesus on the first day. Some of the Gentile Christians evidently attended the first-day celebration of the resurrection, but did not observe the seventh-day rest. In actual fact, the seventh-day Sabbath was no longer binding. God, Jesus, and the apostles had warranted first-day worship, and, implicitly, a first-day Sabbath.

But the apostles did not stress a full day of resting on the first day of the week, because it was not possible for most Christians during that time to take off a full day of work on the first day. In chapter 29, I argued that one may support his family by working on the Sabbath if there is no other way to do it, a work of necessity. I believe the apostles respected that principle, even though it meant that the Gentile Christians did not observe the first-day Sabbath in its full meaning. But Paul did not intend to impose the seventh-day Sabbath upon them either. The attempt to impose that observance was part of the Judaizing movement that Paul contravenes so emphatically in Galatians and elsewhere.

It is better, Paul thought, to observe practically no Sabbath at all, than to accept the Judaizers' practice as something necessary to salvation.

But there are other ways of reading these passages:

1. Some Reformed interpreters believe that in these passages Paul is not talking about weekly Sabbaths at all (either seventh-day or first-day), but about other feast days of the Jewish calendar, some of which are called "Sabbaths," as in Leviticus 16:31; 23:24, 32. The phrase "days and months and seasons and years" in the Galatians passage suggests that possibility, as does "a festival or a new moon or a Sabbath" in Colossians 2:16. Note that Colossians 2:16 speaks of "a" Sabbath, which would naturally refer to something other than the weekly Sabbath, rather than "the" Sabbath, which would naturally refer to the weekly Sabbath. The texts do not necessitate this understanding, but it cannot be entirely ruled out.

2. The Romans and Galatians passages do not mention any "Sabbath," so the possibilities for interpreting them are fairly broad. Even pagan observances are not out of the question. The context of Galatians 4:9–10 makes reference to the Gentile Christians' pagan past and warns them not to return to it. But more likely Paul is rebuking them for accepting a Judaizing practice which he finds deeply *analogous* to paganism.

3. Any interpretation of Galatians 4:9–10 must be qualified by an understanding of the overall message of the letter: Paul's insistence that no Jewish observances, indeed, no works of any kind, are necessary for our justification before God. In Galatians 5:2–4, Paul says that "if you accept circumcision, Christ will be of no advantage to you." But in Acts 16:3, Paul himself circumcised Timothy. The difference is that in Galatians 5, Paul is denying circumcision as a requirement for salvation. In Acts 16, Paul is affirming circumcision as a way to avoid offense. But if we had only Galatians 5:2–4, we might conclude that circumcision is forbidden for any purpose at all. Similarly, Galatians 4:9–10 might be thought to exclude any kind of day keeping. But clearly what Paul has in view there is the keeping of days as a necessary means of salvation. The passage is not relevant to questions about keeping days with other purposes in mind.

4. Colossians 2:16–17 is the most difficult of the three passages for Sabbatarians, because, unlike the other two passages, it contains the word "Sabbath."[23] A rather ingenious Sabbatarian understanding of this passage is found in the "Report of the Committee on Sabbath Matters," which was presented to the Thirty-ninth General Assembly of the Orthodox Presbyterian Church in 1972.[24] The Report observes that "food and drink" (v. 16) are often taken

---

23. Although, again, it speaks of "a" Sabbath, not "the" Sabbath.

24. It is published in the *Minutes of the Fortieth General Assembly of the Orthodox Presbyterian Church* (1973), 92–112, now available at http://www.opc.org/GA/sabbath.html.

to refer to Old Testament dietary laws, but in fact there are no dietary laws referring to drink. It is more likely, then, that "food and drink" refers to food and drink *offerings* made at the temple in Jerusalem. That sets the context for "a festival or a new moon or a Sabbath." This triad is found with references to meat and drink *offerings* in Ezekiel 45:17: "And upon the prince [of the ideal Israel] shall be the obligation of the burnt offerings, and the meat (offerings), and the drink (offerings), in the feasts, and in the new moons, and in the sabbaths, in all the appointed times of the house of Israel."[25]

The triad of "feast, new moon, and Sabbath" is found in other texts referring to offerings (1 Chron. 23:31; 2 Chron. 2:4; 8:13; 31:3; Neh. 10:33; Hos. 2:11). The Report comments, "All of these are quite clearly derived from Numbers 28, 29." In Numbers, it continues, "the subject is *not* the individual worshipper's offerings, nor his personal acts of worship on those days, but the system of official sacrifices to be made for all Israel." Therefore, the Report says:

> We can only conclude that for Paul, "feast, new moon, and sabbath" meant those same official sacrifices the phrase denotes in the Old Testament usage. There is nothing in the phrase to require us to understand that Paul meant to abrogate the Fourth Commandment for Christians. What Paul did mean was that support of the temple sacrifices by Christians was a matter of indifference ("Let no man judge" applies both ways). These sacrifices were part of a "shadow" whose "body is Christ's." They were God-given for that purpose and thus permissible at least for Christians, but were no longer required since the reality had come.
>
> This interpretation parallels quite closely the import of Hebrews 10 where similar language about the "shadow" is found, and where the context demands that "shadow" be understood in terms of Old Testament sacrifices. (p. 101)

This interpretation is not the last word, and I still prefer to regard this passage as a reference to a church debate about the keeping of the seventh-day Sabbath. But the Report's interpretation is a possible one.

Of course, it is my Sabbatarian belief, taken from other parts of Scripture, that leads me to seek an exegesis of these passages compatible with continued Sabbath keeping. The same sort of exercise is necessary on the other side. Those who believe that these three texts exclude new covenant Sabbath keeping must try to find interpretations of other texts, such as Genesis 2:2–3, Exodus 20:8–11, and Revelation 1:10, that are compatible

25. The brackets and parentheses are inserted in the Report.

with the Sabbath's abrogation. All of us are seeking to compare Scripture with Scripture in order to gain the best understanding of the texts. There should be no embarrassment about that on either side. It is not, at least generally, that one side or the other is trying to press texts into a dogmatic mold. At least we should not accuse one another of that.

I do believe, however, that the anti-Sabbatarians have a more difficult task on their hands. Given our ignorance of the controversies that Paul is addressing, it is more likely that the three Pauline texts have a meaning compatible with new covenant Sabbath observance than that all the other texts we have considered can be construed in an anti-Sabbatarian framework.

Having said that, I should add that I don't believe the argument is watertight on either side. People within the Reformed community have differed on this issue since Calvin, and I don't see any argument that will put the debate completely to rest. There should be tolerance among Reformed Christians over this issue. The Orthodox Presbyterian Church and Presbyterian Church in America have refused ordination to some for holding Calvin's view of the Sabbath, implying that Calvin himself was not sufficiently orthodox to minister in that denomination. I recognize that the Westminster standards, to which the Orthodox Presbyterian Church subscribes, holds a view other than Calvin's, but I think that to insist on Westminster distinctives as a test of orthodoxy in this case is sectarian.[26]

FEASTS, SABBATH YEARS, AND JUBILEE

I have noted that in the Old Testament the weekly Sabbath is part of a system that also includes special festival Sabbaths, Sabbath years, and the Jubilee following seven sevens of years. Do these other Sabbaths have any bearing on new covenant life?

I believe that these other Sabbaths are not literally binding on new covenant believers. The festivals are celebrations of various events in Old Testament history: the deliverance from Egypt (Passover), the giving of the law (Pentecost), and the wilderness wanderings (Tabernacles). The Feast of Trumpets and the Day of Atonement bring the Israelite near to God, to bring sacrifice for the forgiveness of sins. These feasts are observed in Jerusalem, where God dwells in the temple.

But in the new covenant, God no longer dwells in a temple in Jerusalem, and the Old Testament redemptive events prove to be only shadows of the

---

26. Such sectarianism, in this case, is the necessary outcome of strict subscriptionism.

final redemption achieved by Christ. The animal sacrifices, which are the centerpiece of these Old Testament celebrations, are now transcended by the ultimate sacrifice of Christ.

The Sabbath years and the Jubilee also depend on the fact that Israel dwells with God in a particular land. In the Sabbath year, Israel is to rest that land (Ex. 23:10–11; Lev. 25:1–7), and in the Jubilee (Lev. 25:8–34) Israel is to return the land to its original family owners. But in the new covenant, we have no divine title to land in Palestine. Our promised land is the whole earth, into which Christ has sent us to bring the gospel (Matt. 28:18–20). Eventually, we will hold title to land in the new heavens and new earth.

Nevertheless, Israel's Sabbath calendar has much to teach us. For one thing, the Sabbath years mandate ecological responsibility. God is concerned, not only with people, animals, and plants, but with land. As Adam was to guard and keep the garden (Gen. 2:15), so Israel is to give rest to the land, so that it can continue to bear plants for food. Although the cultural mandate tells us to have dominion over the earth, that dominion is, like God's, to be a benevolent dominion. We are not to exploit the land, but to preserve it. God takes this responsibility very seriously. One reason why God sent Israel into exile was that they had not been resting the land as he commanded. The exile continued "until the land had enjoyed its Sabbaths" (2 Chron. 36:21).

This does not imply, as in much secular environmentalism, that any land is to be kept pristine, untouched by human hands. God has given the earth to human beings. But we are to deal with it responsibly, which means in our time to control pollution and to use the land in ways that will bless, not curse, future generations.

Another application of the Sabbath calendar for contemporary life is its concern for the poor. We have seen that mercy is an important aspect of the meaning of the Sabbath. This is also true of the Sabbath years. In the seventh year, the land is to "lie fallow, that the poor of your people may eat" (Ex. 23:11). In the seventh year, what grows by itself is for all people, rich and poor, owners and servants. The seventh year becomes an image of heaven in which everybody has enough. The Sabbath years also bring release of debts and freedom to Hebrew servants (Deut. 15:1–6, 12–18). And in the Jubilee, had Israel kept it, God intended a wholesale reorganization of the economy, a new beginning for many who had lost their possessions.

I shall say more about poverty under the eighth commandment. But Scripture is pervasively and passionately concerned about the way we treat the poor, even in its teaching on the Sabbath. We have seen how Isaiah 58, far from being a polemic against Sabbath recreation, is a powerful call to justice in society in keeping with the meaning of the Sabbath. Similarly, Amos 8:4–8 says:

Hear this, you who trample on the needy
 and bring the poor of the land to an end,
saying, "When will the new moon be over,
 that we may sell grain?
And the Sabbath,
 that we may offer wheat for sale,
that we may make the ephah small and the shekel great
 and deal deceitfully with false balances,
that we may buy the poor for silver
 and the needy for a pair of sandals
 and sell the chaff of the wheat?"
The Lord has sworn by the pride of Jacob:
"Surely I will never forget any of their deeds.
Shall not the land tremble on this account,
 and everyone mourn who dwells in it,
and all of it rise like the Nile,
 and be tossed about and sink again, like the Nile of Egypt?"

Israel's Sabbatarians kept the letter of the law, we should assume. But while keeping the Sabbath, they were plotting ways of oppressing the poor on the other six days.

God does not require us any longer to keep the system of sabbatical years. But he certainly will not tolerate among us the attitudes toward the land and the poor that that system sought to prevent. Still today there are those who use the land without any thought for the future, or for the use of it by others. And there are those who buy and sell and rest and worship without any thought of how their actions affect the poor. That is not only sin in general, but Sabbath breaking in particular.

We see how the fourth commandment, like the others, stretches out to cover all of human life. Narrowly, it teaches us to maintain a certain rhythm in our lives: six days of work and one of rest. But this is to look at all of life from a temporal perspective. Six days and one day: that includes everything. To act during the six days in a way that is inappropriate to the six days is a violation of the fourth commandment. The same is true of our behavior on the seventh. So the Sabbath commandment mandates not only rest, but worship (the attitude that is appropriate toward to God) and mercy (the attitude that is appropriate toward our fellow men). And mercy extends to both the land and the poor. So the fourth commandment covers everything. Like the others, it is equivalent to the command to love God and one another. Although it focuses on our attitude toward God, it also governs our attitudes and actions toward one another.

CHAPTER 31

The Fifth Commandment: Honoring Authorities

The fifth commandment, in Exodus 20:12, is as follows: "Honor your father and your mother, that your days may be long in the land that the LORD your God is giving you." The Deuteronomic version is a bit longer: "Honor your father and your mother, as the LORD your God commanded you, that your days may be long, and that it may go well with you in the land that the LORD your God is giving you" (Deut. 5:16). It reminds us again of the source of the command, and it adds a second blessing to the Exodus version, promising not only long life, but also prosperity.[1] Of course, long life is not a blessing without prosperity, so, as with the fourth commandment, Deuteronomy merely spells out what is already implicit in Exodus.

With this commandment, we move from what is sometimes called "the first table" of the law to the "second"—from the first four commands, which focus on our duty toward God, to the last six, which focus on our duty toward one another.[2] The transition is from an emphasis on loving God with all our heart to an emphasis on loving our neighbor as ourselves.[3] Of course, we have seen that the first four commands have much to say about our relationships with other people. Even the Sabbath command is deeply

---

1. Thus it completes the Star Trek benediction, "Live long and prosper."
2. For qualifications of this understanding of the two tables, see the opening paragraph of chapter 23.
3. WLC, 122, cites the love command, and also the Golden Rule, "Whatever you wish that others would do to you, do also to them" (Matt. 7:12).

575

concerned with mercy and justice. We do not serve (worship) God from the heart unless we are also expressing his love to one another.

The fifth commandment makes this very point in a striking way, by its parallel to, and contrast with, the first. The first commandment tells us to worship God alone. The fifth commandment, however, requires a kind of "honor" for human beings as well. So the second table, like the first, begins with the specification of a heart attitude, a deference that leads to service. But how does the honor due only to God differ from the honor due to our parents and other people?

In what follows, I shall discuss the nature of "honor" in Scripture and then consider the other terms used in the fifth commandment.

HONOR

"Honor" is the action verb of the fifth commandment, the action God wishes us to perform. The Larger Catechism sees honor as the respect that an "inferior" offers to a "superior":

> Q. 126. *What is the general scope of the fifth commandment?*
> A. The general scope of the fifth commandment is, the performance of those duties which we mutually owe in our several relations, as inferiors, superiors, or equals.

> Q. 127. *What is the honor that inferiors owe to their superiors?*
> A. The honor which inferiors owe to their superiors is, all due reverence in heart, word, and behavior; prayer and thanksgiving for them; imitation of their virtues and graces; willing obedience to their lawful commands and counsels; due submission to their corrections; fidelity to, defense, and maintenance of their persons and authority, according to their several ranks, and the nature of their places; bearing with their infirmities, and covering them in love, that so they may be an honor to them and to their government.

> Q. 128. *What are the sins of inferiors against their superiors?*
> A. The sins of inferiors against their superiors are, all neglect of the duties required toward them; envying at, contempt of, and rebellion against, their persons and places, in their lawful counsels, commands, and corrections; cursing, mocking, and all such refractory and scandalous carriage, as proves a shame and dishonor to them and their government.

The language of "superiors" and "inferiors" is politically incorrect in the contemporary context. It should not be taken to mean that some people are worth more than others. But, as I shall argue, God has, according to Scripture, given different gifts to different people, and has given real authority to some people over others. The Catechism expresses that authority in the language of superiority and inferiority. To "honor" someone, then, means to relate to superiors as described. In the contemporary world, where equality is emphasized, it is especially important to recognize the respects in which Scripture says that we are *not* equal. Of course, the Catechism later discusses relationships among equals as well, and we shall consider that in due course.

I shall, however, expound the concept of honor using a simpler scheme. Calvin, in his exposition of the Decalogue, usefully explains the concept as including reverence, obedience, and gratitude.[4] By "gratitude," he refers to concrete acts of thanksgiving, particularly financial and material support. Although Calvin didn't put it this way, these three concepts represent the existential, normative, and situational perspectives, respectively. Let us examine each of these aspects of honor.

Reverence (Existential Perspective)

In Scripture, as we have seen, both sin and righteousness begin in the heart. So honor is first of all a heart attitude, expressing reverence or respect. Leviticus 19:3 expresses this attitude toward parents with the word *yare'*, "fear" or "reverence" (cf. the use of *phobos*, "fear," in Rom. 13:7; 1 Peter 2:18). Scripture often uses the language of honor and fear to describe how we should relate to God. For "the fear of the Lord," see chapter 19. Scripture often speaks of honoring God (see Prov. 3:9; John 8:49; 1 Tim. 1:17; 6:16; Heb. 2:9; Rev. 4:9–11). This is indeed the language of worship.

Scripture contrasts sharply the deference due to God with that due to human beings (Acts 4:19; 5:29), even with that due to father and mother (Matt. 10:35–37; Mark 10:29–30; Luke 9:59–60; 14:26). That Jesus places loyalty to himself above loyalty to father and mother (even though he emphatically endorses the fifth commandment in Matthew 15:4–6) is a momentous claim to deity. That loyalty to God transcends loyalty even to parents is an implication of the first commandment.

But the fifth commandment and similar Bible passages use the vocabulary of fear, honor, and worship, on a human level, to indicate the proper

---

4. Calvin, *Institutes*, 2.8.36.

attitude of children to parents. And, moreover, they demand such reverence for parents as a consequence of our reverence for God. Our reverence for parents is not in spite of our reverence for God, but because of it. Deuteronomy 5:16 adds, "as the LORD your God commanded you." Leviticus 19:32, Ephesians 6:1–3, and Colossians 3:20 also invoke divine sanction for the content of the fifth commandment. Jesus too, as I just mentioned, strongly defends the fifth commandment, even though he demands for himself a higher honor than for parents. Against the Pharisees and scribes, he says:

> For God commanded, "Honor your father and your mother," and, "Whoever reviles father or mother must surely die." But you say, "If anyone tells his father or his mother, What you would have gained from me is given to God, he need not honor his father." So for the sake of your tradition you have made void the word of God. (Matt. 15:4–6; cf. Mark 7:9–13)

Mark 7:11 describes this practice by the Aramaic term *Corban*. By making a pledge to give money to the temple, a person could avoid the responsibility to support his parents. Even if he did not fulfill the pledge, he was considered to be free of the parental burden. Jesus condemns this practice as a violation of the fifth commandment. People who pretend in this way to honor God in fact dishonor him, by dishonoring his image.

So Scripture tells us often to express deference and respect to others, in thoughts, words, and actions (Gen. 31:35; 1 Kings 2:19; 1 Tim. 5:1). And it stresses the seriousness of cursing another human being (Ex. 21:17; Lev. 20:9; Prov. 20:20; 30:11).

There needs to be a balance, therefore, between the supreme honor we owe to God alone and a real, but subordinate honor that we owe to our parents (and, as we shall see, to others).[5] Protestants have historically accused Roman Catholics of having a reverence for Mary, the saints, and the church hierarchy, that belongs only to God. Roman Catholics have replied that they reserve the highest honor, worship (*latreia*) exclusively for God, giving lower honors to Mary (*hyperdouleia*) and the saints (*douleia*). They do not pray *to* Mary and the saints, but they invoke the help of Mary and the saints to bring their prayers to Jesus. They regard the titles given to clergy (Holy Father, Right Reverend, Father) as expressing still lower forms of honor.

---

5. In previous books, I have emphasized that even while we participate in the worship of God we should be concerned for the needs of people. See my *Worship in Spirit and Truth* (Phillipsburg, NJ: P&R Publishing, 1996), 7–8, and *Contemporary Worship Music* (Phillipsburg, NJ: P&R Publishing, 1997), 15–16. It sounds pious to say that when we worship we should forget everyone except God, but that sentiment is unbiblical.

Protestants reply that the issue is not, at bottom, terminological. It is, rather, the scriptural basis of these practices. And it is also a question of whether a real distinction exists between one's attitude toward human beings and his attitude toward God. When a Catholic kneels and addresses Mary, is there a real difference between that and a prayer to God? This is not a rhetorical question. In some cases, there may be a real difference. But there is here a dangerous open door to idolatry.

Yet Protestants also need to consider themselves. For them, the danger of idolatry exists less in their relations to Mary and the saints, but more in their regard for church leaders and traditions of the past and present, doctrinal and denominational. When people regard Calvin or the Westminster standards, say, as virtually infallible, there also is a grave danger of idolatry. When they use such traditions to determine how the Bible should be read, making it impossible for the Bible to correct the traditions, then Jesus' words in Matthew 15:6 apply to them: "For the sake of your tradition you have made void the word of God."[6]

Nobody can give an exhaustive list of words, expressions, attitudes, or body movements appropriate and inappropriate for honoring people. The issue is one of the heart, of motive (see chapters 18–21). We must be critical of our own actions and attitudes, learning to "see as" (chapter 20), to see ourselves in biblical categories, even when those categories (like "idolater") are unflattering.

Submission (Normative Perspective)

The second aspect of honor in Calvin's discussion is obedience, but I have chosen a broader term, for reasons that will become evident.

Submission may be understood as part of respect or reverence. When we respect someone, we *hear* him with respect, not assuming from the outset that we know more than he. From those we respect, we expect to learn, and we are willing to change out of respect for their words. When we must disagree, we do so reluctantly, and we express even that disagreement in respectful language.

So Scripture regularly presents parents as teachers (Deut. 6:6–7; Prov. 1:10; 2:1; 3:1). Accepting the wisdom of parent-teachers tends to long life (Prov. 3:1–2; 4:10), the blessing of the fifth commandment. Not every older

6. Compare the discussion of *sola Scriptura* in chapter 11. On denominational traditions, see my *Evangelical Reunion* (Grand Rapids: Baker, 1991), now available at http://reformedperspectives.org/search.asp/keyword/Thchsac/category/th; scroll to my name. On traditionalism in theology and church life, see my "Traditionalism," at http://reformedperspectives.org/search.asp/keyword/THall/category/th; scroll down to the article title.

person is wise, of course. Those who are not wise are considered pathetic cases: "There is no fool like an old fool." But the normal expectation is that age brings wisdom, and that wisdom should be heeded.

Submission is not necessarily a blind obedience. Paul tells Timothy not to "rebuke an older man but encourage him (parakaleō) as you would a father" (1 Tim. 5:1). There are times when a child must take issue with his father's words or actions. But even that admonition must at the same time express respect. The child's approach to his father must be positive, encouraging. He should exhort in such a way as to remain on his father's side. Even in such exhortation, the father-son relationship (and, analogously, the age difference between pastor and older believer) makes a difference in how we speak (cf. 1 Peter 5:5). Note also the negative example of Rehoboam, who refused to listen to the wise counsel of his father's advisers (1 Kings 12).

Now obedience is a form of submission. Submission is the broader category, obedience the narrower one. We express submission in ways other than by obedience. We show submission in our demeanor, our respectful way of listening, our willingness to hear teaching or rebuke, our gentle manner when we must exhort. But sometimes, the proper way to submit is by literal obedience.

This is true especially in the case of young children. Most of us who were raised in the church learned to equate the fifth commandment with the principle "Obey your parents." Indeed, that is what Paul does when he addresses children in Ephesians 6:1 and Colossians 3:20. For a child in the home of his parents, "Honor your father and mother" and "Obey your parents" are virtually synonymous. But as a child grows older, especially when he leaves his parents' home and starts a family of his own, Scripture applies the fifth commandment to him, not in terms of obedience, but rather in terms of respect/reverence and financial support.[7] Yet in a larger sense he still is bound to be submissive, by faithfully listening to their wisdom.

The obligation of obedience exists in other relationships as well, which, as we shall see, are significantly analogous to the parent-child relationship. Scripture requires obedience to civil authorities (Rom. 13:1; Titus 3:1; 1 Peter 2:13–14) and church officers (Phil. 2:12; 2 Thess. 3:14; Heb. 13:17). It urges wives to obey their husbands (1 Peter 3:6), and servants their masters (Col. 3:22–25; 1 Peter 2:18–20). We shall, of course, discuss these relationships in greater depth later on.

---

7. In some parts of the world, adult children, even those who live thousands of miles away, are expected to obey their parents' every whim. That is not biblical. When a man leaves his father and mother and cleaves to his wife (Gen. 2:24), his parents naturally recede in their influence on his life. But he still has responsibilities to them under the fifth commandment.

Obedience to other human beings, however, is always limited. God's authority alone is supreme and limits every form of human authority. When human authorities command us to disobey God, or they forbid us to do what God commands, then we must reply with Peter and John, "We must obey God rather than men" (Acts 5:29). When we sin against God, we may not offer as an excuse that we were commanded to do so by lawful authority. This was the "Nuremberg defense" of Hitler's associates: they claimed they were "only following orders." But Scripture requires the believer to follow God, even when that action amounts to civil disobedience or revolt (see Ex. 1:17, 19–21; 1 Sam. 22:17–23; 2 Kings 18:3; Dan. 3; 6; Acts 4:18–20). Jesus was submissive to his parents (Luke 2:51), but he did not follow them when his heavenly Father called him elsewhere (Luke 2:49). Of course, it is almost too easy for us, when we simply disagree with an authority, to concoct reasons as to why God would have us disobey. We should remember that for us God's will is limited to Scripture, and that we need to be rigorously careful in our determinations of God's will from Scripture.

FINANCIAL SUPPORT (SITUATIONAL PERSPECTIVE)

For the third aspect of honor, I have chosen to use a title more specific than Calvin's "gratefulness." The words for honor in Hebrew (*kavad*) and Greek (*timaō*) have as distinct senses "render financial value." The roots of these terms sometimes refer quite specifically to wealth (see Gen. 13:2; Prov. 13:18; Isa. 43:23; Mal. 1:6–7 [cf. 3:8]; 1 Tim. 5:17).

We have seen how Jesus applies the fifth commandment against the scribes and Pharisees for their *Corban* tradition. One does not honor his parents if one refuses to support them, even under a pious pretense. And Paul says:

> But if a widow has children or grandchildren, let them first learn to show godliness to their own household and to make some return to their parents, for this is pleasing in the sight of God. . . . Command these things as well, so that they may be without reproach. But if anyone does not provide for his relatives, and especially for members of his household, he has denied the faith and is worse than an unbeliever. (1 Tim. 5:4–8)

Note the strong language of verse 8. Clearly we have a responsibility to support our parents—and grandparents—in meeting their needs for finances, and, I assume, also for housing, health care, mental stimulation, emotional support, and so on. When parents grow old and children achieve maturity, honor becomes less a matter of obedience and more a matter of respectful support. This is a "return," as Paul says, a matter of simple justice. When we were unable to do anything for ourselves, our parents met all our needs. Later in life, there is often a reversal of roles. Children and grandchildren must then be prepared to do for their parents what the parents can no longer do for themselves.[8]

Paul does imply that in cases where children and grandchildren simply cannot meet all the needs of elderly relatives, or when there are no children or grandchildren to meet these needs, the church (the extended family) should step in. In the larger context, verses 3 and 5–6 speak of the church's support for those who are "truly widows." But church support, he says, ought to be a last resort. Welfare is first of all a family responsibility.

The nature of the "return" will vary from one family to another. In some cases, there may be no alternative but to make space in one's home for aged parents who can no longer live independently. That is often the best environment in which to express familial love in the fullest way.

But in a fallen world, no situation is perfectly ideal. Home care for elderly relatives is often a difficult situation, both for the older person and for the younger family. So the younger adults often seek alternatives, but they often feel a sense of guilt about the prospect of sending their parents to live somewhere other than their family home.

Nursing homes, particularly, have developed bad reputations over recent decades. Studies have revealed deplorable care in many such institutions, as well as the tendency for younger relatives to abandon the nursing home residents. Many of those residents experience extreme loneliness and neglect. So Christians sometimes ask whether it is ever legitimate to put an aged relative in a nursing home. Is such a decision ever in keeping with the fifth commandment?

There are several principles that bear on this issue:

1. It is not wrong in itself for parents to live apart from their children. Indeed, the original ordinance of marriage in Genesis 2:24 describes a man "leaving" his father and mother in order to "hold fast to his wife." This principle does not rule out multigenerational living arrangements, but it does mean that marriage creates a new authority relationship that is normally expressed by the couple living apart from their parents. As long as a parent is able to live independently, such separation is desirable, though there are certainly advantages to parents and children living fairly close to one another.

2. Even when parents are ill or infirm, we should value their independence. If they can afford and obtain the care they need while living inde-

---

8. Verse 8 implies a priority to the nuclear family, but verse 4 extends obligation beyond that. Verse 8 also requires the obvious, that parents should support their children. But at the moment we are considering the less obvious, opposite relation.

pendently, and they prefer to do that, nobody ought to object. Children, of course, should monitor such situations closely, with a willingness to step in when needed.

3. There are some medical needs that preclude either independent living or living in a family home. These are becoming more common, as people live longer and medicine becomes more sophisticated. Sometimes these needs can best be met through a long-term nursing facility. We should be thankful to God that such institutions exist.

4. Of course, there are wide disparities in the quality and cost of nursing homes. One responsibility of children is to help their parents make wise decisions among alternatives.

5. Children should never abandon parents who have been institutionalized, but should visit often, providing prayer and emotional support.

6. When a nursing home patient has recovered to the point that such care is no longer needed or advantageous, the children should take responsibility to make other arrangements for their parents.

In short, nursing homes can play an important role in the life of Christian families. But children must take responsibility for determining how to use them in an overall context of love and care. Nursing homes should never be places to dump people whom nobody wants to have around. Rather, they should serve to supplement, when needed, a broad relationship of family care, motivated by love and honor.

FATHER AND MOTHER

We have examined the biblical concept of honor, and now we come to the phrase "your father and your mother" in the commandment. The meaning of this phrase may seem obvious. I have been discussing fathers and mothers extensively already, without seeing any particular need to define terms. But the Larger Catechism leads us to a closer look:

> Q. 124. *Who are meant by* father *and* mother *in the fifth commandment?*
>
> A. By *father* and *mother*, in the fifth commandment, are meant, not only natural parents, but all superiors[9] in age and gifts; and

9. The Catechism's references to "superiors" and "inferiors" in its exposition of the fifth commandment come across today as politically incorrect. Theologically speaking, there are certainly senses in which all human beings are equal. But the Catechism focuses on biblically based inequalities, and I find that refreshing.

especially such as, by God's ordinance, are over us in place of authority, whether in family, church, or commonwealth.

Again, the Catechism stretches our minds to consider what "father" and "mother" mean, beyond the obvious. Can this rather broad understanding be justified by Scripture? I think it can be, by means of the following considerations:

The structure of family metaphors in Scripture. Scripture uses *father* and *mother* for a wide number of relationships beyond the literal family. These terms designate rulers (Gen. 45:8; Judg. 5:7; Isa. 49:23), military chiefs (2 Kings 5:13), prophets (2 Kings 2:12), wisdom teachers (Ps. 34:11; Prov. 1:8, 10, 15), church leaders (1 Cor. 4:15; Gal. 4:19; 1 Tim. 1:2; Titus 1:4),[10] and older people (Lev. 19:32;[11] 1 Tim. 5:1, in effect).

Indeed, fifth commandment language applies to God himself: "A son honors his father, and a servant his master. If then I am a father, where is my honor? And if I am a master, where is my fear? says the LORD of hosts to you, O priests, who despise my name" (Mal. 1:6). God, of course, can invoke the first commandment to demand honor for himself. But here in Malachi he chooses to invoke the fifth commandment instead. So any sin against God—that is, any sin at all—is a violation of the fifth commandment. That is the "broad meaning" of the fifth commandment: a mandate to honor God as Father. That aspect of the commandment takes on a richer meaning for New Testament believers, who are taught by Jesus to address God specifically as Father (Matt. 6:9; Eph. 3:14–15).

These metaphorical uses of *father* and *mother* extend the reach of the fifth commandment into many spheres of society and many different authority structures.[12] As we shall see, every authority structure carries an obligation similar to the obligations of children to parents. And faithfulness in each of these relations results in the divine promise of long life and prosperity.

The family is the fundamental sphere from which all others are derived. This is true historically, developmentally, and logically. Historically speaking, in the first family, Adam played all the roles that were later divided among different spheres of authority. He was prophet, priest, and king, and employer, teacher, and so forth. The same was true of Noah, as God

---

10. So they are to receive "esteem" or honor (1 Thess. 5:12–13).

11. Note the comparison here between honoring old people and honoring God.

12. Given what Paul says in Eph. 3:15, the use of "Father" as a title of God is more than a metaphor. It is the reality that gives meaning to all other forms of fatherhood, including the "literal" form.

reconstituted the human race following the flood, and the patriarchs Abraham, Isaac, and Jacob. But when the sons of Jacob become a great nation, a division of labor was needed. The roles become differentiated. But Israel was still essentially a family. The new covenant community in Christ is also a family, with a Father, brothers, and sisters (Matt. 12:48–50; Mark 10:29–30; Rom. 14:10; Eph. 1:5). Church government is essentially family government.

The family is also the fundamental sphere developmentally. Even today, parents perform in the home all the functions of society. For young children, their parents are their authoritative source of teaching, discipline, employment, and religious leadership.

And, logically speaking, rule in all spheres is similar to that of the family. Paul argues that the ability to rule one's family shows ability to rule in the church (1 Tim. 3:4–5).

All forms of authority deserve honor similar to the honor of parents. According to Ephesians 5:22–24, wives are to submit to their husbands as the church submits to Christ. So the wife-husband relationship, in this respect, is like the child-parent relationship. This submission, like the submission of children, is out of reverence for Christ (v. 21) and respect for her husband (v. 33), as is the submission of servants to masters (6:5–9). Ephesians 6:5 speaks of this submission in highly reverential terms: as "fear and trembling." As in the fifth commandment, this submission is not a grudging obedience, but from a heartfelt respect. The same is true in Colossians 3:23–24. In 1 Peter 2:17, we are to honor the emperor out of the fear of God, as in Proverbs 24:21. Psalm 82:6 even uses the word "gods" to designate rulers, suggesting the high level of respect to which even unworthy rulers are entitled. These passages show that the reverence enjoined in the fifth commandment is not limited to the parents of a nuclear family, but extends to all legitimate authorities as well.

All obedience to legitimate authority leads to covenant inheritance. Even more significantly, the promise of prosperity, which distinguishes the fifth commandment, motivates our obedience to authorities beyond the family. In Proverbs 3:1–2, the teacher of wisdom speaks:

> My son, do not forget my teaching,
>   but let your heart keep my commandments,
> for length of days and years of life
>   and peace they will add to you.

The teacher of wisdom here speaks as a father, and no doubt he stands as a model to fathers in Israel. But the passage applies to all of those who communicate truly the wisdom of God. Even if one's own parents are fool-ish, keeping the commandments of God's wisdom will result in long life and prosperity. Note also Colossians 3:23–24: "Whatever you do, work heart-ily, as for the Lord and not for men, knowing that from the Lord you will receive the inheritance as your reward. You are serving the Lord Christ." Here servants inherit the covenant promise by means of hearty service to their masters, not only to their parents.

All people deserve honor. But in one sense the honor of the fifth com-mandment extends even more broadly than this. For it applies, not only to "superiors," as the Larger Catechism puts it, but to "equals" as well. Although the Catechism restricts "honor" to "superiors," it recognizes that the fifth commandment applies to relationships of equality:

> Q. 126. *What is the general scope of the fifth commandment?*
> A. The general scope of the fifth commandment is, the per-formance of those duties which we mutually owe in our several relations, as inferiors, superiors, or equals.

Scripture does speak of honor being due to equals. In a context deal-ing with submission to authority, Peter says, "Honor everyone. Love the brotherhood. Fear God. Honor the emperor" (1 Peter 2:17). The object of "honor" here certainly extends as far as "the brotherhood" in the next clause. So Peter calls us to honor all believers, whether or not they have authority over us. For Peter, the honor we owe to all believers is a fifth commandment honor, as is our honor to God and the emperor.

In Romans 12:10—"Love one another with brotherly affection. Outdo one another in showing honor"—Paul indicates that the scope of honor is the same as that of love. And in Romans 13:7 he tells Christians to pay what they owe and to honor everyone who deserves honor. But then in verses 8–9 he generalizes his exhortation, describing a sense in which our one debt, even after we pay all the others, is to love everyone, to love our neighbor as ourselves. All the other commandments, he says (v. 9), are summed up in the love commandment. So the honor required in the fifth commandment is also a universal honor. It extends to all human beings made in God's image, and, in a special way, to all our brothers and sisters in Christ.

Superiors should honor inferiors. An important theme in the New Testa-ment is that honor is *reciprocal.* That is, not only must the "inferior" honor the "superior," but the reverse as well. So the Catechism says:

Q. 129. *What is required of superiors towards their inferiors?*

A. It is required of superiors, according to that power they receive from God, and that relation wherein they stand, to love, pray for, and bless their inferiors; to instruct, counsel, and admonish them; countenancing, commending, and rewarding such as do well; and discountenancing, reproving, and chastising such as do ill; protecting, and providing for them all things necessary for soul and body: and by grave, wise, holy, and exemplary carriage, to procure glory to God, honor to themselves, and so to preserve that authority which God hath put upon them.

Q. 130. *What are the sins of superiors?*

A. The sins of superiors are, besides the neglect of the duties required of them, an inordinate seeking of themselves, their own glory, ease, profit, or pleasure; commanding things unlawful, or not in the power of inferiors to perform; counseling, encouraging, or favoring them in that which is evil; dissuading, discouraging, or discountenancing them in that which is good; correcting them unduly; careless exposing, or leaving them to wrong, temptation, and danger; provoking them to wrath; or any way dishonoring themselves, or lessening their authority, by an unjust, indiscreet, rigorous, or remiss behavior.

In Ephesians 5:21, Paul asks the church to "submit to one another out of reverence for Christ," and then describes how this mutual submission operates in different relationships: husband/wife, parent/child, master/slave. Contrary to some feminist and liberationist literature, the mutual submission does not eliminate the authority structure, so that, e.g., wives and husbands have equal authority over one another. Paul does teach the existence of a hierarchy. The wife is to submit to the husband, not vice versa (vv. 22–24). Children are to obey their parents, not vice versa (6:1–3). And slaves are to obey their masters, not vice versa (6:5–8).

Some interpreters think that "submitting to one another" in Ephesians 5:21 simply means that the inferiors in these different relationships should submit to their superiors. That may be true, but it does not exhaust the reciprocity described in the larger passage. For in each of these relationships Paul describes a responsibility of the superior to the inferior, as well as the other way around. We saw that in 5:22–24 the wife is to submit to her husband. But Paul also says, in verses 25–33, that husbands should love their wives as Christ loved the church. The same is true in 1 Peter 3:1–7: the wife must submit even to an unbelieving husband, respecting him as her "lord" (v. 6). But the husband must live with her "in an understanding way" (v. 7). In Ephesians 6:1–3, Paul teaches children to obey their parents, but in verse 4 he tells fathers not to "provoke [their] children to anger, but bring them up in the discipline and instruction of the Lord." In verse 5, he tells slaves to obey their masters, but in verse 9 he says, "Masters, do the same to them, and stop your threatening, knowing that he who is both their Master and yours is in heaven, and that there is no partiality with him."

Paul, who is often accused of male chauvinism, sometimes goes out of his way to emphasize reciprocity in the relations between men and women. Note 1 Corinthians 7:2–4:

> But because of the temptation to sexual immorality, each man should have his own wife and each woman her own husband. The husband should give to his wife her conjugal rights, and likewise the wife to her husband. For the wife does not have authority over her own body, but the husband does. Likewise the husband does not have authority over his own body, but the wife does.

In one sense, the husband "owns" his wife, but she also owns her husband. The wife, as a male chauvinist might say, owes conjugal rights to her husband, but Paul affirms the reverse as well, and affirms it before the husband's rights. And, most remarkably, he balances the husband's *authority* over the wife's body with her *authority* over his.

Paul also balances the relations between the sexes in 1 Corinthians 11. He begins by stressing hierarchy: the husband is "the head" of the wife (v. 3), and the wife should wear a covering when praying or prophesying in church, to acknowledge that relationship. He stresses hierarchy also in verses 7–10. But then Paul is quick to balance this teaching by emphasizing reciprocity: "Nevertheless, in the Lord woman is not independent of man nor man of woman; for as woman was made from man, so man is now born of woman. And all things are from God" (vv. 11–12). There is hierarchy, but Paul wants to keep his readers from drawing any false inferences from that fact. Man and woman are mutually dependent.

The reciprocity of these relationships reminds us of the general structure of rule in the church, as Jesus sets it forth in Matthew 20:25–28:

> But Jesus called them to him and said, "You know that the rulers of the Gentiles lord it over them, and their great ones exercise authority over them. It shall not be so among you. But whoever would be great among you must be your servant, and whoever would be first among you must be your slave, even as the Son

of Man came not to be served but to serve, and to give his life
as a ransom for many.

Jesus here rebukes his disciples, who wanted to be placed close to him in
his kingdom. Theirs, he says, is the attitude of secular rulers, who want
authority so that people will serve their own interests. In the church, the
opposite should be the case: those with greater authority should serve
those with less. The greatest will be those who humble themselves the
most. Here Jesus himself is the model, for although he has all authority in
heaven and earth (no question of hierarchy here!), he comes as a servant
to die for his people.

Compare John 13:12–15:

> When he had washed their feet and put on his outer garments and
> resumed his place, he said to them, "Do you understand what I
> have done to you? You call me Teacher and Lord, and you are right,
> for so I am. If I then, your Lord and Teacher, have washed your feet,
> you also ought to wash one another's feet. For I have given you an
> example, that you also should do just as I have done to you.

Again, there is no compromise to the hierarchic superiority of Jesus. He is
Lord and Teacher, and they are right to call him so. But, as such, he washes
the feet of his disciples. Compare also Jesus' words about himself as the
Good Shepherd, who gives his life for the sheep (John 10:1–18).

I conclude that the honor of the fifth commandment is a complex honor.
Certainly the inferior must show honor to the superior, in all spheres of
legitimate authority. There is a hierarchy, an authority structure. But in
the overall relationship, the superior must care most, not for himself, but
for his inferiors. Like Jesus, the Lord who came to die, the ruler (in any
sphere) must lay down his life for his subjects.

This is the basic principle of government in Scripture. It rejects both
egalitarianism and authoritarianism. It does not regard authority as
demeaning, as in some feminist thought, but as a blessing. It does not
claim that everybody is the same, in gifts or status. But neither does it
allow authority to become oppression.[13]

"Father and mother," therefore, is a fairly broad category in Scripture.
Certainly we should not neglect its narrow, literal meaning, which governs
relations in the nuclear family. Children must obey their parents (Eph.
6:1). But the principle of the fifth commandment applies to all authority

---

13. Compare the argument of chapter 4 that non-Christian thought vacillates between
anarchy and totalitarianism. Egalitarianism, taken consistently, is a form of anarchy, for any
authority at all could be construed as inequality.

structures. We are to honor all authorities, giving them respect, submission, and financial support as appropriate. And, beyond that, we are also to honor those who are subject to our authority. So like all the commandments, the fifth commandment has both narrow and broad applications.

THE PROMISE OF PROSPERITY

Paul calls the fifth commandment "the first commandment with a promise" (Eph. 6:2). This is literally the case. The second commandment (Ex. 20:6) does include a statement that God shows "steadfast love to thousands of those who love me and keep my commandments," but it doesn't specify what blessings that love brings to us. Exodus 20:6 is a statement of God's love in the present, but not quite a promise, for it is not a prediction of something specific that will happen in the future to those who are obedient.

So within the Decalogue, the promise is somewhat distinctive to the fifth commandment. Nevertheless, this promise is not an isolated passage in Scripture as a whole. It is a general principle of biblical law that obedience to God brings the blessings of long life and prosperity. In Deuteronomy 5:32–6:3, God tells Israel:

> You shall be careful therefore to do as the LORD your God has commanded you. You shall not turn aside to the right hand or to the left. You shall walk in all the way that the LORD your God has commanded you, that you may live, and that it may go well with you, and that you may live long in the land that you shall possess. Now this is the commandment, the statutes and the rules that the LORD your God commanded me to teach you, that you may do them in the land to which you are going over, to possess it, that you may fear the LORD your God, you and your son and your son's son, by keeping all his statutes and his commandments, which I command you, all the days of your life, and that your days may be long. Hear therefore, O Israel, and be careful to do them, that it may go well with you, and that you may multiply greatly, as the LORD, the God of your fathers, has promised you, in a land flowing with milk and honey.

There are many texts that say that keeping God's law brings "life" (see Lev. 18:5; Deut. 4:1; 5:29; 6:3, 18, 24; 10:13; 12:28; 30:15–20; 1 Kings 3:14; Neh. 9:29; Ps. 1; Isa. 55:3; Ezek. 18:9; 20:11; Amos 5:4–6; Mal. 3:8–12; Matt. 19:17). This principle doesn't explain the process by which sinners receive God's forgiveness. Rather, it describes the rewards of covenant keeping. Deuteronomy 28:1–14 describes in great detail the blessings Israel will receive if it is faithful to God's covenant. The context also specifies curses for disobedience in 27:9–26 and 28:15–68.

As I have mentioned in chapter 7 and elsewhere, Christian ethics is not a Kantian deontology, in which we grit our teeth and do our duty only for duty's sake. Rather, we do our duty also for the rewards that God has promised and to avoid the curses.

This promise continues into the New Testament. Although there is much in the New Testament about persecution and suffering for those who trust Jesus, there is also the promise of prosperity. The balance between these two themes appears in Mark 10:29–31:

> Jesus said, "Truly, I say to you, there is no one who has left house or brothers or sisters or mother or father or children or lands, for my sake and for the gospel, who will not receive a hundredfold now in this time, houses and brothers and sisters and mothers and children and lands, with persecutions, and in the age to come eternal life. But many who are first will be last, and the last first."

Note that there are indeed to be persecutions, and many who are first will be last. But there is here a promise for this life as well as the life to come.

The new covenant, unlike the old, does not give the believer title to land in Palestine (as in the fifth commandment's reference to the "land"). The "houses," "brothers," "sisters," and so on evidently refer to the body of Christ, considered as an extended family. The "lands," I think, are the kingdoms, tongues, and nations that are to be brought under the gospel. That is to say, the new covenant gives believers title to much more land than Israel had: for Christians, the promised land is the whole earth.

It may be that Paul also has this principle in mind when he applies the fifth commandment promise to Christian children: "'Honor your father and mother' (this is the first commandment with a promise), 'that it may go well with you and that you may live long in the land'" (Eph. 6:2–3). "In the land" is *epi tēs gēs* in Greek, which normally means "upon the earth." The phrase may be nothing more than a Greek rendering of the Hebrew of Exodus 20:12, referring to Canaan as the Promised Land. But I am inclined to think that Paul here recontextualizes the promise of Exodus 20:12 and applies it to the land promised to Christians—the whole earth.

Other New Testament promises of prosperity to God's people include 1 Timothy 4:8 and 1 Peter 3:8–12.

The fulfillment of this promise is not always easily visible. One of the mysteries of Scripture is that despite these promises the wicked often prosper and the righteous are oppressed (Jer. 5:28; 12:1). The book of Job is about this mystery, and many psalms are preoccupied with it, such as Psalms 10, 12, 13, 22, 37, 73, and 88. The fullness of blessing awaits the next life.[14] The mystery is why the wait is so long.[15] For now, prosperity comes "with persecutions." But even for the poor and needy, a day in the Lord's house is better than a thousand elsewhere (Ps. 84:10). God does not forsake the righteous (Ps. 37:25), and fellowship with God is the essence of true prosperity.

Given that this is a general biblical principle, why, in the Decalogue, is it connected especially to the fifth commandment? Why does God mention the promise here, rather than in another commandment? I think it has to do with the transition in the Decalogue from "our duty toward God" to "our duty toward man." It is plain enough in Scripture that prosperity comes from honoring God. In the Decalogue, that promise is implicit in the second commandment (where the blessing may attach to the first two commands as a unit, as we saw in chapter 23, note 1). But as we move toward a more anthropocentric focus in commandments five through ten, God wants to tell us that the same blessing comes through honoring other people. Especially, God wants us to know that covenant prosperity depends on our submission to his representatives, as well as to himself. The covenant blessing depends not only on obeying God's law in general, but in submission to parents, teachers of wisdom, church elders, and civil magistrates.

---

14. Although Scripture often describes the covenant blessing as long life, there are occasions when God shortens lives as a covenant blessing: see 1 Kings 14:13; 2 Kings 22:20. He sometimes takes his best servants early, so they will not have to experience the disasters to come. In the light of the whole Bible, the "long life" is eternal life with God. But a long earthly life in friendship with God is in Scripture often a symbol and an anticipation of that eternal life.

15. For a longer discussion of the problem of evil, see DG, 160–82.

CHAPTER 32

The Fifth Commandment: Family, Church, and State

We have seen that God has not left human beings to live as isolated individuals, but has placed them within communities. Over each community is a government, which the members of that community must honor. So there are structures of authority, in which "inferiors" must submit to "superiors." Of course, in some respects, human beings are equal: all are equally in the image of God, equally fallen, equally in need of redemption. And all who are in Christ receive the same salvation in him, though with varying rewards (see chapter 16).

The chief communities discussed in the Bible and in our own time are the family, the church, and the state. In this chapter, I shall seek to define these biblically and describe how they are related to one another.

THE FAMILY

The family began when God created man "male and female" (Gen. 1:27). Genesis 2:18–25 gives a longer account of the creation of woman, and makes it clear that the two sexes are designed for marriage (vv. 24–25). In the marital relationship, the woman relieves Adam's aloneness and serves as a "helper" to the man (v. 18). This is not a disparagement, nor does it, by itself, suggest any subordination. God is man's "help" in Genesis 49:25, Exodus 18:4, Deuteronomy 33:7, and many other passages.

The woman helps the man in many ways. Proverbs 31 gives a number of examples. But the emphasis of Genesis 1–2 is on the bearing of children. The two are to "be fruitful and multiply" (1:28), so as to fill and subdue the earth. So the family is, first of all, the means God has given to carry out the cultural mandate. As I indicated in chapter 17, the cultural mandate cannot be carried out by one person alone. It requires the labors of many people—families and families of families.

The fall estranged man from God, and also from his fellow man (see chapter 15). It marked a breakdown in the relationship between Adam and Eve (3:6–7, 12, 16). Nevertheless, it is through the family that God promises to redeem mankind: the offspring of the woman will bruise the head of the serpent (Satan) (v. 15).

In Genesis 4, God gives children to the first couple. The effects of the fall on the family are terrible: brother kills brother and must go into exile. But in the time of Seth's son Enosh, "people began to call upon the name of the LORD" (Gen. 4:26). So there is a line of faith that runs through Noah, Abraham, Isaac, Jacob, and their descendants. In time, the deliverer, Jesus, is born to fulfill the promise of Genesis 3:15. In both Testaments, God calls families, as well as individuals, to the blessings of salvation and to responsibilities in his kingdom. So in the Old Testament, the male children of believers are circumcised, signing and sealing their membership in the covenant. In the New Testament, I believe, baptism serves the same function. But in any case it is plain that in the New Testament, as well as the Old, God calls families (households) to himself (Acts 11:14; 16:15, 31; 18:8; 1 Cor. 1:16; 16:15).

So there is godly seed as well as ungodly. Scripture is much concerned with raising children in the fear and knowledge of God. A godly household is one that is saturated with the Word of God. Following the Shema, Israel's great confession of the lordship of God and the first great commandment, the Lord says:

> And these words that I command you today shall be on your heart. You shall teach them diligently to your children, and shall talk of them when you sit in your house, and when you walk by the way, and when you lie down, and when you rise. You shall bind them as a sign on your hand, and they shall be as frontlets between your eyes. You shall write them on the doorposts of your house and on your gates. (Deut. 6:6–9)

This is the great charter of Christian education.[1] God wants children to be raised in an atmosphere full of his word, with parents who teach by

---

1. Review here the critique of secular education in chapter 24.

word and example. Scripture says much about discipline as well. Corporal punishment is sometimes necessary (Prov. 10:13; 13:24; 22:15; 23:13–14; 26:3; 29:15). Christians should resist much more strongly the present movement to forbid spanking, or even to define it as child abuse. In biblically ruled households, children honor their parents, and they learn to honor authorities beyond the family as well—indeed, to honor all people as honor is due.

The family, then, is God's means, both of dominion and of redemption. It is as families that people replenish and subdue the earth, and it is as families that we serve as ambassadors for Christ.

So the family is the basic unit of human society. As I indicated in chapter 31, all the institutions of society—prophetic, priestly, and kingly—begin in the family. To children, parents are rulers, educators, providers, and evangelists. All other forms of authority are extended forms of fatherhood and motherhood. Historically, developmentally, and logically, the family is, as I said in the previous chapter, "the fundamental sphere from which all others are derived." Honor in all spheres is derived from parental honor.

The family is also crucial to economic well-being. Honor to parents brings inheritance. It brings long life and prosperity. Rousas Rushdoony points out that "throughout history the basic welfare agency has been the family."[2] Government policies that weaken the family lead to poverty and cultural decline.

THE TWO FAMILIES

If the family is the fundamental sphere from which all others are derived, there are implications for the ongoing discussion of the relation of church and state. It is important, first, that we see the church and the state as extensions of the family. They come into being when the family gets too large to govern itself as a nuclear family or as an extended family.[3]

"State," first of all, is a problematic category in Scripture. It is not a biblical category in the sense that "family," "people of God," "Israel," and "church" are biblical categories. The word *state* is rarely, if ever, found in English translations of the Bible. Scripture speaks of powers and authorities in general, and in some contexts it is plain that these authorities are civil—what we would call the state. It also speaks of

2. Rousas John Rushdoony, *The Institutes of Biblical Law* (Nutley, NJ: Craig Press, 1973), 181. Much of Rushdoony's discussion here is instructive.

3. What follows is a condensation and revision of my article, "Toward a Theology of the State," *Westminster Theological Journal* 51 (1989): 199–226.

kings as distinct from priests and prophets, indicating a realm of distinctive authority that we may choose to call the state.

But the Bible does not explicitly or implicitly define the state, nor does it record any divine authorization of it. God established the family at creation (Gen. 2:24). In Exodus 19–24, God established Israel as a nation, as the people of God. The church is, in one sense, the whole people of God from Adam to the present; in another sense, it is a fresh historical expression of that community, based specifically upon the apostolic confession of Christ (Matt. 16:18–19). But when did God establish the state?

Some have found divine warrant for the state in Genesis 4:15, where God offers Cain protection from violence, or in 9:6, where God commands Noah's family to return bloodshed for bloodshed.[4] But in these passages, God gives responsibilities to a *family*. There is no indication in either passage of any new institution being established. And under the law of Moses, the execution of murderers is carried out, not by anything that might be called "the state," but by "the avenger of blood," kin of the murder victim (Num. 35:19, 21; Deut. 19:12). The family, here, is the instrument of justice. We have no reason to believe, therefore, that any special institution beyond the family for the establishment of justice was created in Genesis 9:6.[5]

What we see in Scripture, rather, is a kind of gradual development from family authority to something that we tend to call a state. The borderline between family and state is not sharp or clear.

We have seen that there is an authority structure within the nuclear family: husband over wife, parents over children. In the patriarchal period, families became extended, but they maintained an authority structure, under the senior males or patriarchs. Abraham watched over Lot's family, as well as his own. Isaac and Jacob maintained close relationships with their children, even after they had grown. Job is another example, perhaps from the patriarchal

4. In chapter 29, I criticized Meredith Kline's view that Gen. 4–9 shows the emergence of a "common grace order" ruled by the divine institution of the state.

5. In *The Institutes of Biblical Law*, 358–62, Rushdoony argues that God withholds the death penalty from the family and gives it exclusively to the state. He bases this argument on the mark of Cain, which he sees as a protection against vengeance from within the family, and upon Deut. 21:18–21, in which, although the parents are required to bring complaints against incorrigible children, "the men of the city," not the parents, execute the death penalty, contrary to the usual order, in which the accusers are the executioners. Rushdoony is right, I think, about the *nuclear* family. Not only the natural ties of love, but the need to bring more objective witnesses into the process would militate against the use of the death penalty within the nuclear family. But in a broader sense, "the men of the city" were family too. Notice also that in Israel the death penalty for murder is executed by "the avenger of blood," a representative of the victim's family (Num. 35:19). And, again, there were no institutions other than the family when God prescribed the death penalty to Noah.

period. The three-generation family continues throughout the Bible. As we saw earlier, Paul, in 1 Timothy 5:8, tells younger people to be responsible, not only for their aged parents, but their grandparents as well.

When Israel was in Egypt, they became too numerous to be subject to a single patriarch. In Exodus 6:14–25, there is a listing of the heads of families within Israel: the tribe of Reuben is divided into four "clans," and so on. These may be "the elders of Israel," referred to in Exodus 3:16–22; 4:29; 12:21; 17:5–6; 18:12. In Exodus 18:21–26, Moses, on the advice of Jethro his father-in-law, sets judges over "thousands," "hundreds," "fifties," and "tens" (v. 25). Is this a new organization of the clan elders, or is it a new set of officers? The relationship between the elders and the Mosaic judges is not clear. Certainly the eldership continued beyond the time of Moses. But equally clearly Israel's government had become much more complicated than it was in Jacob's time.

Another complication is that God established an official priesthood in Israel, under Aaron, Moses' brother.

Moses himself was the ruler over the whole nation, the one who made the judgments that could not be made by lower officials, the one who solved the "hard" cases (Ex. 18:26). His authority came directly from God as a prophet and, virtually, a king.

The picture to this point, then, is that as Israel developed from nuclear family to extended family to clan to nation, family authority became more elaborate and complicated. In time, God introduced new institutions. The heads of extended families were no longer exclusively responsible for prophetic and priestly ministries, as were the patriarchs. Rather, God relieved them by assigning many religious duties to the priests, Levites, and prophets.

Was there, at this point in history, also a divinely appointed "state"? I would say no, if, again, "state" refers to something above and beyond the natural authority of the family. As far back as Genesis 9, as we have seen, God called the family to execute vengeance for bloodshed, and so no new order was needed to administer capital punishment. There was, of course, in Moses' time, a national army to be commanded, but even that had its precedents in patriarchal tradition (Gen. 14).[6] New machinery, of course, was put in place (by some combination of tribal tradition and Mosaic appointment) to resolve disputes, but that too was essentially a family function.

The anointing of Saul as the first king of Israel (1 Sam. 9:15–10:1) marked the beginning of something new. For the first time, there was to

---

6. And note that even the nuclear family retained the use of force for self-defense (Ex. 22:2).

be in Israel a continuing line of monarchs, normally linked by heredity (though of course God often disrupted the hereditary pattern for his own purposes). The institutional change, however, was not a radical one. God ordered the anointing of Saul, but Saul did not rule until that anointing was ratified by the tribal elders (1 Sam. 10:17–24; 11:15). The same was true of David (2 Sam. 5:1–5). David placed his son Solomon on the throne, but for him too there was a popular consensus (1 Kings 3:28; 4:29–34). Very different was the situation with Rehoboam, Solomon's son, who, having failed to satisfy the demands of "all the assembly of Israel" (12:3), and having rejected the advice of the elders (12:6, 8), lost the allegiance of ten tribes. God had promised to make Jeroboam a king (11:29–39), and the ten tribes "made him king over all Israel" (12:20).

So, although Israel's government became more elaborate with its growth, there was no sharp line between family authority and the later authority of prophets, priests, judges, and kings. God set the standards for these officers, appointed some of his own choice, and removed others for their unfaithfulness. At the same time, Israel itself continued to acknowledge its leaders, as they had always recognized the authority of patriarchs and tribal elders.

What we call the "state" is simply a certain level of complexity in the government of a large family. It is not wrong to describe the state as ordained by God, because God clearly approves this development toward greater complexity, and he explicitly designates civil magistrates as his "servants" or "ministers" (Rom. 13:4, *diakonos*; v. 6, *leitourgos*). But it is not as if the family and the state have radically different powers, or that they rule over different spheres of human life.

Now here is another complication. This increasing complexity has taken place both in believing and unbelieving contexts. Lamech, the descendent of Cain, sings a song of vengeance in Genesis 4:23–24. As family head, he sings to his two wives about how he will execute vengeance for bloodshed. Unlike the simple reciprocity implied in Genesis 9:6 and in the Mosaic law of talion (Ex. 21:23–25), Lamech boasts that he will avenge seventy-seven times! This may have been "family justice," but it was exaggerated far beyond anything our God would recognize as just. Still, we can see that, as in the believing line, the mentality of kingship springs up in the context of the nuclear and extended families.

Meredith Kline argues that this theme is resumed in Genesis 6:1–4. He believes that the offense which draws forth God's condemnation is the exercise of royal polygamy: earthly kings ("sons of God") accumulating harems ("daughters of men").[7] Whatever we may say about that exegesis, it is likely that the table of nations in Genesis 10, like the genealogy of the believing line in Genesis 5, is not a complete record of all who lived on the earth, but rather a record of notable leaders, perhaps kings. At any rate, it is clear that the development of kingship was rapid in the world in general, compared to its development in Israel. When Israel first asked for a king, it seemed to them, at least, that "all the nations" already had them (1 Sam. 8:5).

Kings in the other nations were known for conscripting laborers, soldiers, and wives, and for collecting extortionate taxes for private gain (Deut. 17:16–17; 1 Sam. 8:10–18). History reminds us of the terrible, Lamech-like cruelties imposed by pagan kings in the name of royal vengeance. Still, the formal institutional picture is not different from what we have seen in Israel. The pagan kings abused their powers, but so did the Israelite kings. The pagans did not have greater powers than did the kings of Israel. Even outside the covenant, the powers of the king came from God (cf. Rom. 13:1–7). And the pagan kings, like the Israelite kings, had essentially the power of tribal elders, however widespread their territory might be.

The difference between Israel and other kingdoms was that Israel was in covenant with the true God. So it had institutions and civil laws appropriate to its uniqueness. Its temple, priesthood, feasts, and sacrificial system anticipated the coming of Christ to redeem God's people from sin. But the majority of Israel rejected Jesus. So they lost their special status with God.

But the people of God continued in a new form. The church, composed of Jews and Gentiles (with, of course, their families) as equal members of one body, was "the Israel of God" (Gal. 6:16). The olive tree of Abraham continued, but with some old (Jewish) branches broken off and some new (Gentile) branches grafted in (Rom. 11:11–24). The church received the titles of Israel: "a chosen people, a royal priesthood, a holy nation, a people for his own possession" (1 Peter 2:9–10; cf. Ex. 19:6; Titus 2:14).

The new form of the people of God involves many new things. No longer is there a literal tabernacle or temple; Jesus himself is the temple, and he dwells, by his Spirit, within his people, so that in a sense they become the temple (John 2:19–21; 1 Cor. 3:16–17; 6:19; 2 Cor. 6:16). Nor are the new people of God identified, even roughly, with a particular group of clans

---

7. Kline, "Divine Kingship and Gen. 6:1–4," *Westminster Theological Journal* 24 (1962): 187–204. In Kline's view, "kingship" is one of the major unifying themes of the early chapters of Genesis: God himself as royal creator, the sun and moon "ruling" day and night (1:16), man to have dominion over the earth (1:28; 9:1–3), man's failure to exercise godly rule (chap. 3), the genealogies (see text).

or tribes; it is an international body destined to cover the globe (Matt. 28:19–20). It has a government, as did Israel, but that government does not possess the power of the sword (Matt. 26:51–52), but rather "the sword of the Spirit, which is the word of God" (Eph. 6:17). It conquers through love and persuasion, rather than by violence (Matt. 5:38–48; Rom. 12:9–21).

No modern nation, or its government (state), then, will ever play the distinctive role filled by Old Testament Israel. God's purposes now are wider and broader; the whole world is the promised land (Matt. 28:19–20; 1 Cor. 3:21–23; Eph. 6:3). We no longer need the types and shadows of the tabernacle and temple, for we have the reality in Christ (Heb. 8–10). Modern nations continue to act as God's servants to maintain justice and order. But even believing nations, if such there be, will not play the distinctive role of Israel, and neither will their governments. These states need not take Israel's distinctive purposes into account as they rule.

In the modern world, then, each Christian is a citizen of two nations: an earthly nation and the heavenly nation (Eph. 2:6), which is not of this world (John 18:36), the church. Although we belong entirely to Christ, we do not on that account renounce our citizenship in the earthly nations, any more than we leave our earthly families. Indeed, we seek to be good citizens, for those earthly nations themselves, and their rulers, receive their authority from God (Rom. 13:1–7).

The church has its national and tribal leaders, its elders and deacons (1 Tim. 3), who not only preach and teach, administer sacraments, and so on, but also provide services that the elders and kings provided in Israel. They resolve disputes (1 Cor. 5:1–6:8) and lead in battle (Rom. 13:12; Eph. 6:10–18; 1 Thess. 5:8).

The state also has its own leaders, who perform the corresponding services for their clans. We seek as much as possible to be obedient to both, though we are first of all citizens of heaven. When we have disputes we can't settle with other believers, we take them to the church elders (1 Cor. 6:1–8); when we have similar disputes with unbelievers, we take them to the state. When we seek leadership in the battle against Satan, we turn to the rulers of the church, for the state can't help us there; when we seek physical defense against physical attacks, we turn to the state, for the church has no swords, and we, being also citizens in good standing of the earthly nations, have as much right to their protection as anyone (Acts 25:11).[8] We know, however, that when the church wins *its* battle, no more swords will be needed; so the spiritual battle is still the ultimate one.

---

8. We do go to the church to pray and to seek the prayers of others, and those prayers are more effective than the physical weapons wielded by the state.

The church and the earthly nations are related, then, like two different families with overlapping members, occupying the same territory. They both serve the kingdom of God, but it is misleading, in my view, to describe them as two institutional forms of the kingdom coordinate with one another, as is often done in Reformed literature. The church is the organization whose goal is the spreading of God's kingdom throughout the earth. The state, if it is not a Christian state, does not share that goal at all, but may in spite of itself perform some services for the kingdom of God. If the state *is* Christian, it will represent the church in its earthly concerns, using earthly tools denied to the church as such, defending it from physical attack and so forth. It will be a kind of adjunct tool for the church, not an institution coordinate with it.

In short, there are two families: the family of Adam and the family of Christ. Each has grown very large, and has therefore developed complicated governmental structures. These structures are similar. Both have written laws. Both have title to territory on the earth. Both are ruled by "elders" and other officers. Both have judicial functions. Both are religious, for they both operate according to ultimate values.[9] There are also, of course, differences between these two families. The family of Christ may not bear the sword to advance its territory. The family of Adam is not authorized to administer the sacraments.

Believers are both children of Adam and children of Christ. So they live in both kingdoms. But on the last day the only children of Adam who will survive God's judgment are those who are also children of Christ. The family of Jesus will overshadow the family of Adam, so that only one family will continue into the eternal state.

What we call "states," then, are the governmental structures of the family of Adam. "Church government" is the ruling body of the family of Christ.

Should the state be Christian? Certainly. Every human being and every human institution ought to be Christian. First Corinthians 10:31 tells us to do all things to the glory of God. Christians in state government should bring their Christian values to bear on that institution. A government made up of Christians who apply their faith will be a Christian government. To say this, of course, is not to prejudge in detail what sort of government will result. I have rejected the view that modern governments should follow the Mosaic civil law in exhaustive detail. So the process of making a government Christian has many open questions.

9. Some states of the family of Adam actually have established religions. Others, like the United States, embrace secular humanism, which is also a religion. (Recall my discussion of religion in chapter 5.)

Should the state be governed by Scripture? Certainly. All of life should be governed by God's Word. Scripture does not give us a detailed manual of modern statecraft, but it contains principles that should be followed. As we shall see, some believe that the state should be governed only by natural law or natural revelation. I see no reason for such a limitation, though there may be pragmatic reasons at times for Christians to defend their views of government by reference to nature, rather than to Scripture.[10]

Should the state recognize Jesus Christ as king? Yes, for that is who he is—the King of kings and the Lord of lords.[11]

OTHER VIEWS OF THE STATE

EARLY NON-CHRISTIAN THOUGHT

In chapter 4, I indicated that non-Christian thought always finds itself in the dilemma of rationalism and irrationalism. When applied to questions of government, the rationalist side leads to totalitarianism and the irrational- ist side to anarchy. The rationalist believes that very smart people are able to, and should be allowed to, control all aspects of life in a society. The irrationalist prefers no government at all, for he denies the competence of any human mind to govern the lives of others. Many non-Christian think- ers, of course, are unsatisfied with either alternative, at least for practical reasons: who would really like to live either in a totalitarian despotism or in an anarchy? But they are not able to argue persuasively for a middle ground. Arguments for law and order, carried out consistently, lead to totalitarianism. Arguments for freedom lead to anarchy.

Plato carries out his rationalism to defend a totalitarian rule by philoso- pher kings. The irrationalist Sophists teach their students to say anything that will ingratiate them to higher authorities. They seek a middle ground, but they renounce the use of any standards that could provide a normative definition of that middle ground. Aristotle's thought also has totalitarian tendencies, since for him the state is the partnership that includes and governs all other partnerships. But he tries to moderate the implications of

10. See appendix F, "Is Natural Revelation Sufficient to Govern Culture?"

11. When I began thinking about family, church, and state, I first planned to discuss these as three perspectives: family (existential), church (normative), and state (situational). I still think there is truth in this account. In the present world, this is how the three institu- tions come together in our experience. But it seemed to me that the Bible is more redemp- tive-historical in its presentation of these institutions, telling two stories of two families.

this view with talk of avoiding extremes (the golden mean). Later, Machiavelli argued that a ruler should use methods contrary to traditional (i.e., Christian) morality to increase his own glory and to secure his political goals. Today, most readers consider these approaches at best unpersuasive and at worst terrifying. What they share is the lack of a normative standard that sets forth the nature and limitations of state power.

SOCIAL CONTRACT THEORY

Among non-Christian (and some Christian) ethical theorists, the most common way of defining and justifying the authority of government is social contract theory. This approach is attributed to Socrates in Plato's writings, and Epicurus also develops his view of justice along these lines. More recent exponents of a social contract approach are Hobbes, Bodin, Locke, Rousseau, and, in our own time, John Rawls and David Gauthier. One of the Westminster divines, Samuel Rutherford, developed a biblically based version of the social contract in his book *Lex, Rex*.

On a social contract view, the authority and character of government is defined by an agreement of people to be ruled by a particular system of institutions and laws. Some have thought that such an agreement actually took place as a historical event, but David Hume expressed doubts that such an event ever happened,[12] and his doubts have prevailed. The common view among modern contract theorists is that the contract is "hypothetical." That is, we should act "as if" we had subscribed to a contract. But why? Even if there had been an actual historical contract, questions would arise as to why it would bind the descendants of those people who actually agreed to it. But if the contract is only hypothetical, then there is even less reason for those who question its terms to abide by it.

Contract theorists have differed among themselves as to "the state of nature," the nature of society before the contract (or, hypothetically, what it would have been like if the contract were not in force). To Hobbes, the state of nature is a state of war, a war of all against all, making life "solitary, poor, nasty, brutish, and short."[13] To Rousseau, however, the state of nature was far better than any form of civilization. For him, civilization is responsible for the evils of life. Locke, under the influence of Samuel Rutherford's *Lex, Rex*, maintains a middle ground: the state of nature is a state of liberty and equality, in which human beings seek to administer the natural law

---

12. Hume, "Of the Original Contract," available at http://www.constitution.org/dh/origcont.htm.
13. Hobbes, *Leviathan*.

in their own lives and those of others.[14] However, it lacks an established, public law and a generally acknowledged, impartial authority.

Contract theorists also disagree as to the nature of the government formed by the social contract. In Hobbes and Rousseau, contracting individuals give up all their natural rights, except self-defense, to a totalitarian commonwealth (which Hobbes called Leviathan). In Locke, the contract restricts the powers of government. For him, the power of government extends no farther than necessary to protect the life, liberty, and property of the governed, and no farther than is determined by the consent of the governed. To maintain this limitation of government power, Locke advocates checks and balances. He opposes absolute monarchy and warns that even the legislature may be tempted to exercise capricious and arbitrary power.

Locke's position is familiar, for it is echoed in the founding documents of the United States of America. His view of government itself is arguably Christian. But as a basis for the existence and powers of government, the social contract is as unpersuasive in Locke as it is in Hobbes and Rousseau. The differences among social contract thinkers as to the state of nature and the state of society under government indicates that the so-called social contract is not an objective reality that we can investigate to gain certainty about our rights and responsibilities. It is rather an empty vessel into which philosophers pour those ideas that seem right to them on other grounds. The move to a hypothetical view of the contract makes it even less persuasive as a basis for government.

Rutherford, however, in *Lex, Rex*, develops a social contract theory based on the Bible, which gives the idea a much more substantial basis. He argues from Scripture (as I did above in the section on "The Two Families") that Israelite kings had a dual authorization: from God, by anointing, and from the elders of Israel. The involvement of the elders creates a kind of contract, which can be defined historically (contra Hume). In Rutherford's view, the people are free from their obligations if the king breaks the contract. I shall have more to say on this idea at a later point.

Roman Catholic Thought

So I move on to consider distinctively Christian views of the state. As opposed to secular writers, Christians necessarily deal in some way with what Scripture teaches about the state. They also have to reckon with the relationship between the state and the church.

14. Locke, *Two Treatises of Government*.

The Roman Catholic view is a consequence of its general distinction between nature and grace, which I discussed in chapter 17.[15] For Thomas Aquinas, the doctrine of the state can be determined by natural (Aristotelian) reason: the state is the highest social entity to which all citizens belong. It governs the natural life of mankind. Even if the fall had not happened, some such organization would have been necessary. But after the fall, God appoints another agency, the church, to bring saving grace to man.

To most Protestants, such as Luther, the opposite is the case: for them, even before the fall, there was a worshiping community, a church, but no state, because the state is an instrument of force, and before the fall no force was needed. Only after the fall does the state become necessary. Depending on how one defines "church" and "state," either view is possible. If the church is merely a worshiping community, then it is a prefall institution. If it is a dispenser of saving grace, then it is uniquely postfall. If the state is merely a pattern of social authority, then it would appropriately exist in an unfallen world. But if it is distinctly an instrument of force, then it can exist only after the fall.

So Aquinas's view of how the fall affects church and state is biblically possible. But his choice of that possibility reflects his view that the state governs human society apart from grace, while the church has the responsibility of dispensing grace to sinners for their salvation. The state helps us to find earthly happiness, while the church guides us to eternal happiness. The state governs our natural life, while the church governs our supernatural life. Or, as it is sometimes put (rather simplistically), the state governs the affairs of the body, while the church governs the affairs of the soul.

For Aquinas, the church and the state govern distinct spheres of human life, and each is basically autonomous in its own realm. Nevertheless, the church is the higher of the two governments. It is, indeed, the extension of the incarnation of Christ. So where there is conflict between church and state, the church ought to prevail.[16] The state operates according to natural law, the church according to Scripture. But Scripture contains a better knowledge of natural law than anyone can have without it. So the

15. I have discussed many other ramifications of this distinction, which I consider to be unbiblical: the Lutheran distinction between law and gospel (chapter 12), the natural-law approach to ethics (chapter 14), the doctrine of the twofold end (chapter 17), the distinction between religious and nonreligious (chapters 5, 26), and Kline's distinction between the holy and the common (chapter 29). More will follow.

16. In his epistemology, Aquinas teaches that natural reason can operate adequately apart from revelation. But when there is a conflict between revelation and natural reason, the former must prevail. So Scripture has a veto over reason, but does not govern its day-to-day operations.

church, expert in Scripture, has the right and obligation to instruct the state as to the meaning of natural law.

In some historical situations, this view has led the Roman church to assert direct power in the political realm. Pope Boniface VIII believed that a pope could remove a heretical ruler from his secular office. Others, such as Bellarmine, argued that the church, because of its spiritual character, should express its superiority by enlightenment and persuasion, not by exercising physical force. The twentieth-century Thomist Jacques Maritain argued that since the church is by nature spiritual, it fulfills its nature most perfectly in a democracy, where it has no coercive power.

In Roman Catholic thought, the state may assist the church, by creating conditions of order, by acknowledging God, and by seeing that the church has the freedom to worship and teach its doctrines. But the state gets its bearings from natural law, not from Scripture. On this view, the state is secular, not religious. Its government is based on natural reason, not revelation.

Against this sort of view, I have argued four points: (1) All of human life, even reason, is to be governed by God's revelation. (2) Scripture does not warrant the Roman Catholic distinctions between nature and grace, natural reason and revelation, or the doctrine of the twofold end of man. (3) Scripture does not give divine authorization for a "state" as defined by Aquinas, but only for the family. One family development leads to the state and another to the church, but these have essentially the same prerogatives, although God has denied the sword to the church. (4) So Scripture does not distinguish between one institution limited to natural law and another one with access to the fullness of God's revelation in Scripture.

ANABAPTISM

The Thomistic distinction between church and state becomes far more radical in the Anabaptist branch of the Reformation.[17] The Schleitheim Confession, article 6, says:

> The sword is ordained of God outside the perfection of Christ. It punishes and puts to death the wicked, and guards and protects the good. In the Law the sword was ordained for the punishment

17. There was much variety in the views of those originally called "Anabaptist." Thomas Munzer's violent warriors, though also called Anabaptists, certainly held a different view from the Schleitheim Confession and John Howard Yoder. But the most prevalent view of that tradition today is the one discussed here.

of the wicked and for their death, and the same (sword) is (now) ordained to be used by the worldly magistrates.

In the perfection of Christ, however, only the ban is used for a warning and for the excommunication of the one who has sinned, without putting the flesh to death—simply the warning and the command to sin no more.

A modern representative of this tradition is John Howard Yoder, author of *The Politics of Jesus.*[18] Yoder denies that God has granted any legitimate authority to the state. Rather, the state is satanic. Yoder notes that in Matthew 4, the temptation story, "Jesus did not challenge the claim of Satan to be able to dispose of the rule of all nations."[19] He also appeals to Revelation 13, where he finds "an image of government largely comparable to the one we referred to in the earliest portions of the Gospels. The 'Powers' are seen as persecuting the true believers; the same is true in the assumed background of Peter and James."[20]

But what of Romans 13:1–7, which, on the usual interpretation, speaks of the civil magistrate as a "minister of God," appointed by the Lord to punish evil and reward good? Yoder thinks this traditional interpretation fails to see the relationship of the passage to its context in 12:14–21 and 13:8–10, in which the apostle urges Christians to respond in love to persecution. In fact, Yoder says, all three chapters, 12–14, focus on "Christian nonconformity and suffering love as driven and drawn by a sense of God's triumphant movement from the merciful past into a triumphant future."[21] So, "any interpretation of Rom. 13:1–7 that would make it the expression of a static or conservative undergirding of the present social system would therefore represent a refusal to take seriously the context."[22]

In 12:19, God forbids Christians to exercise vengeance, but in 13:4 that is exactly what the state does. Yoder says, "It is inconceivable that these two verses, using such similar language, should be made to be read independently of one another."[23]

In Yoder's view, "The subordination that is called for [in Rom. 13] recognizes whatever power exists, accepts whatever structure of sovereignty happens to prevail. The text does not affirm, as the tradition has it, a divine

18. Grand Rapids: Eerdmans, 1972.
19. Ibid., 195.
20. Ibid., 196.
21. Ibid., 198.
22. Ibid.
23. Ibid., 199.

act of institution or ordination of a particular government."[24] This distinction is something like the distinction in Reformed theology between God's decretive and preceptive wills. The state exists by God's rule of history: he allows or permits it to exist for his good purposes.[25] But he gives the state no normative authority. The state is, in this respect, like Satan himself: "God is not said to *create* or *institute* or *ordain* the powers that be, but only to *order* them, to put them in order, sovereignly to tell them where they belong, what is their place."[26]

But don't verses 4 and 6 speak of these powers as God's servants (*diakonoi*, v. 4) and ministers (*leitourgoi*, v. 6)? In verse 6, Yoder takes the view that *leitourgoi* is actually the subject of the sentence: "The ministers of God are there for this very purpose, as they persist"—referring to those who pay taxes in the first part of the verse. So the ministers are the Christian believers, not the civil powers.

This exegesis of Romans 13 fits into Yoder's larger theses: the state is wrong to bear the sword, and the Christian should not support or participate in the state's use of force. The state is one of the tribulations God allows to afflict Christians, and they should respond to it in suffering love, as in Romans 12:14–21 and 13:8–10. But they should not regard the state as having any divine authority. We are called to be subordinate, not to obey.[27]

I don't find this argument persuasive. Yoder's view of Romans 13:6 is convoluted. He admits that it is "subject to the risks of probability."[28] And he doesn't discuss how it coheres with the very similar language of verse 4.

Contrary to Yoder, further, the contexts of 12:14–21 and 13:8–10 certainly do not exclude the traditional interpretation. Paul there calls believers to follow the law of love, and part of that is to be obedient to civil law. The notion that the civil government is an enemy of the gospel can be found nowhere in Romans 12 or 13.

As for the contrast between Romans 12:19 and 13:4, it is simply the case that individual Christians are not permitted to take vengeance, for vengeance is the Lord's, a common biblical theme (e.g., Deut. 32:35, 41, 43; Ps. 94:1; Isa. 35:4; 61:2). God has also, as we have seen, withheld the sword from the church. But the apparent meaning of Romans 13 is that God has appointed the civil magistrate to bear the sword, serving as his agent of

24. Ibid., 200. The passage is in italics in the original, since Yoder uses this whole sentence as a section heading.

25. Of course, in Reformed theology God not only permits or allows evil, but decrees its existence, without condoning it. See *DG*, 160–82.

26. Yoder, *The Politics of Jesus*, 203 (emphasis his).

27. Ibid., 212.

28. Ibid., 210.

vengeance, as Israel brought his vengeance against the Canaanite tribes. So, as individuals, we should abstain from taking vengeance, but civil magistrates have a special commission from God to take vengeance in his name in certain situations. I see no reason to question that apparent meaning.

Revelation 13 presents various earthly powers under Satan's control, but it doesn't identify these specifically as states. They could just as easily be (and, I think, in some cases are) religious organizations or false churches. As for Matthew 4, we should not assume that Satan tells the truth when he claims some sort of dominion over kingdoms. But if he is telling the truth, he is not the legitimate ruler of the kingdoms of the world. Jesus and his followers came to deliver the nations from his dominion.

Yoder's analysis does illustrate the difficulties involved in identifying a specific divine warrant for state authority. But I have argued that what we call the state is simply a set of functions exercised by the family of Adam. Yoder should have given more consideration to the authority of the family, especially to its statelike functions. Whatever plausibility may attach to the idea that the state is satanic, it is utterly implausible to make the family an arm of Satan's empire. It is rather the case that some family-states are under Satan's dominion, others are under God's dominion, and still others (most, I think) are in a struggle between these two powers.

Genesis 9:6, as I indicated, gives statelike powers to Noah's family. The Anabaptist tradition generally sees the Old Testament negatively, as a divine accommodation to spiritual immaturity. But Genesis 9:6 is a divine command. God also commands the Canaanite conquests and reproves Israel for not being sufficiently warlike. So it is not biblically possible simply to link all civil authority with Satan.

We shall consider the pacifist implications of Yoder's position under the sixth commandment. For now, we had better consider other alternatives.

LUTHERANISM

Luther's Large Catechism, like the Westminster Larger Catechism, derives the state from the family, agreeing with the perspective of this chapter: "The primary locus of authority resides with parents, and that all other human authority derives from that."[29] But I am less sympathetic with his developed view of church and state.

The Lutheran view, like the Roman Catholic, sees church and state as governing two distinct spheres of human life, and, like the Roman Catholic view, it regards the sphere of the state as governed by reason and natural

---

29. Section on the fourth commandment (our fifth).

law,[30] rather than by the whole content of Scripture. As in the Roman view, Scripture instructs the state as to natural law, and it may contradict the interpretations of that law given by political authorities.

The Lutheran approach, however, recognizes better than the Roman the extent to which sin can corrupt both state and church. In this regard, there is some affinity between the Lutheran view and the Anabaptist view. Lutherans, however, deny the Anabaptist view that the state is satanic. Rather, the state has a divinely given authority over its subjects. Yet it is something less than God's best. God's justice is his "strange work," compared to his grace and mercy. Like the Anabaptists, Lutherans find it hard to understand how the God of love could be involved in bloodshed and war. Anabaptists, in the end, deny that God authorizes such an institution. Lutherans accept that he does, but they find it paradoxical.

The distinctively Lutheran formulation is found in the context of "Luther's distinction between the two kingdoms (or the two reigns) of God: the earthly or left-hand kingdom and the heavenly or right-hand kingdom."[31] God reigns over the left-hand kingdom (the state) by the law, and over the right-hand kingdom (the church) by both the law and the gospel.[32] The state is distinctly a postfall institution (contrary to the Roman Catholic understanding), for it uses the forces unleashed by the fall in the interest of God's justice. This is another affinity between Lutheranism and Anabaptism, though Lutheranism is far more moderate.

Lutherans argue that it is impossible to impose upon fallen creatures the law of love given in the gospel. We cannot turn unbelievers into Christians by force. God evangelizes the lost only through the Word. Nor should we imagine that civil society can be governed by the law of love and forgiveness. So various writers have said that it is wrong to try to Christianize unbelieving culture. Rather, the general society should be governed entirely by natural revelation.

In my judgment, there are a number of problems with this view:

1. Natural revelation itself commands all people to worship the true God. Paul in Romans 1 says that idolatry is a sin against the knowledge given in natural revelation. But the two-kingdoms view rejects the notion that government should instruct people to worship the true God. So the two-

---

30. Luther himself was skeptical of the idea of natural law, but it took root in later Lutheranism. At least, it has always been the case that in Lutheranism the state is governed by law, not gospel.

31. Lutheran Church of Australia, "The Two Kingdoms," available at www.lca.org.au/resources/csbq/twokingdoms.pdf.

32. Recall my discussion of the law-gospel distinction in chapter 12.

kingdoms view not only denies the relevance of special revelation to government, but also denies the foundational aspects of natural revelation.

2. Scripture does not warrant a two-kingdoms view. In the Bible, Christ rules, not only over human hearts, not only over the church, but also over nations. "Jesus is Lord" had a clear, political meaning in ancient Roman culture: it was the announcement of the coming of a new king. The gospel itself is the news that the kingdom of God is at hand. Although Jesus' kingdom is "not of this world" (John 18:36), it is over this world, over everything in heaven and on earth (Matt. 28:18). So Scripture teaches a "one-kingdom" view.

3. Making the Bible authoritative for civil government does not imply that government should force unbelievers to become Christians, or to behave as Christians. The Bible doesn't require government to do that (but see point 6 below). Even in the Israelite theocracy, people were not penalized for worshiping false gods as such. Scripture condemns the unbelieving heart, but it never makes unbelief a civil crime. Indeed, there are many sins (pride, envy, etc.) that God abhors, but which cannot and should not be made civil crimes on a biblical understanding.

4. A one-kingdom view does not mean that civil society should be governed by love and forgiveness, rather than by force. Scripture itself denies that that is so. As we have seen, Scripture withholds the sword from the church, but gives it to the civil government. Note again the comparison between Romans 12:14–21 and 13:1–7 in my earlier discussion of Anabaptism.

5. Nor does a one-kingdom view imply that non-Christians are disqualified from government positions. Scripture acknowledges the authority of pagan kings, including the Roman emperors, as representatives of God in the civil realm, deserving of obedience. But faith in the true God certainly does give to some people special wisdom for public service, even in unbelieving societies—witness Joseph and Daniel.

6. Old Testament law does restrict some external manifestations of unbelief, such as idolatry. In my judgment, idolatry should not be a civil crime today (see chapter 13). But we should consider this matter in perspective. All lawbreaking comes from false religion. When someone steals or murders, it is because he is not faithful to his Creator. So any legislation of justice limits the freedom of false religion. It is impossible for government to be religiously neutral, as the two-kingdoms view requires.

7. Similarly, any genuine improvement in society comes from true religion. Those who oppose "Christianizing" society in effect oppose most of the good developments in science, the arts, the care for the poor, and so forth, of the last two thousand years under the impetus of the gospel. To

influence society in a Christian direction is not to force unbelievers to be Christians, but it is to favor justice over injustice, good over evil, mercy over cruelty. As I said in point 3 above, there are, of course, right and wrong ways to Christianize. But it is hard to imagine that anyone, Christian or non-Christian, would want to live in a society devoid of the benefits that Christianity has brought to civilization.

8. Many have argued that the two-kingdoms view opened up the German Lutheran churches to Nazi domination. For on the two-kingdoms view, the church may not demand that the state bow to the kingship of Christ. The church, then, becomes privatized, concerned with its individual and corporate piety, but not with society in general. That criticism is not entirely fair. Certainly Lutheran thinkers have encouraged Christians as individuals to take an active part in politics and to oppose injustice by appeal to natural law. And some Lutherans did participate in the resistance to Hitler. But, as we have seen, a right knowledge of natural law presupposes Scripture (chapter 14). Denial of the right of Scripture to criticize government opens the door wide to injustice, even atrocity.

9. It has always perplexed me that the two-kingdoms view, which emphasizes the distinctive spirituality of the church, has historically been hospitable to an Erastian view of church government, in which a civil ruler becomes the head of the church. The Erastian tendency in Lutheranism is historically understandable, because of the role of the German princes in protecting Luther from persecution by the Roman church. Certainly any Christian would agree that one role of the state is to protect the church. But the notion of the state-church, in which the church becomes an agency of the state, is hard to reconcile with a two-kingdoms understanding. On the other hand, perhaps Erastianism is an extreme implication of the proposition that, even in the church, rule is a matter of law, not gospel. So rule, even in the church itself, is something best performed by a secular officer.[33] I find that idea biblically impossible, given the spiritual qualifications of church rulers in 1 Timothy 3, but it is a measure of the anomalies to which the two-kingdoms view can lead.

10. The two-kingdoms view is very much like the view of Meredith G. Kline that I discussed in chapter 29. On the basis of Genesis 4–9, Kline argues for a "realm of common grace," common rather than holy, and therefore religiously neutral. Kline's argument may be the best one available to show that Scripture teaches divine authorization for a secular state, Luther's "kingdom of the left hand." But in that discussion I gave reason to believe that such a realm does not exist.

---

33. Thanks to my friend John Barber for this suggestion.

11. In Scripture, contrary to Luther, there is nothing "strange" or para-doxical about the fact that God judges wickedness. Indeed, nothing is more typical of him. If anything, it is God's grace to undeserving sinners that is hard to understand.[34]

12. Finally, the two-kingdoms view assumes that God has ordained the state as an institution distinct from the family. I have shown that there is no evidence for that in Scripture. So there is no evidence of any institu-tion that is bound only by natural law and not by the fullness of God's revelation in Scripture.

CALVIN AND RUTHERFORD

John Calvin more or less adopted the two-kingdoms view of Luther, although he is more explicit on the need for Christians to be active in the political order. He also has a more positive view of government than either the Anabaptists or the Lutherans. While they saw government as satanic (Anabaptism) or "God's left hand" (Lutheranism), Calvin discusses at length the benefits that come to Christians because of God's ordination of government.[35] He stresses also that government must attend to both tables of the Decalogue, not only the second, but he does not explain how such a duty is compatible with the secularity of the state.[36]

Calvin, like others in the Reformed tradition, opens the door to forc-ible resistance to injustice. He is cautious about opening this door. But after several sections of the *Institutes* urging believers to be subject even to wicked rulers, he adds this:

> For if there are now any magistrates of the people, appointed to restrain the willfulness of kings (as in ancient times the ephors were set against the Spartan kings, or the tribunes of the people against the Roman consuls, or the demarchs against the senate of the Athenians; and perhaps, as things now are, such power as the three estates exercise in every realm when they hold their chief assemblies), I am so far from forbidding them to withstand, in accordance with their duty, the fierce licentiousness of kings, that, if they wink at kings who violently fall upon and assault the lowly common folk, I declare that their dissimulation involves nefarious

---

34. To be sure, "God is love" is a defining concept (1 John 4:8). But so is "the LORD, whose name is Jealous" (Ex. 34:14). On the notion of a fundamental attribute of God, see *DG*, 392–94.

35. *Institutes*, 4.20.2–5.

36. Ibid., 4.20.9.

perfidy, because they dishonestly betray the freedom of the people, of which they know that they have been appointed protectors by God's ordinance.[37]

Here he declares that if the king behaves lawlessly, lesser magistrates must hold him accountable. Thus he opposes absolute monarchy and places all rulers under law. Then in the final section of the *Institutes* he urges Christians not to obey rulers when they command sin against God: "If they command anything against God, let it go unesteemed."[38]

Samuel Rutherford (1600–1661), in *Lex, Rex*, goes further. In his view, government is ordained by God, but is also a matter of contract between ruler and people, as we saw earlier in the case of Saul, David, Rehoboam, and Jeroboam. When the ruler breaks the contract, he loses his authority to rule, and may be resisted, even overthrown. Like Calvin, Rutherford insists that such resistance or deposition be led by magistrates, people who themselves have legitimate civil authority. Thus, to overthrow a ruler in such cases does not violate Romans 13. It is rather obedience to a legitimate authority over against one who has forfeited that authority.

This view contributed to the religious wars in England and Scotland. Puritans and Scottish Covenanters appealed to these arguments to resist what they considered to be the unjust decrees of the king and the state church. Many Christians of Calvinistic persuasion were also among those who rebelled against the rule of George III over the American colonies. In England, the American Revolution was sometimes called "the Presbyterian revolt." Among Reformed believers on the side of the colonies, the rationale for revolution was essentially that of Calvin and Rutherford: the king had ruled lawlessly, and so the lesser magistrates in the colonies had a right to resist him and ultimately to overthrow his rule.

ABRAHAM KUYPER

Kuyper (1837–1920) was a remarkable Reformed leader, who emphasized that Christ was Lord of all aspects of human life.[39] He himself entered many fields of endeavor, writing and teaching theology and philosophy, leading a separatist movement from the state church which became the Reformed (*Gereformeerde*) Churches in the Netherlands, founding the Free University of Amsterdam, founding two newspapers and writing often

37. Ibid., 4.20.31.
38. Ibid., 4.20.32. Cf. John Calvin, *Commentaries on the Book of the Prophet Daniel* (reprint, Grand Rapids: Baker Book House, 1979), at 6:22.
39. See especially his *Lectures on Calvinism* (Grand Rapids: Eerdmans, 1943).

for them, and leading the Anti-revolutionary Party. As a politician, he served as prime minister of the Netherlands from 1901 to 1905.

All the thinkers considered previously in this section thought of government in terms of a nature/grace contrast. Kuyper broke with this kind of thinking. For him, family, church, and state were simply three spheres of authority ordained by God. God has given each one authority over its own sphere of life; so Kuyper and his disciples spoke of "sphere sovereignty," *souvereiniteit in eigen kring.*[40]

So the state has authority from God, defined by God's Word. It has the responsibility to compel mutual respect in society, to defend the weak, and to collect taxes for national purposes. The state should respect the domains of other spheres: that is the basis of freedom. The state must not interfere in the "internal workings" of the family or the church.

Kuyper believes, like Luther and the Anabaptists, that the state is a postfall institution. The state uses force to make people do what they would rather not do. If man hadn't fallen, Kuyper believes, such force would never have been necessary. Rather, human beings would do the right thing from the workings of conscience and moral suasion. The latter motivation Kuyper described as "organic," the use of force "mechanical." Kuyper (as also in his account of biblical inspiration) placed great emphasis on the organic, as opposed to the mechanical.

The state must observe God's law in Scripture, according to Kuyper, but it should not be a theocracy. A theocracy would be a government with direct access to God, as ancient Israel consulted God through the Urim and the Thummim (Ex. 28:30; Num. 27:21). The government nevertheless has an obligation to protect the church, and it should also punish blasphemy, not because of its impiety, but because it impugns God as the foundation of the state. The state should not, however, attempt to extirpate false religion, because it is not competent to make judgments as to which churches are true and which are false.

Unlike the two-kingdoms view, Kuyper places both church and state under the authority of special revelation, as well as general revelation. Herman Dooyeweerd and his disciples, generally Kuyperian in their orientation, later reverted to a natural law view of ethics and government, since they came to believe that the Bible dealt only with matters of faith.[41]

---

40. This is the title of Kuyper's 1880 Inaugural Lecture at the founding of the Free University. That lecture is the source of Kuyper's famous words, "There is not a square inch in the whole domain of our human existence over which Christ, who is Sovereign over all, does not cry 'Mine.'"

41. See John Frame, *The Amsterdam Philosophy* (Phillipsburg, NJ: Harmony Press, 1972), available at www.frame-poythress.org.

Kuyper's emphasis on the comprehensiveness and sufficiency of biblical revelation was developed by the theonomic movement, which I discussed and criticized in chapter 13.

My own view is closer to Kuyper's than to any other figures we have discussed in this chapter. We must determine the nature and prerogatives of the state from Scripture—*sola Scriptura*. The nature/grace dichotomy is not helpful in determining the legitimacy and competencies of these institutions. But I do not agree with Kuyper that family, church, and state are radically distinct spheres. The state is the family of Adam; the church is the family of Christ. Both families are trying to accomplish the same things for their members, but in the end only the family of Christ will prevail. We must expect conflict between these families, as each tries to claim for its own lord "the whole domain of human existence" (see footnote 40).

SHOULD CHURCHES BE POLITICALLY ACTIVE?

Churches today are in a quandary as to how they should be involved in the political process. Much has been said about the "separation of church and state."[42] Some have advocated a militant stance against social and political evil; others have argued that the job of the church is to preach the gospel, and so the church should avoid politics altogether.

The task of the church is set forth in the Great Commission, which involves not only baptizing, but also discipling, "teaching them to observe all that I have commanded you" (Matt. 28:20). God has not given the sword to the church; our only weapon is the sword of the Spirit, the Word of God. But the Word of God speaks comprehensively to all aspects of human life (1 Cor. 10:31). The Great Commission does not restrict the church to preaching a simple gospel, the way to escape divine judgment. Rather, the preaching of the church presents to the world a way of life that transforms everything, including politics. Christians are not saved, of

42. I agree with John Jefferson Davis, in *Evangelical Ethics* (Phillipsburg, NJ: P&R Publishing, 1993), that the U.S. Constitution does not mandate the separation of church and state as that is usually defined today. It says in effect that Congress shall make no law to create a state church. At the time of the ratification of the Constitution, a number of states had established churches. The writers of the Constitution did not intend to eliminate these, but to keep the federal government from creating its own state church. Of course, "in recent years the federal courts have taken this to mean a virtual separation of Christian *values* from government, rather than a separation of church and state as *institutions*, but that is, as we shall see, an understanding quite foreign to the intention of the framers of the Constitution and Bill of Rights" (p. 10).

course, by political action. But they must bring their faith with them into their families, their workplaces, and their politics.

Of course, in some cultures (like the ancient Roman, in which the New Testament was written) there is not much that Christians can do, other than pray, to influence political structures and policies. But when they can influence them, they should. In modern democracies, all citizens are "lesser magistrates" by virtue of the ballot box. Christians have an obligation to vote according to God's standards. And, as they are gifted and called, they should influence others to vote in the same way.

This is not to say that political choices are always obvious. Often we must choose the lesser of two evils (chapter 13). Candidate Mershon may have a better view of one issue than Candidate Beates, while Beates has a better view on a different issue. It is an art to weigh the importance of different issues and to come to a godly conclusion. Each of us should have a large amount of tolerance for other Christians who come to conclusions that are different from ours. Rarely will one issue trump all others, though I must say that I will never vote for a candidate who advocates or facilitates the killing of unborn children.

But what of the institutional church? Should the church, as church, ever take positions on political issues? Well, certainly, for many "political" issues are straightforward questions of morality. If the church is to preach the whole Word of God, it must preach against abortion, homosexuality, relativism, and so on.[43]

Ethical and political preaching do become problematic when specifics are involved. Now I have argued (in chapter 11) that *sola Scriptura* does not limit us to speaking on matters explicitly presented in Scripture. Preaching, like theology, is the *application* of the Word to situations in our own experience. We are to preach, not only that stealing is wrong, but that it is wrong for Phil to steal from Judy. But specificity does introduce new levels of difficulty. When issues become more specific, it often becomes more difficult to be sure of the biblical position. Certainly the church must oppose drunk driving, for example. But should it support a law that lowers the blood alcohol level to .07 percent for conviction of driving under the influence of alcohol? It may be useful for pastors to bring such issues before their congregations, but it might be difficult for them to be sure that one position or another is the will of God.

But in other specific cases the applications are so clear that there is no room for doubt. For example, if Jack assaults Bill, he should pay the legal

---

43. If anyone is troubled by the dangers of "moralism" in this context, review chapter 16.

penalty. If abortion is murder, then unborn children should be protected by law. At times we should be reluctant to apply God's Word to political issues, because of our own uncertainty. But there is no way to delineate precisely in advance when and where we should and should not make such applications.

Another danger, of course, is that churches will get so caught up in political activism that they lose sight of Christ. The solution is not to avoid political issues, but to see politics as Kuyper did, as an opportunity to promote the claims of King Jesus. It is also important that the church's message, including its political statements, exude the grace of Christ. Grace is not only the center of God's Word, but a vital element of our communication, even of law. Denunciation of the evils of the world only takes us so far. It can, indeed, be counterproductive, because people come to resent constant scolding. Law and gospel must be wrapped up in one another. Political preaching should show how God's grace itself impels us to live by standards that are different from those of the world (Ex. 20:2; Titus 2:11–13).[44]

There are other issues that we should be aware of. Churches can lose their tax exemptions, for example, if they are seen to be too political, especially if they endorse particular candidates for office. I think it is rarely useful to promote a particular candidate from the pulpit, because few candidates are entirely good. Within some limits, Christians should agree to disagree with one another in love over political matters. But there are extreme situations where the differences between candidates are clearly differences between good and evil. If another Hitler were running for office, for example, I believe that Christian preachers should oppose him from the pulpit, regardless of questions of tax exemptions. So God does not prohibit the church from entering even the most specific areas of political debate, but wisdom should often lead to restraint.

CIVIL DISOBEDIENCE AND REVOLUTION

Given that Christians, and even churches, have the right to seek political change, do they ever have the right to disobey existing political rulers—or even to rebel against them?

The general stance of the Christian, as Calvin eloquently points out in the last chapters of the *Institutes*, should be one of obedient submission, even to unjust and cruel rulers. Romans 13:1–7 and 1 Peter 2:13–17 are decidedly antirevolutionary in their emphasis.

44. Thanks to Pastor Tim Keller for this insight.

But, as Calvin also stressed, with Rutherford and later Reformed writers, there are limits to political obedience:

1. When the ruler requires us to sin against God, or forbids something that God commands, we must refuse (see chapter 31).

2. In some cases, especially emergencies, it is necessary to violate written laws so as to achieve higher social ends (see chapter 13, under "Priorities").

3. In some systems of law, including that in the United States, the only way to establish the unconstitutionality of a law is by means of a test case. Someone must break that law, undergo trial, and then use as a defense that the law is unconstitutional. Such test-case lawbreaking is not a violation of the overall *system* of law (see chapter 13), but rather attempts to purify the system by eliminating inappropriate legislation.

4. When the ruler himself violates the law, he is not immune from prosecution. "Lesser magistrates" should enforce the law against him. If the law requires him to leave office, he should be made to do so. If deposition of a ruler under such conditions requires force, then force should be used. If that happens, a sort of revolution has taken place, and Christians should support it.

5. Sometimes it is unclear who are "the governing authorities" of Romans 13:1. During the Vietnam War, for example, there were places where the Saigon government controlled territory by day and the Viet Cong controlled it by night. In such cases, to whom is the Christian to "be subject"? Questions as to which group has the right to govern can be hard to resolve, as are judgments as to who is likely to win the conflict. I would say that a Christian living in such areas should make his best judgment as to which contending army is most in accord with God's standards of justice and give his allegiance to them. But in doing so, he may find himself supporting what some might call a revolutionary movement.

Under some circumstances, then, Christians may find themselves supporting revolutionary movements. But their goal should always be the establishment of a stable government that they can honor in fifth commandment terms, giving their respect, submission, and financial support.

OPERATION RESCUE: A CASE STUDY IN CIVIL DISOBEDIENCE

From 1986 to 1994, members of Operation Rescue sat in front of the doors of abortion clinics, preventing people from entering. When authorities cited trespassing and other laws, Operation Rescue declined to obey, and many accepted imprisonment. Operation Rescue was disbanded after Planned

Parenthood won an $880,000 judgment against them in 1994,[45] but it has been replaced by Operation Rescue West and other organizations, which have generally used more conventional tactics in opposing abortion.

In this section, I will consider the legitimacy and value of the original (pre-1994) program of civil disobedience. Operation Rescue placed demonstrators in the entrances of abortion clinics to block them or at least to make it difficult and embarrassing for women to enter clinics to obtain abortions. In doing so, they violated trespassing laws and court orders of various kinds. But the protesters argued that these laws must be broken for the greater good of saving the lives of unborn children.

I believe that Operation Rescue was correct in its argument that we have an obligation to protect the innocent from unjust destruction (Prov. 24:11). I also agree that the unborn are proper objects of such concern. Sometimes, however, the Operation Rescue presentation of this argument went beyond Scripture. I heard representatives of that organization argue that every Christian must be involved in rescues, since otherwise they would be condoning evil and violating the biblical command to rescue the innocent. But of course we also have obligations to rescue drowning swimmers at the beach. Does that mean that every Christian must spend his time at the beach rescuing swimmers? I think not. The command to rescue is given (1) to individuals as the opportunity naturally arises in their lives (cf. the Good Samaritan) and (2) to the whole church, that each member might make some contribution to defeat the evil of abortion.[46] Those contributions depend upon gifts and opportunities, and therefore they vary a great deal from one Christian to another. To maintain that every Christian must participate in a particular project is to maintain that every Christian must participate in *all* worthy projects, which is an impossible burden for every individual. No, God recognizes our finitude. Our obligations before him take our finitude into account.

Having said this, I still believe that the rescue of unborn babies is a high priority for Christians today. A swimmer drowning by the beach has at least some physical resources to preserve his life. A baby in the womb, by contrast, is the weakest of the weak. He depends entirely on other people to defend his life.

But, contrary to the original Operation Rescue rhetoric, there are other ways to join the battle for the unborn. There is still much room for educational, political, and religious approaches that do not break the law. There are many legal ways of making life difficult for abortionists, especially if a

45. "History of Operation Rescue West," at http://www.operationrescue.org/?p=64.

46. In this respect, our obligation to rescue the dying is like the cultural mandate and the Great Commission: a responsibility of the church as a whole, rather than of every Christian individually (chapter 15).

community can be persuaded that it does not want abortion to be practiced in its midst. Proverbs 24:11 can be fulfilled by other means than by rescues. Indeed, it is arguable that in the long run (which is the most important perspective) these other methods will be more effective than rescues. Rescues certainly aroused public resentment. People who didn't understand the ethical issue easily sympathized with the clinics, the doctors, and the women who were being "harassed." Rescuers become identified with the general lawlessness in our country or with the disruptiveness of many "rights" organizations. The results have been (1) legislation and court decisions that have created special legal protections for abortionists and (2) more pro-choice politicians being elected and appointed to high office. Less dramatic activity might have been more effective in the long run.

But is it sinful to participate in a rescue? I believe not. Some would argue that we should never break the law as long as there are *some* legal means of accomplishing our purposes. But that principle is of doubtful scripturality, and it has the result of enfeebling Christian witness. When the Sanhedrin told Peter and John to stop preaching Christ, they might have come up with a "creative alternative," such as preaching Christ in some other place. But they answered that they would have to obey God and continue preaching (Acts. 4:19–20; cf. 5:29).

But even if we accept the principle of disobeying the law only when legal remedies are absent, I would have to say that even that principle falls short of ruling out all rescues. Granted, as I said above, there are other methods of dealing with the problem, ways which could have great effect upon the future of abortion. But we must focus on the short run as well as the long run. When Betty Groman makes a decision to have an abortion today, the long-range approach will not have much effect on her, however much it may affect other women later on. Those working on long-range solutions have done their best to change Betty's mind, and they have not succeeded. Now they have no more time. Her baby will die unless something more drastic happens. For that baby, there are *no* legal remedies. The mother, the doctor, and the law are all united to deprive that baby of life. The only answer is a rescue. And when rescuers are taken to prison because of their opposition to abortion, the rescuers are in the right and the law enforcers are in the wrong, for they are forbidding what God commands.

I therefore have supported Operation Rescue with money and prayers, and I do not believe it is wrong to participate in rescues if one counts the cost. But I do not think that this method is required of all Christians, and I do not myself now participate in such events. I believe that other, legal methods are more effective in the long run, and I believe I am ethically free to pursue those, rather than participating in rescues.

CHAPTER 33

The Fifth Commandment: Man and Woman

The fifth commandment applies to relations between "superiors" and "inferiors," but it also applies to "equals," according to the Larger Catechism:

> Q. 131. *What are the duties of equals?*
> A. The duties of equals are, to regard the dignity and worth of each other, in giving honor to go one before another; and to rejoice in each other's gifts and advancement, as their own.

> Q. 132. *What are the sins of equals?*
> A. The sins of equals are, besides the neglect of the duties required, the undervaluing of the worth, envying the gifts, grieving at the advancement of prosperity one of another; and usurping preeminence one over another.

The commandment is relevant to equals because, as we've seen, we owe "honor" to all people (1 Peter 2:17). The reason is that human life is something wonderfully precious, God's very image. We should respect that image, even in the worst of human beings.

Now the relation of man and woman[1] is a kind of transition between the relations of "superiority and inferiority" which we considered in the

---

1. I shall consider the distinctively sexual aspects of this relationship under the seventh commandment. Here we shall look at relationships of authority and submission.

previous chapter and those relations of equality to be considered in the next chapter. Men and women are fundamentally equal before God, because they are both made in his image. But in the home and in the church they enter into relationships of authority and submission partly based on gender. I shall therefore consider first their equality as God's image and then discuss their relationships of authority and submission.

MEN AND WOMEN IN THE IMAGE OF GOD[2]

Christian thinking on human dignity, including our dignity specifically as men and as women, begins with the teaching of Genesis 1:27: "So God created man in his own image, in the image of God he created him; male and female he created them." The idea that we are made in the image of God has given comfort and moral stimulus to many. In chapter 18, I argued that this doctrine defines our fundamental ethical responsibility as the imitation of God. But what does it mean to be in God's image?

Theological interpretations of the image have often been complicated and technical. But whatever value there may be in these theological developments, the basic idea is a simple one. The writer of Genesis did not consider the terms "image" and "likeness" (1:26) to be problematic; he made no attempt to explain them.[3] Evidently he was using a concept familiar to his readers.

The ancient world was full of images. Images were simply statues or pictures, intended to represent someone, often a god or a king. As we saw in our discussion of the second commandment, God forbids the worship of images. Yet there is an image of the true God, ourselves.[4] Scripture also calls us to honor one another in a way that is analogous to the way we honor God (see chapter 31).

Meredith G. Kline has shown us that the Bible presents three aspects of the image, which correspond to the lordship attributes and to the three

2. Portions of this section are taken from my article by the same name, published in *Recovering Biblical Manhood and Womanhood*, ed. John Piper and Wayne Grudem (Wheaton, IL: Crossway Books, 1991), 225–32. Used by permission of Crossway Books, a ministry of Good News Publishers, Wheaton, Illinois 60187, www.crossway.com.

3. Although theologians have sometimes drawn distinctions between "image" and "likeness," I believe that the terms both refer to the same thing, our resemblance to God. See John Murray, "Man in the Image of God," in *Collected Writings of John Murray*, vol. 2 (Edinburgh: Banner of Truth Trust, 1977), 34, who argues that the second term is "explanatory or definitive rather than supplementary" to the first.

4. Recall my argument in chapter 25 that the second commandment guards the dignity of man as well as of God, by making man God's only true image.

perspectives I discussed in chapter 3.[5] First, the image of God is physical, bodily. The human eye is an image of God's power to see, as the psalmist says: "He who formed the eye, does he not see?" (Ps. 94:9). God doesn't have literal eyes, but our eyes reflect his power of sight. Similarly, Scripture speaks of God's "arm" and "hand," indicating his power to act and showing that our arms and hands are also images of him. People sometimes object to saying that the image of God is physical, because God doesn't have a body. But that is shortsighted. God doesn't have a body, but our bodies certainly reflect his power. This aspect of the image of God reflects his lordship attribute of *control,* or what we have called the situational perspective.

A second aspect of the image is what Kline calls the official aspect. As God holds the office of king, so he makes us his assistant kings, his vicegerents or regents, to have dominion over the earth (Gen. 1:26, 28). This reflects God's lordship attribute of *authority,* or the normative perspective.

The third element is the ethical element. The New Testament tells us that we reflect God especially in our knowledge, righteousness, and holiness (Eph. 4:24; Col. 3:10). Throughout Scripture, God tells us to "be holy, for I the LORD your God am holy" (Lev. 19:2) or, as Jesus said in Matthew 5:48, to "be perfect, as your heavenly Father is perfect." So the image of God extends to our inmost character. It corresponds to God's lordship attribute of *presence,* or the existential perspective.

In none of these respects is there any difference between men and women. Both sexes image God physically.[6] God charges men and women together to have dominion over the earth (Gen. 1:28), so they share the official aspect of God's image. And he calls both to obedience, implying their equality in the ethical dimension of the image. In the fall, both the man and the woman disobey God, and God brings curses, mingled with blessing, upon them equally (Gen. 3:14–19). It is significant that the curse applies somewhat differently to the man and the woman. The woman will have pain in childbearing; the man will have pain and toil as he works the ground. But both are cursed and equally fallen. Although Scripture mentions that the woman was first deceived (1 Tim. 2:14), it never suggests that women are more or less sinful than men. Christ's redemption, therefore, applies equally to both. Scripture never suggests that women are more or less sanctified than men by the grace of Christ.

5. Meredith G. Kline, *Images of the Spirit* (Grand Rapids: Baker, 1980).

6. Karl Barth argued that sexual differentiation (as a form of social differentiation) *is* the image of God, because he saw an equation between the two in Gen. 1:27. I disagree with this view, and have argued against it in my article "Man and Woman in the Image of God," cited earlier.

Positively, Scripture teaches that both men and women are made in God's image and that they are equally in the image of God:

BOTH MEN AND WOMEN MADE IN GOD'S IMAGE

Genesis 1:27 makes this point quite explicitly, and 2:20 ("helper fit for him") and 2:23 ("bone of my bones and flesh of my flesh") underscore their unity of nature in contrast to the relationship between man and animals (2:19–20; see also 5:1–2). Hurley points out that "man" in 1:26 and 27 is a collective noun (*adam*, "mankind"). The plural membership is indicated by the phrase "male and female" in verse 27, and then to both male and female is given the task appropriate to those created in the image of God (v. 28).[7] This is the uniform teaching of Scripture. Re-creation in the image of Christ applies equally to all believers without distinction (Col. 3:9–11); in fact, that renewal, that sonship (Gal. 3:26), is given to believers so indiscriminately that in this respect "there is neither male nor female" (Gal. 3:28).

MEN AND WOMEN EQUALLY IN THE IMAGE OF GOD

Nothing in Genesis would lead anyone to suppose otherwise. But some have come to another conclusion based on Paul's statement in 1 Corinthians 11:7, "A man ought not to cover his head, since he is the image and glory of God, but woman is the glory of man." Why does Paul omit speaking of woman as "the image of God," after he has applied that title to man? One might even suppose that Paul is here denying that woman is the image of God and is attributing to her a lesser image, that of man.

I agree with C. K. Barrett that "in this context Paul values the term image only as leading to the term glory."[8] The reference to "image" is incidental to Paul's purpose, and therefore not applied to woman, but it notifies his readers of the Old Testament basis for saying that man is the glory of God, "glory" and "image" being roughly, but not entirely, synonymous. Paul's emphasis is on "glory," which focuses on the honor that one person brings to another. Man, he says, was made to honor God. Of course, woman was also made to honor God, but she is also made for a second

---

7. James B. Hurley, *Man and Woman in Biblical Perspective* (Leicester: Inter-Varsity Press, 1981), 172. He points out further that Gen. 1 is concerned about the creation of various types of reality, not with hierarchical differentiations within those types. Therefore, Gen. 1:27 grants the image to the whole human race, not to man as distinguished from woman.

8. C. K. Barrett, *A Commentary on the First Epistle of Paul to the Corinthians* (New York: Harper and Row, 1968), 252.

purpose, namely, to honor man. God made her specifically to be a helper for Adam (Gen. 2:18, 20; cf. Prov. 12:4; Eph. 5:25–29).[9] Man honors and glorifies God by uncovering his head, for covering the head connoted subservience to another creature.[10] Such subservience to men is especially inappropriate for a male prophet, whose whole function is to speak for God. Woman, however, must not only honor God, but also honor man. Indeed, she honors God when she honors the specific task of "helper" for which God made her. Unlike the man, then, she honors God best by displaying her subordination to her fellow creature.

So Paul's point in 1 Corinthians 11:7, then, is not that woman does not image God; it is rather that in addition to imaging God, she also is made to honor man, and that her appearance must be appropriate to that latter function. Nor is there any need to speak of her imaging God in some lesser sense than does man.

Does her subordination itself detract from her capacity to image God? That is an important question, but the answer must surely be negative. Men too are always placed in relations of subordination to other people (Ex. 20:12; Rom. 13:1; Heb. 13:17),[11] but that fact does not prejudice their being the image of God.

Jesus himself became subordinate to his Father, even subordinate to human authorities, in order to redeem us. Human authority, therefore, imaging Jesus, is to be a servant-authority (Matt. 20:20–28).[12] A willingness to subordinate oneself to others for God's sake is, indeed, itself a component of the image, not a compromise thereof.[13] Even submission to unjust authority shows a special likeness to Christ (1 Peter 2:12, 19–25; 3:14–18).[14] It is often by submitting to

9. I agree with those who say that "helper" does not in itself connote any subordination. God is himself the helper of Israel (e.g., Ps. 30:10). However, it is significant that Eve was made after Adam, for the specific purpose of helping him. That cannot be said of God's relationship to Israel. That fact, I believe, lies behind Paul's statements in 1 Cor. 11:8–9 and in 1 Tim. 2:13.

10. Leon Morris, *The First Epistle of Paul to the Corinthians* (Grand Rapids: Eerdmans, 1958), on 11:4. Also James B. Hurley, "Did Paul Require Veils or the Silence of Women?" *Westminster Theological Journal* 35 (1973): 205.

11. Even kings are usually answerable to someone, and even "absolute" monarchs get toppled if they do not succeed in pleasing other powerful members of society.

12. Cf. my discussion of this in chapter 31.

13. Underscoring this point: the head covering of the woman, by which she honors male authority, also establishes her as an honorable woman. Thus, Paul is able to speak of that head covering as a sign of (her own!) authority (1 Cor. 11:10). That head covering gives her the moral authority to prophesy in God's name. See Morris, *The First Epistle of Paul to the Corinthians*, on 11:10.

14. Noel Weeks chides the feminist movement for confusing worth with ruling power. See his *The Sufficiency of Scripture* (Edinburgh: Banner of Truth Trust, 1988), 137. The reader might also usefully peruse Royce Gruenler's *The Trinity in the Gospel of John* (Grand

others that we best display the ethical components of the divine image. How better to demonstrate God's love, his long-suffering, his gentleness, his self-control, than by submitting to others?

SEXUAL DIFFERENTIATION ITSELF IMAGES GOD

As indicated in an earlier footnote, I don't agree with Karl Barth that sexual differentiation *is* the image of God. But I do believe that our sexual qualities, like all other human qualities, image God. The point is not that God is male, female, or both. To say that our eyes image God, remember, is not to say that God has eyes; it is rather to say that our eyes picture something divine. Similarly, our sexuality pictures God's attributes and capacities:

1. Human sexuality mirrors God's creativity. By sexual capacities, we bring forth sons and daughters; God does the same by other means (John 1:12; Rom. 8:14–17; Gal. 4:4–7; Heb. 2:10; 1 John 3:1–2).

2. Love between husband and wife pictures God's love for his people (Ezek. 16; Hos. 1–3; Eph. 5:25–33), which begins with a love within the Trinity itself (John 17:26).

3. The covenant relationship between husband and wife (Prov. 2:17; Mal. 2:14) pictures the covenant relationship between God and man.

4. Scripture describes God both in male and in female terms, though the overwhelming preponderance of imagery is male. The reason, I think, is basically that Scripture wants us to think of God as Lord, and lordship, in Scripture, always connotes authority.[15] Since, in the biblical view, women are subject to male authority in the home and the church, as we shall see, there is some awkwardness in speaking of God in female terms. Our need today, in my view, is for a far greater appreciation of the lordship of God and of Christ. Therefore, the movement to use unisex or female language in referring to God is fundamentally wrongheaded from a biblical perspective.

5. Nevertheless, the very submission of the woman also images God. God the Lord is not too proud to be our "helper." Christ the Lord is not unwilling to be a servant. Godly women stand as models, often as rebukes, to all who would be leaders (Matt. 20:20–28).[16]

Rapids: Baker, 1986), in which he explores the relations of "mutual deference" within the Trinity. I don't agree with some of his points, but there is much stimulus here. Cf. *DG*, 694–96.

15. Scripture also, of course, emphasizes God's masculinity over against the polytheism and degradation of pagan goddess worship. For more considerations of this question, see *DG*, 378–86.

16. For this reason I disagree with Hurley's statement that, according to 1 Cor. 11:7, "the woman is not called to image God or Christ *in the relation which she sustains to her*

MEN AND WOMEN EQUALLY REPRESENT GOD

The image of God is both resemblance to God and representation. We have been discussing the image as resemblance; now we look at the image as representation. The distinction is between structure and function, between nature and task.

King Nebuchadnezzar set up an image of himself to represent him. When people worshiped the image, they were thereby expressing loyalty to the king (Dan. 3:1–6). Images were understood this way in the ancient world. Clearly, a similar notion is expressed in Genesis 1:28, for there God gives Adam the task of filling and subduing the earth.

These tasks are similar to what God himself does in the world. God wants to be known as Lord, which I have expounded in terms of control, authority, and presence. In Genesis 1:28, God gives to Adam a "dominion," a kind of lordship subordinate to God's own. Man (generic!) is the vassal king of the universe. Subduing the earth is to extend human *control* over the world. It also involves *authority*: God gives Adam the right to name the animals, which in the ancient world was an exercise of authority (Gen. 2:19–20; cf. v. 23; 3:20). Mankind is also to "fill" the earth, that is, to make his *presence* felt everywhere. As we have seen, these correspond with the three aspects of the image proposed by Kline and with the lordship attributes.

Whether we consider this dominion an aspect or a consequence of the image does not much matter. Scripture is not interested in such a distinction. It is clear that dominion is a status and a task commensurate with our unique nature as God's image. The Socinians were wrong in limiting the image to man's dominion, for, as we have seen, the image includes much more. But image and dominion certainly do go together.

That this dominion mandate continues after the fall is clear from Genesis 9:1–3. However, sin greatly hinders the accomplishment of God's purpose in the mandate, which was to fill the earth with, and put it under the control of, people who would glorify him. Thus, the New Testament puts emphasis on the Great Commission (Matt. 28:18–20), which is also a command about filling and subduing, but in this case by the saving gospel of Jesus Christ. Through the sovereign authority of Jesus (v. 18), the people of God are to extend their control, authority, and presence throughout the earth. We are "ambassadors for Christ, God making his appeal through us" (2 Cor. 5:20; cf. Phil. 2:14–15).[17]

---

husband" (*Man and Woman*, 173 [emphasis his]). The imaging is not precise, but, as we have seen, imaging never is. I think there are better ways to handle 1 Cor. 11:7; see my earlier discussion.

17. For a fuller account of these mandates, see chapter 17.

Hence, we have the biblical doctrines of sonship, adoption, and inheritance (John 1:12; Rom. 8:14–17; Gal. 3:26–29; Heb. 2:10; 1 John 3:1–3). In these respects, man and woman share equally. Scripture makes no sexual distinction. Indeed, Galatians 3:26 ("for in Christ Jesus you are all sons of God, through faith") precedes by two verses the famous "There is neither male nor female." And, as we have seen, male and female are equally given the original dominion mandate (Gen. 1:27–28).

Does this fact conflict with the authority of men over women in the home and in the church? I think not. Authority and subordination are not, in the abstract, inconsistent with one another. Someone may have authority over one sphere, but not over another; or he may be an authority in one respect, but subordinate in another. Men individually rule in some areas, but must be subject to those in authority over them. Jesus himself is both Lord and Servant.

So, as we saw in chapter 31, human authority itself is always a servant authority, an authority with responsibility for those under authority, as in Matthew 20:25–28, John 13:12–17, and Ephesians 5:22–6:9. So when Scripture speaks of the primacy of man over woman, it often coordinates that teaching with reflections on the mutual dependence of the sexes, as in 1 Corinthians 7:3; 11:11–12.

Women certainly share in the authority given to Adam. Together with men, they are made to rule the earth (Gen. 1:27–28; 1 Cor. 3:21).

Individually, women are given authority in various spheres. Mothers govern children (Ex. 20:12), and older women train the younger ones (Titus 2:4). In some cases, women manage a family business (Prov. 31:10–31). Women exercise authority over everyone as prophets of God (Judg. 4:4; Acts 2:17; 21:9; 1 Cor. 11:5, 10 ["symbol of authority"]). They are also under human authority, to be sure, but so are men.

Citing Matthew 8:9, Stephen B. Clark well observes that one's own authority, far from conflicting with submission to higher authority, often finds its source in such submission.[18] The prophets had authority because they stood under God's authoritative word. Kings, priests, and parents also have authority because God has ordained it. The apostles had authority because of their obedience to Jesus' commission. Recall my earlier note to the effect that the head covering of the woman (1 Cor. 11:10), a sign of submission, is also a sign of her own authority as a prophet.

18. Stephen B. Clark, *Man and Woman in Christ* (Ann Arbor: Servant Books, 1980), 171.

SUMMARY AND CONCLUSION

Women and men equally image God, even in their sexual differences, even in their differences with regard to authority and submission. The reason is that the image of God embraces everything that is human. Both men and women, therefore, resemble God and are called to represent him throughout the creation, exercising control, authority, and presence in his name. This doctrine is not at all inconsistent with the subordination of women to men in the home and in the church. All human beings are under authority, both divine and human authority. Their submission to authority, as well as their authority itself, images God.

MEN AND WOMEN IN THE FAMILY

As I indicated in chapter 32, although the woman is a "helper" to the man (Gen. 2:18) in many ways, the emphasis of the passage is on her role as childbearer.[19] Hence, the Bible emphasizes that women are called to be wives and mothers. This is an emphasis, not an absolute rule. I shall have more to say later about single women and women in vocations other than that of homemaker. Scripture certainly does not forbid women to enter other fields. Indeed, part of the reason that Scripture focuses on homemaking as the woman's role is cultural: with some exceptions, ancient society did not accept women in other positions. But there is also something transcultural in the biblical emphasis, something we would do well to recover today, even though we should also recognize wider applications of the biblical principles.

First, then, we should be aware of the Bible's emphasis on the woman's role as homemaker. In Genesis 1:27–28, there is a correlation between human nature in the image of God and the cultural mandate as the distinctive and comprehensive task of mankind. God makes man "male and female" and then presents the task in two aspects: replenishing and ruling.[20] By reading the passage chiastically, we receive the suggestion that replenishing is especially connected with the female and ruling with the male, although of course we cannot derive any absolute distinction from this language. Thus it is natural that the marital union of "one flesh" should

19. In my thinking about this thesis, I am dependent on some lectures given many years ago by my colleague Mark Futato. I take full responsibility, however, for the following discussion.

20. Note that God created us "male *and* female," not a male-female androgyny, as in modern feminist and New Age thought. Men and women are not interchangeable; their diversity is built into them. And we should not be surprised if they are given different tasks.

lead to offspring. Malachi 2:15 emphasizes that God made couples "one" in order to produce "godly offspring." This rough correlation continues into Genesis 3: after the fall, Adam is cursed in his agricultural labor and Eve in childbearing. Each is cursed in his or her distinctive contribution to the divine mandate. Yet the curse does not overcome the blessing. Man's labor will keep the human race alive until the Messiah comes, and woman's childbearing will in time lead to the birth of the Savior. The name given to the woman in 3:20 (Eve), then, is also based on her function as mother.

Thus we can also understand the strong biblical blessing of children, the cursedness of barrenness, the doctrine of children as "a heritage from the Lord" (Ps. 127:3), Jesus' blessing of the children (Matt. 19:13–15), and the covenantal argument for infant baptism (God calls *families*, not just individuals). We can understand why adultery is such a terrible sin (treason against the *family*, which is far more important to God than the state). We can understand why the education of young women in the church has especially to do with their work as wives and mothers (1 Tim. 5:14; Titus 2:4).

Thus there is a general division of labor between husband and wife, although the division is not rigid. The husband works in the fields and serves as an elder in the gates (Prov. 31:23). The wife works primarily at home, bearing and nurturing the children, teaching them and providing a good environment for their early years. However, it is also true that the woman cannot have children without male "help," nor raise them properly without male fathering, and the man cannot accomplish his cultural tasks without the help of the woman. Proverbs 31 presents a kind of balance: the woman focuses on the home as the major sphere of her activity. She does not sit "in the gates" as a ruler of the people, as does her husband (v. 23);[21] rather, she focuses on household tasks and the needs of her children. But she does also help her husband, not only by typical home-maker work, but also by contributing to the family's economic well-being. She earns money and purchases property (vv. 16, 18). She works hard, so that all her household will have their needs met. Similarly, Ruth gleaned in the fields of Boaz to support herself and her mother-in-law, but when her opportunity came to marry, she saw it as deliverance. Also note the description "working at home" in Titus 2:5. I don't think that proves that a woman should never work outside the home, however. Men too are to be busy at home in their work of family headship (cf. 1 Tim. 3:4–5). But the home is the focus of women's distinctive labor.

---

21. This passage does not imply that women should never rule in society. Deborah was certainly a ruler in Israel, and she glorified God in her work. But she became a ruler when men failed to take on their responsibilities. Male rule was not an absolute principle, but it was the usual and normal fact of Israelite culture, and Scripture does not call for resistance to that pattern.

This is not demeaning to women, nor is it the result of sexist oppression. The bearing and raising of children is as important to God as anything that is typically done by males. Our covenant theology indicates the centrality of the godly home and of godly families. A woman may be called by God to do something other than homemaking. We should honor such callings, but we should never suggest that these callings are more noble or useful than the task of homemaking. Our goal in honoring women should not be to set them free from the home, to do supposedly more important tasks; rather, we should honor them by honoring the tremendously important task that God has given especially to them.

Natural revelation confirms what we have said. Political correctness aside, it is simply the case that, as a general rule, men are more suited than women to tasks requiring upper-body strength. Thus, in the ancient world, when most men worked in agriculture or other back-breaking tasks, a division of labor was natural, one which brought benefits to women as well as to men. In that time, too, women had many more children than they usually do today, and they had less ability to be active in society during menstrual periods. Thus, the traditional division of labor was virtually a physical necessity, though even in those days there were exceptions like Deborah.

Has the modern trend toward less physical labor erased the necessity for such a distinction? No. Recent studies indicate that women in the workforce are absent from their jobs more often than men, on account of illness, menstrual problems, and family responsibilities. These facts are not negligible to employers. Doubtless, again, there are exceptions. But the physical differences between men and women still justify, in general, the traditional division of labor.

These factors must be understood when we consider the biblical principles denying church office to women and requiring of them subordination to their husbands in the home. But more significant than the physical limitations of women is their distinctive calling from God. The scriptural restrictions placed upon them exist, not because they are inherently less gifted than men (even as administrators), but simply because their distinctive work is so important. Here God's wisdom differs radically from modern intellectual (especially feminist) fashions. Indeed, the attitude of many in the church, who despise nursery service and consider the teaching of children a second-rate ministry, also receives a challenge from God's Word. Children are so important that God has reserved the best gifts of half the population for their benefit.

Why should we imagine that working for, say, General Motors, is more important than raising children? Is the former any more important to society, any more rewarding when carried out responsibly? Is it somehow more "liberating" to work in business than to work in one's own home? Or shall we compare working at home to "positions of authority" such as political office and church eldership? Why should working at home be considered less rewarding? Most people who are not in "positions of authority" don't realize how boring, how unrewarding, administrative work can be. We need to reconsider our basic values.

God wants to spread his kingdom, even today, not only through mission work, but through childbearing and nurture. He wants to raise up godly families to glorify him. A family consists of a father, a mother, their children, and, by extension, grandparents, uncles, aunts, and cousins, though of course not all families have all these classes of members. The husband is the "head" of the wife (1 Cor. 11:3–5; Eph. 5:23).[22] The wife is to obey her husband; the children are to obey their parents.[23] The husband is to be the servant-leader of them all.

Although God offers special protection to widows and orphans, single parenthood is not the biblical ideal. Again, natural revelation concurs. Statistics show that children of single-parent homes and homes where both parents work, especially "latchkey" kids, are much more likely to get into trouble (gangs, drugs, illegal activities) than children with traditional families and one parent remaining at home.

Yet our society and governments, more interested in being politically correct than in helping children, subsidize single parenthood through marriage penalties (in the welfare and tax codes), special benefits to working mothers (which are not given to those who remain home), subsidized day care, persecution of homeschooling families, and the like, not to mention creating economic conditions that virtually require two incomes per family.

Many of our churches err here. Christian women often want to escape the routines of child care and to spend their time in other ways. When churches provide organizations for women to spend their time in various activities, they often unintentionally lead them away from their responsibilities in the home. God may call some wives and mothers to vocations (including ministries) outside the home, but churches should not assume that that is the rule.

22. "Head" refers to authority, not "source," as feminists often claim. See Wayne Grudem, "The Meaning of *Kephale* ('Head')," in *Recovering Biblical Manhood and Womanhood*, ed. Piper and Grudem, 425–68. But of course even if it did mean "source," that would connote authority, for God is our source and therefore our authority. Fathers and mothers bring forth their children and thus acquire authority over them. Jesus is the source of the church and therefore has authority over it. So Eve was created from the rib of Adam, and must obey her source.

23. The woman's "desire" in Gen. 3:16 is to usurp her husband's authority; cf. 4:7. See Susan Foh, *Women and the Word of God* (Phillipsburg, NJ: Presbyterian and Reformed, 1979).

The biblical pattern for "women's organizations" in the church is Titus 2. There Paul tells Titus to bring certain messages to older men, younger men, and older women. Significantly, he does not give Titus a message for the younger women.[24] Rather, he asks Titus to teach the older women, who in turn will teach the younger women.[25] For obvious reasons, a young male pastor ought not to devote himself to teaching young women. That job is given to older women, and Titus is to work through them. What are the older women to teach the younger? "They are to teach what is good, and so train the young women to love their husbands and children, to be self-controlled, pure, working at home, kind, and submissive to their own husbands, that the word of God may not be reviled" (Titus 2:3–5).

A women's organization that functions this way will not suggest that young women should undertake jobs more important than that of homemaking, even if those jobs be in church ministries. Rather, it will support and help them with the distinctive task that God has given to women, without demeaning those with different callings. The older women, rather than opting out of the world of children and homemaking, will be teachers in these areas, working alongside the younger mothers to make their job easier. So often in our churches today, the younger women feel unsupported, as the older women, happy to be free from the responsibilities of caring for children, move on to other things and offer no assistance. That should not be. Older women should be taught a different system of values.

There is no more important need in our churches than for ministry to families. Most people in our churches have no idea what the biblical family is to be like, because they have been inundated with modern anti-Christian ideology. They need to be taught about authority relationships, gender-differentiated tasks, and the need to create an atmosphere that saturates children with the Word of God (Deut. 6:6–9).[26]

Churches committed to "church growth" are often tempted to ignore family ministry. It seems easier to minister to rootless individuals as individuals and to push the children aside as distractions. But that mentality is shortsighted. Besides neglecting important biblical priorities, it loses one substantial opportunity for church growth. Many families today are hungry for counsel. Having bought into the dominant modern thinking, and having seen its failure, they are looking for something better. They

24. Thanks to Dennis Johnson for helping me to see this point.
25. Note that there is an important place for the teaching gifts of women in the church, even though women are denied the office of teaching elder. Indeed, besides being the principal teachers of children, women are charged with the major role in teaching about one fourth of the congregation (the "younger women").
26. Cf. the discussion of Christian schools in chapter 24.

watch with broken hearts as their children are eaten alive spiritually by the public schools, the media, and peer pressure. To these the message of Christ can come as the best news imaginable. Churches that minister effectively to families and children often experience substantial growth as more and more families seek their help.

MEN AND WOMEN IN THE CHURCH

The question of women's ordination to church office has become in recent years something of a watershed, distinguishing "evangelical feminists" from others. It is important at this time to be clear on just what Scripture says and does not say about women's role in the church. First, the negatives:

1. Scripture does not say that women may not teach. Titus 2 commissions older women to teach younger women, putting them in charge of teaching one quarter of the adult church membership (i.e., younger women), in addition to their accepted role as teachers of children (as in 2 Tim. 1:5).

2. Scripture does not say that women may not teach men. Acts 18:26 indicates that both Priscilla and her husband Aquila were involved in teaching Apollos, mentioning Priscilla's name first.

3. Scripture does not say that women may never speak in a church meeting. First Corinthians 11:5 refers to women praying and prophesying in worship. The attempt of some to argue that Paul mentions but does not approve this practice, is not persuasive. He requires women who are praying and prophesying to wear a covering while doing so. If he disapproved of them praying and prophesying as such, it would be like saying, "If you rob a bank, be sure to wear a coat and tie."

4. Scripture does not say that women can teach only under divine inspiration. First Corinthians 11:5 probably does refer to charismatic, inspired praying and prophesying. But Titus 2 and Acts 18:26 certainly do not.

5. Scripture does not say that women may teach in informal settings, but not in Lord's Day worship. First Corinthians 11:5 clearly deals with the Lord's Day gathering. And there is no difference between "informal" worship and "formal" worship, so far as regulation is concerned. The regulative principle (chapter 26) governs all occasions when Christians meet to worship God and hear his Word.

What, then, is the nature of the restriction placed on women's activity in such passages as 1 Corinthians 14:33b–36 and 1 Timothy 2:11–14? The former passage reads:

As in all the churches of the saints, the women should keep silent in the churches. For they are not permitted to speak, but should be in submission, as the Law also says. If there is anything they desire to learn, let them ask their husbands at home. For it is shameful for a woman to speak in church. Or was it from you that the word of God came? Or are you the only ones it has reached?

The context of 1 Corinthians 14 has to do with authoritative teaching. In verses 26–28, that teaching comes through inspired prophecy ("a revelation"), "a lesson," tongues (which are uninterpreted prophecy), and the interpretation of tongues. After two or three prophets have spoken, there is a period of evaluation. Paul tells the church to "let the others weigh what is said" (v. 29). This too is an authoritative action. Those who weigh the prophecies are to judge whether the prophets are true or false. But women are excluded from the weighing of prophecies. When the time comes for this evaluation, women are to keep silent.

The weighing of prophecy is not the work of all Christians, but the work of church leaders whose gifts for this task the church has recognized. Today, such recognition is called ordination. In Presbyterian theology, such tasks are given to elders; in other traditions, to bishops, pastors, or ministers.[27] These ordained officers differ from other Christians, not in that they teach, but in that they teach in the name of the church, with the church's explicit approval. So the implication of this passage is that women are not eligible for the teaching *office* of the church, whether that office be called elder, pastor, or bishop.[28]

First Timothy 2:11–14 also deals with authoritative, official teaching, although that is not entirely evident on the surface: "Let a woman learn quietly with all submissiveness. I do not permit a woman to teach or to exercise authority over a man; rather, she is to remain quiet. For Adam was formed first, then Eve; and Adam was not deceived, but the woman was deceived and became a transgressor." According to Douglas Moo:

> While the word can be used more broadly to describe the general ministry of edification that takes place in various ways . . . , the activity usually designated by *teach* is plainly restricted to certain individuals who have the gift of teaching (see 1 Corinthians

27. In many Baptist churches, such responsibilities are given to "deacons." In those churches, women should not be ordained to the office of deacon. I shall later argue, however, that they should be ordained to that office if it is defined differently and more biblically.

28. Here I follow D. A. Carson, "'Silent in the Churches': On the Role of Women in 1 Corinthians 14:33b–36," in *Recovering Biblical Manhood and Womanhood*, ed. Piper and Grudem, particularly pp. 151–53, and also Hurley, *Man and Woman*.

12:28–30; Ephesians 4:11). This makes it clear that not all Christians engaged in teaching. In the pastoral epistles, teaching always has this restricted sense of authoritative doctrinal instruction.[29]

Moo adds that Paul is concerned with the integrity of this type of teaching as he nears the end of his own life and passes the torch to Timothy (1 Tim. 4:11–16; 2 Tim. 2:2; 4:2). And "while perhaps not restricted to the elder-overseer, 'teaching' in this sense was an important activity of these people (see 1 Timothy 3:2; 5:17; Titus 1:9)." So, as in 1 Corinthians 14:33b–36, what Paul forbids to women here is *official* teaching, teaching that is part of the teaching office of the church.

And what of the "authority over a man" which verse 12 says is not to be exercised by women? Moo says:

> But, within these spheres of authority [God and the Scriptures], we may . . . speak legitimately of a governing or ruling function exercised *under* God by some Christians over others (see 1 Thessalonians 5:12; Hebrews 13:17). In the pastoral epistles, this governing authority is ascribed to the elders (see 1 Timothy 3:5; 5:17). Clearly, then, Paul's prohibition of women's having authority over a man would exclude a woman from becoming an elder in the way this office is described in the pastoral epistles.[30]

On this interpretation, to which I subscribe, the fundamental restriction on women's role in the church is the same in both passages: women are not to be elders, or to bear whatever offices in the church entitle them to be official teachers of men.[31]

Is Paul's ruling based on merely local situations in Corinth or Ephesus, as some evangelical feminists have alleged? It would be understandable if Paul were to deal with a local problem by excluding from office those who were causing the problem. But it is not easy to understand why the people causing such a problem would all be of one gender. Actually, however, Paul explicitly denies in these contexts that his concern is merely with local issues. He says in 1 Corinthians 14:33 that he gives the same orders in every

29. Moo, "What Does It Mean Not to Teach or Have Authority over Men?" in *Recovering Biblical Manhood and Womanhood*, ed. Piper and Grudem, 185.

30. Ibid., 187.

31. However, this passage opens another interesting question: might it be legitimate to ordain women to an office that gives them the authority to speak in the name of the church to other women? Titus 2:3–4 teaches that older women have a special responsibility in that regard. Normally such gifts and responsibilities are recognized in the New Testament by the laying on of hands (1 Tim. 4:14; 5:22; 2 Tim. 1:6). And, as I shall mention later, there is a good argument for the ordination of women deacons.

church. And in 1 Timothy 2:13–15 he bases his policy on the created order and the nature of the fall, events which condition all human beings, all local situations, and all human history.

What, then, are we to make of Galatians 3:28, which says that in Christ "there is neither Jew nor Greek, there is neither slave nor free, there is neither male nor female"? Well, obviously Christ has not removed sexual differences in *every* respect! Nor has he removed in every respect the distinction between Jew and Greek. And Paul does not oppose, but rather reinforces in various contexts, the obligations of slaves to obey their masters (as in Eph. 6:5–9). So we must make some distinctions. Clearly the passage is emphasizing the oneness of the church across barriers of nationality, social status, and gender. All believers are equal in the salvation that they have received by grace. But Paul never suggests that national distinctions, sexual differences, or even the master/slave distinctions disappear because of Christ. Nor does he deny that there are differences of office and authority that should be respected in the church.

Why does Paul deny to women the office of elder? The point is not that women have fewer gifts than men, or even that they have lesser gifts of teaching and administration. Titus 2:3–4 indicates that women's teaching gifts play a valuable role in the church. And, as I indicated in the previous section, their teaching of children in the home is, arguably, as important to the kingdom of God as any official teaching role could be.

Paul's grounds for his restriction are as follows: He mentions in 1 Timothy 2:13–14 (1) that Adam was created first, and (2) that Eve, not Adam, was deceived. That Adam was created first, and Eve was made later to be his helper, implies that it was her purpose in life to assist her husband. That Eve was deceived disqualified her from being Adam's official teacher. In the mystery of federal headship, our solidarity with our first parents, these divine determinations are passed on to their descendants.

(3) Another reason for the restriction of the eldership to men is that the church is (as I argued in chapter 32) an extended family, the family of Christ. Paul does not mention this reason in the two passages we have considered, but it is implicit in the overall perspective of the New Testament. If husbands are to be heads of their wives in the family, the same should be the case in the extended family of believers. It would be anomalous if a wife were to be subject to her husband in the nuclear family, but rule over him in the extended family.

(4) Somewhat less obvious, but also implicit in Scripture, is the fact that women have distinctive roles that are at least as important as official teaching and administration. They are homemakers and teachers, both of children and of other women, and they are informal teachers of men

(below). God values those roles as much as any others. And without the responsibilities that attach to the teaching office, women are free to carry on ministries that clergy cannot do nearly as efficiently.[32]

Now besides the official teaching office, sometimes called the "special office," there is a "general" teaching office, held by every believer. As Moo says in the first quote above, the word *teach* can be used in a broader sense, as in Colossians 3:16, where everybody is "teaching and admonishing" one another. Certainly, Scripture does not deny this kind of teaching to women. As unofficial teachers, women have as much right and obligation as anybody to edify their fellow believers, whether men, women, or children. It was in this capacity that Priscilla instructed Apollos in Acts 18:26. It was within the general office that women prayed and prophesied in the church service in 1 Corinthians 11.

General-office teaching, like general-office prayer, is important. The writer to the Hebrews expresses great disappointment that his readers are so immature that they have not become "teachers" (Heb. 5:12). God's plan is that we hear the Word of God, not only once a week from the pulpit, but also from the lips of our brothers and sisters in Christ throughout our life together (as in Heb. 10:24–25).

It is not impossible to imagine that some general-office teachers may have more useful knowledge on certain subjects than special-office teachers. It seems to me that if the elders of a church think it would be helpful for an unordained person to address the congregation on the Lord's Day, they may invite that person to speak. There is no hard and fast rule in Scripture that only ordained men may speak in worship, or even that only ordained men may preach the Word of God. Unordained ministerial candidates often preach the Word at the invitation of the elders. But if the elders may ask general-office Christians to teach the Word in worship, I see no reason why they may not ask a woman to do so. She is not forbidden to teach, or even to teach men; she is only forbidden to occupy the special office.[33]

Indeed, according to the teaching of Romans 12, 1 Corinthians 12–14, and Ephesians 4:1–16 concerning the gifts of the Spirit, all spiritual gifts

32. My wife does much more person-to-person ministry than I, partly because she does *not* teach classes, write books, attend ministers' meetings, and work on committees.

33. May she stand behind the pulpit as she exhorts the congregation from the Word of God? Scripture does not forbid that, for Scripture does not mention pulpits. In some congregations, the pulpit is a symbol of the special office, so the use of it by unordained people confuses the congregation as to who the elders are. In those cases, rather than restricting the pulpit to ordained men, it seems to me, the congregation should be instructed not to take that symbolism too seriously. It is interesting that some Presbyterians who place much weight on the symbolism of the pulpit simultaneously want to exclude other (equally extrabiblical) symbols from the worship area.

are given for the edification of the whole body of Christ. How can we imagine that God would give to women gifts of wisdom, knowledge, and communication that are for the edification of the church *except* for the adult male members? Most all of us men can testify to the great insight of godly women into the Scriptures and their application of Scripture to the Christian life. Can we really believe that we have sinned on those occasions when we have profited from the teaching of women?

In general, a woman may do in the church anything an unordained man may do. So there are vast areas of service in the church for all believers, women and men alike. As one instance, I think that women may contribute much to the church as biblical scholars, and it is appropriate for women who are expert in Scripture and other relevant fields to instruct men preparing for ordination. I have no objection to women as seminary professors. I do believe that most seminary professors should be ordained males, for I think that that teaching should come, for the most part, from elders, those authorized to speak for the church. But often unordained people of both sexes can add great resources to the training of ministers, and we should recognize such gifts and knowledge. But we should be reminded that women also have important duties in the home that legitimately limit their participation in church activities and ministries. Churches should not have as a goal that all lay ministries be staffed equally by men and women.

So far, we have focused on the relation of women to the office of elder. But Scripture also speaks about the office of deacon (1 Tim. 3:8–13). Now although women should not be elected to the office of elder, I believe there is a biblical argument for women deacons. The diaconate, as understood in the Reformed community,[34] is a serving office, rather than a ruling-teaching office. Historically, the diaconate has focused on the ministry of mercy, and women in the New Testament were prominent in that ministry. Robert Strimple's argument for women deacons is a strong one, and churches should give heed to it.[35]

This chapter, nevertheless, will strike many as very restrictive and conservative in the current discussion, because it denies that women should be ordained as elders. But I think this is a clear teaching of Scripture.[36] It

34. In many Baptist communions, deacons are the ruling office, in effect the same as what Presbyterians call elders. In such a context, I would oppose the election of women deacons.

35. Strimple sets forth his position in "Report of the Minority of the Committee on Women in Church Office," *Minutes of the Fifty-fifth General Assembly of the Orthodox Presbyterian Church* (1988), 356–73. It can be found at http://www.opc.org/GA/women_in_office.html#APPENDIX.

36. I have more respect for the argument that women should be silent in worship services than for the argument that women should be ordained to the eldership. That is,

is not a difficult point, and I think it cannot be evaded unless one wishes to reject at that point the authority of Scripture.

William Webb has attempted to reconcile biblical authority with fairly liberal views on homosexuality and the roles of women, by his "redemptive movement hermeneutic."[37] That hermeneutic says that New Testament ethics, while higher than those of the surrounding culture, do not represent God's ideals. They do indicate a direction, and we must adopt an ethic that moves in that direction beyond the New Testament itself. The resulting ethical principles may contradict the explicit commands of Scripture, while affirming its "trajectory" or "direction." Wayne Grudem has provided a nearly exhaustive analysis and critique of this position, and I will not add to it here.[38] It is evident to me that Webb's approach violates the authority of Scripture (chapter 10), since it allows us to do what Scripture forbids, and denies the sufficiency of Scripture (chapter 11), since it requires us to find ultimate principles of ethics outside Scripture—principles of authority equal to or greater than those of Scripture. The chief example that Webb puts forth is that of slavery. But there are better ways of dealing with that issue (see chapter 34).[39] So Webb's approach, like many others, substitutes modern fashion for the authority of Scripture.

But if one rejects that authority here, where does one accept it? Limited inerrantists used to say that Scripture is authoritative on matters of faith and practice, but not on matters of historical detail, scientific accuracy, and so forth. But church office is certainly a matter of "faith and practice." If Paul has erred here, and some feminists of evangelical background are quite candid in saying he did,[40] where can we ever accept his word against some other current fashion?

---

although my position stands between more conservative and more liberal alternatives, I think the conservative alternative is more plausible than the liberal, and I could more easily be persuaded of the former. The more conservative view fails to note that the context of our two passages is one of official teaching. The more liberal view, in my estimation, rejects the teaching of these passages altogether.

37. See William J. Webb, *Slaves, Women and Homosexuals* (Downers Grove, IL: Inter-Varsity Press, 2001).

38. Grudem, "Shall We Move Beyond the New Testament to a Better Ethic?" *Journal of the Evangelical Theological Society* 47 (2004): 299–346. Also published in Grudem, *Evangelical Feminism and Biblical Truth* (Sisters, OR: Multnomah, 2004), 600–645. He abbreviates his critique in *Journal of Biblical Manhood and Womanhood* 10.1 (Spring 2005): 96–120.

39. Jesus does teach in Mark 10:2–9 that Moses' tolerance of divorce was less than God's ideal. He finds the ideal, however, in Scripture, not in some ethical consciousness beyond Scripture, nor by means of some "trajectory" or "redemptive movement" that points to something beyond the text. For Jesus, Scripture is sufficient to set forth ultimate moral norms.

40. E.g., Paul K. Jewett, *Man as Male and Female* (Grand Rapids: Eerdmans, 1975), 112–13.

This matter is serious. Women's ordination has become an accepted doctrine among many professing evangelicals, to such an extent that disagreement with this position is considered bigotry. The position of this chapter, which is the historic position of most of the Christian church, is becoming more and more isolated, even among evangelical and Reformed brothers and sisters. Much prayer is needed. I have no doubt that God will rebuke unbelief in his time, but the immediate future appears ominous.

WOMEN AS ADULT SUNDAY SCHOOL TEACHERS: A CASE STUDY

What follows is my edited and revised version of a committee report presented to South Coast Presbytery of the Presbyterian Church in America. I was the chief author, though I received important help from other committee members. I take full responsibility for the formulation here. The report begins by distinguishing the general and special offices of the teacher in the church, and it then presents the teaching of 1 Corinthians 14:33b–35 and 1 Timothy 2:11–15, as I have done above. Then it discusses a question posed to the presbytery by one of its congregations, New Hope Church: "Is it biblically permissible for a woman to teach men and women in an adult Sunday school class if she is submitted to the session?" I will exclude the initial material and join the report where it begins to discuss that specific issue:

It is important to keep in mind that "Sunday school" as such is not mentioned in Scripture. As an institution, it is a product of the last hundred years. This does not mean that Sunday school is illegitimate. It is, we believe, a legitimate way of carrying out the biblical command to teach people "to observe all that I have commanded you" (Matt. 28:20). But Scripture does not give us a definition of Sunday school, nor a detailed methodology as to how that work must be carried on.

"Adult Sunday school" can mean many things: consider President Jimmy Carter lecturing to hundreds in the Baptist churches of the nation's capital. At the other extreme, in a tiny, newly planted church, adult Sunday school might mean two or three people sitting around a table, discussing questions of importance to them. In some cases, one person might be delegated as "the teacher"; in other cases, a topic might be thrown to the group for free discussion, with no single person controlling the discussion. There are many degrees in between these extremes; some classes are more authoritarian than others.

Sometimes Sunday school is much like a formal worship service, especially in those Sunday schools that emphasize "opening exercises." Sometimes the pastor leads the adult class; sometimes the adult class is even an extension of the sermon. But that is not always the case. Sometimes there is no singing or liturgy at all, no offering, no special role for the teaching elders.

In Acts 18:24–28, do we not have something *like* an adult Sunday school class? To be sure, there are only three members: Priscilla, Aquila, and Apollos. Priscilla and Aquila were trying to teach Apollos the Word of God more completely and accurately; Apollos admitted his need and was learning from them. Granted the many forms that adult Sunday school can take, may it not take this form among others? But if it does, surely it cannot be denied that a woman may in that class use her general-office gifts of teaching. That is plain in Acts 18.

One could argue that when Sunday school approximates formal worship and/or where leadership is generally monopolized by the ordained elders, it could be inappropriate for a woman (or an unordained man!) to step into such a leadership role.[41] There are dangers in *confusing* the special office with the general.

On the other hand, granted the many things that "Sunday school" can mean, the committee is unable to say that women should *never* use their general-office teaching gifts in a mixed group. There may be occasions such as the Priscilla-Aquila-Apollos discussion where the insight of a woman is much to be desired and where there is no confusion created between the general office and the special office.

Our conclusion, then, is that Scripture does not forbid under all circumstances a woman to teach men and women in an adult Sunday school class. Three cautions, however, are important:

1. Such use of women's gifts should not be used in such a way as to blur the distinction between the special and general offices. Appearances are important in this regard. When a woman teaches in church in such a way that she "acts like an elder" or claims the same authority as the elders, or even appears to be doing so to reasonable people in the congregation, then the session should act in gentleness and love to remove the danger. What appears wrong or causes confusion may vary from congregation to congregation and from situation to situation. We cannot, therefore, furnish a final, exhaustive list of what precisely can be done and not done. Application of the biblical principles to specific situations is something we all must do, especially those in leadership positions. God expects the church's leaders to be sensitive to dangers in specific situations and to act, speaking the truth in love.

41. However, I would say that it is not *necessarily* inappropriate, as I argued earlier. Here my personal views differ somewhat from those that prevailed on the committee.

2. The New Hope session rightly draws our attention to the importance of women teachers being "submitted to the session." Submission, of course, is not just literal obedience; it is an attitude, a fruit of the Spirit. Scripture requires such submission of all teachers in the church, especially those who are unordained. Unordained teachers must take pains to make plain that they do not rule in the church, that they teach only by the delegation of others. But perhaps this principle has special application to women who teach. First Timothy 2 stresses the attitude of women in the church, that they are not to be seeking or claiming inappropriate authority over others, but responding in quietness and submission to the teaching authorities. It is not easy to maintain such quietness and humility while at the same time teaching others.

3. Consider the responsibilities given to women in Scripture: bearing and teaching children, teaching other women, working at home, being "helpmeets" to their husbands. Making suitable allowance for differences in gifts and calling, it should be evident that most married women will have their hands full carrying out their scripturally mandated tasks, if those tasks are taken seriously. Many today believe that a woman cannot fulfill her God-given potential unless she is involved in church tasks normally carried out by men. On the contrary: Scripture calls women to a very rich variety of tasks that are of vast importance and which can challenge the most gifted. After carrying out such responsibilities, most people would be simply too tired to aspire to anything else. While we cannot condemn women teaching men in every circumstance, we reject the notion that women are unfulfilled without such experience or that the predominance of male teachers in adult Sunday schools amounts to "oppression" of women.

MEN AND WOMEN IN THE WORKPLACE

I have stressed so far what Scripture emphasizes, that women have special responsibilities in the home, bearing and nurturing children, and caring for the home in submission to their husbands. But not all women are married, and not all married women are mothers. Many women are single, because they are too young for marriage, or because they are widowed or divorced. And to some, God simply has not provided mates. Further, some married women, like the ideal woman of Proverbs 31, have opportunities to buy and sell in the marketplace (Prov. 31:14, 16–18, 24) and to help the needy (v. 20).

Deborah, the wife of Lappidoth (Judg. 4:4), was a prophet in Israel and a judge who resolved cases that came before her (v. 5). When she called on Barak, the military commander, to attack Sisera, general of the army of

Jabin, the Canaanite king, Barak refused to go unless Deborah accompanied him (v. 8). She did, and God gave them the victory. But because of Barak's reluctance to fight without Deborah at his side, God gave Sisera, not into his hands, but into the hands of another woman, Jael, who killed him in her tent (vv. 17–22).

There is certainly a gender subtext to the story. God reveals his will through a female prophet. The male leader will not obey God, unless the woman risks her own life. But God gives victory through her, and the decisive blow in the battle comes from still another woman.

Other women also serve as prophets of the Lord in Scripture. Peter in Acts 2:16–17 appeals to the prophecy of Joel 2:28 to explain the events of Pentecost. Through Joel, God said that at that time both the sons and the daughters of Israel would prophesy. The four daughters of Philip the evangelist were prophets in the early church (Acts 21:8–9), and, as we saw earlier, female prophets addressed the church of Corinth (1 Cor. 11:4–16). I noted earlier as well that women functioned as general-office teachers in the New Testament church.

Clearly, then, although God has given to women a special role in the making of the home, he has not restricted them to that role. He calls some women to other tasks, either to supplement their homemaking or as an alternative to it. Sometimes, as with Deborah and Jael, this calling comes through the failure of a man, in part to bring him shame. At other times, as in Proverbs 31, these additional callings simply express an abundance of gifts. And, in the case of single women, there is often no alternative.

So it is not necessarily wrong for a woman to work outside the home, even when the men in her life are acting responsibly. Many women will hesitate to do this, not wishing to neglect their families, and that is a legitimate concern. In some cases, that concern should prevent a woman from working outside the home, but not necessarily in all cases. Situations and motives will vary.

In the workplace, men and women are generally equal and therefore should relate to one another as WLC, 131, says: "to regard the dignity and worth of each other, in giving honor to go one before another; and to rejoice in each other's gifts and advancement, as their own." If even the master-slave relationship is subject to the principle of servant leadership (Eph. 6:5–9), then that principle surely governs all other relationships in the workplace.

Of course, in the workplace, just as in ancient slavery, there is hierarchy. There are bosses and workers. These should be related as their job descriptions determine, but Christians in the workplace can infuse all these relationships with self-sacrificing love.

I mentioned earlier that we should not expect equal numbers of men and women in the workplace or in specific jobs. There are real gender-based differences in abilities and weaknesses that employers should be able to take into consideration. We should expect more men to be lumberjacks, and more women to produce designs of fine detail. I don't expect in my lifetime to see a woman playing in the National Football League. But these differences are general rules or guidelines, rather than absolute exclusions. Women who want to be lumberjacks and who have the physical abilities should have the opportunity. Hiring decisions, therefore, may legitimately be based on abilities or disabilities that are gender-specific, but not upon gender as such.

Despite Deborah's example, it is generally unwise for women to be placed in combat roles in the military, or in positions that could become combat roles. A soldier must have the physical ability to carry a wounded comrade off the battlefield, and most women don't have that ability. Further, the need for soldiers to live away from their spouses for long periods of time, in close proximity to other soldiers, brings temptation to sexual immorality. The pregnancy rate among women soldiers in such situations has been appalling. But these principles, too, are less than absolute. Arrangements can be made to minimize the moral temptations, and judgments of physical abilities can be made independently of gender.

The role of women in government also deserves reflection. Deborah's example suggests that God may call women to serve as judges and rulers, but the gender subtext of the story indicates, as we have seen, that this was an irregular arrangement. Isaiah 3:12 indicates that the rule of women is a mark of Israel's spiritual decline, a principle well illustrated by the stories of Jezebel, wife of King Ahab (1 Kings 21; 2 Kings 9), and of Athaliah, mother of King Ahaziah (2 Kings 11; 2 Chron. 22). And it is reasonable to ask, if women are to be subordinate in the family and church, and government is an extension of the family somewhat parallel to the church, should not women (as a general rule) be subordinate also in government rather than taking positions of rule?

I don't think we should extrapolate from Isaiah 3:12 and the examples of Jezebel and Athaliah the idea that any woman in public office is a symptom (let alone a cause) of a nation's spiritual decline. We should note that Jezebel and Athaliah were powers behind the throne, not anointed rulers. And certainly Israel was equally disobedient under many of its male rulers, even those not subject to inordinate female influence. Still (politically incorrect as it may be to say this), I do think that it should be considered irregular for women to hold public office, given the home-centered responsibilities God has given to women and the parallel structures of family, church, and state (chapter 32).

But there is no clear biblical prohibition of women rulers in Scripture, and there is no biblical principle that forbids women to participate in a democratic political process (where all people are, in one sense, rulers). I think it is good for women's voices to be heard in political debate and for their gifts to be used in some workings of government, if not at the highest levels, when such work does not conflict with their God-given responsibilities.

As in other fields of labor, we should not expect a certain quota of women members of government. Nor should we give any credit to the argument that only women legislators can represent women citizens. Gender does not have such comprehensive importance. Most people would rather be represented by someone of opposite gender who shares their values than by one who shares their gender but not their values.

CHAPTER 34

The Fifth Commandment:
Equalities, Racial and Otherwise

As we have seen, all people are equal before God, but all are not the same. We equally bear the divine image. But we come in all sizes, shapes, colors, and genders. We differ greatly from one another in abilities and disabilities, intellect, personality, emotional makeup, manner of speech, tastes and preferences, education, experience, and vocations. We also differ morally and spiritually, depending on regeneration and level of spiritual maturity.

Because we are all made in the image of God, we should treat everyone with dignity. Note again, from the Larger Catechism:

> Q. 131. *What are the duties of equals?*
> A. The duties of equals are, to regard the dignity and worth of each other, in giving honor to go one before another; and to rejoice in each other's gifts and advancement, as their own.

> Q. 132. *What are the sins of equals?*
> A. The sins of equals are, besides the neglect of the duties required, the undervaluing of the worth, envying the gifts, grieving at the advancement of prosperity one of another; and usurping preeminence one over another.

But we are not to treat everybody alike. A great pianist should be honored as a great pianist. A great violinist who cannot play the piano should be honored as a great violinist, but not as a great pianist. One called to be a judge should be honored as a judge; whether he should also be honored as a good man is a different question. We owe special honor to our fathers and mothers, to church leaders, to civil authorities, and, above and beyond all these, to Jesus Christ. So the Catechism says that although we should honor the dignity and worth of everyone, we should also recognize differences among people, so as to "rejoice in each other's gifts and advancement" as our own. If everyone had the same gifts, of course, that exhortation would be unnecessary.

The problem is that as sinners we are prone to exaggerate the sameness of people or to exaggerate their differences. Political liberals tend toward the former misunderstanding, and conservatives toward the latter. Liberals often insist, for example, that all sexual orientations are morally equal, and that it is bigotry to discriminate among people on that basis. Conservatives, in the past at least, have discounted the contributions of women and minorities to human thought and culture, exaggerating the differences.

These issues arise, not only in the area of race, but in many others as well. There have been movements to minimize testing in schools, lest one group of students be made to feel superior to another. Qualifications for some occupations, especially in military, police, and fire-fighting professions, have been lowered, in order to maximize the participation of women. Such developments compromise excellence in order to achieve participation by all groups, emphasizing our sameness and minimizing our differences. It almost seems as though we should assume that all people have equal gifts, that people of all groups, backgrounds, and educational attainments are equally qualified for every position. Or, if they are not equally qualified, they should be made equally qualified by a reduction of the qualifications.

Of course we know that not everybody has the same gifts, and not everybody is qualified for every job. Not everyone is qualified to teach nuclear physics or to play linebacker in the NFL. On the whole, fewer women than men are competent to be lumberjacks. And, although one coach was actually fired for saying so, more blacks than whites are competent to play in the NBA. On the other hand, if someone were to exclude whites from professional basketball on the basis of this generalization, he would be taking an extreme position, exaggerating difference at the expense of sameness.

A rational and biblical understanding of these matters requires a more precise understanding of the nature of human sameness and difference. In what follows, I shall focus on racial and national differences, and later on differences in "enablement." But the principles discussed here are applicable to other kinds of differences as well.

THE NATIONS IN SCRIPTURE

In the most fundamental sense, all human beings belong to one race. As Paul said, God "made from one man every nation of mankind to live on all the face of the earth, having determined allotted periods and the boundaries of their dwelling place" (Acts 17:26). Adam is the father of us all, and, following the great flood, Noah is the father of us all.

Nevertheless, Paul also refers to different "nations." The nations are first of all the descendants of the three sons of Noah: Shem, Ham, and Japheth. In his final prophecy, Noah pronounces a blessing on Shem, who turns out to be the ancestor of the Israelites and other Semites (Gen. 10:21–31; 11:10–32), and a secondary blessing on Japheth, that he will dwell in the tents of Shem (Gen. 9:20–27). Japheth is considered to be the ancestor of the great Gentile nations (10:2–5), and this prophecy is wonderfully fulfilled in Jesus, for in him the blessings of Israel are given to the Gentiles. In this prophecy, nothing is said about Ham, but Ham's son Canaan is cursed for Ham's sin of looking at his father's nakedness. Canaan, of course, is the ancestor of the Palestinian tribes that God later calls Israel to destroy (10:15–20).

The nations, therefore, are not equal in every respect, though individuals in those nations are all made in God's image. God gives to the nations different roles to play in history. The blessing on Shem anticipates the special role of Israel in bringing salvation to the world. The blessing on Japheth anticipates the dependence of all nations on the Christ who comes through Israel. The curse on Canaan shows the truth of Exodus 20:5, that God visits the sins of the fathers upon the children.[1]

God begins the actual division of the nations at the Tower of Babel (Gen. 11:1–9). Human beings sometime after the flood sought to maintain a unified civilization around an idolatrous structure, rather than obeying God's command to fill the earth. God cursed their project by confusing their languages. The diversity of language is one of the main differences between nations. In this story, sameness yields even more to difference.

The story of Abraham in Genesis 12 continues the progressive narrowing of God's redemptive blessing to one nation, Israel, and ultimately to one person, Jesus Christ. But from the beginning God indicates that the blessing of Abraham is ultimately for all the nations of the world: "And I will make of you a great nation, and I will bless you and make your name great, so that you will be a blessing. I will bless those who bless you, and him who dishonors you I will curse, and in you all the

---

1. For a discussion of the apparent unfairness of this, see chapter 25.

families of the earth shall be blessed" (Gen. 12:2–3; cf. 18:18; 22:18; 26:4; 28:14; Jer. 4:2; Acts 3:25; Gal. 3:8, 16).

Isaiah actually foresees a spiritual equality between Israel and its great enemies:

> And the LORD will strike Egypt, striking and healing, and they will return to the LORD, and he will listen to their pleas for mercy and heal them.
>
> In that day there will be a highway from Egypt to Assyria, and Assyria will come into Egypt, and Egypt into Assyria, and the Egyptians will worship with the Assyrians. In that day Israel will be the third with Egypt and Assyria, a blessing in the midst of the earth, whom the LORD of hosts has blessed, saying, "Blessed be Egypt my people, and Assyria the work of my hands, and Israel my inheritance." (Isa. 19:22–25)

Although God reminds Israel regularly of his concern for the nations, much of the law given through Moses aimed at isolating Israel from the other nations, protecting her from the sinful influences of other cultures. But even the law was given as a witness:

> See, I have taught you statutes and rules, as the LORD my God commanded me, that you should do them in the land that you are entering to take possession of it. Keep them and do them, for that will be your wisdom and your understanding in the sight of the peoples, who, when they hear all these statutes, will say, "Surely this great nation is a wise and understanding people." For what great nation is there that has a god so near to it as the LORD our God is to us, whenever we call upon him? (Deut. 4:5–7)

The purity of Israel, separated as it was from the other nations, was to be a witness to the nations, inciting their jealousy, enticing them also to worship the true God.

But many Israelites took their divinely imposed isolation as permission to despise other nations. The Pharisaic movement of Jesus' time promoted the notion that other nations were dogs and dirt. Jesus himself, however, reached out to Gentiles. Of him, Matthew 12:18–21 quotes the promise of Isaiah 42:1–3: "Behold, my servant whom I have chosen, my beloved with whom my soul is well pleased. I will put my Spirit upon him, and he will proclaim justice to the Gentiles . . . and in his name the Gentiles will hope" (cf. Luke 2:32).

Jesus ministers to a Roman centurion in Matthew 8:5–13, and finds in him a faith greater than that in anyone in Israel. In Matthew 15:21–28, he grants the request of a Canaanite woman, after a conversation that emphasizes her non-Jewish ancestry and includes an ironic reference to her status as a "dog" at the Jewish table. In the Great Commission, Matthew 28:18–20, Jesus declares that the primary responsibility of the church is to take the gospel to the whole world. As I emphasized in chapter 13, the Great Commission reverses the centripetal movement of the Old Testament (the nations coming to Jerusalem) to a centrifugal movement (God's people bringing the gospel to the nations), and it removes those Old Testament laws that aimed at isolating God's people from other nations.

Nevertheless, even after Pentecost, the early Christians are reluctant to minister to Gentiles. Even Peter hesitates until God gives him a vision and a direct command (Acts 10:1–33). He responds obediently: "So Peter opened his mouth and said: 'Truly I understand that God shows no partiality, but in every nation anyone who fears him and does what is right is acceptable to him'" (vv. 34–35). Then the Holy Spirit comes upon the Gentiles gathered to hear Peter, and he responds, "Can anyone withhold water for baptizing these people, who have received the Holy Spirit just as we have?" (v. 47). The church also welcomes the Gentile believers (Acts 11:1–18). Yet at a later time, Peter's behavior is not consistent with his openness to Gentile believers, and Paul has to rebuke him (Gal. 2:11–14).

God appointed Paul as an apostle, with the special responsibility of taking the gospel to Gentiles (Acts 9:15). Paul preached in synagogues wherever he went, but when the Jews rejected his message, he went to Gentiles (Acts 13:46–48; 18:6; 22:21; 26:17–20; 28:28). In subsequent history, God established churches throughout the world, anticipating the great anthem of Revelation: "And they sang a new song, saying, 'Worthy are you to take the scroll and to open its seals, for you were slain, and by your blood you ransomed people for God from every tribe and language and people and nation'" (Rev. 5:9; cf. 7:9).

The early church had to overcome a high racial barrier between Jews and Gentiles. Some of the Jewish Christians insisted that the Gentiles had to keep the whole law in order to be saved: to be Christians, they needed first to become Jews. Circumcision was, therefore, a particularly difficult issue (Rom. 2:26–29; 3:30; 4:9–12; 1 Cor. 7:19; Gal. 5:2–3, 6, 11; 6:12–15; Col. 3:11). But the Jerusalem council of Acts 15:1–35 declared that Gentiles were free from such requirements, though they should "abstain from the things polluted by idols, and from sexual immorality, and from what has been strangled, and from blood" (v. 20) in order to avoid offending Jews. So both Gentiles and Jews had to bend, to leave their comfort zone. The Gentiles needed to give attention to avoiding offense, and the Jews needed to forego their legalism and exclusiveness.

The New Testament doesn't mention other possible racial or national tensions, such as between Greeks and Romans or between Athenians and Corinthians. But the apostles certainly would have said that if Christ can tear down the barrier between Jews and Gentiles, he can also break down any lesser barrier. Recall Galatians 3:28, "There is neither Jew nor Greek, there is neither slave nor free, there is neither male nor female, for you are all one in Christ Jesus." This is not to say that these differences no longer exist, but this verse proclaims that in Christ all barriers to fellowship among groups of people are removed. Everyone in Christ ought to love everyone else in Christ. Differences between us on a human level are small compared to our unity in Christ. As we have seen, even the tension between leaders and followers is relieved when the leader is a servant leader and the follower is a servant follower.

Romans 12:3–13 and 1 Corinthians 12:4–31 do not focus on racial or national differences, but they mention other differences among us that sometimes cause tension. These passages celebrate those differences: they are gifts. God has given each of us distinct gifts, to build up the whole body. The foot should not complain, "Because I am not a hand, I do not belong to the body" (1 Cor. 12:15). Nor can the eye say to the hand, "I have no need of you" (v. 21). Every part of the body needs every other part. So God does not erase differences among us. In some ways, he increases them, by gifting each of us in a different way. But he expects us, not in spite of those differences, but because of them, to love each other all the more deeply. So Paul's consideration of gifts in 1 Corinthians 12 leads to his hymn to love in chapter 13.

So the Catechism is right to emphasize that Christians have a duty to "regard the dignity and worth of each other, in giving honor to go one before another; and to rejoice in each other's gifts and advancement, as their own." It is hard to recognize dignity and worth in people who are very different from ourselves. But we must make the effort, relying on God's grace. He calls us to honor all people, as we have seen, without making any exceptions for racial and cultural differences. And he calls us, both in the fifth commandment and in the tenth, not to covet the gifts and achievements of others, but to rejoice in them. If we could do that, divisions in the church over race and nationality could be overcome.

SLAVERY

In the United States, there have been conflicts historically between many ethnic and national groups. Waves of immigration from Germany,

Ireland, Italy, Eastern Europe, and the Far East have encountered disrespect from the immigrants who came before them. And the earliest immigrants, the Native Americans, have arguably been treated worst of all.

But the largest racial problem, in terms of its impact on society, has existed between African-Americans, descendants of slaves, and whites, whose ancestors either owned slaves or largely tolerated the existence of slavery. The history of slavery continues to create hostility between black and white, and subsequent history has heightened that tension. After the Civil War, promises of restitution, whether travel back to Africa or "forty acres and a mule," were broken, and the former slaves, denied education, property, and even family ties during their bondage, were left to fend for themselves. For many decades, American society, abetted by laws and courts, segregated the races, relegating blacks to separate and unequal schools, housing, and other facilities, backed up by violence even to the point of lynching.

School segregation ended officially in 1954, and later civil rights legislation protected voting rights and required equality in public accommodations. Desegregation, even affirmative action, has since been the rule in the marketplace, and businesses have reached out to African-Americans as a significant market for their products and services. But discrimination, including informal distrust and disparagement of blacks, continues in many circles.

There also remain gaps in education and economic achievement. Rates of illegitimacy, fatherless homes, and crime are unacceptably high among African-Americans. Liberals tend to explain these facts as the residue of slavery, segregation, and discrimination. Conservatives see them to some extent as an abdication of personal responsibility, using history as an excuse. On a biblical view, there is truth in both of these explanations. Slavery, segregation, and discrimination are horrible crimes against a people, one for which there has not been suitable restitution or reconciliation. One can and should understand "black rage," the anger of African-Americans over these events.[2] And white Christians need to be far more sympathetic, even empathetic.[3] On the other hand, even these great crimes are not an excuse for violating God's law.

We can make a start toward understanding the problem if we ask what Scripture teaches about slavery.

---

2. It's important to note in many areas of ethical discussion that understanding is not condoning. To understand is to recognize human solidarity, to recognize how we would feel if we were in the same situation. Such understanding is often necessary if we are to know how to deal with people.

3. If any readers disparage this advice as sentimental or romantic, I would refer them back to the discussion of emotions in the concluding section of chapter 21.

The chief biblical words translated "slave" are the Hebrew *'ebed* and the Greek *doulos*. These words are often translated "servant" and have a broad range of meaning. It is often unclear whether they refer to bondservice or to a form of employment. We should remember also that the vassal of the covenant was called a "servant." The covenant is a relationship between Lord and servant. So the people of Israel generally are God's servants (Lev. 25:55). And within God's people, some leaders are servants of God in a special way. God says, for example, that Moses is "my servant" (Num. 12:7–8; Josh. 1:2). Paul likewise identifies himself as a servant of Christ (Rom. 1:1). As such, he is also a servant to the church (1 Cor. 9:19), expressing the idea of servant-leadership we considered earlier. This idea gives intensity and seriousness to the common figurative use of the word *servant* to indicate humility and willingness to please someone else, as in Genesis 18:3, 5.

Nevertheless, Scripture does refer clearly to some forms of service for which the English term *slavery* is appropriate: "the state of one bound in servitude as the property of a slaveholder or household."[4] In the Old Testament, there were two distinct forms of slavery: the slavery of foreigners, and the slavery of Israelites. We shall also consider Greco-Roman slavery and slavery in the American South.

Foreign Slaves

God authorized Israel to take slaves in some cases from conquered cities. In Deuteronomy 20:10–11, he says, "When you draw near to a city to fight against it, offer terms of peace to it. And if it responds to you peaceably and it opens to you, then all the people who are found in it shall do forced labor for you and shall serve you." God prescribes no termination to this "forced labor" or slavery. These conquered people are slaves for life, unless they escape or somehow manage to purchase their freedom. In a way, however, this sort of slavery is a mercy. This provision applies to "cities that are very far from you" (v. 15), beyond the land of promise. But as for the cities within the Holy Land, Israel may not take slaves from them, because all the inhabitants of these cities are to be killed (v. 16). Slavery was the fate of the Gibeonites who deceived Israel into believing that they lived far beyond the Holy Land and persuaded Israel to take an oath not to attack them (Josh. 9). But no doubt the Gibeonites relished their slavery in comparison to the alternative.

God also permitted Israel to buy slaves from the nations around them and from foreigners who lived in Israel (Lev. 25:44–46). This also was a

---

4. *The American Heritage College Dictionary*, 3d ed. (Boston: Houghton Mifflin, 2000), 1280.

permanent form of slavery. A father could bequeath slaves to his children "to inherit as a possession forever" (v. 46).

Taking slaves from conquered nations was a common practice in the ancient world. In Israel, however, it was a by-product of holy war (see Deut. 20). Certainly these slaves fell under the general provisions in the law for Israel to show kindness. As we have seen, the fourth commandment specifically mandates weekly rest for slaves, as well as family. Often in the law, God reminds Israel that they too were slaves in Egypt, so they should deal with their slaves differently from how other nations deal with theirs. Significantly, the law forbids Israelites to return escaped slaves to their masters (Deut. 23:15–16). And it requires masters to set a slave free if he loses an eye or a tooth from a beating (Ex. 21:26–27).

There is no reason to think that this institution continues after the time of the theocracy. The provision for slavery in Deuteronomy 20 (vv. 11–14) is an outworking of God's promise to give Israel victory because they are his holy people (vv. 3–4). God takes pains to make clear that this victory is supernatural, by urging Israel to keep the army as small as possible (vv. 5–9). No nation today shares the covenant status of ancient Israel. So God has not promised victory in war to any modern nation, nor has he authorized the taking of slaves on that basis. He has not specifically forbidden it either. But nothing in Scripture stands in the way of its abolition, and, as we shall see, there are substantial biblical principles that encourage its abolition.

HEBREW SLAVES

Another form of slavery in the Old Testament was limited to covenant members. Exodus 21:1–11, Leviticus 25:39–55, and Deuteronomy 15:12–18 contain what is called "Hebrew servant legislation." I have some reservation about describing this relationship as slavery, because Leviticus 25:39–40 says that in this relationship the master "shall not make him serve as a slave; he shall be with you as a hired servant and as a sojourner." Nevertheless, as with slavery, this relationship begins with the sale of one person to another (v. 39a; Ex. 21:2; Deut. 15:12). A person might sell himself into servitude, or a master might purchase a Hebrew servant from someone else. Typically, a person would sell himself to pay a debt, or simply because he had become too poor to support himself and his family (Lev. 25:39). The master, then, could sell him to someone else if he wished. So I do believe that the term *slavery* is appropriate to describe this relationship. The point of Leviticus 25:39 is that the kind of service required of Hebrew slaves should be more like that of hired servants than that of foreign slaves.

What is most notable about this kind of slavery, in contrast to the first kind I discussed, is that it has a termination. In Exodus 21:2, the Hebrew slave "shall serve six years, and in the seventh he shall go out free, for nothing." The same provision is found in Deuteronomy 15:12. In Leviticus 25:40, the termination is the Jubilee. It is not entirely clear how these two provisions fit together. Perhaps the resultant teaching is that the slave is to be released either in the seventh year or in the Jubilee, whichever comes first. It is also unclear how the seventh-year release is related to the sabbatical year in which Israel was to give rest to the land. Deuteronomy 15 deals with the former in the context of the latter. But Exodus 21 does not mention the sabbatical year and says that a term of slavery will always last six years, rather than lasting for whatever period remains until the next sabbatical. In any case, the themes of rest and liberation that we noted under the fourth commandment are found in these contexts as well, together with the six/one pattern.

So, in this legislation, the slave can look forward to freedom. Slavery in Israel is not a perpetual state. Further, the slave is to be treated, according to Leviticus 25:40, "as a hired servant and as a sojourner." And when he is released, "you shall not let him go empty-handed. You shall furnish him liberally out of your flock, out of your threshing floor, and out of your winepress. As the LORD your God has blessed you, you shall give to him" (Deut. 15:13–14). These gifts are evidently to celebrate his freedom, and also to give him a new beginning in a trade.[5]

The emphasis here is that the slave is a fellow Israelite who has fallen on hard times, whether or not of his own making. The master is to be generous to his poor brother. This kind of slavery is a blessing, a help to someone in need. Deuteronomy 15 places this provision in the context of other provisions regarding poverty (vv. 7–11).

In this institution, there is no division of existing families. If a man enters slavery with his wife, she shall be released with him (Ex. 21:3). However, "if his master gives him a wife and she bears him sons or daughters, the wife and her children shall be her master's, and he shall go out alone" (v. 4). This provision may sound cruel to our ears, but we need to remember that the wife also has a debt to pay and the duties of her term of slavery

---

5. James B. Jordan, in "Slavery in Biblical Perspective" (Th.M. thesis, Westminster Theological Seminary, 1980), available at http://www.biblicalhorizons.com/catalogue.htm, says that this bondage is a kind of apprenticeship. Often habits of irresponsibility lead to poverty. The apprenticeship trains the slave in new habits of godly labor. This form of slavery in effect puts the slave through a second childhood, giving him the discipline that he should have learned while growing up. Jordan's insights on slavery have been very helpful to me.

to fulfill. She too will be released after six years of service, and then she is free to return to her husband. A modern analogy would be to a man who marries a woman who is in prison. She will remain in prison until her term is completed, but afterward she will be free to join him. But if the man cannot bear to wait even a few years to establish his household with his wife and children, and if he genuinely loves his master, he may voluntarily accept a status of permanent slavery (Ex. 21:5–6; Deut. 15:16–17).

Other provisions of this legislation include the special rights of slave women (Ex. 21:7–11) and provision for redeeming Jews who are sold to non-Jews in the land (Lev. 25:47–55).

This form of slavery, unlike others, is truly a benevolent institution. It is a remedy for poverty and an opportunity for a new start in life. Most significantly, its goal is freedom.

Like the first form of slavery, this one is deeply connected to specifically Israelite institutions, in this case the sabbatical years and the Jubilee. New covenant believers, therefore, do not have a divine mandate to continue this form of slavery. But it is well worth asking the pragmatic question whether the modern world would be better off if something like Hebrew servant-hood were in place. Bankruptcy is the usual modern way of dealing with unmanageable debt. But at some point there should be a system in which people not only receive debt relief, but also receive training in godly habits that can lead to a debt-free existence. It should not, of course, be called slavery; that would be a public relations nightmare. But Scripture itself, as we have seen, distinguishes this practice in some respects from slavery. A phrase like "debt-relief apprenticeship" would aptly describe this practice and recommend it to thoughtful citizens. Such apprenticeships could be offered, not only by private households, but also by corporations.

GRECO-ROMAN SLAVERY

The references to slavery in the New Testament generally refer to Greco-Roman practices, though Paul's references to himself and Christians as slaves of Christ reflect more the covenantal language of the Old Testament. Greco-Roman slavery had many variations, but it is possible to list some general features. As in the first form of slavery in Israel discussed above, many became slaves as prisoners of war. As in the second form, many also became slaves through poverty. Parents who could not care for their children often sold them into slavery. And many people were born slaves: the children of slaves were slaves themselves. Their duties were varied, but were more often domestic than agricultural. They cleaned and cooked, guarded the household, and even handled financial matters for the family. Many were highly intelligent and were trusted with great responsibility. Among them were musicians, government figures, philosophers, and poets.

Masters often freed their slaves. A slave could purchase his freedom, or someone else could do it for him. Or a master would free a slave as a reward for some special service.

Paul tells slaves to obey their masters with sincerity of heart (Eph. 6:5–9; cf. Col. 3:22–4:1). Peter adds that they should be subject to their masters, "not only to the good and gentle but also to the unjust" (1 Peter 2:18)—emphasizing, as with other relationships, the merit of unjust suffering. In this connection, he invokes Christ's sufferings as the model (vv. 21–25). Peter and Paul here accept the institution of slavery as it exists. They do not encourage rebellion. Paul urges such contentment also in 1 Corinthians 7:21, though he also says there that "if you can gain your freedom, avail yourself of the opportunity."

But Paul gives commands also to masters. In his letter to Philemon, Paul asks his friend to receive back Onesimus, a runaway slave who has recently become a Christian. Paul offers to pay anything that Onesimus may owe. He wants Philemon to accept Onesimus "no longer as a slave but more than a slave, as a beloved brother" (v. 16). Paul here says that Christian brotherhood transcends the institution of slavery. And Paul's admonitions to masters call the very idea of slavery into question. In Ephesians 6:9, he says, "Masters, do the same to them"—evidently, "rendering service with a good will as to the Lord" (v. 7)—"and stop your threatening, knowing that he who is both their Master and yours is in heaven, and that there is no partiality with him" (cf. Col. 4:1).

Here again is the principle of servant leadership that we explored in chapter 31. Masters are to serve their slaves. They are not even to threaten them! These commands of Paul undermine the whole institution of slavery. Slavery without threats is scarcely slavery. One characteristic that distinguishes slavery from other employment is the right of the master to beat the slave, and it is the constant threat of beating that supports the relationship. Servant leadership, applied to the institution of slavery, virtually reverses the roles of master and slave.[6]

So the overall thrust of New Testament teaching is toward the abolition of Greco-Roman slavery. Christians did not carry on a political campaign to end it. They did not have the power for that. And it was many centuries

---

6. As with the relations of husband and wife and of parents and children, Paul does not remove the element of authority. The master still has the right to tell the slave what to do. But servant leadership certainly revolutionizes this relationship, since serving is what it is all about.

before the church fully implemented this implication of the gospel. But eventually slavery fell to the gospel, not to secular egalitarianism.

SLAVERY IN THE AMERICAN SOUTH

During the seventeenth to nineteenth centuries, slavery in the West was almost entirely the result of kidnapping. Western nations continued to fight wars, but they did not enslave their prisoners, as in the ancient world. Slaves came, rather, from the slave trade. This trade began primarily in Africa, where people were kidnapped and forced to go on board ships. They were transported, under hideous conditions, to various countries, including America, where they were sold as slaves. Whites were involved in the slave trade, but also Arabs and black Africans themselves.[7]

The lot of slaves in this system was more degrading than in any of the three forms of slavery described above. Family members were often separated and sold to different households. Education, even learning to read, was forbidden. Further, this institution was based on an unscriptural racist theory, that God made black Africans to be slaves,[8] and qualified them only for domestic work and heavy labor. So there was no provision for their liberation, as in the Hebrew servant legislation. Slaves were not trained for the responsibilities of a free life.

Though some Christians defended this kind of slavery by reference to Scripture, it is clear that Scripture condemns it. In the Bible, kidnapping is a capital crime. Exodus 21:16 reads, "Whoever steals a man and sells him, and anyone found in possession of him, shall be put to death." And Deuteronomy 24:7 says, "If a man is found stealing one of his brothers, the people of Israel, and if he treats him as a slave or sells him, then that thief shall die. So you shall purge the evil from your midst."

What is most saddening, in a way, is that even though many slaves became Christians, their professing Christian masters rarely treated them as brothers and sisters in Christ. Worship was racially segregated. Servant leadership was rare in the relations of whites to blacks within the Christian

7. Many African-Americans have become Muslims, or have adopted Muslim names, thinking of the Arabs as fellow Africans, not tainted by the sins of America against them. Many of these people are unaware of the role that Muslim Arabs played in the history of the slave trade. See, for example, "The Forgotten Holocaust: The Eastern Slave Trade," at http://www.geocities.com/CollegePark/Classroom/9912/easterntrade.html.

8. Some defenders of slavery saw black Africans as descendants of Ham, cursed by God for Ham's sin in Gen. 9:22. But in the biblical text, verses 25–27, the curse passes on to Ham's son Canaan, and Canaan is the progenitor, not of Africans, but of the tribes of Palestine prior to Israel's conquest. This defense of slavery was a transparent rationalization for a biblically abhorrent practice.

community. We recall Old Testament warnings against treating fellow Israelites harshly, and New Testament admonitions that masters are to "stop threatening." In the Hebrew servant passages, the slave is to be prepared for freedom. But American slave owners rarely observed those principles.

So my earlier commendations of the Hebrew servant relationship should not be misunderstood as approving of slavery in the American South. The latter form of slavery was contrary to God's will, and we may thank God for its eradication.[9]

The crime of modern slavery has never been adequately punished. When slavery ended, slaves should at least have received substantial reparations from anyone who owned slaves or was involved in the slave trade. (On a more literal application of the Old Testament statute, slave owners and traders should have been put to death.[10]) The broader society also bore responsibility for tolerating this crime for centuries. At the very least, former slaves should have received sufficient wealth and education to succeed in American society, or to return to Africa, whichever they chose. None of that took place. Rather, the former slaves were mostly left to make it on their own, relegated to the status of second-class citizens, often in danger of violence. The aftermath of slavery, then, was a second crime against African-Americans.[11]

9. Recall from chapter 33 that William Webb uses slavery as a crucial illustration of his approach of deriving ethical norms from the "trajectory" or "redemptive movement" of Scripture, even when his understanding of that movement contradicts the literal teaching of Scripture. My method here is different. I think that Scripture does not require us to maintain any form of slavery in our day, and that larger principles of Scripture are incompatible with it (except for Hebrew servanthood). So the teaching of Scripture is sufficient to ground opposition to modern slavery. One need not appeal to some trajectory that contradicts the commands of Scripture.

10. Some capital crimes in Old Testament law were subject to ransom (Ex. 21:30; Num. 35:31–32). In the present case, it would have been best if the slave owner had agreed to pay his slaves a substantial ransom for his life.

11. Native Americans were treated as badly, or worse. In terms of Old Testament law, they should have received double restitution for everything stolen from them, and a treaty should have been arranged to give them sovereign control over a large part of North America. And that treaty, unlike other treaties made with Native Americans, should have been honored. Why, then, should they not have been acknowledged as rulers of the whole continent? Because the Indians, before the whites arrived, had not developed effective organizational control of that large a region. They did not "own" the land in the modern sense. There was much ungoverned territory. And in the early days Indians profited from the presence of whites in these areas. In many cases, they welcomed white settlers. So something can be said for the rights of those whites (like the Pilgrims) who settled in America, on the assumption that they were welcome and could enter into mutually beneficial relationships with Indians. And some consideration must be given to white families that were attacked and killed without negotiation or warning. There is plenty of blame to go around, but on the whole Native Americans were far more sinned against than sinning. The present reservation system compounds the injustice.

It is hard to know what might be done today to remedy this injustice. Lawsuits have been brought against corporations thought to have profited from slavery, but such responsibility is very difficult to assess after more than a century. Affirmative action, both by government and private enterprise, has helped many blacks obtain educational and employment benefits. But affirmative action has been a mixed blessing, for it often places a stigma on those it helps. Even when recipients of affirmative action are well qualified for their benefits, observers often assume that they are not. And affirmative action places a disadvantage on people who do not receive such benefits, many of whom have no demonstrable connection to slavery or the evils connected with it.[12]

The goal (for all groups of people) is surely for success to be based on accomplishments, rather than on charity based on race. But the history of slavery, segregation, and discrimination is still among the reasons for the economic gap between blacks and whites. Society still has an obligation to narrow that gap.

The gap is narrowing, in any case, and we should thank God for that. As legal and social discrimination lessen, the forces of free markets are set free to reward real accomplishment. African-Americans now have unprecedented opportunities for employment in many fields and unprecedented achievements in those fields. Welfare reform, once thought to be an impending disaster for African-Americans, has brought many into the workplace.

So it may be that the best way for society to pay its debt is to (1) allow the free market to reward genuine qualifications and achievement, (2) provide for those of all races who cannot afford the basic necessities of life (see later discussion of the eighth commandment), and (3) maintain law and order in all strata of society, without racial discrimination. The church, moreover, needs to present the gospel of Christ according to its original intention, as a gospel for all nations (see discussion later in this chapter). For the root of racial injustice is in the heart.

PREJUDICE

Although legal barriers to minority advancement have been largely erased, and social barriers have also decreased, racial and other minorities

---

12. Affirmative action tends to be more beneficial on a small scale than on a large one. When a teacher, for example, singles out a disadvantaged student and works with him so that he is motivated to study and able to reach higher levels, that teacher deserves commendation. The same is true for employers and others. But when a university routinely adds points to the test scores of applicants, based on race alone, without any plan to bring people admitted on that basis up to the level of other students, there is no reason to think that they are doing anybody any good, and there are many reasons to think they are doing harm.

are often disparaged in informal ways. People of one race are often prejudiced against those of another. There is also prejudice between people of different genders, religions, and nationalities. This prejudice is sometimes expressed in words that disparage a group of people. Sometimes the disparagement is real, sometimes only imagined. Sometimes people mean not to disparage, but their language carries unpleasant connotations that they are not fully aware of. Sometimes such comments are made in jest. Ethnic humor is not necessarily a bad thing, but it should not be used in situations where it is likely to bring hurt. And it is often the case that ethnic humor masks a real hostility.

Attitudes, acts, and words perceived to be prejudicial are often described as racist, sexist, and so forth. Prejudice means, literally, judging or evaluating someone before such judgment is appropriate. In one sense, everyone has the same value, for everyone is made in God's image. But, as we have seen, there are moral and spiritual differences among people, different kinds of gifts (both natural and spiritual), and different levels of training and accomplishment. So we often find ourselves evaluating one another on moral and spiritual matters, and also on whether a person has the ability necessary for a specific task. But such judgments should be made fairly, on the basis of evidence and careful thought. Prejudiced thinking makes such evaluations too hastily, without sufficient evidence or thought, because of some assumptions that precede any fair examination of the evidence. Prejudice against an individual is sometimes based on evaluation of a group to which the person belongs. If it is based on judgments about race, we call it racial prejudice or racism. If it is based on sex, it is sexism.

As always in human knowledge, there is an ethical factor in our judgments of other people. Scripture teaches that we should think the best of one another. Criminal judgments in the Old Testament required two or three witnesses (Deut. 17:6; 19:15; Heb. 10:28), and that rule continues in New Testament church discipline (Matt. 18:16; 2 Cor. 13:1; 1 Tim. 5:19). So Paul tells Timothy, "In the presence of God and of Christ Jesus and of the elect angels I charge you to keep these rules without prejudging, doing nothing from partiality" (1 Tim. 5:21). James also opposes partiality (James 2:4; 3:17). *Partiality* is the biblical term for prejudice. It involves treating someone badly, not because the person deserves it, but because of an irrational preference.

So in our relations with one another, our love "bears all things, believes all things" (1 Cor. 13:7). We should evaluate others favorably unless there is strong evidence to the contrary. In personal relations as well as legal ones, the burden of proof is always on the accuser. People are innocent until proved guilty.

That is the rule in moral and spiritual judgments. It is different, of course, in judgments of people's gifts and abilities. We cannot assume that someone is a skilled tennis player simply because we lack evidence to the contrary. It is appropriate in such cases to require some evidence before making a judgment. So when Paul lists the requirements for deacons, he requires them to be "tested first" (1 Tim. 3:10). Elders, too, must give evidence of moral and spiritual maturity before they are appointed to office (vv. 1–7). But in this area too, we should make judgments based on people's accomplishments, not our own prejudices.

Is it ever legitimate to judge or evaluate people based on the groups to which they belong? Sometimes group membership itself is a disqualification. A Muslim, for example, is *ipso facto* unqualified to be an elder in a Presbyterian church. Membership in organizations dedicated to crime and/or violence is itself prohibited by law. To join such an organization is to support crime, and governments rightly penalize that.

In other cases, the relationship between group membership and the individual is not so clear. Is it right, for example, to be suspicious of all Muslims in the wake of the atrocities of modern terrorism? I shall not say much here about the teaching of the Qur'an itself, though such an investigation is relevant to our question. The Qur'an sometimes encourages violence against enemies of Islam, and sometimes promotes peaceful coexistence. The Bible also contains warlike passages, which Christians treat either metaphorically or as references to the divinely authorized conquest of Canaan by Israel. Although I am not a Qur'an scholar, it seems to me that the Qur'an warrants peaceful coexistence of Muslims with non-Muslims (especially the Jewish and Christian "peoples of the Book"), except in a struggle over the governance of "Muslim lands," which are variously defined.

Clearly, however, there are some Muslims today who justify violence against innocent civilians in pursuit of their religious and political objectives. This brand of Islam is a popular movement in many places. By way of comparison: a few lone gunmen in recent years have killed abortion providers in the name of Christ, but they have received almost no support from Christians who are opposed to abortion. In contrast, when New York and Washington were attacked on September 11, 2001, large numbers of Palestinians danced in the streets. Although many Muslims have expressed abhorrence of these attacks and of terrorism generally, only recently (in August 2005) have some Muslim leaders pronounced *fatwas* (in effect, excommunication) against terrorists. Many imams throughout the world continue to advocate violence, without much resistance from fellow Muslims. And Muslims have done little to discourage the extremist teaching of Wahhabism, either in its home country of Saudi Arabia or in the many madrasas (Islamic schools) throughout the world that promulgate such views. Kathleen Parker says that Muslim organizations "are quick to point out that fanatics are a tiny minority and account for only about 1 percent of Muslims worldwide."[13] But, she adds, one percent of the 1.2 billion Muslims in the world is 12 million, roughly the population of Ohio. Statements of condemnation by Muslim leaders are not enough. "Zero tolerance is what we're looking for here. . . . Until the hatred that breeds that kind of cultic dementia is eliminated by the moderate Muslims that insist on the West's understanding, Islam has a problem."[14]

Christian believers should not prejudge individual Muslims to be terrorists or their sympathizers because of their religious affiliation. Still, it is not irrational or prejudicial to give extra scrutiny (in airport security, for example) to Muslim men between the ages of 18 and 50. Such extra scrutiny is not a judgment of guilt, but a reasonable law-enforcement precaution. There is a large, worldwide conspiracy to destroy innocent life that consists mostly of Muslim males in this age group. If police knew that a Caucasian between 25 and 30 with a mustache was about to rob a bank, it would not be prejudicial for them to give special scrutiny to men of this description near banks. And it would make no sense for them to give equal scrutiny to African-American women over 70, especially when time is important. Certainly such extra scrutiny would be a hassle for Muslims, but the solution is not to demand equal treatment of every ethnic group, but to redouble efforts to eliminate terrorist movements, efforts in which Muslim cooperation is invaluable.

Nor is it unreasonable to take special precautions in other situations where evidence indicates the presence of danger. In a high-crime area, one has to be suspicious of people, much as one may try to dissociate that suspicion from race itself. New York's former mayor, Edward I. Koch, says:

> Today, most whites, myself included, would feel very uncomfortable in a totally black neighborhood, particularly at night. What has happened in the last thirty years? Well, Jesse Jackson summed up the reasonableness of white fear in black neighborhoods when he recently said, "There is nothing more painful to me at this stage in my life than to walk down the street and hear footsteps and start thinking about robbery—then look around and see somebody white and feel relieved."[15]

13. In "There *Might* Be Something About Islam," *Orlando Sentinel*, July 17, 2005, G3.
14. Ibid.
15. Edward I. Koch in *National Review*, May 16, 1994, 34. Available at http://www.mugu.com/cgi-bin/Upstream/Issues/race/blacks.html.

One can become extra cautious in such situations without prejudging the character of any individual.

But, given the legitimacy of reasonable caution, Christians ought to press the envelope, take risks, in bringing Christ to people. There are always risks in dealing with people, especially in seeking to show the love of Christ to them. The apostle Paul certainly chose a risky life when God called him to be apostle to the Gentiles:

> Are they servants of Christ? I am a better one—I am talking like a madman—with far greater labors, far more imprisonments, with countless beatings, and often near death. Five times I received at the hands of the Jews the forty lashes less one. Three times I was beaten with rods. Once I was stoned. Three times I was shipwrecked; a night and a day I was adrift at sea; on frequent journeys, in danger from rivers, danger from robbers, danger from my own people, danger from Gentiles, danger in the city, danger in the wilderness, danger at sea, danger from false brothers; in toil and hardship, through many a sleepless night, in hunger and thirst, often without food, in cold and exposure. And, apart from other things, there is the daily pressure on me of my anxiety for all the churches. (2 Cor. 11:23–28)

This was Paul's "moral heroism" (chapter 12). Paul accepted all kinds of danger, including that of witnessing to dangerous people, both Jews and Gentiles.

RACISM AND SEXISM IN CURRENT DEBATE

In contemporary secular discussions of ethics, the issue of relationships between groups overshadows nearly all others. The groups in view are denominated by race, gender, nationality, creed, sexual preference, age, ability (what we used to call "handicap"), etc., and they are classified, in quasi-Marxist terms, as oppressor groups and victim groups. The oppressor group is usually identified as white, middle-class, Christian, heterosexual males. The issue is the unfair or unequal treatment of the victim group by the oppressor group.

Most all other ethical questions eventually get reduced to this one. Even the abortion issue, which at first glance seems rather far removed from these intergroup issues, gets defined in terms of "choice." And "choice" is defended on the basis of gender autonomy: restricting abortion is sexist, the oppression of women by men.

The attitude of the oppressor group toward the victim group is variously described as racist, sexist, age-ist, weight-ist, homophobic, and so on. These attitudes are seen to be at the root of all social and ethical problems.

Issues of such great concern to people should be discussed, not only with sensitivity, but also with care and precision. Unfortunately, most treatments of them are burdened by ambiguity, confusion of distinct issues, and the substitution of rhetoric for argument. There are many things that can be meant by racism, sexism, and so forth, and many practices are condemned as racist or sexist without much careful thought. In this section, I hope to contribute something to the cause of clarification.

I will be writing primarily about racism, though what I say will often apply to other "isms," *mutatis mutandis*. The issue of sexual preference is rather distinct from the others, however. On a scriptural view, homosexuality is a sin, while it is not a sin to belong to a particular race, gender, or other group. The rest of this chapter, therefore, will not apply, in most cases, to questions of "homophobia."[16]

What does "racism" mean, and what are its manifestations? Let us consider some possibilities, taken from current discussions.

1. Racism is often equated with hatred, so it may be defined as "hating people because of their race or color." Hatred, of course, is something inward.[17] We should be quick to recognize it in ourselves and slow to accuse others of it. Unfortunately, in the current discussion, the reverse is often true. People quickly accuse others of racial hatred, but they almost never admit such hatred in themselves. That is one thing that goes wrong in current discussions of race.

Certainly it is sinful, and irrational, to hate someone merely because of ancestry or skin color. A person cannot help who his ancestors were, and ancestry alone never makes a person worthy of hatred.

I do not doubt that such irrational racial hatred exists, but I suspect it is more rare than many ethical writers and news commentators suppose.

---

16. In general, my view is that Christians should relate to homosexuals as people like themselves, in the image of God and therefore precious, but also fallen and therefore under God's judgment apart from the grace of Christ. We should lovingly present Christ in such a way that brings repentance from sexual and other sins and that leads to a godly lifestyle. In the meantime, we should not support special rights for homosexuals. We should have the right to keep our children from homosexual influences in schools and in the general culture.

17. I am taking *hatred* here to refer to emotional revulsion. I realize that Scripture typically uses the term differently, to indicate practical opposition to the goals of another person. On that definition, (a) hatred is not entirely inward, (b) it is not always wrong, and (c) it is not incompatible with love. But in this chapter I am trying to use the term as it is used in the contemporary discussion.

Most of the time, what we call "racial hatred" is really something more subtle, and with a greater initial claim, at least, to rationality. I explore those possibilities below.

2. One distinct form of "racial hatred" is hating members of a particular race because of perceived wrongs done by that racial group. This is not racial hatred pure and simple. Here the hatred is not directed toward people merely because of their ancestry, but because of unreconciled grievances. African-Americans often continue to resent whites because of the history of slavery and segregation. Whites often resent blacks because of the high incidence of crime, illegitimacy, and drug use in their communities, and because of the rhetoric of some black leaders who blame these problems on white society. The problem in either case is not ancestry or skin color as such; the problem is behavior.

With simple racial hatred (#1 above), the solution is obvious: biblical repentance. In this second case, finding solutions is more difficult. Of course, we must certainly, as in the previous case, set aside our hatred. For one thing, it is not fair to blame an entire race for the activities of some of its members, especially when those activities were done in the past, by members of earlier generations.

Some have said that although it is illegitimate for an oppressor group to hate or resent an oppressed group, the reverse is legitimate. But we should reject that argument. If there is anything wrong with racism, sexism, and the like, it is that people are hated or discriminated against or judged, not for what they have done, but solely on the basis of their membership in a group. If that moral principle is correct, it must be applied universally. It is wrong for any racial group to hate any other racial group as a group, regardless of past grievances.

But, as we saw earlier, lingering hatreds and resentments going back many years, even centuries, are not likely to be overcome by any social or political policy. Consideration of such intractable problems should lead us to turn all the more to God's grace in Christ, which alone can produce forgiving hearts. In the final analysis, only the forgiveness of Christ can heal these wounds.

3. But "racism" does not always refer to hatred. Sometimes the term is applied to certain beliefs, such as the belief that one race is inferior to another, either generally or in some particular way.

The belief that one race is generally inferior to another is plainly irrational. Considering all the different abilities and disabilities, all the different virtues and vices, existing in the human race, it is not even clear what would be meant by saying that one human being is "generally superior" to another, let alone saying that one *race* is generally superior or inferior.

And even if we could agree on what a superior race would look like, how could that superiority be measured or verified?

Sometimes these discussions focus on whether members of one race are, on the average, more "intelligent" than another. But intelligence is an extremely complicated matter. There are many different kinds of intelligence. Anyone who is skilled at anything can be called "intelligent." That includes quarterbacks, boxers, and musicians, as well as rocket scientists. IQ and other "intelligence" tests do not measure intelligence as such, but only certain kinds of intelligence relevant to academic success.

Sometimes "superiority" in such discussions refers to *moral* superiority. But Scripture consigns all mankind to the status of sinners before God. The argument of Romans 1–3 is that all races, Jews and Gentiles, are equally guilty before God, hopeless apart from divine grace. Paul rebukes those Jews who believed that they had a higher standing with God because of their ancestry.

The biblical teaching about the differences of supernatural gifts in the body of Christ (Rom. 12; 1 Cor. 12) suggests a similar way of looking at the natural gifts in the human race in general. No individual, no race, has all possible human abilities. And the "lesser" abilities are just as necessary to the whole society as are the "greater" ones. Indeed, those that are most widely acclaimed may be less valuable in the sight of God.

4. However, it is not wrong, in my view, to believe that some races generally excel others *in some particular respects*. One coach at a Midwestern college was fired because he asserted that black athletes are, on average, better sprinters and jumpers than whites. His superiors claimed that his remarks were racist. In my view, that was an injustice. The coach's views, in this case, were very probably true, and he should have had freedom to express them.

Earlier I said that it is very unlikely that one race is "generally" superior to another in any meaningful sense. But it is just as unlikely that all races are equal in every particular ability. The diversity of gifts I mentioned above would suggest that neither individuals nor races nor nations are equal in every human ability or skill.

But in contemporary secular discussions it is considered heresy to assert that people of one race or nationality are superior to others, even in some specific respect. Even scientists who conduct studies of genetic influences upon, e.g., IQ, are often dismissed as racist. That is, in my view, a wrong use of the term *racist*. However it may benefit the self-esteem of particular groups, the assumption that everyone is equal in every way is false and certainly detrimental to the progress of science. Clearly there are genetic factors (among many others) influencing human abilities and disabilities, and scientists should be free to study them.

We should remember, however, that these kinds of racial superiorities and inferiorities should not be held against individuals. I have no doubt that proportionately there are more blacks than whites with the ability to play basketball in the NBA. But the cases of Larry Bird and Steve Nash are sufficient to refute the notion that only blacks should be allowed to compete. Perhaps there are even some whites who could compete with the best blacks in sprinting and jumping. Competition should be open to all, within reason,[18] and we should be willing to be surprised at finding exceptions to our generalities.

Similarly, I have no doubt that, on the whole, men make better lumberjacks than women. But it is quite possible that some women may be better than some men at this kind of work. So even if there are group-based superiorities or inferiorities, we should not use them to justify prejudice against individuals.

5. Another kind of belief that is sometimes called racist is the belief that disproportionate numbers of people in a particular racial group are guilty of some kind of wrongdoing. Earlier we discussed belief in the moral superiority of one group over another. Here I am interested in something somewhat different. The present question is an empirical one. It is not a question of overall moral superiority, but of specific practices. Nor am I here concerned, as I was earlier, with historical grievances. Rather, I here speak of *present* grievances.

For example, it is quite evident that among people living in the United States illegally, a disproportionate number are Latino. Americans prominent in the Mafia are mainly of Sicilian ancestry.[19] The defendants at the Nuremberg trials were predominantly German. Recent terrorists have been predominantly Muslim. The number of illegitimate births is disproportionately high in the black community. And slave owners were predominantly white, as are most white-collar criminals in our time.

Scripture does not dispute the fact that certain kinds of sins abound in certain national groups and result in the judgment of those nations. The Canaanites worshiped idols, and their culture degenerated into the worst forms of wickedness. Israel was not *better* than the Canaanites, but at one point in history, the iniquity of the Canaanites was judged to be full.

People are often judged as racist for holding such empirical beliefs. Yet, ironically, pleas for more border security are often attacked as "anti-Hispanic," and cries for stiffer penalties against violent crime are often stigmatized as "anti-black." Some attack the very phrase "law and order" as

---

18. It is OK to exclude overweight, 66-year-old seminary professors.

19. Russian mafia are becoming more prominent these days, if the gangster film genre is to be believed.

a "code word for racism." Thus the victim groups themselves recognize their own disproportionate involvement in some of the problems of society.

It is time for greater honesty about these matters, even when that honesty requires us to reflect critically upon ourselves and our own people—as when Jesse Jackson, as noted earlier, confessed to his own fear of black-on-black crime.

It is not wrong to recognize these realities for what they are. We must not use them as excuses for racial prejudices, however. It should not be assumed that all Mexican-Americans are here illegally, any more than that all Italian-Americans are connected with the Mafia. But we should, in humility, recognize the sins that are characteristic of our own groups and exhort one another to repent of them. It is, of course, easier and more credible for us to deal with the sins of our own races and nationalities than to deal with the sins of other races and nationalities.

6. Other beliefs sometimes called racist include beliefs about what should be done in response to racial problems. Here are some examples:

(a) Belief that racial intermarriage is wrong. The Old Testament, of course, forbade Israelites to marry people of other nations. But this was a religious, not an ethnic requirement. Israel itself was a "mixed multitude," including not only the physical sons of Jacob, but also many Egyptians, Midianites, and even Canaanites such as Rahab and Ruth. Anyone who confessed the God of Israel (and who, if male, underwent circumcision) was an acceptable candidate for marriage.

I know of no biblical principle which discourages interracial marriage as such. Surely, people entering such unions should be prepared to accept the social consequences of their decision without illusion, though I believe that prejudice against such unions has rather drastically declined in recent years.

(b) Belief that races should be separate. Certainly Scripture does not require the physical separation of races, or the kind of *apartheid* once enforced in the Union of South Africa. If no biblical principle excludes racial intermarriage, then certainly Scripture does not require separation of races.

There are, to be sure, places in the world where antagonism is so intense that separation of ethnic groups may be the only workable solution for the present. As of this writing, I know of no other solution for the ethnic conflict in Bosnia, Central Africa, Palestine, or areas of Armenia and Azerbaijan. To advocate racial separation in these areas should not be condemned as racist. But we should never regard such separation as an end in itself, or a final solution.

Does Scripture place before us the goal of an "integrated society"? Yes, certainly, in the sense of a society in which love and respect exist between races. Yes, in the sense of the dream of Martin Luther King, in which people are judged by their character rather than by the color of their skin. But I do not believe there will ever be, or should be, in this world, a society in which racial differences are abolished, or in which people do not prefer to associate with people like themselves. I shall return to that subject below.

(c) "Politically incorrect" *views*, such as opposition to bilingualism, restrictions on welfare and immigration, and so forth. These are complicated political and social questions. It should not be assumed that holding such views amounts to hatred of minorities or even opposition to their best interests.

7. The term *racism*, as we've seen, can be used to designate certain kinds of hatreds and beliefs, emotions, and thoughts. But it also refers to actions and choices. Emotions, thoughts, and actions correspond to the existential, normative, and situational perspectives.

One action frequently called racist is associating with people of one's own race or nationality, rather than others. Later we will address more formal kinds of "discrimination." Here, we will consider our natural tendency to want to be with people like ourselves. I have called this tendency natural, because I believe that most all of us have it to some degree. We find it easier to talk to people who share our culture, who best understand us, who are least likely to become hostile, who are more likely to become good friends. Those people are more often found among those of similar ethic and cultural background.

This tendency is not generally sinful, in my opinion. It was God who placed human beings in families, so that our most intimate associations are generally those with whom we are closest genetically. Usually we turn to our own cultural groups to find spouses and close friends. There *is* a higher level of mutual understanding and appreciation within ethnic and culture groups than between them. With your own people, it is usually easier to let your hair down, to joke, to cry, even to worship. With people very different from yourself, you often feel that you are "walking on eggs." You are never quite sure when something you say or do will be found offensive, so you tend not to intrude too far into the emotional space of the other group. It is no accident that blacks refer to one another as "soul brothers." It is not that people outside one's ethnic group have no souls, but it sometimes seems like that. The outsiders seem stiff and formal, or their language of friendship seems incomprehensible. You do what you need to do, and then you run back to your home base.

It is this natural human phenomenon, rather than "racism" in the objectionable senses discussed earlier, that results in much of the informal racial and cultural segregation in our society. Why is it, for example, that blacks and whites worship in separate churches? For the most part, it is not because white Christians hate black Christians, or vice versa. Nor is it because they bear continued grudges or believe in the superiority of their own group, though some of these motives may at times be present. Churches tend to belong predominantly to one race or another, because worship is one of those times in which it is important to understand one another on an intimate level. The church is like a family; indeed, it is the family of God. Much of its ministry involves communication, and communication is almost always better within ethnic limits. Blacks and whites tend to speak different languages in worship—a difference that is evident in their choice of music and of preaching style.

Much has been said about how Sunday at 11:00 a.m. is "the most segregated hour of the week." But can it be doubted that *both* blacks and whites prefer to worship with people of their own race? Would black Christians willingly give up their black churches to become, say, 20 percent minorities within white churches? Such "integrated" churches might try hard to include gospel music and black-style preaching occasionally, but it would never be quite the same.

The phenomenon is not limited to differences between whites and blacks. In the United States, there are churches of people that are predominantly of Dutch ancestry, as well as German, Scandinavian, Korean, Chinese, Mexican, etc. Each of these ethnic churches is somewhat distinct in style and emphasis. In the general culture, as immigrants' families have learned English, these ethnic differences have become less important. But in the churches they persist, and they persist because many people want to keep them.

But doesn't the gospel break down racial barriers, bringing people of every kindred, tongue, tribe, and nation into one great new family? Certainly it broke through the barriers between Jew and Gentile, so that the uncircumcised could have full fellowship with God in Christ. And surely the various ethnic groups within the church are to love one another and to accept one another as joint heirs of God's grace.

On the other hand, there is no suggestion in the New Testament that every house church must have representation of both Jews and Gentiles. In many localities, such equality would have been unlikely. And as the church moves throughout the world, congregations are segregated by language differences. Nothing in Scripture suggests that this is wrong.

I therefore defend "freedom of association" within some limits. I don't believe that we are obligated to seek friends of all ethnic groups on an egalitarian basis. Nor do I believe that it is wrong for a church to be predominantly Dutch, or African-American, or Anglo. However, I wish to make a couple qualifications:

(a) *Evangelism*. Church growth literature used to advocate the "homogeneous unit principle," which is that churches should reach out primarily to people in society who are like themselves, ethnically, culturally, and economically. This literature points out, as I have pointed out above, that it is much easier to communicate the gospel within cultural groups than across them. The conclusion, then, is that cross-cultural evangelism is largely a waste of time, and that the church's efforts should be more sharply focused on those with whom they can more effectively communicate.

There is much truth in this principle. Certainly speakers of German can be more effective evangelists among Germans than those who do not speak that language. If I am incapable of learning German, it would probably not be wise for me to dedicate my life to the evangelization of the German people. Other cultural trappings, such as music, dress, and foods, can also be used more effectively by cultural natives.

But we cannot forget that conversion is God's work, a supernatural event, in which God's grace can overcome the inadequacies of our presentation. And Scripture teaches that in our own proclamation the gospel is to be offered freely to all. This does not mean that we should be careless about the quality of our communication. But we need to display God's love for people of all backgrounds, lest our churches be confused with ethnic clubs.

For example, an Anglo church may have many Spanish-speaking neighbors, but may have few members who are able to communicate well with them. I don't believe that they should barge into the Hispanic neighborhoods and bombard them with English gibberish. But they ought to find some way to demonstrate their love and concern for their salvation. Perhaps they should seek partnership with a Spanish-speaking congregation, providing resources, teaching, and encouragement where needed.

After all that has been said in favor of freedom of association, we must recognize that unless some Christians are willing to press the cultural envelope, to get beyond the comforts of our own community, to take risks to bring the gospel to other cultures, races, and nations, we will never fulfill Jesus' Great Commission. I don't believe that every Christian is called to cross-cultural witness, but all of us are called to support the overall ministry of the church. And make no mistake: that ministry is cross-cultural and cross-racial.

(b) *Welcome*. Churches do not have to seek a certain quota of every ethnic or national group in their vicinity. But they must welcome everyone.

Some years ago, *Christianity Today*, whose readership is predominantly white, asked a number of African-American Christians what they most wanted to say to their white brothers and sisters in Christ.

The article intrigued me, because I was not at all sure what they would say. Would they demand greater proportional membership and leadership in white churches? Would they like to see religious "affirmative action"? Would they demand that white churches endorse Jesse Jackson's political agenda?

Not at all. What the black Christians seemed most concerned about was lack of welcome from white churches. One told of how his family moved into a new neighborhood and visited a predominantly white church. The pastor visited them later that week and suggested that the family "might feel more comfortable" at a predominantly black church, some distance away. The black Christian took some offense that the pastor had not welcomed them to the white church and sought their involvement there.

I suspect that the white pastor had the best of intentions. Knowing that, as I have said, people tend to prefer worship with others like themselves, the pastor probably thought that the black family would prefer to worship in a black church, and he sought to serve them by giving them information about a black church in the area.

Nevertheless, his attempt to help was taken as a slight. One may criticize the black Christian for imputing evil motives to the pastor without justification. On the other hand, history imposes on white Christians the obligation to be extra sensitive with blacks on matters of race.

The point here is not to assess blame with any precision, but to underscore to white readers the importance of welcoming *everyone* to our churches. Our primary response to anyone coming to our church should be strongly positive. Yes, it may be that in time black visitors will seek out black churches and Hispanics will seek out Hispanic churches. We cannot condemn this. But in the meantime they should know that they have a home with us, a Christian family that really loves them. And if the black family decides to join our white church, we should be delighted. While Scripture does not require multiculturalism or multiethnicity in every congregation, we should be joyful when it happens. When the church becomes multiethnic, it becomes an emblem of God's worldwide kingdom and it gives the church new gifts, the better to reach out to a broader diversity of people. And if we can encourage such multicultural growth by varying somewhat our language of worship and style of ministry, we should certainly do so.

8. The next type of action we shall consider is *discrimination*, that is, the exclusion of people from jobs, housing, or public accommodations because of race. In the earlier discussion, I pointed out that whatever intellectual or moral disparities there may be among the races should not be assumed of individuals. Both Scripture and American legal tradition call us to

consider people innocent until proved guilty. There are also economic considerations, though these are, of course, less weighty: when businesses exclude people from employment, or even as customers, because of race, they cut themselves off from important markets, usually to the detriment of their profit.

Nondiscrimination, therefore, should be the general rule. But again some qualifications ought to be made:

(a) Is it wrong to have a family business, in which all the employees are members of one household and are therefore, most likely, of one ethnic background? What about a business run by a group of friends, who are all of the same ancestry? Are we always obligated to publicize job openings so that members of all ethnic groups have equal opportunity to be hired? I do not believe that Scripture requires that level of equality. Nor do I believe that government should force all businesses to be equal-opportunity employers in that sense. (And if people want to start a Christian business, they should not be forced to hire Muslims.)

As I argued above, there is a natural human tendency to associate with people like oneself, and Scripture never rebukes that tendency in itself. Of course, limiting employees to one's own family and friends may be economically disadvantageous; such a policy may prevent you from getting the best employees. But in some cases that disadvantage may be overcome by other factors, such as a better sense of unity, a better *esprit de corps*. To do this is not necessarily to hate those outside one's group, or to believe they are inferior. It is simply to prefer association with those most like oneself.

By extension, it is often valuable for people to be educated in schools of one race or one gender. There has never been any proof that racial or gender diversity is a major positive factor in education. Such schools are not right for everybody, but it is not morally wrong to establish them.

(b) We have seen that exercising special caution in high-crime areas is a rational decision and does not deserve to be called racist. Suppose a cab driver is asked to take a passenger into a dangerous part of a city, in which there has been a rash of cab robberies and murders of drivers. Let us say that the driver is white and that the dangerous part of town is predominantly black. If he refuses to go there, is he guilty of racism? Or is he merely making a rational judgment, protecting his own safety?

We can see how the presence of sin in our world complicates moral decisions. In this case, the driver is not discriminating against blacks as such. He is discriminating against some people who may be innocent, because of the additional factor of likely violence. Jesse Jackson's comments cited earlier are to the same effect: in some situations our normal human fear of violence may have a racial context.

There are reasons why we should sometimes take the risk of entering a dangerous situation, as in carrying out the Great Commission, but I don't believe that we are always obligated to do so. Certainly the goal of providing cab service to all parts of the city is desirable, but drivers should not be required to risk their lives in order to bring that about. If the lack of service inconveniences people of certain neighborhoods, that should motivate them to seek better law enforcement and to cooperate more fully with police and civic leaders.

Fear is not always a bad thing. But we need frequently to take stock of our fears to assess their rationality. It would be wrong to use the above kind of example to justify a general policy of racial discrimination, even though much such discrimination may be motivated by an analogous kind of fear. We should support law enforcement to eliminate the justifications of such fears. Where doubt remains, we should stretch ourselves as much as possible, by God's grace, to give others the benefit of the doubt.

Some Concluding Thoughts

We have seen that the term *racism* is something of a wax nose. It means different things to different people. In fact, it tends to be used most often as an undefined term of abuse, to attack people who disagree with the speaker in a vaguely conservative direction. I propose a moratorium on the use of the term. When you get into a discussion of these matters, insist on distinguishing these issues clearly from one another.

Race is certainly a compelling issue to many people today. Therefore, terms like *racism* tend to be used as overarching terms for everything one considers bad in society.

In discussions of race, it never seems to occur to people that we should identify ourselves as anything other than white, black, Hispanic, Asian, or whatever. But that seems to me to be a crucial issue. I'm not only a white man, but also a father, a brother, a husband, a pianist, a theologian, and, most importantly, a Christian. When I vote, I never think what government policies are in the best interests of white people. Rather, I consider what policies are best for Christians, what policies are most biblical.

Of course, if I were black, my history would force me to reflect on my race more often. If I were a woman, I would reflect more often on my gender. But it is important for all Christians to remember that for us race and gender are secondary issues. The families of this earth are one day to be overshadowed by the kingdom of God, in which there will be no more marrying or giving in marriage. Our intimacy will be with Jesus and with all his people.

I have tried to reflect seriously on matters of race, as every Christian teacher should. But one of the greatest mistakes we make is to make racism, sexism, and so forth, the most important issues of human life.

MINORITIES AND THE REFORMED CHURCHES

Why are there so few African-Americans, Native Americans, and Latinos in Reformed churches? This is, I think, an important question. The church of Jesus Christ is to embrace all nations, as God fulfills in Jesus his promise to Abraham (Gen. 12:3; Matt. 28:19). This does not mean, as we saw in the last section, that each congregation must strive to reach a quota of members from every ethnic group, but it does mean that the church as a whole should reach out to everybody.

Some would argue that since the Presbyterian Church in America (PCA), to use one example (others would do equally well), is only one denomination of the church, it shouldn't be expected to try to reach all types of people. They would recommend that the PCA focus on middle class, well-educated whites, with whom they typically have the most rapport. Leave the poor and minorities to the Baptists, independents, and charismatics.

But this approach will not do. In the first place, denominations are unscriptural (see my *Evangelical Reunion*[20]). The church should be one, organizationally as well as spiritually, and that one organization should be ministering to people of all nations and social strata.

Second, denominations typically claim to function as the church. That is, they claim to have a complete message, complete sacraments, a complete organizational structure. They claim to be sufficient as "churches" to carry out the Great Commission. They must make this claim; otherwise, they have no reason to exist. Jesus assigned the work of the Great Commission to the church, not to some religious club. If the PCA wants to do the work of the church, without organic connection to other denominational expressions of the church, then it must do *all* the work of the church. That means, in the present context, that it must reach out to all nations and socioeconomic groups.

Third, the Reformed denominations have claimed to have a sounder formulation of the gospel than non-Reformed bodies, as well as sounder methods of evangelism and nurture. They claim, therefore, to be better equipped than others to carry out the Great Commission. If they are not reaching some ethnic and social groups, that is cause for concern.

20. Grand Rapids: Baker, 1991. Available at www.reformedperspectives.org.

I have no statistics on the success of Reformed churches in reaching out to American minorities, but my observation (and I trust the reader's as well) is that we have been very weak in this respect. I am not entirely clear on the reasons for this, but I mention the following possibilities:

1. Historically, the Reformation has been a movement of scholars (see chapter 21). In the churches, preaching has followed something of an academic model in style and content. This approach appeals to the well-educated, who are also often the relatively wealthy members of society. It tends to turn away others, in the present case the relatively poor minorities.

2. Being an intellectual movement, the Reformation in some circles disparaged feelings, in my judgment to an unscriptural extent (see again chapter 21). This attracted rather stoic kinds of personalities and discouraged those who have greater need of emotional support. It discouraged also the emotionally demonstrative. That is one source of our ethnic uniformity.

3. Similarly, the minimalist aesthetic of Reformed worship (questionably derived from the second commandment: see chapters 25 and 26) limited the churches' ability to communicate effectively to some cultures.

4. Some Reformed theologians, particularly R. L. Dabney, have made statements deemed racist.[21] These are largely forgotten today, but Reformed churches in America must bear the burdens of the history of slavery, segregation, and discrimination against African-Americans. Other denominations and traditions bear the same burdens.

5. The Reformed emphasis on objective, absolute truth has sometimes been misused. It is one thing to insist on the absolute truth of Scripture. But Reformed theologians have often insisted also on the unchangeable divine truth of various traditions of worship and church life. Music is a conspicuous example today. This traditionalism is ironically closer to Roman Catholic theology than to the Reformation *sola Scriptura*, and it forms a major barrier to communication between the Reformed churches and minority cultures.[22]

6. One of these traditions has been the tradition of a "learned ministry," which I will discuss at greater length. The academic emphasis of the

---

21. See, for example, Dabney's "Ecclesiastical Equality of Negroes," in *Discussions: Evangelical and Theological* (1891; reprint, London: Banner of Truth Trust, 1967), 2:199–217. In a loose sheet inserted in the book, the publisher commends Dabney's work in a general way, but adds, "There is, however, one element in Dabney's thought which demands our comment. We have specific reference to his injurious comments about the Negro race. His degrading opinion of the Negro is offensive and deplorable. It is not representative of the Reformed position and has no Biblical warrant. As those who stand in the general stream of Dabney's thought, we apologize to the American Negro community for the attack made upon them by our brother."

22. See my *Contemporary Worship Music: A Biblical Defense* (Phillipsburg, NJ: P&R Publishing, 1997), and my "Traditionalism" at www.reformedperspectives.org and at www.frame-poythress.org.

Reformed movement has led to an emphasis on academic qualifications for pastors. Reformed denominations typically demand a college degree plus some seminary training. And they give to pastoral candidates rigorous examinations in biblical languages, church history, and theology. Members of minority groups typically don't have the financial or educational prerequisites for this kind of study. The result is that very few minority people qualify to become Reformed pastors. But to attract minority church members, it is necessary to ordain minority church officers. This is, I think, a major barrier to minority participation in Reformed churches.

There is much to be said for the concept of a learned ministry. The parson of early American villages was often the one member of the community with academic training. He became the *de facto* local expert, not only on theology, but also on science, history, and other academic subjects. Some would like to see the Christian church regain this cultural ascendancy.

But it can hardly be argued that such a degree of learning is a biblical requirement for ministry. The New Testament requirements do include the provision that an overseer be "able to teach" (1 Tim. 3:2), and we may infer from 2 Timothy 4:2 that he should be able to "preach the word; be ready in season and out of season; reprove, rebuke and exhort" (cf. Titus 1:9). Surely these responsibilities require some head knowledge as well as heart knowledge. But they do not require, even in our present-day culture, a college degree. The apostles themselves were perceived to be "uneducated, common men" (Acts 4:13). With the exception of Paul, they were not trained in the rabbinic schools, let alone what we would now describe as the disciplines of the liberal arts. Luke, alone of the gospel writers, was a cultured man, with training as a physician. The New Testament writers express themselves, not in the Greek of the poets and philosophers, but in the *Koine* of the common people.

Western missionaries planting tribal churches in areas new to the gospel often encourage these churches to install indigenous leadership as early as possible. Such leaders need to know the gospel and the basics of the Bible. But no one insists that a young church, say, in Ghana, need wait until some members of the tribe earn college degrees before they can become pastors or elders. Yet Reformed churches routinely insist on such educational requirements (with some flexibility) in preparing people for ordination in America.

Why should there be such a discrepancy between our standards for mission churches and our standards for home churches? The mission field exists on American territory today. Educational expectations differ greatly in different ethnic and cultural communities. It still makes some sense to require college or university education of those called to be senior pastors of largely white, suburban churches. It makes no sense at all to require such education of those called to work, say, with Hispanic migrant farm workers.

So my suggestion is that we recognize a broader range of educational requirements for different kinds of ministry, rather than having a common set of requirements for everybody who is to be ordained. Of course, some requirements must be met by all candidates: all must have a good knowledge of Scripture and Reformed theology. All must have good ability to communicate these truths in preaching, teaching, and counseling. (I would actually elevate the requirements in these areas.) But there should be no requirements as to *how* this knowledge is obtained (whether by seminary, tutoring, or private study). And of course there should be an emphasis on the qualities of character that dominate the Pauline lists of qualifications for church office (1 Tim. 3:1–10; Titus 1:5–9), qualities that need to be emphasized far more in Reformed churches. But there is no reason also to require college preparation of all ordinands.

It may be that those who are ordained with lesser preparation will need more supervision when they enter ministry. Normally in Presbyterianism we assume that once a man is ordained to the teaching ministry he has all the tools: he is fully prepared to take any responsibility in the church, without any additional help. Of course, in our hearts we know that is wrong. Every pastor needs help, especially in his first years in ministry. In Presbyterianism, supervision of young pastors is supposed to come through presbytery, but that supervision is often very slow in coming. For this purpose, one is attracted to something like Episcopacy, in which one man is charged with supervising the ministries of other men. Presbyteries can approximate this by energizing their committees on "the Minister and His Work." Through some such mechanism, it could be recognized that the education of ministers is an ongoing thing; it doesn't end with ordination. Given such a system, those who enter ministry with less educational preparation than others could receive regular guidance and counsel from more experienced and knowledgeable church leaders.

Does this mean that minority pastors would hold a second-class ordination? No. In my judgment, *every* pastor should be under authority, under supervision. We should not assume that ordination gives the right to autonomous ministry, following the supervised trial period of licensure. Ordination rightly confers some privileges: rights of participation in session and presbytery; rights to administer the sacraments. But it should not be the end of accountability. If *every* teaching elder is accountable to some fellow presbyter(s), then we need not worry that this process would distinguish some as second-class.

I have focused on this sixth barrier between Reformed churches and minorities, for I have had some specific suggestions for overcoming it that needed to be presented at length. But the other problems should also be addressed. If they are, I think we might at least make some progress toward making Reformed churches more multiethnic: that is, toward making Reformed churches more like the church.

THE DISABLED

If we are "to regard the dignity and worth of each other, in giving honor to go one before another; and to rejoice in each other's gifts and advancement,"[23] then we must treat disabled people properly. Here is another minority in great need of Christian love, treated badly by society, and often absent from Reformed churches.

Many people with illnesses and injuries, even serious problems like cancer and heart disease, are well accepted in society and in the churches. Those I have in mind, however, are those that pose special problems in relationships: people who are blind or deaf, others unable to communicate clearly, and still others who, because of neurological injury, are unable to do anything for themselves. "Abled" people tend to avoid them, even in churches. It is not so much that they regard disabled people as inferior, though there are doubtless some subconscious feelings to that effect. More often the problem is that conventionally abled people do not understand how to communicate with the disabled, or how best to show love.

Nancy Eiseland writes:

> The history of the church's interaction with the disabled is at best an ambiguous one. Rather than being a structure for empowerment, the church has more often supported the societal structures and attitudes that have treated people with disabilities as objects of pity and paternalism. For many disabled persons the church has been a "city on a hill"—physically inaccessible and socially inhospitable.[24]

After quoting Eiseland, Michael Beates, himself the father of a severely disabled daughter, says, "The more vital problem is that the Christian community generally tends to keep people with disabilities marginalized in the church."[25]

---

23. WLC, 131.

24. Nancy Eiseland, *The Disabled God* (Nashville: Abington Press, 1994), 20.

25. Michael Beates, "Wholeness from Brokenness: Disability as a Model for the Transforming Power of the Gospel" (D.Min. diss., Reformed Theological Seminary, Orlando,

In chapter 15, I affirmed the Americans with Disabilities Act, with some criticism of the inequities to which it has led. ADA has been better than nothing, but a national law is incapable of dealing justly with all individual cases. The church is in a better position to assess individual needs and act on them. The advantage of churches and other smaller organizations is that they can actually get to know the disabled and minister to their specific needs, without overministering or unfairly disadvantaging others. They can help, while encouraging the disabled to do what they are able to do. (Most all disabled people want and need, not only help, but encouragement to exercise their abilities.) And the church can minister and encourage through the love of Christ.

Certainly church people need to be taught much more about people with various disabilities. They need to know the difference between helping and overhelping. They need to know how to communicate. But most of all, they need to be motivated to reach out.

That motivation is to be found in Scripture, which speaks of disablement in gospel terms. Note: (1) All people are made in the image of God. (2) Disablement is part of the curse that comes after the fall. (3) But the curse affects all of us, not just those who are severely disabled. All of us experience pain and frustration in this fallen world. It is not until we recognize our own disablements that we can reach out to those who are physically disabled. (4) Sin itself is a disability, from which we cannot escape, apart from God's free grace. (5) In the Old Testament, God has a special concern for the disabled. He prohibits abuse of them (Lev. 19:14) and gives them a prominence in his redemptive promises (Ps. 34:18; Isa. 35:3–6). (6) Jesus showed his concern for physical healing as well as for healing in other dimensions of life. Jesus spent much of his time with the disabled (Luke 5:12–13; 14:15–24).

Beates points out that "all the major human characters in the Scriptures are not heroes first. Rather, they are weak, marginalized, unlikely candidates for any noteworthy achievements. Spiritual brokenness is often linked with physical weakness."[26] To accept God's grace is first to recognize ourselves as desperately weak, unable to do anything for ourselves. The world's neglect of the disabled comes from its desire to appear strong, without uncomfortable reminders of its need. But those who come to Christ find in the disabled a picture of their own weakness. Beates says, "People with disabilities are essential in the church, since their presence reminds us that we are all weak and broken before a holy and compassionate God."[27]

2003). Beates's work is the main source of my thoughts in this section, though I take sole responsibility for their formulation.

26. Ibid., 52.
27. Ibid., 138.

CHAPTER 35

The Sixth Commandment: Respecting Life

We come now to a group of three commandments that are very short, In Hebrew, each one consists of one verb with the negative word *lo*: no murder, no adultery, no stealing. Yet each of these raises questions that require lengthy treatment.

The theological background of "You shall not murder" is that God is the Lord of life. He made the waters, indeed the whole world, to "swarm with swarms of living creatures" (Gen. 1:20) and gave to all these creatures "the breath of life" (1:30). His creation of man was very dramatic in this respect: he took dust and personally breathed the breath of life into that dust, whereby "the man became a living creature" (2:7).[1] Life, symbolized by the tree of life in the Garden (2:9), sums up the fullness of man's existence with God: not only physical life, but also spiritual life—his righteousness and holiness.

The word that most fully summarizes the result of Adam's fall is *death*. This was God's threat in Genesis 2:17. So the curse pronounced on the earth following man's sin leads to death: "For you are dust, and to dust you shall return" (3:19). In the new, postfall environment, the first son of Eve kills the second, and "the book of the generations of Adam" (5:1) follows each genealogical entry (except that of Enoch!) with the words "and he

---

1. Compare his meticulous care in forming the living child in his mother's womb, Ps. 139:13–16.

died." Genesis 6 begins with a limitation of the human life span (v. 3) and ends with the destruction of nearly all life on earth. Unfaithfulness to God separates us from life and brings death, and death pervades human history after the fall.

Death, like life, is physical and spiritual. Physical death ends our participation in earthly life. Spiritual death (Eph. 2:5) is a loss of fellowship with God, the Lord of life. Unless interrupted by God's grace, spiritual death leads to eternal death, to permanent separation from God and therefore from his blessing (John 3:36). To be spiritually dead implies that we can do nothing to escape eternal death.

But God sent his Son to endure death in the place of his spiritually dead people. When Jesus died, his people died with him to sin (Rom. 6:2). When he rose, his people rose with him to newness of life (Rom. 6:4).

So throughout Scripture God continues to offer life. We saw in the fifth commandment that God offers long life and prosperity to those who honor their parents. In Deuteronomy 30:19–20, the Lord says through Moses:

> I call heaven and earth to witness against you today, that I have set before you life and death, blessing and curse. Therefore choose life, that you and your offspring may live, loving the LORD your God, obeying his voice and holding fast to him, for he is your life and length of days, that you may dwell in the land that the LORD swore to your fathers, to Abraham, to Isaac, and to Jacob, to give them.

This promise explicitly offers only earthly life. But it is life in fellowship with God, who is life itself. Jesus too is "the Author of life" (Acts 3:15). In him is that life which is "the light of men" (John 1:4). The rest of John's gospel makes clear that fellowship with Jesus leads, not only to earthly prosperity, but to eternal life (John 3:15–16; 4:14; 5:26; 6:35–58; 10:10; 12:50; 14:6; 20:31).

God delights in life. It is a measure of the seriousness of sin that death pervades it. It is a measure of the greatness of salvation that in Christ death is swallowed up by life (2 Cor. 5:4). So the Bible is a book about life and death.

In ethics, then, our attitude toward life and death is an important issue. What the sixth commandment basically says is that life and death are God's business. He is Lord of life and death, and we may not take life without his authorization. Rather, we must respect life as an aspect of our reverence for God. We should especially respect human life because it is the image of God, that image that grounds the first prohibition of bloodshed in Scripture (Gen. 9:5–6).

Somewhat more expansively, the Larger Catechism says:

Q. 135. *What are the duties required in the sixth commandment?*
A. The duties required in the sixth commandment are, all care-ful studies, and lawful endeavors, to preserve the life of ourselves and others, by resisting all thoughts and purposes, subduing all passions, and avoiding all occasions, temptations, and practices, which tend to the unjust taking away the life of any; by just defense thereof against violence, patient bearing of the hand of God, qui-etness of mind, cheerfulness of spirit; a sober use of meat, drink, physic, sleep, labor, and recreations; by charitable thoughts, love, compassion, meekness, gentleness, kindness; peaceable, mild, and courteous speeches and behavior; forbearance, readiness to be rec-onciled, patient bearing and forgiving of injuries, and requiting good for evil; comforting and succoring the distressed, and protect-ing and defending the innocent.

Q. 136. *What are the sins forbidden in the sixth commandment?*
A. The sins forbidden in the sixth commandment are, all taking away the life of ourselves, or of others, except in case of public jus-tice, lawful war, or necessary defense; the neglecting or withdrawing the lawful and necessary means of preservation of life; sinful anger, hatred, envy, desire of revenge; all excessive passions, distracting cares; immoderate use of meat, drink, labor, and recreations; provok-ing words, oppression, quarreling, striking, wounding, and whatso-ever else tends to the destruction of the life of any.

Some readers may be surprised to learn that a lack of cheerfulness vio-lates the sixth commandment! But, as with the other commandments, I defend the expansiveness of these applications. The Larger Catechism has recognized a logic in the biblical teaching that justifies these, that even makes the commandment a perspective on all sin and righteousness. The Puritans saw, among other things, that "a joyful heart is good medi-cine, but a crushed spirit dries up the bones" (Prov. 17:22). As modern medicine is discovering anew, cheerfulness has physical consequences. It promotes life. So the sixth commandment calls us, among many other things, to be cheerful.

The language of the commandment itself leads us to such broad applica-tions. The Hebrew verb *ratsakh* found in this commandment is translated "murder" or "kill." We are familiar with "Thou shalt not kill" from the KJV. The ESV, which I have been using regularly in this book, translates "You shall not murder." Most often, *ratsakh* refers to killing that is unlawful or forbidden. It is not used for the killing of animals or for killing in war. That would suggest that the best translation here is "murder," not the more general "kill." However, the term differs from our English word *murder* in that it applies to manslaughter and negligent homicide.[2]

Deuteronomy 19:5 describes a case "when someone goes into the forest with his neighbor to cut wood, and his hand swings the axe to cut down a tree, and the head slips from the handle and strikes his neighbor so that he dies." The implication is that the killing here is accidental, so the killing is not what we normally call murder. Nevertheless, the word that describes the person responsible is a form of the verb used in the sixth commandment. The ESV translates it "manslayer" (v. 4), which is somewhat archaic, but may be the best choice. So *ratsakh* in the sixth commandment is narrower than "kill," but somewhat broader than "murder."

A closer look at the Old Testament manslaughter texts (Ex. 21:12–14; Num. 35:9–34; Deut. 19:1–13; Josh. 20:1–9) may get us deeper into the theological and ethical implications of the sixth commandment. In Israel, capital punishment for murder was administered by the family of the victim.[3] The avenger of blood represented the victim's family and pursued the slayer in order to kill him. But if the killing was not intentional, the slayer had the opportunity to flee to one of the cities of refuge that God established in the Promised Land. If he succeeded in reaching such a city, the "congregation" (represented by the elders or judges) would "judge between the manslayer and the avenger of blood" (Num. 35:24). If the elders concluded that the killing was unintentional, the avenger was forbidden to kill the slayer as long as the slayer remained in the city of refuge.[4] But "if the manslayer shall at any time go beyond the boundaries of his city of refuge to which he fled, and the avenger of blood finds him outside the boundaries of his city of refuge, and the avenger of blood kills the manslayer, he shall not be guilty of blood" (Num. 35:26–27). To remain under the protection of the city, then, the slayer must remain in its bounds "until the death of

---

2. Contemporary legal use of the terms *murder* and *manslaughter* is somewhat variable. Usually, murder involves both intent to kill and premeditation. Voluntary manslaughter includes intent to kill, without premeditation, as when someone kills another person in a rage. In involuntary manslaughter, there is no intent to kill, but someone behaves in a way that is likely to kill someone (as in reckless driving). Negligent homicide is the failure to take adequate precautions (as in Ex. 21:29; Deut. 22:8). The example of Deut. 19:5, where an axe head flies off its handle and kills someone, may fall under the category of negligent homicide. Further distinctions lead to categories of first-, second-, and third-degree murder, which sometimes overlap the other categories mentioned above, but these vary from country to country and from state to state.

3. For a discussion of the relationship between the family and the state, see chapter 32.

4. If the judgment goes against the slayer, the elders must turn him over to the avenger, who will kill him (Deut. 19:11–13).

the high priest" (v. 28). After that, the slayer may return to his home, and the avenger may no longer threaten his life.

In the Mosaic law, penalties are appropriate to crimes, reflecting the justice of God. The Lord says in Obadiah 15, "As you have done, it shall be done to you; your deeds shall return on your own head" (cf. Ex. 21:23–25; Jer. 50:29; Ezek. 35:15; Hab. 2:8).[5] But what is the appropriateness of having cities of refuge? How does a penalty so complex relate to the act of manslaughter? The best answer I have is that the slayer is assumed to have been careless with human life. He had no hostility toward the victim or any intention of killing him, but he failed to take adequate precautions. His crime is carelessness. So the slayer is allowed to live, but there is a penalty: now he must be extra cautious about his own life.

We see here how seriously Scripture takes the loss of human life. It is significant that the slayer is not finally released until the death of the high priest, indicating that, even in the case of accidental killing, only death can deal with death. The high priest here stands in effect as a substitute for the slayer, foreshadowing Christ. (Note the atonement language of Num. 35:32–33.) It is only because the priest dies that the slayer may live in freedom.

So the commandment does not tell us just to abstain from murder. It also commands us to take precautions against the loss of life. We must guard against the possibility that someone might be killed, being alert to correct life-threatening elements in situations. I will refer to this principle as the doctrine of carefulness.

The doctrine of carefulness forms a bridge between the Mosaic law and the teaching of Christ. Jesus also tells us to eliminate the causes that can lead to loss of life. But, as he always does, he traces those causes to the heart:

> You have heard that it was said to those of old, "You shall not murder; and whoever murders will be liable to judgment." But I say to you that everyone who is angry with his brother will be liable to judgment; whoever insults his brother will be liable to the council; and whoever says, "You fool!" will be liable to the hell of fire. So if you are offering your gift at the altar and there remember that your brother has something against you, leave your gift there before the altar and go. First be reconciled to your brother, and then come and offer your gift. Come to terms quickly with your accuser while you are going with him to court, lest your accuser hand you over to the judge, and the judge to the guard, and you be put in prison.

5. Vern Poythress uses this principle to expound the meaning of the penalties of the law, in *The Shadow of Christ in the Law of Moses* (Brentwood, TN: Wolgemuth and Hyatt, 1991).

Truly, I say to you, you will never get out until you have paid the last penny. (Matt. 5:21–26)

Here Jesus teaches that the sixth commandment forbids anger[6] and verbal abuse,[7] as well as acts of killing. Since Cain's murder of Abel in Genesis 4, it has been plain that murder begins in the heart. Leviticus 19:16–17 draws the same connection: "You shall not go around as a slanderer among your people, and you shall not stand up against the life of your neighbor:[8] I am the LORD. You shall not hate your brother in your heart, but you shall reason frankly with your neighbor, lest you incur sin because of him." Murder begins in hate or anger. John even says, "Everyone who hates his brother is a murderer, and you know that no murderer has eternal life abiding in him" (1 John 3:15; cf. James 1:20).

In Matthew 5:23–26, following the order of thought in Leviticus 19:17, Jesus places a high priority on the resolution of anger, that is, on reconciliation. Being reconciled with a brother takes precedence even over worship. People who allow hostilities to fester, who don't try to overcome them, have violated the sixth commandment, because lack of reconciliation leads to death.[9] On a larger social scale, we can see how the lack of racial reconciliation, for example, has led to catastrophe. Among individuals, the same is true. We need to keep accounts short with one another. When someone sins against us and we cannot simply ignore it (allowing love to "cover" the sin, Prov. 10:12; 1 Peter 4:8), we should deal with the other person face to face, and then, if

6. There are legitimate forms of anger, for God himself is indignant ("angry" in the KJV) with the wicked (Ps. 7:11). Jesus cleansed the temple with a whip (John 2:13–17). God's anger in defending his own cause is often called jealousy. God is jealous (Deut. 32:21), and even declares that his name is Jealous (Ex. 34:14). So it is not wrong for human beings to be jealous against adulterous spouses (Num. 5:11–31). Nor is it wrong for human beings to be angry at those with whom God is angry (see the imprecatory psalms, such as Pss. 69; 109; 137; 139:19–22), or to be angry temporarily with someone who has offended us (Eph. 4:26). Titus 1:7 says that we should be *slow* to anger, as God is (Ps. 103:8), implying that there is such a thing as righteous anger. Cf. DG, 458–68. Nevertheless, much of the anger to which we are naturally prone is wrong, however easy it is for us to rationalize it as righteous indignation. We need God's Spirit to show us what kind of anger we are harboring, to see our thoughts and feelings in their proper biblical categories. Review our discussion of "seeing as" in chapter 20.

7. On verbal abuse, cf. 1 Sam. 25:9–42; 2 Sam. 16:7–8; 19:16–23; Prov. 12:18.

8. The NIV translates this clause, "Do not do anything that endangers your neighbor's life."

9. This principle applies in an even stronger way to our relationship with God. When we become aware that God has something against us, it is imperative that we seek reconciliation with him. Of course, in this case, when we seek reconciliation, we discover that he has already taken the first step.

necessary, with the help of the church, as in Matthew 18:15–20 and Galatians 6:1–2.

Note that Scripture requires that both the person charged with an offense and the one offended seek one another out. In Matthew 5:23–24, the burden is on the one who hears that someone else has something against him. In Matthew 18:15–20, the burden is on the one who believes another has offended him. Neither should wait, thinking that the other should come first.

A still broader conclusion emerges: when hate and anger are thoroughly purged away, only love remains. So the sixth commandment is the equivalent of the law of love. Note the broader context of a passage cited earlier:

> We know that we have passed out of death into life, because we love the brothers. Whoever does not love abides in death. Everyone who hates his brother is a murderer, and you know that no murderer has eternal life abiding in him. By this we know love, that he laid down his life for us, and we ought to lay down our lives for the brothers. (1 John 3:14–16)

Since the commandment mandates love, its ramifications are exceedingly broad, broad enough to cover the whole of ethics from its distinct perspective. So, as the Larger Catechism says, the commandment calls us, not only to avoid murdering people, but also to seek ways of preserving our lives and those of others. That means guarding our passions by the grace of God, and even seeking to be cheerful.

LOVE, VENGEANCE, AND SELF-DEFENSE

The ethic of love is not unique to the New Testament. Jesus proclaims it by quoting Old Testament texts (Matt. 22:34–40; cf. Deut. 6:5; Lev. 19:18).[10] Even the teaching that we should love our enemies appears in both testaments. Leviticus 19:18 proscribes bearing grudges, so its main concern is that we love neighbors with whom we have differences, that is, our enemies. According to Exodus 23:4, if we meet our enemy's ox or donkey going astray, we should return it to him. We are not to rejoice at our enemy's misfortune (Prov. 24:17). In Romans 12:20, Paul quotes Proverbs 25:21–22, which advises us,

> If your enemy is hungry, give him bread to eat,
>   and if he is thirsty, give him water to drink,

10. For the general role of love in biblical ethics, see chapters 12 and 19.

for you will heap burning coals on his head,
    and the Lord will reward you.

What the New Testament adds is an emphasis on showing love to those outside our own community. The Mosaic law does extend the commandment of love to "strangers," people sojourning within Israel (Lev. 19:34). But it is the New Testament that extends the covenant community to all nations. The Great Commission mandates love to all peoples as we bring good news to them. So we are to be neighbors to anyone in our path who is in need, as was the Good Samaritan in Luke 10:25–37. The Samaritan did not impose any religious or ethnic test on the victim of robbery; he simply loved him.

Leviticus 19:18 contrasts loving our neighbor as ourselves with seeking vengeance. Lamech's song is a negative example: "Adah and Zillah, hear my voice; you wives of Lamech, listen to what I say: I have killed a man for wounding me, a young man for striking me. If Cain's revenge is sevenfold, then Lamech's is seventy-sevenfold" (Gen. 4:23–24). Unlike Lamech's glorification of vengeance and violence, the wisdom teacher urges us, "Do not say, 'I will repay evil'; wait for the Lord, and he will deliver you" (Prov. 20:22), and, "Do not say, 'I will do to him as he has done to me; I will pay the man back for what he has done'" (Prov. 24:29). Similarly Paul teaches:

> Bless those who persecute you; bless and do not curse them. Rejoice with those who rejoice, weep with those who weep. Live in harmony with one another. Do not be haughty, but associate with the lowly. Never be conceited. Repay no one evil for evil, but give thought to do what is honorable in the sight of all. If possible, so far as it depends on you, live peaceably with all. Beloved, never avenge yourselves, but leave it to the wrath of God, for it is written, "Vengeance is mine, I will repay, says the Lord." To the contrary, "if your enemy is hungry, feed him; if he is thirsty, give him something to drink; for by so doing you will heap burning coals on his head." Do not be overcome by evil, but overcome evil with good. (Rom. 12:14–21)

Vengeance is the work of God (see Deut. 32:35; Ps. 94:1; 1 Thess. 4:6), and we can trust him to do it well. He cannot be otherwise than just. As we saw in chapter 32, God appoints the family/state to execute vengeance on his behalf, in cases defined by the law (Rom. 13:1–7; cf. Gen. 9:6; Ex. 21:23–25). But God forbids individual human beings to carry out vengeance. When people oppress us, our response should be the very opposite of vengeance, loving and serving our enemies.

It is in this vein that Jesus says:

> You have heard that it was said, "An eye for an eye and a tooth for
> a tooth." But I say to you, Do not resist the one who is evil. But if
> anyone slaps you on the right cheek, turn to him the other also.
> And if anyone would sue you and take your tunic, let him have
> your cloak as well. And if anyone forces you to go one mile, go
> with him two miles. Give to the one who begs from you, and do
> not refuse the one who would borrow from you. (Matt. 5:38–42)

The Anabaptist tradition sees here a prohibition of self-defense. This
view is linked to that tradition's rejection of the state as satanic, which
we considered in chapter 32. As we saw there, writers like John Howard
Yoder think that the Bible prohibits all use of force, whether individual
self-defense or the use of the sword by the state. But I disagree with this
general view of biblical teaching, and I think it leads to a misunderstanding of the present passage. The situations described in these verses are not
physical attacks. The slap on the cheek is a traditional insult, not a threat
to life and limb. The second example is a challenge in a court of law. The
third is a response to a Roman soldier who demands a Jew's services as a
guide or interpreter, and the fourth is a response to a beggar.

Scripture does not say much about individual self-defense as such,
though Exodus 22:2–3 sanctions the killing of someone who invades
your home after dark. But, as I indicated in chapter 32, Scripture says a
lot about the responsibility of the family/state to defend the lives of its
citizens, by force if necessary. In any case, those issues do not arise in
Matthew 5:38–42.

What this passage prohibits is, not self-defense, but vengeance. The
context clearly favors this understanding. Jesus is commenting on the law
of talion ("An eye for an eye and a tooth for a tooth," v. 38; cf. Ex. 21:24),
a general principle of justice to be observed in the courts of Israel. The
Pharisees used this law to justify and limit individual vengeance. Jesus
says in reply that individuals should not take vengeance at all. Then the
succeeding context tells us to love our enemies (vv. 43–48). The opposite
of love for enemies is not self-defense, but vengeance.

Understood in this way, Matthew 5:38–42 coheres with the many other
texts to that effect that we have considered. When someone insults us, or
sues us in court, or forces us to go on a journey, or asks us for a loan, our
response should not be to plan how we can impose commensurate pain
on the other person or gain some sort of payback for ourselves. Rather,
difficult as it seems, Jesus wants us even in such situations to love and
serve our enemies, to find some way to help one who wishes to hurt us.

Peter adds that when such an oppressor has authority over us, we should honor that authority, being willing to endure unjust suffering, as did Jesus (1 Peter 2:13–3:17).

If someone seeks to kill you, or a family member, and there is no help available, it is right for you to ward off the attack, by force if necessary. It is significant, however, that Exodus 22:2–3 permits such defensive killing only when the sun has not risen. The presumption seems to be that if the sun has risen, less lethal remedies, including help from others, are available. (The availability of such alternate remedies, in this and analogous cases, would be a subject for deliberation in court, as judges are asked to assign levels of guilt.) So the law of love limits our response even to a home invader. But it does not forbid us to defend our lives, our families, and our possessions by force, to the extent that is necessary.

Exodus 22:2–3 is a case where the law of Moses negotiates a subtle interface between self-defense and vengeance, proposing criteria to allow the first, but prohibit the second. Individuals may sometimes fight or even kill, to preserve life, but they should not use more force than is necessary in a given situation.

But the important thing is to find ways to bless our persecutors, to do what is honorable, to live peaceably, to give food and drink to our enemies. Christ has set us free from the desire to get back at people. God will exact vengeance; we do not need to worry about it. Christ has set us free to love even our enemies. So even our response to persecutors should be a gospel response, the good news manifested in our lives. We will likely astound our persecutors. That will motivate some, by God's grace, to consider Christ.

CHAPTER 36

The Sixth Commandment:
War and Punishment

The title of this chapter provides (besides an ironic cross between Tolstoy and Dostoyevsky)[1] a way into two topics that are much discussed in connection with the sixth commandment. War and punishment often involve the shedding of blood, even the taking of life. Some have thought that such killing is contrary to the sixth commandment. Of course, it is not literally opposed to the sixth commandment, for, as we have seen, the commandment does not forbid all killing. It forbids killing that is illegitimate according to the law, killing not authorized by God. To find out what kinds of killing God does and does not authorize, we must look elsewhere than the sixth commandment. As throughout the Decalogue, we must go outside the commandment to find out how to apply it. So the shortness of the commandment does not necessarily lead to a short discussion.

THEORIES OF PUNISHMENT

Punishment puts teeth into the concept of authority. An authority cannot function well unless there are consequences for those who disobey. Indeed, it is arguable that an authority that cannot punish is not an

1. With apologies to Jane Austen and Woody Allen.

694

authority at all. Family, church, state, schools, businesses, military services, sports teams—indeed, all organizations structured as authoritative hierarchies—have some way to discipline those who fail to meet their standards. Of these, as we have seen, only the family/state has the right and power to shed blood. But in order to understand this prerogative, it is important for us to understand something of what punishment is.

Why do we punish those who disobey authority? There are several different motives for punishment. I shall mention some that are commonly discussed today, comparing them with the motives for punishment in biblical law.

Motives for Punishment

Deterrence. In deterrence, society punishes an offender (let's call him Josh Clark) as a lesson to the rest of society. We punish thieves in the hope that others will be deterred from thievery. Similarly for murderers, tax evaders, and slanderers. Some punishments presented in the Bible have this purpose (though rarely if ever is this the only purpose). Deuteronomy 13, for example, says that an Israelite who worships other gods should be stoned to death, and then adds, "And all Israel shall hear and fear and never again do any such wickedness as this among you" (v. 11). Also, the cleansings and offerings prescribed in the Mosaic law have in part the function of discouraging certain sins. These are in part pedagogical devices. In fact, since they have no power in themselves to cleanse of sin, their chief purpose is pedagogical. As Israelites watch the priest transfer a person's sin to an animal, kill the animal, and burn it (Lev. 1:1–17), they may come to a greater understanding of the seriousness of sin and its consequences. And they may turn their attention to the full atonement promised by God in the future, seeking divine forgiveness through God's grace. So, motivated by deterrence, we punish Josh to discourage others from committing the same crime.

Reformation. Another, and rather different, justification of punishment is reformation. In this case, we punish Josh, not to deter others in society, but for his own good. Here the goal of punishment is to make Josh a better person, so that he does not commit his crime again. This motive can also be found in biblical law. Church discipline, for example, has the goal of restoration. Against an incestuous church member, Paul prescribes excommunication: "You are to deliver this man to Satan for the destruction of the flesh, so that his spirit may be saved in the day of the Lord" (1 Cor. 5:5). Paul wants the offender to be saved as the result of this discipline, so that he does not have to suffer eternal punishment. So when this man, or perhaps another offender, does in fact come to repentance, Paul asks the Corinthians to forgive him and comfort him (2 Cor. 2:5–11).

Punishment of children in the home, of course, should always have this motivation: "Folly is bound up in the heart of a child, but the rod of discipline drives it far from him" (Prov. 22:15).[2]

Restitution. In the Mosaic law, someone responsible for the loss of property must make restitution to the owner. Often the amount is not specified (Ex. 22:5–6, 12). Presumably in those cases he merely restores what was lost, because the loss was unintentional: for example, when the owner of an animal lets it loose and it grazes in another man's field (22:5). Theft, however, requires double restitution (Ex. 22:4, 7, 9). If Josh steals ten oxen from Lisa, he must pay her twenty. In some cases, there are higher penalties: fivefold restitution for an ox that is killed or sold, fourfold for a sheep (Ex. 22:1). If the thief cannot pay, he is sold into slavery (the Hebrew slavery we discussed in chapter 34).

We have seen that in deterrence the focus is on the general society; in reformation, it is on the offender. In restitution, the focus is on the victim. Here we punish Josh so that Lisa can be made whole again.

Restraint. Punishment also aims sometimes at removing the perpetrator from society. Here our goal is mainly to keep Josh away from us. Like reformation, this motive of punishment focuses on the offender, but this one is very different. Restraint often appears when hope of reformation is lost. For example, sex offenders today are thought to be beyond the normal possibility of rehabilitation. Therefore, they are subject to various restrictions intended simply to keep them away from potential victims.

Imprisonment today is often justified as restraint. Whatever effects prison has on offenders, it does at least to keep them off the streets for a time. This motive is rarely found in the Mosaic law, though the term "cut off" (e.g., Ex. 12:19; 30:33, 38; 31:14) may sometimes refer to exile from the people of God. If Israel did indeed exile some of its people from the borders of the country, it would have the effect of restraining them from further wrongful activities within the community.

2. There is a strong tendency in contemporary society to outlaw the corporal punishment of children, declaring it to be child abuse. Christians should strongly resist this trend. Parents should of course be careful to avoid injuring their children when spanking them. But we cannot compromise for a moment with secular theories that equate corporal punishment with psychic harm. The benefits, indeed the necessity, of physical punishment are a major theme in Proverbs: see 10:13; 13:24; 18:6; 19:18, 29; 22:15; 26:3; 29:15, 17. Prov. 23:13–14 addresses our hesitations: "Do not withhold discipline from a child; if you strike him with a rod, he will not die. If you strike him with the rod, you will save his soul from Sheol."

Taxation. This is the motive behind many speed traps. The speed limit may be utterly unrealistic and the fines may be far too high to fit the crime, but the law is profitable enough for the municipality to build a new city hall. In this motive of punishment, the town makes Josh its financier.

I don't know of any passage in the Bible that authorizes punishment for a profit motive. That has not, however, deterred a number of American towns and counties.

Retribution. Under this motive, we punish Josh simply because he deserves it. We presume that there is an objective moral order in the universe, according to which Josh *ought* to be punished when he commits a crime. This *ought* exists, whether or not the punishment deters, reforms, or performs any other function. Of course, in a Christian worldview, the source of this objective moral order is the triune God. Apart from him, there is no basis for this or any other moral order (review chapter 4 on this point).

OBSERVATIONS

Just as physicists would like to reduce gravity, electromagnetism, and the weak and strong nuclear forces to a single force, creating a "theory of everything," so ethicists have often wanted to reduce these motives to a single theory of punishment. Theories of punishment sometimes reduce all these motives to one, or they seek to show how they relate to one another.

It is not easy to draw these motivations together into a single theory. Deterrence and reformation, for example, push in rather different directions in their applications to specific crimes. If a penologist primarily seeks deterrence, he will tend to make the punishment as harsh as possible, to maximize its effect on the general public. If, on the other hand, he favors reformation, he would probably devise punishments that are milder, perhaps a system of carrots and sticks that not only discourage bad behavior but encourage good. If restraint is the main issue, still different punishments are likely to emerge—perhaps exile, imprisonment, or house arrest—that have little to do with reformation and do not maximize deterrence.

And how does restitution fit into all this? Restitution has long been a major component of civil law, but for many years it was neglected in criminal law. Victims' rights movements in recent years have, however, brought it more to the fore. It may, perhaps, be defended as an aspect of deterrence or reformation, but it is most often in addition to these, rather than combined with them in a unified viewpoint.

Retribution is, I think, the key to a unified understanding of punishment. Many have criticized retribution as a relic of our barbarous past, a kind of mythology without any penological value. I sense, however, that in the last fifty years, under the influence of various articles like C. S. Lewis's "The Humanitarian Theory of Punishment,"[3] it has become possible to discuss retribution in penology without becoming a laughingstock.

As Lewis pointed out, other motives for punishment become unjust if they are not based on a theory of "just deserts." If deterrence is the only consideration, one can justify punishing innocent people for the deterrent value.[4] On that basis, it is not important that the person punished be guilty, only that he appear guilty to the public. If reformation is the only issue, one can argue that everyone should be punished, since we could all use a bit of reforming. But clearly such a reformation program is unjust unless the law identifies which people *deserve* to be placed in a program of reform. The same analysis holds for restitution and restraint—and even taxation.

The primacy of retribution agrees with the law of talion in Scripture: eye for eye, tooth for tooth. Another name for retribution is justice. People should receive the punishment they deserve—not more, not less. Deontological forms of secular ethics (see chapters 4–7) endorse this principle over against teleological and existential systems, but, as we saw in chapter 7, deontological forms of secular ethics cannot locate a plausible authority to determine absolute norms of retribution.

This is another way of saying that just punishment presupposes Christian theism.

PRISON

In the Mosaic law, punishments include restitution (sometimes double or more), capital punishment (sometimes with a ransom provision), beating (Deut. 25:1–3; Prov. 19:29), ceremonial sacrifices, and possibly exile. Those who could not pay restitution would be sold into Hebrew slavery (see chapter 34). There are also unique arrangements for particular situations, like the availability of cities of refuge for manslaughter (chapter 35) and the requirement that a seducer marry the woman if her father consents, but otherwise pay a large penalty (Ex. 22:16–17). Judges evidently had considerable flexibility in determining penalties.[5] The case laws do not

---

3. In *God in the Dock: Essays on Theology and Ethics*, ed. Walter Hooper (Grand Rapids: Eerdmans, 1970), 287–94.

4. Stalinists are known to have done this sort of thing intentionally.

5. It is interesting that, although Deut. 25:1–3 mentions beating as a possible penalty, there is no case law that explicitly mandates this penalty. So judges were free to prescribe it without

cover every possible situation, but rather present representative precedents. Many laws do not have penalties attached, such as the provisions against partiality in lawsuits (Ex. 23:3), failure to rescue an enemy's wandering animals (Ex. 23:4–5), and many others. But failure to keep these provisions sometimes became a ground for God's judgment against the nation, as in Israel's failure to rest the land every seven years.

Significantly, imprisonment, the major form of punishment today, is entirely absent from the Mosaic law. Scripture mentions prisons in Egypt (Gen. 39:19–40:23), Philistia (Judg. 16:21), Assyria (2 Kings 17:4), and Babylon (2 Kings 25:27). Later Israelite kings used prisons to detain their opponents (2 Chron. 16:10; 18:26), as did rulers of the New Testament period (e.g., Matt. 4:12; Acts 5:18). But the law of Moses never specifies a prison term as the penalty for a crime.

Crimes punished today by imprisonment were punished then by beating, restitution, enslavement, and, in many cases, capital punishment, which I shall discuss below. Even in the eighteenth century, prisons were mainly places of detention, not punishment.[6] Prison terms as punishment were a later development, intended to reduce the need for capital punishment, beatings, and other punishments that were considered inhumane. The original idea was that prisons would be places of reformation, hence the names "penitentiaries" and "correctional facilities." As such, however, prisons have been dismal failures, as indicated by the recidivism rate. Indeed, it is arguable that prisons have worsened the problem of crime, for in prisons older criminals influence younger ones. For that reason and for others, released prisoners often can do nothing to make a living except to commit further crimes. So a vicious cycle develops.

Clearly the solution is not to keep building more and more prisons, and the Mosaic law should stimulate our thinking toward better alternatives. I don't believe the Mosaic laws can be applied literally and comprehensively today (see chapter 13), because modern nations are not in covenant with God, as ancient Israel was, and because people today are not much motivated to understand and obey God's standards in their lives. Still, I believe that many of the crimes that contribute the most to prison occupancy should be handled differently: (1) The primary penalty for theft, as in Moses' time, should be that the thief work to repay the victim, if necessary in a kind of forced apprenticeship labor (chapter 34). Double restitution is strict justice: the thief loses what he had sought to gain. It cannot be argued that the appropriateness of this penalty is limited to the Mosaic theocracy.

---

explicit biblical sanction. Their job was to apply general principles of the law to situations that the law itself did not mention, sometimes arriving at penalties not mentioned in the law.

6. R. J. Rushdoony, *The Institutes of Biblical Law* (Nutley, NJ: Craig Press, 1973), 515.

(2) The use of drugs, particularly the possession of small amounts of marijuana, should not be punished by imprisonment. It is debatable whether drug use should be criminalized at all. In my view, it should be regulated like tobacco and alcohol. I will have more to say on this subject at a later point. (3) Beatings, especially in public, are of great deterrent value, and they are far preferable to prison sentences in that they deal with the issue quickly and do not expose the offender to prison culture. My judgment is that this form of punishment has had much to do with the low crime rate in places like Singapore.

Capital punishment should be used more often (see below), both because of its inherent justice and because executing the worst criminals prevents the development of a criminal class. Particularly, society should consider the death penalty for the incorrigible criminal, the one who expresses contempt for the system of justice, as in Deuteronomy 17:12: "The man who acts presumptuously by not obeying the priest who stands to minister there before the LORD your God, or the judge, that man shall die. So you shall purge the evil from Israel."

At least, career criminals should be removed from the general population, even the population of lawbreakers. Removing such people from the prison system would decrease the violence in prisons and the pressure on prisoners to become career criminals. The most common characteristic of lawbreakers is not poverty, poor education, or broken families, much as these influence bad behavior. The most common characteristic is disrespect for law. Persistent contempt of court is much more common and far more serious than most people imagine it to be.

I cannot say that imprisonment should *never* be used as a penalty. As I said earlier, legislators and judges should be free to apply the principles of Scripture to new cases and, if necessary, propose penalties not mentioned in Scripture itself. In the case of imprisonment, however, this freedom has been much overused. Certainly at the present moment it is necessary to keep dangerous and career criminals locked up, until a social consensus emerges to broaden the use of other penalties.

Crowded conditions in prisons have led governments to transfer some inmates to private institutions, some under religious auspices. I would encourage Christians to support "Christian prisons," which can become (like ancient Hebrew slavery) means of genuine rehabilitation. In such a facility, inmates can both hear the gospel and also learn habits of godly living. Inmates of government prisons also hear the gospel and can receive Christian nurture through outside ministries and Christians within the system. But in a Christian prison, the whole system can be attuned to the principles of Scripture, to encourage regeneration and sanctification. This was the original purpose of incarceration, but the advent of secularism made it impossible for prisons to enforce appropriate standards of conduct and to prepare inmates for freedom.

Christians should support ministries to those in conventional prisons as well: evangelistic and diaconal work, visitation (Matt. 25:36–40),[7] ministry to prisoners' families, and halfway houses.

CAPITAL PUNISHMENT

The Old Testament warrants capital punishment for a great many crimes: murder (Lev. 24:17; Num. 35:16–21, 30–33; Deut. 17:6), adultery (Lev. 20:10; Deut. 22:21–24), incest (Lev. 20:11–14), bestiality (Ex. 22:19; Lev. 20:15–16), sodomy (Lev. 18:22; 20:13), rape (Deut. 22:25), false witness in capital crimes (Deut. 19:16–20), kidnapping (Ex. 21:16; Deut. 24:7), fornication by a priest's daughter (Lev. 21:9), witchcraft (Ex. 22:18), human sacrifice (Lev. 20:2–5), striking or cursing father or mother (Ex. 21:15, 17; Lev. 20:9), incorrigible juvenile delinquents (Deut. 21:18–21), blasphemy (Lev. 24:11–14, 16, 23), Sabbath desecration (Ex. 35:2; Num. 15:32–36), false prophecy (Deut. 13:1–10), sacrificing to false gods (Ex. 22:20), contempt for the priest or the judge (Deut. 17:12).[8]

Clearly, then, the language of the sixth commandment cannot be taken in a way that excludes capital punishment. As we have seen, "Thou shalt not kill" is a somewhat misleading translation of the commandment. It forbids killing that is not authorized by God, and the list above indicates some killings that God indeed authorizes.

The capital penalties for blasphemy, witchcraft, and other false religious practices are based on the special holiness of Israel, living in the very presence of God. These should not be enforced by present-day governments.[9] People convicted of other capital crimes could evidently ransom their lives

---

7. I believe that in this passage the people in prison are Christians who are being persecuted for their faith. Nevertheless, it is clear that those who visit and supply the needs of prisoners are doing a good thing. Paul wrote the letter to the Philippians to thank the church for sending a gift to him in prison. (In ancient times, most of the needs of prisoners had to be supplied by family and friends on the outside.) So the love of Christ should motivate his people to help people in prisons, whatever their crimes or religious orientation. And with help should come the gospel.

8. I have taken this list, with only a few verbal changes, from Rushdoony, *The Institutes of Biblical Law*, 77.

9. See the argument of Vern Poythress in *The Shadow of Christ in the Law of Moses* (Brentwood, TN: Wolgemuth and Hyatt, 1991), esp. 311–61. See also my discussion of theonomy in chapter 13.

by a payment (see Ex. 21:30; Num. 35:31–32). But murder has a special position in the list. Numbers 35:31–33 says:

> Moreover, you shall accept no ransom for the life of a murderer, who is guilty of death, but he shall be put to death. And you shall accept no ransom for him who has fled to his city of refuge, that he may return to dwell in the land before the death of the high priest. You shall not pollute the land in which you live, for blood pollutes the land, and no atonement can be made for the land for the blood that is shed in it, except by the blood of the one who shed it.[10]

Verse 33 echoes Genesis 9:5–6: "And for your lifeblood I will require a reckoning: from every beast I will require it and from man. From his fellow man I will require a reckoning for the life of man. Whoever sheds the blood of man, by man shall his blood be shed, for God made man in his own image."

It could be debated whether many of the capital penalties of the Pentateuch should be adopted in modern societies. Many of them seem to be given in view of the special holiness of Israel. But there should be no debate about the appropriateness of the capital penalty for murder. For one thing, it antedates the law of Moses by many centuries. For another, it displays strict justice: blood for blood, life for life. Finally, it is based on man's nature as the image of God, a status given to him before the fall. One made in the image of God is so precious in God's sight that the only appropriate penalty for taking that life is death. So, although there would be no need for capital punishment (or any other punishment) in a sinless world, there is a sense in which capital punishment is a creation ordinance.

The New Testament does not repeal the death penalty. Paul says in Acts 25:11, "If then I am a wrongdoer and have committed anything for which I deserve to die, I do not seek to escape death." In Romans 13, as we saw in chapter 32, Paul justifies the right of the civil government to bear the sword. Both testaments, as we have seen, urge individual believers to love their enemies and not to seek vengeance. But God's requirements of individual believers are not the same as his requirements of civil governments. In both testaments, God gives to the civil government, the government of the family of Adam, the right to take the lives of those who take the lives of others.

Secular objections to capital punishment today usually spring from a generalized view of the sanctity of life, without the biblical distinction between

---

10. Note that, as we saw in chapter 35, manslaughter is a form of "slaying" equivalent to murder except for the city-of-refuge provision.

murderers and victims.[11] The Bible does teach that human life is sacred, but it does not teach that murderers and nonmurderers have the same right to life. Objectors often assume, furthermore, that death is the absolute end of human existence, whereas Scripture teaches that there is a life to come. Murderers who repent of their sins and embrace Christ will spend an eternity in glory. Capital punishment is not an absolute deprivation of existence. It is rather a means of turning a person over to God for final judgment.

People often argue that capital punishment does not deter murder and other crime. States and countries that enforce a death penalty often have as many murders per capita as states and nations that have no death penalty. However, deterrence is not the decisive consideration. As we have seen, the principle that should determine punishment is retribution (i.e., justice), not deterrence. Also, deterrence depends on the swift and sure execution of a penalty. But the execution of murderers in the United States is anything but swift and sure. Statistics on swift and sure capital punishment are hard to come by, so present statistics are hardly definitive. Finally, Singapore is an arguable example of a country in which capital punishment deters murder.

The strongest arguments against the death penalty in our time are its inequitable administration and its use against innocent people. In 1972 (*Furman v. Georgia*), the Supreme Court invalidated federal and state capital punishment provisions on the ground that they gave too much discretion to judges and juries, discretion that was "arbitrary and capricious" in its administration. One of the major issues was racial bias. That court decision was perhaps the only way to rectify a major evil. Since then, many new capital punishment laws have been enacted, with safeguards against arbitrariness that have passed court tests.

More recent opposition to the death penalty has arisen from the fact that DNA evidence has shown some people to have been wrongly convicted of capital crimes. Yet it seems odd that just as we have gained a new scientific tool that will greatly improve the justice of capital cases, some people use this tool as a ground for eliminating the death penalty.

It may seem cruel to put it this way, but the execution of some innocent people does not prove the general injustice of the death penalty. We should mourn with people whose loved ones have been wrongly executed, and we should advocate substantial help for such families. We should also fully utilize every tool that can achieve greater fairness. But justice is never perfect in this world, whatever the penalties at issue.

---

11. This misunderstanding of the sanctity of life often includes as well an equation between the rights of animals and the rights of human beings. But many who hold this generalized view exclude the rights of unborn human beings.

Remember that God instituted capital punishment centuries before DNA evidence was available. Doubtless in the time of the patriarchs and the Mosaic administration, some innocent people were executed and some guilty people went free. But God judged that, despite human inadequacies in administering justice, it was still best to have capital punishment as a principle of law. In the final analysis, of course, human judgment must give way to God's. As I said above, the death penalty is not final in an absolute sense; it is the handing over of someone to God for final disposition. God's judgment never makes mistakes. Ultimately, God's Word teaches us, perfect justice will be done. Capital punishment is not perfect justice, but it is part of the process by which God brings his judgments to bear on a sinful world.

WAR

It is difficult to discuss war in the context of a *sola Scriptura* ethic, because Scripture says little about the actual ethics of warfare. It does recognize war as a result of sin: "What causes quarrels and what causes fights among you? Is it not this, that your passions are at war within you? You desire and do not have, so you murder. You covet and cannot obtain, so you fight and quarrel" (James 4:1–2).

The consummation of history is a time of peace, not war (Isa. 2:4; 9:6–7; 11:6). Until then, Scripture gives special honor to those who seek peace (Ps. 46:9; 120:6–7; Matt. 5:9). Although David is a man after God's own heart, God does not permit him to build the temple, for he is also a man of war (1 Chron. 22:18–19; 28:3). The temple anticipates God's final peace. Its builder must be a man of peace, David's son Solomon, whose very name means peace. So Jesus, the fulfillment of the temple, is "Prince of peace" (Isa. 9:6): "Of the increase of his government and of peace there will be no end, on the throne of David and over his kingdom, to establish it and to uphold it with justice and with righteousness from this time forth and forevermore. The zeal of the LORD of hosts will do this" (v. 7).

Under the new covenant, the kingdom of God is not to be advanced by war, though Christians have not always understood this principle. Jesus has withheld the sword from his family (Matt. 26:52; John 18:1–11). There is a war to be fought by Christians, but it is a spiritual war, not a war to be fought with physical weapons (Eph. 6:10–20). Those weapons have no power against spiritual enemies, Satan and his troops. Only truth, righteousness, the gospel, faith, salvation, the Word of God, and prayer can vanquish Satan's armies. So war is an important metaphor for the life of the Christian (2 Cor. 10:3; 1 Tim. 1:18; 2 Tim. 2:4; 1 Peter 2:11).

Scripture also teaches that the gospel will provoke violence among people, much as we may seek to avoid it (Matt. 10:34–38; Rev. 11:7; 12:7, 17; 13:7; 19:19). There will be persecution for those who honor Christ (2 Tim. 3:12). But such warfare is initiated by opponents of Christ. The individual believer is not to take the offensive. We may defend ourselves and others against physical attack, but our overall mandate is to return good for evil (see chapter 35). We should be lovers of peace (Ps. 34:14; 1 Peter 3:11; Rom. 12:19, 21; 14:19). Even those conducting a lawful war should not delight in killing others. God judges Edom because of its lack of compassion in war (Amos 1:11; cf. Ps. 68:30).

Nevertheless, Scripture recognizes that warfare is sometimes necessary in a fallen world. As we have seen, God has given the sword to the civil magistrate (Acts 25:11; Rom. 13:4). The sword is an instrument of bloodshed and death. God is the one who enables the devout warrior to prevail (Ps. 144:1).

Scripture respects the military vocation. John the Baptist told soldiers not to rob others, but did not tell them to leave the army (Luke 3:14). Roman centurions tend to be positive models in the New Testament (Matt. 27:54; Luke 7:9; Acts 10:2, 22, 35).

In the Old Testament, Abraham rescued his nephew Lot by raising a military force (Gen. 14:13–16). Later, God commanded Israel to make war. Deuteronomy 20 distinguishes two different kinds of war. One is against the Canaanite tribes within the land of promise; the other is against "cities that are very far from you, which are not cities of the nations here" (v. 15). The first kind of warfare[12] is sometimes called *herem* warfare, from a verb used in Deuteronomy 7:2 (cf. Ex. 22:20; Lev. 27:29; Num. 21:2–3).[13] *Herem*, sometimes translated "ban," is a war of total destruction:

> But in the cities of these peoples that the LORD your God is giving you for an inheritance, you shall save alive nothing that breathes, but you shall devote them to complete destruction, the Hittites and the Amorites, the Canaanites and the Perizzites, the Hivites and the Jebusites, as the LORD your God has commanded, that they may not teach you to do according to all their abominable practices that they have done for their gods, and so you sin against the LORD your God. (Deut. 20:16–18; cf. Deut. 7:1–5)

Obviously, God ordained *herem* warfare for a specific situation, the fulfillment of his promise to Abraham, to give the land of Canaan to his

---

12. I am reversing the order in which the chapter presents these.
13. The basic meaning of *herem* is devotion to God. So Scripture also applies the term to various things given to God (Lev. 27:21, 28), even without destruction.

descendants (Gen. 17:8). God does not command us to continue these practices beyond the time of the Israelite theocracy.

The other form of warfare mentioned in Deuteronomy 20 is war against cities that are far away. Here the treatment of Israel's opponents is a bit more lenient, but still severe by modern standards. Israel must offer peace, and if the city accepts that offer, Israel must allow the people to live, but in slavery (vv. 10–11).[14] If the city does not accept this offer, Israel will kill all the males, but take the women and children (presumably as slaves) and enjoy the plunder (vv. 12–14; cf. Deut. 21:10–14).

It is important to remember that even this second kind of warfare is holy war. All of Israel's wars are holy. Before the battle, the priest proclaims a divine promise of victory (vv. 2–4).[15] The people are to be ritually clean (Deut. 23:9–14). Then the officers grant liberal deferments: to men who have built new houses, planted new vineyards, or been recently married (20:5–7). Even cowardice is ground for deferment (v. 8)! (See also Deut. 24:5, concerning a newly married man.) God wants it to be plain that Israel gains its victories, not through numbers, but through God's power. God has not made a similar covenant with any modern nation and has not given to anyone today a promise of victory in war. So neither of the forms of warfare described in Deuteronomy 20 provides an ethical model for modern war.

Nor to my knowledge is there any other Bible passage that provides explicit ethical criteria for entering and waging war.

PACIFISM

Since there is so little explicit reflection in Scripture on the ethics of war, various theories have emerged to try to discern principles implicit in the biblical text or in natural revelation that might help us to make decisions in this area. The two most influential have been pacifism and just war theory. Both of these take various forms.

Typically, pacifism denies that war is ever legitimate or justifiable. This is the view of John Howard Yoder, Ronald Sider, and others of Anabaptist background. In chapter 32, I discussed Yoder's view of the state, which is that it is a satanic opponent of the kingdom of God. Since the state opposes God, on this view, Christians should never be allied with it, especially in warfare. War, indeed, is inherently contrary

---

14. So the offer of "peace" is not an offer of a negotiated settlement!

15. The promise is conditional on Israel's faithfulness to the Lord. God allows Israel to be defeated, even in *herem* warfare, when someone disobeys his commands (Josh. 7:10–12).

to the law of love, in which God commands us to love our enemies and to return good for evil.

I rejected Yoder's view of the state in chapter 32. Romans 13 and other passages do give to the civil ruler a legitimate authority as God's minister to wield the sword against wickedness. He is to oppose attacks on the peace arising both from within and from outside the nation. Further, we have seen in chapter 35 that the law of love requires us as individuals to return good for evil, but it does not require the civil magistrate to do so.

Pacifism is particularly weak in its understanding of war in the Old Testament. In the pacifist view, God permitted war during that time as a concession to Israel's hardness of heart, as he then permitted divorce (Mark 10:2–9). Ideally, Israel should never have fought a war, just as there should have been no divorce among them. In my view, the parallel breaks down. Ideally, in an unfallen world, there would be no divorce and no war. So God's toleration of divorce in the Old Testament (Deut. 24:1–4), and his approval of some warfare, are indeed, in one sense, accommodations to man's hardness of heart. But there is one important difference. God never commanded divorce, except in the unique situation of Ezra 10, but he did command Israel to go to war, as we have seen. Indeed, he rebuked Israel for her failure to drive the Canaanites completely out of the Promised Land (Judg. 2:1–5). Later, God through Samuel rebuked Saul for failing to carry out the *herem* against Amalek (1 Sam. 15). For this failure, God removed Saul's mandate to rule (vv. 16–23). Divorce is rarely a necessity, even in a fallen world, but war is often a necessity.

Pacifists also appeal to some of the church fathers, who opposed Christian participation in the military. But their reasons for opposing it are not always clear. Some, like Lactantius, saw war as violating the law of love. Others, like Justin Martyr and Origen, opposed Christians entering the army, but they prayed that these armies would be victorious. For some, like Tertullian, a major problem for Christians in military service was subjection to pagan oaths and ceremonies. I don't think one can derive from the writings of the Fathers a clearly thought-out pacifism. Arthur Holmes summarizes the teachings of the church fathers as follows:

> They do not deny to government the right to use force, and for all their aversion to violence they do not assert that killing is under all circumstances morally wrong. Their overt objection to soldiering is to the imposition of pagan rites and oaths. Their attitude to war is different from popular pagan attitudes; instead of excitement and glorying in war, they lament its tragic

character and yearn for peace. Yet they are grateful for military action that secures both peace and order.[16]

That seems right to me, though there are individual differences among the Fathers. In any case, the church fathers are not our final authority in these matters. They are only a guide for us in the application of Scripture.

The strongest argument for pacifism, in my view, is that in a war one might easily be required to kill a fellow Christian believer on the other side. Is not Christ our highest allegiance, transcending any responsibility we have to the state? Is not our commitment to Christian brothers and sisters higher than our commitment to fellow citizens of the state? The answer, I think, is that just as in capital punishment one may have to support the execution of a fellow believer who is guilty of murder, even if he is repentant, so in war (presuming that the war is just) one may have to kill a fellow believer who is allied with an aggressor. Again, the distinction between the obligations of the individual and those of the civil ruler must be observed. A Christian in the armed forces becomes part of the civil government, a minister of God to dispense justice, even by force.

JUST WAR THEORY

Just war theory deals with questions of war by invoking natural law.[17] Like the natural-law tradition in general, it originates in Greek and Roman sources. Cicero is the first to set forth a list of criteria to determine what constitutes a just war. A modern Christian philosopher, Arthur Holmes, sets forth a list that is somewhat typical of this approach:

1. Just cause. All aggression is condemned; only defensive war is legitimate.
2. Just intention. The only legitimate intention is to secure a just peace for all involved. Neither revenge nor conquest nor economic gain nor ideological supremacy are justified.
3. Last resort. War may only be entered upon when all negotiations and compromise have been tried and failed.
4. Formal declaration. Since the use of military force is the prerogative of governments, not of private individuals, a state of war must be officially declared by the highest authorities.

16. Holmes, "The Just War," in *War: Four Christian Views*, ed. Robert G. Clouse (Downers Grove, IL: InterVarsity Press, 1981), 127.

17. For my general evaluation of natural law ethics, see chapter 14.

5. Limited objectives. If the purpose is peace, then unconditional surrender or the destruction of a nation's economic or political institutions is an unwarranted objective.
6. Proportionate means. The weaponry and the force used should be limited to what is needed to repel the aggression and deter future attacks, that is to say to secure a just peace. Total or unlimited war is ruled out.
7. Noncombatant immunity. Since war is an official act of government, only those who are officially agents of government may fight, and individuals not actively contributing to the conflict (including POW's and casualties as well as civilian nonparticipants) should be immune from attack.[18]

Other writers have appealed to additional principles, such as these:

8. Comparative justice. War should not be waged unless the evils that are fought are grave enough to justify killing.
9. Probability of success. There must be a reasonable likelihood that the war will achieve its aims.[19]
10. Good faith in treaties and agreements.

In just war theory, these principles must be applied both to the question of whether to go to war and also, where applicable, as in items 5–7 and 9, to the question of how to conduct a war, once the war has begun.

Just war theory is not so much a theory as a set of questions we should ask about any war. I think the questions are good questions. But they almost never lead to a consensus. Those who favor a war can usually argue that it is being fought for a just end, with public declaration, prospect of victory, and so forth. Those who are against it can usually find flaws in the argument. Of course, a nation going to war never does so from absolutely pure motives, is never completely sure about the prospect of victory, and so forth. So these arguments usually end indecisively.

And there is also room for argument about the ideas lying behind the questions themselves. Consider the following responses to the just war principles:

1. *Just cause*. For Holmes, only defensive wars are just. For others, like Harold O. J. Brown,[20] who writes in the same volume, it is sometimes

18. Holmes, "The Just War," 120–21.
19. J. Budziszewski, "New War, Old Principles," *World*, September 29, 2001, 28. The date is significant.
20. Brown identifies himself as one who favors a just war theory, in "A Preventive War Response" (to Holmes), in *War: Four Christian Views*, ed. Clouse, 147.

legitimate to launch a "crusade" or "preventive war."[21] Brown defines preventive war as a war that "intends to forestall an evil that has not yet occurred."[22] A crusade is "begun not in response to a present act of aggression, but as the attempt to set right a past act."[23] The difference of opinion between Holmes and Brown leads to questions about what constitutes defense. I doubt that it is possible to gain certainty on these questions from natural law alone.

Scripture notes at least one case of a justified war that is not defensive. Siege warfare was well known in the ancient world. Deuteronomy 20 describes a siege war in which Israel is the aggressor. The passage does not indicate the reasons that would justify such a conflict. It may be a preventive war or a crusade, but even that is not stated. As I have said, I think Israel's wars do not furnish us with an ethic of modern warfare, but I hesitate to adopt ethical criteria that would classify those wars as unjust. So I am inclined to side with Brown rather than Holmes on this issue. But my resolution of this issue comes down to Scripture, not natural law.

2. *Just intention.* I am sympathetic with Holmes's view that a "just peace" should be the only goal of war. Certainly, Scripture places a high priority on achieving peace (Ps. 34:14; 1 Peter 3:11; Rom. 14:19). It would be wrong to fight for economic gain alone, though if one nation has stolen resources from another, I think the second, as a last resort, may fight back. Yet it occurs to me that revenge (which can be another name for retributive justice), conquest, and ideological supremacy, which Holmes considers unjust motives, all figured in Israel's wars on Canaan. Further, most every revolutionary war in history can be charged with such motives. The winners of both world wars, too, achieved all of these purposes and certainly intended to. Sometimes it is part of justice to gain revenge from a past wrong, to replace an obnoxious regime (i.e., to conquer), and to eradicate an obnoxious ideology (as in denazification).

3. *Last resort.* The biblical emphasis on peace implies that we should seek to resolve issues peacefully in preference to war (Prov. 3:31–32; 15:1; Rom. 12:18). The 2003 war in Iraq raises the question of when available peaceful measures become redundant and a waste of valuable time. The United States could have postponed its attack indefinitely, so that the United Nations Security Council could pass more and more resolutions,

21. Brown, "The Crusade or Preventive War," in *War: Four Christian Views,* ed. Clouse, 153–68.
22. Ibid., 155.
23. Ibid.

expecting them to be rejected by the Iraqi government, and waiting for weapons inspectors to comb every square inch of the Iraqi desert.

4. *Formal declaration.* I certainly agree that war should not be fought by private individuals with no official standing. But modern governments are very complicated entities. The U. S. Constitution forbids war without a congressional declaration. But courts have ruled that the executive branch has the right to engage in some level of conflict without that sanction. It is not at all clear to me whether the Korean War, the Vietnam War, or the two Gulf Wars met this requirement.

5. *Limited objectives.* Unconditional surrender and a drastic overhaul of the nation's economic and political institutions were the demands of the Allies against both Germany and Japan at the end of World War II. Given the situation, I think no lesser demand would have been appropriate. The same was true of the American Civil War and of Israel's wars as described in Deuteronomy 20.

6. *Proportionate means.* Certainly we should avoid unnecessary killing, even in time of war (Deut. 20:10–11; Amos 1:3, 11, 13). But this principle has sometimes been used to limit military means to some kind of bare minimum. Many have argued that Lyndon Johnson's attempt to restrict military means to the minimum necessary, increasing it gradually by small increments, led to U.S. failure in Vietnam. The same has been said about the U.S. military force fighting in Iraq.

A different view of appropriate means is the doctrine of "overwhelming force" advocated by Colin Powell as the strategy of the first Gulf War, which was successful. The nuclear blasts ending the war against Japan were also overwhelming and, in the view of many, tragically disproportionate; but many have defended them, as we shall see later. In any case, it does not seem obvious to me that minimum necessary force is the best policy, either for military success or for human compassion. Arguably, overwhelming force can shortens wars and can even minimize killing.

Further, it is very difficult to judge in advance of a battle how much force will be necessary to achieve an objective. For the sake of the mission and its prompt completion, I think, it is best to err on the side of too many resources, rather than too little. Once the battle has begun, it is easier to cut back than to add.

7. *Noncombatant immunity.* I agree that an army should never directly target noncombatants. However, it is very difficult in many wartime

situations to avoid killing and wounding them. When a government puts military installations next to hospitals, for example, its military opponents must make a hard decision. And sometimes it is difficult to know who is a combatant and who is not. During the Vietnam War, children sometimes welcomed American servicemen, then threw grenades at them. Teenage girls have been suicide bombers in Israel. Guerillas often do not wear uniforms, and they enlist women and children for their services. Soldiers must be wary of "civilians." In many cases, they will legitimately have no suspicions of civilians and will let them get on with their lives. But in other cases they should be suspicious. Criteria for those decisions (i.e., of what should create suspicion) are best developed by the military, not by theologians.

When the enemy uses civilians as human shields, we have a choice: (1) avoid the encounter and try to achieve the objective by other means, (2) seek by precision targeting to eliminate the military contingent while minimizing civilian deaths, (3) where necessary, carry out a broad-based attack, knowing that many civilians will die. I think that we should be biased against the third option. But there is no absolute principle prohibiting the killing of any civilians at all. In Israel's wars, many civilians were killed, sometimes by divine order.

There is a corporate principle that people die for the sins of their representatives. There is something tragic about this, but it's inevitable. When a father sins, he endangers his family. When a ruler sins, he endangers his people. Further, the civilian population is not entirely blameless, for a despot often enjoys popular support in his rise to power and martial exploits.

8. *Comparative justice.* I agree with the principle at a very general level, but its application to specifics is very difficult. It is plausible to say that no evil is grave enough to justify the taking of even one life. That would be a pacifist position. Short of that, this principle forces us to make judgments about the relative value of individual human lives, which leads, I think, to insoluble logical and moral problems.

9. *Probability of success.* Of course, nobody wants to sacrifice lives for a lost cause. But often (as in the American Revolution) the situation provoking war is so difficult as to produce a kind of heedlessness about consequences, as in Patrick Henry's "Give me liberty, or give me death!" What probability of success would anyone have calculated when the American colonies began their war against England? Should the *spirit* of the colonists have been added to the equation? How does one evaluate that factor?

10. *Good faith in treaties and agreements.* God through Amos (1:9) charges Tyre with delivering captives to Edom, despite a "covenant of brother-hood." Certainly a nation is obligated to keep formal agreements with other nations. But there is a place for deceit in warfare, which I shall explore under the ninth commandment.

Just war theory, then, leads to valuable discussions about the ethics of war, but it is rarely if ever definitive. Even its criteria are often problematic and difficult to apply to real situations.

SOME IDEAS FROM SCRIPTURE

So, in matters of war, it is difficult to find definitive answers. As we have seen, Scripture says little on the subject. But the situation is not helped much by recourse to natural law. So we may have to be content with gen-eralities, rather than specifics.

There are some biblical principles that bear on war: the sanctity of life, first of all. We should seek as many ways as possible to protect lives during a war, on both sides. But Scripture is pretty realistic about war. It recognizes that it is not always possible or desirable to protect all noncombatants, for example. Basically, it recognizes that war is hell and that for the most part you just have to put everything into a war and end it quickly. The Bible is helpful in that it loosens things up. It doesn't require the ethicist to micromanage how many weapons are used, for example.

Obviously a Christian will never advocate war unless it is a genuine responsibility of the civil magistrate, pursuing his office to protect the nation against hostile enemies. Such a war should be carried out with a serious regard for human life, even knowing that some human life must be sacrificed to attain the objective.

Here are a few thoughts arising from meditation on the biblical principle of the sanctity of human life:

1. There may indeed be wars in which a Christian cannot conscien-tiously participate. For this reason, I believe that the state should provide the opportunity of conscientious objection to those opposed to a particular war, rather than limiting this option, as today, to those who are opposed to all wars.

2. I think the civil magistrate may sometimes, in order to protect his own people, make a preemptive strike. Nothing in Scripture contradicts this principle, and it is characteristic of the wars of Israel. He may be able to neutralize the enemy with less loss of life by a preemptive strike, than by waiting for the enemy to attack. So I supported the American attack on

Iraq. The agreement of the United Nations would have been a nice thing, but it is morally irrelevant.

3. Regarding the immunity of noncombatants, the distinction between civilian and military is not made in Scripture itself. It is a distinction that we have made to honor the general biblical principle of the sanctity of life. That is to say, even in war we seek to minimize the loss of life, and the best way to do that while achieving the war's objective is to try to identify those in the enemy country who can be left alive without endangering the war effort. So a civilian is someone who is not likely to kill members of the invading army and should therefore ordinarily be spared. But this distinction is only a rough one.

4. War often gives opportunities for humane gestures, such as giving soldiers an opportunity to surrender, and giving civilians an opportunity to escape from impending attack (as the British did in southern Iraq in 2003). It is good to offer such opportunities. But those who choose not to accept them, even for morally good reasons, must accept the consequences.

The Bible recognizes that war is a terrible thing, stemming from lusts and anger. In wars, people die who do not personally deserve death. In contrast to just war theory, however, Scripture does not try to micromanage humanitarianism in time of war. Rather, within some broad limits, it justifies doing whatever is needed to achieve a legitimate military objective. There are opportunities during war to minimize killing, and it is good to take advantage of them when we can. But the military objective comes first.

NUCLEAR WAR AND DETERRENCE

A particular problem of modern warfare is that of weapons of mass destruction: biological, chemical, and nuclear weapons. Such weapons have the power to kill, injure, or sicken great numbers of people, making no distinction between combatants and noncombatants. The use of such weapons has been said to violate a number of provisions of just war theory: limited objectives, proportionate means, noncombatant immunity, and even probability of success. In what follows, I shall focus on nuclear weapons, believing that similar principles may be applied to other means of mass destruction.

Many have argued that if the use of nuclear weapons provokes retaliation, it is unclear who would win and likely that nobody would. Some have even argued that nuclear war would bring an end to life on earth, at least as we know it. A chain of events would lead to "nuclear winter," which could be the end of life itself.

From a biblical standpoint, many have argued that nuclear warfare can only be a *herem* war, aimed at total destruction. It would be a scorched-earth war, destroying not only human beings, but natural resources.[24]

Certainly great efforts should be made to avoid the use of such weapons. These are unprecedented in their destructive power and in the natural and social catastrophe they can create. But two questions are not easy to answer: (1) Do wars ever necessitate the use of such weapons? (2) Should nations maintain supplies of such weapons as deterrents?

With regard to the first question, it is hard to imagine any wartime situation that would require such terrible destruction. Yet the case has been made that the use of atomic bombs against Hiroshima and Nagasaki at the end of World War II destroyed fewer lives than would have been lost in a land attack on Japan, which otherwise would have been inevitable. I am not competent to resolve this military question, and neither, I think, are most theologians. But I am not prepared to say that the use of nuclear weapons is *never* appropriate.

As for the second question, it is obvious that such weapons exist, and it is not always possible for a nation to keep them out of the hands of its enemies. So it is an important question whether a nation should maintain a supply of such weapons as a deterrent to their use by others.

This was the rationale of the U.S. nuclear stockpile during the Cold War with the Soviet Union. American leaders argued that the purpose of these weapons was not, principally, to use them, but to deter others from using them. Opponents of this policy described it by the acronym MAD, "mutual assured destruction." But that phrase summarized well the hope that, given the U.S. arsenal, the Soviets would understand that any nuclear attack would result in their own devastation.

Many arguments were made for and against this policy. Many claimed that the sheer quantity of weapons had grown too large—a question outside the theologian's competence. But, in the final analysis, the strategy worked. No nuclear weapon was used between 1945 and the collapse of the Soviet Union in 1991. Nor has one been used since, as of this writing.

Was this policy too risky? I think not. Alternatives were not promising, and the dangers were sometimes exaggerated. Consider:

24. We recall that Deut. 20:19–20 forbids even the destruction of the enemy's fruit trees. In my view, however, this provision does not forbid the destruction of any natural resources at all, but only those that are unnecessary to the war effort. Israel may cut down other trees to use for battlements (v. 20), but to deliberately cut down the fruit trees would not help Israel and could only serve a vindictive purpose. The besieged city could not use them anyway, until the siege was ended. Arguably, the destruction of fruit trees in a modern nuclear attack would, as part of the general devastation, serve a military purpose.

1. Other proposed policies, such as a unilateral nuclear freeze and unilateral disarmament, would also have been risky. Given Soviet ambitions, it was likely that such policies would have led to their conquest of America's allies and perhaps the U.S. itself. Some writers thought that risking Soviet conquest of America was preferable to risking nuclear war. I have little sympathy with that argument. The government is responsible for preserving the nation and its way of life. Those who are moved by Patrick Henry's "Give me liberty or give me death!" cannot assume that slavery is preferable to death.

2. Even moderate American restraints in arms building were not reciprocated by the Soviet Union. So it was not likely that greater restraint would have reduced the danger at all—even the danger of nuclear war.

3. Treaties did not help much. Until the 1980s, the only treaty accomplishments (the SALT documents) were mutual agreements to increase stockpiles at lesser rates. The Reagan administration took a new direction: the START talks aimed at actual reductions in nuclear arsenals. But it was never clear whether this process would ever reduce nuclear stocks to zero, or whether the Soviets could be trusted to keep any agreements reached.

4. An antiballistic missile system might have been a viable alternative. But the Soviet Union regarded that idea as provocative, as did many in the U.S., and it has proved very difficult even in the 2000s to develop adequate technology for it.

5. There has been no scientific consensus on the "nuclear winter" hypothesis, or other predictions of worldwide disaster following a major nuclear exchange. So the risk of destruction in nuclear exchange, though great, was never proved to be as bad as some claimed.

So I conclude that it was wise for the U.S. and its allies to maintain stockpiles of nuclear weapons as a deterrent to nuclear attack. In a sinful world, there is of course no guarantee that such a strategy will always work. But government always has the responsibility to guard the safety of its people, using the best imperfect strategy at its disposal. I am convinced that in some situations nuclear deterrence is the best strategy, and I know of no biblical principle that forbids it in those situations.

CHAPTER 37

The Sixth Commandment: Protecting Life

The title of this chapter might have been given to either of the previous two chapters, since the sixth commandment has an overall concern for the protection of life. However, this chapter has a somewhat different focus. For one thing, chapter 36 dealt primarily with government decisions, and this chapter will deal mainly with personal, individual decisions. Of course, in some ways, all issues of life and death are both social and personal. For another thing, chapter 36 mainly focused on identifying situations where killing is permissible (capital punishment and just war), while this chapter will focus on areas where God does not permit killing, however much society tolerates it.

Liberal secularists tend to oppose killing in war and capital punishment, but to accept abortion and euthanasia. Biblical ethics, in my view, teaches the reverse. We must grant, of course, that war and capital punishment are not always just. We must also grant that there are times when we should not try to keep people alive. There are times when people approaching death (even if unborn) should be allowed to die. So there are complications here that deserve careful thought.

ABORTION[1]

The Bible does not mention abortion specifically, but it does speak implicitly about the value of unborn children. When I worked on a denom-

---

1. For a longer discussion of abortion, see "Report of the Committee to Study the Matter of Abortion," in the *Minutes of the Thirty-eighth General Assembly of the Orthodox Presbyterian*

inational committee dealing with the issue, some argued that the church should not take a stand on abortion, because the Bible does not explicitly condemn it. They said that the principle of *sola Scriptura* forbade the church to speak on any subject not mentioned in the Bible. But, as we saw in chapter 11, this is to misunderstand the sufficiency of Scripture. That principle does not restrict the church's proclamation to explicit statements of Scripture. Rather, it says that Scripture alone provides us with divine words, and therefore that all the church's teaching must be applications of those divine words. But the very nature of application is to take the words of Scripture and show their relevance to situations outside Scripture. If we are forbidden to make such applications, then we cannot use Scripture at all—only read it. "You shall not steal," therefore, implies that you shall not take the wallets of seminary professors without their consent. And "You shall not murder" implies that you shall not kill unborn children; that is, that you shall not abort a pregnancy.

Exodus 21:22–25

Among the passages of Scripture most clearly relevant to this question is Exodus 21:22–25:

> When men strive together and hit a pregnant woman, so that her children come out, but there is no harm, the one who hit her shall surely be fined, as the woman's husband shall impose on him, and he shall pay as the judges determine. But if there is harm, then you shall pay life for life, eye for eye, tooth for tooth, hand for hand, foot for foot, burn for burn, wound for wound, stripe for stripe.

This passage describes two possible situations, the first in verse 22 (which I shall call "Case A") and the second in verses 23–25 ("Case B"). I shall mention three interpretations, the "live-birth" interpretation, the "miscarriage" interpretation, and the "later Kline" interpretation. Although some have thought that the second interpretation is somewhat favorable to abortion, I regard all three as pro-life.

The live-birth interpretation is the one I favor. In Case A, the Hebrew phrase translated "her children come out" most naturally describes a premature birth. (The plural is a bit puzzling, but it evidently takes into account

---

Church (1971), 135–57. It is available at the OPC website, www.opc.org/GA/abortion.html. I was the chief author of this report, and it is reproduced as an appendix to my *Medical Ethics* (Phillipsburg, NJ: Presbyterian and Reformed, 1988). In a somewhat condensed and edited form, it may also be found in "Abortion from a Biblical Perspective," in *Thou Shalt Not Kill*, ed. Richard L. Ganz (New Rochelle, NY: Arlington House, 1978), 43–75.

the possibility that there may be more than one child in her womb.) So what happens is that a woman somehow gets involved in a brawl between men, and one strikes her so as to cause her to give birth prematurely. Nevertheless, beyond the pain and difficulty of the premature birth itself, there is "no harm." That Hebrew phrase is indefinite, not specifying who is not harmed. But since it is indefinite, we should take it as meaning harm to the mother, the child, or both. Since there is no harm, the legal issue deals entirely with the induced birth itself and the pain and suffering associated with it (compare the similar case in 21:18–19). The woman's husband determines the penalty, in association with judges, who also determine the procedure for payment.

The only difference between Case A and Case B is that in Case B there is harm. Again, the harm is indefinite, so we should take it as applying to the mother, the child, or both. Here the law guides the judges by a long statement of the law of talion: life for life, eye for eye, and so on. In the worst case, where there is a death, the striker must pay with his life. Note, then, that on this interpretation killing an unborn child is as serious a crime as killing a pregnant woman. Indeed, killing an unborn child is a capital offense.

Note that the text does not say that the striker intended to do harm. If the blow killed the child, the child's death was to some extent accidental.[2] Had the striker intended to kill the child, his crime would have been even more serious. Now abortion is the intentional killing of an unborn child. So abortion is even worse than the action said here to be a capital crime. So on the live birth interpretation, this passage has strong pro-life implications.

Some have thought that the second interpretation, the miscarriage interpretation, is more favorable to abortion, but I don't believe it is. On this interpretation, in Case A, "her children come out" describes a miscarriage or still birth.[3] "No harm," then, applies only to the mother, not the

2. Since the killing is accidental, it might trigger the process leading to a trial at a city of refuge (Num. 35:9–29; see chapter 35). That provision, however, is not mentioned here. Perhaps this particular kind of "accidental killing" was considered so serious that the striker was not allowed to evade the penalty by fleeing to the city of refuge. If so, the implication is that the accidental killing of an unborn child is a more serious matter than any other accidental killing—a strongly pro-life conclusion. On this understanding, the law here would give a stronger protection to pregnant women and their children than it gives to other Israelites. Nevertheless, it may be that the death penalty implicit in this passage may be subject to a ransom provision, as we have seen in other capital cases.

3. I think this interpretation is unlikely. Although some have argued for it on the basis of the similarity of this passage to miscarriage texts in other nations, it seems to me that in the Hebrew there is no suggestion of a miscarriage. The term translated "children" is the same word used of children already born. Other terms, like *nefel* and *shakol*, would have been more appropriate to describe a stillbirth.

child, for there has certainly been maximum harm to the child. In Case A, then, the killing of the child is punished by a fine, to be determined by the husband and the judges. In Case B, however, harm comes to the mother. Then the law of talion takes effect. So killing the mother in this situation is a capital crime, but killing the child is not. The latter is punished only by a fine.

Now people who hold to this interpretation often say that it justifies abortion. They reason that the difference in penalty implies a difference in status: since killing the mother is a capital crime, but killing the child receives only a monetary penalty, the child is not a human person with a full right to life. Therefore, at least in some circumstances, abortion is justified.

Even on this interpretation, however, the passage has no such implication. In the Mosaic law, we cannot reason from penalty to personhood. In verse 32 of this same chapter in Exodus, there is a monetary penalty for killing a slave, for in one sense a slave is considered to be property (see also v. 21). Certainly it would not be justified, however, to infer that the slave is less than a person, or that he does not have a right to life. From the miscarriage interpretation of Exodus 21:22–25, therefore, one cannot infer that the unborn child is anything other than a human person with a right to life.

Far more significant than the difference in penalty, on this view, is the fact that, as on the previous interpretation, it is a crime to destroy an unborn child. On both interpretations, this passage gives a special protection to pregnant women and their unborn children. So even on the miscarriage interpretation the implications of this text are pro-life.

The third interpretation I call the "later Kline view," because for a time Meredith Kline advocated (in an unpublished paper) the miscarriage view. But in 1977 he published an article in which he adopted an interpretation that was strongly pro-life, but different from either interpretation we have considered so far.[4] This interpretation depends on some fairly difficult exegetical arguments, so I will mention only the salient points. In Case A, on this view, there is "no harm" to the child, but there is a blow to the mother (*nagaf*) that kills her. The fine is in effect a ransom for the life of the striker. In Case B, the child suffers injury or death, and the law of talion applies up to or including the death penalty. Like the first interpretation, this view prescribes the same penalty for killing the child as for killing the mother, and it implies that the two should be regarded equally as persons with a right to life.

4. Meredith G. Kline, "Lex Talionis and the Human Fetus," *Journal of the Evangelical Theological Society* 20 (1977): 193–201.

On all three interpretations, then, Exodus 21:22–25 protects the unborn child by the force of law. Note also that on none of these interpretations is there any distinction based on the age of the fetus. This legislation treats all unborn life the same. To apply this law to our present context, therefore, we should protect unborn life from the point of conception onward, contrary to those who would protect it only from some point after conception. Note also that on none of these interpretations does the passage deal with abortion itself, the intentional killing of an unborn child. Such intentional killing would have to be regarded as even worse than the offenses described in our passage. Meredith Kline's comment on this fact is worth noting:

> As we observed at the outset, induced abortion was so abhorrent to the Israelite mind that it was not necessary to have a specific prohibition dealing with it in the Mosaic law. The Middle Assyrian laws attest to an abhorrence that was felt for this crime even in the midst of the heathendom around Israel, lacking though it did the illumination of special revelation. For in those laws a woman guilty of abortion was condemned to be impaled on stakes. Even if she managed to lose her own life in producing the abortion, she was still to be impaled and hung up in shame as an expression of the community's repudiation of such an abomination. It is hard to imagine a more damning commentary on what is taking place in enlightened America today than that provided by this legal witness out of the conscience of benighted ancient paganism![5]

Psalm 139:13–16

In this passage, David describes God's dealings with him in the womb of his mother:

> For you formed my inward parts;
>   you knitted me together in my mother's womb.
> I praise you, for I am fearfully and wonderfully made.
> Wonderful are your works;
>   my soul knows it very well.
> My frame was not hidden from you,
> when I was being made in secret,
>   intricately woven in the depths of the earth.

5. Ibid., 200–201.

> Your eyes saw my unformed substance;
> in your book were written, every one of them,
> > the days that were formed for me,
> > when as yet there were none of them.

The important thing here is that in this reflection David refers to his unborn life as fully personal. He designates the fetus with first person pronouns. It was he, David, whom God formed in the womb. So David was a person before his birth.

One must be careful not to press this data too far. It could be argued that this is just a convenient way to refer to his past fetal existence and is not intended to make any metaphysical or ethical assertions about personhood or the right to life. Language is often anachronistic in this way. When we say that the Pilgrims landed on Plymouth Rock, of course we know that the rock did not bear that name when the Pilgrims landed there. But how else can we identify it, without being pedantic? So perhaps in Psalm 139 David refers to himself as a person anachronistically, in order to praise the providence of God who prepared him for life in the world.

However, I have brought up Psalm 139, not because as an isolated text it proves the personhood of the unborn, but because it represents a general biblical usage. In fact, there are many texts that speak of unborn children as persons (see Job 31:15–18; Ps. 22:9; Hos. 12:3; cf. Gen. 25:23–26; 38:27–30). And, significantly, there are no texts that speak of them as anything other than persons. That pattern of language is a significant datum, especially when combined with the evaluation of unborn life in the Mosaic law, discussed above.

Psalm 51:5

In Psalm 51, David confesses sin to God. The heading identifies the sin as his adultery with Bathsheba. In verse 5, he says, "Behold, I was brought forth in iniquity, and in sin did my mother conceive me." Here he is tracing his sin back to its origin. He recognizes that he has always been a sinner before God. Some might have the superficial impression that the sin in verse 5 refers to that of David's mother, but that is impossible in the context. The psalm deals with David's sin, and his alone.

This text, like others we have noted, has personal pronouns referring to David's unborn life. But there is more: the unborn David was also a sinner. Sin in Scripture is a personal quality, never an impersonal one. It is never a property of things, only of persons. It is personal estrangement from God on account of disobedience. Of what sins was the unborn David guilty? The

Christian church has found in this text one of the chief Old Testament witnesses to the doctrine of original sin: that each of us inherits the guilt of Adam's sin and his sinful nature.

Note also that this text explicitly teaches that the sin of David goes back to his very conception. So in this passage (1) David refers to his unborn self as a person, using first person pronouns, (2) he refers to his unborn self as a sinner, and (3) he traces that sin back to his very conception. Clearly he regards himself here as a person from conception.

JUDGES 13:3–5

This passage teaches that Samson is to be a Nazirite from birth, and even before birth.[6] Before Samson's conception, we read:

> And the angel of the LORD appeared to the woman and said to her, "Behold, you are barren and have not borne children, but you shall conceive and bear a son. Therefore be careful and drink no wine or strong drink, and eat nothing unclean, for behold, you shall conceive and bear a son. No razor shall come upon his head, for the child shall be a Nazirite to God from the womb, and he shall begin to save Israel from the hand of the Philistines." (Num. 13:3–5)

Note that Samson's mother, during her pregnancy, has to keep the Nazirite restrictions (v. 4), because her son is a Nazarite even before he is born and must not be defiled. These restrictions apply from his conception.

Just as one must be a person to be a sinner (Ps. 51:5), so one must be a person to be a Nazirite. Thus, Samson, like David, is a person from conception. As there is no reason to think that Samson and David are exceptions to the general rule, we should conclude that all unborn children are persons from conception.

LUKE 1:35

The angel says to the Virgin Mary in Luke 1:35, "The Holy Spirit will come upon you, and the power of the Most High will overshadow you; therefore the child to be born will be called holy—the Son of God." The Holy Spirit brought about the conception of Jesus in Mary's womb, and then she had a normal pregnancy, bearing the child, I presume, about nine months later. But the great miracle here, strictly speaking, was not the virgin birth

6. Nazirites were men who were specially consecrated to God for a period of time. See Num. 6:1–21.

of Jesus, but his virginal conception. It was at his conception that the Spirit acted supernaturally to bring the Son of God into the world.

Jesus, then, was the incarnate Son of God, the second person of the Trinity, from the moment of his conception by the Holy Spirit. Was he, then, anything less than a person at any point in his conception? Certainly not. From conception onward, he was a divine-human person.

This fact does not prove by itself that every human being is a person from conception, but it would be difficult to show from Scripture how and why Jesus should be different from us in this particular respect. To say that he is like us as a person from conception fits the larger biblical pattern we have seen, that the unborn are persons from the beginning, and also fits the pattern of Hebrews 2:17–18; 4:15, that Jesus is like us in all things except sin, that he shares our experiences to the full.

THE DOCTRINE OF CAREFULNESS

In chapter 35, I argued from the manslaughter legislation of the Mosaic law the principle that we should not only avoid murder, but should also be very careful to guard against the *possible* destruction of human life. Of course, in one sense it is always possible for someone to die; I am not talking here about *bare* possibility. But where it is evident that carelessness can lead and has led to tragedy, we must take precautions. So when we swing an axe, we should make sure that the head is securely connected to the handle (Deut. 19:5). When we are angry with a brother, we should take great pains to be reconciled (Matt. 5:22–24).

Now someone may read the above arguments that human beings are persons from conception and not be fully persuaded. He may believe that although these arguments establish their conclusion with a high degree of probability, they are not airtight. To conclude less than that high degree of probability is in my judgment simply unreasonable. But how should we behave, if we consider the conclusion somewhat less than definitive?

The answer is that we should protect all unborn life. For even if the above arguments are only, say, 80 percent certain, they make it highly probable that abortion destroys human lives. And God's law clearly tells us not to take that risk. So our practical response should be exactly the same as if we were persuaded 100 percent.[7] We must be biased in favor of

---

7. This principle obviously does not apply to situations where there is, say, only a 2-percent probability that our action will destroy human life. All of life involves risks and therefore some degree of uncertainty. Nor can I state a mathematical cutoff point where the principle should be applied. But the probabilities in the case before us are very high

life. When faced with uncertainty as to whether or not to kill, we must choose life rather than death.

In the early 1970s, I debated abortion with a senior, respected colleague who held a more liberal view. I will call him Prof. Gottfried. Gottfried thought that we could not prove for sure from Scripture that the unborn child is a person from conception. So he thought that abortion, though undesirable, was permissible in extreme cases like rape or incest. Implicit in his argument was the premise that we could kill anyone whose personhood could not be absolutely proved from Scripture.

In response, I asked the audience to imagine Prof. Gottfried and me on a hunting trip. Those who knew both of us laughed, for they knew that neither of us was likely to go hunting, and that two more unlikely hunting partners could hardly be imagined. Anyway, the story went that we separated at some place in the woods. Then I saw a rustling in the bushes, and I raised my gun, thinking that my deer was in the vicinity. But the thought came to me: What if the movement is not a deer, but is actually Prof. Gottfried? I cannot prove that the movement is caused by a person; certainly I cannot prove that from Scripture. So, on Gottfried's principle, I would be free to shoot first and ask questions later.

But of course every Christian (certainly including Prof. Gottfried) would repudiate such an act. When in doubt, we avoid any action that might destroy human life. This is a biblical principle, and it necessitates a pro-life stance, even for people who are not persuaded by the texts I have presented.

SCIENTIFIC EVIDENCE

The relevant scientific data confirm the argument from Scripture that unborn children are persons. From the point of conception, unborn children have a full complement of chromosomes, half from the father and half from the mother. Therefore, the unborn child is not "part of his mother's body." His genetic makeup is different from hers. So we should not treat the unborn child as we treat hair or fingernails, or even as we treat organs like the gall bladder or liver. The unborn child is a separate and unique human being.

It is also true that the unborn child is dependent on his mother for life support: oxygen, nutrition, and immunity. In this sense, the unborn child is similar to the parts of the mother's body. But this dependence is not essential to his existence. Technology has been able to provide life

---

indeed. (I entertain the possibility of a less than 100-percent probability only for the sake of argument.) Beyond this, I leave the issue to the reader's conscience.

support for very young fetuses, and it is certainly possible that future technology will be able to support the embryo/fetus through the whole gestation period. Furthermore, even after birth children are dependent on adults for life support. So dependence does not count against the independent personhood of the child.

It is also significant that science is no more able than theology to pinpoint a time during gestation at which the unborn becomes a person. There is no point at which a mere physical collection of cells turns into a person with a right to life. The various points that have been suggested—implantation, detectable heartbeat, detectable brainwaves, quickening, viability, and ability to feel pain—are significant developments, but none of them persuasively marks a transition from nonpersonhood to personhood.

In these ways, science agrees with our previous argument from Scripture. But I would caution readers that this is not fundamentally a scientific issue. The chief issue here is the personhood of the unborn, for that conveys a right to life. Personhood is a metaphysical, religious, theological, and ethical category, not a scientific one. There are no scientific observations or experiments that can detect a difference between a person and a nonperson. To reason from scientific premises alone to a conclusion about the rightness or wrongness of abortion is therefore to commit the naturalistic fallacy (see chapters 5–7).

Here I take issue with some pro-life writers who argue from natural law.[8] I do believe that abortion is contrary to nature in the sense that it is the killing of an innocent person. Even people who have never read the Bible understand that it is wrong to do this. And in their hearts, I think most people know that you cannot exempt the unborn from the category of innocent persons. But this conclusion is an intuition based on God's natural revelation, not a demonstration from scientific premises alone. If one desires an argument for this conclusion, one really needs to bring in biblical premises.

Roman Catholics and some others typically say that this issue is scientific, not religious. They are sensitive to the criticism that pro-life Christians are trying to force their religion on others. So they want to insist that the issue is something other than religious. But in my judgment the religious dimension cannot be escaped. Scripture alone (*sola Scriptura*) gives us an adequate argument against the sin of abortion.

CAN ABORTION EVER BE JUSTIFIED?

Much discussion of abortion centers on the hard situations: abortion in cases of rape, incest, or to save the life of the mother. Some have argued

8. Review my general treatment of natural law ethics in chapter 14.

that although abortion should generally be avoided, it is warranted in these situations, and even in other cases, such as: to deal with the physical or psychological health of the mother, possible or actual deformity, population control, or economic need.

Certainly people often seek abortion in the midst of great difficulty, and Christians should sympathize with women who think they have no other alternative. But we cannot compromise the biblical principle that unborn children should be treated the same as those already born. It would certainly be wrong to kill an infant or child because he is deformed, or as a means of population control. So killing an unborn child for these reasons is also wrong. The same, I believe, is true of the more serious issues of rape and incest. We should sympathize with women who do not want to bear children that remind them of such tragic experiences. Such women need much love and counsel. But in the final analysis we must not kill someone because that person is born of rape or incest. We must not kill a child for the sins of his father. The father is guilty; the child is innocent.

In such situations, it may be necessary to give a child up for adoption, though I believe it is best if such a child can be raised by his own mother. For her to undertake such a task, or even to give up the child to adoptive parents, is moral heroism, a great love (chapter 12). But to kill the child is to choose death, not life.

I would make one exception to my generally pro-life stance. That is in the case where the continued existence of the child threatens the physical life of the mother. This situation happens rarely, but it does occur. In an ectopic pregnancy, for example, where the fertilized egg implants itself in the fallopian tubes rather than in the womb, the child cannot live in any case. The physician must remove the child (destroying it) to preserve the woman's life. Some pro-life people do not like to describe this procedure as an abortion, but it is the killing of an unborn child, which fits the definition of the term. I think we should simply be honest in calling the procedure by its proper name.

I consider this procedure ethically right, because there is no possibility of saving the child's life and the child at that point is an unjust aggressor, threatening the life of its mother. Thus, the procedure is the mother's self-defense (see chapter 35).

Our Obligation to Defend the Weak and Helpless

One more group of biblical passages should impress upon us the priority of abortion among the ethical issues the Christian confronts today. Our God cares about the poor and needy:

> For he delivers the needy when he calls,
>   the poor and him who has no helper.
> He has pity on the weak and the needy,
>   and saves the lives of the needy.
> From oppression and violence he redeems their life,
>   and precious is their blood in his sight. (Ps. 72:12–14)

So God wants his people to do likewise. Many passages call on us to help those who are too weak to help themselves:

> Give justice to the weak and the fatherless;
>   maintain the right of the afflicted and the destitute.
> Rescue the weak and the needy;
>   deliver them from the hand of the wicked. (Ps. 82:3–4; cf.
>   Lev. 19:16; Ps. 41:1; Prov. 24:11; Isa. 1:17; 58:5–7, 9–10;
>   Amos 4:1)

The New Testament also emphasizes the care of the poor and needy (see Luke 10:30–37; Acts 4:34–37; 2 Cor. 8:1–15; 9:1–15; Gal. 2:10).

Arguably the unborn are the weakest, poorest, most helpless people that there are. They have no political or economic strength, not even voices to plead their own cause. They are under vicious attack today by the dominant forces of society: the educational establishment, the media, and the government, including the courts, which should be demanding justice. Even the most influential ethical thought of modern society stands against them.

And the most terrible part of this is that these children are under attack from their own mothers. God's plan is that the parents of a child should be his defenders. Our tradition regards a mother's love for her child as something very deep, indeed fierce in its defense of the child's life. The mother is the child's last line of defense. If the mother forsakes her child, who will help? Who indeed? Psalm 27:10 gives the answer: "My father and my mother have forsaken me, but the LORD will take me in." Isaiah speaks in horror about the possibility that a mother might forget her child. But, through Isaiah, God says, "Even these may forget, yet I will not forget you" (49:15). God is the helper of the poor, the husband of the widow, the father of the fatherless. He cares about those for whom the world has no care. And he calls his people to be his agents: "Seek justice, correct oppression; bring justice to the fatherless, plead the widow's cause" (Isa. 1:17). The unborn represent humanity in its most helpless form, under merciless attack. They have, therefore, a *unique* claim upon the mercy of God's people.

Christian maturity is tested by its willingness to go against the odds, to go against intellectual and practical fashions in the service of our King.

It is easy enough to be a Christian when that merely requires us to be nice people. But *love* for Jesus, that love which is motivated by his great sacrifice, requires far more. It calls upon us to renounce what Scripture calls the "wisdom of the world," the fashionable ideas and practices of our society, and to count them as rubbish for the sake of Christ. We honor those like Noah, who built his ark though the world scoffed; like Abraham, who set aside the evidence of his senses and the laughter of his own wife to believe that God would miraculously provide a son; like Moses, who stood up against Pharaoh and brought him the word of God; like Daniel, who faced lions rather than worship an earthly king; like Peter and John, who told officials that "we must obey God rather than men" (Acts 5:29).

Defending Unborn Life in the Present Social Context

I mentioned that today considerable forces are lined up against the unborn. We should understand something of what we are up against.

After *Roe v. Wade* in 1973, a consensus rapidly developed among evangelicals, joining the already existing Roman Catholic consensus, to condemn abortion. Some evangelical theologians, like Bruce Waltke and Meredith Kline, who had earlier defended abortion in some circumstances, became strongly pro-life. Even secular thinkers came more and more to acknowledge that abortion was the taking of human life.

It seemed until the late 1980s that a few changes in the Supreme Court would rapidly return this nation to its historic legal prohibition of abortion. The pro-life movement sensed victory within its grasp, after a hard struggle. But something happened, roughly during the period of the first Bush administration (though I do not blame it on President Bush) to take the victory out of our hands, and it is important that we understand what happened.

As the Soviet Union collapsed, paradoxically, Marxism (perhaps out of self-defense) entrenched itself even more firmly than before in American universities and intellectual circles. In Marxist thought, amid its ethical relativism, there is one evil that is presented in absolute ethical terms: the "oppression" of one group by another. In our time, the dominant application of this ideology is to condemn the oppression by white male Christians of others on the basis of race, nationality, gender, religion, sexual orientation, height, weight, intelligence, habits, and so on. Thus we hear of "political correctness": the attempt of various institutions, especially universities that once made plausible claims to be defenders of intellectual freedom, to police the words, thoughts, and behavior of people so that not one of these oppressed people would endure the slightest offense.[9]

I don't mean to ridicule a genuine concern with injustice; such concern is biblical. But in our society today, the single issue of group oppression is presented in a highly distorted way, which in effect multiplies injustice by gratuitously condemning white Christian males and which blinds us to other kinds of evil.

My main point, however, is that since the late 1980s the pro-abortion movement has linked itself tightly to the Marxist movement for political correctness. The present argument is not that unborn children are less than persons. The presently dominant argument is that to restrict abortion is to oppress women by limiting their choices. That argument has been made, of course, since the 1970s, when the term *pro-choice* was born. But in more recent years it has really caught fire.

In passing, I would point out how pervasive the very word *choice* has become in our time. I carry a "Choice" credit card. I once listened to a radio station that called itself "the classical choice." A major corporation for some years described itself as "the right choice." Nutrition gurus tell us now, not what foods we should eat, but what foods are "the best choices." I generally don't fuss about terminology, and I don't like to hear others doing so. But I must say I am coming to hate the very sound of that word *choice*, because its popularity is, I am convinced, largely the result of an ungodly and murderous mentality. Imagine talking casually about the choice of a woman to murder her own child, as if it were like a choice between two shades of lipstick.

This explains why the pro-abortion movement has become so extreme. Most Americans, polls indicate, favor legal abortions, but oppose abortion on demand; they want restraints and restrictions. But the pro-choice movement will tolerate no restrictions at all. A teenage girl must have parental permission to miss three days of high school, but the abortion advocate will tolerate no involvement of parents in a girl's decision to abort a child. There can be no requirement of parental consent or even notification. President Clinton campaigned on the slogan that abortion should be "safe, legal, and rare," but his policies encouraged abortion, even the horrible procedure called "partial-birth abortion," for he was politically allied to the pro-choice ideologues. To these, any restriction on abortion is the oppression of women, a denial of their autonomy.

That word "autonomy" gets us to the heart of the matter. It locates precisely the contradiction between pro-choice ideology and the Christian

9. For a discussion of some of these issues, see chapter 34.

message. The Bible teaches that we are not autonomous, that we belong body and soul to another, and that we are at his disposal. A human being demanding autonomy is like a fish demanding freedom from water, freedom to live on land. Such freedom is destructive to his nature, and the autonomy of modern, secular thought is equally destructive to human nature. It is not the way to self-fulfillment; it is the way of death. The way to self-fulfillment is, paradoxically, the way of death to self, death with Christ, and eternal life through faith in him. The way to abundant life is the way of the servant of God. This is God's word to the pro-choice movement today. This is the message we must bring in our ministry of mercy.

The message is a judgment on our time, to be sure. We bring to our age a prophetic accusation, that our society has broken God's covenant. But our message is also one of mercy. The element of mercy, I think, needs to be stressed far more than it has been in the pro-life movement. When we deal with women who are facing this awful choice, we must come to them as ministers of mercy, and therefore we must make our message *sound* merciful—far more than we have in the past. The world rightly resents our shrillness and stridency, our quickness to condemn. Jesus was harsh with the Pharisees, but not with the woman of Samaria—though, to be sure, his gentle words convicted her of sin.

The gospel brings mercy to unborn children, of course. But it also speaks mercy to women with their "problem pregnancies." Never before have these women, in all their heartache, fear, and often despair, been so subject to ideological manipulation. The self-appointed feminist spokespersons do not want women with problem pregnancies to know all the relevant facts. They do not want these women to know that their fetus is a baby, that there are dangers in abortion, or that there are alternatives. An article in *National Review* reports that the fashionable ideologues are now trying to discredit adoption, raising images of wicked stepfathers and child molestation, even though most adoptions work out well.[10] They fear, unbelievably, that if adoption becomes more widely accepted, abortion may be discouraged, and that would be a bad result. In the face of such manipulation, the Christian offers grace. We say, "No, you don't have to kill your baby. Yes, there are alternatives; yes, there is help; yes, indeed, there is abundant life in the family of God." And it is our job to make sure this help is available.

This issue makes a strong demand on the Christian's attention, time, passion, and energy. We need to do something. None of us alone can do the job that needs to be done, but we can all do something. Support your

---

10. Marvin Olasky, "Forgotten Choice," *National Review*, March 10, 1997. Available at http://www.findarticles.com/p/articles/mi_m1282/is_n4_v49/ai_19208899.

local pro-life crisis pregnancy center. These organizations are under legal and moral attack from Planned Parenthood and the pro-choice establishment. Volunteer as a counselor, if you are gifted for that. Preach sermons on this subject, if you are a pastor, for many in our churches are confused as to what the Bible teaches, and like wayward sheep they are getting their moral standards from talk shows and magazines. Demonstrate; carry the sign "Abortion Kills Children," for that sign tells the simple truth. Plead with women as they enter abortion clinics. Write to newspaper editors and government officials. Support pro-life candidates for office, and withhold support for otherwise promising candidates who favor abortion.[11] Use legal means to harass abortionists and make it difficult for them to practice. Abortion may be legal, but we don't have to have it in our communities if we don't want it, any more than we have to have landfills or strip clubs.[12]

Be principled and flexible at the same time. If a bill is proposed that restricts abortion in only some cases, support it. Don't take the position that you will support only a total ban. An army takes territory an inch at a time. The important thing is to make progress.

But even more important is to be faithful. In Christ, God has shown us incalculable mercy. We cannot measure the depth, and width, and breadth, and height of his love. Surely love so amazing, so divine, demands our souls, our lives, our all. Let us therefore go forth aggressively, to love others as Christ has loved us.

DEATH[13]

Our attention now shifts from the beginning of life to its end. We have, to be sure, already considered death in the above section: death before birth. But now we must deal with it more generally.

The Bible speaks of life and death in three senses: physical, spiritual, and eternal, as I distinguished these in chapter 35. Here we focus on the physical. Human physical life begins in Genesis 2:7: God "formed the man of dust from the ground and breathed into his nostrils the breath of life, and the

11. Normally I oppose single-issue politics. But we are dealing here with a kind of holocaust: roughly 1.5 million lives a year. In my judgment, this issue outweighs all others in the current political discussion.

12. For a discussion of Operation Rescue's approach, see chapter 32.

13. On this topic and other topics to be considered in this chapter, I have written more extensively in *Medical Ethics* (Phillipsburg, NJ: Presbyterian and Reformed, 1988). In that book, I have also commented on matters that I will not deal with here, such as informed consent.

man became a living creature."[14] This life is passed from parents to children, so we should recognize that any child of Adam and Eve is a living person.

Cessation of breathing is the usual criterion of physical death in Scripture (Job 9:18; 27:3; Pss. 104:29; 135:17; Dan. 10:17; Hab. 2:19; Matt. 27:50; Mark 15:37; Luke 23:46; John 19:30; Acts 5:5, 10). In Hebrew and Greek, the words translated "breath" are also translated "spirit." So there is a felt correlation between the cessation of breath and the separation of spirit from body. If we are to formulate in general terms how people in Bible times determined death, we should add the term "irreversible" to the phrase "cessation of breathing." Presumably even then some people began to breathe after having stopped for a while. So it would take some amount of time before people could be sure that death had occurred.

This criterion is an assumption of Scripture, rather than an explicit norm. That is, Scripture makes use of this criterion, but it doesn't require us to make use of this criterion exclusively. Rather, it leaves the door open for advances in our medical understanding of death.

In modern medicine, the usual criterion is something like that proposed in the "Uniform Declaration of Death Act" (UDDA): "An individual who has sustained either (1) irreversible cessation of circulatory and respiratory functions, or (2) irreversible cessation of all functions of the entire brain, including the brain stem, is dead."[15] The second of these indications is usually called brain death. This condition is generally detected by a flat EEG, but not always. A flat EEG can sometimes be restored. But when it is irreversible, then there is brain death. Of course, the two criteria are closely linked. The three major life systems, governed by heart, lungs, and brain, are mutually dependent.[16] If one is irreversibly lost, the others will follow eventually.

This does not contradict the biblical criterion of the cessation of breathing. It rather identifies causes of this cessation and thereby helps us better to understand when a cessation of breathing is actually irreversible.

The fact that the heart and other organs can be "kept alive" indefinitely by artificial means despite brain death should not lead us to question in these cases whether the patient is truly dead. Clearly a corpse does not

---

14. Cf. Job 12:10; 33:4; Ezek. 37:5–10; Dan. 5:23. This language is also used of non-human living beings (Gen. 6:17; 7:15; 7:22; Acts 17:25; note especially Eccl. 3:19), but Adam is unique in his dramatic intimacy with God in Gen. 2:7. He alone receives breath (figuratively, of course) from God's own nostrils.

15. "Guidelines for the Determination of Death," *Journal of the American Medical Association* 246 (1981): 2184–86. This formula has influenced legislation in many states.

16. One might even say that these are perspectivally related, since each is necessary to the functioning of the others. So the brain is part of the circulatory system, the heart is part of the respiratory system, and so on.

become alive when we move its heart back and forth. A distinction must be drawn between natural and artificial sources of function. Artificial life support may be a means of restoring natural function, but it does not replace that function, even for purposes of determining death.

It is important to recognize that the term "irreversibility" is dependent on technology. It is the responsibility of medical science to seek ways of reversing presently irreversible cases. It is also important to recognize that "irreversibility" is somewhat subjective. Doctors are not always sure whether they can reverse a loss of basic function.

KILLING AND LETTING DIE

The distinction between killing someone and letting him die is important to ethical discussions. Most ethical writers look at the latter more favorably than the former. But letting someone die is not always right, and we need to make some further distinctions in order to deal with the issue.

In one sense, we are all letting others die at every moment of our lives. That is to say, there are people dying all over the world, and for the most part we take no action to preserve their lives. Sometimes this inaction is sin on our part. Surely, for example, we could do far more than we do to help starving children throughout the world. But even when sin is involved, it is not right to say that we have murdered those we have failed to help. So in this case there is a fairly clear distinction between killing someone and letting him die.

It is also the case that even when we choose to help, for example, a drowning swimmer, we may, by making that choice, be letting another person die. In this example, assuming that we are doing all we can, no guilt occurs from letting someone die.

But there are other cases where letting someone die is the same as murder. In the familiar movie scenario, a villain, Hort Bashian, who stands to inherit vast wealth from his uncle Mose, stands by as Mose clutches his heart, begging for his medicine. Hort refuses to give it to him and watches Mose die. Certainly in this case letting him die is morally indistinguishable from murder. We would say the same, certainly, if Mose were in the hospital on life support which could restore him to life, and Hort were to unplug the ventilator and pull the IV systems out of Mose's body.

In general, it is wrong to let someone die when we have the power to keep him alive. But modern medicine complicates the question still more. For today technology can often keep people technically alive indefinitely—people who in past ages would have quickly died from injuries or illnesses.

So our principle must be this: we should never murder anyone, but neither should we prolong the process of dying.[17] Scripture does recognize that death is an inevitable part of the curse. With a few exceptions, such as Enoch (Gen. 5:22–24) and Elijah (2 Kings 2:1–14), and those alive at the return of Christ, everyone experiences death. Attempts to prolong physical life, though often laudable, will ultimately be unsuccessful. That attempt, therefore, is not an absolute priority of the Christian life. Sometimes it is right for one person to give his life for others (John 10:11; 15:13; 1 John 3:16), or to accept great danger for the sake of a divine mission (2 Cor. 4–5; 11:21–27). Biblical heroes of faith undertake such risk, knowing that death is not the end, but only an entrance into glory (2 Cor. 5:6–9; Phil. 1:20–26).

That perspective should also inform our efforts to preserve the lives of others. In general, these efforts are good. But we must acknowledge that God is in control of life and death. So there will come times when we must give up our efforts to save lives and leave people in God's hands.

When is it right, then, to let someone die? When he is dying. But what is dying? It is possible to define death, as we have seen, but dying is much more difficult to identify. In one sense, we are all dying, since death is our destiny. In another sense, the victim in the parable of the good Samaritan was dying until he received care (Luke 10:30). The text calls him "half dead." But in the present context, I use the term *dying* to refer to a condition in which medical help is unable to restore circulation, respiration, and brain activity to normal functioning. It is a state in which medical care is unable to prevent death as defined earlier. Note the following:

1. Dying in this sense is not death. A dying patient is still alive and should be treated with the respect, love, and care due to any other human being. Ordinarily, I do not think it is right to withhold water and nutrition from dying patients.[18]

2. Dying is not the same thing as terminal illness. A person may have a terminal illness (such as cancer or heart disease), yet live with it for many years, often with a significant quality of life.

3. Dying in this sense is often hard to determine. We often do not know for sure whether a particular treatment will restore a patient. Often we must simply accept the judgments of physicians on this score. Not only do they know better than laymen the possibilities of treat-

---

17. I'm well aware of someone's parody, "Thou shalt not kill, but should'st not strive officiously to keep alive." Doubtless that line is intended to trivialize our present train of thought. But I think there is serious biblical substance to this reasoning.

18. My qualification has to do with nasogastric tubes. I am told that often these cannot be inserted without terrible pain to the patient. If a patient is near death, and the tube will cause more distress than benefit, then I would not urge its insertion.

ment, but they have had far more experience with dying and nondying patients, which often gives them a kind of intuition as to whether a patient has fallen beyond the point of medical help. In some cases, it is good to get more than one opinion. But it is important to recognize our fallibility, even the fallibility of medical professionals, in making these determinations.

CARE FOR THE SICK AND INJURED

The general principle is that when a patient is dying we should continue ordinary care (nutrition, water, protection against infection, etc.), but discontinue extraordinary or heroic care. The distinction between ordinary and extraordinary is not precise, and it shifts with the changes in technology. But we may think of extraordinary care as care that is very expensive, difficult, or scarce.

Morally sensitive people sometimes find it hard to understand why any care should be withheld at all. Does not the sanctity of human life demand maximum care at all times?

There are several reasons for withholding care:

1. The purpose of medicine is not only to prolong life, but also to relieve suffering. These two goals usually reinforce one another, but sometimes they are inconsistent. Some treatments for pain may actually reduce lifespan in some patients. So one goal must be weighed against the other. If a patient is dying, a higher value may legitimately be put on the relief of suffering than on lengthening life, for to lengthen life in such cases may only be to prolong the process of death.

2. As the end of life approaches, treatments to prolong life tend to become progressively more expensive and therefore burdensome to families and other supporters, such as church diaconates. Some may object that financial considerations have no place in ethical judgments. Should we not go all out to save life? But consider again the biblical perspective, in which the length of physical life is less than an ultimate priority. The apostle Paul, in Philippians 1:20–24, expresses a desire to leave this world and to be with Christ. He wants to stay in this world only for the sake of the church. It is hard for me to imagine that Paul would have consented to treatment that would have bankrupted the church, while allowing him only a few more days of life. And consider that those few days would be spent in bed, not in ministry. The attitude Paul expresses here and elsewhere is incompatible with that kind of expensive, heroic treatment, given only to prolong a final period of suffering.

3. We should also take into account the scarcity of some means of treatment, like transplants. In the interest of making the best use of them, it may be right to withhold them from dying patients.

EUTHANASIA

Euthanasia, or mercy killing, is killing someone for his own good, to minimize suffering, or to end what someone thinks is an irreversibly low quality of life. We should sympathize with people who undergo such terrible suffering that they, or someone else, think their lives are not worth living. But people make very different judgments in this regard. Some have thought that quadriplegia is such a condition. But quadriplegics like Joni Eareckson Tada have lived wonderfully fruitful lives. God sets no standards in Scripture for a "quality of life" that gives a person a right to life and an obligation to live. In current discussion, quality of life is in the eye of the beholder. It should not be made a standard of who shall live and who shall die. All children of Adam, made in God's image, have a right to life and an obligation to live as long as God allows.

So God's command, "You shall not murder," applies to people who are suffering. We have seen that we have some freedom as to what medical care should be given to suffering patients, but we do not have the freedom to kill them.

A recent case in Florida dealt with Terri Schiavo, a woman who suffered massive brain damage and was unable to communicate with others for over a decade. Physicians determined that she was in a "persistent vegetative state." Her husband Michael sought to have her feeding and hydration tubes removed so that she would die of thirst and starvation.

Terri Schiavo, however, was not dead, nor was she dying, nor was she in a coma. Nor was she terminally ill. Her condition can best be described as "severely disabled." She did respond to visits from her parents, and they sought custody of her from the courts, being willing to bear the expenses of her continued care. The courts, however, responded negatively, despite the attempts of legislative and executive branches of government to save her life. Her feeding tubes were removed, and she died on March 31, 2005.

In my judgment, this was an injustice. There were inconclusive discussions of Terri Schiavo's own wishes and of prospects for improvement in her condition. But the relevant ethical point is that we must not refuse ordinary care to a patient simply because he or she is disabled. In this case, removal of the tubes was equivalent to murder.

To some, this level of disablement turns a person into a nuisance. But we saw in chapter 34 that God has a special care for the disabled and calls us to love them as he does. And those who are patient and open to the disabled often find them to be wonderful friends and partners, as did Terri Schaivo's parents. A friend of mine has a daughter, now over twenty years old, who has been severely disabled from birth. The woman cannot walk or talk or do anything for herself. Yet she does respond emotionally to music, to human touch, and to the emotions of those around her. She has greatly enriched the Christian fellowship of her church. Those who know her would be appalled at the notion that she should be put to death.

SUICIDE

It follows from what I have said that suicide is also a violation of the sixth commandment. Scripture makes no exception for self-murder. Murder is wrong because it destroys the image of God (Gen. 9:6). Suicide does the same thing and is wrong for the same reason.

Scripture does not say explicitly that suicide is wrong, but it places the act in a context of shame and defeat. There are five instances recorded in Scripture: Abimelech (in effect, Judg. 9:52–54), Saul (1 Sam. 31:3–5), Ahithophel (2 Sam. 17:23), Zimri (1 Kings 16:18–19), and Judas (Matt. 27:3–5). All of these came to this end through disobedience to God.

Some more noble Bible characters experienced such frustration that they asked God to take their lives: Moses (Num. 11:12–15), Elijah (1 Kings 19:4), and Jonah (Jonah 4:1–11), but God did not grant those requests. Scripture implies that these requests were not godly. They understandably emerged out of perceptions of defeat, but those perceptions were exaggerated and ultimately wrong. God had more blessings in store for his prophets.

We should try to understand the extremes of sadness, confusion, suffering, and defeat that lead people to want to take their own lives. People who contemplate suicide are in special need of the compassion of the body of Christ and the grace of the cross. Our first approach should not be to judge, but to point to a better way, as God himself did with his weary prophets. God never forsakes his children. He never leads them to a situation where sinful self-destruction is the only option (1 Cor. 10:13).

Sometimes suicidal thoughts and behavior are associated with drugs or clinical depression. In the section "Living with Ourselves" in chapter 15, I explored the relationships between moral choices and our physical makeup. Physical and mental conditions never excuse sin, though they enable others to understand it better and to have greater compassion on the sinner.

A good friend of mine was a long-time missionary to Africa. He returned home with some sort of affliction that threw him into deep depression and led him to attempt suicide several times, eventually with success. While he was in the hospital, a friend asked him whether he continued to trust God's grace in Jesus. He replied, "More than ever before."

Suicide is a sin, but it is not unforgivable. My friend knew that his thoughts of suicide were wrong, and he placed them under the blood of Christ. Eventually they overcame him. But I have no doubt that I will see him in heaven.

We should not confuse suicide with laying down one's life for others. Jesus indicates that to lay down one's life for his friends, as indeed he himself was to do, is the greatest form of love (John 15:13). So Paul's acceptance of danger (2 Cor. 4:7–18; 11:16–33) was not suicidal, but expressed his love for the church. I would place this interpretation also on Samson's "suicide" in Judges 16:28–31. When he pulled down the temple of Dagon, killing many Philistines, he accomplished God's judgment and empowered the people of God. In this one case, God answered affirmatively a prayer for death (v. 30). There was indeed something shameful about Samson's death, as in the cases of Saul and Judas, for Samson was often disobedient to God's will. But his last moments were full of faith. In a small way, he anticipated Jesus, gaining God's victory by dying for his friends.

This principle has ramifications also for medical ethics. It is not wrong for a Christian to refuse medical treatment, out of a recognition that the treatment could be burdensome to his family and fellow believers. I suspect that the apostle Paul, had he lived in our time, would not have wanted to be kept indefinitely on artificial life support, when the expense of that could have been used for ministry. His desire to go on living was only for the sake of ministry (Phil. 1:20–26); otherwise, he preferred to leave this world and be with Christ.

HEALTH AND SAFETY

Our discussion of suicide reminds us that the sixth commandment calls for us to preserve our own lives as well as the lives of others. The Mosaic law does contain public health provisions (Lev. 13–15; Num. 5:1–4; Deut. 24:8–9). So we should take precautions to safeguard our own health and safety. But, just as we distinguished between suicide and sacrificial living, so we should also distinguish between right and wrong concerns for our personal well-being.

ALCOHOL

Scripture warns against the abuse of wine and strong drink (Prov. 20:1; Isa. 5:11, 22; 28:1; 56:12), the drugs of choice in ancient Near Eastern culture. Scripture does speak positively of the use of wine in proper circumstances (Ps. 104:15; Eccl. 10:19; Isa. 55:1; John 2:3–11; 1 Tim. 5:23), and of course wine is an element of the Lord's Supper, following the Passover custom. The positive benefit of wine is not only its nutritional value and its medicinal properties (1 Tim. 5:23) but also its ability "to gladden the heart of man" (Ps. 104:15). So Scripture approves of the ability of wine to alter our mood. We should not think, then, that we must stop drinking before the wine affects our moods; that is its natural and good function.

People abuse wine and strong drink by allowing it to become an addiction. As Isaiah puts it, "Woe to those who rise early in the morning, that they may run after strong drink, who tarry late into the evening as wine inflames them!" (Isa. 5:11), and "Woe to those who are heroes at drinking wine, and valiant men in mixing strong drink" (v. 22). So Isaiah's critique of wine abuse fits well with Paul's saying, "'All things are lawful for me,' but I will not be enslaved by anything" (1 Cor. 6:12).

Alcoholic beverages should also be used with sensitivity to the situational perspective. In some contexts we should restrict our use of wine beyond the limits noted above. Leviticus 10:9 says that priests should not drink wine or strong drink when they go into the tabernacle of God, for in their priestly work they must not impair their ability to distinguish between the holy and the common (v. 10).[19] Proverbs 31:4–5 says that wine and strong drink are not for kings (presumably in the context of their official duties). But strong drink and wine are especially good for those who are perishing or in distress (vv. 6–7). Such passages encourage us to evaluate the appropriateness of the use of such drinks in other situations as well. Scripture itself does not anticipate the effects of alcohol in modern highway traffic. But certainly the driver of an automobile needs to be able to make sound judgments, as did the priest in ancient Israel. Applying the normative perspective to the situational, we can say that it is biblically wrong to drink and drive.

19. The Nazirite must abstain from wine and strong drink for the duration of his vow (Num. 6:3–4). As with the priest, this may have something to do with his specific duties, but I suspect that it is purely ceremonial, for he is also forbidden to eat unfermented juice or anything that comes from the grapevine (v. 3). Fermentation sometimes symbolizes sin in Scripture, and the Nazirite is a kind of walking symbol of consecration to God.

TOBACCO

Tobacco smoking was not known during the biblical period, and its dangers were not fully known until the twentieth century. It is addictive, as the use of alcohol sometimes is, but it doesn't produce the changes in behavior than alcohol does. So the use of tobacco is a danger mainly to the smoker himself, though some illnesses have been associated also with secondhand smoke. There is no benefit to smoking proportionate to the genuine benefits of the use of alcohol, though those used to smoking do get some pleasure from it and much displeasure when they stop.

Given the seriousness of the health problems connected with smoking, beginning with cancer and heart disease, it seems to me to be foolish for anyone to begin smoking. Young people should be informed of the dangers and disciplined to abstain from this practice. Those already addicted to smoking, however, generally find it very difficult to quit. Attempting to quit smoking can be quite disruptive to one's life, and the smoker may need to weigh the benefits of quitting against the distraction of the quitting process. Christians should be gracious and understanding to those who smoke. It is wrong to begin smoking, but if someone is already a smoker, it may be a godly choice not to try to quit.

I must say a word against the common depiction of Reformed theology, by both friends and foes, as a smokers' movement. I have often heard Reformed people boast about their freedom to smoke over against their supposedly legalist fundamentalist brothers and sisters.[20] Some understand a discussion among Reformed theologians to be incomplete without cigars, pipes, and cigarettes. There is even a Reformed theological publication called the *Nicotine Theological Journal*.[21] But some of the men I've known who have been most insistent on their freedom to smoke have died of emphysema and lung cancer.

DRUGS

The abuse of drugs (both prescription and illegal) has become a major problem in modern society. The dangers vary greatly among the different drugs, involving the altering of the mind, addiction, health risks, association with organized crime, and so on. In general, the biblical principles governing alcohol pertain to drugs as well. In some cases (such as medical

---

20. For my own account of Christian freedom, the sufficiency of Scripture, and the adiaphora, see chapter 11.

21. The title, though certainly tongue-in-cheek, opens them wide to gibes by opponents that their content is poisonous.

marijuana and many prescription drugs), there are benefits to be gained, and those benefits should be received with thanks. (I do not believe, for example, that the medicinal use of marijuana should be outlawed.) As we have seen with alcohol, Scripture also approves of a certain level of mood alteration in situations where one does not have to give close attention to one's environment. But the biblical writers who counsel against addiction to alcohol would certainly also disapprove of addiction to heroin and cocaine. The principles are no different, but the danger of addiction is much greater. So to use such highly addictive substances is not biblically wise. Further, Christians should obey the civil laws governing the use of such substances.

They should also, however, seek to influence the civil government toward making wise judgments in this area. As the civil government is rightly concerned with the safety of its people, it should restrict the use of drugs (as alcohol) in driving and other situations where insobriety can cause the loss of life. It is another question, however, whether certain substances should be banned entirely. There are no biblical principles that require such legal bans. Nor has that been the common practice of government with regard to alcohol. When the U.S. did attempt to ban alcohol, that attempt was unsuccessful, creating a huge black market in the forbidden substances. So far, the U.S. war on drugs has been similarly unsuccessful, and it is responsible for creating a large criminal drug industry.

I would counsel consideration of other strategies, parallel to the government restriction of alcohol and tobacco. There should be tough penalties for driving under the influence of drugs and for other drug-induced violence. Drugs should be kept from people under a certain age. But I cannot see what benefit it brings to imprison someone for carrying a small amount of marijuana.[22] Such small-time drug users and sellers, when arrested, learn to associate with more hardened criminals, and upon release they often become full-fledged members of the drug culture.

The argument has been made in conservative journals, as well as in liberal ones, that the possession and use of drugs should in most cases be decriminalized. I do not know if that would be wise; certainly it should not be done without transitional steps. But such an approach would certainly be a blow to the criminal drug industry, which seems now to be doing more harm to society than the drugs themselves. It is time to consider drastic changes in our society's approach to this issue. Here the relative silence of Scripture encourages us to think creatively.

---

22. Cf. the discussion of prisons in chapter 36.

FOOD, DRINK, AND EXERCISE

As we have seen, we have a prima facie biblical responsibility to preserve our own lives,[23] and that implies a regard for physical health. Today we know more than past generations about what promotes health. Thus, many people put large efforts into crafting proper diets and patterns of exercise. This is fine up to a point. In general, these practices contribute to our witness for Christ. But I would remind my readers of a point made earlier, that the length of physical life is not an ultimate priority in Scripture. If health and safety were ultimate priorities, then we would guard them above all else. But the apostle Paul did not do that. As we have seen, he voluntarily undertook a dangerous existence to minister the gospel (2 Cor. 11:16–33). That heedlessness to personal safety was also characteristic of the saints of Hebrews 11. And behind all these examples is the figure of Jesus himself, who left the heavenly glory, hungered, thirsted, risked violence, and in the end gave himself up to beating and crucifixion for us.[24] God has ordained for all of us that this life is to be a time of suffering, as we await the glory to come (1 Peter 4:12–13).

THE ENVIRONMENT

The term *ratsakh* in the sixth commandment applies only to the killing of human beings. Yet, as we have seen, animals also have the breath of life. God cares for all life on earth (Job 39–40; Ps. 104:11–30; Jonah 4:11; Matt. 6:26–30). Even though God gives man the right to eat animals as food (Gen. 9:2–3), he also calls us to be kind to them (Ex. 20:10; 23:5, 12; Deut. 22:4; 25:4; Prov. 12:10; Jonah 4:11; John 10:11). There is a strong analogy between different kinds of life. Those who do not care about the loss of animal life will likely not care much about human life either.

And as we saw earlier, God requires Israel to preserve the enemy's fruit trees when besieging a city (Deut. 20:19). Animal images appear in the divine theophany (Ezek. 1), and biblical eschatology includes descriptions of plants and animals in the new heavens and new earth (Isa. 11:6–8; Rev. 22:2). We have seen also that God requires Israel to give rest to the land

23. See chapter 13.

24. In the cases of both Paul and Jesus, to say that they "risked" danger is not to deny that God (indeed Jesus as God) had full control of every situation. It is not to suggest that we are ruled by chance. But some human decisions are risky in that they increase the probability of danger, and that is true both in Jesus' case and in ours.

every seventh year (Ex. 23:10–11). Israel's failure to do this was a major reason for the exile (2 Chron. 36:20–21).

So although God has a special concern for human life, he is concerned analogously for the whole creation, for all forms of life. He made man to have dominion over the world. But man is not only the lord of creation; he is himself a creature, made of dust. And he is dependent on the rest of creation for his sustenance. So man is to use the resources of the world, but is not to exploit or deplete them. If those resources are depleted, the natural consequence is that man himself suffers. Man must be a responsible steward of the earth if he is to preserve his own life.

In Genesis 2:15, God calls Adam to "work" and "keep" the garden. "Work" (*'abad*) implies that Adam is to be a servant of the land, suggesting the concept of servant leadership (Matt. 20:25–28) that we discussed in chapter 31. To "keep" (*shamar*) the garden is to guard it against intrusion, to defend it.[25] So the sixth commandment requires us to care for the environment.

The cultural mandate does not justify destruction of the environment,[26] as some non-Christian writers have suggested.[27] Man cannot fill and subdue the earth if he destroys the earth's resources. Rather, he is to develop and increase the earth's resources. His own welfare and the welfare of the earth go hand in hand.

Nevertheless, there are differences between a biblical concern for the earth and secular environmentalism:

1. Scriptural environmentalism rejects pantheistic religions of the earth that have motivated some non-Christian activists. The earth is not God. It is not our mother or father. We should not worship it or seek mystical union with it, but we should respect it as God's creation and seek to carry out his will for the planet.

2. Scripture does not teach that all forms of life are equal. Secularists often maintain that animals have the same right to life as human beings. While Scripture mandates kindness to animals, it also allows the eating of meat. Man alone is the image of God, and he alone is to exercise dominion over the earth. As we saw under the fifth commandment, servant leadership is not inconsistent with hierarchy. Man is to be a servant leader to the earth, and he is also the lord of the earth.

---

25. This language is similar to that of Num. 1:53 and elsewhere, which speaks of priests guarding God's sanctuary. Eden was, as we have seen, a sanctuary of God. In a broader sense, the whole creation is a temple of God's dwelling (Isa. 66:1).

26. Readers may wish to review at this point the discussion of the cultural mandate in chapter 17.

27. Most famously, Lynn White Jr., "The Historical Roots of Our Ecologic Crisis," *Science* 155 (1967): 1203–12. Francis Schaeffer replied to White in *Pollution and the Death of Man* (Wheaton, IL: Tyndale House, 1970).

This is not to say that we should always give priority to human industry over the preservation of nature. Human dominion over the earth does not mean paving it over or replacing all forests with factories. The human race itself has an interest in preserving species (some, at any rate), forests, wetlands, and the beauties of God's world. But neither does Scripture justify the generalized suspicion of technology that is common in the secular environmental movement. So the cultural mandate calls us to plan for balanced use of the earth's resources, for the well-being of mankind and for the glory of God.

Rational planning of the use of earth's resources becomes very difficult after the fall, when sinful human beings seek greater portions of the earth at the expense of others. Certainly a balanced environmental policy requires of people and nations a level of cooperation that seems impossible now. Such cooperation is difficult even in the scientific attempt to define problems and needs. I am not competent, for example, to judge literature about the reality, extent, causes, consequences, and remedy for global warming. But even scientific discussions often appear to be biased by ideology on one side or another.[28] Without scientific work in which all have confidence, it is very difficult to know what to do to preserve the environment. Only a regenerate society will find agreement on the worldview questions sufficient to save the earth. So the chief need of the environment is evangelism.

28. This is true in many areas of ethical discussion, such as the question of a genetic basis for homosexuality, or the need for using embryonic stem cells. Science itself is not religiously neutral. Like all human thinking, it must be taken captive to the obedience of Christ (2 Cor. 10:5).

CHAPTER 38

The Seventh Commandment: Sexual Purity

In chapter 33, I considered the male-female relationship in the context of authority structures. Here, I shall discuss sexual ethics as such. The Hebrew of Exodus 20:14, *lo' tin'af*, is straightforward: "You shall not commit adultery." It means, quite specifically, that one should not have sexual intercourse with another person's spouse. That is, we may say, the narrow meaning of the commandment (see chapter 22). But, as we have seen, these narrow meanings can take wings. We saw under the sixth commandment that if we really want to avoid murder, we should ask God to form in us such respect for life that we will not even become angry with another person. But that respect for life can be nothing other than love, which is the essence of all godliness. So the sixth commandment becomes a perspective on all of life. Does the seventh commandment have that same capacity, the ability to broaden out and cover all aspects of human life?

The Westminster divines thought it did. They wrote in the Larger Catechism:

> Q. 138. *What are the duties required in the seventh commandment?*
> A. The duties required in the seventh commandment are, chastity in body, mind, affections, words, and behavior; and the preservation of it in ourselves and others; watchfulness over the eyes and all the senses; temperance, keeping of chaste company,

modesty in apparel; marriage by those that have not the gift of continency, conjugal love, and cohabitation; diligent labor in our callings; shunning all occasions of uncleanness, and resisting temptations thereunto.

Q. 139. *What are the sins forbidden in the seventh commandment?*

A. The sins forbidden in the seventh commandment, besides the neglect of the duties required, are, adultery, fornication, rape, incest, sodomy, and all unnatural lusts; all unclean imaginations, thoughts, purposes, and affections; all corrupt or filthy communications, or listening thereunto; wanton looks, impudent or light behavior, immodest apparel; prohibiting of lawful, and dispensing with unlawful marriages; allowing, tolerating, keeping of stews, and resorting to them; entangling vows of single life, undue delay of marriage; having more wives or husbands than one at the same time; unjust divorce, or desertion; idleness, gluttony, drunkenness, unchaste company; lascivious songs, books, pictures, dancings, stage plays; and all other provocations to, or acts of uncleanness, either in ourselves or others.

The Larger Catechism always goes to the heart, as does Jesus. If we wish to avoid committing adultery, the Catechism says, we should cultivate purity of heart in sexual matters, avoiding occasions of temptation, replacing such occasions with "diligent labor in our callings." Such diligent labor might not seem at first to be an implication of the seventh commandment, but for those who seek sexual purity it is indispensable.

We can follow this line of thinking still further, however. Scripture represents marriage as a reflection of our covenant relationship with God. To violate marriage is to violate that covenant, and unfaithfulness to God is adultery. All sin is unfaithfulness to God, spiritual adultery. So the seventh commandment, like the others, actually covers all of life from its particular perspective. Whenever we sin, we can think of it as marital unfaithfulness. And we should think of it that way, better to understand our radical need of forgiveness from our heavenly husband. The seventh commandment's perspective on sin is a radically personal perspective, presented in vivid, sexual imagery. It yields a powerful motivation for repentance.

Below, we shall consider more fully the narrow and broad meanings of this commandment.

MARRIAGE

As we saw in chapter 33, sexual differentiation is an aspect of the image of God. It is the first distinction mentioned after man's creation: "So God created man in his own image, in the image of God he created him; male and female he created them" (Gen. 1:27). I said in the earlier chapter that we should not identify the image of God with sexual diversity, but one can see from this text the attractiveness of such an idea.

Gender is fundamental to human life. There are, of course, many differences among people, such as differences in age, height, weight, health, ethnicity, interests, personality, strength, and speed. But the sexual difference commands our attention in a more fundamental way than the others. When we first meet someone, their gender is usually the first thing we notice. It is signaled by name, clothing, voice, hair style, skin tone, and body shape, so that one can tell from a distance, even over the telephone (though not over the Internet!), which gender the person is. Once we know the sex of a person, we relate to him or her in certain ways, even in business conversation, different from the ways in which we would relate to a person of the opposite gender. And when we think about another person, according to various surveys, his or her sexuality often comes to mind—more often than many of us would readily admit.

That is, of course, only the beginning. The urge for sexual relations is deep and powerful. God placed that desire in us as a motivation for marriage and reproduction, and as a precious intimacy shared between married partners. But since the fall it has been a great occasion of temptation. In the modern world, sex, even sinful sex, is a pervasive preoccupation, as we can see on billboards all around us, in electronic and print media, in music and art. But sex is also a preoccupation of Scripture, for different reasons.

In Genesis, the sexual difference qualifies human beings to carry out the fundamental task of mankind, the cultural mandate, which is, first, to "be fruitful and multiply and fill the earth" (Gen. 1:28). There must be reproduction if there is to be dominion. So marriage is a creation ordinance. After God makes a woman from the rib of Adam, we read: "Then the man said, 'This at last is bone of my bones and flesh of my flesh; she shall be called Woman, because she was taken out of Man.' Therefore a man shall leave his father and his mother and hold fast to his wife, and they shall become one flesh" (Gen. 2:23–24).

To "leave" is to begin a new household, with its own authority structure. Of course, as we saw under the fifth commandment, leaving father and mother does not end our responsibility to parents, but the honor we owe them takes on a new form in which honor to our spouse takes precedence.

To honor the spouse in this passage is to "hold fast," sometimes translated "cleave." This is not primarily a reference to sexual union. The Hebrew term refers to nonsexual relationships, as when Ruth "clung" to her mother-in-law (Ruth 1:14) and when the men of Judah followed David steadfastly (2 Sam. 20:2). To hold fast is to maintain the company of another person, in loyalty to him. So "leave" and "hold fast" have overlapping meanings. Both refer to location and loyalty, or (recalling our three perspectives) to situation and norm. Husband and wife are to share a situation, a life story, and they are to establish a new authority structure.

The existential perspective is found in the phrase "they shall become one flesh" (v. 24). Here the reference is distinctly sexual. But Paul uses the phrase equally to refer to nurture in Ephesians 5:28–31:

> In the same way husbands should love their wives as their own bodies. He who loves his wife loves himself. For no one ever hated his own flesh, but nourishes and cherishes it, just as Christ does the church, because we are members of his body. "Therefore a man shall leave his father and mother and hold fast to his wife, and the two shall become one flesh."

So marriage creates a new situation, a new norm, and a new deeply personal relationship, including mutual care and sexual fulfillment. This understanding coheres with our triperspectival analysis of love in chapter 12: allegiance, action, and affection.

It should not be surprising, then, that God calls marriage a "covenant" in Ezekiel 16:8 and Malachi 2:14. A covenant is a relationship governed by oath, so it is right that marriage be solemnized in a ceremony. Contrary to much public opinion today, the oath is important.[1] A marriage creates obligations and promises, without which a sexual relationship has no long-term foundation. But only long-term relationships (families) are suitable for raising children and providing protection against the storms of life.[2]

The marriage covenant, therefore, is an image of the covenantal relationship between God and his people. The two covenants are closely related. This way of understanding marriage pervades Scripture. In Genesis 3, our

---

1. I do not entirely reject the idea of common-law marriage. That phrase should be used to indicate a relationship in which a man and a woman, over a period of living together, show themselves publicly to be fully committed to one another, just as if they had taken formal vows. In this case, the vow exists, though implicitly and informally, and it is witnessed by the couple's acquaintances. (Without the public witness, there is no vow.) Nevertheless, such marriages begin in sin as nonmarriages. Only over a period of time can there be public witness to their commitment.

2. Compare the discussion in chapter 32 of the family as the fundamental form of social organization.

first parents' disobedience to God disrupts their marriage relationship. After the fall, sexual shame appears for the first time (3:7), and the man blames his troubles on the woman (v. 12). God announces a curse on her childbearing (v. 16) and his labor (v. 17). So the prosperity of the marriage covenant depends on faithfulness to the divine covenant.

The marriage covenant is also an image of the divine covenant. The prophets frequently draw a parallel between adultery and idolatry. When people worship idols, they violate their covenant with God, just as an adulterer violates his covenant with his wife. So idolatrous Israel is the unfaithful wife of God (Jer. 3:6–10; Ezek. 16; 23; Hos. 2–3). Paul teaches, too, that even outside Israel, when people suppress the truth about God (Rom. 1:18), the first result is idolatry (vv. 23, 25), and the next result is sexual sin (vv. 24, 26–27).

Modern people sometimes wonder why the Bible is so negative toward adultery. Why should a brief, pleasurable encounter be such a serious matter?[3] The deepest answer, I think, is that adultery is covenant treason. Most people can understand why treason against one's government in time of war should be punished severely, even by death. But the family is more fundamental than the nation. It is the root of all corporate relationships (see chapters 31–32). As such, it reflects our fundamental relation to God, so that the mentality of rebellion is the same in both covenants. One who would cheat on his spouse would also cheat on God. The same attitude leads to both kinds of sin.

But Scripture also uses the parallel between these covenants in a positive way. When God promised redemption to Adam and Eve (Gen. 3:15), he also renewed their marriage. He removed the sexual shame of the first couple, as he made garments for them and dressed them himself (v. 21). And throughout Scripture, when God redeems his people, marriage imagery appears:

> As the bridegroom rejoices over the bride,
> so shall your God rejoice over you. (Isa. 62:5)

> Therefore, behold, I will allure her,
> and bring her into the wilderness,
> and speak tenderly to her.
> And there I will give her her vineyards
> and make the Valley of Achor a door of hope.
> And there she shall answer as in the days of her youth,
> as at the time when she came out of the land of Egypt.

---

3. Note the death penalty in Deut. 22:23–24.

And in that day, declares the LORD, you will call me "My Husband," and no longer will you call me "My Baal." For I will remove the names of the Baals from her mouth, and they shall be remembered by name no more. And I will make for them a covenant on that day with the beasts of the field, the birds of the heavens, and the creeping things of the ground. And I will abolish the bow, the sword, and war from the land, and I will make you lie down in safety. And I will betroth you to me forever. I will betroth you to me in righteousness and in justice, in steadfast love and in mercy. I will betroth you to me in faithfulness. And you shall know the LORD. (Hos. 2:14–20)

Husbands, love your wives, as Christ loved the church and gave himself up for her, that he might sanctify her, having cleansed her by the washing of water with the word, so that he might present the church to himself in splendor, without spot or wrinkle or any such thing, that she might be holy and without blemish. In the same way husbands should love their wives as their own bodies. He who loves his wife loves himself. For no one ever hated his own flesh, but nourishes and cherishes it, just as Christ does the church, because we are members of his body. "Therefore a man shall leave his father and mother and hold fast to his wife, and the two shall become one flesh." This mystery is profound, and I am saying that it refers to Christ and the church. However, let each one of you love his wife as himself, and let the wife see that she respects her husband. (Eph. 5:25–33; cf. 1 Cor. 6:15–20; 2 Cor. 11:2)

Jesus' first miracle in the gospel of John is to turn water into wine at a wedding feast (John 2:1–11). Supplying wine was the task of the bridegroom. So Jesus implicitly identified that wedding with his own. In Matthew 22:1–14, he compares his kingdom to a wedding feast, and in Matthew 25:1–13 his coming inaugurates that feast. In Revelation 19:6–9, the consummation of history is "the marriage supper of the Lamb" (v. 9).

Adultery, therefore, is not only covenant treason, but also a rejection of redemptive grace. Within this perspective, other biblical teachings fall into place. A believer should not marry an unbeliever (Gen. 24:1–4; 27:46; Deut. 7:3–4; Ezra 9–10; 1 Cor. 7:39; 9:5; 2 Cor. 6:14–18). A candidate for church eldership must be "above reproach, the husband of one wife" (1 Tim. 3:2). For the elder speaks for God, the husband of the church. An elder must image God's faithfulness in marriage. The same is true for older widows (1 Tim. 5:9), whom the church supports in their ministries of mercy and prayer.

Marriage, therefore, is a good thing. It is part of God's cultural mandate and an image of his own love for his people. Those who forbid marriage do not speak for God, but for deceitful spirits and demons (1 Tim. 4:1–3). They are "liars whose consciences are seared" (v. 2).

Contrary to Roman Catholicism, there is no suggestion in Scripture that church leaders should be unmarried. Priests and Levites in the Old Testament, and apostles in the New, had the right to marry. Although Paul was unmarried through at least much of his ministry, he too had the right to marry (1 Cor. 9:5). There are advantages to singleness in ministry, as 1 Corinthians 7 and 9 indicate. But not everybody has the gift of celibacy (1 Cor. 7:7), and God does call noncelibates into ministry.

It is not sinful to be unmarried, and singleness may be a divine calling, either for a time or for life (Matt. 19:12; 1 Tim. 5:3–10). Paul says in 1 Corinthians 7 that during "the present distress" (v. 26) it is best for people not to enter into new marriages, unless they cannot contain their sexual desire (vv. 8–9). But if they do marry, even in that difficult situation, they have not sinned (v. 28). When he wrote 1 Corinthians, Paul himself was evidently unmarried (7:7), and he believed the single status had advantages in ministry. But in a different context, he urges younger widows to marry and raise children (1 Tim. 5:14).

It is good to have sexual relations within marriage. Scripture does not regard sex as something dirty or morally degrading. It is true that emissions of semen (Lev. 15:16–18) and menstrual fluid (vv. 19–24) were ceremonially unclean, according to the Mosaic law. But cleanness and uncleanness in biblical law are not primarily moral categories. A woman is unclean for a time after bearing a child (Lev. 12:1–8), but of course bearing a child is a good thing, not a sin. Cleanliness laws have to do with tidiness, orderliness, or literal cleanness, and in some cases risks to health, rather than to morality as such. Sex is not evil, but it does sometimes create a mess.

On a couple occasions, sexual activity is seen as incompatible with holy matters (Ex. 19:15; 1 Sam. 21:4–5). And in 1 Corinthians 7:5, Paul suggests that couples might briefly abstain from sex to devote themselves to prayer. Some ancient religions incorporated fornication, even prostitution, into their worship, but the true God prohibited that, doubtless to maintain the purity of marriage and to focus the attention of the worshiper on the Lord. So even in the new covenant, sex and concentrated prayer do not fit well together. But Paul's implication is that such abstinence should be rare.

Scripture emphasizes, however, the delights of godly sex, and it often does so more graphically than some readers would prefer. One whole book of the Bible, the Song of Songs, is devoted to this subject, but I shall quote Proverbs 5:18–19:

Let your fountain be blessed,
> and rejoice in the wife of your youth,
> a lovely deer, a graceful doe.

Let her breasts fill you at all times with delight;
> be intoxicated always in her love.

When Abimelech saw that Isaac and Rebekah were "laughing" together, he knew they were man and wife (Gen. 26:8). Sexual delight and play are a mark of marriage. We should never regard sex in marriage, as Christians sometimes have, as some sort of necessary evil. Husband and wife should delight in it. It should be a constant in marriage, when physically possible. Paul urges married couples not to withhold sex from one another, except for brief times of prayer, as I mentioned above. He even speaks of "conjugal rights" (*opheilē*) (1 Cor. 11:3), indicating that husband and wife have a duty to give themselves sexually to one another. But in the context of the whole Bible, this duty is clearly a pleasure, not a duty for duty's sake (chapter 7).

In the biblical period, parents often chose mates for their children,[4] in the hope and expectation that love would develop after marriage. There is nothing wrong with this practice. God never tells us that marital love must exist before marriage. Rather, he calls spouses to love one another after the marriage has taken place (Eph. 5:25).

But we read also of marriages based on love, which doubtless included sexual attraction. Certainly that was true of the first marriage (Gen. 2:23), also that between Jacob and Rachel (29:1–30), and David and Michal (1 Sam. 18:20–29). David's marriage to Bathsheba (2 Sam. 11) was also motivated by love, though their relationship began in sin.

So marriage, and sex within marriage, are parts of God's good provision for human beings. Marriage and sex enable us to carry out God's cultural mandate, they provide the great pleasure of intimacy, and they image God's own relation to us. Adultery defiles that wonderful blessing and rejects God's good purpose for us.

---

4. In some Christian circles, there is a movement to abolish dating and replace it with "biblical courtship," in which a young man comes to know a young lady in the company of her family and under their supervision. There are many evils associated with unsupervised dating, and from a biblical standpoint there are many attractions in courtship. Aside from the danger of sexual temptation, which is great, we should also consider that what makes a good date is very different from what makes a good marriage. I cannot say, however, that the Bible *commands* a courtship approach, or that Christians who go on unsupervised dates necessarily commit sin. Courtship was the practice in biblical times, a practice superior in many ways to that of modern culture. (It was not an absolute constant, even of biblical culture. Isaac did not court Rebecca.) But it is not a biblical norm. Nevertheless, Christian parents, especially those with daughters, should give it serious consideration as they plan for their children's eventual marriages.

POLYGAMY

We have seen that adultery violates the marriage covenant and shows contempt for our covenant with God. But there are other practices that also compromise the marriage covenant, and we shall consider some of them in the remainder of this chapter.

Polygamy is not a great problem in modern Western countries, mainly because of the influence of Christianity. (Polygamy in the West tends to be serial, not simultaneous!) The advance of polygamous Islam into Europe and America, however, may make this question more important to Western Christians in years to come. But in other parts of the world, young churches find this to be one of the major ethical issues. When a society has a tradition of polygamy, how should the church treat those polygamists who become Christians?

Some churches have taken the position that polygamists professing faith should not be accepted as church members, nor admitted to the sacraments. Yet these churches do seek to give pastoral care to such people.[5] By this policy, they seek to defend the biblical view of the family and to give a clear witness to their culture of their faith in Christ.

While admiring the motivations of this policy, I must say that it is unscriptural. The New Testament was written in a culture that tolerated polygamy, and its own stance is clear. Polygamists were denied church office (1 Tim. 3:2), but there is no evidence that they were denied church membership or sacraments. The implication, rather, is that there were some church members who might have been considered for church office except that they were polygamous.

The Old Testament, of course, is rather tolerant of polygamy, and many of the great Old Testament saints had more than one wife. Jesus states that God's original intention for marriage was one man and one woman (Matt. 19:1–12). Thus we may infer that the Old Testament tolerated polygamy, as it tolerated divorce, because of the "hardness of heart" of the people (v. 8). First Timothy 3:2 also opposes polygamy, for Scripture does not require elders to follow different moral principles than other Christians. If polygamy is wrong for church officers, it is wrong for everybody.

Scripture does not treat polygamy as adultery, however, though in one sense it is that. If a man swears exclusive love to one woman, and then

5. Although they do withhold membership from polygamists who profess Christ, they tend to regard them as believers and treat them as such. But that stance is inconsistent. The door of the church should not be narrower than the door of heaven. All who belong to Christ should be admitted to the church and to the sacraments. If they have committed sins that lead to excommunication, they should then not be regarded as Christians.

takes a second wife, he has broken his original vow. The second wife enters into a sexual relationship with another woman's husband.

Commitment within marriage, like commitment to God, is exclusive. It excludes rival commitments, rival loves (Deut. 6:4–5). A polygamous marriage compromises that exclusiveness. In such a marriage, the spouses share less of one another than in monogamy. And we get the impression from polygamous saints in the Old Testament that jealousy among plural wives was a common thing. So polygamy is a sin. It violates both the letter and the spirit of the seventh commandment, which is to protect the exclusive love of marriage. And since polygamy violates God's norms, it is unfaithful to our heavenly husband. Thus it violates the deepest intention of the seventh commandment.[6]

But though Scripture upholds monogamy as God's pattern, it does not reject polygamists from the kingdom of grace. The reason is obvious. Polygamy is not like other sins. A thief can stop being a thief immediately upon his conversion, and if he does not stop after a reasonable period of pastoral attention, he can and should be removed from the church. But a polygamist cannot simply stop being a polygamist. He has incurred obligations to his wives, and he cannot simply cast them off. A sinful divorce does not remedy the sin of polygamy.

So I believe that churches should admit to membership and to the sacraments people who, though polygamous, otherwise give a credible profession of faith in Christ. But, following the New Testament example, they should not consider such people for church office.

PROSTITUTION

Prostitution is another sexual sin that the Old Testament appears to tolerate in some degree. Judah, the son of Jacob, had sexual relations with a woman he thought was a prostitute in Genesis 38. As it turned out, she was his daughter-in-law. The passage condemns him for his failure to provide for her, but not for having sex with her in the first place. The same is true

---

6. Why doesn't the Old Testament explicitly equate polygamy with adultery? I suspect that it was understood this way: When a married man entered into a marriage covenant with a second woman, he in effect promised exclusive sexual loyalty to a group of two (similarly with larger numbers). Adultery, then, would be understood to be a sexual relationship with someone outside that group. So even plural marriage was seen as an exclusive commitment of love and loyalty, rather than an arrangement that violates that loyalty. In that sense, plural marriage is not as bad as simple adultery, since it is bounded by marital vows. But we see nonetheless that such marriage violates God's original intention and breaks his seventh commandment.

of Samson in Judges 16:1–3. There is no specific command in the Mosaic law forbidding men to consort with prostitutes.

But references to women who are prostitutes are overwhelmingly negative (Prov. 7:10–20). A woman found to have prostituted herself before marriage is to be stoned to death (Deut. 22:20–21).

We saw earlier that God through the prophets describes Israel's idolatry as spiritual adultery. That metaphor becomes even more severe: Israel is not only an adulteress, but a prostitute (Ex. 34:15–16; Deut. 31:16; Judg. 2:17; 8:27, 33; 1 Chron. 5:25; Isa. 1:21; Jer. 2:20; 3:1, 6–14; Ezek. 16:15–58; 23:1–49; Hos. 2:1–13). Her unfaithfulness is not a momentary fling; rather, she actually goes into the business of soliciting lovers. That is, these Israelites do not just turn to Baal to help them in a pinch of difficulty; rather, they passionately seek out more and more false deities to worship, finding them anywhere they can.

The wisdom teacher in Proverbs instructs his son to turn away from the seductions of prostitutes (7:10–20) and other forbidden women (5:1–23; 6:20–35; 7:6–9; 9:13–18; 23:27–28). Adultery and/or prostitution in Proverbs is the antithesis of wisdom.[7] "Lady Wisdom" calls to the young man to learn prudence and truth (8:1–12). "Lady Folly" (9:13) calls him to a place of death (v. 18). Such are the way of the wicked and the way of the righteous (Ps. 1:6) as they appear to a boy on the brink of manhood. He can follow the way of lawless sexual gratification, or he can seek God's wisdom. For many young men and women today, these are precisely the alternatives before them, the two live options.

"Whoring," in Numbers 15:39, is a synecdoche for all sin, a picture of autonomous living. There God tells Israel to wear tassels to remind them to "look at and remember all the commandments of the LORD, to do them, not to follow after your own heart and your own eyes, which you are inclined to whore after." Here we see clearly the broad meaning of the seventh commandment, as a perspective on all sin and righteousness. Satan, working through the fallen desires of our own senses (as in Gen. 3:6), is a seductress, tempting us to turn away from our faithful husband.

Paul unhesitatingly condemns the use of prostitutes:

> Do you not know that your bodies are members of Christ? Shall I then take the members of Christ and make them members of a prostitute? Never! Or do you not know that he who is joined to a

---

7. It is not always clear when the text is speaking specifically of prostitution and when it is speaking of adultery per se. The woman who tries to seduce the boy is always brazen, like a prostitute. And she is married (7:19), so in this case the sexual relation is both prostitution and adultery.

prostitute becomes one body with her? For, as it is written, "The two will become one flesh." But he who is joined to the Lord becomes one spirit with him. (1 Cor. 6:15–17)

If either the prostitute or the client is married, the sexual relationship is literal adultery, as in Proverbs 7:19. Whether or not it is literally adulterous, it is joining members of Christ to a prostitute, figuratively making the Lord himself a client. The very image borders on blasphemy, but it is Paul's, not mine. This act is a terrible offense against the Lord Jesus, and also against God the Spirit: since the Christian's body is the temple of the Spirit, this sin is a defilement of the temple, contempt for the very dwelling place of God. In the Old Testament, entering the holiest part of the temple without God's authorization brought death. Note how sharply God separates his temple in Israel from any association with prostitution (Deut. 23:17–18).[8] So even if a relationship with a prostitute is not literally adulterous, it is a violation of our marriage to Christ and therefore a violation of the seventh commandment.

But this too is not an unforgivable sin. Rahab, the Canaanite woman who welcomed and protected the Israelite spies (Josh. 2), is one of the heroes of faith in Hebrews 11 (v. 31; cf. James 2:25). Scripture regularly identifies her as "the prostitute" (Heb. 11:31; James 2:25; cf. Josh. 2:1). The biblical writers do this, not to stain her memory, but to magnify the grace of God.

HOMOSEXUALITY

The Bible often condemns sexual relations between people of the same sex. In Genesis 19, the men of Sodom demanded that Lot turn over his guests "that we may know them" (v. 5). The Hebrew word "know" (*yada‘*) often refers to sexual intercourse, as in Genesis 4:1, where it is said that Adam "knew" his wife. Lot's response, that these men were acting "so wickedly" (v. 7), indicates that their desire was for homosexual rape. Lot even offers his daughters to them, as if that were a lesser evil (v. 8). This is the event that leads to the total destruction of Sodom and Gomorrah.

The law of Moses says, "You shall not lie with a male as with a woman; it is an abomination" (Lev. 18:22). Also, "If a man lies with a male as with

---

8. Prostitution, like many sins, is more serious when it is done in connection with the temple. Prostitutes in Israel were generally not subject to civil penalties. But if the daughter of a priest engages in prostitution, she is to be burned (Lev. 21:9). Similarly a priest is not to marry a prostitute (Lev. 21:7).

a woman, both of them have committed an abomination; they shall surely be put to death; their blood is upon them" (Lev. 20:13). Paul, in Romans 1, after indicating that pagans repress the truth of God clearly revealed to them (vv. 18–21), sets forth the consequences. These are first idolatry (22–23) and then sexual sin:

> Therefore God gave them up in the lusts of their hearts to impurity, to the dishonoring of their bodies among themselves, because they exchanged the truth about God for a lie and worshiped and served the creature rather than the Creator, who is blessed forever! Amen. For this reason God gave them up to dishonorable passions. For their women exchanged natural relations for those that are contrary to nature; and the men likewise gave up natural relations with women and were consumed with passion for one another, men committing shameless acts with men and receiving in themselves the due penalty for their error. (vv. 24–27)

Afterward, Paul lists other sins that result from unbelief (vv. 28–32). But among all the sins listed in the chapter, homosexuality has a place of prominence. (Note also 1 Corinthians 6:9.)

Now I am fully aware that there is a "gay exegesis" that interprets these texts in ways favorable to homosexuality. In the Sodom story, some have suggested that the men of the city merely wanted to get acquainted with Lot's guests, not to rape them, taking "know" in a nonsexual sense. But such clearly was not Lot's understanding, who charged the crowd with great wickedness, a wickedness even greater than the likely abuse of his own daughters, who had not "known any man" (Gen. 19:8). Jude agrees with Lot's assessment, stating explicitly (in Jude 7) that the sins of Sodom were "sexual immorality" and "unnatural desire."

The new exegesis also reinterprets the other condemnations of homosexuality in the Bible, claiming (1) that they are ceremonial, not moral, and (2) that they apply to specific kinds of homosexuality, rather than homosexuality in general, such as temple prostitution, pedophilia, homosexual promiscuity, or "unnatural" homosexuality (i.e., homosexual acts by people who are heterosexual by nature).

I do not intend to discuss these in detail, however, because I find them utterly implausible. There is not a hint in Scripture itself that these verses teach anything other than their apparent meaning.[9] If anyone wants to

---

9. We should always be suspicious of exegesis that seeks to bring the Bible into line with some contemporary social or political movement. It is true that such movements sometimes alert us to teachings of the Bible that we would otherwise miss. Examples are the movement against slavery and the civil rights movement. But in my judgment "movement

consider these interpretations more seriously, I recommend they consult Greg Bahnsen, *Homosexuality: A Biblical View*,[10] and Robert A. J. Gagnon, *The Bible and Homosexual Practice*.[11] These scholars have given as thorough a refutation of gay exegesis as can be imagined—far more thorough, indeed, than this position deserves.

What is so bad about homosexuality? If either or both partners are married, then the act is literally adulterous. But even if no marriage vow exists, homosexual acts violate God's purpose for sex as part of marriage. Marriage in Scripture is always between a man and a woman, and, as we shall see, God limits the sexual function to the context of marriage.

In Ephesians 5:22–33, the difference between man and woman is crucial to the meaning of marriage. The man (so very inadequately) represents Christ, and the woman represents the church. The church must never be confused with Christ. But in homosexuality, there is no such distinction between the partners. Although one partner may be more passive than the other, there is no clear distinction between husband and wife, between bridegroom and bride. Ultimately, the roles are interchangeable. But symbolically, this suggests that God and man are interchangeable. And that notion is not only wrong, but the root of all sin—the primal heresy.

There are also pragmatic reasons to avoid homosexuality. As I have often said, the godly life is the good life. People who follow God's ways receive earthly blessings and those who disobey suffer curses. The homosexual community is highly promiscuous and homosexuals are prone to violence, suicide, and depression. Gays in Western nations are disproportionately affected by sexually transmitted diseases, especially the life-destroying and currently incurable HIV-AIDS. Are these diseases God's punishment? Paul says in Romans 1:27 that men who commit "shameless acts with men" receive "in themselves the due penalty for their error." Of course, HIV and other diseases are found in heterosexuals as well, and in babies conceived in that condition. These natural consequences do not belong to homosexuals alone, but they do affect homosexuals in large numbers. We should remember that AIDS and other tragic occurrences are not in direct proportion to the sins of an individual. The book of Job and Luke 13:1–5 make that plain.

---

exegesis" must bear a heavy burden of proof, since movements are typical sources of bias. I believe that bias appears also in egalitarian feminist exegesis, and in attempts to bring the Bible into line with current science. And, while we are at it, yes, denominational and theological traditions are sources of bias for similar reasons.

10. Grand Rapids: Baker, 1978.

11. Nashville: Abingdon, 2002. See also Robert A. J. Gagnon and Dan O. Via, *Homosexuality and the Bible: Two Views* (Minneapolis: Augsburg Fortress, 2003).

Much discussion in this area has focused on the distinction between act and orientation. Scripture itself does not explicitly make such a distinction. But, granting that Scripture condemns homosexual acts, are there principles in Scripture for evaluating homosexual orientation?

Orientation, here, is a somewhat slippery idea. Evidently it designates a more or less constant kind of sexual desire. Many people experience sexual desire for people of both sexes. There are probably more "bisexuals" (people who have sexual experience with both genders) than those whose desires are exclusively homosexual. So for many, orientation is a matter of degree.

Another ambiguity is that some desires demand immediate fulfillment, while others can be postponed. Some desires we recognize as wrong, and we turn aside from them; others we embrace.

If homosexual orientation is simply a strong pattern of temptation, it is not wrong in itself. Temptation is not sin. Jesus himself "in every respect has been tempted as we are, yet without sin" (Heb. 4:15). Certainly Jesus experienced sexual temptation, since that is such a pervasive form of temptation to human beings after the fall. But it is possible to reject temptation without sin, and Jesus did reject it.

Christians should be sympathetic to other Christians who are enduring any kind of temptation, especially one that besets them day after day. We do not all have the same patterns of temptation, but we are all tempted in one way or another. Many Christians experience no temptation to abuse alcohol, but some do, and they need brothers and sisters to encourage and pray with them when the temptation is strong. Our attitude toward people with homosexual temptations should be the same. Our disgust with the sin should not turn us from the responsibility to love and counsel one who happens to be tempted in different ways from ourselves.

If a Christian brother or sister gives in to homosexual temptation, but seeks forgiveness and restoration, we should welcome the person and do what we can to help.

On the other hand, if "orientation" refers to lust, a desire that is contrary to God's law (see the discussion of lust below), then it is sinful in itself. Often it is difficult, to be sure, to distinguish between temptation and lust, even for the person tempted. We should not be quick to judge, but quick to love. But if it becomes evident that "orientation" represents the desire of a person's heart, so that he does not want to be subject to God's commands, then rebuke may be necessary to motivate his repentance and save his soul.

On the argument that sexual orientation cannot be overcome, and that therefore we should recognize homosexuality as natural and normal for those with that orientation, see the section "Living with Ourselves" in chapter 15. I reject that argument, as does Scripture.

Homosexuals have become a major political force in modern Western society, and they have made it their goal to exclude criticism of their lifestyle from the public square, even to declare such criticism a "hate crime." They also demand an end to any discrimination based on sexual orientation, on the analogy of racial justice. But of course the analogy between sexual orientation and race is a false one. It is wrong for people to deny equal opportunity to others based on ethnicity or skin color, qualities having nothing to do with moral character. But sexual orientation is a moral issue. People quite rightly have an interest, for example, in keeping their children away from people who commit and defend sexual sin. It is not wrong to exclude homosexuals from positions of teaching, Boy Scout leadership, and so on. And Christians must demand that government protect the right to preach and teach biblical positions on this matter. We must not allow government to silence the preaching of the Word of God.

But, as with other forms of sexual sin, I wish to close on a note of hope. After Paul lists homosexuality among the sins that keep people out of the kingdom of God, he adds, "And such were some of you. But you were washed, you were sanctified, you were justified in the name of the Lord Jesus Christ and by the Spirit of our God" (1 Cor. 6:11). Most likely, then, there were repentant homosexuals in the church at Corinth. If there were not, Paul implies, there could have been, and these would have been washed, sanctified, and justified by Christ and the Spirit. God's grace is able to transform homosexuals and give them the full blessings of the kingdom.[12]

The church should show the grace of God to people caught up in this sin by leading them to Christ and helping them to overcome their sin by God's power. We should also learn how to minister to AIDS patients, without looking down on them. All human beings bear the curse of the fall, and all of us deserve far worse than we have received. AIDS patients have a special need for the compassion of God's people. Remember that the disease is not spread through casual contact or even by nonsexual touching. It is hard for the church to convince homosexuals that we love them, while, like Scripture, condemning their practices. One way is to reach out to those who are the most afflicted.

---

12. For more discussion of the question whether the sin of homosexuality can be overcome, see chapter 15.

INCEST

Leviticus 18:1–18 prohibits sexual relations between "close relatives" (v. 6). That includes blood relatives, such as father, mother, and sister, but also relatives by marriage, such as the uncle's wife (v. 14). In 1 Corinthians 5:1, Paul condemns one who "has his father's wife" (v. 1). The man's partner is evidently not his mother, but another wife of his father. Paul's language reflects Leviticus 18, where the "father's wife" (v. 8) is distinguished from the "mother" (v. 7).

The modern argument against incest is based on the risk of birth defects in children and of psychological trauma to the partners. Perhaps those consequences were also known in biblical times. But Scripture does not mention them. There is a hint of Scripture's own motivation for these laws in Leviticus 18:10, where the law forbids uncovering the nakedness of one's granddaughters because "their nakedness is your own nakedness."

"Uncovering nakedness," the phrase used many times in Leviticus 18, is partly a euphemism for sexual intercourse. But there is more to it. In a family, there is a kind of intimacy shared by all members, even among those who are not married to one another. When extended families live together, or even visit frequently, they express love, embrace, speak with great familiarity, joke, pray together, exhort one another, share secrets, and help one another with problems that would not be mentioned outside the household. In such a context, some are tempted to turn family intimacy into sexual intimacy. Given such close proximity, it might be thought that sexual relations are only a short additional step. God's intention, however, is to distinguish family intimacy from sexual intimacy. Sexual intimacy is for husband and wife alone, for all the reasons noted earlier, including the symbolic image of Christ and the church. So even in the closeness of family reunions, there must be a zone of privacy reserved only for husband and wife. Therefore, intimacy among family members must be nonsexual. And, among single members of the family, it must not be the kind of intimacy that could lead to marriage.

Since the fall, nakedness brings shame (Gen. 2:25; 3:7, 10–11, 21). Even between man and wife, nakedness should not be the normal state of affairs. Certainly God intends that in society human beings should wear clothes and not approach one another sexually apart from marriage. But Leviticus 18:10 suggests that there is a special restriction within the family, intended both to safeguard marriage and to define the limits of family intimacy. All within a family share in a common "nakedness."

When a family member "uncovers the nakedness" of another for sexual relations, he violates that nonsexual trust which is an essential ingredient of family intimacy. He shames the other one, but he also shames himself. Her nakedness is also his. As he has despised his relative, so the rest of the family will despise him. In typical incest, an older relative takes advantage of a younger one, abusing his superior strength and authority. Leviticus 18:10 warns that to do that is to abuse oneself as well. Once family trust is broken, it is difficult, if not impossible, to restore. So incest violates both marital and family intimacy: marital, because it fails to respect the special zone of privacy reserved for husband and wife alone; family, because it compromises the trust that binds families together.

Of course, in the case of blood relations, the prohibition of incest carries other advantages, particularly reducing the risk of birth defects. As we have seen, there are earthly blessings for those who obey God. But there are broader considerations as well, valid in our time as well as in the time of Moses and Paul. Today, no less than in Bible times, incest destroys the intimacy of the family. And, as we have seen, the family is important to God.

PEDOPHILIA

The Bible does not specify an "age of consent" for marriage or (therefore) for sexual intercourse. During biblical times, people evidently married younger than they do today. There are advantages to teenage marriage, especially when the couple has the support of an extended family. Male sexual desire reaches its peak around age 18, and the biblical means of fulfilling that desire is marriage. If teenagers regularly married, there would certainly be far less illegitimacy and single-parent homes.

But young marriage does not fit in well with modern culture. Those who marry early often cannot reach the level of education expected by modern employers, and young people themselves, without the discipline of Christian values, often insist on a period of sowing wild oats before settling down.

So teenagers, and even younger children, are prone to sexual experimentation and exploitation, often by older people. Scripture does not deal with this as a distinct problem. Clearly, however, it is a kind of fornication (see the following section), and if one partner is married it is adulterous. It is an especially wicked kind of fornication, first, because it takes advantage of one who may have little understanding of what is happening, and, second, because it imposes trauma upon the victim, with lifelong consequences.

The recent discovery of rampant pedophilia by Roman Catholic priests has brought the name of Christ into the worst disgrace. The Roman Church is not alone guilty of this crime, but it has by far the largest number of clergy implicated in it. To non-Catholic observers, there are two obvious causes: First, the requirement of celibacy for Catholic clergy. There is no principle in Scripture or even in the Catholic theological tradition that requires celibacy.[13] When the church forbids marriage, God's ordained means of sexual fulfillment, it can expect sexual sin to follow. Second, the Roman Church must come to grips with the Bible's teachings about homosexuality. Most pedophilia is homosexual—men preying on boys. The Vatican has recently made a wise decision to forbid homosexuals to enter the priesthood. It should go beyond this and give counsel to all homosexuals in its fellowship and exercise church discipline when that counsel fails.

FORNICATION

We have seen that the seventh commandment forbids, not only adultery per se, but also other sins that are not literally adulterous. Prostitution, homosexuality, and incest are sometimes, but not always, literally adulterous, in that they violate existing marriage vows. But even when neither party is married, such sexual relations violate one's marriage relation to God.

So the question arises as to sexual relations between unmarried people, relations that are neither prostitution nor homosexuality. In theology, such acts are called "fornication," a term found often in the KJV, as in 1 Corinthians 6:18. But it is not always clear what actions are included in this category.

The Greek term translated "fornication" is *porneia*, which the ESV usually renders "sexual immorality." The term is broader than "adultery," so that all adultery is fornication, but not all fornication is adultery. *Porneia* includes prostitution (Hos. 2:2 lxx), incest (1 Cor. 5:1), and homosexuality (Jude 7), but as a general term it should not be limited to these. I believe, with most Christian writers, that fornication includes all sexual intercourse outside of marriage.[14] But that range of meaning is not evident in 1 Corinthians 6:18. To see the term's full range of meaning, we must look to other passages.

In Exodus 22:16–17: "If a man seduces a virgin who is not engaged to be married and lies with her, he shall give the bride-price for her and make her

13. As we have seen, Paul's advocacy of singleness in 1 Cor. 7 is not for all situations, and Paul even there makes it clear that if people marry they do not sin.

14. The term, like the words for adultery and prostitution, is also a metaphor for unfaithfulness to God (Num. 14:33 lxx; Isa. 1:21 lxx; Heb. 12:16; Rev. 17:4; 19:2). In its metaphorical use, it includes sins other than sexual ones.

his wife. If her father utterly refuses to give her to him, he shall pay money equal to the bride-price for virgins." Here, the penalty for seduction is that the man must marry the woman and pay the bride-price, unless her father disallows the marriage. Deuteronomy 22:29 adds that if he marries her in this situation, he may never divorce her.

Otherwise, a woman found not to be a virgin before marriage is considered in the same category as the prostitute (Deut. 22:13–21) and must be killed. In this case, it is assumed that she consented to premarital sex, because she failed to bring the matter to anyone's attention.

So premarital sex is wrong, both for men and for women. Paul agrees with this assessment, for, in 1 Corinthians 7:9 and 36–38, he prescribes only marriage as a means of controlling sexual desires. It is somewhat remarkable that Paul would take such a position, for the church of Corinth was in a difficult situation ("the present distress," v. 26), in which single people had substantial advantages over married people (vv. 32–35). If it were legitimate for people to control their sexual desire by nonmarital relationships, one would have expected Paul here to mention that alternative. But he does not. Even in difficult circumstances, marriage is to be the exclusive context for sexual relations.

So fornication, or *porneia*, includes all sexual relations outside of marriage. And Scripture judges this sin severely:

> Flee from sexual immorality. Every other sin a person commits is outside the body, but the sexually immoral person sins against his own body. Or do you not know that your body is a temple of the Holy Spirit within you, whom you have from God? You are not your own, for you were bought with a price. So glorify God in your body. (1 Cor. 6:18–20)

This passage follows the condemnation of prostitution that we discussed earlier. It describes fornication in the same terms as prostitution: as a sin against one's own body, which is the temple of the Holy Spirit. It is a defiling of the temple of God. So even though fornication is not always adultery on the human level, it nevertheless violates the exclusiveness of our marriage relation to God. In that deeper sense, fornication violates the seventh commandment.

The Mosaic law does not always treat fornication as seriously as it treats adultery. In the case of Exodus 22:16–17, there is no death penalty, as there would be in a case of adultery. We can understand how, on the human level, unmarried sex is not as disruptive as adultery can be. But Scripture does not wink at fornication. It presents it as a grievous sin. God forgives this sin, as others we have discussed, on the basis of the blood of Christ.

But it is good to remember that only the blood of Christ can remove such a breach in our relationship with God.

In 1 Corinthians 6:20, quoted above, the fact that we are "bought with a price," and therefore belong to another, is the motivation for glorifying God in our bodies.

LUST

We have discussed a number of sexual acts mentioned in Scripture, but there are others as well that trouble us today. Christians often ask their pastors about kissing, necking, and petting outside marriage. And what about masturbation and the use of pornography?[15] We have so far been thinking mainly about sexual intercourse, but what about sexual acts that fall short of it? These sorts of issues did not come up as often in the biblical period, for in those days unmarried women were chaperoned and protected. Unmarried couples did not have much time alone to engage in such activity.

We have seen, however, that actions not mentioned in Scripture (for example, abortion) are often covered by broader principles of Scripture. In such questions involving sexuality, I think the best place to find biblical guidance is in its treatment of lust.[16]

Jesus' commentary on the seventh commandment is this: "You have heard that it was said, 'You shall not commit adultery.' But I say to you that everyone who looks at a woman with lustful intent has already committed adultery with her in his heart" (Matt. 5:27–28). As always, Jesus goes to the heart. Murder comes from anger; adultery comes from lust. God is concerned not only about the actions of murder and adultery, but also about the motives that lead to these actions. And one who wants to please God needs to deal with the condition of his heart, not only with his actions.

But what is lust? Negatively:

1. Lust is not sexual desire as such. That is something good, a God-given incentive to marriage, to intimacy within marriage, and to reproduction. A single person who has a sexual desire for another single person

---

15. Some have thought that Scripture condemns masturbation in the story of Onan (Gen. 38:6–10). However, that is not the case. Onan's act was not masturbation, but *coitus interruptus*. Furthermore, his sin was not his sexual practice itself, but his unwillingness to beget a child in his brother's name (cf. Deut. 25:5–10). So we shall have to evaluate masturbation, not by any specific biblical reference to it, but by broader biblical principles.

16. There are other approaches to these issues. Masturbation, for example, has been condemned on the ground that it is essentially selfish and nonrelational. Certainly the Bible presents sex chiefly as relational, but it is difficult to find biblical ground for condemning and prohibiting all sex acts that occur outside that context.

who might be a marriage candidate is not thereby guilty of sin. First Corinthians 7:9 does not condemn the desire itself, but only a desire that cannot be controlled.

2. Nor is lust a general recognition of another person's sexual attractiveness. Usually when we describe another person as "beautiful" or "handsome," there is a sexual aspect to our judgment. Biblical writers do this often (see Gen. 29:17; 1 Sam. 16:12; 25:3; 2 Sam. 11:2). The human form is one of the beauties of God's creation, given to all for aesthetic enjoyment.

3. Nor is it lustful merely to view or imagine sexual relationships, though there are great dangers here. Scripture itself provokes our imagination by describing sexual events of various kinds. If it is wrong even to think about such matters, then sex education would be impossible. If we are to avoid evil and do good, we must to some extent know about things that are evil and good.

4. Nor, again, should we confuse lust with temptation (see the previous discussion of homosexuality). One can be tempted to sin without sinning, as was Jesus (Heb. 4:15). This does not mean that we should seek out opportunities to be tempted. In the Lord's Prayer, we ask God not to "lead us into temptation" (Matt. 6:13). But temptation is a part of life, and we should pray also that God will enable us to be steadfast in trial. God promises the crown of life to those who persevere (James 1:12; cf. 1 Peter 1:6–9).[17]

What, then, is the positive meaning of lust? Lust is specifically the desire to engage in sexual acts that are contrary to God's law. That is the line that shouldn't be crossed. Eve was not wrong to believe that the forbidden fruit was "good for food, and that it was a delight to the eyes, and that the tree was to be desired to make one wise" (Gen. 3:6). Doubtless the fruit was all these things, and it was not wrong for Eve, even under Satan's influence, to take notice of them. But at some point her appreciation of the fruit's natural qualities slipped into something else—a desire to take that fruit in defiance of God's law. So when a man, for example, thinks about the sexual attractiveness of a woman who is forbidden to him, he often slips across a line in which his attitude becomes "lustful intent" (Matt. 5:28). This lustful intent is not necessarily a decision to commit sexual sin. The man may be far from that. Lust is a desire, rather than an actual decision. But the lust itself is wrong, even if the decision is never made.

Now in my own view of the matter, it is very unlikely that sexual kissing and petting, masturbation, or viewing pornography (with someone other

---

17. *Peirasmos* in these passages is translated "temptation" in the KJV, but most modern translations render it as "trial." But the two ideas are closely related. For these writers, the main problem with undergoing trial is that in doing so one may be tempted to compromise one's confession of Christ.

than a spouse as the focus of one's attention) can be done without lust. That is, such activities lead us into a desire for sexual intercourse contrary to God's will for us. It is, of course, abstractly possible for someone to study pornography merely as an academic subject, or to masturbate with no fantasy at all. I will not claim that such detached involvement never exists. It is also possible that one can engage in deep kissing or petting without having any desire to go further. But I believe that in the vast majority of cases these activities generate the kind of lust that falls under Jesus' condemnation of Matthew 5:27–28.

So Christians who are seeking to please God, rather than to determine how much they can get away with, should avoid these activities. Even among single people, lust is adulterous, for it violates the covenant with our divine spouse.

But these sexual sins, like others, are not unforgivable. After speaking much of Israel's spiritual adultery, God promises to take her back:

> I will heal their apostasy;
>> I will love them freely,
>> for my anger has turned from them.
> I will be like the dew to Israel;
>> he shall blossom like the lily;
>> he shall take root like the trees of Lebanon;
> his shoots shall spread out;
>> his beauty shall be like the olive,
>> and his fragrance like Lebanon.
> They shall return and dwell beneath my shadow;
>> they shall flourish like the grain;
> they shall blossom like the vine;
>> their fame shall be like the wine of Lebanon. (Hos. 14:4–7)

And Paul's words apply here, as in earlier discussions: "And such were some of you. But you were washed, you were sanctified, you were justified in the name of the Lord Jesus Christ and by the Spirit of our God" (1 Cor. 6:11). Through Christ, God performs the miracle of restoring our virginity (2 Cor. 11:2). Christ loved his church and gave himself for her, "that he might sanctify her, having cleansed her by the washing of water with the word, so that he might present the church to himself in splendor, without spot or wrinkle or any such thing, that she might be holy and without blemish" (Eph. 5:26–27; cf. Rev. 21:2).

CHAPTER 39

The Seventh Commandment:
Divorce and Remarriage

From our previous discussion, it should be evident that marriage is a lifetime commitment. Jesus says of marriage in Matthew 19:6, "What therefore God has joined together, let not man separate." Marriage reflects the eternal covenant between God and his elect. It images that covenant by its permanence.[1] And in Malachi 2:14–16 God answers the question why he no longer regards with favor the offerings of Judahites:

> Because the Lord was witness between you and the wife of your youth, to whom you have been faithless, though she is your companion and your wife by covenant. Did he not make them one, with a portion of the Spirit in their union? And what was the one God seeking? Godly offspring. So guard yourselves in your spirit, and let none of you be faithless to the wife of your youth. "For the man who hates and divorces, says the Lord, the God of Israel, covers his garment with violence, says the Lord of hosts. So guard yourselves in your spirit, and do not be faithless."[2]

1. Jesus does, however, teach that earthly marriage does not continue into the afterlife (Matt. 22:30). Cf. Rom. 7:2–3; 1 Cor. 7:39. So marriage images the eternal permanence of God's covenant by its own relative permanence. As God is greater than we, so his covenant is greater than our covenants.
2. I don't understand the quotation marks that the ESV adds to verse 16, but I include them as published.

The NIV adopts the translation "I [the LORD] hate divorce" at the beginning of verse 16. The ESV puts a similar rendering in a footnote. The translations are problematic, but in all of them God expresses a strong disdain for divorce.

Nevertheless, both testaments allow divorce in some cases. Why is this? Jesus teaches that the provision for divorce in Deuteronomy 24:1–4 was "because of your hardness of heart" (Mark 10:5). That is to say, God determined that a prohibition of all divorce would be, for fallen people, unbearable, and therefore counterproductive to good social order. Sin would certainly lead to divorce; the law could not be expected to prevent that. The best thing that law could accomplish would be to regulate divorce, to mitigate its oppressiveness and maintain the rights of those cast aside.

But divorce always represents a failure to achieve God's ideal. It is never something to celebrate. Churches should show love and grace (and, at times, church discipline) to the divorcing and the divorced, but the notion of a "blessing on divorce" is bizarre. A divorce is, rather, cause for mourning, a symptom of failure.

This is not to say that to divorce a spouse is always sinful. Divorce can be a necessary recognition of a separation of heart that has already taken place. It is sometimes like disconnecting life support to someone who is already dead. Divorce, when performed according to biblical principles, is not sin, but the result of sin. In this respect, it is like just war or capital punishment.

So as we consider biblical principles relevant to divorce, let us remember the overall negative evaluation that God places upon it. Divorce is not a blessing that we should seek by meeting various conditions. It is part of the curse. And until it becomes a necessity, we should do all in our power to prevent it from happening.

Even when someone has valid grounds for divorce, he is not obligated to file for divorce. Those who forgive their spouse's adultery and who choose to continue a marriage after periods of desertion are "moral heroes" (chapter 12) who deserve the honor and support of God's people. God's reconciliation with Israel, despite her spiritual adultery, is a striking display of his grace (Hos. 3:1–5). But when a person has biblical grounds for divorce, he is not obligated to remain in the marriage. To divorce in this case is not sin.[3] Before the reconciliation noted above, God himself

---

3. In the past, I was persuaded by the argument that if an adulterous spouse repents, the innocent spouse should not only forgive his sin, but should welcome him back as a marriage partner. It seemed as though to really forgive someone is to restore the relationship to the *status quo ante*, as though the sin had never taken place. On this view, forgiving entails forgetting. I no longer hold that view, for these reasons: (1) God himself does not literally forget the sins he has forgiven, for he is omniscient. (2) Even forgiven sin has

figuratively divorced Israel, saying she was "not my people" (Hos. 1:9). See also Jeremiah 3:8, in which God "sent [Israel] away with a decree of divorce," recalling the language of Deuteronomy 24:1.

Bearing these qualifications in mind, I shall in the remainder of this chapter discuss biblical grounds for divorce. I have no original thoughts on this subject. My intent is simply to set forth the traditional Reformed teaching as summarized in the Westminster Confession and to discuss some of its applications to contemporary questions.[4] The confessional statement reads:

> Although the corruption of man be such as is apt to study arguments unduly to put asunder those whom God hath joined together in marriage: yet, nothing but adultery, or such willful desertion as can no way be remedied by the church, or civil magistrate, is cause sufficient of dissolving the bond of marriage: wherein, a public and orderly course of proceeding is to be observed; and the persons concerned in it not left to their own wills, and discretion, in their own case. (WCF, 24.6)

DEUTERONOMY 24:1–4

In what follows, I shall consider the main biblical texts discussed in connection with the subject of divorce. Deuteronomy 24:1–4 reads:

> When a man takes a wife and marries her, if then she finds no favor in his eyes because he has found some indecency in her, and he writes her a certificate of divorce and puts it in her hand and sends her out of his house, and she departs out of his house, and if she goes and becomes another man's wife, and the latter man hates

---

natural consequences that play out in the world. A forgiven thief must serve his sentence and make restitution. Those who commit sexual sin and repent must still deal sometimes with STDs. (3) The Bible does not place such an obligation on the victim of adultery. Rather, it regards adultery as in itself ground for divorce.

4. The main sources for this discussion are John Murray, *Divorce* (Philadelphia: Presbyterian and Reformed, 1953); Jay Adams, *Marriage, Divorce and Remarriage* (Phillipsburg, NJ: Presbyterian and Reformed, 1980); "Report of the Ad Interim Committee on Divorce and Remarriage," presented to the Twentieth General Assembly of the Presbyterian Church in America (1992), available in the minutes of that assembly and also at http://www.pcanet.org/history/pca/index.html. Murray's book is a thorough (and I think definitive) exegetical study of the relevant biblical texts. Adams puts essentially the same argument into a more popular form. The PCA report summarizes that position, interacts with many writers in the Reformed tradition, and explores issues such as spousal abuse.

her and writes her a certificate of divorce and puts it in her hand and sends her out of his house, or if the latter man dies, who took her to be his wife, then her former husband, who sent her away, may not take her again to be his wife, after she has been defiled, for that is an abomination before the LORD. And you shall not bring sin upon the land that the LORD your God is giving you for an inheritance.

This passage is case law (see chapter 13), which describes a certain situation (vv. 1–3) and then issues a commandment that bears upon that situation (v. 4). Verses 1–3 are an "if" clause, setting forth the hypothesis, and verse 4 is the "then" clause, indicating the consequence.

The hypothesis is complicated: a man divorces his wife because of "some indecency," she marries another man, and then the second husband either divorces her or dies.[5] The meaning of "some indecency" is unclear and has been endlessly debated from biblical times until now.

It is important that in both divorces there is a "certificate." That is to say, the divorce is official. Documentation of the divorce protects the wife if and when her marital status is in question.

The conclusion in verse 4, therefore, says that when a woman is officially divorced from one man and marries another, she may not, after the second marriage ends, return to the first husband. This is the whole teaching of the passage. Explicitly, it neither encourages nor discourages divorce, but only recognizes its existence and regulates it in a single case.

Why is the first husband forbidden to take her back? Verse 4 connects this prohibition to the fact that the woman is "defiled," though the nature of the defilement and its connection with the prohibition is not entirely clear. Evidently the woman has been defiled by her second marriage, which, after divorce, is adulterous. That would be in line with the teaching of Matthew 5:32, Mark 10:11–12, and Luke 16:18.

In that situation, her first husband is responsible for defiling her. When he divorced her, he determined that her second marriage would be adulterous. So, after the second marriage ends, the original husband may not take back the wife he has defiled. This provision also prevents men from divorcing and remarrying at will, a pattern that offends the dignity and seriousness of the marriage relationship.

---

5. In most of the biblical texts we are considering, it is the husband who initiates divorce proceedings, as was the general custom of the time. Clearly, though, the same principles apply when a wife seeks divorce, as often happens in modern society. Mark 10:12 and 1 Cor. 7:10 mention the latter case.

I said that the passage neither encourages nor discourages divorce explicitly. But there is an antidivorce subtext here. Implicitly, the text is saying that divorce has serious consequences to both parties. Obviously that is true in the woman's case. But the man must live with his decision, and the implications of that decision may not be to his liking. In a fallen world, broken relationships cannot always be restored. One should not pursue a divorce without counting that cost.

MATTHEW 5:31–32; MARK 10:2–12; LUKE 16:18; MATTHEW 19:3–9

Jesus teaches in Matthew 5:31–32, Mark 10:2–12, Luke 16:18, and Matthew 19:3–9 that remarriage is prohibited. There is one exception to this rule, which we shall consider in the next section. Matthew 5:31–32 reads, "It was also said, 'Whoever divorces his wife, let him give her a certificate of divorce.' But I say to you that everyone who divorces his wife, except on the ground of sexual immorality, makes her commit adultery. And whoever marries a divorced woman commits adultery."

Some of the Pharisees taught that a man could divorce his wife for any number of reasons, and that his only responsibility was to give her the certificate of divorce mentioned in Deuteronomy 24:1 and 3.[6] Jesus replies (as Deut. 24:1–4 implies) that divorce is a far more serious matter. It breaks the one-flesh unity of marriage that God established in Genesis 2:24. So God rarely recognizes divorce. And, as we saw in Deuteronomy 24, one who divorces his wife (except for sexual immorality) makes her commit adultery. When the woman marries another man (as she surely would in that society), her sexual relationship with him violates her vows to her first husband, which are still in effect. Thus she becomes an adulteress. And her second husband is also guilty of adultery.

The man who remarries after divorcing his wife also commits adultery: "And he said to them, 'Whoever divorces his wife and marries another commits adultery against her, and if she divorces her husband and marries another, she commits adultery'" (Mark 10:11–12; cf. Matt. 19:9). Luke 16:18 speaks to both the original and subsequent partners: "Everyone who divorces his wife and marries another commits adultery, and he who marries a woman divorced from her husband commits adultery." So divorce and

---

6. Jesus evidently refers to the school of Hillel, which held a lenient position on divorce, rather than that of Shammai, which was more restrictive.

remarriage typically lead to adultery by four people: the original husband and wife (in their new marriages) and their new partners.

THE EXCEPTION OF MATTHEW 5:32 AND 19:9

We have only briefly touched on the one exception to Jesus' teaching on divorce and remarriage: "except for sexual immorality." That exception has, of course, been the subject of much discussion.

The exception clause occurs only in Matthew. Mark 10:11–12 and Luke 16:18 present Jesus' teaching without the exception. The silence of Mark and Luke may be due to the fact that the exception was taken for granted. The PCA Report says: "Both pagan and Jewish culture took adultery as a ground for divorce for granted."[7] In Jeremiah 3:8 and Hosea 1:9, mentioned earlier, God himself divorces Israel for her spiritual adultery. In the Old Testament, adultery was a capital crime (Lev. 20:10). In the political context of the New Testament, such capital punishment was not permitted, but it may well have been assumed that one is not obligated to remain with a spouse who, according to God's law, would be divorced by death.

However, there is a problem with this explanation. The term translated "sexual immorality" is *porneia*, which, as we saw in chapter 38, is broader than "adultery." It can refer to a number of sexual sins, of which adultery is only one. In Matthew 15:19 and Hebrews 13:4, *porneia* is distinguished from *moicheia* (adultery). *Porneia* is also used figuratively for unfaithfulness to God, as we saw earlier (Num. 14:33; Isa. 1:21), and therefore for nonsexual sins, such as Esau selling his birthright (Heb. 12:16). It is unlikely that such figurative meanings are relevant here. If divorce is legitimate for every sin that can figuratively be called *porneia*, then Jesus' view of divorce is very liberal indeed. However, his view was clearly more restrictive than that of most teachers of his time. Matthew 19:10–11 states, "The disciples said to him, 'If such is the case of a man with his wife, it is better not to marry.' But he said to them, 'Not everyone can receive this saying, but only those to whom it is given.'" So we should understand *porneia* here to refer to specifically sexual sins, which would include fornication, prostitution, incest, homosexuality, and bestiality, as well as adultery.[8]

---

7. "Report of the Ad Interim Committee on Divorce and Remarriage," 219.

8. Note that all these sins received the death penalty in the Mosaic law. So people whose spouses were guilty of such sins would have been divorced, in effect, by death. Even in Old Testament times, however, there was likely, in these cases, the possibility of ransom for the life of the guilty person. And in the time of Jesus' earthly ministry, the Jews were not permitted by the Romans to carry out capital punishment. In that context, it is understand-

Note, however, that all of these sins are adulterous when performed by a married person. For example, when a married person commits fornication, that is, has sex with an unmarried person, he breaks his marital vow and violates the one-flesh relationship with his spouse. His conduct is adulterous. So in this way *porneia* and *moicheia,* sexual immorality and adultery, are equivalent terms in the present context, though in other contexts they are distinguishable.

The PCA report cited earlier suggests that the range of *porneia* here may be even broader:

> The committee would argue that masturbation and the destructive sin of pornography per se are not grounds for divorce, because they do not unmistakably break the one-flesh relationship; but if a person becomes so obsessed with them that they become a substitute for fulfilling the conjugal rights of the spouse, then they could be understood to break the one-flesh union. Other examples of habitual sexual sin could be cited. But all of these are unclear cases, and judgment will have to rest with the Session in their application of biblical principles.
>
> The guiding principle should be whether the sexual sin does indeed break the one-flesh relationship. Some sexual sins may hurt the marriage union without necessarily breaking it. But when sexual sin becomes externalized in such a way that it becomes a substitute for the one-flesh relation with one's spouse, then the Session may judge it as being the equivalent of *porneia.*[9]

Normally we do not think of habitual masturbation and use of pornography as adulterous, for they are done alone. However, as the committee indicates, they can become substitutes for normal marital sex.[10] And, perhaps more to the point, we should not forget Jesus' teaching in Matthew 5:28 that lust is adulterous. In chapter 38, I argued that masturbation and pornography are almost always accompanied by sexual intentions, and when these are directed to someone other than a marriage partner, they

---

able that divorce would be understood as a substitute for the dissolution of the marriage by death. If the sexually immoral person does not deserve to live, certainly he or she does not deserve to remain in the marriage. The capital penalty indicates that the innocent spouse should be relieved of his or her marital responsibilities.

9. "Report of the Ad Interim Committee on Divorce and Remarriage," 224–25.

10. I'm not sure what to say about the report's contention here. It may be true that deprivation of conjugal rights is ground for divorce, but I think more argument is needed to establish that contention. My argument is simpler: masturbation and the use of pornography, accompanied by lustful thoughts about people other than one's spouse, are adulterous, and for that reason are grounds for divorce.

constitute the sin of lust. So even in these activities, *porneia* and *moicheia* coincide. Practically, of course, it would be difficult to use "lustful thoughts" as a ground for divorce, since they are hidden in the mind. But habitual masturbation and use of pornography are often externalizations of lust, evidence for it, especially (1) when they serve as substitutes for marital sex, and (2) when the person, during these activities, fantasizes of someone other than his spouse. So I agree with the PCA report that sexual sins of this sort can break the one-flesh relationship of marriage and can therefore be grounds for divorce.[11]

In effect, then, for married persons, *porneia* is *moicheia*: sexual immorality is adultery. The PCA Report, therefore, is right to say that the exceptive clauses in Matthew 5:32 and Matthew 19:9 go no further than the common Jewish and pagan understanding that adultery is ground for divorce. We may assume, then, that Mark 10:2–12 and Luke 16:18 omit this exception because they take it for granted. But though Jesus agrees with the common teaching, he also goes beyond it because of his deeper understanding of adultery.

Again, the fact that divorce is permitted for sexual immorality does not mean that it is commanded, necessary, or even desirable. Even in this situation, God hates divorce and loves reconciliation. But, in such a situation, it is not sinful to divorce.

REMARRIAGE AFTER DIVORCE
FOR SEXUAL IMMORALITY

Let us review Matthew 19:9: "And I say to you: whoever divorces his wife, except for sexual immorality, and marries another, commits adultery." Does the phrase "except for sexual immorality" apply only to the prohibition of divorce, or also to the prohibition of remarriage? In the former case, Jesus would be allowing divorce for sexual immorality, but forbidding the divorced partners to marry other spouses. In the latter case, Jesus would be allowing both divorce and remarriage.

John Murray argues that the sentence has one subject ("whoever") and one verb ("commits adultery"). So the man commits adultery because he both divorces and remarries. The structure of the sentence, then, requires

11. Since anger is a form of murder (Matt. 5:21–26) as lust is a form of adultery, some might ask if our reasoning here implies that anger should be penalized as murder. In some cases, behavioral evidence of anger is literally in the category of attempted murder. Such behavior should be punished accordingly. Other times, as with lust, anger is hidden in the heart, and so is not susceptible to human judgment. We should note also one difference between anger and lust: there is godly anger (Ps. 7:11; Eph. 4:26), but there is no such thing as godly lust.

the exception clause to apply to both divorce and remarriage.[12] Further, as the PCA Report says, divorce, if legitimate, entails the right to remarry, because it abrogates the original marital obligations.[13]

So, after divorce on the ground of sexual immorality, the parties may remarry. With John Murray, I agree that remarriage is permitted to both parties, both the innocent party and the guilty party. While it may be best in many cases for the two to be reconciled and remarried to one another, they are not obligated to do this. It is not wrong for them to seek other partners, for divorce has annulled the original marriage bonds. In this case (which, I reiterate, is an exception to the general rule), a second marriage is not adulterous.

How does Deuteronomy 24:1–4 apply in this exceptional case? In this case, a second marriage does not "defile" the divorced person, for the second marriage is not adultery. So if the second marriage ends in death or divorce for sexual immorality, and the original partner is free, then the original partners may remarry one another. Recall that Deuteronomy 24:1–4, like Mark 10:11–12 and Luke 16:18, describe nonexceptional divorce situations.

1 CORINTHIANS 7:10–15

Here, the apostle Paul speaks about divorce and remarriage in the life of the early church:

> To the married I give this charge (not I, but the Lord): the wife should not separate from her husband (but if she does, she should remain unmarried or else be reconciled to her husband), and the husband should not divorce his wife. To the rest I say (I, not the Lord) that if any brother has a wife who is an unbeliever, and she consents to live with him, he should not divorce her. If any woman has a husband who is an unbeliever, and he consents to live with her, she should not divorce him. For the unbelieving husband is made holy because of his wife, and the unbelieving wife is made holy because of her husband. Otherwise your children would be

12. See Murray, *Divorce*, 40; see also Thomas Edgar, "Divorce and Remarriage for Adultery or Desertion," in *Divorce and Remarriage: Four Christian Views*, ed. H. Wayne House (Downers Grove, IL: InterVarsity Press, 1990), 156–62.

13. "Report of the Ad Interim Committee on Divorce and Remarriage," 220. On pp. 206–7, the report points out that in the Mishnah, the essential text of a bill of divorce read, "Lo, thou art free to marry any man." This represents the custom that prevailed in the time of Jesus' earthly ministry.

unclean, but as it is, they are holy. But if the unbelieving partner separates, let it be so. In such cases the brother or sister is not enslaved. God has called you to peace.

Verses 10–11 simply repeat the teaching of Jesus ("not I, but the Lord") that believers should not divorce, and if they do they should not remarry other partners. Paul does not mention the exception of Matthew 5:32 and 19:9, so his teaching here is practically equivalent to that of Mark 10:11–12 and Luke 16:18. We should assume, in line with our earlier discussion, that he would have taken that exception for granted.

Verses 12–15 deal with a situation not mentioned by Jesus in the gospel accounts. Hence, Paul ascribes it to "I, not the Lord."[14] This is the situation of marriage between a believer and an unbeliever.[15] In Paul's teaching, the believer is not to initiate divorce. Verse 14 teaches that the presence of an unbelieving spouse does not contaminate the household in God's sight. Rather, the household is holy to God. Even the unbelieving spouse is "holy" in one sense because of his relationship to the believing spouse. Exegetes and theologians have debated the meaning of this holiness. Clearly Paul is not saying that the unbeliever becomes a holy person (that is, a believer, a saint) simply by having a believing spouse. Rather, he, with the rest of the household, is set apart to God.[16] In Scripture, God claims households as well as individuals (Josh. 24:15; Acts 11:14; 16:31). So the household in 1 Corinthians 7:14 is holy to the Lord, and it should not be broken by divorce.

Verse 15, however, deals with a divorce initiated by the unbeliever. The PCA Report comments as follows:

> Again, the verb "leaves" (*chorizo*) is referring to divorce. Herein lies an interesting point. Paul is referring to a situation in which the deserted spouse is the passive victim of the unrighteous termination of a marriage. This suggests that what we have here is not another ground for divorce, but from the perspective of the

14. Paul does not hereby disclaim inspiration or authority. He is an inspired apostle, and his teaching is no less the word of God than was the teaching of Jesus. He merely distinguishes between what Jesus said in his earthly ministry and what he, Paul, is adding to that teaching.

15. The general teaching of Scripture is that believers should not marry unbelievers (Deut. 7:3; Ezra 10:10; 1 Cor. 7:39; 2 Cor. 6:14–7:1). The patriarchs took pains to keep their sons from marrying Canaanite women (Gen. 24:3; 28:1). But in Paul's missionary labors, there were evidently many situations in which one spouse was converted and the other was not, leaving a *de facto* mixed marriage. Paul's commands here are relevant to all mixed marriages, however they come about.

16. "Set apart" is the root meaning of *holy*.

offended spouse, a *fait accompli.* We are reminded that there are various views attempting to reconcile the desertion of 1 Corinthians 7 with the *porneia* (sexual immorality) of Matthew 19. Some hold that desertion is simply another ground for divorce; Jesus was not giving us an exhaustive list. Others hold that desertion is simply a subset of *porneia, porneia* being a term which has broader connotations than illicit sexual sins. But it seems reasonable to argue that Paul views desertion as the destruction of the marriage which the Christian spouse was unable to prevent. The question Paul raises is, what should a Christian do if an unbelieving spouse leaves the marriage?[17]

I generally agree with the Report on this point. I do, however, think that *porneia* enters into this situation. When an unbeliever divorces a believer, he does not, most likely, intend to remain celibate. His intention is to seek sexual fulfillment elsewhere. So for the Christian to accept this divorce is, among other things, to recognize that the original sexual relationship has been, or will inevitably be, defiled by *porneia.*

How, then, does Paul answer the question that he raises? He says that the believer is not "enslaved," as the ESV puts it. That is a literal rendering of the Greek *douleuō,* and here it means, if somewhat metaphorically, that the divorce has dissolved the obligations of marriage.[18] The "peace" of verse 15 is not a paradoxical peace in the midst of a struggle against divorce action, but an acceptance of that divorce and the freedom it brings.

Must the unbeliever's divorce action be a formal one? Among the Jews, the "certificate of divorce" provided the formal, official record that the divorce had taken place. However consistently the Jews observed this custom, it was not universally practiced among the Gentiles. A man could divorce his wife simply by telling her that she was divorced, or by requiring her to leave his house. A man divorced his wife simply by renouncing his marriage obligations. So divorce was a less formal affair than it is today.

But people today often engage in the same kind of informal separations. For example, an unbelieving man may leave his believing wife and go to live with another woman, without filing divorce papers. Where does that leave the innocent, believing spouse? She may accept the situation of a broken marriage, as Paul says. Thus, she may regard herself as free from the original marriage obligation. But in order to secure recognition of that freedom, she may need herself to file divorce papers with the state. In this case, from a legal standpoint, she is the one initiating the divorce. But,

---

17. "Report of the Ad Interim Committee on Divorce and Remarriage," 227.
18. On the difference between *douleuō* here and *deō* in verse 39, see ibid., 228.

biblically speaking, it is the unbeliever who has instigated divorce, and the believer is merely accepting the status quo. When she files for divorce, she is asking the state to recognize that status quo.

So when the WCF speaks of divorce for "willful desertion" (24.6), we should take that as shorthand for "acceptance of an action by an unbelieving spouse renouncing his marital obligations, that acceptance being ratified as necessary by legal process."

Now it might appear as though verse 15 is irrelevant to marriages between believers. Certainly the verse doesn't mention such marriages; Paul has dealt with them in verses 10–11. But situations are often fluid. Through the discipline of the church, a person recognized as a believer at one time can, through excommunication, be later regarded as an unbeliever. So a marriage between two believers can, by the action of the church, become a marriage between a believer and an unbeliever. Then verse 15 can enter the picture.

As an example, consider Mike, who deserts his wife Jane. Both are professing believers, members of Grace Presbyterian Church. This desertion does not literally fall under the terms of 1 Corinthians 7:15, for Mike and Jane are fellow Christians. But Jane is not without recourse. She has the privilege and the responsibility to call on the church for help. The elders offer counsel and try to restore the marriage. But Mike is adamant. So the church institutes discipline against Mike, following the procedure of Matthew 18:15–20. Admonitions and rebukes are insufficient, and so the procedure leads to excommunication: "If he refuses to listen even to the church, let him be to you as a Gentile and a tax collector" (Matt. 18:17). From that point on, Jane and the church regard Mike as an unbeliever, and their marriage becomes a mixed marriage. Then Mike's desertion of Jane falls under the provision of 1 Corinthians 7:15, and Jane may recognize the fact of that desertion by filing divorce papers.

It is important for us to keep in mind the context of the church fellowship, as we explore other questions, for example that of spousal abuse as a ground of divorce. Although it might seem as though marriage and divorce are transactions only between two individuals, that is not the case. Marriage is a covenant with public vows. Divorce, too, involves people other than the couple directly involved. There are children, relatives, and indeed the whole church fellowship who have an interest in the situation. Both marriage and divorce can have consequences for many people, and those consequences can rebound upon the couple themselves.

Consider the debate as to whether spousal abuse can be a ground for divorce. Certainly physical abuse is a violation of the sixth commandment. So a husband and a wife sometimes, tragically, must be removed from one another to preserve life. The church should facilitate such separation when that is necessary and provide counseling to encourage reconciliation. But if, say, Jack, will not be persuaded to quit harming his wife Linda, the church should institute discipline against Jack. If this discipline leads to excommunication, the question could well arise as to whether Jack has in effect deserted Linda, in terms of 1 Corinthians 7:15.

Although we (with the WCF) speak of "desertion" as the action taken by the unbeliever in 1 Corinthians 7:15, what Paul actually speaks of there is divorce, whether official or unofficial. The "separation" in verse 15 may or may not be geographical. The important thing is that it is a renunciation of one's marital vows. So even if Jack remains in the same house with Linda, the question arises whether his actions amount to a *de facto* divorce.

Each case of this kind must be decided on its merits. It is possible that Jack, even though he is abusive, may still consider himself bound to Linda by marriage. He may claim that in other ways he is still faithful to her. But the session, or other ruling body of a church, must make its own assessment of the situation. Spousal abuse is inconsistent with marital fidelity. Not every inconsistency is ground for divorce, surely. But sometimes violation of marital vows becomes so severe that no real commitment remains. When the church judges that Jack no longer respects his marriage vows, it may declare that he has divorced Linda, and that she may consider the marriage ended. At that point, she may file divorce papers to make the termination official.

The PCA Report says that divorce may be necessary "to protect a blameless spouse from intolerable conditions."[19] But, realizing that this principle could open the floodgates to all sorts of grounds for divorce, the Report then insists that "the list of sins tantamount to desertion cannot be very long."[20] Obviously, what is tolerable to one person may be intolerable to another. So the Report tries to distinguish between objective and subjective sources of intolerability, a very difficult distinction to make with any cogency. I am not satisfied with the Report's reasoning at this point. What is needed is a focus on the question of whether the unbeliever makes a credible claim to be upholding his marital vows. When that claim is no longer credible, because of physical or verbal abuse, emotional entanglements with people other than the spouse, failure to provide, literal desertion, and so on, the church may declare the original marriage null and void and the partners free to remarry. But, as the WCF says, these forms of "desertion" must be such as "can no way be remedied by the church, or civil magistrate." The church should recognize divorces in these cases only when all available remedies have failed.

19. "Report of the Ad Interim Committee on Divorce and Remarriage," 229.
20. Ibid.

CHAPTER 40

The Seventh Commandment: Reproduction

It is difficult, in a system of ethics based on the Ten Commandments, to know exactly where to deal with the ethics of reproduction. Certainly the subject is relevant to the family (fifth commandment). And many of the problems in this area are matters of life and death, questions about preserving the lives of the unborn (sixth commandment). I have chosen to deal with these issues here, however, not only because sex and reproduction are related in an obvious way, but also because in this location my discussion can draw on principles discussed under the fifth and sixth commandments.

BIRTH CONTROL

The first question we shall consider is whether couples may ever take steps to have fewer children than the maximum possible. As we have seen, one purpose of marriage is to bring forth children in obedience to the cultural mandate, "Be fruitful and multiply" (Gen. 1:28). On the other hand, many couples have thought that for various reasons (special callings, health problems, economic pressure, etc.) they should limit the number of children they have.

Some believe that such limitation is wrong. The argument from natural law is that since sexual intercourse leads to conception,[1] we have a moral obligation not to impede that result. But like other natural-law arguments that we have considered (see chapters 14, 37), this one is not persuasive. It is also natural for hair to grow indefinitely long. Long hair, indeed, can be a beautiful thing, a divine blessing (1 Cor. 11:15). But that doesn't prove that hair should never be cut. As I argued earlier, natural law is a revelation of God's moral standards. But one cannot argue moral conclusions from natural law apart from Scripture, without committing the naturalistic fallacy.

So we should ask, as always, what the Bible teaches on this subject. There is much in Scripture to encourage reproduction, beginning with the cultural mandate of Genesis 1:28 and 9:1. Conception is a gift of God (Gen. 4:1; 29:31; 30:22; Judg. 13:3; 1 Sam. 1:5; Ps. 113:9; Isa. 54:1), and barrenness is a curse (Gen. 11:30; 25:21; Ex. 23:26; Deut. 7:14). A large family is a blessing from God:

> Behold, children are a heritage from the LORD,
>   the fruit of the womb a reward.
> Like arrows in the hand of a warrior
>   are the children of one's youth.
> Blessed is the man
>   who fills his quiver with them![2]
> He shall not be put to shame
>   when he speaks with his enemies in the gate. (Ps. 127:3–5)

Further, as we saw under the fifth commandment (especially chapter 32), the family is quite central to God's redemptive purposes. God calls families, not just individuals, to fellowship with him through Christ. In

---

1. Some argue more than this: that nature declares conception to be the "essential purpose" of sex, or, perhaps, one of several essential purposes. Now, as we have seen, sexual relations in marriage do have other functions as well: they seal and define the marriage commitment, and they represent the height of marital intimacy. How can we show which purposes are essential and which are nonessential? I know of no way to determine this through an examination of natural revelation alone. Only Scripture is competent to tell us what is essential. In Scripture, procreation is essential in the sense that it is God's ordained means to a necessary end, the filling of the earth. But it is not essential in that every sexual act must have procreation as its purpose. Remember that the cultural mandate is given, not to each individual, but to the human race as a whole. The human race certainly has an obligation to procreate, and individuals should contribute as they are gifted to achieve this goal. But not everyone is equally gifted. If reproduction were essential to the purpose of each individual sexual relationship, then sex would be forbidden to those who are either too old or otherwise unable to reproduce. So far as I know, nobody has ever argued this position.

2. I heard somewhere that a quiver of the time carried six arrows. On that understanding, most of us today have not had our quivers filled.

those families, children are taught the ways of God (Deut. 6:6–9). Thus God's kingdom grows. Children who learn about God at home lead others to Christ and bring about change in culture and society.[3]

So in Scripture, reproduction is a divine command (Gen. 1:28; 9:1), a divine blessing, and a means to the fulfillment of God's purposes.[4] Some have argued from these data that the Bible implicitly forbids birth control. Certainly at least there is a large biblical presumption in favor of having children. It may seem that limiting conception amounts to (1) disobedience to God's command, (2) rejection of a divine blessing, and (3) rejection of a means to fulfill God's purposes.

However, the issue is not as simple as it may seem. First, the cultural mandate, as we saw in chapter 13 and 17, is not a command given to every individual alone. It is given to the whole human race as a corporate body. God calls some people to singleness (chapter 38), and some who are married are unable to have children, in God's providence. But even these can and should contribute to the fulfillment of the cultural mandate. They should do what they can to encourage the multiplication of the human race over all the earth and its dominion to the glory of God. But their individual contribution may not include marriage and childbearing.

Is it possible, then, that God may call some people to be married, but not to have the maximum number of children they can have? I don't see how we can rule out this possibility. In 1 Corinthians 7, as we saw in chapter 38, Paul says that "in the present distress" (v. 26) it is best for people to be unmarried, even though some might think from a literal reading of Genesis 1:28 that everybody should be married. Is it not possible that some situations might be distressful in such a way that married couples should put off having children? I think Scripture allows for such a possibility.

Is birth control a rejection of a divine blessing? Yes, in a sense. But we saw earlier that, although long hair can be a blessing, it is not wrong to cut it sometimes. Wealth is also a divine blessing (1 Sam. 2:7). Nevertheless, Proverbs 23:4 advises, "Do not toil to acquire wealth; be discerning enough to desist." And Scripture says much about the dangers of riches. Marriage is also a blessing of God, as we have seen, but not every single person should seek marriage (1 Cor. 7:8). The fact that a certain condition is a blessing of God does not mean that everyone should seek it in every situation. Scripture tells us to take situational factors into account and to

---

3. We shall see under the eighth commandment that the family is also centrally important to the economic welfare of people and societies.

4. These three motivations to reproduce are normative, existential, and situational, respectively.

use wise judgment in these matters. It seems to me proper, then, for married couples to use discernment in judging whether to have children and how many children to have.

Finally, does birth control reject a means for the fulfillment of God's purposes? Does it necessarily work against the expansion of his kingdom, against his glorification? I don't believe so. Each of us is to do all things to the glory of God (1 Cor. 10:31). But there are many ways of doing that, of which begetting children is only one. Begetting children is, to be sure, more central in Scripture than many other means to this end. But there are also ways for single people to contribute to God's kingdom, and for those who are barren, though married. Similarly, it seems to me that some married people may conscientiously decide to limit the size of their families, in order better to glorify God by other means.

This is not to say, of course, that people may limit their families for any reason whatever. It is wrong to limit conception merely in order to have money for more luxuries, for example. Reasons for birth control bear a high burden of proof. But it does seem to me that people might legitimately control births in order to guard the health of the mother or more effectively to minister to people in dangerous parts of the world. Such decisions should be made in the light of biblical principles, including those cited above, situational factors, and heart motives.

People today sometimes justify birth control as a means to slow or stop the "overpopulation" of the earth. That argument, I believe, is simply wrong. Most parties to this debate agree that the earth is not overpopulated in the sense that every space is filled up with people. Actually, there are vast unpopulated spaces, as anyone can see who rides an airplane across the U.S. In the debate, rather, overpopulation means that there are insufficient resources to meet the needs of the inhabitants. The issue is economics, not density of population as such. New Jersey is more densely populated than India, but India is more overpopulated in the economic sense.

People debate the answers to economic overpopulation, but it is simplistic to claim that more birth control will in itself make a difference, or that less will make the situation worse. When people advocate birth control as a solution to overpopulation, they are thinking of children almost exclusively as consumers. On this view, each child is nothing more than another empty mouth to feed. But this is wrong. People are not only consumers, but also producers of resources. When children grow up to produce more resources than they consume, they lessen the problem of overpopulation, rather than exacerbate it.

This is all the more reason for Christians to have children. A child raised in a Christian family is more likely than others to have a strong work ethic and a system of values that enables him to provide for others. Christian children, in other words, are more likely to be part of the solution than part of the problem.[5]

So it seems to me that birth control is permissible in many situations, but it bears a high burden of proof. It can be a responsible choice, but it is probably overused.

MEANS OF BIRTH CONTROL

The Roman Catholic Church insists that only "natural" means of birth control are legitimate. So they permit the "rhythm" method (abstinence during the wife's fertile period), but not condoms, diaphragms, intrauterine devices, or pills. It is odd that the Roman Church allows for any method of birth control at all, since she follows the natural-law argument that reproduction is an essential purpose of sex.[6] If indeed reproduction is an essential purpose of sex, then we should never interfere with it, by any means at all. The distinction between natural and artificial means in this context is morally irrelevant. In both cases, there is a human intention to have sexual relations while preventing conception. If that intention is morally wrong, then carrying out that intention by periodic abstinence is just as wrong as carrying it out by the use of condoms.

This is not to say that the means of birth control are indifferent. Some kinds of birth control pills, for example, should not be used, since they in effect produce abortions. They do not prevent fertilization, but they kill fertilized eggs, either directly, or by preventing their implantation. The same is true of the intrauterine device (IUD), and (more obviously) the "morning after pill," marketed in many parts of the world. And it should be even more obvious, from our discussion in chapter 37, that abortion may not be justified as a means of birth control.

But in cases where birth control is morally justified, I see no objection to the rhythm method or to condoms or diaphragms. The rule is that birth control should prevent conception, not kill a human being already conceived.

5. For more on this issue, see R. J. Rushdoony, *The Myth of Overpopulation* (Nutley, NJ: Craig Press, 1969).

6. Some have argued that it is legitimate to prevent reproduction between one sexual act and another, but not during one. That would legitimize the timing of sexual relations, but not doing something during the act itself to prevent conception. But this distinction is artificial. In both cases, there is a human intention, a plan, accompanied by various actions with the goal of having sexual relations without conception. It seems to me irrelevant when those intentions, plans, and actions occur. For example, condoms are usually worn before the sex act is consummated, but nobody thinks that particular time-interval makes a moral difference.

Vasectomy and tubal ligation have become more popular recently as means of birth control, and certainly they have in their favor that they do not take human life. I know of no biblical principle that would rule out these operations in all cases, but situational factors are significant, especially the difficulty of reversing the operation should a person later wish to have children. Success rates in reversing these procedures are increasing, but such success cannot be guaranteed. The relative permanence of these operations is what makes them attractive to many. But it is very difficult, often presumptuous, to be sure that one will never want to have children following such an operation, especially in view of the strong biblical encouragements to be fruitful and multiply. Scripture warns us against being too sure of what the future will bring (James 4:13–17).

Still, in cases where pregnancy would impose serious physical risks on a woman, tubal ligation may be wise. The same result can be obtained by the husband undergoing a vasectomy, assuming that the woman has sexual relations only with her husband. But it should be remembered that men generally have more years of fertility than women, so that a man must look farther into the future than a woman, in contemplating such a step. If a thirty-year-old man gets a vasectomy, and his wife lives only until he is fifty, then he may well marry again and want to beget children in his second marriage.

THE NEW REPRODUCTION

Recent developments in science have created new alternatives in human reproduction. We will consider here (1) artificial insemination by the husband (AIH), (2) artificial insemination by a donor (AID), (3) surrogate motherhood (SM), and (4) in vitro fertilization (IVF). These may be combined in various ways. In AIH, AID, and SM, fertilization usually takes place in vitro (a petri dish), and resulting embryos are implanted in the womb of a woman.

Very little of ethical importance can be said about AIH. This is simply a way around certain difficulties in fertilization, and we can be thankful that it is available. AID, of course, is another question. It has been criticized as a form of adultery, because it brings a third party into the reproduction process. I don't agree with that assessment. Adultery in Scripture always involves sexual intimacy; that is why it is offensive. In AID there is no physical intimacy.

There is a problem, however, with the man who makes the donation of semen. In making that donation, he is opening up the possibility that he will beget children, but he will, in most cases, not know those children or take any responsibility for them. That raises questions about the principle that a man should support his relatives (1 Tim. 5:8). He may, of course, claim that he is providing for his children by placing them in the homes of others—giving them up for adoption, as it were. That claim is not necessarily wrong, but it is hard to credit it when the man gives a blind gift to a sperm bank and has no idea what will be done with it. I think it would not be wrong for a man to donate sperm to a family of which he has some knowledge, a family that he can reasonably trust to care for his offspring. But as this procedure is normally carried out, the identity of the sperm donor is kept from all other parties, and their identities from him.

The method of gathering that semen, normally masturbation, also raises some issues. My discussion in chapter 38 (under "Lust") implies that in most cases it is wrong for a person to masturbate, unless his object of fantasy is his spouse.

SM is like AID, in that a third party enters the reproductive process. In this case, it is a woman, who agrees to carry the child and give it up at birth. As in the case of AID, there are usually no sexual relations, so I don't believe that SM is adultery. As in AID, however, SM raises the question of how a woman can bear a child without subsequently providing for him. This is, I think, particularly difficult if the surrogate's own egg is used, for then she is the biological mother of the child. As with AID, one may defend the procedure as analogous to adoption. But as in the previous case, the "adoption" here should be informed by knowledge of the adopting family.

Another difficulty is that SM fails to take account of the bonding process between a woman and the child in her womb. It is often very difficult for a surrogate mother to give up the child after its birth. That often creates legal, as well as emotional, difficulties.

IVF is good in itself, as a method of conception when others will not work. There is no scriptural reason why a human egg should not be fertilized outside the mother's body and later implanted in her womb, or even to be grown entirely outside the womb when and if that becomes technologically feasible. However, in the usual practice, several eggs are fertilized, and after some observation one is chosen for implantation. The others are destroyed. On a biblical view of the personhood of the unborn child from conception, this procedure is the destruction of human life. Christian women should tell their physicians either to fertilize only one egg and implant that, or to fertilize several and implant them all. Several women have been reported in the press who have chosen the latter alternative, and one, under this procedure, carried quintuplets to term. Given the danger of such a large multiple birth, one must regard that decision as moral heroism.

GENETIC MANIPULATION AND PLAYING GOD

Readers of my work know that science is not my long suit, and I am certainly not up to date on the fast-moving science of genetics, a science which raises a multitude of ethical issues. But, based on biblical teachings and previous discussions in this book, I would like to state some broad guidelines.

When the prospect of genetic engineering became realistic, some Christians gave dire warnings against it: that to tamper with the human genome was to "play God." "Playing God," in this discussion, refers to human beings trying to usurp God's unique prerogatives. In this sense, certainly, playing God is a sin. It is what Satan does, and what he tempts human beings to do, as in Genesis 3. Also, fiction about monsters (e.g. Frankenstein) and global catastrophe have made many people hesitant to support new developments in science that may seem to impinge on God's sovereignty. Even non-Christian writers regularly warn that our scientific and technological sophistication has outpaced our moral maturity.

But people who discuss this principle rarely try to show in a disciplined way what the unique prerogatives of God are. It is obvious that the creation of the world out of nothing is God's unique prerogative, as is the ultimate control of events in nature and history. God is also, uniquely, the ultimate authority over his creatures and the one most personally and intimately involved with all those creatures. These are the unique prerogatives of our covenant head, which we have described elsewhere as the lordship attributes. Other such prerogatives also exist, which may be implications of the lordship attributes. Because God is Lord, for example, he is also our unique and only Savior from sin (Isa. 43:11; John 14:6).

But I know of no passage or principle of Scripture that ascribes to God alone the right to bring about changes in the human genome. On the contrary, the cultural mandate encourages human beings to be involved in the development of all the earth's resources for God's glory and for their own dominion. Surely they cannot achieve that kind of dominion without also mastering themselves, without understanding and controlling developments within their own bodies. This becomes all the more important after the fall, when disease, injury, pain, and death enter the picture. To take dominion over the realm of microscopic organisms, for example, is surely to limit their power to harm human beings. Such is the divine charter for the medical profession. If someone wants, therefore, to claim that some part of the human body, such as the genome, is off limits to scientific exploration, he bears a large burden of proof.

Although we should condemn playing God in the sense defined above, we should recognize at the same time that carrying out the cultural mandate is a work deeply analogous to God's. God is king over all; man is the vassal king. God has all dominion, but man is to seek dominion under him. Although man should not play God, it is important that he image God. And imaging God involves doing many things that God himself does.

So in discussing genetic issues, I tend to avoid rhetoric about playing God and seek to develop more precise criteria that can be derived more straightforwardly from Scripture:

1. Any genetic research or procedure that intentionally destroys unborn human life is wrong (chapter 37).

2. Any research or procedure that creates human beings with an abnormally high risk of injury, disease, or premature death is also wrong. The point is not that it is better not to exist than to be disabled, but rather that we should not use a method of creating human life that we know is likely to create a disability, when there are other methods that reduce this risk.

3. Genetic manipulation should not be used intentionally to create human embryos that lack the power to achieve full human potential. That is to say, for example, that embryos should not be conceived merely to provide "spare parts" for other human beings.

4. If it can be shown through research on animals, and then human subjects, that genetic manipulation can remedy illnesses and other disabilities, we should welcome that as a good thing, even if the procedure is not entirely risk free. In other words, we should not be any more suspicious of genetic remedies than we are of other medical procedures.

5. Similarly, we should be no more suspicious of genetically engineered foods than we are of any other developments in nutrition. If research shows that they are no riskier than other elements of the human diet, they should be accepted.

6. If genetic engineering can be used (safely!) to improve certain kinds of intelligence or skills in people, or to improve the possibility that such gifted people will be conceived, we should accept that as a good thing. There is no difference ethically between improving skills through schooling and improving them through genetic engineering.[7] But in a world

---

7. I am not saying that athletic teams should accept genetic enhancements for athletic performance, or for that matter any other kind of enhancement such as through drugs. The important thing in athletics is that all players perform on an equal playing field. If a league permits performance-enhancing drugs or medical procedures for one player, it must

where such practices become customary, we would need to become extra compassionate to those who do not have such genetic enhancements. And we should come to appreciate better the unique ways in which the relatively weak and disabled contribute to society and to the body of Christ (chapter 34).[8]

7. Would it ever be legitimate to introduce genes of another species into a human being? That would, I think, depend on the purpose and the result. If such a procedure were a means of preserving human life or enhancing human potential, it could be defended, much as the use of an animal heart to keep a human patient alive for a time. If, however, it were to harm the human being or bring a net decrease to his quality of life or human potential, it should not be performed.[9] I see no principles of Scripture or nature that would forbid in all circumstances such use of animal genetic material. God has ordained for man to take dominion over the animal kingdom and to use animals for food, clothing, sacrifice, and other legitimate human purposes.

In general, then, it seems to me that there are no ethical issues in genetic procedures that do not also arise in other medical contexts.

STEM CELLS

Stem cells are cells that can take on various forms used to construct different parts of the body: blood, lungs, arms, eyes, etc. A "pluripotent" stem cell is one that "can become any tissue in the body."[10] This remarkable property gives to stem cells great potential in the fight against many human diseases and injuries.

One plentiful source of stem cells is human embryos. But these are collected from embryos that have died.[11] Now, the killing of embryos, through abortion, reproductive medicine, or experimentation, is biblically

---

permit them for all. Given the great risks of steroids, and the inequities they create among players, it is right for leagues to prohibit their use. It might similarly be right for a league to forbid certain kinds of genetic procedures. My own point here, however, is that one cannot rule out genetic treatments in all circumstances, any more than one can declare all use of steroids immoral.

8. The film *Gattaca* is cautionary in this regard.

9. I speak vaguely here, since it is difficult to know at this point what sorts of purposes and results may be in view.

10. Nigel M. de S. Cameron, "Stem Cells Without Guilt," *Washington Times*, August 26, 2005. I rely greatly on this article in the following discussion.

11. After writing this, I have read of research intended to find a way of removing stem cells from embryos without killing them. If that can be done, I would have no objection to the gathering of stem cells in that way.

wrong, as I have argued (chapter 37). It is not wrong in principle, however, to collect stem cells from an embryo that has already died. But it is wrong to kill embryos for any purpose, including the purpose of gathering stem cells. The problem, then, with the use of embryonic stem cells is that if stem cells are gathered from dead embryos, there will likely be an industry to produce and kill embryos for this purpose. That is morally intolerable.

The U.S. government, under the Bush administration, tried to draw a fine line here, making government funding available for research on already existing stem cell lines, that is, on lines already taken from embryos, but not for additional lines that would require the killing of more embryos.[12] Nevertheless, other governments and private companies are still free to destroy embryos for the purpose of gathering stem cells.

Embryos are not the only source of stem cells. Stem cells can be found in adult tissue as well, but these are not pluripotent. However, recent research has developed other sources of pluripotent ("embryonic-type") stem cells. Cameron says:

> The president's Council on Bioethics recently suggested several options. One would use cells from embryos that have died naturally. Another would focus on a procedure fusing an adult cell, such as a skin cell, with an egg cell after reprogramming the genes of one or both cells. The result would be "embryonic-type stem cells" produced without an embryo—no embryos would be created and none destroyed. These stem cells could generate new cell lines for research, without raising the emotive moral issue of destroying tiny human embryos.[13]

He adds, "The hottest topic is umbilical cord blood, which is rich in stem cells and in the past has been thrown away." A still more recent development is the discovery of a way to get pluripotent stem cells from adult skin. This development reduces to zero the need to kill human embryos in order to obtain stem cells. So Christians need not fear that by opposing the destruction of embryos for stem cells they are holding back the prospect of finding cures for disease and injury. There are viable alternatives that should be supported.

12. The administration did not "ban stem cell research" or even "ban embryonic stem cell research," as they are often accused of doing. All they did was to ban government funding for stem cell research that presupposes additional killings of embryos. They encouraged and funded some stem cell research, but gave no encouragement to the development of an industry to produce stem cells from further destruction of embryos. Of course, they also encouraged the use of stem cells from nonembryonic sources, such as adult tissue and umbilical cord blood.

13. Cameron, "Stem Cells Without Guilt."

CLONING

To clone a human being is to imprint a human egg with genetic material taken entirely from a single person, producing a genetic replica of that person. This is different from normal reproduction, in which genetic material from two persons, mother and father, is combined in a third, their child.

A clone, though a *genetic* replica, is not an exact duplicate of his parent, as in the Michael Keaton movie *Multiplicity*. Although the genetic material of the two persons is identical, the clone will be much younger, and will inevitably be raised in a different environment from the parent. Identical twins, who also share a common genetic makeup, differ from one another significantly, and no doubt a cloned child would be even more different from his "parent."[14] Identical twins often have their similarities reinforced by being raised in the same household, receiving the same education, and being subject to similar influences. A cloned child would not have anywhere near that level of environmental sameness with his parent.

It seems almost inevitable that in the near future someone will succeed in cloning a human being. Indeed, that may already have been achieved. The technique is available, having succeeded with Dolly the sheep and many other animals. So the ethical treatises are flowing thick and fast.

There are some good reasons for Christians to oppose the cloning of humans at this time:

1. Research into the cloning of humans today involves the destruction of many fertilized eggs and embryos. Given the pro-life premise that the fertilized egg is a human person, with the right to life protected in the sixth commandment, such research involves murder, and Christians should not condone it.

2. As of now, the process of cloning as performed on animals produces a high risk in the clones of birth defects and other serious health problems. It is wrong to conceive a human being in such a way as to virtually ensure such problems.

3. It is hard to imagine a good motive for creating a clone of oneself, rather than reproducing normally or using other artificial means of conception (AIH, AID, SM, IVF, etc.; see earlier discussion). Some may secretly wish thereby to achieve some kind of immortality, but of course that is foolish and wrong. Others may want to see someone live after them who has exactly their same personality, talents, and virtues. But these may have as much to do with environment and training as genetics, and the ultimate source for all of these is God's sovereign grace. The same questions

---

14. Actually, the one who donates the genetic material is not a parent, but in effect a twin brother or sister. The father of the cloned child is the father of his donor.

arise about someone's attempt to make a perfect genetic copy of somebody else—say, a spouse or someone they admire—from genetic material that has been frozen or otherwise preserved.

I can, however, imagine one good motive. Consider this case: A married couple can't have biological children because one spouse is incurably infertile. But they wish to have a child who carries on the genetic inheritance of *one* of them, without bringing a third party (AID or SM) into the picture. Certainly the desire to continue one's genetic inheritance is not a bad thing, and the desire to keep third parties out of a couple's reproductive life is certainly a godly desire, though AID and SM are not wrong in all cases.

So the question does arise: if research on cloning reaches a point of success, where clonal reproduction is no more risky than natural reproduction, should Christians approve of it (given the godly motivation described above)?

Here many invoke the argument we discussed earlier: isn't cloning a form of playing God? Consider some arguments against cloning even in the best-case scenario noted above:

1. "God has restricted the right to govern human reproduction." Well, of course God governs everything. But where has he said that he forbids cloning?

2. "Cloning is an unnatural process." Yes, in a way, but so is birth control. So are artificial insemination and surrogate motherhood. So is healing by antibiotics. So is surgery. But God does not call us to leave nature as it is, but to take dominion of nature for his glory (Gen. 1:28–30). It is relevant, perhaps, also to mention that something like cloning does occur in nature: when one fertilized egg divides into two, creating genetically identical twins.

3. "Cloning is *creating*, while natural reproduction is *begetting*. Creating is God's prerogative; begetting is ours." To my knowledge, Scripture does not make any moral distinctions along these lines. Certainly we have creative powers that are part of the divine image in which we are made. We are not, of course, creators in the sense of making the first genetic material. God did that in Genesis 2:7. But it is not clear from Scripture that we should abstain from using the creative powers we do have, that he has given us. Note the parallel between Genesis 1:27; 5:2 and Genesis 5:3.

4. "A cloned child is given an identity not freely chosen by him."[15] But none of us freely chooses his or her identity. We all must take the

---

15. See my review of Hessel Bouma III, Douglas Diekema, Edward Langerak, et al., *Christian Faith, Health, and Medical Practice* (Grand Rapids: Eerdmans, 1989), which makes this argument. The review is appendix J in this volume.

genetic cards we are dealt. The argument may seek to make the point that the cloned child of a pianist might be forced to become a pianist against his will. But that is by no means a necessary consequence of cloning, and parents of normally conceived children often impose similar pressures. Further, nobody can become a really great pianist (or anything else) wholly against his will.

5. "Even when carried out with the best motives, the cloning process uses a technique that has been perfected at the loss of much human life, the destruction of human embryos." This argument gives one pause, but I don't think it is determinative. Certainly the history of weaponry has advanced at the cost of much unjust destruction of human life. But is it therefore wrong for us to use that technology to pursue *just* war or to hunt deer? We cannot evaluate an action merely on the basis of the history of similar actions. To do so is to engage in the genetic fallacy. Something that was once done with a sinful purpose and result may be done again with a godly purpose and result.

So I am not convinced that there is any principle of Scripture that rules out cloning in all cases. Cloning, in the best case, is "playing God" only in the sense that we should always play God: imaging his creativity by taking dominion of natural processes for his glory.

CHAPTER 41

The Eighth Commandment: Respecting Property

The eighth commandment is another short commandment: "You shall not steal." But, like all the commandments, it has many applications. In the case of the sixth and seventh commandments, Jesus' Sermon on the Mount guides us toward the broader implications, but he does not directly comment on this commandment (or on the ninth or tenth). Yet his teaching, and that of the rest of Scripture, leads us to see many sins in the perspective of the eighth commandment. The Westminster divines presented their analysis in the Larger Catechism as follows:

> Q. 141. *What are the duties required in the eighth commandment?*
> A. The duties required in the eighth commandment are, truth, faithfulness, and justice in contracts and commerce between man and man; rendering to everyone his due; restitution of goods unlawfully detained from the right owners thereof; giving and lending freely, according to our abilities, and the necessities of others; moderation of our judgments, wills, and affections concerning worldly goods; a provident care and study to get, keep, use, and dispose these things which are necessary and convenient for the sustentation of our nature, and suitable to our condition; a lawful calling, and diligence in it; frugality; avoiding unnecessary lawsuits, and suretyship, or other like engagements; and an endeavor, by all just and

lawful means, to procure, preserve, and further the wealth and outward estate of others, as well as our own.

Q. 142. *What are the sins forbidden in the eighth commandment?*

A. The sins forbidden in the eighth commandment, besides the neglect of the duties required, are, theft, robbery, man-stealing, and receiving anything that is stolen; fraudulent dealing, false weights and measures, removing land marks, injustice and unfaithfulness in contracts between man and man, or in matters of trust; oppression, extortion, usury, bribery, vexatious lawsuits, unjust enclosures and depopulations; engrossing commodities to enhance the price; unlawful callings, and all other unjust or sinful ways of taking or withholding from our neighbor what belongs to him, or of enriching ourselves; covetousness; inordinate prizing and affecting worldly goods; distrustful and distracting cares and studies in getting, keeping, and using them; envying at the prosperity of others; as likewise idleness, prodigality, wasteful gaming; and all other ways whereby we do unduly prejudice our own outward estate, and defrauding ourselves of the due use and comfort of that estate which God hath given us.

We see here how ingenious fallen man becomes at finding ways to take what belongs to others.[1]

PRESUPPOSITIONS

PRIVATE PROPERTY

The eighth commandment assumes that God has given to human beings ownership of property. Of course, ultimately all property belongs to God (Ex. 19:5; Pss. 24:1; 50:10). But he does call human beings to take dominion over the earth in his name (Gen. 1:28–30; Pss. 8:6; 115:16). We are, in other words, stewards of God, given responsibility to care for God's creation. To his stewards, God also gives the right to enjoy that creation. We are to administer this inheritance to God's glory as well as to our own benefit.

God also gives specific property to specific people. He gave the land of Canaan to Israel, and within Israel a certain portion of land to each tribe. But the land given to Israel as a possession was also the holy land of the

---

1. I note that vexatious lawsuits were a form of stealing even in the seventeenth century.

Lord, the place of God's special presence. So families in Israel were not allowed to sell their land in perpetuity (Lev. 25:10–55). This provision of the law reminded them that their land was ultimately God's, and that God maintained the right to administer its use. Similarly, God ordered them to rest the land every seven years (Lev. 25:4). The land is Israel's (Ex. 33:1–3), but ultimately God's (Hos. 9:3).

Outside the borders of Israel, God also enables people to possess parts of the creation. When Abraham bought a burial plot for his wife Sarah, he respected the property rights of the Hittite people (Gen. 23:1–20). Scripture often affirms the property rights of human beings (1 Kings 21:3–6; Acts 4:37; 5:4). People own houses as well as lands (Acts 12:12; 16:14–15; 21:8).

So Scripture endorses the concept of private property, always with the proviso that God is the ultimate owner of creation and the one who has the ultimate authority over it. The eighth commandment assumes this concept. Stealing would have no meaning, unless there were a clear distinction between what belongs to me and what belongs to someone else.

We should not sharply separate property rights from human rights. To steal someone's property is to take his inheritance and to assault his dignity and freedom.

WORK ETHIC

The eighth commandment also presupposes a work ethic. We have already seen this in the fourth commandment's requirement to work six days, and still earlier in the cultural mandate (Gen. 1:28–30; cf. 2:15). After the fall, work becomes toilsome (Gen. 3:17–19; cf. Ps. 90:10; Eccl. 2:18–26), but it is still necessary and beneficial (Deut. 16:15; 1 Thess. 4:11–12). So we are not to be lazy (Prov. 6:6–11; 12:24, 27; 15:19).[2] Paul warns the Thessalonian church against idleness, a warning he identifies as an element of the apostolic tradition (2 Thess. 3:6). The apostles themselves set the example, working hard so as not to burden the church (2 Thess. 3:7–9; cf. 1 Thess. 2:9). They decreed, "If anyone is not willing to work, let him not eat" (2 Thess. 3:10). That is, anyone who is able to work, but will not, may not presume on the generosity of his fellow believers.

Work is the antithesis of theft: "Let the thief no longer steal, but rather let him labor, doing honest work with his own hands, so that he may have something to share with anyone in need" (Eph. 4:28). Labor replaces theft as a means of sustenance. And more than that: it turns

---

2. This is a frequent theme in Proverbs. Look up references to "sloth," "sluggard," etc.

the thief into a benefactor. Rather than taking what belongs to others, he gives to others what is his. So the eighth commandment mandates a lifestyle of generosity, of compassion, of love. In this way, we begin to see the "broader meaning" of the eighth commandment as a perspective on all sin and all righteousness. To keep the eighth commandment is both to give everyone his due and, beyond that, to sacrifice our own goods in love for others, as Jesus gave his life for us. The eighth commandment mandates both justice and mercy.

In the narrow sense, Scripture notes the following forms of theft:

1. Property theft, normally requiring double restitution (Ex. 22:4, 7)
2. Kidnapping or manstealing, a capital crime (Ex. 21:16; Deut. 24:7; 1 Tim. 1:10)
3. Swindling (Jer. 22:13–17; Amos 8:4–6; Hab. 2:9–12)
4. Stealing from widows and orphans, which is especially heinous (Matt. 23:14)
5. Defrauding employees (James 5:4)
6. Land theft (Isa. 5:8)
7. Unjust weights (Lev. 19:35–36; Deut. 25:15)
8. Misleading someone for economic gain (Prov. 20:14)

In the broader sense, Scripture speaks of theft in metaphorical, but important ways:

1. Stealing affection (2 Sam. 15:6)
2. False prophets, who steal God's word from the people and proclaim their own words as God's (Jer. 23:30)
3. False religious leaders as thieves and robbers (John 10:1)
4. Merchandising in the temple (Matt. 21:13)
5. Robbing God of tithes and offerings (Mal. 3:8; cf. Josh. 7:11)

If theft includes robbing God of his due, then we can understand how, in a sense, all sin is theft. So the eighth commandment is a broad mandate upholding God's whole law.

I shall not spend much time on stealing in the narrow sense. It is quite obvious that, according to Scripture, one may not take for himself something that belongs to someone else, without the permission of the other person. That is true even if one is hungry:

> People do not despise a thief if he steals
>   to satisfy his appetite when he is hungry,
> but if he is caught, he will pay sevenfold;
>   he will give all the goods of his house. (Prov. 6:30–31)

According to the wisdom teacher, people in general are sympathetic to someone who steals in order to eat, but the owner of the food feels differently! In context, this is a natural consequence, which the teacher compares to the consequences of adultery. And like adultery, stealing even to satisfy an intense need is wrong.

So theft is wrong in a fairly obvious way. As I have been writing this book, I have noted that one of the most effective ways to show something is wrong is to compare it to theft. One should not take the property of someone else. There are, however, situational complications, for it is not always easy to determine what constitutes property, what belongs to whom in the first place, and what limitations that ownership places on the use of the property by others.[3]

TITHING

As we have seen, Malachi 3:8 says that failure to tithe is actually robbing God. So we should consider the biblical obligation of the tithe and how it affects us. The Mosaic law mentions tithes in several places, and there is some dispute about how many tithes there were and what percentage of one's income was finally required. Rushdoony presents one possible interpretation of the data:

> The regular tithe, ten percent of one's income (Deut. 14:22) was then tithed to the priests, who received ten percent of the tithe (Num. 18:21–28). Thus, the church tithe was a fraction of the total tithe. The poor tithe, paid every other year (Deut. 14:28; Amos 4:4), alternated with the rejoicing tithe (Deut. 14:22–26) on each six-year cycle out of seven. Thus, the combined poor tithe and religious tithe, averaged out to about 15 percent per year; some say 18 percent. Some of the regular tithe went for levitical services to worship, and to music; much of it went to general social financing, i.e. to godly education and a number of other related services.[4]

Of course, the priests had income from other sources as well. Portions of grain (Lev. 2:3, 10; 7:14) and meat (Lev. 7:31–36) from the sacrifices were

---

3. My position on intellectual property (copyrights, patents, etc.) is pretty far from the mainstream. See my "The Other Shoe: Copyright and the Reasonable Use of Technology," available at http://www.frame-poythress.org/frame_articles/1991OtherShoe.htm. See also Vern Poythress, "Copyrights and Copying: Why the Laws Should be Changed," at http://www.frame-poythress.org/poythress_articles/2005Copyrights.htm.

4. Rousas J. Rushdoony, *The Institutes of Biblical Law* (Nutley, NJ: Craig Press, 1973), 510.

eaten by the priests, and they also ate the shewbread after it was removed from its stand in the tabernacle or the temple (Lev. 24:9). The census tax (Ex. 30:11–16) also went "for the service of the tent of meeting."

The tithe was not a tithe on wealth, or even on income generally, but on agricultural produce.⁵ So the tithes are not deposited in a bank, but in a storehouse (Mal. 3:10). The tithe is holy, and its holiness seems to be connected with the holiness of the Promised Land: "Every tithe of the land, whether of the seed of the land or of the fruit of the trees, is the LORD's; it is holy to the LORD" (Lev. 27:30). It might be argued, therefore, that the tithe is not appropriate in the new covenant, in which the promise of Canaan fades away into the greater promise of the new heavens and the new earth. We note, however, that Abraham, who owned no land in Canaan, paid a tithe to Melchizedek, the mysterious priest-king who in Hebrews foreshadows Christ (Gen. 14:20; Heb. 7:4–10), indicating that tithes were sometimes appropriate even apart from Israel's ownership of the Promised Land. Can we give anything less to the Christ who fulfills the priesthood of Melchizedek?

The New Testament does not explicitly require the tithe,⁶ although it says much about giving. Its emphasis, in passages like 2 Corinthians 8–9, is that giving should be voluntary and cheerful (2 Cor. 9:7–8), but also generous. In Acts 4:34–37, we read of Christians selling property to meet the needs of their poor. We shall look at their view of poverty in the next chapter. But radical giving seemed to be a rule for them—and a joy.

Newcomers sometimes ask church members how much money they should give to the church. The question seems crass, and church people often find various ways to avoid answering it. But for someone who is new to the Christian community, it is a reasonable question. What would be a good ball-park figure? Well, in one sense God demands all that we have, and sometimes he demands that in literal ways, as when he calls someone to martyrdom or to the poor widow's moral heroism (Luke 21:1–4). But our inquirer is interested in what would be considered a normal amount, a base from which one may proceed to greater gifts. When I talk to such inquirers, I cannot get out of my head that again and again in the Old Testament the figure of 10 percent recurs. That is the Lord's portion. It may be that in the New Testament that amount is not strictly required. But surely the "cheerful" giving of 2 Corinthians 9:7 cannot be much less than that. So I unashamedly recommend to inquirers the tithe, as a beginning of financial discipleship.

5. The rejoicing tithe could be turned into money (Deut. 14:25).

6. Jesus does say, in Matt. 23:23, that the Jews were right to tithe mint, dill, and cumin, though they neglected other matters that were more important. But these Jews were, of course, living under the old covenant and under its distinctive obligations.

TAXATION

In the Old Testament, the tithe was the Lord's tax, as it were. To with-hold it was to rob God. Gifts to God were of the firstfruits (Ex. 23:16; Deut. 26:2); that is, the believer gave to God before he took anything for himself. In modern law, however, our obligation to the state takes priority over everything else. What does Scripture say about that? Is the state analogous to God in such a way that failure to pay taxes amounts to robbery? Or is it possible for the state to rob its citizens?

As we have seen, there is provision under the Israelite theocracy to support the priests and Levites, but little is said about the support of elders, judges, or kings. Rushdoony believes that "the basic civil tax in Scripture, the only tax, is the poll or head tax, paid by every man twenty years of age and older (Ex. 30:11–16)."[7] The tax of Exodus 30:11–16 does occur during a census. But the passage does not say it was used by the civil government. Rather, the half shekel is "the LORD's offering to make atonement for your lives" (v. 15). This "atonement money" is given "for the service of the tent of meeting, that it may bring the people of Israel to remembrance before the LORD, so as to make atonement for your lives" (v. 16). This tax has a religious purpose. For each man counted in the census, the money is "a ransom for his life to the LORD" (v. 12).

For the most part, the civil officers of Israel made their living as everyone else did, by herding animals, growing crops, and other regular occupations. Those recognized as elders were the heads of families (chapter 32). They may have continued to work, or they may have lived off the accumulated wealth of their lifetimes. They may also have been supported by their families to some extent. The same may have been the case with the judges whom God appointed by filling them with the Spirit.

Taxation as such became an issue only with the institution of the monarchy. God promised Abraham that kings would be among his descendants (Gen. 17:6, 16; cf. 35:11), and Deuteronomy legislates concerning kings in Israel (17:14–20). The latter passage warns the king against acquiring many horses (v. 16) and wives (v. 17), like the kings of other nations, and he is to be under the law, like his fellow Israelites (vv. 18–20). Nevertheless, a monarchy is expensive. A king must be able to hire an army, since his main function is to wage the nation's wars. And as he represents the nation as head of state, he must have some visible preeminence. Given the ancient understanding of kingship, it was expected that the king would have substantial palaces

7. Rushdoony, *The Institutes of Biblical Law*, 510.

and consume luxuries. So when Israel asked to have a king "like the other nations," the prophet-judge Samuel warned:

> These will be the ways of the king who will reign over you: he will take your sons and appoint them to his chariots and to be his horsemen and to run before his chariots. And he will appoint for himself commanders of thousands and commanders of fifties, and some to plow his ground and to reap his harvest, and to make his implements of war and the equipment of his chariots. He will take your daughters to be perfumers and cooks and bakers. He will take the best of your fields and vineyards and olive orchards and give them to his servants. He will take the tenth of your grain and of your vineyards and give it to his officers and to his servants. He will take your male servants and female servants and the best of your young men and your donkeys, and put them to his work. He will take the tenth of your flocks, and you shall be his slaves. And in that day you will cry out because of your king, whom you have chosen for yourselves, but the LORD will not answer you in that day. (1 Sam. 8:11–18)

Samuel's words are a warning: kingship leads to oppression. In part, this oppression punishes the people for desiring a king in the place of the Lord (vv. 7–9). But to some extent Samuel is simply describing the normal ways of kings. Even at its best, in a fallen world, kingship requires a people to make sacrifices of their sons, daughters, and goods. For the most part, what the king acquires in 1 Samuel 8:11–18 is actually necessary to his function.[8] Even if Israel's request had not been the expression of unbelief, and even if God had fulfilled the promise of kings in some other context, the king would have done essentially the same things. And this is the essence of taxation.

Scripture does not prescribe any maximum or minimum tax.[9] In general it assumes that the king may assess whatever he needs, both for official

---

8. The only exception I can see is the reference to slavery in verse 17. Certainly kings did not generally have the right to turn all their free subjects into slaves. But I think the term "slave" here is metaphorical. Samuel warns Israel that living under a king will *feel* like slavery. Ancient kings did not literally enslave everybody, for that would have erased the distinction between slave and free. Of course, the authority of the king and the authority of the slave master were closely analogous.

9. Some have said that the state should collect no more than 10 percent of a person's income, because otherwise it would be taking more than God's tithe and thus would be supplanting God's authority. I think that argument is weak. One could as easily argue that an employer should not ask his employees to work more than one day in seven, for otherwise they would be giving the employer more of their time than they give to the Lord's Sabbath.

purposes and to maintain his kingly lifestyle. At times, Scripture criticizes taxation as oppressive. Jeroboam, though he disobeyed the Lord in many ways, was right to claim that Solomon's reign had been especially oppressive (1 Kings 12:4). And Solomon's son Rehoboam was wrong in his refusal to lighten his people's burden (12:12–24). God later brought evil on King Ahab and his wife Jezebel for killing Naboth in order to seize his vineyard (1 Kings 21). The murder, of course, was more serious than the seizure. But the text implies that Ahab should have accepted Naboth's refusal to sell. Again, Scripture affirms that the king is subject to the law. He may tax, but he may not steal or murder. The difference between taxing and stealing is that taxation is a regular procedure set forth in law. A monarch steals when he takes property over and above that standard tax without compensation, and when he singles out individuals to make this sacrifice, rather than distributing the burden fairly.

Jesus taught his followers to pay taxes to Caesar (Matt. 22:17–22), as did Paul (Rom. 13:6–7), even though Caesar worshiped idols and claimed deity for himself and former emperors. He used tax money to fund his own cult.

I personally believe that the U.S. government has far overstepped the limits originally established in the Constitution. Thus, it has become far more expensive than it should be. I also believe that lower taxes, on the whole, benefit the economy, while higher taxes discourage economic growth. Since government should be under law, the Bible supports efforts to bring the scope of government back to its constitutional limits or, alternatively, efforts to amend the Constitution to make it justify current practice. But the Bible does not quantify in general how much income government may require of its citizens.

I believe that the law should recognize the priority of our obligations to God (the tithe) and family (1 Tim. 5:8) over our obligations to the state. The tax code provides for this by making contributions to nonprofit organizations deductible and by making similar provision for family expenses such as healthcare. But people have still sometimes been required to sell their homes and businesses in order to pay taxes, and that seems to me to be contrary to biblical priorities. The estate tax is particularly unjust in this regard.

In general, however, taxation is not theft. It is theft when it violates the laws of the land and when its demands conflict with the spheres of family and church. And people who withhold taxes are guilty of theft, depriving the government of its due.

Or, one could argue that a man should spend no more than 10 percent on his family, lest his family become an idol. Of course, everything we have belongs to God, but God authorizes us to spend more money on other things than we give specifically to the church.

BOYCOTTS

The discussion of taxes leads us to consider the use of our money in other areas. Churches and other organizations often urge us to take religious and ethical considerations into account in our use of money, and we should take that exhortation seriously. Sometimes people will organize boycotts, urging citizens to avoid doing business with companies implicated in some kind of evil. An offending business may be charged with despoiling the environment, unfairness to its employees, encouraging abortion, promoting homosexuality, or providing questionable entertainment.

The Christian should weigh these appeals individually, but they must be weighed against other ethical considerations. In general, Scripture does not forbid us to give money to organizations implicated in sin. We have seen that Jesus told his disciples to pay taxes to Caesar, even though some of that money went to support false religion. A similar question arose in Corinth (1 Cor. 8–10), where some believers urged a boycott of pagan meat markets for fear that some of the meat may have been offered to idols. Paul replied, "Eat whatever is sold in the meat market without raising any question on the ground of conscience." He did not even raise the issue of whether some of the money paid for the food would be used to finance pagan worship.

So we should not take the position of boycotting every company implicated in sin. Part of the reason, of course, is that *everyone* is implicated in sin. If we boycott all sinners, we will not be able to buy anything at all. Further, boycotts do not normally have a large impact on a company's profits or policies.

Still, there are times when a boycott may be a useful strategy in our cultural struggle. Certainly boycotts often receive publicity that would not otherwise be available. And, even more than letters protesting a corporate practice, boycotts help a company to understand the extent and depth of public indignation. All businesses want to have good public relations, and they do try to avoid boycotts. A boycott sends a message, at least.

But individual Christians need to make individual judgments in such areas. Pastor Ashby may urge his people to avoid using physicians who perform abortions or refer patients to other doctors for abortion. But a member of his church, Mrs. Miller, may find she has a condition that no one can treat except a doctor who refers patients for abortions. In my judgment, she does not sin if she violates the congregation's boycott.

FINANCIAL RESPONSIBILITY

Moving to somewhat broader applications of the commandment, I would maintain that the eighth commandment mandates responsible use of the funds God has entrusted to us. We have seen that we have responsibilities to our families (1 Tim. 5:8), to the church (2 Cor. 8–9), to the state (Matt. 22:17–22), and to ourselves (2 Thess. 3:10). These responsibilities, in turn, require a seriousness about the use of money.

In Luke 14:28, Jesus takes it as a generally acknowledged fact that when someone builds a tower, he must first count the cost. So he argues that people should consider the cost of discipleship. He also commends the servants in Matthew 25:14–30 who invested their master's money and made it grow, rather than the servant who buried his portion in the ground. His main point, of course, concerns not just the use of money, but of all our resources to advance the kingdom of God. But he uses an illustration that commends prudent investment.

As we shall see in the next chapter, Scripture does not condemn the expenditure of money for relaxation, for entertainment, or even for the consumption of luxuries. But these must be balanced by a concern for others and for one's own future well-being.

There are certain concerns that outweigh financial considerations. Jesus' parable of the rich fool (Luke 12:13–21) is about coveting treasure for oneself, without being rich toward God (v. 21). There is more to be said about this principle under the tenth commandment and in our discussion of wealth and poverty in the next chapter.

GAMBLING

Gambling is often treated as a case of financial irresponsibility. There are many arguments used to justify total abstinence from the practice, such as:

1. It can be linked to the worship of fate or chance.
2. It can be psychologically addictive (1 Cor. 6:12).
3. It can involve covetousness.
4. It can be a waste of time and money, hence a cause of poverty.
5. It can be thought of as a substitute for useful work.
6. Even where legal, it often falls under the control of organized crime.

These are strong arguments. In my judgment, the fourth one is the strongest, and it is linked to others. Much of the allure of gambling (and the advertising on its behalf) is a false promise of quick riches, a promise to which the poor are especially susceptible. But in most cases, gambling (especially when it becomes an addiction) makes the poor only poorer. (The chance of winning the Florida Lottery, for example, is only about one in eighty million.) Scripture warns strongly against the oppression of the poor, as we shall see. So I always vote against state-sponsored gambling, no matter how good a cause it supports.

This is not to say, however, that it is always wrong for an individual to gamble. There are cases in which not one of the above six arguments applies; that's why I use the words "can" and "often" in them. Participation in an office football pool, for example, may involve none of those evils (although at times it too may involve covetousness, etc.). If one enters the pool using only money earmarked for recreation, without addiction or false worship, it can be a harmless bit of fun, strengthening personal relationships. It does not necessarily involve covetousness, because (1) most people expect to lose their money in the process, and (2) if they win, the money becomes theirs legitimately (so they are not coveting anything that is not theirs).

I think also that it is not necessarily wrong for a Christian to buy a state lottery ticket, even after he has voted against the establishment of a state lottery. In the best-case scenario, as in the above example, he is not addicted, worshiping chance, or coveting. He is not wasting money he needs for other purposes or gambling as a substitute for useful work. Rather, he acknowledges God as sovereign, even over what appears to be random (Prov. 16:33), he promises God that he will use the money for the kingdom, and he enjoys the random variations, the play of numbers that God has ordained.

As I have indicated, I have a special interest in this book to define those things that the Bible explicitly or implicitly declares to be sinful in all circumstances. I don't believe that gambling is one of those, any more than drinking alcohol. But a book on ethics needs to give guidance, not only as to what is always sinful, but also as to what is often or generally sinful, given the conditions in which we live (the situational perspective). So the use of alcohol should be subjected to careful limits, and gambling should be carefully controlled as well.[10]

---

10. A friend of mind had an uncle and aunt who lived in Santa Rosa, California, and each year took a trip with fifty dollars to gamble at Reno. They agreed ahead of time to give any winnings to the church. Most years, they had fun trying to beat the system and losing their fifty dollars, and returned home content. But one year they did win several thousand dollars and gave it to the church.

CHAPTER 42

The Eighth Commandment: Wealth and Poverty

We have seen that the eighth commandment challenges us to look at all of life from an economic perspective: to what extent are we giving God his due, and to what extent are we robbing him? Under the rubric of the eighth commandment, we have been taking special notice of our use of wealth. In this chapter, I will consider more directly the biblical teachings about wealth and poverty. It has been said that Jesus taught more about the use of money than about any other subject. That judgment depends on how one categorizes various sayings of our Lord, but it does awaken us to an important theme that we may tend to overlook, especially if we are relatively prosperous.

WEALTH

On the whole, Scripture has a favorable attitude toward wealth. Wealth is a covenant blessing, the prosperity promised to those who obey God (Deut. 8:18; 29:9; Josh. 1:7–8; 1 Kings 2:2–3; 2 Chron. 26:5; 31:21; Pss. 1:3; 112:1–3; Mark 10:29–30). Both wealth and poverty come from God (1 Sam. 2:7; Job 1:21), but human effort is one means that God uses to bring financial success (Prov. 10:4).

A number of great saints were wealthy: Abraham (Gen. 13:2), Job, and David are examples. People of means ministered to Jesus (Luke 8:3). Paul says that there were "not many" wealthy in the church, implying that there were some (1 Cor. 1:26).[1] So it is not sinful as such to be wealthy. Nor is it sinful to desire and enjoy God's material blessings. God commanded Israel to feast before him (Deut. 12:6–7, 17–19; 14:22–23; cf. Job 1:1–5). Jesus attended a wedding feast and supplied additional wine (John 2:1–11). He also ate with wealthy people (Luke 7:36–50; 11:37; 14:1, 12). He praised Mary's extravagant homage to him, despite Judas' insincere argument that her gift should have been sold for the poor instead (John 12:4–8). Indeed, as Paul says, in the context of a warning to the wealthy, God "richly provides us with everything to enjoy" (1 Tim. 6:17).

Nevertheless, many Bible passages present wealth as a snare. Sinners tend to be preoccupied with wealth above everything else. Jesus warns us not to lay up treasures on earth, but in heaven (Matt. 6:19–20). He warns against trying to serve both God and money (Matt. 6:24). He tells a parable about a rich fool who put up one barn after another, without considering his eternal soul (Luke 12:13–21), and another about a rich man who goes to Hades and pleads for his family (Luke 16:19–31). After a rich man refuses to give up his wealth to follow Jesus, Jesus remarks, "It is easier for a camel to go through the eye of a needle than for a rich man to enter the kingdom of God" (Matt. 19:24).

Paul says:

> But those who desire to be rich fall into temptation, into a snare, into many senseless and harmful desires that plunge people into ruin and destruction. For the love of money is a root of all kinds of evils. It is through this craving that some have wandered away from the faith and pierced themselves with many pangs. (1 Tim. 6:9–10)

Not money, but the love of money, is a root of all kinds of evil. Similarly, Paul later adds, it is not wrong to have riches, but to set your hopes on them: "As for the rich in this present age, charge them not to be haughty, nor to set their hopes on the uncertainty of riches, but on God, who richly provides us with everything to enjoy" (1 Tim. 6:17).

James condemns in strong terms the sins connected with wealth:

> Come now, you rich, weep and howl for the miseries that are coming upon you. Your riches have rotted and your garments are moth-eaten. Your gold and silver have corroded, and their corrosion will be evidence against you and will eat your flesh like fire. You have

---

1. I am told that the Countess of Huntington, patron of George Whitefield's ministry, gave thanks to God for the letter "m." She rejoiced that Paul said "not *many* noble," rather than "not *any*."

> laid up treasure in the last days. Behold, the wages of the laborers who mowed your fields, which you kept back by fraud, are crying out against you, and the cries of the harvesters have reached the ears of the Lord of hosts. You have lived on the earth in luxury and in self-indulgence. You have fattened your hearts in a day of slaughter. You have condemned; you have murdered the righteous person. He does not resist you. (James 5:1–6)

Jesus does command the young man in Matthew 19 to give up his riches, but this is not the usual biblical remedy for the problem. Evidently Jesus perceived that this particular young man needed to make a clean break with his own idol, that of wealth. But other Scripture passages don't demand renunciation of riches, but rather godly uses of them and attitudes toward them.

The biblical ideal is certainly not that we all become poor. Rather, it is, first, "godliness with contentment" (1 Tim. 6:6). The wisdom teacher recognizes that there are temptations in both wealth and poverty, so he asks God to give him just enough: "Give me neither poverty nor riches; feed me with the food that is needful for me" (Prov. 30:8; compare "our daily bread" as the Christian's request in Matt. 6:11). But if God does give poverty, or riches, we must expect temptation and be ready to deal with it.

Besides urging contentment, Scripture exhorts the rich to be generous. Jesus tells the rich young man not only to give up his wealth, but to give it to the poor (Matt. 19:21). As we shall see, the Old Testament calls Israel in many ways to show generosity to the poor. In the New Testament, some members of the early church were extravagant in their compassionate use of wealth (Acts 2:44–45). As we saw in the last chapter, the fruit of repentance for theft includes giving to others (Eph. 4:28). And Paul is rarely more eloquent than when in 2 Corinthians 8–9 he urges the Corinthian Christians to respond generously to the need of fellow believers in Jerusalem.

POVERTY IN THE COVENANT COMMUNITY

One of the most pervasive teachings of Scripture is that we should care for the poor. We have seen that already in the above discussion. But it will do us good to listen to some other passages of God's Word:

> If among you, one of your brothers should become poor, in any of your towns within your land that the LORD your God is giving you, you shall not harden your heart or shut your hand against your poor brother, but you shall open your hand to him and lend him sufficient for his need, whatever it may be. (Deut. 15:7–8)

Blessed is the one who considers the poor!
  In the day of trouble the LORD delivers him. (Ps. 41:1)

Whoever oppresses a poor man insults his Maker,
  but he who is generous to the needy honors him. (Prov. 14:31)

Whoever is generous to the poor lends to the LORD,
  and he will repay him for his deed. (Prov. 19:17)

Open your mouth, judge righteously,
  defend the rights of the poor and needy. (Prov. 31:9)

Wash yourselves; make yourselves clean;
  remove the evil of your deeds from before my eyes;
cease to do evil,
  learn to do good;
seek justice,
  correct oppression;
bring justice to the fatherless,
  plead the widow's cause. (Isa. 1:16–17)

The LORD has taken his place to contend;
  he stands to judge peoples.
The LORD will enter into judgment
  with the elders and princes of his people:
"It is you who have devoured the vineyard,
  the spoil of the poor is in your houses.
What do you mean by crushing my people,
  by grinding the face of the poor?"
  declares the Lord GOD of hosts. (Isa. 3:13–15)

Woe to those who decree iniquitous decrees,
  and the writers who keep writing oppression,
to turn aside the needy from justice
  and to rob the poor of my people of their right,
that widows may be their spoil,
  and that they may make the fatherless their prey! (Isa. 10:1–2)

There shall come forth a shoot from the stump of Jesse,
  and a branch from his roots shall bear fruit.
And the Spirit of the LORD shall rest upon him,
    the Spirit of wisdom and understanding,
    the Spirit of counsel and might,
    the Spirit of knowledge and the fear of the LORD.

And his delight shall be in the fear of the LORD.
He shall not judge by what his eyes see,
    or decide disputes by what his ears hear,
but with righteousness he shall judge the poor,
    and decide with equity for the meek of the earth;
and he shall strike the earth with the rod of his mouth,
    and with the breath of his lips he shall kill the wicked. (Isa.
        11:1–4)

Is not this the fast that I choose:
    to loose the bonds of wickedness,
    to undo the straps of the yoke,
to let the oppressed go free,
    and to break every yoke?
Is it not to share your bread with the hungry
    and bring the homeless poor into your house;
when you see the naked, to cover him,
    and not to hide yourself from your own flesh?
Then shall your light break forth like the dawn
    and your healing shall spring up speedily;
your righteousness shall go before you;
    the glory of the LORD shall be your rear guard.
Then you shall call, and the LORD will answer;
    you shall cry, and he will say, "Here I am."
If you take away the yoke from your midst,
    the pointing of the finger, and speaking wickedness,
if you pour yourself out for the hungry
    and satisfy the desire of the afflicted,
then shall your light rise in the darkness
    and your gloom be as the noonday.
And the LORD will guide you continually
    and satisfy your desire in scorched places
    and make your bones strong;
and you shall be like a watered garden,
    like a spring of water,
    whose waters do not fail.
And your ancient ruins shall be rebuilt;
    you shall raise up the foundations of many generations;
you shall be called the repairer of the breach,
    the restorer of streets to dwell in. (Isa. 58:6–12)

A concordance study of *poor, needy, widow, orphan, oppress*, and related words will reveal that the passages quoted above are only the tip of a great iceberg. The Scriptures are full of exhortations to God's people to care for the poor, to show compassion to them. For another example, one thing that Job and his friends agree upon, despite their general dispute, is that a man's righteousness is defined by his treatment of the poor (Job 5:15–16; 20:10, 19; 24:4, 9, 14; 29:12, 16; 30:25; 31:16, 19; 34:28). The Psalms are full of references to God's saving the poor from wicked oppressors (Pss. 9:18; 10:9–14; 12:5; 14:6; 34:6; 35:10; 37:14–15; etc.). And this is one of the chief concerns of the prophets as they bring God's covenant lawsuit against Israel (in the above texts and many more).

I mentioned earlier the teaching of Jesus, Paul, and James that wealth brings temptation to sin. The temptation is not to have compassion for the poor. Jesus asks the rich young man in Matthew 19 not only to give away his wealth, but to give it to the poor. The rich man who goes to Hades in Luke 16 is there, not because he was wealthy, but because he showed no compassion for poor Lazarus (vv. 20–21).[2] When the disciples appointed Paul and Barnabas as missionaries to the Gentiles, they laid upon them one condition: "Only, they asked us to remember the poor, the very thing I was eager to do" (Gal. 2:10), a condition that Paul fulfilled as he requested contributions from newly planted churches for the saints in Jerusalem (2 Cor. 8–9). And in the midst of James's strong condemnation of the rich, quoted in the last section, we see the substance of their sin: "Behold, the wages of the laborers who mowed your fields, which you kept back by fraud, are crying out against you, and the cries of the harvesters have reached the ears of the Lord of hosts" (James 5:4). Their sin is not that they are rich, but that they have gotten their riches by oppressing the poor. Earlier, James includes the care of the poor in his definition of true religion: "If anyone thinks he is religious and does not bridle his tongue but deceives his heart, this person's religion is worthless. Religion that is pure and undefiled before God and the Father is this: to visit orphans and widows in their affliction, and to keep oneself unstained from the world" (James 1:26–27).

In considering this matter, these words of Jesus should constantly ring in our ears:

> When the Son of Man comes in his glory, and all the angels with him, then he will sit on his glorious throne. Before him will be gathered all the nations, and he will separate people one from another as a shepherd separates the sheep from the goats. And he

---

2. The text doesn't say this explicitly, but it seems to me to be implicit in the structure of the narrative. Note especially verse 25.

will place the sheep on his right, but the goats on the left. Then the King will say to those on his right, "Come, you who are blessed by my Father, inherit the kingdom prepared for you from the foundation of the world. For I was hungry and you gave me food, I was thirsty and you gave me drink, I was a stranger and you welcomed me, I was naked and you clothed me, I was sick and you visited me, I was in prison and you came to me." Then the righteous will answer him, saying, "Lord, when did we see you hungry and feed you, or thirsty and give you drink? And when did we see you a stranger and welcome you, or naked and clothe you? And when did we see you sick or in prison and visit you?" And the King will answer them, "Truly, I say to you, as you did it to one of the least of these my brothers, you did it to me."

Then he will say to those on his left, "Depart from me, you cursed, into the eternal fire prepared for the devil and his angels. For I was hungry and you gave me no food, I was thirsty and you gave me no drink, I was a stranger and you did not welcome me, naked and you did not clothe me, sick and in prison and you did not visit me." Then they also will answer, saying, "Lord, when did we see you hungry or thirsty or a stranger or naked or sick or in prison, and did not minister to you?" Then he will answer them, saying, "Truly, I say to you, as you did not do it to one of the least of these, you did not do it to me." And these will go away into eternal punishment, but the righteous into eternal life. (Matt. 25:31–46)

To minister to a poor Christian[3] is to minister to Jesus himself. And ministering to poor believers here determines our eternal reward or punishment.[4]

Who are the poor in Scripture? We should not have to ask that question, but people sometimes do. They are first of all the ones who have few resources. People do sometimes get into this condition because of their own laziness. Scripture does recognize laziness as a problem: we have seen condemnations of it in Proverbs and 2 Thessalonians 3:6–12, for example. But it is interesting that Scripture does not describe lazy people as "poor." Rather, they are "sluggards" or "busybodies." Biblical exhortations to com-

---

3. The reference to "my brothers" in verse 40 indicates that Jesus is speaking of the poor within the body of Christ. As we shall see, however, Christians also have a responsibility to the poor outside the church.

4. Of course, the reward is by grace (chapter 12). But those who receive saving grace also receive the grace of loving others.

passion don't apply to sluggards, except in the general sense that we should be compassionate to everybody. That is to say, compassion, as in the case of the Good Samaritan (Luke 10:25–37), does not wait for a detailed account of the reasons for someone's distress. But there is a special compassion that we should express to the truly poor, not to sluggards.

The "poor" in Scripture are not poor because they are lazy, but because of circumstances to some extent beyond their control. Most often, they are poor because they have been oppressed by the rich and powerful. This economic deprivation then leads to hunger, health crises, and even homelessness. The disabled are often poor.[5] The most common examples of poor people in Scripture are orphans and widows. They often have no reliable income and nobody to speak for them against oppressors.

This last fact adds a theological dimension to poverty. Since the poor have no advocate, they often turn to God. They join the remnant of faithful people who trust God despite the general unbelief and idolatry around them. Indeed, in this way poverty often becomes a metaphor for faithfulness. Even King David, who had plenty of financial resources, could say, when under attack, "As for me, I am poor and needy, but the Lord takes thought for me" (Ps. 40:17; cf. Pss. 70:5; 86:1; 109:22). Although he had money, he realized that his enemies were far too powerful to be bought off. Only the Lord could save him. In this respect, there was no difference between David and the lowliest peasant. So David claimed God's promise to the poor. I suspect that this is related to Jesus' beatitude, "Blessed are the poor in spirit, for theirs is the kingdom of heaven" (Matt. 5:3).[6]

In this sense, it is true that "God is on the side of the poor." However, that slogan has sometimes been misused by theologians of liberation and others. Certainly it should not be taken to mean that God is against the rich merely because they are rich, or that he favors the poor simply because they are poor. The larger context is crucial. God sides with the poor when they are *unjustly* poor, that is, oppressed. He sides with them because they have a just case, but are unable to make their argument through human channels.

It is in this sense that we should equate compassion for the poor with justice. It is wrong to say that justice requires an equal distribution of resources as such. It does not. But when the rich oppress the poor, to defend the poor against them is simple justice. Insofar as human courts can improve the situation, they are not, then, to be biased in favor of the poor. Rather,

---

5. Cf. my discussion of the disabled in chapter 34.

6. The parallel in Luke 6:20 says simply, "Blessed are you who are poor, for yours is the kingdom of God." The formulation in Matthew makes more explicit that Jesus intends also to commend metaphorical poverty, faithfulness to God in the midst of oppression.

they should be biased neither for the rich nor for the poor. Judges should make their decisions according to God's justice. Exodus 23:2–3 presents the balance: "You shall not fall in with the many to do evil, nor shall you bear witness in a lawsuit, siding with the many, so as to pervert justice, nor shall you be partial to a poor man in his lawsuit." Similarly, Leviticus 19:15 says, "You shall do no injustice in court. You shall not be partial to the poor or defer to the great, but in righteousness shall you judge your neighbor."

The courts should not be biased in favor of either rich or poor (or, as in Ex. 23:2, in favor of an oppressive majority). A truly unbiased judicial system, however, is the best ally of the poor. The poor of society are unfairly treated more often than the rich, as the prophets indicate. A court system that welcomes their petitions on an equal basis is one of the most powerful tools that society has to remedy this injustice. But if courts are biased in favor of the poor, they lose credibility and power, as well as justice.

So one way that society can show compassion to the poor is through a just legal system. But this is only the beginning of the ways in which Scripture exhorts us to care for the poor. Some of the other biblical provisions are as follows:

The family. The family was then, and today remains, the first and most solid defense against poverty. In Israel, it was understood that parents would provide for their children, that children would provide for parents in their old age, and that parents would leave an inheritance for their children (see chapter 31). Had Israel observed the Jubilee year (Lev. 25:8–17), that would have provided a periodic restoration of family holdings that were sold to avoid poverty.[7] In Israel, this pattern was not compromised by income or estate taxes. In modern society, the breakdown of the family through illegitimacy and divorce is one of the major causes of poverty. Nothing can do more to alleviate the problem than the restoration of a biblical family structure.

The seventh-year release. In the Sabbatical year, debts were remitted, so that everyone got a new economic start:

> At the end of every seven years you shall grant a release. And this is the manner of the release: every creditor shall release what he has lent to his neighbor. He shall not exact it of his neighbor, his brother, because the LORD's release has been proclaimed. Of

7. I argued in chapter 30 that the Jubilee does not carry over into the new covenant. But it is an example of Scripture's larger understanding that the family is the chief guardian of wealth.

a foreigner you may exact it, but whatever of yours is with your brother your hand shall release. (Deut. 15:1–3)

Christians today are not required to follow Israel's calendar of sabbatical years, but it is good to keep debt agreements to relatively short-term levels and to forgive debts that threaten to destroy a person's financial solvency. Bankruptcy laws have the intent of carrying out this principle, though, to be sure, it is easy for people to abuse them. It is significant that following this passage the Lord says, "But there will be no poor among you" (v. 4).

The kinsman-redeemer. Leviticus 25:25 says, "If your brother becomes poor and sells part of his property, then his nearest redeemer shall come and redeem what his brother has sold." This provision is in addition to the Jubilee legislation and shows again how central is the family as the biblical remedy for poverty. In the book of Ruth, Boaz becomes her kinsman-redeemer, when another man refuses the obligation. The word translated "redeem" here, *ga'al*, is also used in passages describing Yahweh as the Redeemer (for example, Isa. 44:23; 48:20; 49:7; 52:9). This is the background of the New Testament concept of redemption in Christ. So New Testament believers have often seen in the kinsman-redeemer an anticipation of Christ.

Tithes. As I mentioned in chapter 41, a major portion of the tithe went to meet the needs of the poor. Here we see how the extended family of Israel helps to meet needs that individual families cannot meet. Although the tithe may not be literally binding upon the New Testament church, I argued that it is at least a starting point for responsible giving. Most Christians today fall lamentably short of this starting point. If all Christians tithed, I doubt that any material needs within the body of Christ would be unmet.[8]

Interest-free charitable loans. "If among you, one of your brothers should become poor, in any of your towns within your land that the LORD your God is giving you, you shall not harden your heart or shut your hand against your poor brother, but you shall open your hand to him and lend him sufficient for his need, whatever it may be" (Deut. 15:7–8). God's people should be generous to those poor who request loan assistance. Leviticus 25:35–37 adds that the lender should not require interest or seek any profit from the transaction. This provision has led to a continuing discussion of "usury"

8. In the Mormon sect, which I regard as a cult, tithing is mandatory. However reluctantly, one cannot help but admire the achievements of this organization in providing ministries of mercy to their own people.

among Christian ethicists, but it is obvious that these passages are not forbidding interest or profit in general. These passages pertain to charitable loans, not commercial or housing loans. As I see it, there is nothing about this provision that would limit it to the old covenant. Rather, Christian believers, too, should be openhanded in providing loans to the poor.

Gleaning. In Leviticus 19:10 and 23:22, the law requires a limitation on the harvest for the sake of the poor. Landowners are not to harvest their crops to the very edge of the field, but are to leave some for the poor to gather for themselves. Gleaning is hard work, harder than a regular harvest in which the produce is easier to reach. But it is a means for people to escape the extremes of poverty. We recall that Ruth gleaned in the fields of Boaz to support herself and her mother-in-law Naomi (Ruth 2:2). So the gleaning provision preserved her to be the great-grandmother of King David and an ancestor of Jesus Christ. In a related statute, Exodus 23:11 provides that in the sabbatical year, when the fields should lie fallow, all may eat of what grows by itself, "that the poor of your people may eat; and what they leave the beasts of the field may eat."

It is hard to relate these statutes to modern societies, in which agriculture plays a smaller role. But this principle suggests that part of the products of industry should go to the poor, and also that it is a good thing to ask the poor to work for it when possible. Many grocery stores and restaurants offer food to organizations that feed the poor. Rushdoony mentions Goodwill Industries as an even closer modern parallel to ancient gleaning, since the actual work of restoring the donated items is often done by people who are in need.[9] One could also mention the Salvation Army and other similar organizations. An especially significant parallel is Habitat for Humanity, which asks poor people to help build houses for others in the hope that eventually others will build a house for them. These organizations deserve the support of Christian believers.

Penology. When people in Israel were unable to pay financial obligations, they were often sold into a kind of slavery that I discussed in some detail in chapter 34. This "Hebrew slavery" was very different from other forms of slavery, such as slavery in the American South. It was in fact a kind of household apprenticeship, where offenders, for a period not exceeding six years, learned habits of discipline and ways of making a living. Like others we have noted, this was a family-centered remedy: in this case, a family virtually adopted the servant for a time, and he learned

9. Rousas J. Rushdoony, *The Institutes of Biblical Law* (Nutley, NJ: Craig Press, 1973), 249.

the kind of disciplines that are best learned in a good family environment. This element of Israelite law, together with the absence of imprisonment as a penalty, worked to make people productive, law-abiding members of society. I suggested in the earlier chapter how this institution might instruct us today.

The work ethic. I said in chapter 41 that the eighth commandment presupposes a work ethic. "If anyone is not willing to work, let him not eat" (2 Thess. 3:10). When a society stresses this principle, it motivates people to take responsibility for their financial situation. The revision of welfare legislation under the Clinton administration in the U.S. sent a large number of welfare recipients into the work force. In my judgment, that was largely a good thing, although I believe there should not have been pressure on single mothers to leave the care of their children. Child care is as useful as any other kind of work, and it deserves the support of society. The problem, however, is that support of child care can encourage illegitimate births—which was itself a major factor contributing to the welfare crisis. I believe, nevertheless, that mothers should have been encouraged to stay with their children, and at the same time to perform tasks at home that provide an income for their families.

Financial wisdom. Jesus' words about counting the cost of building a tower (Luke 14:28) are among the biblical statements of economic wisdom, although he uses this admonition to make a larger point (cf. Prov. 24:27). Teaching such wisdom to our children is one way to keep them out of poverty.

Massive sharing. As we have seen, the New Testament urges on us a generous spirit, almost heedless of consequence. Recall the moral heroism of the poor widow who put all she had into the temple treasury (Mark 12:42–44). Recall also Paul's reference to "cheerful" giving (2 Cor. 9:7). Care for the poor was at the heart of the Christian ethic. John asks, "But if anyone has the world's goods and sees his brother in need, yet closes his heart against him, how does God's love abide in him?" (1 John 3:17).

The most startling example is the attitude of the Christians described in the early chapters of Acts:

> And all who believed were together and had all things in common. And they were selling their possessions and belongings and distributing the proceeds to all, as any had need. (Acts 2:44–45)

> Now the full number of those who believed were of one heart and soul, and no one said that any of the things that belonged to him was his own, but they had everything in common. (Acts 4:32)

> There was not a needy person among them, for as many as were owners of lands or houses sold them and brought the proceeds of what was sold and laid it at the apostles' feet, and it was distributed to each as any had need. Thus Joseph, who was also called by the apostles Barnabas (which means son of encouragement), a Levite, a native of Cyprus, sold a field that belonged to him and brought the money and laid it at the apostles' feet. (Acts 4:34–37)

This is not, of course, a warrant for Marxist communism, for it has nothing to do with state ownership of the means of production. Nor does it conflict with the doctrine of private property implicit in the eighth commandment. In Acts 4:32, the phrase "they had everything in common" must be balanced by the phrase "the things that belonged to him." Possessions still belonged to individuals and families until they were given away. Peter makes that plain when he deals with Ananias and Sapphira, who lied to the church and the Holy Spirit about how much they had given: "While it remained unsold, did it not remain your own? And after it was sold, was it not at your disposal? Why is it that you have contrived this deed in your heart? You have not lied to men but to God" (Acts 5:4). Ananias and Sapphira genuinely owned their land. Their sin was not in failing to give it all to the church, but rather in lying about it. Nevertheless, as a body, the believers were so generous that for practical purposes there was indeed common ownership of property. When a need arose, nobody *said that his property was his own.*

Hospitality. Part of massive sharing is hospitality (Rom. 12:13; 1 Tim. 3:2; Titus 1:8; 1 Peter 4:9). Hospitality is opening one's home to others. The essence of it is not entertainment, as in modern society, but a willingness to let others live with us for a time as needed. So the natural recipients of hospitality are the poor, as well as Christian travelers. Hospitality in this sense is one of the character traits required for the eldership in Timothy and Titus, and John identifies a troublemaker in the church by his refusal to exercise it:

> I have written something to the church, but Diotrephes, who likes to put himself first, does not acknowledge our authority. So if I come, I will bring up what he is doing, talking wicked nonsense against us. And not content with that, he refuses to welcome the

brothers, and also stops those who want to and puts them out of the church. (3 John 9–10)

One should not open one's home to false teachers (2 John 10), but one should be openhanded to those who travel to carry the message of the gospel.

The result of the church's massive sharing was that "there was not a needy person among them" (Acts 4:34). We are reminded of God's promise to Israel that "there will be no poor among you" (Deut. 15:4). The generosity of these new covenant Christians fulfilled, for a while, the promise of Deuteronomy. In the Old Testament, God's promise to abolish poverty was conditional: "But there will be no poor among you; for the LORD will bless you in the land that the LORD your God is giving you for an inheritance to possess—if only you will strictly obey the voice of the LORD your God, being careful to do all this commandment that I command you today" (vv. 4–5).

Israel did not meet those conditions, as the prophets make plain. God anticipated Israel's failure, and in verse 11 he said "there will never cease to be poor in the land." The same, alas, is true also of the new covenant community (Matt. 26:11). But when God's people, by his grace, rise to the occasion of serving their brothers and sisters, poverty in the church can be eliminated.

WORLD POVERTY

So far I have discussed the issue of poverty primarily within the Christian community. Do Christians also have a responsibility to alleviate poverty in the world at large? Paul in Galatians 6:10 gives us general direction: "So then, as we have opportunity, let us do good to everyone, and especially to those who are of the household of faith." Notice that "the household of faith" has priority. As we have seen, caring for our immediate family is the top priority, then caring for our extended family, the church. But far from ruling out giving to unbelievers, Paul urges us to do good to them as well, "as we have opportunity." He presupposes that many Christians will be so blessed by the Lord that even after supporting their families and the needs of the church they will still have resources to help people outside the church.

In terms of this verse, we would not expect our giving to unbelieving people to be as lavish as our giving to fellow believers. But "as we have opportunity," we should give to everyone in need.

The parable of the good Samaritan in Luke 10:25–37 describes such an opportunity. The Samaritan meets a man left "half dead" by robbers (v. 30). He does what he can to care for the victim. He imposes no creedal test, and he is limited by no ethnic bias. He simply acts as a neighbor.

So Christians should try to help any needy person who enters their lives in such a way. They should try to meet those needs from their own resources, or from those of the church.

Beyond the nuclear family and the extended family of Christ, there is also the family of Adam (which I discussed in chapter 32). Christians are members both of the family of Christ and of the family of Adam. Our responsibilities to the family of Christ take precedence, but they don't exclude responsibilities to the family of Adam.

But a problem emerges here. It is one thing to meet the needs of someone we encounter on the road. But today we have become aware of the vast needs of people all over the world. Books like Ronald Sider's *Rich Christians in an Age of Hunger*[10] display the terrible statistics: millions of people don't have enough calories to live, die of preventable diseases, or live on only a few hundred dollars a year.[11] Eliminating hunger in the Christian community seems, given the biblical principles, a practical possibility. But eliminating world poverty may appear virtually impossible.

Well, the individual Christian is not commissioned to eliminate world poverty! But we should do what we can, both as individuals and as communities. It is not easy to know what to do, because the causes of world poverty are complex. Some attempts to analyze the reasons for poverty are as follows:

Unequal distribution of natural resources. Certainly resources are divided unequally. But some nations that are relatively poor in natural resources are among the wealthiest, like Japan, Taiwan, and Germany, which import nearly all of their oil.

Population density. Population growth has been cited as a reason for poverty, but many of the more densely populated countries are comparatively rich, such as Japan and the urban areas of the U.S. As I indicated in chapter 40, overpopulation is a much-abused term, since many regard human beings

10. Nashville: World Publishing, 1997.

11. Sider and others also include statistics about the disparity between Western incomes and those of the poor of other nations. While that disparity gives us pause, I don't think that it places the same burden on us as the other statistics I mentioned. We don't have a biblical mandate, in my judgment, to "narrow the gap between rich and poor," as an end in itself. We do, however, have a mandate to feed hungry people.

only as consumers, rather than also as producers of wealth. An increase in the number of productive, motivated, compassionate citizens would be a great help to alleviating poverty anywhere.

Ethical and religious failure. It may be that in some parts of the world there is a failure to recognize the importance of work. In general, however, it seems to me that in the poorest parts of the world people work very hard indeed, or at least are willing to work hard when given the opportunity. One related problem, however, is that in many cultures people are not taught to save for the future, to educate themselves and their children for higher income, or to provide an inheritance for their children.[12] They are content to work for daily subsistence. Here religion plays a role. The Bible has taught people in the West a "future orientation," a concern for later generations. Other religions often fail to do that. For example, Buddhism teaches people to seek annihilation, Hinduism has an inflexible caste system, and Islam often seeks to impose the limitations of seventh-century culture on modern people.

Consumption by the rich nations. People sometimes argue that the rich nations are to blame for the poverty of the rest of the world. The case has been made, for example, that the large U.S. consumption of beef raises grain prices in the rest of the world. But if Americans were to stop eating beef, the result would be less production of grain or larger surpluses. It is not clear that the price of grain for people in Africa would be lower.

Others have claimed that multinational corporations take advantage of third world nations by hiring cheap labor there. But what are the alternatives? (1) If these corporations left the third world, that would only contribute to unemployment. (2) If they stayed and paid higher wages, that would result in higher prices, which the third world, as well as the rest of the world, would have to pay. (3) If they provided goods at lower cost to the third world, that would discourage local production and create a situation of permanent dependence. (4) If they gave food for work (Sider's suggestion), that would limit the economic freedom of the workers. A monetary wage gives the means to buy other things. If their work is profitable for the company, workers should earn enough to buy food; if it is not profitable, then that kind of industry should be discouraged.

12. Liberal economist John Kenneth Galbraith, in *The Nature of Mass Poverty* (Cambridge, MA: Harvard University Press, 1979), says that the main problem in poor nations is *accommodation* to poverty, the perception of the people that nothing can be done about it and that they should resign themselves to a destitute future.

In general, there is no reason to suppose that wealth in one part of the world creates poverty elsewhere, at least in any simplistic sense. America's success has not prevented Taiwan or Korea from being successful, or vice versa. Economic prosperity is not a zero-sum game.

Bad government. Certainly bad government policies contribute to poverty within their countries. That includes fraud, corruption, tariffs, resistance to outside investment, restricting dissemination of information, political authoritarianism, socialism, and other ideologies. But some nations, such as China, have developed strong economies despite political repression.

In my judgment, there is no quick or easy answer to the problems of world poverty. All of the above factors and others should be considered further; my analysis is far from final, or even thorough. But since Scripture promises relative prosperity to those who obey the Lord, and since much of the prosperity of Europe and America comes from the influence of the gospel, I would say that the best thing we can do for the third world is to bring the gospel of Jesus Christ to them.

What can be done in the short term? Certainly the church should take the lead in ministering to people in the midst of famine and natural disaster. We should take the lead in ministering to "the poorest of the poor," who can find help nowhere else. We should engage in gospel-centered mercy ministries that not only meet immediate needs but also teach academic skills, profitable trades, and more productive means of agriculture. We should create communities in the poorest parts of the world to demonstrate how Christ makes a difference in family and church life. And we should encourage government policies that allow other nations to trade and compete with ours on an equal basis.

The mention of government raises the more general issue of its role in dealing with poverty. I believe, and will argue later, that government has no mandate to control a nation's economy, and that in general a free enterprise system, unencumbered by government, provides the best engine for producing jobs, which are in turn the best means for getting people out of poverty. So I tend to be skeptical of government welfare programs, to say nothing of "wars on poverty." At the same time, rulers, like all people, should have a deep concern for the poor. We have seen, for example, that Scripture urges courts are to be fair, not biased toward either rich or poor. Their neutrality in fact generally brings benefit to the poor. Civil rulers have a special responsibility to call the oppressors of the poor to account. So Daniel says to King Nebuchadnezzar, "Therefore, O king, let my counsel be acceptable to you: break off your sins by practicing righteousness, and your iniquities by showing mercy to the oppressed, that there may perhaps be a lengthening of your prosperity" (Dan. 4:27).

Rulers are tempted to show favoritism to their rich cronies at the expense of the poor. God, through Daniel, tells the king to show mercy instead. This is not a mandate for government welfare, but an exhortation to deal judicially with those who oppress the poor.[13]

I do not believe, however, that we should oppose government welfare in all circumstances. The state is the government of the family of Adam, just as the institutional church is the government of the family of Christ (see chapter 32). Families take care of their own. In general, I think that capitalism is the best system of economic organization for both rich and poor. But capitalism does not guarantee that all will succeed. People "fall through the cracks." Some cannot make it on their own, and churches often turn a blind eye. For such, often the poorest of the poor, there is a place for government support. But that support should be light-handed. It should, when possible, prepare recipients and their children to earn their own living. It should encourage them to find work when they are able. It should turn their care over to families and religious bodies whenever possible. It should not seek to monopolize or dominate the nation's care-giving system, or place barriers in the way of others who have resources to help. It should revise the tax system to strengthen the family, to encourage rather than discourage inheritance.

ECONOMIC SYSTEMS

To enlarge on these remarks about government welfare, I will say a bit more about socialism and capitalism as systems of economic organization. Since the eighth commandment presupposes private ownership of property,

---

13. Meredith Kline argues for a still larger role for the king in providing welfare, based on a comparison between divine and human kingship. The psalms that emphasize God's kingly role, he observes, often present him as "father of the fatherless, intervening in behalf of those bereft of paternal support; who upholds and provides justice for the widow, gives food to the hungry and preserves the sojourner; who is the helper of the helpless (cf., e.g., Pss. 10:14, 16; 27:10; 68:5, 6; 146:7–10; cf. Ps. 72)" (*Kingdom Prologue* [privately printed, 1991], 108). Kline's application to human kingship and civil government is something of a stretch in my view. God's kingship differs from human civil rule in that God's is (rightly) totalitarian. He rules family and church as well as state. So his rule is comprehensive, unlike any human institution. Human rulers do not have such power, and their authority is limited by other institutions, such as family and church. So it is not obvious from these Scripture texts that human rulers must emulate God's work of feeding the hungry, though as we have seen it is certainly the function of government to provide justice for the widow. Nevertheless, I do agree with Kline that Scripture doesn't forbid a state role in welfare. However, I think it should be a last resort. It is dangerous for a civil ruler to try to emulate God's comprehensive role as authority and provider.

it rejects systems of economics that deny that principle. Marxism, in particular, argues that property belongs to the nation as a whole, represented by the state. Therefore, on that view, the state has the right to control all means of production, all products, and all wealth. In other words, the state should control the whole economy. In effect, then, for Marxism, the state replaces God as the ultimate owner and controller of the world. This view falls under the biblical description of idolatry.

We have seen in recent years the collapse of the Soviet Union, a huge experiment in Marxian communism. China remains totalitarian as of this writing, but its economy has become less and less socialist over the last few decades and more open to individual enterprise. The remaining Marxist strongholds of Cuba and North Korea are impoverished. So the pragmatic argument for Marxism is no longer credible. Nor is the moral argument, that socialism brings people out of poverty.[14] Capitalist economies in the West have been far more efficient at alleviating poverty, though that task is not over by any means.

Further, when the Soviet Union collapsed, the rest of the world breathed a sigh of relief. For socialism has an inner drive toward world conquest. Since the economies of nations are interdependent, a state cannot fully control its own economy without controlling the economy of the whole world. Another way to say this is that once the state replaces God as the owner and controller of the world, the deity of the state must be expressed universally, just like God. So the state becomes omnipresent, as well as omnipotent, omniscient, and omnibenevolent.

The main ethical argument for socialism is that it is more compassionate than capitalism.[15] Short-term gains in equality do sometimes result from socialism. Literacy has increased in Cuba, but Cuba was the most literate nation in Latin America before communism, and it is not clear how much of the advance is due to socialism. Socialist states have decreased the gap between rich and poor, but more by impoverishing the rich than by enriching the poor.[16] But selfishness abounds in socialist states as much as in capitalist. The main difference is that in socialism the way to accumulate benefits is political rather than entrepreneurial: by supporting the policies of the governing party. There is no reason to suppose that politicians are any less selfish than entrepreneurs.

14. I would remind the reader of my earlier critique of Marx in chapter 6, to the effect that his ethics are actually relativist. Marxists who follow their mentor in this respect, therefore, have no basis for making an ethical argument for their position.

15. But the point of the previous footnote applies here as well.

16. And before we praise socialism for its compassion, let us not forget the millions of people who have been murdered because they resisted, or even disagreed with, socialist doctrine.

Capitalism is often said to be built on selfishness, and there is truth in that statement. But there is also a moral case for capitalism, as developed in recent years by such writers as Michael Novak and George Gilder.[17] A successful entrepreneur is one who discerns a need or want among people and seeks to fill that need.[18] So there is an altruistic spirit that accompanies the selfish desire for profit. One cannot say, surely, that capitalism is purely altruistic, but neither can one say that it is purely selfish. And of course individual entrepreneurs are usually better able to determine the material needs of fellow citizens than are government economic planners. So whatever the motives of entrepreneurs and companies, a capitalist system is more efficient at supplying needed goods.

The Bible does not directly address the question of how a society should organize its economy. As we have seen, it does affirm private property and the principle that one should meet his own needs and his family's through work. When it deals with civil government, it presents it as limited, both by divine sovereignty and by other institutions. The Bible's doctrine of divine sovereignty rejects totalitarianism. But among nontotalitarian systems, the Bible leaves various options open to us. Our choice among these should, however, take larger biblical values into consideration.

I tend to vote for conservative candidates, because conservatives tend to have more respect for Christianity than do liberals. And I honestly believe that free enterprise is better for the poor, on the whole, than is a government management of human welfare. In the last section, however, I argued that government welfare is not wrong in all situations, and in some cases at least can be defended. So I do not believe that government involvement in welfare is wrong per se. And if I believed that a liberal government program would improve the condition of the poor, that would go a long way toward persuading me to vote accordingly. The issue is empirical and pragmatic more than specifically theological: does a particular political program seem likely to help the poor? If that program is in accord with a generally biblical view of the scope of government, then it may well deserve the support of Christian voters.[19]

17. George F. Gilder, *Wealth and Poverty* (New York: Basic Books, 1981). A distinctively Christian argument along the same line is Ronald H. Nash, *Poverty and Wealth* (Westchester, IL: Crossway Books, 1986). See also John Jefferson Davis, *Your Wealth in God's World* (Phillipsburg, NJ: P&R Publishing, 1994).

18. We must, of course, grant that often entrepreneurs *create* needs and wants for their own advancement.

19. In general, single-issue voting is a bad thing. We should weigh all the programs and policies of parties and candidates before deciding whom to vote for. But some issues are so serious that they dominate all others. For me, abortion is such an issue, and it is one issue that keeps me voting on the conservative side. But from a biblical standpoint, the care of the poor is nearly as important. I think it is somewhat less important than abortion, because

Pundits and politicians, even Christian writers, often assume that anyone who cares for the poor will vote liberal. I do not believe that argument is fair.[20] But the issue is important, perhaps one of the most important. We should not equate the Scriptures with any political program. But as Christians determine who to vote for, the issue of poverty should be one of their central concerns.[21]

HOMELESSNESS

There are a great many individual issues under the general heading of poverty. I've chosen to end the chapter by mentioning one of them. Homelessness is poverty at its worst. I do not believe that Christians should be concerned about poverty as a mere "gap between rich and poor." Rather, Christians should be concerned when people don't have the essentials of life: food, clothing, housing, health care. We discussed world hunger earlier. Health care is somewhat relative to culture. Nakedness is not a world problem. But homelessness is a major concern.

There are different causes of homelessness. Some are homeless by choice, and that fact must not be overlooked. This choice may be a perfectly rational one. One student who attended seminary in California during an August term years ago decided to live in his car while he was there. With the money he saved on rent, he joined a health club, where he had a locker for some belongings and facilities for bathing and so on.

---

abortion is literally a matter of life and death. As I indicated in chapter 37, unborn children are the most helpless of citizens, what we may now call the poorest of the poor. And they are being killed, not merely oppressed or neglected. (We recall that Mother Teresa not only championed care for the poorest, but also—to the distress of some of her supporters—care for the unborn. These concerns proceeded from the same ethical impulse.) But we must also be concerned about those who have survived into infancy and have remained poor.

20. In the 2004 U.S. election campaign, only John Edwards, the Democratic vice presidential candidate, addressed the issue of poverty. All the other candidates appealed to the "middle class" and avoided like the plague any reference to the needs of the poor. The reason is obvious: the middle class is a far more potent electoral bloc than the poor, and the middle class tends to be suspicious of anyone who seeks improvement in the condition of the poor. I did not vote for John Edwards, or support his particular policies. But I pray that future generations of Christian "compassionate conservatives" will come to have *priorities* more like those of Edwards than like those of the other candidates.

21. For analyses and strategies for fighting poverty within a framework of biblical Christianity and free enterprise economics, see E. Calvin Beisner, *Prosperity and Poverty* (Westchester, IL: Crossway Books, 1988); David Hall, ed., *Welfare Reformed* (Phillipsburg, NJ: P&R Publishing, 1994); Marvin Olasky, *The Tragedy of American Compassion* (Washington: Regnery, 1992); George Grant, *In the Shadow of Plenty* (Ft. Worth: Dominion Press, 1986); id., *Bringing in the Sheaves* (Brentwood, TN: Wolgemuth and Hyatt, 1988); id., *The Dispossessed* (Westchester, IL: Crossway Books, 1986).

Others are homeless for equally rational, but less admirable reasons. My wife and I invited four otherwise homeless people to stay with us for a while several years ago. All of them could have had homes elsewhere, had they been willing to live a "straight life." They had preferred to get into drugs and other illegal things, and therefore could not return to their families. Now they were trying to turn their lives around with the help of God, and we were led to help them do this. I do believe that many of the homeless are homeless because they have rejected the values of families and others who care for them.

Another cause of homelessness is government policy. Rent control laws have, ironically, caused a shortage of housing in many places. Such laws discourage new rental housing and drive up the cost of home ownership. Other laws similarly affecting the housing market are zoning regulations, environmental and appearance regulations, and other building codes. Whether or not these laws promote valid social goals, they do adversely affect the housing market, and Christians should take an interest in such things as part of their concern for the homeless.

Another cause of homelessness is poverty, which, as we have seen, has many causes, governmental and otherwise. George Grant's books offer some valuable suggestions for churches that seek to make an impact on the problem at this level. Work, training, and evangelization can have a large impact here. The traditional rescue mission has a legitimate place, and I certainly applaud the compassion and courage of such ministries over many decades. But organizations are most helpful when they offer job training, counseling, and accountability to homeless people who are converted, with the goal of a comprehensive change in lifestyle. Churches themselves can carry on this sort of ministry up to a point, but there is a need for cooperative efforts among churches to deal with the magnitude of the problem today.

Finally, many who live on the streets are mentally ill.[22] For years, the majority of the mentally ill were institutionalized. Eventually, this practice ended, condemned as unjust imprisonment. Unfortunately, however, many people with psychological afflictions were simply dumped on the streets without any continuing treatment or supervision. These people have a major claim on the compassion of families, churches, and, in the last resort, government.

---

22. I use this phrase, aware of the objections advanced against it by those in the nouthetic counseling community (with whom I usually agree). I use it, however, mainly to include conditions like schizophrenia and bipolar disorder, which most nouthetic counselors agree can be treated in some degree by medical science. "Mental illness" is the most common way of labeling such afflictions.

CHAPTER 43

The Ninth Commandment:
Truthfulness

The ninth commandment is a bit longer than the previous three: "You shall not bear false witness against your neighbor" (Ex. 20:16).[1] As it is usually taught, we might have expected it to read simply, "You shall not lie." But the longer formulation sets a context with some qualifications that we need to be aware of. That context defines the narrow meaning of the commandment and gives us some guidance in drawing broader meanings from it.

The context is that of legal testimony. The sin of false witness is that of distorting the facts in such a way as to harm one's neighbor. That witness may take place in a formal court hearing or elsewhere, as Leviticus 6:1–7 indicates:

> The LORD spoke to Moses, saying, "If anyone sins and commits a breach of faith against the LORD by deceiving his neighbor in a matter of deposit or security, or through robbery, or if he has oppressed his neighbor or has found something lost and lied about it, swearing falsely—in any of all the things that people do and sin thereby—if he has sinned and has realized his guilt and will restore what he

---

1. The only difference between the formulation of the ninth commandment in Ex. 20:16 and that in Deut. 5:20 is the word translated "false." In Exodus, it is *sheqer*, "falsehood"; in Deuteronomy, *shav'*, "vanity." As we saw in the discussion of the third commandment (chapter 27), these terms are somewhat interchangeable, though their nuances differ.

took by robbery or what he got by oppression or the deposit that was committed to him or the lost thing that he found or anything about which he has sworn falsely, he shall restore it in full and shall add a fifth to it, and give it to him to whom it belongs on the day he realizes his guilt. And he shall bring to the priest as his compensation to the LORD a ram without blemish out of the flock, or its equivalent for a guilt offering. And the priest shall make atonement for him before the LORD, and he shall be forgiven for any of the things that one may do and thereby become guilty."

Here false witness is a form of theft. So property is a major issue in the ninth commandment. We can see, then, that the eighth through tenth commandments all deal in some way with property law. One may even summarize the "second table of the law" by saying that the fifth commandment requires respect for others, which means that we may not unjustly take life (sixth commandment), a spouse (seventh), or property (eighth through tenth).

But in the ninth commandment, the focal concern is witness, which deals with matters other than property crime. In Scripture, legal witnesses hold sway even over life and death (1 Kings 21:13; Matt. 26:60–61; Acts 6:13–14). The law required the witnesses to a capital offense to cast the first stones against the convicted criminal (Deut. 17:7). A witness found to be false receives the penalty he sought to impose upon the accused (Deut. 19:16–19). So the ninth commandment continues the emphasis of the eighth on the integrity of the justice system.

It also promotes a general concern for truthfulness within the covenant community. Hosea 4:1–2 lists a number of the sins of Israel, evidently with the Decalogue in view:

Hear the word of the LORD, O children of Israel, for the LORD has a controversy with the inhabitants of the land. There is no faithfulness or steadfast love, and no knowledge of God in the land; there is swearing, lying, murder, stealing, and committing adultery; they break all bounds, and bloodshed follows bloodshed.

"Lying" seems in this list to represent the meaning of the ninth commandment, as other terms on the list refer clearly to other commandments of the Decalogue. So we may understand the ninth commandment to be the foundation of the general biblical polemic against lying (Pss. 12:2; 31:18; 63:11; 101:7; 119:29, 163; Prov. 6:17, 19; 12:22; 13:5; 19:5, 9; Zech. 8:16; Eph. 4:25; 1 John 2:21; Rev. 21:27; 22:15). Satan is a liar and the father of lies (John 8:44). Lying is a regular characteristic of the unregenerate (Rom. 1:25; 3:8–18; 2 Cor. 4:2–4; 2 Thess. 2:9–12). Sinners actually take delight in lying (Prov. 18:8; 26:22). We recall that false prophets were stoned to death (Deut. 13:1–5).

Lying also sums up many ways in which we harm one another by words: gossip and slander (Ps. 15:3; Prov. 11:13; 16:28; 20:19; 25:23; 26:20; Rom. 1:29–30; 2 Cor. 12:20; Gal. 5:19–20; 1 Tim. 5:13; 3 John 10), judging rashly (2 Sam. 16:4 and 19:24–28; Matt. 7:1–3; John 9:2), and twisting someone's words (Matt. 26:61 and John 2:19).[2] So Scripture speaks often about the power of the tongue to do evil (Gen. 11:6–7; Rom. 3:13–14; James 3:2–10).

Thus, in a broad sense, false witness covers many kinds of sins. In addition, witnessing itself has broader meanings. Israel bears witness of God's nature and mighty deeds to the nations (Isa. 43:10, 12). Christians are Jesus' witnesses (Acts 1:8). Jesus himself is the true witness of God, a witness for the truth (John 18:37), a witness against the sins of the church (Rev. 3:14).

Witness is not only what we say, but what we are and do. I recall years ago preparing a message for young people, urging them to "witness" to non-Christians concerning their faith. I searched diligently through concordances, trying to find passages in which God commands believers to witness. I couldn't find any. Scripture does command us to preach, teach, proclaim, and so on, but not to witness. The reason, I think, is that, as in Isaiah 43:10, 12 and Acts 1:8, God has already made us witnesses; we have no choice in the matter. He does not command us to be witnesses, because we already are. We can witness truly or falsely, but we cannot avoid witnessing.

If that is true, witness in the broader sense includes, not only our words, but all of life. So the ninth commandment, like the others, is a perspective on all righteousness, and false witness is a perspective on sin.

So the Westminster Larger Catechism finds in this, as in other commandments, a perspective on all human sin and righteousness. Note especially the last sentence of WLC, 144:

> Q. 144. *What are the duties required in the ninth commandment?*
> A. The duties required in the ninth commandment are, the preserving and promoting of truth between man and man, and the good

---

2. We have the responsibility to put the best construction on other people's words and behavior, unless there is cogent witness to the contrary, what the Bible calls "two or three witnesses." That means we are to give one another the benefit of the doubt, on the principle of "innocent until proved guilty." I suspect that adherence to this principle would substantially reduce the amount of theological controversy.

name of our neighbor, as well as our own; appearing and standing
for the truth; and from the heart, sincerely, freely, clearly, and fully,
speaking the truth, and only the truth, in matters of judgment and
justice, and in all other things whatsoever; a charitable esteem of
our neighbors; loving, desiring, and rejoicing in their good name;
sorrowing for, and covering of their infirmities; freely acknowledging
of their gifts and graces, defending their innocency; a ready receiving of a good report, and unwillingness to admit of an evil report,
concerning them; discouraging talebearers, flatterers, and slanderers;
love and care of our own good name, and defending it when need
requireth; keeping of lawful promises; studying and practicing of
whatsoever things are true, honest, lovely, and of good report.

Q. 145. *What are the sins forbidden in the ninth commandment?*

A. The sins forbidden in the ninth commandment are, all preju-
dicing the truth, and the good name of our neighbors, as well as our
own, especially in public judicature; giving false evidence, suborn-
ing false witnesses, wittingly appearing and pleading for an evil
cause, outfacing and overbearing the truth; passing unjust sentence,
calling evil good, and good evil; rewarding the wicked according
to the work of the righteous, and the righteous according to the
work of the wicked; forgery, concealing the truth, undue silence in
a just cause, and holding our peace when iniquity calleth for either
a reproof from ourselves, or complaint to others; speaking the truth
unseasonably, or maliciously to a wrong end, or perverting it to a
wrong meaning, or in doubtful and equivocal expressions, to the
prejudice of truth or justice; speaking untruth, lying, slandering,
backbiting, detracting, talebearing, whispering, scoffing, reviling,
rash, harsh, and partial censuring; misconstructing intentions,
words, and actions; flattering, vainglorious boasting, thinking or
speaking too highly or too meanly of ourselves or others; denying the gifts and graces of God; aggravating smaller faults; hiding,
excusing, or extenuating of sins, when called to a free confession;
unnecessary discovering of infirmities; raising false rumors, receiving and countenancing evil reports, and stopping our ears against
just defense; evil suspicion; envying or grieving at the deserved
credit of any, endeavoring or desiring to impair it, rejoicing in their
disgrace and infamy; scornful contempt, fond admiration; breach of
lawful promises; neglecting such things as are of good report, and
practicing, or not avoiding ourselves, or not hindering what we can
in others, such things as procure an ill name.

MUST WE ALWAYS TELL THE TRUTH?

A number of Reformed theologians, such as John Murray, have seen the ninth commandment as a testimony to "the sanctity of truth" in a very general sense.[3] On Murray's view, it is never right to say anything that does not correspond with fact. This is also the view of Augustine. In view of the biblical and confessional data mentioned above, we should take this position seriously. I think, however, that other biblical data should move us in a different direction.

The ninth commandment itself, as we have seen, does not mandate truth in an abstract way, but in the concrete relationships between believers and their neighbors. The Larger Catechism, though applying the commandment very broadly, like other commandments, focuses too on human relationships.[4] To obey the ninth commandment is to promote truth "between man and man, and the good name of our neighbor as well as our own."

The same conclusion arises from considering the nature of lies. A lie is not simply an untrue statement. A mistake is not a lie.[5] A parable is not a lie, even though it may describe events that did not happen historically.[6] A fictional story is not a lie, unless the author pretends it is factual. A hyperbolic statement (e.g., "It took me forever to get here") is not a lie, but a regular linguistic convention. The same is true for the flatteries that are part of normal social discourse: "Sincerely yours," "I had a good time," and so on. They may be literally untrue, but everybody understands that, and such language serves an edifying purpose, as a kind of glue that holds civilized society together. In these ways and others, statements that are literally untrue may be means of communicating truth, and nobody would claim that they are lies.

In games (whether board games or athletic contests), strategy often dictates deception. Everyone understands this and participates with that understanding. That is part of the fun of it. When the quarterback hides the ball and thereby misdirects the defense, he deceives them, but nobody would call him a liar.

---

3. John Murray, *Principles of Conduct* (Grand Rapids: Eerdmans, 1957), 123–48.

4. This is the main thrust of the WLC's exposition. To be fair, however, I should add that it also mentions "speaking the truth, and only the truth, in matters of judgment and justice, and in all other things whatsoever," the latter phrase suggesting a more abstract and universal concept of speaking the truth. But even this sentence has mainly to do with justice in society.

5. Some mistakes, of course, arise out of sin. Sometimes ignorance is culpable. But it is not always so. See *DKG*, 21, n. 4.

6. Of course, in larger senses, parables convey truths.

Similarly, people often deceive one another in a joking manner and nobody finds any fault with it. Proverbs 26:18–19, however, warns us of dangers here:

> Like a madman who throws firebrands, arrows, and death
> is the man who deceives his neighbor
>   and says, "I am only joking!"

Sometimes "jokes," especially practical jokes, are not funny: they can hurt. But sometimes they are only harmless jokes. "Magic," based on sleight of hand, also relies on deception, but everybody knows that, and, given that understanding, displays of it can be delightful.[7] The same is true for special effects in films that create dramatic illusions.

Sometimes misdirection can have an edifying purpose. In Luke 24:28, Jesus is walking with two disciples on the road to Emmaus. The verse says that he "acted as if he were going farther." Of course, he knew even then that the disciples would want him to stay longer, and that he would accede to their request. So his "acting" was to some extent deceptive. But it stirred up the disciples to request of his presence, a holy desire. The misdirection was, therefore, a blessing.

What, then, is a lie? I would say that a lie is a word or act that intentionally deceives a neighbor in order to hurt him. It is false witness *against* a neighbor. That excludes untruths that come from edifying devices, honest mistakes, honest fictions, games, magic tricks, and, for the most part, jokes. In some of these cases, we describe the untruths as "little white lies," but most of the time we don't describe them as lies at all.

But then we must give some attention to the term "neighbor." Is everybody a neighbor? If so, then the commandment would forbid us to mislead anybody in order to hurt that person. But Scripture does not teach that everybody is our neighbor. Certainly the parable of the good Samaritan in Luke 10:25–37 greatly expanded the Jews' concept of a neighbor. They wanted to construe it narrowly, at least to exclude Gentiles, so as to limit their responsibility. But Jesus taught that the chief question is not "Who is my neighbor?" but "To whom will I be a neighbor?" And he answered the latter question by saying that we should be neighbors to anyone we find to be in need.

But even that parable does not universalize the concept of neighbor. Not everyone we meet on the road is a person in need of care. Some may be thieves and murderers—our enemies. In chapter 19, I discussed a form of love that is due even to our enemies. But I also emphasized that love of

---

7. I am not, of course, here speaking of the magic of the occult (see chapter 24).

enemies is not incompatible with a desire to bring God's judgment upon them.[8] And we have seen in other chapters that such love is not incompatible with self-defense, punishment, or just war.

It is in this way that I would understand the rather substantial number of Bible passages in which someone misleads an enemy, without incurring any condemnation, and sometimes even being commended:

1. Exodus 1:15–21—the Israelite midwives in Egypt.
2. Joshua 2:4–6; 6:17, 25; Hebrews 11:31; James 2:25—Rahab's deception. Note that apart from what Rahab *told* her countrymen, even *hiding* the spies amounted to a deception.
3. Joshua 8:3–8—the ambush at Ai. As John Murray recognizes, God himself authorized this deception.
4. Judges 4:18–21; 5:24–27—Jael and Sisera.
5. 1 Samuel 16:1–5—Samuel misleads Saul as to the reason for his mission.
6. 1 Samuel 19:12–17—Michal deceives her father's troops.
7. 1 Samuel 20:6—David's counsel to Jonathan.
8. 1 Samuel 21:13—David feigns madness.
9. 1 Samuel 27:10—David lies to Achish.
10. 2 Samuel 5:22–25—another military deceit.
11. 2 Samuel 15:34—Hushai counseled to lie to Absalom.
12. 2 Samuel 17:19–20—women deceive Absalom's men.
13. 1 Kings 22:19–23—God sends a lying spirit against Ahab.
14. 2 Kings 6:14–20—Elisha misleads the Syrian troops.
15. Jeremiah 38:24–28—Jeremiah lies to the princes.
16. 2 Thessalonians 2:11—God sends powerful delusion so that his enemies will believe a lie.

In these passages, there is deceit, and that deceit brings harm. But the harm comes to an enemy, not to a neighbor.

Nevertheless, the predominant view among Reformed Christians is that of Augustine and Murray, that we should never tell lies under any circumstances. Murray explains the above passages by the following principles: (1) In some of them, such as passage #2, Scripture commends what the liar accomplished without commending his or her lie. (2) As in passage #5, he says it is legitimate to withhold the whole truth from someone, but not to misrepresent the truth. (3) As in passage #3, we need not always act in ways that are consistent with

---

8. God's own jealousy and anger is not incompatible with his general love for all his creatures. See *DG*, 458–68.

the mistaken interpretations of our actions made by others (in this case, the residents of Ai).

The first explanation is inadequate with regard to Rahab, for what Scripture commends is precisely her *concealment*, her creating a false impression in the minds of the Jericho officials.

As for the second principle, we can grant that it is sometimes right to withhold truth. But the question is whether it is ever right to withhold truth when that may reasonably be expected to create a false impression in someone else's mind. If it does, as it did in 1 Samuel 16:1–5 and other passages on our list, then it can scarcely be distinguished from explicit deception.

And the third principle depends on a sharp distinction between words that mislead and acts that mislead. Murray is saying in effect that we should never mislead people with our words, but we may mislead them by the way we behave. That distinction is not cogent.

And none of these explanations helps us to understand why God himself deceives people in passages #13 and #16.

Charles Hodge recommends an approach that is different from that of Murray:

> It is generally admitted that in criminal falsehoods there must be not only the enunciation or signification of what is false, and an intention to deceive, but also a violation of some obligation. If there may be any combination of circumstances under which a man is not bound to speak the truth, those to whom the declaration or signification is made have no right to expect him to do so.[9]

In Hodge's view, we are not obligated to tell the truth in certain specifically defined relationships and situations. He mentions military strategy, for example, as one area in which there is no such obligation: we are not required to tell the truth to the enemy. Just as the sixth commandment does not rule out all killing, but forces us to look elsewhere in Scripture to find out what killing is legitimate, so the ninth commandment requires us to look elsewhere to determine when we are and are not obligated to tell the truth.

I don't disagree with this last point. However, I think that Hodge is placing the burden of proof too much on those who wish to *require* truthfulness. That skews the discussion too much in favor of exceptions to that requirement. I think the ninth commandment places the burden of proof on those who seek to justify deception.

9. Charles Hodge, *Systematic Theology* (New York: Charles Scribner's Sons, 1872), 3:441.

Further, many of Hodge's examples of exceptions are taken from extra-biblical ethical literature. He makes little attempt to derive them from Scripture, or even to show what biblical principles enable us to judge their legitimacy. To remedy this inadequacy, I have tried to show that the language of the ninth commandment itself, with the applications of it in the sixteen passages listed above, shows us the nature and limits of our obligation to tell the truth.

In still another approach to the issue, Meredith Kline explains the biblical examples of deception as "intrusion."[10] In his view, the ethics of the end times differ from the ethics that God has given to us in the law and in Jesus' teaching. In normal times, we are to love our enemies and protect them. But in the end times, the enemies of God will have neither a right to life nor a right to truth. Now sometimes, Kline says, the end times enter our present time (and so "intrude"). The intrusion is a time of divine judgment, and, in that time, God authorizes his people to kill the opponents of God (as did Joshua and David) and also to withhold truth from them. In these times, God himself authorizes exceptions to the principles of the Decalogue.

Kline denies that principles of intrusion ethics can be part of normal Christian ethics:

> Ignorance of [the intrusion principle] is fraught with danger for the formulator of Christian ethics, for he will be likely to found matters of present Christian duty upon cases of Intrusion ethics. And thereby he would become unwittingly guilty of assuming the prerogative of God to abrogate the principle of common grace.[11]

Scripture, however, does not distinguish two different ethics. Some of God's commands (like his command to Joshua to kill the Canaanites) are for temporary situations. And Kline is right to say that often those situations are instances of special divine judgments. But capital punishment and just war are also subjects of regular, normative ethics. There are times even in advance of final judgment when the wicked deserve to lose their lives. Perhaps even such "normal capital punishment" can be assimilated to the intrusion model, but if so, we should note that, contrary to Kline, intrusion is a normal part of our ethical life, as limited and defined by God's revelation.

Capital punishment and just war are, as we have seen, not exceptions to the principles of the Decalogue. The commandments of the Decalogue,

---

10. Kline, "The Intrusion and the Decalogue," in his *The Structure of Biblical Authority* (Grand Rapids: Eerdmans, 1972), 154–71.

11. Ibid., 170–71. Here, as elsewhere, Kline overworks the concept of common grace (see chapters 29 and 32).

as we saw in chapter 13, are republications of creation ordinances, not to be repealed. But exegesis of the commandments shows that they are sometimes less sweeping than they initially appear to be. For example, the sixth commandment does not rule out all killing. Similarly, I would argue that the prohibition of "false witness against your neighbor" does not rule out all deception. So we do not need a principle of intrusion to justify, for example, deception in wartime, though theologians may legitimately analyze such deception as a kind of divine judgment in advance of the last day.

It does appear that the Bible passages listed above, which justify deception in certain cases, all have to do with the promotion of justice against the wicked, especially when they seek innocent life. Whether or not we speak of these as intrusions, we should recall that in the ninth commandment the requirement to tell the truth is conditioned on a relationship, that of "neighbor." In other passages, too, we are forbidden to lie because of a relationship. In Ephesians 4:25, the relationship is our union with one another in Christ.

I have questioned whether a neighborly relationship exists between a believer and someone who seeks to murder. At least, I doubt that those who misled others in the sixteen passages mentioned earlier were in a neighborly relationship with their opponents. Certainly those who deceived in those passages didn't think so. And I think Scripture concurs in their judgment.

So we have no obligation to tell the truth to people who, for example, seek innocent life. In many volumes and essays on ethics, authors refer to perhaps the most famous of all ethical dilemmas: During World War II, a Christian is sheltering Jews in his home, protecting them from the Nazis. SS officers come to the door and ask him directly whether he is hiding Jews. The dilemma appears to be that either he breaks the sixth commandment, by turning the Jews over to their would-be murderers, or he breaks the ninth commandment, by telling a lie to the SS. This kind of incident actually took place a number of times in the Nazi era, and many were troubled by having to make this choice. A choice to be silent would not have solved the problem, for it would have been, in effect, to invite a search and to hand the Jews over to their murderers.

I argued in chapter 13 that there are no tragic moral choices, no insoluble ethical dilemmas, though there are certainly many situations in which Christians have been perplexed about what to do. In this case, however, I think the obligation of the believer is clearly to deceive the SS. Of course, in this situation deception might not do much good; SS officers were not easily dissuaded from their suspicions. But if there were any chance to mislead the SS officers, as Rahab misled the officers of her own people, I think the Christian should have availed himself of that strategy.[12]

This is not to deprecate the heroism of those who believed they were obligated to tell the truth in such cases. God honors their hospitality to the Jews, often at great cost and risk, and we should honor them too. Although they misunderstood their ethical obligation, they did what they did out of conviction, trying to glorify God, in the midst of a situation of unparalleled difficulty. Most of us would have done much worse.

PROTECTING OTHERS' REPUTATIONS

As we have seen, one of the major emphases of the ninth commandment and the confessional expositions of it is that we should not distort the truth in order to hurt a neighbor. Scripture emphasizes this concern in many contexts. Like American law, for example, it insists that when someone is accused of wrongdoing, the burden of proof is on the accuser: people are innocent until proved guilty. In the Old Testament, this burden is expressed by the requirement of "two or three witnesses." This principle bears obviously on capital crimes (Deut. 17:6), but also on all other charges of wrongdoing: "A single witness shall not suffice against a person for any crime or for any wrong in connection with any offense that he has committed. Only on the evidence of two witnesses or of three witnesses shall a charge be established" (Deut. 19:15; cf. Heb. 10:28).

Jesus incorporates this teaching into his plan for discipline within the church:

> If your brother sins against you, go and tell him his fault, between you and him alone. If he listens to you, you have gained your brother. But if he does not listen, take one or two others along with you, that every charge may be established by the evidence of two or three witnesses. If he refuses to listen to them, tell it to the church. And if he refuses to listen even to the church, let him be to you as a Gentile and a tax collector. Truly, I say to you, whatever you bind on earth shall be bound in heaven, and whatever you loose on earth shall be loosed in heaven. Again I say to you, if two of you agree on earth about anything they ask, it will be done for

12. Note that even before the SS officer arrived, the family had already engaged in deception by the very act of hiding the Jews from the authorities. By this act, they placed themselves in a position of combatants against the Nazi regime. In that role, continuing deception is not only warranted, but required.

them by my Father in heaven. For where two or three are gathered in my name, there am I among them. (Matt. 18:15–20)

It is, of course, possible and legitimate for a Christian sometimes to ignore the sins of others, for "love covers a multitude of sins" (1 Peter 4:8). If we made an issue of every sin that someone else commits, we would be tied up continually in confrontation and ecclesiastical litigation. But when we see a definite need to correct the other person, either for his own good or for the good of the church, Jesus gives us the pattern for doing it. That pattern is not to talk about the sinner behind his back (gossip), but to confront him directly.[13] If that confrontation doesn't bring restoration, then the accuser is to bring "two or three witnesses" (cf. 2 Cor. 13:1; 1 Tim. 5:19). If that second confrontation fails, the accuser should pursue formal church discipline, trusting the promise of Christ's presence (Matt. 18:20) even through this distasteful process.

But note especially here how the accused is protected: by open confrontation rather than gossip, by a burden of proof on the accuser, by many in the church participating in the process, and by the presence of Christ, who judges all things rightly.

A further protection is this: Paul urges those who would confront others to confront themselves at the same time: "Brothers, if anyone is caught in any transgression, you who are spiritual should restore him in a spirit of

---

13. A couple of qualifications need to be made: (1) If I think my neighbor has committed a serious sin, I may have to talk to a third party about it to get counsel. He could help me understand how best to apply Matt. 18 and Gal. 6:1, or perhaps he could dissuade me from pressing the matter. Such consultation is not gossip, as long as it is kept confidential. A good rule is: in such a situation, speak to a third party only if that party can help resolve the problem in a biblical way. (2) Matt. 18 is talking about sin that begins in private, one person sinning against another. The situation is somewhat different when sin is widely known. For example, if a liberal theologian Dr. Deutschmann publishes a heretical book, and that book does harm in a congregation, the elders do not need to speak to Deutschmann privately before criticizing the book and warning the congregation. Deutschmann has renounced his right to privacy by committing his sin in public. Nevertheless, we should not push this distinction between private and public sins too hard. Consider a case in which Bert writes an article accusing Ernie, his colleague on a seminary faculty, of vile heresy. Bert avoided talking to Ernie about the matter beforehand, even though the two had adjoining offices, because Bert claimed that Ernie's sin was public and that Matt. 18 therefore didn't apply. But the matter could have been resolved far more quickly and peacefully if Bert had first called Ernie on the phone or sat down with him to chat. Bert's unwillingness to do this calls in question his desire to restore Ernie and to maintain the unity of the church. It also calls Bert's spiritual maturity into question. Bert should have at least considered the possibility that he was wrong and that a conversation with Ernie might have resolved the dispute. Matt. 18 not only provides a way of dealing with private sins, but also sets forth a system of values relevant to any controversy: work it out at the most private level possible; deal with it in the church courts, if possible; seek peace and unity, to the extent these are possible.

gentleness. Keep watch on yourself, lest you too be tempted" (Gal. 6:1). One who would correct others should, as Jesus says, take the plank from his own eye before removing a speck from someone else's (Matt. 7:3–5). One who would correct someone else should not sit on a high horse; he should set aside his pride, understanding that sin afflicts us all. Indeed, Satan uses the very process of correction to tempt the accuser to pride.

According to Galatians 6:1, harshness is another barrier to godly correction. When we are dealing with someone else's sin, we need to ask regularly if we are approaching him *gently*. Gentleness is an important character trait in Scripture, and it is often compromised in the anger of confrontation.

The reputation of a person is a delicate thing, not easily restored after it is compromised. When someone accuses another of wrongs through gossip, inadequate testimony, and/or harsh confrontation, he does great harm. Note the concern that God himself has for his own great name (Ex. 32:11–14; Josh. 7:9).

I believe that this is one area where Christians today have often grieved the Lord. Many churches today have no formal church discipline, so there are no protections for those who are accused, and often the local gossip determines the outcome of a dispute. People start whispering, a negative consensus develops, and the target of the criticism leaves the church.

Further, Christians have often attacked one another with a total neglect of biblical standards of evidence. One might think that theologians, at least, would be careful to judge disputes fairly, gently, and cautiously, but in my judgment they are often the worst offenders.[14] In theological controversy, writers often delight in distorting the words of one another, reading them in the worst possible (or worse than possible) sense. Many writers invoke the rhetoric of anathema and condemnation, without any adequate argument, and without any meaningful attempt to seek peace.

Such controversialists often invoke the example of Luther and Calvin in this regard. I think these Reformers were themselves too quick with insulting epithets and anathemas. But for the most part, they justified these epithets with careful biblical argumentation. I do not see a similar care in many of the self-appointed modern guardians of orthodoxy. It is true, also, that the prophets, Jesus, and Paul often used strong language against their opponents. They used that strong language against oppressors of the poor, against Pharisees who burdened the people with unbiblical moral standards, and against Judaizers, who wanted to force Gentiles to become Jews before receiving the grace of God in Christ. But they were very gentle with others

---

14. For more discussion of this issue, with many examples, see my article, "Machen's Warrior Children," in *Alister E. McGrath and Evangelical Theology*, ed. Sung Wook Chung (Grand Rapids: Baker, 2003), 113–47. See also *DG*, 751–68.

with whom they disagreed: Jesus with the woman of Samaria (John 4) and Paul with Christian vegetarians and observers of days (Rom. 14). Present-day defenders of the faith often fail to make such distinctions.

Many theological controversialists today set themselves up as Internet gurus, declaring brothers and sisters to be excommunicate on their say-so alone, showing contempt for the authority of the church, which alone has been authorized by God to make such judgments, and violating God's standards requiring protection of the accused. Many of these have no scruples about spreading lies to anybody who will listen. It never occurs to them that they have a responsibility to protect the reputations of fellow Christians, even those with whom they disagree.

In part, the problem is due to the failure of church discipline in most contemporary congregations. Denominationalism has played a role in this failure (cf. chapter 24). An accused person or a false accuser can easily leave one church and join another if he is threatened by discipline. Or he can express his opinions on the Internet, with little or no church oversight.

It is time for Christians to recognize that this behavior is sin. It is gossip, often slander, and Christians should not support it. The church needs to wake up to the problem. Theology, especially on the Internet, needs to become accountable to the body of Christ. We need to demonstrate to the world that we adhere to God's standards of evidence, and that we deal with sin in a way that is principled, but also gentle and winsome.[15]

---

15. The reader may discern from my tone of voice that I speak from personal experience, having been burned by some criticism that in my view ignored biblical standards. Of many cases of this, I cite an Internet guru who a couple years ago announced to everyone who would listen that John Frame was one of a group of writers trying to "change the Reformed doctrine of justification." This was a gross mischaracterization, for there is nothing in any of my writings that might suggest this. For the record, my view on justification is nothing more or less than that of the Westminster Standards, as may be clearly seen from my book *Salvation Belongs to the Lord* (Phillipsburg, NJ: P&R Publishing, 2006). I accused the guru of bearing false witness, but he denied it. Sadly, I must say that I was not surprised by his denial. His response was that since I supposedly want to change other elements of the Reformed tradition, I surely want to change this one, too. I would fail any seminary student who used such an argument in a term paper. Such reasoning, or lack of reasoning, invalidates any claim to theological understanding. And the spiritual immaturity of this person clearly disqualifies him as a teacher in the church of Jesus Christ.

CHAPTER 44

The Tenth Commandment: The Desires of the Heart

The tenth commandment can be stated very simply, as Paul does in Romans 7:7 and 13:9, "You shall not covet." But its original Old Testament formulations include numerous applications: "You shall not covet your neighbor's house; you shall not covet your neighbor's wife, or his male servant, or his female servant, or his ox, or his donkey, or anything that is your neighbor's" (Ex. 20:17; cf. Deut. 5:21).

This list is like that of the fourth commandment, which tells us to give rest to every family member, servant, and animal in our households. The longer formulations discourage us from trying to find exceptions to the universality of this commandment. "You shall not covet anything" would not be enough, for our sinful hearts (and the heart is the culprit here) covet in specifics as well as generalities. So God gives us both, and, as with the ninth commandment, focuses on relationships between the believer and his neighbor—relationships disrupted by coveting. Those relationships, indeed, are the main focus of the whole "second table" of the law. The first table focuses on another relationship, between ourselves and God, the relationship on which all others are modeled.

I mentioned that the tenth commandment focuses on the heart. All the others do as well, as we have seen, especially in the light of Jesus' teaching about them. To murder someone, we must first desire to murder him, and Jesus finds in unrighteous anger that desire to murder. To commit adultery, one must first desire someone else's spouse, and Jesus identifies that desire with lust. So to steal, one must first desire to steal. Jesus does not mention that specific point, but the tenth commandment brings it out. And the tenth commandment also says implicitly that all desire for sin is itself sinful.

So the tenth commandment vindicates Jesus' reading of the Decalogue. The focus on the heart is not a New Testament innovation. It is also an Old Testament concern. From the beginning, God wanted Israel to write his words on her heart (Deut. 5:29; 6:5–6; 10:16; 11:18; etc.). And the tenth commandment forms a fitting climax to the Decalogue by reducing all sin to the motives of the heart.

The Larger Catechism takes a broad view of this commandment, as it does of the others:

> Q. 147. *What are the duties required in the tenth commandment?*
> A. The duties required in the tenth commandment are, such a full contentment with our own condition, and such a charitable frame of the whole soul toward our neighbor, as that all our inward motions and affections touching him, tend unto, and further all that good which is his.

> Q. 148. *What are the sins forbidden in the tenth commandment?*
> A. The sins forbidden in the tenth commandment are, discontentment with our own estate; envying and grieving at the good of our neighbor, together with all inordinate motions and affections to anything that is his.

Two themes are prominent in the Catechism's formulations. First, they emphasize the virtue of contentment, which I mentioned in connection with the eighth commandment (see especially Ps. 78:18–19; Luke 3:14; 2 Cor. 9:8; Phil. 4:11; 1 Tim. 6:6–8; Heb. 13:5). We need to recognize that what God has provided is enough and to be thankful for it. If we are truly satisfied by God's provision, we will not covet. And how can we be dissatisfied with God's provision, considering his infinite wisdom and his love for us in Christ?

The other theme in the Catechism is interpersonal: the sin of "envying and grieving at the good of our neighbor." It is bad enough to be dissatisfied with God's provision. It is worse when someone else's prosperity upsets us. We should be thankful for God's blessings, not only on us, but on others as well. And, I would add, it is still worse for us to hate someone else because he is more prosperous than we are. That hatred is what Nietzsche called *ressentiment*. This hatred of the successful has been a major force in modern politics, particularly in socialist and populist movements. For some, it is not adequate in politics to help the poor, unless at the same time one hurts the rich.[1]

COVETING AND OTHER DESIRES

But we must look more closely at the nature of coveting, lest we confuse it with other desires. The Bible does not condemn all human desires, as does Buddhism. As we saw in chapter 17, Scripture motivates our obedience by promising rewards, thus legitimizing our desire for God's blessings. God himself is the chief desire of the believer's heart (Pss. 42:1–2; 73:25; Phil. 1:23). He promises prosperity to those who keep his covenant, and we should desire that. These blessings are earthly as well as heavenly (Mark 10:29–31), material as well as spiritual. It is not wrong for us to desire food (Matt. 4:2), drink (John 19:28–29), sleep (Luke 8:23), sex (Gen. 2:22–23; Song), children (Gen. 30:22–23; 1 Sam. 1:17; Ps. 127:3–5), or a better dwelling (Prov. 24:27).

What, then, is that special kind of desire called coveting? In discussing the seventh commandment (chapter 38), I defined lust as the desire to have a sexual relationship in a way that involves breaking God's law. Lust is sexual coveting. It is not wrong, say, for Chuck to desire a sexual relationship with Alice, given that both are single. That is a God-given incentive toward marriage. It is wrong for him to desire sex with her apart from marriage, for that is a desire to violate God's law. Similarly, it is not wrong for Louise to admire a beautiful vase in someone else's home, or even to wish that it were hers. It would be wrong for her to wish that she could steal it.

The theological tradition has distinguished several stages of desire:[2]

1. Spontaneous desire (one that catches you off guard)
2. Nursing that desire (sometimes called *titillatio*)
3. Making a plan to achieve it
4. Accomplishing the desire (the deed)

Douma cites studies that try to locate coveting within this process:

> The tenth commandment uses a word most often translated "covet." A somewhat more accurate rendering, suggested by

---

1. For some helpful discussions of *ressentiment*, see R. J. Rushdoony, *Politics of Guilt and Pity* (Nutley, NJ: Craig Press, 1970); Herbert Schlossberg, *Idols for Destruction* (Nashville: Nelson, 1983).

2. I have paraphrased this list from J. Douma, *The Ten Commandments* (Phillipsburg, NJ: P&R Publishing, 1996), 340.

Semitic language scholar J. P. Lettinga and others, would be, "You shall not set your desire(s) on your neighbor's house, wife, etc." If we set our desire upon something, we are out to get what we desire. Thus, to set our desire on something *already* involves forming a *plan* . . . ready to be put into motion as soon as opportunity arises. . . .

Stated briefly, we could also say it this way: Anyone who sets his desire(s) on his neighbor's house, wife, employees, or animals will not be able to keep his hands off. With premeditation he intends to strike. That is the primary meaning of the tenth commandment.[3]

As evidence for this meaning, Douma cites several passages that describe coveting not only as inward desires, but also as attempts to grab something illicitly (Ex. 34:24; Deut. 7:25; Josh. 7:21; Mic. 2:2).

On this analysis, coveting occurs at stages 2 and 3. Douma notes that on this view coveting, though a desire of the heart, is not found only in the heart, but extends to behavior as well. People sometimes say that coveting is such a private sin that neither the state nor the church can take disciplinary action against it. But plans are often expressed in words, in documents, and in actions. Often, objective evidence is available, not only of murder or rape, but of *intent* or *attempt* to murder or rape. So even when someone fails to accomplish an evil deed, the state or the church may sometimes prosecute him for his intention.

Nevertheless, Douma is unwilling to go along with the typical Roman Catholic position, which says that stages 2–4 are sinful, but that stage 1 is not. Rather, he follows Calvin, who argues that other commandments deal with stages 3–4, but that this one deals with stages 1–2.[4] Here Douma goes beyond what he considers to be the narrow meaning of "covet" to a broader meaning of the term, informed by other principles of Scripture.

How can we be held responsible for a spontaneous desire, one that captures us off guard? Douma answers by referring to the doctrine of total depravity. Our evil desires, even spontaneous ones, come "from an evil heart."[5] He agrees with the Heidelberg Catechism, which states:

> Q. 113. *What does the tenth Commandment require?*
> A. That not even the least inclination or thought against any commandment of God ever enter our heart, but that with

3. Ibid., 340–41 (emphasis his).
4. It seems to me, however, that the other commandments also deal with stages 1–2. That is the implication of my previous discussions of them.
5. Douma, *The Ten Commandments*, 351.

our whole heart we continually hate all sin and take pleasure in all righteousness.

I agree with Douma and with the Catechism, but I would stress again my earlier point, that we are talking, not about desires for things as such, but about desires to get things by breaking God's law. The Catechism guards this qualification, for it speaks only of inclinations or thoughts "against any commandment of God." The relevant thought here is not the thought of obtaining and eating a candy bar, but the thought of stealing one.

So Scripture speaks of secret sins (Pss. 19:12; 90:8; 139:23–24; Jer. 17:9), and of evil imaginations and thoughts (Gen. 6:5; 8:21).

The New Testament, like the Old, condemns covetousness, as in Luke 12:15 and Romans 7:7–8. Note the references to "desires" in Galatians 5:16–17, 24 and 1 John 2:16–17. The New Testament connects covetousness with other sins, such as sexual license (Eph. 4:19; 5:3) and false prophecy (2 Peter 2:3, 14). Covetousness is idolatry, according to Colossians 3:5.

So if the narrow meaning of the commandment is that all intentions and attempts to take what belongs to someone else is forbidden, then the broad meaning is that all sinful intentions, and therefore all sin, is forbidden. All sin comes from the heart. If the heart is pure, there will be no sin at all. So this commandment in effect includes all the others, as a perspective on all sin and righteousness.

Much more could be said about the tenth commandment, but I will stop here. To apply this commandment in depth is to search one's own heart for desires that displease the Lord. It is also important to review from our studies of the other commandments the ways in which external sins arise from inner motivations.

SUMMARY OF THE TEN COMMANDMENTS

The Decalogue is the primary governing document of God's covenant with Israel at Mt. Sinai. Like secular covenant documents, it serves as the highest law. So God orders it to be placed in the most holy part of his sanctuary, "by the side of the ark of the covenant" (Deut. 31:26). If Israel obeys these laws, she will be blessed; otherwise, she will be cursed.

The document begins with the name of the Lord, Yahweh. He identifies himself as covenant head and specifically as the author of the document. Since these are God's words, they have absolute authority. God's name also identifies him as the one "who brought you out of the land of Egypt, out of the house of slavery" (Ex. 20:2). The covenant is law, but it begins with redemptive grace. God chose Israel from among all the nations to be his special people, not because of their numbers (Deut. 7:7) or their righteousness (Deut. 9:5–6), but simply because of his love for them. That love motivated him to redeem them from slavery. They are to obey him out of gratitude for that deliverance. We who have a greater deliverance, from all our sin in Christ, also obey out of gratitude, not to earn our way to heaven.

The first four commandments focus on our relationship with God; the last six, on our relationships to one another. But our obligations to God have implications for our relationships with our fellow men, and we keep our obligations to them out of loyalty to God. For example, one who has no gods before the Lord (first commandment) must seek to bring his fellow men also under the exclusive sway of Yahweh. And honoring our father and mother (fifth commandment) includes honoring our heavenly Father.

Since Jesus is Yahweh in the flesh, the source of our ultimate redemption, we keep the commandments for his sake. We worship in no other name than his (first commandment; John 14:6), we regard him as the only image of God worthy of worship (second commandment; Heb. 1:3), and so on (see chapter 22).

The commandments have both narrow and broad meanings. Each focuses on a particular area of human life, but each also serves as a perspective on all sin and all righteousness:

1. The first commandment teaches us to worship only Yahweh. More broadly, it teaches us that nothing is more important than him in any area of human life. Particularly, it calls us to honor Jesus as king, as individuals and in society.

2. The second commandment forbids us to make idols as objects of worship. Broadly, it teaches us to live exclusively by God's revelation in all that we do, especially by his revelation in Jesus, the ultimate image of God.

3. The third commandment teaches us not to use God's name irreverently or falsely. Broadly, it forbids us to misuse anything in God's revelation, that is, in the whole world. We should especially honor the name of Jesus, which is above every name.

4. The fourth commandment tells us to observe one day in seven as God's holy day. Broadly, it tells us to use all our time for his glory and to seek the fullness of his redemptive rest in Christ.

5. The fifth commandment tells us to honor our parents. Broadly, it tells us to honor all authorities whom God has ordained, including God himself and Jesus as king.

6. The sixth commandment tells us not to take innocent human life. Broadly, it tells us to honor the Lord of life and to bring to all his promise of eternal life.
7. The seventh commandment tells us to respect the marriage bed. Broadly, it calls us to be faithful to God as our holy husband, to Jesus Christ as the bridegroom of the church.
8. The eighth commandment tells us not to take what belongs to others. Broadly, it warns us against taking to ourselves what belongs to God alone.
9. The ninth commandment forbids us to distort the truth in order to hurt a neighbor. Broadly, it calls us to be witnesses of Jesus, the true witness.
10. The tenth commandment tells us not to desire anything contrary to God's will. Broadly, it teaches us that all sin begins in the desires of the heart.

PART FIVE

CHRIST AND CULTURE

CHAPTER 45

What Is Culture?

Part 4, which may be considered my "treatise on ethics," is by far the largest part of this book. But, as I mentioned at the beginning, ethics is not all there is to the doctrine of the Christian life. So I have chosen to supplement this presentation of ethics from the normative perspective by considering in part 5 the situational perspective (living in God's world: Christ and culture) and in part 6 the existential perspective (living by God's grace: spiritual maturity). The two remaining perspectives can be discussed in fewer words, because much of their territory has already been covered. The three perspectives, as I have argued, cover the same territory; indeed, each perspective includes the other two. So I have already said much about our situation and our personal growth. What remains is to take up some issues that I have missed.

I shall consider the topic of Christ and culture in five chapters.[1] In the first, I'll ask, "What Is Culture?" The next chapter, "Christ and Culture," will consider how the Bible describes the relation of Christ to all the cultures of the world. In the third chapter, "Christ and *Our* Culture," I will get more specific, applying what we've learned to the culture we live in, that of the present-day Western world. The fourth chapter, "Christians in Our Culture," will discuss how *we* should relate to present-day culture: do we flee, fight, set up an alternative, or what? The fifth chapter, "Culture in

1. These chapters are based on lectures that I presented at McIlwain Memorial Presbyterian Church in Pensacola, Florida, in the summer of 2001, for the Pensacola Theological Institute.

the Church," will discuss what use the church can make of culture in its evangelism, in its nurturing of believers, and in its worship.

So what is culture? Scripture does not contain a definition of culture. Indeed, it does not contain definitions of any English words. So we have to understand how the word is typically used among us, and then ask if that concept matches anything in the Bible, and what the Bible says about it. Etymologically, the word *culture* comes from the Latin verb *colere*, which refers literally to agriculture, tilling the ground in order to grow things. By a slight extension, it applies also to growing or raising things that don't begin in the ground. So equiculture is the raising of horses, and aviculture is the raising of birds.

Beyond these more literal uses, we use the term *culture* to describe anything that human beings work at to achieve. So culture is not only what we grow, but also what we make, both with our hands and with our minds. It includes our houses, our barns, our tools, our cities and towns, our arts and crafts. It also includes the systems of ideas that we build up: science, philosophy, economics, politics, theology, history, and the means of teaching them, education: schools, universities, seminaries. Indeed, it includes all our corporate bodies and institutions: families, churches, governments, business enterprises. And culture also includes our customs, games, sports, entertainment, music, literature, and cuisine.

So definitions of culture tend to be fairly comprehensive. The Lausanne Committee on World Evangelism defined *culture* as "an integrated system of beliefs, values, customs, and institutions which binds a society together and gives it a sense of identity, dignity, security, and continuity."[2] Ken Myers writes that culture is "a dynamic pattern, an ever-changing matrix of objects, artifacts, sounds, institutions, philosophies, fashions, enthusiasms, myths, prejudices, relationships, attitudes, tastes, rituals, habits, colors and loves, all embodied in individual people, in groups and collectives and associations of people (many of whom do not know they are associated), in books, in buildings, in the use of time and space, in wars, in jokes, and in food."[3]

From definitions and descriptions of this sort, you might come away thinking that culture is everything. But that would be a mistake. We should make an important distinction between creation and culture. Creation is what God makes; culture is what we make. Now of course God is sovereign, so everything we make is also his in one sense. Or, somewhat better: creation is what God makes by himself, and culture is what he makes through us. The sun, moon, and stars are not culture. The light and darkness are not

2. *The Willowbank Report: Consultation on the Gospel and Culture.* Available at http://community.gospelcom.net/Brix?pageID=14322.

3. Ken Myers, *All God's Children and Blue Suede Shoes* (Wheaton, IL: Crossway Books, 1989), 34.

culture. The basic chemistry of the earth, and the original genetic structure of life forms are not culture; they are God's creation.

So our discussion leads us back to Genesis. Although we get our basic definition of culture from our understanding of the English language, we must as Christians go to Scripture if we are to understand what is most important about culture, namely, what God thinks about it. In Genesis, we learn that God made the heavens and the earth and everything in them, including man and woman, in six days (however long those days may have been).

At the end of those six days, culture began. Scripture doesn't say that God makes or creates culture, though he does in a sense. Rather, he commands Adam and Eve to make it. Culture is not a creation, but something that God has commanded, or "mandated," us to make: "God blessed them. And God said to them, 'Be fruitful and multiply and fill the earth and subdue it and have dominion over the fish of the sea and over the birds of the heavens and over every living thing that moves on the earth'" (Gen. 1:28).

I will refer to that command from time to time, as many other Reformed theologians have, as the "cultural mandate." It is very important. The first human experience recorded in Scripture is the experience of hearing this command. This command governed everything Adam and Eve would do thereafter. It defines the very purpose of human life.[4]

There are two elements to it: filling and rule. First, filling: Adam and Eve are to have children, grandchildren, and so on. They are not to stay in Eden. Genesis 2:24 says that a man will leave his father and mother and live with his wife, so there is to be a multiplication of homes, ultimately throughout the world.

As they fill the world, they are to rule it. They are not to be terrified by the natural world—neither by the wild animals, nor by electrical storms, nor by earthquakes, nor by the desert heat. Rather, they are to march through the world as kings and queens, taking possession of everything. They are to harness the animals, the heat and cold, the electricity and seismic energy, to serve their own purposes. That means development. Adam and Eve are not to leave the world untouched, as some radical environmentalists would prefer. Rather, they are to *use* the resources of God's creation, to bring out the potential of the heavens and the earth, to facilitate their rule under God. They are to turn the creation into a culture, into a home for human society.

Of course, use is one thing, and exploitation is something else. Adam's family had to remember that they were made of dust. They were not God;

4. For a fuller discussion, see chapter 17.

they were finite, not infinite. To live, they needed to eat. So, although God gave them the right to rule the earth, in one sense they were subordinate to the earth. They needed the earth for their food and shelter. That's another difference between creation and culture. God creates the world, but he does not depend on the world at all. The world depends entirely on him. But in human life, there is mutual dependence between ourselves and the world. The world depends on us to fill and rule it, but we depend on the world for our very existence.

Just as Adam was to take care of the garden (Gen. 2:15), so Adam's family was to take care of the earth. God wanted them to use it and also to preserve it—to use, but not to use up. So God later told Israel to rest the land after six years of cultivation. Man is to rule the earth, but also to serve it. He is to be a servant-king. That is the basis of biblical environmentalism.

So culture is what we make, and it begins right after creation, in response to God's command. But once we see that, we must expand our definition of culture a bit. Culture is not only a fact, but a value. It is not only something that happens; it is also something that God desires, something he values.

God gave this command to Adam and Eve for the same reason, ultimately, that he does everything else: for his own glory. God's glory is that beautiful, intense light that shines out from him when he makes himself visible to human beings. In the beginning, God created us as his "image and glory" (1 Cor. 11:7).[5] So he wanted Adam's family to spread that glory through the whole world. Adam was not to rule merely for himself, but for God, glorifying God in all he did. So culture is based on a divine command. Adam must develop culture because that is God's desire. Culture is for God's sake. So it is subject to his commands, his desires, his norms, his values.

So as we go back to look again at the various definitions of culture that people have offered, we can see that there is almost always a *value* element, a *normative* element. In the Lausanne statement, for example, culture is not only crops, farms, and artifacts, but "an integrated system of beliefs, values, customs, and institutions." Note especially the term "values." And Lausanne goes on to say that this system is one "which binds a society together and gives it a sense of identity, dignity, security, and continuity."[6] My own feeling is that the Lausanne statement supposes more unity than there usually is. You might well ask whether our own culture is an "integrated system." Is it integrated, or is it a collection of many systems, often battling one another for supremacy? Is there any system of values that

---

5. See also the correlations between *image* and *glory* in Rom. 1:23; 2 Cor. 3:18; Heb. 1:3.
6. *The Willowbank Report: Consultation on the Gospel and Culture.*

"binds our society together and gives it a sense of identity, dignity, security, and continuity"? Perhaps at one time Christianity provided that unity; perhaps at another time the ideas of the Founding Fathers, such as those of the Declaration of Independence and the U.S. Constitution, provided that sense of unity in the United States.

But surely cultures always involve values. If we no longer have unified values, perhaps the conclusion to draw is that we no longer have a single culture. But culture always includes evaluation, a common understanding, not only of what is, but also of what is good and right. So Matthew Arnold, for example, defines culture as "the pursuit of our total perfection by means of getting to know, on all the matters which most concern us, the best which has been thought and said in the world."[7] And T. S. Eliot understood culture "simply as that which makes life worth living. And it is what justifies other people and other generations in saying, when they contemplate the remains and the influence of an extinct civilisation, that it was worth while for that civilisation to have existed."[8]

Are you a "cultured" person? In a descriptive sense, we are all cultured, for no human being exists outside of culture. But in a normative sense, sad to say, not all of us are cultured, or at least not all of us are equally cultured. As my high school buddies used to say, there is a difference between "culture" and "culchah." To be "culchah'd" is to be refined, to be educated, to have good taste, to be among the elite. If you are culchah'd, you prefer opera to rock and roll, filet of sole to hamburgers, and Van Gogh to Norman Rockwell. It's sometimes hard to draw the line between a respect for cultural norms and mere snobbery. But the word *culture* traditionally refers to something that's good, something that's better. So William Herridge wrote, "The cultured man is he who is thoroughly matured in every part, so as to be able to fulfil the purpose of his creation."[9]

The definitions of Arnold, Eliot, and Herridge are perhaps unbalanced on the normative side, to the neglect of the descriptive. A better definition would say that culture is both what human society is and what it ought to be, both real and ideal. Culture is what a society has made of God's creation, together with its ideals of what it ought to make of it.

Or perhaps we should put the ideal first. People make things, because they already have a plan in view—a purpose, a goal, an ideal. The ideal comes first, then making things. First the norm, then the cultivation, the culture.

---

7. Arnold, *An Essay on Political and Social Culture*, in *Culture and Anarchy* (New York: Macmillan, 1882), xi.

8. Eliot, "Notes Towards the Definition of Culture," in *Christianity and Culture* (New York: Harcourt Brace Jovanovich, 1968), 100.

9. William T. Herridge, "Christianity and Culture," *The Presbyterian Review* 9 (1888): 389.

So now we can see how culture is related to religion. When we talk about values and ideals, we are talking about religion. In the broad sense, a person's religion is what grips his heart most strongly, what motivates him most deeply. It is the value that transcends all other values. So Henry Van Til says that "culture is simply the service of God in our lives; it is religion externalized."[10] It is interesting that that Latin term *colere*, from which we get the word *culture*, also refers to religious service, and comes into English as *cult*, *cultic*, and so on. Culture and cult go together.

If a society worships idols, false gods, then that worship will govern the culture of that society. If a society worships the true God, that worship will deeply influence, even pervade, its culture. If, like ours, a society is religiously divided, then it will reveal a mixture of religious influences.

Religions are totalitarian. They govern everything. That's certainly true of biblical Christianity. Scripture says, "Whether you eat or drink, or whatever you do, do all to the glory of God" (1 Cor. 10:31). Romans 14:23 says, "Whatever does not proceed from faith is sin." And Colossians 3:17 tells us, "And whatever you do, in word or deed, do everything in the name of the Lord Jesus, giving thanks to God the Father through him." So everything we do in culture will reflect our faith in some way. The same is true if you're a Muslim: you will seek to express your Islamic faith in everything you think, say, or do. The same is true for Buddhists, Hindus, atheists, philosophical skeptics, rationalists, modernists, postmodernists, and neo-pagan monists. (For these purposes, I'll use *religion*, *philosophy*, and *worldview* synonymously.) Every worldview, every philosophy, even if it professes to be nonreligious, has this totalitarian influence on human life, and, followed consistently, will dictate a certain kind of culture. Culture, therefore, is never religiously neutral. Everything in culture expresses and communicates a religious conviction: either faith in the true God or denial of him.

When we think about cultures, or elements of culture, that deny the true God, we must go beyond Genesis 1 and 2, to Genesis 3. For Scripture teaches that we have fallen into sin and that our cultures reflect that fall. God's original purpose is to fill the world with human culture that glorifies him. And today we do see people filling and ruling the earth, but in human cultures that often express hatred for the Creator.

In the garden of Eden, Eve, and then Adam, had a clear-cut choice: whether to obey Satan or God. Did she really imagine that Satan knew something God didn't know, or that Satan had a higher level of authority? Or did she imagine that she herself had a higher level of authority than

10. Henry R. Van Til, *The Calvinistic Concept of Culture* (Philadelphia: Presbyterian and Reformed, 1959), 200. Cf. the discussion of Clouser's view of religion in chapter 5.

either of them—the "right to choose"? Perhaps these boil down the same thing. For when you claim authority for yourself, *autonomy*, you are playing Satan's game. That's exactly what Satan wants you to believe. Certainly, believing in our own autonomy is very foolish. But Adam accepted that foolishness, and it spread throughout their family.

We sin when we pretend to be our own boss, when we claim to be the final authority in place of God. In our sinful condition, we claim to be the supreme judges of what is true and what is right. As sinners, we seek our own glory, rather than the glory of God. It's not that sinners don't know God. Paul in Romans 1 tells us that sinners do know God very well. But they don't like the knowledge of God. They suppress it; they exchange it for a lie. Then they think and behave as if God didn't exist. So Paul emphasizes that God-denying cultures are full of idols and every kind of wickedness. At one point, God destroyed mankind with a flood, showing mercy only to Noah and his family. Genesis 6:5 tells us, "The Lord saw how great man's wickedness on the earth had become, and that every inclination of the thoughts of his heart was only evil all the time." But the flood didn't do away with sin. In Genesis 8:21, after the flood, God says it is still the case that "every inclination of his heart is evil from childhood."

So we might be led to think that there is nothing good in human culture after the fall. Certainly the stories of Babel and of Sodom and Gomorrah don't give us much hope. But other parts of Scripture point to elements of goodness even in fallen culture. Genesis 4 narrates how Adam and Eve's first son, Cain, murdered his brother Abel. But later in the chapter, we learn that Cain's family developed a culture. They built a city. Some descendants lived in tents and raised livestock. Others made musical instruments and metal tools. In Scripture, these are all good things.

Moses was "instructed in all the wisdom of the Egyptians," according to Stephen in Acts 7:22. Stephen does not condemn this pagan education as evil, but, as Dennis Johnson puts it, "concurs with the Jewish tradition's *positive* assessment of Moses' intellectual engagement with pagan wisdom."[11] Compare the positive estimate of pagan wisdom in the time of Solomon: Solomon's wisdom is greater than that of any of the pagan sages (1 Kings 4:29–34), but that assessment assumes that the wisdom of the pagan sages is worth something.

In Samuel, Kings, and Chronicles, we read about Hiram, king of Tyre. Tyre and Sidon in Scripture are usually examples of wicked cities. But some citizens of these places were expert carpenters and stonemasons. David

---

11. Dennis E. Johnson, "Spiritual Antithesis, Common Grace, and Practical Theology," *Westminster Theological Journal* 64 (2002): 82.

accepted their help in building his palace, and Solomon accepted their help in building the temple of the Lord. 1 Kings 5:6 says that nobody in Israel could fell timber like the Sidonians. Now that's good. That's a good skill, and God used it in producing his temple.

Remember, of course, that a person can be skilled and wicked at the same time.[12] You may know a car repairman who's great at fixing cars, but who overcharges and cheats and lies. Being a good plumber or a good writer or a good pianist doesn't make you a good person. The word *good* can be confusing here. It can mean "ethically good," or merely "useful" or "skilled."

Nevertheless, there are some kinds of goodness even in pagan culture: good products, good skills, real wisdom. The reason is the grace of God. God shows his mercy and kindness to us by bringing us blessings even in wicked cultures. There are two forms of God's grace that we need to distinguish at this point: common grace and special grace. The basic difference between these is that special grace brings salvation, and common grace does not. But let us look at these a bit more closely.

Common grace,[13] nonsaving grace, is a difficult concept to get hold of. The phrase is not biblical; indeed, I don't know of any passage of Scripture that uses the term *grace* in this way. But Scripture does speak of certain blessings of God that fall short of salvation:

1. God restrains human sin. He keeps people from doing all the wickedness they otherwise would do. For example, he confused the languages of people at the Tower of Babel to keep them from accomplishing their wicked purposes (Gen. 11:6–9). He even keeps Satan on a short leash. God allowed him, for instance, to harm Job up to a point, but no further (Job 1:12; 2:6).

2. He gives some blessings to everybody without exception, such as the rain and the sunshine (Matt. 5:43–48; Acts 14:17). He gives food to all living things (Pss. 65:5–13; 145:15–16). He gives civil government "for your good" (Rom. 13:4), "that we may lead a peaceful and quiet life, godly and dignified in every way" (1 Tim. 2:1–2).

3. God gives skills and knowledge to unbelievers, so that they can do good in society. An unbeliever can do no good in the highest sense of *good*. Paul says that "those who are in the flesh cannot please God" (Rom. 8:8). To please God, our works must be done for the glory of God, obedient to the Word of God, and motivated by faith and love of God. Unbelievers never do good works in this sense; indeed, even believers' works always fall short, according to this standard. But unbelievers are able to do things

---

12. Cf. the discussion in chapter 2.
13. For a more thorough discussion of common grace, see *DG*, 429–37.

that *look* good to us. They don't look good to God, for he knows the heart. But they look good to us, and they often bring benefits to society. So non-Christians often improve society through their skills and ideas. They make scientific discoveries, produce labor-saving inventions, develop businesses that supply jobs, and produce works of art and entertainment.

That's common grace. You can see how God's common grace leads to many good things even in unbelieving culture.

The other source of goodness, of course, is God's special grace, his work of saving the world through Christ. This work of God goes far beyond common grace. For God sent Jesus, not just to keep us from being as bad as we could be, but to make us as good as creatures can be, to transform us into the glorious image of Christ himself. Jesus died for his people and rose again, so that they might be raised with him, dead to sin and alive to righteousness in Jesus. The gospel calls people of all nations to turn from their sins, believe in Jesus, and receive God's saving grace, his free gift of eternal life.

Does God's saving grace make an impact on culture? Certainly it does. When you believe in Jesus, your whole life changes direction: your thoughts, words, and deeds. Whether you eat, or drink, or whatever you do, you seek to do it for God's glory. So whether you are a car repairman, a homemaker, a poet, a plumber, a pianist, a civil magistrate, or a pastor, you try to do your work for the glory of God. You'll fail, because you won't be perfect until glory. But you'll try. And sometimes trying can make a huge difference. You can influence your culture, as many Christians have.

If you read a book like *What If Jesus Had Never Been Born?* by D. James Kennedy and Jerry Newcombe,[14] you should be impressed by the great influence of the Christian gospel, and specifically Calvinism, upon Western culture. I don't want to minimize the wickedness of modern culture, and I will have much more to say about that. But for now I'm making the point that there is good as well. Kennedy and Newcombe emphasize that Christians, for distinctively Christian motives, have greatly influenced Western culture in such areas as help for the poor, teaching of literacy, education for all, political freedom, economic freedom, science, medicine, the family, the arts, and the sanctity of life. Without Jesus, without his gospel, without the influence of his people, all these areas of culture would be vastly different and very much worse.

The gospel, you see, is not only a message for individuals, telling them how to avoid God's wrath. It is also a message about a kingdom, a society, a new community, a new covenant, a new family, a new nation,

14. Nashville: Thomas Nelson, 1994.

a new way of life, and, therefore, a new culture. God calls us to build a
city of God, a New Jerusalem.

Remember the cultural mandate. Sin does not abrogate it. God repeated
it to Noah's family in Genesis 9:1–7. Nor does Jesus abrogate it. Indeed,
he restates it for his church in the Great Commission (Matt. 28:19–20).
Theologians have often debated how the cultural mandate and the Great
Commission fit together.[15] For now, just remember that both of these call for
a renewed culture: "Go therefore and make disciples of all nations, baptizing them in the name of the Father and of the Son and of the Holy Spirit,
teaching them to observe all that I have commanded you. And behold, I
am with you always, to the end of the age."

Do you see how comprehensive that is? The Great Commission tells us
not only to tell people the gospel and get them baptized, but also to teach
them to obey everything Jesus has commanded us. Everything. The gospel
creates new people, who are committed to Christ in every area of their
lives. People like these will change the world. They will fill and rule the
earth for the glory of Jesus. They will plant churches and establish godly
families, and they will also establish hospitals, schools, arts, and sciences.
That is what has happened, by God's grace. And that is what will continue
to happen until Jesus comes.

Does that mean that culture is OK, after all—that we don't need to worry
about it? Certainly not. It means that the relation of Christ and culture is
more complicated than you may have thought. It's certainly not warfare,
pure and simple. There is a war, but the war is between Christ and Satan,
Christ and unbelief, not Christ and culture. Nor is it a mutual embrace.
Culture is an ambiguity, a mixture of sin and righteousness, of good and
bad, of love of Christ and hatred of Christ. That picture leaves us much to
explore in the next four chapters.

---

15. For a more thorough treatment of this question, see chapter 17.

CHAPTER 46

Christ and Culture

In the last chapter, I defined culture as what we make of God's creation, or rather what God makes through us. Culture is the human response, in obedience or disobedience, to the cultural mandate, God's command to Adam and Eve to replenish the earth and subdue it. As such, culture expresses our religion, our service to God or to an idol. Since the fall into sin, described in Genesis 3, culture expresses unbelief, rebellion against God. But there is also good in culture, because of God's common grace and his special grace. By his common grace, God restrains human sin. By his special grace, he sends Christ to save us. And Jesus' saved people spread over the earth, preaching the gospel, winning others to Christ, and bringing the influence of Jesus into the cultures of the world. So in any human culture, we can expect to find both good and bad.

Here I want to look more closely at the relationship between Christ and human culture as Scripture presents it. I will be looking at five different historical models of this relationship, five ways in which Christians have understood the relation of Christ to culture. These are not my models. Everybody who discusses Christianity and culture discusses these. The first one to formulate them was H. Richard Niebuhr, in his book *Christ and Culture*,[1] probably the most influential twentieth-century work on the subject.

But I will try to evaluate these models biblically. When we're thinking about culture, of course, we must think about a lot of things outside the Bible. But the Bible is our ultimate norm, and our only ultimate norm—*sola*

1. New York: Harper, 1951.

Scriptura. As Christians, we should not seek to be autonomous, as Eve did in Genesis 3, to make our own wisdom supreme. To God, the best of human wisdom is foolishness. We must listen to him first, for the fear of the Lord is the beginning of true wisdom.

I say that at this point, first, because it's always good to be reminded of it, and second, because it seems to me to be especially important to discussions of Christ and culture. When Christians evaluate culture, they often give a great deal of weight to various theories of historical development, of sociology and psychology, of aesthetic excellence, and so on. While knowledge in these fields and others can help us to *apply* scriptural principles, extra-biblical theories are never the final criterion. Only Scripture has the final word. And we must always be open to let Scripture criticize our theories. We must never force Scripture to say what our theories demand; rather, we must continually revise and even abandon our theories as we interact over and over again with God's Word.[2]

Niebuhr's five models are these: (1) Christ against culture, (2) the Christ of culture, (3) Christ above culture, (4) Christ and culture in paradox, and (5) Christ the transformer of culture. Let's look at these individually. Hardly anybody is a pure example of just one of these. Most of us mix up these models in our thinking. But they are guideposts by which we can compare our views to those of others and identify emphases in the great thinkers of the church over history.

CHRIST AGAINST CULTURE

In the early days of Christianity, there were many conflicts between the Christians, the Jews, and the pagans, often rising to the level of persecution. Christians often saw themselves at war with the surrounding culture. A number of the church fathers, the earliest Christian writers after the New Testament period, described the Christians as a "third race," distinct from both Jews and Gentiles. The Christians worshiped a different God, lived by a different law, and had a different inward character. The world was simply wicked. Tertullian (ca. 160–220) argued that Christians could not participate in the military, in politics, or in trade with the world. After we become Christians, Tertullian said, we have no need of Greek philosophy. Jerusalem and Athens have nothing to do with one another.

You can see the main outlines of this picture: Christianity and culture are opposites, opposed to one another, at war with one another. This view became

---

2. Cf. the discussion of the authority and sufficiency of Scripture in chapters 9–11.

less common after the Roman Empire became officially Christian under Constantine. But this sort of language emerged often later, in Anabaptist groups, among the Amish, and among some varieties of American evangelicals.

These groups have been able to appeal to some themes of the Bible. In the Old Testament, God wanted Israel to be strictly separate from the pagan nations. God's people were to be different from the pagan world, not only in their worship, but also in their diet, their clothing, their calendar, their patterns of work and rest, their planting and resting the land, and their laws. They were to be God's special people, his "peculiar" people, a holy nation, different from all other nations on earth (Ex. 19:5–6).

In the New Testament, we read of another holy nation, another special people of God, distinct from all the nations, but also different from the Jews. These are the people of Christ. In the New Testament, there is much emphasis on the conflict between Christians and the world.

Now the Bible uses the term *world* in different ways. Sometimes the world is simply the whole creation of God, the inhabited earth, without reference to sin or salvation. But Scripture often reminds us that the human world has fallen into sin. So it often uses the term *world*—either the spatial term *kosmos* or the temporal term *aion*—to designate everything opposed to God. The world hates Jesus, because he testifies that its works are evil (John 7:7). Jesus' Jewish opponents are "of this world," but he is not (John 8:23). Satan is the ruler of this world (John 12:31; 14:30; 16:11; 2 Cor. 4:4; 1 John 5:19). The world cannot receive the Holy Spirit (John 14:17). The world will rejoice when Jesus is killed (16:20). In the world, the disciples will have tribulation; but take heart, Christ has overcome the world (16:33). Jesus has chosen his disciples out of the world (John 17:6). He prays for them, but not for the world (17:9). The disciples are not of the world, even as he is not of the world (17:14).

Paul picks up the theme: don't be conformed to the world (Rom. 12:2). The wisdom of the world is foolishness with God (e.g., 1 Cor. 1:20–21; 2:6–8). Remember that the saints will judge the world (1 Cor. 6:2). Paul says the world is crucified to him, and he to the world (Gal. 6:14). James says that true religion is to visit widows and orphans and to keep oneself unspotted from the world (1:27). But the most arresting antithesis is in 1 John:

> Do not love the world or the things in the world. If anyone loves the world, the love of the Father is not in him. For all that is in the world—the desires of the flesh and the desires of his eyes and pride in possessions—is not from the Father but is from the world. And the world is passing away along with its desires, but whoever does the will of God abides forever. (2:15–17)

So there is an antithesis, an opposition, between Christ and the world, and therefore between the believer and the world. Significantly, however, Scripture never tells Christians to leave the world. Obviously we can never leave the world in the sense of God's creation. But should we try to stay away from other human beings, from human society contaminated by sin? Perhaps a little surprisingly, the Bible's answer is no. Jesus prays, not that the Father will take the disciples out of the world, but that he will keep them from the Evil One (John 17:15). They are not of the world, but as the Father sent Jesus into the world, so he sends his disciples into the world (17:11–18). Paul. did not forbid the Corinthians to associate with people who are immoral, greedy, swindlers, or even idolaters, for, he says, "then you would need to go out of the world" (1 Cor. 5:10). Like Jesus, we are to shine as lights of the world (Matt. 5:14; cf. Phil. 2:15). So we are to be *in* the world, but not *of* the world—a very difficult balance to maintain, to be sure.

So there is a biblical basis for thinking in terms of antithesis. Should we, then, adopt the model of "Christ against culture"? Well, for one thing, *culture* and *world* are not synonymous. As I argued in the previous chapter, culture is a mixture of good and bad. It includes the effects of sin as well as the effects of God's grace. But *world,* used in that negative ethical sense, is entirely bad. The *world* is the kingdom of the Evil One, and Christians should not be conformed to it even a little bit. We should not have any love for it. Our only concern should be to rescue people out of it. The world is a great snare and delusion.

Culture is a broader term than *world. World* is the bad part of culture. It is the culture of unbelief, taken in its essence, without the effects of common grace and special grace. The early church, looking out on a world untouched by the gospel, often saw worldliness as something pervasive and inescapable. It was a systematic kind of unbelief that tried to bring everything under its sway. So Christians didn't always make fine distinctions between the evils of the world and the mixed good and evil of culture.

But sometimes they did. In 1 Corinthians 9, for example, Paul says that to the Jews he becomes as a Jew, to the Greeks as a Greek. To the weak (to people with special religious scruples) he becomes weak, in order to gain the weak. Paul accommodates his behavior to the customs of different groups, to their culture, so that he can win them to Christ. He doesn't commit sin, but he conforms his behavior to their cultural expectations in nonsinful ways. This assumes that not everything in Jewish and Gentile cultures is evil. And, as I mentioned before, every culture contains some good products, customs, and institutions, such as crops, marriage, government, and language. The Greek language is a product of Greek culture, for example. But it's not wrong for Paul to use it in his preaching and teaching. The Greek language is cultural, but it is not *worldly.*

So: Christ against the world, yes; Christ against culture, no. There is, of course, much for us to oppose in culture, but God doesn't call us to oppose culture as such.

THE CHRIST OF CULTURE

As we've seen, the church fathers tended to see Christ and culture in conflict. But they were not entirely consistent about that. When they defended Christians against the attacks of the pagans, they tended to seek common ground. They pointed out how Christians were a vital part of the larger society and brought many benefits to the general culture. So even Tertullian says to the pagans:

> We sojourn with you in the world, abjuring neither forum, nor shambles, nor bath, nor booth, nor inn, nor weekly market, nor any other places of commerce. . . . We sail with you, and fight with you, and till the ground with you; and in like manner we unite with you in your traffickings—even in the various arts we make public property of our works for your benefit.[3]

Niebuhr, however, quotes this section and adds: "This, however, is said in defense. When he admonishes believers his counsel is to withdraw from many meetings and many occupations, not only because they are corrupted by their relation to pagan faith but because they require a mode of life contrary to the spirit and the law of Christ."[4]

But Tertullian's attempt to seek common ground with paganism was not isolated. Justin Martyr, for example, and later Clement of Alexandria recommended Christianity to the pagans as the fulfillment of Greek philosophy. Plato, they thought, lived according to the *logos*, according to rational speech; and of course the *Logos* in John 1:1–14 is Jesus Christ. So, said Justin, Socrates and Plato were Christians. Just as the Old Testament prepared the Jews for Christ, so Greek philosophy prepared the Greeks for Christ. Jesus is the fulfillment of all that is highest and best in the philosophies of men. The Greeks should have no problem in accepting Christ, because, in effect, they are Christians already.

Niebuhr also mentions the medieval thinker Peter Abelard and the liberal Protestants who followed Albrecht Ritschl in the nineteenth century as examples of this tendency. They presented Jesus exclusively as a moral

---

3. *Apology*, xlii.
4. H. Richard Niebuhr, *Christ and Culture* (New York: Harper, 1951), 55–56.

teacher. To them, Jesus doesn't oppose human culture; rather, he teaches all that is noblest and best in the cultural traditions of mankind.[5]

Certainly these thinkers are not wrong in saying that Christ affirms what is right and good in all human culture. But it is unbiblical to limit Jesus to those things he shares with human culture. Jesus' wisdom is far greater than any Greek philosopher or modern moralist ever dreamed. And, indeed, he is far more than a philosopher or moralist. No moral teacher can save us from sin, for we have in ourselves no power to act morally. But Jesus died to satisfy the wrath of God, so that we might live eternally and so that we might be able to please God. And the preaching of this good news makes foolish the wisdom of the world.

Further, the "Christ of culture" position tends to neglect the biblical doctrine of sin. It identifies Christ with culture, because it doesn't see how bad culture is under the influence of the fall and the curse.

Nevertheless, Christians have often had a hard time distinguishing between Christ and culture. One common criticism of Western missionaries over the last two centuries has been that they have tried to impose Western culture on other countries in the name of Christ. They have brought not only the gospel, but also Western clothing, Western hymns, and Western politics. But drawing these lines is not always easy. When a missionary counsels a tribe about clothing, where does he draw the line between a biblical concern for modesty and Western aesthetic standards? When he recommends music for their worship, how much of his thinking is governed by biblical standards and to what extent is he merely homesick for the music he grew up with? When you grow up in a Christian society, or in a culture deeply influenced by the gospel, it's tempting to want all other societies to be like that.

This problem even enters into our understanding of Scripture. When Paul says that women praying or prophesying should have a particular hairstyle or head covering, is this command limited to a particular culture, or is it a universal norm? It's easy for us to criticize Abelard and Ritschl for their easy equation of Christ and culture, but we face the same problem.

CHRIST ABOVE CULTURE

Niebuhr has special names for views three through five. Those who hold the third view are "synthesists," those who hold the fourth are "dualists," and those who hold the fifth are "transformationalists."

5. Ibid., 89–101.

The third view recognizes that Christ and culture are different, and, unlike the first view, recognizes that there is good in both. Thomas Aquinas (1225–1274) is the chief representative of this view, and the Roman Catholic Church adopted his position in a somewhat official way. At the heart of Roman Catholic theology is the distinction between nature and grace. Nature is the world as God made it. Grace is the name for special gifts that God gives to human beings beyond nature.[6]

Natural reason, for example, is part of our nature, as God created us. It enables us to understand the world around us—and even to prove the existence of God, according to Aquinas. But by natural reason, we can never understand the Trinity or understand how to be saved from sin. For that we need a higher means of knowledge, divine revelation and faith. Natural reason belongs to nature; faith belongs to grace.

By our natural abilities, we plow the soil, marry and raise families, and achieve various kinds of earthly happiness. But to reach our highest purpose, a supernatural purpose, we need God's grace.

We must make the same distinction among authorities. The state administers nature; the church administers grace.

So how does Christ relate to culture? Generally speaking, culture is man's development of nature. Christ supplements nature with something higher. The higher then mingles easily with the lower, in a "synthesis."

This doesn't sound so bad when you first hear of it; in fact, it seems to make good sense. The trouble is that the way it is sometimes put is that you really don't need Christ at the lower level, only at the higher level. Natural reason, for example, works perfectly well without the help of divine revelation. Aristotle learned many valuable things through his natural reason. His problem was not so much that he was wrong, though sometimes he was. His problem was that he needed to know more than his reason could tell him. He needed a supplement.

And you can do just fine at making your living and raising your family without Christ. But if you're interested in eternal life, then you need something more. Indeed, if you're *really* interested in eternal life, you'll quit your job, promise never to marry, and become a monk, taking vows of poverty, chastity, and obedience.

The problem, however, is that it is unbiblical to separate nature and grace in this sort of way. Remember that God intends us to live our natural lives for his glory. When we eat and drink, do our jobs, and raise our families, we should be doing that for the glory of God. But apart from grace, we are sinners. "Every intention of the thoughts of [our] heart [is] *only*

---

6. Cf. the discussions of nature and grace in chapters 17 and 32.

evil continually" (Gen. 6:5). So without grace we cannot live our natural lives as God intended. We need far more than a supplement. We need a complete change of direction.

The same is true for natural reason. Yes, it's true that we can know God through the world around us. But without faith, we hate that truth and suppress it. We cannot rightly understand the world, then, apart from God's grace, his revelation.

The state can maintain order through force. But it has no sense of its true powers and limits apart from God's Word. Without that, its force becomes tyranny.

So in Scripture, nature and grace are quite inseparable. Grace is not just a higher level, a supplement to nature. Rather, nature is hopeless, apart from grace. And so we must understand culture. Sodom and Gomorrah, Tyre and Sidon, and the degenerates of Romans 1 are examples of what culture is like without Christ.

CHRIST AND CULTURE IN PARADOX

Each view that we've discussed recognizes something important about the relation of Christ and culture. The first view recognizes the reality of spiritual warfare. The second recognizes that there is good in culture. The third recognizes that Christ is different from even what's best in culture. The fourth view, now, what Niebuhr calls "dualism," recognizes far more than the third the intense sinfulness of culture. This view is usually associated with the Lutheran tradition, but it has been held by many Reformed people too, especially in recent years. I confess I find it harder to understand and to describe than the other views, but I will do my best.[7]

The heart of this view is that, as Gene Veith puts it, God exercises a "double sovereignty."[8] He has "two Kingdoms." He rules one way in the church and a different way in the world in general: "In the church, God reigns through the work of Christ and the giving of the Holy Spirit, expressing his love and grace through the forgiveness of sins and the life of faith."[9] In the world in general, God "exercises his authority and providential

7. This position is closely related to the Lutheran view of law and gospel (which I discussed in chapter 12), natural law ethics (chapter 14), the doctrine of the twofold end (chapter 17), Kline's view of common grace (chapter 29), and his view of the state (chapter 32).

8. Gene Edward Veith, "Christianity and Culture: God's Double Sovereignty," from *Modern Reformation*, 6.1 (January–February, 1997): 15–19, available at http://www.issuesset. org/resource/archives/veith2.htm.

9. Ibid., 5–6.

control" through "natural laws" (of physics, chemistry, etc.). "Similarly, God rules the nations—even those who do not acknowledge him—making human beings to be social creatures, in need of governments, laws, and cultures to mitigate the self-destructive tendencies of sin and to enable human beings to survive."[10] Veith also describes these two sovereignties or two kingdoms as gospel versus law and spiritual versus secular. Luther used the metaphor of the spiritual as God's "right hand," and the secular as God's "left hand."

So far, I can agree with most all of this. Certainly God does rule the church somewhat differently from the way he rules the secular world. I do miss something, though. Of Veith's two divine sovereignties, neither one is what we usually call "divine sovereignty" in Reformed theology. In Reformed theology, God's sovereignty is comprehensive. All things come to pass according to the good pleasure of his will (Eph. 1:11). And God's general sovereignty is not exercised primarily through natural laws, though those may play a role, but primarily by his own direct involvement in history, by Christ, in whom all things hold together, and the Spirit, who makes life abound on the earth.[11] Scripture never speaks of natural laws in the sense of impersonal forces through which God works. It may be useful in science to speak of such things, but that can only be a way of speaking in shorthand of God's direct, personal action. So I think there is a unity in God's sovereignty that the two-kingdom doctrine somewhat obscures.

A more serious problem is that the two-kingdom doctrine claims a duality, not only in God's providence, but also in God's standards. There are secular values and religious values, secular norms and religious norms. Secular society is responsible only to follow natural laws, the morality found in nature. So, he says, "morality is not a matter of religion."[12] The church, however, is subject to the whole Word of God. Therefore, although the Christian can participate in the general culture, he should not seek to Christianize it, to turn it into a Christian culture. There is no such thing as a Christian culture; there is only secular culture and a Christian church. Nor, of course, should he try to bring secular standards (e.g., secular music) into the church.

Secular society is governed by the principle of justice, and therefore by the sword. The church is governed, not by the sword, but by God's Word and Spirit. Veith argues that we should not ask civil governments to show forgiveness to criminals, but to punish them according to justice. Justice is the natural morality; forgiveness is found only in the church. So there is some inconsistency between the secular ethic and the ethic of the church.

10. Ibid., 6.
11. For more on this, see *DG*, chapters 13–14.
12. Veith, "Christianity and Culture," 6.

Now, I have all sorts of problems with the idea that there are two different sets of divine norms:

1. To be sure, non-Christians have what might be called a "natural knowledge of morality"; and, to be sure, that knowledge consists of law rather than gospel. But there is no inconsistency between what God commands through this natural knowledge and what he commands us in Scripture. God's moral standards are one, even though they come through two media.

2. Contrary to Veith, morality certainly is a matter of religion. The moral law is binding because the true God requires it of us. If God did not exist, there would be no right or wrong. That includes natural morality. In Romans 1, people know right and wrong, because they know that the true God exists, however much they try to repress that knowledge. So even in the non-Christian's conscience, morality is a matter of religion. And insofar as they do repress that knowledge, they fall into idolatry and unnatural lust, says Paul. Errors in religion lead to errors in morality. Nevertheless, enough of that natural knowledge shines through that nonbelievers often do pay lip-service to it even when they are violating it (Rom. 1:32).

3. Through the Scriptures and through their regenerate insight, Christians have available to them a fuller understanding of God's law than non-Christians have. They ought to bring that Christian understanding and insight to bear upon culture and government as best they can. But when we do that, aren't we in one sense working to "Christianize culture"?

4. It is true that the state has the power of the sword and that the church does not. But that is not because there are two different moralities, one secular and one Christian. Rather, that distinction comes out of the Word of God. God tells us in Scripture that the state has the power of the sword and the church does not. This doctrine is what we earlier called "sphere sovereignty" (chapter 32), and although people sometimes try to make more out of this principle than it deserves, it certainly is the case that God gives to the church and to the state different areas of authority and different means of enforcing that authority. There is no inconsistency here, no paradox. It is simply a distinction that God in his Word has asked us to make. The relation between Christ and culture is often confused, I think, with the relation between church and state. Although these two distinctions are related, they are not synonymous.

5. So the use of the sword by the state is not an alternative to Christian morality, but part of Christian morality. It is not an impediment to a Christian state, but the very essence of a Christian state. A Christian state would not be a state where love and forgiveness replace justice. It would be a state that expresses the justice of God.

6. This does not mean that the state may force people to become Christians, even though some Christians in the past have mistakenly drawn this implication. That is not a proper role for the state in a biblical understanding.

7. Similarly, the Christian should seek to bring biblical standards to bear in all areas of society and culture. Our motive is not to try to make non-Christians live the Christian life, but simply to work out the implications of our faith in all areas of life.

8. The conventional criticism of the two-kingdom theory is that it is too conservative. According to this criticism, the two-kingdom view avoids any kind of Christian activism, because it wants to just let the secular be the secular. So some have blamed the two-kingdom view for the passivity of the German church in the Nazi era. Veith defends the two-kingdom view against this criticism by saying that it does permit Christians actively to promote justice in society, if that justice is seen in a properly secular way. Here I tend to agree with Veith rather than with the critics. But I wonder what standard the two-kingdom Christians are to use for their activism. May they use the Scriptures to define the nature of justice in society, or are they somehow limited to natural revelation? And how do we distinguish between what is scriptural and what is merely natural? The two-kingdom doctrine leaves it unclear. And perhaps that very lack of clarity has kept Christians in some situations from being as active as they should have been.[13]

9. Veith says that just as we should not bring the standards of the church to bear on culture, so we shouldn't let secular standards—for example of art and music—invade the church. On the other hand, this theory also says that there are no distinctively Christian standards of art and music, only secular standards. Veith says, "There is no need for a distinctively Christian approach to music, plumbing, computer science, physics, or wood-carving,"[14] so we have no choice but to employ the standards used in secular art and music schools. Most who write in this way advocate a kind of artistic conservatism, holding to classical standards in church music and so on. But the secular world is very confused about what constitutes "good" music, for example. If we must listen to them, who should we listen to, and why should we listen only to the conservative voices, rather than the radical ones? This whole position is very confusing. I shall have more to say about standards for church music in a later chapter.[15]

13. Recall Budziszewski's admission that statements about natural law must be verified by the Scriptures (chapter 14).

14. Veith, "Christianity and Culture," 8.

15. See also my articles, "In Defense of Christian Activism" and "Is Natural Revelation Sufficient to Govern Culture?" appendices E and F in this volume.

CHRIST, THE TRANSFORMER OF CULTURE

So, by process of elimination, but not only that, I find myself supporting the fifth view, that Christians should be seeking to transform culture according to the standards of God's Word. This simply means that if you are a Christian artist, car repairman, government official, or whatever, you should be seeking to do your work as a Christian, to apply God's standards to your work. As Paul says, "Whether you eat or drink, or whatever you do, do all to the glory of God." Christians have always sought to do this, and in seeking to do this, they have had a huge impact on culture. They haven't turned earth into heaven, or the world into the church. And sometimes they have made tragic mistakes. But they have also done a great deal of good, as a book like the one by Kennedy and Newcombe indicates.[16] Here are a few responses to common criticisms:

1. Seeking to transform culture in this way does not mean trying save the world apart from God's grace. It simply means obeying God as our thankful response to his grace.

2. A transformational approach does not assume an unrealistic optimism about what is possible in fallen society. We know, just as much as the dualists do, that the world is fallen, deeply sinful, and totally depraved. But we also have confidence in God's common grace and his special grace. Real change for the better can occur, and history shows that it has occurred—not perfection, but real change for the better.

3. To apply Christian standards to art, for example, does not mean that we must turn our artistic works into salvation tracts. The Bible doesn't require that. I do believe that the gospel of salvation is a fit subject, indeed a glorious subject for artistic treatment. Bach's Passions and Da Vinci's *Last Supper* are proof of that. But art should deal with all aspects of God's creation.

4. A transformational approach does not mean that every human activity practiced by a Christian (e.g., plumbing, car repair) must be obviously, externally different from the same activities practiced by non-Christians. There is always a difference, but often the difference is that of motive, goal, and standard, rather than anything external. The Christian seeks to change his tires to the glory of God, and the non-Christian does not. But that's a difference that couldn't be captured in a photograph. When changing tires, Christian and non-Christian may look very much alike.

5. Critics have often bemoaned the lack of high standards in Christian art, music, and other cultural activity. To some extent, these crit-

---

16. D. James Kennedy and Jerry Newcombe, *What If Jesus Had Never Been Born?* (Nashville: Thomas Nelson, 1994).

ics are right. But the answer to this problem is not to accept secular standards uncritically. (Again, even if we did, which ones should we accept?) The answer is rather to be more faithful to God, both in his special and in his general revelation. We ought to be humble enough to learn what we can from the knowledge in these areas that God has given to unbelievers. But we should always be challenging it on the basis of our knowledge of the true God.

CHAPTER 47

Christ and *Our* Culture

So far, we've been talking about culture generally and somewhat theoretically. In chapter 45, we discussed "What Is Culture?" and in chapter 46 we discussed the general relationship between Christ and any culture at all. Now we must focus in on culture as it actually is and has been, culture as we actually experience it.

GOD, THE CRITIC OF CULTURE

Analysis and evaluation of culture has been going on a long time. God himself was the first critic of culture. As he looked at the culture of Noah's day, "The LORD saw that the wickedness of man was great in the earth, and that every intention of the thoughts of his heart was only evil continually. And the LORD was sorry that he had made man on the earth, and it grieved him to his heart" (Gen. 6:5–6).

So God sent the flood in judgment. But the flood didn't make everything right.[1] Shortly thereafter, some of Noah's descendants built a tower in the plain of Shinar, an attempt to make a name for themselves and a headquarters that would keep the human race from scattering over the earth as God

---

1. After the flood, in Gen. 8:21, we read, "And when the LORD smelled the pleasing aroma, the LORD said in his heart, 'I will never again curse the ground because of man, for the intention of man's heart is evil from his youth. Neither will I ever again strike down every living creature as I have done.'" Clearly, the flood did not wash away human sin.

876

commanded. God disapproved the project and confounded their language to prevent them from finishing it. Then in the time of Abraham we read of God's destruction of the wicked cities of Sodom and Gomorrah.

We might reason that because of the fall, all human culture stands equally under God's judgment. But that would not be true. Three chapters before the destruction of Sodom, God says to Abraham that his descendants will possess the Promised Land, but not until several generations have passed. Why must they wait? The answer God gives is that "the iniquity of the Amorites is not yet complete" (Gen. 15:16). In Genesis, God makes distinctions. Sodom and Gomorrah are ready for judgment, but the Amorites are not yet ready. The Amorite culture is not yet depraved to the extent that the Sodomite culture is. There is still some good there. Even in Sodom, God makes distinctions. He tells Abraham that he will save the city if he finds ten good men there. He doesn't find them, but there is righteous Lot, and God rescues him from the fire and brimstone.

But several hundred years later, the iniquity of the Amorites is full. God gives the land to his people, because of his promise, but also because of the wickedness of the nations that are there. Israel conquers, not because of her own righteousness, but because of the wickedness of the other nations (Deut. 9:4–5). Moses says to Israel in Deuteronomy 18:9–12:

> When you come into the land that the LORD your God is giving you, you shall not learn to follow the abominable practices of those nations. There shall not be found among you anyone who burns his son or his daughter as an offering, anyone who practices divination or tells fortunes or interprets omens, or a sorcerer or a charmer or a medium or a wizard or a necromancer, for whoever does these things is an abomination to the LORD. And because of these abominations the LORD your God is driving them out before you.

Notice the extent to which God's critique of this ancient culture is based on their religion. We recall the quote from Henry Van Til that "culture is religion externalized." And when Israel herself forsakes the true and living God, her own culture deteriorates so that it becomes even worse than that of the pagan nations, and thus ripe for God's judgment. God sends to them prophet after prophet, but there is no real and lasting change. Finally, he sends his own beloved Son, Jesus. But still the cities of Israel will not hear. Jesus says in Matthew 11:20–24 that if the mighty works done in Chorazin, Bethsaida, and Capernaum had been done in Tyre, Sidon, or Sodom, the latter cities would have repented. But the Israelite cities had become even more ripe for judgment than those pagan cities that have been proverbial for their wickedness.

Paul also brings out the religious basis of cultural depravity in Romans 1. It is when people exchange the truth of God for a lie that they begin worshiping idols. Worshiping idols leads to other sins, especially sexual ones, but, Paul adds, "all manner of unrighteousness" (v. 29) as well.

Still, for Paul, the depravity of culture does not mean that you can never use its products or follow its customs. He advises the Corinthians to freely buy what is sold in the meat markets, even if it may have been offered to idols (1 Cor. 10:25). They are to pay good money to the idolaters, even though that means that the merchant may take that money and use it to support the idol's temple. Paul is also willing to be like the Jews sometimes, to win the Jews, and like the Greeks sometimes, to win the Greeks (1 Cor. 9:19–23). So he shows that not everything in culture is bad, that not everything in culture is forbidden to the Christian. How could it be? We can no more escape from culture than we can escape from our own skins. Even the Amish reflect a culture, though it is the culture of some years in the past.

So Scripture gives us God's point of view on human culture. In general, it is a depressing picture. People rebel against God, and they end up practicing every kind of wickedness. Nevertheless, God makes distinctions between what is good and bad and between what is less bad and more bad.

CHRISTIAN CRITICISM OF CULTURE

Outside the Bible, too, many have made evaluations of human culture in general and of specific cultures. We can find criticism of culture among ancient pagan writers, both historians and philosophers, and among the early church fathers, as we saw in our earlier discussion. Augustine had much to say about the culture of ancient Rome in his *City of God*, in which he compared the heavenly city to the earthly city. Not much of this criticism took place in the medieval and Reformation periods, however, and it wasn't until the eighteenth and especially the nineteenth centuries that sociology and cultural anthropology became academic disciplines.

Roman Catholics and Anglicans in the late nineteenth and early twentieth centuries developed critiques of culture that are still valuable today. One thinks of G. K. Chesterton, Evelyn Waugh, J. R. Tolkien, Dorothy Sayers, C. S. Lewis, and Malcolm Muggeridge. Many liberal theologians, such as Paul Tillich, also wrote on the theme of Christianity and culture. In the Netherlands, Abraham Kuyper and others had important things to say about culture, but their contributions tended to focus on the theology of culture (the subject of chapters 45 and 46) or on the Christian's participation in culture (the subject of chapters 48 and 49). They had relatively little to say about our current subject, the nature and value of present-day culture.

Among evangelical Christians in America, the analysis of culture was slow to develop. However, more recently a lot of work has been done in this area. Let me mention some important names.

FRANCIS SCHAEFFER

In our own Reformed evangelical circles, certainly we must give a lot of credit to Francis Schaeffer. In his personal witnessing to intellectual skeptics, and later in his writings, especially *The God Who Is There*[2] and *How Should We Then Live?*[3] Schaeffer drew a picture of the history of Western thought and culture from the ancient world to our own time, drawing especially on his knowledge of philosophy, theology, and art. Schaeffer was not a professional scholar, but he gained a lot of knowledge in many fields, both from friendly scholars like the art historian Hans Rookmaaker and just from talking to students and others who visited him in Switzerland. Thus he became a rather remarkable intellectual generalist. Not specialized in a single field, he developed a remarkable ability to draw connections between developments in philosophy, art, science, theology, and literature. And he won people to his viewpoint, and, more importantly, to Jesus Christ, through open dialogue and through the radical hospitality of his home, in which his wife Edith played the crucial role.

Schaeffer's overall analysis of culture went like this: In ancient Greece, there was respect for objective truth and for the power of human reason to discover truth. The Greeks understood truth straightforwardly as the opposite of error. Therefore, they respected logic: if A was true, A could not be false.

In the modern period, however, that confidence waned. Philosophers of the eighteenth century moved from rationalism to skepticism. Schaeffer believed that the early nineteenth-century philosopher Hegel played an important role. Unlike the Greeks, who taught a clear-cut antithesis between truth and falsehood, Hegel, in Schaeffer's account, believed that truth and falsehood somehow had to be synthesized, brought together. Traditional logic lost its importance. Then in later thinkers like Kierkegaard and Nietzsche, there is a rejection of the whole idea of objective truth. For them, the ultimate is not truth as opposed to falsehood, a truth that can be

2. London: Hodder and Stoughton, 1968.
3. Old Tappan, NJ: F. H. Revell, 1976.

stated in clear language. Rather, the truth is something ineffable, indescribable, a final experience. To reach what is ultimate, you must escape from reason, get beyond it and above it.

At this point, Schaeffer liked to say, there was a large historical transition. Human thought passed over what Schaeffer called "the line of despair." On one side of that line was a real confidence that objective truth was obtainable. On the other side, that hope was lost. Thus, twentieth-century thought was significantly different from any thought in the past, and radically different from the thought of ancient Greece. When someone passes over the line of despair, Schaeffer taught, the usual forms of evangelism are meaningless to him. Before a modern person will even listen to the gospel, you need to convince him that there is such a thing as objective truth. This is preevangelism. You must show him that the biblical God offers himself, not as an irrational "final experience," but as someone who is really there, who exists as opposed to not existing.

Schaeffer, then, saw a movement of history, from confidence in reason in the ancient world to irrationalism in the present day. And he was able to link these philosophical developments to the twentieth-century trends in art and music, liberalism and neoorthodoxy in theology, and the novels of Camus. All human intellectual life in the twentieth century, thought Schaeffer, was dominated by a sense of despair, of meaninglessness, to which only biblical Christianity could provide an answer.

OS GUINNESS

Schaeffer inspired quite a number of younger intellectuals to do this kind of cultural analysis and evangelism. Os Guinness in 1973 published a brilliant book called *The Dust of Death*,[4] which presented a history of the 1960s counterculture and its continuing effects on Western culture. Guinness agreed with Schaeffer that the twentieth century was essentially post-Christian, but that Western culture continued to flourish for a while on the residual moral principles taught by Christianity (what Van Til called "borrowed capital"). So many in the culture were optimistic about the future, without any good reason for being optimistic. Now in the sixties, there was a great disruption of this optimistic confidence. The intellectual elite and the counterculture came to reject this optimism and the Christian values, even the borrowed Christian values, that that optimism represented. So pessimistic humanism replaced optimistic humanism as the most influential cultural movement.

4. Downers Grove, IL: InterVarsity Press, 1973.

Guinness speaks of the surprise of these intellectuals at finding that a world without God "is a hell, rather than a paradise."[5] Nevertheless, the pessimists saw this disenchantment as irreversible, because they had accepted "the death of God as a cultural fact."[6] This disenchantment attached to technology: people no longer thought that technology was the road to comfort and ease; they began to see it as a monster that could destroy the human environment and community. The pessimists saw violence becoming increasingly prominent in society. Granting the death of God, they sought some measure of relief in sexual liberation, Eastern religions, drugs, and the occult. In the end, the counterculture influenced the larger culture to accept many of these things as legitimate.

Like Schaeffer, Guinness sees this as a post-Christian society, and the endpoint of a movement from rationalism to irrationalism. Others who wrote in the Schaeffer tradition included Donald Drew, Jerram Barrs, and Udo Middelmann.

DAVID WELLS

In more recent years, however, the most prominent evangelical critics of culture have been historians: Mark Noll, George Marsden, Thomas Oden, Alister McGrath, and many others.[7] The most important of these, in my estimation, is David Wells.

Wells's approach is somewhat similar to that of Schaeffer and Guinness. Wells was not pleased when I said that in print,[8] but I stick by my guns; I think the parallels are significant. Like Guinness and Schaeffer, Wells sees the present time as being vastly different from any other time in history. His book *No Place for Truth* begins with a long discussion of how his hometown of Wenham, Massachusetts, changed over two hundred years. He titles the chapter, nostalgically, "A Delicious Paradise Lost."[9] In his judgment, the history of Wenham, like the history of the United States in general, is a story of decline into that culture we call "modern." Wells

5. Ibid., 20–21.

6. Ibid., 21; cf. 72.

7. For some background to the developing prominence of church historians among evangelical scholars, see my paper, "Traditionalism," available at http://www.frame-poythress.org/frame_articles/1999Traditionalism.htm.

8. Frame, "In Defense of Something Close to Biblicism," *Westminster Theological Journal* 59 (1997): 269–318, with replies by David Wells and Richard Muller and a further reply by me. Also published (without the replies) as an appendix to my *Contemporary Worship Music* (Phillipsburg, NJ: P&R Publishing, 1997).

9. Wells, *No Place for Truth* (Grand Rapids: Eerdmans, 1993), 17–52.

characterizes modern culture, first, as *subjectivist* or irrationalist: basing one's life on human experience, rather than upon objective truth. Here he echoes the theme of Schaeffer's analysis: modern culture as an escape from reason and truth.

Modern culture also, he says, is *psychologistic*, believing in psychotherapy as the best way to deal with human problems. It is preoccupied with *professionalism*: business management and marketing techniques as the model for achieving any kind of common enterprise. It is *consumerist*, believing that we must always be willing to provide for people what they want, or what they can be induced to buy. It is *pragmatist*, holding that results are the ultimate justification for any idea or decision.

Wells's main interest is not so much to analyze culture as to indict the church for its capitulation to culture. In chapter 49, I will focus on that issue.

KENNETH A. MYERS

Another Reformed Christian who seeks to accuse the evangelical church of capitulation to the worst in modern culture is Ken Myers, once a producer and editor for National Public Radio and more recently host of the Mars Hill tape ministry and author of a brilliant and highly influential volume called *All God's Children and Blue Suede Shoes: Christians and Popular Culture*.[10] Myers bases his analysis on a distinction between three kinds of culture: high, folk, and popular. He captures the differences between these in some catchy illustrations. In food, high culture would be a gourmet restaurant. Folk culture would be good home cooking. Popular culture would be a fast-food restaurant. You can see how this distinction would apply to music: Beethoven is high art, African-American spirituals are folk art, and Metallica is pop art.

Popular culture, Myers thinks, began during the Industrial Revolution, when there were mass movements from farms to cities. Folk culture didn't fit the city, lacking the supportive community necessary to sustain it. The new urbanites felt that something else was needed to offset the monotony of work and to fill the new leisure hours they were gaining. That something else had to be exciting and diverting. Indeed, Myers thinks it is fair to describe popular culture as "a culture of diversion."[11] But in this situation many became obsessive about diversion, compulsive about excitement, and passionate about instant gratification. This meant, of course, liberation from traditional values and restraints.

10. Wheaton, IL: Crossway Books, 1989.
11. Ibid., 56.

The key to Myers's analysis is the value judgments he makes about these. High culture, he says, has the ability to provide a transcendent perspective. It has, he says,

> its roots in antiquity, in an age of convictions about absolutes, about truth, about virtue. However corrupted it has become over the centuries (and it has become quite corrupted in our own century), its essential features make it capable of maintaining and transmitting more about human experience in creation, and about God's redemptive intervention in history, than its alternatives.

Then he adds, "Folk culture, while simpler in manner and less communicable from one folk to another, has the virtues of honesty, integrity, commitment to tradition, and perseverance in the face of opposition."[12]

Myers, however, has almost nothing positive to say about popular culture. He does say that not everything about popular culture is bad, and that it can provide "innocent pleasures." And at one point he admits that within the scope of popular art, "there are numerous films, television programs, rock songs, or detective novels that are splendid productions as entertainment and as art."[13] But, he adds, "its principal attributes are . . . obstacles to enjoying the best of American experience."[14]

As Myers sees it, popular culture is governed largely by marketing considerations, not artistic ones. It is not concerned to communicate truth or insight or great values. It tries to discover successful *formulas*, formulas that people will buy into again and again. And Myers quotes Abraham Kaplan as saying, "Popular art uses formulas, not for analysis, but for the experience itself."[15] Its values are those of entertainment, not of art. As with entertainment, pop artists never want their audience to feel they must *work* to enjoy it; everything must be immediately accessible. And pop art "cannot bear the sustained attention that high art can."[16]

So, Myers tells us, it's not wrong to occasionally enjoy popular art, but it would be wrong for us to get addicted to it or to spend large amounts of time in it. And we certainly should not adopt the values of popular culture which, as Myers sees it, are essentially the same values that Wells attaches to modern culture in general.

12. Ibid., 59.
13. Ibid., 86.
14. Ibid., xiii.
15. Ibid., 80.
16. Ibid., 83.

PREMODERN, MODERN, AND POSTMODERN

Many recent analyses of culture have employed the threefold distinction of premodern, modern, and postmodern.[17] The modern period has roots in the Renaissance, but most people date its beginning in the Enlightenment of the seventeenth and eighteenth centuries. At that time, leading thinkers abandoned religion and tradition, seeking to build up the whole edifice of human knowledge on a foundation of human reason. So during the modern period, science and technology have flourished and have been models for all other knowledge to follow. Modernism has encouraged skepticism about religion and about the supernatural in general.

Postmodernism, however, has rejected many of the assumptions of modernism. Anticipated by earlier thinkers like Pascal, Kant, and Nietzsche, postmodernists have developed a certain critical or skeptical attitude toward human reason itself and a greater openness to other avenues toward knowledge. Richard Pratt summarizes the three movements as follows:

I. Standard of Truth
   A. Premodern: Truth is discerned primarily through religious institutions and mythology under the guidance of religious leaders.
   B. Modern: Truth is discerned primarily through rational and scientific investigation under the guidance of rationalistic philosophers and scientists.
   C. Postmodern: Truth is discerned both through mythology and rational-scientific means.

II. Ultimate Reality
   A. Premodern: Ultimate reality is spiritual and deeply influences events in the ephemeral physical world.
   B. Modern: Ultimate reality is the physical world. If a spiritual world exists at all, it is ephemeral and uninvolved in the events of the physical world.
   C. Postmodern: Ultimate reality is both physical and spiritual (personal and impersonal); these dimensions of reality interact in countless ways.

17. One useful summary of postmodernism is Stanley J. Grenz, *A Primer on Postmodernism* (Grand Rapids: Eerdmans, 1996).

III. Seeker of Truth
  A. Premodern: Individuality is discouraged and conformity to community traditions is highly prized.
  B. Modern: Individuality of the independent objective scholar (transcendent subject) is prized over conformity to received traditions.
  C. Postmodern: Individuality is disdained as self-deceptive, but individuals are encouraged to defy oppressive traditions.

IV. Modes of Communication
  A. Premodern: Heavy reliance on oral, ritualized and iconographic communication due to widespread illiteracy and primitive publishing techniques.
  B. Modern: Heavy reliance on written communication, especially paper, due to rising literacy and publishing technologies (printing press).
  C. Postmodern: Written communication is lowered to the level of other formats, especially the iconographic, due to widespread electronic technologies.

V. Historical Progress
  A. Widespread mythic meta-narratives depict history in never-ending cycles.
  B. Widespread rational and scientific meta-narratives depict history as progressing toward utopia.
  C. Fragmented, heteromorphic multi-narratives depict history as cycles and counter-cycles of cacophony and harmony.[18] (Meta-narratives are suspected as attempts to oppress victim groups.)

Many have felt that the problems of modern culture are due to the effects of modernism and postmodernism, so understood. Indeed, we can see in architecture and art, music, philosophy, and entertainment, a struggle between the values of modernism (systematic rationality) and those of postmodernism (holistic acceptance of experience, criticism of reason and worldviews). Postmodernism tends to be very skeptical and very open at the same time: open to experience, yet skeptical of dogmatic accounts of experience; open to many interpretations of literature from many points of view, but dogmatically critical of ideas that are deemed oppressive, not politically correct. Many see postmodernism as the dominant ideology today on university campuses and among the elite opinion-making class of our society.

18. Pratt, "Postmoderns: Opponents or Opportunities?" (unpublished lecture outline), 1.3–8. Used by permission.

CORNELIUS VAN TIL

Cornelius Van Til was professor of apologetics at Westminster Theological Seminary in Philadelphia from 1929 to 1975. So his writings take us back to an earlier part of the twentieth century. He was one of Schaeffer's teachers, and he died in 1987, before the books of Wells and Myers were published. He never wrote about culture, as his nephew Henry did, but he did write much about philosophy, about worldviews, and about ways of determining ethical value. That is all, of course, quite relevant to the analysis and evaluation of culture. In these areas, I believe, he had unparalleled biblical insight and presents a very helpful perspective for our consideration, one rather different from the other thinkers we have considered.

Van Til knew a great deal about the history of human thought, but he made very little of historical turning points. This is one noticeable difference between him and the thinkers we have so far considered. Schaeffer, Guinness, Wells, Myers, and the chroniclers of postmodernism all make a case against present-day culture, based on historical developments. For Schaeffer, the turning point was the "line of despair"; for Guinness, the counterculture of the 1960s; for Wells, modernism; for Myers, the Industrial Revolution; for many others, postmodernism. So for these thinkers it is some relatively recent historical development that is responsible for most of the ills of present-day culture.

Van Til knew only one turning point: the fall of Adam and Eve in the garden of Eden. History since that time, in his view, has been replay after replay. Eve was rationalist and irrationalist, modernist and postmodernist, oppressive establishment and countercultural rebel, an idolater of value and a destroyer of it, all at the same time. Picture the scene. Eve knows what God has said, but she has also heard a word from Satan that claims God is a liar. How will she make up her mind? It should have been obvious, of course. God is the Creator; he has perfect knowledge and understanding; he has the right to speak with absolute authority. Eve should have trusted God, too, because he loved her.

But something happened in her consciousness. Somehow, she no longer accepted God's word as the final word. As Van Til explains, Eve was shut up to two remaining alternatives: either there is no final authority or she was the final authority. As a rationalist, she believed that she had the authority to decide what was true or false, right or wrong. But if she was the final authority, then there was no God, nobody who could speak a word more authoritative than hers. And if there was no God, there was no meaning, no rationality, no structure, no ground for any other word, including hers, to be authoritative. So Eve was both a rationalist and an irrationalist. She thought she was the supreme authority, but she also believed there was no supreme authority. These two beliefs were inconsistent, of course. But both are necessary to the unbelieving mind-set.

Van Til analyzed the history of philosophy to show that all non-Christian thinkers, from ancient Greece to the present, were both rationalists and irrationalists at the same time. Van Til did not agree with Schaeffer that the ancient Greeks had an adequate view of truth. The Greeks believed with Eve that truth could be known through the autonomous human intellect, and that was no better than subjectivism or irrationalism. Nor did he take the position of Wells and others that the ills of culture come from modernism, the Industrial Revolution, the sixties' counterculture, or postmodernism. Eve was both a traditionalist and a modernist, a modernist and a postmodernist. History is not a movement from rationalism to irrationalism, but a dialogue, a dance, between them. When rationalism gets out of hand, irrationalism jumps in, and vice versa.

So the problem is not history; the problem is sin. Culture is bad today, but Sodom and Gomorrah were probably not any better, nor were Tyre, Sidon, Nineveh, Babylon, Rome, Capernaum, Chorazin, or Bethsaida.

Popular culture is bad, but high culture is too. Beethoven was a devotee of the secularism of the French Revolution, Wagner of German mythology, and their music makes a powerful case for these false worldviews. The problems of high culture go back a long way. It is not that high culture has been infected by popular culture; if anything, the reverse is true. And folk culture has always had alongside its humble virtues a lot of bawdy tales, class warfare, ignorant populism, and disrespect for the holy.

It is always wrong to try to single out one element of culture as pure, even relatively pure, and blame all of society's ills on some other element. That is almost always self-serving: we like what we like, and we want to blame the evils of life on the culture we dislike. But perhaps we need to have a more biblical view of sin. Sin is not limited to one segment of society or one segment of culture. It pervades everything. And whatever good there is comes from God's common and special grace.

CHAPTER 48

Christians in Our Culture

In the last three chapters, I've been arguing that culture (and our culture in particular) is both good and bad. It is bad because of human depravity, and good because of God's common grace and special grace. Now we need to get more personal. How should we as Christians interact with the culture in which God has placed us?

The general biblical formula is that we are to be "in" the world (John 17:11, 15; Titus 2:12), but not "of" the world (John 15:19; 17:14, 16). As we saw earlier, it is wrong to identify the "world" as "culture." The world is the negative side of culture. But that negative side is inescapable, and this biblical principle is crucial for Christians who are trying to live godly lives. Yet to say that we should be "in the world," but not "of the world," is obvious in a way. Of course we are "in" the world: we are ourselves part of the world, and the world constitutes our whole environment. Escaping the world is inconceivable. Similarly, it is obvious that we should not be "of" the world, for to be of the world is to accept the world's values and its opposition to God.

In this chapter and the next, I will explore some specific ways of being in the world but not of it. First I will examine the question of whether Christians should strive to be part of the cultural elite. Then I will discuss Christian involvement in the film industry. In the next chapter, I will consider music, especially in Christian worship.

SHOULD CHRISTIANS JOIN THE CULTURAL ELITE?

There was a time when Christianity was the dominant force in Western culture (education, scholarship, the arts, literature, science, law, treatment of the poor, etc). That time included the medieval and Renaissance periods, the Reformation and the post-Reformation periods, until around 1750 (the death of J. S. Bach). Even during this period of dominance, other factors were also influential: Greek and Roman culture and Islam, for example. From 1750 to about 1920, Christians were a significant, though not a dominant influence. In many places, the pastor, priest, or rector was the most educated man in the area. People would come to him, not only for spiritual advice, but also as an expert on history, science, philosophy, and the arts.

After 1920 (and I speak from an American perspective, of course) that influence went through a rather drastic decline. The Scopes trial, in which the Christian critique of evolution became a laughingstock, was the symbolic, if not the actual, point of decline. For the next twenty years or so, much (though certainly not all) of American evangelicalism became explicitly anti-intellectual, and that anti-intellectualism determined its reputation in the society at large. Many Christians thought that the contemporary academic world was what Paul called in Colossians 2:8 "philosophy and empty deceit," a spiritual snare to be avoided. This view was shallow and harmful to the church's witness. But one can still admire the fundamentalists for putting their loyalty to Christ ahead of cultural fashions, intellectual and otherwise.

From 1925 to 1945, there was little serious evangelical (sometimes called "fundamentalist") participation in academics, the arts, or sciences. It is to this period that Mark Noll's comments about "the scandal of the evangelical mind" (he says that scandal is "that there is no evangelical mind") actually apply.[1] The development of Reformed theology at Princeton Seminary (Westminster after 1928) was one exception to this general rule. In that movement there was, if anything, an overemphasis on intellectual rigor (see my discussion of "The Pathos Game" in chapter 21).

After World War II, however, there was something of an evangelical renaissance. Younger Christian leaders like Carl F. H. Henry and Billy Graham, together with Harold J. Ockenga, Charles E. Fuller, and financier J. Howard Pew, joined together to try to form an evangelicalism that would be informed by sound scholarship and be apologetically powerful and socially relevant. Fuller Seminary, *Christianity Today*, and the Billy Graham Evangelistic Association were elements of the "new evangelical" movement, as it was

---

1. Mark A. Noll, *The Scandal of the Evangelical Mind* (Grand Rapids: Eerdmans, 1994).

called. Westminster was the model for Fuller in the early days, and Westminster graduates like Edward J. Carnell and Paul K. Jewett joined the early Fuller faculty. Gordon Clark was also a significant influence: Henry, Graham, Edmund Clowney, and others were students of his at Wheaton. Clark's intellectualism played a major role in the self-image of the new evangelicalism.

The new evangelicalism was somewhat ashamed of its fundamentalist past. It repudiated the idea of an antithesis between Christianity and secular learning and determined to take a positive role in the affairs of society. Cornelius Van Til tried to inject a different note: we should be positive about intellect and science per se, but we should also be aware of the effects of sin upon the life of the mind. Van Til even spoke of antithesis between Christianity and secular learning. He did not mean to say that everything in secular philosophy and science was false, but that it was deeply flawed by an anti-Christian epistemology and could never be taken for granted. Van Til was no obscurantist. He had earned a Ph.D. in philosophy at Princeton and had a knowledge of history, philosophy, and culture that few could equal. But the main body of evangelicalism saw his emphasis to be too much a reversion to the fundamentalist anti-intellectualism.

The new evangelical movement, committed as it was to mainstream scholarship, came to grief in the 1960s on the question of biblical inerrancy. On that issue, evangelicals had to choose between mainstream scholarship and Christian orthodoxy. The movement divided between those alternatives.

More recently, these two strains have drawn closer together again. Noninerrantists and limited inerrantists have taken fairly conservative stands on matters of biblical criticism, while inerrantists have become hermeneutically more sophisticated. Yet the two branches often diverge, especially on questions of feminism and homosexuality, which in the end are doctrinal questions. The limited inerrantists had originally said that they accepted the full authority of Scripture on doctrinal matters, but not on matters of history and science. But Paul Jewett, in *Man as Male and Female*, said that Paul's view of women in the church was wrong[2]—and that was certainly a matter of doctrine, not merely of history or science.

From 1970 to the present, there has been a constant effort to get evangelicals involved in mainstream academics, the arts, and in the debates of the public forum. Evangelicalism has become an important factor in social and political discussions. The previously secular academic domain of philosophy has been invaded by many Christians, including distinguished figures like Alvin Plantinga, Richard Swinburne, and Paul Helm. "Faith-based"

2. Paul K. Jewett, *Man as Male and Female* (Grand Rapids: Eerdmans, 1975), 112–13.

mercy ministries have again taken the initiative to alleviate social problems. Christian schools and Christian homeschooling have become an important element of American education. Even the Christian critique of evolution has become more respectable in the hands of the "intelligent design" writers, such as Phillip Johnson, Michael Behe, and William Dembski. *World Magazine*, with its Christian editorial position, has become the fourth-largest selling news magazine. Christian music ("CCM") and book publishing have become major industries, attracting the investment of secular publishers and distributors. Every U.S. President since Dwight Eisenhower has befriended Billy Graham and has given some lip service, at least, to evangelical faith. There is much talk (both by advocates and opponents) of the Republican party being taken over by the Christian Right.

American evangelicalism, therefore, is today a cultural force to be reckoned with. Yet many still perceive evangelicalism as it was perceived from 1925 to 1945, as an anti-intellectual cultural backwater. These critics (like Noll, David Wells, Michael Horton, Os Guinness, Ken Myers, Frank Schaeffer, and D. G. Hart) think that CCM is poor-quality music, that evangelical art is largely kitsch, that evangelical literature is aesthetically inferior, that evangelical social action is a hopeless attempt to Christianize fallen society, that evangelical thinking is relativist and subjectivist, inadequately focused on objective truth.

In the remainder of this section, let me address one question that emerges from such discussions: should Christians be patrons of "high art"? That is, should Christians renounce popular culture and embrace what our culture recommends as the highest forms of art and literature? This question is linked with questions dealing with other areas of interaction between Christ and culture, but I must focus on the narrower question here.

In responding to this question, I adopt my customary *sola Scriptura* principle. In my judgment, these discussions have been governed far too much by autonomous analysis of historical trends and routine acceptance of secular standards (see my articles on "Biblicism" and "Traditionalism"[3]). I think that the postwar new evangelicals should have paid more attention to Van Til and less to Clark. Then they would have sensed more of the ambiguity of Christian involvement in scholarship and society.

To the question of whether we should embrace high art, my answer is yes and no. High art is an admirable tradition, nurtured in the past by great Christians like Bach, Rembrandt, and Dürer. But it has always been subject to non-Christian influences and has been dominated by them since 1750 or so. In Beethoven, Wagner, Cage, and others, "classical" music has been

---

3. Both articles are available at www.frame-poythress.org.

an instrument of anti-Christian ideology. The same is true of much art, literature, drama, and film. Ken Myers, as we saw in chapter 47, admits that all is not right with high art, but he thinks the problem is that high art has been corrupted by popular art, by the profit motive, and so on. As I see it, the problem is not the influence of popular culture; the problem is original sin.

Myers distinguishes between high art, folk art, and popular art. He rather likes the first two, but despises the third. Folk art, like high art, he thinks, has been corrupted by popular art. With William Edgar (see his review of *All God's Children*[4]) and others, I think Myers's thesis is greatly exaggerated. There is much good in popular art (though we tend not to recognize it until it becomes old-fashioned: ragtime, blues, big bands, Elvis, the Beatles, and so on). The problem is not with one genre or another, but, as Van Til emphasized, the sin that corrupts everything.

Myers's assessments of quality are not unquestionable, but this is a legitimate subject for discussion. A second area, however, is power of communication. Even if high art is objectively "better than," say, folk art, there is a vast difference between the two as to communication. Some people can appreciate one of them far more than the other. That question is especially important when we consider the use of art in worship. A Latin Mass may be objectively better musically than a Southern gospel hymn, but if in a particular church the former is incomprehensible and the latter clearly conveys the biblical gospel, then certainly the choice must be made in favor of the folk art, rather than the high art. There are those who say that we should teach our churches to appreciate high art. But is it really the job of the church to give to its members an education in aesthetics? Perhaps even in the aesthetic realm, the academic prejudice comes to bear. Perhaps evangelicals in this area are still trying to overcome their shame at their fundamentalist heritage. I consider this a distraction from the work of the church. Where high art is appreciated and understood, we should use it. Where we can make it appreciated and understood by a bit of intellectual stretching, let's do that. But where the people speak an entirely different aesthetic language and have little inclination to change their tastes, let us not seek to change them. Let us not fight battles over aesthetics.

Francis Schaeffer used to chide fellow evangelicals for their failure to attend art exhibits and the like. I would encourage fellow Christians with gifts and interests in high art to become acquainted with it and to tell the rest of us, as Schaeffer did, what challenges and opportunities the art world presents to us. But I don't think the Bible requires every Christian to be

4. *Westminster Theological Journal* 53 (1991): 377–80.

an expert in high culture, or even to appreciate it. The fundamentalists were wrong to think that the Bible forbade such cultural involvements. But it would be equally wrong to argue that evangelicals must be zealous advocates of art or experts in it. We need to recognize more the diversity of the church, the differences in culture, gifts, and interests. These differences are not necessarily sinful. They simply indicate the richness of God's image and of the Spirit's endowments.

It is not wrong to try to push ourselves to higher achievement and appreciation of higher excellences. But it is wrong to criticize one another for failing to meet those levels of achievement and excellence. We should encourage one another to higher standards, but we should also be willing to start where people are in order to help them go higher. And our definition of "higher" must not be borrowed from fallen culture, but must recognize the dimensions of worldview and communication.

SHOULD CHRISTIANS GO TO MOVIES?

Can we be yet more specific? Let's take a specific form of culture and look at it more closely. We could look at science, business, advertising, politics, economics, music, the fine arts, or many other elements of culture. I prefer to look at film, since I've done some thinking about that in the past, and since I think it may be a live issue for many of us. Like rock music and other entertainments, film is a form of culture that our children know a great deal about, and it poses great temptations to them and to us. As we think about film, perhaps we will develop some biblical criteria that we can apply to other forms of culture as well.

Some Christians may wonder how a fellow believer can give any support to the film industry, notorious as it is for anti-Christian bias and moral relativism. I would note that there is also a view on the opposite extreme: some Christian critics of culture insist that all Christians have a responsibility to become culturally aware, to become knowledgeable about cultural trends in art, music, literature, film, drama, and so on.

I reject both of these extremes. If we are to be "in" the world, but not "of" the world, that means that we not only may, but should, be willing to live amid secular (i.e., anti-Christian) influence without ourselves compromising the faith. In this respect, it doesn't matter whether that secular influence comes from film or from involvement in business, labor, neighborhood, politics, or whatever. Nor, within the general realm of media entertainment, does it matter whether we are talking about Beethoven or modern rock, Jane Austen or William Faulkner, Ernest Hemingway or

Jackie Collins, news or business magazines, TV or film, Disney films or films by Martin Scorsese. To avoid non-Christian influence altogether, we would have to live as hermits (assuming that we could even find some place in the world beyond the reach of modern communications and government). In all modern experience, there is a heavy component of antibiblical teaching and influence. But complete isolation is not a live option for biblical Christians. Even the Christian hermits of the ancient and medieval periods justified their existence as a life of prayer, and thus as a life which was in and for the world. How can we pray for a world we know nothing about? We must not seek to isolate ourselves from the world, but rather to be "salt" and "light" in our fallen culture, to carry out our Lord's Great Commission.

That balance, of being "in" but not "of" the world, is sometimes difficult to maintain. One's choices in this area should be based in part upon his or her own moral and spiritual maturity. Some people, especially children or those who are young in the faith, or those with special problems like alcohol addiction or unusual susceptibility to sexual temptation, should limit their exposure to some parts of secular culture in appropriate ways. But at the same time they should be trained in Christian maturity, so that eventually they can enter the secular arena more fully, not fearing that they will be compromised by the culture, but expecting to influence the culture positively for Christ.

These decisions should also be based on one's gifts, calling, and station in life. I do not believe, with the Christian "culturalists," that every Christian, or even every mature Christian, has an obligation to attend art exhibits, concerts, films, and so forth. Christians should seek to influence the world for Christ in some way—that is the Great Commission. But the precise way in which they reach out to the world may differ greatly from one believer to another. My brother-in-law is the pastor of a church in the inner city of Philadelphia. He does not normally go to films, dramas, or art exhibits. But he is definitely "in" the world, the real world, and he ministers to it with all the strength that God provides him. A knowledge of entertainment media would be of little use to him in his ministry, and I would be the last person to urge him to become "culturally aware."

Yet there are others (such as myself, I believe) who are called of God to devote some of their energy to the criticism of culture. Many pastors, as well as youth workers, scholars, teachers, writers, parents, and others are in this category. For them it is not wrong, I believe, within sensible limits, to expose themselves to modern film or other media. The apostle Paul said that he was not ignorant of Satan's devices (2 Cor. 2:11). For that purpose, if for no other, we may be called to learn what filmmakers have to say to us.

Some arguments used by Christians who are opposed to moderate attendance at films are as follows:

1. "Graphic acts of violence debase those who watch them, making
the viewers more prone to violence." On this proposition there is mixed
statistical evidence. Some people, especially children, do seem to resort
more quickly to violence, or to imitate violence, as the result of viewing
simulated violence on TV or film. I do advocate that parents limit and
monitor the use of these media by their children. But I find it hard to
believe that everybody should for this reason drastically curtail their film
attendance. I have never myself (even in childhood, as best I can recall)
felt the least bit inclined toward violence as the result of watching it on
film. For the most part, viewing such violence increases my resolve to
find nonviolent solutions to problems. I think that many other people are
similar to me in this respect.

Further, if we maintain a proper critical distance from the films we watch
(a distance which is necessary for many other reasons), we can see that film
violence is essentially choreography. No one really gets hurt. And for the
most part in films, even today, unjustly violent people are not rewarded
or glorified.

It is important to maintain perspective: lack of perspective is one of
the most prevalent defects in Christian thought today, in my view. And
the larger perspective is that violence is all around us and unavoidable.
To avoid it entirely would be to depart from the world. Indeed, Scripture itself contains descriptions of terrifying, even gory violence; just read
the book of Judges. Since Scripture includes such descriptions, we must
assume that there are good reasons for it—reasons conducive to edification
(2 Tim. 3:16–17). It is not hard to imagine what those reasons might be.
The violence of the wicked shows us what the fall has done to us, and the
violence of divine judgment summons us to repentance (Luke 13:1–5). On
this basis, we cannot deny that some exposure to depictions of violence
can be edifying.

2. "Sexual scenes in movies excite impure lusts." Again, I think this is
true of some viewers, but not others. If sex scenes in films have that effect
on you, then don't go to films until God gives you a greater mastery over
temptation. But I don't think this is a problem for every Christian.

But some might go further and insist that, even for those who are not
tempted toward sin by screen sex, it is wrong to view actors in the process
of doing things that are sinful in themselves. (The same point has been
made with regard to the use of unwholesome or blasphemous language in
movie scripts: see chapter 27.) I grant that some scenes in the movies cross
over that line of being "sinful in themselves." True, screen sex is usually,

for the actors and actresses involved, not very "sexy." The filming of such scenes is done bit by bit, with all sorts of technical intrusions, and usually without actual genital contact. Still, if I were married to an actress who chose to engage publicly in deep kissing and simulated intercourse with a third party, I would consider myself to have been violated. In my view, that is a scriptural view of the matter.

So some movie sex is certainly sinful in itself. And one cannot, certainly, justify watching sin for its own sake. I would not go to a film for the purpose of watching an actor and actress in a nude sex scene (thus I avoid "XXX" flicks), any more than I would take a walk in the park to spy on kids making love behind the bushes. On the other hand, I would not stay away from the park out of fear that I might happen to observe some illicit sex. Similarly, if film actors wish to commit sin before the camera, that is their responsibility. I don't believe I commit sin when I, in the normal course of my cultural pursuits, observe what they, without consulting me, have chosen to do in public. Still, I avoid films in which the nudity and simulated sex are the main point, or in which they overwhelm the whole atmosphere of the film.

3. "Modern films promote, very effectively, a non-Christian philosophy of life." This is true, and it is the most profound of all arguments against Christian attendance at films. Sex, foul language, and violence are incidental elements in film, but the non-Christian world-and-life view is often at its core. That worldview does more damage in society than any cinematic portrayals of sex, violence, and ungodly speech. Indeed, that worldview is what makes the sex, violence, and language in movies unwholesome, in contrast to biblical depictions of such things.

But again, perspective is in order. Non-Christian philosophy has dominated the arts and general culture for the last three centuries. To avoid exposure to non-Christian worldviews and values, we would have to avoid exposure to Mozart and Beethoven, Emerson and Thoreau, Hume and Kant, Paine and Jefferson, D. W. Griffith and Charlie Chaplin, and so on, not to mention Plato, Aristotle, Sophocles, Euripides, Cicero, and other ancients. We tend to discount older exponents of non-Christian values, viewing them with the halo that comes with long cultural acceptance. For that reason, these older thinkers are often more dangerous than those who are more contemporary and more obviously anti-Christian. Indeed, for similar reasons, we must beware of G-rated films as much as R- and X-rated films. Yes, let us limit our exposure to all of these influences, but not to the extent of leaving the world, or to the extent of becoming ignorant of Satan's devices (2 Cor. 2:11).

4. "We should not give our money to an industry that encourages immorality and unbelief." Scripture does not require believers to support only

industries and institutions that are morally and religiously pure. Jesus taught his disciples to pay taxes to Caesar, taxes which supported the emperor cult, among other things. Paul taught the Corinthians to buy food in the marketplace without asking whether or not it had been offered to idols. Scripture is realistic enough to know that if we had to inquire about the religion or morals of every merchant before doing business with him, we could not buy at all.

I do not think it is wrong for Christians to boycott industries or companies which they believe are doing social and/or religious harm in the world. They are certainly free to withhold their economic support of them. On the other hand, I do not believe that Scripture requires us to boycott such organizations. We really could not do that in every case without completely isolating ourselves from the world.[5]

I would conclude, therefore, that a moderate amount of moviegoing is legitimate for most Christians. I don't think we should be ashamed of that or even ashamed of enjoying it. Moderation, of course, requires careful thought about priorities. Even activities that are good in themselves can become wrong if they crowd out of our lives things that are more important. Each of us needs to do some self-examination in this area. Choices about exposure to entertainment and culture are not religiously neutral. But those who are conscientious about pleasing God and keeping his commandments need not feel guilty about moderate movie attendance.

FILM AND CULTURE

Harvie Conn has described film as a "cultural mirror," a valuable reflection of contemporary attitudes, philosophies, values, and lifestyles. Others, such as Michael Medved, have placed more emphasis on the idea of film as a *former* of culture.

As I see it, both emphases are true. The relation between film and culture is a chicken-and-egg relationship. Film is of course a product of culture, for the makers of films are people of their own time. On the other hand, within their own culture, filmmakers are often atypical. They tend to be more liberal politically, less inclined to practice religion, and more open to radical social attitudes and movements, than the general population. Thus, their films tend to support radicalism and to subvert traditional, especially Christian, values. When those filmmakers answer criticisms of the content of their films by saying, "We are only reflecting the broader culture," they

5. Cf. the discussion of boycotts in chapter 41.

either are naive or are being dishonest. In the broader culture, there is far more interest in religion, far more family integrity, far more clean language, and far more honest work than one would ever guess from films.

In any case, it is important when we go to the movies to take with us some understanding of what is happening in the general culture: both what is considered traditional and what is considered avant-garde.

One cannot adequately summarize the current cultural situation in a brief essay, but I will offer a summary here simply to show the reader where I am coming from in my reviews. As I see it, Western culture has moved in the last three hundred years from a time of Christian dominance to a time of anti-Christian secular dominance. Even today, however, there is in Western culture quite a bit of "borrowed Christian capital," and, every now and then, Christian teaching is heard with respect.

It is possible to overestimate the role of secular liberalism in contemporary society. From the portrayals of the 1960s in popular media, especially film, one would get the impression that everybody in the United States was "dropping out," taking drugs, protesting the war, and supporting radical leftist causes. Perhaps that is what most filmmakers and their friends were doing. But most Americans were fed up with all the protests, drugs, and pompous young moralizers. They elected Richard Nixon president in 1968, and they overwhelmingly reelected him in 1972 against George McGovern, who was the voice of the radical left. Arguably, the populace moved rightward through the 1970s, resulting in the election of Ronald Reagan in 1980 and 1984. During the last thirty years, the only Democrats elected president were Carter and Clinton, both Southern governors who persuaded the electorate of their moderation. The overt liberals—McGovern, Mondale, and Dukakis—were soundly defeated.

Liberal ideas, therefore, are not nearly as pervasive within the general culture as they are in the press, higher education, and the entertainment industry. Still, they do leave their mark in important ways, largely because these institutions—together with the influence of government—have so much power.

Today the focus of the liberal movement can be summarized by the term equality. That movement especially emphasizes, in a quasi-Marxist way, equality between men and women, between races, cultures, and religions, and between rich and poor.

Christianity also endorses equality of all persons in the eyes of divine and human law (see chapter 34). God is no respecter of persons, and human law must not give preference to people based on wealth, gender, or race. But the liberal consensus endorses unbiblical forms of equality: identical roles for men and women, abolition of any "gaps" between rich and poor, elimination of any moral sanction against homosexuality. Ultimately, liberal equality amounts to moral relativism. But it is a moral relativism that becomes very dogmatic and very nonrelativist in asserting its own egalitarianism. Anyone who disagrees, who is not "politically correct," must be smeared and ostracized from polite society.

The God of the Bible treats people equally in some respects, but, in other ways, he is the great divider. He separates the righteous from the wicked in his terrible judgments. He sets the nonrelative moral boundaries for creatures by revealing his law. He has no interest in abolishing economic differences between people in this world. He establishes institutions of family, state, and church, and gives different people different roles within these institutions: husband/wife/child, magistrate/citizen, elder/member.

The biblical God is able to make choices among people because he is a person. One distinctive of personhood is rational choice. The problem with secular liberalism is that it has abandoned belief in the personal God of the Bible. In the secular view, the most ultimate features of the universe are impersonal, not personal. But an impersonal force cannot make choices. It must act on all other realities equally. An electrical current will shock anyone or anything that comes up against it. But a person can choose how he will respond to other persons and objects in its environment.

Rejection of the personal God of Scripture inevitably brings universalism: either all are saved or all are lost. And it brings egalitarianism.

The moral relativist side of secular liberalism stems from the fact that, as Dostoyevsky noted, if God doesn't exist, anything is permitted. But such universal permissiveness is a recipe for chaos, one which even secularists cannot easily accept. Thus they seek to replace God with another supposed absolute. (Scripture calls this process "idolatry.") That absolute is, in most cases, their own autonomous moral judgment. Hence, there is the dogmatic side of secularism. But when that dogmatism fails, when the secularists' own judgment proves untrustworthy, then they revert to relativism: "Oh well, nobody really knows." Relativism and dogmatism: these are the Scylla and Charybdis of secular liberalism. Strictly speaking, these are inconsistent with one another. But they supplement and need one another. The secularist bounces back and forth from one to the other as on a pendulum.

Cornelius Van Til calls relativism and dogmatism "irrationalism" and "rationalism," respectively, thereby relating these themes to the traditional concerns of philosophical epistemology. Os Guinness, in *The Dust of Death*, describes them as "pessimism" and "optimism," thus relating these motifs to practical attitudes. It is important, especially in the context of film, that we do not see these themes only as elements of a theoretical worldview or ethical system, but that we see them as attitudes that affect all areas of human life. For if someone has adopted a relativist ethic, that person will likely be in despair and pessimistic when it comes to making choices in any area of life. He has rejected God, the source of all meaning. What ground can he possibly have for optimism? On the other hand, he can become a dogmatic secularist instead of a relativist, even though these are two sides of the same coin. Then he may well be optimistic; but it will be a false hope.

In films, then, we must reckon with the presence both of moral relativism and of secular dogmatism. But we may also find traces, sometimes more than traces, of Christian ideas which, in spite of the present resistance of the general culture and of the film industry, have managed to assert themselves. One will find large elements of Christian teaching and values in older stories set to modern films, such as the plays of Shakespeare and medieval legends. And one will also find films of recent vintage where Christian values are prominent. *Chariots of Fire, Tender Mercies, A Trip to Bountiful, Shadowlands, The Exorcism of Emily Rose, The Passion of the Christ,* and the Narnia series are recent films which, if not distinctively Christian, nevertheless present distinctively Christian ideas in a favorable light. Sometimes one finds Christian themes and symbolism in films, even films that are not in themselves supportive of Christian values. Christians should be ready to be surprised when they attend films, and not only negatively.

Sometimes it is easy to explain these authentically Christian elements in films, by the Christian convictions of a writer, director, or other member(s) of the filmmaking team. Other times it is not easy to explain. Sometimes it just seems as though the non-Christian filmmakers were unable to overcome the dramatic, intellectual, and moral force of the Christian revelation, and so, for once, they let it have its way.

In my film reviews, I try to bring out the messages of the filmmakers.[6] In them I focus on the themes of equality, relativism, and dogmatic idolatry. And I also bring out those elements in which I think God's word has overcome cultural resistance to speak its cinematic piece.

QUESTIONS TO ASK OF FILMS

In my discussion of film and culture, I identified the general thrust of modern secular liberalism and its antithesis to Christianity. My reviews

6. My movie reviews are available at www.frame-poythress.org. Click on "Books," then scroll to *Theology at the Movies.*

deal with those themes in general. Here I wish to be a bit more specific. What follows are certain questions that are always in my mind when I go to films. I would recommend that other Christian viewers ask the same questions. I don't go through this whole list in each review; I only discuss the ones that I think are most important to the particular film.

1. Who wrote the film? Who produced it? Who directed it? Do we know anything about their philosophy of life? The previous works of actors are also important. Actors contribute much to the quality of a film, though little to its fundamental conception. But actors do tend to sign on to projects with which they have some ideological affinity (assuming financial rewards are not otherwise determinative). Mel Gibson almost never takes on films with a heavy sexual element; Mickey Rourke almost always does. The presence of certain actors, granting that they sometimes go "against type," can tell you something about the message of a film.

2. Is it aesthetically well made? Are the production and acting values of high quality? These factors may have little to do with the message. But they do tend to determine the extent of the film's cultural impact, and that is important for our purposes. If a film is well made, it can have a large impact upon the culture for good or ill. (Of course, some bad films also have a major impact!)

3. Is it true to its own position? This is another mark of quality. Generally speaking, an honest film, regardless of its point of view, will have a larger cultural impact than one which blunts its points.

4. What kind of film is it? Fantasy? Biography? Realistic drama? Comedy? Obviously each film must be judged according to its purpose and genre. We don't demand of a fantasy the kind of historical accuracy that we demand of a supposedly literal biography.

5. What is the worldview of the film? Is it theistic or atheistic? Christian or non-Christian? If non-Christian, is its main thrust relativistic or dogmatic? How does it employ the theme of equality? Is there any role for providence, for God? Is the film pessimistic or optimistic? Does the action move in a deterministic fashion, or is there a significant role for human choice?

6. What is the plot? What problems do the characters face? Can these problems be correlated in some way with the fall of mankind in Adam? Does the film in effect deny the fall, or does it affirm it in some way?

7. Are the problems soluble? If so, how? What methods are available to the characters, so that they can find the answers they need?

8. What is the moral stance of the film? Is it relativistic, dogmatic, or both in some combination? What are its attitudes toward sex, family, human life, property, truth, and heart attitudes? What is the source of moral norms, if any? Does justice prevail?

9. In comedy, what is it that is funny? What are the typical incongruities? Who is the butt of the jokes—Christians, traditional values, the wicked, the righteous, God, Satan? Is the humor anarchic? Is it rationality gone awry? Is it bitter or gentle? Does it rely on caricatures? If so, of whom?

10. Are there allusions to historical events, literary works, other films, famous people, Scripture, and so on, that would give us some idea where the filmmakers are coming from? We should remember, of course, that allusions may be negative, positive, ironic, or merely decorative. A biblical allusion does not necessarily indicate acceptance of biblical values.

11. What are the chief images of the film? Is there anything interesting about the lighting, the camera angles, the sound, or the timing that would reinforce a particular theme? Are there significant symbols?

12. Are there any explicitly religious themes? Christ figures?[7] Does the film express significant attitudes toward Christ, the clergy, or the church? Does it distort Christianity or present it at its worst? Or does it present it with some insight and/or sympathy? Does it recognize the element of personal piety in people's lives?[8] If so, does it approve or disapprove of it? What about Satan, the demons, the occult? Does the film recognize their activity in some way? Is the devil taken seriously? If so, how is he dealt with?

---

7. Steven Spielberg's character E.T. is, I think, a genuine Christ figure: recall the themes of preexistence, growth, teaching, miracle, healing, death, resurrection, and ascension. Spielberg denied this parallel, but in my view it is objectively there, even if Spielberg was unconscious of it. The reason is that the human mind has a need for a gospel like that of the New Testament. Those who don't accept that gospel often instinctively give to their idolatrous inventions powers parallel to those of Christ.

8. The character of Frank Burns in the original M*A*S*H was a pious fellow who knelt to pray at his bedside, to the scorn of his fellow soldiers. Eventually, it turned out that he was an adulterer and a hypocrite. That is fairly typical of the way Hollywood portrays Christian piety.

CHAPTER 49

Culture in the Church

We have seen that culture is a mixed affair, the result of sinful human activity on the one hand, and God's grace (common and special) on the other (chapter 45). Christians are not to leave culture alone or to limit their influence to the content of natural law. Rather, they are to seek a transformation of culture through the whole Word of God (chapter 46). To do that, they need to understand the peculiarities of the culture they are part of, while understanding that in some ways culture has always been the same: rationalistic and irrationalistic, naive and degenerate, afflicted by selfishness, oppression, and hatred of life and truth, and yet also confronted by the gospel (chapter 47). So Christians should enter the dialogue over cultural objects, such as film, armed with the whole revelation of Christ (chapter 48).

I conclude the discussion of culture here by asking in what way the products and activities of culture should be used in the ministry of the church itself. I am not asking here *whether* these should be used in the church. The church is itself part of culture, and culture is inseparable from the church. Primarily the church is its people, and those people and their cultural activities, good and bad, are activities of the church. The language we use, the ways we approach people, our style of teaching, our dress, our hospitality, our church architecture, and, yes, our music, are profoundly influenced by culture. To some extent, that culture comes from past ages, and to some extent from the contemporary scene. But the church fools itself if it thinks it can operate apart from cultural influences.

If those influences are necessarily bad, then any ministry at all would be for that reason sinful. But, as we have seen, culture has itself been influenced by both common grace and the gospel. Paul does not hesitate to accept some cultural distinctives of Jews and Greeks (1 Cor. 9:20–23), so that he can bring the gospel to both. But of course there are many cultural distinctives of Jews and Greeks that Paul does not adopt: among the Jews, sinful pride, falsifications of God's word, hatred of Gentiles; among the Gentiles, idolatry, sexual sin, and so on. That is the issue also before us today: which elements of culture to adopt and which to reject as sinful.

I would like now to focus on music used in worship, which is a frequent battleground today in the church. The approach I recommend, however, has applications to the use of other arts in the church, as well as to styles of preaching, evangelism, and nurture.

I am encouraged that in many circles today the "worship wars" seem to be ending, as churches adopt blended forms of worship, drawing together the traditional and the contemporary, and as Christians of all ages and backgrounds seem to be blessed by the songs and other liturgical elements. I hope this chapter will in some small measure encourage this development.[1]

The main argument today about church music is over the claim that contemporary worship songs are a product of the worst elements of contemporary culture. We saw in chapter 47 the Wells-Myers critique of contemporary popular culture, that it is subjectivist, humanist, anti-intellectual, psychologistic, professionalist, consumerist, pragmatist, and focused on entertainment. The fear that many writers have is that by adapting hymns and songs from this culture the church will encourage these non-Christian values, rather than standing against them.

This argument does carry some weight. Music powerfully affects the heart, for good or ill. Doubtless Scripture puts such a strong emphasis on song in worship because music contributes great vividness and memorability to a text. Sometimes, indeed, the music overwhelms the text, creating a mood that might be at odds with the words. That does sometimes happen when

---

1. For more thorough consideration of these matters, see my two worship books, *Worship in Spirit and Truth* (Phillipsburg, NJ: P&R Publishing, 1996) and *Contemporary Worship Music: A Biblical Defense* (Phillipsburg, NJ: P&R Publishing, 1997). The latter book was written at a time and place when the polemics were pretty fierce. My concern then was to defend brothers and sisters who were under attack because they abandoned some traditions in order to reach the lost. But I would write today in a more irenic spirit. I also recommend *With One Voice*, by my esteemed colleague Reggie Kidd (Grand Rapids: Baker, 2005), who places these matters in a biblical balance. I like to think of my first book as reflecting the normative perspective, my second one as situational (engaging with the debates of the time), and Reggie's book as adding to these an existential perspective: the actual experience of biblical worship. But it would be wrong to see *With One Voice* as a mere supplement to my books.

contemporary music is used in church, but it is maddeningly difficult to analyze and evaluate this process. Years ago, I felt that electric guitars inevitably detracted from the purity of praise. It seemed to conjure up a world of secular rock and roll, with all its illicit sexuality, drug addiction, and anarchic atheism. But today the electric guitar often leads me to praise of an extreme sort (and what other kind of praise is fit to honor God?), challenging me to mobilize everything in my heart, body, and voice to honor the Lord of all. Many worshipers, I believe, feel the same way. But there are certainly others who feel about the electric guitar the way I felt many years ago. So how does one design worship that will minister to both groups?

The other side of it is that for some it is the classical traditions, the old hymns, the ancient liturgies, the smells and bells, that overwhelm the words of the gospel. So the answer is certainly not to retreat to an exclusively traditional approach to worship.[2]

Nor is the answer to develop a kind of mechanical balance between tradition and contemporaneity. For the effect of music varies from person to person. What communicates the gospel powerfully to one person will destroy worship for another. The ideal thing would be for everyone to bend a little bit. Those who find high art or traditional liturgy to be their natural language of worship should accept contemporary forms of music, if not for themselves, as a service to other members of the body. Those who find real worship only in the contemporary style should likewise defer to those on the other side. That is the way it should be in the body of Christ: people washing one another's feet, serving one another rather than themselves.

I used the phrase "language of worship" intentionally, for I think that the issue is largely one of communication. First Corinthians 14 is the one passage in the New Testament that describes in some detail the postresurrection worship of the early church. In that chapter, the burden of the apostle Paul is to encourage intelligible communication in worship. People who speak in tongues without interpretation may be speaking to God (v. 2), but they do not build up the church (v. 3). Paul uses the term "build up" (edify) six times in the chapter (vv. 3, 4, 5, 12, 17, 26). The whole thrust of Paul's instruction is that worship should edify the congregation.

We know from other biblical considerations that the chief purpose of worship is to glorify God and to obey the requirements of his revelation (cf. chapters 24–26). But in 1 Corinthians 14, there is also a horizontal dimension. Worship should teach, nurture, challenge, and motivate God's people. Hebrews 10:24–25 also emphasizes this aspect: "And let us consider how to stir up one

2. As I argued in chapter 26, the regulative principle of worship based on the second commandment does not require a traditionalist style of worship. On the contrary, it is best used as a tool to criticize traditions that are contrary to Scripture or add to it.

another to love and good works, not neglecting to meet together, as is the habit of some, but encouraging one another, and all the more as you see the Day drawing near." This is what Paul calls edification. And he emphasizes that if worship is to edify, it must use language that is intelligible to the congregation. The Protestant Reformers inferred from this principle that worship should not be in Latin, but in the vernacular languages of the nations, such as German, French, Dutch, and English. Someone who understands no Latin may well glorify God in a Latin service, but he will not be edified by the words spoken.

But music is analogous to language in important ways. It communicates content, both by its association with words and in its own right. It communicates emotions of all sorts—exciting, calm, and in between. But as I indicated above, a single piece will communicate different things to different people. The communication value of music depends highly on contexts: the physical setting, what happens before and after, the background of the hearers, and so forth.

Just as we should not conduct a service for English speakers entirely in Latin, so we should not arrange worship in a nursing home consisting entirely of songs written after 2000. The music, most likely, will not "speak to" that congregation; or, if it does communicate, it will communicate something other than the gospel. But neither should worship in a Young Life camp consist entirely of traditional hymns. It would not be wrong in either case to use some music that would not be immediately appreciated by the audience, in order to help them grow in their ability to worship in different ways and to respect people different from themselves. Teaching unfamiliar styles of music may also edify by exposing people to the insights of different eras.

It is wrong, however, to ignore the whole question of edification, of communication, as if it didn't exist. In his book *A Better Way*, Michael Horton quotes Lee Strobel as saying, "I begin in the real world, connecting with (the seekers') needs, and show them that I do understand where they've been and where they are. Based on that, I show the relevance of Scripture. I build a bridge from the real world into the world of Scripture."[3] Then Horton replies, "But that is just the question, isn't it: Do we even know what the 'real world' is apart from its divine description? . . . Furthermore, hasn't God built that bridge from the Word to his hearers by sending us preachers who announce his judgment and pardon?"[4]

3. Michael Horton, *A Better Way* (Grand Rapids: Baker, 2002), 215. Strobel is speaking about preaching, but his comments, and Horton's reply, apply as easily to music as communication. I have been assuming that the importance of communication in preaching is obvious; it is also important in music. That Horton fails to appreciate the importance of communication even in preaching is deeply troubling.

4. Ibid.

I do not doubt the truth of Horton's assertions that God has called preachers of the Word, and that without that Word we cannot understand what the real world is.[5] I doubt that Strobel would disagree with them either. Here and elsewhere in his writings, Horton magnifies unnecessarily the differences between his own ideas and those of other evangelicals. So I disagree with Horton's implication that one who acknowledges God's sovereignty in revelation need not be concerned with human communication (Strobel's "building a bridge"). It is generally wrong to pit divine sovereignty against human responsibility.[6] Those preachers whom God sends to announce his judgment and pardon must explain that revelation to their hearers in order to edify them. And that task may be described metaphorically as "building a bridge."

Music is part of that bridge building. Just as a church must speak the language of its congregation, so it must find worship music that can be understood by its congregation and will edify them. As we have seen, most congregations include people who speak different musical languages.

This problem is like that of churches where different national languages are spoken. In a church where some speak Spanish and others English as a primary language, various things can be done. One can have separate services for each language group, or longer services in which there is something in each language (or in which there is translation). In some cases, it may be wise to split into two churches.

These alternatives exist also for churches in which people speak and understand different musical languages.[7] But the case of musical diversity is actually a little easier than that of linguistic diversity. It is easier to learn unfamiliar musical forms than to learn a new language. If we learn how to defer to one another in humility, we can usually, after a time, find value in other musical languages, without formal teaching. That is, certainly, the best alternative.

It is true that some music is more effective at edifying immature Christians than mature Christians, and some vice versa. So some have argued that music should be geared to the mature, to communicate with them and to challenge the immature to grow up. But that is to misunderstand the nature of education/edification. The way to teach mathematics to a child is not to put him in a college calculus course. It is, rather, to bring him along step-by-step, through addition, subtraction, and so on. Similarly, in worship there should be words, and songs, that communicate with people

5. This is the normative perspective. But there are situational and existential perspectives as well, which Horton either overlooks or denies.

6. See *DG*, 119–25.

7. Even the translation approach has a musical equivalent. Worship leaders can explain what is happening in a particular musical arrangement.

at every level: child, adolescent, adult, unbeliever, new convert, growing believer, mature Christian. And these should also be words and songs that challenge people of each level to grow to the next level of maturity.

So worship music, like sermons and prayers, must edify people in their own languages. Like all language, musical language is part of culture. Worship music has never been completely distinctive to the church. Bach's secular music and his sacred music have much in common. Church music has always used the styles and techniques of its culture, just as preaching has always used the language of the culture. In the West, only chant is distinctively religious, but that is not distinctively Christian, since it is found also in Jewish, Muslim, and Hindu worship.

There is no sound argument to the effect that Christian worship music should be in a particular style, or that some styles are forbidden to it. As I have argued (chapter 26), the second commandment excludes traditionalism as a principle of worship. Some have argued that some kinds of music are too low in quality to use in worship, but the concept of quality here is difficult to define. And there is no consensus, even among musically knowledgeable people, as to what music is of sufficiently high quality for worship.[8] There are some styles of music that some people associate with non-Christian ideas and contexts, but those associations are not shared by everybody. And the argument that a song is inappropriate because its style is influenced by a particular genre is a classic example of the genetic fallacy.[9]

So there is no simple answer to the question of how cultural styles of music should be used in the worship of the church. Elders and worship leaders must weigh many factors, including the specific composition of their congregations, to determine what will be most edifying for all. Cultural influences cannot be avoided, and they should not be. To avoid the culture is to avoid the Great Commission. So we must carry on as best we can, recognizing that we will sometimes make mistakes, and what we decide will not be the most perfect decision for all worshipers.

But we can be encouraged that this kind of worship leadership is pleasing to God. He has called us to edify people even in our praise to him. We can be thankful that even in worship he is concerned to bless us with the mercies of Christ. He, too, is the one who has brought many types of people together in the body of Christ. He wants us to seek to communicate with all of these, even if the communication is not perfect. And it is he who has provided us with the cultural resources for doing so.

8. See my *Contemporary Worship Music*, 107–28.

9. The genetic fallacy, a cousin to the naturalistic fallacy (chapter 5), argues that something is good because it comes from a good source, or, as in this case, that something is bad because it comes from a bad source.

PART SIX

PERSONAL SPIRITUAL MATURITY

CHAPTER 50

Growing in Grace

I am not a specialist in the doctrine of sanctification or in the disciplines of what is now called "spiritual formation." But this book is called *The Doctrine of the Christian Life*, so something must be said about the way we grow in likeness to Christ. Without this concluding discussion, some might get the impression that the road to Christian maturity is simply to grit your teeth and obey God's law. That image is not entirely wrong, as we shall see. But it is only one perspective!

We considered the normative perspective in part 4, "The Ten Commandments." Then, in part 5, I discussed the situational perspective of Christ and culture. Now we come to the final chapter, which presents the existential perspective of the entire book. Of course, within each of these three divisions there are other triperspectival distinctions.

So I conclude the book with a one-chapter analysis of this important subject. My brevity should not be taken to express my view of the relative importance of this matter. It is very important, and it should certainly be discussed in books at least as thick as this one. It is as important as anything else in this volume, if not more so. But my own limitations and the already formidable length of this book require me to sum up this topic in a brief fashion.[1] Sometimes brevity can be an advantage. Brief discussions

---

1. My mentor, Cornelius Van Til, did something similar in his *Christian Theistic Ethics* ([Ripon, CA:] den Dulk Christian Foundation, 1971). In that book, he distinguished the goal, motive, and standard of ethics (one major source of my three perspectives). He presented a thorough analysis of the goal and standard, but only a minimal reflection on the motive. Van Til's example does not excuse what I have done, but some will regard it as a mitigating circumstance.

911

often pack more punch than longer ones, putting the essential points more strongly. Whether or not that is the case here, that is my goal.

Another excuse for my brevity here is that much about this topic has been said already. In chapter 9, I emphasized that God reveals himself, not only through creation and Scripture, but also in the human heart, made in his image. In chapter 12, I discussed the relationships between law and grace, law and love, and law and gospel, stressing that, although God's law is the norm for the Christian, we are not saved by keeping the law. We are saved entirely by God's grace, and that grace upholds us throughout our walk with God. What good things we do are the work of God's Spirit within us. In chapter 15, I discussed "Living with Ourselves," and in chapter 16 the already/not-yet tension in which we must make moral decisions. In chapter 17, we learned something of the biblical doctrine of vocation and the processes by which God calls us to specific roles in life. Then, in chapters 18–21, I discussed the existential perspective of ethical decision making. Chapter 20, especially, contains much description of the process or experience of God's ethical guidance. And in the discussion of the commandments, I have not avoided discussion of the actual experience of making decisions, especially the need for us to confront the idols of our hearts. Each commandment, as we have seen, requires certain behavior. But it also requires a change of heart.

The chapters focusing on culture (chapters 45–49) also challenged us to purity of heart. Often, the question is not whether to participate in this or that cultural activity, but with what motive we will participate.[2] Our decisions in this area should be determined by Jesus' Great Commission, as we become all things to all men in order to save some.

Finally, in this concluding chapter, I will try to summarize how we grow in holiness, given God's standards and our created and cultural environment.

THE DYNAMIC OF THE BIBLICAL ETHIC

John Murray, whom I have quoted often in this book, says that one of the most important elements of biblical ethics "may be stated broadly as union and communion with Christ. More specifically it is the truth of union with Christ in the virtue of his death and the power of his resurrection."[3] Briefly, when Jesus died on the cross, his people died to sin (Rom. 6:1–3, 6, 11). When he rose from the dead, his people rose with him to newness of life

2. Of course, there are some kinds of cultural participation that are sinful in themselves.
3. John Murray, *Principles of Conduct* (Grand Rapids: Eerdmans, 1957), 203.

(Rom. 6:4–5, 11; Col. 3:1–3). Our death to sin has destroyed the "old man" of sin and corruption (Rom. 6:6; cf. Gal. 5:24; Eph. 4:20–24; Col. 3:9–10). Because we died and rose with Jesus, Paul says, "sin will have no dominion over you, since you are not under law but under grace" (Rom. 6:14).

At first glance, it might seem that this teaching implies our present sinlessness. But, of course, Paul and many other biblical writers affirm that believers commit sin. John says, "If we say we have no sin, we deceive ourselves, and the truth is not in us. If we confess our sins, he is faithful and just to forgive us our sins and to cleanse us from all unrighteousness. If we say we have not sinned, we make him a liar, and his word is not in us" (1 John 1:8–10). Jesus likewise taught that even after we are cleansed of sin, we still need to ask God for forgiveness (Matt. 6:12). He puts it metaphorically that we still need to wash our feet daily, though our whole bodies are clean (John 13:10). And Paul, having taught that we are dead to sin, exhorts believers, "Let not sin therefore reign in your mortal bodies, to make you obey their passions" (Rom. 6:12).

So the question arises, what good is it that we have been crucified and risen with Christ? Murray cites Romans 6:14, "For sin will have no dominion over you, since you are not under law but under grace." He comments, "This is not exhortation. It is categorical assurance and means that the person who is under grace is not and cannot be the bondservant of sin."[4] The exhortations of 6:11–12 presuppose the reality of the statement of verse 14. Paul's argument is that we should reckon as a fact the assurance of verse 14, and this assurance will motivate us to turn from sin. The indicative underlies the imperative.[5]

So our death to sin and resurrection to life in union with Christ do not immediately keep us from ever committing sin. There is an "already" and a "not yet." We have died to sin, but the effects of it linger, and we must continue to struggle against it—and still even "put [it] to death" (Rom. 8:13; Col. 3:5).[6] Christ has broken in us the *dominion* of sin, but has not

---

4. Ibid., 219.

5. This is a common biblical theme. See the comments on the history of redemption as a motivation for good works in chapter 3 and the discussion of redemptive history in chapter 16.

6. I consider it a bit odd that Murray does not deal with these passages, which would seem to raise a question about his understanding of Rom. 6. He has argued that the old man has been put to death in the past, and that he is not in any sense still alive. Yet Rom. 8:13 and Col. 3:5 urge us to put sin to death, assuming that in some sense sin is still alive within us. That would suggest that our death to sin is both already and not yet (see chapter 16), not merely already, as Murray claims. But I think Murray's position can still be defended. Although the image of death and life is used both in Rom. 6 and in these two passages, there is a difference. Rom. 6 describes the death of our old man of sin. Rom. 8:13 and Col. 3:5 describe a different death, the death

eliminated all sin from our lives. But the fact that sin's dominion is broken motivates us to change. It gives us the confidence that at heart we are no longer sinners, and that God has placed in our hearts all the resources that we need to be godly people.

Murray relates these resources to the power of the Spirit within us: "It is by reason of the resurrection that Christ is given the promise of the Spirit and it is the resurrected Lord who sends forth the Holy Spirit."[7]

He cites in this connection Acts 2:32–33; John 16:7; 15:26. So the Holy Spirit is the Spirit of Christ (Rom. 8:9; 1 Peter 1:11; cf. Acts 16:7; Phil. 1:19; Gal. 4:6); Christ is the Lord of the Spirit (2 Cor. 3:18; cf. 1 Cor. 15:45). So our union with Christ in his resurrection is "in that pneumatic conditioning, endowment, and power which are his."[8] The Spirit gives life, not only in the physical sense, but also in the spiritual-ethical sense (Rom. 8:2, 10; 1 Cor. 15:45; 2 Cor. 3:6; Gal. 6:8). So we can do nothing good without the continuing work of the Spirit within us (Rom. 7:6; 8:5–13; Gal. 5:16–17, 25). Christian virtues are the fruit of the Spirit (Gal. 5:22–24). The love of Christ, which fulfills the law, comes from the Spirit (Rom. 15:30; Gal. 5:22; cf. Col. 1:8; Gal. 5:14–16; Rom. 13:8–14). Through the Spirit we are saved by washing and renewal (Titus 3:5). Murray sums it up: "And this is to say, in New Testament terms, that the man of God is 'Spiritual', indwelt, governed, and directed by the Holy Spirit."[9]

The "dynamic" of the Christian life, therefore, is our union and communion with Christ in his death and resurrection, which is at the same time a union and communion with the Spirit. When Christ died, we died with him to sin, making a decisive breach with sin called "the death of the old man."[10] Our responsibility is, first, to recognize this death as a fact, and, second, to turn away from sin daily under the motivation of that fact. When temptation comes, we should say, "No, I'm dead to that."

I note that in this picture of sanctification there is both grace and works, both divine sovereignty and human responsibility. All our goodness (always

---

of our present sins, a death which we ourselves bring about, with God's help. Putting all of this together, we should conclude that there is an already and a not yet to our sanctification in general, but that Paul's language about the crucifixion of the old man describes only the already.

7. Murray, *Principles of Conduct*, 221.

8. Ibid., 223.

9. Ibid., 224. Murray goes on to make some useful observations about the Spirit as the Spirit of truth and love.

10. Murray elsewhere refers to this breach as "definitive sanctification." See his essay of that title in *Collected Works of John Murray*, vol. 2 (Edinburgh: Banner of Truth Trust, 1977), 277–84, and the next four essays in the volume: "The Agency in Definitive Sanctification" (285–93), "Progressive Sanctification" (294–304), "The Pattern of Sanctification" (305–12), and "The Goal of Sanctification" (313–17).

imperfect in this life) comes from God's grace, through Christ and the Spirit. But our role is not to wait passively for God to work in us. We too have a responsibility: to reckon ourselves dead to sin, to put to death the sin that remains in us, and in that context to choose what is good. Scripture does not teach us to "let go and let God." Rather, it calls us actively to fight the spiritual warfare. We are to put on the armor of God (Eph. 6:10–20) and stand against Satan, extinguishing his fiery darts.

This relation of grace and works is what we saw in the Decalogue. It begins with God's grace: "I am the Lord your God, who brought you out of the land of Egypt, out of the house of slavery" (Ex. 20:2), and then tells Israel to keep God's commands in response to that grace. And we have seen in the New Testament that we are to obey God because of the grace he has given us in Christ. Grace motivates our obedience, by giving us the power to obey (the situational perspective), by eliciting our gratitude (the existential perspective), and by giving us the knowledge that our attempts to obey will not be in vain (the normative perspective).

So we can summarize the dynamic of the biblical ethic by saying that grace motivates obedience.

THE GOSPEL DEEPENS THE LAW

It is wrong, therefore, to pit grace against law in the process of sanctification. Of course, there are right and wrong ways of expressing the relationship between them. But we should reject the notion (cf. chapter 12) that we should live only according to the gospel and not according to the law. All our goodness is by grace. But the gracious work of the Spirit enables us to keep "the righteous requirement of the law" (Rom. 8:4).

It would be equally wrong, however, to imagine that once we have trusted Christ for salvation we may then forget about the gospel and go about trying to obey the law. It is important, not only to obey the law, but to obey it for the right reasons, which include the grace given in the gospel.[11] We can never forget what Jesus has done for us, and his great work changes the way we look at God's law.[12]

---

11. In chapter 3, I listed three "biblical reasons to do good works," correlated with my three perspectives: (1) the history of redemption (grace, the gospel), (2) the authority of God's commands, and (3) the presence of the Spirit. Christians are often tempted to focus so exclusively on one of these that they forget the others.

12. In this discussion, I have been helped by Richard F. Lovelace, *Dynamics of Spiritual Renewal* (Downers Grove, IL: InterVarsity Press, 1979); Jerry Bridges, *The Discipline of Grace* (Colorado Springs: NavPress, 1994); Bryan Chapell, *Holiness by Grace* (Wheaton, IL: Crossway Books, 2003); Neil H. Williams, *The Theology of Sonship* (Jenkintown, PA:

We have seen that justification and sanctification are different. In justification, our works play no role. God accepts us as righteous solely on the basis of Christ's atonement. In sanctification, God's grace is equally pervasive, but there is a role for our efforts. All our goodness comes from God, but it is still important for us to take up arms against Satan and do what is right.

So Protestants have maintained that justification is "by faith alone." Sanctification is also by faith, but not by faith alone. It is important to emphasize both parts of this statement about sanctification. It is not by faith alone, for human effort is necessary to achieve it. Of course, it is God's grace that gives us the ability to put in that effort. But human effort is necessary for sanctification in a way that it is not necessary for justification.

Even though sanctification is not by faith alone, it is certainly by faith. In our quest for holiness, we must above all trust God. We must remember what God has done for us. We must reckon ourselves dead to sin and alive to God. We must remember that because of Christ we are the people of God, sons and daughters of God, friends of God, the bride and body of Christ, and the temple of his Spirit. In other words, we must remember the gospel.

The gospel deepens our understanding of the Christian life. For example, we have seen that love is central to both Old and New Testament ethics. But the gospel of the New Testament unveils a new dimension: "that you love one another: just as I have loved you, you also are to love one another. By this all people will know that you are my disciples, if you have love for one another" (John 13:34–35). Now the standard of love is Jesus giving himself up for us on the cross. Love is still a divine command, part of the law. But the work of Christ has deepened that command in a radical way.

Similarly, as we have seen, Jesus' teaching in the Sermon on the Mount directs God's commandments to the heart. The Old Testament also addresses the heart. God calls us there to apply his words to our heart (Deut. 4:29; 6:5–6; 10:12, 16; 11:18; etc.), and the tenth commandment especially shows us that sin and obedience begin in the heart.

So the gospel as presented in the New Testament presents the law as something even more demanding than it might have appeared to Old Testament believers. It shows clearly how it is impossible to keep the law in our own strength. So the gospel deepens the law. It shows that we can never be satisfied with a moderate level of goodness, for God will never be satisfied with that.

World Harvest Mission, 2002), setting forth the "sonship" teaching of the late C. John Miller. I have also benefited much from lectures and sermons by pastors Tim Keller, Dick Kaufmann, and Douglass Swagerty. I do not, however, endorse everything in these sources, and I take full responsibility for the formulations here.

At the same time, the gospel will not allow us to fall into despair, for it points us to Jesus, who has kept the law in our place and who has redeemed us forever from the wrath of God. As goes the slogan of the Sonship movement, "Cheer up, for you are much worse than you think you are." We are so bad that only God can save us—and he does! And in Christ, we are much better than we have ever imagined ourselves to be.

This approach to sanctification does not pit gospel against law.[13] In the Christian life, the law continues to be the standard of goodness and right-ness. It defines what we seek to achieve. But the gospel sheds a new light on it, showing how hard its requirements are, and turning us to seek again and again the grace of God in Christ. Turning to grace is itself a require-ment, a law. But it is a law that illumines all other law, deepening it and lightening it at the same time.

So, without neglecting other requirements of the law, it is important to recognize the truth of Jesus' statement that "this is the work of God, that you believe in him whom he has sent" (John 6:29). Our chief work (and it is a work) is to believe, to really believe, in Jesus. Our initial faith in him must be renewed day by day. We should be preoccupied with his promises, the blessings of his salvation.

The opposite side of faith is repentance. And the gospel shows us the need for a life of deeper repentance. God calls us to repent even of our righteousness. As Isaiah 64:6 says, "All our righteous deeds are like a pol-luted garment." Or, as Jesus puts it, "Unless your righteousness exceeds that of the scribes and Pharisees, you will never enter the kingdom of heaven" (Matt. 5:20). God wants us to be holy as he is holy (Lev. 19:2), perfect as he is perfect (Matt. 5:48). So, although the Spirit has enabled us to grow in righteousness, we fall woefully short. Even the good things we do are in the service of the idols of our heart, particularly our own pride. As New Testament accounts of the Pharisees show us, the more we achieve reputations as righteous people, the more prone we are, often, to ungodly pride and contempt for others. So we never reach a point where we can stop repenting.

So the gospel is not opposed to law, nor vice versa. As I indicated in chapter 12, law and gospel come wrapped inside one another. Neither can be properly understood without the other. The law defines our need that the gospel satisfies. The gospel shows us the true depths of the law and turns us to lives of repentance and faith.

---

13. Review my critique (in chapter 12) of the opposition of law to gospel found in the Formula of Concord.

THE MEANS OF GRACE

The Reformed tradition has stressed certain resources that God has given us to help us grow in grace. They are called "the means of grace," because God actually works through them to sanctify us, to bring us to spiritual maturity. Through these, we learn to obey God, to live by faith, and to repent of sin.

First, let us examine what a means of grace is.[14] We know what grace is: God's unmerited favor, indeed, his unmerited favor where we deserve wrath. Without God's grace, we are lost. But we need God's grace, not only at the beginning of the Christian life, but throughout it. So where can we go to find God's continuing grace? Where do we go to get the resources for sanctification, for continuing spiritual growth? The short answer is that there are three places: the Word, fellowship, and prayer.

Except for the second, we can find those resources either privately or publicly. The second, of course, is by definition public. But we can receive the Word either by individual Bible study or through the public preaching and teaching of the church. And we can pray, of course, either privately or publicly. But in our private use of the means of grace, we come to God as members of the church, that is, as members of the body of Christ. Apart from that body, our Bible study and prayer will not help us. Indeed, we need other members of the church to help us understand the Bible, and to teach us how to pray. So, in an important sense, even the private means of grace are within the church.

Let's think a bit more about that triad, the Word, fellowship, and prayer. It ties in with other threefold distinctions I've made in this book. The Word is normative, fellowship is situational (interacting with fellow believers in our environment), and prayer is existential (interacting with God in the depths of our hearts). Some might wonder why I haven't mentioned worship, and especially the sacraments. But I think these and other means are subdivisions of one of my three headings. Sacraments, I believe, are forms of church fellowship. Worship is an overarching category that includes all three.

It is not typical in Reformed theology to regard fellowship as a means of grace. But I think it clearly is. Many passages in the New Testament speak of "one anothering" (John 13:34–35; Rom. 12:10; 13:8; 15:5; 16:16; 1 Cor. 12:25; Gal. 5:13; Eph. 4:2, 32; 5:21; Col. 3:13, 16; 1 Thess. 3:12; 4:9, 18; 5:11; Heb. 3:13; 10:24–25; James 5:16; 1 Peter 1:22; 3:8 [KJV, NIV]; 1 John 3:11, 23; 4:7, 11). We are to love one another, forgive one another, pray

14. The rest of this chapter is a revised version of chapter 20 of my book *Salvation Belongs to the Lord: An Introduction to Systematic Theology* (Phillipsburg, NJ: P&R Publishing, 2006).

for one another, edify one another, and so on. These make it plain that our spiritual health depends on one another: both what other believers do for us and what we do for them. The larger concept that includes all those one-anotherings is the concept of fellowship. More on that in a little bit.

THE WORD

First let's think about the Word of God as a means of grace. God's Word is powerful, authoritative, and self-expressive. (Note the three perspectives.)[15] It is "the power of God for salvation" (Rom. 1:16). People come to Christ through the Word, not just by reading it, but by hearing it in preaching and teaching (Rom. 10:17). Most people, historically, have not come to Christ just by sitting at home and reading the Bible, though some have. Far more have come to Christ through another person preaching, teaching, witnessing, and answering questions (1 Cor. 1:21). Most people in the ancient world, of course, were not able to read at all. So it became especially important that believers reach out and *tell* them what God's Word says. So communication of the Word comes by mission. It is a corporate enterprise, not just an individual experience. It is a means of grace brought through the church.

Of course, God also is involved in the communication of the Word. God never leaves his church alone. He comes with the church to reach and save the lost. So, as we've seen, the Holy Spirit accompanies the Word, enabling people to receive it, "not only in word, but also in power and in the Holy Spirit and with full conviction" (1 Thess. 1:5).

Because the Spirit accompanies the Word in saving power, it is a "living and active" word (Heb. 4:12). So when more and more people come to faith, Scripture speaks of "the word" increasing (Acts 6:7; 13:49).

But the Word is active not only in our initial salvation, but throughout our lives, especially in our sanctification. Psalm 19:7–9 says:

> The law of the LORD is perfect,
>   reviving the soul;
> the testimony of the LORD is sure,
>   making wise the simple;
> the precepts of the LORD are right,
>   rejoicing the heart;
> the commandment of the LORD is pure,
>   enlightening the eyes;

15. I have discussed God's Word in *DG*, 470–75, and in chapters 4 and 5 of *Salvation Belongs to the Lord*. I will discuss it at much greater length in *The Doctrine of the Word of God* (forthcoming).

the fear of the LORD is clean,
    enduring forever;
the rules of the LORD are true,
    and righteous altogether.

Many Scripture passages (e.g., Ps. 119:105; Matt. 4:4; Acts 20:32; Rom. 15:4; 2 Tim. 3:16; Heb. 4:12–13; 2 Peter 1:19) tell us that God's Word changes us, sanctifies us, drives us to repentance, and incites us to love God and one another. It's so important, therefore, to read the Word, to study it, indeed to meditate on it:

Blessed is the man
    who walks not in the counsel of the wicked,
nor stands in the way of sinners,
    nor sits in the seat of scoffers;
but his delight is in the law of the LORD,
    and on his law he meditates day and night.
He is like a tree
    planted by streams of water
that yields its fruit in its season,
    and its leaf does not wither.
In all that he does, he prospers. (Ps. 1:1–3)

The word for "meditate" there can also refer to an animal chewing its cud, over and over again. That's what we need to do, figuratively speaking. (Don't chew the pages of your Bible.) We need to run the Bible passages through our mind over and over again, until we take it to heart. Look at the blessing of doing this: "He is like a tree planted by streams of water that yields its fruit in its season, and its leaf does not wither. In all that he does, he prospers" (Ps. 1:3). This is the way to fruitfulness and prosperity in the Lord—meditating on his Word.

FELLOWSHIP

The second means of grace is fellowship with God and other believers. We usually think of fellowship as parties and dinners, but in the New Testament it is much more. The Greek word for fellowship is *koinonia*, which comes from the adjective *koinos*, "common." Fellowship is having in common; it is sharing something with someone else. In the New Testament, it sometimes means sharing goods. In 2 Corinthians 8:4 and Philippians 1:5, it refers to giving gifts to help needy fellow Christians. In that sense, the early church had a truly radical fellowship. In Acts 4:32, we read, "Now the full number of those who believed were of one heart and soul, and no one said that any of the things that belonged to him was his own, but they had everything in common." They shared their hearts, they shared their souls, and they shared their property, as we saw in chapter 42. Some of the Christians sold property and gave the proceeds to the apostles for the needs of fellow Christians. That is a kind of fellowship we rarely see in the church today, but it is simply an expression of the love that Jesus taught us. He told us to love one another as he loved us. That means being ready to lay down your life for another Christian.

Koinonia in the New Testament also refers to a religious sharing, a religious commonness (1 Cor. 1:9; 10:20; 2 Cor. 6:14; Gal. 2:9; 1 John 1:3). To have fellowship is to worship together—together with God, with Jesus, with other believers in the Lord. Finally, fellowship is a heartfelt sense of brotherhood, of closeness, of belonging to one family in the Lord (Phil. 2:1).

So fellowship refers to all the kinds of one-anothering mentioned earlier in this chapter: loving one another, encouraging one another, and so on. So let's look at some specific forms of fellowship:

1. As I mentioned earlier, fellowship in the New Testament involves *worship*. Fellowship is a religious commonness, a worshiping together. In worship, we fellowship with God. We come to be with him, and he comes to be with us (Ps. 22:25; Rom. 15:9; 2 Chron. 5:13–14; 1 Cor. 14:25; James 4:8). But worship is also a fellowship with other believers, in which God builds us up. In worship, we often come to insights that we haven't been able to attain in any other way. In Psalm 73, the writer says that he despaired in his heart, because he saw the prosperity of the wicked and the oppression of the righteous, until, he says, "I went into the sanctuary of God; then I discerned their end" (v. 17). It was in the sanctuary, in worship, that the psalmist was convinced that the prosperity of the wicked was temporary, that God would bring the wicked into his terrible judgments in his own time.

So one form of fellowship is worship. The sacraments are a special part of that. In baptism, God admits people to the visible church. The symbolism of baptism presents the gospel to us. The water symbolizes our cleansing from sin, and that in turn indicates our union with Christ in his death and resurrection (Rom. 6:3–4). The Lord's Supper also pictures the gospel: the bread representing the body of Christ, given for us; the cup representing his blood, shed for the forgiveness of our sins. The supper renews the covenant (Luke 22:20; 1 Cor. 11:25). So in the sacraments, God reminds us vividly of his gospel promises. And he seals the promises to us, guaranteeing that he will fulfill his promises.

2. Fellowship is also *giving*. I mentioned earlier the radical sharing of the church in Acts 4–5. This giving, as Paul says, is first a giving of oneself, then of one's wealth (2 Cor. 8:5). After all, if you have given yourself away to the Lord and to your brothers and sisters, it shouldn't be too much to give your wealth. This may sound masochistic, but the Lord is not Moloch. He doesn't call on us to destroy ourselves. When you give yourself away, you receive back all the rich blessings of the Lord. There is a reward. Paul says in 2 Corinthians 9:6–12:

> The point is this: whoever sows sparingly will also reap sparingly, and whoever sows bountifully will also reap bountifully. Each one must give as he has made up his mind, not reluctantly or under compulsion, for God loves a cheerful giver. And God is able to make all grace abound to you, so that having all sufficiency [*or* contentment] in all things at all times, you may abound in every good work. As it is written,
>
>> "He has distributed freely, he has given to the poor;
>> his righteousness endures forever."
>
> He who supplies seed to the sower and bread for food will supply and multiply your seed for sowing and increase the harvest of your righteousness. You will be enriched in every way for all your generosity, which through us will produce thanksgiving to God. For the ministry of this service is not only supplying the needs of the saints, but is also overflowing in many thanksgivings to God.

There's the language of the means of grace, in spades. Verse 8 says, "And God is able to make all grace abound to you, so that having all sufficiency [*or* contentment] in all things at all times, you may abound in every good work." Through giving, we reap bountifully; we will experience hilarious joy; we will have plenty of seed, plenty of bread. And what we do will lead people to thank God. Giving is a source of the most wonderful blessings!

Scripture tells us, first, to give to our own families: "But if anyone does not provide for his relatives, and especially for members of his household, he has denied the faith and is worse than an unbeliever" (1 Tim. 5:8). That is some of the strongest condemnation in the whole New Testament.

Then, we should do good to all people, but especially to "the household of faith" (Gal. 6:10). The household of faith is the church, our extended family. So God has called us to take care of the poor members of the body of Christ. 1 John 3:17 says, "But if anyone has the world's goods and sees his brother in need, yet closes his heart against him, how does God's love abide in him?" The love of Christ puts us in a special relationship with our poor brothers and sisters, so that God's love constrains us to give them help (Gal. 2:10; James 2:16; 1 John 3:17).

But remember that in Galatians 6:10, Paul says to do good "especially" to those of the household of faith. He doesn't say "only," but "especially." That means we have a biblical mandate to meet the needs of the poor outside the body of Christ. Galatians 6:10 does state a priority: family first. But it doesn't restrict us from doing good to others. Indeed, it encourages us to do good to "all" people.

Here we may cringe a bit. How can I, you might ask, who can barely afford to feed my kids, have a responsibility to help the poor of the whole world? Well, one example Scripture gives us is the parable of the good Samaritan in Luke 10:25–37. When the Samaritan sees a man dying by the side of the road, he does not pass by on the other side, as did the priest and the Levite. Nor does he ask questions about the victim's religious allegiance. He simply gives what help he can. The Bible doesn't ask us in an abstract way to divide our resources up among all the millions of people throughout the world who are in need. Rather, what Paul has in mind in Galatians 6:10 is being ready to help those whom God brings across our path. When we have resources that can be used to help someone, we should be generous; that's all.

But I suspect that if all of God's people tithed, that is, gave a tenth of their income to the work of the Lord, the church would be in a far better position to help the needy within the church and outside as well (see Mal. 3:8–10). And "offerings" in Scripture are something above and beyond the tithe. Let that be a word to the wise.

3. The word *fellowship* also applies to our relation to the Spirit (2 Cor. 13:14) and his gifts. The work of evangelism is closely connected with that. Paul speaks of the Philippians' fellowship with him in the gospel (Phil. 1:5). Those who are filled with the Spirit engage in evangelism (Acts 2:4, 14–36; 4:8, 31; 9:17, 20; 13:9, 52).

Nurture is obviously part of our fellowship with one another. In Ephesians 4:29, Paul says that the talk that comes out of our mouths must always seek to build up one another. When a brother sins, we seek to reclaim him (Gal. 6:1; James 5:20). When someone is in need, we help. When someone is sick, we pray (James 5:14). The negative side, of course, is that when a brother or sister will not repent after teaching and admonition, we must sometimes exercise formal discipline against him, even, as we've seen, to the point of excommunication. But even that is for his benefit (1 Cor. 5:5).

So we can understand fellowship as worship, sharing goods, and that intimacy with one another in the Spirit that nurtures and edifies. In terms of our threefold pattern, we can think of worship as normative, sharing goods as situational, and nurture as existential.

PRAYER

We have talked about the Word and fellowship as means of grace. The third category is prayer. Grudem defines prayer as personal communication with God, corporate or individual.[16] The aspects of prayer are: (1) adoration, when we praise God for who he is and what he has done; (2) confession of sin, in which we humble ourselves before God, who sees our hearts as they really are;[17] (3) thanksgiving, in which we acknowledge that everything we have comes from him, and that without him we have no good thing; and (4) intercession (supplication), making requests for ourselves and for others. Here, we should not confine ourselves to praying for individuals. The great concerns of the kingdom of God also demand our attention. We should remember especially the work of missions and the bringing of everything human under the dominion of Christ.

Over a period of time, our prayer should include all four elements (abbreviated by the acronym ACTS). But we shall focus on intercession here, since most of the theological questions center around that.

Why should we pray? People often ask this question out of a concern for the sovereignty of God. If God is in control of everything, then what difference can our prayers make? God already knows and has planned what he will do; we can't change his eternal plan. So why should we bother to pray?

First, there is the normative reason: because God commands us to pray. First Thessalonians 5:17 says, succinctly, "Pray without ceasing," and this is one of many biblical commands to pray. Even if we don't understand how prayer and God's sovereignty work together, we should pray simply because our heavenly Father wants us to. But why does he want us to pray, if praying is not going to change his eternal plan?

That takes us to the second reason, which I call the "existential" reason: prayer is a means of fellowship with our heavenly Father. We saw earlier the importance of fellowship, and prayer is a form of fellowship as well. In Luke 11:9–13, Jesus says that prayer is like a child going to his earthly father (cf. Matt. 6:9). The child wants something, and the father is eager to give. But the father does not give until the child asks. Any of us who are fathers or mothers understand the dynamic here. We want to give good things to our children, but even more we want to have a good relationship with them.

16. Wayne Grudem, *Systematic Theology* (Grand Rapids: Zondervan, 1994), 376.
17. Don't forget the earlier teaching in this chapter about how the gospel calls us to lives of radical repentance.

Our heavenly Father wants the same. He does not want to be an automatic dispenser of goods, but to really be our Father, a real person. We saw early in the book how important it is that God is a person, not an impersonal or abstract being. How good it is to be able to talk to the ruler of the universe! How good it is that he delights to have this conversation!

But there's a third reason as well. If our prayers could not change anything, then the relationship would be rather hollow. If a child had no hope that his father could change anything on his behalf, he would not be motivated to ask. So there is also what I call a situational motive for prayer, and that is that prayer changes things. Or, to put it more theologically, God ordains prayer as a means to change history. There are things that happen because of prayer, and things that do not happen because of no prayer. In 2 Chronicles 7:14, God says that if his people will humble themselves and pray, then he will forgive their sin and heal their land. In Luke 11:9–10, Jesus says that he who seeks, finds. And James 4:2 says that if we don't have things we need, it is because we do not ask. Prayer really does work.

Now of course prayer doesn't change the eternal plan of God. But within that eternal plan are many plans for means and ends. God ordains that crops will grow, but not without water and sun. He ordains that people will be saved, but (ordinarily) not without the teaching of the Word. And he ordains that we will have everything we truly need, but not without prayer. God's eternal plan has determined that many things will be achieved by prayer, and that many things will not be achieved without prayer.

But since prayer is part of a personal relationship with God, it does not operate mechanically or automatically. We know that prayer sometimes disappoints, and that too is part of the relationship. When we pray, we ought to trust that God, like a loving father, is much wiser than we are, and that in the end he does what he knows is best. There is mystery here, as we can well understand. How many four-year-olds understand why their fathers do and do not choose to honor their requests?

But the Bible does give us some insight into why some prayers are better than others. Wayne Grudem, whose theology has been very helpful to me in this chapter, says that good prayer, effective prayer, prayer that honors God and that God honors, typically occurs in several "spheres."[18] That is, good prayer is *in* Jesus' name, *in* the Spirit, *according to* his will, and so on. Figuratively speaking, these are the locations of prayer. Let's look at these briefly.

Good prayer, first of all, is in Jesus' name. This is not a mechanical expression that we tag on to the end of a prayer. Sometimes it is a good

18. Grudem, *Systematic Theology*, 382–91.

thing to add on. At other times, it's a mere form, perhaps somehow intended to make the prayer more powerful or to impress people with our piety. But whether we use that formula or not, the important thing is that our prayer really be in Jesus' name. That means recognizing that he is our only mediator with God (1 Tim. 2:5), our one and only high priest (Heb. 4:14–15). He is the only person who can give us access to the Father. We come through him because he has made the final sacrifice. When he died, the veil of the temple was torn in two, so the Lord opened wide our access to him (Heb. 10:22). The New Testament tells us not to be timid and scared, afraid that God will destroy us if we come too close. That actually was the situation in the Old Testament. He wants us, rather, to be bold in coming before God, bold in prayer, asking for big things. As our high priest, Jesus is also our intercessor. He is the one who brings our prayers to the Father.

So when you pray, come with Jesus' authorization. Tell God, either verbally or by your attitude of heart, that you are coming only because of Jesus. Jesus has said, "In that day you will ask nothing of me. Truly, truly, I say to you, whatever you ask of the Father in my name, he will give it to you. Until now you have asked nothing in my name. Ask, and you will receive, that your joy may be full" (John 16:23–24; cf. Eph. 5:20).

So we pray in Jesus' name. We also pray in the Holy Spirit (Rom. 8:26–27). The Spirit dwells in our hearts and knows our inmost thoughts. He bears witness to us that we are, in fact, children of God through faith in Christ. When we don't know what to pray for, he brings his own prayers to the Father, out of his own infinite wisdom. Sometimes a loved one is terribly ill, and we don't know whether to pray for healing or for God to take the person home. We call on God to act according to his love and wisdom. Within us, the Spirit is praying the prayer that needs to be offered.

Good prayer is according to God's will. First John 5:14–15 says, "And this is the confidence that we have toward him, that if we ask anything according to his will he hears us. And if we know that he hears us in whatever we ask, we know that we have the requests that we have asked of him" (cf. Matt. 6:10). So we should not pray anything contrary to the Scriptures. Usually we do not know God's decretive will, his eternal plan. So I may pray for God to heal a friend, not knowing if that is what God ultimately wants to do. That's all right, if in our hearts we also pray that the Lord's will be done.

Scripture also tells us to pray in faith (Matt. 21:22; Mark 11:24; James 1:6). These passages refer not only to saving faith in Christ, but also to faith that we will receive what we have prayed for. This principle follows from the last. If prayer is according to God's will, then of course he will grant it. If we believe that our prayer is according to God's will, then we must believe that he will grant it. Of course, we may be wrong in our belief about God's will. So if, along with our prayer for what we want, we pray that God's will be done, then we know that our prayer will always be answered.

Scripture also presents obedience as a condition of answered prayer, or perhaps as another "sphere" of prayer: "If I had cherished iniquity in my heart, the Lord would not have listened" (Ps. 66:18); "Beloved, if our heart does not condemn us, we have confidence before God; and whatever we ask we receive from him, because we keep his commandments and do what pleases him" (1 John 3:21–22; cf. Prov. 15:8, 29; 28:9; 1 Peter 3:7, 12). Now these verses don't teach that we must be sinless for God to answer our prayers. None of us is sinless, but God answers the prayers of many of us. Yet sin does sometimes stand in the way. If we are complacent about sin, "cherishing iniquity," as the psalmist says, we had better repent before we do any other business with God. So confession of sin is a vitally important part of prayer (Matt. 6:12; 1 John 1:9; James 5:16).

And when we pray, God not only wants us to request forgiveness for ourselves, but also to grant forgiveness to those who have sinned against us (Matt. 6:14–15; Mark 11:25). Lack of forgiveness can hinder our petitions to the Lord.

Scripture also describes various attitudes appropriate to prayer. Humility is one (Matt. 6:5; Luke 18:11–13). How inappropriate it is for us to be proud of ourselves when we are standing before almighty God. His greatness should show us how small we are, how trivial our abilities and accomplishments are. He should make us aware that everything we are and everything we have accomplished comes from him.

In Jesus' parable of the Pharisee and the tax collector (Luke 18:9–14), a Pharisee is very proud before God. But he expresses his pride in the form of thanks. Formally, at least, he acknowledges that all his virtues have come from God: "I thank you that I am not like other men." But the pride just billows from his heart: "God, I thank you that I am not like other men, extortioners, unjust, adulterers, or even like this tax collector. I fast twice a week; I give tithes of all that I get" (vv. 11–12). We should be like the tax collector in the parable, recognizing that we have nothing to boast of: "Nothing in my hand I bring; simply to thy cross I cling."[19] That's one reason confession of sin is so important. Nobody can be proud who really understands how much he has sinned against God, and what a great price God paid to bring forgiveness.

19. This is a line from the hymn "Rock of Ages," by Augustus Toplady.

Persistence is another virtue in prayer (Gen. 32:26; Deut. 9:25–26; Mark 14:39; Luke 6:12; 2 Cor. 12:8. Col. 4:2; 1 Thess. 5:17). If God doesn't answer, you should ask again whether your prayer is according to the will of God. But if you still believe it is, keep going. God may have his reasons for postponing the answer that he still intends to give. And wait for his answer (Pss. 27:14; 38:15; 130:5–6).

Earnestness is a quality that we see in the prayers of many of God's people in Scripture. See how passionate they are in prayer, how urgent: "O Lord, hear; O Lord, forgive. O Lord, pay attention and act. Delay not, for your own sake, O my God, because your city and your people are called by your name" (Dan. 9:19; cf. Heb. 5:7). People sometimes ask why we need to be passionate in prayer. Does God need to be aroused? Does he respond more to emotional appeals than nonemotional ones? Well, remember that our relationship to God is personal. He is our Father, not a favor-dispensing machine. Our emotions and our repetitions show our persistence; they show that our hope is only in God. And sometimes our requests are shown to be shallow by an unemotional approach to God.

After all this, what happens when God doesn't answer our prayers, or doesn't answer them right away? He may indeed be planning to answer, but other things have to happen first. Think of how many years God's people prayed for him to redeem them from Egypt. Think how many years they prayed for the coming of the Messiah. Think how many years we have been praying for his return, "Even so, come, Lord Jesus." But God chose the right time to send Moses, and the right time to send Jesus—in "the fullness of time," as Paul says in Galatians 4:4. And his answers will always come—at the right time.

Our sin may be another reason why God has not answered (James 1:6–8; 4:3). We may not be in the right sphere when we pray for something. Or, as mentioned earlier, we may be complacent with some area of our life that violates God's standards.

But there is still a third reason for unanswered prayer, and that is God's sovereign purposes. As I said earlier, we don't know God's secret decree, and so, when we pray, we should always say under our breath or in our hearts, if not openly, "Thy will be done." Jesus qualified his prayer that way in the garden before his crucifixion (Luke 22:42).[20] Surely we too must qualify our prayers that way. The apostle Paul prayed to the Lord three times to remove the impediment that he called his "thorn in the flesh." But the Lord said no: "My grace is sufficient for you, for my power is made perfect in

---

20. I mention this passage, not to imply that Jesus was ignorant of God's sovereign purpose. He was not. But the passage authorizes us to qualify our prayers in submission to that sovereign purpose.

weakness" (2 Cor. 12:9). Paul could not have known all the ways in which his thorn in the flesh would magnify God's power. But God did, and he did what was best for Paul's ministry, which was also what was best for Paul.

So prayer is a means of God's grace to us, both individual prayer and public prayer. Public prayer in worship brings all the members of the body together in agreement. In Matthew 18:19, Jesus says, "Again I say to you, if two of you agree on earth about anything they ask, it will be done for them by my Father in heaven." So when two or three or more agree in prayer, as in public worship, their prayers have a special power. We see in the New Testament how the prayer meeting of Acts 4 led to a powerful witness for the gospel. Verse 31 says, "And when they had prayed, the place in which they were gathered together was shaken, and they were all filled with the Holy Spirit and continued to speak the word of God with boldness." Corporate prayer is a fellowship with the Holy Spirit, something we do in him (Eph. 6:18; Jude 20). In the sphere of the Spirit, we draw upon his power, his love, and his wisdom, as he intercedes for us.

ETHICS AND BIBLICAL EVENTS

These brief comments will supplement the discussion of redemptive history in chapter 16.

Some may wonder why I have chosen to write an ethical treatise focusing on law, rather than on the great events of biblical history. Why not an ethic of creation? Or incarnation? Or atonement, resurrection, or eschatological expectation?

An ethic of creation would, of course, focus on the biblical concern for the environment. But since the environment includes everything, such an ethic could use the environment as a perspective on other ethical teaching in the Bible: God as our worship environment, the Sabbath as our temporal environment, the family as our nurturing environment, and so forth.

An ethic of incarnation might focus on how we should follow Jesus' example by entering fully into the lives of others, loving them by empathy and sympathy. An ethic of atonement would focus on self-sacrificing love as the paradigm of love. An ethic of resurrection would stress bringing God's renewal into our own lives and those of others. An eschatological ethic would see everything in the light of our future hope, including the rewards of heaven.

I have no objection to ethical treatises of these types. They can be very helpful, useful perspectives on the discipline. I have chosen, however, to focus on the law, for reasons such as the following:

1. The focus on law enables us to interact with our theological traditions, for it is the focus of the confessions of various denominations.

2. The law has been the main focus of my own study of ethics, so I find it easier to work in this conceptual milieu.

3. Despite its historic centrality, the authority of the law is under attack in some Christian circles (not to mention secular circles). Many Christians think that attention to the law is spiritually detrimental, or that it detracts from grace. In my judgment, this view confuses the legal with the legalistic. This whole book, I trust, is an antidote to that kind of thinking.

4. An ethic based on one or more redemptive-historical events inevitably reverts to law when it seeks to define its specific standards. In an ethic of creation, an author will want to say that we should care for the environment. But how does he know that, from the bare fact that God created the heavens and the earth? God has not charged rats or tigers with the care of the earth, only human beings. And he has given us that responsibility, not just by creating things, but by giving us a mandate to care for them. *Mandate* is another word for law. Similarly, whatever we may want to derive ethically from incarnation, etc., will have to be verified in God's law. To derive it from the event simply in itself is a case of the naturalistic fallacy.

5. It may be that in some cases the desire to turn from law to some other aspect of Scripture as an ethical focus is related to the desire for human autonomy. As sinners (and often as modern theologians), we don't want God telling us what to do. It may seem that by moving away from a legal focus we can avoid the stark voice of God commanding good and forbidding evil. But, as I have indicated, the focus on biblical events depends on the law for its ethical authority and credibility.

APPENDIX B

___

ZWINGLI AND REFORMED ETHICS

In this volume, I have not said much about historical figures. In this appendix and the next, the reader may discern something of the way I approach them. These were originally published in *Baker's Dictionary of Christian Ethics*, edited by Carl F. H. Henry (Grand Rapids: Baker, 1973), and are used by permission of the publisher (with slight changes).

The Reformed branch of Protestantism (as contrasted with the Lutheran and Radical branches) began with the work of Ulrich Zwingli (1484–1531) in Zurich, Switzerland.

Zwingli was not an ethical theorist in the formal sense, but he was a practical man who valued actions above talk, and whose writings display a profound ethical concern. This practical bent, more than his "humanistic" background, led him to a greater emphasis than Luther on the positive functions of the law of God in the Christian life. To Zwingli, the law is not only a threat, but a gift of God's grace. It reveals the believer's sinfulness, not to slay him, but to kindle in him love for the gracious lawgiver and therefore true repentance. The Ten Commandments stand as an eternally valid standard of Christian conduct, not annulled, but vindicated by the grace of God in Christ. They represent God's fundamental demand upon all men, a demand known "by nature" even to those men unacquainted with the written law. Zwingli did not feel, however, that the law made life easy for the Christian. He was deeply aware of the inner conflicts pictured in Romans 7, and of the tensions between joy and sorrow, struggle and satisfaction, conflict and peace in the Christian life. In his catalogue of

Christian virtues, he laid particular stress upon discipline, temperance, and sobriety—traits which fit the believer for the fierceness of the spiritual battle. He regarded the law, moreover, as bearing not only upon individuals, but upon society as a whole. The civil magistrate is a minister of God who is called upon to bring both believers and unbelievers into external conformity with God's law as much as possible, though of course true inward conformity to the law is possible only through the working of faith in the heart by the power of the Holy Spirit.

Since Zwingli, Reformed ethics has maintained his basic emphases. It has generally rejected his view that salvation is open to the heathen on the basis of natural law alone, and thereby has set itself off more sharply in distinction from Roman Catholic ethics while underscoring more emphatically Zwingli's own emphasis on the necessity of written Scripture. Reformed ethics maintains the distinctive Reformation teaching that man is unable to please God in any way apart from the grace of God in Christ and the regenerating power of the Holy Spirit. Yet, in contrast with other forms of Protestantism (and in sharp antithesis with modern liberal thinking), Reformed ethics maintains a distinctive emphasis upon the eternal authority and relevance of God's moral law. Reformed thinkers are, of course, not blind to the fact that God often requires different things of different people in different situations, but they will not concede that this fact in the least diminishes our responsibility to obey these requirements. Nor do they concede the objection that such a position is "legalistic." Recent studies have confirmed that law is an indispensable element in the very concept of a covenant between God and man. Obedience to divine commands is an essential requirement of both old and new covenants (Deut. 6:1–9; Matt. 5:17–20; John 13:34–35; 14:15, 21, 23; 15:10; 1 John 5:3; 2 John 6). Keeping the law cannot save a man, but those who are saved will want to keep the commandments of the Lord who redeems them.

It is an oversimplification, however, to describe Reformed ethics as purely and simply an ethics of law. The Reformed confessions and theologies emphasize other aspects of ethics in addition to the legal aspect: (1) Reformed ethics is "situational" in the sense that it sees the ethical task as one of directing present circumstances toward a future goal (that of the kingdom of God), and therefore as one which requires an analysis of the present "situation." It recognizes that present situation as already structured by God's great redemptive acts in the past, and as being directed by God's providence toward the final consummation. The Christian life, therefore, is characterized by a tension between the "already" and the "not yet." Unlike modern "situationism," however, Reformed ethics recognizes that the most important factor in the present situation is the ever-living God who continues to speak his will to us through the Scriptures of the Old Testament and New Testament. (2) Reformed ethics is also "existential," in that it sees faith and love as necessary and sufficient conditions for genuine good works, and therefore sees the ethical task as that of purifying the inner man, that his righteousness may be more than merely external. Unlike modern "existential" ethics, however, the Reformed position recognizes the power of God's commands to purify the soul (Ps. 19) when addressed to a believing heart.

G. W. Bromiley, ed., *Zwingli and Bullinger*, Library of Christian Classics XXIV, Philadelphia, Westminster, 1953; J. Murray, *Principles of Conduct*, Grand Rapids, Eerdmans, 1955; C. Van Til, *Christian Theistic Ethics*, unpublished class syllabus privately reproduced, 1970.

SCHLEIERMACHER AND PROTESTANT ETHICS

Like appendix B, this article appeared in *Baker's Dictionary of Christian Ethics*, edited by Carl F. H. Henry (Grand Rapids: Baker, 1973). It is used by permission of the publisher (with slight changes).

Friedrich D. E. Schleiermacher (1768–1834) is sometimes called "the father of modern theology." Perhaps the most important of his influential innovations is his view that the final authority in religious matters is not Scripture (as in orthodox Protestantism), or natural reason (as in pre-Kantian rationalism), or a combination of these plus tradition (as in Roman Catholicism), but intuitive religious feeling. For Schleiermacher, "Christian doctrines are accounts of the Christian religious affections set forth in speech."[1] The influence of this principle upon modern liberal Protestantism, and not least upon modern liberal Protestant ethics, is incalculable. Schleiermacher's specifically ethical writings, however (*Grundlinien einer Kritik der bisherigen Sittenlehre, Grundriss der philosophischen Ethik*), have had comparatively little impact on recent thought. This fact would have disappointed Schleiermacher, for he regarded his ethical works as in one sense the capstone of his theological labors and even regarded dogmatics itself as a kind of subdivision of ethics.[2]

Schleiermacher virtually identifies ethics with what we would ordinarily call "history"—i.e., a descriptive account of the ways in which man's reason acts upon nature to accomplish its purposes. Specifically Christian ethics,

---

1. *The Christian Faith* (Edinburgh: T. and T. Clark, 1928), 76.
2. Ibid., 3.

then, describes the ways in which the Christian's communion with God through Christ influences his actions. In line with this conception, Schleiermacher presents detailed "descriptions" of various goods, virtues, and duties and the relations between them. Essentially he sees the ethical life as a struggle to attain "unity" or "peace" between apparently (but in his view not actually) conflicting realities—spirit and flesh, ideal and real, reason and nature, individual and universal, production and appropriation, etc. In this spirit, he supports the development of "unity" in the political and social realms—the developing Prussian state and the Lutheran-Reformed ecclesiastical union—at least insofar as he feels that these unions have a firm basis in the popular cultural consciousness. He advocates broad social reforms, particularly improvements in the condition of the poor.

Schleiermacher contrasts this "descriptive" approach most often with what we might call a "normative" approach—i.e., the exposition of an eternal, authoritative standard which demands man's obedience.[3] Like the modern "situationist," Schleiermacher belittles the value of "law" to exalt that of "love." In his view, law "does not pierce behind the outward act" and thus cannot deal with inward motives. This view leads him to the paradoxical position that the two great commandments of the law (Matt. 22:36–40) are not commandments at all. Such a view has a substantial weakness: if consistent, it has no basis for declaring *anything* to be right or wrong. Mere description cannot yield such evaluations, which require a biblical appreciation of the law of God (Deut. 6:1–9; Matt. 5:17–19; John 14:15).

---

3. Ibid., 517.

GENTLENESS IN THE PASTORATE

This is a chapel talk I gave at a theological seminary. It will supplement the treatment of Christian virtues in chapter 19 and the emphasis on the passions in chapter 21. I have long felt that in Reformed circles there is a great need for pastors and theologians to cultivate the virtue of gentleness.

I would like to speak on a topic that is often neglected, but of great importance for those who seek the pastoral office. That is the subject of *gentleness* in the pastorate. I think we all know that gentleness is one of the fruits of the Spirit in Galatians 5:22–23. You may know also that it appears again in a similar list of Christian virtues in 1 Timothy 6:11, virtues specifically of Christian leadership. But gentleness is not usually one of the first qualities we look for in a pastor. In fact, I think that gentleness is one of those Christian virtues that seems to fall through the cracks when we are making evaluations of ourselves and of one another.

Indeed, there has been among us, I think, some confusion about what to do with gentleness. Certainly the old liberal theologians distorted the concept when they used it in effect to eliminate the wrath and judgment of God from their preaching. God, they said, was so gentle, so kind, that he would never punish anyone for sinning against him. Thus they robbed God of his justice; indeed, they replaced the biblical God with a grandfatherly, lenient, and indulgent god out of their own imaginations. Together with this distortion of God was a distortion of Jesus. The liberal Jesus was a kindly soul who hugged babies and patted lambs on the head, but who had within him not a drop of righteous anger or jealousy or zeal for the truth.

For the liberal, surely, such a God and such a Christ would not approve of any stern measures to preserve the holiness of his church. In liberal churches, formal discipline for doctrinal matters, indeed even for moral transgressions, became a thing of the past.

Evangelicals understandably reacted against that misunderstanding of the divine gentleness. They heaped ridicule and scorn upon the "gentle Jesus, meek and mild" of the liberal theologians and set forth Jesus as the risen and ascended Lord of heaven and earth, who would soon return in flaming fire to bring his terrible judgments on the earth. C. S. Lewis's Aslan was, he reminded us, not a *tame* lion. Christ is a "tiger." And so, we have argued, there is a place for formal discipline in the church. Sometimes pastors must be stern, strong, and jealous for the righteousness of God. Many Reformed teachers today, fortified by such teaching as Abraham Kuyper's "Life is religion," Van Til's apologetics of antithesis, Jay Adams's nouthetic counseling, and the dominion theology of the Christian Reconstruction movement, especially emphasize that Christians are not to be wimps. We are not to meekly tolerate the wickedness of our society, but we are to be a true Christian army, putting on the whole armor of God, casting down imaginations, bringing every thought captive to Christ, conquering all human enterprises in the name of King Jesus.

So swings the pendulum, from walk-all-over-me liberalism to dominion militancy. I don't want to turn away from the militancy. I see a lot of value in Kuyper, in Van Til and Adams, indeed in the Christian Reconstruction movement as well. (I don't see quite as much value in it as they do.) But what has happened to gentleness in all of this? Again, we know it is part of the Christian life, and especially that it is one of the qualifications of the Christian pastor. But it slips through the cracks. Ironically, the concept of gentleness seems itself to be very gentle. It doesn't shout out at us; it almost seems to hide among those long lists of Christian virtues.

But let's look more closely at Scripture. Look at Exodus 34:6 and 7, where God defines himself, where he explains his name to Moses: "The LORD, the LORD, a God merciful and gracious, slow to anger, and abounding in steadfast love and faithfulness, keeping steadfast love for thousands, forgiving iniquity and transgression and sin, but who will by no means clear the guilty, visiting the iniquity of the fathers on the children and the children's children, to the third and the fourth generation." Yes, there is judgment there. Fearsome judgment. But there is also mercy, long-suffering, and compassion. As the New Testament says, God *is* love. Sin deserves instantaneous infliction of death, but God is so merciful to us. Here is a

God who is gentle with sinners. We learn how gentle when we read in the New Testament that "God shows his love for us in that while we were still sinners, Christ died for us" (Rom. 5:8). The Lord Jesus comes as God's gentle shepherd of his people. Remember Isaiah 40:11? "He will tend his flock like a shepherd; he will gather the lambs in his arms; he will carry them in his bosom, and gently lead those that are with young." Yes, our Lord is gentle.

Jesus did not jump all over people who were guilty of sin. To the immoral woman of Samaria, he offered the living water of eternal life. He offered her a wonderful gift, before her sins even entered the conversation. Yes, he did discuss her sins at a later point, but in a very loving, gentle way. He healed people first, and then said, "Go and sin no more."

And think of how often Paul emphasizes the importance of gentleness in the ministry:

> We could have made demands as apostles of Christ. But we were gentle among you, like a nursing mother taking care of her own children. (1 Thess. 2:6–7)

> I Paul, myself entreat you, by the meekness and gentleness of Christ . . . (2 Cor. 10:1)

> Put on then, as God's chosen ones, holy and beloved, compassion, kindness, humility, meekness, and patience, bearing with one another and, if one has a complaint against another, forgiving each other; as the Lord has forgiven you, so you also must forgive. And above all these put on love, which binds everything together in perfect harmony. (Col. 3:12–14)

> And the Lord's servant must not be quarrelsome but kind to everyone, able to teach, patiently enduring evil, correcting his opponents with gentleness [are you listening?]. God may perhaps grant them repentance leading to a knowledge of the truth. (2 Tim. 2:24–25)

Think of the little book of Philemon, where Paul writes asking his friend to treat well the former slave Onesimus, whom Paul is sending back to Philemon. Onesimus is now a Christian brother. Paul says to Philemon that he could, as an apostle, command Philemon to do the right thing, but instead he humbly entreats on the basis of love. In verse 8, he says, "Accordingly, though I am bold enough in Christ to command you to do what is required, yet for love's sake I prefer to appeal to you." Then in verse 14 he adds, "I preferred to do nothing without your consent in order that your goodness might not be by compulsion but of your own free will." Paul had great authority as an apostle, but, as Jesus taught, Paul did not believe a leader should "lord it over" his flock, commanding them to do this and that, threatening them, coercing them, making life miserable for them. Rather, he sought to resolve problems in the gentlest way possible. Like a good parent, he did not want to provoke his children to wrath. Rather, he wanted to teach them, by word and example, how to love the ways of God from the heart. And loving God from the heart involves *spontaneous* obedience. It was important for Paul to cultivate *spontaneous* obedience among his people.

Certainly here there is no disparagement of justice, no compromise of the holiness of the church. Paul did advocate excommunication for those who could not be reached any other way (1 Cor. 5), but, characteristically, he saw even excommunication as a means to restore, to heal: "You are to deliver this man to Satan for the destruction of the flesh, so that his spirit may be saved in the day of the Lord." But Paul's concept of the pastor is certainly a lot less like a king or general than it is like a shepherd or even a nursing mother.

Another way to put it, perhaps, is that Paul did not see himself as standing in an *adversarial* relationship with his people. He was not their enemy, but their friend, their father, their nursing mother. I guess I've been rather saddened by some reports I have heard lately of elders who have taken an adversarial stance against their own sheep.

We in the Reformed churches and seminaries need to be warned here in a special way. These institutions were founded by academic theologians, and in these bodies there has always been an atmosphere of academic disputation. There is nothing wrong with that in itself. Academic disputation can be useful and fun. We argue with one another, seek to establish different ideas about this or that, and afterwards shake hands and go out for coffee or whatever. There is always an adversarial relationship in academic debate, but that is usually temporary, unless the issues discussed have implications far beyond the academy. Theological issues do have such implications, and so even in the seminary there are dangers in academic theological debate. But even at its best, the atmosphere of academic debate falls far short of what God wants for his church. The church is not an academic debating society, not a place where one seeks by whatever means to prove himself right and to prove the other guy wrong. It is above all a place where we care for one another as nursing mothers care for their babies. And if that atmosphere of caring, protecting, nurturing, loving, is ever replaced by an adversarial climate, no matter how temporary, the very life of the church is in danger.

Reformed seminaries historically have also stood for a tough, militant Christianity which stresses the lordship of Christ and rejects the wimpish God of theological modernism. We stress the need to preach judgment, to stress those doctrines of Scripture like miracles and predestination which are least congenial to modern man. That is all to the good. But it is our task today to determine how all that can be integrated into a church life which is recognizably, atmospherically, loving, nurturing, caring, gentle. If we preach the toughness of God without passionately seeking to maintain that gentleness, we commit an error opposite to that of modernism and one just as bad. Speaking the truth in love—that is the balance God calls us to maintain. Hear Galatians 6:1: "Brothers, if anyone is caught in any transgression, you who are spiritual should restore him in a spirit of *gentleness*. Keep watch on yourself, lest you too be tempted." Restore, reprove, rebuke; but don't let the gentleness of Jesus ever be lost. Likewise Philippians 4:5 NIV: "Let your *gentleness* be evident to all [why gentleness, rather than something else?]. The Lord is near."

What about you? Are you able to nurture others in this way? Maybe you love people, but you don't know how to correct them in a truly gentle way, without harshness, without hurting. If so, find someone who can serve as a model and teacher for you in this area; it is tremendously important. And, for the sake of our Lord Jesus Christ and for the love of his sheep, stay out of the pastorate until you have learned.

APPENDIX E

IN DEFENSE OF CHRISTIAN ACTIVISM

A short form of this article appeared in *Christian Culture*, April 2006, 1–4, and a longer version at www.christianculture.com (April 19, 2006). It is used here by permission (slightly changed).

Christian activism, by which I mean simply any Christian attempt to improve society, has had its ups and downs over the centuries. If you read a book like D. James Kennedy and Jerry Newcombe, *What If Jesus Had Never Been Born*,[1] you should be impressed by the great influence of the Christian gospel, and specifically Calvinism, upon Western culture. I don't want to minimize the wickedness of fallen culture. But for now I'm making the point that there is good as well. Kennedy and Newcombe emphasize that Christians, for distinctively Christian motives, have vastly influenced Western culture in such areas as help for the poor, the abolition of slavery, the teaching of literacy, education for all, political freedom, economic freedom, science, medicine, the family, the arts, and the sanctity of life. Without Jesus, without his gospel, without the influence of his people, all these areas of culture would be vastly different and very much worse.

But from time to time there has been a failure of nerve. None of these efforts by Christians has led to perfection. There is still much evil in the world, and there are many who would silence the Christian voice. So Christians have often been discouraged by the net results of their efforts. We recall the period from around 1925 to 1945, when fundamentalist Christians in America largely retreated from any kind of social action. And

---

1. Nashville: Thomas Nelson, 1994.

943

in the 1990s, the Moral Majority was disbanded, and Christian leaders like Jerry Falwell and columnist Cal Thomas disparaged Christian social activism, saying that it detracted from the Christian's fundamental responsibility to proclaim the gospel.

One can easily understand such retreat psychologically, as a weariness and frustration. But some writers have offered theological rationales for it. One is grounded in premillennialism: Christ may return at any moment, and so we don't have time to try to fix society, only to rescue a few souls from damnation. This world will be destroyed, and, as the old saying would have it, it is a waste of time to polish brass on a sinking ship.

I am not a premillennialist, but even if I were, I could not use this argument. We don't know when Christ is coming. In the meantime, Scripture tells us not only to rescue people from hell by preaching the gospel, but also to care for the poor, the orphan, and the widow. It calls us to "do good to everyone, and especially to those who are of the household of faith" (Gal. 6:10). It calls us not only to bring people to faith and baptism, but also to teach them "to observe all that I have commanded you" (Matt. 28:20), which includes the pursuit of mercy and justice among human beings.

As God's Spirit penetrates people's hearts through the gospel, those people become new creatures (2 Cor. 5:17). They take their faith into every sphere of life, including the workplace, politics, economics, education, and the arts. And in all these realms, they seek to glorify God. They hear Paul's exhortation in 1 Corinthians 10:31, "Whether you eat or drink, or whatever you do, do all to the glory of God." They obey, imperfectly to be sure. But their incipient obedience leads to significant changes in society, as we've seen above.

It is true that the New Testament does not focus on the goal of improving the general society. Most of its social teaching concerns relations of love within the body of Christ. But Jesus taught his disciples to minister to people without regard to their creed or national origin (Luke 10:25–37), and Paul, as we saw, urges believers to do good "especially" to the household of faith, but not exclusively there. The early Christians did not have the power to affect much the politics and culture of the Roman Empire, but they did what they could. For example, they rescued babies who had been exposed to die and brought them up in their homes.

The Romans, at least, felt threatened. *Kyrios Iēsous,* "Jesus is Lord," sounded all too much to them like *kyrios Kaisar,* "Caesar is Lord," their own fundamental confession. Jesus did not come in his first advent to be an earthly king, but he is indeed King of kings and Lord of lords (Rev. 17:14; 19:16), to whom all authority has been given (Matt. 28:18). He is the mighty Son of David, whose kingdom is to stretch "from sea to sea" and "from the River to the ends of the earth" (Ps. 72:8). The Romans persecuted Christians because they believed that Christ's kingship was a threat to Caesar. The Christians protested that Christ was not an earthly king, and that they sought to be good Roman citizens. They said that sincerely. But in time Christianity overwhelmed the Roman Empire, not by the sword, but by the power of the gospel. In time, Scripture teaches, the kingdoms of this world are to become the kingdom of Christ (Rev. 11:15). So the gospel certainly is a political movement. That is not to say that Christians should seek political power by the sword. But they should never imagine that their faith is politically irrelevant.

In time, Christians came to have more and more direct influence on society and its institutions. The Kennedy-Newcombe volume and others trace these influences. Democracy is also a product of Christian thought and influence (see, for example, Samuel Rutherford's *Lex, Rex*). And under democracy, citizens have power, whether they want it or not, to effect changes in the leadership and policies of a nation. The above arguments suggest that Christians would be foolish not to participate in this process. And it goes without saying that Christians should vote, not according to the godless ideologies of the secular world, but according to the standards of the Word of God. And when that happens, even more transformations take place in society.

I have dealt with the basic fundamentalist argument that would have us abandon our social responsibility and just preach the simple gospel. But there is also another argument against Christian social action that has become more popular in our day. This argument has some historical roots, being based in Luther's distinction of "two kingdoms,"[2] and it is used today particularly by confessional Lutherans and some Calvinists, most of whom, though theologically orthodox, would not want to be called fundamentalists.

Michael Horton's article in *Christianity Today*, "How the Kingdom Comes,"[3] is a typical popular presentation of this position. He emphasizes that the kingdom of God comes by God's power, not ours. He points out that Jesus in the New Testament does not commission his people to destroy unbelievers with the sword. So "there are no calls in the New Testament either to withdraw into a private ghetto or to 'take back' the realms of cultural and political activity." The church exists within the world as a community of Word and sacrament, but does not seek influence in the

2. I discuss this distinction, its history and its ramifications, often in this book. See esp. chapters 12, 14, 17, 29, 32, 45–46.

3. 50.1 (January 2006): 42. I am using the version posted at http://www.christianitytoday.com/global/printer.html?/ct/2006/001/2.43.html.

larger society. He says, "There is no 'Christian politics' or 'Christian art' or 'Christian literature,' any more than there is 'Christian plumbing.'" Then he urges the church not to try to be like the world, or to make the world into something like the church.

There is much truth in this position. Certainly God does not call us today to destroy unbelief with the sword, as God called Joshua to destroy the pagan inhabitants of Canaan. But one can certainly renounce the use of the sword against unbelief without renouncing Christian activism in general. Christian activism, remember, is simply the attempt of Christians to improve the general society. Especially today in the democratic West, that can be done by many lawful means, without violence.

So Horton confuses the question of whether we should use violence with the larger question of whether we should seek to influence developments in society. I believe he confuses other questions as well:

1. He brings up the distinction between the church and civil society. But one can surely acknowledge such a distinction without disavowing attempts of the former to influence the latter. So far as I know, nobody in this discussion thinks that the state should administer sacraments, or, again, that the church should lead Christians into armed warfare. So to bring up these issues is to make a straw-man argument.

2. Horton asks whether the kingdom of God is a culture, created by man, or God's sovereign action. Certainly the latter. Again, I know of no evangelical who thinks otherwise. Does this distinction mean that we should take a passive stance, waiting for God to deal with social evils, rather than seeking to alleviate them by our own resources? Scripture never draws this sort of conclusion. The sovereignty of God never excludes human responsibility in this way.

Horton's article, at one point, even argues that we should not make special efforts to reach young people with the gospel. (He chooses some crass examples, but he evidently wants to exclude all such efforts, not just the crass ones.) He says, "The Word creates its own publicity as it is preached. . . . It creates its own relevance." What this suggests is that since God's own Word is sovereign, powerful, and clear, we need make no efforts to *make* it clear to people. That again, is to pit God's sovereignty against human responsibility. If this were true, we would not make any attempt to improve communication in preaching, but should rather just wait for God to communicate. This is unbiblical and foolish. Even to preach the gospel in English rather than Greek is to make a human effort to make God's Word clear.

There are dangers here, to be sure. But the book of Acts shows that Paul spoke differently to Jews than to Greeks. He took differences in language and culture into account (cf. 1 Cor. 9:19–23). Obviously, we do not present the gospel to five-year-old children the same way we present it to campus intellectuals. To say that "the Word creates its own relevance" is true in a sense, but if it is taken to imply that we do not need to take our audience into account in our communication, this statement is a recipe for failure. The application of this to our central discussion is that although the kingdom comes through God's sovereign action, that doesn't exclude human efforts to bring the Word of God to bear on society.

3. Should Christians seek to "transform their workplace, neighborhood, or nation into the kingdom of Christ"? Again, God brings the kingdom in his own time. And again, this fact does not rule out human attempts to improve society. If by "transforming the workplace . . . into the kingdom of Christ" Horton means transforming the workplace into a church, then of course we should not do that. But this is irrelevant to the question of whether to pursue biblical standards in the workplace, neighborhood, and nation. We cannot turn the workplace into a church, but we can certainly make it a better workplace as we accept our responsibility as Christians to take every thought captive to the obedience of Christ (2 Cor. 10:5).

4. Should we support every political or artistic movement that calls itself Christian? Certainly not. But that does not refute the possibility that some such movements may be worthy of Christian support.

5. Should the church "bind Christian consciences beyond Scripture"? No. Horton evidently thinks this is what happens when the church advocates Christian political action. But that is not necessarily the case. On the best view of the matter, Christian political action is simply applying the principles of Scripture to political life: the sanctity of truth and life, the integrity of the family, protection of property, and so on. Christians should not hold these principles in the church and deny them in their public life. Of course, there are legitimate areas of debate as to precisely what policies constitute applications of Scripture. But these debates do not invalidate the attempt to apply Scripture to society. In principle, it is no more difficult to apply Scripture to social issues than to apply it to issues of church doctrine and government.

6. Should the church, then, be like the culture, as it seeks to be an agent of cultural change? (a) In some ways, absolutely not. It should teach and model biblical standards of sexuality, for example, which are quite opposite to those in the world. (b) In other ways, certainly. If we are to carry out the Great Commission, we must, like Paul, speak the language of people around us, "become all things to all people, that by all means I might save some" (1 Cor. 9:22). Given the distinction between (a) and (b), we should not discourage Christian activism on the ground that it makes the church "like the world."

7. Should believers "share with unbelievers in pain and pleasure, poverty and wealth, hurricanes and holidays," until Jesus' return? Sure. But that says nothing against Christian attempts to improve that shared culture by use of God's revealed wisdom.

Horton, therefore, seeks to discourage Christian cultural activism, by linking it up with various evils, such as (1) identifying church and state, (2) denying God's sovereignty, (3) confusing culture with God's kingdom, (4) bad "Christian" art, etc., (5) binding Christian consciences beyond Scripture, (6) Christians adopting the sins of culture, and (7) failure to acknowledge a shared culture. But a right kind of Christian activism entails none of these evils. These are a smokescreen, irrelevant to the conclusion Horton seeks to argue.

So is there such a thing as Christian politics or art? (a) The answer to this question obviously does not follow from the answers to #1–#7 above, as Horton seems to think it does. (b) In the most obvious meaning, "Christian politics" simply refers to Christians making their political decisions on biblical principles. In that sense, there certainly is such a thing as Christian politics. Similarly, there are Christian art and other cultural activities. (c) If Horton means to deny that we should apply biblical standards to public issues, then he certainly holds a very radical position. This does not follow from any of his previous argumentation, and there is no argument for it in the article. In my judgment this conclusion is directly contrary to 1 Corinthians 10:31, "Whether you eat or drink, or whatever you do, do all to the glory of God."

There is one more argument, however, that we should think about, one that I think plays a major role in Horton's own thinking, but which he mentions in the article only very briefly:

> Is Jesus Christ Lord over secular powers and principalities? At least in Reformed theology, the answer is yes, though he is Lord in different ways over the world and the church. God presently rules the world through providence and common grace, while he rules the church through Word, sacrament, and covenantal nurture.

A reader might wonder what this distinction has to do with the question of Christian social activism. Nobody can doubt that God rules the world through providence and common grace, but how does that fact bear on whether or not Christians should try to change society? The answer is that "providence and common grace" are code words for a complicated theological position that Horton works from, but does not express directly, in this article.

That position is the Lutheran "two kingdoms" doctrine, which I mentioned before. In other writings, Horton links this doctrine to Meredith G. Kline's doctrine of a "common grace" realm.[4] The kingdom of "common grace," or of God's "left hand" (Luther), is a realm in which the state rules by natural revelation, rather than by the whole biblical word of God. That realm is religiously neutral. I have criticized this position extensively elsewhere (see footnote 2). I see no biblical basis for suggesting that any sphere of human activity is not to be governed by God's full revelation, or that any human project should not acknowledge God.

To be sure, God brings his common grace to all his creatures, and they are all aware of his natural revelation. But Paul in Romans 1 teaches that the unregenerate repress natural revelation and prefer to live lives of sin. The only remedy is special revelation, the gospel. So Calvin taught that nobody can appreciate natural revelation without the "spectacles" of Scripture. There is, therefore, no human activity that can function as God intended by natural revelation alone. We are to do all things to the glory of God in Christ (1 Cor. 10:31), to bring every thought captive to the Lord (2 Cor. 10:5). Every human institution·must acknowledge him as King of kings and Lord of lords, for that is what he is.

Kline believes that the Israelite theocracy was a "holy" state, but that all other governments are unholy, common, or profane, and thus part of the "common grace realm," and not subject to special revelation. Israel, to be sure, had a special relation to God as God's holy people. But Scripture never suggests that pagan governments are not responsible to God's special revelation. Indeed, Israelite prophets brought God's special revelation to bear against Babylon, Assyria, Moab, Cush, Egypt, Tyre, and Sidon, as well as Israel (as in Isa. 13–23), and against Rome (in the book of Revelation).

To deny the two-kingdoms view is *not* to identify the kingdom of God with fallen culture, or to make any of the other errors discussed in #1–#7 above.

More can be said about the two-kingdoms doctrine. But the important thing to remember here is that Horton has offered no persuasive argument for his very radical conclusion. He writes engagingly, but his discussion is highly confused and unpersuasive.

It is interesting to me, also, that despite their polemic against Christian activism, Horton and others who hold the two-kingdoms view (like Gene Veith) do not hesitate to criticize culture in print, from various biblical perspectives. Are these articles only for the benefit of the church, written without any hope at all that they might influence the unbelieving culture?

---

4. Kline, *Kingdom Prologue* (privately published, 1991).

I doubt it. But then Horton and Veith, like others of us, have engaged in Christian activism, however contrary that may be to their principles.[5]

Beyond the premillennial-fundamentalist arguments and the Horton-Kline common grace argument, I know of no other serious arguments against Christian activism.[6] So I urge Christians to bring the standards of the Word of God to bear on matters of culture and politics, as well as matters that are more narrowly theological.

In taking this position, I follow Abraham Kuyper, the great Dutch statesman, theologian, and journalist. Kuyper of course made the famous statement that there is no square inch of territory in the whole universe over which Christ does not say, "This is mine." See his *Lectures on Calvinism* for his views on how Calvinism has influenced the arts, politics, economics, etc.

I also follow Cornelius Van Til, who taught apologetics at Westminster Seminary in Philadelphia for many years. Van Til was Kuyperian through and through, maintaining that the Bible "speaks about everything" and encouraging his students and readers to apply the Scriptures to every sphere of life. So he supported Christian schools very vigorously. And Van Til quoted passages like 1 Corinthians 10:31 and 2 Corinthians 10:5 all the time, to that effect. He emphasized that the real issues in every sphere of human activity were religious. No doubt he would say that the "common grace realm" of Luther, Kline, and Horton is a sphere of "religious neutrality," a realm where human reason should seek to interpret the data of natural revelation without the aid of Scripture. And Van Til, following Kuyper, believed there was no such realm.

In the Kuyperian view, all the ills of society are essentially religious. They stem from people worshiping false gods. Either sinners worship the gods of some pagan ideology, or they give primacy to their own autonomous thought. It is such false religion that leads to war, violence, disdain for the poor, abortion, adultery, divorce, and homosexuality. Insofar as the Kline-Horton view obscures the religious nature of our cultural and political issues, it confuses Christians as to their responsibilities.

In the general society as well as in the church, Christians should settle for nothing less than the comprehensive lordship of Jesus Christ. He is King of kings and Lord of lords. To say this is not to advocate violent revolution in Jesus' name. He has forbidden us to take that course. But by his Word and Spirit, by his love, and by wise use of the means available to us, we seek to exalt him, not only in the church, but in the whole world.

---

5. Kline, too, wrote an exegetical article opposing abortion. See his "*Lex Talionis* and the Human Fetus," *Journal of the Evangelical Theological Society* 20 (1977): 193–201.

6. There is also the Anabaptist argument that the state is satanic. But Christians of Anabaptist background are among those most involved in Christian activism today.

IS NATURAL REVELATION SUFFICIENT
TO GOVERN CULTURE?

This article appeared in *Christian Culture*, August 2006, 1–3, and is used by permission (with slight changes).

The titular question seems to me to be central in the current discussion in the Reformed camp between Kuyperians and Klineans. Kuyperians argue that Scripture governs all aspects of human life, including culture and government.[1] Klineans[2] believe that politics and general culture are

1. There are some exceptions. The followers of Dooyeweerd in the Toronto Institute for Christian Studies identify themselves with Kuyper, but they believe that Scripture itself does not govern all of culture. Rather, (1) it provides the gospel message by which people are regenerated by the Holy Spirit, (2) it gives us a world-and-life view (creation, fall, and redemption) that we should seek to relate to everything in the world, and (3) it gives specific direction in matters of faith, which on the Dooyeweerdian view is sharply distinguished from other spheres of human learning and social organization. In their view, therefore, Scripture does not give us standards for right and wrong. Rather, those standards are to be found from natural revelation under the impetus of regeneration and a general worldview (creation, fall, and redemption) derived from Scripture. So in fact the Dooyeweerdian movement holds to a natural-law position in ethics, politics, the arts, and other cultural matters, more characteristic of the Klinean-Lutheran view than of the Kuyperian.

2. See Meredith G. Kline, *Kingdom Prologue* (downloadable from http://www.twoagepress. org.htm). Kline's disciples often connect his position with the Lutheran contrasts between law and gospel and between the "two kingdoms." I argue that these views are also similar to the Roman Catholic distinction between nature and grace. See this book, chapter 12 and *passim*.

governed by natural revelation and common grace.[3] On their view, Christians should not urge distinctively biblical principles upon the institutions of the broad society; rather, they should draw people's attention to the demands of natural law, the ethical implications of natural revelation.

I believe that this position is wrong, for the following reasons:

1. *Natural revelation was not sufficient before the fall of Adam.* Even in Paradise, as Cornelius Van Til used to say, our first parents learned truth, not only from their senses and reason from God's revelation in creation, but also from the divine voice itself. According to Genesis 1:28–30, God did not leave it to our first parents to find out his will on their own, by scrutinizing natural revelation. Rather, he spoke to them in his own words, giving them the fundamental task of their existence. Indeed, it is this passage, often called "the cultural mandate," that defines culture for God's people.

He gave them more divine words in Genesis 2:16–17. Adam and Eve had the responsibility of interpreting natural revelation in accord with the audible words God had spoken to them. God's spoken words functioned as a criterion for the truth of any interpretations of natural revelation that might have occurred to them.

2. *Natural revelation is not sufficient after the fall.* Unlike unfallen Adam, fallen man seeks to rule his life by his would-be autonomous knowledge of natural revelation, without obeying God's audible and written words. But to do this is necessarily to distort the meaning of natural revelation. Romans 1 tells us that the sinner represses the truth of natural revelation, exchanging it for a lie. So his use of natural revelation leads only to more sin, and worse. Paul mentions particularly the sins of idolatry and sexual uncleanness.[4]

3. *Natural revelation is not sufficient for salvation.* As Scripture presents it in passages like Psalm 19 and Romans 1, God's revelation in nature tells people that God exists, his nature, and his moral standards. But it does not tell them how they can be forgiven for their violations of these moral standards.

4. *Natural revelation is not sufficient for pleasing God in any sphere.* Since natural revelation does not bring people to salvation, it cannot prevent its

---

3. "Natural revelation" is God's revelation of himself in the created order, apart from such verbal revelations as Scripture, prophecy, and the divine voice from heaven. Scripture speaks of this in passages such as Ps. 19 and Rom. 1. "Special revelation" is God's revealing of himself in words and sentences. The gospel of redemption through Christ is part of special revelation. "Common grace" is nonsaving grace, God's kindness to those who do not believe in him, including his restraint on their sin.

4. Natural revelation is, nevertheless, clear and authoritative, taking away every excuse (Rom. 1:20). Natural revelation declares God's truth, and sinners continue to know that truth at some level of their consciousness even though they distort it. So their distortion is culpable. They adopt an interpretation of natural revelation that justifies their sin, even though they know better.

own distortion in the human heart. With natural revelation alone, nobody can please God.[5]

5. *The only remedy for the distortion of natural revelation is God's grace.* Paul later says, "For all have sinned and fall short of the glory of God, and are justified by his grace as a gift, through the redemption that is in Christ Jesus" (Rom. 3:23–24).

6. *God's grace comes to us through God's special revelation, the gospel of Scripture* (Rom. 10:14–17). Saving faith is trusting in that message, that God will save all who come to him through Christ.

7. *So we cannot understand natural revelation without distortion, unless we view it biblically.* Calvin says (*Institutes*, 1.1.6) that Scripture is like a pair of glasses, which brings into sharp focus what is otherwise blurred.

8. *God has never authorized any social institutions or activities to govern themselves without the use of his spoken and written words.* Kline and others have claimed that God authorized that sort of society between Cain and the Mosaic covenant, a society he describes as a common grace order, governed by natural revelation alone. The Mosaic covenant began a different kind of society, a "holy" society, governed by God's written words. But even during the administration of this covenant, on Kline's view, nations other than Israel were common grace societies. And when the new covenant in Christ replaced the Mosaic, there was no longer any provision, even among God's people, for Scripture to govern society. So all nations today are common grace nations—societies to be governed by natural revelation, not the Bible.

I do not believe, however, that Scripture itself ever makes any such distinction. There is no record in Scripture of any nation or society divinely authorized to govern itself by natural revelation alone. God's arrangement with Cain (Gen. 4:8–16) is by special revelation, God's own words. Similarly, God's covenants with Noah (Gen. 8:20–9:17) and Abraham (12:1–3; also chaps. 15 and 17). God authorizes Noah's family to establish law and order, including the penalty of bloodshed for those who shed blood (9:6). Noah therefore receives this authorization, not by natural revelation, but by supernatural. During the time of the Mosaic covenant, God's prophets address, not only Israel, but pagan nations as well, bringing God's spoken words to them (e.g., Isa. 10–24) and demanding that they live up to God's revealed standards. Given the insufficiencies of natural revelation noted above, this fact should not be surprising.

9. *Natural revelation is not sufficient for our public dialogue with non-Christians.* Some will be surprised at this claim, for it has often been thought

---

5. This is not to say, of course, that unsaved people are as bad as they can be, or to deny that God's common grace restrains human sin. It is simply to say that, apart from grace, nobody can please God (Rom. 8:8).

that the Klinean position is an advantage to public dialogue. Better appeal to nature, it is said, than to sling Bible passages at people. Certainly, this position has some rhetorical advantages in the present climate of unbelief. Many give a hearing, at least, to natural-law ethics that they would not give to Bible exposition. But what we gain in rhetoric, in my view, we lose in cogency.

Romans 1 does say that God clearly reveals his ethical standards in natural revelation. But it doesn't say how he reveals these. Thomas Aquinas and others thought that God reveals them through our ability to construct arguments, deducing conclusions from natural phenomena. That is unlikely, since Paul considers this clear revelation to be universal (see Rom. 3:10–20), and many people (e.g., small children) are incapable of devising arguments. More likely, the knowledge of natural revelation comes to us in an intuitive manner, though some may be able to develop arguments based on that intuited data.

But arguments actually developed from natural-revelation premises ("natural-law arguments," as they are called) are rarely cogent. Roman Catholics, for example, often argue that birth control is forbidden because of the natural connection between sexual intercourse and reproduction. That connection obviously exists, but the moral conclusion is not a necessary one. Indeed the argument (like many natural-law arguments) is a naturalistic fallacy, an attempt to reason from fact to obligation, from "is" to "ought."

Cogent and persuasive ethical reasoning presupposes a worldview and standards of judgment. It is not easy to argue these from nature alone. For Christians, these standards come from Scripture. So apart from Scripture, ethical argument loses its cogency and often its persuasiveness. Nonbelievers, of course, won't usually accept Scripture as authoritative. But they may at least respect an argument that is self-conscious about its epistemological and metaphysical presuppositions.

In public discussion, it may sometimes be desirable to argue a position without directly referring to Scripture. We may, for example, point to the cultural consequences of China's one-child policy, or to the general indifference to human life encouraged by legalized abortion, or to the societal consequences of secularized education. Arguments like these will be persuasive to some non-Christians. They appeal to that knowledge of natural revelation that they are unable fully to suppress. But when someone presses us to ask, for example, why we think that indifference to human life is a bad thing, we must in the end refer to Scripture, for that is the ultimate source of our values.

10. *Jesus Christ rules all spheres of human life (Matt. 28:18), including politics.* He is King of kings and Lord of lords (Rev. 17:14; 19:16; cf. 1 Tim.

6:15). The chief confession of the New Testament is *kyrios Iēsous*, "Jesus is Lord" (Rom. 10:9; 1 Cor. 12:3; Phil. 2:11). This confession opposes the slogan "Caesar is Lord." Although the kingdom of Jesus is different in many ways from earthly kingdoms, the Romans rightly feared Jesus as a rival to Caesar. In time, the empire became Christian, not by the sword, but by the power of the gospel. So, as in many other ways, the gospel, written and preached, transformed society. We should not adopt a theory that limits the social effects of the gospel in our own time.

11. *The gospel will transform the whole creation.* This includes even the inanimate creation. The natural order "waits with eager longing for the revealing of the sons of God" (Rom. 8:19). In Christ, all things will be reconciled to God (Col. 1:20). This makes even less likely the view that the Word of God governs only the institutional church, and not the general culture.

12. *Christians should seek the glory of God in all areas of life* (1 Cor. 10:31). Since the Gospel transforms all things, we should also seek that goal, aligning our own responsible actions with God's sovereign purpose. God intends for all human thoughts to be brought captive to the obedience of Christ (2 Cor. 10:5).

13. *So natural revelation is insufficient in our witness to the lordship of Christ.* In our public dialogue on cultural matters, the most important thing is to be true to the Great Commission, exalting Christ before human beings. Our argument should be a witness, or, at the very least, it should not detract from witness. For this purpose, natural revelation is of some use. Paul, for example, appealed to natural revelation when he dealt with Gentiles in Acts 14:15–17 and 17:22–31. But the climax of the Acts 17 sermon[6] was an appeal to the resurrection of Christ, not a datum of natural revelation.

Too often, in ethical debate, Christians sound too much like unbelievers. They reason as if they and their opponents are both operating on the same principle: human rational autonomy. I believe they almost inevitably give this false impression when they are reasoning according to natural law alone. Only when the Christian goes beyond natural law and begins to talk about Jesus as the resurrected King of kings does his witness become distinctively Christian. At that point, of course, he is reasoning from Scripture, not from natural revelation alone.

So I conclude that Christian reasoning about ethics, whether public or private, should never be based on natural revelation alone. Natural

---

6. I am sure he would have said the same thing in the Acts 14 address, had he had enough time. Perhaps he did, and Luke did not record it. But Paul sought in every place above all to preach Christ and him crucified (1 Cor. 2:2).

revelation is important, certainly, in *applying* the principles of Scripture. And observations of natural facts may make the difference in some cases (e.g., when a public policy choice depends on a statistic). But a complete ethical argument must appeal to the ultimate source of moral authority. And for Protestant Christians that is Scripture and Scripture alone. A further consequence is the conclusion given in the title of this article: natural revelation is not sufficient to govern human society or culture.

This Kuyperian approach should not be taken to imply that state and church should be merged, or that human cultural effort alone brings in the kingdom of God, or that all the arts should devote themselves entirely to evangelism, or that the church should become worldly. A number of people, such as Michael Horton, have charged that the Kuyperian view leads to such errors.[7] But all the Kuyperians want to say is that Christian involvement in all cultural areas should be governed by the Word of God. Of course, if the Word of God says that state and church should be merged, then state and church should be merged. But it doesn't say that. Some Christians in the past have erred in this respect, as when they have tried to achieve power for the church by wielding the sword. But they have erred, not in seeking to bring Scripture to bear on public life, but in misunderstanding what Scripture requires. And, although the errors of our ancestors should motivate more humility on our part when we try to apply Scripture to society, these errors are entirely irrelevant to the question of whether we should today seek to apply Scripture to culture.

I am thankful that God has led the church to debate these issues again, and I hope that this debate will lead Christians to greater clarity on this important matter. The very lordship of Christ is the issue. We are called to confess that lordship in everything we do, and in every sphere of life that we enter.

---

7. See my critique of his position in "In Defense of Activism," *Christian Culture*, April 2006, 1–4. An expanded version is available at http://www.frame-poythress.org/frame_articles/2006InDefense.html, and as appendix E in this volume.

REVIEW OF R. J. RUSHDOONY,
The Institutes of Biblical Law[1]

This review will supplement my discussion of theonomy in chapter 13. It was originally published in the *Westminster Theological Journal* 38 (1976): 195–217, and is used here by permission (with slight changes).

Encouraging me to take on this review assignment, a colleague said, "We'll have to start taking Rushdoony more seriously." Though Rushdoony is one of the most prolific writers in the Reformed camp, though his following is large and increasing, and though his writings contain able exposition and scholarly defense of the Reformed faith, we have pretty much ignored him. His books have not been regularly reviewed and his name has not been frequently mentioned.

I have come to regard this, however, as a premature dismissal of an important Christian thinker. Recent experiences with Rushdoony associates and recent reading, particularly in *The Institutes of Biblical Law*, have convinced me that we must indeed take Rushdoony more seriously. In other fields, I have had trouble at many points with Rushdoony's argumentation; his *Institutes*, however, has convinced me that, whatever may be said in criticism of his work, Rushdoony is one of the most important Christian social critics alive today. It is most necessary, therefore, that we see Rushdoony in perspective, noting both his strengths and his weaknesses, so that we may best benefit from his really substantial insights. I have noticed that most who know Rushdoony's work are either passionately for

1. Nutley, NJ: Craig Press, 1973.

him or passionately against him. This review will not please either group very much, but I am convinced that in our circles we need less passionate advocacy and more sympathetic critical analysis. My goal is not to please the partisans, but to help those who are willing to admit that they need help in these matters.

Let us begin positively: What is it that makes Rushdoony so important as a Christian social critic? Accordingly, on what criteria do I make this evaluation? First, unlike some other "prophetic Christian voices" in modern society, Rushdoony is perfectly clear as to the source and basis of his social critique. In his view, God's law for society is *biblical* law, pure and simple. He argues most cogently against any attempt to replace Scripture with "natural law" (pp. 679–93), human wisdom, or plain lawlessness as a basis for social order. The expression "law-word," ambiguous in the writings of some Christian philosophers, causes no problems in Rushdoony's *Institutes*, despite its frequent appearance there. The law-word is the law of Scripture. Therefore, Rushdoony's method of social criticism is simply to expound the biblical law and to measure human societies by that criterion.

Second, Rushdoony not only affirms scriptural authority, but *knows* Scripture in considerable breadth and depth. Where else can we find a social critic who is so much an exegete? The *Institutes* begins with a 650-page commentary on the Decalogue, which incorporates explanations of nearly every Pentateuchal statute and which traces the applications of these laws throughout the history of redemption. Rushdoony's interpretations are mostly secondhand, but he displays considerable intelligence and scriptural discernment in evaluating various exegetical proposals. There is much comparison of Scripture with Scripture. Some of his more interesting suggestions follow: The *exousia* on the woman's head of 1 Corinthians 11:10 is a symbol, both of her authority and of her submission to authority (p. 346); the mark placed on Cain represented God's determination to withhold the penalty of capital punishment from the family authority structure (pp. 358ff.). He gives a somewhat expanded view of *porneia* in Matthew 5:32 and 19:9, which warrants a somewhat more liberal view of divorce than is typical of the Reformed tradition (pp. 40lff.). He views New Testament elders as leaders of many Christian cultural enterprises beyond the institutional church and the eldership as a "functioning" rather than a merely "voting" office (pp. 743ff.). Because of this exegetical thrust, Rushdoony's work, unlike that of some Christian writers, avoids being a mere pale reflection of the latest fashions in humanist thought. His approach is distinctive, and its distinctiveness arises out of its scripturality.

Third, Rushdoony has a remarkably detailed grasp of the historical background and present condition of human culture. If it is rare to find exegetical skill in a social critic, it is even more rare to find that exegetical skill combined with such knowledge of the world. The extent of Rushdoony's reading is astonishing, and his use of it is always thoughtful and to the point. He is one of the least parochial of Reformed scholars, well acquainted with many ecclesiastical traditions and able to recognize and appreciate biblical elements in non-Reformed and pre-Reformed communions, without compromising his own Reformed convictions (cf., e.g., pp. 339, 345, 401, 513, 549, 849). Many of his anecdotes are amusing. There is always an implicit critique. Rushdoony chooses his illustrations well. One's mind never wanders from the point. At least, my interest did not lag throughout the 849 pages of text. Further, Rushdoony not only knows what happens; he also has a keen sense of why things happen. He displays remarkable insights into the workings of the modern mind: how humanist intellectuals resolve problems about property by defining "property" out of existence (p. 161); the lingering belief in verbal magic whereby American liberals treasured the oratorical skills of Kennedy above the concrete accomplishments of Johnson (pp. 577ff.); the wily ability of sinners to slander one another by telling selected portions of the truth (p. 593). Frequently, he is most effective in demonstrating the foolishness of unregenerate thought. The argument that one "cannot define" pornography assumes that without precise definition nothing can be recognized to exist (the rational is the real). But, as Rushdoony correctly points out, pornography, even if it cannot be defined, can certainly be recognized (as can many other things, such as a friend, love, time, etc.). His philosophical skills, though limited, are often well used in such contexts.

Finally, Rushdoony not only acknowledges biblical authority, knows the Bible, and knows our cultural situation; he is also able to apply biblical principles to our culture in creative and cogent ways. Rushdoony has grasped a hugely important point that theologians rarely acknowledge, namely, that theology must involve the application of the Word of God to the whole world. Otherwise, theology is a "lie," testifying that God himself is irrelevant (p. 597; cf. pp. 308, 652ff.). The *Institutes,* therefore, presents a plan for the reformation of all aspects of human society in accord with biblical law. Rushdoony advocates this reformation in various ways:

1. He sets forth eloquently the beauty of a society governed by biblical law: a society where the power of the state is strictly limited (pp. 429–30, *passim*); where eminent domain belongs to God alone, not to the state (pp. 492–93, 499ff.); where there are no property taxes (pp. 56, 283), no expropriations beyond the tithes (pp. 846ff.), but where welfare is effectively provided through covenantal institutions; where all citizens expose and prosecute criminals (pp. 271, 463ff.); where criminals are responsible

to make restitution to their victims (p. 272); where crime is rare because habitual and serious offenders are promptly executed and because others are caught and forced to make restitution, a society without prisons and the farce of pseudo-rehabilitation (pp. 228ff., 458ff., 514ff.); where war is not permitted to take precedence over every other human activity (pp. 277ff.); where the environment is protected by following the instructions of its Creator (pp. 141ff., 164ff.).

2. Where the biblical laws at first glance appear *not* to be so beautiful, but rather (to our humanist-indoctrinated minds) to be strange, trivial, or even cruel, Rushdoony effectively explains the divine logic underlying them. The denial of full citizenship to eunuchs (p. 100), the execution of blasphemers (pp. 106ff.) and incorrigible juvenile delinquents (pp. 185ff., 481ff.), the prohibition of taking a mother bird together with her young (pp. 169, 257, 267), the levirate (pp. 308–9), the dowry legislation (pp. 185ff., 481ff.), and other perplexing biblical statutes are cogently defended.

3. Besides showing the inherent logic of biblical law, Rushdoony shows how that biblical law has been used through history, how its observance has brought about justice and happiness in many societies, and how its abandonment has brought about cultural disaster. He is quite specific with regard to American culture, and he advocates dramatic changes in our legal and institutional structure. His strongest and most frequent polemic is against "statism," the view that the state has the right to tax, control, and disturb all areas of human life. In that regard, his rhetoric closely resembles that of political conservatism, which, indeed, he acknowledges as resting on Christianity to an extent (p. 289). Yet he strongly opposes *laissez faire* capitalism (pp. 288ff., 432–33, 472) as a deification of the abstract laws of economics. Rushdoony's proposals really do not fit very well under any contemporary label, and that in itself is an index of his zeal to follow Scripture rather than to please men.

All things considered, however, Rushdoony's apologetic for biblical law presents a pleasing picture indeed! Although in theory he seems to disapprove of pragmatic argumentation for biblical principles (p. 140), much of the *Institutes* amounts to precisely that. It presents a society which almost any regenerate person would prefer over existing societies. Well, the Lord himself motivates his people to obey by giving promises (Ex. 20:12; etc.). There is a *biblical* pragmatism. Indeed, even those who cannot accept Rushdoony's view that the Old Testament civil law is normative for contemporary civil government may go away from the *Institutes* wishing that view were true, or perhaps wanting to employ that law despite its nonnormativity. Rushdoony himself seems to take the latter approach with regard to the dietary regulations (pp. 297ff.). Therefore, even if a theological argument is forthcoming to refute Rushdoony's general thesis about the civil law, we must seriously ask ourselves what better law can be found, what wiser proposals can be made for the complex and difficult business of governing a nation (cf. Deut. 4:8).

Those who object to Rushdoony's position on the civil law must examine themselves to make sure that their objections do not arise out of distaste for the law itself. There are various arguments against his view which arise out of legitimate exegetical and biblico-theological concerns (see below), yet it is hard to understand on the basis of those theological arguments alone the horror sometimes expressed at his position. Is it possible that to some extent these reactions arise simply because we don't want a society which executes homosexuals, forbids hybridization and transplants (pp. 253ff.), legislates against sexual intercourse during menstruation (pp. 427ff.), and so forth? If indeed we object to these laws as such, then we are questioning the wisdom of God, and that is sin. Moral offense at these statutes is moral offense at God's Word, his covenant rule. Whatever position we take on the present normativity of these laws, we must learn how to delight in them, to be thankful that God gave them to Israel, to covet the happiness that obedience to such laws must have brought to faithful Israelites. We dare not presume to oppose Rushdoony out of a humanistically tainted moral vision.

According to our four criteria, therefore, Rushdoony is indeed an important Christian social critic. We must listen to him. Let us, then, turn to a fuller consideration of the general structure and argument of the book.

From a formal standpoint, the book is a bit rough-hewn. It began as a series of lectures, and in some respects it is still a series of written lectures rather than a unified book. There is considerable repetition: tithes are discussed in similar ways on pages 51ff. and on pages 28lff., circumcision and baptism on pages 41ff. and on pages 755ff., John 8:1–11 on page 398 and pages 702ff., abortion on pages 268 and 714—reasons for these duplications not being entirely clear. Repetition, of course, is inevitable in a lecture series: some in the audience may not have attended an earlier lecture, or may need reminding; the lecturer may get a new insight on a topic already discussed. But there is less justification for this in a published work. The organization of the book is not always clear. Occasionally Rushdoony jumps from topic to topic quickly without clarifying the connections between the matters discussed (pp. 38, 40, 50, 80, etc.). One wonders why "the negativism of the law" is discussed preceding the exegesis of the third commandment, since it is equally applicable to the first and second and could well have been included in an introductory chapter. I, at least, feel that chapters XI–XV might more logically have preceded than followed the material on the Decalogue. Some quotations are not footnoted (pp. 308, 325, 477, etc.). These criticisms, however, are minor. Since most will use this volume as a reference book, some repetition may be justifiable, as it is in an encyclopedia. The macrostructure of the book is always clear, the index is adequate, and the style is lucid, concise, and vigorous.

Our main concern, then, will be with substance more than with form. Rushdoony intends the book to be "a beginning . . . an instituting consideration of that law which must govern society, and which shall govern society under God" (p. 2). One might take the phrase "govern society" in a broad sense, "function as the dominant ideology of society." In that broad sense, "biblical law" would include the entire Bible, for all of Scripture is given to "govern society" in that sense. Rushdoony sometimes seems to have that broader sense in mind, particularly when he discusses redemption, atonement, the need of regeneration, and the structure of the church. Elsewhere, however, it seems that Rushdoony takes "govern society" in a somewhat more narrow sense, i.e., "function as the basic civil law of society." At one point, he determines not to discuss certain passages in the Sermon on the Mount because he feels that they are "not within the scope of civil law" (p. 636). Sometimes, in other words, he seems to aim at applying Scripture to all aspects of society (a large order, to be sure!); at other times, he seems to want to confine himself to the bearing of Scripture upon the civil law-structure of society. Surely we can say at least that the latter is his main concern and the focus of the book.

This brings us to his major thesis, that almost all of the Old Testament civil law is literally normative for civil governments today (on that "almost," see the discussion below). He defends this position with two sorts of argument. First, he employs many of the traditional arguments against antinomianism familiar to students of Reformed literature: obedience to God's commands is basic to scriptural morality (pp. 670ff.). Law defines the biblical concepts of holiness, righteousness, and sanctification (pp. 306–7). Christ is the "champion" of the law, defending it against human additions, subtractions, and perversions (pp. 698ff.). Apart from biblical law, there is no standard for our behavior in this world; the alternative to obedience is autonomy (pp. 652ff.).

These arguments are cogently presented and effective, I would say, against any position suggesting that God's law as such is not binding. It is possible, however, to renounce antinomianism, to affirm our continuing obligation to obey God's commands, and still to disagree with Rushdoony as to what particular obligations bind us today. The arguments against antinomianism call in question much Lutheran, dispensational, and modernist thinking on these matters, but they do not serve to establish

Rushdoony's distinctive view of the civil law as over against that of, say, Professor Meredith Kline. Those holding the alternative view would agree with Rushdoony that God's law is binding, even upon civil magistrates, even upon political and social institutions, while disagreeing with him as to the specific ordinances now in effect. I am inclined to think that Rushdoony expects too much of the arguments against antinomianism and says too little on the precise question at issue within the Reformed camp, namely, what laws are now binding?

At times Rushdoony expresses himself in such a way as to suggest that there is no change in man's obligation from one age to the next. He speaks of God "whose grace and law remain the same in every age" (p. 2). He quotes a passage from Thielicke which merely raises a question, which is to my mind legitimate and important, as to whether a particular Old Testament statute is binding upon the New Testament believer, and, without argument, he charges Thielicke with having "set aside" the law (p. 423). It would seem here that in Rushdoony's view one is antinomian if he even raises a question about the continuing normativity of an old covenant provision. On the other hand, at various points Rushdoony himself acknowledges divinely authorized changes in the obligations of the people of God: literal frontlets are no longer required (pp. 21ff.); there is no more earthly tabernacle since the ascension of Christ (p. 72); the "details" of the quarantine laws are no longer applicable (p. 293); new covenant believers (as opposed to old covenant believers) are forbidden to enter a state of slavery (p. 485); Paul "revised" the ruling of the apostolic council on meats offered to idols (p. 733). Rushdoony's views on the Sabbath (pp. 128ff., 735, 796), the dietary laws (pp. 297ff., 734–35, 792), the old covenant sacraments (pp. 734, 794) and animal offerings (pp. 782–83), are not altogether clear to me, but they certainly do presuppose some change in obligation from one covenantal order to the next. Thus Rushdoony ought to acknowledge more straightforwardly that there is a question here. The issue is not simply antinomianism versus acceptance of law. The question is also "What law?"

There is a second group of arguments in the *Institutes* that does address this sort of question, defending specifically the present normativity of the Old Testament civil law. Rushdoony argues (1) that it is impossible to distinguish, as has commonly been done, between "civil" and "moral" statutes (pp. 304–5), and (2) that Scripture calls all the nations of the world to account for their obedience or disobedience to this civil-moral law (pp. 657ff., 693). His conclusion is that, if the moral law is binding, as Reformed people have always said, then the civil law is binding too, and upon governments and institutions as well as upon individuals. Rushdoony sets forth these arguments much more sketchily than the arguments against antinomianism, but it is at this point that the issues will have to be worked out within the Reformed camp. Rushdoony's arguments have a prima facie cogency about them which ought to be taken seriously by his critics. On the other hand, I also wish that Rushdoony would confront more directly the arguments offered by other Reformed writers on behalf of other positions. Rushdoony is familiar, for instance, with the writings of Meredith Kline. It would have been most helpful if Rushdoony had interacted with Kline's account of the relation between covenantal and cultural units in the new covenant structure (Kline, *By Oath Consigned*, pp. 99–102; *Structure of Biblical Authority*, pp. 94–110). Kline argues that the new covenant establishes a new "community polity" for the people of God. When the kingdom of God is taken from Israel and given to a new people, a new order is established wherein the authority structure no longer bears the sword and carries out civil penalties. We can imagine, I suppose, what a dialogue between Rushdoony and Kline would be like. Rushdoony might well argue that Kline draws too sharply the distinction between old and new covenant orders. He might also point out that even if Kline's construction be accepted, we must still resolve the question of how nations are to be governed. If the civil magistrate is not a theocratic officer in the Old Testament sense, he is nevertheless a "minister of God" in some sense (Rom. 13:4) and obligated to rule in accord with justice. And how do we define civil justice without reference to the Old Testament law, "moral" and "civil"? Then Kline might ask how on this basis we can avoid furthering the kingdom of God with the sword, and so on. I have said that Reformed scholars will have to take Rushdoony more seriously; but that is a two-way street. He will also have to take them more seriously and address the strongest arguments for positions other than his own. In the *Institutes* he does not even appear to be fully aware what those positions are.

I am not now ready to endorse or refute Rushdoony's position on this issue. In general, I feel that the question is not as simple as either Rushdoony or his critics sometimes suggest. And since I am now reviewing Rushdoony's book, not someone else's, let me suggest some aspects of his formulation which are in need of clarification. Rushdoony's thesis is a thesis about the application of God's law to human society. But "application" of law involves not only law. It involves at least two other things, namely, a "situation" *to which* the law is applied and a "moral agent" capable of *making* that application. Anyone who is concerned, as Rushdoony is, to exalt the role of law in moral and civil life must be especially careful to specify the relation of law to the other two factors which are crucial to legal and moral righteousness. A balanced view will look at the ethical process from the standpoint of each of these elements in relation to the other two. It will look at these matters from, let us say, normative, situational, and existential perspectives. In each of these areas, I find significant confusions in Rushdoony's formulations.

The normative perspective. This perspective, focusing upon the law itself, is the main perspective of the book. Yet when we ask concerning the precise role of God's law in the total process of ethical decision making, Rushdoony's position appears less clear than it seemed at first glance. As mentioned earlier, Rushdoony's *Institutes* is not always clear as to precisely what laws are binding upon us today and in what sense they are binding. His rhetoric sometimes suggests that all Old Testament statutes are currently normative, but he also sets forth explicit exceptions to this principle. Some of the exceptions are a bit hard to construe. On the Sabbath issue, he argues on the basis of Colossians 2:16–17 that "the *formalisms* of the Old Testament observances are ended," while "the essence of the law is in force and is basic to all biblical law" (p. 157); but he never quite makes clear how we are to distinguish between formalisms and essence. There is no mode of Sabbath keeping, after all, which has not been regarded by someone as a "formalism." On the questions of Passover (p. 794) and animal sacrifices (pp. 782–83), Rushdoony is also vague. He speaks with apparent approval of Christians who carry on these practices, but he does not quite say they are obligatory today. Hebrews 10 never enters the discussion.

For a book which intends to restore biblical law to its rightful role in human society, and which is in large part a polemic against antinomianism, the *Institutes* is distressingly unclear in its concepts of antinomianism and legalism. We have seen Thielicke rebuked as antinomian merely for raising a question about the current applicability of a particular Old Testament statute. Similarly, Rushdoony attacks Bruce Waltke, who differs from him on the exegesis of Exodus 21:22–25, and suggests that this exegetical view is a symptom of Waltke's general "antinomian dispensationalism" (p. 263). Well, Waltke was once a dispensationalist, and possibly antinomian in some sense; but his exegesis of Exodus 21 may not be written off as a mere antinomian reflex.[2] Some, like Meredith Kline, have agreed with Waltke's exegesis who cannot be suspected of being antinomians. On the exegetical point, I agree with Rushdoony, but the reference to antinomianism not only is forced but also obscures the concept of antinomianism which is so central to the

---

2. Waltke is no longer a dispensationalist, and he has adopted a strongly pro-life understanding of Scripture.

book. The polemic against antinomianism will lose all force if the reader comes to feel that "antinomian" is a label for anyone who disagrees with Rushdoony's exegesis.

The concept of "legalism" is even more obscure. The book contains at least four definitions of legalism: (i) Legalism is the view that man is justified by keeping the law (pp. 305, 549). (ii) Legalism abuses and, I assume, misinterprets (though Rushdoony doesn't say so) the letter of the law to violate its "spirit" (and also, I assume, its letter rightly interpreted) (p. 636). [As the parenthetical comments indicate, this definition creates problems in and of itself, apart from its relations to the others.] (iii) Legalism substitutes man's law for God's (p. 709). (iv) Legalism is the view that God is bound by the same laws that bind mankind (p. 837). This last definition is not Rushdoony's own, but is found in an appendix by Gary North, which apparently has Rushdoony's general approval. The second may possibly be regarded as a characterization of legalism rather than a definition. There are logical connections between these four accounts. It may fairly be said that if one is a legalist in one sense, he will likely be to some degree a legalist in others; but the four are not synonymous, and the simultaneous use of all of them without adequate specification of the relations among them leads to confusion. In the same appendix where the fourth definition appears, Gary North calls John Murray a "legalist" (p. 840) for disagreeing with him about Rahab's lie in Joshua 2:3ff. I suppose North might plausibly regard Murray as a legalist in the third sense, at this point, since on North's view Murray is here substituting man's law for God's. Even in the third sense, however, it makes little sense to charge Murray with legalism on the basis of this one exegetical issue. All of us are "legalistic" on some point or other—even, I imagine, Gary North. But to call someone a legalist generally implies that the person so labeled is habitually or characteristically legalistic, and North clearly has not demonstrated any such characteristic in Murray. Furthermore, the charge becomes even more absurd if we take it in the fourth sense, which is North's own definition. North says nothing that comes even close to indicting Murray on that score. And would anyone dream of calling Murray a legalist in the first sense?

But there is an even more serious normative unclarity in this book, which, if not remedied, could nullify Rushdoony's otherwise admirable defense of the authority of biblical law. This problem also arises out of the rather strange discussions of truth telling, one by Rushdoony and another by North. Both men defend Rahab's lie, as many other exegetes have done. Whatever we may think of that position, there is nothing strange or unusual about it as such. The problem arises in that it is hard to tell which of the following positions Rushdoony and North wish to advocate:

(i) Lying in some situations is permitted by the law and therefore approved by God—Rahab's lie was lawful and therefore not sinful. (ii) Lying is unlawful and therefore sinful, but in some situations we must do it anyway in order to achieve some higher divine purpose; Rahab was legally guilty for lying, but she was right in allowing herself to incur guilt. Now we may well disagree with the first position, but at least it makes some metaethical sense. It presupposes that the law is the criterion of right and wrong, that obeying it is always right, and disobeying it is always wrong. Whether or not we accept this position, we surely ought to accept its metaethical presupposition, which is good Reformed thinking and one of the basic thrusts of the *Institutes*. The second position, however, suggests that law is not the ultimate criterion of right and wrong, that it is sometimes necessary and good to break the law; or, perhaps, interpreted somewhat differently, it suggests that the law at some points requires sin. I devoutly hope that Rushdoony and North are asserting the first rather than the second position. But if they are not asserting the second, then I don't understand a number of things in these chapters, such as the argument on page 548 against making truth telling an "absolute." In that section, Rushdoony argues that truth telling is not absolute; only God himself is absolute. But he surely ought to know the dangers inherent in setting "God himself" over against God's commandments. Once we do that with one commandment, we must do it with all. If a genuine command of God can be broken out of some extralegal concern for "God himself," then how do we avoid the antinomianism against which Rushdoony so zealously warns us? I am also disturbed by the argument on page 549, where criticism of Rahab's lie is blamed upon an "abstract" concern for "self-perfection" as the goal of sanctification. Well, no one wants an "abstract" concern about anything, whatever that means! But does Rushdoony mean to say here that in order to please God we must be willing to sacrifice our own perfection? Does he mean that we must be willing to incur guilt in order to honor God? I hope not. Such an idea introduces contradiction into the law and into God's very nature. But I find the argument hard to comprehend otherwise. If Rushdoony is arguing the first position, then there is really no need to engage in this obscure and dangerous reasoning. On this position, truth telling *as defined by the law* is indeed absolute, not in the sense of being superior to God, but in the sense of being binding upon men. Further, that law will never require us to compromise our own perfection or holiness, for that perfection and holiness consist precisely in obedience to the law of God. The second position, however, is antinomian, and Rushdoony ought to disown it in no uncertain terms.

The situational perspective. Let us turn now to the question of how the law is to be applied to various life situations. We shall note two sorts of problems. Firstly, Rushdoony never formulates very clearly his view on the extent to which cultural change affects the proper application of biblical law. He does admit some effects of this sort. Commenting on 1 Corinthians 7:11–24, he argues that the Old Testament provisions against mixed marriage could not be simply applied to marriage in Gentile cultures, since the latter form of marriage was "atomistic" or "noncovenantal" in character (pp. 412–13). Presumably, then, all Old Testament statutes ought to be investigated in this way, to see if God intended them to function in cultures which are, as ours, different in many ways from that of Old Testament Israel. But Rushdoony rarely makes use of this sort of principle or carries out this sort of investigation. Might it not at least be useful to supplement the biblical law with additional statutes, applying the broad principles of biblical justice to situations (steel mills, space travel, atomic war, etc.) unknown in biblical times? Here Rushdoony is somewhat unclear. At times he appears to reject all "statute law" (pp. 585, 638, 644, 787) on the basis of the sufficiency of Scripture. One suspects at times that, although to Rushdoony Scripture is not a "textbook of physics or biology" (p. 684), it is indeed a textbook of statecraft in the sense that it includes all the statutes that will ever be needed for any sort of culture. At other times, however, he seems to grant legitimacy to those statutes which are proper applications of biblical law (pp. 499, 517–18, 690ff., 708–9). *The Institutes* would be greatly helped by some explicit consideration of the general problem of how the ancient biblical law is to be applied to current situations. How can we take the "situation" into account without making nature or history normative (one of Rushdoony's major concerns) or lapsing into antinomian pragmatism (another)? We have seen how Rushdoony sometimes disapproves, yet sometimes engages in, a kind of "pragmatic" argumentation. At points he seems to deny that "virtue is always rescued and rewarded, and truth is always triumphant" (p. 543; cf. pp. 259ff., 841); at other times, he insists on the basis of biblical promises that obedience brings blessing and disobedience brings disaster (the second paragraph of p. 508 is especially relevant here; cf. also pp. 255, 367, 821–22). I think there is truth on both sides of this apparent contradiction, but that truth must be much more clearly defined to be helpful. The answer is to be found, I would say, in the integration of general and special revelation advocated by Van Til. Nature and Scripture interpret one another. When we have properly interpreted our "situation" in the light of Scripture, then we may properly make moral decisions on the basis of an expected divine blessing within the situation. If, however, that expectation of blessing is not scripturally grounded, then any moral appeal to it is an autonomous pragmatism.

Secondly, it is hard, sometimes, to apply the law to life situations even when cultural change is not a major consideration. Most theologians agree that the biblical case laws, for instance, are intended to exemplify principles which apply to cases other than those explicitly stated. Certainly the apostle Paul adopts this approach to the statute concerning ox muzzling (1 Cor. 9:9; Deut. 25:4). But how do we determine the principles exemplified in case laws? How did Paul know that Deuteronomy 25:4 exemplified the principle of fair reimbursement rather than, say, merely the principle of kindness to animals or the evil of greed? Doubtless the key is to compare Scripture with Scripture, to compare this statute with other scriptural teachings about man's status in the creation. Then by an *a fortiori* argument: if God requires fair reimbursement to animal laborers, how much more to human? Rushdoony also uses *a fortiori* arguments cogently at various points. For example, if a habitually delinquent son is to be executed, then (*a fortiori*) all habitual criminals deserve that punishment (p. 187; cf. also pp. 430, 482, 594). At other times, the argument is not *a fortiori*, but the derivation of principle is fairly obvious. For example, if a husband may not slander his wife, then a wife may not slander her husband either, and the penalty is the same in both cases (pp. 591). At other points, however, Rushdoony's derivations of principles are controversial indeed. Some which trouble me follow:

(1) Although he argues via parity against a wife's slander of her husband, as we have seen, he argues that female and male homosexuality are very differently regarded in the law, male homosexuality being a capital crime, female homosexuality being an "uncleanness" justifying divorce (p. 425). I cannot understand why the case for parity here is not as strong as in the other case. Rushdoony raises no clear scriptural considerations against the parallel.

(2) Both Rushdoony and North argue that bribery is a crime only for the one who takes a bribe, not for the one who offers it (pp. 535–36, 842–43). But elsewhere the book presents sound biblical grounds against encouraging, indulging, and consenting to evil (pp. 425, 483, 544, 832). Surely, to offer a bribe is to encourage someone else to commit a crime. In this biblical context, it would certainly seem necessary to take the bribery statute as forbidding both taking and giving of bribes. North might still be able to defend what he calls "biblical bribery" on some sort of "intrusion" principle (Kline), but he ought at least to address the strong prima facie case for the other position and to avoid suggesting that offering bribes is warranted by the statute in question.

(3) In discussing "The Negativism of the Law," Rushdoony argues that since the Decalogue is largely negative, our civil laws ought to be negative too, i.e., directed against specific evils, rather than setting forth ideals for society to attain. However, on pages 110–11, 220–21, 241, and elsewhere, he follows the Westminster catechisms in setting forth the "positive" implications of the commandments. So far as I can tell, he says nothing adequately to reconcile the two emphases.

More briefly: (4) Does the commandment against removing landmarks really justify a general social conservatism, as Rushdoony seems to think (p. 328)? If so, to what degree? (5) Does the requirement of corroboration in legal testimony really rule out *all* use of lie detectors (pp. 565ff.)? (6) Does the protection of fruit trees in war really warrant the general proposition that "production is prior to politics" (p. 280)? (7) Does the fifth commandment really require instant obedience to parents of such a sort that the child may never ask questions about the justification for the command (p. 193)? (8) Does the separation of Paul and Barnabas into separate spheres of labor really justify separation from an ecclesiastical fellowship to avoid formal discipline (p. 769)? (9) If Rahab's treason is justifiable in terms of some special wartime ethic (pp. 837ff.), then on what basis do we condemn participation in revolution, as Rushdoony wants to do (pp. 76, 722–23, etc.)? (10) If it was wrong to import rabbits into Australia (p. 261), why was it right to import martins into Griggsville (p. 259)? (11) Does the law against transvestism really forbid an able-bodied man to be supported by his wife (p. 436)? If it is really wrong, as Rushdoony suggests, for a man to do "woman's work" (p. 437), why is it not wrong for the woman of Proverbs 31 to go into business?

Other examples could be given. There are a lot of proposed applications in the book which are implausible in themselves and not adequately argued in the text. This fact suggests to me that Rushdoony has not given sufficient thought to just what is involved in applying a law to a situation. Perhaps these examples merely indicate that the book was written too hurriedly. In any case, the book could benefit greatly, not only from more consistency and better arguments, but also from a discussion of the specific question of applicatory methodology.

The existential perspective. We now focus upon the moral agent, the person who applies the law to situations. It is in this area that Rushdoony's book is weakest of all. In fairness, it should be said that Rushdoony may well have regarded this area as outside the proper scope of the book. He declines to discuss the teachings of the Sermon on the Mount concerning lust and hatred on the ground that they are "not within the scope of the civil law"

(p. 636). He might argue, therefore, that we should not demand of him, in this already lengthy book, a full account of moral agency, motive, heart attitude, etc. I must, however, venture into this area, first, because what he does say about these matters is often misleading and, second, because his inadequacies in this area generate serious problems elsewhere in his system. The three "perspectives" are so interrelated that it is really not possible to treat one of them properly without some attention to both the others.

To his credit, Rushdoony emphasizes strongly man's need of regeneration as the prerequisite for law keeping (pp. 706, 709, 725, 43, 113, etc.). He also emphasizes eloquently and cogently the personalism of biblical ethics—the fact that Scripture treats man as a responsible person rather than as an environmentally determined victim (pp. 24ff., 272, 339, 434, 446, 467, 486, 507, 570–71, etc.). He shows quite well in these sections how the fashionable "personalisms" of secular thought actually depersonalize man by denying his responsibility. We should note also Rushdoony's refreshing defense of the passions as over against stoicized forms of Christianity (p. 635). Regeneration, personalism, a positive view of the passions—these are important first steps in the formulation of a biblical doctrine of moral agency.

However, almost everything else he says—about the emotions, regeneration, conscience, and even love—is negative. There is in the book a rather pervasive polemic against "emotionalism," "sentimentality," and so on (pp. 121ff., 213, 247, 251, 483, 463, 634ff., etc.). Taken in the best sense, this polemic justifiably rebukes those who would substitute emotion, sentiment, "sensitivity," and so on, for God's law. But in these passages, one looks in vain for any recognition of the positive functions of conscience, of feeling, and of sensitivity. The defense of the passions on page 635 noted above is almost entirely isolated and is somewhat compromised in its own context. Nowhere is there any suggestion that the love ethic of Scripture requires godly emotions, a renewed conscience, or a renewed sensitivity to the concerns of others. Rushdoony seems at one point, for instance, to disparage a moral appeal to gratitude, simply because there is not in the immediate context any reference to law (p. 213). But, on that ground, the Decalogue itself would be "sentimental," since it motivates obedience chiefly through gratitude to God for the redemption from Egypt. New Testament ethics, too, rarely urges believers to obey simply because God has commanded obedience. The basis of obedience is, most commonly, gratitude for what Christ has done. Apart from law, to be sure, there would be no way of knowing how such gratitude ought to be expressed. But Rushdoony's account would lead one to think that gratitude as such is unsuitable as a motive for good works, and that is simply not the teaching of Scripture. It is better to say that only through the law of God may we distinguish true and false gratitude and thus live lives of true thankfulness.

The same sort of problem arises when Rushdoony considers the question of how to define good works, sanctification, and righteousness. He is most insistent that these concepts be defined in terms of law. He reproaches Berkhof because the latter's definition of good works focuses upon their origin in regeneration and only secondarily points out that they must conform to the law (pp. 553–54). He finds the definition in terms of regeneration to be "too vague." Well, that all depends on what you are looking for. Scripture itself defines and characterizes good works in various ways. Good works are in obedience to God's commands, but they are also "fruits of the Spirit." Sin is transgression of law, but it is also lack of faith (Rom. 14:23). Scripture looks at good works from many angles, and does not, so far as I can see, define one angle as better than another, or one angle as more vague than another. It is just as important, I would think, to see good works in their relation to regeneration as to see their relation to the law. A definition of good works in terms of regeneration may seem vague if you are looking for an account of the relation of good works to law, but the reverse is also true. What one misses in Rushdoony is any appreciation for the importance of defining good works in relation to moral agency, regeneration, gratitude, love, and so forth. It is, I agree, wrong to make any of these a substitute for law. But the opposite error is just as bad.

Rushdoony frequently makes use in various forms of the slogan, "Justification is by grace through faith; sanctification is by law" (pp. 304–5, 549, 674, 714, 732–33, 751). The slogan is somewhat misleading, for it could be taken to suggest that law plays no role in justification and grace no role in sanctification—a plainly unbiblical idea. We would simply write off this slogan as a slip of the pen, except that (1) Rushdoony uses it so frequently, and (2) the slogan is symptomatic of a serious weakness: he really seems to have little appreciation for the role played by grace in the area of sanctification. This is a fairly serious criticism, and I would certainly like to believe that his own convictions are more adequate than what comes out in the book. But we have seen how he treats only negatively the relation of sanctification to regeneration and its fruit, gratitude. We shall see it also in Rushdoony's treatment of the central concept of biblical ethics, namely love.

If love is the fulfilling of the law, one would expect that a top priority item in any account of biblical law would be a full discussion of the biblical view of love. Amazingly, however, Rushdoony takes the same approach with regard to love as what we have seen him take toward other basic concepts. His discussion of love is almost exclusively negative. He issues a polemic against substituting love for law, an admonition to keep love subordinate to law (pp. 173, 254, 284, 467, 303–4, 336, 346, 432). Compare, however, page 360, where love is almost given its due in the marital context. The reciprocity of the law-love relation in Scripture is completely missing from this account. Yes, we must not substitute love for law, but we had better not substitute law for love, either. Yes, love may be defined in terms of law, but the requirement of the law is also summarized and defined in the love commandment. The language of subordination between law and love, unless it specify mutual subordination, is in my view most inadequate here. Love must indeed conform to law, but obedience to law must arise from and manifest love. Without love, the first fruit of the Spirit, there can be no good works or sanctification.

This serious inadequacy has further consequences. The biblical doctrine of love to one's enemies in particular receives most inadequate treatment. It is acknowledged briefly on pages 599–600 as part of a general exhortation to further a godly order of law where everyone will receive his legal deserts. Compare also page 247, on restoring the enemy's ox. But note also the following. At a number of points in the book, there is a rather imprecise polemic against "sympathy" for criminals. In Rushdoony's view, sympathy for criminals, together with the tendency to blame society for a criminal's misdeeds, is a kind of sentimentality which is disobedient to God (pp. 188, 384, 421, 572). But surely more distinctions have to be made here. It is certainly true that Scripture forbids "pity" in the judging process; i.e., a judge ought not to reduce the sentence required by the law out of pity for the offender. But this biblical provision surely does not forbid every sort of "sympathy" for criminals, as seems to be suggested by Rushdoony's rather sweeping formulations. If it did, then Jesus would have broken the law in ministering to the woman taken in adultery (a passage to which Rushdoony attaches considerable importance, despite the textual problem) or to the thief on the cross. And since there is such a thing as "community responsibility" (pp. 270ff.), is there not some sense in which we must blame society for crime? Not, of course, in any sense which removes responsibility from the criminal, but in a sense wherein the community must face up to its own particular sort of responsibility? Rushdoony here, as elsewhere, uses a meat-ax where a scalpel is needed; his imprecision rather distorts the overall biblical teaching on this matter. In my view, if Rushdoony had given more thought to the positive scriptural teaching on love, especially love of the enemy, he would not have been so confused at this point.

Gary North argues that certain commandments in the Sermon on the Mount are "recommendations for the ethical conduct of a *captive* people" (p. 845, italics his). The commands to agree with adversaries quickly, to go the second mile, and to turn the other cheek, in North's view, are exhortations telling us how to ingratiate ourselves to unbelieving rulers while we ourselves are out of power. But once the unbelieving ruler loses power, that ethic no longer holds. In the latter situation, says North, the Christian should not go the second mile or turn the other cheek, but rather "should either bust him in the chops or haul him before the magistrate, and possibly both." He says, "It is only in a period of civil impotence that Christians are under the rule to 'resist not evil.'" Interesting exegesis! I had always thought these passages had something to do with loving our enemies! And I had also thought that we should love our enemies even when we are in power. These passages do appear in the same context as the command to love our enemies (Matt. 5:43ff.). On North's view, the sayings of Matthew 5:25 and 5:39–42 have very little to do with love of enemies; rather, they urge cynical political acts, policies to be repudiated once we get some political muscle. Well, I am not ready to condemn this exegesis, but I consider it strange in the extreme that North does not even mention the command to love one's enemies or try to fit that into his interpretation. In fact, one wonders what positive bearing the command to love one's enemies can have in such a framework. But North does not even seem to recognize the existence of a problem here. It seems to me that both Rushdoony and North need to do a lot more thinking in this area if the scripturality of their approach is to be demonstrated.

There are other problems too. I think the confusion noted earlier about the negative and positive sides of the law might have been avoided through more reflection on the role of love in biblical law. It is precisely the love commandment which imparts a positive thrust to negatively formulated statutes. I think that consideration of moral agency would make Rushdoony a bit more positive on the matter of "self-perfection" as an ethical goal (p. 549). I also think that if he were more aware of the personal, subjective aspects of biblical morality, he might have been a bit less dogmatic about rather dubious applications of laws and more aware of his own fallibility as a human moral agent. It would also have motivated him to show a bit more "sympathy" in his analyses of various problems. For example, his treatment of the civil rights movement is wholly disapproving (pp. 121, 157), and he sanctions racial and cultural discrimination of various sorts which were opposed by that movement (pp. 257, 531). At the same time, one looks in vain through this book to find any sympathetic account of the human suffering which preceded the civil rights protests. Now it may be true that Scripture permits us to associate with whom we will, that it does not require us to "integrate" with those of different cultures; but what of those situations where millions of people of one race, by exercising their right of free association, effectively deprive another race of opportunity in employment, housing, education, and so on? Rushdoony does oppose the "oppression" of one group by another, on racial as well as other grounds (p. 537), but what remedy does he have for the kind of hurt done to people through apparently legal means in this situation (cf. p. 636)? A bit more "sympathy" with people and a bit less preoccupation with legal rights would greatly improve his treatment of these matters. Scripture does not always require us to make full use of our "rights"—quite the contrary (1 Cor. 9), but Rushdoony doesn't give us much help on the question of when to demand our rights and when not to.

Finally, I must say that this book displays little "sympathy" for those who disagree with Rushdoony's positions. Over and over again, Rushdoony accuses some Christian thinker or other of "nonsense" (pp. 14, 764, 551), even "pharisaic nonsense" (with reference to John Murray, p. 546) and "heretical nonsense" and "silly, trifling reasoning" (with reference to Calvin, pp. 9, 653), and "blasphemy" (with reference to Bucer, p. 682). Some are even "proponents of pauperization, encouragers of usury . . . middlemen of economic whoredom . . . financial pimps" (p. 819—North's assessment of pastors who fail to preach his application of the usury statutes). The term "sanctimonious ostrich" applies to some (p. 842—North's characterization of a "legalist" like John Murray). It may be that some of these epithets are appropriate, but I don't believe most of them are. At a number of points, Rushdoony quotes an opponent and then places upon that quotation the worst possible interpretation, often in my view with little justification (pp. 253, 336, 483–84, 423, 510, 681, 841). He tends to see unambiguous evil where it is possible to demonstrate only confusion. In criticizing opponents, he sometimes sets forth dubious, even unclear hypotheses as if they were obvious proven fact: dispensationalism teaches two ways of salvation (p. 18); voodoo is the traditional religion of the American Negro (p. 61); the goal of the civil rights movement is "not equality but power" (p. 60); pietism disparages the passions (but is also too emotionalist!) (pp. 635–36). At best, these are oversimplifications; at worst, simply false. I cannot help but point out here Rushdoony's own complaint against the "sinful intolerance of human frailties" in some circles (p. 630). Even granting that everything Rushdoony teaches is right (and that assumption should be in question), it just might be that some of those who disagree with him are not Pharisees, hypocrites, sanctimonious ostriches, and the like, but sincere Christian believers who simply have not yet discovered what Rushdoony has learned. For such who are trying to learn from him, the book displays little tolerance of their failings, little appreciation of their need, little winsomeness.

In Calvin's (not Rushdoony's) *Institutes* (III, vii, 6) there is a beautiful passage setting forth the Christian's obligations to show love to all men. In a book published in 1971, *The One and the Many*, Rushdoony attacked that passage as coming close to liberalism and containing a "vein of antinomianism" (p. 263). In my view, Rushdoony has been so preoccupied with the question of the authority of the law that he has missed some very weighty elements of biblical teaching, and that has distorted both the content and the style of his own *Institutes*. I do wish he would go back and read that Calvin passage again and open himself up to the sheer scripturality of it. That could help a great deal.

In conclusion, Rushdoony's *Institutes of Biblical Law* is a big book, with great strengths and great weaknesses. I have tried to keep this review balanced between strong praise and strong criticism. As it has turned out, the first part has been almost all positive and the last part almost all negative. In case the first part has been forgotten, I would reiterate that Rushdoony is a most important thinker, possibly the most important contemporary Reformed social critic. But he needs to develop much more intellectual self-discipline and self-criticism, particularly in the metaethical area, in order to define clearly what it means to accept biblical law as normative. And he needs to give much more attention, both analytical and personal, to the biblical teaching on moral agency, regeneration, and its fruits, particularly love. In developing his approach in these areas, it would certainly be an advantage for him to become less isolated from the mainstream of Reformed ecclesiastical and theological life. My impression is that he tends to set himself off so sharply from other Reformed thinkers that he is not in a very good position to benefit from their counsel. Nor are they in a good position to benefit from his. Rushdoony's isolation is probably not entirely his own fault, and if that isolation is to be overcome, the initiative will have to be mutual. It is a matter of making the fullest use of the gifts of the Spirit, and on that matter the Lord will not allow us to be indifferent.

REVIEW OF PETER RICHARDSON,
Paul's Ethic of Freedom[1]

This review (with slight changes) was originally published in *Transformation* 1.4 (October–December, 1984): 28. It is used here by permission.

Peter Richardson argues that the apostle Paul taught and lived a concept of freedom only described in his own writings. This concept includes the freedom of Gentiles from Jewish law and customs (pp. 40ff.), freedom of women from male domination (pp. 57ff.), freedom of believers to be "inconsistent" in their ethical behavior (p. 90; cf. pp. 79ff.), and freedom of the church to follow the Spirit without a fixed order or structure in its worship or government (pp. 142ff.). Richardson finds this concept most clearly expressed in the earlier writings of Paul. Later on, he thinks, Paul compromised these principles under the pressure of various practical problems in the churches. He developed a greater concern for order, structure, and principles as he came to realize that the return of Christ would not be imminent.

The scholarship of the book is sophisticated and subtle, but the formulations are not overly technical. Most helpful to me were (1) the discussion of Paul's principle of "adaptability" (pp. 79ff.), especially Richardson's account of the quarrel between Paul and Peter (pp. 90–97); (2) the description of the "Corinth radicals" and the possible relation of these to Gnosticism (pp. 99–108); (3) Richardson's discussion of the "mutuality" of concern and service between slave and master (pp. 51–55)

1. Philadelphia: Westminster Press, 1979.

and husband and wife (pp. 68–70, 117); (4) his analysis of the Pauline contrast between "strong" and "weak" (pp. 126–41).

On the concept of freedom itself, however, I find the book rather confusing, perhaps confused. Sometimes it seems that this freedom excludes any authority relationship: Richardson thinks Paul is not fully consistent when he gives commands to the churches (pp. 78–82, 115) and when he tells wives to obey their husbands (pp. 70–78). Sometimes, though, it seems that Pauline freedom permits an authority relationship as long as "in Christ" the difference between parties "does not matter" (p. 49—the discussion of slavery). Sometimes Richardson argues as if Christian behavior is to be totally unprincipled, except for its evangelical goal (p. 87: does he *really* mean to suggest that for Paul the end justifies any means whatsoever?). At other times, it seems that Christian freedom is subject to all sorts of limits: love (p. 80), the "law of Christ" (p. 80), the content of the gospel (pp. 95, 139), the "territorial imperative" (p. 96), and others (e.g., pp. 122–23). At times, even the principle of adaptability itself becomes an absolute principle which limits freedom (pp. 90ff.). Richardson's frequent mention of the Spirit as the one who "directs the Christian life" (p. 79) is not much help. He assumes a kind of antithesis between Spirit and law (pp. 79, 97, 171), which is by no means obvious. (Why cannot the Spirit motivate us to obey the law? Note how Paul speaks of obedience to commands as a test of spirituality in 1 Corinthians 14:37.) Much more care must be devoted to the *meaning* of freedom and the relation of freedom to law, limits, the Spirit, and authority.

I am not persuaded that Paul's concept is as unique in Scripture as Richardson says. His analysis of the Old Testament background (pp. 17ff.) says nothing about the Abrahamic covenant, even though he concedes that that covenant was basic to Paul's thinking (pp. 15–16). He does recognize fundamental agreements between Paul and Peter (pp. 90–97) in this area. Nor does Richardson do justice to the Gospels and Acts.

I can mention other problems only briefly for lack of space: (1) a tendency to infer far too much from what Paul does or does not emphasize or mention in a certain context (instances of this problem on pp. 70, 77, 144, 164); (2) a tendency to draw historical conclusions from inadequate data (pp. 22, 23, 91, 146, 163)—but Richardson is moderate in this respect, compared with other liberal New Testament scholars; (3) a tendency to make gratuitous value judgments (pp. 55–56, 66, 73, 115, 118, 165, 167, 169).

REVIEW OF MARGARET HOWE,
Women in Church Leadership[1]

I wrote this review at the request of a friend. It will supplement the discussion of men and women in chapter 33.

The author's credentials are very respectable, and the book contains some interesting and helpful ideas. I would agree with her, for instance, that there is a strong argument for women deacons (pp. 29ff.) and that women may teach in church under some conditions (pp. 58ff.). I'm also pleased to see her work out an idea which I have always suspected to be true, namely, that the New Testament terms for office are flexible and that church government varied considerably from place to place (pp. 67ff.). I also agree that the concepts of the church leader as priest and as celibate have done a great deal of harm in the church and indeed have degraded the status of women in the church (pp. 83ff., 105ff.). I also like Howe's emphasis on servant leadership (Matt. 20:25–28), which she stresses at various points throughout the book. In all of these areas, I think that Reformed people have much to learn from her.

Chapters 7–11 contain some interesting information about present attitudes in the churches over "women's issues." That data is good to have, though I don't agree with all the author's criteria for evaluating it.

That brings me to my areas of reservation. My main problem is that the book is weak in its argument for women's ordination to the eldership. In general, my own position is that of James Hurley, who argues in *Man*

---

1. Grand Rapids: Zondervan, 1982.

and Woman in Biblical Perspective[2] that women may serve as deacons and may teach under the supervision of the eldership, but that they may not themselves be elders: i.e., the church, like the home, is to be ruled by men under God. That book, I think, is superior to Howe's in the fullness of its exegetical work and its biblical theology.

The first chapter, "Inconsistencies," is thought provoking. I would agree that there is no detailed description of church office in the New Testament, and that the statements of the New Testament must be understood in their cultural context. I would agree that Jesus' relationships with women were very unusual for their time (pp. 18–19), and that the head covering was part of the cultural pattern of the time, not necessarily binding on us today (pp. 20–21). If, then, the restriction of the pastorate to males is based only on cultural tradition, I would agree that that tradition could be changed as customs change (pp. 24ff.). Of course, even in that case, I think Paul's teaching suggests that the church should be somewhat conservative in the spectrum of social tradition and change. He did, after all, recommend that the women observe the custom of head covering, even though some were abandoning it. But my major problem here is that I don't think that the male eldership is like the head covering. I don't believe that the male eldership is merely a cultural tradition. Therefore, I don't think the author's arguments here apply to the matter of eldership.

Therefore, I don't find as many "inconsistencies" as Howe finds in the present-day church. I do believe that women may sing in church (p. 26) and serve as missionaries (pp. 26–27), without their being qualified to serve as elders. I don't believe that position is at all inconsistent. Women may do anything that men who are not elders may do.

In chapter 2, I think she makes a strong case for the ordination of women to the diaconate; it isn't airtight, but I think that on balance it is pretty good. I would agree with her exegesis of Romans 16:1, 1 Timothy 3:11, and Romans 16:7. The historical arguments at the end of the chapter are interesting, but of course they don't prove anything. Our standard of truth is Scripture, not church history.

Chapter 3 is the main exegetical section of the book, and here it is that I have the most severe problems. Indeed, I disagree not only with Howe's exegesis here, but also with the view of biblical authority that seems to underlie it, if I rightly understand her. She begins with the common liberal assumption that there are two different creation accounts which contradict one another (pp. 45–46). She doesn't

2. Grand Rapids: Zondervan, 1981.

even argue the matter. (For a contrary view, see E. J. Young, *In the Beginning.*[3])

Then she proceeds, as I see it, not to exegete 1 Timothy 2:11–13, but to argue against what the passage says. She says that Paul (or whoever she regards as the author of 1 Timothy) misunderstood Genesis 1–3: he contradicts Genesis 1 in favor of Genesis 2 (pp. 46–47), he is wrong about the significance of Adam being created first (p. 47), and he is wrong about the woman being deceived (p. 47).

Now I agree that 1 Timothy 2:11–13 is a difficult passage. But if we accept the Bible as the word of God, we must read it obediently, not finding fault with it as Howe does. If we read obediently, I don't see how we can escape the conclusion that there is a subordination of woman to man which derives from creation, not merely from culture, and which ought to be reflected in the life of the church. Hurley, in the book I mentioned earlier, does as good a job with this as I have seen. Howe, in my opinion, doesn't even begin to deal with these issues.

On pages 49ff., she asks whether there is any "submission" implied in Genesis 1–3. I would agree that the term "helper" does not necessarily denote inequality or subordination. On page 50, I would disagree with Howe as to the meaning of the woman's "desire" for her husband (p. 52). Susan Foh's book *Women and the Word of God*[4] argues that the woman's "desire" is not sexual desire (as Howe points out, that wouldn't make much sense in the context), but rather the desire to dominate the man (cf. Gen. 4:7, where God tells Cain that sin "desires to have him"). Therefore, I believe that Genesis 1–3 does describe a pattern of authority and subordination, contrary to Howe's conclusion. That certainly is Paul's conclusion in 1 Timothy 2, but Howe, like most feminists, simply brushes that passage aside, as we've seen.

I agree that Genesis 3 describes the woman as "aggressive" and the man as "passive" (p. 53). And I would say that those attitudes had something to do with leading them into sin! If the Bible as a whole teaches that man is the head of the woman (and it does!), then certainly the behavior of Adam and Eve in Genesis 3 fall below the biblical norm for marriage.

Her discussion of Ephesians 5:21–23, also, is quite inadequate (pp. 54ff.). She point out rightly that there is *mutual* submission in marriage, even as Christ humbled himself to serve his people. That note needs to be sounded more often. However, that is not the only teaching of Ephesians 5:21–23. After all, even though there is "mutual submission" between Christ and

3. Edinburgh: Banner of Truth Trust, 1976.
4. Phillipsburg, NJ: Presbyterian and Reformed, 1980.

the church, the two are clearly not on the same level. Christ is *Lord*. Though Jesus rules gently, for the good of his people, by his suffering love, he also demands obedience: John 12:48; 14:21; 15:10; etc. Clearly, Paul is drawing a parallel here to the marriage situation. Husband and wife are to "mutually" submit, to be sure, but there is also an authority structure here. Paul does say that wives should be *subject* to their husbands, not the other way around.

The same goes for 1 Peter 3 (pp. 55–56). Clearly, the title "lord" here is not just a general title of respect. Peter clearly uses it to indicate that the woman should be "subject" to her husband. This is not only the "mutual" submission mentioned earlier; it is unilateral, clearly, in this context. This does not, of course, exclude the wife from all decision making, suggestion making, etc. (p. 56). And there are indications in Genesis of Sarah's submissiveness—going along with Abraham's deceptions, etc.

The first part of the discussion of 1 Corinthians 11 is pretty good (pp. 58ff.). I agree in general with the point about the clothing, though I think Hurley's treatment is more thorough and more accurate on a number of points. I do disagree with her understanding of the "apparent hierarchy" (God-Christ-man-woman) on page 60. She says it indicates not "rule," but "source." But headship elsewhere in the Pauline Epistles clearly indicates rule. And, indeed, throughout the Scriptures there is a parallel between "source" and "rule." God is in authority because all things come from him. (A student of mine did a very elaborate paper tying these ideas together.)[5]

As for 1 Corinthians 14—again, I think Hurley does a much better job. Howe just raises problems and then evades them by saying that Paul must be referring to a purely local problem (pp. 62–63). But she doesn't even deal with Paul's statement in 1 Corinthians 14:33 (cf. v. 36) that the issue was *not* merely local, that Paul gave the same rule to *all* the churches.

Again, I think there is much good in the book, but also a lot of bad exegesis and some views that are simply incompatible with the infallible authority of Scripture. I have read a number of "evangelical feminist" books, and I have yet to see one that treats all the biblical data as truly authoritative, with the seriousness that Scripture deserves.

---

5. Today (in 2005) I rely on Wayne Grudem's definitive study of *kephalē* (head): see appendix 1 in *Recovering Biblical Manhood and Womanhood*, ed. John Piper and Wayne Grudem (Wheaton, IL: Crossway Books, 1991), 425–68. He argues that "head" means "authority," not "source."

REVIEW OF HESSEL BOUMA III ET AL.,
Christian Faith, Health, and Medical Practice[1]

This review supplements my treatment of the sixth and seventh commandments on various issues of medical ethics. It deals also with questions of ethical method, which bear on most everything in the present volume. The article was originally published by *Christian Renewal*, June 18, 1990, 16–17, there entitled "Calvin Center Book Mirrors Secular Thinking." I reprint it here (with slight changes) with permission.

This book was written by an "interdisciplinary team of scholars" gathered under the auspices of the Calvin Center for Christian Scholarship. Of the five authors, Bouma works in the field of biology, Diekema in medicine, Langerak in philosophy, Rottman in sociology, and Verhey in religion. In the book, however, they speak as "we" throughout, not distinguishing in any explicit way their individual contributions or viewpoints. We are therefore authorized to hold all members of the group responsible for the content of the book. In what follows I shall refer to the book as *CFHMP* and to the authors generally as "the authors" or "the team."

Thomas L. Jipping reviewed the book's position on abortion in the November 28, 1989, issue of *Christian Renewal*. I agree, on the whole, with Jipping's analysis and strongly negative evaluation. In the present article, I intend to look at the book as a whole, focusing on issues other than abortion.

1. Hessel Bouma III, Douglas Diekema, Edward Langerak, Theodore Rottman, and Allen Verhey, *Christian Faith, Health, and Medical Practice* (Grand Rapids: Eerdmans, 1989).

First, it is important that we understand the methods and criteria by which the team seeks to reach conclusions on ethical matters. For Protestant Christians, the most serious issue here is the team's view of Scripture. The book's only systematic reflection on the nature of Scripture is in a long footnote on page 19. Here the authors begin by saying that "Scripture is the Word of God *and* the words of men" (emphasis theirs). They follow this statement by misusing an analogy between Scripture and Christ: "The human words—with all their historical particularity—may be neither identified and confused with the Word of God nor divided from and contrasted with the divine Word." Evidently, however, the team is not much worried here about people who "divide" or "contrast" the human words from the divine. That issue never gets defined; indeed, it never comes up again. They are, rather, concerned with some ("fundamentalists"? "conservatives"?) who, in their estimation, "identify" or "confuse" the human words with the Word of God.

Though they cite the Council of Chalcedon as the source of this parallel, they have quite misunderstood the relationship. The Chalcedon declaration speaks of the two natures of Christ, the divine and the human. It says of those natures that they may not be confused, changed into one another, divided, or separated. Now if we apply this language to Scripture, we would have to say that in the case of Scripture also, its human character may not be confused, changed into, divided, or separated from its divine character. But our team of authors adds a new element not found anywhere in the Chalcedon formula. They identify the "human element" with "the human words—with all their historical particularity." Had Chalcedon included such a thought about Christ, it would have had to say that the human Jesus "with all his historical particularity" was so purely human that he could not be identified or confused with God. Actually, however, Chalcedon said nothing like that about Jesus. The closest Chalcedon came to speaking about Jesus "with all his historical particularity" was to speak of his "person," *prosopon*. And Chalcedon affirms that the *person* of Jesus was (and is) *both* God and man. The implication of this is that while Jesus' *human nature* is not to be identified with God, his "historical particularity," his *person*, may indeed be identified both with God and with man.[2] And if we make the precisely parallel point about Scripture, we must conclude that its words in their "historical particularity" are *both* divine *and* human, not merely human. They may indeed, then, be "identified with" the words of God. The word of God in Scripture is not something hidden above, within,

2. Interestingly, in another context, *CFHMP* does accept this view, and even presses it to somewhat controversial lengths when it speaks of "God, suffering" on the cross (p. 10).

or below the actual words of the Bible in their historical particularity.[3] Rather, those words *are* the word of God. So says Scripture itself and the confessions of the church (both ancient and Reformed).

Since the *CFHMP* team refuses to identify the words of the Bible with the word of God, they assume they have freedom to criticize the content of Scripture (in its historical particularity, of course!). If we ask of Scripture certain kinds of questions about nature, we can expect only "quaint and curious replies" (p. 19, n. 5). In the "ancient Mediterranean," we are told, "the demonological understanding of sickness and psychosis was widespread" (p. 18). The context makes clear that the biblical authors, even Jesus, shared this misunderstanding of illness. While the "demonological" theory does contain the truth that the sick do not have control of themselves (p. 19), in general it cannot be accepted today, according to *CFHMP*. The Bible, of course, is not really at fault for promoting this misunderstanding, because "the biblical stories are not addressed to twentieth-century scientific or clinical questions and may not be used to prescribe either the way to understand such suffering today or the way to provide therapy" (pp. 18, 19).

In my view, the volume greatly overstates its case by speaking of a "demonological understanding of sickness." Scripture never suggests that *all* sickness, or even all psychosis, is the result of demonic activity. Indeed, most New Testament narratives concerning miraculous healing do not mention demons at all. And in some passages, such as Matthew 4:24, a clear distinction is drawn between diseases and demon possession. The fact is that the biblical writers did not hold to any generalized "demonological understanding of sickness." The difference between them and modern secularists is that they believed that *some* human infirmities were caused or made worse by demonic influence. So stated, I think the biblical view is not at all unreasonable; certainly it does not deserve to be maligned as "quaint" and "curious."

Even in matters of theology, the Bible is not wholly reliable, according to *CFHMP*. Some biblical authors, it says, insisted "that suffering is always in some sense deserved" (p. 10). The team is glad, however, that other sources help us to transcend such a naive view. At this point they cite, not the book of Job, but an article by D. Smith.

---

3. Where *is* the word of God, according to *CFHMP*? I gather that it is in the words of Scripture, but not "in their historical particularity." But where is that? I hate to carp, but *all* the words of my Bible are historically particular. I cannot even imagine a word that is other than historically particular, unless it is "timeless and general," and I doubt if *CFHMP* intends to identify the word of God with timeless generalities—or am I wrong? Or is "historical particularity" just an intentionally vague and pretentious expression intended to throw critics off the scent of what is happening here?

The same is true of ethics. "Within the realm of moral inquiry, furthermore, questions concerning what concrete deed I should do or leave undone in a particular context may receive only a quaint reply from Scripture" (p. 19, n. 5). No examples are given here. But I gather the team is opposing at this point a particular way of using Scripture found in some Christian ethical writings (including my own!). In the more conservative treatments of medical ethics, such as those of J. Jefferson Davis, Franklin E. Payne, the nouthetic counseling movement of Jay E. Adams and others, and the theonomic movement of R. J. Rushdoony and others, the usual approach to ethical problems is to find in the Bible explicit or implicit divine commands which relate to the problems at issue. The attempt is then made to *apply* those commands to the issues under discussion. The process of application, of course, requires some extrabiblical knowledge as well, namely, knowledge of the situation to which the command is to be applied. In such a way, the commands of God shed light upon the believer's path (Ps. 119:105).

Nowhere in *CFHMP* is there any suggestion that the believer is subject to biblical commands (even the commands of Jesus), though the book tries to make much use of Scripture in other ways. My suspicion is that those who try to justify concrete decisions on the basis of biblical commands would be among those who, in the eyes of the Calvin team, are receiving only "quaint" replies from Scripture.

How, then, does *CFHMP* suggest that we make our ethical decisions? Despite the authors' deficient view of scriptural authority, Scripture does play a large role in their ethical method. Not that Scripture provides commands to be applied to life situations; but it does provide other things. Primarily, they view Scripture as "story" or "narrative" (pp. 67, 124ff.), following the approach of what today is often called "story theology." Story theology is different things to different theologians. To some, it simply means that when we interpret the Bible we should remember that the Bible is not a mere list of doctrinal truths or moral commands, but that it is in many respects a story. Stories may teach doctrinal or historical truths, they may also teach moral lessons, but they also influence our lives in many other ways: by motivating us, by providing vivid illustrations and pictures of the truth, by giving us insight into the character of God and of human beings. Sometimes stories affect us in ways that are difficult to put into words.

To other story theologians, the importance of story theology is to undermine the traditional concern with historical, doctrinal, and moral accuracy in Scripture. On such views, it is not important whether biblical narratives convey accurate historical information. Rather, we accept the story, historical or not, as containing various models for our behavior, suggesting new situations which stimulate our thoughts and our ethical motives, and so on. Biblical narrative, in other words, is treated much as the church has customarily treated parable. Similarly, it is not important whether the ethical injunctions and doctrinal teachings of Scripture are "true" in the sense of "correct." Rather, they too are simply part of the story, to be evaluated according to broader criteria. It seems to me that the story theology of *CFHMP* is of the second variety, rather than the first. As we have seen, the book denies the inerrancy of biblical doctrine and the significance of biblical ethical injunctions. They therefore see story, not as a *supplement* to other functions of Scripture, but as a *substitute* for them.

But how do you get ethics out of the Bible if Scripture gives only "quaint" answers to ethical questions, if scriptural assumptions about disease are incorrect, and if scriptural authority has exclusive reference to a story that may be true only as parables are true?

CFHMP does also appeal to certain broad, general *teachings* of Scripture, especially creation out of nothing (pp. 3ff.), the reality of evil (pp. 7ff.), providence (pp. 8–9), suffering (pp. 9–10), God's faithfulness and care (pp. 11–12), human faithfulness and freedom (pp. 13ff.), faith in God (pp. 16–17), watchfulness and healing (pp. 17ff.), our obligation to the poor (pp. 21ff.), the "already" versus the "not yet" (pp. 23ff.), and "imaging" God (pp. 27ff.).[4] Their most central biblical concept is "covenant" (esp. pp. 67ff.). They urge as an alternative to secular "deontological" and "teleological" ethics a "covenantal" ethic. The "covenantal" ethic affirms human rights (like the deontologist) and considers consequences (like the teleologist), but it sees our primary relationships to one another more in terms of love and family responsibility than in terms of autonomous individuals considering "rights" and "consequences."

We might say, therefore, that the method of *CFHMP* is narrative or story theology plus appeal to some very general scriptural concepts. Sometimes, as with the concept of "covenant," their accounts of these concepts are illuminating, but often their formulations are questionable at least. Take "human freedom," for example. To their credit, the *CFHMP* team maintains an essentially Augustinian (as opposed to Pelagian or Arminian) understanding of human freedom, thus resisting some bad tendencies within current theology. Human freedom presupposes an established self, which chooses consistently and predictably by virtue of its own character. Hence, divine providence is no threat to human freedom (pp. 12ff.). But then the authors try to turn the fact of freedom into a norm, so as to imply that we

---

4. See Jipping's excellent critique of their concept of imaging in his article in the November 28, 1989, issue of *Christian Renewal*.

should never give medical treatment without a person's "informed consent" (p. 14).[5] Now I agree that Scripture requires informed consent, but my argument is very different. It is that God has not given authority to medical people analogous to the authority he gives to parents or civil government. Scripture contains no divine warrant allowing physicians to force care upon a person. That fact, however, is not based on the patient's metaphysical freedom. On the contrary, there are other human authorities (such as civil government and parental authorities mentioned about) who *do* have the right in some situations to make decisions for a person against that person's will. The biblical point is not (as CFHMP suggests) that a person's will may never be overruled, but rather that God has not authorized the medical community to overrule it. CFHMP's methods, however, would never have led them to the proper argument. To find that argument we need to have, not a vague focus on story and broad biblical concepts, but a detailed analysis of biblical *precepts* to see what God has or has not required. CFHMP's team could not engage in such analysis, because they believe that biblical moral precepts give us only "quaint" answers to ethical problems.

One mistake leads to another. The CFHMP team's argument against cloning, for example, is that it "establishes an identity for the child that is not freely owned by the child and that does not invite anyone to nurture and engage the child's capacities for agency" (p. 184). How many of us have identities that are "freely owned" by ourselves? I, for one, had no role in choosing my genetic makeup. Yet I certainly do not consider that an imposition on my freedom. If my genetic makeup and environmental training push me in a certain career direction and rule out others, even that, certainly, cannot be meaningfully said to violate my freedom. And is it really true that no one will ever nurture the capacities for free choice in a cloned child? CFHMP assumes that if a child is cloned from a great pianist, society will give him no choice but himself to become a pianist (pp. 184–85). But that is simplistic. For one thing, we may well doubt whether anyone can become a pianist (or anything else) unless at some point he affirms that vocation freely from within. If society wants the child in question to become a great pianist, it *must* nurture his/her capacity for choice, even at the risk that the child will respond by choosing some other vocation. For another thing, the motive of cloning a child from the cells of a great pianist might not be specifically to create another great pianist; the

5. I will not here go into the philosophical problems raised by CFHMP's attempt to derive norms from facts, though readers trained in philosophy can profitably meditate on that issue also. While I don't quite agree with Hume and Moore about the so-called naturalistic fallacy, I do think that ethical writers have an obligation to show the basis of their "oughts." CFHMP is far too often negligent in supplying such bases.

motive might rather be to create a person who, regardless of his vocation, exhibits the creativity and discipline of his clone-predecessor.

CFHMP tries, in other words, to make the concept of freedom carry much too much moral weight. In doing so, the authors miss out on some of the complications of the issues with which they deal. (I do feel that one of the *strengths* of CFHMP is that on the whole they are very much aware of complication, of nuance. But their method, at times, restricts the scope of their moral vision.) Were they able theologically to make more use of Scripture's "quaint" answers to specific problems, they might have observed that God in Scripture does not consider human freedom in every case inviolable (consider the "rod" in Proverbs), and they might have seen too that there are principles in Scripture relevant to cloning other than freedom.

The story-concept approach of CFHMP reminds me of the theological situation back in the 1940s and 1950s. Then the liberal and neoorthodox theologians were insisting obsessively that God never reveals himself by giving us "information." If, then, Scripture contains no information about God, how can a theology be based on Scripture? The liberal theologians answered with a kind of narrative theology known as *Heilsgeschichte*, or "acts of God theology," plus an intensive investigation into broad, general biblical concepts. God does not give us theological information directly, they thought, but we can develop theologies based on the narratives (regardless of their historical value) and on broad scriptural concepts.

It was James Barr, himself very much a liberal, who called an end to it all. He pointed out, in his *Semantics of Biblical Language*,[6] that communication by language is primarily by sentences (or longer units), rather than individual words. Therefore, he argued, if we are unable to trust the sentences of Scripture (i.e., the information), we should not claim to derive our theologies from scriptural words (concepts). Words mean nothing except in the context of sentences, and concepts have meaning only in the context of information. Further, he pointed out, from a theological point of view, "revelation" in the Bible does include revelation of information; to exclude information from revelation may meet the desires of modern thinkers, but it cannot be justified on the basis of Scripture itself.

Similar principles apply to CFHMP's story-concept approach. In attempting to escape the "quaintness" of Scripture's actual moral teachings and ethical injunctions, CFHMP seeks to develop a Christian ethic out of biblical stories and broad concepts. But the concepts and stories have ethical meaning only as aspects of biblical moral teaching. The bare

6. Oxford: Oxford University Press, 1961.

fact that man is free has, in itself, no moral implications. It gains moral implications when we see in Scripture not only that man is free, but also that God requires us to nurture and respect that freedom in certain ways. But then to find the moral implications of human freedom, we must go to the biblical moral injunctions. *CFHMP* cannot do this, I gather, because they suppose that these injunctions are merely "quaint." But without the injunctions, the stories and the concepts yield no moral conclusions.

This is why the arguments of *CFHMP* are often weak, even when they are presented in defense of sound conclusions. Examples: (1) Over and over, *CFHMP* invokes the concept of "watchfulness" to enforce a particular conclusion (pp. 17ff., *passim*): "A watchful medicine will" do this or that. I am not clear as to what they mean by "watchful"; in most contexts, it seems to mean something like "reasonable" or "thoughtful." I confess, however, that I am rarely persuaded by this sort of argument. Often they seem to be telling me that if I am thoughtful, I will do this or that, without leading me through the relevant "thoughtful" reasoning process.

(2) While they have a rather "middle of the road" view of abortion,[7] and though they do not exclude the killing of embryos in the course of in vitro fertilization, nevertheless they absolutely exclude "the use of embryos procreated in vitro for experimental purposes" (p. 204). The reason is that "it is wrong to begin human life with the intention of discarding it once we have used it." But elsewhere they are unwilling to say that the embryo *is* human life. So the basis of this dogmatic exclusion is obscure.

(3) They also absolutely exclude "commercial contracts for surrogacy," though against surrogacy itself they only raise "caution" (p. 204). The argument against the contracts (p. 203) is not that surrogacy involves parenting without commitment to raise the child; it is rather that commercial contracts for surrogacy will drive a greater wedge between the rich and the poor. Concern for the poor is a major theme in *CFHMP*, as well it should be (cf. pp. 156–70). But *CFHMP* does not ever present a careful biblical analysis of what the relations of rich and poor should be. Rather, they operate on rather vague intuitions of a generally egalitarian (though not specifically Marxist) sort and various sorts of prejudices against the commercialization of medicine. It is that vague intuition that seems to underlie their aversion to surrogacy contracts, but it does not, certainly, make their case very plausible.

(4) Following on the last point: Much is said in the book about the "rights" of the poor to various sorts of things and the "requirements of justice" (pp. 82, 162ff.). Even a woman's "right" to abortion is defended on the

7. Again, see Jipping's article.

ground that women should not be asked to make "unequal" sacrifices (pp. 214–16). This talk about rights and equality is mostly unargued; the team evidently thinks that their readers will find it obvious. I do not, though I certainly do believe that we should help the poor to receive health care. The biblical basis for helping the poor is not abstract rhetoric about rights or equality, but the demands of Christian love and the biblical injunctions commanding us to care for the poor. But perhaps that point is too "quaint" for *CFHMP*.

(5) They use slippery-slope arguments at a number of points. These are arguments to the effect that society should forbid A because it could lead to B. So, "benevolent killing of those who are dying can too easily justify the benevolent killing of other mortals, even those who are not yet dying" (p. 299). But they are unwilling absolutely to prohibit abortion, even though the slippery-slope argument from abortion to euthanasia is more plausible than the slopes that they themselves invoke.

(6) Their view of "tragedy" is unbiblical, in my view.[8] I grant that we often have to choose between incompatible goods or between "evils": sometimes any decision will bring harm to someone. Such "tragedies" occur in decisions about the allocation of medical care. This does not mean, however, that in such situations it is impossible for us to do our duty, impossible to do what is right before God. Although at times we must choose between evils, we are never in such a position that we must choose between two wrongs. This, at any rate, is Scripture's teaching. If, by living in a fallen world, human beings are forced by circumstances to make sinful choices, then Jesus must also have been a sinner. But Scripture proclaims his sinlessness, and it promises us also that God will "provide the way of escape" from temptation (1 Cor. 10:13). But *CFHMP* ignores this quaint reply to their dilemma and waxes eloquent about the "gathering of evils" and the "colliding of goods" (pp. 132ff.). By this they do not mean simply that we must sometimes choose between evils; it means that in some situations we cannot do our duty before God (p. 196).

(7) The last chapter of the book (pp. 308ff.) is a discussion of AIDS, but it carries out its analysis with no reference to the moral right or wrong of homosexuality! A footnote explains that this chapter was written after the team had ceased to meet together, and therefore they could not be expected to deal with this issue, though they were able to discuss AIDS purely as a disease. I confess bafflement. If anything, the reverse ought to be true. What Scripture says about homosexuality is plain as a pikestaff, as Cornelius Van Til used to say. It is the complicated nature of

---

8. See chapter 13 of the present volume.

the disease itself which should have required further meetings and team interaction. The chapter isn't entirely bad, certainly. It does make the point several times that sexual faithfulness in monogamous relationships will prevent one from the sexual transmission of AIDS (pp. 308, 322), and that certainly needs to be said. But in dealing with the homosexual factor, the chapter generally emphasizes the evils of what has been called (though not in CFHMP) "homophobia," rather than the evils of homosexuality itself. (How did they decide, I wonder, without further team meetings, that "homophobia" was bad?) They are opposed to any kind of quarantine, any movement to "control" people with AIDS, any "arbitrary diminishing of their freedom," any refusal to treat, any "shunning" or "stigma." In general, I agree with these positions,[9] but I think it must also be said, for example, that people who knowingly infect others with the disease should be punished severely and isolated from the public. The book advocates that gay lovers of AIDS patients be used as proxies to give informed consent to treatment when the patient is unable to do it himself (p. 339), and it suggests that genuine faithfulness can be present in homosexual relationships (p. 333). All of this, without any balancing critique, presents homosexuality in a very flattering light. In my view, this is unworthy of a Christian publication.

Therefore, the method of the book, in my opinion, often leads to confusion and unpersuasive arguments. I would not say that on this account the book is valueless. On the contrary, it contains a great deal of interesting information and ethical wisdom. It is well informed. But it clearly is not adequate as a Reformed ethic, for it is not adequately biblical. The CFHMP team surely cannot say with the Belgic Confession that "we believe without a doubt all things contained in (the Scriptures)."

And because the book does not forthrightly embrace the Christian church's authoritative standard, its ethical work is disappointing. Apart from the specific criticisms already noted, I am disappointed in that this book almost never reaches distinctively Christian conclusions. In view of what Scripture says about the antithesis between the wisdom of God and the wisdom of the world, we would certainly expect that a book of Christian ethics would differ sharply, in both its method and its conclusions, from secular ethical thinking. But since CFHMP compromises on the presuppositions of Christian ethics, its conclusions most often find agreement with the secular traditions. The sad thing is that it is difficult (if it is even possible) to find even one topic on which CFHMP recom-

---

9. I do think that those who get the disease by voluntary homosexual activity rightly deserve a "stigma" in some sense. But even that stigma should belong only to the unrepentant.

mends a conclusion that is different from the consensus of secular ethicists. It differs from them only in its reasoning, which is, as I have indicated, its least valuable feature.

There are basically two kinds of ethics books which claim to be Christian. One kind, such as those of Franklin E. Payne and others, which I mentioned earlier,[10] seeks to apply the commands of Scripture to ethical problems, assuming that Scripture is nothing less than God's word to us. The other kind is what I sometimes call (with an intentional tone of slight deprecation) "love and justice books." These books derive certain values from the Bible, such as love and justice, but they do not accept the whole Bible as God's word, and thus they feel free to accommodate its ethical teachings to current fashion.

CFHMP is most clearly a "love and justice" book, although, to be sure, it makes use of more biblical concepts than merely those of love and justice. The team in effect disparages the conclusions of the first group of authors as "quaint." Indeed, CFHMP's very elaborate bibliography (pp. 376–400: 24 pages!) contains no references at all to ethical works of the first type I have mentioned, except for Clifford Bajema's *Abortion and the Meaning of Personhood*.[11] (Evidently they felt a need to refer to at least one strongly pro-life author.)

The first group of authors, which one might call the "biblical ethics" group, does read the love and justice books. But, as with CFHMP, the love and justice people almost never read the works of the biblical ethicists. The problem, then, is not just that the CFHMP authors are on the wrong track; rather, they are not even teachable. They are not even listening to those who argue another view. Ironically (and this has often been true in other contexts), here it is the "liberals" who are illiberal, closed minded, while the "conservatives" are the ones seeking to learn what they can from those in other camps.

Any member of the Christian Reformed Church must ask seriously why such a book would be produced under the auspices of the Calvin Center—a book that decisively rejects—even ridicules, in effect—the Church's creedal position on Scripture, and which is not even in dialogue with those whose thinking is self-consciously biblical and Reformed. Discipline, according to Calvin, is a mark of the true church. A church that cannot enforce its own doctrinal standards is surely in deep trouble.

---

10. My own *Medical Ethics* (Phillipsburg, NJ: Presbyterian and Reformed, 1988) attempts to follow in this tradition—as does now, of course, *The Doctrine of the Christian Life*.

11. It is, of course, possible that I have missed something among these many titles.

REVIEW OF R. F. R. GARDNER,
Abortion: The Personal Dilemma[1]

This review was published in the *Westminster Theological Journal* 35 (1973): 234–37, and is used by permission (with slight changes). It supplements the discussion of abortion in chapter 37 of this book.

This *might* have been the ideal Christian book on the difficult question of abortion. For one thing, it would be hard to imagine anyone better qualified to write such a book. The author is not only a consultant obstetrician and gynecologist, but also an ordained minister of the United Free Church of Scotland. (The back cover states that the combination of minister and gynecologist is "possibly unique"!)

And the man is quite a scholar. His reading, as indicated by the footnoted quotations and references, has been amazingly comprehensive. Mr. Gardner has a quotation for every occasion—not only to substantiate facts, but to express opinions he agrees with, opinions he disagrees with, opinions in between, humorous asides, common wisdom, etc. One wishes at times that there were fewer quotations and more critical analysis of the quotations chosen, but one can be grateful that here is a virtually exhaustive survey of the best things that have been said on all sides of the issue.

And the book is loaded with information too. The author believes that "facts are the scarcest commodity in the abortion debate" (p. 16), and, well, they are certainly not scarce in his book! We learn, for instance, that "in Taiwan despite the illegality of all abortion, a questionnaire to obstetri-

1. Exeter: Paternoster Press, 1972.

cians suggest [*sic*] that for every thousand births there are 180 abortions, usually to 'correct' contraceptive failure" (p. 34). We learn the number of bed-days spent in Chilean hospitals by patients with illegal terminations (p. 35), the recent change in the Rumanian abortion law (p. 38), the percentage of atheists and agnostics in the British Abortion Law Reform Association (p. 54), the Salvation Army's view of the British 1967 abortion act (p. 104), and, well, it seems like hundreds and hundreds of other pieces of information.

Now maybe you don't want to learn all those facts, even granting the relative scarcity of that commodity! But don't let me give you the wrong impression. This is not merely a compendium of unrelated "items of interest." Mr. Gardner has done a lot of thinking as well as a lot of reading. The closing bibliography, for instance, is, considering the huge number of references in the body of the book, remarkably concise and carefully selected. And if indeed the quotations of various opinions are at times annoyingly superfluous (and perhaps my American bias shows at this point!), the information is really not, for Mr. Gardner subjects that information to very careful analysis indeed and does a masterful job of giving shape to it. This book takes the history of the abortion debate, the contemporary situation throughout the world, and the prognosis, and efficiently focuses on what is most important. The various reasons for aborting and not aborting in every conceivable situation are dissected with remarkable scrutiny. In this respect, the very multiplicity of cited facts has a point: the author wants us to see how complicated these issues are. A former missionary doctor and teacher in Africa, he wants us to transcend our cultural provincialism (hence the information on Taiwan, Chile, Rumania, and even Zanzibar! [p. 34]) and our ideological simplemindedness as well. He incisively debunks the oversimplifications of pro-abortionists, antiabortionists, and middle-of-the-roaders alike.

So, the author is a gynecologist, a minister, a scholar—and also a Christian! He is indeed an *evangelical* Christian, unashamed to express the most unqualified views of biblical inspiration and authority (pp. 114–15), notably inhospitable to modern "situation ethics" (pp. 103ff.), and affirming fully biblical views of sex and marriage (pp. 248ff.). Further, he maintains that Christianity is fully relevant to the practice of gynecology.[2] Gardner is at his best when he lambastes those who wish to discuss the abortion issue without mention of religion or morality (pp. 15ff., 89ff.). However, I think that many evangelicals, especially

---

2. And, interestingly, Christianity is relevant to psychology too. Gardner quotes with approval the advice from a letter of C. S. Lewis: "Keep clear of psychiatrists unless you know that they are also Christians" (p. 233).

in America, will find Mr. Gardner a bit too ecumenical in his choice of theological "authorities": he quotes Francis Schaeffer and John A. T. Robinson, Hudson Taylor and Dietrich Bonhoeffer, D. Martyn Lloyd-Jones and Harvey Cox, Carl F. H. Henry and the Jesuit Gregory Baum, with apparently equal approval and enthusiasm. Yet one cannot read the whole book without seeing clearly where his heart is.

Mr. Gardner's heart commitment is particularly obvious in the profound Christian compassion which permeates this volume. That compassion is most infectious: it is hard to read this book without at some point being convicted of one's own lack of love. Many will come to this book with neat, precise ideas on how people requesting abortion should be "handled." But Gardner will lead them through case after case after case—laboring with, agonizing with, each sad woman. What will happen to the woman if abortion is refused? If it is granted? What of her other children? What of her husband? What of the economic situation? The psychological? The medical? What of the morale of the doctors and nurses? For the reader, this can be an exhausting business. It is hard work to do so much thinking, but then love is hard work. The aforementioned comprehensiveness of Gardner's scholarship is in a sense a measure of his love, and of the love he wishes to arouse in his readers. The reader of this book can expect to experience a certain amount of agony, if he reads with any seriousness, and in God's providence such agony can yield spiritual fruit.

Scholarly, evangelical, compassionate. One would expect, therefore, this book to be ideal as a Christian study of abortion. I must, however, sadly decline to recommend it as such. The tragic flaw in this otherwise heroic volume is its inadequate treatment of the biblical teaching. It is hard to imagine why a scholarly evangelical with access to such biblical scholars as James Barr and Donald Wiseman (p. 11), and with such a passion for scripturality, would include in his book such a superficial treatment of the biblical texts. For example, in discussing the crucial passage in Exodus 21:22–25, Gardner explains that there have been three basic interpretations of the passage, the second one being "that the fine is payable for the blow, providing that no harm follow to mother or child" (pp. 118–19). After merely listing the three interpretations, with no analysis or discussion, he concludes: "It would seem fairly obvious that in any case the text implies a difference in the eyes of the law between the fetus and a person" (p. 118). But that conclusion is precisely what the "second view" denies. Gardner's treatments of other texts are equally cursory. Further, there is no mention in this book of what, in my opinion, is the most crucial scriptural consideration, namely, the obligation of the believer to avoid even the *probable* taking of human life.[3]

On such a slender biblical foundation, Gardner declares his view that "while the fetus is to be cherished increasingly as it develops, we should regard its first breath at birth as the moment when God gives it not only life, but the offer of Life" (p. 126). He therefore advocates abortion in a great many situations, though he is not an advocate of "abortion on demand." Just where he draws the line is a bit difficult to explain, but there are *some* cases where he clearly advocates refusal of abortion. In fact, he closes the book, rather strangely, with a strong endorsement of the Birthright organization, the creed of which is that "it is the right of every pregnant woman to give birth, and the right of every child to be born" (p. 275). On the next page, he does hint that there may be some slight difference between his approach and that of Birthright, but it is indeed strange that he should quote the creed of that organization with no criticism, for surely that creed is not *his* creed. Still, he seems to have a sort of emotional attachment to the "antiabortion" side of the debate, and he evidently wants to leave the reader with a kind of antiabortion-ist thrust, even though that thrust is undercut frequently in other parts of the book.

Thus, the book as a whole leaves one somewhat confused, and the weakness of the exegetical discussion undermines the authority of much that is said. We are still waiting for that "ideal" book on abortion. But for the present, anyway, Gardner's book is indispensable. Weak as it is at the crucial point, it still says a great many things that need saying, and it says them very well. In dramatizing the problems, there is nothing better: this book actually makes you *feel* them. And the answers, though incomplete, are often laden with a most uncommon Christian wisdom.

3. Cf. my article, "Abortion—and Some Christian Assumptions," *Banner of Truth* no. 100 (January 1972): 29–31.

REVIEW OF BEVERLY WILDUNG HARRISON,
Our Right to Choose: Toward a New Ethic of Abortion[1]

This review first appeared in *Eternity* 35 (October 1984): 43–44. It supplements the discussion of abortion in chapter 37 of the present volume.

This book is a learned and eloquent presentation of a radical feminist position on abortion. If in the final analysis her positions and even arguments are predictable and sharply at odds with evangelical Christianity, nevertheless there is much that we can learn along the way.

The book contains both historical and ethical analysis. The historical material argues the feminist positions about the oppression of women—familiar enough—but also presents some interesting points about the history of the abortion debate. The author points out that not all the condemnations of abortion in the history of Christian theology can be proven to have arisen chiefly out of respect for fetal life. Other considerations, too, played a role, notably a correlation between abortion and sexual looseness. Pro-life writers now will have to respond to Harrison's challenge. It will not be as easy as before to prove that the positions of the church fathers are identical with the modern pro-life view. She also discusses the theological debates over when the soul enters the body and the distinctions between "formed" and "unformed" fetuses.

The heart of the book, however, is the ethical analysis. Harrison argues well the case that abortion is a moral issue and cannot, therefore, be settled (as some pro-lifers have tried to settle it) by historical and scientific

1. Boston: Beacon Press, 1983.

observation alone. That the fetus has a unique set of chromosomes from conception is an important scientific fact, but the issue is how we value that fact. Harrison says that such judgments take not only scientific expertise, but also ethical sensitivity, and I agree.

Harrison's own ethical sensitivities, however, are not governed by biblical authority. Where they do come from is left rather unclear. Most often, she merely asserts her values without argument, though she does buttress them from time to time by appeals to other thinkers, especially to liberation and process theologians. The bottom line, for her, is that in a world where women are oppressed and denied control of their bodies, the mother's right to choose must be the decisive consideration. Although the fetus has some value, especially after viability, abortion can never be excluded if the woman involved can somehow construe it to be in her best interest.

Bibliography

Adams, James E. *War Psalms of the Prince of Peace*. Phillipsburg, NJ: P&R Publishing, 1991.

Adams, Jay. *Marriage, Divorce and Remarriage*. Phillipsburg, NJ: Presbyterian and Reformed, 1980.

———. "Reflections on Westminster Theology and Homiletics." In *The Pattern of Sound Doctrine*, edited by David VanDrunen, 261–68. Phillipsburg, NJ: P&R Publishing, 2004.

Allen, Diogenes. *Philosophy for Understanding Theology*. Atlanta: John Knox Press, 1985.

The American Heritage College Dictionary. 3d ed. Boston: Houghton Mifflin, 2000.

Arnold, Matthew. *Culture and Anarchy: An Essay on Political and Social Culture*. New York: Macmillan, 1882.

Ayer, A. J. *Language, Truth, and Logic*. New York: Oxford University Press, 1936.

Bahnsen, Greg L. *Homosexuality: A Biblical View*. Grand Rapids: Baker, 1978.

———. *Theonomy in Christian Ethics*. Phillipsburg, NJ: Presbyterian and Reformed, 1977.

———. *Van Til's Apologetic*. Phillipsburg, NJ: P&R Publishing, 1998.

Barker, William S., and W. Robert Godfrey, eds. *Theonomy: A Reformed Critique*. Grand Rapids: Zondervan, 1990.

Barr, James. *Semantics of Biblical Language*. Oxford: Oxford University Press, 1961.

Barrett, C. K. *A Commentary on the First Epistle of Paul to the Corinthians*. New York: Harper and Row, 1968.

Bauckham, R. J. "Sabbath and Sunday in the Protestant Tradition." In *From Sabbath to Lord's Day*, edited by D. A. Carson, 311–41. Grand Rapids: Zondervan, 1982.

Beates, Michael S. "Wholeness from Brokenness: Disability as a Model of the Transforming Power of the Gospel." D.Min. diss., Reformed Theological Seminary, Orlando, 2003.

Beisner, E. Calvin. *Prosperity and Poverty*. Westchester, IL: Crossway Books, 1988.

Bentham, Jeremy. *An Introduction to the Principles of Morals and Legislation*. Reprint, London: Athlone Press, 1970.

Bouma, Hessel, III, Douglas Diekema, Edward Langerak, Theodore Rottman, and Allen Verhey. *Christian Faith, Health, and Medical Practice*. Grand Rapids: Eerdmans, 1989.

Bradley, F. H. *Ethical Studies*. Oxford: Clarendon Press, 1927.

Brandt, Richard B. *Ethical Theory*. Englewood Cliffs, NJ: Prentice Hall, 1959.

Bridges, Jerry. *The Discipline of Grace*. Colorado Springs: NavPress, 1994.

Bromiley, G. W., ed. *Zwingli and Bullinger*. Library of Christian Classics 24. Philadelphia: Westminster Press, 1953.

Brown, Harold O. J. "A Preventive War Response" (to Holmes). In *War: Four Christian Views*, edited by Robert G. Clouse, 146–50. Downers Grove, IL: InterVarsity Press, 1981.

———. "The Crusade or Preventive War." In *War: Four Christian Views*, edited by Robert G. Clouse, 153–68. Downers Grove, IL: InterVarsity Press, 1981.

Brown, P. D. "Science and Sodomy." *Credenda Agenda* 5.3 (1993): 18.

Brunner, Emil. *The Divine Imperative*. Philadelphia: Westminster Press, 1947.

Budziszewski, J. "New War, Old Principles." *World*, September 29, 2001, 28.

———. *The Revenge of Conscience*. Dallas: Spence Publishing Co., 1999.

———. *What We Can't Not Know*. Dallas: Spence Publishing Co., 2003.

———. *Written on the Heart*. Downers Grove, IL: InterVarsity Press, 1997.

Bushell, Michael. *The Songs of Zion*. Pittsburgh: Crown and Covenant Publications, 1980.

Calvin, John. *Commentaries on the Book of the Prophet Daniel*. Translated by Thomas Myers. 2 vols. Reprint, Grand Rapids: Baker Book House, 1979.

———. *Institutes of the Christian Religion*. Edited by John T. McNeill. Translated by Ford Lewis Battles. The Library of Christian Classics 20–21. Philadelphia: Westminster Press, 1960.

Cameron, Nigel M. de S. "Stem Cells Without Guilt." *Washington Times*, August 26, 2005.

Carson, D. A. "'Silent in the Churches': On the Role of Women in 1 Corinthians 14:33b–36." In *Recovering Biblical Manhood and Womanhood*, edited by John Piper and Wayne Grudem, 140–53. Wheaton, IL: Crossway Books, 1991.

———, ed. *From Sabbath to Lord's Day*. Grand Rapids: Zondervan, 1982.

Chapell, Bryan. *Holiness by Grace*. Wheaton, IL: Crossway Books, 2003.

Christ or the Lodge, available at http://opc.org/GA/masonry.html.

Chung, Sung Wook, ed. *Alister E. McGrath and Evangelical Theology*. Grand Rapids: Baker, 2003.

Clark, Gordon H. *Religion, Reason, and Revelation*. Philadelphia: Presbyterian and Reformed, 1961.

———. *Thales to Dewey*. Boston: Houghton Mifflin, 1957, 46–48.

Clark, Stephen B. *Man and Woman in Christ*. Ann Arbor: Servant Books, 1980.

Clouse, Robert G., ed. *War: Four Christian Views*. Downers Grove, IL: InterVarsity Press, 1981.

Clouser, Roy. *The Myth of Religious Neutrality*. Notre Dame, IN: University of Notre Dame Press, 1991.

Clowney, Edmund. *The Unfolding Mystery*. Colorado Springs: NavPress, 1988.

Dabney, R. L. "Ecclesiastical Equality of Negroes." In *Discussions: Evangelical and Theological*, 2:199–217. Reprint, London: Banner of Truth Trust, 1967.

Davis, John Jefferson. *Evangelical Ethics*. Philadelphia: P&R Publishing, 2004.

———. *Your Wealth in God's World*. Phillipsburg, NJ: P&R Publishing, 1994.

Dennison, Charles G., and Richard C. Gamble, eds. *Pressing Toward the Mark*. Philadelphia: Committee for the Historian of the Orthodox Presbyterian Church, 1986.

Dennison, James T. "Building the Biblical-Theological Sermon, Part One: Perspective." At http://www.kerux.com/documents/KeruxV4N3A3.asp.

———. "What Is Biblical Theology?" In *Creator, Redeemer, Consummator*, edited by Howard Griffith and John Muether, 187–91. Jackson, MS: Reformed Academic Press, 2000.

Dewey, John. *Ethics*. New York: Holt, 1932.

———. *Reconstruction in Philosophy*. New York: New American Library, 1950.

Dooyeweerd, Herman. *In the Twilight of Western Thought*. Philadelphia: Presbyterian and Reformed, 1960.

Douma, J. *Responsible Conduct*. Phillipsburg, NJ: P&R Publishing, 2003.

————. *The Ten Commandments*. Phillipsburg, NJ: P&R Publishing, 1996.

Edgar, Thomas. "Divorce and Remarriage for Adultery or Desertion." In *Divorce and Remarriage: Four Christian Views*, edited by H. Wayne House, 156–62. Downers Grove, IL: InterVarsity Press, 1990.

Edgar, William. Review of *All God's Children*, by Kenneth A. Myers. *Westminster Theological Journal* 53 (1991): 377–80.

Editorial. *National Review*. Aug. 9, 1993, 17.

Eiseland, Nancy. *The Disabled God*. Nashville: Abington Press, 1994.

Eliot, T. S. *Christianity and Culture: The Idea of a Christian Society and Notes Towards the Definition of Culture*. New York: Harcourt Brace Jovanovich, 1968.

Elwell, Walter A., ed. *Evangelical Dictionary of Theology*. Grand Rapids: Baker, 1984.

Ewing, Curtis Clair, and Charles Wesley Ewing. *Israel's Calendar and the True Sabbath*. Velma, OK: National Message Ministry, 1958.

Fletcher, Joseph F. *Situation Ethics: The New Morality*. Philadelphia: Westminster Press, 1966.

Foh, Susan T. *Women and the Word of God*. Phillipsburg, NJ: Presbyterian and Reformed, 1980.

"The Forgotten Holocaust: The Eastern Slave Trade." At http://www.geocities.com/CollegePark/Classroom/9912/easterntrade.html.

Frame, John M. "Abortion—and Some Christian Assumptions." *Banner of Truth*, no. 100 (January 1972), 29–31.

————. "Abortion from a Biblical Perspective." In *Thou Shalt Not Kill*, edited by Richard L. Ganz, 43–75. New Rochelle, NY: Arlington House, 1978.

————. *The Amsterdam Philosophy*. Phillipsburg, NJ: Harmony Press, 1972.

————. *Apologetics to the Glory of God*. Phillipsburg, NJ: P&R Publishing, 1994.

————. *Contemporary Worship Music: A Biblical Defense*. Phillipsburg, NJ: P&R Publishing, 1997.

————. *Cornelius Van Til: An Analysis of His Thought*. Phillipsburg, NJ: P&R Publishing, 1995.

————. *The Doctrine of God*. Phillipsburg, NJ: P&R Publishing, 2002.

————. *The Doctrine of the Knowledge of God*. Phillipsburg, NJ: P&R Publishing, 1987.

————. *The Doctrine of the Word of God*. Forthcoming.

————. *Evangelical Reunion: Denominations and the Body of Christ*. Grand Rapids: Baker, 1991.

———. "Greeks Bearing Gifts." In *Revolutions in Worldview: Understanding the Flow of Western Thought*, edited by W. Andrew Hoffecker, 1–36. Phillipsburg, NJ: P&R Publishing, 2007.

———. "In Defense of Christian Activism." *Christian Culture*, April 2006, 1–4. Expanded version at http://www.frame-poythress.org/frame_articles/2006InDefense.html.

———. "In Defense of Something Close to Biblicism." *Westminster Theological Journal* 59 (1997): 269–91. Replies by David F. Wells ("On Being Framed," pp. 293–300) and Richard A. Muller ("Historiography in the Service of Theology and Worship," pp. 301–10), followed by Frame's response ("Reply to Richard Muller and David Wells," pp. 311–81).

———. "Machen's Warrior Children." In *Alister E. McGrath and Evangelical Theology*, edited by Sung Wook Chung, 113–47. Grand Rapids: Baker, 2003.

———. *Medical Ethics*. Phillipsburg, NJ: Presbyterian and Reformed, 1988.

———. "Men and Women in the Image of God." In *Recovering Biblical Manhood and Womanhood*, edited by John Piper and Wayne Grudem, 225–32. Wheaton, IL: Crossway Books, 1991.

———. *No Other God*. Phillipsburg, NJ: P&R Publishing, 2001.

———. "The One, the Many, and Theonomy." In *Theonomy: A Reformed Critique*, edited by William S. Barker and W. Robert Godfrey, 89–99. Grand Rapids: Zondervan, 1990.

———. "The Other Shoe: Copyright and the Reasonable Use of Technology." *Antithesis* 2.4 (July–August, 1991): 10–12.

———. *Salvation Belongs to the Lord: An Introduction to Systematic Theology*. Phillipsburg, NJ: P&R Publishing, 2006.

———. "Toward a Theology of the State," *Westminster Theological Journal* 51 (1989): 199–226.

———. "Traditionalism." At http://reformedperspectives.org and http://www.frame-poythress.org.

———. *Worship in Spirit and Truth*. Phillipsburg, NJ: P&R Publishing, 1996.

Gaffin, Richard B., Jr. *Calvin and the Sabbath*. Fearn, Ross-shire: Christian Focus, 1998.

———. *Perspectives on Pentecost*. Phillipsburg, NJ: Presbyterian and Reformed, 1979.

———. "A Sabbath Rest Still Awaits the People of God." In *Pressing Toward the Mark*, edited by Charles G. Dennison and Richard C. Gamble, 33–51. Philadelphia: Committee for the Historian of the Orthodox Presbyterian Church, 1986.

————. "Systematic Theology and Biblical Theology." In *The New Testament Student and Theology*, edited by John H. Skilton, 32–50. Nutley, NJ: Presbyterian and Reformed, 1976.

Gagnon, Robert A. J. *The Bible and Homosexual Practice*. Nashville: Abingdon, 2002.

———— and Dan O. Via. *Homosexuality and the Bible: Two Views*. Minneapolis: Augsburg Fortress, 2003.

Galbraith, John Kenneth. *The Nature of Mass Poverty*. Cambridge, MA: Harvard University Press, 1979.

Ganz, Richard L., ed. *Thou Shalt Not Kill*. New Rochelle, NY: Arlington House, 1978.

Gardner, Edmund G. "Dante Alighieri." In *The Catholic Encyclopedia*, online edition, 2003. At http://www.newadvent.org/cathen/04628a.htm.

Gardner, R. F. R. *Abortion: The Personal Dilemma*. Exeter: Paternoster Press, 1972.

Garlington, Don. *Law and Gospel: The Contribution of the New Perspective on Paul*. Forthcoming.

Gerstner, John, Arthur Lindsley, and R. C. Sproul. *Classical Apologetics*. Grand Rapids: Zondervan, 1984.

Gilder, George F. *Wealth and Poverty*. New York: Basic Books, 1981.

Grant, George. *Bringing in the Sheaves*. Brentwood, TN: Wolgemuth and Hyatt, 1988.

————. *The Dispossessed*. Westchester, IL: Crossway Books, 1986.

————. *In the Shadow of Plenty*. Ft. Worth: Dominion Press, 1986.

Greidanus, Sidney. *Sola Scriptura: Problems and Principles in Preaching Historical Texts*. Toronto: Wedge Publishing Foundation, 1979.

Grenz, Stanley J. *A Primer on Postmodernism*. Grand Rapids: Eerdmans, 1996.

Griffith, Howard, and John Muether, eds. *Creator, Redeemer, Consummator*. Jackson, MS: Reformed Academic Press, 2000.

Grudem, Wayne. *Evangelical Feminism and Biblical Truth*. Sisters, OR: Multnomah, 2004.

————. "The Meaning of *Kephalē* ('Head')." In *Recovering Biblical Manhood and Womanhood*, edited by John Piper and Wayne Grudem, 425–68. Wheaton, IL: Crossway Books, 1991.

————. "Shall We Move Beyond the New Testament to a Better Ethic?" *Journal of the Evangelical Theological Society* 47 (2004): 299–346.

————. *Systematic Theology*. Grand Rapids: Zondervan, 1994.

Gruenler, Royce. *The Trinity in the Gospel of John*. Grand Rapids: Baker, 1986.

"Guidelines for the Determination of Death." *Journal of the American Medical Association* 246 (1981): 2184–86.

Guinness, Os. *The Dust of Death.* Downers Grove, IL: InterVarsity Press, 1973.

Hall, David, ed. *Welfare Reformed.* Phillipsburg, NJ: P&R Publishing, 1994.

Harrison, Beverly Wildung. *Our Right to Choose: Toward a New Ethic of Abortion.* Boston: Beacon Press, 1983.

Hegel, Georg Wilhelm Friedrich. *Early Theological Writings.* Translated by T. M. Knox and Richard Kroner. Chicago: University of Chicago Press, 1948.

Herridge, William T. "Christianity and Culture." *The Presbyterian Review* 9 (1888): 389.

Hick, John. *God Has Many Names.* Philadelphia: Westminster Press, 1982.

Hill, Charles E. "N. T. Wright on Justification." At http://www.thirdmill. org/files/english/html/nt/NT.h.Hill.Wright.html.

"History of Operation Rescue West." At http://www.operationrescue. org/?p=64.

Hodge, Charles. "The General Assembly." *Biblical Repertory and Princeton Review* 17 (1845): 428–71. The section on "Romish Baptism" (pp. 444–71) is available as "Do Roman Catholic Clergy Count as Ministers of the Gospel?" At http://www.hornes.org/theologia/content/charles_ hodge/do_rc_clergy_count_as_gospel_ministers.htm.

———. "Is the Church of Rome a Part of the Visible Church?" *Biblical Repertory and Princeton Review* 18 (1846): 320–44. At http://www. hornes.org/theologia/content/charles_hodge/is_the_church_of_rome_ a_part_of_the_visible_church.htm.

———. *Systematic Theology.* Reprint, Grand Rapids: Eerdmans, n.d.

Hoffecker, W. Andrew, ed. *Revolutions in Worldview: Understanding the Flow of Western Thought.* Phillipsburg, NJ: P&R Publishing, 2007.

Holmes, Arthur. "The Just War." In *War: Four Christian Views,* edited by Robert G. Clouse, 115–35. Downers Grove, IL: InterVarsity Press, 1981.

Hooykaas, R. *Religion and the Rise of Modern Science.* Grand Rapids: Eerdmans, 1972.

Horton, Michael. *A Better Way.* Grand Rapids: Baker, 2002.

———. "How the Kingdom Comes." *Christianity Today* 50.1 (January 2006): 42.

House, H. Wayne, ed. *Divorce and Remarriage: Four Christian Views.* Downers Grove, IL: InterVarsity Press, 1990.

Howe, Margaret. *Women in Church Leadership.* Grand Rapids: Zondervan, 1982.

Hume, David. "Of the Original Contract." At http://www.constitution. org/dh/origcont.htm.

Hurley, James B. "Did Paul Require Veils or the Silence of Women?" *Westminster Theological Journal* 35 (1973): 190–220.

———. *Man and Woman in Biblical Perspective*. Leicester: Inter-Varsity Press, 1981.

"Is There a 'Gay Gene'?" *Chalcedon Report*, no. 466 (September 2004), 14.

Jacob, Charles L. "Eat the Fat, Drink the Sweet, and Be Merry." At http://reformedperspectives.org/newfiles/cha_jaboc/TH.Jacob.Sabbath.html.

Jewett, Paul K. *The Ordination of Women*. Grand Rapids: Eerdmans, 1980.

Jipping, Thomas L. "CCCS Team Builds on Faulty Foundation: Study on Abortion Falls Flat." *Christian Renewal* 8.6 (November 28, 1989): 10–12.

Johnson, Dennis E. "Spiritual Antithesis, Common Grace, and Practical Theology." *Westminster Theological Journal* 64 (2002): 73–94.

Jones, Peter. *Capturing the Pagan Mind*. Escondido, CA: Main Entry Editions, 2003.

———. *The Gnostic Empire Strikes Back*. Phillipsburg, NJ: P&R Publishing, 1992.

———. *Spirit Wars: Pagan Revival in Christian America*. Escondido, CA: Main Entry Editions, 1997.

James B. Jordan. "Concerning Halloween." *Open Book*, no. 28 (August 1996). At http://www.biblicalhorizons.com/open-book/no-28-concerning-halloween/.

———. "Jephthah's Daughter." *Biblical Horizons*, no. 86 (June 1996). At http://www.biblicalhorizons.com /biblical-horizons/no-86-jephthahs-daughter/.

———. *Judges: God's War Against Humanism*. Tyler, TX: Geneva Ministries, 1985.

———. *Sabbath Breaking and the Death Penalty*. Privately printed.

———. "Slavery in Biblical Perspective." Th.M. thesis, Westminster Theological Seminary, 1980.

Kaufmann, Walter, ed. *Existentialism from Dostoyevsky to Sartre*. New York: New American Library, 1975.

Keil, C. F., and F. Delitzsch. *Commentary on the Old Testament*. Reprint, Grand Rapids: Eerdmans, 1949.

Kennedy, D. James, and Jerry Newcombe. *What If Jesus Had Never Been Born?* Nashville: Thomas Nelson, 1994.

Kim, Ezra Hyun. "Biblical Preaching Is Apologia." D.Min. project, Westminster Theological Seminary in California, 2000.

Kline, Meredith G. "Divine Kingship and Gen. 6:1–4." *Westminster Theological Journal* 24 (1962): 187–204.

———. *Images of the Spirit*. Grand Rapids: Baker, 1980.

————. "The Intrusion and the Decalogue." *Westminster Theological Journal* 16 (1953–54): 1–22.

————. *Kingdom Prologue.* Privately printed, 1991.

————. "*Lex Talionis* and the Human Fetus." *Journal of the Evangelical Theological Society* 20 (1977): 193–201.

————. *The Structure of Biblical Authority.* Grand Rapids: Eerdmans, 1972.

Koch, Edward I. Column in *National Review*, May 16, 1994, 34.

Krauthammer. Charles. Column in *Escondido Times-Advocate*, July 25, 1993.

Kushner, Harold S. *When Bad Things Happen to Good People.* New York: Schocken Books, 1981.

Kuyper, Abraham. *Lectures on Calvinism.* Grand Rapids: Eerdmans, 1943.

Lampe, G. W. H. *A Patristic Greek Lexicon.* Oxford: Clarendon Press, 1961.

Leithart, Peter J. *Natural Law: A Reformed Critique.* Niceville, FL: Biblical Horizons, 1996.

LeVay, S. "A Difference in Hypothalamic Structure Between Heterosexual and Homosexual Men." *Science* 253 (1991): 1034–37.

Lewis, C. S. "The Humanitarian Theory of Punishment." In *God in the Dock: Essays on Theology and Ethics*, edited by Walter Hooper, 287–94. Grand Rapids: Eerdmans, 1970.

Lincoln, A. T. "From Sabbath to Lord's Day: A Biblical and Theological Perspective." In *From Sabbath to Lord's Day*, edited by D. A. Carson, 343–412. Grand Rapids: Zondervan, 1982.

————. "Sabbath, Rest, and Eschatology in the New Testament." In *From Sabbath to Lord's Day*, edited by D. A. Carson, 197–220. Grand Rapids: Zondervan, 1982.

Lovelace, Richard F. *Dynamics of Spiritual Renewal.* Downers Grove, IL: InterVarsity Press, 1979.

Longman, Tremper, III. *Immanuel in Our Place: Seeing Christ in Israel's Worship.* Phillipsburg, NJ: P&R Publishing, 2001.

Lutheran Church of Australia. "The Two Kingdoms." At www.lca.org. au/resources/csbq/twokingdoms.pdf.

Machen, J. Gresham. *Christianity and Liberalism.* New York: Macmillan, 1923.

————. *What Is Faith?* New York: Macmillan, 1925.

MacIntyre, Alasdair. *A Short History of Ethics.* New York: Macmillan, 1966.

McLaughlin, Ra. "Is the Sabbath Saturday or Sunday?" At http://reformed answers.org/answer.asp/file/99959.qna/category/th/page/questions.

Meyers, Jeffrey J. "*Vere Homo*: The Case for Pictures of the Lord Jesus Christ." Niceville, FL: Biblical Horizons, 1993.

Mill, John Stuart. *Utilitarianism and Other Essays.* London: Penguin Books, 1987.

Miller, C. John. *Repentance and Twentieth-Century Man*. Fort Washington, PA: Christian Literature Crusade, 1980, 1998.

"Minority Report of the Committee on Song in the Public Worship of God." *Minutes of the Fourteenth General Assembly of the Orthodox Presbyterian Church* (1947), 58–66.

Montgomery, John Warwick. *The Suicide of Christian Theology*. Minneapolis: Bethany Fellowship, 1970.

Moo, Douglas. "What Does It Mean Not to Teach or Have Authority over Men?" In *Recovering Biblical Manhood and Womanhood*, edited by John Piper and Wayne Grudem, 179–93. Wheaton, IL: Crossway Books, 1991.

Moore, G. E. *Principia Ethica*. Cambridge: Cambridge University Press, 1903.

Morris, Leon. *The First Epistle of Paul to the Corinthians*. Grand Rapids: Eerdmans, 1958.

Motyer, J. A. "Imprecatory Psalms." In *Evangelical Dictionary of Theology*, edited by Walter A. Elwell, 554. Grand Rapids: Baker, 1984.

Murray, John. "The Agency in Definitive Sanctification." In *Collected Writings of John Murray*, 2:285–93. Edinburgh: Banner of Truth Trust, 1977.

———. "Definitive Sanctification." In *Collected Writings of John Murray*, 2:277–84. Edinburgh: Banner of Truth Trust, 1977.

———. *Divorce*. Philadelphia: Presbyterian and Reformed, 1961.

———. "The Fall of Man." In *Collected Writings of John Murray*, 2:67–76. Edinburgh: Banner of Truth Trust, 1977.

———. "The Goal of Sanctification." In *Collected Writings of John Murray*, 2:313–17. Edinburgh: Banner of Truth Trust, 1977.

———. "Man in the Image of God." In *Collected Writings of John Murray*, 2:34–46. Edinburgh: Banner of Truth Trust, 1977.

———. "The Pattern of Sanctification." In *Collected Writings of John Murray*, 2: 305–12. Edinburgh: Banner of Truth Trust, 1977.

———. *Principles of Conduct*. Grand Rapids: Eerdmans, 1957.

———. "Progressive Sanctification." In *Collected Writings of John Murray*, 2:294–304. Edinburgh: Banner of Truth Trust, 1977.

———. "Song in Public Worship." In *Worship in the Presence of God*, edited by Frank J. Smith and David C. Lachman, 179–92. Greenville, SC: Greenville Presbyterian Theological Seminary Press, 1992.

Myers, Kenneth A. *All God's Children and Blue Suede Shoes*. Wheaton, IL: Crossway Books, 1989.

Nash, Ronald H. *Poverty and Wealth*. Westchester, IL: Crossway Books, 1986.

Niebuhr, H. Richard. *Christ and Culture*. New York: Harper, 1951.

Nietzsche, Friedrich. *Beyond Good and Evil*. London: Allen and Unwin, 1967.

————. *The Birth of Tragedy and the Genealogy of Morals*. New York: Anchor Books, 1990.

————. *The Joyful Wisdom*. New York: Ungar, 1960.

————. "On Truth and Lies in a Nonmoral Sense." In *Philosophy and Truth: Selections from Nietzsche's Notebooks of the Early 1870s*. Translated and edited by Daniel Breazeale. Atlantic Highlands, NJ: Humanities Press, 1990.

Noll, Mark A. *The Scandal of the Evangelical Mind*. Grand Rapids: Eerdmans, 1994.

Olasky, Marvin. "Forgotten Choice." *National Review*, March 10, 1997.

————. *The Tragedy of American Compassion*. Washington: Regnery, 1992.

Pagels, Elaine. *The Gnostic Gospels*. New York: Vintage, 1989.

Palmer, Donald. *Looking at Philosophy*. Mountain View, CA: Mayfield Publishing Co., 1988.

Parker, Kathleen. "There Might Be Something About Islam." *Orlando Sentinel*, July 17, 2005, G3.

Piper, John. *Brothers, We Are Not Professionals*. Nashville: Broadman and Holman, 2002.

————. *Desiring God*. Sisters, OR: Multnomah Publishers, 2003.

————. *The Purifying Power of Living by Faith in Future Grace*. Sisters, OR: Multnomah Books, 1995.

———— and Wayne Grudem, eds. *Recovering Biblical Manhood and Womanhood*. Wheaton, IL: Crossway Books, 1991.

Poythress, Vern S. "Copyright and Intellectual Property: Why the Laws Should Be Changed." At http://www.frame-poythress.org/poythress_articles/2005Copyrights.htm.

————. *The Shadow of Christ in the Law of Moses*. Brentwood, TN: Wolgemuth and Hyatt, 1991.

Pratt, Richard. "Postmoderns: Opponents or Opportunities?" Unpublished lecture outline.

Prichard, H. A. *Moral Obligation*. London: Oxford, 1949.

Rawls, John. *A Theory of Justice*. Cambridge, MA: Harvard University Press, 1971.

"Report of the Ad Interim Committee on Divorce and Remarriage." *Minutes of the Twentieth General Assembly of the Presbyterian Church in America* (1992). At http://www.pcanet.org/history/pca/index.html.

"Report of the Ad Interim Committee to Study Freemasonry." *Minutes of the Fifteen General Assembly of the Presbyterian Church in America* (1987). At http://www.pcanet.org/history/pca/2-300.pdf.

"Report of the Committee on Sabbath Matters." *Minutes of the Fortieth General Assembly of the Orthodox Presbyterian Church* (1973), 92–112.

"Report of the Committee on Song in the Public Worship of God." *Minutes of the Thirteenth General Assembly of the Orthodox Presbyterian Church* (1946), 101–7, and *Minutes of the Fourteenth General Assembly of the Orthodox Presbyterian Church* (1947), 51–58.

"Report of the Committee to Study the Matter of Abortion." *Minutes of the Thirty-eighth General Assembly of the Orthodox Presbyterian Church* (1971), 135–57.

"Report of the Minority of the Committee on Women in Church Office." *Minutes of the Fifty-fifth General Assembly of the Orthodox Presbyterian Church* (1988), 356–73.

Richardson, Peter. *Paul's Ethic of Freedom*. Philadelphia: Westminster Press, 1979.

Riddlebarger, Kim. "Reformed Confessionalism and the 'New Perspective' on Paul." At www.alliancenet.org.

Rockwell, Llewellyn H. "Wheelchairs at Third Base." *National Review*, July 7, 1993, 47–50.

Rushdoony, Rousas J. *The Institutes of Biblical Law*. Nutley, NJ: Craig Press, 1973.

———. *The Myth of Overpopulation*. Nutley, NJ: Craig Press, 1969.

———. *Politics of Guilt and Pity*. Nutley, NJ: Craig Press, 1970.

Sartre, Jean-Paul. *Being and Nothingness*. New York: Philosophical Library, 1956.

Schaeffer, Francis. *The God Who Is There*. London: Hodder and Stoughton, 1968.

———. *How Should We Then Live?* Old Tappan, NJ: F. H. Revell, 1976.

———. *Pollution and the Death of Man*. Wheaton, IL: Tyndale House, 1970.

Schleiermacher, Friedrich D. E. *The Christian Faith*. Edinburgh: T. and T. Clark, 1928.

Schlossberg, Herbert. *Idols for Destruction*. Nashville: Nelson, 1983.

Schwertley, Brian. "The Sabbath and Modern Industrial Civilization." *The Counsel of Chalcedon* 23.5–6 (October–November, 2001): 36–40.

Sidgwick, Henry. *The Methods of Ethics*. New York: Macmillan, 1901.

Skilton, John H., ed. *The New Testament Student and Theology*. Nutley, NJ: Presbyterian and Reformed, 1976.

Smith, Frank J., and David C. Lachman, eds. *Worship in the Presence of God*. Greenville, SC: Greenville Presbyterian Theological Seminary Press, 1992.

Stevenson, C. L. *Ethics and Language*. New Haven: Yale University Press, 1944.

Stonehouse, N. B., and Paul Woolley, eds. *The Infallible Word*. Philadelphia: Presbyterian Guardian Publishing Corporation, 1946.

Trueblood, D. Elton. *The Humor of Christ*. New York: Harper, 1964.

Tsoukalas, Steven. *Masonic Rites and Wrongs*. Phillipsburg, NJ: P&R Publishing, 1997.

Van Til, Cornelius. *Christian Theistic Ethics*. [Ripon, CA:] den Dulk Christian Foundation, 1971.

———. *A Christian Theory of Knowledge*. Philadelphia: Presbyterian and Reformed, 1969.

———. *Christianity and Barthianism*. Philadelphia: Presbyterian and Reformed, 1962.

———. *An Introduction to Systematic Theology*. Nutley, NJ: Presbyterian and Reformed, 1974.

———. "Nature and Scripture." In *The Infallible Word*, edited by N. B. Stonehouse and Paul Woolley, 263–301. Philadelphia: Presbyterian Guardian Publishing Corporation, 1946.

———. *The New Modernism*. Philadelphia: Presbyterian and Reformed, 1946.

———. *Why I Believe in God*. Philadelphia: Committee on Christian Education, Orthodox Presbyterian Church, n.d.

Van Til, Henry R. *The Calvinistic Concept of Culture*. Philadelphia: Presbyterian and Reformed, 1959.

VanDrunen, David, ed. *The Pattern of Sound Doctrine*. Phillipsburg, NJ: P&R Publishing, 2004.

Veith, Gene Edward. "Christianity and Culture: God's Double Sovereignty." *Modern Reformation* 6.1 (January–February, 1997): 15–19.

Vos, Geerhardus. *Biblical Theology, Old and New Testaments*. Grand Rapids: Eerdmans, 1954.

———. *The Pauline Eschatology*. Grand Rapids: Eerdmans, 1953. Reprint, Phillipsburg, NJ: Presbyterian and Reformed, 1986.

———. *The Teaching of Jesus Concerning the Kingdom of God and the Church*. Nutley, NJ: Presbyterian and Reformed, 1972.

Waltke, Bruce. *Biblical Theology*. Forthcoming.

Warfield, Benjamin Breckinridge. "The Emotional Life of Our Lord." In *The Person and Work of Christ*, 98–145. Philadelphia: Presbyterian and Reformed, 1950.

———. *Perfectionism*. Philadelphia: Presbyterian and Reformed, 1958.

Webb, William J. *Slaves, Women and Homosexuals*. Downers Grove, IL: InterVarsity Press, 2001.

Weeks, Noel. *The Sufficiency of Scripture*. Edinburgh: Banner of Truth Trust, 1988.

Wells, David. *No Place for Truth*. Grand Rapids: Eerdmans, 1993.

Wenham, Gordon J. *The Book of Leviticus*. Grand Rapids: Eerdmans, 1979.

White, Lynn, Jr. "The Historical Roots of Our Ecologic Crisis." *Science* 155 (1967): 1203–12.

Williams, Neil H. *The Theology of Sonship*. Jenkintown, PA: World Harvest Mission, 2002.

The Willowbank Report: Consultation on the Gospel and Culture. At http://community.gospelcom.net/Brix?pageID=14322.

Wittgenstein, Ludwig. *The Blue and Brown Books*. Oxford: Blackwell, 1964.

―――. "Lecture on Ethics." 1929. At http://www.kolumbus.fi/m.sipola/ethics.htm.

―――. *Philosophical Investigations*. New York: Macmillan, 1953, 1968.

―――. *Tractatus Logico-Philosophicus*. London: Routledge and Kegan Paul, 1921, 1963.

Wright, N. T. "Paul's Gospel and Caesar's Empire." At http://www.ctinquiry.org/publications/wright.htm.

Yoder, John Howard. *The Politics of Jesus*. Grand Rapids: Eerdmans, 1972.

Young, E. J. *In the Beginning*. Edinburgh: Banner of Truth Trust, 1976.

Index of Names

Index of Subjects

Index of Scripture

4:1—416
4:2—458
4:2–3—353, 355, 485
4:7—918
4:7–21—193, 334, 336
4:8—318, 613n34
4:8–10—386
4:9–10—337
4:9–11—134
4:9–12—199
4:10—193
4:11—918
4:12—456
4:13–17—355
4:16—318
4:18—347
4:19–20—334
4:20—456
5:2—30
5:3—3, 23, 146, 181, 195, 934
5:14–15—926
5:16—225
5:19—865
5:20—352
5:21—459

2 John
5–6—195
6—146, 181, 934
7—485
8—283
10—821

3 John
3–4—352
9–10—821
10—269, 832

Jude
7—758, 764
9—255
20—929

Revelation
1:5—337
1:7—458
1:10—401, 516, 554, 560, 562, 571
1:17—26
2:5—331, 434
3:14—832
3:16—431, 434
3:19—424
4:6–8—255
4:9–11—577
5:9—652
5:11–12—411
6:10—339
7:9—211, 652
7:9–10—463
7:10—411
9:20—459
10:5–6—498
11:7—705
11:15—945
11:18—283

12:7—255, 705
12:17—705
13—609
13:6—490
13:7—705
13:13—543
15:3–4—346
16:13—416
17:4—764n14
17:14—944, 954
18:20—339
19:2—764n14
19:6—463
19:6–9—751
19:9—553, 751
19:10—256
19:16—944, 954
19:19—705
20—282
20:3—419
21:1—270
21:2—768
21:3—21, 24
21:8—459
21:23—133
21:27—831
22:2—202n6, 743
22:8–9—256
22:15—459, 831
22:18–19—158
22:20—282